Microsoft® Official Academic Course

Microsoft Exchange Server® 2007 Configuration (70-236)

Jason W. Eckert, triOS College

WILEY

Credits

EXECUTIVE EDITOR	John Kane
DIRECTOR OF MARKETING AND SALES	Mitchell Beaton
MICROSOFT STRATEGIC RELATIONSHIPS MANAGER	Merrick Van Dongen of Microsoft Learning
EDITORIAL PROGRAM ASSISTANT	Jennifer Lartz
PRODUCTION MANAGER	Micheline Frederick
PRODUCTION EDITOR	Kerry Weinstein
CREATIVE DIRECTOR	Harry Nolan
COVER DESIGNER	Jim O'Shea
TECHNOLOGY AND MEDIA	Lauren Sapira/Elena Santa Maria

This book was set in Garamond by Aptara, Inc. and printed and bound by Bind Rite Graphics.
The covers were printed by Phoenix Color.

ISBN 978-0-470-38029-1

Printed in the United States of America

10 9 8 7 6 5 4 3 2 1

Foreword from the Publisher

Wiley's publishing vision for the Microsoft Official Academic Course series is to provide students and instructors with the skills and knowledge they need to use Microsoft technology effectively in all aspects of their personal and professional lives. Quality instruction is required to help both educators and students get the most from Microsoft's software tools and to become more productive. Thus our mission is to make our instructional programs trusted educational companions for life.

To accomplish this mission, Wiley and Microsoft have partnered to develop the highest quality educational programs for Information Workers, IT Professionals, and Developers. Materials created by this partnership carry the brand name "Microsoft Official Academic Course," assuring instructors and students alike that the content of these textbooks is fully endorsed by Microsoft, and that they provide the highest quality information and instruction on Microsoft products. The Microsoft Official Academic Course textbooks are "Official" in still one more way—they are the officially sanctioned courseware for Microsoft IT Academy members.

The Microsoft Official Academic Course series focuses on *workforce development*. These programs are aimed at those students seeking to enter the workforce, change jobs, or embark on new careers as information workers, IT professionals, and developers. Microsoft Official Academic Course programs address their needs by emphasizing authentic workplace scenarios with an abundance of projects, exercises, cases, and assessments.

The Microsoft Official Academic Courses are mapped to Microsoft's extensive research and job-task analysis, the same research and analysis used to create the Microsoft Certified Technology Specialist (MCTS) exam. The textbooks focus on real skills for real jobs. As students work through the projects and exercises in the textbooks they enhance their level of knowledge and their ability to apply the latest Microsoft technology to everyday tasks. These students also gain resume-building credentials that can assist them in finding a job, keeping their current job, or in furthering their education.

The concept of life-long learning is today an utmost necessity. Job roles, and even whole job categories, are changing so quickly that none of us can stay competitive and productive without continuously updating our skills and capabilities. The Microsoft Official Academic Course offerings, and their focus on Microsoft certification exam preparation, provide a means for people to acquire and effectively update their skills and knowledge. Wiley supports students in this endeavor through the development and distribution of these courses as Microsoft's official academic publisher.

Today educational publishing requires attention to providing quality print and robust electronic content. By integrating Microsoft Official Academic Course products, *WileyPLUS*, and Microsoft certifications, we are better able to deliver efficient learning solutions for students and teachers alike.

Bonnie Lieberman

General Manager and Senior Vice President

Preface

Welcome to the Microsoft Official Academic Course (MOAC) program for Microsoft Exchange Server 2007. MOAC represents the collaboration between Microsoft Learning and John Wiley & Sons, Inc. publishing company. Microsoft and Wiley teamed up to produce a series of textbooks that deliver compelling and innovative teaching solutions to instructors and superior learning experiences for students. Infused and informed by in-depth knowledge from the creators of Exchange Server 2007, and crafted by a publisher known worldwide for the pedagogical quality of its products, these textbooks maximize skills transfer in minimum time. Students are challenged to reach their potential by using their new technical skills as highly productive members of the workforce.

Because this knowledgebase comes directly from Microsoft, architect of the Exchange Server 2007 operating system and creator of the Microsoft Certified Technology Specialist and Microsoft Certified Professional exams (www.microsoft.com/learning/mcp/mcts), you are sure to receive the topical coverage that is most relevant to students' personal and professional success. Microsoft's direct participation not only assures you that MOAC textbook content is accurate and current; it also means that students will receive the best instruction possible to enable their success on certification exams and in the workplace.

▪ The Microsoft Official Academic Course Program

The *Microsoft Official Academic Course* series is a complete program for instructors and institutions to prepare and deliver great courses on Microsoft software technologies. With MOAC, we recognize that, because of the rapid pace of change in the technology and curriculum developed by Microsoft, there is an ongoing set of needs beyond classroom instruction tools for an instructor to be ready to teach the course. The MOAC program endeavors to provide solutions for all these needs in a systematic manner in order to ensure a successful and rewarding course experience for both instructor and student—technical and curriculum training for instructor readiness with new software releases; the software itself for student use at home for building hands-on skills, assessment, and validation of skill development; and a great set of tools for delivering instruction in the classroom and lab. All are important to the smooth delivery of an interesting course on Microsoft software, and all are provided with the MOAC program. We think about the model below as a gauge for ensuring that we completely support you in your goal of teaching a great course. As you evaluate your instructional materials options, you may wish to use the model for comparison purposes with available products.

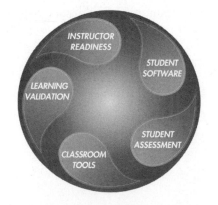

■ Pedagogical Features

The MOAC textbook for Microsoft Exchange Server 2007 Configuration is designed to cover all the learning objectives for that MCTS exam, which is referred to as its "objective domain." The Microsoft Certified Technology Specialist (MCTS) exam objectives are highlighted throughout the textbook. Many pedagogical features have been developed specifically for *Microsoft Official Academic Course* programs.

Presenting the extensive procedural information and technical concepts woven throughout the textbook raises challenges for the student and instructor alike. The Illustrated Book Tour that follows provides a guide to the rich features contributing to *Microsoft Official Academic Course* program's pedagogical plan. Following is a list of key features in each lesson designed to prepare students for success on the certification exams and in the workplace:

- Each lesson begins with an **Lesson Skill Matrix**. More than a standard list of learning objectives, the Domain Matrix correlates each software skill covered in the lesson to the specific MCTS objective domain.

- Concise and frequent **Step-by-Step** instructions teach students new features and provide an opportunity for hands-on practice. Numbered steps give detailed, step-by-step instructions to help students learn software skills. The steps also show results and screen images to match what students should see on their computer screens.

- **Illustrations:** Screen images provide visual feedback as students work through the exercises. The images reinforce key concepts, provide visual clues about the steps, and allow students to check their progress.

- **Key Terms:** Important technical vocabulary is listed at the beginning of the lesson. When these terms are used later in the lesson, they appear in bold italic type and are defined. The Glossary contains all of the key terms and their definitions.

- Engaging point-of-use **Reader aids**, located throughout the lessons, tell students why this topic is relevant (*The Bottom Line*), provide students with helpful hints (*Take Note*), or show alternate ways to accomplish tasks (*Another Way*). Reader aids also provide additional relevant or background information that adds value to the lesson.

- **Certification Ready?** features throughout the text signal students where a specific certification objective is covered. They provide students with a chance to check their understanding of that particular MCTS objective and, if necessary, review the section of the lesson where it is covered. MOAC offers complete preparation for MCTS certification.

- **Knowledge Assessments** provide progressively more challenging lesson-ending activities.

▪ Lesson Features

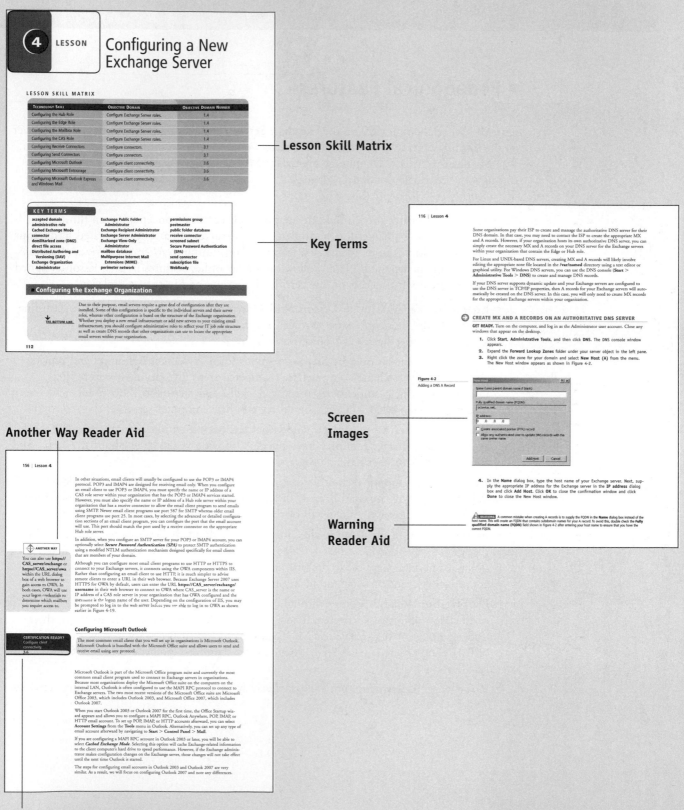

Lesson Skill Matrix

Key Terms

Screen Images

Another Way Reader Aid

Warning Reader Aid

MCTS Certification Objective Alert

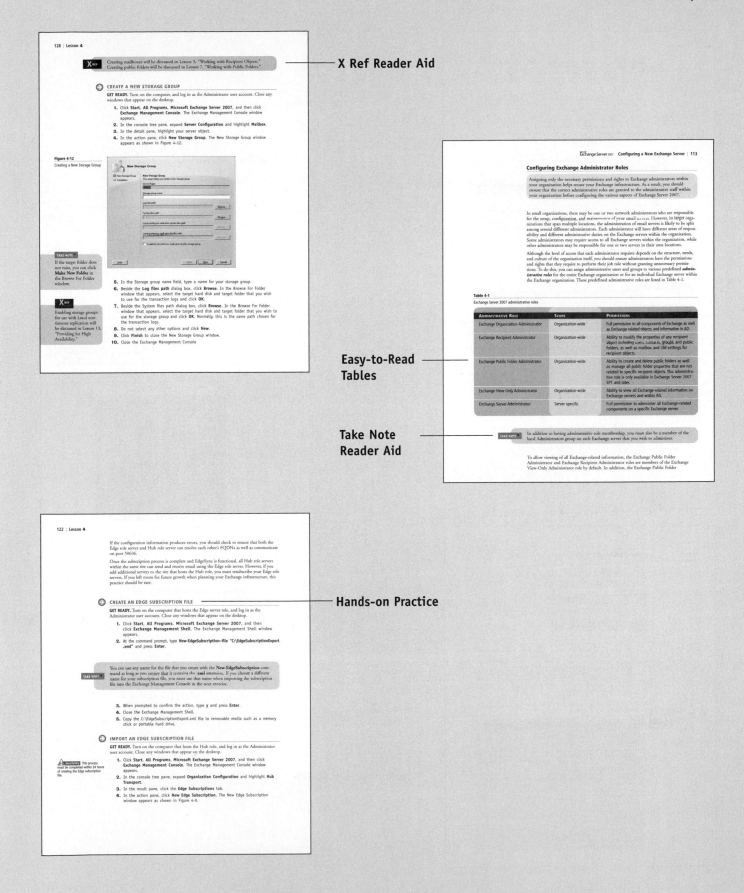

X Ref Reader Aid

Easy-to-Read Tables

Take Note Reader Aid

Hands-on Practice

The Bottom Line Reader Aid

Informative Diagrams

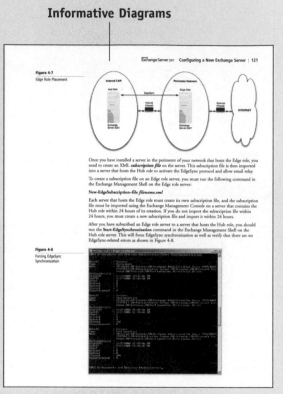

Summary Skill Matrix

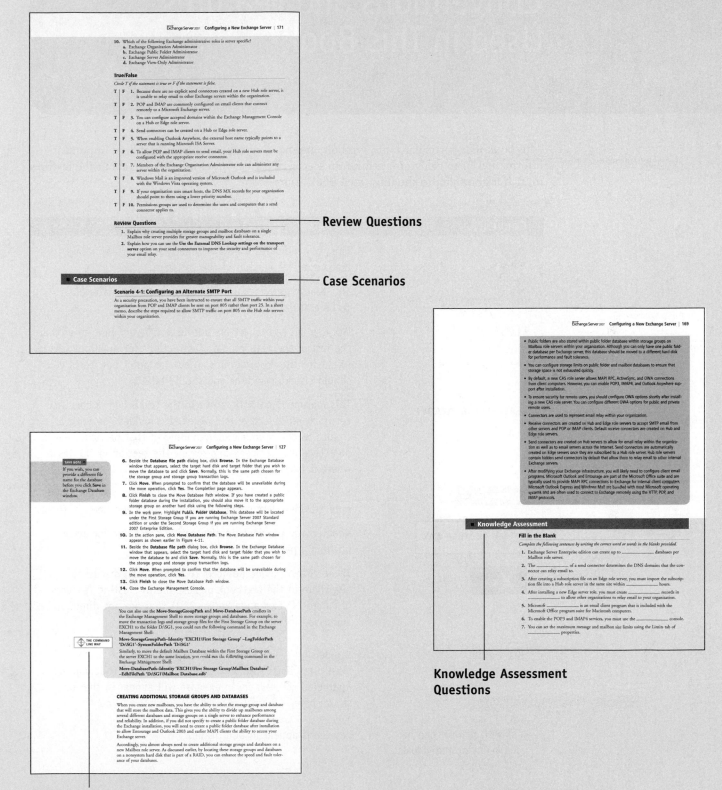

Review Questions

Case Scenarios

Knowledge Assessment
Questions

Command Line Way

Conventions and Features Used in This Book

This book uses particular fonts, symbols, and heading conventions to highlight important information or to call your attention to special steps. For more information about the features in each lesson, refer to the Illustrated Book Tour section.

CONVENTION	MEANING
NEW FEATURE	This icon indicates a new or greatly improved Windows feature in this version of the software.
↓ THE BOTTOM LINE	This feature provides a brief summary of the material to be covered in the section that follows.
CLOSE	Words in all capital letters and in a different font color than the rest of the text indicate instructions for opening, saving, or closing files or programs. They also point out items you should check or actions you should take.
CERTIFICATION READY?	This feature signals the point in the text where a specific certification objective is covered. It provides you with a chance to check your understanding of that particular MCTS objective and, if necessary, review the section of the lesson where it is covered.
TAKE NOTE	Reader aids appear in shaded boxes found in your text. *Take Note* provides helpful hints related to particular tasks or topics.
✦ ANOTHER WAY	*Another Way* provides an alternative procedure for accomplishing a particular task.
X REF	These notes provide pointers to information discussed elsewhere in the textbook or describe interesting features of Mircrosoft Exchange Server 2007 that are not directly addressed in the current topic or exercise.
Alt + Tab	A plus sign (+) between two key names means that you must press both keys at the same time. Keys that you are instructed to press in an exercise will appear in the font shown here.
A *shared printer* can be used by many individuals on a network.	Key terms appear in bold italic.
Key **My Name is.**	Any text you are asked to key appears in color.
Click **OK.**	Any button on the screen you are supposed to click on or select will also appear in color.

Instructor Support Program

The *Microsoft Official Academic Course* programs are accompanied by a rich array of resources that incorporate the extensive textbook visuals to form a pedagogically cohesive package. These resources provide all the materials instructors need to deploy and deliver their courses. Resources available online for download include:

- The **MSDN Academic Alliance** is designed to provide the easiest and most inexpensive developer tools, products, and technologies available to faculty and students in labs, classrooms, and on student PCs. A free 3-year membership is available to qualified MOAC adopters.

  Note: Microsoft Exchange Server 2007 can be downloaded from MSDN AA for use by students in this course

- The **Instructor's Guide** contains Solutions to all the textbook exercises as well as chapter summaries and lecture notes. The Instructor's Guide and Syllabi for various term lengths are available from the Book Companion site (www.wiley.com/college/microsoft) and from *WileyPLUS*.

- The **Test Bank** contains hundreds of questions in multiple-choice, true-false, short answer, and essay formats and is available to download from the Instructor's Book Companion site (www.wiley.com/college/microsoft) and from *WileyPLUS*. A complete answer key is provided.

- **PowerPoint Presentations and Images.** A complete set of PowerPoint presentations is available on the Instructor's Book Companion site (www.wiley.com/college/microsoft) and in *WileyPLUS* to enhance classroom presentations. Tailored to the text's topical coverage and Skills Matrix, these presentations are designed to convey key Microsoft Exchange Server concepts addressed in the text.

  All figures from the text are on the Instructor's Book Companion site (www.wiley.com/college/microsoft) and in *WileyPLUS*. You can incorporate them into your PowerPoint presentations, or create your own overhead transparencies and handouts.

  By using these visuals in class discussions, you can help focus students' attention on key elements of Windows Server and help them understand how to use it effectively in the workplace.

- When it comes to improving the classroom experience, there is no better source of ideas and inspiration than your fellow colleagues. The **Wiley Faculty Network** connects teachers with technology, facilitates the exchange of best practices, and helps to enhance instructional efficiency and effectiveness. Faculty Network activities include technology training and tutorials, virtual seminars, peer-to-peer exchanges of experiences and ideas, personal consulting, and sharing of resources. For details visit www.WhereFacultyConnect.com.

WileyPLUS

Broad developments in education over the past decade have influenced the instructional approach taken in the Microsoft Official Academic Course program. The way that students learn, especially about new technologies, has changed dramatically in the Internet era. Electronic learning materials and Internet-based instruction is now as much a part of classroom instruction as printed textbooks. *WileyPLUS* provides the technology to create an environment where students reach their full potential and experience academic success that will last them a lifetime!

WileyPLUS is a powerful and highly-integrated suite of teaching and learning resources designed to bridge the gap between what happens in the classroom and what happens at home and on the job. *WileyPLUS* provides instructors with the resources to teach their students new technologies and guide them to reach their goals of getting ahead in the job market by having the skills to become certified and advance in the workforce. For students, *WileyPLUS* provides the tools for study and practice that are available to them 24/7, wherever and whenever they want to study. *WileyPLUS* includes a complete online version of the student textbook, PowerPoint presentations, homework and practice assignments and quizzes, image galleries, test bank questions, gradebook, and all the instructor resources in one easy-to-use Web site.

Organized around the everyday activities you and your students perform in the class, *WileyPLUS* helps you:

- **Prepare & Present** outstanding class presentations using relevant PowerPoint slides and other *WileyPLUS* materials—and you can easily upload and add your own.

- **Create Assignments** by choosing from questions organized by lesson, level of difficulty, and source—and add your own questions. Students' homework and quizzes are automatically graded, and the results are recorded in your gradebook.

- **Offer context-sensitive help to students, 24/7.** When you assign homework or quizzes, you decide if and when students get access to hints, solutions, or answers where appropriate—or they can be linked to relevant sections of their complete, online text for additional help whenever—and wherever they need it most.

- **Track Student Progress.** Analyze students' results and assess their level of understanding on an individual and class level using the *WileyPLUS* gradebook, or export data to your own personal gradebook.

- **Administer Your Course.** *WileyPLUS* can easily be integrated with another course management system, gradebook, or other resources you are using in your class, providing you with the flexibility to build your course, your way.

Please view our online demo at **www.wiley.com/college/wileyplus.** Here you will find additional information about the features and benefits of *WileyPLUS*, how to request a "test drive" of *WileyPLUS* for this title, and how to adopt it for class use.

MSDN ACADEMIC ALLIANCE—FREE 3-YEAR MEMBERSHIP AVAILABLE TO QUALIFIED ADOPTERS!

The Microsoft Developer Network Academic Alliance (MSDN AA) is designed to provide the easiest and most inexpensive way for universities to make the latest Microsoft developer tools, products, and technologies available in labs, classrooms, and on student PCs. MSDN AA is an annual membership program for departments teaching Science, Technology, Engineering, and Mathematics (STEM) courses. The membership provides a complete solution to keep academic labs, faculty, and students on the leading edge of technology.

Software available in the MSDN AA program is provided at no charge to adopting departments through the Wiley and Microsoft publishing partnership.

As a bonus to this free offer, faculty will be introduced to Microsoft's Faculty Connection and Academic Resource Center. It takes time and preparation to keep students engaged while giving them a fundamental understanding of theory, and the Microsoft Faculty Connection is designed to help STEM professors with this preparation by providing articles, curriculum, and tools that professors can use to engage and inspire today's technology students.

Contact your Wiley rep for details.

For more information about the MSDN Academic Alliance program, go to:

msdn.microsoft.com/academic/

Note: Microsoft Exchange Server 2007 can be downloaded from MSDN AA for use by students in this course.

Important Web Addresses and Phone Numbers

To locate the Wiley Higher Education Rep in your area, go to the following Web address and click on the "*Who's My Rep?*" link at the top of the page.

www.wiley.com/college

Or Call the MOAC Toll Free Number: 1 + (888) 764-7001 (U.S. & Canada only).

To learn more about becoming a Microsoft Certified Professional and exam availability, visit www.microsoft.com/learning/mcp.

Student Support Program

Book Companion Web Site (www.wiley.com/college/microsoft)

The students' book companion site for the MOAC series includes any resources, exercise files, and Web links that will be used in conjunction with this course.

WileyPLUS

WileyPLUS is a powerful and highly-integrated suite of teaching and learning resources designed to bridge the gap between what happens in the classroom and what happens at home and on the job. For students, *WileyPLUS* provides the tools for study and practice that are available 24/7, wherever and whenever they want to study. *WileyPLUS* includes a complete online version of the student textbook, PowerPoint presentations, homework and practice assignments and quizzes, image galleries, test bank questions, gradebook, and all the instructor resources in one easy-to-use Web site.

WileyPLUS provides immediate feedback on student assignments and a wealth of support materials. This powerful study tool will help your students develop their conceptual understanding of the class material and increase their ability to answer questions.

- A **Study and Practice** area links directly to text content, allowing students to review the text while they study and answer.

- An **Assignment** area keeps all the work you want your students to complete in one location, making it easy for them to stay on task. Students have access to a variety of interactive self-assessment tools, as well as other resources for building their confidence and understanding. In addition, all of the assignments and quizzes contain a link to the relevant section of the multimedia book, providing students with context-sensitive help that allows them to conquer obstacles as they arise.

- A **Personal Gradebook** for each student allows students to view their results from past assignments at any time.

Please view our online demo at www.wiley.com/college/wileyplus. Here you will find additional information about the features and benefits of *WileyPLUS*, how to request a "test drive" of *WileyPLUS* for this title, and how to adopt it for class use.

Wiley Desktop Editions

Wiley MOAC Desktop Editions are innovative, electronic versions of printed textbooks. Students buy the desktop version for 50% off the U.S. price of the printed text, and get the added value of permanence and portability. Wiley Desktop Editions provide students with numerous additional benefits that are not available with other e-text solutions.

Wiley Desktop Editions are NOT subscriptions; students download the Wiley Desktop Edition to their computer desktops. Students own the content they buy to keep for as long as they want. Once a Wiley Desktop Edition is downloaded to the computer desktop, students have instant access to all of the content without being online. Students can also print out the sections they prefer to read in hard copy. Students also have access to fully integrated resources within their Wiley Desktop Edition. From highlighting their e-text to taking and sharing notes, students can easily personalize their Wiley Desktop Edition as they are reading or following along in class.

Microsoft Exchange Server 2007 Software

As an adopter of a MOAC textbook, your school's department is eligible for a free three-year membership to the MSDN Academic Alliance (MSDN AA). Through MSDN AA, full versions of Exchange Server 2007 are available for your use with this course. See your Wiley rep for details.

Preparing to Take the Microsoft Certified Technology Specialist (MCTS) Exam

The Microsoft Certified Technology Specialist (MCTS) certifications enable professionals to target specific technologies and to distinguish themselves by demonstrating in-depth knowledge and expertise in their specialized technologies. Microsoft Certified Technology Specialists are consistently capable of implementing, building, troubleshooting, and debugging a particular Microsoft Technology.

For organizations, the new generation of Microsoft certifications provides better skills verification tools that help with assessing not only in-demand skills on Exchange Server, but also the ability to quickly complete on-the-job tasks. Individuals will find it easier to identify and work towards the certification credential that meets their personal and professional goals.

To learn more about becoming a Microsoft Certified Professional and exam availability, visit www.microsoft.com/learning/mcp.

Microsoft Certifications for IT Professionals

The new Microsoft Certified Technology Specialist (MCTS) and Microsoft Certified IT Professional (MCITP) credentials provide IT professionals with a simpler and more targeted framework to showcase their technical skills in addition to the skills that are required for specific developer job roles.

The Microsoft Certified Professional (MCP), Microsoft Certified System Administrator (MCSA), and Microsoft Certified Systems Engineer (MCSE) credentials continue to provide IT professionals who use Microsoft Exchange Server 2003, Windows XP, and Windows Server 2003 with industry recognition and validation of their IT skills and experience.

Microsoft Certified Technology Specialist

The new Microsoft Certified Tehnology Specialist (MCTS) credential highlights your skills using a specific Microsoft technology. You can demonstrate your abilities as an IT professional or developer with in-depth knowledge of the Microsoft technology that you use today or are planning to deploy.

The MCTS certifications enable professionals to target specific technologies and to distinguish themselves by demonstrating in-depth knowledge and expertise in their specialized technologies. Microsoft Certified Technology Specialists are consistently capable of implementing, building, troubleshooting, and debugging a particular Microsoft technology.

You can learn more about the MCTS program at www.microsoft.com/learning/mcp/mcts.

Microsoft Certified IT Professional

The new Microsoft Certified IT Professional (MCITP) credential lets you highlight your specific area of expertise. Now, you can easily distinguish yourself as an expert in engineering, designing, and deploying messaging solutions with Microsoft Exchange Server 2007.

By becoming certified, you demonstrate to employers that you have achieved a predictable level of skill in the use of Microsoft technologies. Employers often require certification either as a condition of employment or as a condition of advancement within the company or other organization.

You can learn more about the MCITP program at www.microsoft.com/learning/mcp/mcitp.

The certification examinations are sponsored by Microsoft but administered through Microsoft's exam delivery partner Prometric.

Preparing to Take an Exam

Unless you are a very experienced user, you will need to use a test preparation course to prepare to complete the test correctly and within the time allowed. The *Microsoft Official Academic Course* series is designed to prepare you with a strong knowledge of all exam topics, and with some additional review and practice on your own, you should feel confident in your ability to pass the appropriate exam.

After you decide which exam to take, review the list of objectives for the exam. You can easily identify tasks that are included in the objective list by locating the Lesson Skill Matrix at the start of each lesson and the Certification Ready sidebars in the margin of the lessons in this book.

To take the MCTS test, visit www.microsoft.com/learning/mcp/mcts to locate your nearest testing center. Then call the testing center directly to schedule your test. The amount of advance notice you should provide will vary for different testing centers, and it typically depends on the number of computers available at the testing center, the number of other testers who have already been scheduled for the day on which you want to take the test, and the number of times per week that the testing center offers MCTS testing. In general, you should call to schedule your test at least two weeks prior to the date on which you want to take the test.

When you arrive at the testing center, you might be asked for proof of identity. A driver's license or passport is an acceptable form of identification. If you do not have either of these items of documentation, call your testing center and ask what alternative forms of identification will be accepted. If you are retaking a test, bring your MCTS identification number, which will have been given to you when you previously took the test. If you have not prepaid or if your organization has not already arranged to make payment for you, you will need to pay the test-taking fee when you arrive.

Student CD

The CD-ROM included with this book contains practice exams that will help you hone your knowledge before you take the MCTS Microsoft Exchange Server 2007 Configuration (Exam 70-236) certification examination. The exams are meant to provide practice for your certification exam and are also good reinforcement of the material covered in the course.

The enclosed Student CD will run automatically. Upon accepting the license agreement, you will proceed directly to the exams. The exams also can be accessed through the Assets folder located within the CD files.

Jason W. Eckert is a technical trainer, consultant, and best-selling author in the Information Technology (IT) industry. With over 20 IT certifications, 20 years of IT experience, and 18 published textbooks covering topics such as UNIX, Linux, Exchange Server, BlackBerry, Windows Server 2003, and Windows Vista, Jason brings his expertise to every class that he teaches at triOS College. Jason is also the triOS College Technology Faculty Head, where he continues to refine and improve the college technology programs. You can find more information about Jason @ http://www.jasoneckert.net.

Acknowledgments

MOAC Instructor Advisory Board

We thank our Instructor Advisory Board, an elite group of educators who has assisted us every step of the way in building these products. Advisory Board members have acted as our sounding board on key pedagogical and design decisions leading to the development of these compelling and innovative textbooks for future Information Workers. Their dedication to technology education is truly appreciated.

Charles DeSassure, Tarrant County College

Charles DeSassure is Department Chair and Instructor of Computer Science & Information Technology at Tarrant County College Southeast Campus, Arlington, Texas. He has had experience as a MIS Manager, system analyst, field technology analyst, LAN Administrator, microcomputer specialist, and public school teacher in South Carolina. DeSassure has worked in higher education for more than ten years and received the Excellence Award in Teaching from the National Institute for Staff and Organizational Development (NISOD). He currently serves on the Educational Testing Service (ETS) iSkills National Advisory Committee and chaired the Tarrant County College District Student Assessment Committee. He has written proposals and makes presentations at major educational conferences nationwide. DeSassure has served as a textbook reviewer for John Wiley & Sons and Prentice Hall. He teaches courses in information security, networking, distance learning, and computer literacy. DeSassure holds a master's degree in Computer Resources & Information Management from Webster University.

Kim Ehlert, Waukesha County Technical College

Kim Ehlert is the Microsoft Program Coordinator and a Network Specialist instructor at Waukesha County Technical College, teaching the full range of MCSE and networking courses for the past nine years. Prior to joining WCTC, Kim was a professor at the Milwaukee School of Engineering for five years where she oversaw the Novell Academic Education and the Microsoft IT Academy programs. She has a wide variety of industry experience including network design and management for Johnson Controls, local city fire departments, police departments, large church congregations, health departments, and accounting firms. Kim holds many industry certifications including MCDST, MCSE, Security+, Network+, Server+, MCT, and CNE.

Kim has a bachelor's degree in Information Systems and a master's degree in Business Administration from the University of Wisconsin Milwaukee. When she is not busy teaching, she enjoys spending time with her husband Gregg and their two children—Alex, 14, and Courtney, 17.

Penny Gudgeon, Corinthian Colleges, Inc.

Penny Gudgeon is the Program Manager for IT curriculum at Corinthian Colleges, Inc. Previously, she was responsible for computer programming and web curriculum for twenty-seven campuses in Corinthian's Canadian division, CDI College of Business, Technology and Health Care. Penny joined CDI College in 1997 as a computer programming instructor at one of the campuses outside of Toronto. Prior to joining CDI College, Penny taught productivity software at another Canadian college, the Academy of Learning, for four years. Penny has experience in helping students achieve their goals through various learning models from instructor-led to self-directed to online.

xviii |
www.wiley.com/college/microsoft *or*
call the MOAC Toll-Free Number: 1+(888) 764-7001 (U.S. & Canada only)

Before embarking on a career in education, Penny worked in the fields of advertising, marketing/sales, mechanical and electronic engineering technology, and computer programming. When not working from her home office or indulging her passion for lifelong learning, Penny likes to read mysteries, garden, and relax at home in Hamilton, Ontario, with her Shih-Tzu, Gracie.

Margaret Leary, Northern Virginia Community College

Margaret Leary is Professor of IST at Northern Virginia Community College, teaching Networking and Network Security Courses for the past ten years. She is the co-Principal Investigator on the CyberWATCH initiative, an NSF-funded regional consortium of higher education institutions and businesses working together to increase the number of network security personnel in the workforce. She also serves as a Senior Security Policy Manager and Research Analyst at Nortel Government Solutions and holds a CISSP certification.

Margaret holds a B.S.B.A. and MBA/Technology Management from the University of Phoenix, and is pursuing her Ph.D. in Organization and Management with an IT Specialization at Capella University. Her dissertation is titled "Quantifying the Discoverability of Identity Attributes in Internet-Based Public Records: Impact on Identity Theft and Knowledge-based Authentication." She has several other published articles in various government and industry magazines, notably on identity management and network security.

Wen Liu, ITT Educational Services, Inc.

Wen Liu is Director of Corporate Curriculum Development at ITT Educational Services, Inc. He joined the ITT corporate headquarters in 1998 as a Senior Network Analyst to plan and deploy the corporate WAN infrastructure. A year later he assumed the position of Corporate Curriculum Manager supervising the curriculum development of all IT programs. After he was promoted to the current position three years ago, he continued to manage the curriculum research and development for all the programs offered in the School of Information Technology in addition to supervising the curriculum development in other areas (such as Schools of Drafting and Design and Schools of Electronics Technology). Prior to his employment with ITT Educational Services, Liu was a Telecommunications Analyst at the state government of Indiana working on the state backbone project that provided Internet and telecommunications services to the public users such as K-12 and higher education institutions, government agencies, libraries, and healthcare facilities.

Wen Liu has an M.A. in Student Personnel Administration in Higher Education and an M.S. in Information and Communications Sciences from Ball State University, Indiana. He used to be the director of special projects on the board of directors of the Indiana Telecommunications User Association, and used to serve on Course Technology's IT Advisory Board. He is currently a member of the IEEE and its Computer Society.

Jared Spencer, Westwood College Online

Jared Spencer has been the Lead Faculty for Networking at Westwood College Online since 2006. He began teaching in 2001 and has taught both on-ground and online for a variety of institutions, including Robert Morris University and Point Park University. In addition to his academic background, he has more than fifteen years of industry experience working for companies including the Thomson Corporation and IBM.

Jared has a master's degree in Internet Information Systems and is currently ABD and pursuing his doctorate in Information Systems at Nova Southeastern University. He has authored several papers that have been presented at conferences and appeared in publications such as the Journal of Internet Commerce and the Journal of Information Privacy and Security (JIPC). He holds a number of industry certifications, including AIX (UNIX), A+, Network+, Security+, MCSA on Windows 2000, and MCSA on Windows 2003 Server.

We thank Scott Elliott, Christie Digital Systems, Inc., for his diligent review, providing invaluable feedback in the service of quality instructional materials.

Focus Group and Survey Participants

Finally, we thank the hundreds of instructors who participated in our focus groups and surveys to ensure that the Microsoft Official Academic Courses best met the needs of our customers.

Jean Aguilar, Mt. Hood Community College

Konrad Akens, Zane State College

Michael Albers, University of Memphis

Diana Anderson, Big Sandy Community & Technical College

Phyllis Anderson, Delaware County Community College

Judith Andrews, Feather River College

Damon Antos, American River College

Bridget Archer, Oakton Community College

Linda Arnold, Harrisburg Area Community College–Lebanon Campus

Neha Arya, Fullerton College

Mohammad Bajwa, Katharine Gibbs School–New York

Virginia Baker, University of Alaska Fairbanks

Carla Bannick, Pima Community College

Rita Barkley, Northeast Alabama Community College

Elsa Barr, Central Community College–Hastings

Ronald W. Barry, Ventura County Community College District

Elizabeth Bastcdo, Central Carolina Technical College

Karen Baston, Waubonsee Community College

Karen Bean, Blinn College

Scott Beckstrand, Community College of Southern Nevada

Paulette Bell, Santa Rosa Junior College

Liz Bennett, Southeast Technical Institute

Nancy Bermea, Olympic College

Lucy Betz, Milwaukee Area Technical College

Meral Binbasioglu, Hofstra University

Catherine Binder, Strayer University & Katharine Gibbs School–Philadelphia

Terrel Blair, El Centro College

Ruth Blalock, Alamance Community College

Beverly Bohner, Reading Area Community College

Henry Bojack, Farmingdale State University

Matthew Bowie, Luna Community College

Julie Boyles, Portland Community College

Karen Brandt, College of the Albemarle

Stephen Brown, College of San Mateo

Jared Bruckner, Southern Adventist University

Pam Brune, Chattanooga State Technical Community College

Sue Buchholz, Georgia Perimeter College

Roberta Buczyna, Edison College

Angela Butler, Mississippi Gulf Coast Community College

Rebecca Byrd, Augusta Technical College

Kristen Callahan, Mercer County Community College

Judy Cameron, Spokane Community College

Dianne Campbell, Athens Technical College

Gena Casas, Florida Community College at Jacksonville

Jesus Castrejon, Latin Technologies

Gail Chambers, Southwest Tennessee Community College

Jacques Chansavang, Indiana University–Purdue University Fort Wayne

Nancy Chapko, Milwaukee Area Technical College

Rebecca Chavez, Yavapai College

Sanjiv Chopra, Thomas Nelson Community College

Greg Clements, Midland Lutheran College

Dayna Coker, Southwestern Oklahoma State University–Sayre Campus

Tamra Collins, Otero Junior College

Janet Conrey, Gavilan Community College

Carol Cornforth, West Virginia Northern Community College

Gary Cotton, American River College

Edie Cox, Chattahoochee Technical College

Rollie Cox, Madison Area Technical College

David Crawford, Northwestern Michigan College

J.K. Crowley, Victor Valley College

Rosalyn Culver, Washtenaw Community College

Sharon Custer, Huntington University

Sandra Daniels, New River Community College

Anila Das, Cedar Valley College

Brad Davis, Santa Rosa Junior College

Susan Davis, Green River Community College

Mark Dawdy, Lincoln Land Community College

Jennifer Day, Sinclair Community College

Carol Deane, Eastern Idaho Technical College

Julie DeBuhr, Lewis-Clark State College

Janis DeHaven, Central Community College

Drew Dekreon, University of Alaska–Anchorage

Joy DePover, Central Lakes College

Salli DiBartolo, Brevard Community College

Melissa Diegnau, Riverland Community College

Al Dillard, Lansdale School of Business

Marjorie Duffy, Cosumnes River College

Sarah Dunn, Southwest Tennessee Community College

Shahla Durany, Tarrant County College–South Campus

Kay Durden, University of Tennessee at Martin

Dineen Ebert, St. Louis Community College–Meramec

Donna Ehrhart, State University of New York–Brockport

Larry Elias, Montgomery County Community College

Glenda Elser, New Mexico State University at Alamogordo

Angela Evangelinos, Monroe County Community College

Angie Evans, Ivy Tech Community College of Indiana

Linda Farrington, Indian Hills Community College

Dana Fladhammer, Phoenix College

Richard Flores, Citrus College

Connie Fox, Community and Technical College at Institute of Technology West Virginia University

Wanda Freeman, Okefenokee Technical College

Brenda Freeman, Augusta Technical College

Susan Fry, Boise State University

Roger Fulk, Wright State University–Lake Campus

Sue Furnas, Collin County Community College District

Sandy Gabel, Vernon College

Laura Galvan, Fayetteville Technical Community College

Candace Garrod, Red Rocks Community College

Sherrie Geitgey, Northwest State Community College

Chris Gerig, Chattahoochee Technical College

Barb Gillespie, Cuyamaca College

Jessica Gilmore, Highline Community College

Pamela Gilmore, Reedley College

Debbie Glinert, Queensborough Community College

Steven Goldman, Polk Community College

Bettie Goodman, C.S. Mott Community College

Mike Grabill, Katharine Gibbs School–Philadelphia

Francis Green, Penn State University

Walter Griffin, Blinn College

Fillmore Guinn, Odessa College

Helen Haasch, Milwaukee Area Technical College

John Habal, Ventura College

Joy Haerens, Chaffey College

Norman Hahn, Thomas Nelson Community College

Kathy Hall, Alamance Community College

Teri Harbacheck, Boise State University

Linda Harper, Richland Community College

Maureen Harper, Indian Hills Community College

Steve Harris, Katharine Gibbs School–New York

Robyn Hart, Fresno City College

Darien Hartman, Boise State University

Gina Hatcher, Tacoma Community College

Winona T. Hatcher, Aiken Technical College

BJ Hathaway, Northeast Wisconsin Tech College

Cynthia Hauki, West Hills College–Coalinga

Mary L. Haynes, Wayne County Community College

Marcie Hawkins, Zane State College

Steve Hebrock, Ohio State University Agricultural Technical Institute

Sue Heistand, Iowa Central Community College

Heith Hennel, Valencia Community College

Donna Hendricks, South Arkansas Community College

Judy Hendrix, Dyersburg State Community College

Gloria Hensel, Matanuska-Susitna College University of Alaska Anchorage

Gwendolyn Hester, Richland College

Tammarra Holmes, Laramie County Community College

Dee Hobson, Richland College

Keith Hoell, Katharine Gibbs School–New York

Pashia Hogan, Northeast State Technical Community College

Susan Hoggard, Tulsa Community College

Kathleen Holliman, Wallace Community College Selma

Chastity Honchul, Brown Mackie College/Wright State University

Christie Hovey, Lincoln Land Community College

Peggy Hughes, Allegany College of Maryland

Sandra Hume, Chippewa Valley Technical College

John Hutson, Aims Community College

Celia Ing, Sacramento City College

Joan Ivey, Lanier Technical College

Barbara Jaffari, College of the Redwoods

Penny Jakes, University of Montana College of Technology

Eduardo Jaramillo, Peninsula College

Barbara Jauken, Southeast Community College

Susan Jennings, Stephen F. Austin State University

Leslie Jernberg, Eastern Idaho Technical College

Linda Johns, Georgia Perimeter College

Brent Johnson, Okefenokee Technical College

Mary Johnson, Mt. San Antonio College

Shirley Johnson, Trinidad State Junior College–Valley Campus

Sandra M. Jolley, Tarrant County College

Teresa Jolly, South Georgia Technical College

Dr. Deborah Jones, South Georgia Technical College

Margie Jones, Central Virginia Community College

Randall Jones, Marshall Community and Technical College

Diane Karlsbraaten, Lake Region State College

Teresa Keller, Ivy Tech Community College of Indiana

Charles Kemnitz, Pennsylvania College of Technology

Sandra Kinghorn, Ventura College

Bill Klein, Katharine Gibbs School–Philadelphia

Bea Knaapen, Fresno City College

Kit Kofoed, Western Wyoming Community College

Maria Kolatis, County College of Morris

Barry Kolb, Ocean County College

Karen Kuralt, University of Arkansas at Little Rock

Belva-Carole Lamb, Rogue Community College

Betty Lambert, Des Moines Area Community College

Anita Lande, Cabrillo College

Junnae Landry, Pratt Community College

Karen Lankisch, UC Clermont

David Lanzilla, Central Florida Community College

Nora Laredo, Cerritos Community College

Jennifer Larrabee, Chippewa Valley Technical College

Debra Larson, Idaho State University

Barb Lave, Portland Community College

Audrey Lawrence, Tidewater Community College

Deborah Layton, Eastern Oklahoma State College

Larry LeBlanc, Owen Graduate School–Vanderbilt University

Philip Lee, Nashville State Community College

Michael Lehrfeld, Brevard Community College

Vasant Limaye, Southwest Collegiate Institute for the Deaf – Howard College

Anne C. Lewis, Edgecombe Community College

Stephen Linkin, Houston Community College

Peggy Linston, Athens Technical College

Hugh Lofton, Moultrie Technical College

Donna Lohn, Lakeland Community College

Jackie Lou, Lake Tahoe Community College

Donna Love, Gaston College

Curt Lynch, Ozarks Technical Community College

Sheilah Lynn, Florida Community College–Jacksonville

Pat R. Lyon, Tomball College

Bill Madden, Bergen Community College

Heather Madden, Delaware Technical & Community College

Donna Madsen, Kirkwood Community College

Jane Maringer-Cantu, Gavilan College

Suzanne Marks, Bellevue Community College

Carol Martin, Louisiana State University–Alexandria

Cheryl Martucci, Diablo Valley College

Roberta Marvel, Eastern Wyoming College

Tom Mason, Brookdale Community College

Mindy Mass, Santa Barbara City College

Dixie Massaro, Irvine Valley College

Rebekah May, Ashland Community & Technical College

Emma Mays-Reynolds, Dyersburg State Community College

Timothy Mayes, Metropolitan State College of Denver

Reggie McCarthy, Central Lakes College

Matt McCaskill, Brevard Community College

Kevin McFarlane, Front Range Community College

Donna McGill, Yuba Community College

Terri McKeever, Ozarks Technical Community College

Patricia McMahon, South Suburban College

Sally McMillin, Katharine Gibbs School–Philadelphia

Charles McNerney, Bergen Community College

Lisa Mears, Palm Beach Community College

Imran Mehmood, ITT Technical Institute–King of Prussia Campus

Virginia Melvin, Southwest Tennessee Community College

Jeanne Mercer, Texas State Technical College

Denise Merrell, Jefferson Community & Technical College

Catherine Merrikin, Pearl River Community College

Diane D. Mickey, Northern Virginia Community College

Darrelyn Miller, Grays Harbor College

Sue Mitchell, Calhoun Community College

Jacquie Moldenhauer, Front Range Community College

Linda Motonaga, Los Angeles City College

Sam Mryyan, Allen County Community College

Cindy Murphy, Southeastern Community College

Ryan Murphy, Sinclair Community College

Sharon E. Nastav, Johnson County Community College

Christine Naylor, Kent State University Ashtabula

Haji Nazarian, Seattle Central Community College

Nancy Noe, Linn-Benton Community College

Jennie Noriega, San Joaquin Delta College

Linda Nutter, Peninsula College

Thomas Omerza, Middle Bucks Institute of Technology

Edith Orozco, St. Philip's College

Dona Orr, Boise State University

Joanne Osgood, Chaffey College

Janice Owens, Kishwaukee College

Tatyana Pashnyak, Bainbridge College

John Partacz, College of DuPage

Tim Paul, Montana State University–Great Falls

Joseph Perez, South Texas College

Mike Peterson, Chemeketa Community College

Dr. Karen R. Petitto, West Virginia Wesleyan College

Terry Pierce, Onandaga Community College

Ashlee Pieris, Raritan Valley Community College

Jamie Pinchot, Thiel College

Michelle Poertner, Northwestern Michigan College

Betty Posta, University of Toledo

Deborah Powell, West Central Technical College

Mark Pranger, Rogers State University

Carolyn Rainey, Southeast Missouri State University

Linda Raskovich, Hibbing Community College

Leslie Ratliff, Griffin Technical College

Mar-Sue Ratzke, Rio Hondo Community College

Roxy Reissen, Southeastern Community College

Silvio Reyes, Technical Career Institutes

Patricia Rishavy, Anoka Technical College

Jean Robbins, Southeast Technical Institute

Carol Roberts, Eastern Maine Community College and University of Maine

Teresa Roberts, Wilson Technical Community College

Vicki Robertson, Southwest Tennessee Community College

Betty Rogge, Ohio State Agricultural Technical Institute

Lynne Rusley, Missouri Southern State University

Claude Russo, Brevard Community College

Ginger Sabine, Northwestern Technical College

Steven Sachs, Los Angeles Valley College

Joanne Salas, Olympic College

Lloyd Sandmann, Pima Community College–Desert Vista Campus

Beverly Santillo, Georgia Perimeter College

Theresa Savarese, San Diego City College

Sharolyn Sayers, Milwaukee Area Technical College

Judith Scheeren, Westmoreland County Community College

Adolph Scheiwe, Joliet Junior College

Marilyn Schmid, Asheville-Buncombe Technical Community College

Janet Sebesy, Cuyahoga Community College

Phyllis T. Shafer, Brookdale Community College

Ralph Shafer, Truckee Meadows Community College

Anne Marie Shanley, County College of Morris

Shelia Shelton, Surry Community College

Merilyn Shepherd, Danville Area Community College

Susan Sinele, Aims Community College

Beth Sindt, Hawkeye Community College

Andrew Smith, Marian College

Brenda Smith, Southwest Tennessee Community College

Lynne Smith, State University of New York–Delhi

Rob Smith, Katharine Gibbs School–Philadelphia

Tonya Smith, Arkansas State University–Mountain Home

Del Spencer – Trinity Valley Community College

Jeri Spinner, Idaho State University

Eric Stadnik, Santa Rosa Junior College

Karen Stanton, Los Medanos College

Meg Stoner, Santa Rosa Junior College

Beverly Stowers, Ivy Tech Community College of Indiana

Marcia Stranix, Yuba College

Kim Styles, Tri-County Technical College

Sylvia Summers, Tacoma Community College

Beverly Swann, Delaware Technical & Community College

Ann Taff, Tulsa Community College

Mike Theiss, University of Wisconsin–Marathon Campus

Romy Thiele, Cañada College

Sharron Thompson, Portland Community College

Ingrid Thompson-Sellers, Georgia Perimeter College

Barbara Tietsort, University of Cincinnati–Raymond Walters College

Janine Tiffany, Reading Area Community College

Denise Tillery, University of Nevada Las Vegas

Susan Trebelhorn, Normandale Community College

Noel Trout, Santiago Canyon College

Cheryl Turgeon, Asnuntuck Community College

Steve Turner, Ventura College

Sylvia Unwin, Bellevue Community College

Lilly Vigil, Colorado Mountain College

Sabrina Vincent, College of the Mainland

Mary Vitrano, Palm Beach Community College

Brad Vogt, Northeast Community College

Cozell Wagner, Southeastern Community College

Carolyn Walker, Tri-County Technical College

Sherry Walker, Tulsa Community College

Qi Wang, Tacoma Community College

Betty Wanielista, Valencia Community College

Marge Warber, Lanier Technical College–Forsyth Campus

Marjorie Webster, Bergen Community College

Linda Wenn, Central Community College

Mark Westlund, Olympic College

Carolyn Whited, Roane State Community College

Winona Whited, Richland College

Jerry Wilkerson, Scott Community College

Joel Willenbring, Fullerton College

Barbara Williams, WITC Superior

Charlotte Williams, Jones County Junior College

Bonnie Willy, Ivy Tech Community College of Indiana

Diane Wilson, J. Sargeant Reynolds Community College

James Wolfe, Metropolitan Community College

Marjory Wooten, Lanier Technical College

Mark Yanko, Hocking College

Alexis Yusov, Pace University

Naeem Zaman, San Joaquin Delta College

Kathleen Zimmerman, Des Moines Area Community College

We also thank Lutz Ziob, Merrick Van Dongen, Jim LeValley, Bruce Curling, Joe Wilson, Rob Linsky, Jim Clark, Jim Palmeri, and Scott Serna at Microsoft for their encouragement and support in making the Microsoft Official Academic Course programs the finest instructional materials for mastering the newest Microsoft technologies for both students and instructors.

Brief Contents

Contents

Exchange Server 2007 Basics

LESSON SKILL MATRIX

TECHNOLOGY SKILL	OBJECTIVE DOMAIN
Identify the purpose and usage of Exchange Server 2007.	Supplemental
Describe standard email terminology.	Supplemental
Understand email relay and DNS MX record usage.	Supplemental
Explain the various types and uses of email protocols.	Supplemental
Identify previous versions of Exchange Server and their features.	Supplemental
List the new features introduced in Exchange Server 2007.	Supplemental
Describe the function and usage of Exchange Server 2007 server roles.	Supplemental

KEY TERMS

Active Directory (AD)
ActiveSync
Client Access Server (CAS)
cmdlets
Domain Name System (DNS)
Edge Transport Role (Edge)
EdgeSync
Exchange Management Console
 (EMC)
Exchange Management Shell
 (EMS)
Extended Simple Mail Transfer
 Protocol (ESMTP)
Hub Transport Role (Hub)

Hypertext Transfer Protocol
 (HTTP)
Internet Message Access
 Protocol Version 4 (IMAP4)
Mail Delivery Agent (MDA)
Mail Transfer Agent (MTA)
Mail User Agent (MUA)
Mailbox Role
MAPI clients
Messaging Application
 Programming Interface (MAPI)
Messaging Records Management
 (MRM)
Outlook Anywhere

Outlook Web Access (OWA)
Post Office Protocol Version 3
 (POP3)
PowerShell
public folders
round robin
RPC over HTTP/HTTPS
Secure Socket Layer (SSL)
Simple Mail Transfer Protocol
 (SMTP)
smart host
Transport Layer Security (TLS)
Unified Messaging (UM)

■ Understanding Course Requirements

THE BOTTOM LINE Exchange Server is a messaging and collaboration software product from Microsoft. Exchange Server 2007 is the most comprehensive and feature-rich version of Exchange Server to date.

Microsoft Exchange Server is a messaging software product that is used in many organizations today. Although its main use is to provide email services, Exchange Server can also be used for collaboration such as scheduling and calendaring.

Exchange Server 2007 provides a new interface that is easier to use and a new role-based structure that is scalable to very large organizations. Whether you are new to Exchange Server or have experience maintaining a previous version of Exchange Server or other email system, you will be introduced to many new concepts and procedures as you learn Exchange Server 2007.

In this course, we examine how email systems work to deliver email across networks and the Internet as well as how Exchange Server 2007 works with the Windows Active Directory service to provide for email delivery within an organization.

You will learn how to install, configure, maintain, and troubleshoot Exchange Server 2007 in a variety of different environments and scenarios. More specifically, you will learn how to configure email clients, user settings, mailboxes, public folders, email protocols, address lists, and the Active Directory service. Additionally, you will learn how to backup, restore, monitor, secure, and cluster email servers.

■ Email Fundamentals

THE BOTTOM LINE

Because email plays an important role in our lives, it is exciting to learn how Microsoft Exchange Server 2007 works within an organization to relay email across the Internet. However, you must first have a solid grasp of email terminology and concepts. Additionally, it is vital to understand how email is sent from your email client to email servers around your organization and the Internet. More specifically, this includes understanding how emails are relayed using the DNS system on the Internet, as well a general knowledge of the various email protocols that work together to relay emails from one computer to another.

How Email Works

Email is one of the oldest applications of the Internet. Understanding how MUAs, MTAs and MDAs work together to relay email will help you understand how Microsoft Exchange Server 2007 relays email in various environments.

Electronic mail (email) consists of written messages that are sent between people on a computer or computer network. Long before the Internet, universities and other academic institutions that had large computer systems used forms of email. Since 1965, Massachusetts Institute of Technology (MIT), for example, used email as a means of collaboration between computer programmers.

When ARPANET became popular as an interuniversity computer network in the 1980s, email was considered its main application. ARPANET eventually became known as the Internet in the 1990s and is the largest interconnected series of networks in the world. Email was its first "killer application."

Today, nearly everyone who has a computer and Internet access from an ***Internet Service Provider (ISP)*** sends email to communicate with friends and family.

More important, email is used by nearly every organization as its main form of internal and external communication. Organizations in the past communicated almost exclusively by meetings or telephone, which can be time consuming for certain tasks that can be quickly communicated via email.

For users who send email (called ***senders***), email is typically created and sent using an email client program called a ***Mail User Agent (MUA)***. Common MUAs include:

- Microsoft Outlook
- Microsoft Outlook Express
- Windows Mail
- Microsoft Entourage
- Mozilla Thunderbird
- Apple Mail
- Eudora
- Web browsers such as Internet Explorer and Mozilla Firefox (if connecting to web-based email systems like Gmail, Hotmail, and Yahoo Mail)

Each of these MUAs has different user interfaces and configuration options. We will examine the configuration of different MUAs in a later lesson.

Once an email is written using an MUA and addressed to a target user (called a ***recipient***), it must be sent to an email server. Common email servers include:

- Microsoft Exchange
- Lotus Domino
- Novell GroupWise
- Sendmail
- Postfix

The email server contains a program called the ***Mail Transfer Agent (MTA)*** that decides where to send the email that it receives from the MUA.

If the email needs to be delivered to a recipient in another organization, then the MTA sends the email across the Internet to the target email server for the other organization (see Figure 1-1). The target email server contains a program called a ***Mail Delivery Agent (MDA)*** that it uses to deliver the mail to the correct mailbox on the email server. Recipients will then use their MUA to obtain the email from their mailbox.

Figure 1-1

Internet Email Relay

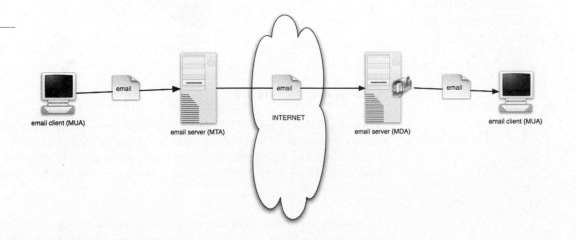

email client (MUA)   email server (MTA)   INTERNET   email server (MDA)   email client (MUA)

Alternatively, if the email needs to be delivered to a user within the same organization, then the MTA sends the email to its own MDA, which it then uses to deliver the email to the correct mailbox for the recipient. Recipients can then use their own MUA to retrieve the email as shown in Figure 1-2.

Figure 1-2

Internal Email Relay

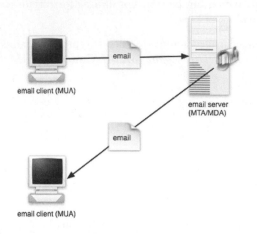

Regardless of whether the MTA and MDA are within the same organization, the process whereby an MTA sends email to an MDA is commonly called *email relay*.

To send email back and forth, email servers typically have both an MTA and an MDA. Furthermore, MUAs can connect across the Internet to an email server to send and receive emails. This is common for remote and home users who connect across the Internet to the email server at their company or ISP. This organization is shown in Figure 1-3.

Figure 1-3

Internet Mail Relay and Access

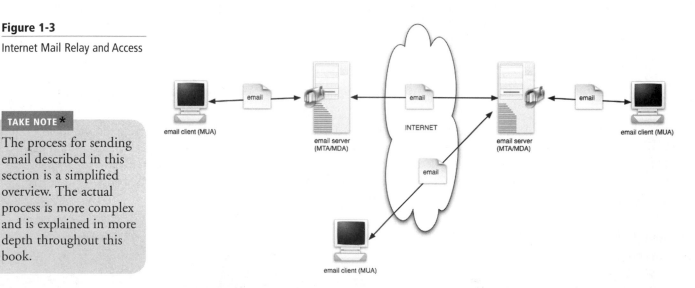

TAKE NOTE *

The process for sending email described in this section is a simplified overview. The actual process is more complex and is explained in more depth throughout this book.

DNS and Email Relay

Domain Name System (DNS) provides a robust means of locating resources on local and remote networks such as the Internet. As a result, DNS is used to locate destination email servers by using special records. Understanding how these DNS records work enables you to understand how email is relayed across networks to remote email servers and smart hosts.

To connect to another computer on a TCP/IP network such as the Internet, you need to obtain the IP address of the destination computer. Unfortunately, IP addresses are numbers, and numbers are hard to remember.

Domain Name System (DNS) provides us with an easy way around this problem. DNS has a hierarchical naming convention (also called a namespace) that starts with an imaginary root (referred to with a period "."). and several top-level domain names that describe the type of organization.

The most common top-level domain names in DNS include:

- com (commercial)
- org (nonprofit organization)
- net (an organization that maintains a network)
- edu (educational institution)
- gov (government)
- *abbr* (a two-letter *abbreviation* for the country; for example *us* refers to the United States and *ca* refers to Canada)

A DNS name also contains a second-level domain name that refers to the actual name of the organization. For example, microsoft.com is the commercial organization called Microsoft.

Under the second-level domain can be other subdomain names or the names of individual computer hosts. For example, www.microsoft.com refers to the computer called www (running the web server service) in the commercial organization called Microsoft. Similarly, server1.north.bell.ca refers to the computer called server1 in the north division of a Canadian organization called Bell. Both www.microsoft.com and server1.north.bell.ca are called *Fully Qualified Domain Names (FQDNs)* because they contain the name of the host computer.

To simplify resource location, each FQDN must be matched to a corresponding IP address on a DNS server on the Internet. The records on a DNS server that match an FQDN to an IP address are called *A (host) records.*

Because the DNS namespace is hierarchal, each domain in DNS has its own DNS server(s). For example, Microsoft will have one or more DNS server that holds the FQDNs and IP addresses for computers within the microsoft.com domain. Furthermore, all DNS servers, including the DNS servers at your company or ISP, know how to query other DNS servers within the DNS hierarchy.

Thus, when you type www.microsoft.com into a web browser, your computer contacts the DNS server listed in TCP/IP properties for your network interface and resolves the name www.microsoft.com to the correct IP address using the appropriate A record. This process is called *DNS name resolution*. Next, your web browser contacts the Microsoft web server by IP address to obtain a web page. The whole process is illustrated in Figure 1-4.

Figure 1-4

DNS Name Resolution

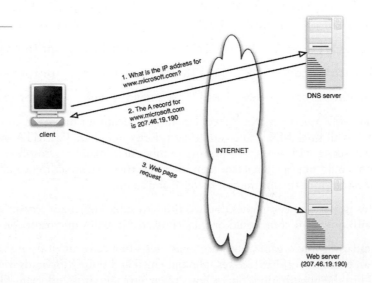

When configuring an MUA, you need to specify the MTA that it will use by IP address, NetBIOS name, or FQDN. If you specify the MTA using an FQDN, then a DNS server on your network must have an entry that will resolve the name to an IP address.

Alternatively, when sending email, you never address the target email server using an FQDN. Instead, email addresses are typically sent to the target domain and not the target email server. For example, to email Bob Jones at Microsoft, you would use an email such as bob .jones@microsoft.com instead of bob.jones@mailserver1.microsoft.com.

To accommodate this, DNS servers contain *Mail eXchanger (MX) records* that are used to indicate the email server for a particular domain to which email should be forwarded.

When an MUA sends an email (addressed to a recipient such as bob.jones@microsoft.com) to an MTA, the MTA uses the DNS server listed in its own TCP/IP properties to resolve the MX record for the target domain (i.e., microsoft.com). After the MX record has been resolved to the IP address of a target email server using the associated A record, the MTA forwards the email to the MDA on the target email server, which then delivers the email to the correct mailbox based on the recipient's name in the email address (i.e., bob.jones). The recipient can then access the email from his mailbox as shown in Figure 1-5.

Figure 1-5

Resolving MX Records

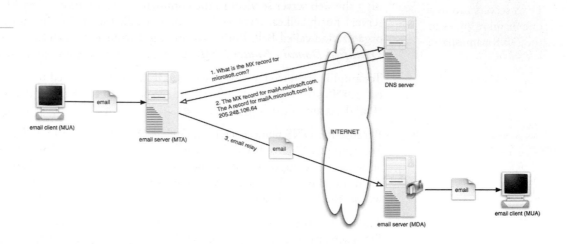

Because there may be more than one email server in a particular organization, domains may have more than one MX record. Each MX record is given a *priority number* when created. The lower the priority number, the greater the chance that it will be a target for email. Consider the following MX records for the microsoft.com domain:

```
microsoft.com    MX    mailA.microsoft.com    priority=10

microsoft.com    MX    mailB.microsoft.com    priority=20

microsoft.com    MX    mailC.microsoft.com    priority=30
```

If an MTA queries a DNS server for the MX record for microsoft.com, the DNS server returns all three MX records and their priority numbers. The MTA then tries to contact the email server with the lowest priority number first (mailA.microsoft.com). If mailA.microsoft .com could not be contacted, then the MTA tries to contact the email server with the second lowest priority (mailB.microsoft.com), and so on.

This is useful in companies that wish to have a backup email server. In the previous example, mailB.microsoft.com would only be contacted if mailA.microsoft.com was unavailable.

Similarly, some organizations use smart hosts to receive email from the Internet. A *smart host* is an email server that receives inbound email and simply forwards it to another email server within the organization. Smart hosts often have antivirus and spam-filtering software that stops malicious and unsolicited email from entering the company.

The MX record for the smart host should have a lower priority number than other MX records. In the earlier example, mailA.microsoft.com could be the smart host email server and would receive all emails by default. If mailA.microsoft.com was unavailable, then email would be sent to the internal mail server (mailB.microsoft.com) or to the backup internal mail server (mailC.microsoft.com) if mailB.microsoft.com was unavailable.

In larger organizations, there may be several MX records for different email servers that have the same priority:

```
microsoft.com     MX     mailA.microsoft.com     priority=10

microsoft.com     MX     mailB.microsoft.com     priority=10

microsoft.com     MX     mailC.microsoft.com     priority=10
```

Just as before, when the MTA queries a DNS server for the MX record for microsoft.com, the DNS server returns all three MX records. Because the priority numbers are the same on all three records, the MTA tries to contact the email server that is first in the list (mailA.microsoft.com). If mailA.microsoft.com could not be contacted, then the MTA tries to contact the email server that is second in the list (mailB.microsoft.com), and so on.

Although this initially achieves the same result, DNS will rotate the list of MX records each time an MTA sends an MX record query. This feature of DNS is called *round robin*. Thus, the next time an MTA queries the MX records for microsoft.com, it will receive the following list:

```
microsoft.com     MX     mailB.microsoft.com     priority=10

microsoft.com     MX     mailC.microsoft.com     priority=10

microsoft.com     MX     mailA.microsoft.com     priority=10
```

Now, the first email server to be contacted is mailB.microsoft.com. Similarly, the third MX record query will return a list with mailC.microsoft.com at the top of the list and the fourth MX record query will return the original list with mailA.microsoft.com at the top of the list.

By keeping the same priorities on MX records, you can balance the load of traffic evenly across each of the three email servers. These three email servers may be internal email servers, or they may be smart hosts that will forward email to internal mail servers.

XREF

Creating MX records in DNS is a common task after installing Exchange Server 2007. As a result, MX record creation is discussed in Lesson 4, "Configuring a New Exchange Server."

 TEST DNS NAME RESOLUTION USING NSLOOKUP

GET READY. Log on to Windows Server 2003, and open a command prompt window.

1. Type nslookup at the command prompt and press **Enter**.

2. At the **nslookup** prompt, type **www.yahoo.com** and press **Enter**. Notice the IP address for the Yahoo web server. The nslookup.exe command queries A records by default.

3. At the nslookup prompt, type **set q=mx** and press **Enter**. This tells nslookup.exe to obtain MX records on future queries.

4. At the nslookup prompt, type **yahoo.com** and press **Enter**. Notice that there are several MX records with the same priority (or preference) for the yahoo.com domain. Record the order of the MX records. Also note that the nslookup.exe command returns the IP addresses for each email server from the associated A records.

5. At the nslookup prompt, type **yahoo.com** and press **Enter**. Notice that the order of the MX records for the yahoo.com domain is different from the previous step due to the round robin feature of DNS.

6. Type **exit** at the nslookup prompt and press **Enter**.

7. Type **exit** at the command prompt and press **Enter**.

ANOTHER WAY

You can also type **set type=mx** at the nslookup prompt to tell nslookup .exe to obtain MX records on future queries.

Email Formats and Protocols

Today, email systems are very complex and involve several different technologies for sending and receiving emails. Possessing knowledge of the many protocols used to send and receive emails is a vital asset when examining the structure of Exchange Server 2007.

When you type an email into an MUA, the text itself is either left unformatted (called *plain text*) or formatted using *Hypertext Markup Language (HTML)* or *Rich Text Format (RTF)* to allow different font, colors, and pictures.

Regardless of the email format, MUAs, MTAs, and MDAs must also use specific *email protocols* when sending email across a network. The most common email protocols include:

- SMTP (Simple Mail Transfer Protocol)
- SMTPS (Secure Simple Mail Transfer Protocol)
- ESMTP (Extended Simple Mail Transfer Protocol)
- ESMTPS (Secure Extended Simple Mail Transfer Protocol)
- POP3 (Post Office Protocol Version 3)
- POP3S (Secure Post Office Protocol Version 3)
- IMAP4 (Internet Message Access Protocol Version 4)
- IMAP4S (Secure Internet Message Access Protocol Version 4)
- HTTP (Hypertext Transfer Protocol)
- HTTPS (Secure Hypertext Transfer Protocol)
- RPC (Remote Procedure Call)
- RPC (Remote Procedure Call) over HTTP/HTTPS
- ActiveSync

> **TAKE NOTE** *
>
> All protocols that end with S (SMTPS, ESMTPS, POP3S, IMAP4S, and HTTPS) use *Secure Socket Layer (SSL)* encryption or *Transport Layer Security (TLS)* encryption to protect the contents of emails.

The protocols available depend on whether the email is being sent from an MUA to an MTA, from an MTA to an MDA, or from a mailbox to an MUA as shown in Figure 1-6. For example, when an MUA sends email to an MTA, one of the following protocols may be used:

- SMTP/SMTPS
- ESMTP/ESMTPS
- HTTP/HTTPS
- RPC
- RPC over HTTP/HTTPS
- ActiveSync

Alternatively, when an MUA receives email from a mailbox, it uses only one of the following protocols:

- POP3/POP3S
- IMAP4/IMAP4S
- HTTP/HTTPS
- RPC
- RPC over HTTP/HTTPS
- ActiveSync

Finally, when an MTA relays email to an MDA, it can use one of the following protocols only:

- SMTP/SMTPS
- ESMTP/ESMTPS
- RPC
- RPC over HTTP/HTTPS

Figure 1-6

Email Protocols

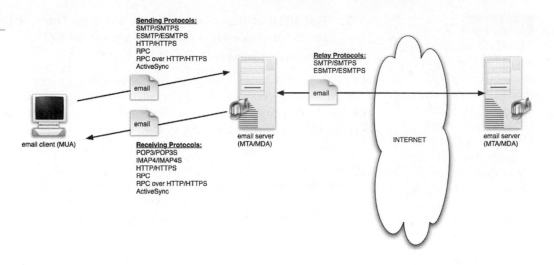

Figure 1-6

Email Protocols

TAKE NOTE *****

You can optionally configure POP3 to leave a copy of emails in your mailbox on the email server.

The POP3 and IMAP4 protocols are very similar and designed for obtaining emails from the mailbox on an email server. By default, POP3 downloads and erases the email from the mailbox on the email server, whereas IMAP4 allows you to view emails while leaving a copy in the mailbox on the email server. In addition, IMAP4 can support larger emails than POP3.

Although IMAP4 was designed as a replacement for POP3, POP3 continues to be one of the most common email protocols on the Internet between ISPs and home clients.

The SMTP and ESMTP protocols were specifically designed to send emails rather than obtain them. When you configure a POP3 or IMAP4 email account in an MUA, you must supply the name or IP address of the email server that hosts the POP3 or IMAP4 service to receive email, as well as the name or IP address of a server that hosts the SMTP service so that you can send email.

ESMTP is an improved version of SMTP that has greater support for embedded graphics and attachments in emails and is the most common form of SMTP used today between email servers. To see which version of SMTP your email server accepts, you can use the telnet.exe program from a client computer to connect to the email server on the SMTP/ESMTP port (25 by default). If the email server accepts the EHLO command in your telnet session, it supports ESMTP. Alternatively, if the email server accepts the HELO command in your telnet session, it only supports SMTP.

TAKE NOTE *****

Although email servers and clients use the term SMTP in most of their configuration options, they actually mean ESMTP. As a result, SMTP is often used when referring to both SMTP and ESMTP.

➔ **VERIFY ESMTP SUPPORT ON AN EMAIL SERVER**

GET READY. Log on to Windows Server 2003, and open a command prompt window.

TAKE NOTE *****

If you are trying this exercise on a home Internet connection and you do not receive any response from a target email server, your ISP may not allow traffic from your home computer on port 25.

1. Type **nslookup** at the command prompt and press **Enter**.
2. At the nslookup prompt, type **set q=mx** and press **Enter**.
3. At the nslookup prompt, type **yahoo.com** and press **Enter**. Record the IP address of the first Yahoo email server.
4. Type **exit** at the nslookup prompt and press **Enter**.
5. Type **telnet** *IP_address* **25** at the nslookup prompt (where *IP_address* refers to the IP address of the first Yahoo email server from Step 3) and press **Enter**.
6. Type **EHLO** at the command prompt and press **Enter**. Notice that the Yahoo email server supports ESMTP.

7. Type **HELO** at the command prompt and press **Enter**. Notice that the Yahoo email server has backwards compatibility support for SMTP.

8. Close your command window.

HTTP is typically used if the email server hosts a Web site that allows you to view and compose emails using your web browser or email client program. Microsoft ***Outlook Web Access (OWA)*** comes with Exchange Server 2007 and may be used with ***Internet Information Services (IIS)*** to provide a way for users to connect remotely using a web browser to check and send email.

RPC-based protocols are used to provide a variety of protocols across a network. Microsoft Outlook and Entourage clients can use RPCs alongside the Microsoft ***Messaging Application Programming Interface (MAPI)*** component of Windows to take advantage of all the features available in Exchange Server. However, RPC-based protocols are not well suited for use with remote clients because RPC traffic is relatively bandwidth intensive compared to other protocols and requires unnecessary ports to be opened on firewalls.

TAKE NOTE *

Because Microsoft email clients such as Outlook and Entourage can use MAPI and RPCs to send and receive emails, these clients are often called ***MAPI clients*** in Exchange Server 2007. Likewise, the term ***MAPI RPC*** usually refers to the MAPI implementation of the RPC email protocol.

As a result of these limitations, Outlook 2003 and later clients can use RPC over HTTP to connect to a remote Microsoft Exchange server. RPCs are encapsulated in HTTP packets in Outlook before they are sent across the Internet to an RPC over HTTP proxy, which removes the encapsulation and forwards the RPCs to the Microsoft Exchange server. In Microsoft Exchange Server 2007, RPC over HTTP is called ***Outlook Anywhere***.

ActiveSync is a protocol based on HTTP and XML that can be used by some browser-enabled cellular telephones (called ***smart phones***) to access emails from a Microsoft Exchange server. Any smart phone running the Windows Mobile operating system can use the ActiveSync protocol.

■ Introducing Exchange Server 2007

THE BOTTOM LINE

Now that you have an understanding of email systems, you can apply that knowledge to Exchange Server 2007. In addition to several new features, Exchange Server 2007 introduces a role-based structure that is radically different from the structure used in previous versions of Exchange. Understanding the features and structure of Exchange Server 2007 compared to its predecessors is vital when deploying and configuring Exchange Server 2007 email servers within your organization.

Exchange Server Overview

Prior to Exchange Server 2007, there were three other major versions of Exchange Server. Understanding their features will help you understand how Exchange Server 2007 operates in a mixed environment.

Exchange Server is Microsoft's email server product. In addition to the typical MTA and MDA functions, Exchange Server has several extra features to enhance business productivity (such as personal calendars, scheduling, and contact management) that work with MUAs.

TAKE NOTE *

Only MAPI clients can take full advantage of all the features in Exchange Server.

There are four main versions of Exchange that are used in organizations today:

- Exchange Server 5.5
- Exchange Server 2000
- Exchange Server 2003
- Exchange Server 2007

Microsoft originally developed Exchange Server for its own internal use to replace its UNIX-based email system. As a result, the first commercial release of Exchange Server started at version 4.0 in 1996. However, Exchange Server didn't gain market momentum until 1997 when Exchange Server 5.5 was released. Exchange Server 5.5 had full support for SMTP as well as the International Telecommunication Union (ITU) X.400 and X.500 standards. *X.400* defines the rules for sending email today, whereas *X.500* defines the structure and use of directory services such as Novell eDirectory and Microsoft *Active Directory (AD)*. In addition, Exchange 5.5 made efficient use of *public folders*, which were storage areas on the email server that could be used to store email and other types of message data such as newsgroup postings for easy organization and sharing among email recipients.

Exchange 5.5 also introduced the OWA web-based email interface to allow remote clients the ability to check their email with their web browser. For fast storage and retrieval of email, Exchange 5.5 stores mailboxes in an email *database* on the hard drive of the Exchange server.

Exchange Server 2000 was released shortly after Windows 2000 and added better clustering support, larger email database sizes, and the ability to combine email databases into *storage groups* for better database management. It was also the first version of Exchange Server that required the Microsoft Active Directory service.

 REF   Exchange Server 2007 is closely integrated with the Active Directory service. For more information on Active Directory, refer to Lesson 2, "Working with Active Directory."

Exchange Server 2003 followed the release of Windows Server 2003 and had tools that could easily upgrade Exchange Server 5.5 and 2000 email servers. As a result, many organizations that deployed Exchange Server 5.5 did not upgrade their email servers until Exchange Server 2003 was available. In addition to the features in previous versions, Exchange Server 2003 added support for disaster recovery using the *recovery storage group (RSG)*, as well as ActiveSync and spam filtering. However, Exchange Server 2003 could be installed only on 32-bit versions of Windows 2000 Server and Windows Server 2003.

Exchange Server 2007 offers many different tools and features compared to previous versions of Exchange Server as will be discussed in the next section.

What's New in Exchange Server 2007

Exchange Server 2007 contains many new features and improvements that make it Microsoft's most advanced email server today. Understanding these features and improvements is essential before deploying Exchange Server 2007 in a Windows network environment.

Like previous versions of Exchange Server, Exchange Server 2007 comes in two editions: Standard and Enterprise. The Enterprise edition contains more support for hardware and extra features that are unavailable in the Standard edition.

Exchange Server 2007 has a vastly different structure compared to previous versions of Exchange Server.

Although you can download a trial 32-bit (x86) version of Exchange Server 2007 for testing purposes, the commercial version only runs on 64-bit (x86-64) computers with a 64-bit version of Windows Server 2003. Because previous versions of Exchange ran only on 32-bit computers, organizations can no longer perform in-place upgrades to Exchange Server 2007. Instead, organizations must purchase new hardware to run Exchange Server 2007 and migrate existing mailboxes to the new servers.

If you want to install Exchange Server 2007 on a 64-bit version of Windows Server 2008, you must install Exchange Server 2007 Service Pack 1 (SP1) or greater. See Lesson 3, "Deploying Exchange Server 2007" for more information.

Exchange Server 2007 has several new features that make it an attractive choice for email relay. These features include:

1. Enhanced performance.

    Because Exchange Server 2007 only runs in 64-bit production environments, it can take advantage of more than 4 GB of physical RAM. Having more than 4 GB of RAM allows Exchange Server to speed up Input/Output (I/O) requests to hard disks as well as support more email databases and storage groups.

    Exchange Server 2007 is limited to 5 databases and storage groups on a single server for Standard edition and 50 databases and storage groups on a single server for Enterprise edition. For comparison, Exchange Server 2003 was limited to 1 database and storage group for Standard edition or 20 databases and 4 storage groups for Enterprise edition.

    Databases also have a faster structure in Exchange Server 2007 than in previous versions of Exchange Server. The smallest writable unit within an email database is called a *page*. A larger database page size increases the likelihood that an entire email will be read using a single I/O request. The 8 KB page size used in Exchange Server 2007 databases is twice the page size used in previous versions of Exchange and adds to the overall speed of Exchange Server.

2. Unlimited database size.

    Previous versions of Exchange Server had a maximum database size of 16 terabytes (TB). Exchange Server 2007 database sizes are theoretically unlimited. In practice, the maximum database size on Exchange Server 2007 is only limited by hardware capability and backup requirements. This allows an email database to grow at the same pace as an organization's email needs.

3. Fax and voice mail integration.

    Using the *Unified Messaging (UM)* feature of Exchange Server 2007, you can integrate voice mail and faxes into your email system. Users can then configure call answering or access their voice mail, faxes, and email from Outlook, Entourage, OWA, or a smart phone running the Windows Mobile operating system.

    Similarly, you can use *Outlook Voice Access (OVA)* to access your mailbox from a telephone. Your emails and calendar appointments can be read to you over the phone line, or you can send or forward email messages using the voice recognition feature of OVA.

4. Improved management tools.

    Exchange Server 2007 has consolidated and refined its graphical tools used for managing the Exchange server as well as provided a new scriptable command-line interface.

✚ MORE INFORMATION

When configuring previous versions of Exchange Server, you typically used a graphical utility such as Exchange Administrator (Exchange 5.5) or Exchange System Manager (Exchange 2000 and 2003). Neither of these utilities exist in Exchange Server 2007.

The new ***Exchange Management Console (EMC)*** in Exchange Server 2007 uses the new and more intuitive Microsoft Management Console (MMC) version 3.0 interface. This interface has four panes as shown in Figure 1-7.

Figure 1-7

The Exchange Management Console

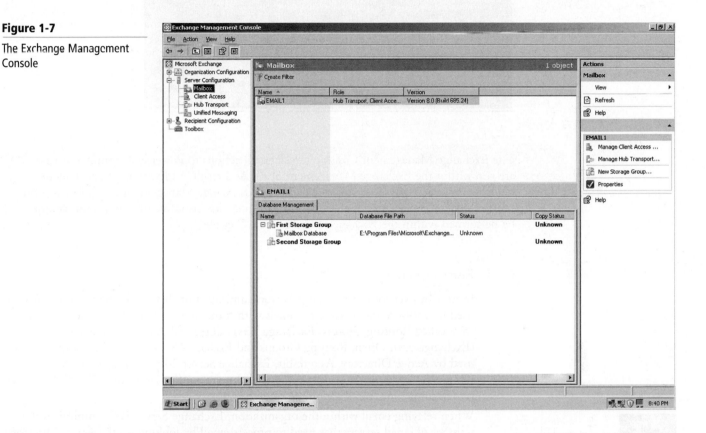

The Console Tree allows you to navigate to different areas of the utility, whereas the Action Pane displays common task shortcuts that correspond to the object highlighted in the Console Tree. You can use the Result Pane to view properties for an object in the Console Tree and the Work Pane to modify those properties.

The Exchange Management Console also provides a centralized graphical interface for administration. To manage email settings for individual users in Exchange Server 2000 and 2003, you needed to open the properties of user accounts in the Active Directory Users and Computers console. All of these tasks can now be done within the Exchange Management Console in Exchange Server 2007.

In addition to the Exchange Management Console, Exchange Server 2007 offers the ***Exchange Management Shell (EMS)***, which is a snap-in for the Windows ***PowerShell*** scripting language. The Exchange Management Console has almost 400 Exchange-specific commands called ***cmdlets*** that may be used to configure and manage Exchange Server 2007. For standardization and easy recall, cmdlets are verb-noun combinations that define the action that is performed (verb) followed by the object or area that is affected (noun). For example, the **Remove-PublicFolder** cmdlet can be used to remove a public folder on an Exchange server, whereas the **Set-Mailbox** cmdlet can be used to set parameters for a user's mailbox. In addition, cmdlets may be combined in useful ways using UNIX-style data redirection or stored in reusable script files to automate complex tasks. An example of the Exchange Management Shell interface is shown in Figure 1-8.

Figure 1-8

The Exchange Management Shell

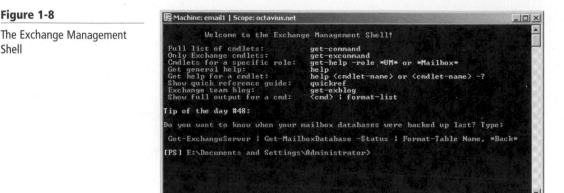

> The Exchange Management Console translates all actions to PowerShell commands that are run within the Exchange Management Shell. As a result, all Exchange Management Console functions may be performed within the Exchange Management Shell. In addition, the Exchange Management Shell can perform some administrative functions that cannot be performed within the Exchange Management Console.

TAKE NOTE *

5. Faster email relay.

   In previous versions of Exchange Server, administrators had to define objects that were used to optimize the delivery of emails within the same organization. These objects were called Routing Groups (Exchange Server 2000 and 2003) and Exchange Sites (Exchange 5.5). Often, Routing Groups and Exchange Sites mirrored the *site* structure used by Active Directory. As a result, Exchange Server 2007 no longer creates Routing Groups or Exchange Sites. Instead, it uses the site configuration from Active Directory to determine how email should be routed.

   When relaying email within the organization, Exchange Server 2007 minimizes the number of email servers that need to process email by looking up the Active Directory site configuration and calculating the quickest route to the destination email server. Email is then routed directly to the destination email server.

   For faster email relay outside the organization, Exchange Server 2007 no longer relies on the SMTP service within the Internet Information Services (IIS) component of Windows. Instead, Exchange Server 2007 ships with its own SMTP service that is optimized to work directly with the new components in Exchange Server 2007.

X REF

The configuration of Active Directory sites is discussed in Lesson 2, "Working with Active Directory."

TAKE NOTE *

Spam is often referred to as junk email. Although it is often used to advertise a product or service, spam includes any email that is unsolicited and not part of normal business or personal communications.

6. Enhanced email protection.

   Exchange Server 2007 comes with improved email filtering to reduce the number of malicious and *spam* messages. Emails that have been scanned by antivirus software are tagged before they are routed within the organization, giving destination computers better control over emails that may be malicious and should be scanned locally for viruses. In addition, Exchange Server 2007 can now use the Junk Email Filter Lists from its Outlook 2003, Outlook 2007, and Entourage clients to filter emails at the server level.

7. Managed folder support.

   Today, many organizations require that important emails be saved for legal or business reasons. In Exchange Server 2007, you can use the *Messaging Records Management (MRM)* feature to create a specific folder within a user's mailbox called a *managed folder*.

You can then specify custom settings for managed folders that prevent emails from being deleted by the Exchange server for a certain period of time. Users can then store important emails in their managed folder to satisfy the needs of their organization.

8. Better user experience.

    Exchange also boasts several improvements that are geared toward the user. The OWA interface now supports ActiveSync and has additional functions as well as a new design that work together to make it easier to use. Outlook and Entourage clients will notice more reliable and efficient calendaring functionality as well as the ability to customize how Out of Office messages are sent.

9. Improved clustering support.

    In Exchange Server 2003, you could provide redundancy for your entire email server by installing a second Exchange server and configuring Windows Cluster Services to create an Exchange Server *cluster*. Both of the Exchange servers, or *nodes*, needed to share the same external storage device for storing emails and had to run in one of two cluster modes. In Active/Passive mode, one of the Exchange servers (the active node) was active and in use on the network, while the other node (the passive node) was only used if the active node became unavailable (a process called *failover*). In Active/Active mode, each node was actively used. Failover would occur if one of the active nodes became unavailable, and the other Exchange server would handle twice its normal load.

    The main downside of failover is that it only protects against the failure of a server and not the data on the shared storage device. As a result, Exchange Server 2007 introduces several new types of clustering based on existing clustering methods used on database servers.

    In *Cluster Continuous Replication (CCR)* and *Standby Continuous Replication (SCR)*, you can configure Exchange Server 2007 to replicate its email data continuously to another Exchange server on a local or remote network. CCR requires that the target Exchange server be installed in the same cluster whereas SCR does not. Because each Exchange server maintains its own storage, the email data is protected when a failure occurs.

    Similarly, you can configure Exchange Server 2007 to replicate its email data continuously to another local hard drive as a form of backup in case the main hard disk fails. This is called *Local Continuous Replication (LCR)*.

10. Role-based deployment.

    To make the deployment of Exchange Server easier in organizations that deploy several email servers, Exchange Server 2007 introduces five *server roles* that define the functions that will be available on a particular email server. In smaller organizations, a single server can be configured with several server roles. However, in larger organizations, you can spread different server roles across multiple email servers to enhance email security and speed up email relay. The five server roles in Exchange Server 2007 are discussed in the next section of this lesson.

TAKE NOTE *

Support for Active/Active mode clustering has been discontinued with Exchange Server 2007. You can still use Active/Passive mode clustering with Exchange Server 2007 by creating a *Single Copy Cluster (SCC)*.

TAKE NOTE *

To use SCR, you must have Exchange Server 2007 SP1.

➕ MORE INFORMATION

Some features that were available in previous versions of Exchange Server are no longer available in Exchange Server 2007. The most important of these include the creation of direct connectors to other email systems such as Novell GroupWise, Lotus Notes, and legacy X.400 MTA. Messages sent to these systems must be relayed across the Internet with all other public email. If you need to create connectors to these systems, you must use an Exchange Server 2003 computer within your organization.

Exchange Server 2007 Roles

Server roles are used by Exchange Server 2007 to refine the services that are available on a particular email server. This allows administrators to adapt Exchange Server 2007 to the particular environment in which it will be used. Before you deploy Exchange Server 2007, you must have a good understanding of the five server roles and how they may be used together within an organization.

As mentioned in the previous section, one of the key differences between Exchange Server 2007 and previous versions of Exchange Server is its role-based architecture. Exchange Server 2007 introduces five server roles that are specifically designed to help email administrators better control how Exchange Server 2007 relays email internally within their own organization. In addition, server roles make it easier for email administrators to deploy multiple Exchange servers within the same organization as well as grow their email infrastructure. Table 1-1 lists the five server roles available in Exchange Server 2007.

Table 1-1

The five server roles in Exchange Server 2007

SERVER ROLE	DESCRIPTION
Client Access Server (CAS)	Allows email clients access to their mailboxes using OWA (HTTP/HTTPS), POP3, IMAP4, Outlook Anywhere (RPC over HTTP/HTTPS), ActiveSync, and MAPI (RPC).
Mailbox	Responsible for hosting and providing access to the databases that contain mailboxes and public folders.
Hub Transport (Hub)	Handles all email relay within the organization and is functionally equivalent to the MTA and MDA in a generic email system. The Hub role is integrated with the Active Directory service and uses Exchange Server 2007 configuration stored in Active Directory to direct and restrict email flow.
Edge Transport (Edge)	Functionally equivalent to the smart host role in a generic email system although it is optional. It offers antivirus and antispam protection to provide extra security at the edge or perimeter of your network. All email sent to or received from the Internet passes through servers that hold this role. For added security, the Edge role cannot directly access Active Directory. Instead, only the information from Active Directory that is used to filter emails is sent from Hub servers to Edge servers via a special protocol called EdgeSync.
Unified Messaging (UM)	Allows users to access email, voice mail, and fax messages from a MAPI client, OWA, smart phone, or telephone. It is optional.

A single Exchange server can run all of the server roles simultaneously with the exception of the Edge role, which must run on its own Exchange server.

Server roles are chosen during the installation of Exchange Server 2007. For more information on the installation of Exchange Server 2007, refer to Lesson 3, "Deploying Exchange Server 2007."

By default, Exchange Server 2007 installs the CAS, Mailbox, and Hub roles to allow email access, storage, and relay as shown in Figure 1-9.

Figure 1-9

The Default Exchange Server Roles

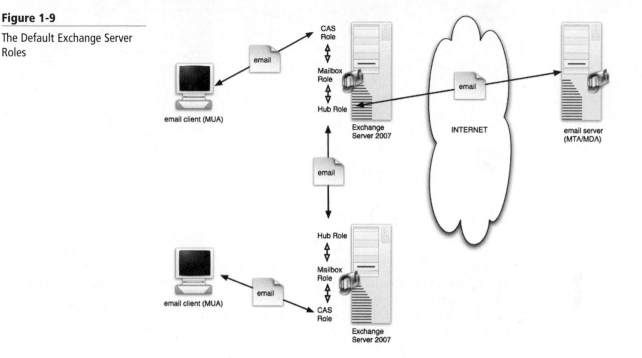

The Hub role performs all internal and external email relay. Internal email is sent to the correct destination email servers using recipient information in Active Directory. Before external email is sent, the Hub role must use DNS MX records to locate the destination email server. Similarly, MX records must exist in DNS for at least one email server in your organization that contains the Hub role to allow external email servers the ability to relay email to your organization. In addition, nearly all organizations use a firewall between their internal networks and the Internet. As a result, you also need to ensure that incoming SMTP/ESMTP traffic (TCP/IP port 25) is allowed to reach the servers that perform the Hub role.

In larger organizations that have more demanding email relay requirements, you can divide the CAS, Mailbox, and Hub roles among several email servers. These servers can be placed strategically to allow for improved email performance. For example, placing servers that have the CAS role close to client computers will speed up email access times.

One of the main problems that organizations face today is security. For email systems, incoming email from the Internet may be malicious (contain viruses) or unsolicited (spam).

As a result, many organizations install antivirus and antispam software on their email servers. However, this software uses a great deal of server resources and will adversely affect the performance of the email server as a result. After installing antispam and antivirus software on an Exchange server that is running the CAS, Mailbox, or Hub role, clients will notice that it takes longer to access the server, obtain email from their mailbox, use their calendar, and send email to others in the same organization.

To solve this problem, you can implement an Exchange server that is running the Edge role on the perimeter of your network to filter Internet-based email traffic using antivirus and antispam software. Figure 1-10 shows how an Edge role may be used to alter email relay.

Figure 1-10

Using the Edge Server Role

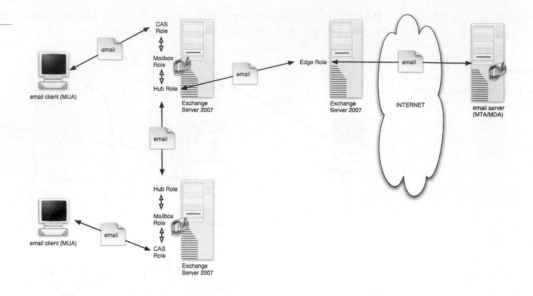

If the Edge role is used within your organization, DNS MX records for your organization should point to the servers that contain the Edge role. This forces all incoming Internet email to be sent to the servers that contain the Edge role. These servers will then filter emails for spam and viruses before they relay the emails to the servers that hold the Hub transport role for delivery to the correct mailbox.

TAKE NOTE *

Larger organizations will likely have multiple servers that contain the Edge role. For round robin load balancing, DNS MX records for these servers should have the same priority number.

The Edge role only deals with Internet-based email and does not affect internal email processed by the CAS, Mailbox, and Hub roles. Because most email sent by an organization is addressed to internal recipients, you will obtain better email performance by using the Edge role to protect Internet-based email rather than installing antivirus and antispam software on other server roles.

TAKE NOTE *

Although the Edge role cannot coexist on the same computer as other server roles, you can install the antivirus and antispam capabilities of the Edge role on an Exchange server that had the Hub role. However, this is not recommended for performance reasons.

Furthermore, the Edge role does not depend on Active Directory to function. As a result, Exchange servers that contain the Edge role do not need to be part of an Active Directory domain. However, the Edge role will need access to some configuration and user information in Active Directory to filter emails. This information is periodically sent to the Edge role server from servers that run the Hub role using a special protocol called **_EdgeSync_**.

➕ **MORE INFORMATION**

To obtain information using EdgeSync, Windows Server 2003 computers that run the Edge role must be running the Active Directory Application Mode (ADAM) service. Similarly, Windows Server 2008 computers that run the Edge role must have the Active Directory Lightweight Directory Services (ADLDS).

You can optionally install one or more UM roles within your organization to allow voice mail, faxes, and email to be accessed by MAPI, OWA, and smart phone clients in your organization. UM functions as a relay between a company's existing internal telephone system, called a ***Private Branch eXchange (PBX)***, and the other email servers within your organization as shown in Figure 1-11.

Figure 1-11

Using the UM Server Role

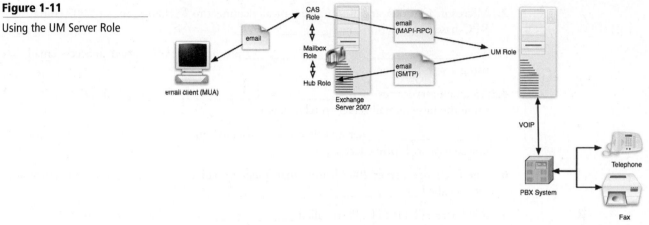

Incoming voice mail and fax messages recorded by the PBX are forwarded to a server running the UM role using the ***Voice Over IP (VOIP)*** protocol. The UM role then searches the Active Directory service to locate the users that match the telephone extension of the incoming voice mail or fax message. Once located, the UM role converts the voice mail or fax message to an email format and forwards it to the Hub role using SMTP for delivery to the correct mailbox.

To provide remote access to mailboxes from a phone line using OVA, the UM role also communicates directly with the CAS role using MAPI and the RPC protocol to access the appropriate information. This information is then converted to synthetic voice by the UM role and sent to the PBX system using VOIP.

SUMMARY SKILL MATRIX

IN THIS LESSON YOU LEARNED:

* Email is composed using an MUA on an email client and relayed to the recipients mailbox using MTAs and MDAs on email servers.

* For email to be routed across the Internet, MX records must exist in DNS to locate destination email servers that host mailboxes for recipients.

* Email clients and servers communicate using email protocols such as SMTP/ESMTP, IMAP4, POP3, HTTP, RPC, and ActiveSync. Different protocols are used to perform different parts of the email relay process.

* There were three widely used versions of Exchange Server before Exchange Server 2007: Exchange Server 5.5, Exchange Server 2000, and Exchange Server 2003. Each version has different features and support.

* Exchange Server 2007 offers better performance, additional security, enhanced tools, and more features than previous versions of Exchange Server.

* To enhance deployment and scalability, Exchange Server 2007 uses five server roles to define the services that are available on a particular Exchange server: CAS, Mailbox, Hub, Edge, and UM.

■ Knowledge Assessment

Fill in the Blank

Complete the following sentences by writing the correct word or words in the blanks provided.

1. The program used to send email on an email client is also called a _____.

2. Microsoft Outlook and Entourage typically connect to Exchange Server 2007 using RPC-based connections and _____.

3. The _____ and _____ protocols are often used to access email using a web browser.

4. An email server uses _____ and _____ records in DNS to determine the target email server to relay email to.

5. The _____ server role must be installed on its own Exchange server and cannot coexist with other server roles.

6. The Exchange Server 2007 feature that integrates voice mail and fax into an email system is called _____.

7. RPC over HTTP/HTTPS is called _____ in Exchange Server 2007.

8. _____ is a new type of clustering in Exchange Server 2007 that can be used to perform continuous backups of data to a local hard drive.

9. If a DNS server returns several MX records with different priorities, the one with the _____ priority is contacted first.

10. Exchange Management Shell is a command-based administration tool in Exchange Server 2007 that is based on _____.

Multiple Choice

Circle the letter that corresponds to the best answer.

1. Which of the following server roles in Exchange Server 2007 handles POP3 connections from client computers?
   - **a.** CAS
   - **b.** Hub
   - **c.** Mailbox
   - **d.** Edge

2. Outlook Web Access (OWA) relies on the _____ component of Windows.
   - **a.** Site
   - **b.** PowerShell
   - **c.** IIS
   - **d.** RPC

3. Which of the following email protocols encrypts data during transfer?
   - **a.** ESMTPS
   - **b.** IMAP4
   - **c.** HTTP
   - **d.** RPC

4. What DNS feature rotates the order of MX records before they are given to the email server that requested them?
   - **a.** Failover
   - **b.** MX ordering
   - **c.** Priorities
   - **d.** Round robin

5. Which of the following is not a valid email message format?
   - **a.** Plain text
   - **b.** RPC
   - **c.** HTML
   - **d.** Rich Text

6. Which of the following protocols can be used to obtain email from an email server? (Choose all that apply.)
   - **a.** SMTP
   - **b.** MAPI RPC
   - **c.** POP3
   - **d.** IMAP4

7. Which of the following priority numbers will most likely be assigned to the DNS MX record that is used to identify a smart host?
   - **a.** 10
   - **b.** 255
   - **c.** 99
   - **d.** 5

8. Which of the following is not a valid cmdlet structure?
   - **a.** Get-PublicFolder
   - **b.** Enable-MailboxDatabase
   - **c.** Email-Send
   - **d.** Update-Content

9. Which of the following allows Exchange Server 2007 to scale from small to large organizations? (Choose all that apply.)
   - **a.** 64-bit architecture
   - **b.** separation of roles
   - **c.** unlimited database size
   - **d.** support for new business requirements such as UM and MRM

10. What must be configured if your organization uses the Edge role?
    - **a.** ActiveSync
    - **b.** EdgeSync
    - **c.** X.400
    - **d.** MAPI

True/False

Circle T if the statement is true or F if the statement is false.

T | F **1.** Servers that contain the Edge role access their configuration information from the Active Directory database.

T | F **2.** Email systems typically adhere to the X.400 directory service standard.

T | F **3.** Exchange servers store mailboxes in a database.

T | F **4.** The Exchange Management Shell (EMS) can only perform a subset of the functions available in the Exchange Management Console (EMC).

T | F **5.** IMAP4 was designed as a more robust replacement for POP3.

Matching

Match the term in Column 1 to its description in Column 2.

- **a.** PBX
- **b.** MTA
- **c.** ActiveSync
- **d.** Edge
- **e.** Thunderbird

_____ **1.** A server role that provides smart host capabilities in Exchange Server 2007.

_____ **2.** A common Mail User Agent (MUA).

_____ **3.** A software program that relays mail across computer networks such as the Internet.

_____ **4.** Sends fax and voice mail to the Unified Messaging (UM) role.

_____ **5.** An email protocol used by smart phones.

Review Questions

1. Outline the process and protocols used to relay email on the Internet.
2. Describe the protocols that email clients can use to obtain email from an email server as well as to send email to an email server.

■ Case Scenarios

Scenario 1-1: Creating a Proposal

You are the network administrator for a medium-sized organization. Currently, your organization has been using Windows 2000 servers running Exchange Server 2000 to provide email services. Your manager has asked you whether the organization should consider replacing its current Exchange servers with new servers that run Exchange Server 2007. Prepare a short proposal outlining the key benefits and costs associated with replacing the current Exchange server with several servers running Exchange Server 2007.

Scenario 1-2: Designing Server Roles

Your company has opened a new division that will employ 200 people and work under its own Internet identity. This new division will need a secure email system that allows internal Outlook clients to check their emails, fax, and voice mail. In addition, mobile clients require the ability to check their email from a telephone or smart phone. In a short memo, diagram the necessary server roles and email protocols that will need to be implemented in this new environment using Exchange Server 2007.

Working with Active Directory

LESSON SKILL MATRIX

TECHNOLOGY SKILL	OBJECTIVE DOMAIN
Describe the purpose and function of Active Directory.	Supplemental
Understand the structure of Active Directory.	Supplemental
Understand the function of groups, functional levels, sites, global catalog, and FSMO roles in an Active Directory environment.	Supplemental
Raise domain and forest functional levels.	Supplemental
Configure Active Directory sites.	Supplemental
Administer FSMOs, global catalog, and Trusts.	Supplemental
Create and manage OU, user, group, and computer objects.	Supplemental
Configure GPOs.	Supplemental

KEY TERMS

Active Directory Domains and
  Trusts
Active Directory Sites and
  Services
Active Directory Users and
  Computers
bridgehead server
container object
directory partitions
distribution group
domain
Domain Controller (DC)
domain functional level
Domain Naming Master
dynamic update
Flexible Single Master
  Operations (FSMO)
forest

forest functional level
forest root domain
global catalog (GC)
Globally Unique IDentifier
  (GUID)
Group Policy Objects (GPOs)
group scope
Infrastructure Master
Kerberos
leaf object
Lightweight Directory Access
  Protocol (LDAP)
PDC Emulator
RID Master
Schema Master
Security Accounts
  Manager (SAM)
security group

Security IDentifier (SID)
service record (SRV)
site link
site object
subnet object
tree
trust relationship
Universal Group Membership
  Caching (UGMC)
User Principle Name (UPN)

■ Understanding the Structure of Active Directory

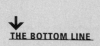

THE BOTTOM LINE

Exchange Server 2007 is tightly integrated with the Active Directory service. As a result, the configuration of Active Directory often affects the deployment and configuration of Exchange Server 2007. Due to the close relationship between users and email, many organizations also require that Exchange Server administrators provide Active Directory administration as part of their job role. Therefore, it is important to understand the function and configuration of Active Directory as an Exchange Server administrator.

What is Active Directory?

Active Directory was introduced with Windows 2000 Server to provide access to user and computer information within a domain. Before examining the various procedures used to administer Active Directory, it is important to first understand its function and features.

Active Directory (AD) is a Windows directory service that stores and retrieves information about users and network resources. The information stored in AD is used by programs and services to validate the identity of users (a process called *authentication*) as well as restrict resource access for users (a process called *authorization*).

Directory services such as AD are designed for network environments where there are more than 10 computers and users require secure access to network resources such as shared files or printers. All client and server computers must be specifically configured to use a directory service. Computers that require the use of AD must be configured to join an AD *domain* as well as use a DNS server that contains records for computers within the domain.

When you use an AD network, you typically log on to a client computer that is part of an AD domain. The client computer then forwards your user logon information to a directory services server in your domain called a *Domain Controller (DC)* that validates your username and password and issues you a *token* that lists your user and group information. Your domain token is destroyed when you log out of your client computer and re-created when you log in again.

TAKE NOTE *

To locate DCs, client computers must query their DNS server for *service records (SRV)* to identify the computers on the network that offer AD services.

➕ MORE INFORMATION

UNIX, Linux, Macintosh, Windows 2000, and later clients use the *Kerberos* ticket-based authentication protocol to log in to a DC and obtain a token. As a result, these tokens are often called *tickets*.

Each domain network resource contains an *Access Control List (ACL)*. The ACL lists the permissions that specific AD users have when accessing the resource. When you access a shared network resource, the server with the shared resource uses your token to verify your identity and enforce your permissions listed in the ACL. Provided that ACLs list only domain users, AD provides secure resource access because users not authenticated to the domain will be rejected when they attempt to access the resource.

TAKE NOTE *

Because remote computers use your token to verify your identity, you are not prompted to log on to other domain computers. As a result, you only need to log on once to a DC to access all the resources that you have permission to within the domain. This feature is often called *single sign-on*.

To allow computers to join domains and issue tokens to users, DCs must contain a *database* of *objects* such as user and computer accounts. This database is hierarchical and conforms to the International Telecommunication Union (ITU) X.500 standard. The AD service uses the *Lightweight Directory Access Protocol (LDAP)* to quickly access object information stored in the database.

Besides authentication and authorization, AD contains a powerful administrative feature called *Group Policy*. Group Policy can be used to automatically configure the software, security settings, and user interface on computers within an AD domain based on the location of the user or computer object within the AD database. Group Policy may also be used to deploy and remove software on domain computers.

To configure Group Policy, administrators create *Group Policy Objects (GPOs)* that have the appropriate settings. A single GPO can be applied to thousands of users and computers within an organization. This reduces the time and effort that it takes to administer a large domain.

Understanding Objects

AD uses leaf objects to represent users and resources, as well as container objects to organize resources. When you work with AD, it is important to understand the different types of objects and their uses.

The AD database can theoretically contain an unlimited number of objects. As a result, AD is scalable to any size of organization.

The total list of all available object types (called *classes*) and their associated properties (called *attributes*) is stored in the AD *schema*. Members of the Schema Admins group in AD can modify the schema to include more object types and attributes.

Objects that represent a user, computer, or resource are called *leaf objects* and contain attributes that are used by applications. For example, the UM role of Exchange Server 2007 uses the telephone extension attribute within each user account object in AD to match incoming voice mail to the appropriate mailbox.

The default leaf object classes that exist in AD include:

- User accounts
- Group accounts
- Computer accounts
- Printers
- Shared folders

Alternatively, some AD objects can contain leaf objects and are primarily used to organize leaf objects for quick location, delegation of administration, and the use of Group Policy. As a result, these objects are called *container objects* and provide the main structure of AD. There are three main container objects:

- Domains
- Organizational units (OUs)
- Sites

A domain object represents a particular organization or business unit and is given a unique DNS domain name as a result. Domain objects can contain leaf objects as well as OUs.

OUs are similar to folders on a hard drive. While folders on a hard drive can contain files or subfolders, OUs can contain leaf objects or other OUs called *child OUs*. Nearly all AD objects are organized into OUs within a domain. Figure 2-1 shows a domain called octavius.net that uses OUs to organize leaf objects by division (East and West) as well as by department (Accounting, Marketing, and Production).

Figure 2-1

The Octavius Domain Structure

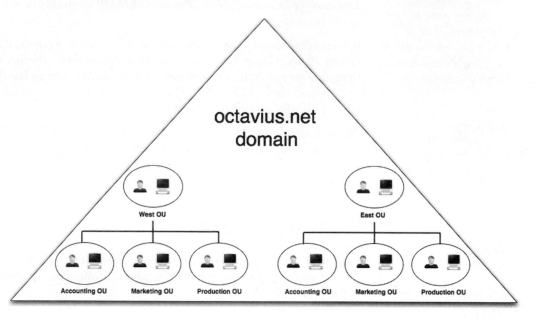

Because objects within the AD database are organized hierarchically and searched using LDAP, each object must have a unique LDAP name called a *distinguished name (DN)*. DNs identify leaf objects using the *common name (CN)* prefix. For example, the DN for a user account called bob in the Accounting OU under the West OU shown in Figure 2-1 would be: CN=bob,OU=Accounting,OU=West,DC=octavius,DC=net

Site objects represent physical locations. A site object can contain DC computer accounts and is primarily used to control the replication of AD data between physical locations. We discuss site objects in more depth later in this lesson.

Understanding Forests and Trusts

To accommodate all sizes of organizations, AD creates a forest for each organization that contains one or more trees. Each tree can contain one or more domains that share a common DNS name structure. Trust relationships are automatically created between domains in a forest to allow resource access across domains. Understanding the AD forest and trust structure is vital when administering DCs.

Domain objects are the base unit of organization in AD. Each domain has a unique DNS name that represents the name of the organization or business unit. In small organizations, there is typically one business unit for the entire organization. However, larger organizations can contain several individual business units.

To accommodate large organizations, AD creates a *forest* that can contain multiple domains that are part of the same organization. When the first DC in an organization is created, it creates the forest as well as the first domain in the forest called the *forest root domain*. As additional DCs are added, they can be configured to participate in the forest root domain or they can be used to create additional domains within the same forest. Figure 2-2 depicts a typical forest.

Although each domain in a forest must have at least one DC to hold the AD database for that domain, you should install additional DCs in each domain. This allows for fault tolerance if a single DC fails as well as provides load balancing for authentication requests. There is no limit to the number of DCs that can be installed in a single domain.

Figure 2-2

Octavius Forest Structure

TAKE NOTE *

In Figure 2-2, octavius .net is typically referred to as a ***parent domain***, whereas asia.octavius .net and europe.octavius .net are called ***child domains***.

TAKE NOTE *

Trust relationships do not give permissions to resources. Instead, they allow users to access resources in other domains that an administrator has granted them permission to. Without trust relationships, permissions on domain resources may only be given to users in the same domain.

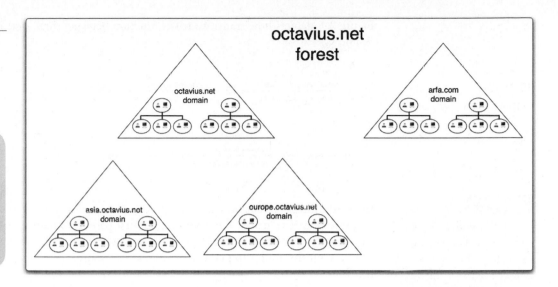

Some business units are related and will likely contain a portion of the same DNS name. In Figure 2-2, the octavius.net domain represents the main offices of the Octavius organization in North America, whereas the asia.octavius.net and europe.octavius.net subdomains represent the Asian and European offices of the Octavius organization. Because all three domains share the same core domain name, we refer to them as the octavius.net ***tree***.

If an organization contains business units that have different public identities or DNS names, these units will be represented by separate trees in the forest. Although the arfa.com domain in Figure 2-2 is part of the Octavius organization, it is part of the arfa.com tree.

Each domain in a forest maintains its own security, administrator user accounts, and resources. To allow users in a domain (the source domain) to access resources that they have permission to in another domain (the target domain), the target domain must trust the source domain. This is called a ***trust relationship*** or simply a ***trust***.

Trust relationships are represented by arrow symbols in a forest diagram. Figure 2-3 shows how trust relationships are drawn between two fictitious domains (domain A and domain B).

Figure 2-3

One-Way Trusts

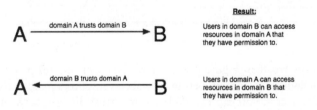

The trust relationships shown in Figure 2-3 are called ***one-way trusts***. If users in each domain require access to resources in the other domain, then a ***two-way trust*** can be used as shown in Figure 2-4.

Figure 2-4

Two-Way Trusts

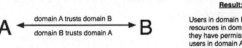

To reduce the number of trust relationships that need to be created in large forests, trust can be ***transitive***. If domain A trusts domain B using a transitive trust, and domain B trusts domain C using a transitive trust, then it is assumed that domain A trusts domain C as well. Users in domain C can then access resources that they have permission to in domain A.

Figure 2-5 depicts how transitive trusts function between three fictitious domains (domain A, B, and C).

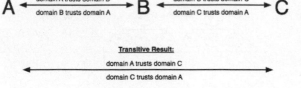

In an AD forest, parent domains in each tree automatically trust their child domains using two-way transitive trusts. Furthermore, the first parent domain in each tree automatically trusts the first parent domain in all other trees within the forest. This allows administrators in any domain the ability to grant permissions on resources to users in any other domain within the forest.

Figure 2-6 shows the default trust relationships for the octavius.net forest.

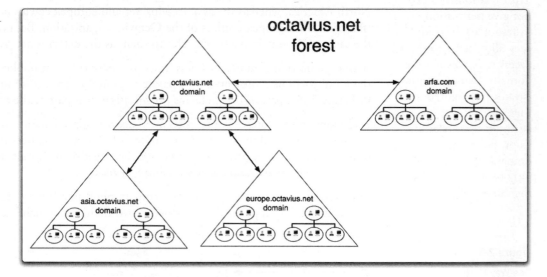

Although the trusts in Figure 2-6 are transitive, users in europe.octavius.net must first contact the octavius.net domain before they access resources in the arfa.com domain. To speed up resource access, you can manually create a trust directly between the europe.octavius.net and arfa.com domains. This trust is called a ***shortcut trust*** and will prevent the octavius.net domain from being contacted when users in europe.octavius.net access resources in arfa.com.

You can also create trusts to entities outside of your forest. For example, ***external trusts*** can be made between a domain in your forest and an NT4 domain and a domain in another Windows forest. Similarly, ***realm trusts*** can be made between a domain in your forest and a UNIX Kerberos Realm, and ***cross forest trusts*** can be made between two Windows Server 2003 machines and newer forests.

Understanding Groups

Global, domain local, and universal security groups are used to simplify permissions assignments on resources within your forest. In order to successfully manage authorization in a forest, you must first understand the different group types and scopes available as well as their intended usage.

TAKE NOTE *

The domain token that you receive during authentication lists the groups your user account belongs to. This enables network servers to grant you permission to resources based on the groups listed in the ACL on the resource.

You can assign permissions on resources within your domain to user accounts in your domain or to user accounts in remote domains that you trust via a trust relationship. However, assigning permissions to specific user accounts is a time consuming and inefficient process in organizations that have several user accounts that require access to the same resources.

To organize and simplify the assignment of permissions on resources, you should place several user account objects in a group object and assign permissions to the group object for the resource. This approach also minimizes the number of entries in the ACL on each resource and increases the speed of resource access. For example, to grant 50 users access to a particular resource, placing those users in a group and assigning permissions on the resource to the group results in a single entry in the ACL.

There are two main types of group accounts in AD:

- Security groups
- Distribution groups

Distribution groups are designed for email distribution only and contain an email address attribute as a result. When you send email to a distribution group, it is sent to the user accounts that are members of the group.

Like distribution groups, ***security groups*** can be used for email distribution. Unlike distribution groups, security groups can be assigned permissions to resources and are the main group type used in AD as a result.

To accommodate resource access across domains in a forest, AD further defines three ***group scopes***:

- Global
- Domain local
- Universal

Although these group scopes may be applied to both distribution and security groups, they mainly serve to simplify permissions assignment across the forest using security groups. Consequently, each security group scope has a different application within the AD forest as described in Table 2-1.

Table 2-1

Active Directory security group scopes

Group Scope	Allowed Group Members	Domains That Can Use the Group
Global	Objects (users accounts, computer accounts, group accounts) from the same domain as the global group	Any domain in the forest
Domain local	Objects (users accounts, computer accounts, group accounts) from any domain in the forest	Only the domain to which the domain local group belongs
Universal	Objects (users accounts, computer accounts, group accounts) from any domain in the forest	Any domain in the forest

TAKE NOTE *

At first glance, you may notice that universal groups provide the most functionality. As a result, they could be used in place of global and domain local groups. Unfortunately, because universal groups are stored in the global catalog, you should limit the usage and membership of universal groups to avoid performance problems in AD. The global catalog is discussed later in this lesson.

Global security groups may be assigned permissions to resources or added as a member to another group in any domain within the forest. However, global groups can only contain objects from the same domain in which the global group was created. Alternatively, domain local groups may be assigned permissions to resources or added as a member to another group in the same domain but can contain objects from any domain in the forest. Universal groups are unrestricted; they can be assigned permissions to resources, added as a member to another group in any domain within the forest, and can contain any object in the forest.

If used properly, these three group scopes organize the assignment of permissions across an entire forest. At minimum, user accounts in each domain should be added to global groups based on job function.

For example, each domain could contain a global group called Sales-GG. The Sales-GG group can then be assigned permissions to resources in the same domain or in other domains within the forest.

To simply the assignment of permissions to all sales users in the forest, you could create a universal group called Sales-U and add the Sales-GG groups from each domain to its membership list. If you assign permissions to the Sales-U group, all sales users in the forest will receive the permissions.

Additionally, you can create domain local groups for specific resources to make permissions assignments easier to identify. For example, if all sales users in the forest must use a printer in your domain called HPLaserJet6, you could create a domain local group called HPLaserJet6-DL and add the Sales-U group as a member. By simply assigning print permission to the HPLaserJet6-DL group, you will have given print permission to all sales users within the organization.

This approach is often called *AGUDLP*:

A—**A**dd users to

G—**G**lobal groups based on job function. Add global groups to

U—**U**niversal groups for forestwide use. Add universal groups to

DL—**D**omain **L**ocal groups that are matched to a particular resource. Assign

P—**P**ermissions to the domain local group.

➕ MORE INFORMATION

Computers that do not participate in AD contain user accounts and group accounts in the Windows Registry that are only used on the local computer. Although these local user accounts and local groups do not exist in the AD database, users who log in to a domain from a client computer can still choose to log in using a local user account rather than authenticate to the domain. In this case, domain resources are unavailable and the user can only access resources that grant access to their local user account and local groups.

Furthermore, when a computer joins a domain, domain groups are automatically added as members to the default local groups. For example, the Domain Users group is added to the local Users group and the Domain Admins group is added to the local Administrators group on each domain computer. This gives domain users the same abilities as local users and domain administrators the same abilities as local administrators on each domain computer.

Understanding Functional Levels

Domains in an AD forest use functional levels to maintain backwards compatibility to Windows NT4 domains or previous versions of AD. Changing your domain functional level affects the features of both AD and Exchange Server 2007. Thus, it is important to understand AD functional levels when supporting Exchange Server 2007 in an AD environment.

Windows domains were first introduced with Windows NT4 Server, yet NT4 domains did not use AD. Instead, Windows NT4 domains stored user, group, and computer accounts in a nonhierarchical database called the *Security Accounts Manager (SAM)*. A read-write copy of the SAM was stored on a single *Primary Domain Controller (PDC)* in each NT4 domain. All additional NT4 DCs were called *Backup Domain Controllers (BDCs)* and obtained a copy of the SAM from the PDC so that they could authenticate users.

AD was introduced with Windows 2000 Server and was a major departure from the SAM structure used in Windows NT4. Although Windows Server 2003 and Windows Server 2008 also use AD, they contain additional AD features that are unavailable in previous versions.

Many organizations have based their network infrastructure on Windows NT4 and Windows 2000 domains in the past. As a result, you can migrate these domains to Windows Server 2003 and 2008 by upgrading or replacing older DCs with new ones. However, this migration may take several months or years. Consequently, domains within your organization can contain a mixture of Windows NT4, Windows 2000, Windows Server 2003, and Windows Server 2008 DCs.

To account for the diverse features and structure between each version of DC, each AD domain contains *domain functional levels* that allow different levels of backwards compatibility by allowing different types of DCs to participate in domain authentication. The domain functional levels for Windows Server 2003 AD domains are described in Table 2-2.

Table 2-2

Windows Server 2003 domain functional levels

DOMAIN FUNCTIONAL LEVEL	DC OPERATING SYSTEMS SUPPORTED WITHIN THE DOMAIN
Windows 2000 Mixed	Windows NT4, Windows 2000, Windows Server 2003
Windows NT4 Interim	Windows NT4, Windows Server 2003
Windows 2000 Native	Windows 2000, Windows Server 2003
Windows Server 2003	Windows Server 2003

By default, Windows Server 2003 AD domains are in the Windows 2000 Mixed functional level to allow backwards compatibility with Windows NT4 and Windows 2000 DCs. By raising the domain functional level to the Windows 2000 Native functional level, you prevent NT4 DCs from participating in domain authentication and enable several Windows 2000 specific features such as the ability to use universal groups. Similarly, to enable the new features introduced in Windows Server 2003 AD, you must raise your domain functional level to the Windows Server 2003 functional level.

 WARNING Raising a functional level is a one-way operation. You cannot return to the previous functional level once it has been raised.

 TAKE NOTE * Domain functional levels only determine the types of DCs that can participate in a particular domain. A domain at the Windows Server 2003 functional level can only contain Windows Server 2003 DCs but can still contain clients that run previous versions of Windows such as Windows NT4 and Windows 2000.

Windows Server 2008 AD does not allow backwards compatibility with Windows NT4 domains. Table 2-3 lists the domain functional levels available in Windows Server 2008.

Table 2-3

Windows Server 2008 domain functional levels

DOMAIN FUNCTIONAL LEVEL	DC OPERATING SYSTEMS SUPPORTED WITHIN THE DOMAIN
Windows 2000 Native	Windows 2000, Windows Server 2003, Windows Server 2008
Windows Server 2003	Windows Server 2003, Windows Server 2008
Windows Server 2008	Windows Server 2008

TAKE NOTE*

Exchange Server 2007 requires that you upgrade your domain functional level to Windows 2000 Native or higher.

By default, Windows Server 2008 AD uses the Windows 2000 Native functional level for backwards compatibility. To take advantage of new features introduced with Windows Server 2003 AD, you must raise your domain to the Windows Server 2003 functional level. Similarly, to enable the new features introduced with Windows Server 2008 AD, you must raise your domain to the Windows Server 2008 functional level.

In a forest that contains multiple domains, each domain may operate at a different functional level. Those domains that have a higher functional level can take advantage of the latest features in AD. Some features of AD require minimum domain functional level of all domains within the forest. As a result, AD contains *forest functional levels* that define the type of DCs allowed within all domains in the forest. Tables 2-4 and 2-5 show the forest functional levels used by Windows Server 2003 AD and Windows Server 2008 AD, respectively.

Table 2-4

Windows Server 2003 forest functional levels

FOREST FUNCTIONAL LEVEL	DC OPERATING SYSTEMS SUPPORTED WITHIN THE FOREST
Windows 2000	Windows NT4, Windows 2000, Windows Server 2003
Windows Server 2003 Interim	Windows NT4, Windows Server 2003
Windows Server 2003	Windows Server 2003

Table 2-5

Windows Server 2008 forest functional levels

FOREST FUNCTIONAL LEVEL	DC OPERATING SYSTEMS SUPPORTED WITHIN THE FOREST
Windows 2000 Native	Windows 2000, Windows Server 2003, Windows Server 2008
Windows Server 2003	Windows Server 2003, Windows Server 2008
Windows Server 2008	Windows Server 2008

TAKE NOTE*

Cross forest trusts require that both forests apply the Windows Server 2003 forest functional level or higher.

To raise your forest functional level, you must first raise your domain function levels. For example, to raise the forest function level to Windows Server 2003, all domains in your forest should first be raised to the Windows Server 2003 domain functional level. As with domain functional levels, you cannot revert to a previous forest functional level once it has been raised.

Understanding Sites and Replication

> Information is replicated between DCs in a domain and forest when new information is added to the AD database or existing information is modified or removed. To control replication within an organization, AD uses site and site link objects. Furthermore, Exchange Server 2007 uses AD sites to control the flow of internal email within an organization.

To ensure the continuous operation of AD if a DC fails, most organizations deploy more than one DC in each domain within a forest. Each DC in a domain will contain a copy of the AD database. To ensure that DCs in the same domain can authenticate users using the same AD database, changes made to the AD database on one DC are replicated to other DCs.

To understand how AD replication works, you must first understand the structure of the AD database stored on each DC. There are three main sections of the AD database called *directory partitions*:

- Schema partition
- Configuration partition
- Domain partition

The schema partition contains the AD schema and must be identical on all DCs in the forest to ensure that objects can be interpreted by any DC. If a change is made to the schema partition, such as the addition of a new object class, the schema partition changes must be replicated to all other DCs in the forest.

Like the schema partition, the configuration partition must be identical on all DCs in the forest as it stores the structure and layout of the AD forest. If you change the structure of the forest by adding a new domain or trust relationship, the configuration partition will be replicated to all other DCs in the forest.

All objects within a particular domain are stored in the domain partition on the DCs. Because of this, the domain partition is the largest directory partition and typically contains thousands of objects. Replicating the domain partition to all DCs in the forest would prove too bandwidth intensive and would increase the size of the AD database unnecessarily. As a result, when a change is made to the domain partition on a DC, such as the addition of a user account object, it is replicated to other DCs in the same domain only. Because each domain maintains its own domain objects, you must contact DCs in a remote domain when you need access to information that is stored within an object in the remote domain.

On a fast network such as a LAN, AD replication occurs quickly. However, many organizations have multiple physical locations that are linked by relatively slow WAN connections via the Internet. Frequent AD replication across these slow WAN connections will consume a great deal of the available bandwidth and likely slow down the organization's access to the Internet.

One way to reduce the impact of AD replication on bandwidth is to ensure that each location within your organization has its own domain. In this case, only replication of schema and configuration changes will occur across the slow WAN connections to DCs in other domains within the forest. Administrators can simply ensure that changes made to the schema or forest structure occur after normal business hours to minimize the impact of any replication outside of the domain.

Unfortunately, using one domain per location is more costly to implement and manage over time. Alternatively, you can implement AD *site objects* to optimize the replication that occurs across slow WAN links between the physical locations within your organization.

TAKE NOTE*

Although changes to the schema and configuration are replicated to all other DCs in the forest, these changes are relatively infrequent. Alternatively, changes to the domain partition are relatively frequent and replicated only to DCs within the same domain.

Consider the octavius.net domain shown in Figure 2-7. DC1 and DC2 contain a copy of all objects in the octavius.net domain yet are physically located at the western offices of the Octavius organization in Cupertino, California. Similarly, DC3 and DC4 contain a copy of the objects in the octavius.net domain. However, they are located in the eastern offices of the Octavius organization in Boston, Massachusetts.

Figure 2-7

Octavius.net Domain Controller Locations

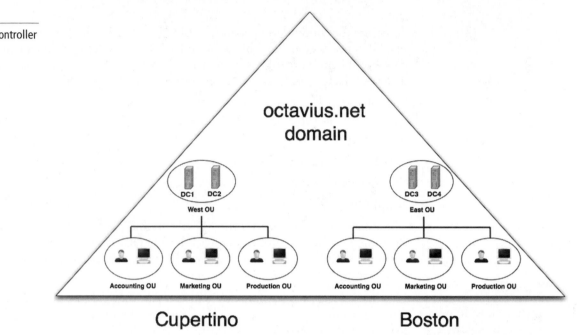

When an AD object such as a user account is created or modified on DC3 in Boston, it is immediately replicated to DC1, DC2, and DC4. Replication to DC4 will take only a few moments on the Boston network, but will take considerably longer to traverse the Internet from Boston to Cupertino in order to reach DC1 and DC2. Assuming that AD objects are modified several hundred times per hour, replication to DC1 and DC2 will likely congest the slow WAN connections in both Boston and Cupertino.

Furthermore, objects created by administrators in Boston will likely be used primarily by the DCs in Boston. For example, if an administrator creates a user account on DC3 for a new hire at the Boston office, only DC3 and DC4 will need to query the user account object to perform authentication unless the user travels to Cupertino.

By creating AD sites that represent the Cupertino and Boston locations, you can create a ***site link*** object between the Cupertino and Boston sites that specifies when replication should occur. Figure 2-8 shows the octavius.net domain configured using sites.

The site link between the Cupertino and Boston sites shown in Figure 2-8 can be configured to schedule replication for certain times or accumulate AD database changes for a certain period of time before replicating them all at once to reduce the effects on WAN bandwidth.

Figure 2-8

Octavius.net Site Structure

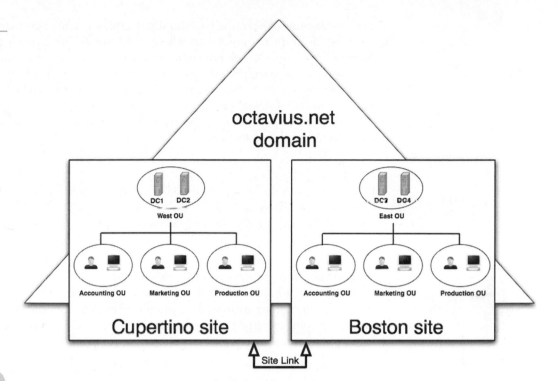

To save bandwidth, replication between sites only occurs between a single DC in each site called a *bridgehead server*. Although AD automatically chooses a DC to become the bridgehead server in each site, you can manually specify the bridgehead server for each site.

Assume that the Cupertino-Boston site link is configured to replicate every hour between 9:00 p.m. and 3:00 a.m., which is after normal business hours in both locations. In this case, a new user account object created on DC3 will immediately replicate to DC4 but will not replicate to DC1 and DC2 until after 9:00 p.m. Because the user account is for a Boston user, the replication delay to Cupertino is negligible.

There is no limit to the number of sites and site link objects that may be created in an AD forest. In large organizations that have several offices, you will likely create many sites and site link objects. In this case, you can change the *cost* value on each site link to encourage the use of certain replication paths. If there are multiple site link objects between a source and destination domain, AD will use the site link objects that have the lowest cost between both domains.

It is important to create your AD site structure carefully. Exchange Server 2007 uses the AD site structure to control how email is relayed within your organization.

Understanding Global Catalog

The global catalog provides quick object access to universal groups and UPNs within an AD forest. After configuring AD sites, you should carefully consider the placement of global catalog servers within your organization to allow quick authentication and resource access. Additionally, Exchange Server 2007 contacts the global catalog to search for email recipients within the organization when relaying email.

For fast resource access in remote domains, you should always ensure that client computers can easily reach a GC server by placing the GC on at least one DC in each site within the forest.

Because forests can grow very large, a list of all object names in the forest is stored on at least one DC to aid in locating objects in the AD. This list is called the *global catalog (GC)* and is hosted on the first DC in the forest by default. The GC is similar to a telephone book. Where a telephone book allows you to quickly locate a telephone number, the GC allows you to quickly locate an object in a remote domain.

For user account objects, the GC also stores a unique name that users can use to log in to their domain from a computer anywhere in the forest. This name is called a *User Principle Name (UPN)* and must be unique in the forest. To log in to a remote domain using a UPN, you simply need to specify *username@domainname* in the User Name dialog box at the Windows logon screen. For example, to log in as the user with the login name bob in the asia.octavius.net domain, you can specify bob@asia.octavius.net at the Windows logon screen. When a UPN is specified at the Windows logon screen, a GC is contacted to locate the right user account in the correct domain.

TAKE NOTE* Only domains at the Windows 2000 Native functional level or higher can access the GC. Consequently, UPNs can only be used during the logon process if the domain is at or above the Windows 2000 Native functional level.

Additionally, universal groups are entirely stored in the GC and can be accessed by domains that are at the Windows 2000 Native functional level or greater. Because authentication tokens list your group membership, you must contact a GC during the logon process to determine your universal group membership. Thus, a GC server is necessary to complete the logon process for domains that are at or above the Windows 2000 Native functional level.

When forest objects are added or removed, the GC in each site must be updated. In a large forest, the GC is replicated frequently and may congest the WAN bandwidth in small branch locations. To solve this problem, you should avoid placing the GC on DCs in sites that have limited WAN bandwidth. For these sites, they must still contact a GC in another site to complete the logon process if the domain is at the Windows 2000 Native functional level.

To speed up the logon process for sites in a Windows 2000 Native functional level domain that do not have a GC, you should enable *Universal Group Membership Caching (UGMC)* on the site to allow DCs in the site the ability to cache the universal group memberships for user accounts. In this case, a remote GC must be contacted the first time a user authenticates to the domain to verify universal group memberships and populate the cache. On subsequent logons, the DC in the site simply uses the universal group membership information for the user stored in the cache to complete the logon process.

TAKE NOTE* Even if a GC is unavailable, domain administrators can still log in to a domain that is at or above the Windows 2000 Native functional level.

Understanding FSMO Roles

Flexible Single Master Operations (FSMO) roles provide specific functions within an AD domain and forest. It is important to understand the placement and function of FSMO roles in order to optimize the performance of AD as well as troubleshoot AD problems.

In any AD environment, certain domain and forest functions must be coordinated from a single DC. These functions are called *Flexible Single Master Operations (FSMO)*. A DC can hold a single FSMO role or can hold all FSMO roles for its domain or forest.

Table 2-6 lists the two forestwide FSMO roles that must be present on a single DC in the forest, as well as the three domainwide FSMO roles that must be on a single DC in each domain within the forest.

Table 2-6

Forestwide and Domainwide FSMO Roles

FSMO ROLE	NUMBER PER DOMAIN OR FOREST	FUNCTION
Schema Master	1 per forest	Replicates changes made to the AD schema to all DCs in the forest. In order to modify the AD schema, the DC that holds the Schema Master FSMO role must be available.
Domain Naming Master	1 per forest	Permits the addition of new domains and removal of existing domains. Before a new domain is added to the forest, the DC that holds the Domain Naming Master FSMO is contacted to ensure that the name is unique. The Domain Naming Master also ensures that the updated forest configuration is replicated to all DCs in the forest. For best performance, the DC that contains the Domain Naming Master FSMO role should also contain the GC.
PDC Emulator	1 per domain	Emulates an NT4 PDC for backwards compatibility to NT4 BDCs that exist in a Windows 2000 Mixed functional level domain. In addition, the PDC Emulator coordinates user password changes and synchronizes time among the computers in a domain.
RID Master	1 per domain	Issues unique **Relative IDentifiers (RIDs)** to DCs within the domain. RIDs are unique numbers that are used to create Security Identifiers (SIDs) for newly created objects in the domain. Because the RID Master generates the RIDs used by all the DCs in a domain when creating new objects, SIDs are guaranteed to be unique among domain objects. The RID Master FSMO generates blocks of 500 RIDs for each DC in the domain. When a DC has exhausted its supply of RIDs, it contacts the RID Master FSMO to obtain another 500.
Infrastructure Master	1 per domain	Coordinates group membership as well as the use of GUIDs and DNs between the current domain and other domains in the forest. Because the GC performs similar functions, the Infrastructure Master FSMO role should be placed on a DC that does not contain the GC.

By default, the first DC installed in the forest contains all five FSMO roles and the first DC installed in all additional domains contains the three domainwide FSMO roles. However, if one of these DCs fail, several FSMO roles will be unavailable. As a result, you should move the default FSMO roles to different DCs for fault tolerance.

It is important to ensure that the DCs that contain FSMO roles are available at all times. For example, if the PDC Emulator FSMO role is unavailable, users could receive an incorrect time that may prevent them from logging in to their domain because the Kerberos authentication protocol requires that the time on a client and DC be no more than five minutes different. Additionally, if the RID Master FSMO is unavailable, you could receive an error message when attempting to create a new object in the AD database.

If a DC that holds an FSMO role fails, you can force another DC to assume the FSMO role. To do this, you must *seize* the FSMO role from a DC that is online. To bring the failed DC back online, you should first reinstall the operating system and configure it as a new DC in the existing domain.

TAKE NOTE ✱

Exchange Server 2007 extends the AD schema. As a result, it is important to ensure that the first Exchange Server 2007 computer deployed can contact the DC that holds the Schema Master FSMO role. It is good practice to move the Schema Master FSMO role to a DC close to the computer that will become the first Exchange server to reduce installation problems and speed the installation process.

■ Installing Active Directory

↓
THE BOTTOM LINE

AD consists of several services and components that run on a Windows Server. To deploy AD in your organization, you must first prepare your servers and network environment as well as run the Active Directory Installation Wizard. Following installation, you should ensure that all components were installed successfully before configuring AD. Alternatively, you can remove AD from a DC to restore it to its previous state.

Preparing for Installation

The common American proverb "failing to plan is planning to fail" is true for any AD installation. To reduce the chance that an AD installation will fail, you should ensure that you have the necessary prerequisites before beginning the installation.

Although you can install Exchange Server 2007 SP1 on a Windows Server 2008 computer, Exchange Server 2007 was originally designed to interoperate in a Windows Server 2003 AD environment. As a result, we will focus on the installation and configuration of Windows Server 2003 AD in this lesson.

Before you begin the installation of AD on a Windows Server 2003, it is important to ensure that you have the necessary prerequisites:

TAKE NOTE ✱

You cannot install AD on a computer running the Web Edition of Windows Server 2003.

- A computer running the Standard Edition, Enterprise Edition, or Datacenter Edition of Windows Server 2003 or Windows Server 2003 R2 with the latest service packs and updates installed. This computer should use the NTFS file system for its system volume and contain at least 250 MB of free space on the NTFS file system for use by AD.

- A DNS server on the network that supports SRV records and is configured with a zone for the AD domain. Alternatively, this DNS server can be created and configured automatically on the first DC in a domain during AD installation.

TAKE NOTE ✱

To support AD, your DNS server must support the **Berkeley Internet Name Domain (BIND)** version 4.9.6 standard to allow SRV record support. To also allow the automatic creation and updating of SRV records using the DNS *dynamic update* protocol, your DNS server should support BIND version 8.1.2. Windows Server 2003 DNS supports BIND version 8.1.2 standard.

TAKE NOTE ✱

For performance reasons, it is considered a poor practice to install AD on a server that provides other business-critical services such as web, email, file, print, or database services.

- A network interface that is connected to a TCP/IP network and configured to use the appropriate DNS server. If you are installing a new forest or tree in an existing forest, you can automatically install and configure DNS on your computer during the AD installation. In this case, you should specify your own IP address in the Preferred DNS server dialog box within TCP/IP properties to ensure that DNS is installed on your computer regardless of whether an external DNS server on the Internet holds a zone for your domain.

- A user account that is a member of the local Administrators group on the Windows Server 2003 computer. To join an existing domain, you also require a user account that is a member of the Domain Admins group in the existing domain. Similarly, to create a new domain in an existing forest, you will also require a user account that is a member of the Enterprise Admins group in the forest root domain.

➡ **CONFIGURE DNS BEFORE ACTIVE DIRECTORY INSTALLATION**

GET READY. Turn on the computer, and log in as the Administrator user account. Close any windows that appear on the desktop.

1. Click **Start, Control Panel,** and then click **Network Connections.** A list of your network connections will appear on the right-hand menu.

2. Click the network connection that is connected to your TCP/IP network. If you have a single network interface, this is called **Local Area Connection** by default. The network interface property screen appears.

3. Highlight **Internet Protocol (TCP/IP),** and click **Properties.** The Internet Protocol (TCP/IP) Properties screen appears.

4. Ensure that the **Preferred DNS server** dialog box lists the IP address of a DNS server on your network that is configured with a zone for the AD domain that you wish to install on your computer. If you are installing a new forest or tree and plan to automatically install and configure DNS during AD installation, ensure that the computer's IP address is listed in the Preferred DNS server dialog box as shown in Figure 2-9.

Figure 2-9

Preparing DNS for Active Directory Installation

Internet Protocol (TCP/IP) Properties ? ✕

General

You can get IP settings assigned automatically if your network supports this capability. Otherwise, you need to ask your network administrator for the appropriate IP settings.

○ Obtain an IP address automatically
● Use the following IP address:

IP address:	192 . 168 . 1 . 42
Subnet mask:	255 . 255 . 255 . 0
Default gateway:	192 . 168 . 1 . 254

○ Obtain DNS server address automatically
● Use the following DNS server addresses:

Preferred DNS server:	192 . 168 . 1 . 42
Alternate DNS server:	. . .

Advanced...

OK   Cancel

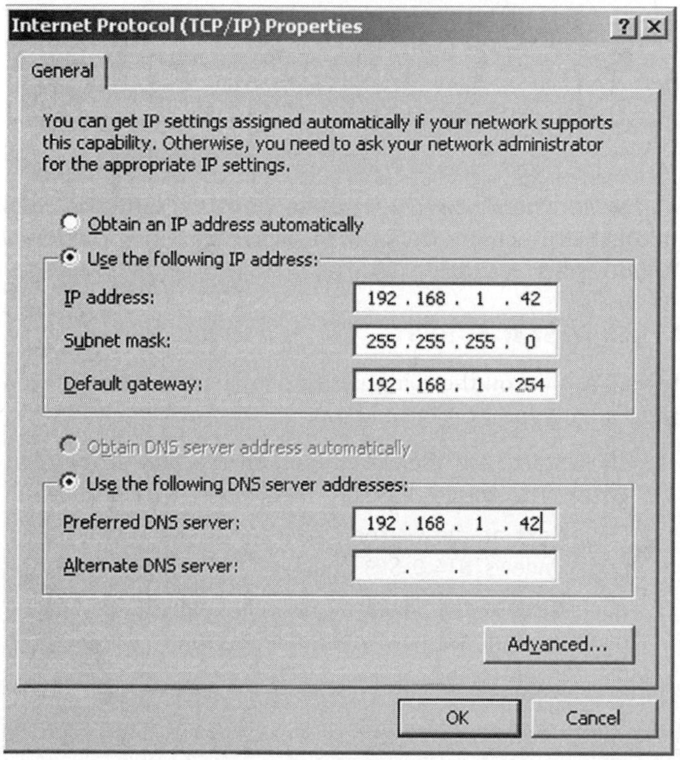

ANOTHER WAY

You can use the IP address 127.0.0.1 to refer to your local computer. Instead of entering your computer's IP address in the Preferred DNS server dialog box shown in Figure 2-9, you can instead enter 127.0.0.1 in the Preferred DNS server dialog box to achieve the same effect.

5. Click **OK** to close the Internet Protocol (TCP/IP) Properties screen.

6. Click **OK** to close the network interface property screen.

Performing the Installation

If you have verified the prerequisites for AD, the installation of a DC will likely proceed without any problems. The methods used to install a DC in a new forest and existing forest are almost identical. Although this section will discuss both methods, we will focus on creating the first DC in a new forest.

When you install AD on a new Windows Server 2003 computer, you must run the *Active Directory Installation Wizard.* This wizard may be used to install an additional DC in an existing domain, a new domain in an existing tree, a new domain in a new tree, or a new domain in a new forest.

To start the Active Directory Installation Wizard, you can simply run the **dcpromo.exe** program from a command window or the Run dialog box. Alternatively, you can use the *Configure Your Server Wizard* to start the Active Directory Installation Wizard by choosing the Domain Controller role when prompted as shown in Figure 2-10.

Figure 2-10

Configure Your Server Wizard

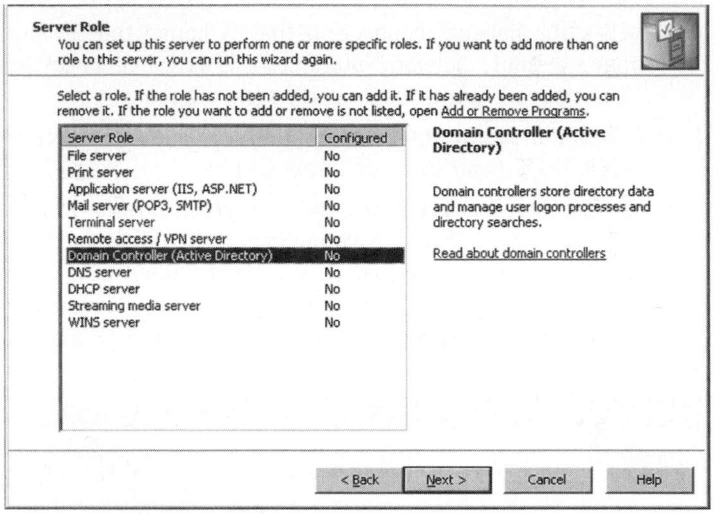

The Configure Your Server Wizard can be started from the Administrative Tools menu on the Windows Start menu or from the Manage Your Server window that appears after you log on to Windows Server 2003.

INSTALL A NEW FOREST

GET READY. Turn on the computer, and log in as the Administrator user account. Close any windows that appear on the desktop.

1. Click **Start**, and then click **Run**. In the Run dialog box, type **dcpromo**, and press **Enter**. The Active Directory Installation Wizard appears.
2. Click **Next** at the Welcome page. You receive a warning indicating that Windows 95 and Windows NT4.0 SP3 clients are no longer supported in AD.
3. Click **Next** at the Operating System Compatibility page. The Domain Controller Type page appears as shown in Figure 2-11.

Figure 2-11

Specifying Domain Controller Type

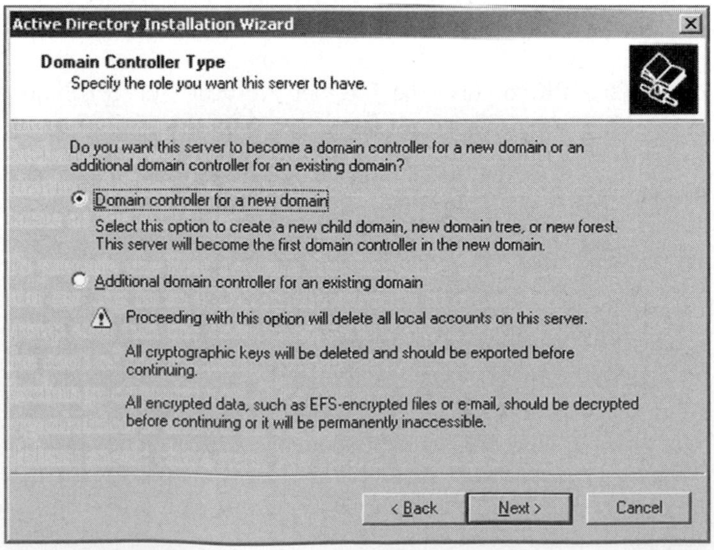

4. At the Domain Controller Type page ensure that **Domain controller for a new domain** is selected and click **Next**. The Create New Domain page is displayed.

➕ **MORE INFORMATION**

If you select **Additional domain controller for an existing domain** in Figure 2-11, you will be prompted to specify the DNS name of the target domain as well as the username and password for a user that is a member of the Domain Admins group in the target domain as shown in Figure 2-12.

Figure 2-12

Specifying the Domain Name and Credentials

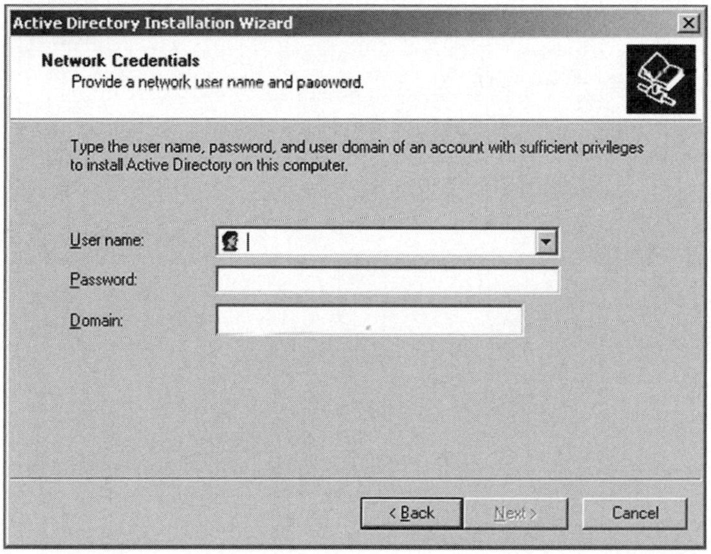

5. At Create New Domain page shown in Figure 2-13, ensure that **Domain in a new forest** is selected and click **Next**. The New Domain Name page appears.

Figure 2-13

Selecting a New Domain

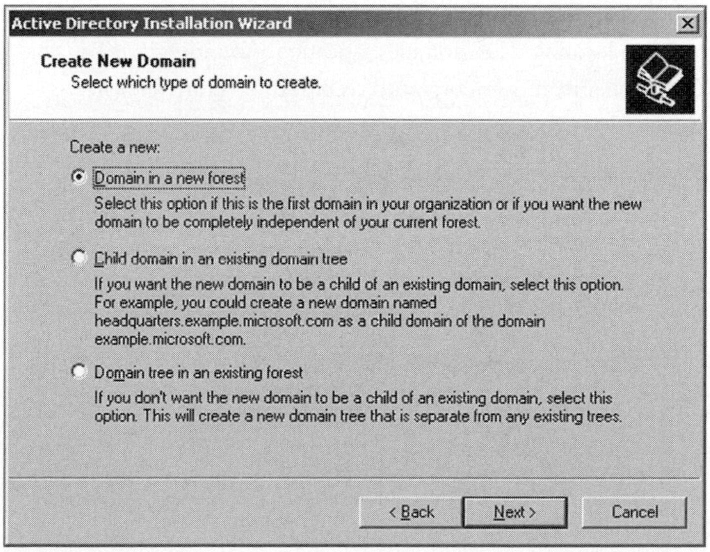

➕ **MORE INFORMATION**

If you select **Child domain in an existing domain tree** or **Domain tree in an existing forest** in Figure 2-13, you will be prompted to specify the DNS name of the new domain as well as the username and password for a user that is a member of the Enterprise Admins group in the target domain as shown in Figure 2-12.

6. At the New Domain Name page, enter the DNS name of the first domain in the forest as shown in Figure 2-14 and click **Next**. The Active Directory Installation Wizard takes a few moments to validate that no other domains exist on the network with the same name. In addition, the Active Directory Installation Wizard contacts the DNS server listed in TCP/IP properties to verify that a DNS zone is properly configured for the new domain. When this process completes, the NetBIOS Domain Name page is displayed.

Figure 2-14

Specifying the Domain Name

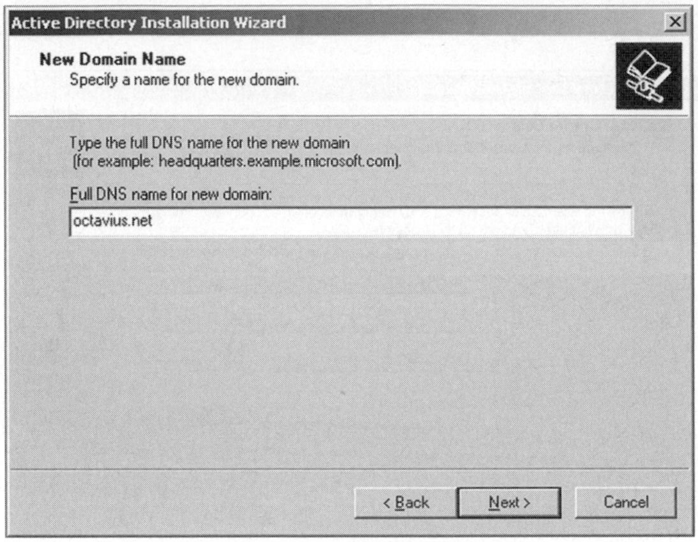

7. At the NetBIOS Domain Name page shown in Figure 2-15, review the NetBIOS name generated from your domain DNS name and click **Next**. The Database and Log Folders page appears.

TAKE NOTE*

By default, the NetBIOS domain name is generated from the first 15 characters of your DNS name before the first period. Windows 9x and NT4 clients use it when joining a domain or when locating a DC for authentication. Accordingly, if you change the default NetBIOS domain name, it is important to record it for future reference.

Figure 2-15

Specifying the NetBIOS Domain Name

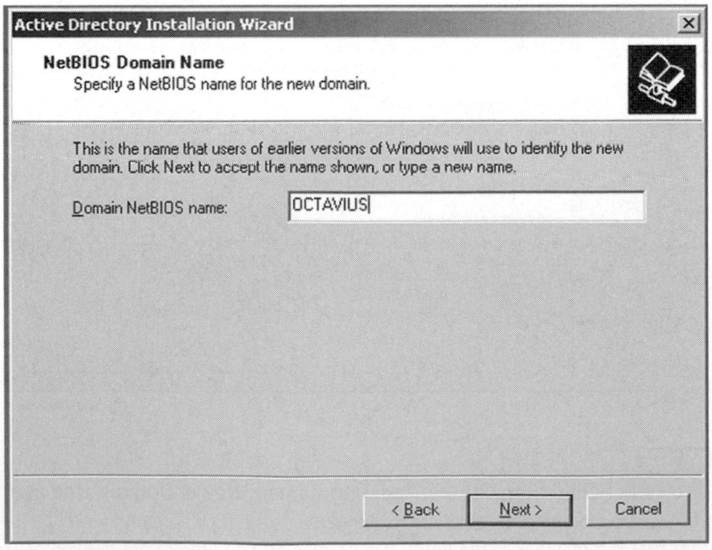

TAKE NOTE*

In a production environment, you typically change the default location of the AD database and logs to a different hard drive. This allows for better performance because AD does not need to compete with the system drive when reading and writing data. The AD database and logs must reside on an NTFS partition.

8. At the Database and Log Folders page, review the default location for the AD database and database logs as shown in Figure 2-16 and click **Next**. The Shared System Volume page is displayed.

Figure 2-16

Specifying the Database and Log Location

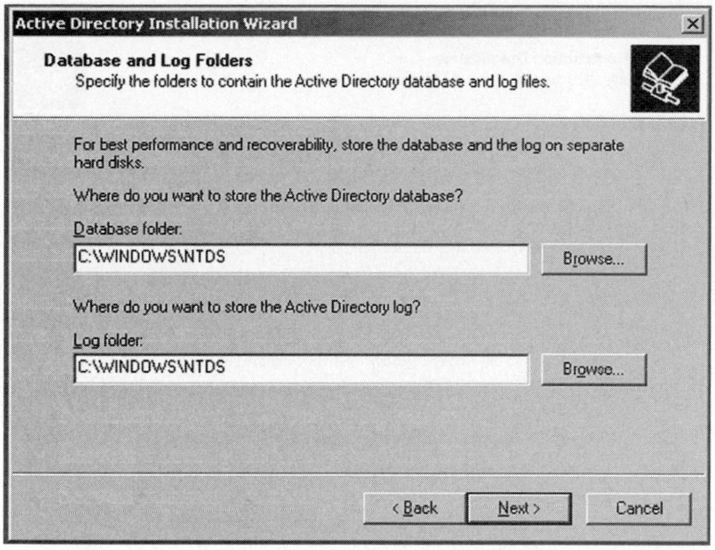

The SYSVOL shared folder is used to deploy GPOs to computers within the domain as well as perform replication. It must reside on an NTFS volume and is typically stored on a separate hard drive in production environments to improve performance.

9. At the Shared System Volume page, review the default location for the SYSVOL shared folder as shown in Figure 2-17 and click **Next**. Following this, the DNS Registration Diagnostics page is displayed.

Figure 2-17

Specifying the SYSVOL Folder Location

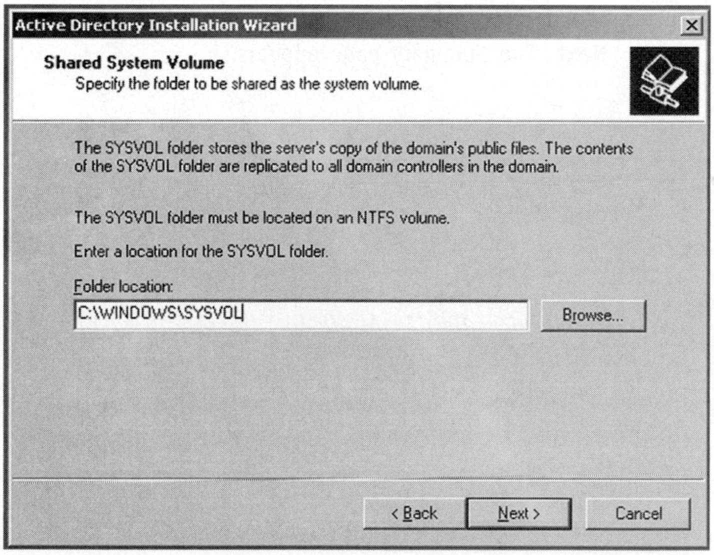

10. At the DNS Registration Diagnostics page, read the results of the DNS diagnostics to identify whether the Preferred DNS server listed in TCP/IP properties is properly configured to support SRV records for your domain. Because you are installing a new forest and have not yet configured DNS, the diagnostic results indicate that DNS is not installed on your DNS server (your computer) as shown in Figure 2-18. As a result, ensure that **Install and configure the DNS server on this computer** is selected and click **Next**. The Permissions page appears.

Figure 2-18

Selecting DNS Options

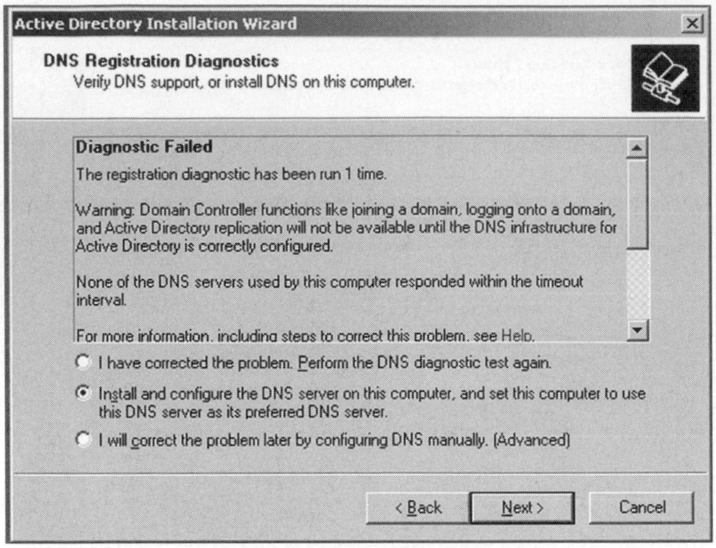

11. At the Permissions page, ensure that **Permissions compatible with Windows 2000 or Windows Server 2003 operating systems** is selected because we will not contain NT4 servers within our forest and click **Next**. The Directory Services Restore Mode Administrator Password page is displayed.

12. At the Directory Services Restore Mode Administrator Password page, enter a complex password in both password dialog boxes as shown in Figure 2-19 and click **Next**. The Summary page appears.

⚠️ **WARNING** Because the Directory Services Restore Mode Administrator password is only set during DC installation, ensure that you write this password down in the event that you need to log in to your DC after it has been booted to Directory Services Restore Mode.

TAKE NOTE *

Directory Services Restore Mode does not load the AD and is typically used to repair problems with the AD database. You can enter this mode by pressing F8 during the boot process and selecting the Directory Services Restore Mode option from the menu that is displayed.

Figure 2-19

Specifying a Directory Service Restore Mode Password

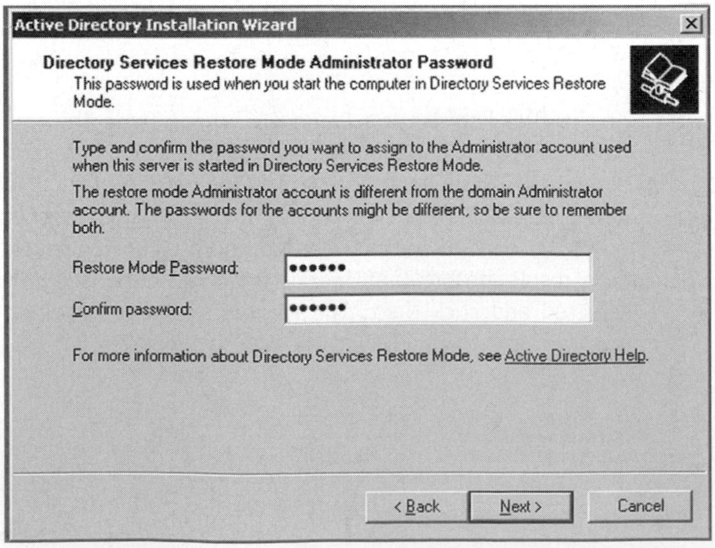

13. At the Summary page, review your installation choices and click **Next** to begin the installation of your DC. The installation typically takes 5 to 15 minutes depending on your hardware and will prompt you for your Windows Server 2003 CD in order to install the files required by the DNS server. After the installation has completed, click the **Finish** button.

14. To finish the installation process, click **Restart Now** on the screen that appears to restart your computer.

Verifying the Installation

After installing a new DC, you should ensure that your domain controller and DNS server are functioning properly before you configure sites, FSMOs, GC, and AD objects.

After the Active Directory Installation Wizard completes, you must reboot your computer to load the AD services. If successful, you should see your domain membership listed on the Computer Name tab of the System utility (**Start** > **Control Panel** > **System Properties**) as shown in Figure 2-20.

Figure 2-20

Verifying Domain Membership

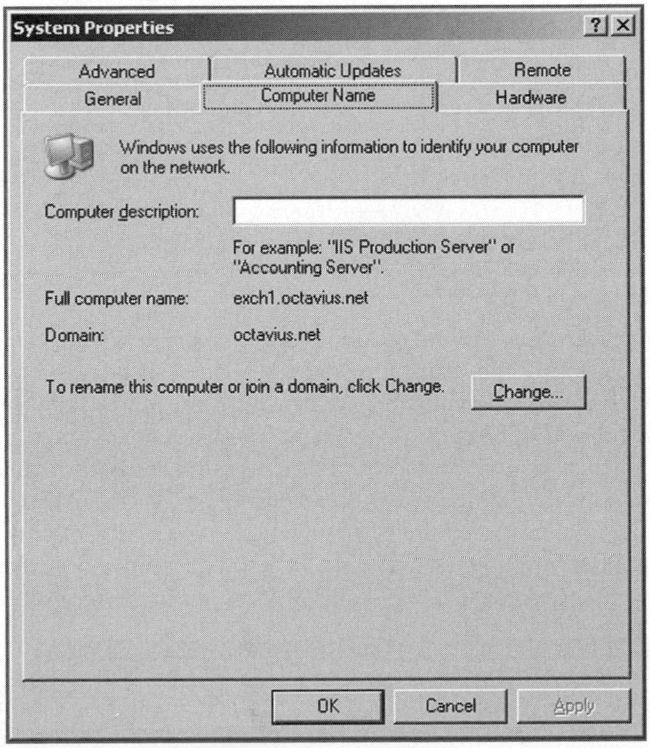

Although your domain membership may indicate the correct information, you should ensure that the AD services are running properly and that no problems were encountered during the installation.

To see any installation-related errors, you can view the **%systemroot%\debug\dcpromo.log** file in a text editor such as notepad.exe as shown in Figure 2-21.

Figure 2-21

Viewing the Active Directory
Installation Log

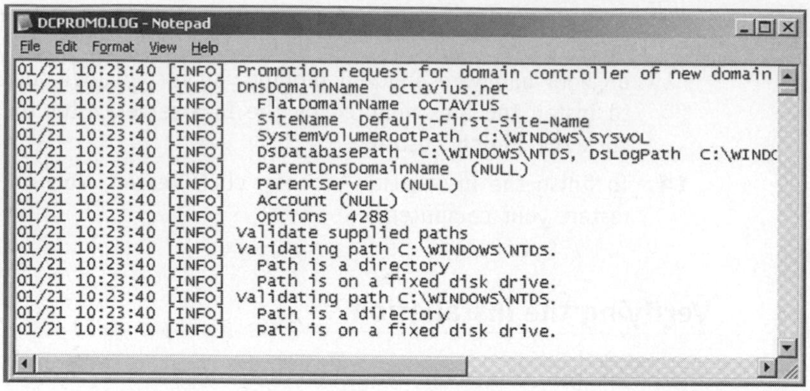

TAKE NOTE*

The %systemroot%
variable refers to the
location of the Windows
operating system direc-
tory. On most systems,
it refers to C:\Windows.

Additionally, you can use the Directory Service log in Event Viewer (**Start** > **Administrative Tools** > **Event Viewer**) to ensure that no errors were encountered during the initialization of AD services at boot time as shown in Figure 2-22.

Figure 2-22

Viewing the Directory Service
Log

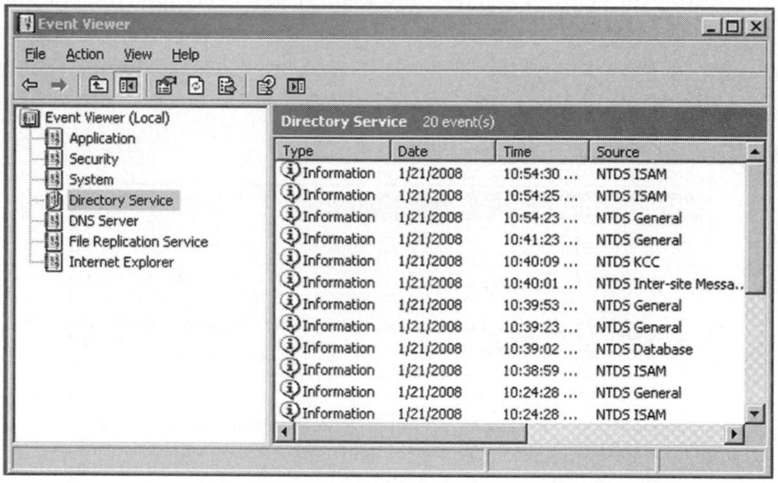

During the first boot following AD installation, your computer contacts the DNS server configured in TCP/IP properties using the DNS dynamic update protocol and creates the necessary SRV records used by clients when locating AD services. To verify the creation of SRV records on a Windows DNS server, simply open the DNS console (**Start** > **Administrative Tools** > **DNS**). Under your server object and the Forward Lookup Zones folder, you should see two zones for your domain (_msdcs.*domainname* and *domainname*) with several subfolders if the dynamic update protocol was successful. The subfolders contain SRV records that describe the services available on DCs in your domain. Figure 2-23 shows the two zones created on the EXCH1 server for the octavius.net domain, as well as the SRV records in the _tcp subfolder of the octavius.net zone.

Figure 2-23

Verifying SRV Record Creation

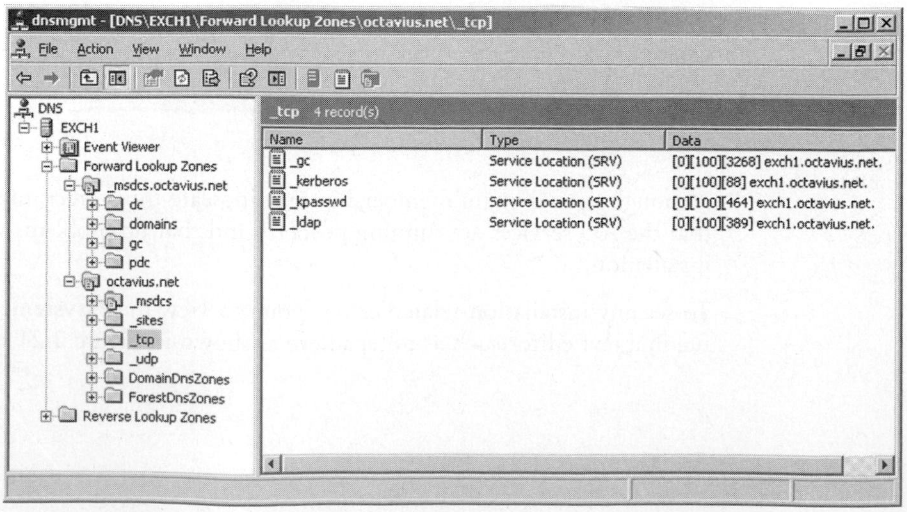

If you do not see any subfolders or SRV records in the DNS console, simply restart the Net Logon service on your DC to rerun the DNS dynamic update process. To restart the Net Logon service, simply open the Services console (**Start** > **Administrative Tools** > **Services**), right click the Net Logon service in the list and select **Restart**. Alternatively, you can restart the Net Logon service from a command window or Run dialog box using the following commands:

net stop netlogon

net start netlogon

If restarting the Net Logon service does not create SRV records, you should ensure that the zone for your domain supports DNS dynamic updates. On a Windows DNS server, simply right click your *domainname* zone in the DNS console and click Properties to view the status of your DNS zone as shown in Figure 2-24.

Figure 2-24

Specifying Dynamic Updates on a Zone

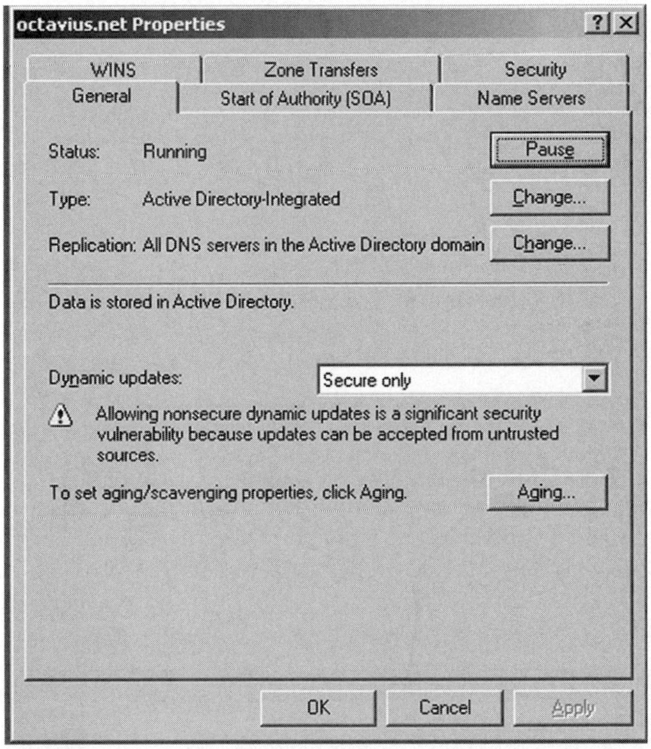

If the Dynamic updates drop-down box is set to None, then you need to change it to allow dynamic updates. Secure dynamic updates are chosen by default if DNS is installed during the Active Directory Installation Wizard and use the Kerberos protocol to ensure that only domain computers are allowed to create records on the DNS server.

TAKE NOTE*

If you used a nonWindows DNS server that does not support dynamic updates to host the DNS zones used by AD, you can manually import the SRV records listed in the %systemroot%\system32\config\netlogon.dns file into the zone file on the nonWindows DNS server.

The dynamic update protocol is not limited to the creation of SRV records in DNS. Computers running Windows 2000 and later in the domain use the dynamic update protocol to automatically create A records for their computers. In large domains, this can create numerous records in the DNS zone and slow down DNS queries as a result. Consequently, you should click on the **Aging** button shown in Figure 2-24 to configure the automatic deletion of outdated DNS records that were added with dynamic update as depicted in Figure 2-25.

Figure 2-25

Enabling DNS Aging and Scavenging

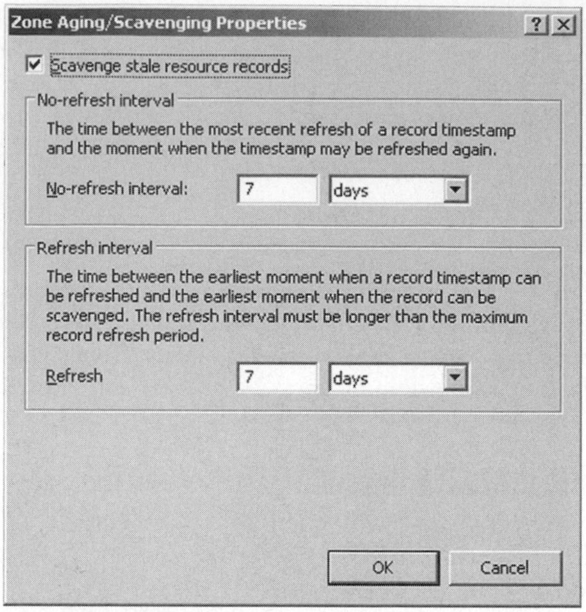

Removing Active Directory

> To remove AD from an existing DC, you can simply run the Active Directory Installation Wizard again.

There may be times when you need to remove AD from a DC in your domain such as the decommissioning of a server. In this case, you can simply run the Active Directory Installation Wizard again on the DC. The Active Directory Installation Wizard detects the configuration of AD on the computer and prompts you to remove AD as shown in Figure 2-26.

Figure 2-26

Removing Active Directory

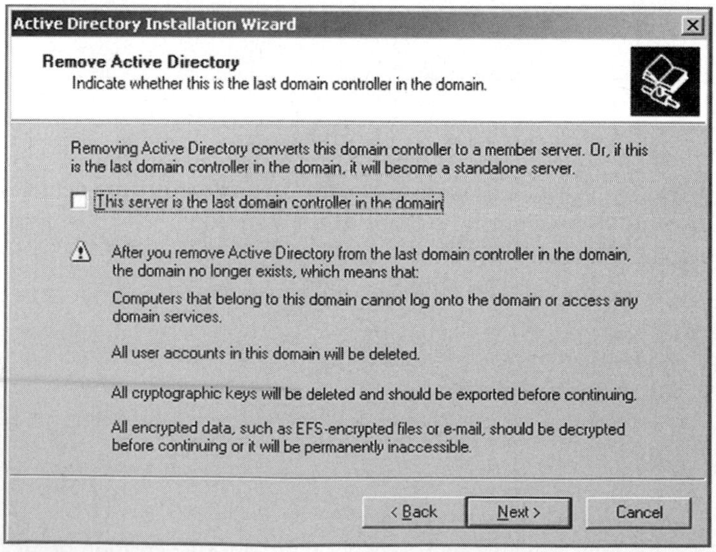

After removing AD from your DC, the computer will still be joined to the domain and will still contain a computer account in the domain unless you select **This server is the last domain controller in the domain** from Figure 2-26.

If the removal of AD fails or you receive an error message during the Active Directory Installation Wizard, you can force the removal of AD by running the **dcpromo/forceremoval** command from a command window or the Run dialog box.

Configuring Active Directory

THE BOTTOM LINE

Following a successful AD deployment, there are several tasks that you should perform to ensure that AD functions properly. More specifically, you should ensure that your domains and forest run at the highest functional level, as well as create a site structure that allows for efficient replication. Additionally, you should examine the placement of FSMOs and GC to optimize AD performance and reliability and create trusts that allow fast resource access between child domains as well as resource access to foreign domains, forests, and Kerberos realms.

Raising Functional Levels

The domain and forest functional level affects the type of DCs that are allowed in the domain and forest. As a result, raising your domain and forest functional level will allow you to use additional features that are available in more recent versions of AD.

By default, new AD domains are set to the Windows 2000 Mixed functional level for backwards compatibility. In general, you should always ensure that all domains and the forest run at the highest possible domain functional level to allow for the most functionality from AD.

Before deploying Exchange Server 2007, you need to ensure that all domains that will contain Exchange Server or email recipients are raised to the Windows 2000 Native functional level or higher.

 RAISE THE DOMAIN FUNCTIONAL LEVEL

GET READY. Turn on the computer, and log in as the Administrator user account. Close any windows that appear on the desktop.

1. Click **Start**, **Administrative Tools**, and **Active Directory Domains and Trusts**. The Active Directory Domains and Trusts console appears.

2. In the left pane, right click the object that represents your AD domain and select **Raise Domain Functional Level** from the menu. The Raise Domain Functional Level window appears as shown in Figure 2-27.

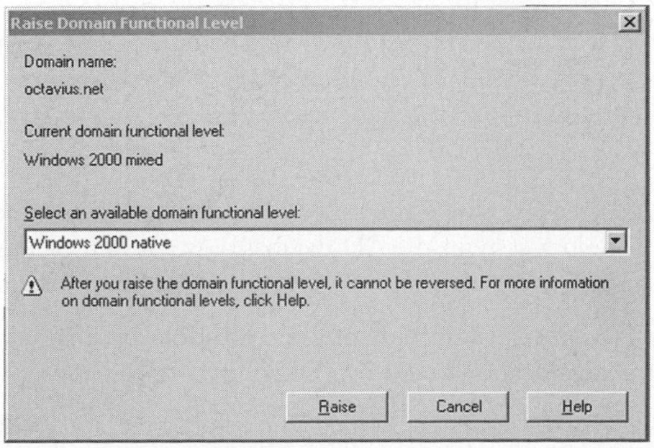

Figure 2-27

Raising the Domain Functional Level

> **Raise Domain Functional Level** ☒
>
> Domain name:
> octavius.net
>
> Current domain functional level:
> Windows 2000 mixed
>
> Select an available domain functional level:
> Windows 2000 native ▼
>
> ⚠ After you raise the domain functional level, it cannot be reversed. For more information on domain functional levels, click Help.
>
> [Raise] [Cancel] [Help]

ANOTHER WAY

You can also raise the domain functional level by right clicking your domain object in the Active Directory Users and Computers console and selecting Raise Domain Functional Level from the menu.

3. Select the appropriate domain functional level from the drop-down box shown in Figure 2-27 and click **Raise**. You will receive a warning indicating that the action is irreversible.

4. Click **OK** to confirm the action.

5. Click **OK** again to close the Raise Domain Functional Level dialog box.

 RAISE THE FOREST FUNCTIONAL LEVEL

GET READY. Turn on the computer, and log in as the Administrator user account. Close any windows that appear on the desktop.

1. Click **Start**, **Administrative Tools**, and **Active Directory Domains and Trusts**. The Active Directory Domains and Trusts console appears.

2. In the left pane, right click Active Directory Domains and Trusts and select **Raise Forest Functional Level** from the menu. The Raise Forest Functional Level window appears as shown in Figure 2-28.

Figure 2-28

Raising the Forest Functional Level

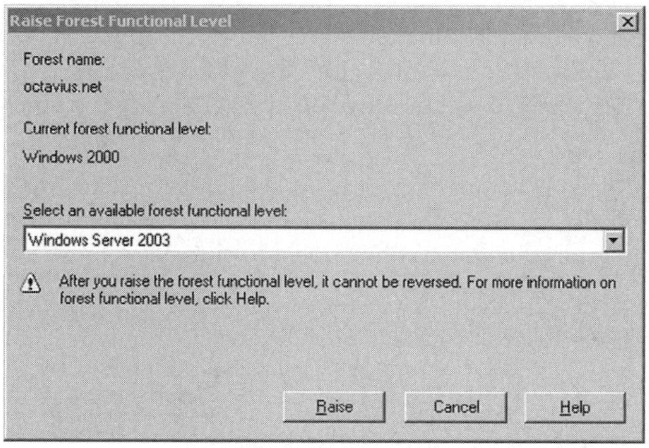

> **Raise Forest Functional Level**
>
> Forest name:
> octavius.net
>
> Current forest functional level:
> Windows 2000
>
> Select an available forest functional level:
> Windows Server 2003 ▼
>
> ⚠ After you raise the forest functional level, it cannot be reversed. For more information on forest functional level, click Help.
>
> [Raise] [Cancel] [Help]

3. Select the appropriate forest functional level from the drop-down box shown in Figure 2-28 and click **Raise**. You will receive a warning indicating that the action is irreversible.

4. Click **OK** to confirm the action.

5. Click **OK** again to close the Raise Forest Functional Level dialog box.

Configuring Sites

> After creating a new domain or forest, you should ensure that you create site and subnet objects that represent the physical locations within your organization. Following this, you should configure site link objects between sites to allow for efficient replication.

By default, AD creates a single site called Default-First-Site-Name that includes all DCs in the forest that hold a copy of the AD database. As a result, AD assumes that all DCs are on the same fast LAN and changes between DCs are replicated frequently.

If your organization spans multiple physical locations, you should create multiple site objects that represent each location and move DC objects to the appropriate site.

To ensure that new DCs that are added to the forest are automatically associated with the correct site, you should create **subnet objects** that represent the physical TCP/IP subnets that are available in each site. When a DC is added to the forest, the IP address on its network interface is associated with the correct subnet object and a DC object is created in the site that the subnet object is coupled with. A single site can be associated with multiple subnet objects if the site has several different interconnected LANs.

TAKE NOTE*

Instead of creating a new site object for the first site in your organization, you can simply rename Default-First-Site-Name.

Once sites and subnets have been configured, you can create site link objects that connect two or more sites together. Site link objects contain the restrictions used when AD data is replicated between bridgehead servers in different sites.

The protocol used to replicate between DCs is called the ***inter-site transport***. Although most replication uses an inter-site transport that uses RPCs over the IP protocol, you can configure SMTP to replicate the AD schema and configuration between domains in the same forest. By default, AD creates a default site link object called DEFAULTIPSITELINK that connects all sites using the IP inter-site transport.

To configure sites, you can use the ***Active Directory Sites and Services*** console (**Start** > **Administrative Tools** > **Active Directory Sites and Services**). Figure 2-29 shows the default site structure following the installation of the first DC (EXCH1) in the octavius.net organization.

TAKE NOTE *

If you wish to configure subnet objects, you must coordinate the TCP/IP configuration within the organization to ensure that each location uses a different TCP/IP subnet.

Figure 2-29

Default Site Structure

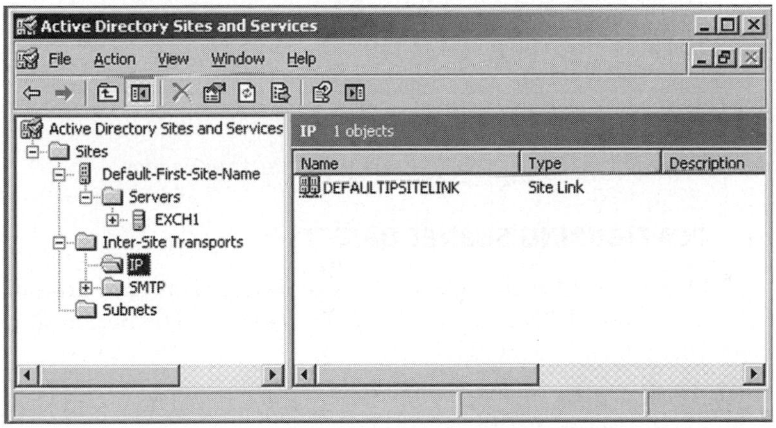

CONFIGURING SITE OBJECTS

Site configuration relies on the details of your actual organization. Although the following exercises use the octavius.net organization introduced in this lesson as an example, they can be performed on any forest for practice. Octavius.net contains two physical locations (Cupertino and Boston) that are linked to each other via the Internet.

CONFIGURE SITE OBJECTS

GET READY. Turn on the computer, and log in as the Administrator user account. Close any windows that appear on the desktop.

1. Click **Start**, **Administrative Tools**, and **Active Directory Sites and Services**. The Active Directory Sites and Services console appears.

2. In the left pane, expand Default-First-Site-Name. Underneath Default-First-Site-Name, expand the Servers folder. Note that an object representing your DC exists within the Default-First-Site-Name site.

3. Right click Default-First-Site-Name and select **Rename** from the menu. Type **Cupertino** beside the site object and press **Enter**.

4. Right click the Sites folder and select **New Site** from the menu. The New Object—Site window appears.

5. Type **Boston** in the Name dialog box. Next, click on **DEFAULTIPSITELINK** to ensure that the new site uses the default site link object as shown in Figure 2-30 and click **OK**. An Active Directory window appears.

Figure 2-30

Creating a New Site

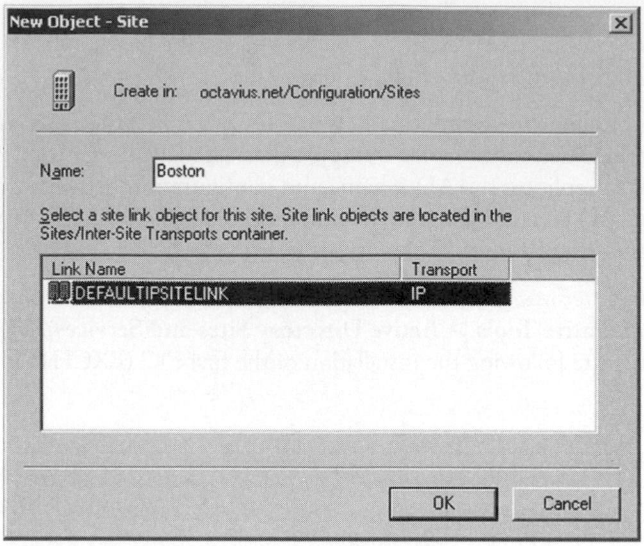

6. Click **OK** to close the Active Directory window.

CONFIGURING SUBNET OBJECTS

Octavius.net has three subnets across the Cupertino and Boston locations. The Cupertino site has a single LAN that uses the 10.1.0.0 subnet. The Boston site has two LANs that use the 10.2.0.0 and 10.3.0.0 subnets.

CONFIGURE SUBNET OBJECTS

GET READY. Turn on the computer, and log in as the Administrator user account. Close any windows that appear on the desktop.

1. Click **Start**, **Administrative Tools**, and **Active Directory Sites and Services**. The Active Directory Sites and Services console appears.

2. Right click the Subnets folder and select **New Subnet** from the menu. The New Object—Subnet window appears as shown in Figure 2-31.

Figure 2-31

Creating a New Subnet

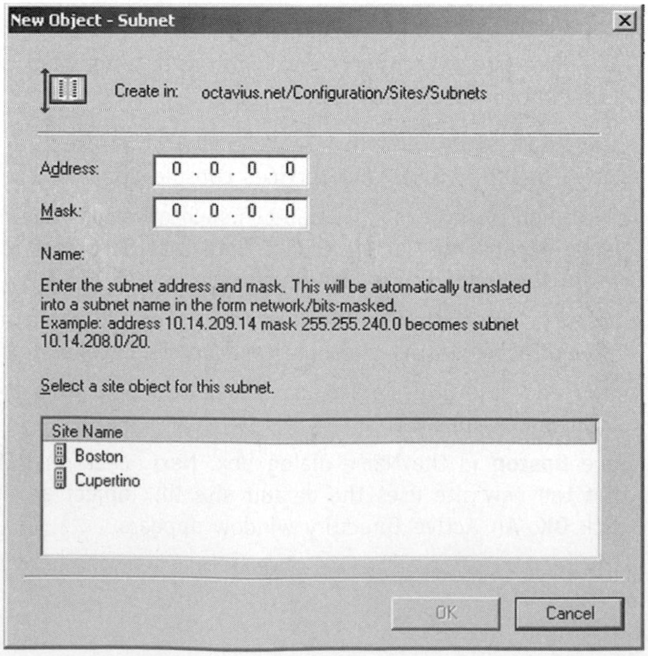

3. In the Address dialog box, enter the IP network **10.1.0.0**. In the Mask dialog box, enter the subnet mask **255.255.0.0**. Next, highlight the **Cupertino** site to associate the 10.1.0.0 network with the Cupertino site and click **OK**.

4. Again, right click the Subnets folder and select **New Subnet** from the menu. In the Address dialog box, enter the IP network **10.2.0.0**. In the Mask dialog box, enter the subnet mask **255.255.0.0**. Next, highlight the **Boston** site to associate the 10.2.0.0 network with the Boston site and click **OK**.

5. Again, right click the Subnets folder and select **New Subnet** from the menu. In the Address dialog box, enter the IP network **10.3.0.0**. In the Mask dialog box, enter the subnet mask **255.255.0.0**. Next, highlight the **Boston** site to associate the 10.3.0.0 network with the Boston site and click **OK**.

CONFIGURING SITE LINK OBJECTS

Octavius.net has different administrative staff members in the Cupertino and Boston locations who are responsible for creating objects for use within their own location. As a result, object replication can occur after business hours without affecting normal operations. You need to ensure that replication only occurs every hour between 9:00 p.m. and 3:00 a.m. Monday to Friday and hourly on weekends.

 CONFIGURE SITE LINK OBJECTS

GET READY. Turn on the computer, and log in as the Administrator user account. Close any windows that appear on the desktop.

1. Click **Start**, **Administrative Tools**, and **Active Directory Sites and Services**. The Active Directory Sites and Services console appears.

2. In the left pane, expand Inter-Site Transports and highlight the **IP** folder. Note the DEFAULTIPSITELINK object within the IP folder.

3. Right click the DEFAULTIPSITELINK object in the right page and select **Delete** from the menu. When prompted to confirm the deletion, click **Yes**.

4. Right click the IP folder in the left pane and select **New Site Link** from the menu. The New Object—Site Link window appears as shown in Figure 2-32.

Figure 2-32

Creating a New Site Link

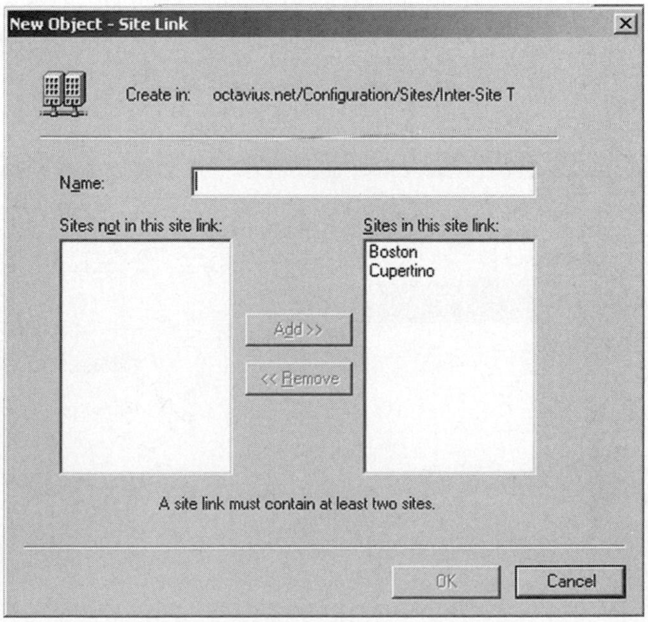

New Object - Site Link

Create in: octavius.net/Configuration/Sites/Inter-Site T

Name:

Sites not in this site link:

Sites in this site link:
Boston
Cupertino

Add >>

<< Remove

A site link must contain at least two sites.

OK   Cancel

5. Type **Cupertino-to-Boston** in the Name dialog box. Ensure that the Boston and Cupertino sites are included within the site link as shown in Figure 2-32 and click **OK**.

6. Right click the Cupertino-to-Boston site link in the right pane and select **Properties** from the menu. The Cupertino-to-Boston Properties screen appears a shown in Figure 2-33.

Figure 2-33

Configuring Site Properties

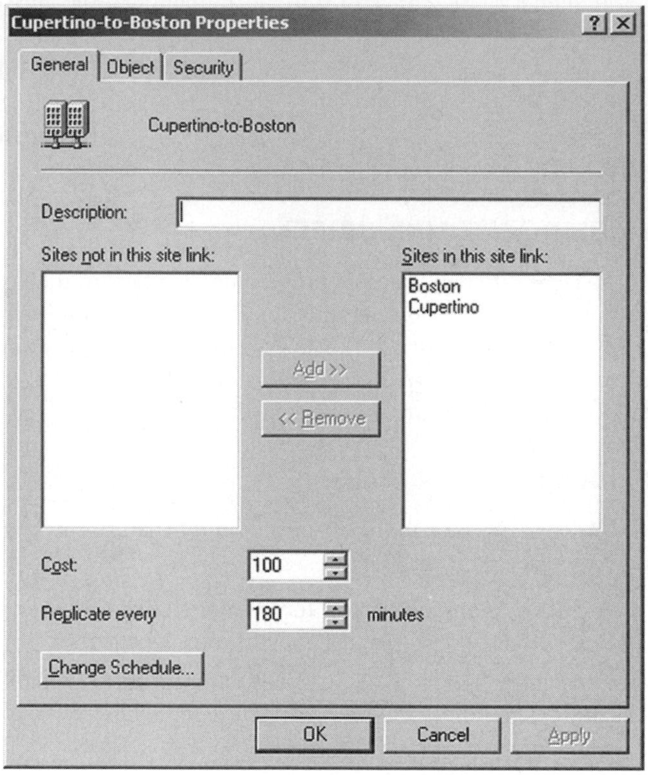

TAKE NOTE*

Because we only have a single site link that can be used to connect the Cupertino and Boston sites, there is no need to modify the cost of this site link to influence the use of a particular site link.

7. Enter **60** in the Replicate every dialog box instead of the default value of 180.

8. Click the **Change Schedule** button. The Schedule for Cupertino-to-Boston window appears.

9. Use your mouse to highlight the cells that indicate 3:00 a.m. to 9:00 p.m. Monday to Friday and choose **Replication Not Available** as depicted in Figure 2-34 and click **OK**.

Figure 2-34

Specifying a Replication Schedule

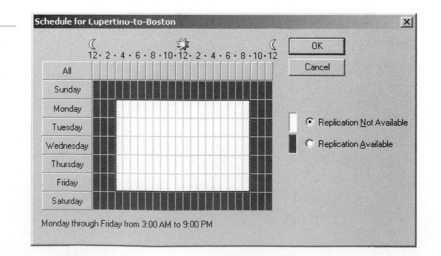

10. Click **OK** to close the Cupertino-to-Boston Properties screen.

CONFIGURING THE PREFERRED BRIDGEHEAD SERVER

Although several DCs will be added to the octavius.net forest in the coming months, you wish to ensure that EXCH1 in the Cupertino site is always used to perform replication using the IP inter-site transport between Cupertino and Boston. The procedures in this section can be used on any server object within the Active Directory Sites and Services console.

 ### CONFIGURE THE PREFERRED BRIDGEHEAD SERVER

GET READY. Turn on the computer, and log in as the Administrator user account. Close any windows that appear on the desktop.

1. Click **Start**, **Administrative Tools**, and **Active Directory Sites and Services**. The Active Directory Sites and Services console appears.

2. In the left pane, expand Cupertino. Underneath Cupertino, expand the Servers folder. Right click the EXCH1 object and select **Properties** from the menu. The EXCH1 Properties screen is displayed as shown in Figure 2-35.

Figure 2-35

Specifying the Preferred Bridgehead Server

```
EXCH1 Properties                                    ? X

 General | Object | Security |

    ▥        EXCH1
    _____

    Description: [                              ]

    Transports available for          This server is a preferred
    inter-site data transfer:         bridgehead server for the
                                      following transports:

    ┌─────────────────┐              ┌─────────────────┐
    │ IP              │  [ Add >> ]   │                 │
    │ SMTP            │               │                 │
    │                 │  [ << Remove ]│                 │
    │                 │               │                 │
    └─────────────────┘              └─────────────────┘

    ┌ Computer ──────────────────────────────────────┐
    │  Computer:  [EXCH1                            ] │
    │                                                 │
    │  Domain:    [octavius.net                     ] │
    └─────────────────────────────────────────────────┘

              [   OK   ]   [ Cancel ]   [ Apply ]
```

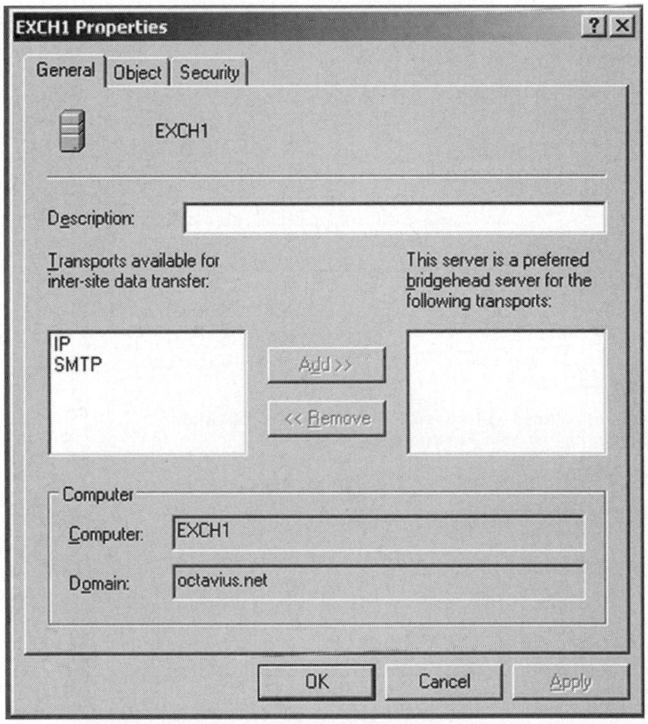

3. By default, all replication protocols are listed in the left dialog box. Highlight **IP** in the left dialog box and click the **Add** >> button to move it to the right dialog box. This will ensure that EXCH1 is used as the bridgehead server for the Cupertino site.

4. Click **OK** to close the EXCH1 Properties screen.

Configuring the Global Catalog

Configuring GC is important to ensure the normal operation of AD and guarantee fast object queries. As a result, it is important to configure GC on the appropriate DCs within your organization.

For best performance, you should ensure that all sites within your organization have at least one DC that contains the GC. Additionally, you must ensure that a GC exists in each site that contains an Exchange server.

If you have a site that is connected to other sites via a slow WAN connection that is ill-suited to GC replication traffic, you may instead choose to enable UGMC on the site to allow fast user logons to a Windows 2000 Native functional level or higher domain.

➡ ADD THE GLOBAL CATALOG TO A DOMAIN CONTROLLER

GET READY. Turn on the computer, and log in as the Administrator user account. Close any windows that appear on the desktop.

1. Click **Start**, **Administrative Tools**, and **Active Directory Sites and Services**. The Active Directory Sites and Services console appears.

2. In the left pane, expand the site that contains your DC object. Underneath the site, expand the Servers folder and expand your DC object to expose the NTDS Settings object. Right click **NTDS Settings** and select **Properties** from the menu. The NTDS Settings Properties screen is displayed as shown in Figure 2-36.

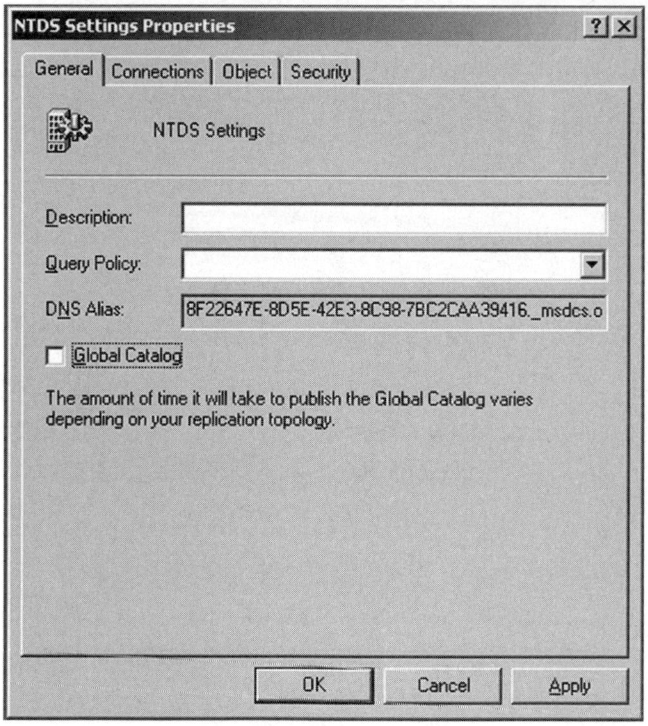

Figure 2-36

Adding the Global Catalog

3. Place a check mark in the Global Catalog checkbox and click **OK** to close the NTDS Settings Properties screen.

➡ ENABLE UNIVERSAL GROUP MEMBERSHIP CACHING ON A SITE

GET READY. Turn on the computer, and log in as the Administrator user account. Close any windows that appear on the desktop.

1. Click **Start**, **Administrative Tools**, and **Active Directory Sites and Services**. The Active Directory Sites and Services console appears.

2. In the left pane, highlight the site that should use UGMC. Right click the **NTDS Settings** object in the right pane, and select **Properties** from the menu. The NTDS Site Settings Properties screen is displayed as shown in Figure 2-37.

Figure 2-37

Enabling Universal Group Membership Caching

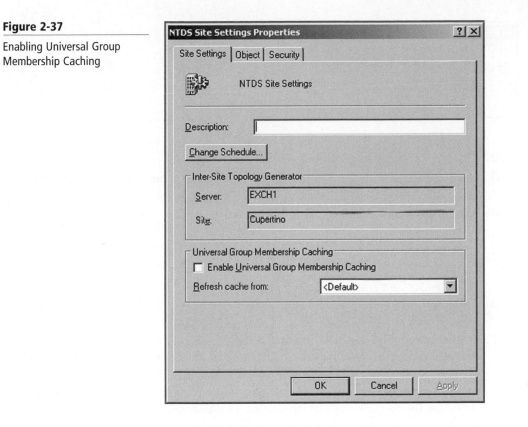

3. Place a check mark in the Enable Universal Group Membership Caching checkbox and click **OK** to close the NTDS Site Settings Properties screen.

Configuring FSMO Roles

FSMO roles provide critical operations in an AD forest and domain. You should become accustomed with the tools used to view and change FSMO roles in order to optimize the performance and reliability of AD.

By default, the forestwide FSMO roles exist on the first DC in the forest and the domainwide FSMO roles exist on the first DC in each domain. After installing new forests, domains, and DCs, you should consider moving the FSMO roles to a DC that is highly visible on the network to allow FSMOs to function normally. You can view and change FSMO roles using one of the following utilities:

- Active Directory Schema MMC snap-in (Schema Master)
- Active Directory Domains and Trusts (Domain Naming Master)
- Active Directory Users and Computers (PDC Emulator, RID Master, Infrastructure Master)

If the DC that holds an FSMO fails, you must use the **ntdsutil.exe** command on a running DC to forcefully seize and assume the FSMO role.

VIEW AND CHANGE THE SCHEMA MASTER

GET READY. Turn on the computer, and log in as the Administrator user account. Close any windows that appear on the desktop.

1. Click **Start**, **Run**, and type **regsvr32 schmmgmt.dll** in the Run box to register the Active Directory Schema snap-in. If successful, you will see the RegSvr32 window shown in Figure 2-38.

Figure 2-38

Registering the Schema DLL

TAKE NOTE*

By registering the Active Directory Schema snap-in, you will be allowed to add it to the MMC.

2. Click **OK** to close the RegSvr32 window.

3. Next, click **Start**, **Run**, type **mmc** in the Run box, and press **Enter** to open the Microsoft Management Console (MMC).

4. In the MMC, click **File** and select **Add/Remove Snap-in**. The Add/Remove Snap-in window appears.

5. Click **Add** and select **Active Directory Schema** from the Add Stand-alone Snap-in window. Click **Add** and then click **Close** to close the Add Stand-alone Snap-in window.

6. Click **OK** in the Add/Remove Snap-in to add the Active Directory Schema to the MMC.

7. In the left pane of the MMC, expand Active Directory Schema. Next, right click Active Directory Schema and select **Change Domain Controller** from the menu. The Change Domain Controller window appears.

8. Select **Specify Name**, enter the DNS name of your current DC in the dialog box and click **OK** to close the Change Domain Controller window.

9. Right click Active Directory Schema and select **Operations Master** from the menu. The Change Schema Master window appears as shown in Figure 2-39.

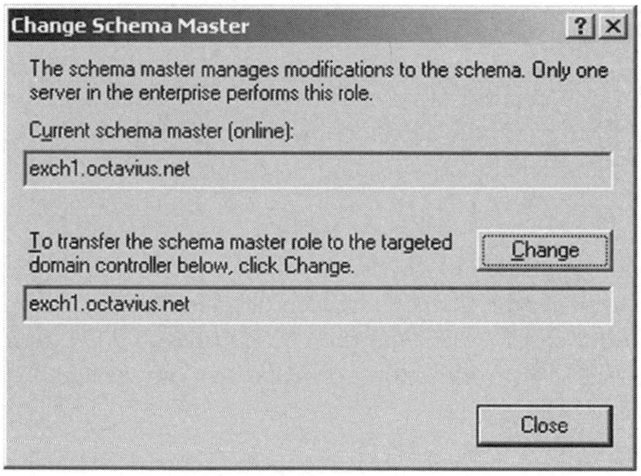

Figure 2-39

Viewing and Changing the Schema Master

> **Change Schema Master** ?|X|
>
> The schema master manages modifications to the schema. Only one server in the enterprise performs this role.
>
> Current schema master (online):
>
> exch1.octavius.net
>
> To transfer the schema master role to the targeted domain controller below, click Change.   [Change]
>
> exch1.octavius.net
>
> [Close]

10. Observe the name of the DC that currently holds the Schema Master FSMO role. If the Schema Master DC is online, you can transfer the role to your DC (listed in the second dialog box). To do this, click the **Change** button shown in Figure 2-39 and click **Yes** when prompted to confirm the change.

11. Click **Close** to close the Change Schema Master window.

➔ **VIEW AND CHANGE THE DOMAIN NAMING MASTER**

GET READY. Turn on the computer, and log in as the Administrator user account. Close any windows that appear on the desktop.

1. Click **Start**, **Administrative Tools**, and **Active Directory Domains and Trusts**. The Active Directory Domains and Trusts console appears.

   2. In the left pane, right click Active Directory Domains and Trusts and select **Connect to Domain Controller** from the menu. The Connect to Domain Controller window appears.

   3. Select your DC from the list and click **OK** to close the Connect to Domain Controller window.

   4. In the left pane, right click Active Directory Domains and Trusts and select **Operations Master** from the menu. The Change Operations Master window appears as shown in Figure 2-40.

Figure 2-40

Viewing and Changing the
Domain Naming Master

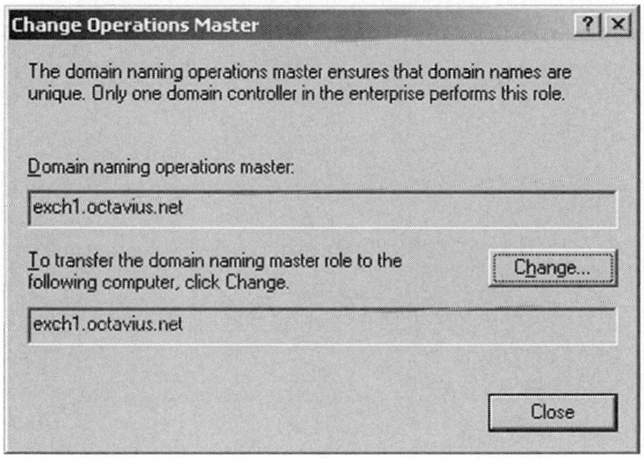

   5. Observe the name of the DC that currently holds the Domain Naming Master FSMO role. If the Domain Naming Master DC is online, you can transfer the role to your DC (listed in the second dialog box). To do this, click the **Change** button shown in Figure 2-40 and click **Yes** when prompted to confirm the change.

   6. Click **Close** to close the Change Operations Master window.

⊙ VIEW AND CHANGE THE DOMAINWIDE FSMO ROLES

GET READY. Turn on the computer, and log in as the Administrator user account. Close any windows that appear on the desktop.

   1. Click **Start**, **Administrative Tools**, and **Active Directory Users and Computers**. The Active Directory Users and Computers console appears.

   2. In the left pane, right click the object that represents your domain and select **Connect to Domain Controller** from the menu. The Connect to Domain Controller window appears.

   3. Select your DC from the list and click **OK** to close the Connect to Domain Controller window.

   4. In the left pane, right click the object that represents your domain and select **Operations Masters** from the menu. The Operations Master window appears as shown in Figure 2-41. Note that there are three tabs for each of the three domain-wide FSMO roles.

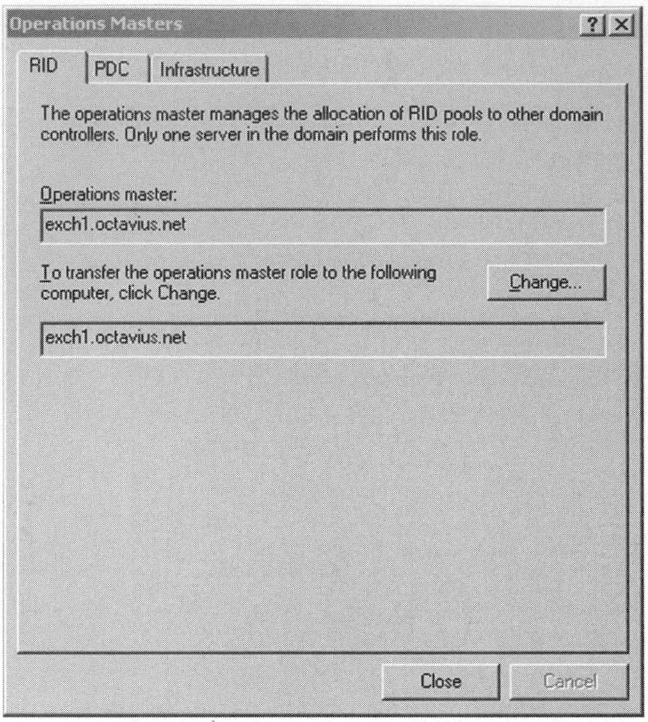

Figure 2-41

Viewing and Changing the
Domainwide FSMO Roles

5. Observe the name of the DC that currently holds the RID Master FSMO role. If the RID Master DC is online, you can transfer the role to your DC by clicking the **Change** button and clicking **Yes** when prompted to confirm the change.

6. Click on the PDC tab and observe the name of the DC that currently holds the PDC Emulator FSMO role. If the PDC Emulator DC is online, you can transfer the role to your DC by clicking the **Change** button and clicking **Yes** when prompted to confirm the change.

7. Click on the Infrastructure tab and observe the name of the DC that currently holds the Infrastructure Master FSMO role. If the Infrastructure Master DC is online, you can transfer the role to your DC by clicking the **Change** button and clicking **Yes** when prompted to confirm the change.

8. Click **Close** to close the Operations Master window.

SEIZE A FAILED FSMO ROLE

GET READY. Turn on the computer, and log in as the Administrator user account. Close any windows that appear on the desktop.

1. Click **Start**, **Run**, type **ntdsutil** in the Run dialog box, and press **Enter**. The ntdsutil.exe prompt appears in a command window.

2. At the ntdsutil.exe prompt, type **roles** and press **Enter** to open the FSMO maintenance prompt.

3. At the FSMO maintenance prompt, type **connections** and press **Enter** to open the server connections prompt.

4. At the server connections prompt, type **connect to server DC** where *DC* is the DNS name of your current DC and press **Enter**. Type **quit** at the server connections prompt, and press **Enter** to return to the FSMO maintenance prompt.

5. At the FSMO maintenance prompt, type one of the following commands to seize the appropriate FSMO role and press **Enter**. You will be presented with the Role Seizure Confirmation Dialog window as shown in Figure 2-42.

- Seize PDC
- Seize RID Master
- Seize schema Master
- Seize infrastructure Master
- Seize domain naming Master

Figure 2-42

Seizing an FSMO Role

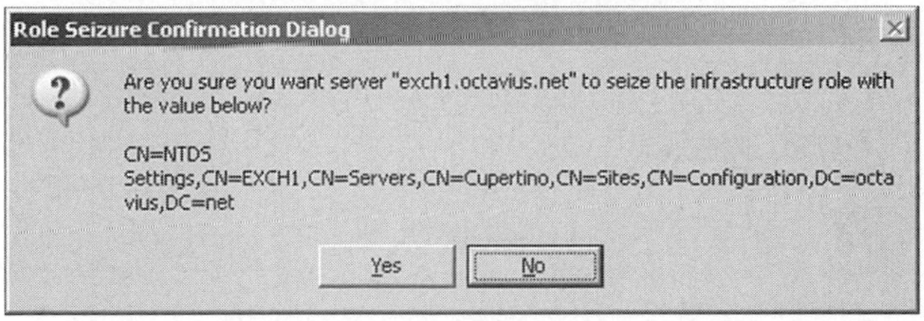

Role Seizure Confirmation Dialog

Are you sure you want server "exch1.octavius.net" to seize the infrastructure role with the value below?

CN=NTDS Settings,CN=EXCH1,CN=Servers,CN=Cupertino,CN=Sites,CN=Configuration,DC=octavius,DC=net

Yes   No

6. Click **Yes** to confirm the role seizure.

7. Type **quit** at the FSMO maintenance prompt, and press **Enter** to return to the ntdsutil.exe prompt.

8. Type **quit** at the ntdsutil.exe prompt, and press **Enter** to close ntdsutil.

Configuring Trusts

You may be required to create a trust relationship between domains in order to speed up authentication and resource access within your own forest to allow group membership and resource access to a remote forest, domain or Kerberos realm. As a result, you should understand how to set up additional trust relationships in your forest.

Two-way transitive trusts are automatically created between the first domains in each tree within a forest as well as between parent domains and their child domains. This gives administrators in a domain the ability to assign permissions to users and groups in other domains within the forest. In addition, trust relationships allow users and groups to become members of groups in another domain within the same forest.

Although the default trusts in a forest cannot be managed using Windows utilities, you can use the Active Directory Domains and Trusts console (**Start** > **Administrative Tools** > **Active Directory Domains and Trusts**) to create additional shortcut trusts between domains in different trees to speed up performance. In addition, the Active Directory Domains and Trusts console can be used to create trusts to domains, forests, and Kerberos realms outside of your forest to allow for remote permissions assignment or group membership.

Before creating a trust relationship, you should ensure that your computer can contact a DC in the target domain, forest, or Kerberos Realm. This often involves ensuring that the DNS server listed in TCP/IP properties for members of the domain is configured to forward requests for the target domain to a DNS server that holds the necessary A or SRV records for the target domain. On a Windows DNS server, you can simply open the DNS console (**Start** > **Administrative Tools** > **DNS**), and highlight the Forwarders tab of your DNS server properties to add a forwarder entry as shown in Figure 2-43.

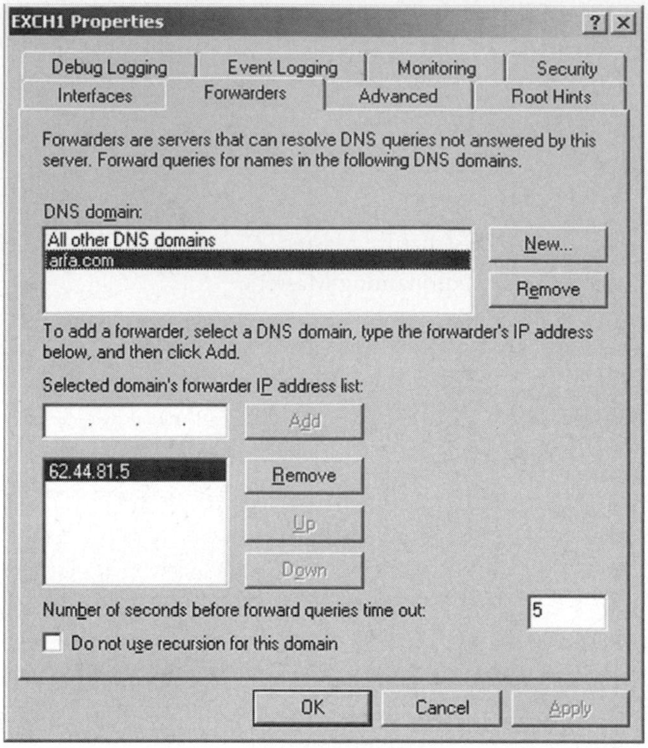

Figure 2-43

Configuring a DNS Forwarding
Entry

The DNS server configured in Figure 2-43 will forward any DNS name resolution requests
for arfa.com to the DNS server with the IP address 62.44.81.5.

Once you are able to resolve names in the target domain successfully, you can right click
the object that represents your domain in the Active Directory Domains and Trusts console,
choose **Properties**, and highlight the Trusts tab as shown in Figure 2-44.

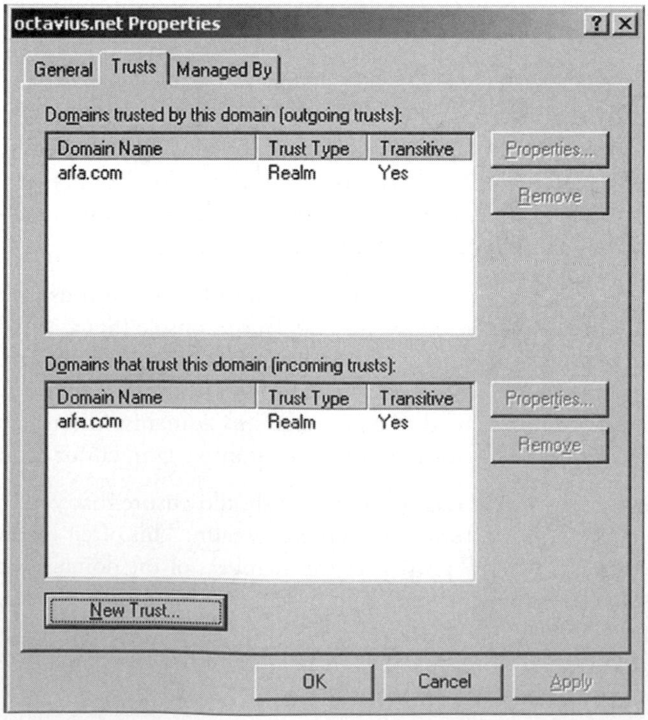

Figure 2-44

Manually Configuring Trust
Relationships

TAKE NOTE * Manually created trusts can become corrupted over time. You can check the validity of a trust in the Active Directory Domains and Trusts console by selecting the **Properties** button beside a trust shown in Figure 2-44.

Figure 2-44 already indicates that a two-way realm trust has been created between your domain and arfa.com (outgoing trust) as well as between arfa.com and your domain (incoming trust). To create additional trusts, you can click on the **New Trust** button shown in Figure 2-44 to open the New Trust Wizard. After specifying the name of the target domain, forest, or Kerberos realm in the New Trust Wizard, the options available will be specific to the type of trust available. You may be prompted for the style of trust (transitive or nontransitive), as well as the direction of the trust (one-way outgoing, one-way incoming, two-way). If you create a one-way incoming or two-way trust, you must contact the remote DC to configure the trust and will need to enter a password to validate the trust or a username and password of the remote Administrator to automatically create the trust.

■ Managing Active Directory Objects

THE BOTTOM LINE The creation and management of OU, user, computer, and group objects is a common daily administrative task for AD and Exchange administrators. In addition, Group Policy is often used to configure the settings applied to users and computers within AD including email configuration. Consequently, it is important to understand the procedures and utilities used to manage AD objects and Group Policy.

Creating and Managing Organizational Units

Before creating objects within a domain, you should ensure that a suitable OU structure exists to organize those objects.

OUs are primarily used to organize objects within a domain and may be created or managed using the Active Directory Users and Computers console (**Start** > **Administrative Tools** > **Active Directory Users and Computers**). The OUs that you create for your domain will depend on the requirements of the organization. As a result, new domains only contain a single Domain Controllers OU by default to contain DC computer accounts. All other objects such as user, computer, and group accounts are organized into default folders and should be moved to the appropriate OUs after they have been created.

Figure 2-45 shows the default Domain Controllers OU and folder structure for the octavius .net domain as well as additional East and West OUs that were created by the domain administrator to suit the organization. The East and West OUs contain subordinate OUs for each of the major departments in octavius.net.

To rename, move, or delete an OU, you can simply right click the OU within the Active Directory Users and Computers console and select the appropriate option. Before deleting an OU, ensure that the objects within the OU have been moved to another location.

TAKE NOTE * OU icons can be easily differentiated from folder icons in the Active Directory Users and Computers console because OU icons contain a picture of a book.

Figure 2-45

Octavius.net Organizational
Unit Structure

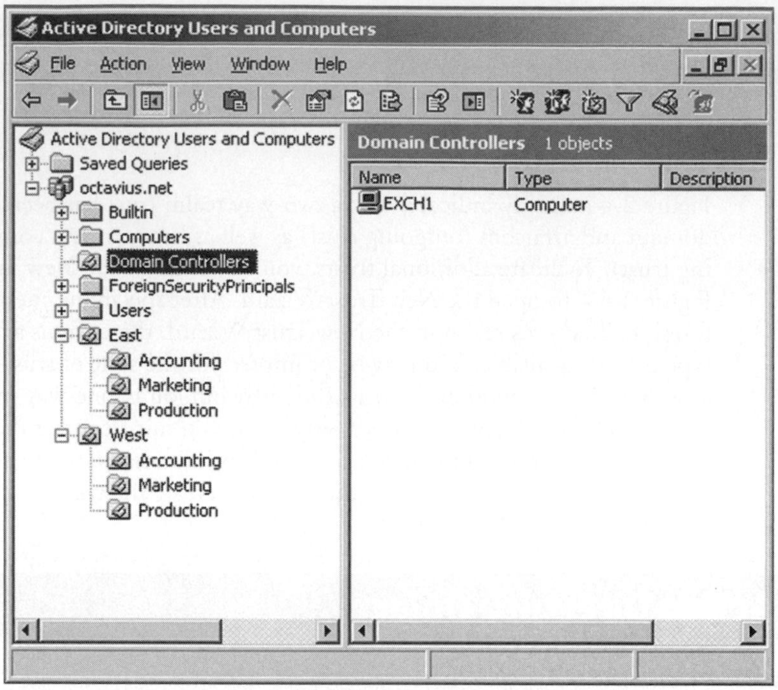

```
Active Directory Users and Computers                          _ □ X
  File   Action   View   Window   Help                        _ ᴮ X
  ⇐ ⇒   🖭 📖   ✂ 🖺 ✕ 🖆 🗗 🗔   🗗 📖   🖫🖫🖫 ▽ 🖫🖫
  Active Directory Users and Computers   Domain Controllers   1 objects
    Saved Queries                          Name        Type        Description
    octavius.net                           🖳EXCH1      Computer
      Builtin
      Computers
      Domain Controllers
      ForeignSecurityPrincipals
      Users
      East
         Accounting
         Marketing
         Production
      West
         Accounting
         Marketing
         Production
```

  CREATE A NEW ORGANIZATIONAL UNIT

GET READY. Turn on the computer, and log in as the Administrator user account. Close any
windows that appear on the desktop.

1. Click **Start**, **Administrative Tools**, and **Active Directory Users and Computers**.
   The Active Directory Users and Computers console appears.

2. In the left pane, right click the object that represents your AD domain and
   select **New** followed by **Organizational Unit** from the menu. The New Object—
   Organizational Unit window appears as shown in Figure 2-46.

Figure 2-46

Creating a New
Organizational Unit

```
New Object - Organizational Unit                               X
    🗀    Create in:   octavius.net/

    Name:
    |

                                            OK         Cancel
```

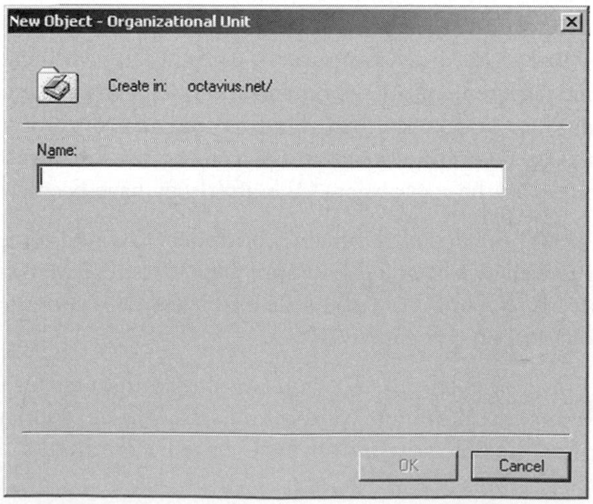

3. Type the name of the OU in the Name dialog box and click **OK**.

Creating and Managing Users

Exchange server relies on the information stored within user accounts when relaying email to mailboxes within the organization and when sending emails outside the organization. In order to manage Exchange Server 2007, it is important to first understand how to create and manage user accounts.

User account objects in AD store a great deal of information that is used by various programs and services. As with OUs, you can create user accounts using the Active Directory Users and Computers console (**Start** > **Administrative Tools** > **Active Directory Users and Computers**). When you create a user account, you need only specify the user's name, UPN, and password information. However, when you view the properties of a user account by right clicking the user account object and selecting **Properties** from the menu, you can navigate the several tabs to specify several more attributes as shown in Figure 2-47 for the user Bob Jones.

Figure 2-47

Editing User Attributes

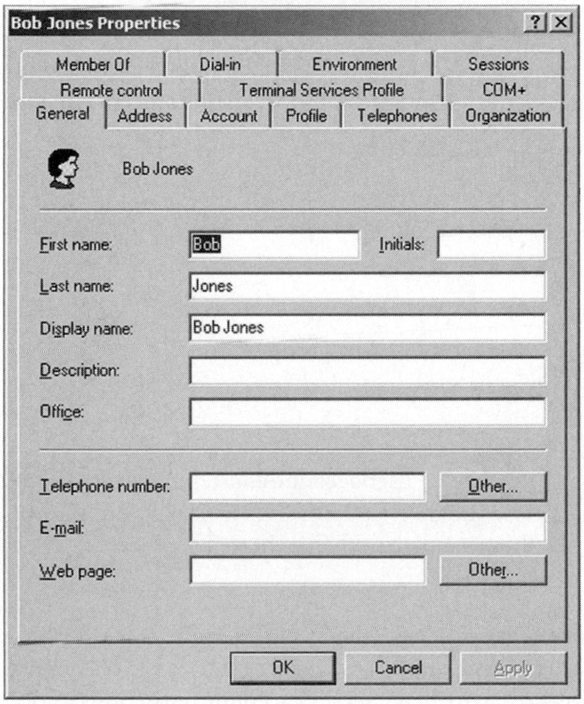

If you need to change the attributes of several user accounts simultaneously, simply select each user account object in Active Directory Users and Computers while holding down the **Ctrl** key on the keyboard, right click the selection, and choose **Properties**. This opens the Properties for Multiple Items window as shown in Figure 2-48. Not all user attributes are available in the Properties for Multiple Items window because many attributes are user specific.

Figure 2-48

Editing the Attributes for
Multiple Users

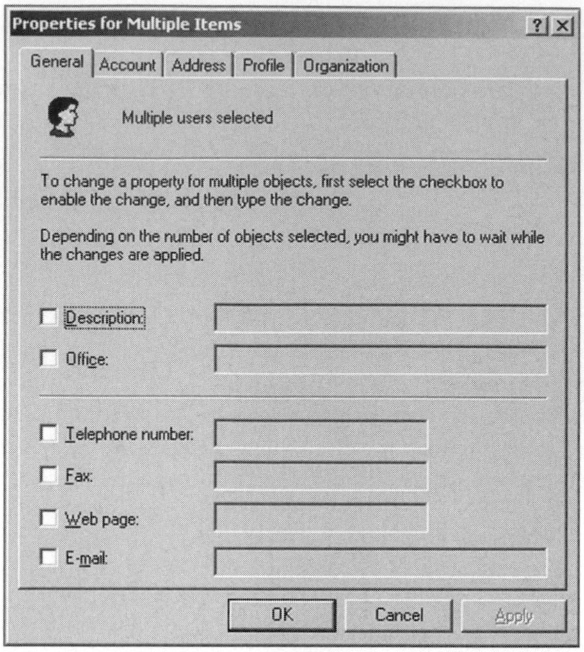

As with OU objects, most user maintenance can be performed by right clicking the user account object and selecting the appropriate option. This includes:

- Renaming the user account
- Moving the user account
- Deleting the user account
- Disabling the user account
- Resetting the user password
- Adding the user account to a group
- Copying the user account

TAKE NOTE *

If you accidentally delete a user account and re-create it, you must reassign all permissions to resources because the deleted user's SID is never reused. As a result, you should disable user accounts rather than delete them when possible.

To save time and ease management, many administrators create a sample user account for a specific department called a *user account template* that contains attributes that are common to all users in the department, such as account restrictions and group membership. When creating users in the future, you can then copy the template user account for that department and supply only the unique user information for the particular user.

⊖ **CREATE A USER ACCOUNT**

ANOTHER WAY

Instead, right click your domain object to create a new user account directly under the domain object. However, this is considered poor organization for AD objects.

GET READY. Turn on the computer, and log in as the Administrator user account. Close any windows that appear on the desktop.

1. Click **Start**, **Administrative Tools**, and **Active Directory Users and Computers**. The Active Directory Users and Computers console appears.

2. In the left pane, locate the OU object that should contain the user account. Right click the OU object and select **New** followed by **User** from the menu. The New Object—User window appears as shown in Figure 2-49.

Figure 2-49

Creating a New User

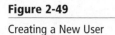

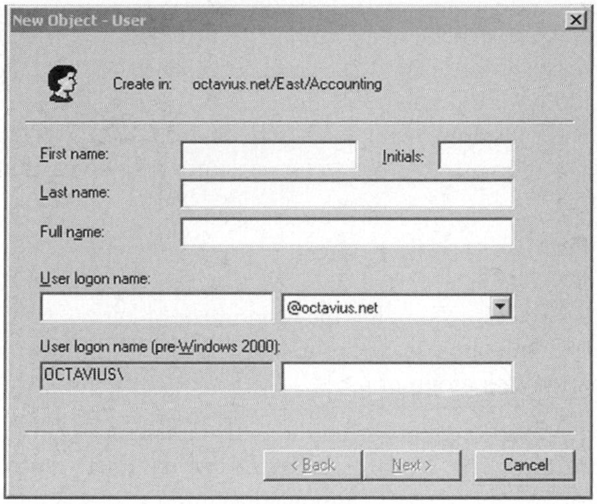

By default, AD domains require complex passwords for user accounts. These passwords must be at least six characters long and contain three of the four different types of characters (uppercase, lowercase, numbers, symbols).

3. Supply the appropriate information in the First name, Initials, and Last name fields as necessary.

4. In the User logon name dialog box, select a logon name that is unique in your domain and ensure that the correct domain name is listed next to it. This will become the UPN for the user account.

5. Observe the User logon name (preWindows 2000) that must be used if the user logs into the domain from a Windows 9x or NT4 client computer, and click **Next**. You will see the screen shown in Figure 2-50.

Figure 2-50

Specifying User Password Configuration

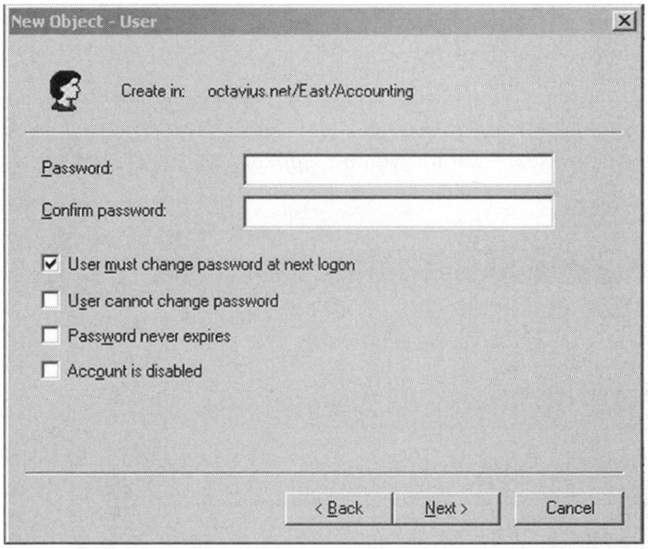

6. Supply the appropriate password information and options for your user account and click **Next**. You will be presented with a summary of your selections.

7. Click **Finish** to create the user account object.

Creating and Managing Groups

Groups are important to reduce the time and effort needed to administer resources in an AD and Exchange Server environment. Consequently, it is important to understand how groups can be created and managed using Active Directory Users and Computers.

TAKE NOTE *
Every domain contains a Domain Admins security group in the default Users folder in the Active Directory Users and Computers console that allows members to administer the domain. In addition, the forest root domain contains an Enterprise Admins group that allows forestwide administration and a Schema Admins group that allows modification of the AD schema. The first Administrator account in the forest automatically belongs to all three groups.

AD uses group objects to simplify the assignment of permissions to multiple user accounts. Exchange Server can also use groups to simplify email administration for multiple users or relay information to a group of users.

You can create group accounts using the Active Directory Users and Computers console (**Start** > **Administrative Tools** > **Active Directory Users and Computers**). When creating a group it is important to use a naming convention that accurately describes the group. For example, **Accounts Payable GG East** can be used to easily indicate a Global Group that contains Accounts Payable users in the East division of the organization.

Once created, you can modify the properties of the group and change its type or scope or group membership. Groups can contain user, group, and computer objects as members. To, rename, move, or delete a group, you can right click the group within the Active Directory Users and Computers console and select the appropriate option.

CREATE A NEW GROUP

GET READY. Turn on the computer, and log in as the Administrator user account. Close any windows that appear on the desktop.

TAKE NOTE *

Deleting a group does not delete the members of the group.

1. Click **Start**, **Administrative Tools**, and **Active Directory Users and Computers**. The Active Directory Users and Computers console appears.
2. In the left pane, locate the OU object that should contain the group account. Right click the OU object and select **New** followed by **Group** from the menu. The New Object—Group window appears as shown in Figure 2-51.

Figure 2-51

Creating a New Group

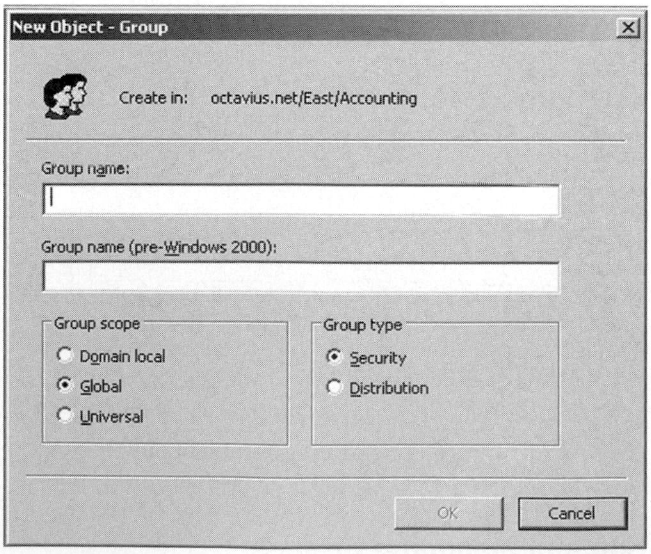

New Object - Group
Create in: octavius.net/East/Accounting
Group name:
Group name (pre-Windows 2000):
Group scope	Group type
○ Domain local	⦿ Security
⦿ Global	○ Distribution
○ Universal	
OK   Cancel

ANOTHER WAY

Instead, right click your domain object to create a new group account directly under the domain object. However, this is considered poor organization for AD objects.

3. Supply a name in the Group name dialog box and select the appropriate group scope and type. Observe the Group name (preWindows 2000) that must be used if the user logs in to the domain from a Windows 9x or NT4 client computer, and click **OK**.

⊕ ADD MEMBERS TO A GROUP

If you want to add the current group as a member of another group, you can highlight the Member Of tab shown in Figure 2-52.

GET READY. Turn on the computer, and log in as the Administrator user account. Close any windows that appear on the desktop.

1. Click **Start**, **Administrative Tools**, and **Active Directory Users and Computers**. The Active Directory Users and Computers console appears.

2. In the left pane, locate the group object that you wish to modify. Right click the group object and select **Properties**. Highlight the **Members** tab of the group's properties as shown in Figure 2-52.

Figure 2-52

Modifying Group Membership

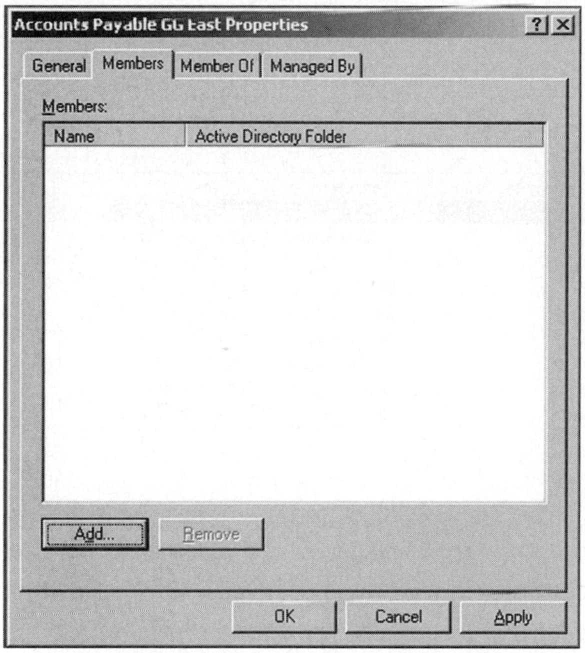

```
Accounts Payable GG East Properties                    ? X
┌─────────┬─────────┬──────────┬────────────┐
│ General │ Members │ Member Of│ Managed By  │
└─────────┴─────────┴──────────┴────────────┘
 Members:
 ┌──────────────┬──────────────────────────┐
 │ Name         │ Active Directory Folder   │
 ├──────────────┴──────────────────────────┤
 │                                          │
 │                                          │
 │                                          │
 │                                          │
 │                                          │
 │                                          │
 │                                          │
 └──────────────────────────────────────────┘
 ┌──────────┐  ┌──────────┐
 │  Add...  │  │  Remove  │
 └──────────┘  └──────────┘

        ┌──────┐  ┌────────┐  ┌────────┐
        │  OK  │  │ Cancel │  │ Apply  │
        └──────┘  └────────┘  └────────┘
```

3. Click the **Add** button. The Select Users, Contacts, Computers, or Groups window appears as shown in Figure 2-53.

Figure 2-53

Searching for Objects

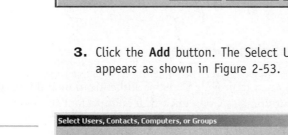

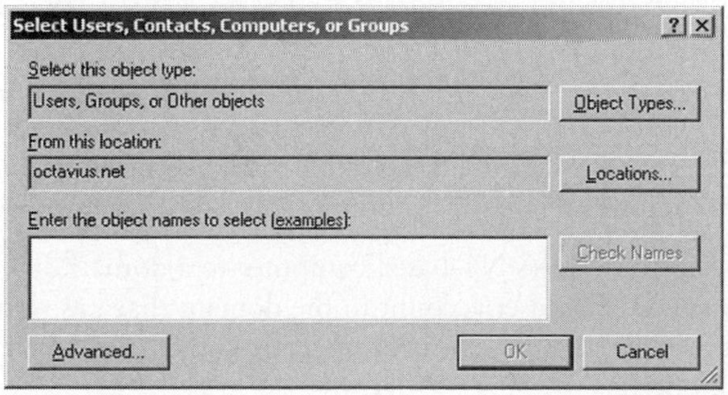

4. If you plan to add computer accounts to your group, you must select the **Object Types** button, place a checkbox beside Computers in the Object Types window, and click **OK.**

5. In the Select Users, Contacts, Computers, or Groups window, you can supply the name of the object or search for the object by clicking the **Advanced** button, supplying optional search criteria, and clicking the **Find Now** button to view an object list as depicted in Figure 2-54.

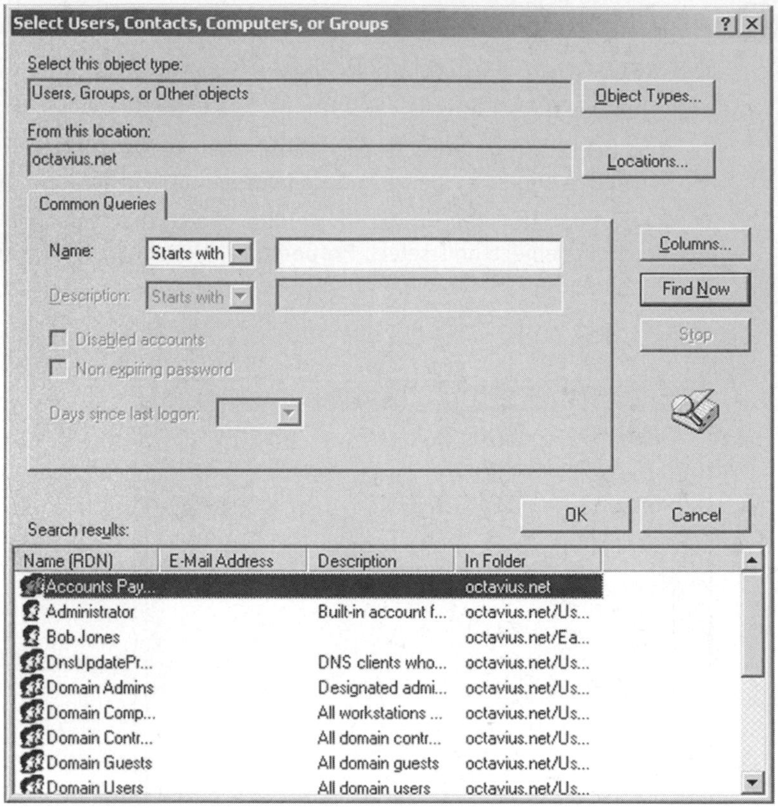

Figure 2-54

Listing Available Objects

TAKE NOTE *

You can select multiple objects by holding down the **Ctrl** key when selecting objects or select a range of objects by holding down the **Shift** key when selecting objects.

6. Select the appropriate object from the list and click **OK** to return to the Select Users, Contacts, Computers, or Groups window.
7. Click **OK** to return to the group properties window.
8. Click **OK** to modify the group membership.

Creating and Managing Computers

TAKE NOTE *

Windows NT-based computers include Windows NT4, Windows 2000, Windows XP, Windows Server 2003, Windows Vista, and Windows Server 2008. Windows 9x computers include Windows 95, Windows 98, and Windows Millennium.

Computer objects are used to provide Kerberos authentication and Group Policy for most computers within your domain. Consequently, it is important to understand how to create and administer computer objects in AD.

Computer objects exist for all Windows NT-based computers within a domain. Although Windows 9x computers can join a domain, they are not represented by computer objects.

When you join a Windows NT-based computer to a domain, you are prompted for the username and password of a user account in the domain that has rights to add computer objects to AD. This user account is then used to create a computer object in the domain that represents the computer.

By default, computer objects are created in the default Computers folder in the domain and named according to the NetBIOS name of the computer. You should always move computer objects to the appropriate OU after they have been created for organization and assignment of Group Policy.

Alternatively, you can create computer objects named after the NetBIOS name of each client computer before the computers are joined to the domain to save time and ensure that the computer accounts are located in the correct OU before the client computer joins the domain. This process is called ***prestaging*** computer objects.

TAKE NOTE * Administrators can create an unlimited number of computer objects within a domain, whereas nonadministrative user accounts have the ability to add up to 10 computer accounts in the domain.

Although the location of computer objects determines the GPOs that the associated computers receive, computer objects are primarily used by the Kerberos authentication protocol. Each computer object contains a system-generated password that is synchronized to the associated client computer and used to secure the Kerberos protocol between the client and DC during authentication. This system-generated password is changed every 14 days and may occasionally become unsynchronized. If a computer object becomes unsynchronized, the client computer will no longer be able to authenticate any user to the domain. In this case, you can right click the computer object in the Active Directory Users and Computers console and select **Reset Account**. Following this, you must remove the domain membership on the computer and then rejoin it to the domain so that it can resynchronize with the associated computer object.

Similarly, to move or delete a computer object, you can right click the computer object within the Active Directory Users and Computers console and select the appropriate option.

⊙ PRESTAGE A COMPUTER OBJECT

GET READY. Turn on the computer, and log in as the Administrator user account. Close any windows that appear on the desktop.

TAKE NOTE *
Only Windows 2000 and later computers can use Group Policy and Kerberos authentication.

1. Click **Start**, **Administrative Tools**, and **Active Directory Users and Computers**. The Active Directory Users and Computers console appears.

2. In the left pane, locate the OU object that should contain the computer account. Right click the OU object and select **New** followed by **Computer** from the menu. The New Object—Computer window appears as shown in Figure 2-55.

Figure 2-55

Creating a Computer Object

ANOTHER WAY

Instead, you can right click your domain object to create a new computer account directly under the domain object. However, this is considered poor organization for AD objects.

New Object - Computer

Create in: octavius.net/East/Accounting

Computer name:

Computer name (pre-Windows 2000):

The following user or group can join this computer to a domain.
User or group:
Default: Domain Admins   Change...

☐ Assign this computer account as a pre-Windows 2000 computer
☐ Assign this computer account as a backup domain controller

< Back   Next >   Cancel

3. Supply the NetBIOS name of the client computer in the Computer name dialog box and select the user that is allowed to join the computer to the domain and use this computer object. For a Windows NT4 computer, the NetBIOS name must match the name in the Computer name (preWindows 2000) dialog box and you must select **Assign this computer account as a preWindows 2000 computer**. If the

computer is a Windows NT4 BDC, you must additionally select **Assign this computer account as a backup domain controller**. Click **Next** to view the Managed window shown in Figure 2-56.

Figure 2-56

Specifying a Managed
Computer Object

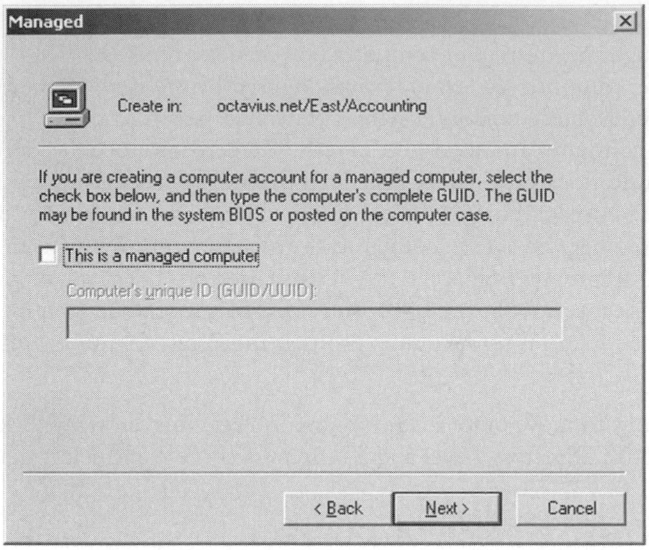

4. If the computer will be installed using Remote Installation Services (RIS) or Windows Deployment Services (WDS), then you should select **This is a managed computer** and enter the GUID that is stored in the BIOS of the client computer and used to perform remote installations.

5. Click **Next** to review your configuration options.

6. Click **Finish** to create the computer account.

RESET A COMPUTER OBJECT

GET READY. Turn on the computer, and log in as the Administrator user account. Close any windows that appear on the desktop.

1. Click **Start**, **Administrative Tools**, and **Active Directory Users and Computers**. The Active Directory Users and Computers console appears.

2. In the left pane, locate the appropriate computer object. Right click the computer object and select **Reset Account**.

3. Click **Yes** when prompted to confirm the reset.

4. Click **OK** to close the confirmation dialog box. Following this step, you must configure the client computer to remove domain membership and then reconfigure the client computer to join the domain again. For Windows 2000 and later computers, you can configure domain membership on the Computer Name tab of System properties in the Control Panel.

5. On the client computer, click **Start**, **Control Panel**, and **System**. The System Properties window appears.

6. Highlight the **Computer Name** tab and click the **Change** button. The Computer Name Changes window appears.

7. Select **Workgroup** and supply a temporary workgroup name that is less than 15 characters long and click **OK**. Enter the credentials of a valid domain user account when prompted and click **OK**.

8. Click **OK** when prompted to reboot your computer. Click **OK** to close the System Properties dialog box and reboot your computer.

9. After your client computer has rebooted, click **Start**, **Control Panel**, and **System**. The System Properties window appears.

10. Highlight the **Computer Name** tab and click the **Change** button. The Computer Name Changes window appears.

11. Select Domain, enter the FQDN of the domain and click **OK**. Enter the credentials of a valid domain user account when prompted and click **OK**.

12. Click **OK** to close the System Properties window and reboot your computer.

Configuring Group Policy

> By configuring Group Policy, Active Directory can be used to configure user and computer settings within your domain.

Group Policy is a versatile administrative tool in AD that can be used to apply software and configure settings on computers within the domain using GPOs. To function, GPOs must be linked to a site, domain, or OU that contains user or computer accounts.

GPO settings are stored in one of two sections within a GPO: the *Computer Configuration* and the *User Configuration*. Windows 2000 or later computers apply the Computer Configuration from all GPOs that are linked to a site, domain, or OU object that contain their computer account. Similarly, when domain users log in to a Windows 2000 or later computer, they apply the User Configuration from all GPOs that are linked to a site, domain, or OU object that contains their user account.

A single user or computer object may receive the settings from several GPOs. To prevent conflicts in the event that two GPOs contain different values for the same setting, GPOs are applied to user and computer objects based on the link in the following order:

1. Site
2. Domain
3. Parent OU
4. Child OUs

Thus, if the User Configuration section of a GPO linked to your domain has a setting that conflicts with the same setting in the User Configuration section of a GPO that is linked to the OU that contains your user account, you will receive the setting that is configured in the GPO that is linked to the OU that contains your user account.

There are two default GPOs in each AD domain. The Default Domain Policy GPO is linked to the domain object and applies to all users and computers in the domain by default. The Default Domain Controllers Policy GPO is linked to the Domain Controllers OU and applies to DC computer accounts.

To create and manage additional GPOs that are linked to a domain or OU object, you can right click the domain or OU object in the Active Directory Users and Computers console, select **Properties**, and highlight the Group Policy tab as shown in Figure 2-57.

Figure 2-57

Managing Group Policy Objects

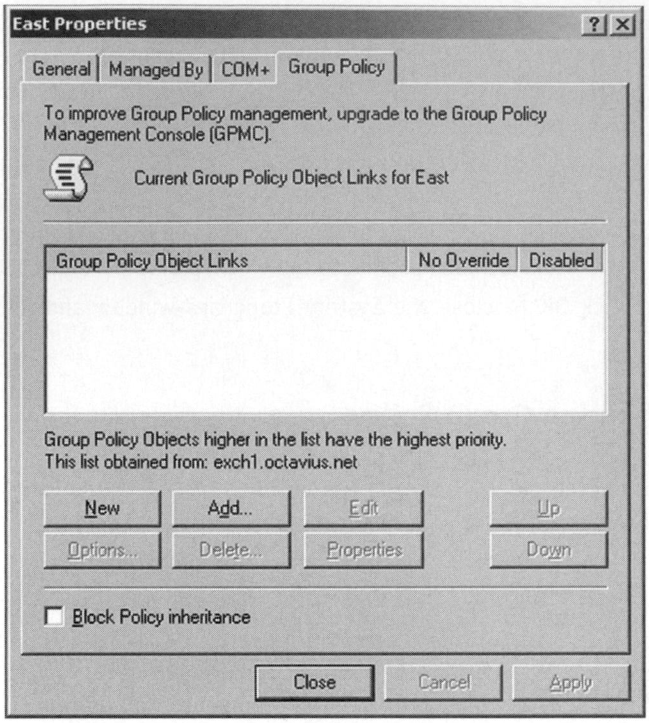

ANOTHER WAY

The *Group Policy Management Console (GPMC)* is a comprehensive tool used to manage GPOs that are linked to sites, domains, and OUs. You can download the GPMC from Microsoft's Web site.

To create a new GPO, you can click the **New** button shown in Figure 2-57. Alternatively, you can link an existing GPO to the current domain or OU object by selecting the **Add** button and selecting the appropriate GPO.

To create and manage GPOs that are linked to sites objects, you can access the properties of a site object in the Active Directory Sites and Services console and select the **Group Policy** tab. The options available are identical to those in Figure 2-57.

To edit a GPO, simply click on the Edit button shown in Figure 2-57 to open the *Group Policy Object Editor* depicted in Figure 2-58. Using the Group Policy Object Editor, you can select the appropriate configuration options under the User Configuration or Computer Configuration section.

Figure 2-58

Modifying Group Policy Object Settings

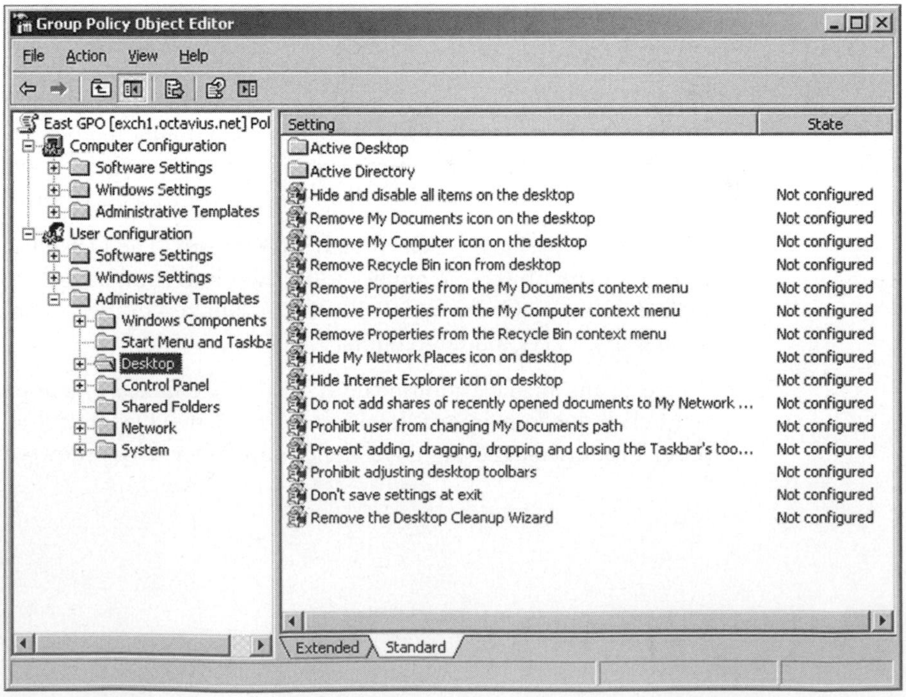

The Administrative Templates sections under the User Configuration and Computer Configuration can be expanded to include additional configuration options available for various software packages. Many software manufacturers allow you to download and install *administrative templates* that can be imported into a GPO and used to configure settings for their software applications.

To import an additional administrative template into a GPO, right click Administrative Templates under the User Configuration or Computer Configuration shown in Figure 2-58, select **Add/Remove Templates**, and specify the templates that you wish to add. Figure 2-59 shows a GPO with the Microsoft Outlook 2007 administrative template added.

Figure 2-59

Configuring Administrative Templates

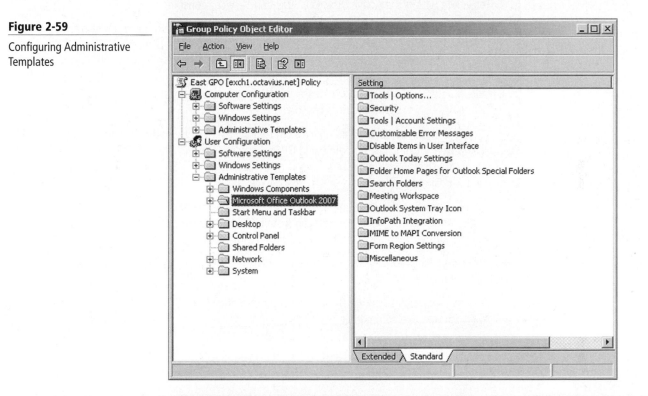

SUMMARY SKILL MATRIX

IN THIS LESSON YOU LEARNED:

- AD is maintained on DCs that contain a database of objects for a domain within a tree in a forest. Each DC also contains a copy of the object schema and forest configuration.

- Leaf objects represent users and network resources, whereas container objects are used to organize leaf objects within an AD database. Most leaf objects can be created using the Active Directory Users and Computers console.

- Domains in a forest provide their own security and use trust relationships to allow the assignment of permissions on resources to users in remote domain. Two-way transitive trusts exist by default between parent and child domains in a forest as well as between the parent domains of each tree in the forest. Additional trusts can be manually created using the Active Directory Domains and Trusts console.

- AD uses security groups with scopes that are global, universal, or domain local to organize the assignment of permissions in the forest.

- Functional levels are used to represent the level of backwards compatibility allowed in a domain and forest. You can raise your functional level to reduce backwards compatibility and enable new domain features. You can raise your domain and forest functional level using the Active Directory Domains and Trusts console.

- Site and subnet objects are used to represent different locations within an AD forest. You can create site link objects between sites that specify restrictions for replication. Site, subnet, and site link objects can be managed using the Active Directory Sites and Services console.

- The GC is a database of all object names, UPNs, and universal groups in the forest. It is used to speed forestwide searching, allow remote logins, maintain universal group membership, and allow logins for Windows 2000 Native and higher functional level domains. You can specify the placement of GC using the Active Directory Sites and Services console.

- UGMC allows for fast user logins in sites that do not contain a GC and may be configured on a site within the Active Directory Sites and Services console.

- FSMO roles provide special functions in an AD forest and domain. Each forest contains a Schema Master FSMO that may be configured using the Active Directory Schema MMC snap-in, as well as a Domain Naming Master FSMO that may be configured using Active Directory Domains and Trusts console. Similarly, each domain contains a PDC Emulator, RID Master, and Infrastructure Master FSMO that may be configured using the Active Directory Users and Computers console.

- Group Policy is a powerful administrative tool for configuring software and settings on computers within your domain using GPOs. You can administer GPOs using the Active Directory Users and Computers console, the Active Directory Sites and Services console, and the GPMC.

- Before installing AD, you should ensure that you have the necessary operating system, login, and DNS requirements. You can install a DC by running the Configure Your Server Wizard or by running the dcpromo.exe command.

- After installing AD on a DC, you should verify the addition of the AD services and DNS SRV records.

- You can remove AD from a DC by running the Configure Your Server Wizard or by running the dcpromo.exe command.

■ Knowledge Assessment

Fill in the Blank

Complete the following sentences by writing the correct word or words in the blanks provided.

1. To begin an AD installation, you can run the _____ command.

2. The authentication protocol used by Windows 2000 and later computers in a domain is called _____.

3. The _____ FSMO role is responsible for time synchronization across the domain.

4. To complete the authentication process in a domain that is at the Windows 2000 Native functional level or higher, a _____ must be contacted.

5. Following an AD installation, you should verify the existence of _____ records on the DNS server that holds the zone for the AD domain.

6. The letters _____ represent the general principle used when assigning users to groups in a large forest.

7. To view the DC that holds the Schema Master FSMO role, you must use the _____ MMC snap-in.

8. A(n) _____ is an LDAP name used to describe each object within AD.

9. To speed up resource access across child domains in your forest, you can create _____ trusts.

10. To enable Universal Group Membership Caching, you must use the _____ console.

Multiple Choice

Circle the letter that corresponds to the best answer.

1. You receive an object-related error when attempting to create a new user account within your domain. What FSMO role should you ensure is online to complete the addition of the user account?
   - **a.** PDC Emulator
   - **b.** Domain Naming Master
   - **c.** Infrastructure Master
   - **d.** RID Master

2. You plan on promoting an existing Windows Server 2003 computer to become an additional domain controller in your domain. To which group must the user account you specify during the AD installation belong at minimum?
   - **a.** Domain Users
   - **b.** Domain Admins
   - **c.** Enterprise Admins
   - **d.** Schema Admins

3. Which of the following utilities must you use to seize an FSMO role?
   - **a.** ntdsutil.exe
   - **b.** dcpromo.exe
   - **c.** Active Directory Domains and Trusts
   - **d.** Active Directory Sites and Services

4. Which of the following are container objects in the AD database? (Choose all that apply.)
   - **a.** Group policy
   - **b.** Site
   - **c.** Domain
   - **d.** OU

5. Which of the following objects is used to locate the correct site for a newly installed DC?
   - **a.** Site link
   - **b.** Subnet
   - **c.** Locator
   - **d.** Bridgehead

6. Several users called you today stating that they could not change their passwords. After investigating, you also noticed that the time on their computers was also incorrect. Which of the following FSMO roles may be unavailable?
   - **a.** PDC Emulator
   - **b.** RID Master
   - **c.** Infrastructure Master
   - **d.** Schema Master

7. Which of the following DCs are allowed to participate in a Windows 2000 Native mode domain? (Choose all that apply.)
   - **a.** Windows NT4 Server
   - **b.** Windows 2000 Server
   - **c.** Windows Sever 2003
   - **d.** Windows Server 2008

8. A single user within your organization calls you for help after having trouble logging on to the domain. After further investigation, you notice that the user is able to log on to the domain from another computer and that no users are able to successfully log on to the domain from the user's original computer. What is most likely the cause of the problem?
   - **a.** The time on the computer is incorrect and must be changed
   - **b.** The user account has been disabled and must be enabled
   - **c.** The user account has been locked and must be unlocked
   - **d.** The computer account for the user's computer has become corrupted and must be reset

9. You wish to create a group that will contain the Marketing staff within your own domain. This group will be assigned permissions to resources in other domains within your forest. What is the most appropriate scope for this new group?
   - **a.** Local
   - **b.** Global
   - **c.** Domain local
   - **d.** Universal

10. When attempting to remove AD from an existing DC that you wish to decommission, you receive an error message. Which switch to the dcpromo.exe command will allow you to remove this DC from the domain?

    a. /force   **b.** /remove

    c. /forceremoval   **d.** /f

True/False

Circle T if the statement is true or F if the statement is false.

T | F   **1.** Tokens are issued to users following authentication and used to provide access to resources that list the user in their ACL.

T | F   **2.** When a domain functional level is set to Windows 2000 Interim, only Windows 2000 and later DCs are allowed to participate in domain authentication.

T | F   **3.** Global groups may only be used in the local domain but can contain objects from any domain in the forest.

T | F   **4.** Computer objects may be managed using the Active Directory Users and Computers console.

T | F   **5.** By default, two-way transitive trusts are between all domains in a forest.

T | F   **6.** To control replication, you configure the properties of site link objects.

T | F   **7.** When possible, you should ensure that each site in the forest contains a DC that contains the GC role.

T | F   **8.** You can configure Group Policy using the Active Directory Domains and Trusts console.

T | F   **9.** The Domain Naming Master FSMO role should be on a DC that contains the GC.

T | F **10.** A single AD domain can contain an unlimited number of objects.

Review Questions

    1. Explain why it is important to create sites after deploying your first domain in the forest.

    2. Detail reasons why understanding the function and location of your FSMO roles will help you troubleshoot AD problems.

    3. Give some reasons why each AD site should contain a DC that hosts the GC.

    4. Explain why AD domains are a security and replication boundary.

■ Case Scenarios

Scenario 2-1: Designing a Forest

You are the network administrator for a shipping company with locations in the United States, Canada, and Japan. There are five offices in the United States, three offices in Canada, and three offices in Japan. In a short memo, diagram a sample forest, domain, and OU structure that will accommodate this organization.

Scenario 2-2: Planning for Sites, GC, and FSMO Roles

In the forest diagram that you created for the company described in Scenario 2-1, label the appropriate sites that should be created to ensure efficient replication. Assuming that each site has a minimum of two DCs, label the location of GC servers and FSMO roles.

Deploying Exchange Server 2007

LESSON SKILL MATRIX

Technology Skill	Objective Domain	Objective Domain Number
Meeting Active Directory Requirements	Prepare the infrastructure for Exchange installation.	1.1
Preparing Legacy Exchange Servers	Prepare the infrastructure for Exchange installation.	1.1
Meeting Hardware Requirements	Prepare the servers for Exchange installation.	1.2
Meeting Software Requirements	Prepare the servers for Exchange installation.	1.2
Performing a Graphical Installation	Install Exchange.	1.3
Performing an Unattended Installation	Install Exchange.	1.3
Finalizing the Installation	Install Exchange.	1.3

KEY TERMS

Exchange Best Practices
  Analyzer
Exchange organization
Just a Bunch of Disks
  (JBOD)
link state
migration

Parallel Advanced Technology
  Attachment (PATA)
Redundant Array of Independent
  Disks (RAID)
routing groups
Serial Advanced Technology
  Attachment (SATA)

Small Computer Systems
  Interface (SCSI)
Storage Area Network (SAN)
Windows Server Update Services
  (WSUS)

■ Preparing for an Exchange Server 2007 Installation

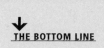

THE BOTTOM LINE

Email infrastructures are among the largest systems within organizations today and should be planned carefully as a result. The deployment of Exchange Server 2007 is no exception to this rule. Before you deploy Exchange Server 2007 in your organization, you will need to plan server roles as well as prepare the appropriate hardware and software. In addition, you will need to prepare AD as well as any legacy Exchange servers for the deployment of Exchange Server 2007.

Planning Exchange Roles

Fundamental to a successful Exchange Server 2007 deployment is the proper planning of Exchange server roles. More specifically, you should focus on the number of Exchange servers required for your organization as well as the number and type of server roles that should be placed on each Exchange server.

Before deploying Exchange Server 2007, you should carefully consider the number and placement of server roles within your organization. In most small organizations, a single Exchange server with the Mailbox, Hub Transport, and CAS roles will usually be adequate for the current email requirements. As a result, a typical Exchange Server 2007 installation includes these roles by default.

Because Exchange servers that hold the Mailbox, Hub Transport, and CAS roles can provide email storage, access, and routing, they are easily scalable. As small organizations grow, they can introduce additional Exchange servers with these same roles to service different areas within the organization as shown in Figure 3-1.

Figure 3-1

Scaling the Default Server Roles

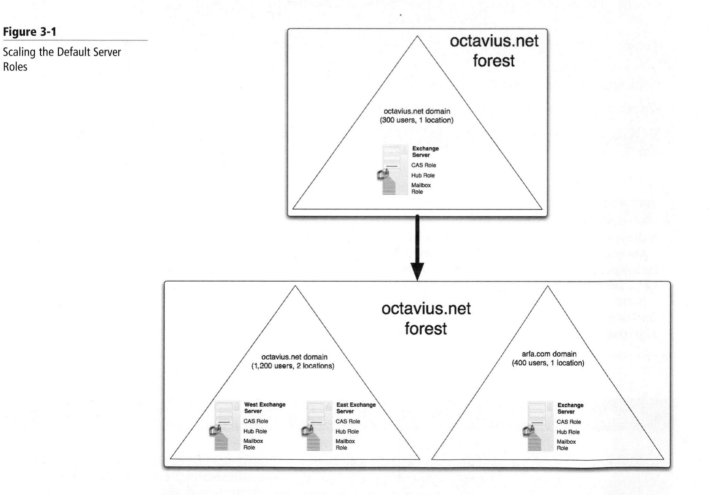

In Figure 3-1, the Octavius organizat ion expanded from a single domain, single location, 300-user structure to a multiple domain, three location, 1,600-user structure by adding two additional Exchange servers. Each Exchange server provides email storage and access for clients within their location, as well as internal and external email routing.

In larger organizations, it is more efficient and cost effective to deploy Exchange servers that have specific server roles and that are strategically placed within an organization to optimize email storage, access, and routing. These Exchange servers need only contain the hardware necessary to support their function. Figure 3-2 depicts an octavius.net domain that contains a diverse Exchange infrastructure spanning two locations.

Figure 3-2

Separating Server Roles

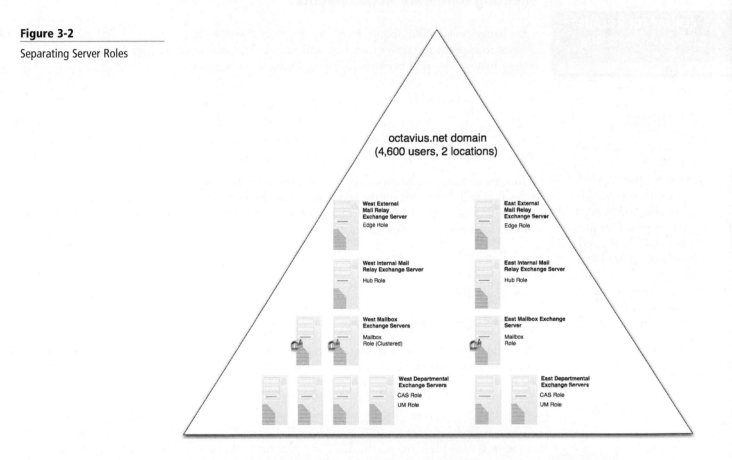

In Figure 3-2, email storage is provided by the Mailbox Exchange servers in the East and West offices. In addition, each location has several Departmental Exchange servers that provide email access to clients in each department. To support internal and external email relay as well as ensure that inbound and outbound email is filtered for viruses and spam, there are separate Exchange servers in each location that provide the Hub role and the Edge role.

Ultimately, the number and placement of Exchange server roles will depend on the needs and structure of your organization, but should support current email requirements and allow for future growth. In addition, the design of your Exchange infrastructure must obey the following rules:

- There must be at least one Hub role per AD site to allow for email relay between Exchange servers in different sites.
- The CAS role should have fast access to the Mailbox role. If the CAS and Mailbox roles are on different servers, you should ensure that the network that separates them has at least 100 Mbps of bandwidth.
- Clustered Mailbox roles cannot share hardware with other roles.
- Edge roles cannot share hardware with other roles.

Although it is not restricted, it is poor practice to install any Exchange role on a server that contains other network functions such as a DC, database server, file server, print server, or proxy server. These functions will require additional resources over time as the company grows and will likely reduce the performance of your Exchange server. Furthermore, if you install Exchange on a DC, you will not be able to change the domain membership or remove AD from the DC until Exchange is removed first.

Meeting Hardware Requirements

Exchange Server 2007 requires a 64-bit platform as well as ample memory and hard disk space to support the server roles that will exist within your organization. As a result, planning hardware is vital prior to deploying Exchange Server 2007.

TAKE NOTE *

In general, it is good practice to purchase more hardware than you think you need to meet your organization's email needs. This prevents any unexpected performance problems as a result of additional load and allows for future growth.

Different organizations have different numbers of users and different email requirements. In addition to planning the number of Exchange servers, you should carefully consider the hardware that each Exchange server will require to support the email demands of the organization.

The type of hardware that you choose for a specific server depends on the Exchange server roles that will be present on the server as well as the number of emails that the server is expected to process. Overall, there are three major hardware categories that you must consider before deploying Exchange Server 2007:

- Processor
- Memory
- Hard disk

PROCESSOR REQUIREMENTS

Regardless of server role, Exchange Server 2007 requires a 64-bit Intel 64 or AMD64 processor. Itanium 64-bit processors are not supported by Exchange Server 2007.

TAKE NOTE *

Although Exchange Server 2007 can be installed on a 32-bit Intel or AMD processor running at 800 MHz or greater, this is not supported for production environments and is intended for product testing only. However, you can install the Exchange management tools on a 32-bit computer to perform remote administration of a computer running a 64-bit version of Exchange Server 2007.

Most server-class computers today ship with a variety of configurations and can contain multiple processors or processors with multiple cores. As a result, it is difficult to determine the minimum number of processors and processor cores required for an Exchange server. In general, the number of processors and processor cores is largely dependent on the number of emails that are sent within your organization as well as the server roles on each Exchange server. Server roles that perform numerous calculations are likely to require multiple processors with multiple cores.

For example, servers that host the Edge role will require multiple processors or processor cores to support the calculation required by the antivirus and antispam software. Similarly, servers that host the CAS role and provide access to email using encrypted protocols such as POP3S will likely require multiple processors or processor cores to handle the calculations needed for the encryption and decryption. Similarly, servers that contain multiple server roles will perform more calculations and will likely require multiple processors or processor cores.

MEMORY REQUIREMENTS

Due to its 64-bit architecture, Exchange Server 2007 can use more than 4 GB of physical RAM. However, the recommended minimum RAM requirements vary depending on the server role as described in Table 3-1.

Table 3-1

Exchange Server 2007 RAM requirements

EXCHANGE SERVER ROLE	RECOMMENDED MINIMUM RAM
Edge Transport (Edge)	1 GB per core (2 GB minimum)
Hub Transport (Hub)	1 GB per core (2 GB minimum)
Unified Messaging (UM)	1 GB per core (2 GB minimum)
Client Access Server (CAS)	2 GB per core (2 GB minimum)
Mailbox	2 GB plus 5 MB per mailbox

If an Exchange server will contain multiple server roles, you should add the appropriate minimum RAM requirements shown in Table 3-1. Thus an Exchange server that hosts the Edge, Hub, CAS, and Mailbox server roles should have at least 8 GB of RAM plus 5 MB per mailbox.

In addition, the amount of RAM on an Exchange server holding the Mailbox server role relates to the number of storage groups used to store email. A server with 2 GB of RAM that hosts the Mailbox server role will adequately support up to 4 storage groups. However, to properly support 50 storage groups, the server hosting the Mailbox server role should have 26 GB of RAM.

In addition to physical RAM requirements, each Exchange server should contain an adequate amount of virtual memory. The amount of virtual memory in Windows is determined by the size of the paging file. In general, you should ensure that the paging file size for any Exchange server is equal to the amount of physical RAM plus 10 MB.

By default, the paging file exists on the Windows system partition. Although not required for Exchange Server 2007, you should move the paging file to a different hard disk. This increases overall system performance because paging requests will not compete with Windows I/O requests on the same hard disk. However, by moving the paging file to another hard disk, Windows cannot create automatic memory dumps in the event of a system crash. Normally, this is not a problem in most environments, but should be considered if your organization has a Microsoft support contract because automatic memory dumps can be sent to Microsoft support for analysis.

TAKE NOTE *

Exchange Server 2007 SP1 has a more efficient storage engine. As a result, you only need 15 GB of RAM to support 50 storage groups in Exchange Server 2007 SP1.

TAKE NOTE *

To move your paging file to a different hard drive, simply specify a **Custom size** for a partition on the target hard drive in the Virtual Memory window and specify **No paging file** for the Windows system partition.

MODIFY THE PAGING FILE

GET READY. Turn on the computer, and log in as the Administrator user account. Close any windows that appear on the desktop.

1. Click **Start**, **Control Panel**, and then click **System**. The System Properties window appears.

2. Highlight the **Advanced** tab. In the Performance section, click the **Settings** button to open the Performance Options window.

3. Highlight the **Advanced** tab. In the Virtual memory section, click the **Change** button to open the Virtual Memory window.

4. Select the appropriate hard drive partition in the selection window at the top of the screen and ensure that **Custom size** is selected.

5. Specify an initial and maximum size for your paging file in the dialog boxes and click **Set**. The initial size for your paging file must be set to the minimum paging file size required by Exchange Server 2007.

6. Click **OK** to close the Virtual Memory window. Click **OK** again to close the Performance Options window and click **OK** once again to close the System Properties window.

HARD DISK REQUIREMENTS

All hard disk partitions that will be used by Exchange Server 2007 must be formatted using the NTFS file system. For installation, Exchange Server 2007 requires a minimum of 1.2 GB of free disk space as well as an additional 200 MB of free space on the Windows system partition.

In addition, Exchange Server 2007 will require ample storage for email queues and storage groups. The amount of space required for the email queues and storage groups depends on the number of emails that your organization typically sends, the average size of email attachments, and whether your organization archives email over time. Because hard disk space is generally inexpensive today, it is best practice to double your maximum expected space requirements to allow for future growth.

To speed email relay, storage, and retrieval, you should ensure that your hard disks have fast transfer rates. *Small Computer Systems Interface (SCSI)* and *Serial Advanced Technology Attachment (SATA)* hard disks generally have faster transfer rates than *Parallel Advanced Technology Attachment (PATA)* hard disks. Many organizations today store important server information such as Exchange mailboxes on external hard disks that can be shared by several servers. This configuration is called a *Storage Area Network (SAN)* and typically involves SCSI or SATA hard disks in an external drive enclosure that are linked to one or more servers with a fast connection.

Furthermore, many servers and SAN devices use several hard disks simultaneously to speed up data transfer and provide fault tolerance in the event of a hard disk failure. This configuration is called a *Redundant Array of Independent Disks (RAID)* and is a good form to use for any Exchange server in your organization that hosts the Mailbox role. Although RAID configurations may be handled by software running on the Windows operating system, it is most often implemented by the hard disk controller on the computer to reduce the strain on the computer's processor and improve performance.

TAKE NOTE*

If your Exchange server will host the UM role, you will also require 500 MB of space for each unified messaging language pack that you install.

⊕ MORE INFORMATION

The three most common RAID implementations are called RAID 0, RAID 1, and RAID 5. RAID 0 configurations are not fault tolerant if a single hard drive fails and include **spanning** and **striping**.

RAID 0 spanning is also called **Just a Bunch of Disks (JBOD)** and consists of two or more hard disks that are seen as one large continuous volume. Thus, if you had two 250 GB hard disks, you could create one volume that is 500 GB in size. When the free space on the first disk is exhausted, the second hard disk is used to store data.

RAID 0 striping also creates a single large volume, but divides data equally among two or more hard disks to speed up read-and-write operations. For example, if you have three hard disks in a RAID 0 striping configuration, a file that is saved to the hard disk would be divided into three sections. Each section is written to a different hard disk concurrently, which allows the file to be saved in one-third the time. This same file can then be read in one-third of time for the same reason. Because RAID 0 speeds read-and-write access, it is appropriate for the Hub, Edge, UM, and CAS roles. The Mailbox role should provide fault tolerance for its email and public folder databases and is better suited for RAID 1 and RAID 5.

RAID 1 is called **mirroring** and provides fault tolerance in the case of a hard disk failure. In this RAID configuration, all information is written to two separate hard disks at the same time. If one hard disk fails, then the system automatically uses the other hard disk exclusively. Because each hard disk contains identical data, no data is lost by the failure of a single hard drive, and the failed hard drive can be replaced and reconfigured as a RAID 1 after working hours.

RAID 5 is called **striping with parity** and is the most common RAID configuration used today. It is similar to striping because it creates a single volume and divides data, yet it requires a minimum of three hard disks. In a RAID 5 configuration that uses three hard disks, files are split into two sections and saved to two of the hard disks. Parity information that can be used to regenerate the file if half of it is missing is saved on the remaining hard disk. During each write operation, the parity information is rotated among all three drives. Thus, if a single hard drive fails, the parity information can be used to quickly generate the missing data. Similarly, in a RAID 5 configuration that uses four hard disks, files are divided into three sections and saved to three different hard disks while the parity information is saved to the remaining hard disk. If a single hard disk fails, then the parity information can be used to regenerate the data that was missing. Because parity information is only written to a single hard drive during a normal write operation, the parity information takes up less overall space in RAID 5 configurations that use more hard disks.

In larger systems, RAID levels are often combined. For example, RAID 15 refers to a RAID 5 stripe with parity configuration that is mirrored (RAID 1) to another RAID 5 stripe with parity, and RAID 10 refers to a RAID 0 stripe that is mirrored (RAID 1) to another RAID 0 stripe.

Meeting Software Requirements

Exchange Server 2007 requires a 64-bit Windows Server 2003 operating system or later. In addition, you must install several software components before deploying Exchange Server 2007. The number and type of software components depends on the server roles that will be hosted on the Exchange Server 2007 computer.

TAKE NOTE*

You should always ensure that your Windows operating system is updated with the latest service pack and contains the latest patches from Microsoft.

Exchange Server 2007 relies on several software components. First and foremost, Exchange Server 2007 must be installed on a computer running the Windows Server 2003, Windows Server 2003 R2, or Windows Server 2008 operating system with the latest updates. If you plan on providing cluster capabilities on Exchange Server 2007, you must use the Enterprise or Datacenter Edition of Windows Server 2003, Windows Server 2003 R2, or Windows Server 2008.

In addition to the operating system software requirements, Exchange Server 2007 also requires several supporting software components:

- Windows PowerShell Version 1.0 or later
- .NET Framework Version 2.0 or later
- MMC Version 3.0 or later

⊘ **INSTALL EXCHANGE SERVER 2007 PREREQUISITE SOFTWARE ON WINDOWS SERVER 2003**

GET READY. Turn on the computer, and log in as the Administrator user account. Close any windows that appear on the desktop.

1. Obtain and install PowerShell 1.0 for your platform. You can download PowerShell 1.0 for your platform from www.microsoft.com/downloads.

Rather than searching the Microsoft Download Web site for software, it is easier to enter a search string into a search engine Web site such as Google.com. For example, entering the phrase **powershell download** into Google.com will present you with a direct link to the download page for the latest version of PowerShell from the Microsoft download Web site. This method will work for any software packages that you need to download in this lesson.

2. Obtain and install the .NET Framework 2.0 and the .NET Framework 2.0 SP1 packages for your platform. You can download these packages from www.microsoft.com/downloads.

If you have Windows Server 2003 R2 or later, the .NET Framework 2.0 package is available using the **Add/Remove Windows Components** section of **Add or Remove Programs** in Control Panel. However, after adding this component using Control Panel, you must download the .NET Framework 2.0 SP1 patch.

3. Ensure that you have the MMC Version 3.0 installed on your computer. You can download the MMC Version 3.0 for your platform from www.microsoft.com/downloads.

Depending on the server roles that are required on your Exchange Server 2007 computer, you may need to install additional Windows software components. These components are listed in Table 3-2.

Table 3-2

Prerequisite software required by server roles

SERVER ROLE	REQUIRED SOFTWARE
Client Access Server (CAS)	IIS (including the WWW service and ASP.NET components) RPC over HTTP proxy
Mailbox	IIS (including the WWW service and COM + components)
Hub Transport (Hub)	No additional software components are required
Edge Transport (Edge)	ADAM SP1 for computers running Windows Server 2003 or Windows Server 2003 R2 Active Directory Lightweight Directory Services (AD LDS) for computers running Windows Server 2008
Unified Messaging (UM)	Windows Media Encoder Windows Media Audio Voice Codec Core XML Services (MSXML) Version 6.0 or later

TAKE NOTE*

If you install IIS on your computer, you must ensure that the SMTP and NNTP components are not selected before installing Exchange Server 2007.

 INSTALL ROLE-BASED PREREQUISITE SOFTWARE FOR EXCHANGE SERVER 2007 ON WINDOWS SERVER 2003

GET READY. Turn on the computer, and log in as the Administrator user account. Close any windows that appear on the desktop.

1. Click **Start**, **Control Panel**, and then click **Add or Remove Programs**. The Add or Remove Programs window appears.

2. Click **Add/Remove Windows Components** tab. After a few moments, the Windows Components Wizard window appears.

3. Place a checkmark beside **Application Server**. This installs IIS with the default components including the WWW service and COM + components. The SMTP and NNTP components are not installed by default.

4. Highlight Application Server and click **Details**. In the Application Server window, place a checkmark beside **ASP.NET** and click **OK**.

5. Highlight Networking Services and click **Details**. In the Networking Services window, place a checkmark beside **RPC over HTTP Proxy** and click **OK**.

6. Click **Next** to install the components. Insert your Windows Server 2003 installation media when prompted and click **OK**. After the installation has finished, click **Finish** and close the Add or Remove Programs window.

7. Obtain and install ADAM for your platform. You can download ADAM for your platform from www.microsoft.com/downloads.

8. Obtain and install the MSXML 6.0, Windows Media Encoder, and Windows Media Audio Voice Codec packages for your platform. You can download these packages for your platform from www.microsoft.com/downloads.

Meeting Active Directory Requirements

Before installing the first Exchange Server 2007 computer in your forest, you must ensure that AD is properly prepared. This involves meeting Schema Master and GC requirements as well as running several commands from the Exchange Server 2007 installation media to prepare the forest and domains for Exchange Server 2007 objects.

Although Exchange Server 2007 operates closely with AD, you must take several steps to prepare your AD forest for the installation of the first Exchange server.

All domains that will contain Exchange Server 2007 computers or email recipients must be running at the Windows 2000 Native or higher functional level.

Furthermore, Exchange Server 2007 requires constant access to the GC. Accordingly, you must ensure that at least one GC server exists in each site that will contain Exchange Server 2007 computers. Moreover, all GC servers used by Exchange Server 2007 must be running Windows Server 2003 SP1 or Windows Server 2003 R2 or later.

Before the installation of the first Exchange Server 2007 computer in the forest, the AD schema must be extended to include new objects. To extend the AD schema, Exchange Server 2007 requires that the DC that contains the Schema Master FSMO role must be running Windows Server 2003 SP1 or Windows Server 2003 R2 or later.

Once you have satisfied the functional level, GC, and Schema Master requirements, you must perform several tasks to prepare AD for Exchange Server 2007 objects. These tasks must be performed in the following order:

1. Prepare legacy permissions.

2. Prepare the Active Directory schema.

3. Prepare the first domain.

4. Prepare all other domains.

TAKE NOTE*

Depending on the size and complexity of your forest, each of these tasks may take a considerable amount of time because the changes may need to replicate to other DCs within the domain and forest.

Although the Exchange Installation Wizard will prompt you to perform these tasks when you install the first Exchange Server 2007 computer in your forest, it is best to perform these actions beforehand for flexibility in large forests as well as to ensure that any problems that arise can be remedied before the installation of Exchange Server 2007. To prepare your AD forest and domains before installing Exchange Server 2007, you can run the **setup.com** program from the root of the Exchange Server 2007 installation media with the appropriate switches.

PREPARING LEGACY PERMISSIONS

ANOTHER WAY

To save typing, you can use the **/pl** switch in place of the **/PrepareLegacy ExchangePermissions** switch.

For any domains in the forest that currently have Exchange 2000 or Exchange Server 2003 deployed, you must prepare the permissions on those domains for the addition of Exchange Server 2007. To prepare all domains, you can run the **setup /PrepareLegacy ExchangePermissions** command as shown in Figure 3-3 from the root of the Exchange Server 2007 installation media while logged in as a user that is a member of the Enterprise Admins group. Alternatively, if you wish to prepare a single domain only, you can log in as a user that is a member of the Domain Admins group and run the command **setup /PrepareLegacyExchangePermissions:** *domainname* from the root of the Exchange Server 2007 installation media where *domainname* is the DNS name of the appropriate domain in your forest.

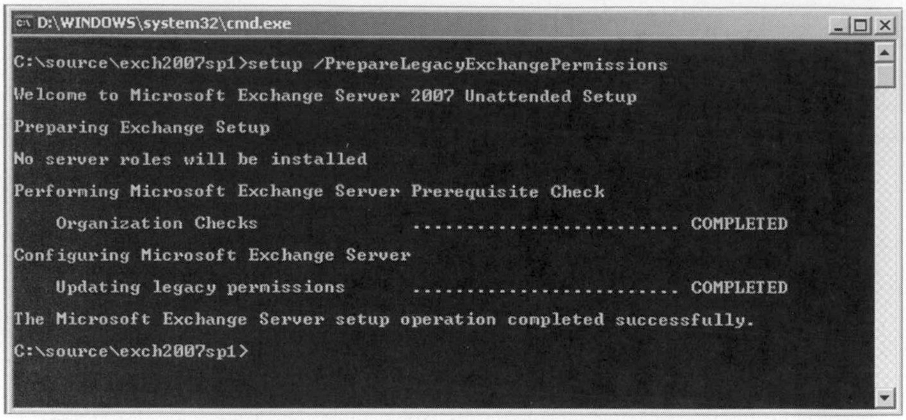

Figure 3-3

Preparing Legacy Permissions

```
C:\WINDOWS\system32\cmd.exe                                    _ |□| X|
C:\source\exch2007sp1>setup /PrepareLegacyExchangePermissions
Welcome to Microsoft Exchange Server 2007 Unattended Setup
Preparing Exchange Setup
No server roles will be installed
Performing Microsoft Exchange Server Prerequisite Check

    Organization Checks              ..................... COMPLETED
Configuring Microsoft Exchange Server

    Updating legacy permissions      ..................... COMPLETED
The Microsoft Exchange Server setup operation completed successfully.

C:\source\exch2007sp1>
```

ANOTHER WAY

To save typing, you can use the **/ps** switch in place of the **/PrepareSchema** switch.

PREPARING THE ACTIVE DIRECTORY SCHEMA

Before the first Exchange Server 2007 computer is installed in your forest, you must extend the AD schema to include new Exchange Server 2007 object classes and attributes. To do this, you must log on as a user that is a member of the Enterprise Admins and Schema Admins groups to a computer that is in the same domain and site as the DC that holds the Schema Master FSMO role. Next, you can run the command **setup /PrepareSchema** command as shown in Figure 3-4 from the root of the Exchange Server 2007 installation media.

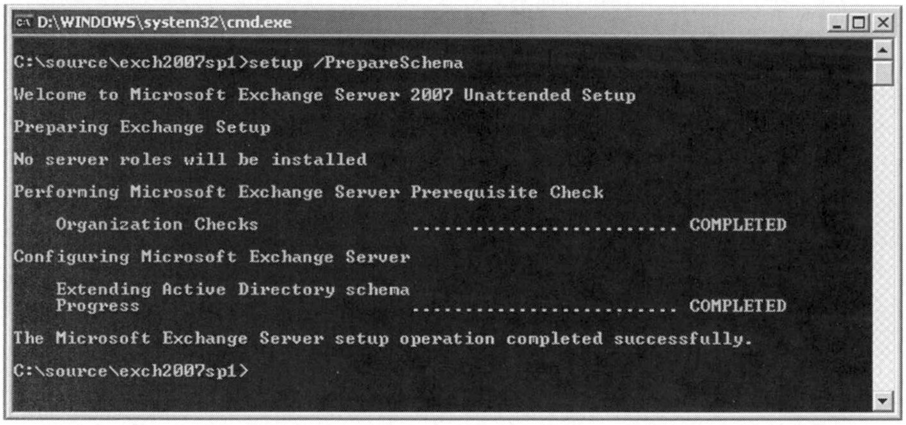

Figure 3-4

Preparing the Active Directory Schema

```
C:\WINDOWS\system32\cmd.exe                                    _ |□| X|
C:\source\exch2007sp1>setup /PrepareSchema
Welcome to Microsoft Exchange Server 2007 Unattended Setup
Preparing Exchange Setup
No server roles will be installed
Performing Microsoft Exchange Server Prerequisite Check

    Organization Checks              ..................... COMPLETED
Configuring Microsoft Exchange Server

    Extending Active Directory schema
    Progress                         ..................... COMPLETED
The Microsoft Exchange Server setup operation completed successfully.

C:\source\exch2007sp1>
```

TAKE NOTE *

Because the Exchange organization is stored in the configuration partition of AD, you can only create one Exchange organization per AD forest in Exchange Server 2007.

PREPARING THE FIRST DOMAIN

After extending the AD schema, you can prepare the first domain for the addition of the first Exchange Server 2007 computer and create an ***Exchange organization***. The Exchange organization defines the scope of management for Exchange server and is typically set to the same name as the AD forest.

To prepare the first domain for Exchange Server 2007 and create the Exchange organization, you can log in to a DC in the domain as a user that is a member of the Enterprise Admins group and run the command **setup/PrepareAD/OrganizationName:** *name* command from the root of the Exchange Server 2007 installation media where ***name*** is the name of the Exchange organization. The preparation of the first domain in the Octavius Exchange organization is shown in Figure 3-5. The Exchange organization name must only contain alphanumeric characters. No special characters, symbols, or punctuation characters are allowed.

To save typing, you can use the **/p** switch in place of the **/PrepareAD** switch as well as the **/on** switch in place of the **/OrganizationName** switch.

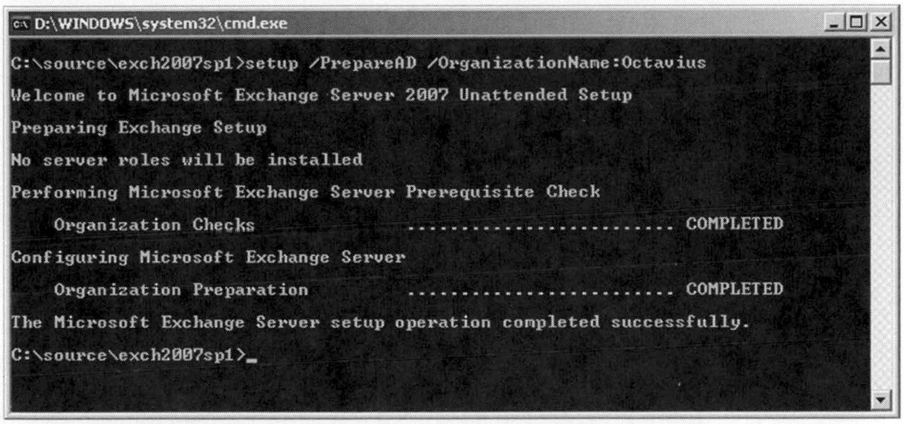

Figure 3-5

Preparing the First Active Directory Domain and Exchange Organization

If you are adding Exchange Server 2007 to an existing Exchange Server 2003 environment, an Exchange organization already exists in the AD forest. As a result, you do not need to specify the **/OrganizationName** switch to the **setup** command. However, you still need to be logged in as a user that is a member of both the Enterprise Admins group and the Exchange Server 2003 Full Administrator role.

After preparing the first domain for Exchange Server 2007, you will notice a new OU called Microsoft Exchange Security Groups in the Active Directory Users and Computers console as shown in Figure 3-6. This OU contains the following universal security groups:

- **Exchange Organization Administrators**—Contains administrative user accounts that can administer all components of Exchange.
- **Exchange Public Folder Administrators**—Contains administrative user accounts that can administer Exchange public folders.
- **Exchange Recipient Administrators**—Contains administrative user accounts that can administer AD user accounts and manage user mailboxes.
- **Exchange Servers**—Contains the computer accounts for all Exchange servers.
- **Exchange View-Only Administrators**—Contains administrative user accounts that can read Exchange configuration information for auditing purposes.
- **ExchangeLegacyInterop**—Used to maintain interoperability between Exchange Server 2007 and Exchange Server 2003 computers in the forest.

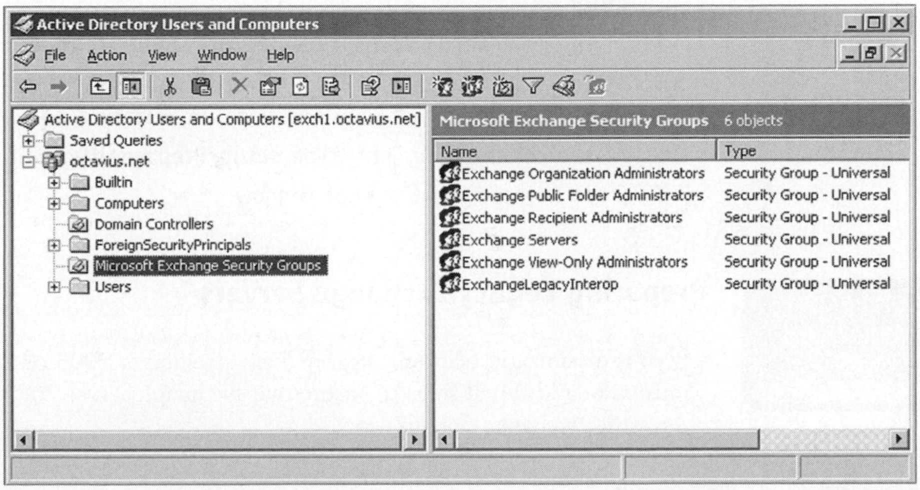

Figure 3-6

Exchange Universal Security Groups in the Forest Root Domain

ANOTHER WAY To save typing, you can use the **/pd** switch in place of the **/PrepareDomain** switch as well as the **/pad** switch in place of the **/PrepareAllDomains** switch.

PREPARING ALL OTHER DOMAINS

After preparing the first domain for Exchange Server 2007, you can prepare other domains in the forest as a member of the Enterprise Admins group by using the command **setup.exe/PrepareDomain:** *domainname* from the root of the Exchange Server 2007 installation media where *domainname* is the name of the target domain. Alternatively, you can prepare all other domains in the forest using the command **setup.exe /PrepareAllDomains** from the root of the Exchange Server 2007 installation media as shown in Figure 3-7.

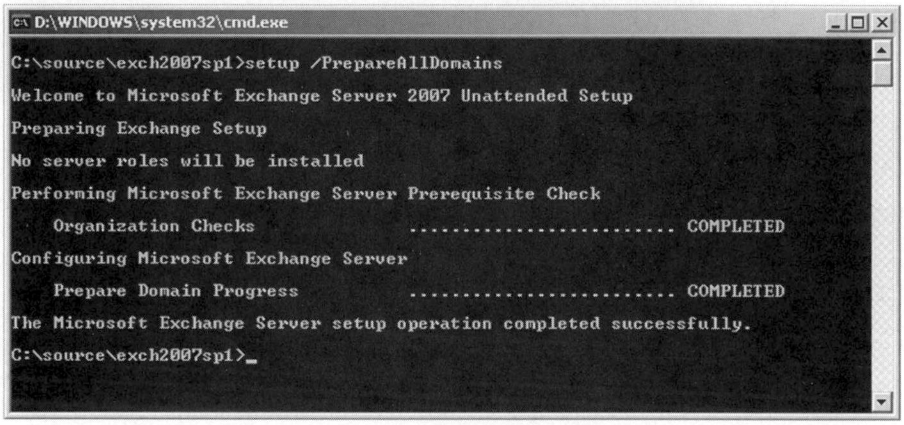

Figure 3-7

Preparing All AD Domains

```
D:\WINDOWS\system32\cmd.exe                                    _ □ X

C:\source\exch2007sp1>setup /PrepareAllDomains
Welcome to Microsoft Exchange Server 2007 Unattended Setup
Preparing Exchange Setup
No server roles will be installed
Performing Microsoft Exchange Server Prerequisite Check

    Organization Checks              ....................... COMPLETED
Configuring Microsoft Exchange Server

    Prepare Domain Progress          ....................... COMPLETED
The Microsoft Exchange Server setup operation completed successfully.

C:\source\exch2007sp1>_
```

→ **PREPARE A FOREST FOR EXCHANGE SERVER 2007**

GET READY. Turn on the computer, and log in as the Administrator user account in the forest root domain. Close any windows that appear on the desktop.

1. Click **Start**, and then click **Command Prompt**. The Command Prompt window appears.
2. Navigate to the root of your Exchange Server 2007 installation media using the appropriate command at the command prompt. For example, if your installation media is identified as D drive in My Computer, simply type **D:** at the command prompt and press **Enter.**
3. At the command prompt, type **setup/PrepareLegacyExchangePermissions** and press **Enter.**
4. At the command prompt, type **setup/PrepareSchema** and press **Enter.**
5. At the command prompt, type **setup/PrepareAD /OrganizationName:***name* where *name* is the name of your Exchange organization and press **Enter.**
6. At the command prompt, type **setup/PrepareAllDomains** and press **Enter.**
7. Close the command prompt window.

Preparing Legacy Exchange Servers

CERTIFICATION READY?
Prepare the infrastructure
for Exchange installation.
1.1

If your organization contains legacy Exchange Server 2003 or Exchange 2000 servers, you must take additional steps to ensure that Exchange Server 2007 can coexist with them in the same Exchange organization.

X REF

Creating and moving mailboxes will be covered in Lesson 4, "Configuring a New Exchange Server" and Lesson 5, "Working with Recipient Objects."

Many organizations that plan to deploy Exchange Server 2007 already have an existing Exchange server infrastructure in place. Due to hardware requirements, you cannot perform an in-place upgrade of previous versions of Exchange to Exchange Server 2007.

Instead, you must introduce Exchange Server 2007 servers to your existing Exchange environment. Following this, you can gradually move the mailbox and public folder resources on the legacy Exchange servers to servers running Exchange Server 2007 and retire the legacy Exchange servers. This process is called *migration* and may take several weeks or months to perform depending on the size and complexity of your organization.

Before adding an Exchange Server 2007 computer to your legacy Exchange infrastructure, you must ensure that AD has been prepared as described in the previous section. Furthermore, you must ensure that:

- No Exchange 5.5 or earlier servers exist within your organization,
- Servers running Exchange Server 2003 have Exchange Server 2003 SP2 or greater, and
- Servers running Exchange 2000 have Exchange 2000 SP3 or greater.

Instead of using AD site objects, Exchange Server 2003 and Exchange 2000 use *routing groups* to identify different physical locations within the same Exchange organization. Internal email in an Exchange Server 2003 or Exchange 2000 infrastructure is routed between routing groups using a *link state* software transport. If your existing Exchange Server 2003 or Exchange 2000 infrastructure contains two or more routing groups, you must disable link state before introducing your first Exchange Server 2007 computer. You can disable link state by adding a REG_DWORD called **SuppressStateChanges** with a value of **1** to the registry key **HKEY_LOCAL_MACHINE\SYSTEM\CurrentControlSet\Services\RESvc\ Parameters** on all Exchange Server 2003 and Exchange 2000 servers.

DISABLE LINK STATE ON A LEGACY EXCHANGE SERVER

GET READY. Turn on the Exchange Server 2003 or Exchange 2000 computer, and log in as the Administrator user account. Close any windows that appear on the desktop.

1. Click **Start** and then click **Run**. In the Run dialog box, type **regedit** and press **Enter**. The Registry Editor window appears.
2. Expand **HKEY_LOCAL_MACHINE\SYSTEM\CurrentControlSet\Services\RESvc\ Parameters**.
3. Right click the Parameters key in the left pane and click **New, DWORD Value**. Type **SuppressStateChanges** in the Name field and press **Enter**.
4. Double click the **SuppressStateChanges** value. In the Edit DWORD Value window, type **1** in the Value data dialog box and click **OK**.
5. Close the Registry Editor window and reboot the computer to reload the Windows registry.

Running the Exchange Best Practices Analyzer

You can run the Exchange Best Practices Analyzer to ensure that you have correctly installed prerequisite software and performed the necessary AD preparation prior to the installation of Exchange Server 2007.

Exchange Server 2007 comes with a utility called the *Exchange Best Practices Analyzer* tool that can help you tune the performance of your Exchange servers and detect configuration errors. After you have prepared the AD forest for the installation of the first Exchange Server 2007 computer, you can download and run the Exchange Best Practices Analyzer to verify that all software and AD prerequisites have been met as well as gauge the size and complexity of your AD forest.

When you run the Exchange Best Practices Analyzer, you are prompted to check for updates and the name of a DC in your forest to connect to. Following this, you can specify a new Exchange 2007 Readiness Check scan as shown in Figure 3-8.

Figure 3-8

Specifying Scan Options

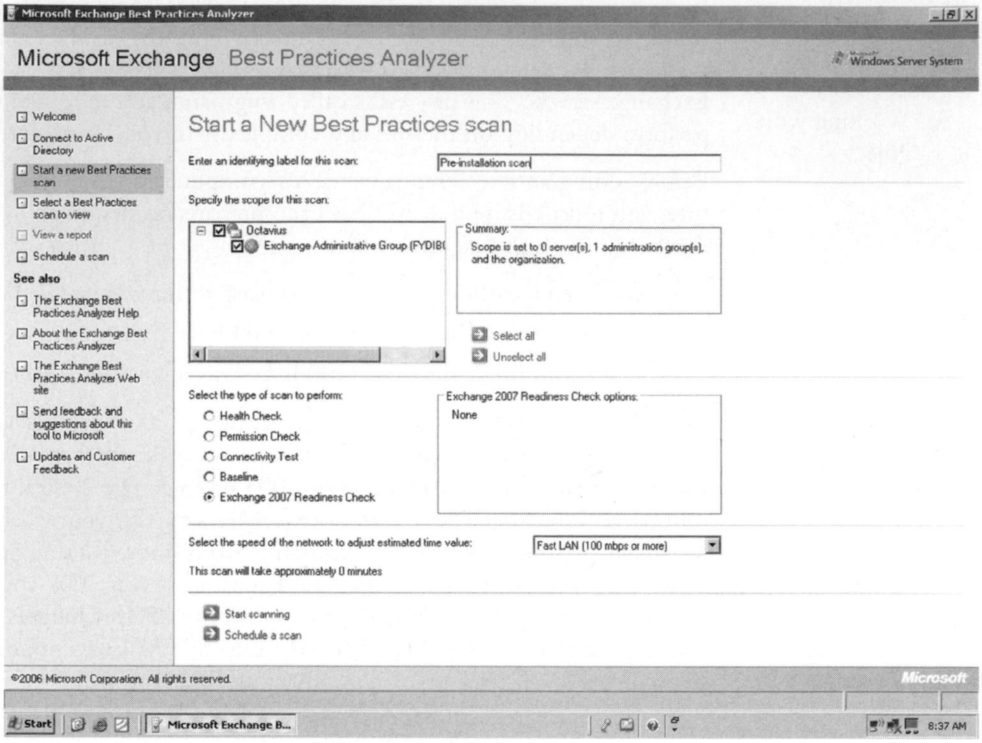

Once you complete a scan by clicking the **Start scanning** link in Figure 3-8, you can view one of several reports to identify the readiness of your AD forest for an Exchange Server 2007 installation. If your AD domain is ready for Exchange Server 2007 installation, the default List Reports view shown in Figure 3-9 should indicate no warnings or errors.

Figure 3-9

Viewing Scan Results

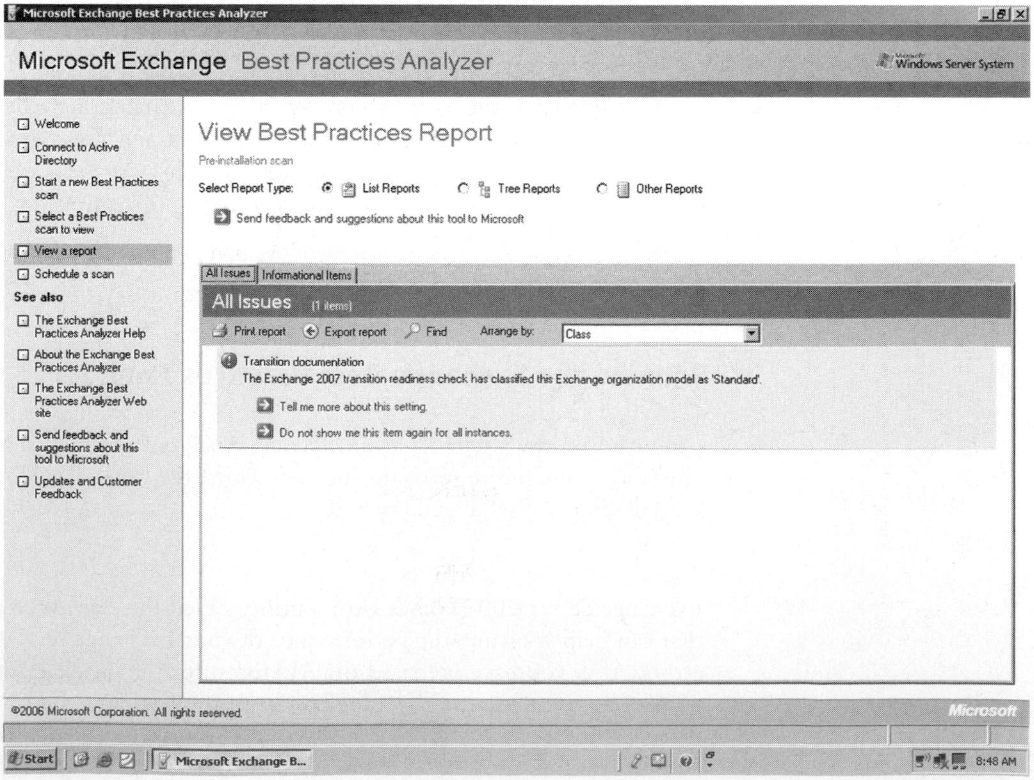

The report shown in Figure 3-9 also indicates that the AD forest uses the Standard *Exchange organization model*. There are four Exchange organization models that describe the relative size and complexity of the AD forest: simple, standard, large, and complex. You can use these Exchange organization models to gauge the complexity required when planning your Exchange Server 2007 server roles.

⊙ RUN THE EXCHANGE BEST PRACTICES ANALYZER

GET READY. Turn on the computer, and log in as the Administrator user account. Close any windows that appear on the desktop.

1. Ensure that you have downloaded and installed the latest version of the Exchange Server 2007 Best Practices Analyzer from **www.microsoft.com/downloads**.

2. Click **Start**, **All Programs**, **Microsoft Exchange**, and then click **Best Practices Analyzer Tool**. The Microsoft Exchange Best Practices Analyzer window appears.

3. On the Welcome page, click **Download the latest updates**. Any updates for the Exchange Best Practices Analyzer will be automatically downloaded and installed. Next, click **Select options for a new scan**.

4. On the Connect to Active Directory page, ensure that the name of your DC is listed in the Active Directory server dialog box and click **Connect to the Active Directory server**. If you receive an Authentication error, click **Show advanced login options**, specify the appropriate user information and click **Connect to the Active Directory server.**

5. On the Start a New Best Practices scan page, type a descriptive name for your scan in the dialog box, select **Exchange 2007 Readiness Check** and click **Start scanning**.

6. On the Scanning Completed page, click **View a report of this Best Practices scan**.

7. On the View Best Practices Report page, note any warnings regarding your AD structure if present and click **Transition documentation** to view your Exchange organization model. Next, highlight the **Informational Items** tab to view your AD summary.

> **TAKE NOTE ✱**
>
> You can print or export your reports using the **Print report** and **Export report** buttons in the summary window or select **Tree Reports** to view detailed reports regarding your AD forest.

8. Close the Microsoft Exchange Best Practices Analyzer window.

■ Installing Exchange Server 2007

> **↓ THE BOTTOM LINE**
>
> After properly preparing for Exchange Server 2007 deployment, the installation process is straightforward. To install Exchange Server 2007 from the installation media, you can run the setup.exe for graphical mode or the setup.com for unattended mode. Following the installation of Exchange Server 2007, you should verify that all components were correctly installed as well as license and update your Exchange servers.

CERTIFICATION READY?
Install Exchange.
1.3

Performing a Graphical Installation

Once you have satisfied the necessary hardware, software, and AD prerequisites, you can start the Exchange Server 2007 installation and select the server roles that should be installed on your email server.

To start an Exchange Server 2007 graphical installation, simply log in to the server using a user account that is a member of the Enterprise Admins group and run the **setup.exe** program from the root of the Exchange Server 2007 installation media.

During the installation, you must select the server roles that will be hosted on the Exchange server. A typical Exchange Server 2007 installation adds the Client Access Server, Hub Transport, and Mailbox roles, whereas a custom Exchange Server 2007 installation allows you to select specific roles. If you select the Edge Transport role or a Mailbox role that is clustered, you cannot add any additional roles to the Exchange server.

The installation procedure is identical for 32-bit and 64-bit versions of Exchange Server 2007 and Exchange Server 2007 SP1. In this lesson and throughout this text, we will focus on Exchange Server 2007 SP1.

⊕ INSTALL EXCHANGE SERVER 2007 SP1

GET READY. Turn on the computer, and log in as the Administrator user account. Close any windows that appear on the desktop.

1. Navigate to the root of the Exchange Server 2007 media and double click the **setup.exe** file. After a few moments, the Exchange Server 2007 welcome screen appears as shown in Figure 3-10.

Figure 3-10

Exchange Server Setup Welcome Screen

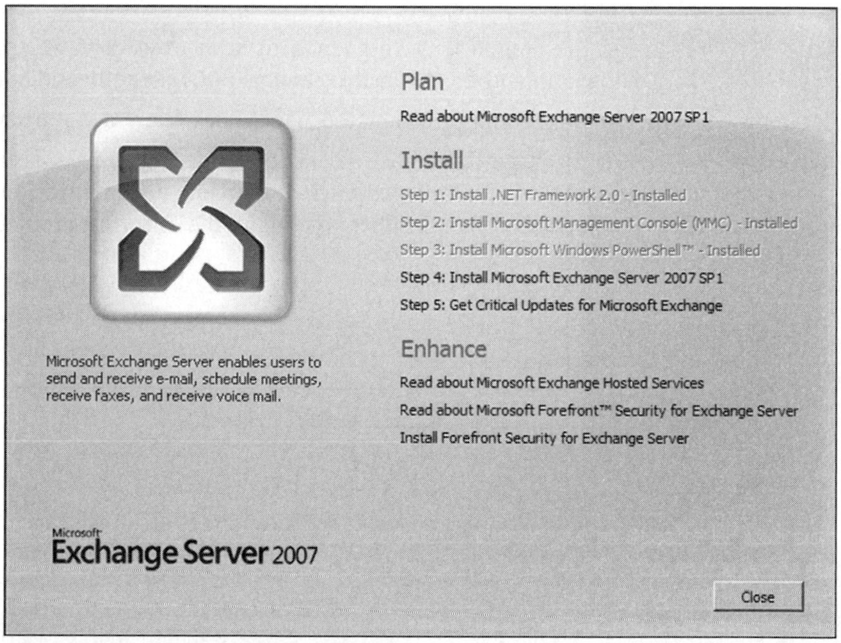

If you have installed the Exchange Server 2007 prerequisite software, the links for Steps 1, 2, and 3 will be unavailable as depicted in Figure 3-10. If these links are available, they direct you to the Microsoft Download Web site.

TAKE NOTE*

2. Click **Step 4: Install Microsoft Exchange Server 2007 SP1.** The Exchange Server 2007 SP1 Setup wizard appears as shown in Figure 3-11.

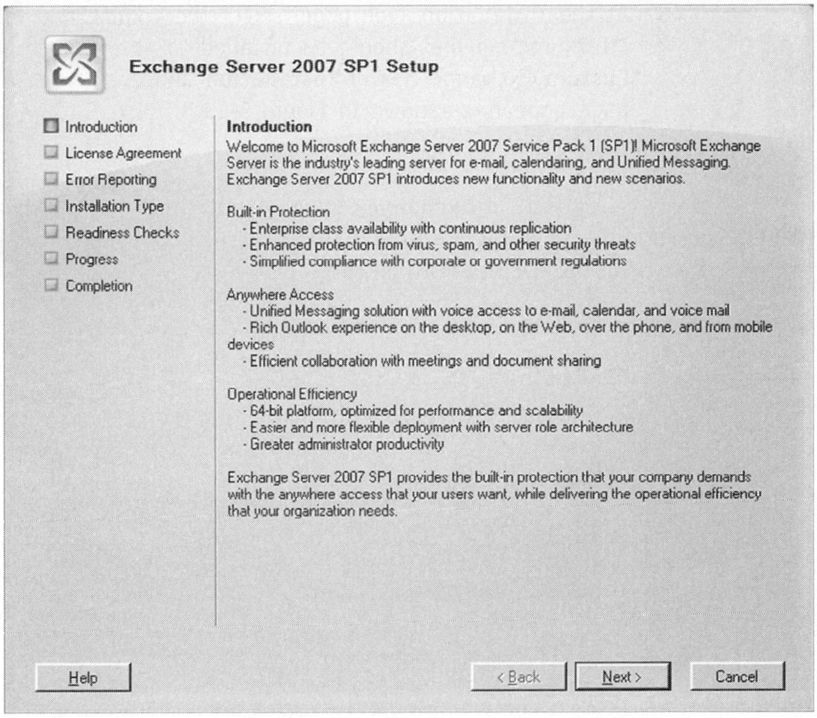

Figure 3-11

Starting the Exchange Server
2007 Installation

Exchange Server 2007 SP1 Setup

- Introduction
- License Agreement
- Error Reporting
- Installation Type
- Readiness Checks
- Progress
- Completion

Introduction
Welcome to Microsoft Exchange Server 2007 Service Pack 1 (SP1)! Microsoft Exchange Server is the industry's leading server for e-mail, calendaring, and Unified Messaging. Exchange Server 2007 SP1 introduces new functionality and new scenarios.

Built-in Protection
   - Enterprise class availability with continuous replication
   - Enhanced protection from virus, spam, and other security threats
   - Simplified compliance with corporate or government regulations

Anywhere Access
   - Unified Messaging solution with voice access to e-mail, calendar, and voice mail
   - Rich Outlook experience on the desktop, on the Web, over the phone, and from mobile devices
   - Efficient collaboration with meetings and document sharing

Operational Efficiency
   - 64-bit platform, optimized for performance and scalability
   - Easier and more flexible deployment with server role architecture
   - Greater administrator productivity

Exchange Server 2007 SP1 provides the built-in protection that your company demands with the anywhere access that your users want, while delivering the operational efficiency that your organization needs.

Help   < Back   Next >   Cancel

3. At the Introduction page, click **Next**. The License Agreement page appears.

4. At the License Agreement page, select **I accept the terms in the license agreement** and click **Next**. The Error Reporting page appears.

5. At the Error Reporting page, ensure that **No** is selected and click **Next**. The Installation Type page appears as shown in Figure 3-12.

ANOTHER WAY

You may instead select **Yes** at the Error Reporting page to participate in Microsoft's quality assurance program. However, this will require added bandwidth and is not recommended for classroom use.

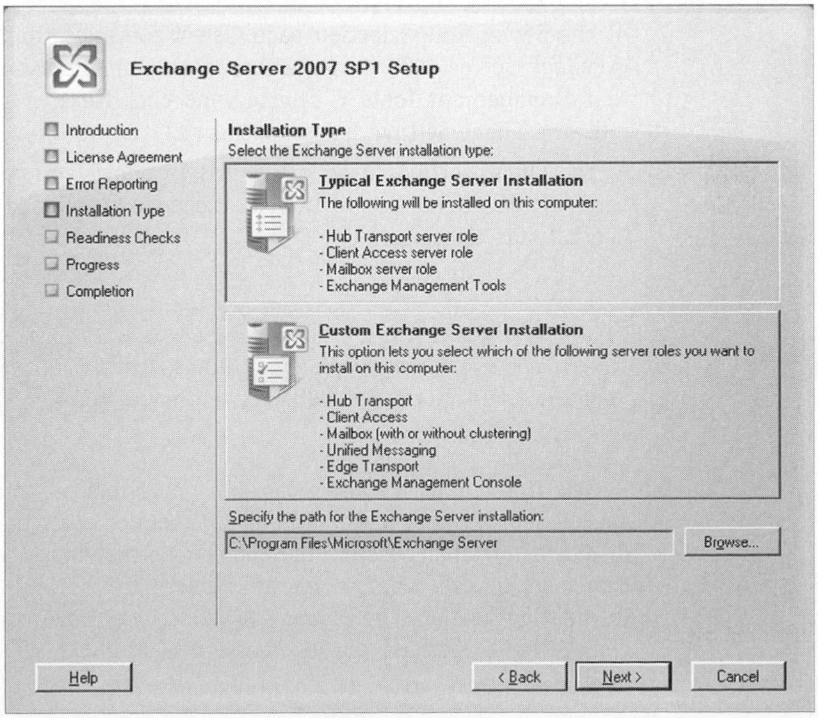

Figure 3-12

Specifying the Installation Type

Exchange Server 2007 SP1 Setup

- Introduction
- License Agreement
- Error Reporting
- Installation Type
- Readiness Checks
- Progress
- Completion

Installation Type
Select the Exchange Server installation type:

Typical Exchange Server Installation
The following will be installed on this computer:

   - Hub Transport server role
   - Client Access server role
   - Mailbox server role
   - Exchange Management Tools

Custom Exchange Server Installation
This option lets you select which of the following server roles you want to install on this computer:

   - Hub Transport
   - Client Access
   - Mailbox (with or without clustering)
   - Unified Messaging
   - Edge Transport
   - Exchange Management Console

Specify the path for the Exchange Server installation:

C:\Program Files\Microsoft\Exchange Server   Browse...

Help   < Back   Next >   Cancel

6. At the Installation Type page, select the volume and folder that Exchange Server 2007 program files should be installed to at the bottom of the screen. Next, select **Custom Exchange Server Installation** and click **Next**. The Server Role Selection page appears as shown in Figure 3-13.

ANOTHER WAY

If you select **Typical Exchange Server Installation** from the Installation Type page, the installation program will install the Hub Transport, Client Access, and Mailbox roles as well as the Exchange Management Tools.

Figure 3-13

Selecting Individual Server Roles

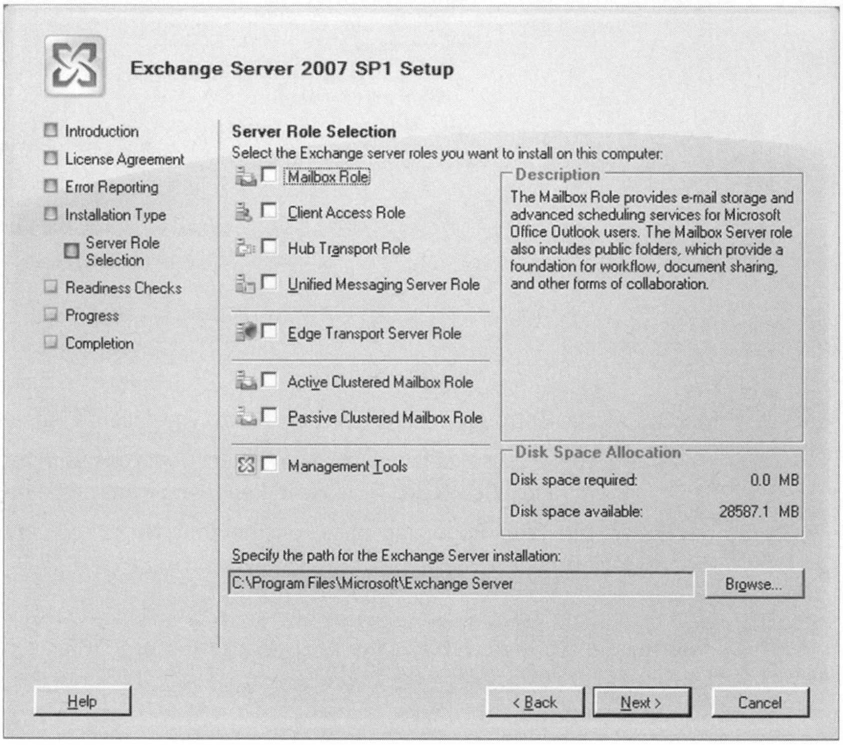

---

7. At the Server Role Selection page, select the roles that you require on your Exchange Server 2007 computer based on your preinstallation plan. Next, ensure that **Management Tools** is selected and click **Next**. If you selected the Mailbox role, the Client Settings page appears.

8. At the Client Settings page, select **Yes** to allow Entourage and Outlook 2003 and earlier MAPI clients access to your Exchange server and click **Next**. The Readiness Checks page appears.

TAKE NOTE*

A public folder database is required by Entourage and Outlook 2003 or earlier clients when connecting to your Exchange server using MAPI. If you select **Yes** at the Client Settings page, a default public folder database is created on your Exchange server.

---

9. Review the Readiness Checks page for any errors or warnings. If you have not met the proper software, hardware, and AD requirements, the Readiness Checks page will display errors that describe the component that must be installed or the action that must be taken before you are allowed to continue the Exchange Server 2007 installation as shown in Figure 3-14. Once you have corrected the errors, you can click **Retry** to perform the readiness checks again.

Figure 3-14

A Failed Readiness Check

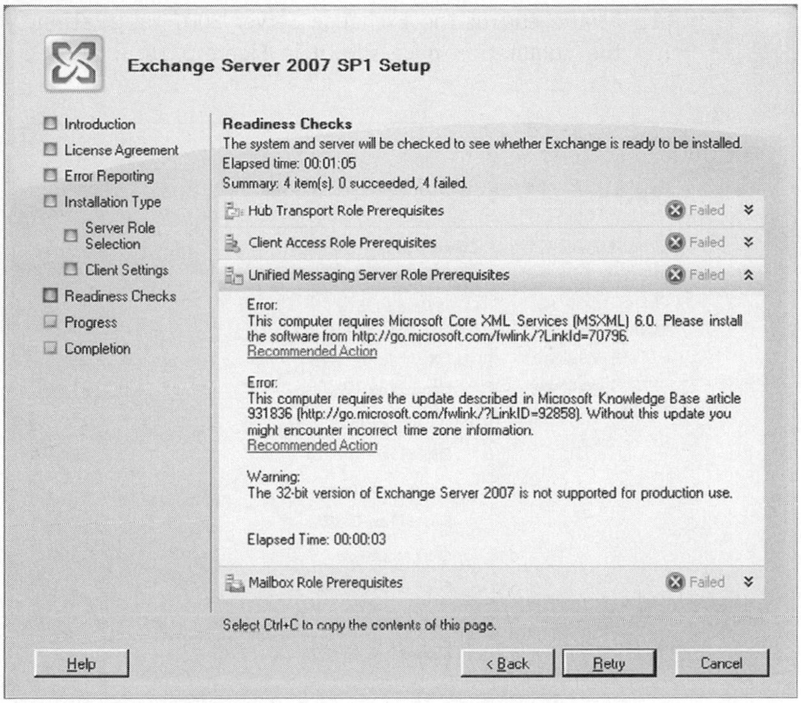

10. Once the Readiness Checks page is free of errors, you can click the **Install** button shown in Figure 3-15 to begin the Exchange Server 2007 installation.

Figure 3-15

Completing the Readiness Checks

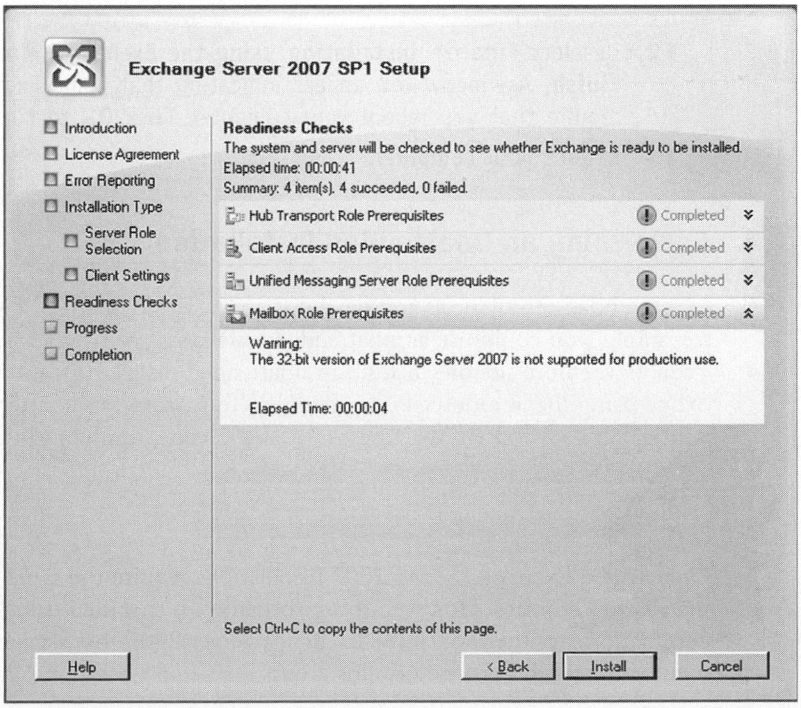

TAKE NOTE*

Figure 3-15 indicates the warning that you receive when you install the 32-bit version of Exchange. Although the installation will proceed, the 32-bit version should not be used in a production environment.

11. At the end of the Exchange Server 2007 installation, you will be presented with the Completion page shown in Figure 3-16.

Figure 3-16

Completing the Exchange Server Installation

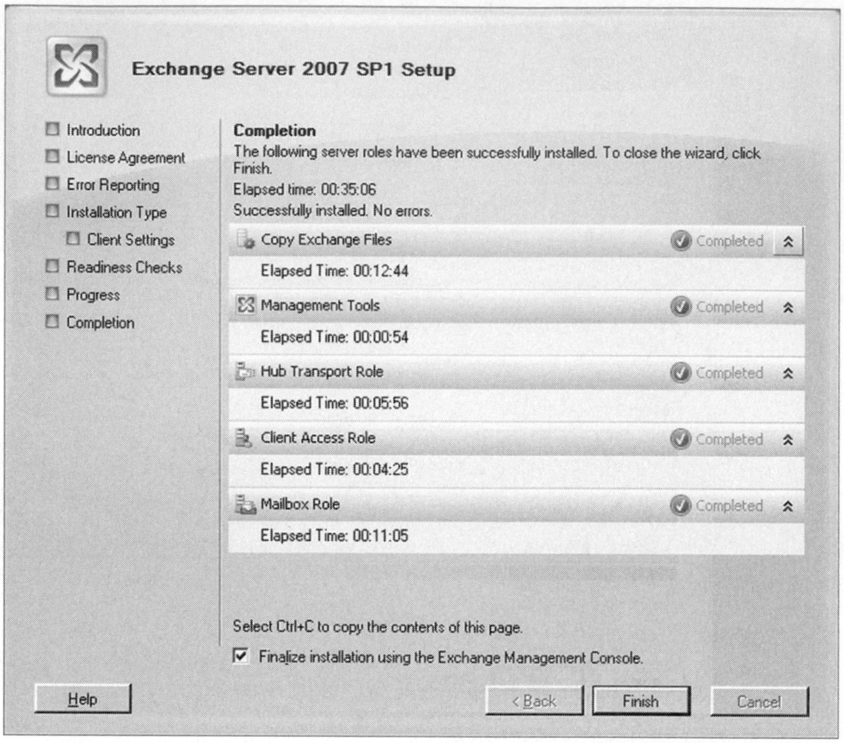

12. Deselect **Finalize installation using the Exchange Management Console** and click **Finish**. A window will appear indicating that some Exchange Server 2007 settings require that you reboot your computer. Click **OK** to close the window.

13. Reboot your computer.

Performing an Unattended Installation

Unattended installations add flexibility to the deployment of Exchange Server 2007. For example, you could use an unattended installation command within a script file that is run at a remote site or schedule an unattended installation command to run at a later time using the Windows Task Scheduler. To perform an unattended installation, you must supply the appropriate switches to the setup.com command in the root of the installation media.

TAKE NOTE*

If any software, hardware, or AD prerequisites have not been satisfied prior to performing an unattended installation, the setup program will fail and list the actions that need to be performed.

Unattended Exchange Server 2007 installations require the same information that a graphical installation requires. However, this information is specified using switches to the **setup.com** command from the root of the Exchange Server 2007 installation media by a user that is a member of the Enterprise Admins group.

For example, consider the following unattended installation command:

setup /mode:Install /roles:HubTransport,ClientAccess,Mailbox /EnableLegacyOutlook / TargetDir:D:\ExchangeServer2007

This command installs (**/mode:Install**) the Exchange Management tools, Hub, CAS, and Mailbox roles (**/roles:HubTransport,ClientAccess,Mailbox**) to the D:\ExchangeServer2007 directory (**/TargetDir:D:\ExchangeServer2007**) as well as creates a public folder database for Entourage and Outlook 2003 or earlier MAPI clients (**/EnableLegacyOutlook**).

If you do not specify a certain switch to the **setup.com** command, the default value will be assumed. Thus, the following command will install the Exchange Management tools, Hub, CAS, and Mailbox roles to the default directory (%systemroot%\Program Files\Microsoft\ Exchange Server\) without creating a public folder database for Entourage and Outlook 2003 or earlier MAPI clients.

setup /mode:Install /roles:HubTransport,ClientAccess,Mailbox

At minimum, you must specify the **/mode** switch to specify the type of installation as well as the **/roles** switch to specify the components to install.

Valid options to the **/roles** switch include:

- **Install** to install the specified roles
- **Uninstall** to remove the specified roles
- **Upgrade** to upgrade roles from Exchange Server 2003 to Exchange Server 2003 SP1

Valid options to the **/roles** switch include:

- **HubTransport**, **HT**, or **H** to specify the Hub Transport role
- **ClientAccess**, **CA**, or **C** to specify the CAS role
- **Mailbox**, **MB**, or **M** to specify the Mailbox role
- **EdgeTransport**, **ET**, or **E** to specify the Edge role
- **UnifiedMessaging**, **UM**, or **U** to specify the UM role

TAKE NOTE *

We have examined the most common switches to the setup.com command in this section. For a complete list of switches to the setup.com command, run the command **setup /?** from the root of the Exchange Server 2007 installation media.

When you install any server role, the Exchange Management tools are automatically installed. If you only want to install the Exchange Management tools to the default location on a computer, you can specify **ManagementTools**, **MT**, or **M** as an option to the **/roles** switch as shown:

setup /mode:Install /roles:ManagementTools

Verifying the Installation

After the installation process has completed, you should verify that all Exchange components were installed successfully before placing your Exchange server in a production environment. This involves reviewing your server configuration and folder structure as well as reviewing Exchange-related logs.

After installation, you should check the configuration of your system to ensure that there were no errors during the installation process. More specifically, you should perform the following tasks:

- Verify the addition of the Exchange management tools and server roles,
- Examine the Exchange folder structure, and
- Examine the Exchange logs.

VERIFYING EXCHANGE MANAGEMENT TOOLS AND SERVER ROLES

After installing the Exchange Server 2007, the Exchange Management Console MMC snap-in is added to the MMC and the Exchange Management Shell snap-in is added to PowerShell. You can open these utilities by selecting them from the Exchange Server menu (**Start**, **All Programs**, **Microsoft Exchange Server 2007**).

If the Exchange Management Shell snap-in was not properly added to PowerShell during the installation of the Exchange Management Tools, you can start PowerShell (**Start** > **All Programs** > **Windows PowerShell 1.0** > **Windows PowerShell**) and run the command **Add-PSSnapin Microsoft.Exchange.Management.PowerShell.Admin** to add it manually.

Similarly, if the Exchange Management Console snap-in was not added to the MMC during installation, you can open the MMC (**Start** > **Run** and type **mmc**), and manually add the Microsoft Exchange snap-in by selecting **File**, **Add/Remove Snap-in** from the MMC window.

Provided the Exchange Management tools were properly installed, you can verify the installation of server roles on your Exchange server by viewing the details pane for your server in the Exchange Management Console or by running the command **get-ExchangeServer | Format-List** from the Exchange Management Shell.

If a particular server role or management tool was not installed properly, you can remove and reinstall the role. You will learn how to remove roles from your Exchange server at the end of this lesson.

⊖ VERIFY EXCHANGE MANAGEMENT TOOLS AND SERVER ROLES

GET READY. Turn on the computer, and log in as the Administrator user account. Close any windows that appear on the desktop.

1. Click **Start**, **All Programs**, **Microsoft Exchange Server 2007**, and then click **Exchange Management Console**. The Exchange Management Console window appears.

2. Click **OK** to close the dialog box stating that you have unlicensed servers.

3. Highlight **Server Configuration** in the console tree pane and view your server object in the detail pane as depicted in Figure 3-17. The Role column next to your server object should list the roles that were successfully installed.

Figure 3-17

Verifying Server Roles Using the Exchange Management Console

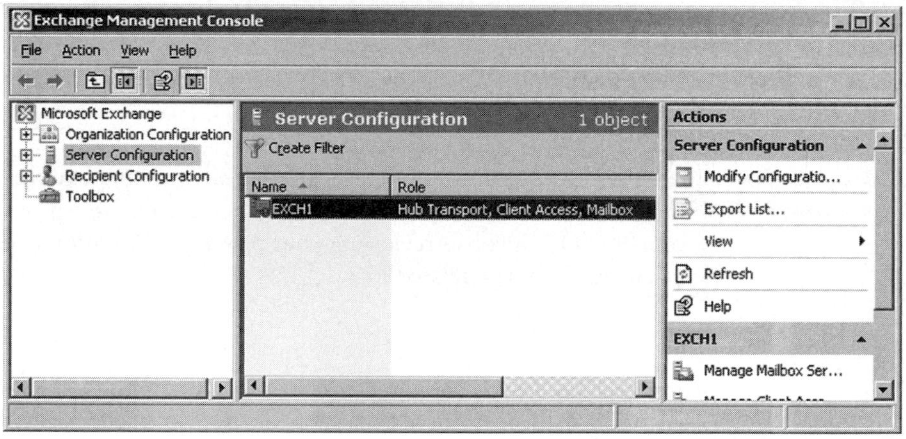

4. Close the Exchange Management Console.

TAKE NOTE*

If you see a red circle icon next to Microsoft Exchange in the console tree pane, the Exchange Management Console cannot connect to the Exchange software on your server. If all Exchange-related services are running on your server, you may need to reinstall the Exchange management tools.

5. Click **Start**, **All Programs**, **Microsoft Exchange Server 2007**, and then click **Exchange Management Shell**. The Exchange Management Shell window appears.

6. At the command prompt, type **get-ExchangeServer | Format-List** and press **Enter** to view a server configuration similar to that shown in Figure 3-18. The ServerRoles section should list your installed server roles.

Figure 3-18

Viewing Server Configuration Using the Exchange Management Shell

7. Close the Exchange Management Shell.

EXAMINING THE EXCHANGE FOLDER STRUCTURE

During the Exchange Server 2007 installation, several new subdirectories are added to the installation directory depending on the roles you have installed. After installing Exchange Server 2007, you should verify the existence of these folders as well as become accustomed to their function for later use.

Figure 3-19 shows the folders present under the installation directory when you install Exchange Server 2007 in the default directory (%systemroot%\Program Files\Microsoft\ Exchange Server). Table 3-3 describes the function and contents of each of these folders.

Figure 3-19

Viewing the Exchange Folder Structure

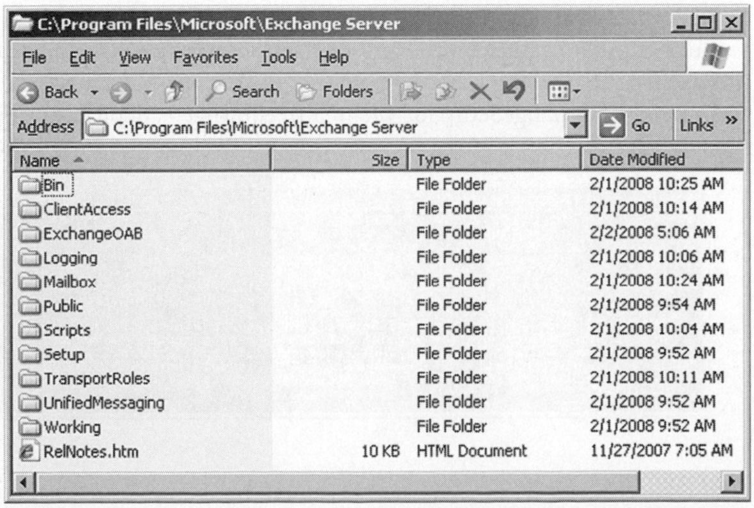

Table 3-3

Exchange Server 2007
installation directory subfolders

EXCHANGE SERVER ROLE	DESCRIPTION
Bin	Contains the programs and program components used by Exchange Server. This directory is present regardless of the server roles installed.
ClientAccess	Contains the configuration files used by the CAS role.
ExchangeOAB	Contains the Exchange offline address book used by the CAS role.
Logging	Contains Exchange server log files. This directory is present regardless of the server roles installed.
Mailbox	Contains the default storage groups and databases used by the Mailbox role for email and public folder storage.
Public	Contains configuration files and drivers used by the Edge and Hub roles when processing email for relay.
Scripts	Contains scripts that may be used to automate Exchange server administrative tasks. This directory is present regardless of the server roles installed.
Setup	Contains Exchange server configuration information. This directory is present regardless of the server roles installed.
TransportRoles	Contains the configuration used by the Hub and Edge roles when relaying and filtering email.
UnifiedMessaging	Contains the configuration files used by the UM role as well as the database used to store UM voice mail.

EXAMINING EXCHANGE LOGS

If you encountered error or warning messages during the Exchange Server 2007 installation process, you can obtain detailed information regarding the messages by viewing the Exchange setup log files. These log files are created in the %systemroot%\ExchangeSetupLogs\ folder and contain information regarding different parts of the installation process:

- ExchangeSetup.log lists the tasks that were performed during the Exchange Server 2007 installation process.
- ExchangeSetup.msilog lists the installation of files from the Exchange Server 2007 installation media.

Because these installation logs contain a great deal of information, you should use the Exchange Management Shell to search and display only messages that have the word "error" in them. For example, you can type **Get-SetupLog %systemroot%\ExchangeSetupLogs\ExchangeSetup.log –error –tree** in the Exchange Management Shell to view only the errors from the ExchangeSetup.log file in a tree format as depicted in Figure 3-20.

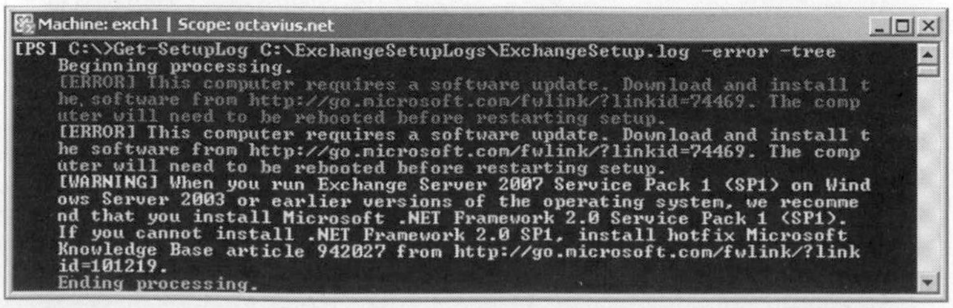

Figure 3-20

Parsing the Exchange
Setup Log

In addition to examining the Exchange setup log files for errors, you should also check for Exchange service errors. The services that comprise Exchange Server 2007 log information, warnings, and errors to the Windows Application Event Log. Exchange-related errors and warnings in the Windows Application Event Log often indicate configuration or installation-related problems.

➡ **VIEW THE EXCHANGE SETUP LOGS AND APPLICATION EVENT LOG**

GET READY. Turn on the computer, and log in as the Administrator user account. Close any windows that appear on the desktop.

1. Click Start, **All Programs**, **Microsoft Exchange Server 2007**, and then click **Exchange Management Shell**. The Exchange Management Shell window appears.

2. Type **Get-SetupLog %systemroot%\ExchangeSetupLogs\ExchangeSetup.log –error –tree** and press **Enter.** Once the log file has been parsed, view the results.

3. Type **Get-SetupLog %systemroot%\ExchangeSetupLogs\ExchangeSetup.msilog –error –tree** and press **Enter.** Once the log file has been parsed, view the results.

4. Close the Exchange Management Shell.

5. Click **Start**, **Administrative Tools**, and then click **Event Viewer**. The Event Viewer window appears.

6. Highlight **Application** in the left pane to view the Application Event Log.

7. Click the **Type** column twice in the right pane to sort the information, warning, and error messages by type and scroll to the top of the list. View any Exchange-related errors and warnings.

8. Close the Event Viewer window.

Finalizing the Installation

CERTIFICATION READY?
Install Exchange.
1.3

Following a successful installation, you should enter the Exchange Server 2007 product key and update your Exchange Server software.

After a successful installation, Exchange Server 2007 is placed in a 120-day evaluation mode. To use Exchange Server beyond this period, you must enter the Exchange product key in the Exchange Management Console and restart the Microsoft Exchange Information Store service. Because the 32-bit version of Exchange Server 2007 is unsupported in production environments, you cannot purchase or enter a product key for it in the Exchange Management Console.

➕ MORE INFORMATION

You can also enter the Exchange Server product key in the Exchange Management Shell using the command **Set-ExchangeServer –Identity** *server_name* **–ProductKey** *xxxxx-xxxxx-xxxxx-xxxxx-xxxxx* where *server_name* is the name of the Exchange Server you wish to license and *xxxxx-xxxxx-xxxxx-xxxxx-xxxxx* is the 25-character Exchange product key. After entering this command, you must still restart the Microsoft Exchange Information Store service.

Because Exchange Server 2007 is a heavily used network resource, it is important to keep it updated to ensure that it maintains a high level of security and reliability. After installing Exchange Server 2007, you should periodically check for and install Exchange Server 2007 updates. By selecting **Step 5: Get Critical Updates for Microsoft Exchange** from the Exchange Server 2007 welcome screen shown earlier in Figure 3-10, you will be redirected to the Microsoft Update Web site where you can scan your computer for updates and install Exchange updates.

Alternatively, you can visit the Microsoft Update Web site manually using Internet Explorer to obtain Exchange updates or configure the *Automatic Updates* feature of Windows to ensure that your Exchange server receives updates on a regular basis.

In many organizations, administrators configure a *Windows Server Update Services (WSUS)* server to automatically download and distribute updates to computers within the organization. WSUS may also be used to update your Exchange servers within the organization.

→ ENTER THE EXCHANGE PRODUCT KEY

GET READY. Turn on the computer, and log in as the Administrator user account. Close any windows that appear on the desktop.

ANOTHER WAY

You can also restart the Microsoft Exchange Information Store by typing the command **net stop "Microsoft Exchange Information Store" /y** followed by the command **net start "Microsoft Exchange Information Store" /y** from a Windows command prompt.

1. Click **Start, All Programs, Microsoft Exchange Server 2007**, and then click **Exchange Management Console**. The Exchange Management Console window appears.

2. Click **OK** to close the dialog box stating that you have unlicensed servers.

3. In the console tree pane, highlight **Server Configuration**.

4. In the result pane, highlight your server. Next, click **Enter Product** Key in the action pane. The Enter Product Key window appears.

5. Input your product key in the Product Key dialog box and press **Enter**.

6. Close the Exchange Management Console. You must now restart the Microsoft Exchange Information Store service to enable the product key.

7. Click **Start, Administrative Tools**, and then click **Services**. The Services window appears.

8. Right click **Microsoft Exchange Information Store** in the right pane and click **Restart**.

9. Close the Services window.

→ UPDATE EXCHANGE SERVER 2007

GET READY. Turn on the computer, and log in as the Administrator user account. Close any windows that appear on the desktop.

1. Navigate to the root of the Exchange Server 2007 media and double click the **setup.exe** file. After a few moments, the Exchange Server 2007 welcome screen appears.

2. Click **Step 5: Get Critical Updates for Microsoft Exchange**. Internet Explorer opens and directs you to the Microsoft Update Web site. Follow the instructions on the Web site to scan for and apply any updates that are required by your version of Windows and Exchange Server 2007.

3. Close all windows on your desktop.

4. Click **Start, Control Panel**, and then click **System**. The System Properties window appears.

5. Highlight the **Automatic Updates** tab and select **Automatic (recommended)**. Select an appropriate time for downloading updates and then click **OK**.

■ Changing and Removing Exchange Server 2007

↓
THE BOTTOM LINE   After deploying Exchange Server 2007, you may need to add additional server roles to an Exchange server or remove existing server roles. Before changing or removing Exchange Server 2007, you should first understand the associated restrictions and procedures.

Over time, you may need to add server roles to an existing Exchange server to provide extra functionality. Alternatively, you may need to remove server roles from an Exchange server to change your server role structure, improve performance, or decommission an Exchange server.

TAKE NOTE*

You must be a member of the Exchange Organization Administrators group to add and remove server roles on existing Exchange servers. By default, the Administrator account in the forest root domain is a member of this group.

To perform these tasks, you can simply select Microsoft Exchange Server 2007 in the Add or Remove Programs tool as shown in Figure 3-21.

Figure 3-21

Changing and Removing Exchange Server

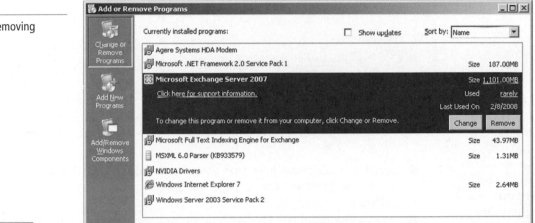

ANOTHER WAY

To start the Exchange Setup wizard in Maintenance mode and add server roles to your existing Exchange server, you can also run the **setup.exe** command from the root of your Exchange Server 2007 installation media.

When you click the **Change** button beside Microsoft Exchange Server 2007 in Figure 3-21, the Exchange Setup wizard starts in Maintenance mode and allows you to add server roles to your existing Exchange server. Similarly, clicking the **Remove** button in Figure 3-21 will start the Exchange Setup wizard and allow you to remove server roles from your Exchange server.

Alternatively, you can use the **/mode:Install** and **/mode:Uninstall** switches of the **setup.com** command to add and remove server roles from an existing Exchange server respectively. For example, to remove the CAS role from your Exchange server, you could run the following command from the root of your Exchange Server 2007 installation media:

setup /mode:Uninstall /roles:ClientAccess

TAKE NOTE*

Before you remove the Mailbox role, you must ensure that all mailbox and public folder databases have been removed or moved to other Exchange servers.

⊕ ADD ADDITIONAL SERVER ROLES TO EXCHANGE SERVER 2007

GET READY. Turn on the computer, and log in as the Administrator user account in the forest root domain. Close any windows that appear on the desktop.

1. Click **Start**, **Control Panel**, and then click **Add or Remove Programs**. The Add or Remove Programs window appears.
2. Highlight **Microsoft Exchange Server 2007** and click **Change**. The Exchange Server 2007 SP1 Setup window appears.

3. At the Exchange Maintenance Mode page, click **Next**. The Server Roles Selection page appears as depicted in Figure 3-22.

Figure 3-22

Adding Exchange Roles

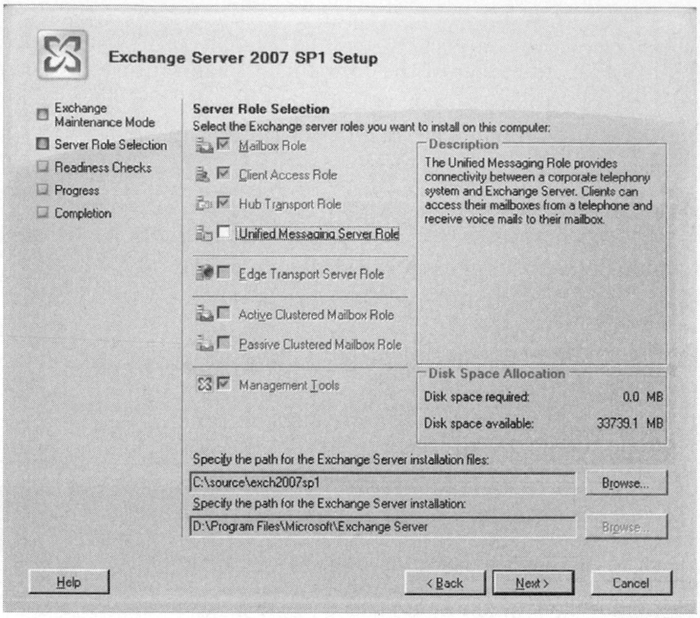

TAKE NOTE*

Only the roles that can be added to your Exchange server may be selected on the Roles Selection page. Because the Edge and Clustered Mailbox roles cannot share hardware with other roles, they cannot be selected.

4. Select the additional roles that you wish to add to your Exchange server and click **Next**. The Readiness Checks page will appear and check your system for prerequisite software.
5. Review the Readiness Checks page for any errors or warnings. If you have not met the proper software, hardware, and AD requirements for the role you wish to add, the Readiness Checks page will display errors that describe the component that must be installed or the action that must be taken before you are allowed to continue the Exchange Server 2007 installation. Once you have corrected the errors, you can click **Retry** to perform the readiness checks again.
6. Once the Readiness Checks page is free of errors, you can click the **Install** button to add the appropriate roles to your Exchange server.
7. On the Completion page, click **Finish**. A window will appear indicating that some Exchange Server 2007 settings require that you reboot your computer. Click **OK** to close the window.
8. Reboot your computer.

REMOVE SERVER ROLES FROM EXCHANGE SERVER 2007

GET READY. Turn on the computer, and log in as the Administrator user account in the forest root domain. Close any windows that appear on the desktop.

1. Click **Start**, **Control Panel**, and then click **Add or Remove Programs**. The Add or Remove Programs window appears.
2. Highlight **Microsoft Exchange Server 2007** and click **Remove**. The Exchange Server 2007 SP1 Setup window appears.
3. At the Exchange Maintenance Mode page, click **Next**. The Server Roles Selection page appears as depicted in Figure 3-23.

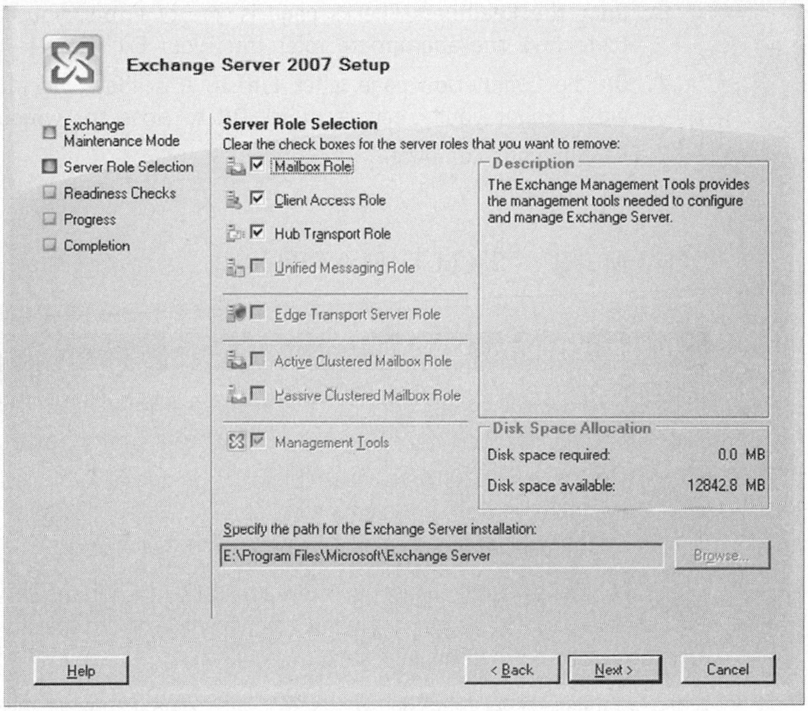

Figure 3-23

Removing Existing Server Roles

4. Select the additional roles that you wish to remove from your Exchange server and click **Next**. The Readiness Checks page will appear and check your system for prerequisite software.

5. Review the Readiness Checks page for any errors or warnings. If you are removing the Mailbox role and have not moved the mailbox and public folder databases to another server, you will see the error shown in Figure 3-24. Once you have corrected any errors, you can click **Retry** to perform the readiness checks again.

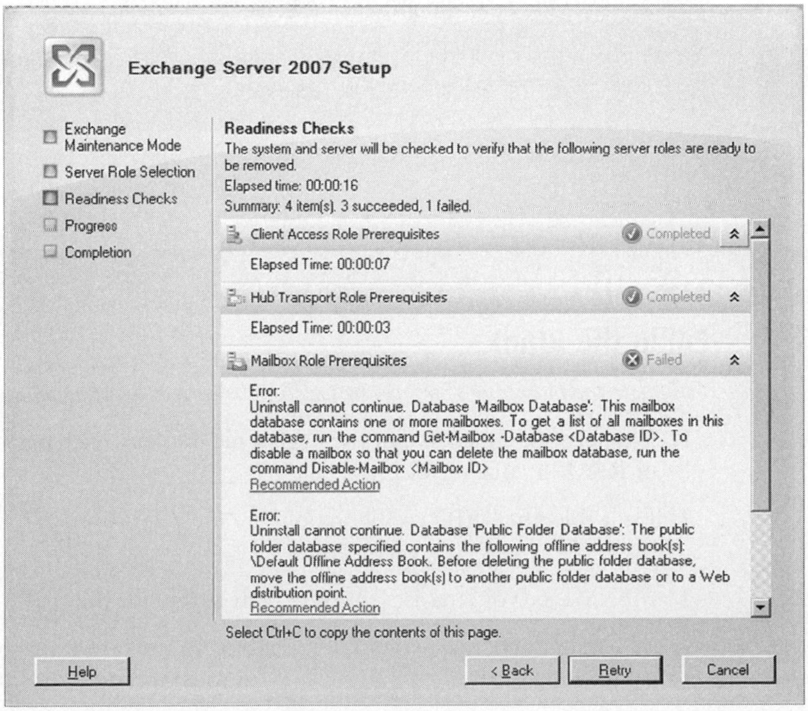

Figure 3-24

Mailbox Role Failed Readiness Checks

6. Once the Readiness Checks page is free of errors, you can click the **Remove** button to remove the appropriate roles from your Exchange server.

7. On the Completion page, click **Finish**. A window will appear indicating that you must reboot your computer. Click **OK** to close the window.

8. Reboot your computer.

SUMMARY SKILL MATRIX

IN THIS LESSON YOU LEARNED:

- Prior to deploying Exchange Server 2007, you should plan the number and placement of Exchange Server 2007 server roles within your organization.

- Exchange Server 2007 supports 64-bit Intel 64 and AMD64 platforms only. The amount of RAM and hard disk space required by Exchange Server 2007 is dependent on the server roles that will be hosted by the Exchange server.

- All Exchange servers must have PowerShell 1.0, .NET Framework 2.0, and MMC 3.0 installed as well as other software components that are specific to the server roles that will be hosted by the Exchange server.

- You must ensure that your existing AD and Exchange environment is compatible with Exchange Server 2007 prior to deployment. More specifically, you must prepare legacy Exchange servers, the AD schema, and AD domains prior to deploying AD. The Microsoft Exchange Best Practices Analyzer can help in Exchange server planning and preparation.

- You can install Exchange Server 2007 in graphical mode by running the **setup.exe** program or in unattended mode by using the appropriate switches to the **setup.com** program. During the installation, you must select the appropriate server roles for your Exchange server.

- Following an Exchange Server 2007 installation, you should review the installed Exchange components, Exchange setup logs, Application Event Log, as well as install an Exchange license and update your Exchange server.

- You can use the Add or Remove Programs utility in Control Panel to modify or remove server roles on existing Exchange servers.

■ Knowledge Assessment

Fill in the Blank

Complete the following sentences by writing the correct word or words in the blanks provided.

1. The recommended size of the paging file on your Exchange server is equal to the amount of RAM in your server plus _____ MB.

2. Fault tolerant RAID configurations are most appropriate for Exchange servers that host the _____ server role.

3. MSXML 6.0 or later is a software prerequisite for the _____ server role.

4. When an Exchange Server 2007 is added to the forest, its computer account is automatically added to the _____ universal security group in the forest root domain.

5. After you license your Exchange server, you must restart the _____ service for the changes to be applied.

6. If your existing Exchange Server 2003 infrastructure contains more than one routing group, you must disable _____ in the registry of the legacy Exchange server prior to deploying Exchange Server 2007.

7. To remove server roles from an existing Exchange Server 2007 computer, you must be a member of the _____ group.

8. To prepare the AD schema for the installation of the first Exchange Server 2007 computer, you can use the _____ command.

9. The Exchange organization name is usually the same as your _____ name.

10. To quickly view your server configuration from within the Exchange Management Shell, you can type the _____ command.

Multiple Choice

Circle the letter that corresponds to the best answer.

1. How much RAM is recommended for a quad-core Xeon computer that will run the Mailbox role only with 800 mailboxes?
   - **a.** 2 GB
   - **b.** 6 GB
   - **c.** 8 GB
   - **d.** 9 GB

2. How much RAM is recommended for a dual-core AMD64 computer that will run the Mailbox, CAS, and Hub roles and plans on hosting 200 mailboxes?
   - **a.** 2 GB
   - **b.** 6 GB
   - **c.** 8 GB
   - **d.** 9 GB

3. How much disk space do you require across all NTFS partitions to install the CAS and UM roles on a new Exchange server with one UM language pack?
   - **a.** 1.7 GB
   - **b.** 1.9 GB
   - **c.** 2.4 GB
   - **d.** 2.6 GB

4. Which of the following are requirements before running the **setup /PrepareSchema** command? (Choose all that apply.)
   - **a.** Your user account must be a part of the Enterprise Admins group
   - **b.** Your user account must be a part of the Schema Admins group
   - **c.** The DC that hosts the Schema Master FSMO must be on a computer running Exchange Server 2003 SP1 or Exchange Server 2003 R2.
   - **d.** Your Exchange server must be in the same AD site as the Schema Master FSMO

5. Which of the following Exchange server roles require the installation of IIS? (Choose all that apply.)
   - **a.** CAS
   - **b.** Mailbox
   - **c.** Hub
   - **d.** Edge

6. Which log in the Windows Event Viewer contains Exchange-related events?
   - **a.** Security
   - **b.** Directory Services
   - **c.** System
   - **d.** Application

7. Which of the following Exchange server roles requires that the RPC over HTTP proxy be installed?
   - **a.** CAS
   - **b.** Mailbox
   - **c.** Hub
   - **d.** Edge

8. Which of the following storage configurations use external hard disks that can be shared by multiple servers?
   - **a.** RAID
   - **b.** SAN
   - **c.** SCSI
   - **d.** PATA

9. Which of the following log files lists the tasks that were performed during the Exchange Server 2007 installation process?
   a. %systemroot%\ExchangeSetup.msilog
   b. %systemroot%\ExchangeSetup.log
   c. %systemroot%\ExchangeSetupLogs\ExchangeSetup.msilog
   d. %systemroot%\ExchangeSetupLogs\ExchangeSetup.log

10. Which of the following directories contains Exchange-related programs following a successful Exchange Server 2007 installation?
    a. %systemroot%\Program Files\Microsoft\Exchange Server\bin
    b. %systemroot%\Program Files\Microsoft\Exchange Server\OAB
    c. %systemroot%\Program Files\Microsoft\Exchange Server\Scripts
    d. %systemroot%\Program Files\Microsoft\Exchange Server\ExchangeMTA

True/False

Circle T if the statement is true or F if the statement is false.

T F 1. A typical Exchange installation installs the CAS, UM, and Mailbox roles by default.

T F 2. You must have at least one Hub role in each AD site that will contain Exchange servers or recipients.

T F 3. Mailbox roles cannot share hardware with other roles.

T F 4. Edge roles cannot share hardware with other roles.

T F 5. All domains that will have Exchange servers or recipient objects must be set to Windows 2000 Native functional level or higher.

T F 6. You must ensure that at least one DC in each domain that will contain Exchange servers hosts the GC.

T F 7. To install the CAS role, you must ensure that the server contains the ASP.NET component of IIS.

T F 8. All Exchange server roles require the .NET Framework 1.0 or later.

T F 9. You cannot perform an in-place upgrade of Exchange Server 2003 to Exchange Server 2007.

T F 10. Exchange Server 2007 cannot be installed on the Itanium 64-bit architecture.

Review Questions

1. Explain why smaller organizations are more likely to implement Exchange servers that contain multiple roles.

2. Give some reasons why the command **setup /PrepareAD /OrganizationName:*name*** would fail (where ***name*** is the Exchange organization name).

■ Case Scenarios

Scenario 3-1: Planning Exchange Server Roles

You are the network administrator for a clothing retailer that has the following locations in the United States, Canada, and Europe:

Denver—500 users across two sites

Miami—1,100 users across three sites

Toronto—600 users in one site

Berlin—400 users in one site

London—800 users across two sites

All locations should perform virus and spam filtering on all incoming email as well as provide encrypted access for employees who check their email from home. In addition, Toronto and Miami require Unified Messaging functionality. Diagram a sample Exchange Server 2007 infrastructure for this organization that lists the number of Exchange servers required in each location and the roles that should be present on each Exchange server. Provide a rationale for all recommendations.

Scenario 3-2: Planning Exchange Hardware and Software

For the servers that you recommended in Scenario 3-1, detail the hardware and software required to support the Exchange Server 2007 server roles and user requirements in a short memo. Justify all of your decisions.

4 LESSON

Configuring a New Exchange Server

LESSON SKILL MATRIX

TECHNOLOGY SKILL	OBJECTIVE DOMAIN	OBJECTIVE DOMAIN NUMBER
Configuring the Hub Role	Configure Exchange Server roles.	1.4
Configuring the Edge Role	Configure Exchange Server roles.	1.4
Configuring the Mailbox Role	Configure Exchange Server roles.	1.4
Configuring the CAS Role	Configure Exchange Server roles.	1.4
Configuring Receive Connectors	Configure connectors.	3.1
Configuring Send Connectors	Configure connectors.	3.1
Configuring Microsoft Outlook	Configure client connectivity.	3.6
Configuring Microsoft Entourage	Configure client connectivity.	3.6
Configuring Microsoft Outlook Express and Windows Mail	Configure client connectivity.	3.6

KEY TERMS

accepted domain
administrative role
Cached Exchange Mode
connector
demilitarized zone (DMZ)
direct file access
Distributed Authoring and
    Versioning (DAV)
Exchange Organization
    Administrator

Exchange Public Folder
    Administrator
Exchange Recipient Administrator
Exchange Server Administrator
Exchange View-Only
    Administrator
mailbox database
Multipurpose Internet Mail
    Extensions (MIME)
perimeter network

permissions group
postmaster
public folder database
receive connector
screened subnet
Secure Password Authentication
    (SPA)
send connector
subscription file
WebReady

■ Configuring the Exchange Organization

THE BOTTOM LINE

Due to their purpose, email servers require a great deal of configuration after they are installed. Some of this configuration is specific to the individual servers and their server roles, whereas other configuration is based on the structure of the Exchange organization. Whether you deploy a new email infrastructure or add new servers to your existing email infrastructure, you should configure administrative roles to reflect your IT job role structure as well as create DNS records that other organizations can use to locate the appropriate email servers within your organization.

Configuring Exchange Administrator Roles

Assigning only the necessary permissions and rights to Exchange administrators within your organization helps secure your Exchange infrastructure. As a result, you should ensure that the correct administrative roles are granted to the administrative staff within your organization before configuring the various aspects of Exchange Server 2007.

In small organizations, there may be one or two network administrators who are responsible for the setup, configuration, and maintenance of your email servers. However, in larger organizations that span multiple locations, the administration of email servers is likely to be split among several different administrators. Each administrator will have different areas of responsibility and different administrative duties on the Exchange servers within the organization. Some administrators may require access to all Exchange servers within the organization, while other administrators may be responsible for one or two servers in their own locations.

Although the level of access that each administrator requires depends on the structure, needs, and culture of the organization itself, you should ensure administrators have the permissions and rights that they require to perform their job role without granting unnecessary permissions. To do this, you can assign administrative users and groups to various predefined *administrative roles* for the entire Exchange organization or for an individual Exchange server within the Exchange organization. These predefined administrative roles are listed in Table 4-1.

Table 4-1

Exchange Server 2007 administrative roles

ADMINISTRATIVE ROLE	SCOPE	PERMISSIONS
Exchange Organization Administrator	Organization-wide	Full permission to all components of Exchange as well as Exchange-related objects and information in AD.
Exchange Recipient Administrator	Organization-wide	Ability to modify the properties of any recipient object including users, contacts, groups, and public folders, as well as mailbox and UM settings for recipient objects.
Exchange Public Folder Administrator	Organization-wide	Ability to create and delete public folders as well as manage all public folder properties that are not related to specific recipient objects. This administrative role is only available in Exchange Server 2007 SP1 and later.
Exchange View-Only Administrator	Organization-wide	Ability to view all Exchange-related information on Exchange servers and within AD.
Exchange Server Administrator	Server specific	Full permission to administer all Exchange-related components on a specific Exchange server.

TAKE NOTE* In addition to having administrative role membership, you must also be a member of the local Administrators group on each Exchange server that you wish to administer.

To allow viewing of all Exchange-related information, the Exchange Public Folder Administrator and Exchange Recipient Administrator roles are members of the Exchange View-Only Administrator role by default. In addition, the Exchange Public Folder

TAKE NOTE*

The Administrator account in the forest root domain is added to the Exchange Organization Administrators group by default.

Administrator role and the Exchange Recipient Administrator role both contain the Exchange Organization Administrator role. This ensures that members of the Exchange Organization Administrator role always have the ability to perform the functions of the Exchange Public Folder Administrator and Exchange Recipient Administrator roles as well as the ability to view all Exchange-related information on Exchange servers and within AD.

Except for the Exchange Server Administrator role, all administrative roles are represented by universal security groups of the same name in the Microsoft Exchange Security Groups OU in the forest root domain. As a result, you can modify the membership of these groups in the Active Directory Users and Computers console to configure administrative roles.

Alternatively, you can use the Exchange Management Console to view, assign, or remove administrative roles. If you assign the Exchange Server Administrator role to a user or group, that user or group is also added to the Exchange View-Only Administrator role because the Exchange Server Administrator role is not a member of the Exchange View-Only Administrator role by default.

ADD AN EXCHANGE ADMINISTRATOR

GET READY. Turn on the computer, and log in as the Administrator user account. Close any windows that appear on the desktop.

1. Click **Start**, **All Programs**, **Microsoft Exchange Server 2007**, and then click **Exchange Management Console**. The Exchange Management Console window appears.
2. In the console tree pane, highlight **Organization Configuration**.
3. In the action pane, click **Add Exchange Administrator**. The Add Exchange Administrator window appears as shown in Figure 4-1.

Figure 4-1

Adding an Exchange Administrator

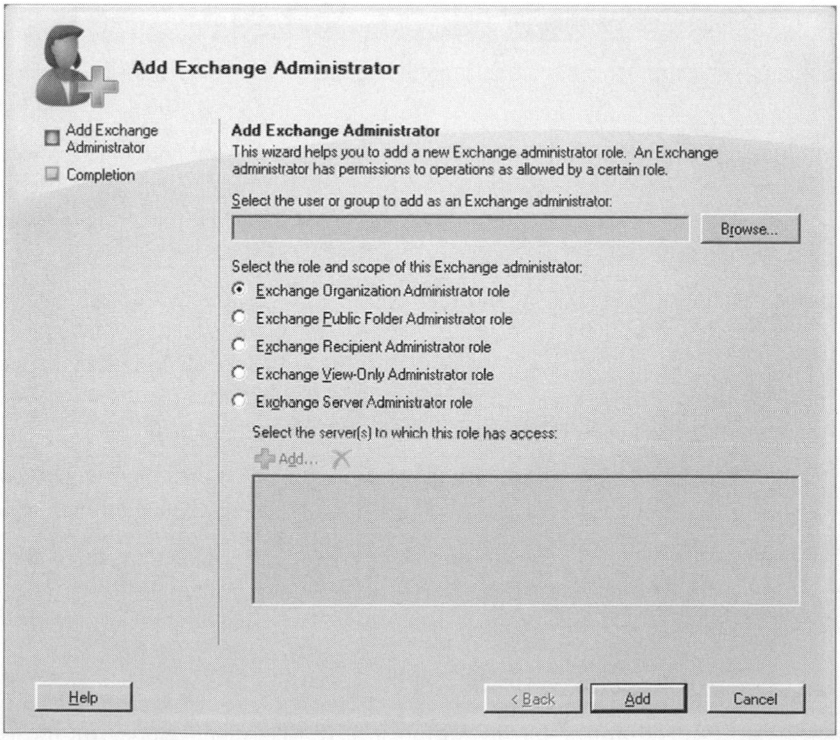

4. Click the **Browse** button, select the appropriate user or group and click **OK.**
5. Select the appropriate administrative role for the user or group. If you select the Exchange Server Administrator role, you must also click the **Add** button underneath Exchange Server Administrator role, select the Exchange server(s) that the role should apply to, and click **OK.**

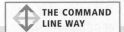

THE COMMAND LINE WAY

You can also use the **Add-ExchangeAdministrator** and **Remove-ExchangeAdministrator** cmdlets in the Exchange Management Shell to add and remove administrative roles. For example, to assign the user with the logon name bob.jones to the Exchange Organization Administrator role for the Exchange organization called Octavius, you could run the following command in the Exchange Management Shell: **Add-ExchangeAdministrator -Role OrgAdmin -Identity Octavius\bob .jones**.

6. Click **Add**. The Completion page appears.
7. Click **Finish** to close the Add Exchange Administrator window.
8. Close the Exchange Management Console.

Configuring DNS Records

After deploying email servers within your organization, you should ensure that external organizations can relay email to your organization. This involves creating DNS records to represent the email servers within your organization that accept email.

Recall that DNS MX and A records are used to locate email servers for organizations on the Internet. The Exchange servers in your organization that host the Edge or Hub roles contact a DNS server when they need to resolve the names and IP addresses of foreign email servers to which they need to relay email.

Similarly, when foreign email servers need to relay email to your organization, they use DNS to resolve the names and IP addresses of the email servers within your organization. For this to occur, DNS must contain MX records that list the names of the Exchange servers in your organization that are configured to receive Internet email as well as A records that list the associated IP address of these servers.

Because the Edge role is responsible for processing incoming email from the Internet, you should ensure that MX and A records exist for each Exchange server in your organization that hosts the Edge role. If your organization has multiple Edge roles, you should balance the load of incoming email across all Exchange servers that host an Edge role using DNS round robin. To allow for DNS round robin, simply ensure that the MX records for each Exchange server have the same priority number.

If your organization does not contain the Edge role, then the Hub role is responsible for processing incoming Internet email. In this case, you must ensure that MX and A records exist for each Exchange server in your organization that contains the Hub role. If your organization has multiple Hub roles, you can also use DNS round robin to load balance the incoming email by ensuring that the MX records for your Exchange servers have the same priority number.

TAKE NOTE✱

Because only the Edge and Hub roles process incoming Internet email, you do not need to create MX records for new Exchange servers that only host the CAS, Mailbox, or UM roles. If your organization uses the Edge role, then all incoming email must pass through the Edge role, and you do not need to create MX records for Exchange servers that host the Hub role.

TAKE NOTE✱

Authoritative DNS servers can be queried by other DNS servers on the Internet provided that their domain is registered on the Internet by a Registrar. To register a domain using a Registrar, you can contact your ISP or visit www.internic.net.

If your organization uses a smart host to filter email before it is sent to your organization, you should ensure that an MX and A record exists for the smart host server and that its MX priority number is lower than the priority number used in the MX records for the Exchange servers that host the Edge or Hub role in your organization. This lower priority number will ensure that all email is first sent to the smart host server, which will be configured to forward email to the servers in your organization. If the smart host server is offline, then incoming email will be sent directly to the email servers in your organization that host the Edge or Hub role.

To create DNS MX and A records, you must first locate an ***authoritative DNS server*** for your organization's domain. An authoritative DNS server hosts the zone file that contains the DNS records for the domain that represents your organization. Other DNS servers on the Internet will query the authoritative DNS server for your organization's domain when they need to resolve the DNS MX and A records for your organization.

Some organizations pay their ISP to create and manage the authoritative DNS server for their DNS domain. In that case, you may need to contact the ISP to create the appropriate MX and A records. However, if your organization hosts its own authoritative DNS server, you can simply create the necessary MX and A records on your DNS server for the Exchange servers within your organization that contain the Edge or Hub role.

For Linux and UNIX-based DNS servers, creating MX and A records will likely involve editing the appropriate zone file located in the **/var/named** directory using a text editor or graphical utility. For Windows DNS servers, you can use the DNS console (**Start** > **Administrative Tools** > **DNS**) to create and manage DNS records.

If your DNS server supports dynamic update and your Exchange servers are configured to use the DNS server in TCP/IP properties, then A records for your Exchange servers will automatically be created on the DNS server. In this case, you will only need to create MX records for the appropriate Exchange servers within your organization.

⊖ CREATE MX AND A RECORDS ON AN AUTHORITATIVE DNS SERVER

GET READY. Turn on the computer, and log in as the Administrator user account. Close any windows that appear on the desktop.

1. Click **Start**, **Administrative Tools**, and then click **DNS**. The DNS console window appears.
2. Expand the **Forward Lookup Zones** folder under your server object in the left pane.
3. Right click the zone for your domain and select **New Host (A)** from the menu. The New Host window appears as shown in Figure 4-2.

Figure 4-2

Adding a DNS A Record

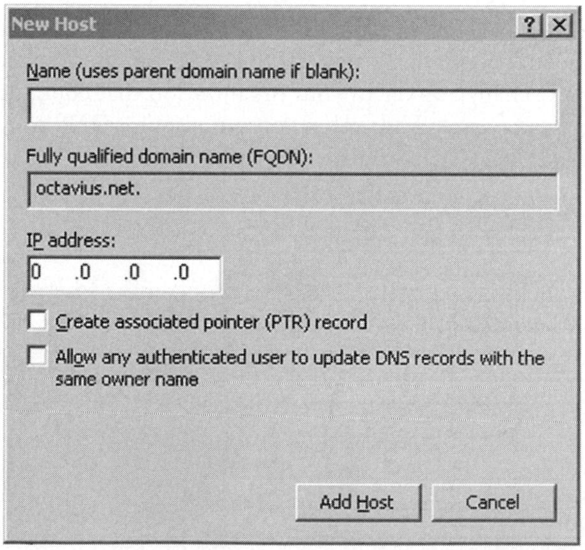

4. In the **Name** dialog box, type the host name of your Exchange server. Next, supply the appropriate IP address for the Exchange server in the **IP address** dialog box and click **Add Host**. Click **OK** to close the confirmation window and click **Done** to close the New Host window.

⚠ **WARNING** A common mistake when creating A records is to supply the FQDN in the **Name** dialog box instead of the host name. This will create an FQDN that contains subdomain names for your A record. To avoid this, double check the **Fully qualified domain name (FQDN)** field shown in Figure 4-2 after entering your host name to ensure that you have the correct FQDN.

5. Right click the zone for your domain and select **New Mail Exchanger (MX)** from the menu. The New Resource Record window appears as shown in Figure 4-3.

Figure 4-3

Adding a DNS MX Record

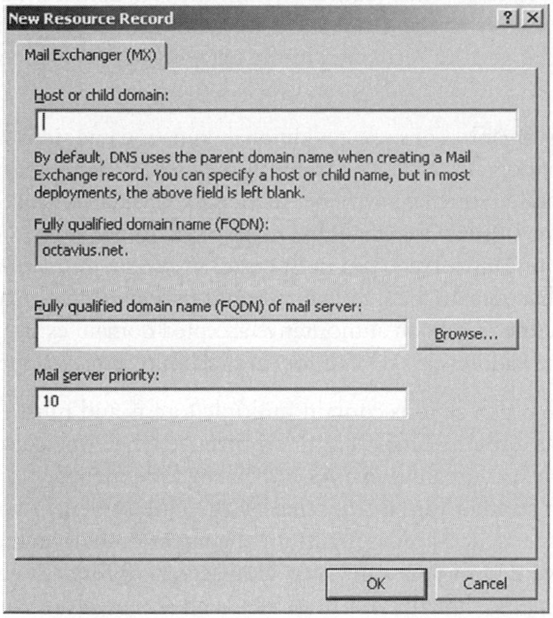

| New Resource Record | ? X |

Mail Exchanger (MX)

Host or child domain:

By default, DNS uses the parent domain name when creating a Mail Exchange record. You can specify a host or child name, but in most deployments, the above field is left blank.

Fully qualified domain name (FQDN):

octavius.net.

Fully qualified domain name (FQDN) of mail server:

Browse...

Mail server priority:

10

OK   Cancel

6. Verify that the authoritative DNS domain that your Exchange server will receive email for is listed in the **Fully qualified domain name (FQDN)** box. If your Exchange server will be configured to receive email for a subdomain, you must enter the appropriate subdomain in the **Host or child domain** dialog box. Normally this dialog box is left empty.

7. Next, supply the FQDN of the Exchange server in the **Fully qualified domain name (FQDN) of mail server** dialog box. If you wish to change the priority number from the default of 10, enter the appropriate priority number in the **Mail server priority** dialog box.

8. Click **OK** to create the MX record.

9. Close the DNS console.

ANOTHER WAY

Instead of entering the FQDN of your email server, you can click the **Browse** button in Figure 4-3 and navigate to the A record for your email server.

■ Configuring Server Roles

↓
THE BOTTOM LINE

Most Exchange Server 2007 configuration depends on the server roles that are present on each email server within your organization. Although much of this configuration is discussed throughout this book, this section focuses on the configuration tasks that are commonly performed for server roles shortly after they have been added to the Exchange organization.

X REF

The structure and configuration of the UM role will be discussed in Lesson 12, "Providing for Mobile Access and Unified Messaging."

Configuring the Hub Role

CERTIFICATION READY?
Configure Exchange
Server Roles.
1.4

After installation, the Hub role is configured to accept and route internal email within the organization. However, you should also configure the domains that the Hub role should accept email from, as well as configure a postmaster account for each server that hosts the Hub role in your organization to ensure that email problems are sent to the appropriate person.

CONFIGURING ACCEPTED DOMAINS

After installing the Exchange Server 2007, the Hub role is configured to receive emails that are addressed to an email address within the AD domain. For example, after install-ing the first Hub role in the octavius.net domain, the Exchange organization is set to accept email that is addressed to recipients in the octavius.net domain and reject email that is not addressed to a recipient in the octavius.net domain.

However, many organizations select additional domain name suffixes for email use by particular users within their organization. For example, the user bob.jones may be configured with the email address bob.jones@research.octavius.net to identify his membership in the research division of the organization. To allow for email that is addressed to bob.jones@research .octavius.net to be processed by your Hub servers, you must create an ***accepted domain*** for research.octavius.net that indicates that your Exchange organization is responsible for email that is sent to recipients in research.octavius.net. Once an authoritative accepted domain exists, the Hub server will locate the recipient by email address in AD and forward incoming email to the correct mailbox.

Similarly, some organizations contain multiple forests and must maintain separate Exchange organizations as a result. This is common practice when one company acquires another yet requires that both companies maintain their own identity. By default, email that is addressed to a domain in another forest is rejected by the Hub servers in your Exchange organization unless you create an accepted domain for the target domain name that specifies how email should be forwarded. If you want your Hub servers to forward email that is addressed to the target domain name directly, you must create an accepted domain that uses ***internal relay***. Alternatively, you can create an accepted domain that uses ***external relay*** to force all email that is addressed to the target domain name to be forwarded to the appropriate email servers across the Internet by the Edge role. To forward email addressed to an accepted domain name to email servers outside the Exchange organization, the Hub and Edge roles must be able to resolve the MX records for the accepted domain name.

You can configure accepted domains within the Exchange Management Console by navigating to **Organization Configuration** > **Hub Transport** and selecting the **Accepted Domains** tab as shown in Figure 4-4.

> **TAKE NOTE***
>
> If used, the Edge role also processes accepted domains. However, you cannot configure accepted domains for the Edge role. Instead, the Hub role replicates its accepted domain information to the Edge role using the EdgeSync protocol.

Figure 4-4

Viewing Accepted Domains

Hub Transport			2 objects
Journaling	Send Connectors	Edge Subscriptions	Global Settings
Remote Domains	Accepted Domains	E-mail Address Policies	Transport Rules

Name ▼	Accepted Domain	Type	Default
octavius.net	octavius.net	Authoritative	True
Arfa	arfa.com	Internal Relay	False

In Figure 4-4, emails that are addressed to recipients in the octavius.net domain are processed by the Hub servers, whereas emails addressed to recipients in the arfa.com domain are forwarded directly by the Hub server to the appropriate email server for the arfa.com domain using internal relay.

 ADD AN ACCEPTED DOMAIN

GET READY. Turn on the computer and log in as the Administrator user account. Close any windows that appear on the desktop.

1. Click **Start**, **All Programs**, **Microsoft Exchange Server 2007**, and then click **Exchange Management Console**. The Exchange Management Console window appears.

2. In the console tree pane, expand **Organization Configuration** and highlight **Hub Transport**.

3. In the result pane, click the **Accepted Domains** tab.

4. In the action pane, click **New Accepted Domain**. The New Accepted Domain window appears as shown in Figure 4-5.

Figure 4-5

Creating a New Accepted Domain

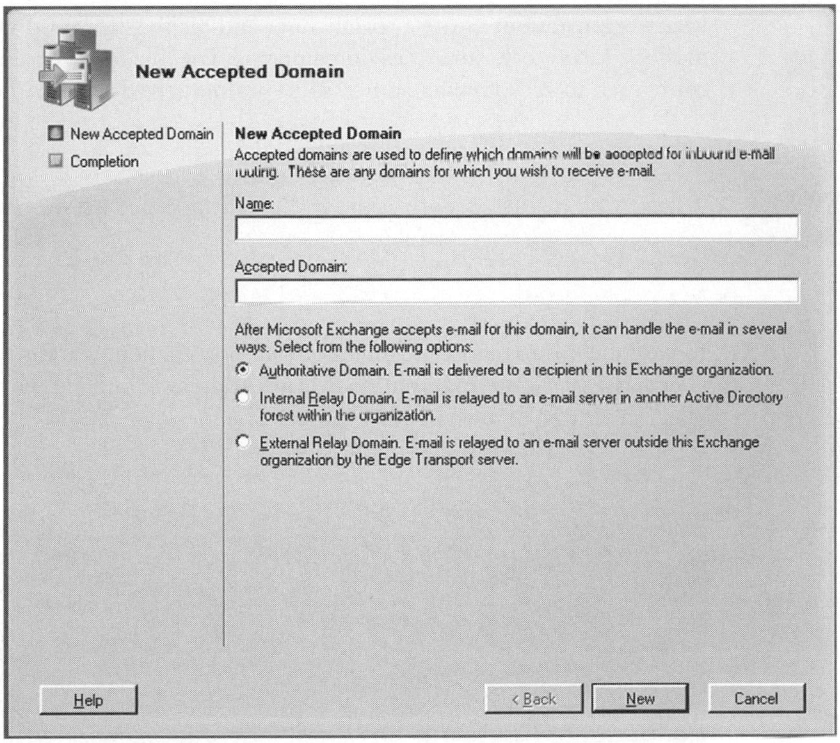

THE COMMAND LINE WAY

You can also use the **New-AcceptedDomain** and **Remove-Accepted Domain** cmdlets in the Exchange Management Shell to add and remove accepted domains. For example, to add the accepted domain for arfa.com shown in Figure 4-4, you could run the following command in the Exchange Management Shell: **New-AcceptedDomain -DomainName arfa.com -Name Arfa–DomainType InternalRelay.**

5. Type a name that represents the accepted domain in the **Name** dialog box. Next, type the domain name for the accepted domain in the **Accepted Domain** dialog box.

6. Select the appropriate method that should be used to handle email sent to the accepted domain:

- **Authoritative Domain** is appropriate for domain names that are used by recipients who have mailboxes on your Exchange servers.
- **Internal Relay Domain** allows your Hub role servers to directly forward email for the domain name to the appropriate email server by resolving its MX records.
- **External Relay Domain** forces your Edge role servers to forward the email for the domain name to the appropriate email server on the Internet by resolving its MX records.

7. Click **New**. The Completion page appears.

8. Click **Finish** to close the New Accepted Domain window.

9. Close the Exchange Management Console.

CONFIGURING A POSTMASTER

Most email servers contain a special email address called the ***postmaster*** that represents the person who is responsible for the ongoing operation of the email server. Users who have problems sending or receiving email will see the postmaster email address on their delivery notifications and can send email to the postmaster to alert them to the problem.

In Exchange Server 2007, the relay of postmaster email is handled by the Hub role. Each server that hosts the Hub role can have a different postmaster, and the postmaster email address is not set by default.

To set the postmaster email address, you can use the **Set-TransportServer** cmdlet in the Exchange Management Shell. For example, to set the postmaster address on the server EXCH1 to Administrator@octavius.net, you could run the following command within the Exchange Management Shell:

Set-TransportServer–Identity EXCH1–ExternalPostMasterAddress Administrator@octavius.net

Many organizations create a specific user and mailbox for postmaster email and set the postmaster address to postmaster@domainname. For this to occur, an existing mailbox must be configured to accept email addressed to postmaster@domainname.

 REF   Configuring mailboxes with additional email addresses will be discussed in Lesson 5, "Working with Recipient Objects."

To view the postmasters configured for your organization, you can use the **Get-TransportServer | Format-List Name,ExternalPostMasterAddress** command within the Exchange Management Shell as shown in Figure 4-6.

Figure 4-6

Viewing Postmasters

Configuring the Edge Role

CERTIFICATION READY?
Configure Exchange
Server Roles.
1.4

After installation, the Edge role is not functional until it is configured to participate in the Exchange organization. To do this, you must create a subscription file on each Edge role server and import it on a Hub role server within your site.

TAKE NOTE*

In a Windows Server 2008 AD environment, AD LDS is used instead of ADAM to obtain configuration information on an Edge role server.

Unlike other Exchange servers within your Exchange Organization, servers that host the Edge role cannot communicate directly with AD. Instead, these Edge role servers must use ADAM to periodically obtain AD and Exchange information using the EdgeSync protocol from a server that hosts the Hub role.

Most organizations have a ***perimeter network*** that is directly connected to the Internet via a firewall. Servers that must provide public access from other servers or clients on the Internet are typically placed in this perimeter network, whereas other servers that maintain sensitive resources are placed on the organization's internal LAN and configured to access the servers in the perimeter network through another firewall.

TAKE NOTE*

Perimeter networks are often called ***demilitarized zones (DMZs)*** or ***screened subnets***.

The Edge role in Exchange Server 2007 is intended for use within a perimeter network whereas all other roles are intended for use within the internal LAN. If your organization places an Edge role server in the perimeter network, it will need to communicate to a Hub role server on the internal LAN across a firewall as shown in Figure 4-7. For this to occur, you must open TCP port 50636 on the internal firewall to allow the EdgeSync protocol as well as ensure that the Edge role server can resolve the FQDN of the Hub role server and vice versa.

Figure 4-7

Edge Role Placement

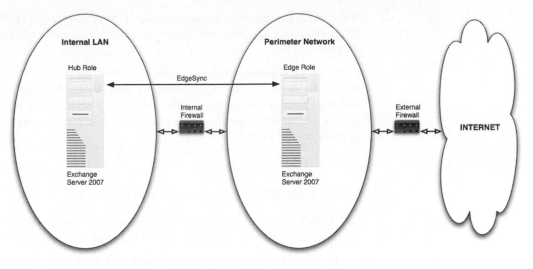

Once you have installed a server in the perimeter of your network that hosts the Edge role, you need to create an XML *subscription file* on the server. This subscription file is then imported into a server that hosts the Hub role to activate the EdgeSync protocol and allow email relay.

To create a subscription file on an Edge role server, you must run the following command in the Exchange Management Shell on the Edge role server:

New-EdgeSubscription–file *filename.xml*

Each server that hosts the Edge role must create its own subscription file, and the subscription file must be imported using the Exchange Management Console on a server that contains the Hub role within 24 hours of its creation. If you do not import the subscription file within 24 hours, you must create a new subscription file and import it within 24 hours.

After you have subscribed an Edge role server to a server that hosts the Hub role, you should run the **Start-EdgeSynchronization** command in the Exchange Management Shell on the Hub role server. This will force EdgeSync synchronization as well as verify that there are no EdgeSync-related errors as shown in Figure 4-8.

Figure 4-8

Forcing EdgeSync Synchronization

```
Machine: exch1 | Scope: octavius.net
[PS] D:\Documents and Settings\Administrator>Start-EdgeSynchronization

Result          : Success
Type            : Recipients
Name            : CN=exch3,CN=Servers,CN=Exchange Administrative Group (FYDIBOHF
                  23SPDLT),CN=Administrative Groups,CN=Octavius,CN=Microsoft Exc
                  hange,CN=Services,CN=Configuration,DC=octavius,DC=net
FailureDetails  :
StartUTC        : 2/17/2008 12:43:46 PM
EndUTC          : 2/17/2008 12:43:46 PM
Added           : 0
Deleted         : 0
Updated         : 0
Scanned         : 2
TargetScanned   : 0

Result          : Success
Type            : Configuration
Name            : CN=exch3,CN=Servers,CN=Exchange Administrative Group (FYDIBOHF
                  23SPDLT),CN=Administrative Groups,CN=Octavius,CN=Microsoft Exc
                  hange,CN=Services,CN=Configuration,DC=octavius,DC=net
FailureDetails  :
StartUTC        : 2/17/2008 12:43:46 PM
EndUTC          : 2/17/2008 12:43:46 PM
Added           : 1
Deleted         : 0
Updated         : 0
Scanned         : 345
TargetScanned   : 0

Result          : Success
Type            : Configuration
Name            : CN=exch3,CN=Servers,CN=Exchange Administrative Group (FYDIBOHF
                  23SPDLT),CN=Administrative Groups,CN=Octavius,CN=Microsoft Exc
                  hange,CN=Services,CN=Configuration,DC=octavius,DC=net
FailureDetails  :
StartUTC        : 2/17/2008 12:43:46 PM
EndUTC          : 2/17/2008 12:43:46 PM
Added           : 1
Deleted         : 0
Updated         : 0
Scanned         : 345
TargetScanned   : 0

[PS] D:\Documents and Settings\Administrator>
```

If the configuration information produces errors, you should check to ensure that both the Edge role server and Hub role server can resolve each other's FQDNs as well as communicate on port 50636.

Once the subscription process is complete and EdgeSync is functional, all Hub role servers within the same site can send and receive email using the Edge role server. However, if you add additional servers to the site that hosts the Hub role, you must resubscribe your Edge role servers. If you left room for future growth when planning your Exchange infrastructure, this practice should be rare.

→ CREATE AN EDGE SUBSCRIPTION FILE

GET READY. Turn on the computer that hosts the Edge server role, and log in as the Administrator user account. Close any windows that appear on the desktop.

1. Click **Start, All Programs, Microsoft Exchange Server 2007**, and then click **Exchange Management Shell**. The Exchange Management Shell window appears.

2. At the command prompt, type **New-EdgeSubscription–file "C:\EdgeSubscriptionExport .xml"** and press **Enter**.

You can use any name for the file that you create with the **New-EdgeSubscription** command as long as you ensure that it contains the **.xml** extension. If you choose a different name for your subscription file, you must use that name when importing the subscription file into the Exchange Management Console in the next exercise.

3. When prompted to confirm the action, type **y** and press **Enter**.

4. Close the Exchange Management Shell.

5. Copy the C:\EdgeSubscriptionExport.xml file to removable media such as a memory stick or portable hard drive.

→ IMPORT AN EDGE SUBSCRIPTION FILE

GET READY. Turn on the computer that hosts the Hub role, and log in as the Administrator user account. Close any windows that appear on the desktop.

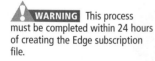
WARNING This process must be completed within 24 hours of creating the Edge subscription file.

1. Click **Start, All Programs, Microsoft Exchange Server 2007**, and then click **Exchange Management Console**. The Exchange Management Console window appears.

2. In the console tree pane, expand **Organization Configuration** and highlight **Hub Transport**.

3. In the result pane, click the **Edge Subscriptions** tab.

4. In the action pane, click **New Edge Subscription**. The New Edge Subscription window appears as shown in Figure 4-9.

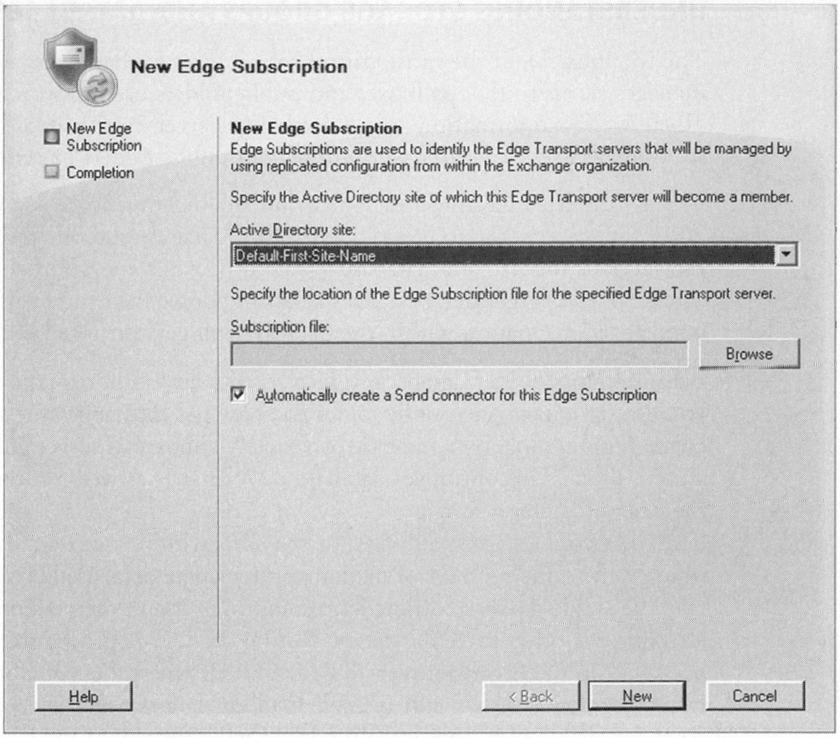

Figure 4-9

Importing an Edge Subscription File

New Edge Subscription

New Edge Subscription
☐ Completion

New Edge Subscription
Edge Subscriptions are used to identify the Edge Transport servers that will be managed by using replicated configuration from within the Exchange organization.

Specify the Active Directory site of which this Edge Transport server will become a member.

Active Directory site:
Default-First-Site-Name

Specify the location of the Edge Subscription file for the specified Edge Transport server.

Subscription file:

Browse

☑ Automatically create a Send connector for this Edge Subscription

Help   < Back   New   Cancel

5. Select the appropriate AD site that your Edge role server should communicate with in the **Active Directory site** drop-down box.

6. Next, click **Browse**, navigate to and select the EdgeSubscriptionExport.xml file that you created on the Edge role server and click **OK**.

7. Click **New**. The Completion page appears.

8. Click **Finish** to close the New Edge Subscription window. The Edge subscription should appear under the Edge Subscriptions tab in the result pane.

9. Close the Exchange Management Console.

10. Click **Start, All Programs, Microsoft Exchange Server 2007**, and then click **Exchange Management Shell**. The Exchange Management Shell window appears.

11. At the command prompt, type **Start-EdgeSynchronization** and press **Enter**. Examine the output for errors.

12. Close the Exchange Management Shell.

THE COMMAND LINE WAY

Although you can import an Edge subscription file within the Exchange Management Console, you can also use the **New-EdgeSubscription** cmdlet in the Exchange Management Shell on a Hub role server. To import the C:\EdgeSubscriptionExport.xml file created earlier on an Edge role server into a Hub role server within the Cupertino site, you could run the following command in the Exchange Management Shell on the Hub role server:

New-EdgeSubscription -FileName 'C:\EdgeSubscriptionExport.xml' -Site 'Cupertino'

Configuring the Mailbox Role

CERTIFICATION READY?
Configure Exchange Server Roles.
1.4

After installation, Mailbox role servers contain a single storage group that contains a single mailbox database. Depending on installation choices, the Mailbox role server may also contain a database for public folders. To optimize information storage on your Mailbox role, you may need to move existing storage groups and databases or create new ones. In addition, these databases should enforce storage limits to prevent certain email recipients from using up all of the available space on your Mailbox role server before your databases are put into production.

UNDERSTANDING STORAGE GROUPS AND DATABASES

The Mailbox role is the most critical role in your Exchange organization because it stores and manages access to the mailboxes and public folders used to store vital company information. To ensure fast information access, Exchange Server 2007 uses a database storage engine that stores mailboxes in *mailbox databases* and public folders in *public folder databases*.

Because the size of a single mailbox or public folder database is unlimited in Exchange Server 2007, you can choose to create one mailbox database and one public folder database per server. However, as the size of a database grows, it becomes more difficult to search and manage. As a general rule, larger database sizes result in poorer Exchange performance and a greater likelihood that information within the database will get corrupted.

Because public folder databases typically store far less information than mailbox databases, you can only have one public folder database per Exchange server. However, you should create multiple mailbox databases on each Mailbox role server and divide mailboxes evenly among them. This optimizes database performance as well as provides for flexible recovery in the case of database corruption. Say, for example, that your Mailbox role server has four databases that contain the mailboxes for the users within your organization and each database has roughly the same number of mailboxes. If a single database becomes corrupted, then you can take the single database offline by dismounting it and then restore it from backup without affecting the other three databases. During the restore procedure, only one-quarter of all the users within the organization will be unable to access their mailboxes. Alternatively, if your Mailbox role server has only a single mailbox database and it becomes corrupted, taking the database offline to restore it from backup will affect all of the users within your organization.

The Standard edition of Exchange Server 2007 allows you to create up to 5 databases per server, whereas the Enterprise edition can create up to 50 databases on a single server.

All databases must be contained within a database storage group that is represented by a folder on a hard disk. Storage groups can contain up to five databases and are used to simplify database management because you can specify similar backup and maintenance schedules for each storage group.

Using the Standard edition of Exchange Server 2007, you can create only a single storage group on each Mailbox role server. As a result, if you create multiple databases on a Mailbox role server that runs Exchange Server 2007 Standard edition, you must place those databases in the same storage group.

Exchange Server 2007 Enterprise edition can create up to 50 storage groups on a single server. Because the Enterprise edition can also create up to 50 databases on a single server, each database can be located in its own storage group for more granular management. Because storage groups can be located on different hard disks, this allows for greater flexibility and fault tolerance in the event of a single hard disk failure.

> **TAKE NOTE**✲ Microsoft recommends that you create one database per storage group in Exchange Server 2007 Enterprise edition.

MODIFYING THE DEFAULT STORAGE GROUPS AND DATABASES

When you install the Mailbox role on an Exchange server, a single mailbox database is created called **Mailbox Database.edb** and stored in a storage group called **First Storage Group** on the hard drive (%systemroot%\Program Files\Exchange Server\Mailbox\First Storage Group). If you chose to allow Entourage and Outlook 2003 and earlier MAPI clients the ability to access your Exchange server during the Exchange Server 2007 installation wizard, then a public folder database called **Public Folder Database.edb** is also created. If you are running the Enterprise edition of Exchange Server 2007, this public folder database will be stored in a separate storage group on the hard disk called **Second Storage Group** (%systemroot%\ Program Files\Exchange Server\Mailbox\First Storage Group).

Recall that Mailbox role servers are likely equipped with additional hard disks and that these additional hard disks are usually combined in some fault tolerant RAID such as RAID 1 or RAID 5. If your Mailbox role server has multiple hard disks or implements RAID, you should move the default storage groups and databases to another hard disk or RAID volume to improve performance and fault tolerance.

When information is stored in a database, it is first written to a transaction log in the storage group to improve performance and allow point-in-time recovery of information that is lost after being written to the database. By default, databases and transaction logs are stored in the same folder on the hard drive that comprises the storage group. However, when you move a storage group, you have the option to select a different folder for the database and transaction logs. Each of these folders still comprises the same storage group, but can be located on separate hard drives to improve performance and fault tolerance. In most cases, administrators store the database and transaction logs in the same folder to simplify organization and administration.

MOVE THE DEFAULT STORAGE GROUPS

GET READY. Turn on the computer, and log in as the Administrator user account. Close any windows that appear on the desktop.

1. Click **Start**, **All Programs**, **Microsoft Exchange Server 2007**, and then click **Exchange Management Console**. The Exchange Management Console window appears.
2. In the console tree pane, expand **Server Configuration** and highlight **Mailbox**.
3. In the result pane, highlight your server object.
4. In the work pane, highlight **First Storage Group**.
5. In the action pane, click **Move Storage Group Path**. The Move Storage Group Path window appears as shown in Figure 4-10.

Figure 4-10

Moving a Default Storage Group

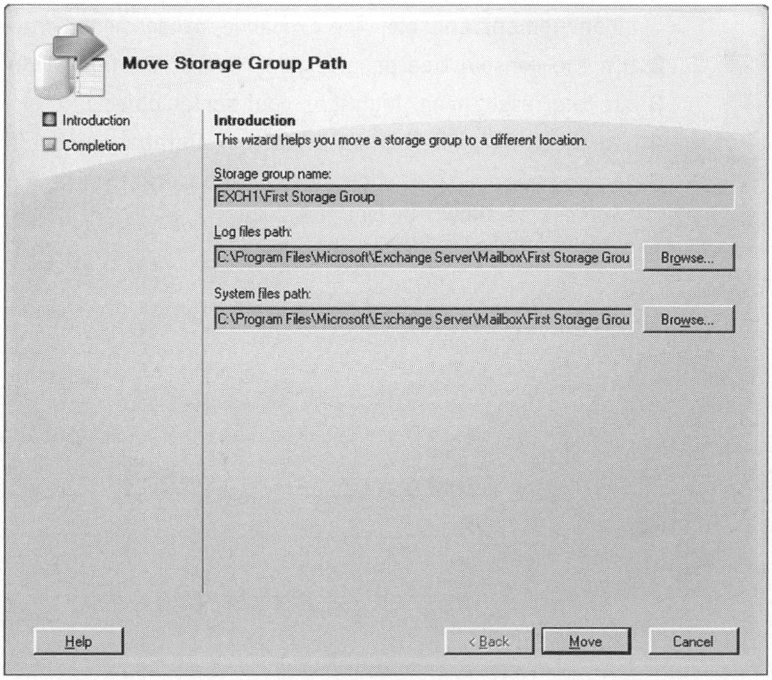

6. Beside the **Log files path** dialog box, click **Browse**. In the Browse For Folder window that appears, select the target hard disk and target folder that you wish to move the transaction logs to and click **OK**.
7. Beside the **System files path** dialog box, click **Browse**. In the Browse For Folder window that appears, select the target hard disk and target folder that you wish to move the storage group to and click **OK**. Normally, this is the same path chosen for the transaction logs.

TAKE NOTE*

If the target folder does not exist, you can click **Make New Folder** in the Browse For Folder window.

8. Click **Move**. When prompted to confirm that databases within the storage group will be unavailable during the move operation, click **Yes**. The Completion page appears.

9. Click **Finish** to close the Move Storage Group Path window. If your server is running Exchange Server 2007 Enterprise edition, and have created a public folder database during the installation, you should also move the Second Storage Group using the following steps.

10. In the work pane, highlight **Second Storage Group**.

11. In the action pane, click **Move Storage Group Path**. The Move Storage Group Path window appears as shown earlier in Figure 4-10.

12. Beside the **Log files path** dialog box, click **Browse**. In the Browse For Folder window that appears, select the target hard disk and target folder that you wish to move the transaction logs to and click **OK**.

13. Beside the **System files path** dialog box, click **Browse**. In the Browse For Folder window that appears, select the target hard disk and target folder that you wish to move the storage group to and click **OK**. Normally, this is the same path chosen for the transaction logs.

14. Click **Move**. When prompted to confirm that databases within the storage group will be unavailable during the move operation, click **Yes**. The Completion page appears.

15. Click **Finish** to close the Move Storage Group Path window.

16. Close the Exchange Management Console.

➔ MOVE THE DEFAULT MAILBOX AND PUBLIC FOLDER DATABASES

GET READY. Turn on the computer, and log in as the Administrator user account. Close any windows that appear on the desktop.

1. Click **Start**, **All Programs**, **Microsoft Exchange Server 2007**, and then click **Exchange Management Console**. The Exchange Management Console window appears.

2. In the console tree pane, expand **Server Configuration** and highlight **Mailbox**.

3. In the result pane, highlight your server object.

4. In the work pane, highlight **Mailbox Database** under the First Storage Group.

5. In the action pane, click **Move Database Path**. The Move Database Path window appears as shown in Figure 4-11.

Figure 4-11

Moving a Default Database

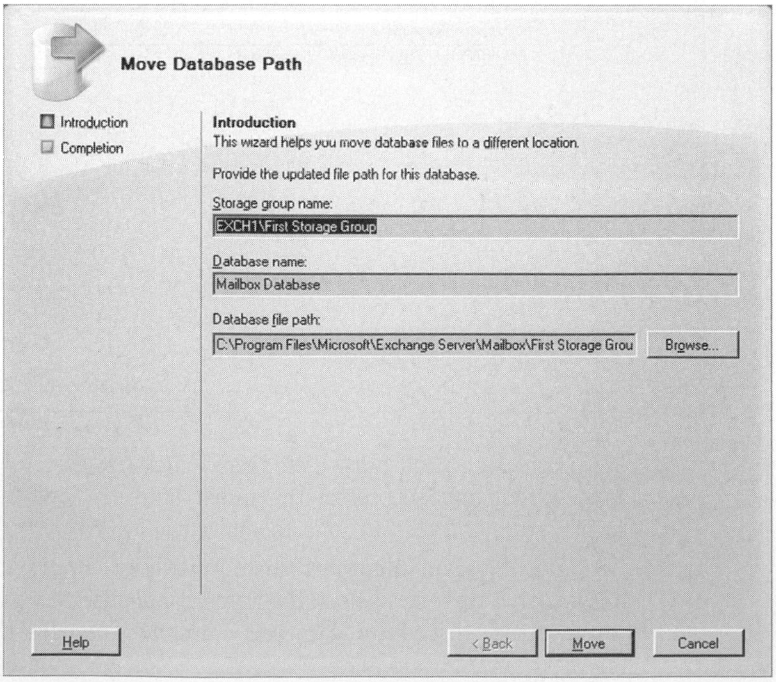

6. Beside the **Database file path** dialog box, click **Browse**. In the Exchange Database window that appears, select the target hard disk and target folder that you wish to move the database to and click **Save**. Normally, this is the same path chosen for the storage group and storage group transaction logs.

7. Click **Move**. When prompted to confirm that the database will be unavailable during the move operation, click **Yes**. The Completion page appears.

8. Click **Finish** to close the Move Database Path window. If you have created a public folder database during the installation, you should also move it to the appropriate storage group on another hard disk using the following steps.

9. In the work pane, highlight **Public Folder Database**. This database will be located under the First Storage Group if you are running Exchange Server 2007 Standard edition or under the Second Storage Group if you are running Exchange Server 2007 Enterprise Edition.

10. In the action pane, click **Move Database Path**. The Move Database Path window appears as shown earlier in Figure 4-11.

11. Beside the **Database file path** dialog box, click **Browse**. In the Exchange Database window that appears, select the target hard disk and target folder that you wish to move the database to and click **Save**. Normally, this is the same path chosen for the storage group and storage group transaction logs.

12. Click **Move**. When prompted to confirm that the database will be unavailable during the move operation, click **Yes**.

13. Click **Finish** to close the Move Database Path window.

14. Close the Exchange Management Console.

THE COMMAND LINE WAY

You can also use the **Move-StorageGroupPath** and **Move-DatabasePath** cmdlets in the Exchange Management Shell to move storage groups and databases. For example, to move the transaction logs and storage group files for the First Storage Group on the server EXCH1 to the folder D:\SG1, you could run the following command in the Exchange Management Shell:

Move-StorageGroupPath–Identity 'EXCH1\First Storage Group' –LogFolderPath 'D:\SG1'–SystemFolderPath 'D:\SG1'

Similarly, to move the default Mailbox Database within the First Storage Group on the server EXCH1 to the same location, you could run the following command in the Exchange Management Shell:

Move-DatabasePath–Identity 'EXCH1\First Storage Group\Mailbox Database' –EdbFilePath 'D:\SG1\Mailbox Database.edb'

CREATING ADDITIONAL STORAGE GROUPS AND DATABASES

When you create new mailboxes, you have the ability to select the storage group and database that will store the mailbox data. This gives you the ability to divide up mailboxes among several different databases and storage groups on a single server to enhance performance and reliability. In addition, if you did not specify to create a public folder database during the Exchange installation, you will need to create a public folder database after installation to allow Entourage and Outlook 2003 and earlier MAPI clients the ability to access your Exchange server.

Accordingly, you almost always need to create additional storage groups and databases on a new Mailbox role server. As discussed earlier, by locating these storage groups and databases on a nonsystem hard disk that is part of a RAID, you can enhance the speed and fault tolerance of your databases.

> **X REF** Creating mailboxes will be discussed in Lesson 5, "Working with Recipient Objects." Creating public folders will be discussed in Lesson 7, "Working with Public Folders."

⊙ CREATE A NEW STORAGE GROUP

GET READY. Turn on the computer, and log in as the Administrator user account. Close any windows that appear on the desktop.

1. Click **Start**, **All Programs**, **Microsoft Exchange Server 2007**, and then click **Exchange Management Console**. The Exchange Management Console window appears.

2. In the console tree pane, expand **Server Configuration** and highlight **Mailbox**.

3. In the detail pane, highlight your server object.

4. In the action pane, click **New Storage Group**. The New Storage Group window appears as shown in Figure 4-12.

Figure 4-12

Creating a New Storage Group

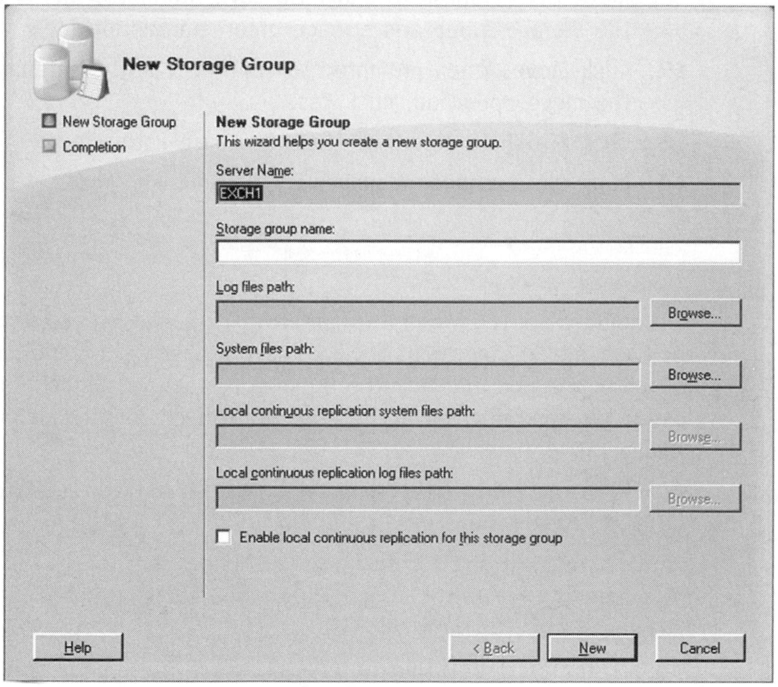

> **TAKE NOTE*** If the target folder does not exist, you can click **Make New Folder** in the Browse For Folder window.

> **X REF** Enabling storage groups for use with Local continuous replication will be discussed in Lesson 13, "Providing for High Availability."

5. In the Storage group name field, type a name for your storage group.

6. Beside the **Log files path** dialog box, click **Browse**. In the Browse For Folder window that appears, select the target hard disk and target folder that you wish to use for the transaction logs and click **OK**.

7. Beside the System files path dialog box, click **Browse**. In the Browse For Folder window that appears, select the target hard disk and target folder that you wish to use for the storage group and click **OK**. Normally, this is the same path chosen for the transaction logs.

8. Do not select any other options and click **New**.

9. Click **Finish** to close the New Storage Group window.

10. Close the Exchange Management Console

THE COMMAND
LINE WAY

You can also use the **New-StorageGroup** cmdlet in the Exchange Management Shell to create a new storage group. For example, to create a new storage group called Third Storage Group on the server called EXCH1, and specify that transaction logs and storage group files should be stored in the folder D:\SG3, you could run the following command in the Exchange Management Shell:

New-StorageGroup–Server 'EXCH1'–Name 'Third Storage Group'–LogFolderPath 'D:\SG3'–SystemFolderPath 'D:\SG3'

Alternatively, you can use the **Get-StorageGroup** cmdlet to obtain information about an existing storage group or the **Set-StorageGroup** cmdlet to change its properties. To remove an existing storage group, you can use the **Remove-StorageGroup** cmdlet. For more information on the **New-StorageGroup, Get-StorageGroup**, **Set StorageGroup,** and **Remove-StorageGroup** cmdlets, search for their names within Exchange Server 2007 Help.

CREATE A NEW MAILBOX DATABASE

GET READY. Turn on the computer, and log in as the Administrator user account. Close any windows that appear on the desktop.

1. Click **Start**, **All Programs**, **Microsoft Exchange Server 2007**, and then click **Exchange Management Console**. The Exchange Management Console window appears.

2. In the console tree pane, expand **Server Configuration** and highlight **Mailbox**.

3. In the result pane, highlight your server object.

4. In the work pane, highlight the storage group that should contain the new mailbox database.

5. In the action pane, click **New Mailbox Database**. The New Mailbox Database window appears as shown in Figure 4-13.

Figure 4-13

Creating a New Mailbox Database

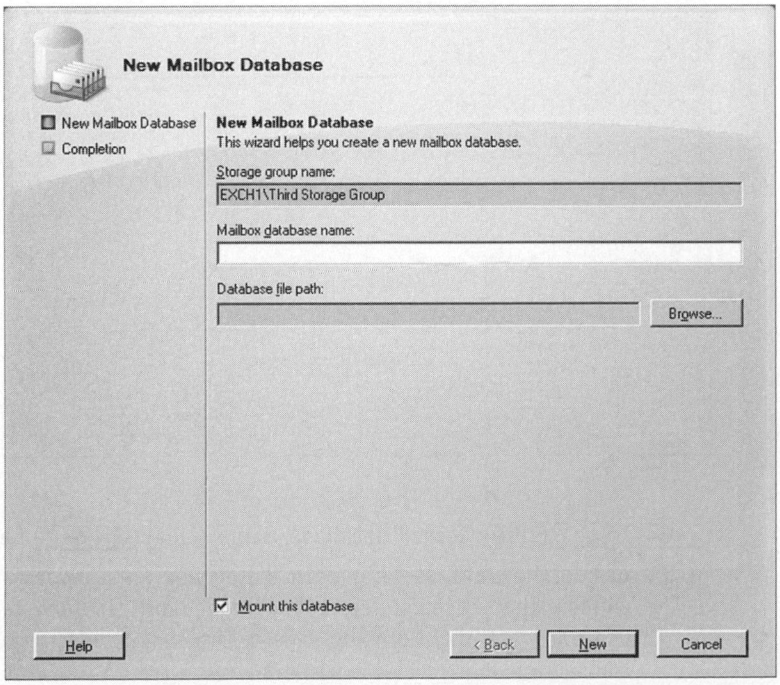

New Mailbox Database

- New Mailbox Database
- Completion

New Mailbox Database
This wizard helps you create a new mailbox database.

Storage group name:

EXCH1\Third Storage Group

Mailbox database name:

Database file path:

Browse...

☑ Mount this database

Help   < Back   New   Cancel

6. In the **Mailbox database name** field, type a name for your mailbox database.

7. Beside the **Database file path** dialog box, click **Browse**. In the Browse For Folder window that appears, select the target hard disk and target folder that you wish to

use and click **OK**. Normally, this is the same folder used for the storage group and transaction logs.

8. Verify that **Mount this database** is selected to ensure that the database will be available for use after creation and click **New**.

9. Click **Finish** to close the New Mailbox Database window.

10. Close the Exchange Management Console.

 CREATE A NEW PUBLIC FOLDER DATABASE

GET READY. Turn on the computer, and log in as the Administrator user account. Close any windows that appear on the desktop.

1. Click **Start**, **All Programs**, **Microsoft Exchange Server 2007**, and then click **Exchange Management Console**. The Exchange Management Console window appears.

2. In the console tree pane, expand **Server Configuration** and highlight **Mailbox**.

3. In the result pane, highlight your server object.

4. In the work pane, highlight the storage group that should contain the new mailbox database.

5. In the action pane, click **New Public Folder Database**. The New Public Folder Database window appears as shown in Figure 4-14.

Figure 4-14

Creating a New Public Folder Database

New Public Folder Database

- New Public Folder Database
- Completion

New Public Folder Database
This wizard helps you create a new public folder database.

Storage group name:
EXCH1\Fourth Storage Group

Public folder database name:

Database file path:

Browse...

☑ Mount this database

Help   < Back   New   Cancel

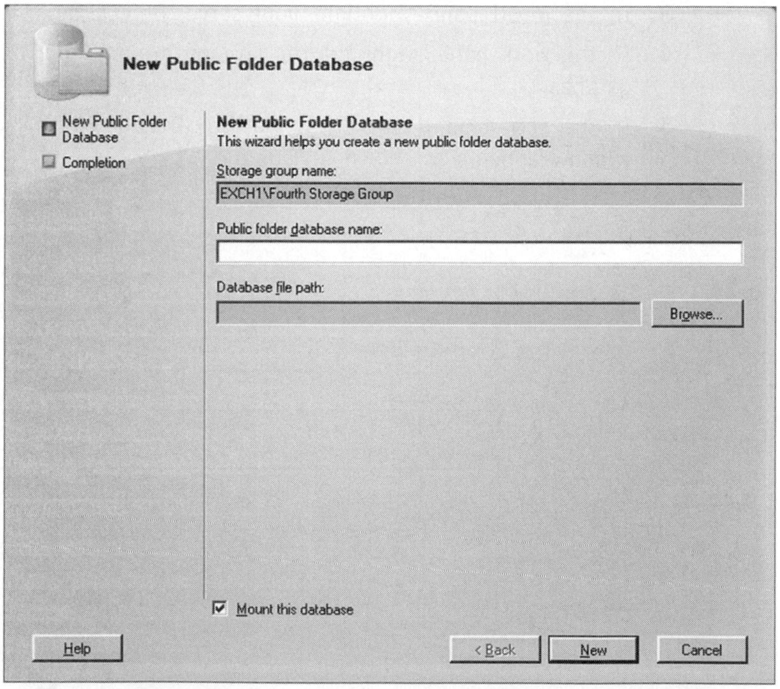

6. In the **Public folder database name** field, type a name for your mailbox database.

7. Beside the **Database file path** dialog box, click **Browse**. In the Browse For Folder window that appears, select the target hard disk and target folder that you wish to use and click **OK**. Normally, this is the same folder used for the storage group and transaction logs.

8. Verify that **Mount this database** is selected to ensure that the database will be available for use after creation and click **New**.

9. Click **Finish** to close the New Public Folder Database window.

10. Close the Exchange Management Console.

⚠ **WARNING** Remember that you can only create one public folder database per Mailbox role server. If you already have a public folder database, you will receive an error message when attempting to create one by clicking the **New** button.

THE COMMAND LINE WAY

You can also use the **New-MailboxDatabase** and **New-PublicFolderDatabase** cmdlets in the Exchange Management Shell to create new mailbox and public folder databases. For example, to create a new mailbox database called Mailbox Database 3 in the storage group called Third Storage Group on the server called EXCH1, and specify that the database file is stored as D:\SG3\Mailbox Database 3.edb, you could run the following command in the Exchange Management Shell:

New-MailboxDatabase–StorageGroup 'EXCH1\Third Storage Group' –Name 'Mailbox Database 3'–EdbFilePath 'D:\SG3\Mailbox Database 3.edb'

Similarly, to create a public folder database called Public Folder Database in the storage group called Fourth Storage Group on the server called EXCH1 and to specify that the database file is stored as D:\SG4\Public Folder Database.edb, you could run the following command in the Exchange Management Shell:

New-PublicFolderDatabase–StorageGroup 'EXCH1\Fourth Storage Group'–Name 'Public Folder Database'–EdbFilePath 'D:\SG4\Public Folder Database.edb'

Once you create a new public folder database using the Exchange Management Shell, you can mount it to make it available on the system using the **Mount-Database** cmdlet or later dismount it using the **Dismount-Database** cmdlet. To mount the databases created in the previous two examples, you could run the following commands within the Exchange Management Shell:

Mount-Database–Identity 'Mailbox Database 3'

Mount-Database–Identity 'Public Folder Database'

You can also use the **Get-MailboxDatabase** and **Get-PublicFolderDatabase** cmdlets to obtain information about an existing mailbox or public folder database. Additionally, the **Set-MailboxDatabase** and **Set-PublicFolderDatabase cmdlets** can be used to modify the properties of an existing mailbox or public folder database, and the **Remove-MailboxDatabase** and **Remove-PublicFolderDatabase** cmdlets can be used to remove a mailbox or public folder database. For more information on the cmdlets used in this section, simply search for their names within Exchange Server 2007 Help.

SETTING STORAGE LIMITS ON A NEW DATABASE

The main form of communication in many organizations today involves email, and email today often contains large attachments such as spreadsheets, presentations, and multimedia. Moreover, if users forget to remove unnecessary emails from their mailbox periodically, their mailboxes will grow continuously over time and use up the available space on your email servers. As a result, nearly all organizations impose some kind of user-based storage limit on email servers to prevent ambitious users from using up all of the available space on the Mailbox role servers. In general, you should enforce storage limits on your mailbox databases so that users are warned when they approach their limits and are not allowed to store emails once their limits have been reached.

To avoid problems, the best time to set up these email restrictions is immediately after creating a new mailbox database. If you highlight your mailbox database in the Exchange Management Console and select **Properties** from the action pane, you can set the default size restrictions for mailboxes that are stored in the mailbox database on the **Limits** tab as shown in Figure 4-15.

Figure 4-15 reflects limits that are appropriate for an organization that allocates a maximum of 1 GB (1048576 KB) for individual user mailboxes. When a user's mailbox reaches 900 MB (921600 KB), the user will receive a warning email at 1:00 a.m. from Exchange indicating that he is approaching his limit and should remove any unnecessary emails. When a user's mailbox reaches 950 MB (972800 KB), he will not be able to send any emails using Exchange server and will receive an additional warning email from Exchange at 1:00 a.m. However, the user will continue receiving emails from others until the mailbox size reaches 1 GB (1048576 KB). As this point, the user can no longer send or receive any emails until he reduces the size of his mailbox.

Figure 4-15

Modifying Mailbox Database
Limits

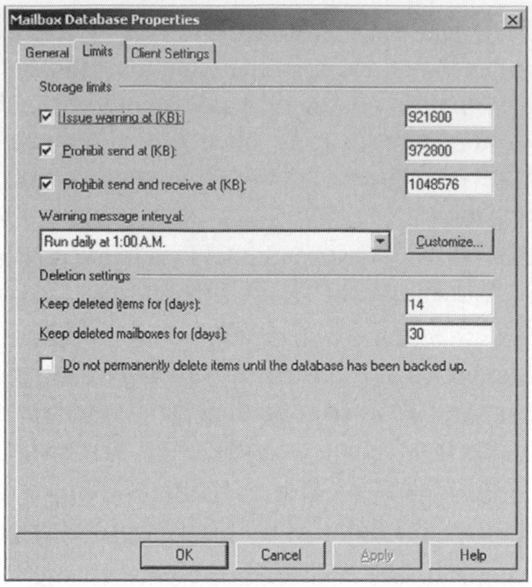

Storage limits can also be applied to public folder databases to prevent users from posting too much data to public folders. As with mailbox databases, to set limits on a public folder database, you can highlight it in the Exchange Management Console, select **Properties** from the action pane, and specify the appropriate settings on the **Limits** tab as shown in Figure 4-16.

Figure 4-16

Modifying Public Folder
Database Limits

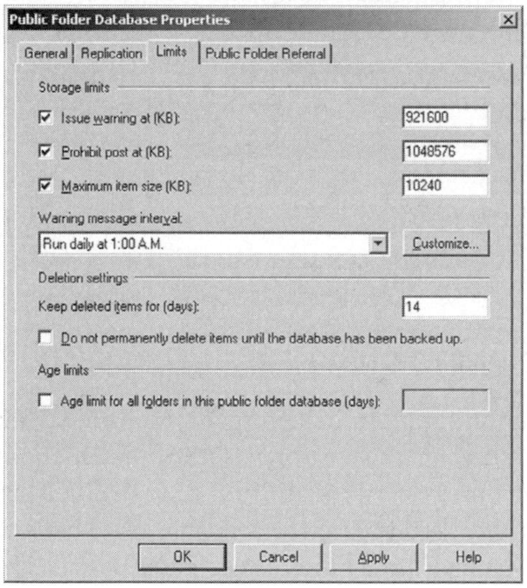

In Figure 4-16, users receive an email warning at 1:00 a.m. if they have posted more than 900 MB (921600 KB) to public folders within the public folder database. After storing 1 GB (1048576 KB) of data within the public folder database, users will receive an error if they attempt to post any additional data. In addition, users will receive an error message if they attempt to post a message or item that is larger than 10 MB (10240 KB) to a public folder that is stored in the public folder database.

THE COMMAND LINE WAY

You can also use the appropriate options alongside the **Set-MailboxDatabase** and **Set-PublicFolderDatabase** cmdlets in the Exchange Management Shell to set limits. For example, to set the limits shown in Figures 4-15 and 4-16, you could run the following commands in the Exchange Management Shell:

Set-MailboxDatabase–Identity 'Mailbox Database'–IssueWarningQuota '921600'–ProhibitSendQuota '972800'–ProhibitSendReceiveQuota '1048576'

Set-PublicFolderDatabase–Identity 'Public Folder Database'–IssueWarningQuota '921600'–ProhibitPostQuota '1048576'–MaxItemSize '10240'

Configuring the CAS Role

CERTIFICATION READY?
Configure Exchange Server Roles.
1.4

Because the CAS role provides client access to the databases maintained by the Mailbox role within your organization, it is important to ensure that the email protocols on the CAS role are properly configured after installation before you set up email clients. This involves enabling Outlook Anywhere, POP, and IMAP, as well as configuring options for OWA.

ENABLING EMAIL PROTOCOLS

Because MAPI takes full advantage of the features in email client programs such as Microsoft Outlook and Entourage, most organizations use the MAPI RPC protocol alongside these programs when configuring internal client computers for email access. In addition, mobile email access using a web browser or smart phone is becoming very popular in many organizations today. As a result, the CAS role is enabled for MAPI RPC, ActiveSync, and Outlook Web Access (OWA) connections by default after installation.

Although OWA is configured to allow client access using the HTTPS protocol, the SSL certificate that is used for HTTPS by IIS is not digitally signed and will give related warnings to users when they connect to OWA on the CAS role server using their web browser.

X REF Providing signed SSL certificates to IIS for use with OWA is covered in Lesson 8, "Configuring Email Protocols and Transport Rules." The configuration of ActiveSync is discussed in Lesson 12, "Providing for Mobile Access and Unified Messaging."

Email client programs that connect to your Exchange servers from across the Internet often use POP3, IMAP4, or Outlook Anywhere (RPC over HTTP/HTTPS) protocols. However, these protocols are not enabled by default on the CAS role after installation.

To enable POP3, you simply need to enable and start the **Microsoft Exchange POP3** service in the Services console (**Start** > **Administrative Tools** > **Services**). After locating the Microsoft Exchange POP3 service in the Services console, right click the service, select **Properties,** and select a Startup type of **Automatic** to ensure that the service is automatically started at boot time as shown in Figure 4-17 . Following this, you can click the **Start** button in Figure 4-17 to start the service and allow POP3 clients access to the CAS role.

Figure 4-17
Enabling the POP3 Service

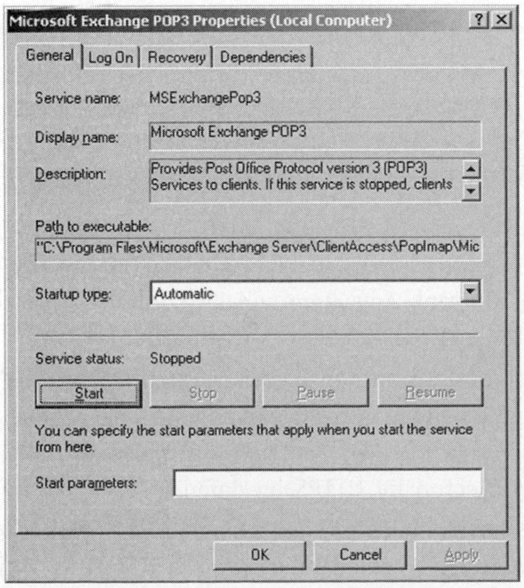

As with POP3, you can enable the IMAP4 service by enabling and starting the Microsoft Exchange IMAP4 service in the Services console. The procedure for this is identical to the one for POP3.

If your organization has remote Outlook 2003 or later clients, you can enable the Outlook Anywhere protocol to obtain all the Exchange features available to MAPI clients. When used with HTTPS, Outlook Anywhere provides secure email access over the Internet using the RPC protocol. Before enabling Outlook Anywhere, secure access to Exchange using the RPC protocol, which requires that other encryption technologies such as IP Security (IPSec) or Virtual Private Networks (VPNs) be set up beforehand.

For extra security, remote Outlook Anywhere clients can connect to a secure proxy server such as *Microsoft Internet Security and Acceleration (ISA) Server*, which can be configured to forward Outlook Anywhere traffic to your CAS role servers.

X REF

Before enabling Outlook Anywhere, you must install the **RPC over HTTP proxy** component of Windows. This was discussed in Lesson 3, "Deploying Exchange Server 2007."

ENABLE OUTLOOK ANYWHERE

GET READY. Turn on the computer, and log in as the Administrator user account. Close any windows that appear on the desktop.

1. Click **Start**, **All Programs**, **Microsoft Exchange Server 2007**, and then click **Exchange Management Console**. The Exchange Management Console window appears.

2. In the console tree pane, expand **Server Configuration** and highlight **Client Access**.

3. In the action pane, click **Enable Outlook Anywhere**. The Enable Outlook Anywhere window appears as shown in Figure 4-18.

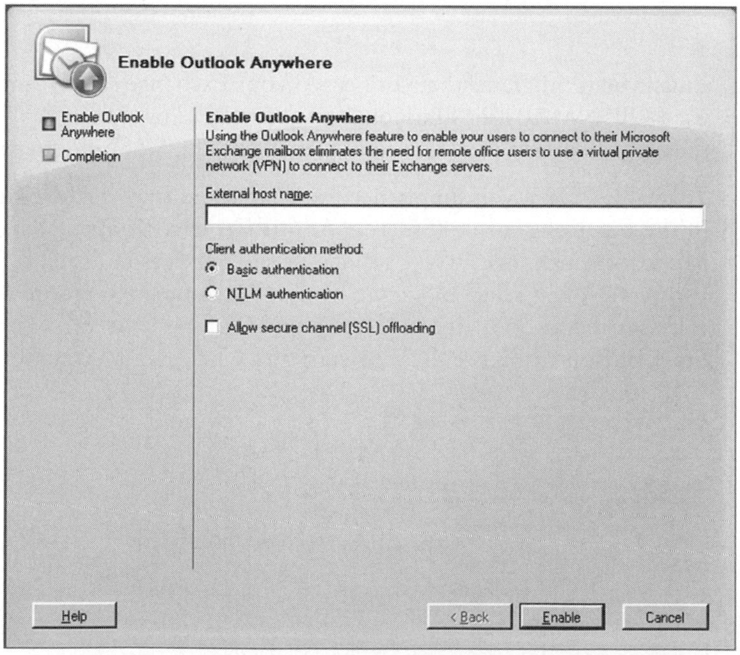

Figure 4-18

Enabling Outlook Anywhere

4. In the **External host name** field, type the FQDN of your CAS role server. Alternatively, if your Outlook Anywhere will be configured to connect via an ISA Server, enter the FQDN of your ISA Server in this field.

5. Select the appropriate authentication method:

   • **Basic authentication** transfers username and password information in plain text. This is adequate for use with Outlook Anywhere because the username and password are protected by HTTPS by default.

   • **NTLM authentication** does not transmit passwords across the network in plain text and is the recommended option as it offers additional protection.

6. If your CAS role server contains a bus mastering network card that supports SSL offloading, you can select **Allow secure channel (SSL) offloading** to ensure that the network card will perform the SSL encryption instead of the computer's processors.

7. Click **Enable**. At the Completion screen, click **Finish**.

8. Close the Exchange Management Console.

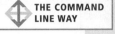

You can also use the **Enable-OutlookAnywhere** cmdlet in the Exchange Management Shell to enable Outlook Anywhere or the **Disable-OutlookAnywhere** cmdlet to disable Outlook Anywhere on a CAS role server. For example, to create enable Outlook Anywhere with NTLM authentication and no SSL offloading on the server EXCH1 and specify an external hostname of proxy1.octavius.net, you could run the following command in the Exchange Management Shell:

Enable-OutlookAnywhere -Server:'EXCH1' -ExternalHostName:'proxy1.octavius.net' -ExternalAuthenticationMethod:'NTLM' -SSLOffloading:$false

You can also use the **Get-OutlookAnywhere** cmdlet in the Exchange Management Shell to view the options that are configured for Outlook Anywhere. Alternatively, you can use several different options and arguments alongside the **Set-OutlookAnywhere** cmdlet to modify Outlook Anywhere options. For more information on the use of these cmdlets, simply search for them in Exchange Server 2007 Help.

CONFIGURING OWA OPTIONS

By providing access from anywhere on the Internet using a web browser, OWA provides flexibility and reliability for the users in your organization. However, this flexibility may also pose a threat to the security of your email system because there is no absolute way to ensure the identity of remote users. A malicious person could use someone else's username and password to access email using OWA from any location on the Internet. Similarly, if a user leaves her computer unattended in an Internet café while connected to OWA, others can gain access to company resources and sensitive information. In short, providing easy remote email access adds several potential security vulnerabilities.

To mitigate these security vulnerabilities, Exchange Server 2007 adds several enhancements to OWA. You can now restrict the user features that are available in OWA as well as the company file servers that OWA users are allowed to access. In addition, you can provide additional restrictions depending on computer location. When users connect to OWA on the CAS role server, they are prompted at the logon screen to select whether they are using a computer in a public or private location as shown in Figure 4-19.

Figure 4-19

OWA Logon Screen

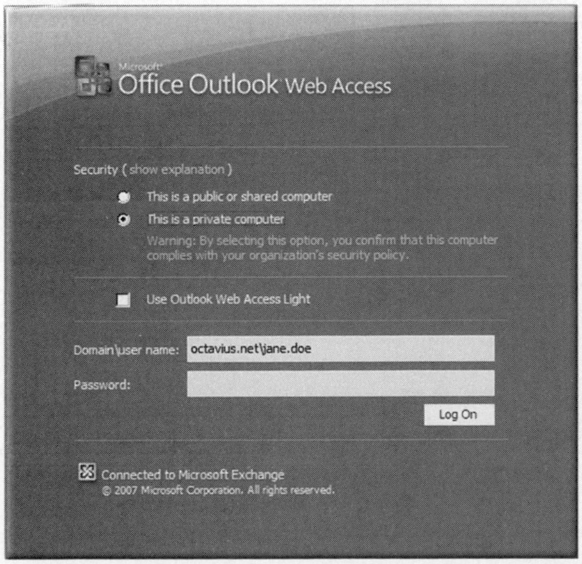

If users select **This is a public or shared computer** in Figure 4-19, you can specify options that prevent them from accessing file servers or the SharePoint infrastructure within your organization while using OWA. This will reduce the chance that a malicious person will gain access to sensitive information at an unattended computer.

To configure OWA options, you must navigate to **Server Configuration > Client Access** within the Exchange Management Console, select your CAS role server in the result pane and highlight the **Outlook Web Access** tab as shown in Figure 4-20.

Figure 4-20

Configuring OWA

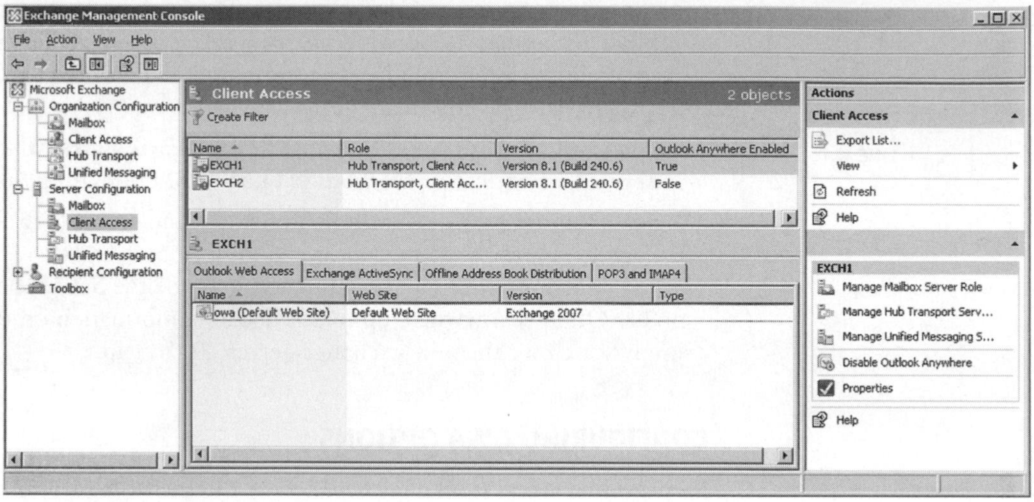

Most OWA configuration is performed within the properties of the owa (Default Web Site) object shown in Figure 4-20. On the Segmentation tab of owa (Default Web Site) properties, you can disable any unwanted OWA features as shown in Figure 4-21.

Figure 4-21

OWA Properties Segmentation Tab

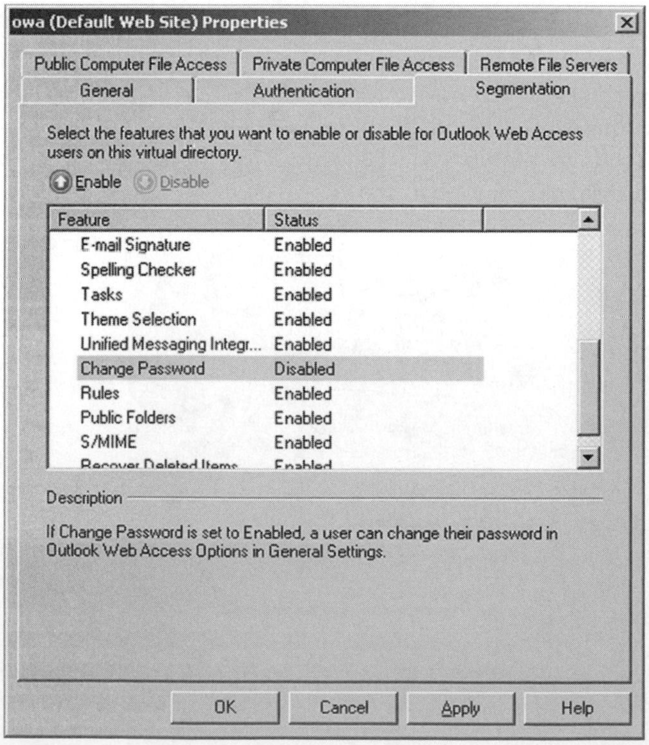

All OWA features are enabled by default. At minimum, most Exchange administrators disable the **Change Password** feature of OWA shown in Figure 4-21. This prevents a malicious user from changing a password using OWA on an unattended system and locking out the real user as a result.

You can also select the Remote File Servers tab of owa (Default Web Site) properties as shown in Figure 4-22 to specify the file servers that OWA users are allowed to access during their session. By default, OWA is blocked from accessing all file servers in the Unknown Servers section. In this case, you can click the **Allow** button in the Allow List section and provide the FQDNs of file servers that you wish OWA clients to access. Alternatively, you can select **Allow** in the drop-down box under the Unknown Servers section to allow access to all file servers by default and then click the **Block** button under the Block List section to provide the FQDNs of file servers that OWA clients should not access. If you specify the same FQDN in the Allow List and Block List sections, OWA clients will be blocked from accessing the server with that FQDN. If you modify the Allow List or Block List sections, you must also click the **Configure** button and add the domain names from all FQDNs to the list of internal servers that OWA uses when accessing network resources.

Figure 4-22

OWA Properties Remote File Servers Tab

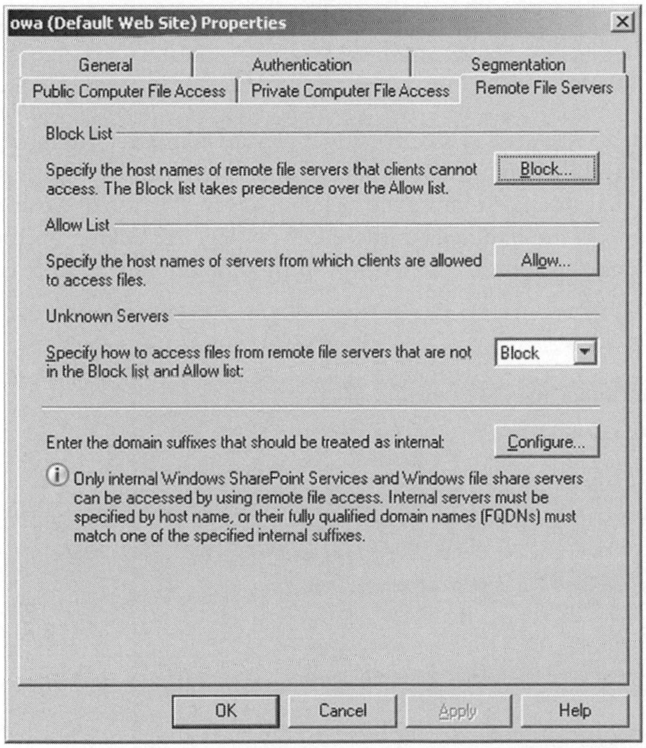

To set OWA options used when a user selects **This is a private computer** at the OWA logon screen shown in Figure 4-19, you can navigate to the Private Computer File Access tab shown in Figure 4-23.

As shown in Figure 4-23, OWA users are allowed to access email attachments (called *Direct file access*) as well as view certain document formats directly in their web browser using the *WebReady* feature of OWA by default. In addition, users are able to access file servers and SharePoint servers provided that they are allowed on the Remote File Servers tab shown earlier in Figure 4-22.

Figure 4-23

OWA Properties Private
Computer File Access Tab

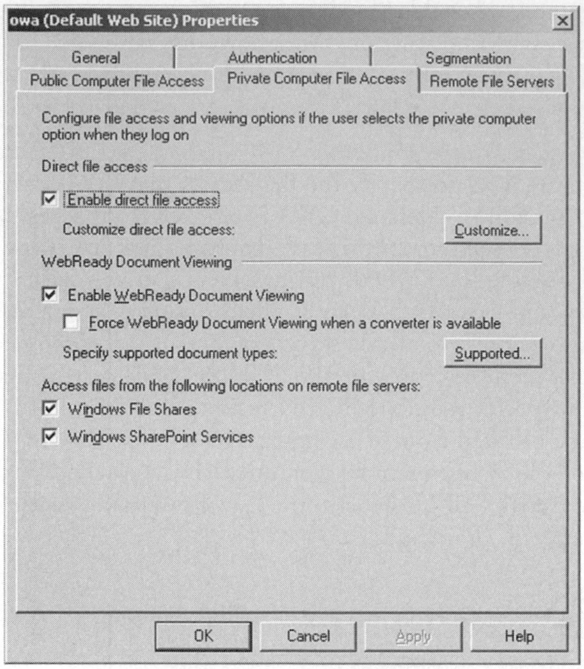

Because OWA users who are using a private computer are more secure than those who are using a public computer, it is safe to allow the default options unless you have a company policy that restricts remote file access. However, you may wish to control the way email attachments are handled for these OWA users by clicking on the **Customize** button and specifying the appropriate settings in the Direct File Access Settings window shown in Figure 4-24.

Figure 4-24

Specifying OWA Attachment
Settings

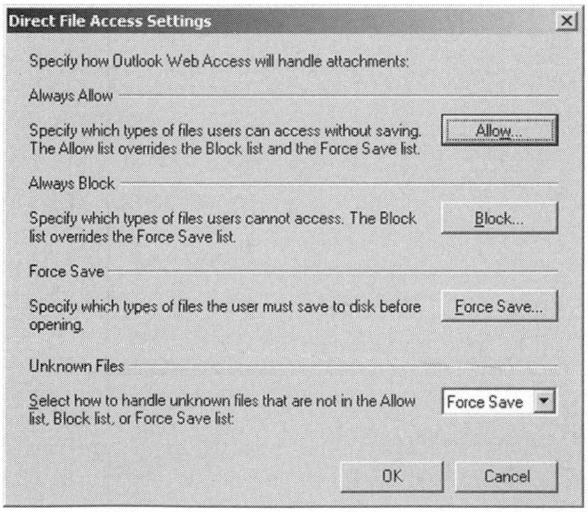

To specify the attachments that OWA users are allowed to open directly from their OWA session, you can click on the **Allow** button. Similarly, you can click the **Block** button to specify attachments that OWA users are not allowed to access or the **Force Save** button to specify attachments that OWA users must first save to their local computer before opening. For example, when you click the **Allow** button, the screen shown in Figure 4-25 appears and allows you to specify the file extensions (such as .avi or .bmp) or file types (GIF, Javascript) that are allowed.

Because email attachment formats are described by the *Multipurpose Internet Mail Extensions (MIME)* standard, you must use a MIME name when specifying file types in Figure 4-25. For example, to specify XML text files, the MIME name would be text/xml.

Figure 4-25

Allowing Attachment Types

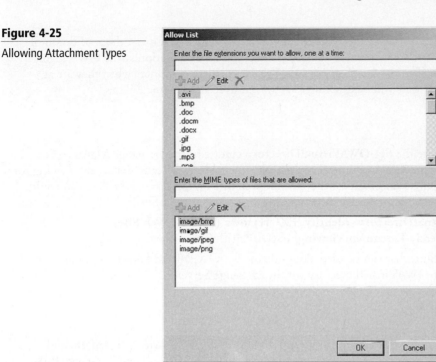

Once you have customized email attachment settings, you can choose to restrict the documents that are available for viewing with WebReady. By default, WebReady can be used to view Microsoft Word, PowerPoint, and Excel files as well PDF and rich text files. However, you can restrict this list by selecting the **Supported** button as shown in Figure 4-23.

By selecting the Public Computer File Access tab of owa (Default Web Site) properties, you can specify OWA options used when a user selects **This is a public or shared computer** at the OWA logon screen shown in Figure 4-19. The options and defaults on this tab are identical to the Private Computer File Access tab. However, you should restrict the default options. This will prevent users who access OWA from a public computer from having the same access level and abilities as those who access OWA from a private computer.

To prevent public OWA users from accessing file servers and SharePoint servers as well as downloading or viewing attachments that may contain sensitive company information, you could simply disable those features by deselecting them as shown in Figure 4-26.

Figure 4-26

OWA Properties Public Computer File Access Tab

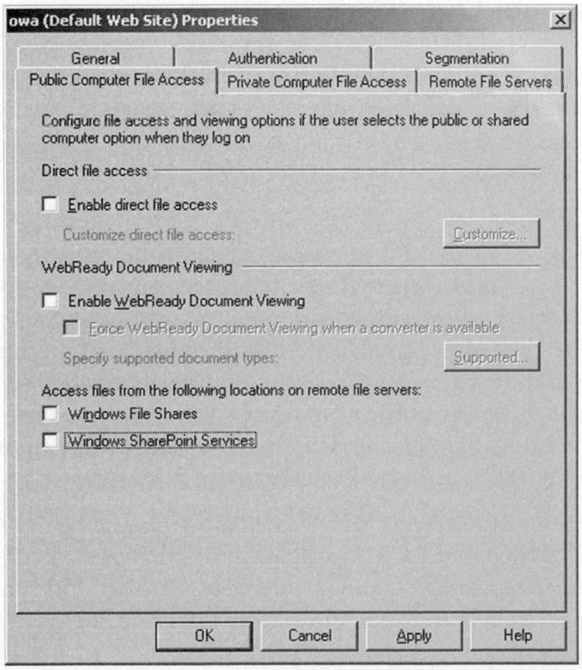

Although you can specify more restrictive options for public OWA users, the application of these restrictions relies on the user's ability to select the correct location at the OWA logon screen shown in Figure 4-19. If users select **This is a private computer** when they are at a public computer, they will be exposing their system to security vulnerabilities.

You can also use the **Set-OWAVirtualDirectory** cmdlet in the Exchange Management Shell to configure OWA options. For example, to enable WebReady document viewing for Private Computers on OWA for the Default Web Site on the server EXCH1, you could run the following command within the Exchange Management Shell:

Set-OWAVirtualDirectory -Identity 'EXCH1\owa (Default Web Site)'
-ForceWebReady DocumentViewingFirstOnPrivateComputers

For more options that can be used alongside the Set-OWAVirtualDirectory cmdlet, simply search for Set-OWAVirtualDirectory within Exchange Server 2007 Help.

We will discuss the detailed configuration of the POP3/POP3S, IMAP4/IMAP4S, and HTTP/HTTPS protocols in Lesson 8, "Configuring Email Protocols and Transport Rules."

Configuring Email Relay

THE BOTTOM LINE

Exchange infrastructures can vary greatly in their composition and function because they are modeled after the needs of the organization. In addition to configuring new server roles that are deployed in your Exchange organization, it is vital to ensure that email is sent and received properly by Hub and Edge role servers. To do this, you must configure the appropriate connector objects that represent email flow within your organization and across the Internet.

Understanding Connectors

In any email system, specific objects form the basis for sending and receiving email. In order to understand how Exchange servers relay email internally and externally, you must first understand the concept of connector objects.

To relay email within your organization and across the Internet, your Hub and Edge role servers must have *connectors* that specify how to send and receive email. Connectors specify how your Exchange server should communicate with other Exchange servers, POP3 clients, IMAP4 clients, and external email servers. In addition, connectors are configured to match a certain type of traffic. *Receive connectors* are stored on a Hub or Edge role server and specify how to handle incoming traffic from other email servers or POP3 and IMAP4 clients. *Send connectors* are stored in AD and determine how to send email to other servers within the organization as well as across the Internet.

Previous versions of Exchange Server could create special connectors that allowed email to be relayed directly to nonExchange email servers that were part of your organization such as Novell GroupWise, Lotus Domino, and Microsoft Mail. In Exchange Server 2007, these special connectors are not available. Instead, email sent to these systems is relayed using SMTP alongside other outgoing email.

Configuring Receive Connectors

Receive connectors contain the configuration information that allows Hub and Edge role servers to process inbound email from email clients and other servers. As a result, you should understand how to create and manage receive connectors to ensure that the email servers within your organization receive the email that is relayed to them.

TAKE NOTE★

Although Edge role servers can receive emails from the Internet and from within the organization by default, they must still be subscribed to a Hub role server before they are able to relay email.

When you install a new Edge role, a receive connector is automatically created that accepts email from the Hub role servers within your organization as well as incoming email from the Internet using the SMTP protocol on port 25.

Similarly, when you install a new Hub role, two receive connectors are automatically created. The first connector is called **Default**. It allows the Hub role server to receive email using SMTP on port 25 from POP3 and IMAP4 clients as well as from other Exchange servers within the organization. Because many POP3 and IMAP4 clients now use port 587 when sending email to the Hub role using SMTP, a second connector called **Client** is also created to allow SMTP connections from POP3 and IMAP4 clients on port 587.

CONFIGURING EXISTING RECEIVE CONNECTORS

To view the default receive connector on an Edge role server, you can simply navigate to **Edge Transport** within the Exchange Management Console, select your server object in the result pane and highlight the **Receive Connectors** tab as shown in Figure 4-27. On a Hub role server, you must navigate to **Server Configuration** > **Hub Transport** within the Exchange Management Console and select the appropriate server in the result pane as shown in Figure 4-28.

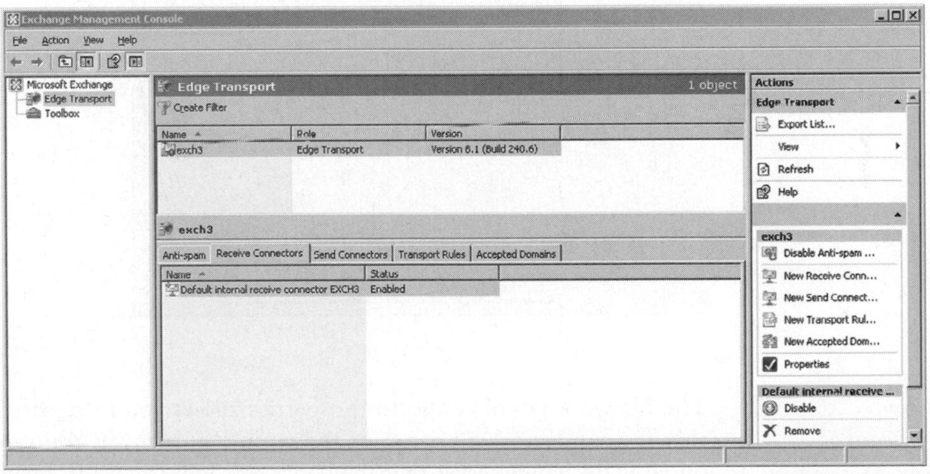

Figure 4-27

Viewing Receive Connectors on an Edge Role Server

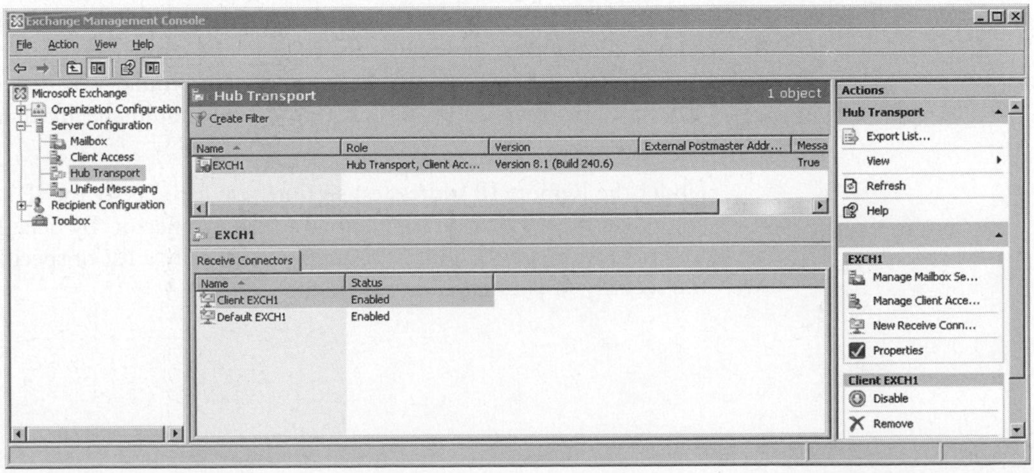

Figure 4-28

Viewing Receive Connectors on a Hub Role Server

You can temporarily prevent a receive connector from being used within the Exchange Management Console by selecting **Disable** in the action pane.

When you select **Properties** in the action pane for an existing connector, you can modify the connector settings. On the General tab of connector properties, you can specify the FQDN used when your email server responds to SMTP connection attempts as well as the maximum message size that your email server will accept as shown in Figure 4-29. If you select **Verbose** in the Protocol logging level drop-down box, information regarding all connections will be logged to files in the C:\Program Files\Microsoft\Exchange Server\ TransportRoles\Logs\ProtocolLog\SmtpReceive directory. Because verbose logging will use a large amount of disk space, you should only enable it for a short period of time when troubleshooting a problem.

Figure 4-29

Receive Connector Properties
General Tab

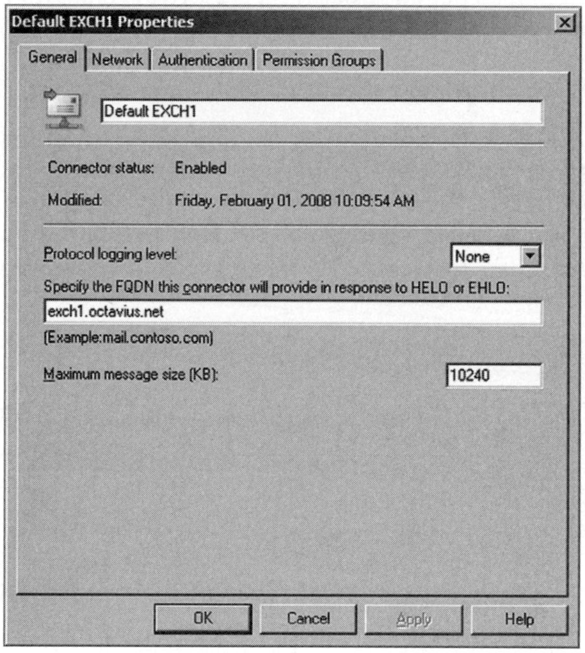

The Network tab of connector properties allows you to specify IP and port information that the connector will match as shown in Figure 4-30. You can specify the IP addresses on your Exchange server that the connector will listen for email on under the Local IP address(es) section as well as the SMTP port under the Port section. By default, receive connectors listen to all IP addresses on your server. If your Exchange server has multiple network interfaces, you may want to limit the connector to the IP address of a specific network interface on which you expect email. Similarly, if the connector should listen on a different port than 25 for SMTP traffic, you should specify the appropriate port under the Port section.

Under the Remote IP address(es) section, you can specify the IP addresses of remote computers and email servers that can send email to this connector. By default, receive connectors listen for email from any IP address, but you can specify a list of specific IP addresses to improve the security of your email infrastructure.

Figure 4-30

Receive Connector Properties
Network Tab

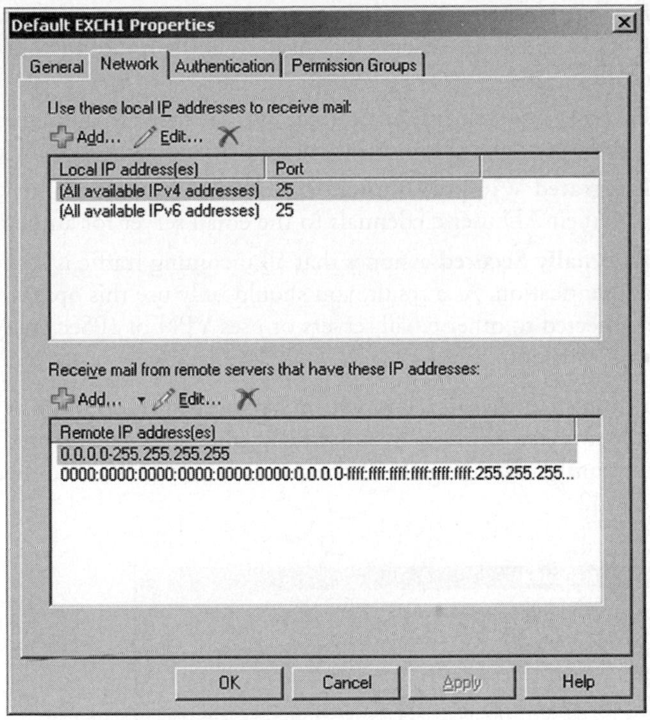

To provide additional security, many computers and email servers will attempt to authenticate to remote email servers before sending them email. The Authentication tab of receive connector properties allows you to specify the supported authentication protocols and mechanisms as shown in Figure 4-31.

Figure 4-31

Receive Connector Properties
Authentication Tab

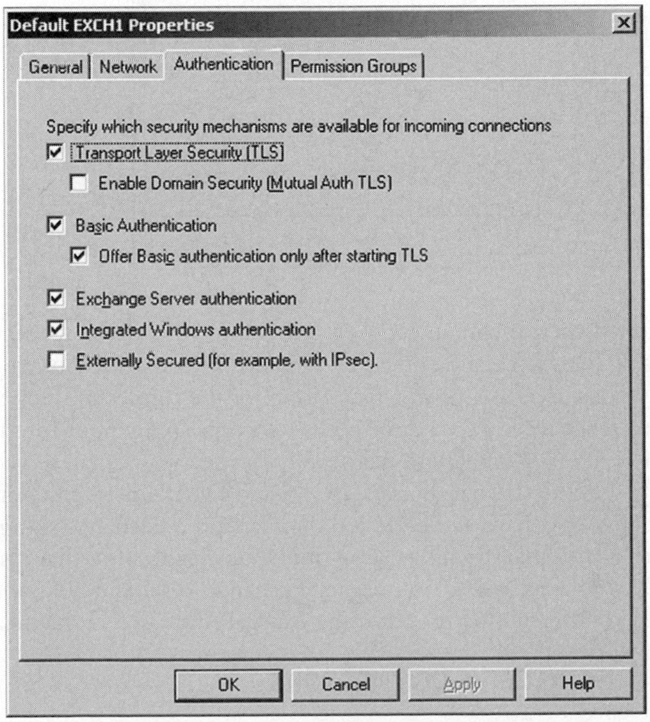

There are several different authentication options that can be selected:

- **Transport Layer Security (TLS)** is based on SSL and can be used to provide encrypted authentication, but requires a TLS certificate on both computers. Mutual Auth TLS is appropriate for providing security between organizations.

- **Basic Authentication** and Basic Authentication combined with TLS is appropriate for POP3 and IMAP4 clients that need to authenticate to your email server before sending email.
- **Exchange Server authentication** uses Kerberos to authenticate email servers and is used when relaying email internally within your organization by default.
- **Integrated Windows authentication** allows POP3 and IMAP4 clients to automatically pass their AD user credentials to the email server for authentication.
- **Externally Secured** assumes that all incoming traffic is secured and doesn't require authentication. As a result, you should only use this option if your network is privately connected to other email servers or uses VPN or IPSec encryption to secure all email transmission.

In addition to authentication, you must specify which users or remote computers can use each connector. These users and computers are represented using *permissions groups* that are configured using the Permissions Groups tab of connector properties as shown in Figure 4-32.

Figure 4-32

Receive Connector Properties Permissions Groups Tab

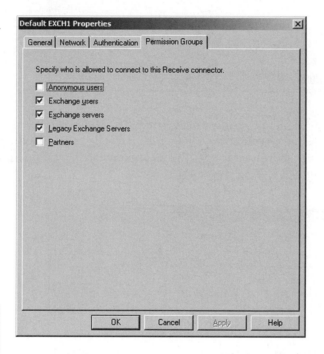

To allow users and computers to relay email to your Exchange server without authenticating using one of the authentication methods listed on the Authentication tab, you can select Anonymous users as a permissions group for the connector. However, this option is only selected if the receive connector needs to accept anonymous Internet email, as it also allows malicious users the ability to relay spam through your email server to protect their identities. By selecting Exchange users, POP3 and IMAP4 users can send email to your Exchange server after they have authenticated. Similarly, the Exchange server and legacy Exchange server options allow email from servers within your organization that run the Exchange 2007 Hub and Edge roles as well as from legacy Exchange 2000 and 2003 servers. The Partners option is only used for email that is sent using Mutual Auth TLS authentication.

CREATING RECEIVE CONNECTORS

Although the default receive connectors on a Hub or Edge role server are configured appropriately to receive email from other servers as well as from POP3 and IMAP4 users, you may need to configure additional receive connectors on a new Hub or Edge role server. For example, if your organization uses port 7299 for internal email relay, you will need to create a new receive connector that allows for traffic from other Exchange servers on port 7299 using Exchange Server authentication.

To simplify specifying authentication methods and permissions groups, you are prompted to select one of the following intended use options when you create a new receive connector:

- **Internet** does not require authentication and is used for receiving email from the Internet because most public email servers do not authenticate when relaying email.
- **Internal** uses Exchange Server authentication and is used for receiving email from existing Exchange servers within your organization.
- **Client** requires Basic, TLS, or Integrated Windows authentication and is used for receiving emails from POP3 and IMAP4 users within your organization.
- **Partner** requires TLS authentication and is used for trusted email servers that are not directly part of your organization.
- **Custom** does not specify a default authentication method or apply to specific users or computers. After creating a custom receive connector, you must edit the connector properties to specify the appropriate authentication and permissions group options.

⊘ CREATE A NEW CUSTOM RECEIVE CONNECTOR

GET READY. Turn on the Hub or Edge role computer, and log in as the Administrator user account. Close any windows that appear on the desktop.

1. Click **Start**, **All Programs**, **Microsoft Exchange Server 2007**, and then click **Exchange Management Console**. The Exchange Management Console window appears.

2. If you are creating a receive connector on an Edge role server, click **Edge Transport** in the console tree, select your server in the result pane and highlight the **Receive Connectors** tab in the work pane. Alternatively, if you are creating a receive connector on a Hub role server, expand **Server Configuration** in the console tree, click **Hub Transport** and highlight your server in the result pane.

3. In the action pane, click **New Receive Connector**. The New SMTP Receive Connector window appears as shown in Figure 4-33.

Figure 4-33

Creating a New SMTP Receive Connector

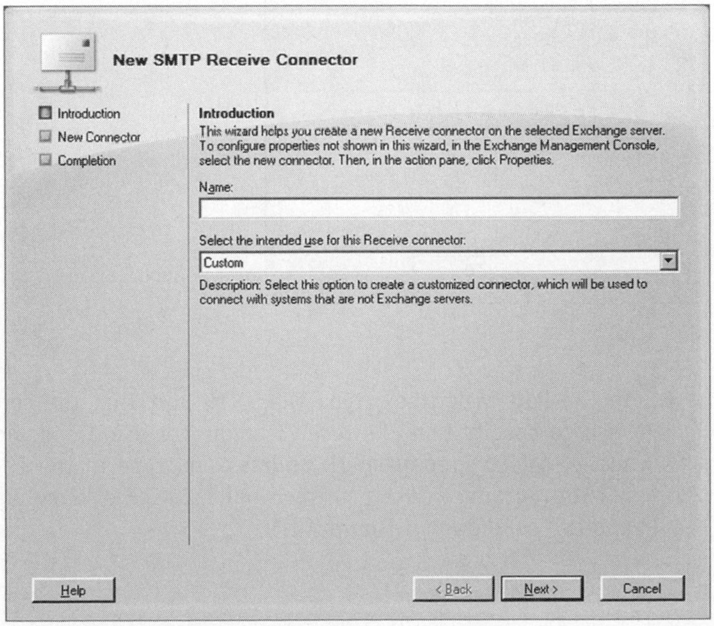

4. In the **Name** field, type a descriptive name for your receive connector. In the **Select the intended use for this Receive connector** drop-down box, ensure that Custom is selected and click **Next**. The Local Network settings page appears as shown in Figure 4-34.

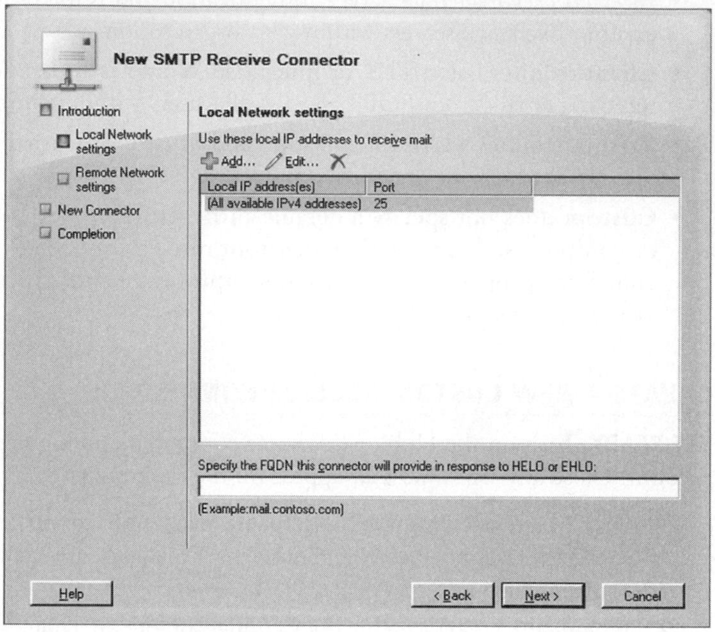

Figure 4-34

Specifying Network Settings

5. Type the FQDN of your server in the dialog box at the bottom of the screen and click **Edit**. The Edit Receive Connector Binding window appears as shown in Figure 4-35.

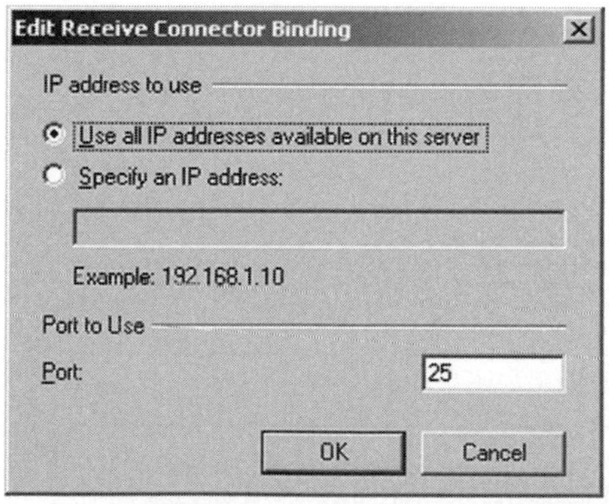

Figure 4-35

Editing Local Network Settings

6. In the Port dialog box, type the SMTP port that the connector will use. If you wish to specify that the receive connector use a specific network interface on your server, select **Specify an IP address** and type in the IP address on the desired network interface. When finished, click **OK**. The Remote Network settings page appears as shown in Figure 4-36.

Figure 4-36

Specifying Remote Network Settings

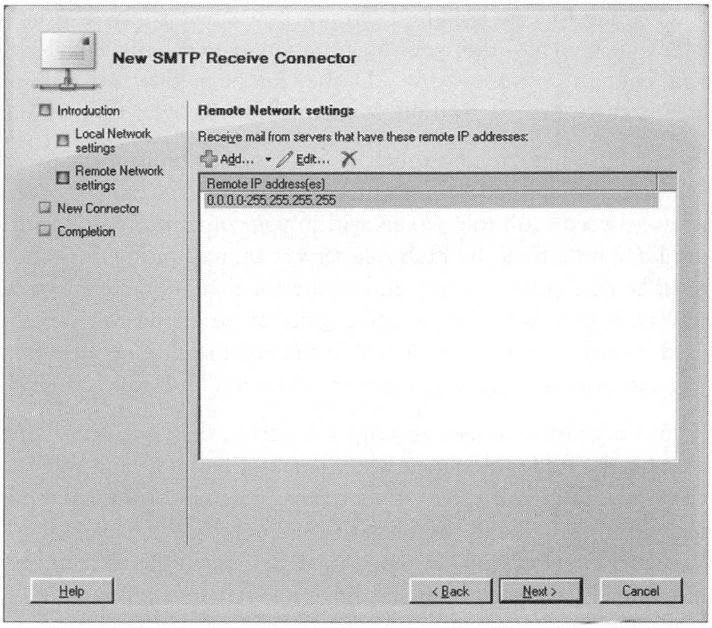

New SMTP Receive Connector

☐ Introduction
  ☐ Local Network settings
  ☐ Remote Network settings
☐ New Connector
☐ Completion

Remote Network settings

Receive mail from servers that have these remote IP addresses:

➕Add... ▾ / Edit... ✕

Remote IP address(es)
0.0.0.0-255.255.255.255

Help   < Back   Next >   Cancel

7. By default, email is accepted from all remote computers. To specify the computers that the connector will accept email from, you can click **Edit** and supply an alternate IP address range or click the arrow next to the Add button, select the appropriate criteria, and supply the appropriate information. When you have finished specifying the appropriate IP information, click **Next**. The New Connector page appears.

8. Review your selections and click **New**. The Completion page appears.

9. Click **Finish** to close the New SMTP Receive Connector window.

10. Close the Exchange Management Console.

THE COMMAND LINE WAY

You can also use the **New-ReceiveConnector** cmdlet in the Exchange Management Shell to create receive connectors. For example, to create a custom receive connector called "SMTP for Port 7299" that accepts SMTP traffic on port 7299 on the network interface on your server with the IP 192.168.1.135 from other computers with IP addresses in the range 192.168.1.1 through 192.168.1.200, you could run the following command in the Exchange Management Shell:

New-ReceiveConnector -Name "SMTP for Port 7299" -Bindings 192.168.1.135:7299 -RemoteIPRanges 192.168.1.1-192.168.1.200

You can also use the **Get-Receive Connector** cmdlet to obtain information about the configuration of an existing receive connector, the **Set-ReceiveConnector** cmdlet to modify an existing receive connector, or the **Remove-ReceiveConnector** cmdlet to remove a receive connector. For more information on the usage of these cmdlets, search for them in Exchange Server 2007 Help.

Configuring Send Connectors

To relay email to other Exchange servers within your Exchange organization as well as to external email servers on the Internet, your Hub and Edge role servers must be configured with the appropriate send connectors. Understanding how to create and modify send connectors is essential for providing email relay within your organization.

Send connectors are used to determine how email is relayed from your Exchange server to other Exchange servers within your organization or to external email servers on the Internet. Because send connectors are stored in AD, they can be used by any Hub or Edge role server within your organization, but are typically configured for use by specific Hub or Edge role servers.

By default, there are no explicit send connectors automatically created on a Hub server. However, hidden send connectors are built into Exchange Server 2007 to allow for email relay between Hub role servers within your organization. If your organization does not use the Edge role, then the Hub role servers are responsible for sending email to the Internet and must be configured with a send connector that allows email to be forwarded to external email servers. When you create a send connector on a Hub role server, that send connector can be used by any Hub role server within the organization because it is stored in AD. Alternatively, you can associate a send connector to specific Hub role servers during creation.

If your organization uses an Edge role server, then two send connectors are automatically created for the Edge role server when it subscribes to a Hub role server. The first send connector allows the Edge role server to send email to all locations on the Internet, whereas the second send connector allows the Edge role server to relay email to the Hub role servers within your Exchange organization. In short, these two default send connectors allow for Internet email functionality on your Hub and Edge role servers.

Because send connectors are stored in AD, the two default send connectors for each Edge role server are replicated from Hub role servers to the Edge role servers using EdgeSync. As a result, to modify a send connector for an Edge role server, you must modify the send connector on a Hub role server and allow the changes to propagate to the Edge role server.

CONFIGURING EXISTING SEND CONNECTORS

As with receive connectors, you must view the properties of a send connector in order to configure it. To locate the send connectors used by Hub and Edge role servers in your organization, you can navigate to **Organization Configuration** > **Hub Transport** within the Exchange Management Console and highlight the **Send Connectors** tab in the result pane as shown in Figure 4-37.

Figure 4-37

Viewing Send Connectors

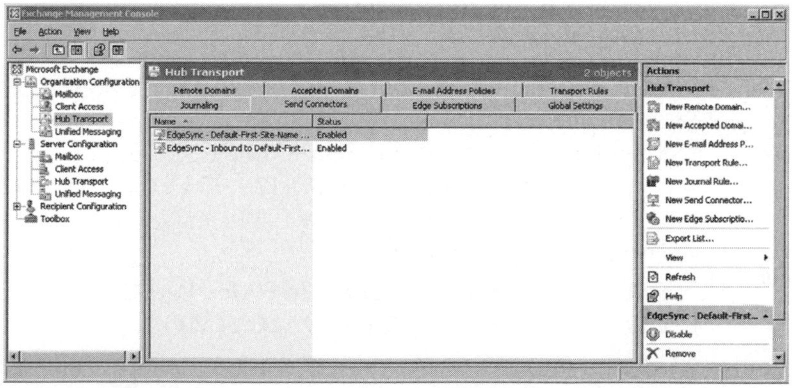

> **TAKE NOTE** * You can temporarily prevent a send connector from being used within the Exchange Management Console by selecting **Disable** in the action pane.

When you select **Properties** in the action pane for an existing connector, you can specify the FQDN used when your email server responds to SMTP connection attempts as well as the maximum message size that your email server will send on the General tab as shown in Figure 4-38. If you select **Verbose** in the **Protocol logging level** drop-down box, information regarding all connections will be logged to files in the C:\Program Files\Microsoft\ Exchange Server\TransportRoles\Logs\ProtocolLog\SmtpSend directory.

Figure 4-38

Send Connector Properties
General Tab

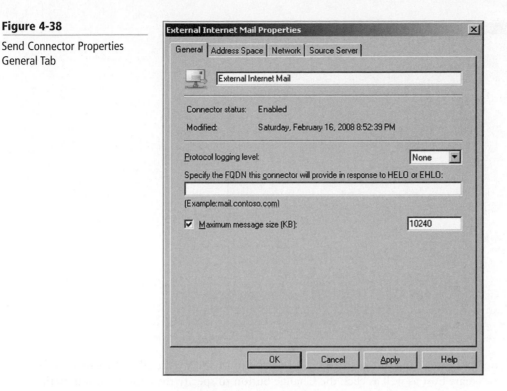

To specify the target DNS domains that the send connector will apply to, you must use the Address Space tab of send connector properties. The Address Space tab as shown in Figure 4-39 applies to all external DNS domains on the Internet (*). Alternatively, to control sent emails, you can specify certain domains on the Address Space tab for each connector and later specify that different Edge or Hub role servers use different connectors. If you add multiple DNS domains to the list, the lines with the lowest cost value are processed first. To specify that only Hub role servers in the same AD site can use the send connector, you can select the **Scoped Send connector** checkbox.

Figure 4-39

Send Connector Properties
Address Space Tab

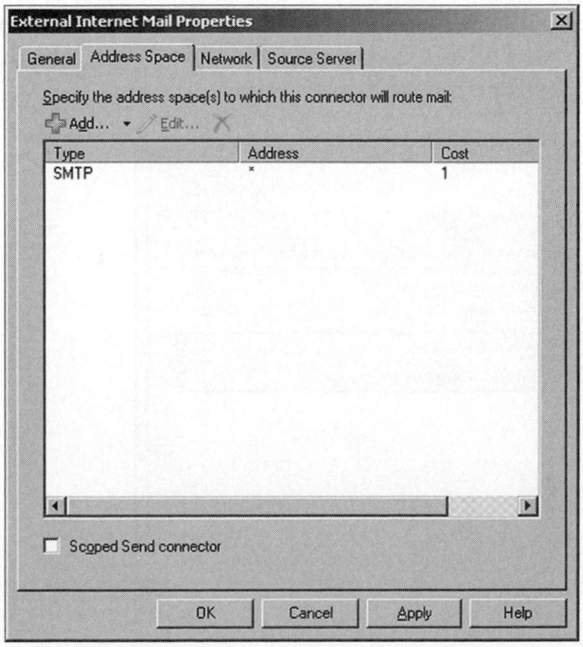

When locating target email servers to relay email to, Hub and Edge servers use DNS MX records by default. However, you can configure your Hub or Edge servers to forward outgoing email to a smart host using the Network tab of send connector properties as shown in Figure 4-40.

Figure 4-40

Send Connector Properties
Network Tab

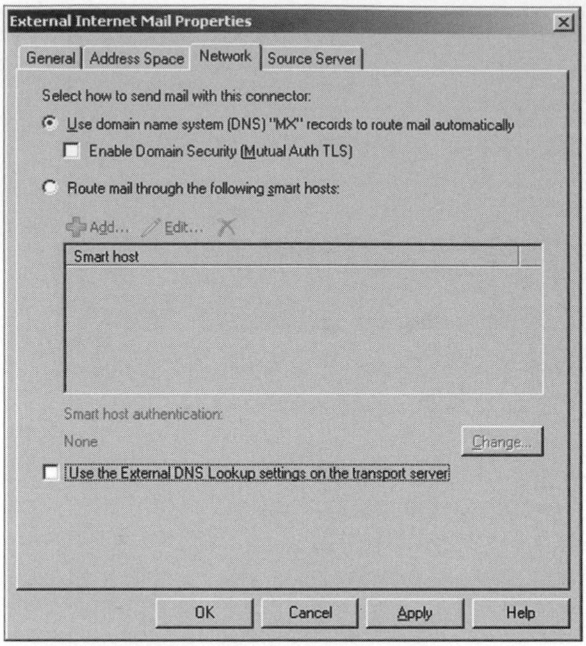

If you configure a smart host in Figure 4-40, you must specify the IP address or FQDN of the smart host as well as click the Change button to specify the authentication method required by the smart host server.

In some organizations, the internal DNS servers within the organization are not configured to resolve names on the Internet. In this case, it is important to ensure that you check **Use the External DNS Lookup settings on the transport server** in Figure 4-40. Following this, you must configure the IP address of at least one external DNS server that can resolve Internet DNS names on the **External DNS Lookups** tab of the Hub or Edge role server in the Exchange Management Console as shown in Figure 4-41. You can access the Edge role server properties by navigating to **Edge Transport** in the Exchange Management Console, highlighting your Edge role server in the details pane and clicking **Properties** in the action pane. To access the properties of a Hub role server, you can navigate to **Server Configuration** > **Hub Transport** in the Exchange Management Console, select your Hub role server in the details pane and click **Properties** in the action pane.

Figure 4-41

Exchange Server Properties
External DNS Lookups Tab

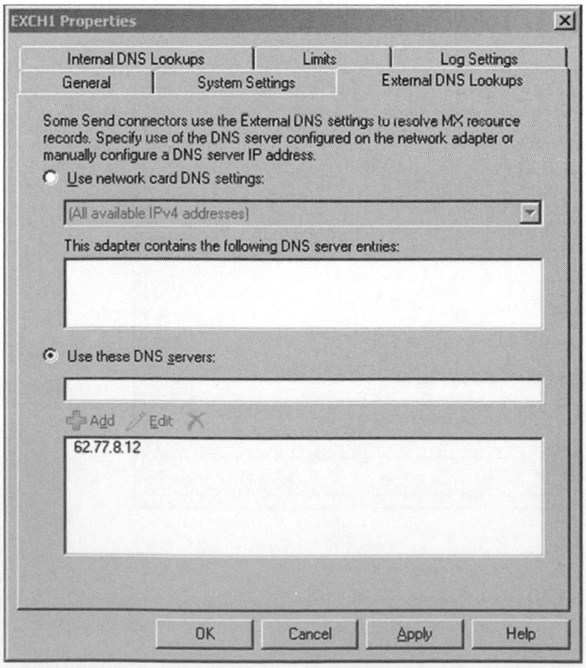

Once you have specified network settings, you can associate a send connector with specific servers on the Source Server tab of send connector properties as shown in Figure 4-42. Although you can add multiple servers to this list, you cannot add Hub role servers as well as Edge role servers to the same connector.

Figure 4-42

Send Connector Properties
Source Server Tab

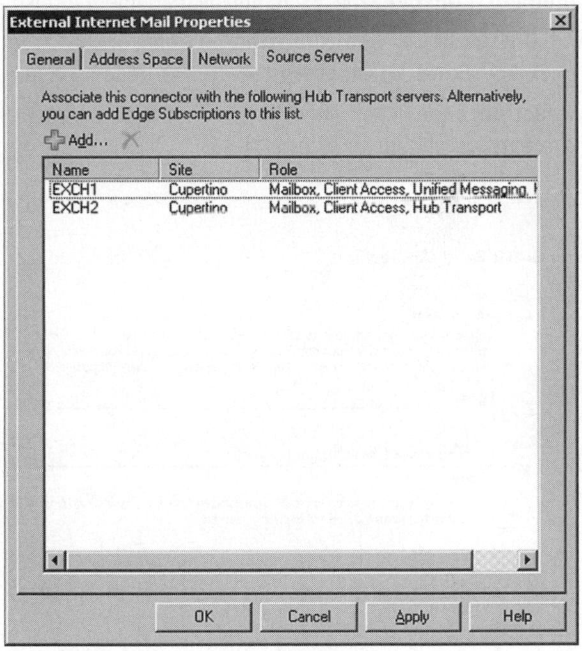

CREATING SEND CONNECTORS

By default, the Hub role servers within your organization can relay email internally. After subscribing an Edge role server to a Hub role server, the Hub role servers within your site can use the Edge role server to relay external Internet email using the default send connectors.

However, you will need to create send connectors on your Hub role servers if your organization does not use the Edge role or if you wish to customize email relay. By creating several send connectors that apply to different DNS domains and apply to different Edge or Hub servers, you can control which email servers relay email to particular DNS domains.

To simplify specifying the address space and source servers, you are prompted to select one of the following intended use options when you create a new send connector:

- **Internal** is used to route email through other Exchange servers within your organization. Because all Exchange servers in your Exchange organization can automatically relay email to one another using AD site information, you only need to select this option if you wish to customize internal email relay.

- **Internet** is used to send email to all domains on the Internet. This option is appropriate when creating send connectors for Hub role servers in your organization when the Edge role is not used.

- **Partner** is used to relay email to specific email servers that are not directly part of your organization.

- **Custom** does not specify a default address space or source server. This option allows you to specify all aspects of a send connector.

⊖ CREATE A NEW CUSTOM SEND CONNECTOR

GET READY. Turn on the Hub role computer, and log in as the Administrator user account. Close any windows that appear on the desktop.

1. Click **Start**, **All Programs**, **Microsoft Exchange Server 2007**, and then click **Exchange Management Console**. The Exchange Management Console window appears.

2. Expand **Organization Configuration** in the console tree, highlight **Hub Transport**, and click the **Send Connectors** tab in the result pane.

3. In the action pane, click **New Send Connector**. The New SMTP Send Connector window appears as shown in Figure 4-43.

Figure 4-43

Creating a New SMTP Send Connector

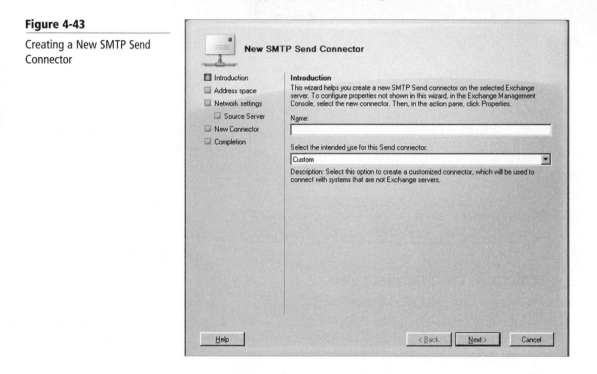

4. In the **Name** field, type a descriptive name for your send connector. In the **Select the intended use for this Send connector** drop-down box, ensure that Custom is selected and click **Next**. The Address space page appears as shown in Figure 4-44.

Figure 4-44

Specifying the Address Space

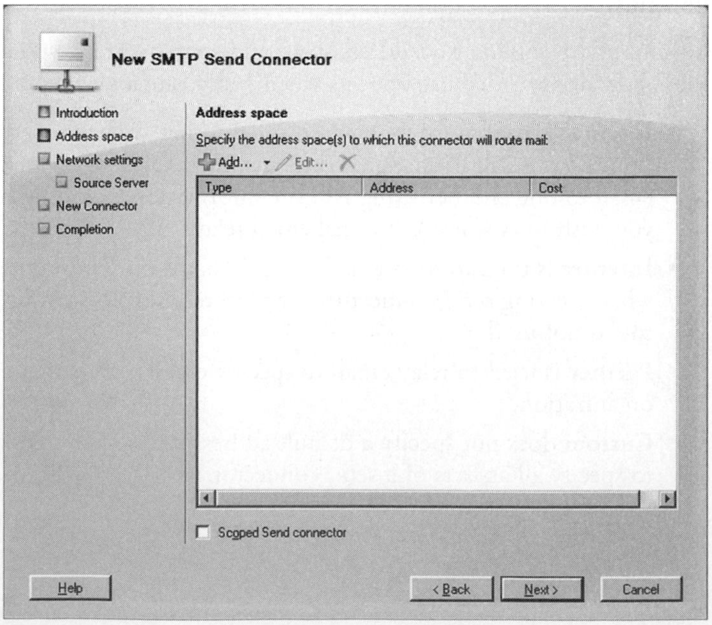

5. Click **Add.** The SMTP Address Space page appears as shown in Figure 4-45.

Figure 4-45

Adding an Address Space

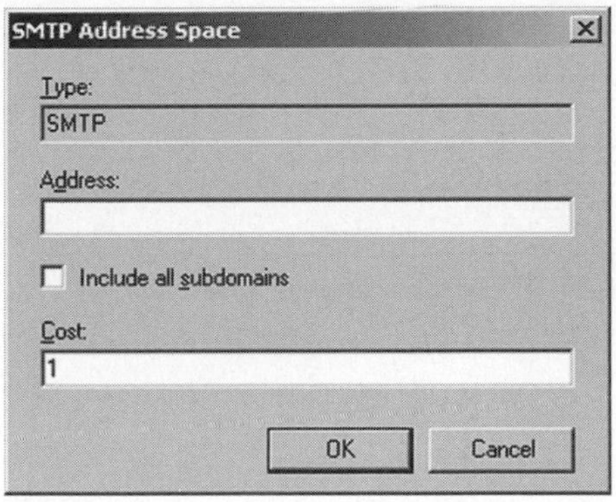

SMTP Address Space   ☒

Type:

SMTP

Address:

☐ Include all subdomains

Cost:

1

OK   Cancel

If you want your connector to apply to all Internet domains, type* in the Address dialog box and select **Include all subdomains.**

6. In the Address dialog box, type the DNS domain name that the send connector should apply to. Select **Include all subdomains** to apply the connector to all subordinate domains of the DNS domain name that you typed in the Address dialog box and click **OK** to close the SMTP Address Space window.

7. If you wish to apply the connector to the Hub servers in your AD site only, select **Scoped Send connector.** Click **Next.** The Network settings page appears as shown in Figure 4-46.

Figure 4-46

Specifying Network Settings

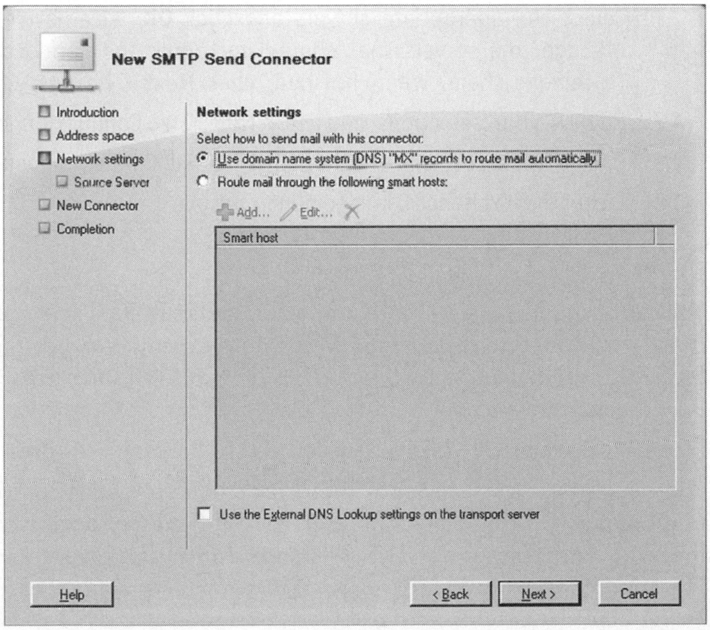

New SMTP Send Connector

☐ Introduction
☐ Address space
☐ Network settings
  ☐ Source Server
☐ New Connector
☐ Completion

Network settings

Select how to send mail with this connector:

◉ Use domain name system (DNS) "MX" records to route mail automatically

○ Route mail through the following smart hosts:

➕ Add... ✏ Edit... ✖

Smart host

☐ Use the External DNS Lookup settings on the transport server

Help   < Back   Next >   Cancel

8. If email sent to the address space on this connector should be forwarded to a smart host, select **Route mail through the following smart hosts** and click **Add.** In the Add smart host window, specify the IP address or FQDN of your smart host and click **OK.**

9. If the connector should use an external DNS server listed in your Hub or Edge role server properties, click **Use the External DNS Lookup settings on the transport server.**

10. Click **Next**. The Source Server page appears as shown in Figure 4-47.

Figure 4-47

Specifying Source Servers

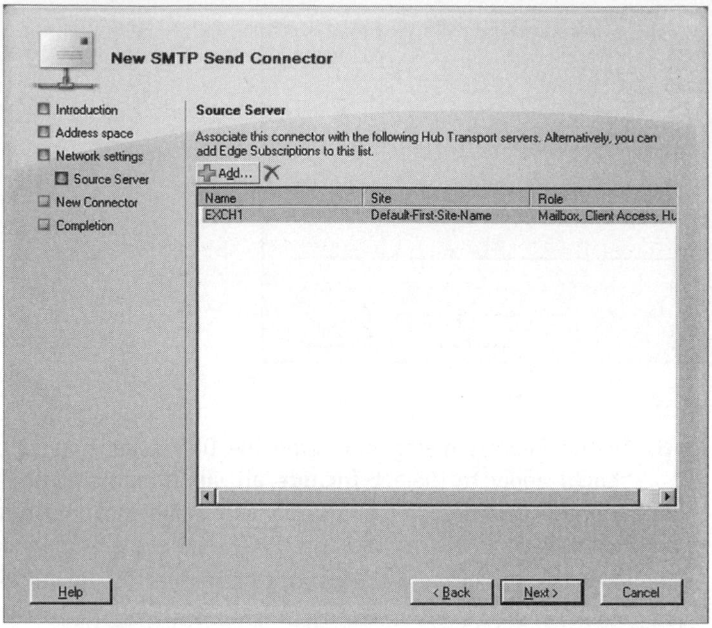

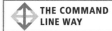

11. To apply the send connector to additional Hub or Edge role servers, click **Add**, select the appropriate servers and click **OK**. Alternatively, you can select any Hub or Edge role servers that should not apply the connector and press the red **X** icon to remove them. When finished, click **Next**. The New Connector page appears.

12. Review your selections and click **New**. The Completion page appears.

13. Click **Finish** to close the New SMTP Send Connector window.

14. Close the Exchange Management Console.

THE COMMAND LINE WAY

You can also use the **New-SendConnector** cmdlet in the Exchange Management Shell to create send connectors. For example, to create a custom send connector called "Internet SMTP Relay" that relays SMTP traffic addressed to all Internet DNS domains using any Exchange server, you could run the following command in the Exchange Management Shell:

New-SendConnector -Name "Internet SMTP Relay" -AddressSpaces*

You can also use the **Get-SendConnector** cmdlet to obtain information about the configuration of an existing send connector, the **Set-SendConnector** cmdlet to modify an existing send connector, or the **Remove-SendConnector** cmdlet to remove a send connector. For more information on the usage of these cmdlets, simply search for them in Exchange Server 2007 Help.

■ Configuring Clients

THE BOTTOM LINE

The configuration of an email system does not stop once the email servers have been prepared. For an email system to work, email clients must be configured to utilize the various email servers within your organization to send and receive email. Regardless of whether you are deploying Exchange for the first time or adding additional Exchange servers to your Exchange organization, you will likely need to configure new email clients or reconfigure existing clients in order for them to take advantage of your new email infrastructure.

Client Considerations

There is a wide variety of email client programs that can be used alongside different email protocols to access email servers from within the organization or from across the Internet. As a result, you should understand the different types of email client configurations possible before configuring email clients.

Configuring client computers varies tremendously in different situations. Email clients can be configured to interact with your email servers using a variety of different email protocols such as POP3 or MAPI RPC. Moreover, different email client programs support different protocols and protocol options. Although there are dozens of available different email client programs on the Internet, we restrict our discussion to Microsoft email client programs in this lesson. Table 4-2 lists these email client programs and their protocol support.

Table 4-2

Common email client programs

EMAIL CLIENT PROGRAM	EMAIL PROTOCOLS SUPPORTED
Microsoft Outlook 2003 Microsoft Outlook 2007	MAPI RPC POP3/POP3S IMAP4/IMAP4S SMTP/SMTPS and ESMTP/ESMTPS Outlook Anywhere (RPC over HTTP/HTTPS) HTTP/HTTPS (to OWA and Windows Live Hotmail only)
Microsoft Entourage 2004 Microsoft Entourage 2008	MAPI RPC POP3/POP3S IMAP4/IMAP4S SMTP/SMTPS and ESMTP/ESMTPS HTTP/HTTPS (to OWA and Windows Live Hotmail only)
Microsoft Outlook Express Windows Mail	POP3/POP3S IMAP4/IMAP4S SMTP/SMTPS and ESMTP/ESMTPS HTTP/HTTPS

TAKE NOTE *

By default, Exchange Server 2007 configures encryption for all POP3, IMAP4, and HTTP connections in favor of greater security. Consequently, you will need to specify the appropriate POP3S, IMAP4S, or HTTPS protocol options within the client email program.

Although most email client programs support multiple email protocols, the protocol that you choose to configure is largely dependent on whether client computers are on the same LAN as your Exchange servers or whether they connect remotely from across the Internet.

Users within an organization typically use the Microsoft Office suite and connect to Exchange servers using a fast LAN. As a result, you will likely configure the MAPI RPC protocol for these clients because it works closely with Microsoft Outlook and Entourage to allow for advanced user features such as time scheduling. This configuration is referred to simply as **Exchange** or **Exchange Server** in Microsoft Outlook and Entourage because the email client connects directly to the Exchange server using the MAPI RPC protocol.

For remote email clients, you will likely set up the email client to connect to the Exchange server using the POP3, IMAP4, SMTP, HTTP, or Outlook Anywhere protocols.

If your remote email clients have Microsoft Outlook installed as part of the Microsoft Office suite, they can be configured to use Outlook Anywhere to take full advantage of the same features that they are accustomed to when connecting with Microsoft Outlook in the office.

In other situations, email clients will usually be configured to use the POP3 or IMAP4 protocol. POP3 and IMAP4 are designed for receiving email only. When you configure an email client to use POP3 or IMAP4, you must specify the name or IP address of a CAS role server within your organization that has the POP3 or IMAP4 services started. However, you must also specify the name or IP address of a Hub role server within your organization that has a receive connector to allow the email client program to send emails using SMTP. Newer email client programs use port 587 for SMTP whereas older email client programs use port 25. In most cases, by selecting the advanced or detailed configuration sections of an email client program, you can configure the port that the email account will use. This port should match the port used by a receive connector on the appropriate Hub role server.

In addition, when you configure an SMTP server for your POP3 or IMAP4 account, you can optionally select **Secure Password Authentication (SPA)** to protect SMTP authentication using a modified NTLM authentication mechanism designed specifically for email clients that are members of your domain.

Although you can configure most email client programs to use HTTP or HTTPS to connect to your Exchange servers, it connects using the OWA components within IIS. Rather than configuring an email client to use HTTP, it is much simpler to advise remote clients to enter a URL in their web browser. Because Exchange Server 2007 uses HTTPS for OWA by default, users can enter the URL **https://CAS_server/exchange/ username** in their web browser to connect to OWA where CAS_server is the name or IP address of a CAS role server in your organization that has OWA configured and the username is the logon name of the user. Depending on the configuration of IIS, you may be prompted to log in to the web server before you are able to log in to OWA as shown earlier in Figure 4-19.

ANOTHER WAY

You can also use **https:// CAS_server/exchange** or **https://CAS_server/owa** within the URL dialog box of a web browser to gain access to OWA. In both cases, OWA will use your logon credentials to determine which mailbox you require access to.

Configuring Microsoft Outlook

> The most common email client that you will set up in organizations is Microsoft Outlook. Microsoft Outlook is bundled with the Microsoft Office suite and allows users to send and receive email using any protocol.

CERTIFICATION READY?
Configure client connectivity.
3.6

Microsoft Outlook is part of the Microsoft Office program suite and currently the most common email client program used to connect to Exchange servers in organizations. Because most organizations deploy the Microsoft Office suite on the computers on the internal LAN, Outlook is often configured to use the MAPI RPC protocol to connect to Exchange servers. The two most recent versions of the Microsoft Office suite are Microsoft Office 2003, which includes Outlook 2003, and Microsoft Office 2007, which includes Outlook 2007.

When you start Outlook 2003 or Outlook 2007 for the first time, the Office Startup wizard appears and allows you to configure a MAPI RPC, Outlook Anywhere, POP, IMAP, or HTTP email account. To set up POP, IMAP, or HTTP accounts afterward, you can select **Account Settings** from the **Tools** menu in Outlook. Alternatively, you can set up any type of email account afterward by navigating to **Start** > **Control Panel** > **Mail**.

If you are configuring a MAPI RPC account in Outlook 2003 or later, you will be able to select **Cached Exchange Mode**. Selecting this option will cache Exchange-related information to the client computer's hard drive to speed performance. However, if the Exchange administrator makes configuration changes on the Exchange server, those changes will not take effect until the next time Outlook is started.

The steps for configuring email accounts in Outlook 2003 and Outlook 2007 are very similar. As a result, we will focus on configuring Outlook 2007 and note any differences.

CONFIGURE A NEW ACCOUNT IN MICROSOFT OUTLOOK 2007

GET READY. Turn on the client computer, and log in as the appropriate domain user account if necessary. Close any windows that appear on the desktop.

1. Click **Start**, **All Programs**, **Microsoft Office**, and then click **Microsoft Office Outlook 2007**. If the Office 2007 Startup wizard appears, click **Next**. Select **No** and click **Next**. Select **Continue with no e-mail support** and click **Finish**.

2. Close Outlook 2007.

3. Click **Start**, **Control Panel**, **Mail**. At the Mail Setup—Outlook window, click **E-mail Accounts**. If prompted to enable RSS feeds, click **Yes**. The Account Settings window appears as shown in Figure 4-48.

Figure 4-48

Outlook Account Settings

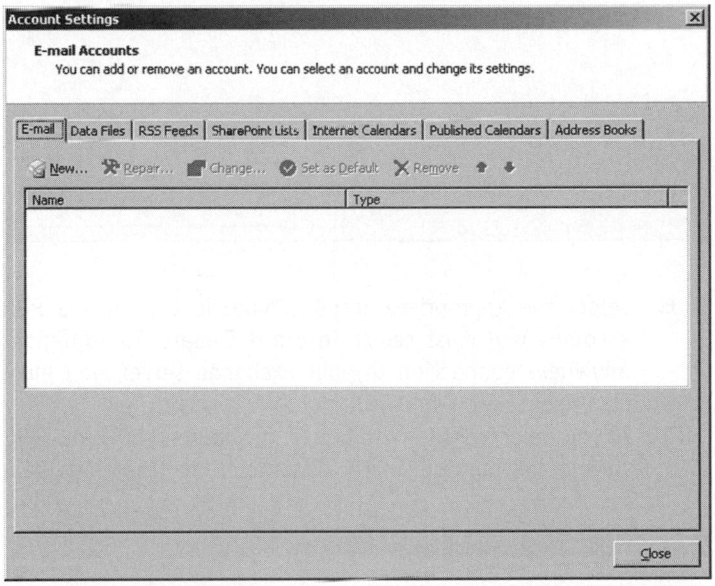

In Outlook 2003, you are prompted to Add a new e-mail account when you click E-mail Accounts at the Mail Setup—Outlook window. Following this, you must select the type of email account (Microsoft Exchange Server using MAPI RPC, POP3, IMAP, or HTTP). Following this, the configuration options for each protocol are nearly identical to those in Outlook 2007.

TAKE NOTE*

4. In the Account Settings window, click **New**. The Add New E-mail Account window appears as shown in Figure 4-49.

Figure 4-49

Adding a New Outlook Account

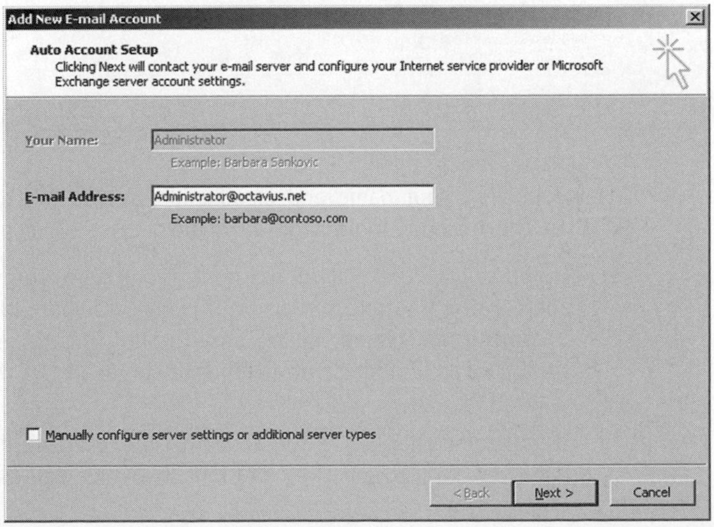

5. Select **Manually configure server settings or additional server types** and click **Next**. The Choose E-mail Service page appears as shown in Figure 4-50.

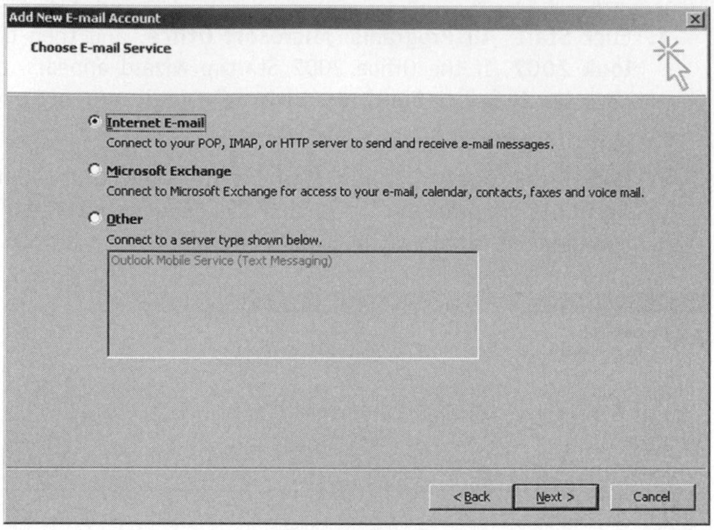

Figure 4-50

Specifying the Account Type

6. Select the appropriate account type. To configure a POP, IMAP, or HTTP-based account, you must select **Internet E-mail**. To configure a MAPI RPC or Outlook Anywhere connection to your Exchange server, you must select **Microsoft Exchange**. Click **Next** when finished.

7. If you selected Internet E-mail in Figure 4-50, you will be prompted to supply the correct information on the Internet E-mail Settings page shown in Figure 4-51.

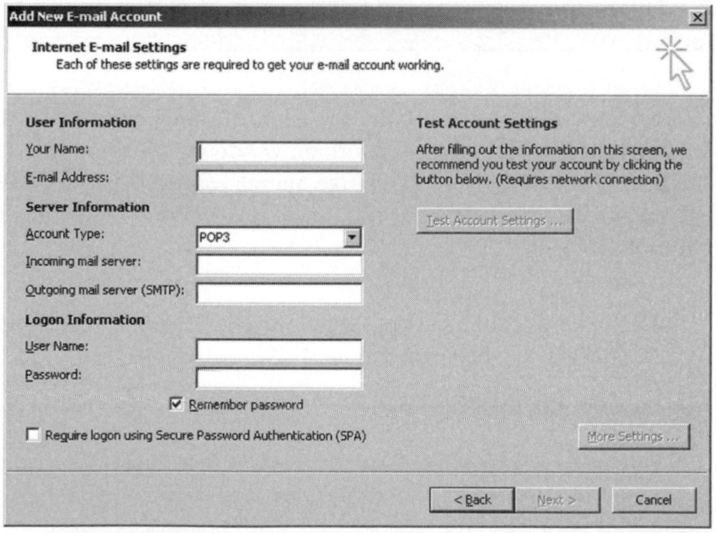

Figure 4-51

Configuring POP, IMAP, and HTTP Settings

After supplying your name and email address, you must select either **POP**, **IMAP**, or **HTTP** in the **Account Type** drop-down box.

a. If you select POP or IMAP as the account type, you must specify the FQDN or IP address of a CAS role server running the associated POP or IMAP service in the **Incoming mail server** dialog box. In addition, to send email you must supply the FQDN or IP address of a Hub role server in the **Outgoing mail server (SMTP)** dialog box.

b. If you selected HTTP as the account type, you will be allowed to select your HTTP service provider (i.e., Hotmail, OWA) as well as the associated URL.

Most email servers require authentication, so you must supply the appropriate username and password in the Logon Information section. If your email client is part of a Windows domain, you can also select **Require logon using Secure Password Authentication (SPA)** to provide additional security when sending email to your SMTP server.

After you have provided the required information, you can optionally click the **More Settings** button to specify different port numbers, credentials for outgoing SMTP traffic, and encryption. Because Exchange Server 2007 uses POP3S and IMAP4S by default, you must click **More Settings**, highlight the Advanced tab, and select the appropriate option to configure SSL. Figure 4-52 shows an SSL configuration for POP3S.

Figure 4-52

Configuring Advanced Account Settings

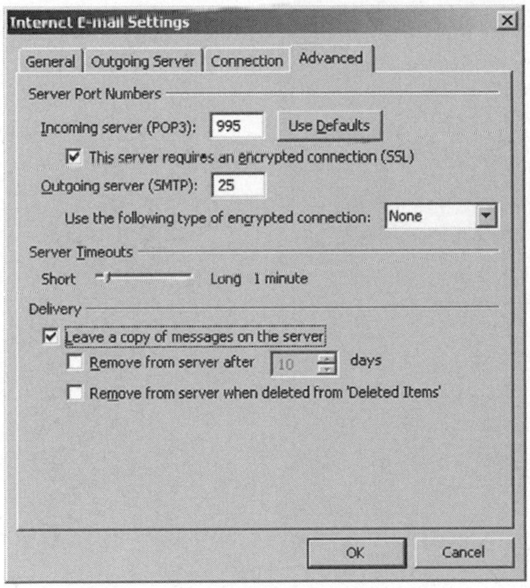

The Advanced tab for a POP connection also allows you to optionally configure POP3 to leave copies of email on the server just as IMAP4 does. Figure 4-52 has this option configured as well. Once you click **OK** in Figure 4-52, you can click **Test Account Settings** as shown in Figure 4-51 to ensure that the email servers can be successfully contacted from your computer.

8. Alternatively, if you selected Microsoft Exchange in Figure 4-50, you will be prompted to supply the FQDN or IP address of a CAS role server as well as your domain user account on the Microsoft Exchange Settings page shown in Figure 4-53.

Figure 4-53

Adding an Exchange Account

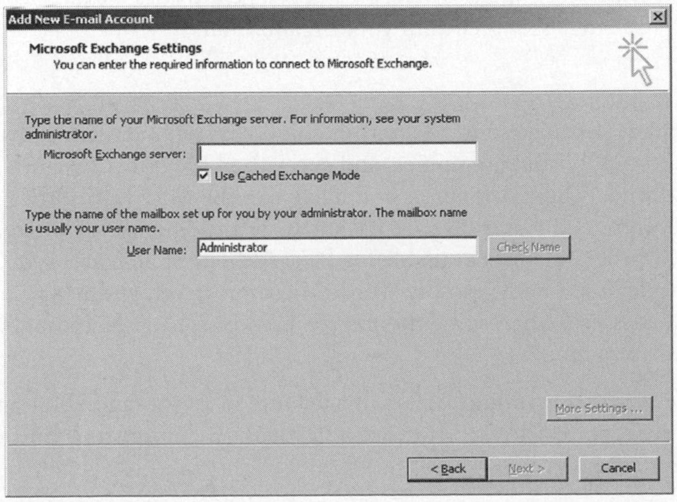

To store a copy of the user's mailbox on the local computer for fast access, ensure that the **Use Cached Exchange Mode** box is selected. Following this, you can click **Check Name** to verify the connection to the Exchange server. If the connection attempt is successful, the FQDN of the server and the user account will be underlined in the Microsoft Exchange Settings window.

To enable Outlook Anywhere, you must click **More Settings** and select **Connect to Microsoft Exchange using HTTP** on the **Connection** tab as shown in Figure 4-54. Following this you must click on the **Exchange Proxy Settings** button and specify the name of the Exchange server or ISA Server computer that is configured to accept Outlook Anywhere connections.

Figure 4-54

Configuring Outlook Anywhere Settings

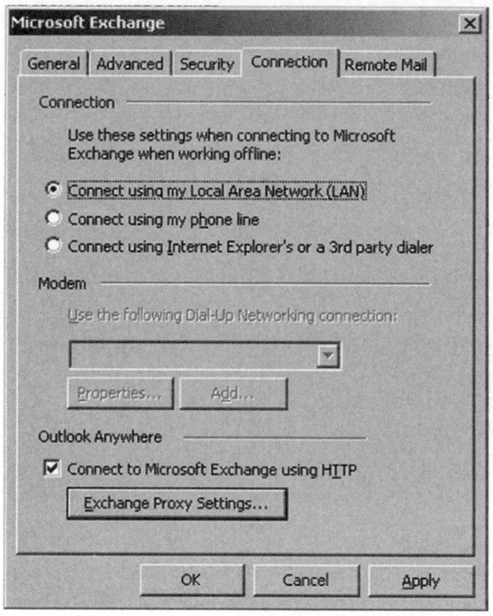

9. When finished specifying account settings, click **Next**. The Congratulations! screen appears.
10. At the Congratulations! screen, click **Finish** to close the Add New E-mail Account window.
11. Close the Mail Setup—Outlook window.

Configuring Microsoft Entourage

CERTIFICATION READY?
Configure client connectivity.
3.6

For Macintosh users, Microsoft Entourage provides a robust email client that can connect to Exchange servers within your organization.

In many organizations, Macintosh computers will be used in departments that perform desktop publishing, graphics, and specialized programs that run only on UNIX-based platforms. These computers will likely run the Microsoft Office 2004 or Microsoft Office 2008 program suites that are analogous to the Microsoft Office 2003 and Microsoft Office 2007 program suites available for PCs. Although the Microsoft Office suites for Macintosh include the same Microsoft Word, Microsoft Excel, and Microsoft PowerPoint programs that PC users use, Microsoft Entourage is used instead of Microsoft Outlook as the main email client program.

The steps for configuring email accounts in Entourage 2004 and Entourage 2008 are nearly identical. As a result, we will focus on configuring Entourage 2008 and note any differences.

CONFIGURE A NEW ACCOUNT IN MICROSOFT ENTOURAGE 2008

GET READY. Turn on the Macintosh client computer, and log in as the appropriate domain user account if necessary. Close any windows that appear on the desktop.

1. Click the Microsoft Entourage icon on the Macintosh OS X dock to open Microsoft Entourage 2008. Alternatively, you can navigate to **Macintosh HD**, **Applications**, **Microsoft Office 2008**, and then click **Microsoft Entourage** to open Microsoft Entourage 2008. If an Account Setup Assistant window appears, close the window.

2. Select the **Tools** menu and click **Accounts**. The Accounts window appears as shown in Figure 4-55.

Figure 4-55

Entourage Accounts Window

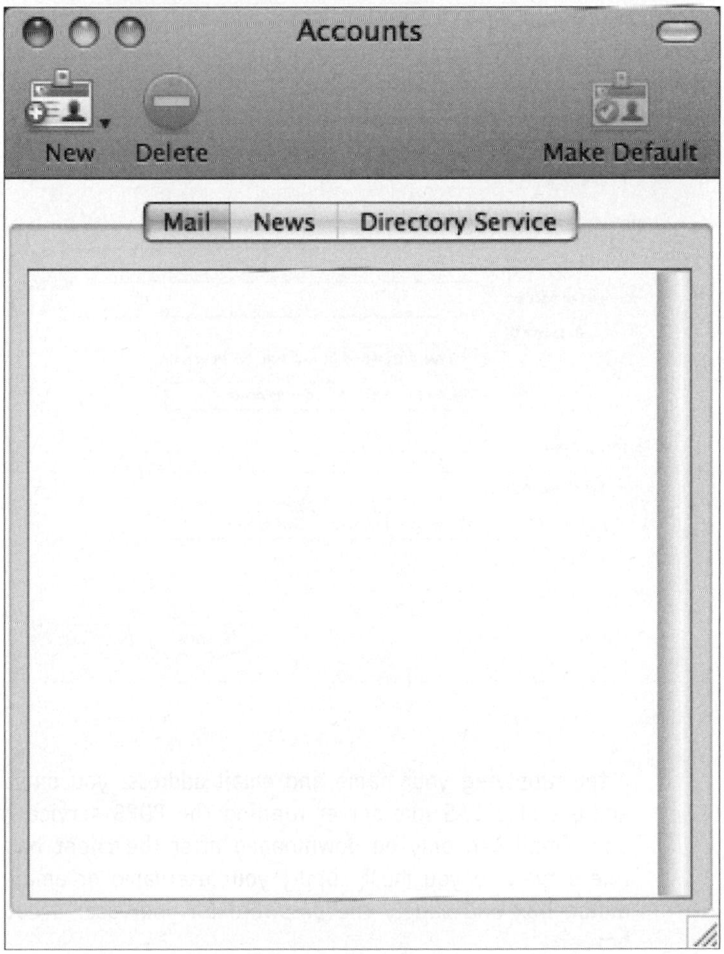

3. In the Account window, click **New**. If the Account Setup Assistant window appears, click **Configure Account Manually**, click **Cancel**, and click **New** from the Account window again. The New Account window appears as shown in Figure 4-56.

Figure 4-56

Adding a New Entourage Account

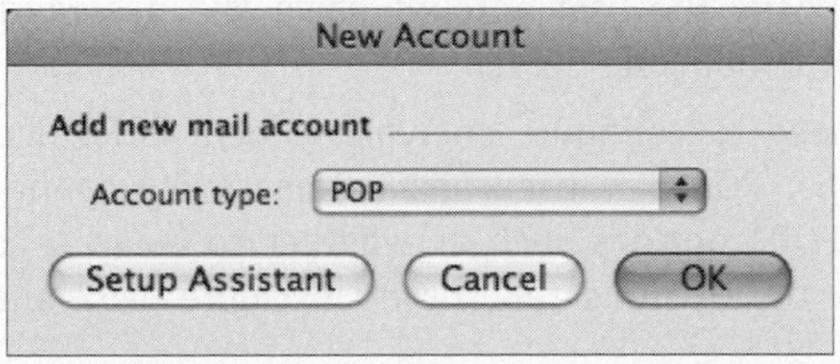

To configure a MAPI RPC account in Entourage 2004, you must first select the **Exchange** tab from the Account window before clicking the **New** button. The Exchange tab is not used in Entourage 2008.

4. Select the appropriate email protocol in the Account type drop-down box. You can select from POP, IMAP, Exchange (MAPI RPC or HTTP/HTTPS), or Windows Live Hotmail (HTTP/HTTPS). The Edit Account window appears.

5. If you selected POP as the account type in Figure 4-56, you will be prompted to supply the correct POP service information as shown in Figure 4-57.

Figure 4-57

Configuring POP Settings

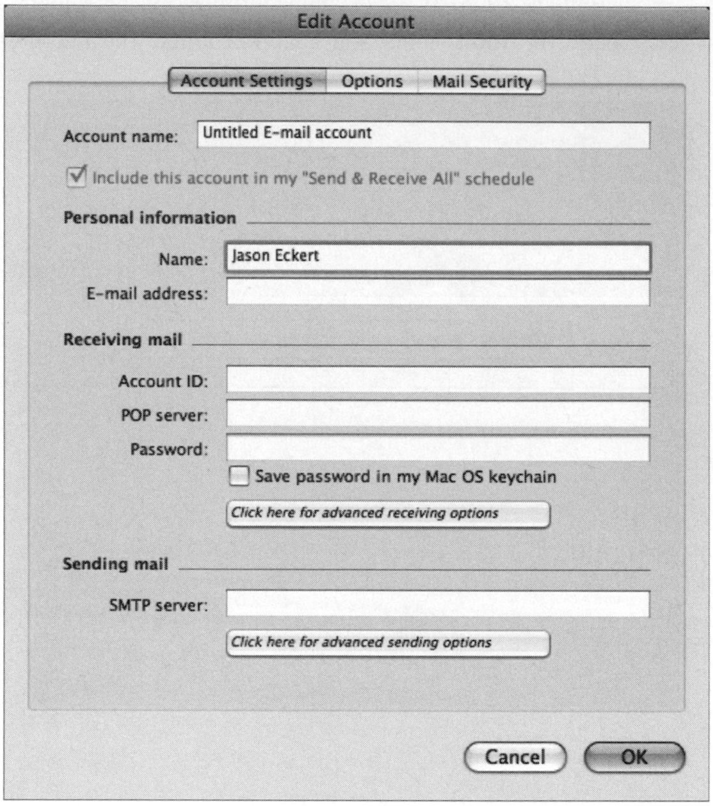

Edit Account
Account Settings   Options   Mail Security
Account name: Untitled E-mail account
☑ Include this account in my "Send & Receive All" schedule
Personal information
Name: Jason Eckert
E-mail address:
Receiving mail
Account ID:
POP server:
Password:
☐ Save password in my Mac OS keychain
Click here for advanced receiving options
Sending mail
SMTP server:
Click here for advanced sending options
Cancel   OK

After supplying your name and email address, you must supply the FQDN or IP address of a CAS role server running the POP3 service in the **POP server** dialog box. Email can only be downloaded after the client has authenticated to the CAS role server, so you must supply your username or email address in the **Account ID** dialog box and supply the password for your user account in the **Password** dialog box.

To prevent Entourage from prompting you for your password each time it is started, you must select **Save password in my Mac OS keychain**.

In addition, to send email you must supply the FQDN or IP address of a Hub role server in the **SMTP server** dialog box and click **Click here for advanced sending options** to specify the user account name and password used to authenticate when sending to your Hub role server.

You do not need to configure encryption for a POP3 account because Entourage detects whether POP3S is used and automatically configures it. However, to configure other POP3 options such as whether to leave a copy of email on the server, you can click the **Options** tab shown in Figure 4-57 and configure the appropriate options.

6. If you selected IMAP as the account type in Figure 4-56, you will be prompted to supply the correct IMAP service information as shown in Figure 4-58.

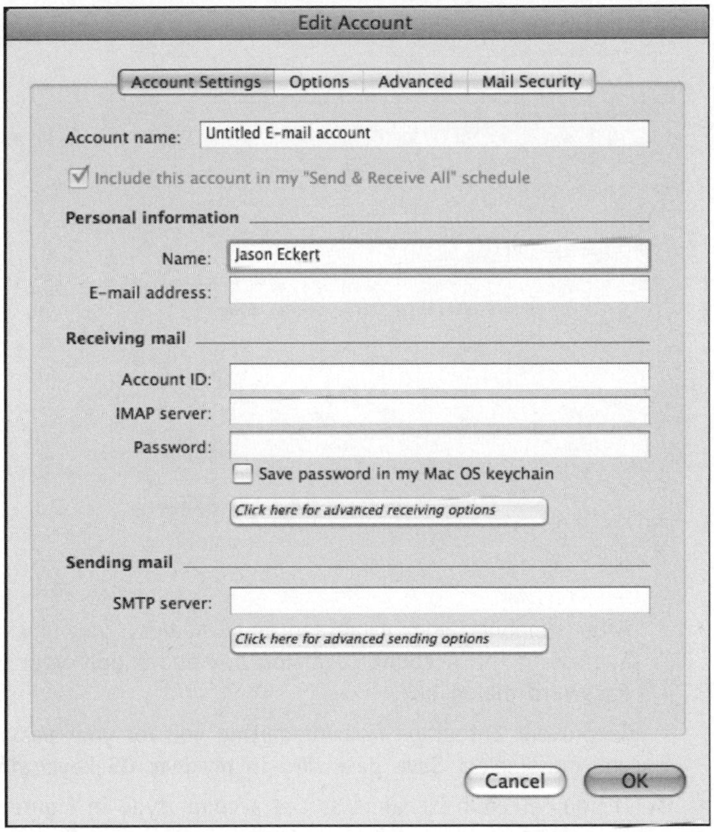

Figure 4-58

Configuring IMAP Settings

After supplying your name and email address, you must supply the FQDN or IP address of a CAS role server running the IMAP4 service in the **IMAP server** dialog box. Email can only be downloaded after the client has authenticated to the CAS role server, so you must supply your username or email address in the **Account ID** dialog box and supply the password for your user account in the **Password** dialog box.

To prevent Entourage from prompting you for your password each time it is started, you must select **Save password in my Mac OS keychain**.

In addition, to send email you must supply the FQDN or IP address of a Hub role server in the **SMTP server** dialog box and click **Click here for advanced sending options** to specify the user account name and password used to authenticate when sending to your Hub role server.

You do not need to configure encryption for an IMAP4 account because Entourage detects whether IMAP4S is used and automatically configures it. However, to configure other IMAP4 options, such as the use of public folders, you can click the **Options** tab shown in Figure 4-58 and configure the appropriate options.

7. If you selected Windows Live Hotmail as the account type in Figure 4-56, you will be prompted to supply the correct information regarding your Hotmail account as shown in Figure 4-59.

Figure 4-59

Configuring HTTP Settings

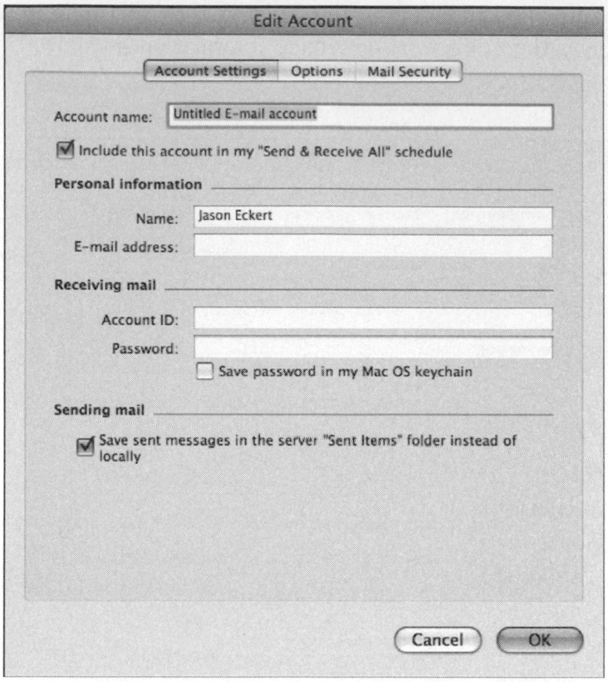

To configure a Windows Live Hotmail account, you must have a Windows Live Plus membership.

After supplying your name and email address, you must supply your Hotmail email address in the **Account ID** dialog box and supply your Hotmail password in the **Password** dialog box.

To prevent Entourage from prompting you for your password each time it is started, you must select **Save password in my Mac OS keychain**.

8. If you selected Exchange as the account type in Figure 4-56, you will be prompted to supply the correct information regarding your Exchange server and user account as shown in Figure 4-60.

Figure 4-60

Configuring Exchange Settings

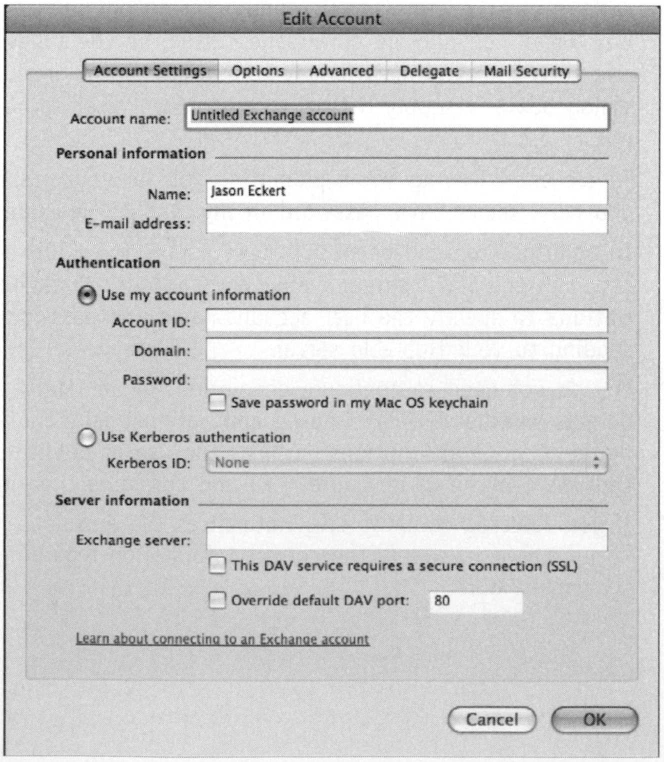

After supplying your name and email address, you must supply your domain credentials. If you select **Use my account information**, you must supply your domain user account name in the **Account ID** dialog box, the DNS name of your Windows domain in the **Domain** dialog box, and your domain user account password in the **Password** dialog box.

To prevent Entourage from prompting you for your password each time it is started, you must select **Save password in my Mac OS keychain**. Alternatively, if your Macintosh computer is a member of an AD domain in your forest, you can simply select **Use Kerberos authentication** and choose your user account from the **Kerberos ID** drop-down box.

Following this, you supply the name of your CAS role server. If you enter the FQDN of your CAS role server in the Exchange server dialog box, Entourage will use the MAPI RPC protocol to send and retrieve email. However, you can also enter the URL for OWA on your CAS role server (**http://FQDN_of_CAS_server/exchange**) to configure Entourage to use HTTP/HTTPS when sending and receiving email using the web-based *Distributed Authoring and Versioning (DAV)* service that is part of OWA.

Exchange Server 2007 uses encryption for all DAV and MAPI connections, so you must also select **This DAV service requires a secure connection (SSL)**.

9. After you have specified the appropriate information for your POP, IMAP, Exchange, or Windows Live Hotmail account, click **OK** to close the Edit Account window.

10. Close the Accounts window.

Configuring Microsoft Outlook Express and Windows Mail

> For home users, Microsoft Outlook Express and Windows Mail allow for the remote access of email using POP, IMAP, or HTTP. Because most Windows operating systems come with either of these programs, you will likely need to configure them at some point or create documentation to allow home users the ability to set up their own accounts to connect to the organization's email servers.

Unlike Microsoft Outlook and Entourage, Microsoft Outlook Express is a part of the Internet Explorer application package. As a result, it is shipped with nearly all Microsoft operating systems such as Windows 98, Windows 2000, Windows XP, and Windows Server 2003.

If your organization has users who require company email access from their PC at home, you will likely need to provide them with instructions on how to configure their Microsoft Outlook Express clients to send and receive email using your organization's Exchange servers and the POP or IMAP protocols. Alternatively, these clients can use OWA to access their email or configure Outlook Express to retrieve email using OWA.

Windows Vista uses an improved version of Microsoft Outlook Express called Windows Mail. Unlike Outlook Express, Windows Mail is not part of the Internet Explorer application package and is available exclusively for Windows Vista clients. The steps for configuring email accounts in Microsoft Outlook Express and Windows Mail are virtually identical. As a result, we will focus on configuring Microsoft Outlook Express because it has a larger install base.

CONFIGURE A NEW ACCOUNT IN MICROSOFT OUTLOOK EXPRESS

GET READY. Turn on the client computer, and log in as the appropriate domain user account if necessary. Close any windows that appear on the desktop.

1. Click **Start**, **All Programs**, and then **Outlook Express**. If you are prompted to make Outlook Express the default mail client on your computer, deselect **Always perform this check when starting Outlook Express** and click **No**. The Outlook Express window appears.

TAKE NOTE *

To configure an Exchange account type in Microsoft Entourage 2008, you must be running the Standard edition of Microsoft Office 2008 or greater.

CERTIFICATION READY?
Configure client connectivity.
3.6

2. Select the **Tools** menu, click **Accounts**. The Internet Accounts window appears as shown in Figure 4-61.

Figure 4-61

Configuring Outlook Express Accounts

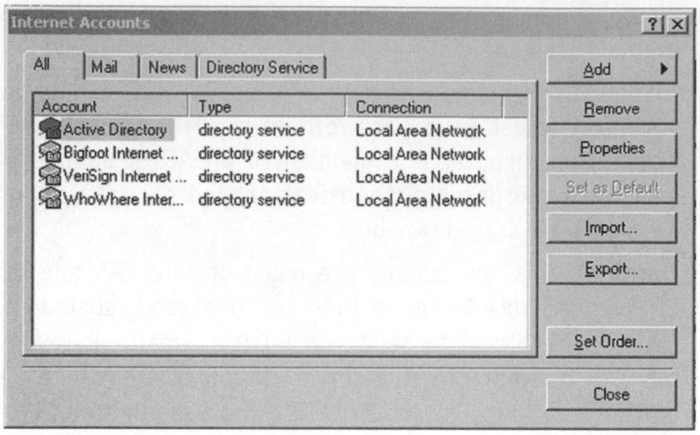

3. Click the **Add** button and select **Mail** from the side menu. The Internet Connection Wizard window appears as shown in Figure 4-62.

Figure 4-62

Setting the Display Name

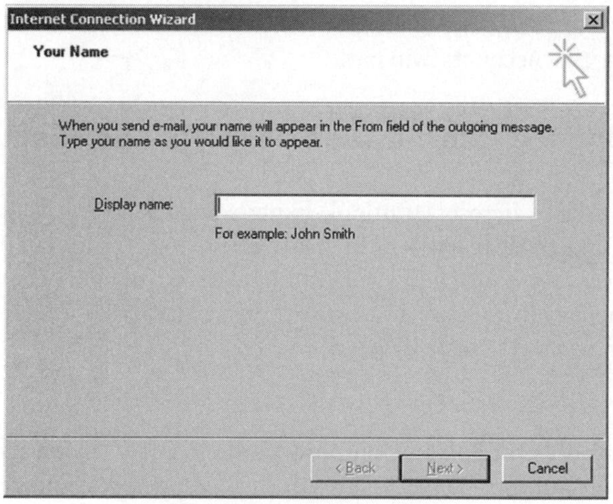

4. Type your name in the **Display name** dialog box and click **Next**. The Internet E-mail Address page appears as shown in Figure 4-63.

Figure 4-63

Setting the E-mail Address

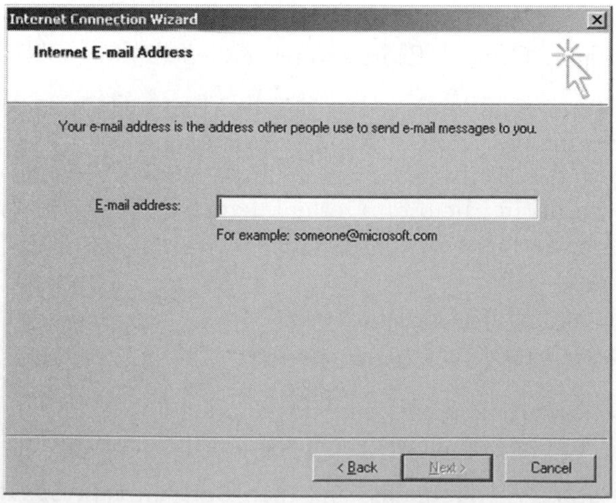

5. Type your email address in the **E-mail address** dialog box and click **Next**. The E-mail Server Names page appears as shown in Figure 4-64.

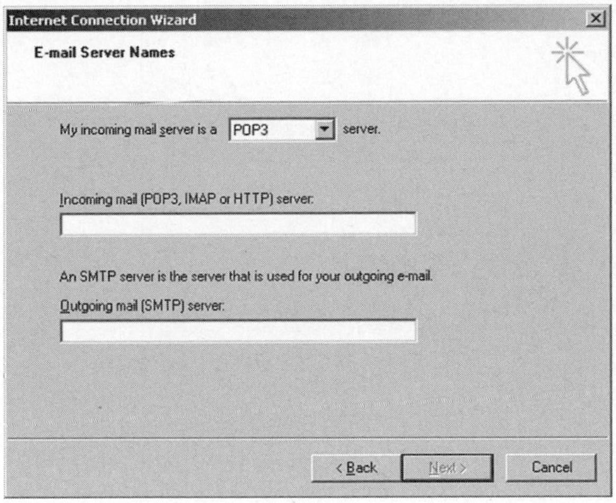

Figure 4-64

Configuring POP and IMAP Settings

6. Select the appropriate account type (**POP**, **IMAP**, **HTTP**) in the drop-down box.

7. Specify the FQDN or IP address of a CAS role server running the associated POP, IMAP, or HTTP (OWA) service in the **Incoming mail (POP3, IMAP, HTTP) server** dialog box.

    a. If you selected a POP or IMAP account type, you must also supply the FQDN or IP address of a Hub role server in the **Outgoing mail (SMTP) server** dialog box in order to send email.

    b. If you selected HTTP as the account type, you will also be allowed to select your HTTP service provider (**Hotmail**, **MSN**, **Other**) as well as the associated URL as shown in Figure 4-65. To configure Outlook Express to use OWA, you must select the **Other** provider and specify the OWA URL in the **Incoming mail (POP3, IMAP, HTTP) server** dialog box.

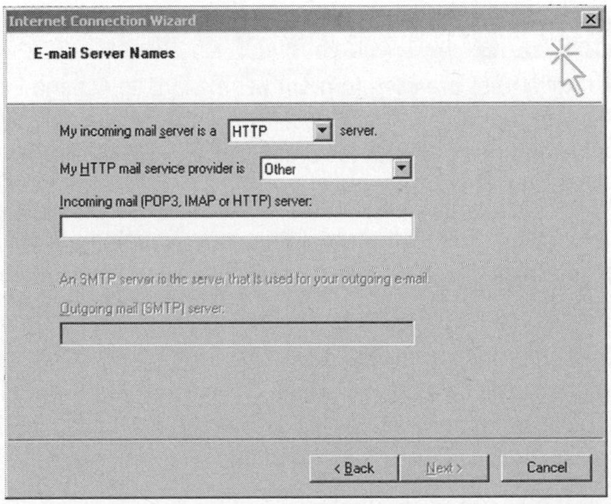

Figure 4-65

Configuring HTTP Settings

8. When finished specifying account settings, click **Next**. The Internet Mail Logon screen appears as shown in Figure 4-66.

9. Enter your user account name in the **Account name** dialog box and the associated password in the **Password** dialog box. Unless the computer is a public computer, ensure that **Remember password** is selected to prevent Outlook Express from prompting for credentials each time it is opened. If your email client is part of a Windows domain, you can also select **Logon using Secure Password Authentication (SPA)** to provide additional security when sending email to your SMTP server.

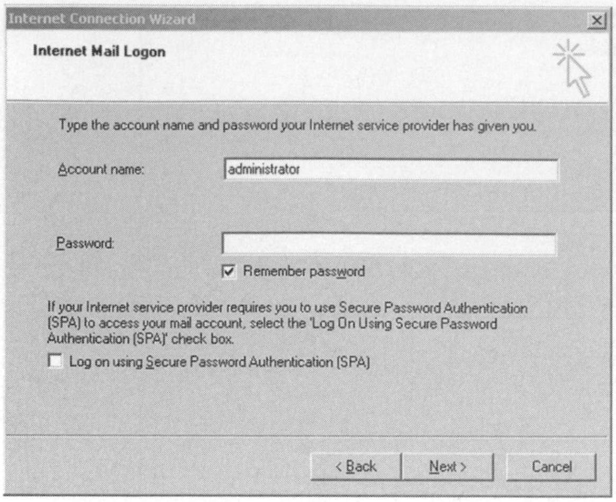

Figure 4-66

Configuring Authentication

10. Click **Next** when finished. The Congratulations page appears.

11. Click **Finish** to close the Internet Connection Wizard window. After you have added a POP3 or IMAP4 account, it is not configured for encryption (POP3S or IMAP4S). Exchange Server 2007 uses encryption by default, so you must configure the properties of the account in the Internet Accounts window afterward.

12. Highlight your POP3 or IMAP4 account in the Internet Accounts window and click **Properties**. On the Advanced tab, select **This server requires a secure connection (SSL)** for the appropriate protocol and click **OK**.

13. Close the Internet Accounts window.

SUMMARY SKILL MATRIX

IN THIS LESSON YOU LEARNED:

- Administrative roles are used to grant permissions to AD and Exchange Server 2007. You should ensure that administrative user accounts are members of the appropriate administrative role within your Exchange organization.

- To allow foreign email servers on the Internet to relay email to your Exchange servers, you should ensure that DNS MX records exist for your domain name. Depending on your email structure, MX records can resolve to the IP address of your Hub role servers, Edge role servers, or smart hosts.

- To accept and process email addressed to domain names that are not part of your AD structure, you must configure accepted domains on your Hub role servers. Email sent to accepted domain names can be sent to mailboxes within your organization or forwarded to email servers outside of your organization by Hub or Edge role servers.

- Each Hub role server can be configured with a postmaster email address that users can email if problems arise with email relay.

- Before an Edge role server can relay email, it must be subscribed to a Hub role server in the same AD site. To subscribe an Edge role server, you can create a subscription file that must be imported into a Hub role server within 24 hours.

- Email is stored in mailbox databases within storage groups on Mailbox role servers within your organization. To speed performance and provide fault tolerance, you should create additional storage groups and mailbox databases on different hard disks, as well as move the default storage groups and mailbox databases to another hard disk.

- Public folders are also stored within public folder database within storage groups on Mailbox role servers within your organization. Although you can only have one public folder database per Exchange server, this database should be moved to a different hard disk for performance and fault tolerance.

- You can configure storage limits on public folder and mailbox databases to ensure that storage space is not exhausted quickly.

- By default, a new CAS role server allows MAPI RPC, ActiveSync, and OWA connections from client computers. However, you can enable POP3, IMAP4, and Outlook Anywhere support after installation.

- To ensure security for remote users, you should configure OWA options shortly after installing a new CAS role server. You can configure different OWA options for public and private remote users.

- Connectors are used to represent email relay within your organization.

- Receive connectors are created on Hub and Edge role servers to accept SMTP email from other servers and POP or IMAP clients. Default receive connectors are created on Hub and Edge role servers.

- Send connectors are created on Hub servers to allow for email relay within the organization as well as to email servers across the Internet. Send connectors are automatically created on Edge servers once they are subscribed to a Hub role server. Hub role servers contain hidden send connectors by default that allow them to relay email to other internal Exchange servers.

- After modifying your Exchange infrastructure, you will likely need to configure client email programs. Microsoft Outlook and Entourage are part of the Microsoft Office suite and are typically used to provide MAPI RPC connections to Exchange for internal client computers. Microsoft Outlook Express and Windows Mail are bundled with most Microsoft operating systems and are often used to connect to Exchange remotely using the HTTP, POP, and IMAP protocols.

Knowledge Assessment

Fill in the Blank

Complete the following sentences by writing the correct word or words in the blanks provided.

1. Exchange Server Enterprise edition can create up to _____ databases per Mailbox role server.

2. The _____ of a send connector determines the DNS domains that the connector can relay email to.

3. After creating a subscription file on an Edge role server, you must import the subscription file into a Hub role server in the same site within _____ hours.

4. After installing a new Edge server role, you must create _____ records in _____ to allow other organizations to relay email to your organization.

5. Microsoft _____ is an email client program that is included with the Microsoft Office program suite for Macintosh computers.

6. To enable the POP3 and IMAP4 services, you must use the _____ console.

7. You can set the maximum message and mailbox size limits using the Limits tab of _____ properties.

8. You would like to ensure that all internal email addressed to your partner organization arfa.com is forwarded directly to the appropriate email servers by your Hub servers. To do this, you must create an accepted domain for arfa.com that uses _____ relay.

9. To access OWA, you can specify the URL https://servername/_____ within a web browser.

10. Edge role servers are typically installed on a _____ network.

Multiple Choice

Circle the letter that corresponds to the best answer.

1. When configuring OWA options, which selections will improve the security of your OWA clients? (Choose all that apply.)
   a. Disabling the change password feature of OWA.
   b. Disabling WebReady content viewing.
   c. Specifying more restrictive options on the Private Computer File Access tab than on the Public Computer File Access tab.
   d. Restricting the attachments that OWA users can download.

2. What intended use should you select in the New SMTP Receive Connector wizard if you wish to create a connector to match SMTP traffic from other Exchange servers within your organization?
   a. Internet   b. Internal
   c. Client   d. Custom

3. Which intended use should you select in the New SMTP Send Connector wizard if you wish to create a connector that applies to all domains on the Internet?
   a. Internet   b. Internal
   c. Custom   d. Partner

4. Which of the following email client programs has support for the MAPI RPC protocol? (Choose all that apply.)
   a. Windows Mail   b. Microsoft Outlook
   c. Microsoft Outlook Express   d. Microsoft Entourage

5. Which port do newer email client programs use when sending email using SMTP?
   a. 23   b. 25
   c. 110   d. 587

6. What could you select when setting up an Outlook 2003 or later client to allow Exchange account information to be cached to the local computer?
   a. Use Cached Exchange Mode
   b. Use security for this connection (SSL)
   c. This DAV port requires a secure connection (SSL)
   d. Enable Client Side Caching

7. Which of the following protocols are enabled by default on a new CAS role server? (Choose all that apply.)
   a. HTTP/HTTPS (OWA)   b. POP3/POP3S
   c. ActiveSync   d. MAPI RPC

8. Which of the following authentication methods on a receive connector are appropriate for POP3 and IMAP4 clients?
   a. Basic   b. Exchange Server
   c. Integrated Windows   d. TLS

9. How many databases can be created on an Exchange Server 2007 Standard edition computer?
   a. 1   b. 5
   c. 50   d. 255

10. Which of the following Exchange administrative roles is server specific?

    a. Exchange Organization Administrator

    b. Exchange Public Folder Administrator

    c. Exchange Server Administrator

    d. Exchange View-Only Administrator

True/False

Circle T if the statement is true or F if the statement is false.

T   F   **1.** Because there are no explicit send connectors created on a new Hub role server, it is unable to relay email to other Exchange servers within the organization.

T   F   **2.** POP and IMAP are commonly configured on email clients that connect remotely to a Microsoft Exchange server.

T   F   **3.** You can configure accepted domains within the Exchange Management Console on a Hub or Edge role server.

T   F   **4.** Send connectors can be created on a Hub or Edge role server.

T   F   **5.** When enabling Outlook Anywhere, the external host name typically points to a server that is running Microsoft ISA Server.

T   F   **6.** To allow POP and IMAP clients to send email, your Hub role servers must be configured with the appropriate receive connector.

T   F   **7.** Members of the Exchange Organization Administrator role can administer any server within the organization.

T   F   **8.** Windows Mail is an improved version of Microsoft Outlook and is included with the Windows Vista operating system.

T   F   **9.** If your organization uses smart hosts, the DNS MX records for your organization should point to them using a lower priority number.

T   F   **10.** Permissions groups are used to determine the users and computers that a send connector applies to.

Review Questions

1. Explain why creating multiple storage groups and mailbox databases on a single Mailbox role server provides for greater manageability and fault tolerance.

2. Explain how you can use the **Use the External DNS Lookup settings on the transport server** option on your send connectors to improve the security and performance of your email relay.

■ Case Scenarios

Scenario 4-1: Configuring an Alternate SMTP Port

As a security precaution, you have been instructed to ensure that all SMTP traffic within your organization from POP and IMAP clients be sent on port 805 rather than port 25. In a short memo, describe the steps required to allow SMTP traffic on port 805 on the Hub role servers within your organization.

Scenario 4-2: Configuring Email Clients

Your organization has recently decided to allow employees to access their company email from home after working hours using the POP3 protocol. In addition, home users will be allowed to send email using the company's SMTP servers. It is your responsibility to provide the necessary information to the people in your organization who wish to configure their home computers for POP3 email access. Assuming that employees use a variety of different operating systems and email client programs, list the steps and information that people in your organization can likely follow to set up their home computers.

Working with Recipient Objects

LESSON SKILL MATRIX

TECHNOLOGY SKILL	OBJECTIVE DOMAIN	OBJECTIVE DOMAIN NUMBER
Working with Mailbox Users	Configure recipients.	2.1
Working with Mail Users and Mail Contacts	Configure recipients.	2.1
Implementing an Exchange Resource Forest	Configure recipients.	2.1
Working with Mail-Enabled Groups	Configure mail-enabled groups.	2.2
Working with Resource Mailboxes	Configure resource mailboxes.	2.3
Moving Mailboxes	Move mailboxes.	2.5
Configuring Resource Booking Policies	Configure policies.	3.4

KEY TERMS

Active Directory Migration Tool
   (ADMT)
alias
Automatic Booking
Book-In Policy
Calendar Attendant
dynamic distribution group
Exchange resource forest
expansion server

Full Access permission
In Policy
linked mailbox user
mail contact
mail user
mail-enabled universal
   distribution group
mail-enabled universal security
   group

master account
Out Policy
recipient object
Resource Booking Attendant
resource mailbox
Send As permission
Send On Behalf permission

■ Understanding Recipient Objects

↓ THE BOTTOM LINE

Recipient objects represent the entities within your organization that use your Exchange servers for email relay and access. Before you understand how to create, configure, and manage recipient objects, you must first understand the various types of recipient objects and their usage within the organization.

When you send email, you provide a target email address in the form alias@domain where the *alias* represents the person or entity that should receive the email and domain represents the DNS domain used by the organization. Although the alias portion of an email typically represents a user within your organization or other organizations on the Internet, it can also represent a group of people, a folder, or a resource. In short, the alias portion of an email address represents the recipient of the email sent to that email address.

In general, recipients are simply objects within Exchange or Active Directory (AD) that contain an email address within your organization that Exchange can relay email to.

There are nine major types of *recipient objects* that can be created in Exchange Server 2007. Table 5-1 lists the major recipient object types and their features.

Table 5-1

Exchange Server 2007 recipients

RECIPIENT OBJECTS	DESCRIPTION
Mailbox user	User accounts within AD that have an email address within the organization as well as a mailbox on a Mailbox role server within the organization. Any email sent to a mailbox user is sent to the mailbox for the mailbox user.
Mail user	User accounts within AD that have an email address within the organization, but do not have a mailbox on any Mailbox role server within the organization. Instead, mail users have a second, external email address that is attached to their AD user account. Any email sent to the email address of a mail user within your organization is forwarded using the external email address to the appropriate email server on the Internet.
Mail contact	Objects within AD that contain an email address within the organization as well as an external email address. Any email sent to the email address of a mail contact within your organization is forwarded using the external email address to the appropriate email server on the Internet. Because mail contacts are not user account objects, they cannot be used to log in to an AD domain.
Mail-enabled universal distribution group	Universal distribution groups in AD that have an email address within the organization. Any email sent to a mail-enabled universal distribution group is forwarded to all recipient objects within the group.
Mail-enabled universal security group	Universal security groups in AD that have an email address within the organization. Any email sent to a mail-enabled universal security group is forwarded to all recipient objects within the group. In addition, mail-enabled universal security groups can be assigned permissions to domain resources such as files and printers.
Dynamic distribution group	Contains an email address within the organization as well as a set of criteria used to automatically determine its group membership. Any email sent to a dynamic distribution group is forwarded to all recipient objects that match the appropriate criteria.
Resource mailbox	Used to simplify resource scheduling when creating meeting requests using the Calendaring feature of MAPI clients such as Outlook. More specifically, resource mailboxes are disabled mailbox users that represent rooms or equipment. Like other mailbox users within your organization, resource mailboxes have an email address within the organization that is used by the Calendaring feature of MAPI clients when scheduling resource usage.
Linked mailbox user	Allows a user in one forest to access a mailbox in another forest across a trust relationship. Linked mailbox users are typically used when Exchange Server 2007 is deployed in a separate forest for security reasons or when several different forests require a single uniform Exchange infrastructure.
Mail-enabled public folder	Public folder objects that contain an email address within the organization. Any emails that are sent to a mail-enabled public folder are stored within the public folder itself.

Mail-enabled public folders will be discussed in Lesson 7, "Working with Public Folders." All other recipient objects will be discussed in this lesson.

To create and manage all recipient objects within your organization, you must be a member of the Exchange Recipient Administrator or Exchange Organization Administrator role. Members of the Exchange Public Folder Administrator role are able to create and manage mail-enabled public folders within your organization.

Working with Mailbox Users

↓
THE BOTTOM LINE

Mailbox users are the most common recipient objects that Exchange administrators work with because they represent users within an organization that have both a user account in AD and a mailbox on an Exchange server. In addition, mailbox users have the most configuration and management options. To work with mailbox users, you must understand how to create them, remove them, configure their properties, and manage their permissions.

CERTIFICATION READY?
Configure recipients.

2.1

Creating Mailbox Users

Mailbox users may be created using the Exchange Management Console or the Exchange Management Shell. During creation, you must specify an existing user account or create a new one as well as specify the mailbox settings and alias for the mailbox user.

Because most members of your organization require a mailbox hosted by email servers within your organization, mailbox users are the most common type of recipient object that you will create in Exchange Server 2007. All mailbox users require an AD user account that is connected to a mailbox within a mailbox database on a Mailbox role server within your organization.

Depending on your organization's structure and policies, Exchange administrators may also be responsible for creating AD user accounts. In that case, you can create and associate a mailbox to a new AD user account at the same time by creating a new mailbox user in the Exchange Management Console. Alternatively, if your organization separates administrative duties and requires that different administrators create new AD user accounts and mailboxes, you can simply create a mailbox and associate it to an existing AD user account in the Exchange Management Console.

Regardless of whether you are creating a new mailbox user or mailbox enabling an existing AD user, you will be prompted to supply the alias used when creating the email address for the mailbox user. Although the alias does not need to match the login name of the user, it usually does for consistency.

⊙ **CREATE A MAILBOX USER**

GET READY. Turn on the computer, and log in as the Administrator user account. Close any windows that appear on the desktop.

1. Click **Start**, **All Programs**, **Microsoft Exchange Server 2007**, and then click **Exchange Management Console**. The Exchange Management Console window appears.
2. In the console tree pane, expand **Recipient Configuration** and highlight **Mailbox**.

3. In the action pane, click **New Mailbox**. The New Mailbox window appears as shown in Figure 5-1.

Figure 5-1

Creating a New Mailbox User

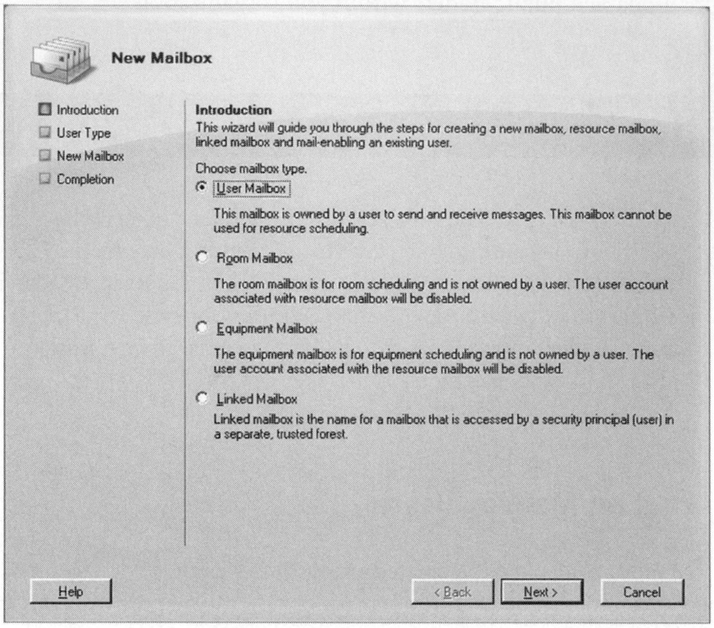

New Mailbox

- Introduction
- User Type
- New Mailbox
- Completion

Introduction
This wizard will guide you through the steps for creating a new mailbox, resource mailbox, linked mailbox and mail-enabling an existing user.

Choose mailbox type.

○ User Mailbox

This mailbox is owned by a user to send and receive messages. This mailbox cannot be used for resource scheduling.

○ Room Mailbox

The room mailbox is for room scheduling and is not owned by a user. The user account associated with resource mailbox will be disabled.

○ Equipment Mailbox

The equipment mailbox is for equipment scheduling and is not owned by a user. The user account associated with the resource mailbox will be disabled.

○ Linked Mailbox

Linked mailbox is the name for a mailbox that is accessed by a security principal (user) in a separate, trusted forest.

Help   < Back   Next >   Cancel

4. Select **User Mailbox** and click **Next**. The User Type page appears as shown in Figure 5-2.

Figure 5-2

Specifying the User Type

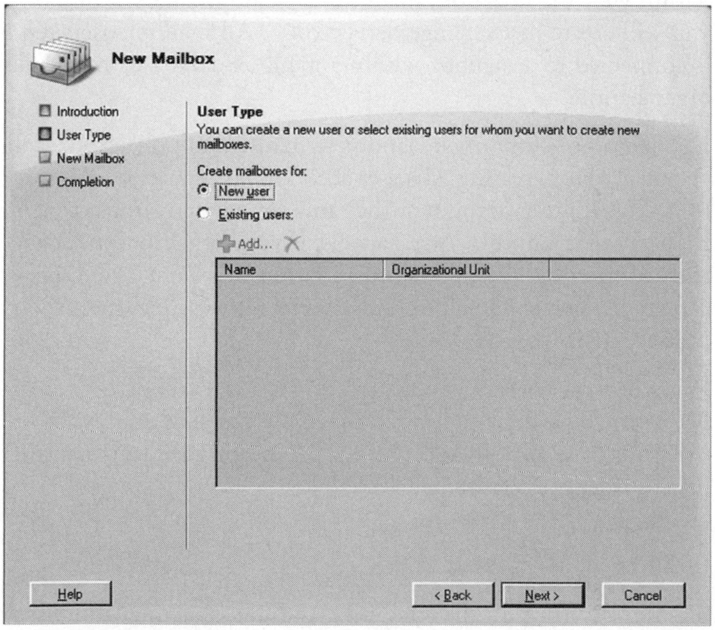

New Mailbox

- Introduction
- User Type
- New Mailbox
- Completion

User Type
You can create a new user or select existing users for whom you want to create new mailboxes.

Create mailboxes for:

○ New user

○ Existing users:

Add... ✕

Name	Organizational Unit	

Help   < Back   Next >   Cancel

5. If you wish to create a new AD user with an associated mailbox, ensure that **New user** is selected. Alternatively, you can choose to mailbox enable an existing AD user. To mailbox enable an existing user, select **Existing users**, click the **Add** button, select the appropriate user in the Select User window that appears and click **OK**.

6. Click **Next**. If you selected New user on the User Type page, you will be prompted to specify the AD user account information on the User Information page as shown in Figure 5-3.

Figure 5-3

Adding User Information

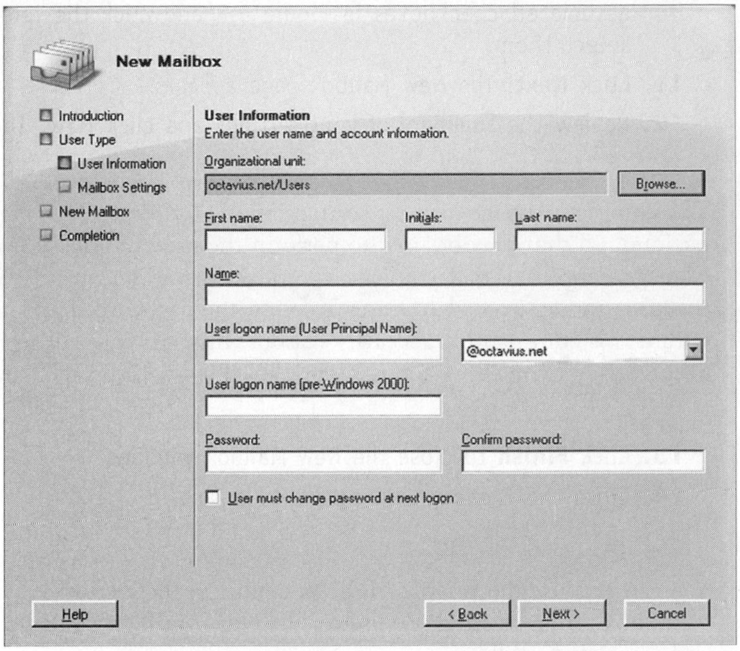

TAKE NOTE *

If you selected **Existing users** on the User Type page, you will skip entering the account information shown in Figure 5-3.

7. By default, the user will be created in the default Users folder in your current domain. Because users are rarely created in this folder, you should click **Browse**, select the appropriate Organizational Unit (OU), and click **OK**. All other account settings on this page are similar in function to the settings that you choose when creating a new user account in the Active Directory Users and Computers console as discussed in Lesson 2. When finished entering the user account information, click **Next**. The Mailbox Settings page appears as shown in Figure 5-4.

Figure 5-4

Configuring Mailbox Settings

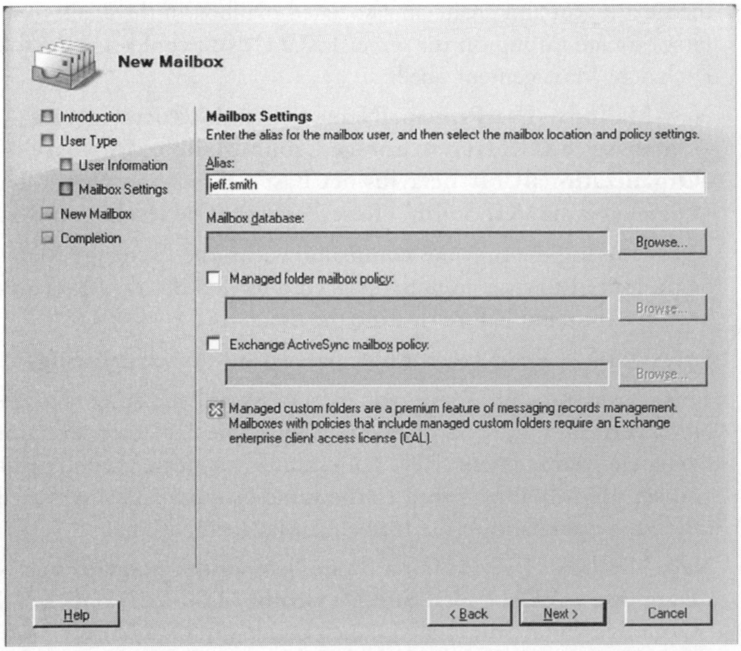

X REF

Managed folder policies will be discussed in Lesson 6, "Address Lists, Policies, and Bulk Management." ActiveSync policies will be discussed in Lesson 12, "Providing for Mobile Access and Unified Messaging."

8. At the Mailbox Settings page, ensure that the **Alias** dialog box contains the recipient name that should appear in the email address. For example, in Figure 5-4, the email address for the user will be jeff.smith@domain.

9. Click **Browse** next to the Mailbox database dialog box, select the Mailbox database in the Select Mailbox Database window that appears, and click **OK**.

10. If you have created a Managed folder mailbox policy or an ActiveSync mailbox policy that you wish to apply to this mailbox user, you can select the

associated checkboxes in Figure 5-4 and click the related **Browse** buttons to select them.

11. Click **Next**. The New Mailbox page appears.

12. Review the summary of your settings and click **New**. The Completion page appears.

TAKE NOTE *

The completion page of most configuration wizards in Exchange Server 2007 displays a command that may be used to perform the same actions from within the Exchange Management Shell that you have executed during the wizard. When creating a new mail box user and associated AD user account, the password that you specify is not shown within this command for security reasons. Instead, you will see the value 'SystemSecurity SecureString' in place of all passwords specified within an Exchange Server 2007 wizard.

---

13. Click **Finish** to close the New Mailbox window.

14. Close the Exchange Management Console.

 **THE COMMAND LINE WAY**

You can also use the **Enable-Mailbox** cmdlet in the Exchange Management Shell to create a mailbox for an existing AD user or the **New-Mailbox** cmdlet to create a new AD user and associated mailbox.

For example, to create a mailbox in the Mailbox Database within the First Storage Group on the server EXCH1 for the existing user with the logon name jeff.smith in the domain octavius.net, you could run the following command in the Exchange Management Shell:

Enable-Mailbox 'jeff.smith@octavius.net'–Database 'EXCH1\First Storage Group\ Mailbox Database'

Alternatively, to create a new AD user for Jeff Smith (logon name = jeff.smith) within the East OU in the octavius.net domain, require that Jeff must change his password on the next logon and create an associated mailbox in the Mailbox Database within the First Storage Group on the server EXCH1, you could run the following command in the Exchange Management Shell:

New-Mailbox -UserPrincipalName 'jeff.smith@octavius.net' –Alias 'jeff.smith' –Database 'EXCH1\First Storage Group\Mailbox Database' –Name 'Jeff Smith' –OrganizationalUnit 'octavius.net/East' –FirstName 'Jeff' –LastName 'Smith' –DisplayName 'Jeff Smith' –ResetPasswordOnNextLogon $true

After entering the previous command within the Exchange Management Console, you will be prompted to type an initial password for Jeff Smith. Alternatively, you could run the following command before creating the user:

$password = Read-Host 'Enter password' –AsSecureString

This command will prompt you for a password and store it in the $password variable. Next, you can use this $password variable when creating several mailbox users in the Exchange Management Shell. For example, to create the Jeff Smith user described earlier and set the initial password to the value of the $password variable, you could run the following command in the Exchange Management Shell:

New-Mailbox –UserPrincipalName 'jeff.smith@octavius.net' –Alias 'jeff.smith' –Database 'EXCH1\First Storage Group\Mailbox Database' –Name 'Jeff Smith' –OrganizationalUnit 'octavius.net/East' –FirstName 'Jeff' –LastName 'Smith' –DisplayName 'Jeff Smith' –ResetPasswordOnNextLogon $true –password $password

---

Configuring Mailbox Users

The configuration of mailbox users can be performed by accessing the properties of the mailbox user within the Exchange Management Console or by running the appropriate cmdlet within the Exchange Management Shell.

Provided that you are a member of the Exchange Organization Administrator or Exchange Recipient Administrator role, you can administer the properties of all mailbox users within the organization, regardless of which Mailbox role server stores their associated mailbox.

To view all mailbox users within your organization, you can navigate to **Recipient Configuration** > **Mailbox** within the Exchange Management Console. Because there may be hundreds or thousands of mailbox users within your organization, you can narrow the list of users shown in the Exchange Management Console by selecting **Create Filter** from the detail pane and specifying the appropriate information. For example, to see the mailbox users on the server called EXCH1, you could specify Server Equals EXCH1 as shown in Figure 5-5 and click **Apply Filter**.

Figure 5-5

Applying Mailbox User Filters

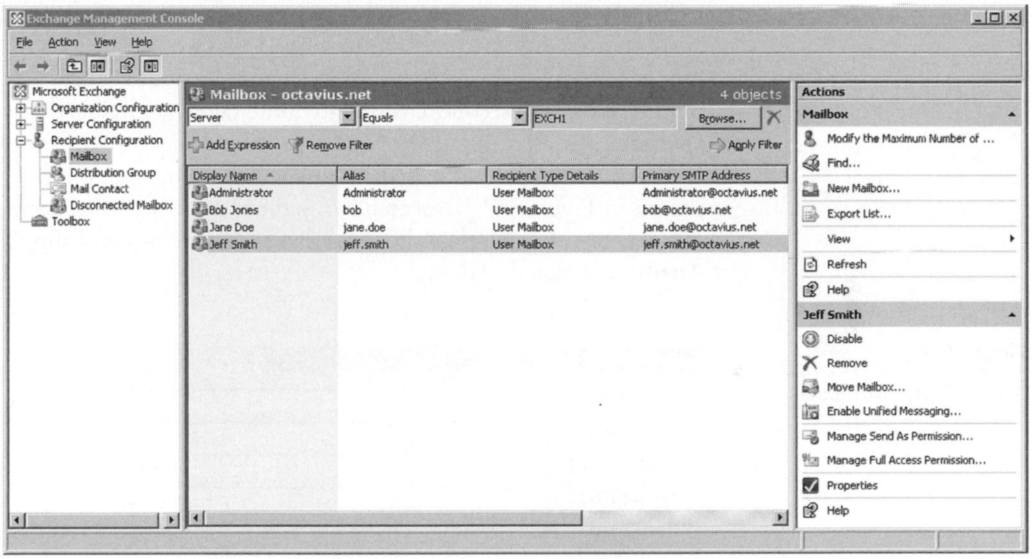

You can add/specify multiple criteria to your view filter in Figure 5-5 by clicking **Add Expression** or remove your filter by selecting **Remove Filter**.

Once you have located the appropriate mailbox user, you can highlight it in the detail pane and select **Properties** from the action pane to view its properties. The properties for the Jeff Smith mailbox user are shown in Figure 5-6.

Figure 5-6

Mailbox User Properties

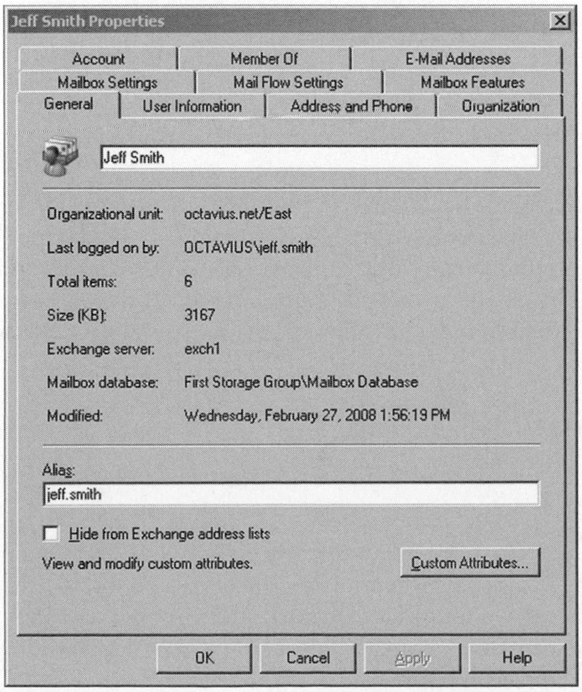

The General tab of mailbox user properties displays the information about the location of the AD user account as well as the location and contents of the mailbox itself. In Figure 5-6, the mailbox for Jeff Smith has 6 items that take up 3167 KB of space on the Mailbox Database in the First Storage Group on the server exch1. In addition, you can modify the alias used to generate the email address for the mailbox user or hide the user from any email address lists that are generated by Exchange to represent groups of mail recipients.

By clicking the **Custom Attributes** button shown in Figure 5-6, you can store up to 15 custom attributes in the mailbox user that may be used later when searching for users or creating dynamic distribution groups. These custom attributes are simply text labels that reflect the job role, project, subdepartment, or status of the mailbox user. You can use these custom attributes to store information that is not normally stored in the properties of a user account. For example, the first custom attribute could represent the team within the organization, the second custom attribute could represent the project, and the third custom attribute could represent the location of the project. If Jeff Smith is part of the TASU team working on the project called Athena in Chicago, you could enter the custom attributes shown in Figure 5-7. To search for mailbox users who are working on project Athena, you can then create a filter as shown earlier in Figure 5-5 and supply the expression Custom Attribute 2 Equals Athena.

Figure 5-7

Adding Custom Attributes

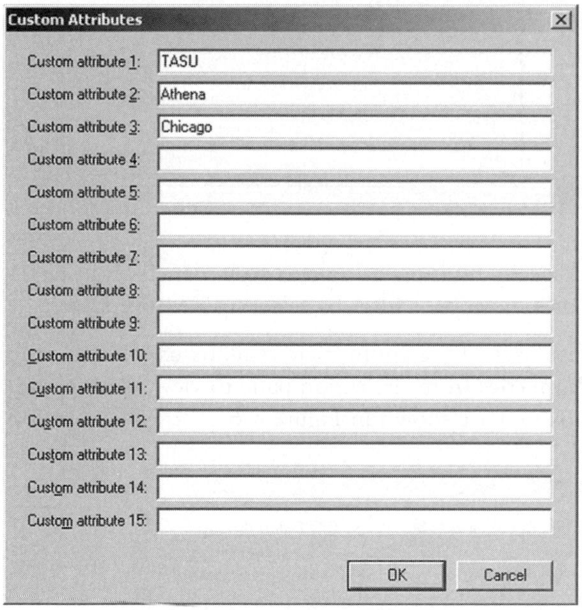

The User Information, Address and Phone, Organization, Member Of, and Account tabs of mailbox user properties contain information about the mailbox user such as logon name, group membership, full name, contact information, and department. This information is taken from the existing AD user account if the account was mailbox enabled, but must be entered manually if the user account was created alongside the mailbox.

TAKE NOTE * Although the Member Of tab lists the groups that the mailbox user is a member of, you cannot modify group membership using it.

The remaining tabs within the properties of a mailbox user contain Exchange-specific configuration for the mailbox user and mailbox. To view and modify the SMTP email address for the mailbox user, you can use the E-Mail Addresses tab. By default, a single email address is added in the form alias@domain. However, you can add additional email addresses to allow the recipient to receive email sent to multiple email addresses.

Figure 5-8 shows the E-Mail Addresses tab for the user Jeff Smith in the octavius.net domain. Because the alias for Jeff Smith is jeff.smith, the SMTP address jeff.smith@octavius.net was added automatically using an email address policy. An additional address, jsmith@octavius.net was added afterward to reflect the email address format that was used by the octavius.net domain in the past. If a remote sender with the old contact information for Jeff Smith addresses email to jsmith@octavius.net, it will still be sent to the mailbox for Jeff Smith. Because the jeff.smith@octavius.net address is bold in Figure 5-8, it will be used as the sending address when Jeff Smith sends or replies to email. Hence, when Jeff Smith replies to an email that was addressed to jsmith@octavius.net, the reply will list jeff.smith@octavius.net as the sender instead of jsmith@octavius.net. The sending address is always defined from the alias set on the mailbox user. To change the sending address, you can deselect **Automatically update e-mail addresses based on e-mail address policy**, shown in Figure 5-8, highlight another email address, and click **Set as Reply**.

Figure 5-8

Configuring Email Addresses

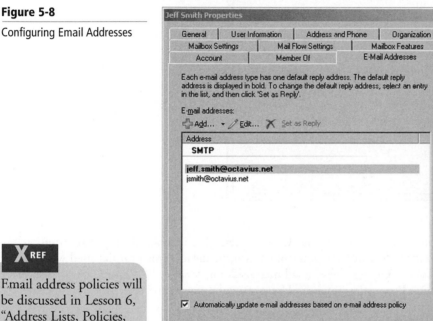

Email address policies will be discussed in Lesson 6, "Address Lists, Policies, and Bulk Management."

Additional addresses are also used when users change their legal surname after marriage. For example, if Sue Wong (sue.wong@octavius.net) changes her surname to Richards, you can modify the alias for Sue Wong's mailbox user to sue.richards on the General tab of her mailbox user properties. This will assign a default SMTP email address of sue.richards@octavius.net and automatically add a secondary SMTP address of sue.wong@octavius.net to ensure that she receives email that is still sent to sue.wong@octavius.net. When Sue Richards replies to any emails that were sent to sue.wong@octavius.net, the reply email will be from sue.richards@octavius.net, and the original sender can then update his or her contact list.

Many organizations specify a postmaster of postmaster@domain on their Hub role servers. To ensure that email sent to postmaster@octavius.net is sent to Jeff Smith, you could set postmaster@octavius.net as the postmaster email address on your Hub role servers and then add the address postmaster@octavius.net as an additional email address on the E-Mail Addresses tab of Jeff Smith's mailbox user object.

Configuring postmaster addresses and accepted domains on Hub role servers was discussed in Lesson 4, "Configuring a New Exchange Server."

Although there is no limit to the number of additional SMTP addresses that you can create for a single mailbox user, you should keep the number to a minimum for manageability and performance. Furthermore, if you add an additional email address that has a different domain, you must add an authoritative accepted domain for the domain on the Hub transport servers within your organization to ensure that your Hub servers will accept email for the domain and forward it to the appropriate mailbox.

To control the protocols and features that the mailbox user is allowed to use, you can enable or disable the appropriate protocols or features on the Mailbox Features tab shown in Figure 5-9.

Figure 5-9

Specifying Mailbox Features

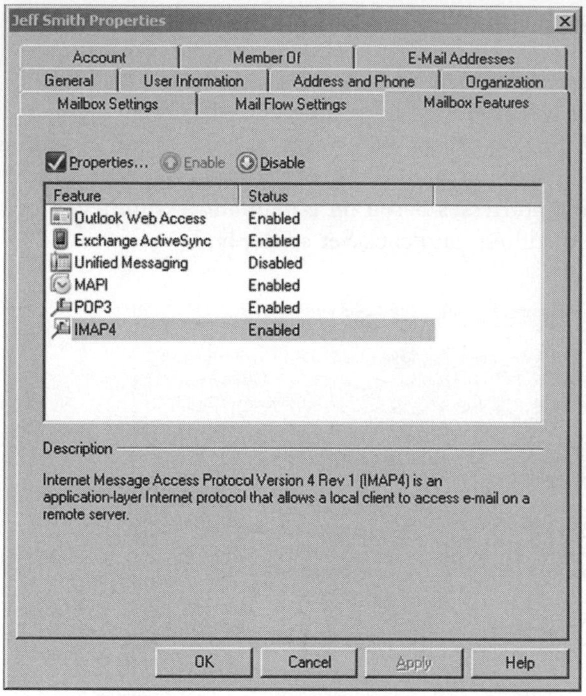

By default, all protocols are enabled and Unified Messaging is disabled. If you are running Exchange Server 2007 SP1 or later, you can control the default email format used when POP or IMAP users compose a new email message. Simply select POP3 or IMAP4 as shown in Figure 5-9, click **Properties**, uncheck **Use protocol default**, and select the appropriate default email format:

- **Text.** Emails are composed in plain text, which means email can be processed by any client or mobile device.
- **HTML.** Emails are composed in HTML format.
- **HTML and alternative text.** Emails can consist of HTML and plain text components.
- **Enriched text.** Emails are composed using Rich Text Format (RTF).
- **Enriched text and alternative text.** Emails can consist of RTF and plain text components.

The Mailbox Settings tab of mailbox user properties shown in Figure 5-10 can be used to change the mailbox settings for the mailbox user. In the properties of Messaging Records Management, you can specify a managed folder mailbox policy or modify the one chosen during the creation of the mailbox user. Similarly, in the properties of Storage Quotas, you can override the mailbox size limits and deleted item retention period set on the mailbox database as shown in Figure 5-11.

In Figure 5-11, deleted items will be retained for the default period of 14 days, and users will receive a warning email when their mailbox reaches 900 MB (921600 KB). When a user's mailbox reaches 950 MB (972800 KB), he will receive an additional warning email and will not be able to send any emails using Exchange. However, the user will continue receiving emails from others until the mailbox size reaches 1 GB (1048576 KB). As this point, the user can no longer send or receive any emails until he reduces the size of his mailbox.

X REF

You can configure default mailbox size limits on the Limits tab of mailbox database properties as discussed earlier in Lesson 4, "Configuring a New Exchange Server."

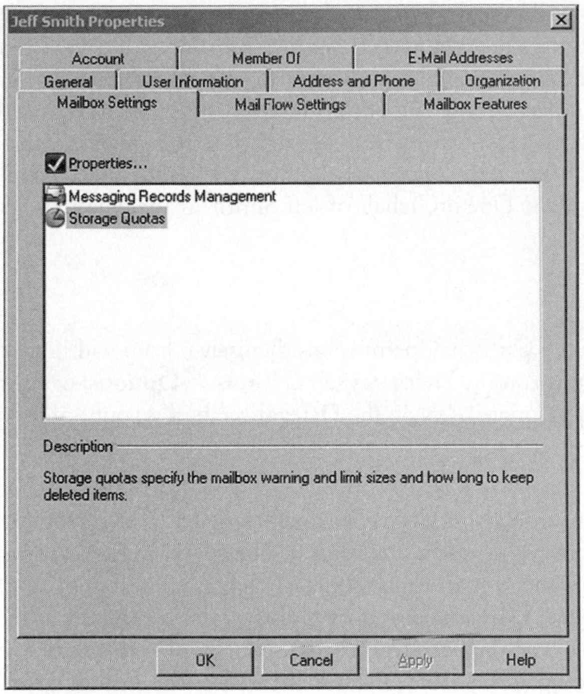

Figure 5-10

Configuring Mailbox Settings

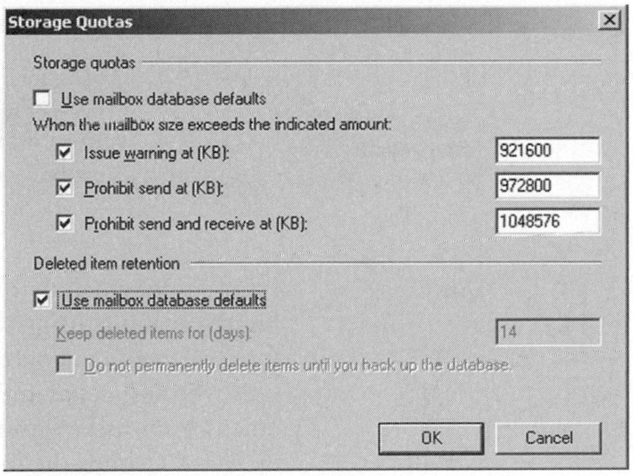

Figure 5-11

Configuring Mailbox Storage Quotas

To allow for greater flexibility and more granular control, you can also alter settings for mail relay on an individual user basis. This information is used by the Mailbox, CAS, and Hub role servers within your organization and can be configured using the Mail Flow Settings tab of mailbox user properties. Figure 5-12 displays the Mail Flow Settings tab for Jeff Smith.

When you access the properties of Delivery Options in Figure 5-12, you can specify ***Send On Behalf permission***, forwarding options, and recipient limits as shown in Figure 5-13.

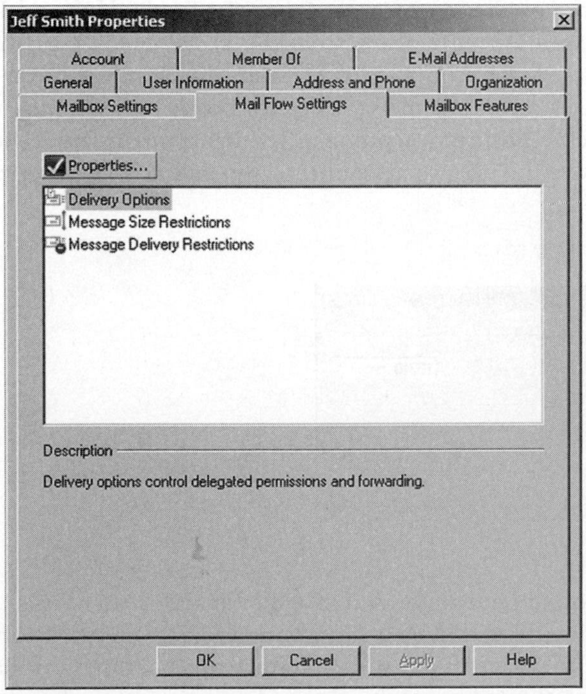

Figure 5-12

Configuring Mail Flow Settings

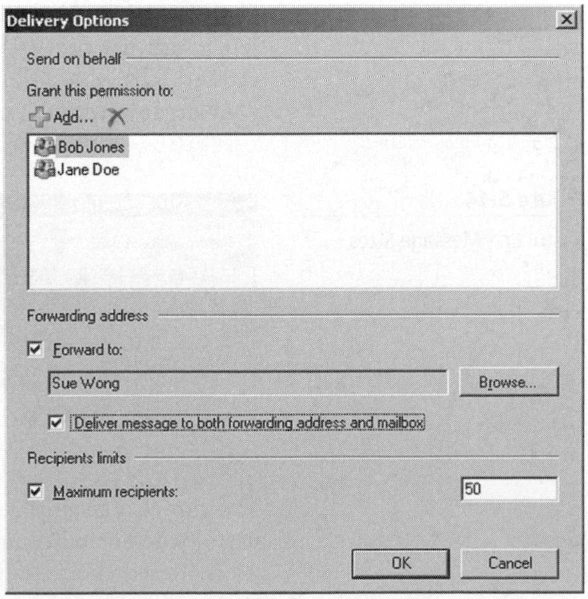

Figure 5-13

Configuring Delivery Options

By default, when Jeff Smith sends email, the From field in the email displays his primary email address (jeff.smith@octavius.net). However, because Bob Jones and Jane Doe have Send On Behalf permission to Jeff Smith's mailbox, they can compose a new email from their own account in Outlook or Entourage, choose the option to view the From box, and then change the contents of the From box to jeff.smith@octavius.net. When the email is sent, it will appear as though it was sent from "Bob Jones on behalf of Jeff Smith" if the email was composed by Bob Jones or from "Jane Doe on behalf of Jeff Smith" if the email was composed by Jane Doe.

TAKE NOTE* Mailbox users can also grant Send On Behalf permissions themselves from within Outlook by specifying the appropriate users on the **Delegates** tab of **Tools** > **Options**, or from within Entourage by specifying the appropriate users on the **Delegates** tab of account properties.

In addition, email that is sent to Jeff Smith's mailbox is forwarded to Sue Wong as well as Jeff Smith's mailbox using the Forwarding address section of Figure 5-13. *Forwarding* is often used when an employee leaves the organization to ensure that emails are sent to the mailbox user who will act as a replacement. In addition, forwarding is also a method of monitoring emails from users within your organization. In this case, you should ensure that the email is delivered to both the forwarding address and mailbox if the user should not be made aware of the monitoring.

In the early days of email, it was not uncommon to send out mass emails that contained hundreds of recipients for advertising purposes. Today, this activity may be negatively interpreted as spam and can be limited by specifying the maximum number of recipients within the Recipient limits section of Delivery Options. As shown in Figure 5-13, any emails with more than 50 recipients that are sent by Jeff Smith will be returned as undeliverable.

Emails with large attachments are difficult to relay and can slow down the email servers within your organization. As a result, you should always restrict the maximum size of emails that are relayed by your email servers. Although you can restrict the maximum message size within the properties of a send or receive connector on the Hub and Edge role servers within your organization, you can also restrict the size of emails on a mailbox user basis. To do this, you can access the properties of Message Size Restrictions on the Mail Flow Settings tab. Figure 5-14 shows the message size restrictions for the mailbox user Jeff Smith. By preventing Jeff Smith from sending or receiving emails larger than 10 MB (10240 KB), you will improve the performance of the Hub and Edge role servers within your organization.

Figure 5-14

Restricting Message Sizes

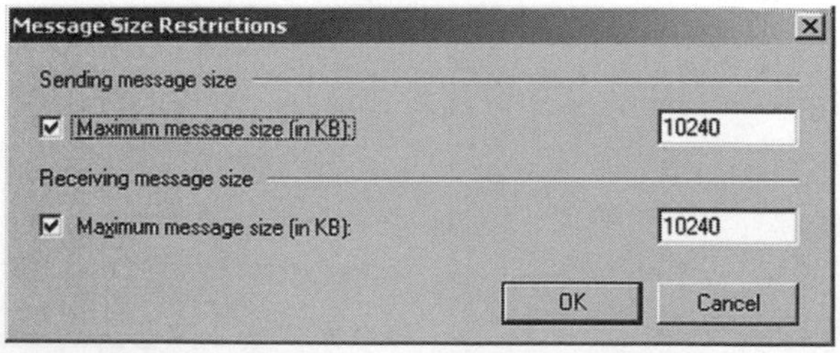

You can also specify the allowed senders for an individual mailbox user. This is often useful when email communication within your organization must be restricted to specific users. Research and development teams are an example of this because information within the team must not be allowed to reach other individuals within the organization by accident.

To specify allowed senders for a mailbox user, you can access the properties of Message Delivery Restrictions in the Mail Flow Settings tab of mailbox user properties as shown in Figure 5-15 for the user Jeff Smith. In Figure 5-15, Jeff Smith allows messages from all authenticated senders except for Billy Martin.

Figure 5-15

Configuring Allowed Senders

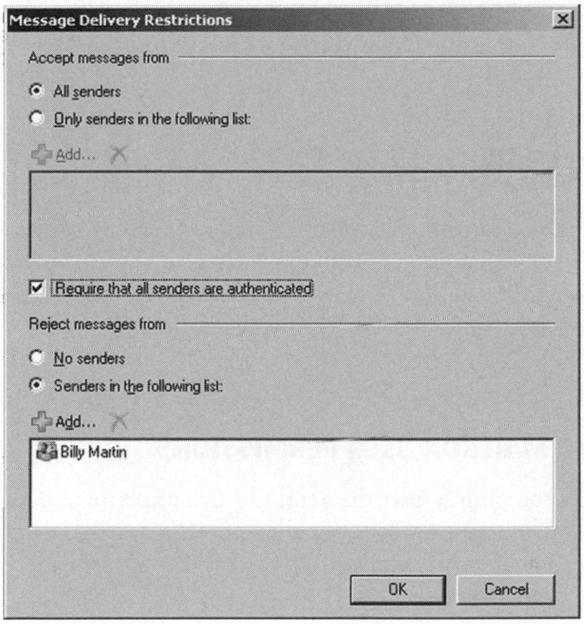

You can also modify the properties of a mailbox user using the **Set-Mailbox** cmdlet within the Exchange Management Shell. For example, to set the maximum size for sent email to 10 MB (10485760 bytes) for the user Jeff Smith, you could run the following command within the Exchange Management Shell:

Set-Mailbox 'jeff.smith@octavius.net' -MaxSendSize 10485760

When you identify the object that you wish to modify within the Exchange Management Console, you can use a variety of different formats. For example, you can identify Jeff Smith using his display name (Jeff Smith), logon name (jeff.smith), or LDAP name (CN=Jeff Smith, OU=East, DC=octavius, DC=net). Because the Exchange Management Shell supports UNIX-style redirection, you can use the pipe (|) symbol to send the name of the object to the appropriate cmdlet. As a result, the following commands perform the same action as the one described earlier:

Set-Mailbox –Identity 'Jeff Smith' –MaxSendSize 10485760

Set-Mailbox –Identity 'jeff.smith' –MaxSendSize 10485760

Set-Mailbox –Identity 'CN=Jeff Smith, OU=East, DC=octavius, DC=net' –MaxSendSize 10485760

'jeff.smith@octavius.net' | Set-Mailbox –MaxSendSize 10485760

'Jeff Smith' | Set-Mailbox –MaxSendSize 10485760

'jeff.smith' | Set-Mailbox –MaxSendSize 10485760

'CN=Jeff Smith, OU=East, DC=octavius, DC=net' | Set-Mailbox –MaxSendSize 10485760

All future cmdlet examples will vary the syntax used to identify recipient objects. This will ensure that you become accustomed to the different formats available within the Exchange Management Shell.

THE COMMAND LINE WAY

These examples only modified a single attribute of the Jeff Smith mailbox user (MaxSendSize). To see other options that can be used alongside the SetMailbox cmdlet to modify other properties of a mailbox user, search for Set-Mailbox within Exchange Server 2007 Help.

To view the settings that you have configured for a mail user, you can use the **Get-Mailbox** cmdlet. For example, the following command within the Exchange Management Shell lists the properties of the Jeff Smith mail user described earlier:

Get-MailUser 'jeff.smith@octavius.net' | format-list

Managing Mailbox Users

After you create and configure the properties for mailbox users, you must manage them over time. This involves granting or denying permissions as well as disabling or removing the mailbox user. In addition, you may need to reconnect the mailbox for a disabled or deleted user to a new or existing mailbox user at a later time.

MANAGING MAILBOX USER PERMISSIONS

Although you can grant a user the Send On Behalf permission to another mailbox user, the Send On Behalf permission does not allow senders to mask their identity. Email sent using the Send On Behalf permission will always list the real sender in the From field or preview pane within the email client.

However, there are two additional permissions that an administrator can grant on a mailbox user to allow other users the ability to assume that user's identity. These permissions are the *Send As permission* and the *Full Access permission*.

The Send As permission is nearly identical to the Send On Behalf permission. However, the Send As permission hides the identity of the original sender. For example, if you grant Bob Jones the Send As permission to the Jeff Smith mailbox user account, Bob Jones can compose a new email from his own account in Outlook or Entourage, choose the option to view the From box, and then change the contents of the From box to jeff.smith@octavius.net. However, when the email is sent, it will appear as though it was sent from Jeff Smith. The recipients of the email message will not know that the email was actually sent from Bob Jones on Jeff Smith's behalf.

You can also grant the Send As permission to a group for a mailbox user to allow all members of the group the ability to send emails as that user. This is often used if your organization requires several users to send certain emails using a single identity. Say, for example, that the Octavius organization creates a dummy mailbox user with the email companyevents@octavius.net and grants Send As permission to several users or groups for this dummy mailbox user. In this case, any user with Send As permission to this dummy mailbox user can send companywide emails regarding special events using a consistent single identity of companyevents@octavius.net.

> **TAKE NOTE**
>
> You should only grant the Send As permission if another person must be trusted to send email using the sole identity of another user.

⊕ MANAGE SEND AS PERMISSIONS FOR A MAILBOX USER

GET READY. Turn on the computer, and log in as the Administrator user account. Close any windows that appear on the desktop.

1. Click **Start**, **All Programs**, **Microsoft Exchange Server 2007**, and then click **Exchange Management Console**. The Exchange Management Console window appears.

2. In the console tree pane, expand **Recipient Configuration** and highlight **Mailbox**.

3. In the result pane, select the user you wish to manage Send As permissions for.

4. In the action pane, click **Manage Send As Permission**. The Manage Send As Permission window appears as shown in Figure 5-16.

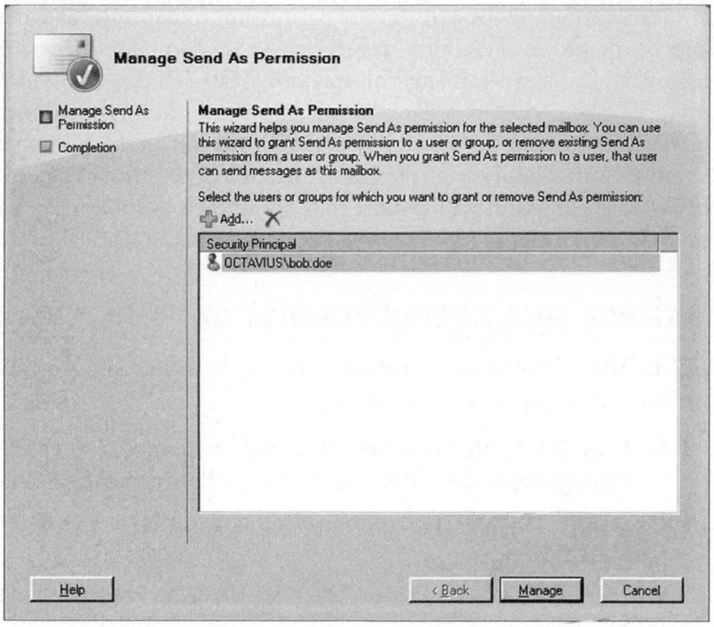

Figure 5-16

Managing Send As Permission

Manage Send As Permission

Manage Send As Permission
Completion

Manage Send As Permission

This wizard helps you manage Send As permission for the selected mailbox. You can use this wizard to grant Send As permission to a user or group, or remove existing Send As permission from a user or group. When you grant Send As permission to a user, that user can send messages as this mailbox.

Select the users or groups for which you want to grant or remove Send As permission:

Add... ✕

Security Principal
OCTAVIUS\bob.doe

Help   < Back   Manage   Cancel

5. To remove the Send As Permission granted to an existing user or group listed in the Security Principle dialog box, highlight the user or group and click the red **X** icon. Alternatively, to grant the Send As permission to a user or group, click **Add**, select the appropriate user or group in the Select User or Group dialog box that appears, and click **OK**.

6. Click **Manage**. The Completion page appears.

7. Click **Finish** to close the Manage Send As Permission window.

8. Close the Exchange Management Console.

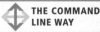 **THE COMMAND LINE WAY**

You can also use the **Add-ADPermission** cmdlet in the Exchange Management Shell to assign Send As permission to a user or group for a mailbox user. For example, to grant Send As permission to Bob Jones (logon name = bob.jones@octavius.net) for the mailbox user Jeff Smith located in the East OU of the octavius.net domain (LDAP name: CN= Jeff Smith, OU=East, DC=octavius, DC=net), you could run the following command in the Exchange Management Shell:

Add-ADPermission –Identity 'CN=Jeff Smith, OU=East, DC=octavius, DC=net' –User 'octavius.net\bob.jones' –ExtendedRights 'Send-as'

Similarly, you can use the **Remove-ADPermission** cmdlet to remove Send As permissions for a mailbox user. For example, to remove the Send As permission added in the previous example, you could run the following command in the Exchange Management Shell:

Remove-ADPermission –Identity 'CN=Jeff Smith,OU=East,DC=octavius,DC=net' –User 'octavius.net\bob.jones' –InheritanceType 'All' –ExtendedRights 'Send-as' –ChildObjectTypes $null –InheritedObjectType $null –Properties $null

Although the Send As permission allows a delegate the ability to send emails as another mailbox user, it does not allow the delegate to view the emails within that user's mailbox. In some organizations, an assistant or colleague must be able to send and receive emails using another user's identity when that user is on a business trip, vacation, or sick leave. To do this, you can grant the Full Access permission to the assistant or colleague for the target mailbox user. Users with Full Access permission to a target mailbox user can open the target mailbox alongside their own mailbox from within Outlook or Entourage. As a result, they will receive emails sent to the target mailbox user and can respond to them using the identity of the target mailbox user.

You can also grant the Full Access permission to a group for a mailbox user to allow all members of the group the ability to receive and send emails as that user. This is often used if your organization has an information mailbox that several users need to have full control of. For example, the Octavius organization can create a dummy mailbox user with the email address hr@octavius.net and grant Full Access permission to the human resources group within the organization. Members of the human resources group will be able to receive emails sent to hr@octavius.net and will be able to reply to the ones that they are individually responsible for in their departments.

→ MANAGE FULL ACCESS PERMISSIONS FOR A MAILBOX USER

GET READY. Turn on the computer, and log in as the Administrator user account. Close any windows that appear on the desktop.

1. Click **Start**, **All Programs**, **Microsoft Exchange Server 2007**, and then click **Exchange Management Console.** The Exchange Management Console window appears.

2. In the console tree pane, expand **Recipient Configuration** and highlight **Mailbox**.

3. In the result pane, select the user that you wish to manage Full Access permissions for.

4. In the action pane, click **Manage Full Access Permission**. The Manage Full Access Permission window appears as shown in Figure 5-17.

Figure 5-17

Managing Full Access Permission

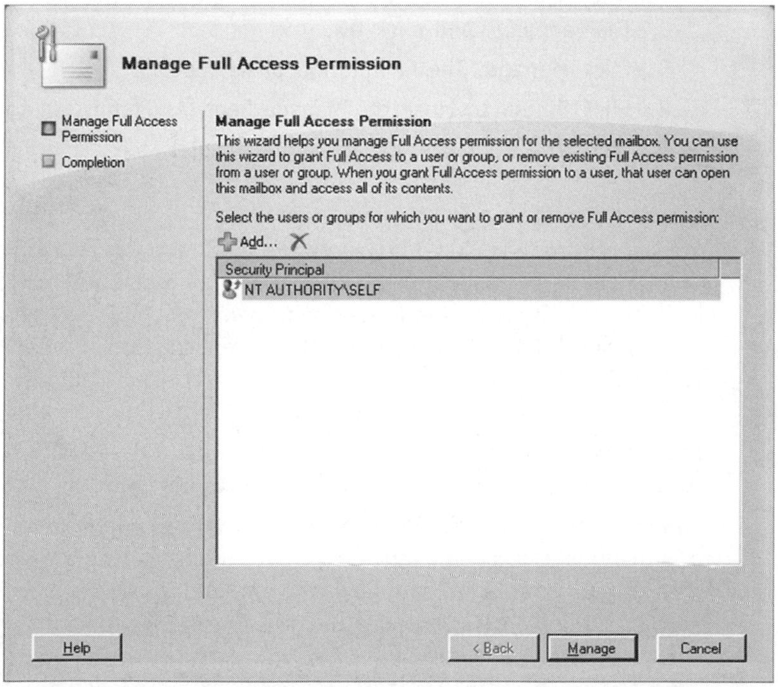

TAKE NOTE*

Do not remove the default **NT AUTHORITY\SELF** security principle shown in Figure 5-17. This security principle is required to allow mailbox users full access to their own mailbox.

5. To remove the Full Access permission granted to an existing user or group listed in the Security Principle dialog box, highlight the user or group and click the red **X** icon. Alternatively, to grant the Full Access permission to a user or group, click **Add**, select the appropriate user or group in the Select User or Group dialog box that appears, and click **OK**.

6. Click **Manage**. The Completion page appears.

7. Click **Finish** to close the Manage Full Access Permission window.

8. Close the Exchange Management Console.

THE COMMAND
LINE WAY

You can also use the **Add-MailboxPermission** cmdlet in the Exchange Management Shell to assign Full Access permission to a user or group for a mailbox user. For example, to grant Full Access permission to Bob Jones (logon name = bob.jones@octavius.net) for the mailbox user Jeff Smith located in the East OU of the octavius.net domain (LDAP name: CN=Jeff Smith, OU=East, DC=octavius, DC=net), you could run the following command in the Exchange Management Shell:

Add-MailboxPermission –Identity 'CN=Jeff Smith,OU=East,DC=octavius,DC=net' –User 'octavius.net\bob.jones' –AccessRights 'FullAccess'

Similarly, you can use the **Remove-MailboxPermission** cmdlet to remove Full Access permissions to a user or group for a mailbox user. For example, to remove the Full Access permission added in the previous example, you could run the following command in the Exchange Management Shell:

Remove-MailboxPermission –Identity 'CN=Jeff Smith, OU=East, DC=octavius, DC=net' –User 'octavius.net\bob.jones' –InheritanceType 'All' –AccessRights 'FullAccess'

Users who have Full Access permission to the target user's mailbox must manually add the target mailbox to the properties of their Exchange account within Outlook or Entourage. To do this from within Outlook 2007, you can navigate to **Tools** > **Account Settings**, double click on your Exchange account, click the **More Settings** button, and add the appropriate mailbox to the Mailboxes section on the Advanced tab shown in Figure 5-18.

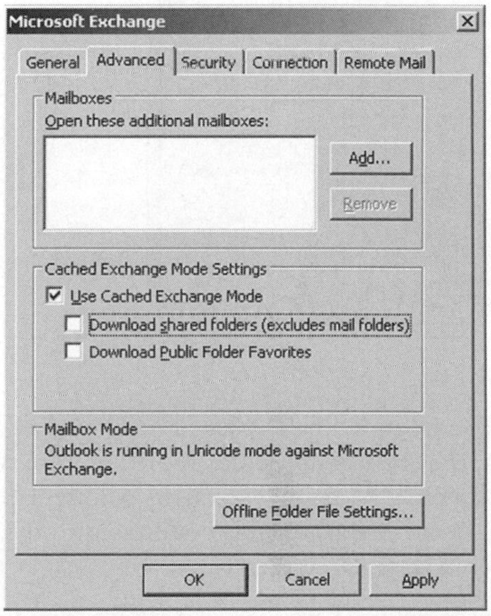

Figure 5-18

Adding Additional Mailboxes to an Exchange Account in Outlook 2007

DISABLING, REMOVING, AND RECONNECTING MAILBOX USERS

When you navigate to **Recipient Configuration** > **Mailbox** within the Exchange Management Console and highlight a mailbox user in the detail pane, you are given the **Disable** or **Remove** options in the action pane.

If you choose to disable a mailbox user, all Exchange-related properties within the AD user account are removed, but the user account is not removed from AD. In general, you should disable mailbox users if the AD account no longer needs email access yet the AD account must still exist for domain authentication.

Alternatively, if you choose to remove a mailbox user, the AD user account is removed completely and the associated user will no longer be able to authenticate to the domain. This option is typically used to save time if the administration of Exchange and AD are performed by the same person. If a user account and mailbox must be removed when a user leaves the organization, then both tasks can be done at the same time from within the Exchange Management Console. Otherwise, the mailbox user would need to be disabled in the Exchange Management Console and the associated user account would need to be removed in the Active Directory Users and Computers console.

Regardless of whether you disable or remove an existing mailbox user, the mailbox is not removed immediately. Instead, the mailbox is simply disconnected and marked for deletion. You can view the disconnected mailboxes within your organization by navigating to **Recipient Configuration > Disconnected Mailbox** within the Exchange Management Console.

By default, disconnected mailboxes are automatically removed after 30 days, but you can change this interval by accessing the Limits tab of mailbox database properties as shown in Figure 5-19. To view the properties of a mailbox database, simply navigate to **Server Configuration > Mailbox** in the Exchange Management Console and select the appropriate server in the detail pane. You can then highlight the appropriate mailbox database in the work pane and click **Properties** in the action pane.

Figure 5-19

Configuring Deletion Settings on a Mailbox Database

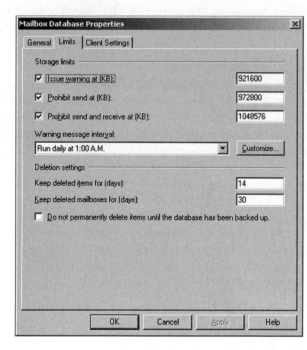

When users leave your organization, the associated mailbox user accounts are either disabled or removed. In addition, the email addresses for those users are typically added as secondary email addresses in the properties of the mailbox users who replace them in their job roles. This allows future emails from external contacts addressed to the original user to be sent to the mailbox of the person who replaced them.

In some cases, the new user will need access to past emails stored in the mailbox of the original mailbox user who left the organization. You can reconnect the original user's mailbox to the new user account after you create an AD user account for them.

TAKE NOTE*

Alternatively, you can disable the AD user account for a user who has left the organization and create a new mailbox user for the person who will act as a replacement. Following this, you can grant the new user Full Access permission to the existing mailbox and add it as a secondary mailbox within Outlook or Entourage as discussed earlier. This will allow the replacement user to receive and reply to emails that are sent to the original user.

⊖ DISABLE A MAILBOX USER

GET READY. Turn on the computer, and log in as the Administrator user account. Close any windows that appear on the desktop.

1. Click **Start**, **All Programs**, **Microsoft Exchange Server 2007**, and then click **Exchange Management Console**. The Exchange Management Console window appears.

2. In the console tree pane, expand **Recipient Configuration** and highlight **Mailbox**.

3. In the result pane, select the appropriate mailbox user, and click **Disable** in the action pane. When prompted to confirm the action, click **Yes**.

4. Close the Exchange Management Console.

THE COMMAND LINE WAY

You can also use the **Disable-Mailbox** cmdlet in the Exchange Management Shell to disable a mailbox user. To disable Jeff Smith (email address jeff.smith@octavius.net), you could run the following command in the Exchange Management Shell:

Disable-Mailbox 'jeff.smith@octavius.net'

⊖ REMOVE A MAILBOX USER

GET READY. Turn on the computer, and log in as the Administrator user account. Close any windows that appear on the desktop.

1. Click **Start**, **All Programs**, **Microsoft Exchange Server 2007**, and then click **Exchange Management Console**. The Exchange Management Console window appears.

2. In the console tree pane, expand **Recipient Configuration** and highlight **Mailbox**.

3. In the result pane, select the appropriate mailbox user and click **Remove** in the action pane. When prompted to confirm the action, click **Yes**.

4. Close the Exchange Management Console.

THE COMMAND LINE WAY

You can also use the **Remove-Mailbox** cmdlet in the Exchange Management Shell to remove a mailbox user from AD and mark the mailbox for deletion. To remove the user Jeff Smith (logon name = jeff.smith) in the octavius.net domain, you could run the following command in the Exchange Management Shell:

Remove-Mailbox–Identity 'octavius.net\jeff.smith'

The Exchange Management Shell allows for additional options when removing users. For example, to remove the mailbox immediately from the mailbox database without waiting the default time period of 30 days, you can append **–Permanent $true** to the Remove-Mailbox command.

⊖ RECONNECT A MAILBOX

GET READY. Turn on the computer, and log in as the Administrator user account. Close any windows that appear on the desktop.

1. Click **Start**, **All Programs**, **Microsoft Exchange Server 2007**, and then click **Exchange Management Console**. The Exchange Management Console window appears.

2. In the console tree pane, expand **Recipient Configuration** and highlight **Disconnected Mailbox**.

3. In the result pane, select the appropriate mailbox and click **Connect** in the action pane. The Connect Mailbox window appears as shown in Figure 5-20.

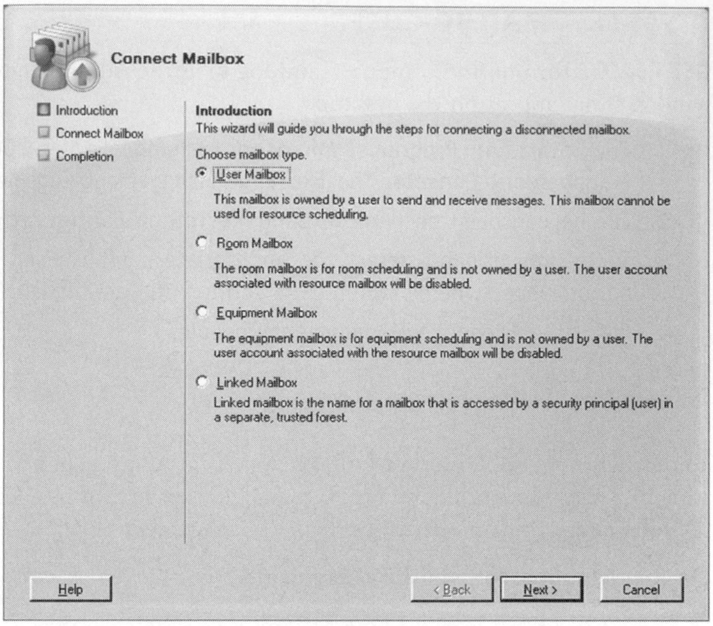

Figure 5-20

Connecting a Disconnected
Mailbox

4. Select the type of mailbox that you wish to reconnect. To reconnect a user mailbox, ensure that **User Mailbox** is selected and click **Next**. The Mailbox Settings page appears as shown in Figure 5-21.

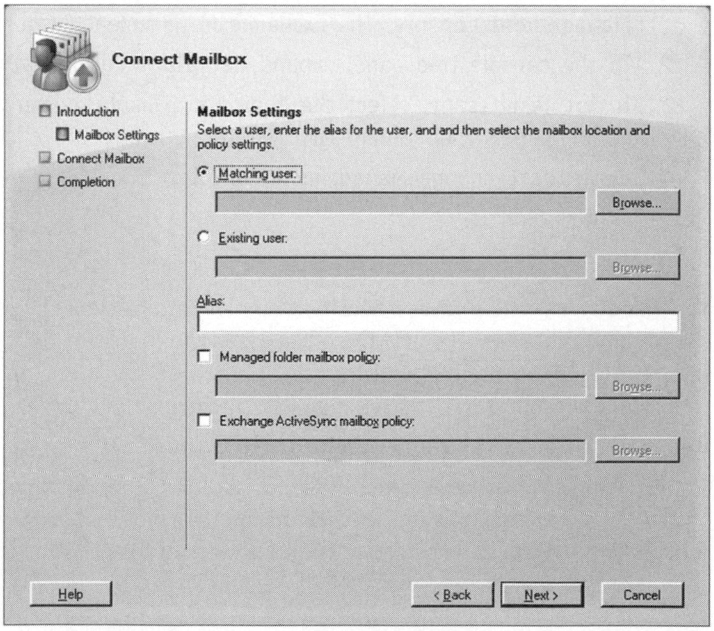

Figure 5-21

Specifying Mailbox Settings

5. If you wish to reconnect the mailbox to an AD user of the same name, select **Matching user**, click **Browse**, select the user account in the Select User window, and click **OK**. Alternatively, to reconnect the mailbox to a different AD user, select **Existing user**, click **Browse**, select the user account in the Select User window, and click **OK**.

6. Ensure that the correct alias is listed in the Alias dialog box. You can optionally specify a managed folder or ActiveSync policy by selecting the associated checkboxes in Figure 5-21 and clicking the related **Browse** buttons to select them.

7. Click **Next**. The Connect Mailbox page appears.

8. Click **Connect**. The Completion page appears.

9. Click **Finish** to close the Connect Mailbox window.

10. Close the Exchange Management Console.

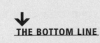

THE COMMAND LINE WAY

You can also use the **Connect-Mailbox** cmdlet in the Exchange Management Shell to recon-nect a mailbox. Before you reconnect a mailbox using the Exchange Management Shell, you must first obtain the GUID for the appropriate mailbox on the Mailbox role server by running the following command within the Exchange Management Shell on the Mailbox role server:

Get-MailboxStatistics | Where {$_.DisconnectDate -ne $null} | format-list

Next, you can locate the value in the **MailboxGuid** field for the appropriate disconnected mailbox and use it alongside the **Connect-Mailbox** cmdlet. For example, to reconnect the mailbox for Jeff Smith (MailboxGuid = 390fa663-db30-46b3-adf4-0dc752fb4e6s) within the Mailbox Database in the First Storage Group on the Mailbox role server exch1.octavius.net to the AD user Jeff Smith (logon name = jeff.smith) with an alias of jeff.smith, you could run the following command in the Exchange Management Shell:

Connect-Mailbox –Identity '390fa663-db30-46b3-adf4-0dc752fb4e6s'-Database 'exch1 .octavius.net\First Storage Group\Mailbox Database' –User 'octavius.net\jeff.smith' –Alias 'jeff.smith'

■ Working with Mail Users and Mail Contacts

↓ **THE BOTTOM LINE**

For users within your organization who do not require a mailbox hosted on an Exchange server, you can create mail users or mail contacts to represent them so that they can participate in your Exchange infrastructure. Because mail users and mail contacts often represent external email recipients, they are configured to forward email to an exter-nal email server. In addition to configuring mailbox users, Exchange administrators must understand how to configure mail users and mail contacts in any Exchange organization.

Creating Mail Users and Mail Contacts

You can create mail users and mail contacts within the Exchange Management Console or the Exchange Management Shell. As with creating mailbox users, you can choose to cre-ate a new mail user or mail enable an existing AD user account. Similarly, you can create a new mail contact or mail enable an existing AD contact.

Nearly all organizations employ external members who are contracted to provide essential ser-vices within the organization, yet are employed directly by another organization. Often, these external members do not require a mailbox in your organization because they already have a mailbox on an email server within their home organization.

Because email is often a primary form of communication between all members of an organi-zation regardless of whether they are directly employed or not, it is important to accommo-date external members within your Exchange infrastructure.

TAKE NOTE*

Only create mail users if the contract member requires an AD user account to access network resources. If the contract member does not require an AD user account, you can create a mail contact to represent them.

If external members require access to network resources, you will need to create AD user accounts for them as well as grant permissions to the appropriate resources for their user accounts. However, instead of creating mailboxes for these users within your organization, you can create email addresses for them that are used to forward email to their organization's email server. User accounts that are used to provide email forwarding in this scenario are called *mail users*.

Alternatively, if external members will not require access to network resources or the ability to authenticate to the domains in your AD forest, you can simply create a *mail contact* for them that contains an email address used to identify them within the organization. When email is sent to the mail contact, Exchange will simply forward it to the external organization's email server.

Regardless of whether you create a mail contact or mail user, you must specify the external email address for the user as well as an alias that will be used to create an email address for the member within the organization. For example, if you create a mail contact or mail user in the octavius.net domain for Kelly Armstrong using an alias of kelly.armstrong and specifying the external email address of karmstrong@mips-in.com, then the mail contact or mail user for Kelly Armstrong will have a primary email address of karmstrong@mips-in.com, secondary email address of kelly.armstrong@octavius.net, and an external email address of karmstrong@mips-in.com. Other users within the organization will quickly find kelly.armstrong when searching for email addresses within their domain using their email client programs. However, when email is sent to kelly.armstrong@octavius.net, it is simply forwarded to karmstrong@mips-in.com using external email relay.

By default, when you create a new mail user, an associated AD user is created as well. Alternatively, you can choose to mail enable an existing AD user account to create a new mail user. This is appropriate for organizations with separate AD and Exchange administrators and administrative duties.

Similarly, when you create a new mail contact, an associated AD contact object is created as well. If your organization separates AD and Exchange administrative duties, you can choose to mail enable an existing AD contact object that another administrator has created to create a new mail contact.

⊘ **CREATE A MAIL USER**

GET READY. Turn on the computer, and log in as the Administrator user account. Close any windows that appear on the desktop.

1. Click **Start**, **All Programs**, **Microsoft Exchange Server 2007**, and then click **Exchange Management Console**. The Exchange Management Console window appears.

2. In the console tree pane, expand **Recipient Configuration** and highlight **Mail Contact**.

3. In the action pane, click **New Mail User**. The New Mail User window appears as shown in Figure 5-22.

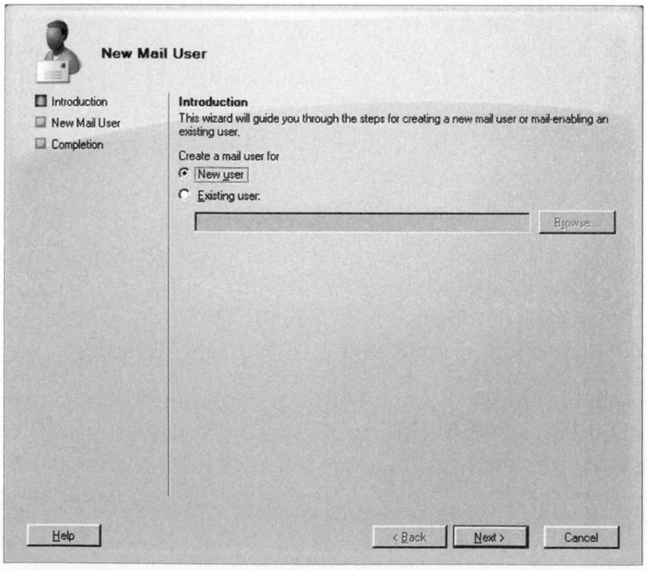

Figure 5-22

Creating a New Mail User

4. If you wish to create a new AD user that is mail enabled, ensure that **New user** is selected. Alternatively, you can choose to mail enable an existing AD user. To mail enable an existing user, select **Existing user**, click the **Browse** button, select the appropriate user in the Select User window that appears, and click **OK**.

5. Click **Next**. If you selected New user on the previous screen, you will be prompted to specify the AD user account information as shown in Figure 5-23.

Figure 5-23

Adding Mail User Information

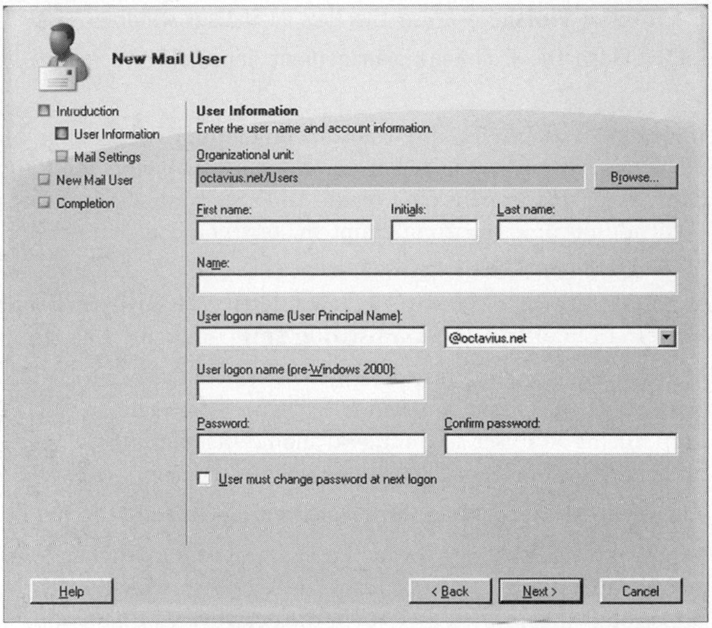

TAKE NOTE*

If you selected **Existing users** in Figure 5-22, you will skip the entering of account information shown in Figure 5-23.

6. By default, the user will be created in the default Users folder in your current domain. Because users are rarely created in this folder, you should click **Browse**, select the appropriate OU, and click **OK.** All other account settings on this page are similar in function to the settings that you choose when creating a new user account in the Active Directory Users and Computers console as discussed in Lesson 2. When finished entering the user account information, click **Next.** The Mail Settings page appears as shown in Figure 5-24.

Figure 5-24

Adding Mail User Settings

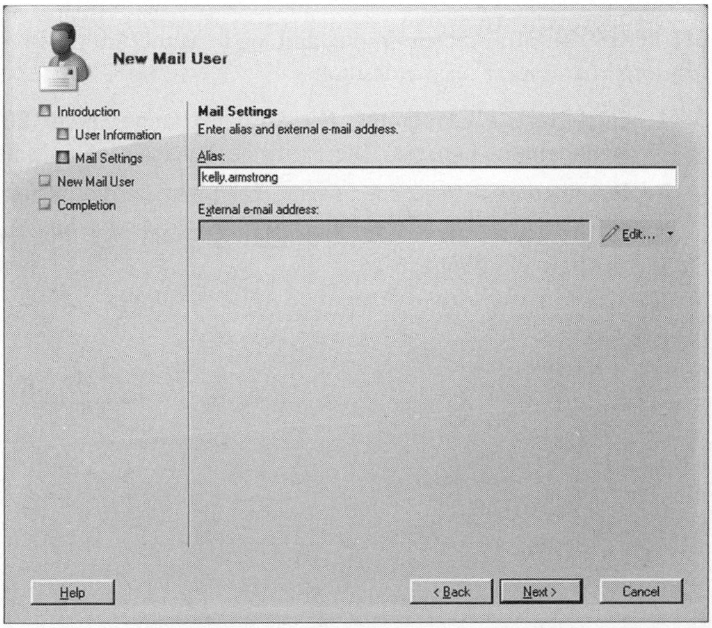

7. At the Mail Settings page, ensure that the **Alias** dialog box contains the recipient name that should appear in the email address. For example, in Figure 5-24, the email address for the user will be kelly.armstrong@domain.

8. Click **Edit** next to the External email address dialog box, type in the external SMTP email address for the mail user in the SMTP Address window that appears and click **OK.**

9. Click **Next.** The New Mail User page appears.

10. Review the summary of your settings and click **New.** The Completion page appears.

11. Click **Finish** to close the New Mail User window.

12. Close the Exchange Management Console.

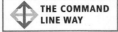

THE COMMAND LINE WAY

You can also use the **Enable-Mailbox** cmdlet in the Exchange Management Shell to mail enable an existing AD user. For example, to mail enable the Kelly Armstrong user in the East OU of the octavius.net domain and specify an alias of kelly.armstrong and external email address of karmstrong@mips-in.com, you could run the following command in the Exchange Management Shell:

Enable-MailUser –Identity 'octavius.net/East/Kelly Armstrong' –Alias 'kelly.armstrong' –ExternalEmailAddress 'karmstrong@mips-in.com'

Alternatively, you can create a new mail user and associated AD user account using the **New-MailUser** cmdlet within the Exchange Management Shell. To specify an initial password for the AD user account, you should first run the following command within the Exchange Management Shell and supply the appropriate password when prompted:

$password = Read-Host 'Enter password' –AsSecureString

Next, you can run the following command in the Exchange Management Shell to create the mail user and AD user account for Kelly Armstrong (alias and logon name = kelly .armstrong) within the East OU in the octavius.net domain, using an external email address of karmstrong@mips-in.com and requiring that the default password supplied earlier be changed on the next logon:

New-MailUser -Name 'Kelly Armstrong' -FirstName 'Kelly' -LastName 'Armstrong' –DisplayName 'Kelly Armstrong' -OrganizationalUnit 'octavius.net/East' –UserPrincipalName 'kelly.armstrong@octavius.net' -Password $password -ResetPasswordOnNextLogon $true –ExternalEmailAddress 'karmstrong@mips-in.com'

→ CREATE A MAIL CONTACT

GET READY. Turn on the computer, and log in as the Administrator user account. Close any windows that appear on the desktop.

1. Click **Start**, **All Programs**, **Microsoft Exchange Server 2007**, and then click **Exchange Management Console**. The Exchange Management Console window appears.

2. In the console tree pane, expand **Recipient Configuration** and highlight **Mail Contact**.

3. In the action pane, click **New Mail Contact**. The New Mail Contact window appears as shown in Figure 5-25.

Figure 5-25

Creating a New Mail Contact

![New Mail Contact window. The left pane lists: Introduction, Contact Information, New Mail Contact, Completion. The right pane shows "Introduction — This wizard will guide you through the steps for creating a new mail contact or mail-enabling an existing contact. Create a mail contact for: ⦿ New contact ◯ Existing contact: [text box] [Browse...]". Buttons at bottom: Help, < Back, Next >, Cancel.]

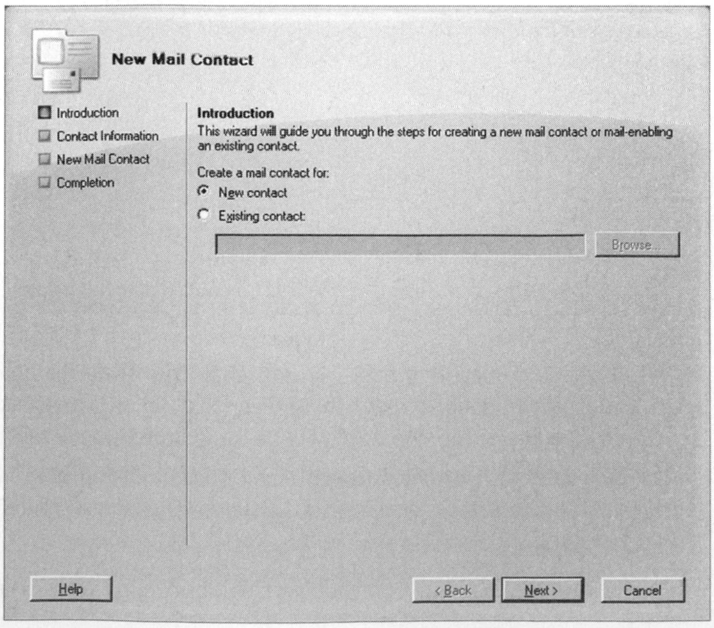

4. If you wish to create a new AD contact object that is mail enabled, ensure that **New contact** is selected. Alternatively, you can choose to mail enable an existing AD contact object. To mail enable an existing contact object, select **Existing contact**, click the **Browse** button, select the appropriate user in the Select Contact window that appears, and click **OK**.

5. Click **Next**. The Contact Information page appears as shown in Figure 5-26.

Figure 5-26

Adding Contact Information

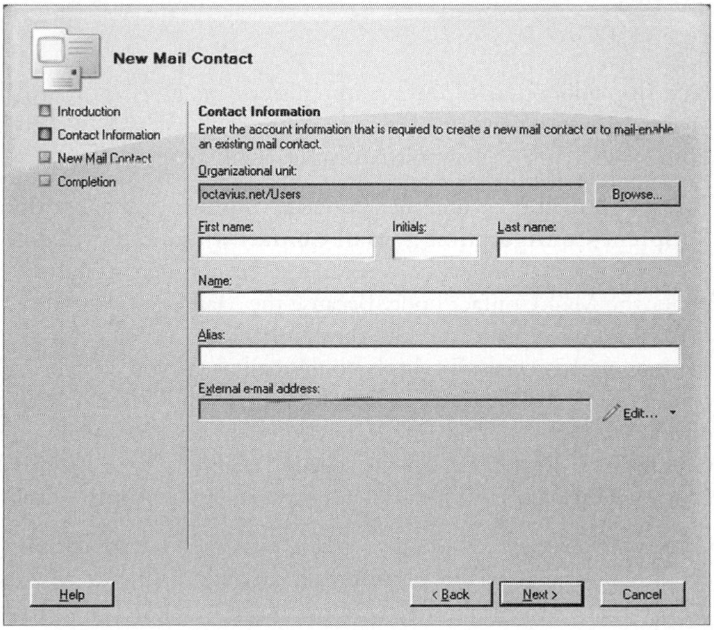

TAKE NOTE*

If you selected **Existing contact** in Figure 5-25, you will only be allowed to change the alias and external email address information shown in Figure 5-26.

6. If you chose New contact in Figure 5-25, the mail contact will be created in the default Users folder in your current domain. Because objects are rarely created in this folder, you should click **Browse**, select the appropriate OU, and click **OK**. For a new contact, you should also enter the name information for the contact.

7. Ensure that the **Alias** dialog box contains the recipient name that should appear in the email address. For example, if the alias is kelly.armstrong, the email address for the mail contact will be kelly.armstrong@domain.

8. Click **Edit** next to the External e-mail address dialog box, type in the external SMTP email address for the mail contact in the SMTP Address window that appears, and click **OK**.

9. Click **Next**. The New Mail Contact page appears.

10. Review the summary of your settings and click **New**. The Completion page appears.

11. Click **Finish** to close the New Mail Contact window.

12. Close the Exchange Management Console.

THE COMMAND LINE WAY

You can also use the **Enable-MailContact** cmdlet in the Exchange Management Shell to mail enable an existing contact object within AD. For example, to mail enable the Kelly Armstrong contact object in the East OU of the octavius.net domain and specify an alias of kelly.armstrong and external email address of karmstrong@mips-in.com, you could run the following command in the Exchange Management Shell:

Enable-MailContact –Identity 'octavius.net/East/Kelly Armstrong' -Alias 'kelly .armstrong' –ExternalEmailAddress 'karmstrong@mips-in.com'

Alternatively, you can use the **New-MailContact** cmdlet to create a new mail contact. For example to create a mail contact for Kelly Armstrong (alias = kelly.armstrong) within the East OU in the octavius.net domain using an external email address of karmstrong@ mips-in.com, you could run the following command in the Exchange Management Shell:

New-MailContact -Name 'Kelly Armstrong' -FirstName 'Kelly' -LastName 'Armstrong' -OrganizationalUnit 'octavius.net/East' -Alias 'kelly.armstrong' -ExternalEmailAddress 'karmstrong@mips-in.com'

Configuring Mail Users and Mail Contacts

Because mail users and mail contacts do not have mailboxes within the organization, there are fewer configuration options for them compared to mailbox users. Like mailbox users, the configuration of mail users and mail contacts is performed using the properties of the recipient object in the Exchange Management Console or the appropriate cmdlet within the Exchange Management Shell.

As with mailbox users, you can administer all mail users and mail contacts within your organization provided you are a member of the Exchange Organization Administrator or Exchange Recipient Administrator role.

To view all mail users and mail contacts within your organization, you can navigate to **Recipient Configuration > Mail Contact** within the Exchange Management Console. As with viewing mailbox users, you can also create filters to narrow the list of objects displayed under the Mail Contact node. Because the Mail Contact node contains both mail user and mail contact recipient objects, you should create a filter to display only the types of objects that you wish to view. To display only mail users, you can click **Create Filter** in the detail pane, specify **Recipient Type Details Equals Mail User** in the appropriate expression drop-down boxes, and click **Apply Filter**. Alternatively, to display only mail contacts, you can click **Create Filter** in the detail pane, specify **Recipient Type Details Equals Mail Contact** in the appropriate expression drop-down boxes, and click **Apply Filter**.

Once you have located the appropriate mail user or mail contact, you can highlight it in the detail pane and select **Properties** from the action pane to view its properties. The properties for the Kelly Armstrong mail user are shown in Figure 5-27; however, the properties of a mail user and mail contact are nearly identical.

Figure 5-27

Mail User Properties

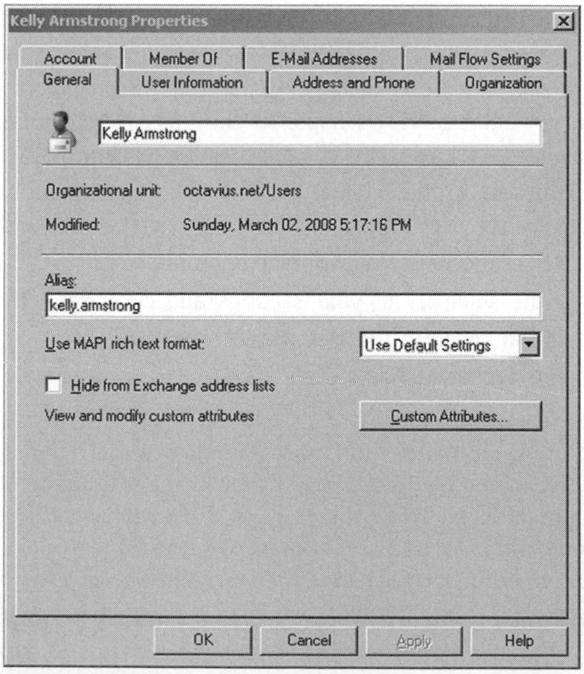

Like the General tab of mailbox user properties, the General tab in the properties of a mail user or mail contact displays the location of the AD object as well as allows you to change the alias, hide the object from email address lists, and create up to 15 custom attributes for use when searching for objects or creating dynamic distribution groups. However, instead of displaying mailbox information, the General tab in the properties of a mail user or mail contact allows you to control whether the mail user or mail contact can send emails from a MAPI client within the organization using rich text format by selecting **Always** or **Never** in the associated drop-down box.

Both mail users and mail contacts have Address and Phone, Organization, and Member Of tabs that contain information about the mail user. Mail users also have User Information and Account tabs that contain information from AD regarding the associated user account. Similarly, mail contacts have a Contact Information tab that lists information regarding the AD contact object. The information from these tabs is taken from the existing AD user or contact object if the object was mail enabled, but must be entered manually if the mail user or mail contact was created by Exchange.

The E-Mail Addresses tab for a mail user or mail contact lists the primary external email address as well as the internal secondary email address generated using the alias. In Figure 5-28, the Kelly Armstrong mail user has an external SMTP email address of karmstrong@mips-in .com that is marked as the primary address so that emails sent by the mail user contain karmstrong@mips-in.com within the From field of the email. Because the mail user was created in the octavius.net domain, a secondary email address of kelly.armstrong@mips-in.com was generated from the alias to allow internal users to quickly locate and send mail to the mail user.

TAKE NOTE*

As with mailbox users, the Member Of tab for a mail user or mail contact object lists the groups that the object is a member of. You cannot modify group membership using it.

Figure 5-28

Configuring Mail User Email Addresses

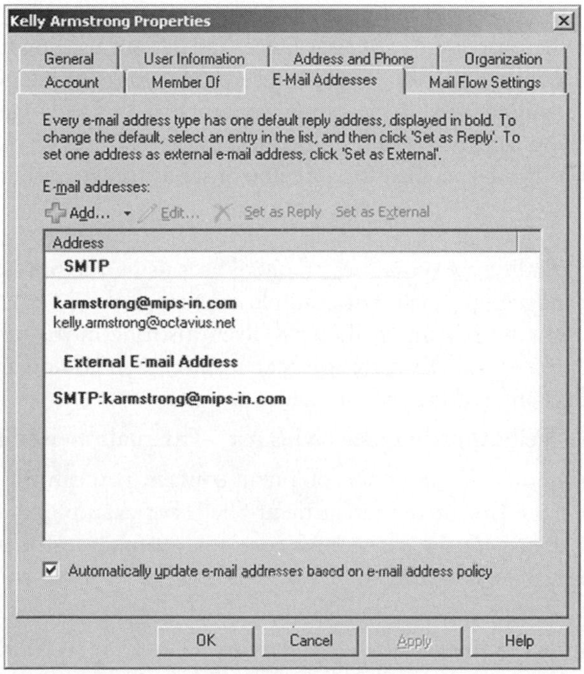

As with mailbox users, you can add additional email addresses to the E-Mail Addresses tab of a mail user or mail contact as well as change the alias. However, you cannot remove the external email address. If the external email address needs to be changed, you can highlight it and click the **Edit** button to modify it.

Because mail users and mail contacts do not have mailboxes, there are no Mailbox Settings or Mailbox Features tabs as seen in the properties of a mailbox user. In addition, the Mail Flow Settings tab of a mail user or mail contact can only be used to limit message size and delivery as shown in Figure 5-29.

Figure 5-29

Configuring Mail Flow Settings

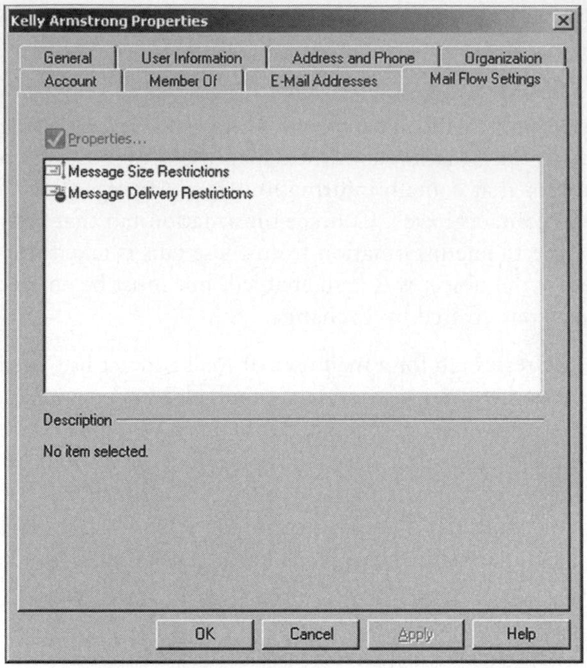

Kelly Armstrong Properties

| General | User Information | Address and Phone | Organization |
| Account | Member Of | E-Mail Addresses | Mail Flow Settings |

☑ Properties...

⊟ Message Size Restrictions
⊟ Message Delivery Restrictions

Description
No item selected.

| OK | Cancel | Apply | Help |

If you access the properties of Message Size Restrictions as shown in Figure 5-29, you can specify the maximum size for messages received by your Exchange servers for forwarding to the external email address. By accessing the properties of Message Delivery Restrictions in Figure 5-29, you can specify allowed senders for a mail user or mail contact. These settings are identical to those specified for a mailbox user as shown earlier in Figure 5-15.

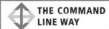
THE COMMAND
LINE WAY

You can also modify the properties of a mail user using the **Set-MailUser** cmdlet within the Exchange Management Shell. For example, to change the external email address to kellya@ mips-in.com for the existing mail user Kelly Armstrong in the octavius.net domain (internal email address = kelly.armstrong@octavius.net), you could run the following command within the Exchange Management Shell:

Set-MailUser 'kelly.armstrong@octavius.net' –ExternalEmailAddress 'kellya@mips-in.com'

Similarly, to modify the properties of a mail contact, you can use the **Set-MailContact** cmdlet within the Exchange Management Shell. For example, to change the display name to Kelly Armstrong for the Kelly Armstrong mail contact in the octavius.net domain (internal email address = kelly.armstrong@octavius.net), you could run the following command within the Exchange Management Console:

Set-MailContact 'kelly.armstrong@octavius.net' –DisplayName 'Kelly Armstrong'

To see more options that can be used alongside the Set-MailUser and Set-MailContact cmdlets, search for Set-MailUser and Set-MailContact within Exchange Server 2007 Help.

To view the settings that you have configured for a mail user, you can use the **Get-MailUser** cmdlet. Similarly, the **Get-MailContact** cmdlet can be used to view settings for a mail contact. For example, the following command within the Exchange Management Shell lists the properties of the Kelly Armstrong mail user described earlier:

Get-MailUser 'kelly.armstrong@octavius.net' | format-list

Managing Mail Users and Mail Contacts

As with mailbox users, you can disable or remove mail users and mail contacts. These tasks can be done using the Exchange Management Console, the Active Directory Users and Computers console, or the appropriate cmdlets within the Exchange Management Shell.

Unlike mailbox users, you cannot grant Send As permission or Full Access permission to a mail user or mail contact. However, you can disable or remove a mail user and mail contact in much the same way you would disable or remove a mailbox user.

If you disable a mail user, all Exchange-related properties within the AD user account are removed, but the user account is not removed from AD. In general, you should disable mail users if users within your organization no longer need to contact the mail user, yet the AD account must still exist for domain authentication.

Similarly, if you disable a mail contact, the Exchange-related properties within the AD contact object are removed, but the contact object is not deleted.

Alternatively, if you choose to remove a mail user or mail contact, the associated AD user account or contact object is removed completely. This option is often used when the contract for a mail user or mail contact has expired. Because mail users and mail contacts do not have associated mailboxes, you can also remove them by deleting their objects directly in the Active Directory Users and Computers console.

⊕ DISABLE A MAIL USER OR MAIL CONTACT

GET READY. Turn on the computer, and log in as the Administrator user account. Close any windows that appear on the desktop.

1. Click **Start**, **All Programs**, **Microsoft Exchange Server 2007**, and then click **Exchange Management Console**. The Exchange Management Console window appears.
2. In the console tree pane, expand **Recipient Configuration** and highlight **Mail Contact**.
3. In the result pane, select the appropriate mail user or mail contact and click **Disable** in the action pane. When prompted to confirm the action, click **Yes**.
4. Close the Exchange Management Console.

You can also use the **Disable-MailUser** cmdlet in the Exchange Management Shell to disable a mail user. To disable Kelly Armstrong (internal email address kelly.armstrong@ octavius.net), you could run the following command in the Exchange Management Shell:

Disable-MailUser 'kelly.armstrong@octavius.net'

Similarly, you can use the **Disable-MailContact** cmdlet in the Exchange Management Shell to disable a mail contact. To disable Kelly Armstrong (internal email address kelly.armstrong@ octavius.net), you could run the following command in the Exchange Management Shell:

Disable-MailContact 'kelly.armstrong@octavius.net'

⊕ REMOVE A MAIL USER OR MAIL CONTACT

GET READY. Turn on the computer, and log in as the Administrator user account. Close any windows that appear on the desktop.

1. Click **Start**, **All Programs**, **Microsoft Exchange Server 2007**, and then click **Exchange Management Console**. The Exchange Management Console window appears.
2. In the console tree pane, expand **Recipient Configuration** and highlight **Mail Contact**.
3. In the result pane, select the appropriate mail user or mail contact and click **Remove** in the action pane. When prompted to confirm the action, click **Yes**.
4. Close the Exchange Management Console.

THE COMMAND LINE WAY

You can also use the **Remove-MailUser** cmdlet in the Exchange Management Shell to remove a mail user from AD. To remove the user Kelly Armstrong (logon name = kelly.armstrong) in the octavius.net domain, you could run the following command in the Exchange Management Shell:

Remove-MailUser –Identity 'octavius.net\kelly.armstrong'

Similarly, you can use the **Remove-MailContact** cmdlet in the Exchange Management Shell to remove a mail contact from AD. To remove the contact Kelly Armstrong (logon name = kelly.armstrong) in the octavius.net domain, you could run the following command in the Exchange Management Shell:

Remove-MailContact –Identity 'octavius.net\kelly.armstrong'

Working with Mail-Enabled Groups

↓
THE BOTTOM LINE

Mail-enabled groups are used to streamline the sending of email to multiple recipients within an organization. As a result, you should create mail-enabled groups after deploying a new Exchange organization and as organizations grow and change over time. In addition, you should understand how to manage and configure mail-enabled groups to ensure that they reflect the needs of users and the organization.

CERTIFICATION READY?
Configure mail-enabled groups.
2.2

Working with Mail-Enabled Universal Groups

Mail-enabled universal groups are simply universal security or distribution groups that have an email address and contain other recipient objects as members. You can create, configure, and manage them using the Exchange Management Console and Exchange Management Shell.

CREATING MAIL-ENABLED UNIVERSAL GROUPS

Creating mail-enabled groups simplifies and organizes the sending of email to multiple recipients. Nearly all organizations are made up of several different departments, teams, projects, and business units. By creating mail-enabled groups to represent these entities and adding the appropriate mailbox users, mail users, and mail contacts to these groups, you can enhance the productivity of the users within your organization. For example, when these users need to communicate to all the members of a specific department, they could send an email to the mail-enabled group for that department. All members of the department will receive a copy of the email message and can reply to it individually.

TAKE NOTE*

In general, it is considered good form to create mail-enabled groups within your organization to represent even the smallest groups of users who share the same function, location, or job role. This allows for the greatest flexibility when sending emails.

You can create security groups and distribution groups within AD that have global, domain local, or universal scope. Security groups may be assigned permissions and rights to network resources, whereas distribution groups cannot. Exchange Server 2007 allows you to mail enable both security groups and distribution groups, however, these groups must have universal scope. If you create a *mail-enabled universal security group*, it can be used to assign permissions and rights to network resources as well as to send email to a group of recipient objects. However, if you create a *mail-enabled universal distribution group*, it can only be used when sending email to a group of recipient objects. In general, you should create mail-enabled universal security groups if the members within the group require the same access to network resources. This allows administrators to use the mail-enabled universal security groups to simplify the assignment of permissions on resources. If the mail-enabled groups should only be used by Exchange, you should create them as mail-enabled universal distribution groups.

Mail-enabled universal security and distribution groups can contain any recipient object other than dynamic distribution groups. This includes other universal security and distribution groups.

To save administration, you can create and mail enable a new universal security or distribution group within the Exchange Management Console. Alternatively, you can choose to mail-enable an existing universal security or distribution group that was created previously. As with creating other recipient objects, you must specify an appropriate alias for the group object during creation that will be used to generate the email address that others will use when contacting group members.

CREATE A MAIL-ENABLED UNIVERSAL GROUP

GET READY. Turn on the computer, and log in as the Administrator user account. Close any windows that appear on the desktop.

1. Click **Start**, **All Programs**, **Microsoft Exchange Server 2007**, and then click **Exchange Management Console**. The Exchange Management Console window appears.

2. In the console tree pane, expand **Recipient Configuration** and highlight **Distribution Group**.

3. In the action pane, click **New Distribution Group**. The New Distribution Group window appears as shown in Figure 5-30.

Figure 5-30

Creating a New Universal Distribution Group

![Screenshot of the New Distribution Group wizard window. The left pane lists the wizard steps: Introduction, Group Information, New Distribution Group, Completion. The main pane shows the Introduction heading with text "This wizard will guide you through the steps for creating a new distribution group or mail-enable an existing group." Below is "Create a Distribution Group for:" with two radio options: "New group" (selected) and "Existing group" with a Browse button. At the bottom are Help, Back, Next, and Cancel buttons.]

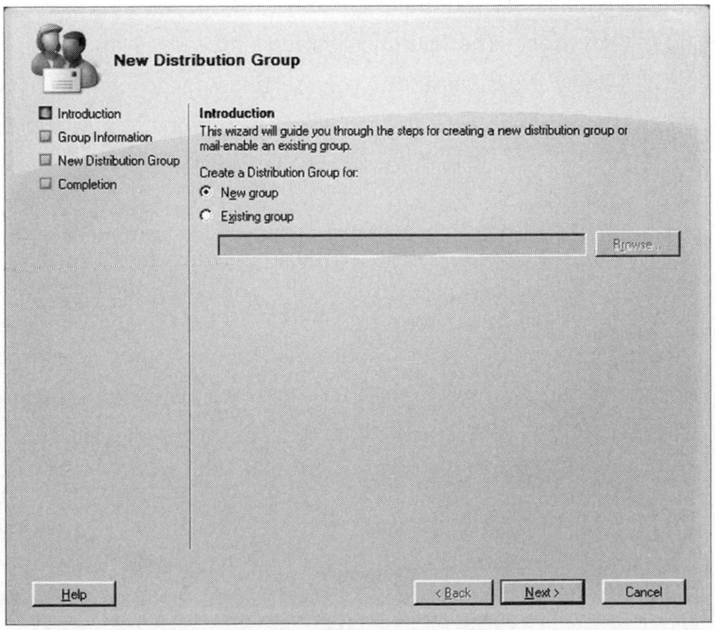

4. If you wish to create a new universal group that is mail enabled, ensure that **New group** is selected. Alternatively, you can choose to mail enable an existing universal group. To mail enable an existing universal group, select **Existing group**, click the **Browse** button, select the appropriate universal security or distribution group in the Select Group window that appears, and click **OK**.

5. Click **Next**. The Group Information page appears as shown in Figure 5-31.

Figure 5-31

Specifying Group Information

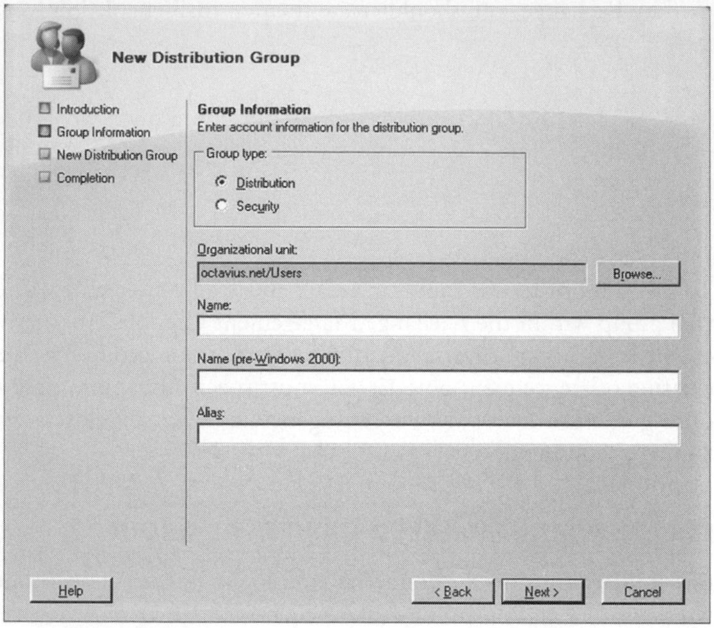

New Distribution Group

- Introduction
- Group Information
- New Distribution Group
- Completion

Group Information
Enter account information for the distribution group.

Group type:
- ⦿ Distribution
- ○ Security

Organizational unit:
octavius.net/Users   Browse...

Name:

Name (pre-Windows 2000):

Alias:

Help   < Back   Next >   Cancel

6. If you chose New group in Figure 5-30, the universal group will be created in the default Users folder in your current domain. Because objects are rarely created in this folder, you should click **Browse**, select the appropriate OU, and click **OK**. For a new universal group you should select the appropriate type (**Distribution** or **Security**) as well as supply an appropriate name in the **Name** dialog boxes.

7. Ensure that the **Alias** dialog box contains the appropriate group name that should appear in the email address. Normally, for simplicity and organization, the alias is the same as the group name.

8. Click **Next**. The New Distribution Group page appears.

9. Review the summary of your settings and click **New**. The Completion page appears.

10. Click **Finish** to close the New Distribution Group window.

11. Close the Exchange Management Console.

THE COMMAND LINE WAY

You can also use the **Enable-DistributionGroup** cmdlet in the Exchange Management Shell to mail enable an existing universal group object within AD. For example, to mail enable the Marketing universal group in the East OU of the octavius.net domain and specify an alias of marketing, you could run the following command in the Exchange Management Shell:

Enable-DistributionGroup –Identity 'octavius.net/East/Marketing' –Alias 'marketing'

Alternatively, you can use the **New-DistributionGroup** cmdlet to create a new mail contact. For example to create a new mail-enabled universal distribution group called Marketing in the East OU of the octavius.net domain with a Pre-Windows 2000 name of Marketing and an alias of marketing, you could run the following command in the Exchange Management Shell:

New-DistributionGroup –Name 'Marketing' –SamAccountName 'Marketing' –Type 'Distribution' –OrganizationalUnit 'octavius.net/East' –Alias 'marketing'

CONFIGURING MAIL-ENABLED UNIVERSAL GROUPS

Mail-enabled groups are displayed under the **Recipient Configuration > Distribution Group** node within the Exchange Management Console and can be administered by members of the Exchange Organization Administrator or Exchange Recipient Administrator role.

If your organization has several mail-enabled groups, you can create a filter to narrow the list of objects displayed under the Distribution Group node. To display only mail-enabled universal security groups, you can click **Create Filter** in the detail pane, specify **Recipient Type Details Equals Mail-Enabled Universal Security Group** in the appropriate expression drop-down boxes, and click **Apply Filter**. Alternatively, to display only mail-enabled universal distribution groups, you can click **Create Filter** in the detail pane, specify **Recipient Type Details Equals Mail-Enabled Universal Distribution Group** in the appropriate expression drop-down boxes, and click **Apply Filter**.

Once you have located the appropriate mail-enabled universal group, you can highlight it in the detail pane and select **Properties** from the action pane to view its properties. The properties options of mail-enabled universal security groups that you can configure are identical to the properties options of a mail-enabled universal distribution group. The properties of the Marketing mail-enabled universal group are shown in Figure 5-32.

Figure 5-32

Universal Distribution Group Properties

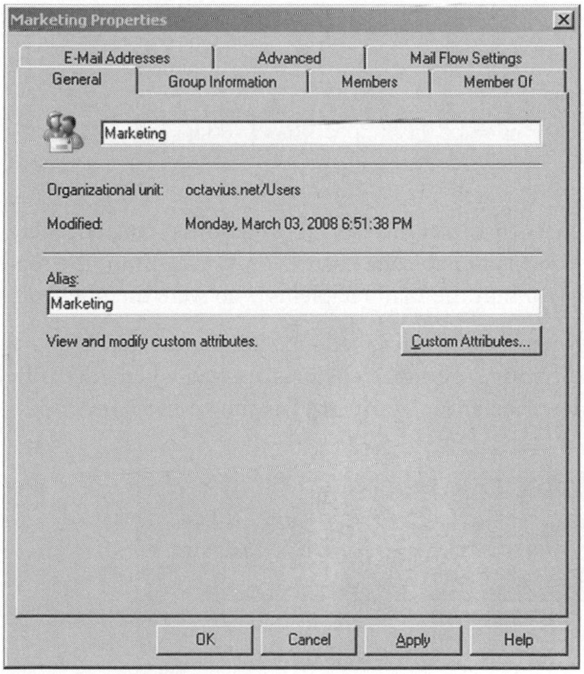

The General tab in the properties of a mail-enabled universal group displays the location of the AD object as well as allows you change the alias and create up to 15 custom attributes for use when searching for the mail-enabled universal group or creating dynamic distribution groups.

The E-Mail Addresses tab of a mail-enabled universal group lists the primary email address for the group that was automatically generated using the alias. As with other recipient objects, you can create additional email addresses for a mail-enabled universal group.

In addition, the Mail Flow Settings tab of a mail-enabled universal group is identical to the Mail Flow Settings of a mail user or mail contact. You can specify the maximum size for incoming messages that are forwarded to the mail-enabled universal group as well as specify allowed senders for the mail-enabled universal group.

Because a mail-enabled universal group can be a member of other groups, the property sheet has a Member Of tab that lists the groups that contain the mail-enabled universal group. However, this list is not modifiable because group membership can only be changed on the parent group. To add members to your mail-enabled universal group or remove existing members, you can use the Members tab shown in Figure 5-33.

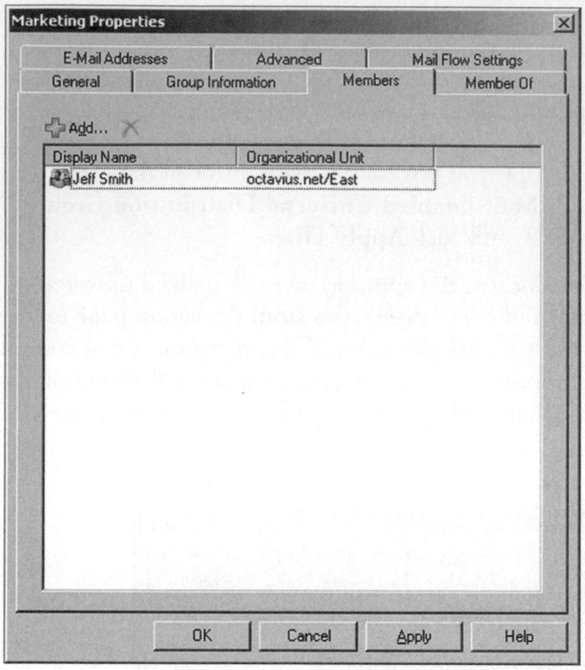

Figure 5-33

Configuring Members

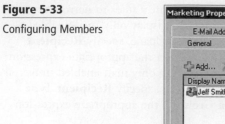

After a new mail-enabled universal group has been created, there are no members by default. However, if you mail-enable an existing universal group, the mail-enabled universal group will automatically contain the mail recipients who were members of the group beforehand.

After adding members to your mail-enabled universal group, it is good form to enter a description for your group that will be displayed when a MAPI client such as Outlook or Entourage views the group's properties as shown in Figure 5-34.

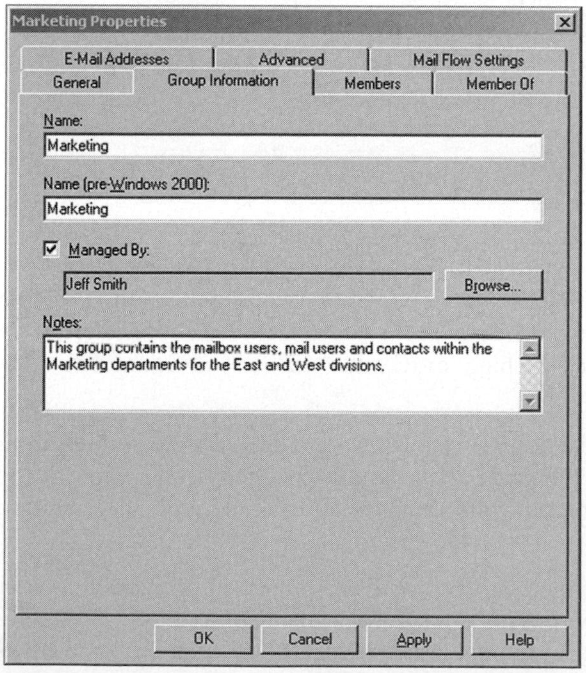

Figure 5-34

Configuring Group Information

You can also select a recipient to act as the ***group manager***. The group manager is typically the person who is responsible for the operation of the department or team within the organization that the group represents. If mail sent to a mail-enabled universal group is rejected by one of its members, a nondelivery report is generated and sent to the sender by default. For mail-enabled universal groups that have several members, there is a greater possibility that the sender will receive multiple nondelivery reports. To prevent this, you can force nonde-livery reports to be sent to the group manager by selecting **Send delivery reports to group manager** on the Advanced tab of mail-enabled universal group properties as shown in Figure 5-35. The group manager can then contact the Exchange administrator to investigate delivery problems.

Figure 5-35

Specifying Advanced Distribution Group Information

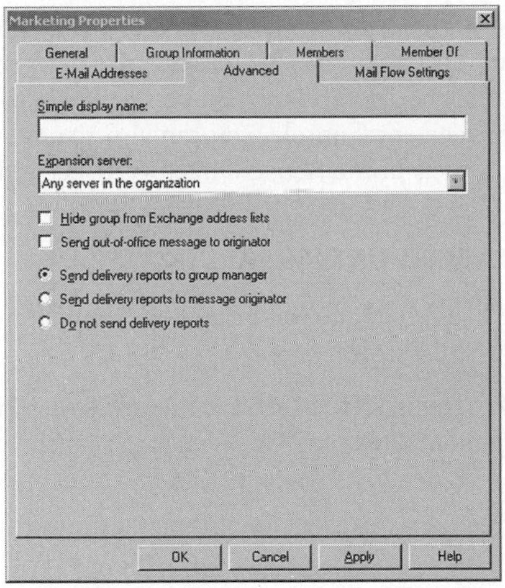

You can specify a display name on the Advanced tab to be used in delivery reports as well as hide the group from address lists and prevent the sender from receiving out-of-office messages from group members.

The *expansion server* is the Exchange server that is responsible for looking up the group membership within AD before routing email addressed to the group. By default, the nearest Hub role server provides this function, but you can choose a specific expansion server in the drop-down box in Figure 5-35.

THE COMMAND LINE WAY

You can add members to a mail-enabled universal group using the **Add-Distribution Gro-upMember** cmdlet and remove existing members using the **Remove-DistributionGroup Member** cmdlet. For example, to add Kelly Armstrong (email address kelly.armstrong@octavius .net) as a member of the Marketing mail-enabled universal group (email address = marketing@ octavius.net), you could run the following command within the Exchange Management Console:

Add-DistributionGroupMember –Identity 'marketing@octavius.net' –Member 'kelly .armstrong@octavius.net'

You can also modify the properties of a mail-enabled universal group using the **Set-Distribution Group** cmdlet within the Exchange Management Shell. For example, to change the display name to Marketing Group for the Marketing mail-enabled universal group within the octavius .net domain (email address = marketing@octavius.net), you could run the following command within the Exchange Management Console:

Set –DistributionGroup –Identity 'marketing@octavius.net' –DisplayName 'Marketing Group'

To see more options that can be used alongside the Set-DistributionGroup cmdlet, search for Set-DistributionGroup within Exchange Server 2007 Help.

To view the properties that you have configured for a mail-enabled universal group, you can use the **Get-DistributionGroup** cmdlet. For example, the following command within the Exchange Management Shell lists the properties of the Marketing distribution group:

Get-DistributionGroup –Identity 'marketing@octavius.net' | format-list

MANAGING MAIL-ENABLED UNIVERSAL GROUPS

To prevent a mail-enabled universal group from being used to relay mail to its members, you can simply disable it. Disabling a mail-enabled universal group will remove all Exchange-related properties within the AD universal group account, but the universal group, its membership list, and its members are not removed. After disabling a mail-enabled universal group, you can mail enabled it again using the same procedure discussed earlier in this lesson.

Alternatively, if you choose to remove a mail-enabled universal group, the universal group is removed completely from AD. If you need to recreate the mail-enabled universal group in the future, you will need to add the appropriate members again. Although they can be removed within the Exchange Management Console, you can also remove mail-enabled universal groups by deleting their objects in the Active Directory Users and Computers console.

→ DISABLE A MAIL-ENABLED UNIVERSAL GROUP

GET READY. Turn on the computer, and log in as the Administrator user account. Close any windows that appear on the desktop.

1. Click **Start**, **All Programs**, **Microsoft Exchange Server 2007**, and then click **Exchange Management Console**. The Exchange Management Console window appears.

2. In the console tree pane, expand **Recipient Configuration** and highlight **Distribution Group**.

3. In the result pane, select the appropriate mail-enabled universal group and click **Disable** in the action pane. When prompted to confirm the action, click **Yes**.

4. Close the Exchange Management Console.

You can also use the **Disable-DistributionGroup** cmdlet in the Exchange Management Shell to disable a mail-enabled universal group. To disable the Marketing mail-enabled universal group (email address = marketing@octavius.net), you could run the following command in the Exchange Management Shell:

Disable-DistributionGroup 'marketing@octavius.net'

→ REMOVE A MAIL-ENABLED UNIVERSAL GROUP

GET READY. Turn on the computer, and log in as the Administrator user account. Close any windows that appear on the desktop.

1. Click **Start**, **All Programs**, **Microsoft Exchange Server 2007**, and then click **Exchange Management Console**. The Exchange Management Console window appears.

2. In the console tree pane, expand **Recipient Configuration** and highlight **Distribution Group**.

3. In the result pane, select the appropriate mail-enabled universal group and click **Remove** in the action pane. When prompted to confirm the action, click **Yes**.

4. Close the Exchange Management Console.

You can also use the **Remove-DistributionGroup** cmdlet in the Exchange Management Shell to remove a mail-enabled universal group. To remove the Marketing mail-enabled universal group (email address = marketing@octavius.net), you could run the following command in the Exchange Management Shell:

Remove-DistributionGroup 'marketing@octavius.net'

Working with Dynamic Distribution Groups

Dynamic distribution groups are better suited for sending email to multiple users if the list of users changes frequently. Unlike universal distribution groups, dynamic distribution groups use criteria to populate their membership when email is relayed to them. To work with dynamic distribution groups, you must understand how to create, configure, and manage them using the Exchange Management Console and the appropriate cmdlets within the Exchange Management Shell.

CREATING DYNAMIC DISTRIBUTION GROUPS

While mail-enabled universal groups simplify the sending of email to multiple recipients, their membership needs to be managed manually. This works well for mail-enabled universal groups that have a fixed membership. However, some organizational groups may have a membership that changes frequently. For these groups, creating and maintaining the membership of the associated mail-enabled universal groups can be time consuming.

For divisions, teams, and other entities within your organization that do not have a fixed membership, you can create a mail-enabled *dynamic distribution group*. Dynamic distribution groups automatically populate their group membership when they are used to relay email by searching AD for recipient objects that match certain criteria. These criteria are specified when you create the group and consist of two components:

- *Conditions* that match the value of an attribute within the recipient object such as Department or Custom Attribute 5
- A *filter* that specifies the location within AD that will be searched for recipient objects as well as the types of recipients to search for (contacts, mailbox users, etc.)

Say, for example, that you need to create a mail-enabled group that contains all of the full-time staff members who are part of the TASU project within the East Marketing department. In addition, your organization creates mailbox users for all full-time staff and stores the project name within the first Custom Attribute within each mailbox user. To perform this task, you could create a dynamic distribution group that specifies conditions that match the mail-enabled users within the East OU (and all subordinate OUs) whose Department attribute equals 'Marketing' and Custom Attribute 1 attribute equals 'TASU.' When email is sent to this group, Exchange performs a search for the appropriate mailbox users and forwards the email to each member.

Unlike other recipient objects, you only create a mail-enabled dynamic distribution group using Exchange tools. The alias that you specify for the mail-enabled dynamic distribution group will be used to generate the email address that others will use when contacting members of the dynamic distribution group.

➡ CREATE A DYNAMIC DISTRIBUTION GROUP

GET READY. Turn on the computer, and log in as the Administrator user account. Close any windows that appear on the desktop.

1. Click **Start, All Programs, Microsoft Exchange Server 2007**, and then click **Exchange Management Console.** The Exchange Management Console window appears.
2. In the console tree pane, expand **Recipient Configuration** and highlight **Distribution Group.**
3. In the action pane, click **New Dynamic Distribution Group.** The New Dynamic Distribution Group window appears as shown in Figure 5-36.

Figure 5-36

Creating a New Dynamic
Distribution Group

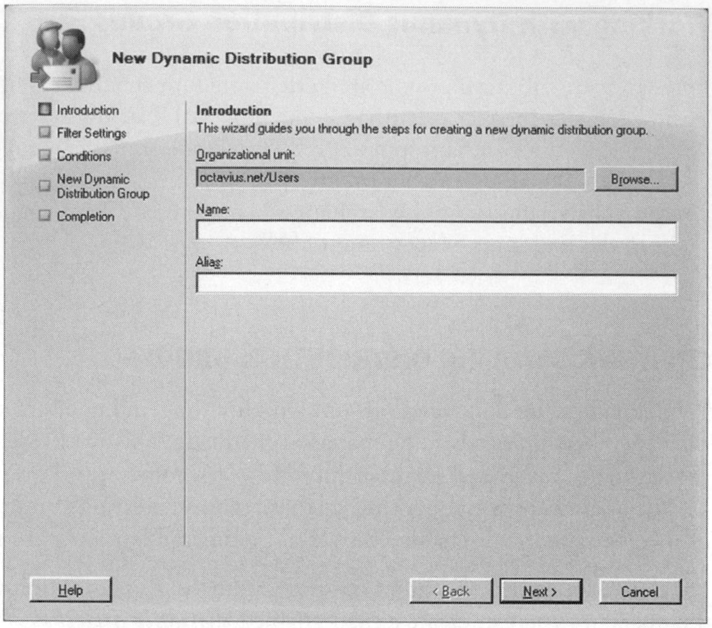

4. By default, the dynamic distribution group will be created in the default Users folder in your current domain. Because objects are rarely created in this folder, you should click **Browse**, select the appropriate OU, and click **OK**.

5. Next, supply an appropriate name for the dynamic distribution group in the **Name** dialog box as well as an appropriate alias used to generate the email address in the **Alias** dialog box. Normally the alias is the same as the group name for simplicity and organization.

6. Click **Next**. The Filter Settings page appears as shown in Figure 5-37.

Figure 5-37

Adding Filter Settings

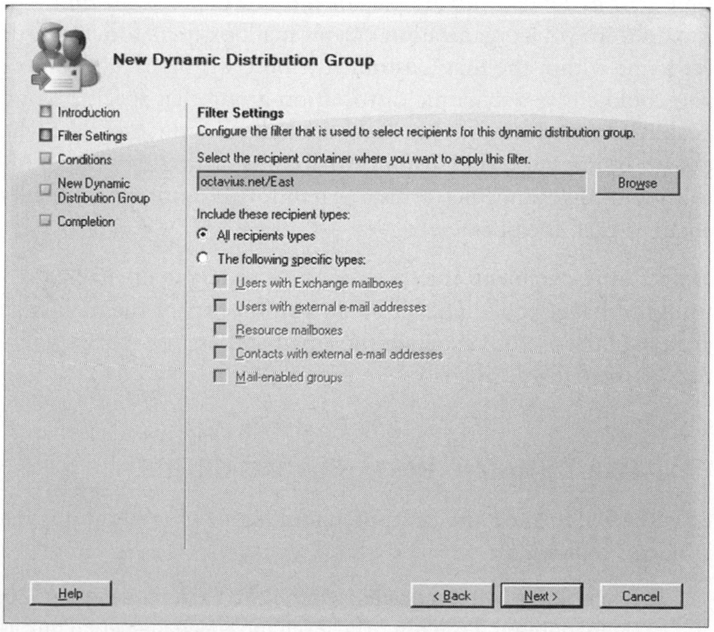

7. Click **Browse**. In the Select Organizational Unit window that appears, select the appropriate domain or OU that the dynamic distribution group will use when searching for recipients and click **OK**.

8. If you wish to restrict the types of recipient objects that the distribution group will apply to, select **The following specific types** and select the appropriate recipient types to include.

9. Click **Next**. The Conditions page appears as shown in Figure 5-38.

Figure 5-38

Adding Conditions

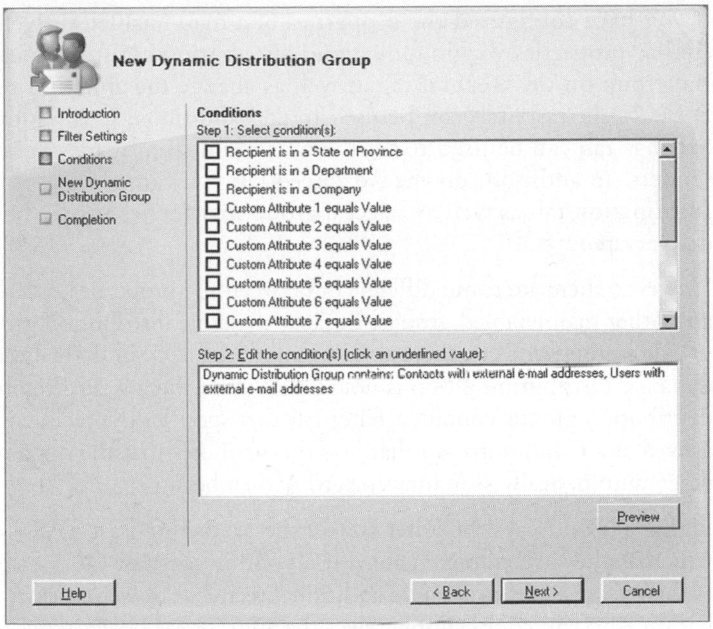

New Dynamic Distribution Group

- Introduction
- Filter Settings
- Conditions
- New Dynamic Distribution Group
- Completion

Conditions

Step 1: Select condition(s):

- ☐ Recipient is in a State or Province
- ☐ Recipient is in a Department
- ☐ Recipient is in a Company
- ☐ Custom Attribute 1 equals Value
- ☐ Custom Attribute 2 equals Value
- ☐ Custom Attribute 3 equals Value
- ☐ Custom Attribute 4 equals Value
- ☐ Custom Attribute 5 equals Value
- ☐ Custom Attribute 6 equals Value
- ☐ Custom Attribute 7 equals Value

Step 2: Edit the condition(s) (click an underlined value):

Dynamic Distribution Group contains: Contacts with external e-mail addresses, Users with external e-mail addresses

Preview

Help   < Back   Next >   Cancel

10. Select the recipient object attributes that the dynamic distribution group will match when searching for group members. Each attribute that you select will add a condition to the Step 2 dialog box. To add a value for each attribute, you must click **specified** within the condition that was added to the Step 2 dialog box, type in the appropriate value in the window that appears, click **Add,** and then click **OK.**

11. To test your settings by searching for the recipient objects that match your filter and conditions, you can click **Preview** in Figure 5-38 and review the information shown in the Dynamic Distribution Group Preview window. When finished reviewing the results, click **OK** to close the Dynamic Distribution Group Preview window.

12. Click **Next.** The New Dynamic Distribution Group page appears.

13. Review the summary of your settings and click **New.** The Completion page appears.

14. Click **Finish** to close the New Dynamic Distribution Group window.

15. Close the Exchange Management Console.

THE COMMAND LINE WAY

You can use the **New-DynamicDistributionGroup** cmdlet to create a new dynamic distribution group. For example, to create a new dynamic distribution group called External Marketing Members (alias = ext-marketing) within the Groups OU of the octavius.net domain that contains mail users and mail contacts within the Marketing department of the octavius.net domain, you could run the following command in the Exchange Management Shell:

New-DynamicDistributionGroup –Name 'External Marketing Members' –Alias 'ext-marketing' –OrganizationalUnit 'octavius.net/Groups' -IncludedRecipients 'MailUsers, MailContacts' –ConditionalDepartment 'Marketing' –RecipientContainer 'octavius.net'

To see more options that can be used alongside the New-DynamicDistributionGroup cmdlet, search for New-DynamicDistributionGroup within Exchange Server 2007 Help.

CONFIGURING DYNAMIC DISTRIBUTION GROUPS

As with mail-enabled universal groups, dynamic distribution groups are stored under the **Recipient Configuration** > **Distribution Group** node within the Exchange Management Console and can be administered by members of the Exchange Organization Administrator or Exchange Recipient Administrator role. To display only dynamic distribution groups under this node, you can click **Create Filter** in the detail pane, specify **Recipient Type Details Equals Dynamic Distribution Group** in the appropriate expression drop-down boxes, and click **Apply Filter.** Once you have located the appropriate mail-enabled universal group, you can highlight it in the detail pane and select **Properties** from the action pane to view its properties.

If you have configured the properties of a mail-enabled universal group, you will find similar properties within a dynamic distribution group. You can view the location of the group on the General tab as well as change the alias and set custom attributes. The E-Mail Addresses tab can be used to add additional email addresses, and the Mail Flow Settings tab can be used to set the maximum size for messages as well as specify allowed senders. In addition, on the Advanced tab you can add a group description to the Group Information tab as well as select a group manager that may be configured to receive delivery reports.

However, there are some differences between the properties of a dynamic distribution group and other mail-enabled groups. Because dynamic distribution groups cannot be a member of other group objects, there is no Member Of tab. Similarly, because the membership of a dynamic distribution group is not statically set, there is no Members tab. Instead, dynamic distribution groups contain a Filter tab that specifies the recipient object types and locations as well as a Conditions tab that lists the attributes that the dynamic distribution will match when automatically searching for group members.

Figure 5-39 displays the Filter tab for the Marketing-East-TASU dynamic distribution group, which applies to mailbox-enabled users within the East OU of the octavius.net domain. If this group needs to include additional recipient object types or apply to a different OU within AD, you could simply select the appropriate object types or click **Browse** and select a different OU.

Figure 5-39

Modifying Filter Settings

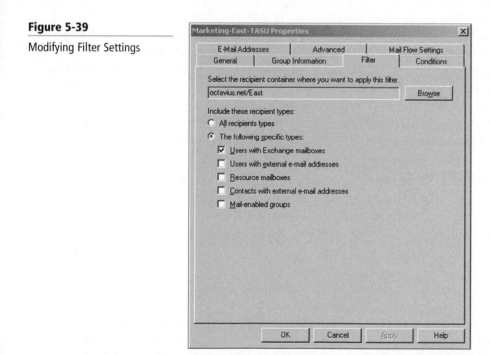

The Conditions tab of the Marketing-East-TASU dynamic distribution group shown in Figure 5-40 further specifies that recipient object members must have a Department attribute equal to Marketing as well as Custom Attribute 1 equal to TASU. To change the value of existing attributes, click on the related blue hyperlink in the Step 2 section and modify the value. For example, to modify the department in Figure 5-40, you would click on the **Marketing** hyperlink and supply a different value or add additional values. Alternatively, you can select additional attributes in the Step 1 section and modify the value in the Step 2 section in the same manner.

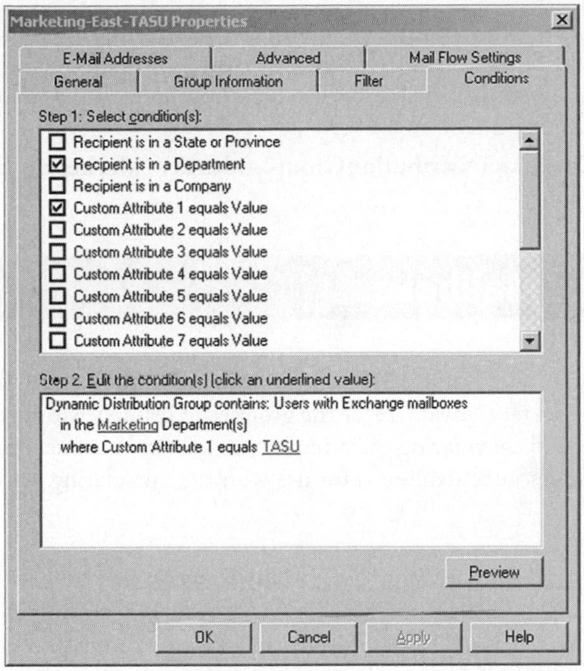

Figure 5-40

Modifying Configuration
Settings

You can also modify the properties of a dynamic distribution group using the **Set-DynamicDistributionGroup** cmdlet within the Exchange Management Shell. For example, to add an additional condition to the Marketing-East-TASU dynamic distribution group that requires the Custom Attribute 2 to have a value of Chicago, you could run the following command within the Exchange Management Console:

Set-DynamicDistributionGroup –Identity 'Marketing-East-TASU' –Conditional CustomAttribute2 'Chicago'

THE COMMAND LINE WAY

To see more options that can be used alongside the Set-DynamicDistributionGroup cmdlet, search for Set-DynamicDistribution Group within Exchange Server 2007 Help.

To view the settings that you have configured for a dynamic distribution group, you can use the **Get-DynamicDistributionGroup** cmdlet. For example, the following command within the Exchange Management Shell lists the properties of the Marketing-East-TASU distribution group:

Get-DynamicDistributionGroup –Identity 'Marketing-East-TASU' | format-list

MANAGING DYNAMIC DISTRIBUTION GROUPS

Because dynamic distribution groups can only be created using Exchange tools, you cannot disable a dynamic distribution group and later mail enable it. Instead, to prevent the dynamic distribution group from being used, you must remove it entirely. If you need to recreate the same dynamic distribution group in the future, you will need to specify the appropriate filter and conditions again.

 REMOVE A DYNAMIC DISTRIBUTION GROUP

GET READY. Turn on the computer, and log in as the Administrator user account. Close any windows that appear on the desktop.

1. Click **Start**, **All Programs**, **Microsoft Exchange Server 2007**, and then click **Exchange Management Console**. The Exchange Management Console window appears.

2. In the console tree pane, expand **Recipient Configuration** and highlight **Distribution Group**.

3. In the result pane, select the appropriate dynamic distribution group and click **Remove** in the action pane. When prompted to confirm the action, click **Yes**.

4. Close the Exchange Management Console.

THE COMMAND LINE WAY

You can also use the **Remove-DynamicDistributionGroup** cmdlet in the Exchange Management Shell to remove a dynamic distribution group. To remove the Marketing-East-TASU dynamic distribution group, you could run the following command in the Exchange Management Shell:

Remove-DynamicDistributionGroup –Identity 'Marketing-East-TASU'

■ Working with Resource Mailboxes

↓ THE BOTTOM LINE

Many organizations deploy MAPI clients such as Outlook and Entourage. These clients are typically used to take advantage of the groupware features within Exchange Server 2007 such as advanced calendaring. As a result, you should become accustomed to the procedures used to create resource mailboxes for use with the calendaring features of MAPI clients.

CERTIFICATION READY?
Configure resource mailboxes.
2.3

Creating and Using Resource Mailboxes

Because resource mailboxes are similar in structure to mailbox users, the procedures used to create them are similar to those used to create mailbox users. Once created, Outlook and Entourage users can use them to hold information used to schedule a room or equipment resource. As with mailbox users, you can use the Exchange Management Console and Exchange Management Shell to create them.

Many organizations today take advantage of the calendaring features within Outlook and Entourage to schedule and manage meetings among email recipients. In a typical scenario, a user will send a new meeting request within Outlook or Entourage to other mail recipients within the organization that lists the time and locations of the meeting. The mail recipients can then choose to accept the meeting details, reject the meeting details, or propose an alternative time. Depending on the choices made within meeting requests, time will automatically be scheduled for each email recipient within the Calendar section of Outlook or Entourage. Additional meeting requests can be sent to change the details of a scheduled meeting or cancel it.

Exchange Server 2007 allows you to create recipient objects to represent rooms or equipment that can also be scheduled within a meeting request. These recipient objects are called **resource mailboxes**. When you create a new meeting request within Outlook or Entourage, you can click the **To** button to select recipient objects that should attend the meeting as well as the resources that the meeting will need as shown in Figure 5-41.

Figure 5-41

Adding Resources to a Meeting Request

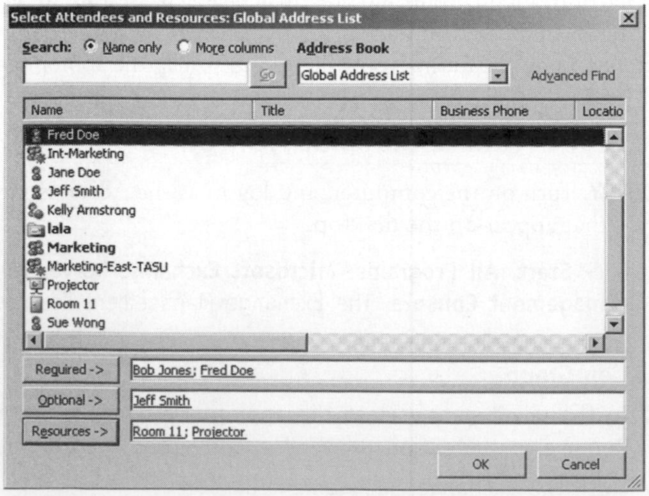

Select Attendees and Resources: Global Address List			
Search: ⦿ Name only ○ More columns **Address Book**			
[ ] Go	Global Address List ▾		Advanced Find
Name	Title	Business Phone	Locatio
👤 Fred Doe			
👥 Int-Marketing			
👤 Jane Doe			
👤 Jeff Smith			
👥 Kelly Armstrong			
📁 lala			
👥 Marketing			
👥 Marketing-East-TASU			
🖥 Projector			
📁 Room 11			
👤 Sue Wong			

Required ->	Bob Jones; Fred Doe
Optional ->	Jeff Smith
Resources ->	Room 11; Projector

OK   Cancel

In Figure 5-41, the Resources dialog box contains two resource mailboxes to represent the need for Room 11 and a projector during the meeting. After selecting the appropriate recipient objects and resource mailboxes, the meeting request will list any room or equipment resource mailboxes within the Location field of the meeting request as shown in Figure 5-42. If the resource mailboxes listed within the email have *Automatic Booking* enabled, the sender will receive immediate notification if the room or equipment resources are already booked for that time when they click Send as shown in Figure 5-42. The sender can then reschedule the meeting as necessary.

Figure 5-42

Scheduling Resources in a Meeting Request

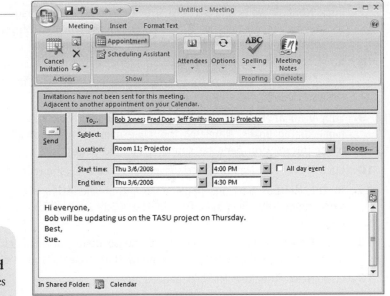

 **ANOTHER WAY**

Instead, add a resource mailbox to the **Required** or **Optional** dialog boxes shown in Figure 5-41. These resource mailboxes will then appear alongside other recipient objects within the **To** field shown in Figure 5-42.

Resource mailboxes are simply mailbox users with a disabled user account in AD and an associated mailbox within a mailbox database on a Mailbox role server within your organization to store meeting information. Because resource mailboxes do not represent users, it is considered good form to create a separate OU for them within your AD domain to allow for organization and quick access.

The process of creating a resource mailbox is nearly identical to that of creating a mailbox user. However, after the creation of a new resource mailbox, the corresponding user account in AD is disabled to prevent logons or mail retrieval. In addition, if you wish to use an existing user account within AD for the resource mailbox, that user account must first be disabled.

Before you create resource mailboxes, you should first create a naming convention for the rooms and equipment within your organization to allow for easy location within Outlook or Entourage. For example, your organization may use a naming convention of BuildingLocation-RoomNumber for rooms and BuildingLocation-Department-EquipmentName for equipment. Thus, Fairway204 could refer to room 204 within the building on Fairway Road, whereas Weber-Accounting-Epson2350Projector would refer to the associated Epson model 2350 projector within the Accounting department on Weber Street.

 CREATE A RESOURCE MAILBOX

GET READY. Turn on the computer, and log in as the Administrator user account. Close any windows that appear on the desktop.

1. Click **Start, All Programs, Microsoft Exchange Server 2007,** and then click **Exchange Management Console.** The Exchange Management Console window appears.

2. In the console tree pane, expand **Recipient Configuration** and highlight **Mailbox.**

3. In the action pane, click **New Mailbox.** The New Mailbox window appears as shown earlier in Figure 5-1.

TAKE NOTE★

If you select **Existing users**, you will only be able to select existing users who are disabled within AD.

TAKE NOTE★

If you selected **Existing users** on the User Type page, you will skip entering the account information shown earlier in Figure 5-3.

TAKE NOTE★

Managed folder policies and ActiveSync policies do not apply to resource mailboxes.

4. To create a resource mailbox that represents a room number, select **Room Mailbox**. Alternatively, you can select **Equipment Mailbox** to create a resource mailbox that represents equipment or devices.

5. Click **Next**. The User Type page appears as shown earlier in Figure 5-2.

6. If you wish to create a resource mailbox alongside a new disabled AD user account, ensure that **New user** is selected. Alternatively, you can choose to use an existing AD user when creating a resource mailbox. To do this, select **Existing users**, click the **Add** button, select the appropriate user in the Select User window that appears, and click **OK**.

7. Click **Next**. If you selected New user on the User Type page, you will be prompted to specify the AD user account information on the User Information page as shown earlier in Figure 5-3.

8. By default, the user will be created in the default Users folder in your current domain. If you wish to store resource mailboxes in a different container, click **Browse**, select the appropriate OU, and click **OK**.

9. Supply an appropriate name in the Name dialog box as well as the two User logon name dialog boxes. Normally, the same name is used for all three dialog boxes. No other information need be supplied on this page.

10. Click **Next**. The Mailbox Settings page appears as shown earlier in Figure 5-4.

11. At the Mailbox Settings page, ensure that the **Alias** dialog box contains the same name that was specified in the Name dialog box on the User Information page.

12. Click **Browse** next to the Mailbox database dialog box, select the Mailbox database in the Select Mailbox Database window that appears and click **OK**.

13. Click **Next**. The New Mailbox page appears.

14. Review the summary of your settings and click **New**. The Completion page appears.

15. Click **Finish** to close the New Mailbox window.

16. Close the Exchange Management Console.

THE COMMAND LINE WAY

The **Enable-Mailbox** cmdlet in the Exchange Management Shell can also be used to create a resource mailbox from an existing disabled user account within AD. To create a room resource mailbox using the existing Room8 user in the East OU of the octavius .net domain, with an alias of Room8 and a mailbox within the Mailbox Database in the First Storage Group on the server EXCH1, you could run the following command in the Exchange Management Shell:

Enable-Mailbox –Identity 'octavius.net/East/Room8' –Alias 'Room8' –Database 'EXCH1\First Storage Group\Mailbox Database' –Room

Alternatively, to create a resource mailbox and associated AD user, you can use the **New-Mailbox** cmdlet. For example, to create an equipment resource mailbox with a Name, Logon Name, and Alias of 3M-Projector within the East OU of the octavius.net domain and create an associated mailbox in the Mailbox Database within the First Storage Group on the server EXCH1, you could run the following command in the Exchange Management Shell:

New-Mailbox –Name '3M-Projector' –Alias '3M-Projector' –UserPrincipalName '3M-Projector@octavius.net' –SamAccountName '3M-Projector' –OrganizationalUnit 'octavius.net/East' –Database 'EXCH1\First Storage Group\Mailbox Database' –Equipment

Configuring Resource Mailboxes

Although resource mailboxes contain the same properties as a regular mailbox user, most options are not configured because resource mailboxes are not used to gain access to the Exchange infrastructure. Instead, you typically configure resource information, automatic booking, and resource booking policies for use by others who schedule a resource using the resource mailbox. Although some of this configuration can be performed in the properties of the resource mailbox in the Exchange Management Console, most of it must be configured using cmdlets within the Exchange Management Shell.

CONFIGURING RESOURCE MAILBOX PROPERTIES

Because resource mailboxes are mailbox users, you can configure them under the **Recipient Configuration** > **Mailbox** node within the Exchange Management Console. Additionally, you can create a filter to narrow the list displayed in this node to specific room or equipment resource mailboxes only. Simply click **Create Filter** in the detail pane, specify **Recipient Type Details Equals Room Mailbox** or **Recipient Type Details Equals Equipment Mailbox** in the appropriate expression drop-down boxes, and click **Apply Filter**. Once you have located the appropriate resource mailbox, you can highlight it in the detail pane and select **Properties** from the action pane to view its properties.

The properties for a resource mailbox contain the same tabs as a mailbox user. However, because resource mailboxes are not used in the same manner as a mailbox user, the information on these tabs is not configured for a resource mailbox. Instead, resource mailboxes contain an additional Resource Information tab that can be used to list additional room or equipment attributes that will help users choose the appropriate resource when scheduling meetings. The Resource Information tab shown in Figure 5-43 indicates that Room 11 has a capacity of 16 seats and contains a projector, wireless network access, and a whiteboard.

Figure 5-43

Configuring Resource Information

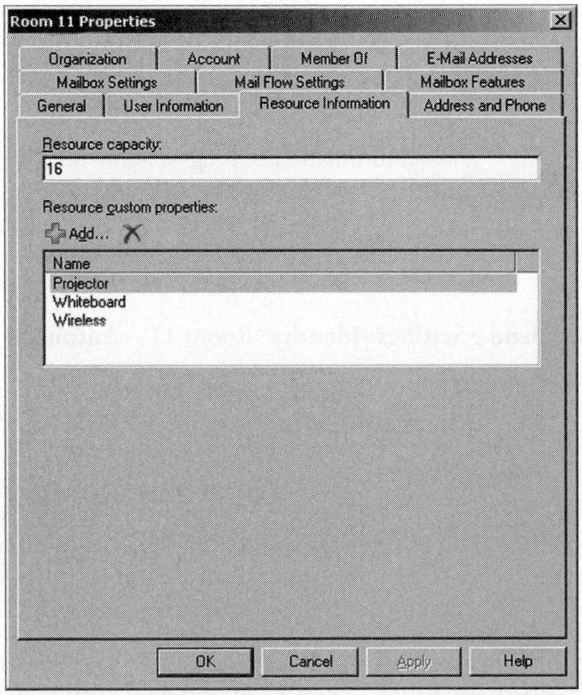

Before you can add custom properties to the Resource Information tab shown in Figure 5-43, you must create custom properties within the AD schema using the **Set-ResourceConfig** cmdlet in the Exchange Management Shell. For example, to create the Projector, Whiteboard, and Wireless custom properties for use with room resource mailboxes using the dc01.octavius. net DC, you could run the following command within the Exchange Management Shell:

Set-ResourceConfig –DomainController dc01.octavius.net –ResourcePropertySchema ('Room/Projector', 'Room/Whiteboard', 'Room/Wireless')

Although custom properties are often used to provide extra information for room resource mailboxes, you can create custom properties for equipment resource mailboxes by specifying **Equipment** in place of **Room** in the previous command. If you wish to create additional custom properties later on, you must also specify the existing properties alongside the Set-ResourceConfig command. Otherwise they will be overwritten.

When Outlook or Entourage users select resource mailboxes to add to a meeting request, they will see the capacity and custom properties under the Capacity and Description field of the selection dialog box as shown in Figure 5-44.

Figure 5-44

Viewing Resource Information

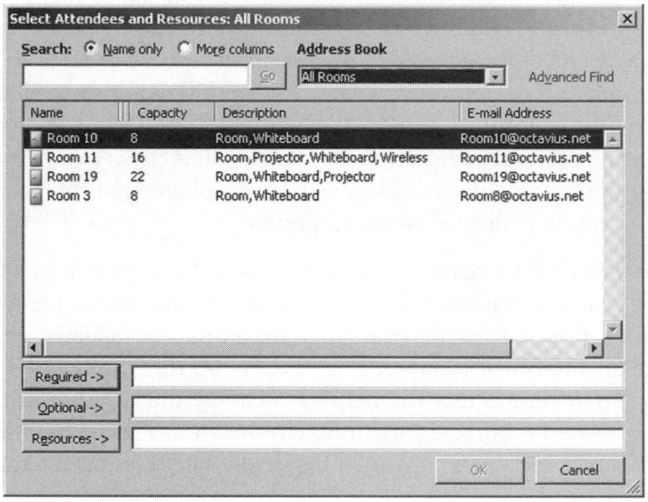

CONFIGURING AUTOMATIC BOOKING

In addition to adding capacity information and custom attributes to a new resource mailbox, you should also enable Automatic Booking to allow users to receive notification when a resource is double booked. To enable Automatic Booking on a resource mailbox, you must use the **Set- MailboxCalendarSettings** cmdlet within the Exchange Management Shell. For example, the following command will enable Automatic Booking on the Room 11 resource mailbox:

Set-MailboxCalendarSettings -Identity 'Room 11' –Automate –Processing:AutoAccept

After enabling Automatic Booking, the **Resource Booking Attendant** in Exchange Server 2007 will then automatically attempt to book the associated resources when a user sends a meeting request that contains resource mailboxes and return an error if the resource is already booked. In addition, Automatic Booking enables the **Calendar Attendant**, which automatically schedules meetings tentatively in a user's calendar even if the user is not currently logged on or accessing email using Outlook or Entourage. To turn off Automated Booking on the Room 11 mailbox, yet still allow the Calendar Attendant to run on the resource mailbox, you could run the following command within the Exchange Management Shell:

Set-MailboxCalendarSettings –Identity 'Room 11' –AutomateProcessing:AutoUpdate

Alternatively, to disable both the Resource Booking Attendant and Calendar Attendant components of Automatic Booking on the Room 11 resource mailbox, you can run the following command within the Exchange Management Shell:

Set-MailboxCalendarSettings –Identity 'Room 11' –AutomateProcessing:None

CERTIFICATION READY?
Configure policies.
3.4

CONFIGURING RESOURCE BOOKING POLICIES

The **Set-MailboxCalendarSettings** cmdlet in Exchange Server 2007 may also be used to create *resource booking policies* that specify which users can automatically book a resource within a meeting request using Automatic Booking. There are three main types of policies that can be applied to users within your organization:

- In Policy
- Out Policy
- Book-In Policy

Users who are defined in an *In Policy* can request a resource, but the request must be approved by a delegate on the resource mailbox before the resource is booked for the time specified in the meeting request. To add jeff.smith@octavius.net and bob.doe@octavius.net to an In Policy for the Room 11 resource mailbox, you can run the following command within the Exchange Management Shell:

Set-MailboxCalendarSettings –Identity 'Room 11' –RequestInPolicy 'jeff.smith@octavius .net', 'bob.doe@octavius.net'

Alternatively, you could apply an In Policy to all users using the following command within the Exchange Management Shell:

Set-MailboxCalendarSettings –Identity 'Room 11' –AllRequestInPolicy:$true

Next, you can specify a delegate for the Room 11 resource mailbox with the ability to approve resource booking requests. This delegate can add the calendar for the resource mailbox to his own Exchange account within Outlook or Entourage and allow or deny booking requests. To set the delegate on the Room 11 resource mailbox to Billy Martin, you could run the following command within the Exchange Management Shell:

Set-MailboxCalendarSettings –Identity 'Room 11' –ResourceDelegates 'Billy Martin'

Alternatively, you can add users to an *Out Policy*. Users who are defined in an Out Policy can automatically book a resource without a delegate provided that there are no resource conflicts. If there is a resource conflict, the request is forwarded to the delegate for approval. To add jeff.smith@octavius.net and bob.doe@octavius.net to an Out Policy for the Room 11 resource mailbox, you can run the following command within the Exchange Management Shell:

Set-MailboxCalendarSettings -Identity 'Room 11' -RequestOutPolicy 'jeff.smith@ octavius.net', 'bob.doe@octavius.net'

Or you can instead apply an Out Policy to all users using the following command within the Exchange Management Shell:

Set-MailboxCalendarSettings –Identity 'Room 11' –AllRequestOutPolicy:$true

To allow the automatic booking of available resources without using a delegate, you can add those users to a *Book-In Policy*. To add jeff.smith@octavius.net and bob.doe@octavius.net to a Book-In Policy for the Room 11 resource mailbox, you can run the following command within the Exchange Management Shell:

Set-MailboxCalendarSettings –Identity 'Room 11' –BookInPolicy 'jeff.smith@octavius .net', 'bob.doe@octavius.net'

Alternatively, you could apply a Book-In Policy to all users using the following command within the Exchange Management Shell:

Set-MailboxCalendarSettings –Identity 'Room 11' –AllBookInPolicy:$true

To view the resource booking policy and Automatic Booking settings that you have configured for a resource mailbox, you can use the **Get-MailboxCalendarSettings** cmdlet. To view the settings for the Room 11 resource mailbox as a list, you can run the following command within the Exchange Management Shell:

Get-MailboxCalendarSettings –Identity 'Room 11' | format-list

Managing Resource Mailboxes

Because resource mailboxes are similar in structure to mailbox users, the procedures and utilities used to manage them are identical.

Because resource mailboxes are simply mailbox users, the procedures and cmdlets used to manage them are identical to those used to manage mailbox users. Although you can grant the Send As and Full Access permissions for a resource mailbox, doing so will give unnecessary permissions to the resource mailbox and, as a result, is seldom done.

As with mailbox users, when you disable a resource mailbox, the associated user account is not deleted and the mailbox is marked for deletion. Similarly, when you delete a resource mailbox, the associated user account in AD is removed and the mailbox is marked for deletion. You can also reconnect the mailbox at a later time to an existing or new user account.

To perform these actions, refer to the procedures and cmdlets described within the "Managing Mailbox Users" section earlier in this lesson.

▪ Moving Mailboxes

THE BOTTOM LINE

There are a variety of different situations that will require the moving of mail boxes between Exchange servers within your organization or to other organizations. Understanding the procedures and utilities used to move mailboxes are key to performing as an Exchange administrator.

CERTIFICATION READY?
Move mailboxes.

2.5

As an Exchange administrator, you will be required to move mailboxes between mailbox databases, storage groups, and servers to meet a variety of different needs. When a user in one department relocates to another department, you may need to move the user's mailbox to a Mailbox role server in the other department to ensure fast email access. In addition, you may need to move mailboxes to provide load balancing for Mailbox access as your organization grows or to comply with structural change within the organization such as the combining of two departments. You can move mailboxes that are connected to mailbox users, linked mailbox users as well as resource mailboxes.

Although you can move mailboxes using the Exchange Management Console, the Exchange Management Shell allows you to specify more options when moving mailboxes. To move a mailbox, you must be a member of the Exchange Recipient Administrator role as well as a member of Exchange Server Administrator role and local Administrators group on the source and target Mailbox role servers at minimum.

After moving a mailbox, CAS role servers will automatically connect to the correct mailbox when providing access to email. However, the first time users access their mailboxes using OWA, they will need to wait several minutes while the OWA message table is rebuilt using the new mailbox location.

Moving Mailboxes Using the Exchange Management Console

If you need to move a small number of mailboxes within the same Exchange organization, the Exchange Management Console can provide a quick and easy-to-use interface.

By default, the Exchange Management Console allows you to move mailboxes with the same Exchange organization and AD forest only. The Exchange Management Console also allows mailboxes to be moved between Exchange servers within your organization running Exchange 2000 or Exchange Server 2003.

You can also move multiple mailboxes at the same time within the Exchange Management Console provided that they are to be moved to the same destination. To do this, you can navigate to **Recipient Configuration** > **Mailbox** and select the appropriate users while holding down the **Ctrl** key before selecting the **Move Mailbox** action. Alternatively, you can select a range of users by holding down the **Shift** key while selecting the first and last user.

After the move operation has completed, you should see the new mailbox location listed on the General tab of mailbox user properties as shown earlier in Figure 5-6.

 MOVE MAILBOXES USING THE EXCHANGE MANAGEMENT CONSOLE

GET READY. Turn on the computer, and log in as the Administrator user account. Close any windows that appear on the desktop.

1. Click **Start**, **All Programs**, **Microsoft Exchange Server 2007**, and then click **Exchange Management Console**. The Exchange Management Console window appears.

2. In the console tree pane, expand **Recipient Configuration** and highlight **Mailbox**.

3. In the result pane, select the appropriate mailbox(es) and click **Move Mailbox** in the action pane. The Move Mailbox window appears as shown in Figure 5-45.

Figure 5-45

Moving a Mailbox

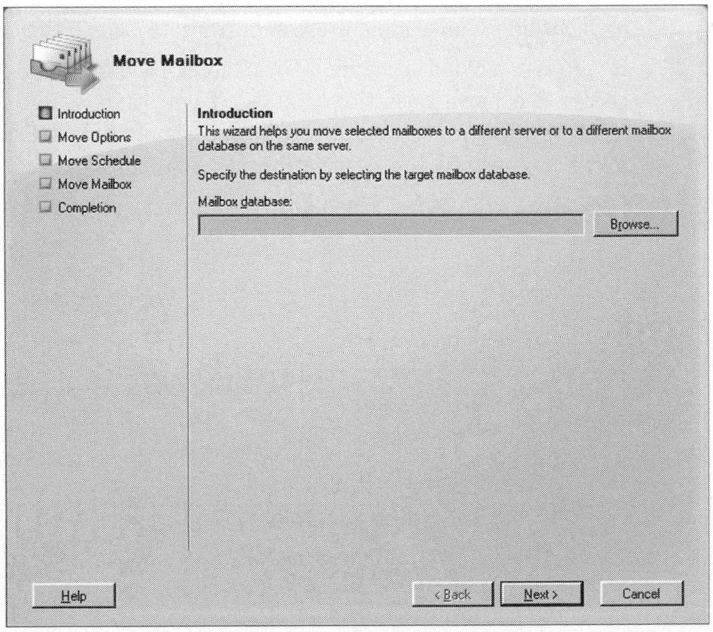

Move Mailbox

- Introduction
- Move Options
- Move Schedule
- Move Mailbox
- Completion

Introduction

This wizard helps you move selected mailboxes to a different server or to a different mailbox database on the same server.

Specify the destination by selecting the target mailbox database.

Mailbox database:

[   ] [Browse...]

[Help]   [< Back] [Next >] [Cancel]

4. Click **Browse**, select the destination mailbox database in the Select Mailbox Database window and click **OK**. Click **Next** when finished. The Move Options page appears as shown in Figure 5-46.

Figure 5-46

Specifying Move Options

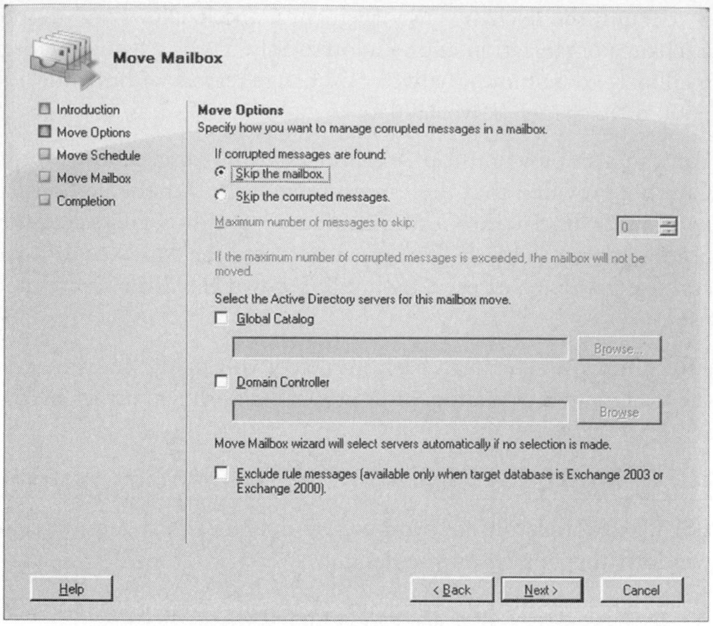

TAKE NOTE*

If you are moving a large mailbox, you must ensure that the mailbox does not exceed the storage limits on the target mailbox database. If it does, the move operation will fail.

5. By default, the move will fail if corrupted messages are detected in the mailbox during the move operation. Alternatively, you can select **Skip the corrupted messages** and specify the number of corrupted messages that you will skip before the move operation fails in the associated dialog box. Because a large number of corrupted messages usually indicate problems with the mailbox itself, you should keep this number to 10 or less.
6. The GC and DC used to provide and modify object information during the move operation are selected by default using the site information stored in AD. You can optionally specify a GC and DC by selecting the associated checkboxes in Figure 5-46 and clicking the related **Browse** buttons to select them.
7. If you are moving a mailbox to a target Exchange 2000 or Exchange Server 2003 server, the move operation will fail if you have mailbox settings that take up more than 32 KB of space. As a result, you should select **Exclude rule messages** to avoid problems if the destination server is not running Exchange Server 2007.
8. Click **Next**. The Move Schedule page appears as shown in Figure 5-47.

Figure 5-47

Scheduling a Move Operation

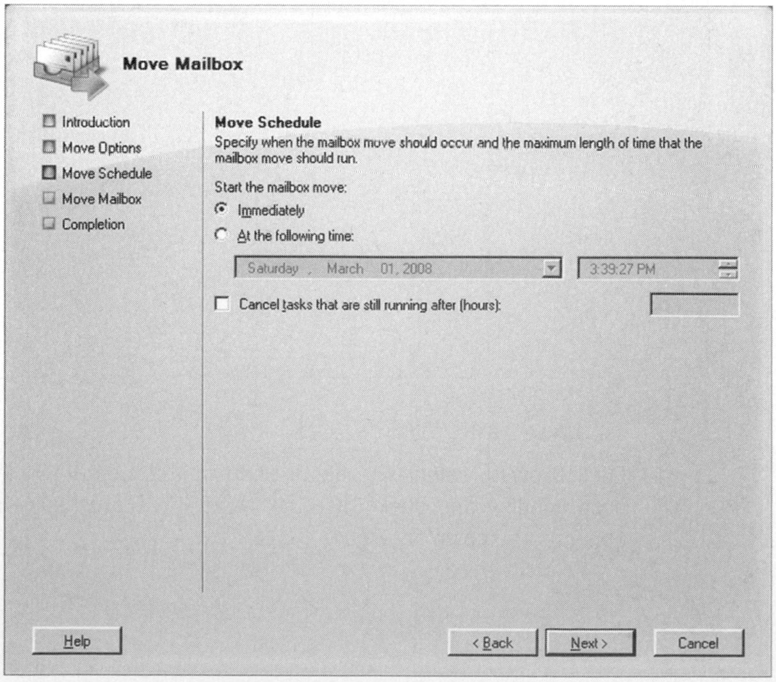

TAKE NOTE*

If you schedule a move operation, the Move Mailbox window remains open at the Move Mailbox page until the specified time is reached. If you want to move other mailboxes during this time, you must open another instance of the Exchange Management Console.

9. By default, the move operation will start immediately following the wizard. To schedule the move to occur at a different time, select **At the following time** and select the appropriate time from the drop-down boxes. Although the amount of time it takes to move a mailbox is large for larger mailboxes, network and service problems may pause a move operation indefinitely. To prevent this, you can click **Cancel tasks that are still running after (hours)** and supply the number of hours before a move operation is cancelled in the associated dialog box.

10. Click **Next**. The Move Mailbox page appears.

11. Click **Move**. Once the move operation has completed, the Completion page appears.

12. Click **Finish** to close the Move Mailbox window.

13. Close the Exchange Management Console.

Moving Mailboxes Using the Exchange Management Shell

To move several mailboxes, move mailboxes between forests, or perform advanced move operations, you must use the Move-Mailbox cmdlet within the Exchange Management Shell.

As with the Exchange Management Console, the Exchange Management Shell allows you to move mailboxes within your organization. However, the Exchange Management Shell can also be used to move mailboxes between forests and Exchange organizations as well as set advanced options for moving a mailbox.

To move mailboxes using the Exchange Management Shell, you can use the **Move-Mailbox** cmdlet. For example, to move the mailbox for Jeff Smith (email address = jeff.smith@octavius.net) to the Mailbox Database in the Third Storage Group on the server exch2.octavius.net within the same Exchange organization, you can use the following command within the Exchange Management Shell:

Move-Mailbox 'jeff.smith@octavius.net' –TargetDatabase 'exch2.octavius.net\Third Storage Group\Mailbox Database'

By default, this mailbox move will assume the default values for all other move options that were specified when moving a mailbox using the Exchange Management Console. However, you can append options to the **Move-Mailbox** cmdlet to override these defaults as well as specify additional move options. Table 5-2 lists the most common options to the **Move-Mailbox** cmdlet.

Table 5-2

Common Move-Mailbox options

RECIPIENT OBJECTS	DESCRIPTION
-BadItemLimit 'n'	Specifies that the move operation will fail only after encountering more than *n* corrupted messages in the source mailbox.
-IgnoreRuleLimitErrors	Ignores mailbox rules during the move operation. This option can only be applied if the destination mailbox is on an Exchange 2000 or Exchange Server 2003 computer.
-GlobalCatalog 'FQDN'	Specifies that the global catalog (GC) server used during the move operation should be FQDN. It this is not specified, a GC server within the same site will be chosen.
-DomainController 'FQDN'	Specifies that the Domain Controller used during the move operation should be FQDN. It this is not specified, a Domain Controller within the same site will be chosen.

(continued)

Table 5-2 (*continued*)

RECIPIENT OBJECTS	DESCRIPTION
-ConfigurationOnly	Changes the location of the Exchange server in the mailbox user without moving the mailbox. This option is only used if the mailbox database has been moved previously to another server without updating the mailbox user properties.
-PreserveMailboxSizeLimit	Prevents the source mailbox from inheriting the mailbox size limits from the destination mailbox database during the move operation.
-RetryInterval 'hh:mm:ss'	Specifies the interval used to display status information during the move operation using the format hours:minutes:seconds (hh:mm:ss).
-RetryTimeout 'hh:mm'	Specifies the amount of time allowed for a mailbox move operation before it automatically fails using the format hours:minutes (hh:mm).
-AttachmentFilename 'arg'	Specifies the attachments that are allowed during the move. Typically *arg* is a wildcard such as '*.txt' to specify attachments that have a txt extension. Multiple *arg* values are allowed provided they are separated by commas.
-ExcludeFolders 'arg'	Specifies the folders that should be excluded from the move operation. To exclude the folder called Work from the move operation, *arg* should be set to '\Work'. Multiple *arg* values are allowed provided they are separated by commas.
-IncludeFolders 'arg'	Specifies the folders that should be included in the move operation. To include the contents of the Inbox folder only during the move operation, *arg* should be set to '\Inbox'. Multiple *arg* values are allowed provided they are separated by commas.
-Locale 'arg'	Specifies the locale of messages that should be included in the move operation.
-ContentKeywords 'arg'	Specifies the keywords that must be present in the message body or attachments for the message to be moved to the target mailbox. Multiple *arg* values are allowed provided they are separated by commas.
-SubjectKeywords 'arg'	Specifies the keywords that must be present in the message subject for the message to be moved to the target mailbox. Multiple *arg* values are allowed provided they are separated by commas.
-AllContentKeywords 'arg'	Specifies the keywords that must be present in the message subject, body, or attachments for the message to be moved to the target mailbox. Multiple *arg* values are allowed provided they are separated by commas.
-StartDate 'mm/dd/yyyy'	Specifies the earliest date for emails that should be included in the move operation using the format month/day/year (mm/dd/yyyy).
-EndDate 'mm/dd/yyyy'	Specifies the latest date for emails that should be included in the move operation using the format month/day/year (mm/dd/yyyy).

Thus, to move items newer than August 15, 2008, within the mailbox for Jeff Smith described in the previous example while preserving the original mailbox size limits and ensuring that five corrupted messages can be skipped before the move operation fails, you could run the following command within the Exchange Management Shell:

Move-Mailbox 'jeff.smith@octavius.net' –TargetDatabase 'exch2.octavius.net\Third Storage Group\Mailbox Database' –BadItemLimit'5' –PreserveMailboxSizeLimit -StartDate '08/15/2008'

You can also move a mailbox to another forest using the Exchange Management Shell. However, the **Move-Mailbox** cmdlet must be run from the target forest. To perform the move operation, you must also be a member of the Exchange Recipient Administrator role in both forests as well as a member of Exchange Server Administrator role and local Administrators group on the source and target Mailbox role servers at minimum.

Before running the **Move-Mailbox** cmdlet, you should create a variable within the Exchange Management Shell to store the credentials of the appropriate user in the source and target forests. To do this, you can enter the following commands within the Exchange Management Shell:

$SourceCredential = Get-Credential

$TargetCredential = Get-Credential

Following each of these commands, you will be prompted to supply the appropriate account and password information. This information will be stored in the $SourceCredential and $TargetCredential variables.

Next, you can run the Move-Mailbox cmdlet from the target forest to perform the move operation. For example, to move the mailbox for the user Jeff Smith in the octavius.net domain to the Mailbox Database within the First Storage Group on exch1.arfa.com in the arfa.com domain, you could run the following command in the Exchange Management Shell on an Exchange server within the arfa.com forest:

Move-Mailbox –Target Database 'exch1.arfa.com\First Storage Group\Mailbox Database' –Identity 'jeff.smith@octavius.net' –DomainController dc15.arfa.com –GlobalCatalog dc15.arfa.com "SourceForestGlobalCatalog dc2.octavius.net –NTAccountOU –OU=North, DC=arfa, DC=com" –SourceForestCredential $SourceCredential -TargetForestCredential $TargetCredential

For the move operation, the DC and GC server used in the target forest is dc15.arfa.com and the GC server used in the source forest is dc2.octavius.net. If you do not specify the DC and GC servers for the target forest, they will be chosen automatically from the site information within AD in the target forest. However, the source forest GC server must always be specified for the move operation to be successful.

In addition, the **Move-Mailbox** command creates a disabled user account of the same name in the target forest within the OU that you specify with the -**NTAccountOU** parameter. If a target mailbox already exists, you can instead use the –**AllowMerge** parameter to merge the source and target mailboxes.

If a mailbox needs to be moved between forests, the user account is often moved to the target forest first using the *Active Directory Migration Tool (ADMT)* in order to preserve account settings and SIDs. If the source user account does not need to be used following the mailbox move, you can also append the –**SourceMailboxCleanupOptions DeleteSourceNTAccount** option to the **Move-Mailbox** cmdlet to remove the source mailbox and AD user account.

■ Implementing an Exchange Resource Forest

THE BOTTOM LINE

To consolidate several Exchange infrastructures or to provide additional security, many organizations deploy Exchange in a separate resource forest to serve the email needs of other forests that comprise your organization. Mailbox users within the Exchange resource forest are created as linked mailbox users to allow users in other forests access to Exchange. You should become familiar with the process used to create a resource forest as well as the procedures and utilities used to create and manage linked mailbox users in the event that you need to deploy or work with Exchange resource forests.

Creating an Exchange Resource Forest and Linked Mailbox Users

Exchange resource forests are created in the same manner as any other forest and connect to other forests using one-way trust relationships. After deploying a resource forest, you must create linked mailbox users to allow email access for users in other forests. Linked mailbox users are created in the Exchange resource forest using the Exchange Management Console or Exchange Management Shell in much the same way that you create mailbox users.

Some organizations must maintain several different forests to allow for different security, business, or schema requirements. These organizations can choose to implement a single forest for use with Exchange only. This forest is called an ***Exchange resource forest*** and will contain all the mailboxes for users within all forests of the organization. Furthermore, because these mailboxes are linked to the appropriate user accounts in each forest for email access, they are called ***linked mailbox users***.

Consider the three forests and domains shown in Figure 5-48. The octavius.net and alphamiata.net forests contain user accounts and function like most other forests. The arfa.com Exchange resource forest contains mailboxes that are linked to the user accounts in the octavius.net and alphamiata.net forests. Because the arfa.com forest trusts both the octavius .net and alphamiata.net forests, user accounts in the octavius.net and alphamiata.net forests can access the Exchange servers in the arfa.com forest when sending and receiving email.

Figure 5-48

The arfa.com Exchange Resource Forest Structure

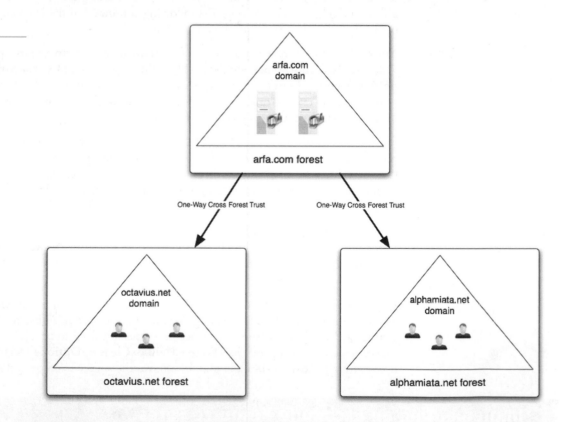

Linked mailbox users are simply mailbox users in an Exchange resource forest that have a disabled user account in the Exchange resource forest as well as a mailbox on a Mailbox role server in the Exchange organization for the Exchange resource forest. As a result, each user in the octavius.net and alphamiata.net forests shown in Figure 5-48 will have a matching user in the arfa.com forest that is disabled. Although users in the octavius.net and alphamiata .net forests can use an email client program to access their email from the Exchange servers in the arfa.com forest, they must supply the credentials for the user account in their own forest because the mailbox user that represents them in the arfa.com forest is disabled and only links to their user account in either the octavius.net or alphamiata.net forests.

X REF

The creation of forests and trust relationships were discussed earlier in Lesson 2, "Working with Active Directory."

To deploy an Exchange resource forest, you must ensure that one-way external or cross forest trusts are created so that the Exchange resource forest trusts all other forests. Next, you must create linked mailbox users in the Exchange resource forest that are linked to target user accounts in other trusted forests. These target user accounts are called ***master accounts*** and must be created in the target forest before a linked mailbox user is created in the Exchange resource forest.

CREATE A LINKED MAILBOX USER

GET READY. Turn on the computer in the Exchange resource forest, and log in as the Administrator user account. Close any windows that appear on the desktop.

1. Click **Start**, **All Programs**, **Microsoft Exchange Server 2007**, and then click **Exchange Management Console.** The Exchange Management Console window appears.
2. In the console tree pane, expand **Recipient Configuration** and highlight **Mailbox.**
3. In the action pane, click **New Mailbox.** The New Mailbox window appears as shown earlier in Figure 5-1.
4. Select **Linked Mailbox** and click **Next.** The User Type page appears as shown earlier in Figure 5-2.
5. If you wish to create a linked mailbox alongside a new disabled AD user account in the Exchange resource forest, ensure that **New user** is selected. Alternatively, you can choose to use an existing disabled AD user in the Exchange resource forest when creating a linked mailbox. To do this, select **Existing users**, click the **Add** button, select the appropriate user in the Select User window that appears, and click **OK.**
6. Click **Next.** If you selected New user on the User Type page, you will be prompted to specify information that will be used to create the disabled AD user account in the Exchange resource forest on the User Information page. Because the user account will be disabled, the password-related information is optional. For consistency and organization, the name information on this page should match the naming convention used for the AD user account in the target forest. For example, the information shown in Figure 5-49 will be used to create a user account for Adel Moore (logon name = adel.moore) in the arfa.com forest that will be later linked to the Adel Moore account in the octavius.net domain (logon name = adel.moore).

TAKE NOTE*

If you select **Existing users**, you will only be able to select existing users who are disabled within AD.

Figure 5-49

Creating a New Linked Mailbox User

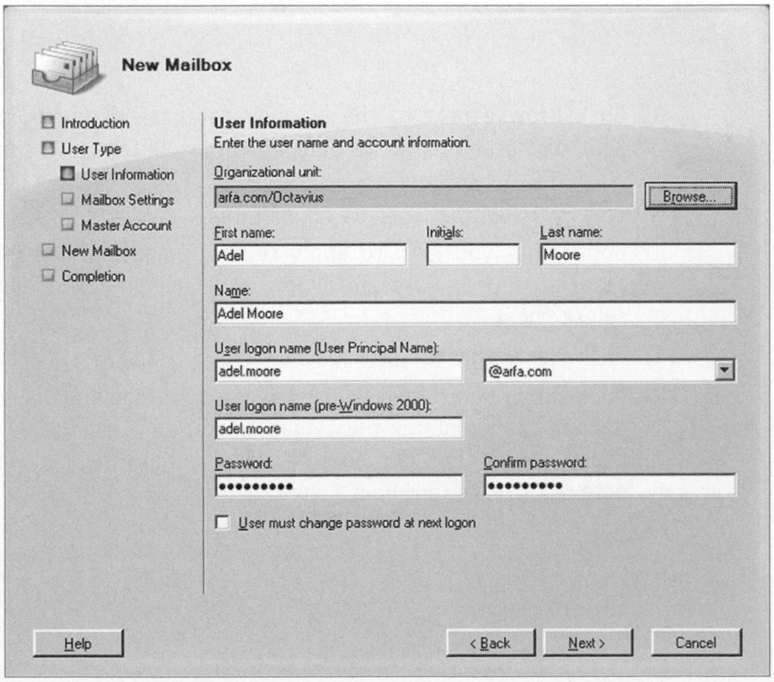

TAKE NOTE*

If you selected **Existing users** on the User Type page, you will skip entering the account information on the User Information page shown in Figure 5-49.

7. By default, the user will be created in the default Users folder in the current domain of the Exchange resource forest. If you wish to store resource mailboxes in a different container, click **Browse**, select the appropriate OU and click **OK**. For organization, it is best to create OUs for each domain or forest that you will create linked mailbox users for. Because the target AD user account for Adel Moore is in the octavius.net domain, the Octavius OU was chosen as the location for the Adel Moore disabled AD user account in the arfa.com domain as shown in Figure 5-49.

8. Click **Next**. The Mailbox Settings page appears. Ensure that the **Alias** dialog box contains the alias that will be used to generate the email address for the linked mailbox user in the Exchange resource domain. The alias shown in Figure 5-50 for the Adel Moore linked mailbox user will generate an email address of adel.moore@ arfa.com.

Figure 5-50

Specifying Mailbox Settings

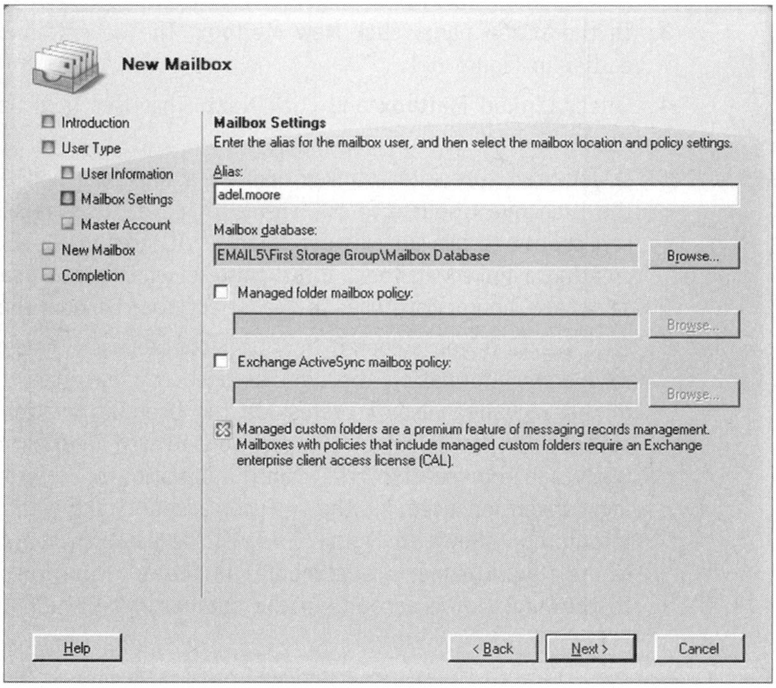

9. Click **Browse** next to the Mailbox database dialog box, select the appropriate Mailbox database in the Select Mailbox Database window that appears, and click **OK**.

10. If you have created a Managed folder mailbox policy or an ActiveSync mailbox policy that you wish to apply to the linked mailbox user, you can select the associated checkboxes in Figure 5-50 and click the related **Browse** buttons to select them.

11. Click **Next**. The Master Account page appears.

12. Click **Browse** next to the Trusted forest or domain dialog box, select the trusted domain that contains the target user account in the window that appears, and click **OK**. For the Adel Moore linked mailbox user described earlier, this domain is octavius.net as shown in Figure 5-51.

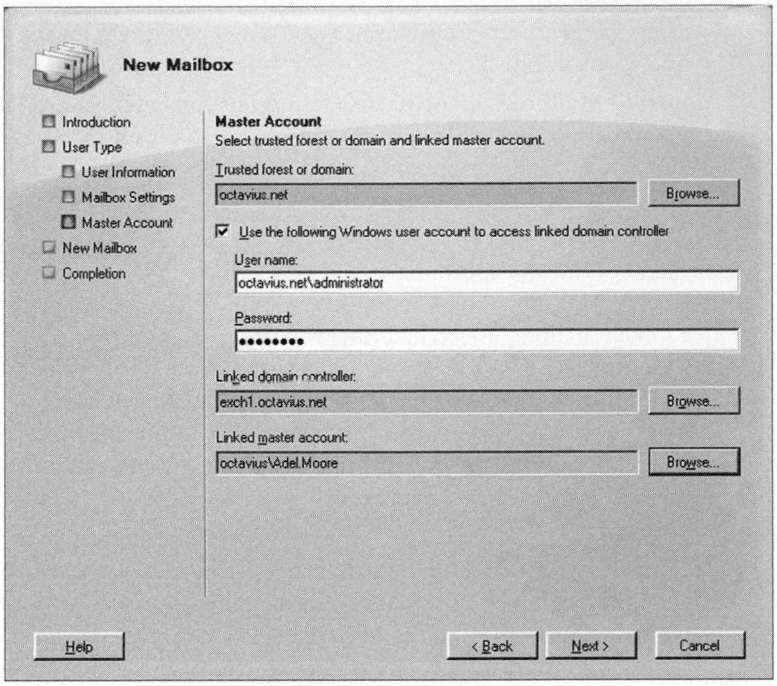

Figure 5-51

Specifying Master Account
Settings

New Mailbox

- Introduction
- User Type
  - User Information
  - Mailbox Settings
  - Master Account
- New Mailbox
- Completion

Master Account
Select trusted forest or domain and linked master account.

Trusted forest or domain:

`octavius.net`   Browse...

☑ Use the following Windows user account to access linked domain controller

User name:

`octavius.net\administrator`

Password:

`••••••••`

Linked domain controller:

`exch1.octavius.net`   Browse...

Linked master account:

`octavius\Adel.Moore`   Browse...

Help   < Back   Next >   Cancel

13. To ensure that the linked mailbox user is created successfully, you should select **Use the following Windows user account to access the linked domain controller** and specify the credentials of a user account in the target domain that is a member of the Domain Admins or Enterprise Admins group.

14. Click **Browse** next to the Linked domain controller dialog box, select a DC that is in the same domain as the target user account in the window that appears, and click **OK**.

15. Next, click **Browse** next to the Linked master account dialog box, select the target user account in the window that appears, and click **OK**. For the Adel Moore linked mailbox user, the Linked master account dialog box should display the octavius\ Adel.Moore account.

16. Click **Next**. The New Mailbox page appears.

17. Review the summary of your settings and click **New**. The Completion page appears.

18. Click **Finish** to close the New Mailbox window.

19. Close the Exchange Management Console.

THE COMMAND
LINE WAY

The **Enable-Mailbox** cmdlet in the Exchange Management Shell can also be used to create a linked mailbox user using an existing disabled user account within the Exchange resource forest. Before running the Enable-Mailbox cmdlet, you should first supply the credentials of a Domain Admin or Enterprise Admin in the target domain by entering the following command in the Exchange Management Console:

$TargetCredential = Get-Credential

Next, you can use the Enable-Mailbox cmdlet to create the linked mailbox user in the Exchange resource forest. For example, to create a linked mailbox user from the existing disabled user Adel Moore (alias and logon name = adel.moore) in Octavius OU in the arfa.com domain within your Exchange resource forest, specify a mailbox in the Mailbox database within the First Storage Group on the server EMAIL5, and link the mailbox to the Adel Moore user account in the octavius.net domain (logon name = adel.moore) using the DC exch1.octavius.net, you could run the following command in the Exchange Management Shell:

Enable-Mailbox –Identity 'arfa.com/Octavius/adel.moore' –Alias 'adel.moore' –Database 'EMAIL5\First Storage Group\Mailbox Database' –LinkedMasterAccount 'octavius.net\adel.moore' –LinkedDomainController 'exch1.octavius.net' –LinkedCredential $TargetCredential

Alternatively, you can use the **New-Mailbox** cmdlet after creating the $TargetCredential variable with the appropriate logon credentials to create the linked mailbox user in the Exchange resource forest alongside a disabled AD user account. For example, to create a linked mailbox user called Adel Moore (alias and logon name = adel.moore) in the Octavius OU of the arfa.com domain within your Exchange resource forest, specify a mailbox in the Mailbox database within the First Storage Group on the server EMAIL5, and link the mailbox to the Adel Moore user account in the octavius.net domain (logon name = adel.moore) using the DC exch1.octavius.net, you could run the following command in the Exchange Management Shell:

New-Mailbox –Name 'Adel Moore' –Alias 'adel.moore' –OrganizationalUnit 'arfa. com/Octavius' –UserPrincipalName 'adel.moore@arfa.com' –SamAccountName 'adel.moore' FirstName 'Adel' –LastName 'Moore' –Database 'EMAIL5\First Storage Group\Mailbox Database' –LinkedMasterAccount 'octavius.net\adel.moore' –LinkedDomainController 'exch1.octavius.net' –LinkedCredential $TargetCredential

Some organizations use Exchange resource forests to consolidate the existing Exchange organizations in several forests. This may be required after two or more organizations merge or when the IT departments within several different forests are combined into a single unit.

In this case, each forest that must be configured to use an Exchange resource forest will already have an Exchange infrastructure with mailbox users for several members of the organization. Luckily, the procedure for migrating to an Exchange resource forest is nearly identical to the procedure used to implement a new Exchange resource forest. To migrate to an Exchange resource forest, you must ensure that one-way external or cross forest trusts are created so that the Exchange resource forest trusts all other forests. Next, you must create linked mailbox users in the Exchange resource forest that are linked to master accounts in other trusted forests using the same procedure discussed earlier.

Because the master accounts in the target domain are already mailbox users, you can move the mailboxes for them in the target domain to the Exchange resource domain using the **Move-Mailbox** cmdlet in the Exchange Management Shell. The **Move-Mailbox** cmdlet must be run from an Exchange server in the Exchange resource forest with the **–AllowMerge** option.

Before running the Move-Mailbox cmdlet, you should specify the credentials for a user who is a member of the Domain Admins or Enterprise Admins group in the target domain by using the following command in the Exchange Management Console:

$TargetCredential = Get-Credential

Next, you can move the mailbox for a target user to the Exchange resource forest. For example, after creating the linked mailbox user for Adel Moore in the arfa.com domain, you can use the following command in the Exchange Management Shell to move the mailbox for the Adel Moore mailbox user in the octavius.net domain (logon name = adel.moore@octavius.net) to the Mailbox Database in the First Storage Group on the server EMAIL5 in the arfa.com domain.

Move-Mailbox 'octavius.net/adel.moore' –TargetDatabase 'EMAIL5\First Storage Group\Mailbox Database' –SourceForestGlobalCatalog 'exch1.octavius.net' –DomainController 'dc4.arfa.com' NTAccountOU 'OU=Octavius, DC=arfa, DC=com' –Sourceforestcredential $TargetCredential –AllowMerge

In this command, the linked mailbox user resides in the Octavius OU of the arfa.com domain in the Exchange resource forest. In addition, the GC server used in the target domain during the move was exch1.octavius.net and the DC used in the Exchange resource forest was dc4.arfa.com.

After the master account mailboxes for all linked mailbox users have been moved to Exchange servers in the Exchange resource forest, you can reconfigure email client programs to obtain email from the Exchange servers in the Exchange resource forest. Users can use the same domain credentials they use to log in to their domain to access email in the Exchange resource forest because the mailbox is linked to their domain AD user account.

Following this, you can disable the mailbox users in the target domains and decommission the Exchange servers. Disabling the mailbox users will not remove the associated user account in AD. As a result, users will still be able to authenticate and access email from the Exchange servers in the Exchange resource forest.

Configuring and Managing Linked Mailbox Users

The procedures used to configure and manage linked mailbox users are identical to those used to configure regular mailbox users. However, all configuration and management must be performed from within the Exchange resource forest.

The configuration and management of linked mailbox users is always performed in the Exchange resource forest. Because linked mailbox users are simply mailbox users who allow access from a master account in a trusted forest, you can configure them under the **Recipient Configuration** > **Mailbox** node within the Exchange Management Console. Additionally, you can create a filter to narrow the list displayed in this node to specific room or equipment resource mailboxes only. Simply click **Create Filter** in the detail pane, specify **Recipient Type Details Equals Linked Mailbox** in the appropriate expression drop-down boxes, and click **Apply Filter**. Once you have located the appropriate linked mailbox user, you can highlight it in the detail pane and select **Properties** from the action pane to view its properties.

The properties for a linked mailbox user are identical to those for a regular mailbox user and are configured in the same way using the same procedures and cmdlets. However, the E-Mail Addresses tab lists email addresses for the trusted domain as well as the domain in the Exchange resource forest as shown for the Adel Moore linked mailbox user in Figure 5-52.

Figure 5-52

Configuring Linked Mailbox
User Email Addresses

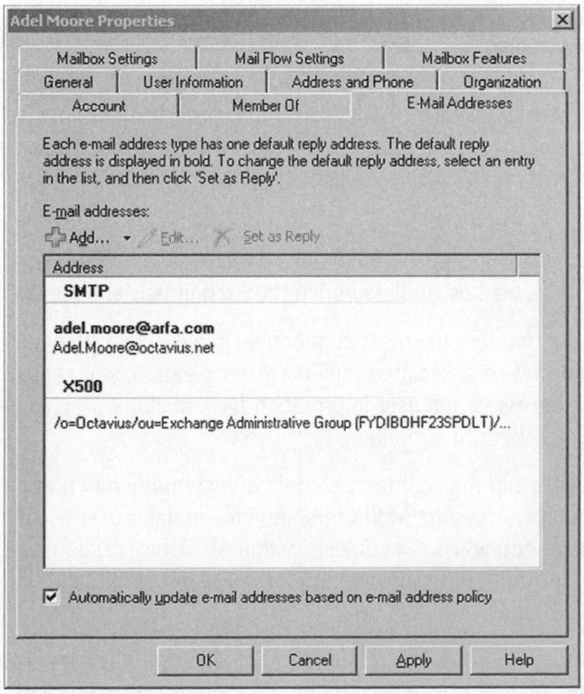

In Figure 5-52, the primary email address (adel.moore@arfa.com) was generated by the alias for the linked user account in the Exchange resource forest (arfa.com), whereas the secondary email address (Adel.Moore@octavius.net) reflects the domain that contains the linked master account (octavius.net). Thus, any email sent from Adel Moore will be addressed from adel.moore@arfa.com. To maintain the original identity of octavius.net in sent emails, you could deselect **Automatically update e-mail addresses based on e-mail address policy**, highlight the Adel.Moore@octavius.net email address, and click **Set as Reply** as shown in Figure 5-52. In addition, an X500 address is added to allow DCs to locate the mailbox across the trust relationship.

To configure the other properties of a linked mailbox user, refer to the procedures and cmdlets described within the "Managing Mailbox Users" section earlier in this lesson.

You can grant the Send As and Full Access permissions for a linked mailbox user using the same procedures used with regular mailbox users. However, by default, linked mailbox users grant Send As and Full Access permission to the linked master account. These default permissions allow for mailbox access across forests and should not be removed. Similarly, to grant Send As or Full Access permission, you should select target users or groups in the trusted domains rather than in the Exchange resource forest. To grant Send As or Full Access permission to a linked mailbox user, refer to the procedures and cmdlets described within the "Managing Mailbox Users" section earlier in this lesson.

Disabling and removing linked mailbox users is also similar to disabling and removing regular mailbox users. When you disable a linked mailbox user, the link to the master account is removed and the mailbox is marked for deletion. However, the disabled user account in the Exchange resource forest is not deleted and the master account in the target domain is not deleted. When you delete a linked mailbox user, the link to the master account is removed, the mailbox is marked for deletion, and the disabled user account in the Exchange resource forest is deleted. However, the master account in the target domain is not deleted. As with mailbox users, you can reconnect a mailbox that is marked for deletion at a later time to a new or existing mailbox user or linked mailbox user. To disable, remove, or reconnect a linked mailbox user, refer to the procedures and cmdlets described within the "Managing Mailbox Users" section earlier in this lesson.

SUMMARY SKILL MATRIX

IN THIS LESSON YOU LEARNED:

- There are nine major recipient object types that contain email addresses within your organization: mailbox users, mail users, mail contacts, mail-enabled universal security groups, mail-enabled universal distribution groups, dynamic distribution groups, resource mailboxes, and mail-enabled public folders.

- Members of the Exchange Organization Administrator or Exchange Administrator role can create, configure, and manage all recipient objects using the Exchange Management Console as well as cmdlets within the Exchange Management Shell.

- Mailbox users are the most common recipient object. They consist of a mail-enabled user account and an associated mailbox. After creation, you can configure the mailbox settings, email addresses, and user information for a mailbox user, as well as disable, remove, or reconnect them to a mailbox.

- Mail users and mail contacts contain an external email address that internal organization email is forwarded to. Mail users are mail-enabled user accounts whereas mail contacts are mail-enabled contact objects within AD. After creation, you can configure email addresses and object information for mail users and mail contacts as well as disable or remove them.

- Mail-enabled universal groups are used when sending email to multiple recipient objects. Mail-enabled universal security groups can also be used to assign permissions and rights whereas mail-enabled universal distribution groups cannot. After creation, you can modify the group membership, group manager and expansion server settings for mail-enabled universal groups as well as disable or remove them.

- Instead of having a static group membership, dynamic distribution groups use criteria to match other recipient objects. These criteria are processed when email is sent to the dynamic distribution group and consist of a filter as well as several conditions. You can modify the filter and conditions for a dynamic distribution group after it has been created, as well as remove it entirely.

- Resource mailboxes are special mailbox users who are used to hold room or equipment resource scheduling information for use with the calendaring feature of Outlook and Entourage. Following creation, you can configure resource information, Automatic Booking, and resource booking policies for a resource mailbox. Like other mailbox users, resource mailboxes can also be disabled, removed, or reconnected.

- You can move mailboxes to other mailbox databases on the same server or another server using the Exchange Management Console or Move-Mailbox cmdlet within the Exchange Management Shell. The Move-Mailbox cmdlet offers more options than the Exchange Management Console and allows mailboxes to be moved between forests.

- To provide email services for multiple forests, or to consolidate email infrastructures, you can deploy an Exchange resource forest to hold Exchange servers that will be used by several forests across trust relationships. Linked mailbox users within the Exchange resource forest allow an associated master account in another forest access to email in a mailbox within the Exchange resource forest. Linked mailbox users are configured and managed like other mailbox users.

■ Knowledge Assessment

Fill in the Blank

Complete the following sentences by writing the correct word or words in the blanks provided.

1. When you configure a new linked mailbox user, you must specify a _____ to identify the remote user account that has the ability to access the mailbox.

2. The _____ US-cmdlet can obtain configuration information for a mail contact.

3. To prevent a mailbox user from using OWA, you can configure the appropriate option on the _____ tab of mailbox user properties.

4. To access the email within an additional mailbox in Outlook or Entourage, you must have _____ permission to the target mailbox.

5. To allow users to schedule a resource mailbox without the use of a delegate, you can create a _____ policy.

6. The default email address that is given to a recipient object is automatically generated from the _____ provided during creation and the domain name suffix of the domain the object was created in.

7. The _____ cmdlet may be used to create a new mailbox user.

8. When a member leaves the organization, you can configure _____ on the associated mailbox user to ensure that another mailbox user receives any email sent to that member.

9. To be notified immediately that a scheduled resource is unavailable when a meeting request is sent, the resource mailbox must have _____ enabled.

10. Before moving a mailbox to another forest in order to relocate an existing mailbox user, you should first migrate the user account to the target forest using the _____.

Multiple Choice

Circle the letter that corresponds to the best answer.

1. If a mailbox user within your organization legally changes his or her name, what actions should you perform on the recipient object? (Choose all that apply.)
   a. Modify the user information
   b. Modify the alias
   c. Change the primary email address
   d. Remove any secondary email addresses

2. Which of the following do dynamic distribution groups use to automatically populate their group membership? (Choose two answers.)
   a. conditions   b. scope
   c. filter   d. range

3. You are attempting to select custom properties within the properties of a resource mailbox, but none are displayed in the selection window. What should you do?
   a. Register them using the AD schema
   b. Configure them first using the Set-ResourceConfig cmdlet
   c. Add them as custom attributes first
   d. Create the custom properties first using the Object tab of resource mailbox properties

4. Which of the following recipient object types contain a disabled user account? (Choose all that apply.)
   a. mailbox users   b. linked mailbox users
   c. resource mailboxes   d. mail users

5. Which cmdlet can you use to reconnect a mailbox to an existing AD user?
   a. Enable-Mailbox
   b. New-Mailbox
   c. Connect-Mailbox
   d. Reconnect-Mailbox

True/False

Circle T if the statement is true or F if the statement is false.

T F   1. By default, disconnected mailboxes are deleted after 30 days.

T F   2. The Send On Behalf permission allows a user to send email using the sole identity of another user.

T F   3. Exchange Recipient Administrators can create and manage all recipient objects within AD.

T F   4. An Exchange resource forest is trusted by other forests using one-way cross forest or external trusts.

T F   5. When you create an In Policy for a resource mailbox, users can automatically book the resource provided there are no conflicts.

T F   6. When you disable a recipient object, the associated AD object is removed.

T F   7. You can create a new mail-enabled universal security group using the SetDistributionGroup cmdlet within the Exchange Management Shell.

T F   8. To provide an outside member of your organization an internal email address and the ability to log in to a domain, you can create a mail user.

T F   9. The Move-Mailbox cmdlet within the Exchange Management Shell can only be used to move mailboxes within the same Exchange organization and forest.

T F 10. The external email address for a mail user cannot be changed after the mail user has been created.

Review Questions

1. Explain why creating resource mailboxes will improve the productivity of your organization.

2. Explain how you can use custom attributes within recipient objects alongside dynamic distribution groups to simplify administration within Exchange Server 2007.

■ Case Scenarios

Scenario 5-1: Configuring an Exchange Resource Forest

Your organization has recently merged with another organization. During the merger, it was decided that both organizations will maintain separate forests and separate AD administrative staff but will combine their Exchange 2007 infrastructures into a single unit by deploying a new Exchange resource forest that will service both forests. You have been tasked with hiring the staff required to create and manage this new Exchange resource forest as well as create an action plan to migrate the existing Exchange infrastructures in both existing forests to the new Exchange resource forest.

In a short memo, describe the procedures that you will need to undertake to transition the current environment to an Exchange resource forest environment in a smooth and efficient manner.

Scenario 5-2: Managing Recipient Objects

Until recently, your organization has used mailbox users exclusively for all members of the organization including contract members. As a result, the available space on your Mailbox role servers is running low. During a meeting, your manager has asked you to provide possible solutions for this problem and recommend procedures to prevent it from happening in the future. You manager wants you to present this at the following meeting in one week.

Prepare a short presentation that you can present at this meeting that outlines some solutions to the disk space problem as well as some procedures that may be used to prevent the problem from reoccurring frequently in the future.

6 | LESSON

Address Lists, Policies, and Bulk Management

LESSON SKILL MATRIX

TECHNOLOGY SKILL	OBJECTIVE DOMAIN	OBJECTIVE DOMAIN NUMBER
Working with Multiple Recipient Objects	Implement bulk management of mail-enabled objects.	2.6
Configuring Message Compliance Policies	Configure transport rules and message compliance.	3.3
Configuring Policies	Configure policies.	3.4

KEY TERMS

address list	Journaling agent	messaging compliance
batch file	managed custom folder	Offline Address Book (OAB)
bulk management	managed default folder	parameter
comma-separated values (CSV) file	Managed Folder Assistant	premium journaling
	managed folder mailbox policy	standard journaling
email address policy	message journaling	template recipient object

■ Configuring Address Lists and Offline Address Books

THE BOTTOM LINE

Email systems today provide the main communication mechanism for users within your organization. As a result, you should ensure that your email system allows users to create emails as quickly as possible in order to maximize the efficiency of your organization. By creating address lists that are stored in Offline Address Books, you will help the users within your organization quickly locate recipient objects that they need to send email to and hence improve their overall email experience.

Creating and Managing Address Lists

Address lists are custom lists of recipient objects that MAPI clients can use within your organization to locate other recipient objects when sending email. You should create address lists for common groups within your organization to ensure that users can locate other recipient objects quickly. Address lists can be created using the Exchange Management Console or the Exchange Management Shell.

Sometimes the most difficult task when sending email is determining who to send it to. In larger organizations that have hundreds or thousands of recipient objects, this task can be very tedious. By creating *address lists*, you can help users quickly locate the email recipients that they need to send email to.

Address lists are simply lists of email recipients. When you compose a new email in a MAPI client such as Outlook or Exchange, you can click the **To** button and select the appropriate address list from the Select Names window to narrow the list of recipient objects that you wish to browse. For example, if you need to send an email to a person in the Accounting department, but you can't remember his last name, you can click **To** in a new email message and select the address list for the Accounting department. Because the Accounting department address list only displays users in the Accounting department, you can quickly locate the appropriate user from the list.

TAKE NOTE*

Don't confuse address lists with mail-enabled groups. Address lists are not recipient objects. They are only used to help locate individual recipient objects within an email client program such as Outlook or Entourage. Mail-enabled groups are recipient objects that can be used to send emails to multiple recipient objects.

You can create and manage address lists using the **Address Lists** tab under the **Organization Configuration** > **Mailbox** node in the Exchange Management Console as shown in Figure 6-1.

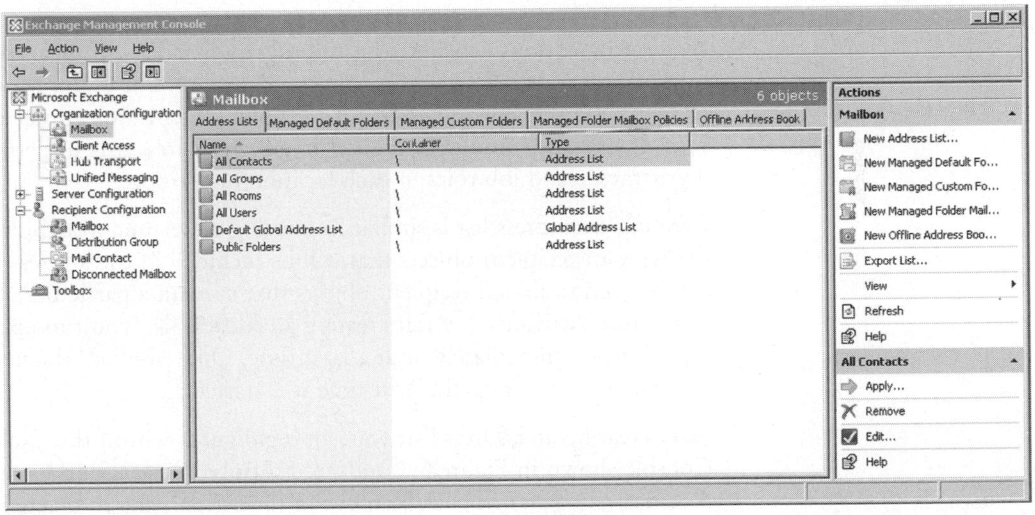

Figure 6-1

Viewing Default Address Lists

Figure 6-1 also contains the default address lists that are created within an Exchange organization:

- **All Contacts**—Mail contacts in the Exchange organization.
- **All Groups**—Mail-enabled universal groups in the Exchange organization.
- **All Rooms**—Room resource mailboxes in the Exchange organization.
- **All Users**—Mailbox users, linked mailbox users, mail users, and resource mailboxes in the Exchange organization.
- **Default Global Address List**—All recipient objects in the Exchange organization.
- **Public Folders**—All public folders in the Exchange organization.

The Default Global Address List cannot be modified, renamed, or removed because MAPI clients require it to function. All other default address lists can be renamed or removed but their list properties cannot be modified.

It is a good practice to retain the default address lists and create additional address lists that represent the structure of your organization so that users can view them to locate recipient objects efficiently. These additional address lists can be created alongside the default address lists or underneath them. For example, you could create an address list called All East Accounting Users and store it underneath the All Users address list. When users compose a new email and select the **To** button, they will see the All East Accounting Users address list under the All Users address list when they select the **Address Book** drop-down box in the Select Names dialog box as shown in Figure 6-2.

Figure 6-2

Accessing Address Lists

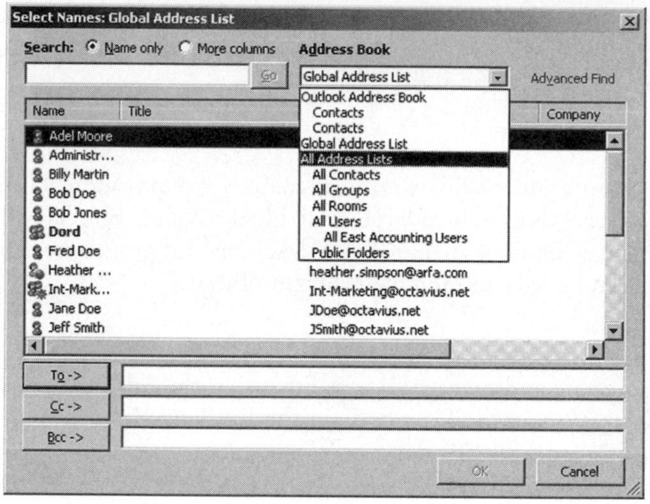

By creating address lists underneath other address lists, you can provide an intuitive organization for the address lists within your organization. For example, you can create new address lists alongside the default address lists that represent the various locations or divisions within your organization and then create specialized address lists underneath them to refer to the departments and job roles in each location or division.

Creating an address list is similar to creating a dynamic distribution group. You can specify the types of recipient objects that will be included in the address list as well as conditions that can be used to match recipient objects that contain a particular attribute such as Department or Custom Attribute 1. After creating an address list, you can apply it to your Exchange organization immediately or at a later time. Once applied, the new address list will appear in Outlook or Entourage the next time it is started.

After creating an address list, you can highlight it within the Exchange Management Console shown in Figure 6-1 and select **Apply** in the action pane to apply the address list. Alternatively, you can click **Remove** in the action pane to delete it or click **Edit** in the action pane to rename it or modify its properties. When you edit an address list in the Exchange Management Console, the configuration wizard used to create the address list appears again to allow you to modify the current address list name and settings.

⊙ CREATE A NEW ADDRESS LIST

GET READY. Turn on the computer, and log in as the Administrator user account. Close any windows that appear on the desktop.

1. Click **Start, All Programs, Microsoft Exchange Server 2007,** and then click **Exchange Management Console.** The Exchange Management Console window appears.

2. In the console tree pane, expand **Organization Configuration** and highlight **Mailbox.**

3. In the action pane, click **New Address List**. The New Address List window appears as shown in Figure 6-3.

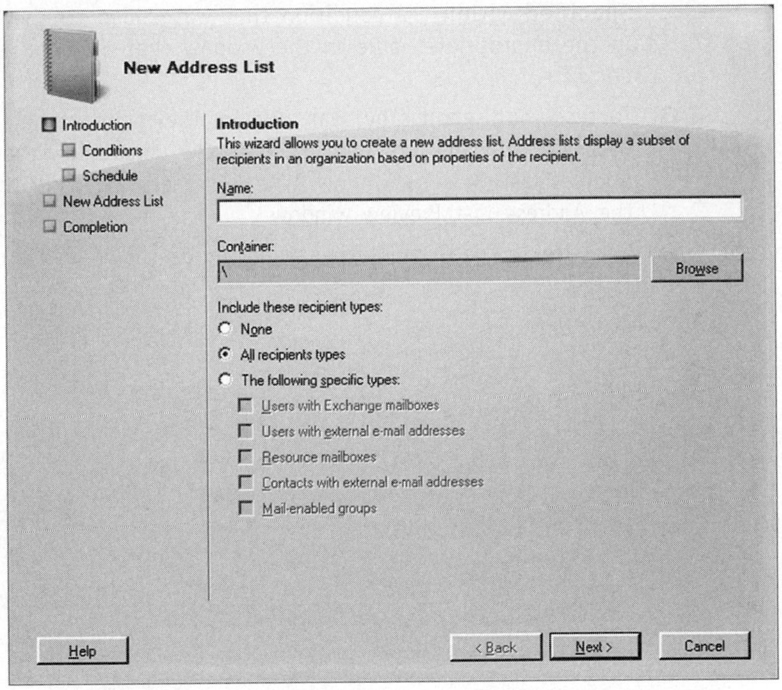

Figure 6-3

Creating a New Address List

New Address List

Introduction
Conditions
Schedule
New Address List
Completion

Introduction
This wizard allows you to create a new address list. Address lists display a subset of recipients in an organization based on properties of the recipient.

N̲ame:

Con̲tainer:
\   Bro̲wse

Include these recipient types:
○ N̲one
◉ All recipients types
○ The following s̲pecific types:
  ☐ U̲sers with Exchange mailboxes
  ☐ Users with e̲xternal e-mail addresses
  ☐ R̲esource mailboxes
  ☐ C̲ontacts with external e-mail addresses
  ☐ M̲ail-enabled groups

Help   < B̲ack   N̲ext >   Cancel

4. Supply an appropriate name in the Name dialog box. If you wish to create the address list under an existing address list, click **Browse** next to the Container dialog box, select the appropriate address list in the Select Address List window that appears, and click **OK**.

5. If you wish to select specific recipient object types to include in the address list, click **The following specific types** and select the appropriate recipient object types. Alternatively, you can click **None** if you wish to later modify the address list and specify recipient object types.

6. Click **Next**. The Conditions page appears as shown in Figure 6-4.

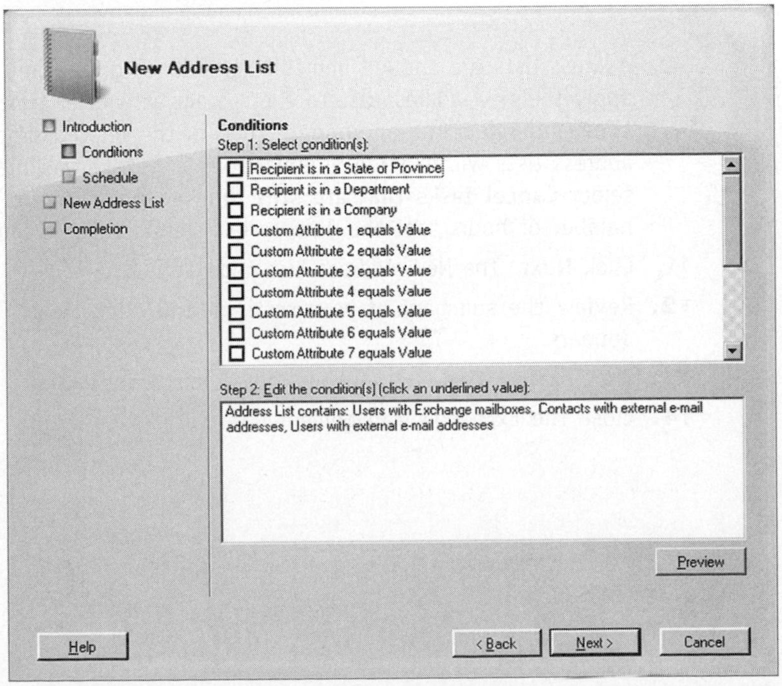

Figure 6-4

Specifying Address List
Conditions

New Address List

Introduction
Conditions
Schedule
New Address List
Completion

Conditions
Step 1: Select c̲ondition(s):

☐ Recipient is in a State or Province
☐ Recipient is in a Department
☐ Recipient is in a Company
☐ Custom Attribute 1 equals Value
☐ Custom Attribute 2 equals Value
☐ Custom Attribute 3 equals Value
☐ Custom Attribute 4 equals Value
☐ Custom Attribute 5 equals Value
☐ Custom Attribute 6 equals Value
☐ Custom Attribute 7 equals Value

Step 2: E̲dit the condition(s) (click an underlined value):

Address List contains: Users with Exchange mailboxes, Contacts with external e-mail addresses, Users with external e-mail addresses

Preview

Help   < B̲ack   N̲ext >   Cancel

7. Select the recipient object attributes that the address list will match when including recipient objects. Each attribute that you select will add a condition to the Step 2 dialog box. To add a value for each attribute, you must click **Specified** within the condition that was added to the Step 2 dialog box, type in the appropriate value in the window that appears, click **Add,** and then click **OK.**

8. To test your settings by searching for the recipient objects that match your address list, you can click **Preview** in Figure 6-4 and review the information shown in the Address List Preview window. When finished reviewing the results, click **OK** to close the Address List Preview window.

9. Click **Next.** The Schedule page appears as shown in Figure 6-5.

Figure 6-5

Scheduling Address List Application

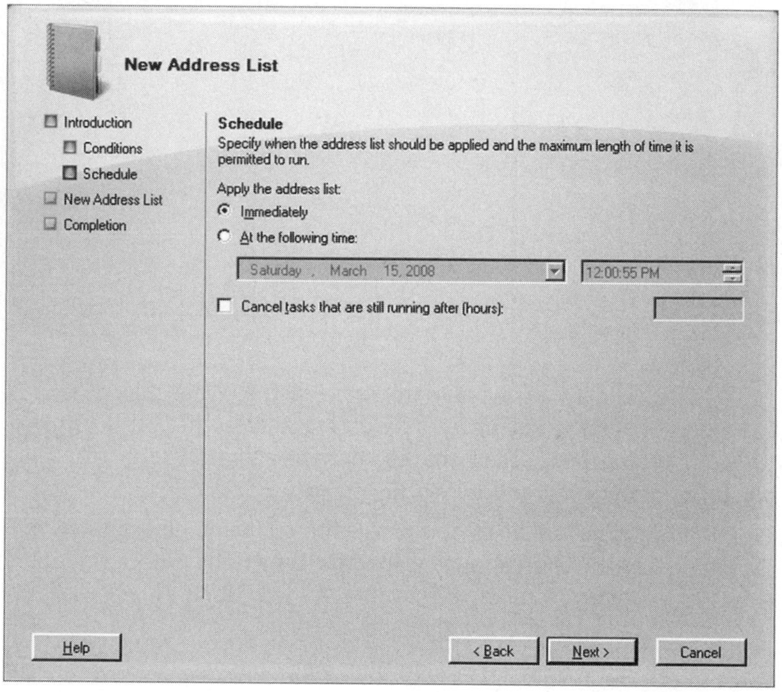

10. Address lists are applied immediately following creation by default. If you wish to apply the new address list to the system at a later time, click **At the following time** and select the appropriate time in the related drop-down boxes. Because large address lists within large organizations may take a while to process, you can also select **Cancel tasks that are still running after (hours)** and supply the maximum number of hours that the address list should take to apply.

11. Click **Next.** The New Address List page appears.

12. Review the summary of your settings and click **New.** The Completion page appears.

13. Click **Finish** to close the New Address List window.

14. Close the Exchange Management Console.

You can also use the **New-AddressList** cmdlet in the Exchange Management Shell to create address lists. For example, to create an address list called All East Accounting Users under the existing All Users address list that includes mailbox users, mail contacts, and mail users that have a Department attribute of Accounting-East, you could run the following command in the Exchange Management Shell:

New-AddressList –Name 'All East Accounting Users' –Container '\All Users' – IncludedRecipients 'MailboxUsers, MailContacts, MailUsers' –ConditionalDepartment 'Accounting-East'

To apply an address list, you can use the **Update-AddressList** cmdlet. To apply the address list created in the previous example, you could run the following command in the Exchange Management Shell:

Update-AddressList –Identity '\All Users\All East Accounting Users'

You can also use the **Get-AddressList** cmdlet to view address list settings or the **Set-AddressList** cmdlet to modify the properties of an existing address list. For example, to rename the All East Accounting Users address list to All Accounting Users and view the properties of the address list afterwards, you could use the following commands in the Exchange Management Shell:

Set-AddressList -Identity '\All Users\All East Accounting Users' -Name 'All Accounting Users'

Get-AddressList -Identity '\All Users\All Accounting Users' | Format-List

To remove the All Accounting Users address list you can use the **Remove-AddressList** cmdlet within the Exchange Management Shell as shown in the following command:

Remove-AddressList -Identity '\All Users\All Accounting Users'

If the All Accounting Users address list has address lists underneath it, you must use the **–Recursive** option alongside the Remove-AddressList command to remove the address lists underneath All Accounting Users.

Creating and Managing Offline Address Books

To ensure that MAPI clients can access important address lists when they are not directly connected to their Exchange server, you should ensure that the address lists are added to an Offline Address Book that is configured on the mailbox databases used by the MAPI clients. Offline Address Books may be created and managed using the Exchange Management Console or the Exchange Management Shell.

Although address lists allow users to locate recipient objects when using a MAPI client, they are only available when the Exchange server that the MAPI client is configured to use is online and available. Thus, users within the organization who use mobile computers may not be able to view address lists when traveling outside the organization. For these mobile users, gaining access to the email address information in their address lists for reference or to send emails using another email client program may be necessary while traveling.

To accommodate this, Exchange Server 2007 uses *Offline Address Books (OABs)*. OABs are downloaded from Mailbox role servers to MAPI clients and can contain one or more address lists. When a MAPI client is not connected to the Exchange server, it can still view the information in address lists using the OAB stored on the MAPI client.

You can create and manage OABs within the Exchange Management Console using the **Offline Address Book** tab of the **Organization Configuration** > **Mailbox** node. After deployment, Exchange Server 2007 creates a Default Offline Address Book that contains the Default Global Address List as shown in Figure 6-6.

Figure 6-6

Viewing the Default Offline Address Book

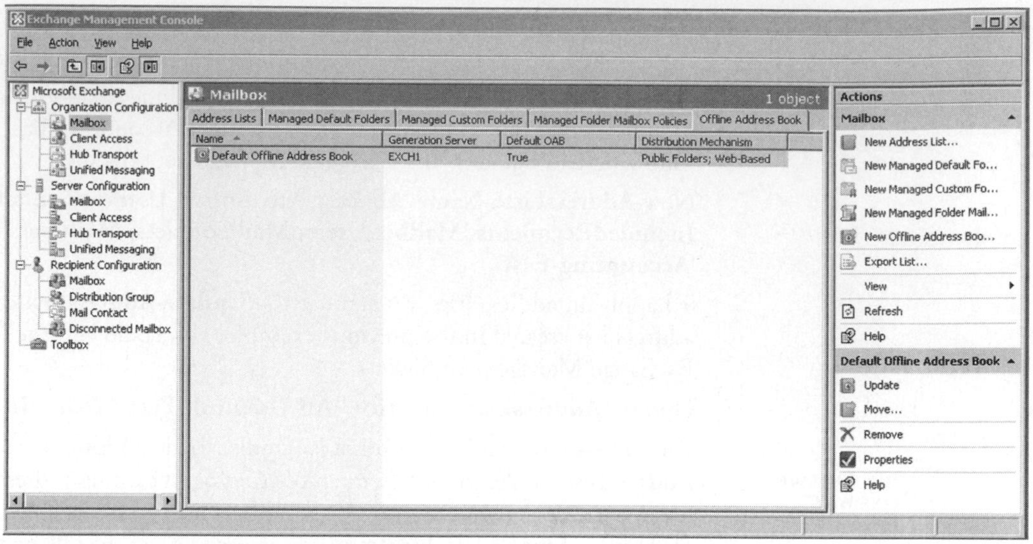

To modify an OAB, simply highlight it in the result pane shown in Figure 6-6 and select **Properties** in the action pane. The properties of the Default Offline Address Book are shown in Figure 6-7.

Figure 6-7

Viewing General Offline Address Book Properties

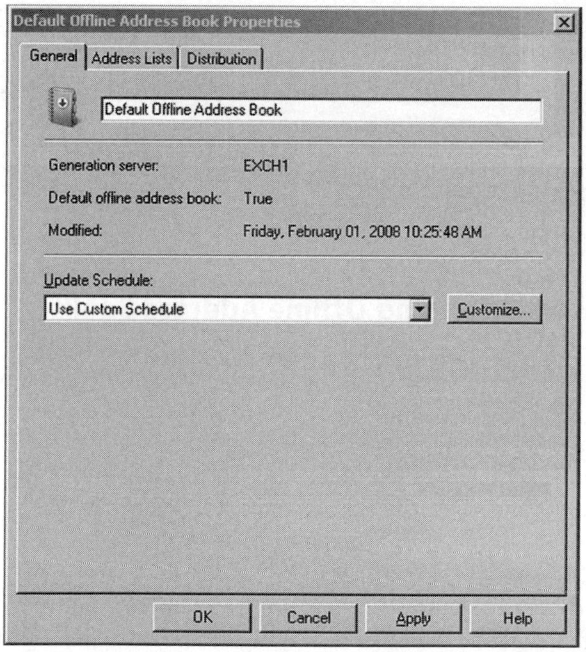

Figure 6-7 indicates the Default Offline Address Book will be generated by the Mailbox role server called EXCH1 and that it is the default OAB used by all mailboxes within the organization. Additionally, you can supply a different name for the OAB in the dialog box shown in Figure 6-7 or modify the Update Schedule section to specify when the information within the OAB will be automatically updated to include new recipients. The Default Offline Address Book is rebuilt each day using a custom schedule of 6:00 a.m. by default. To change the schedule, you can click **Customize** in Figure 6-7 and select a different time period or select a predefined period from the Update Schedule drop-down box.

Although the Default Offline Address Book includes the Default Global Address List, you can also include other address lists to make searching for recipient objects easier. Simply click **Include the following address lists** on the Address Lists tab as shown in Figure 6-8 and add the appropriate address lists using the **Add** button.

OABs are distributed to Outlook 2007 and Entourage 2008 clients using a Web site config-ured on a Mailbox role server by default. For Outlook 2003 and Entourage 2004 and earlier clients, OABs are instead distributed alongside the default public folders. To configure the distribution of OABs, you can navigate to the Distribution tab of OAB properties as shown in Figure 6-9.

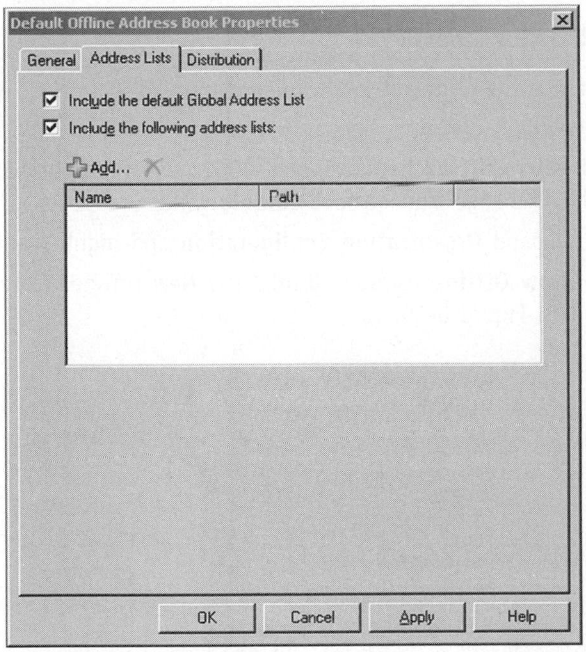

Figure 6-8

Adding Address Lists to an Offline Address Book

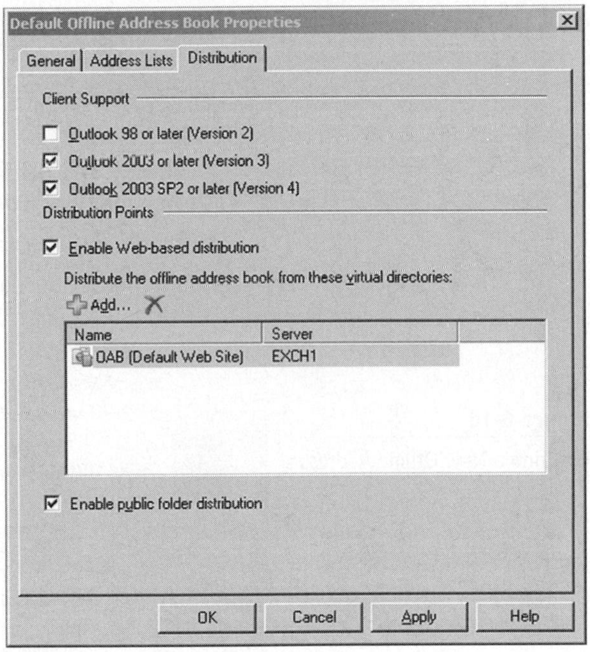

Figure 6-9

Configuring Offline Address Book Distribution

In the Client Support section of Figure 6-9, you can configure the clients that will obtain a copy of the OAB. There are three selections that you can choose from that depend on the OAB versions supported by the MAPI clients deployed within your organization:

- **Outlook 98 or later (Version 2)** applies to Outlook 98, Outlook 2000, Outlook 2002, and Entourage X.
- **Outlook 2003 or later (Version 3)** applies to Outlook 2003 and Entourage 2004.
- **Outlook 2003 SP2 or later (Version 4)** applies to Outlook 2003 SP2, Outlook 2007, and Entourage 2008.

By default, Version 2 and Version 3 MAPI clients require distribution using public folders under the Distribution Points section, whereas Version 4 MAPI clients can use either pub-lic folder distribution or web-based distribution. The Default Web site on the first CAS role server within your organization distributes the OAB to all Version 4 MAPI clients by default. However, you should add the Default Web site on each CAS role server in the organization so that Version 4 MAPI clients can obtain the OAB from the nearest CAS role server.

In addition to modifying the Default Offline Address Book, you can create additional OABs for different departments or job functions. You can specify that these additional OABs be generated by the Mailbox role servers in the appropriate departments as well as configure the OABs for use with the appropriate mailbox databases on your Mailbox role servers in each department.

For example, you could configure an OAB on the mailbox database used by the mailbox users in your Accounting department that includes only the address lists needed by Accounting department staff. You could then configure a second OAB on the mailbox database that contains the mailbox users in the Marketing department. This second OAB will only contain address lists needed by the Marketing department staff. Furthermore, you can specify that the Accounting OAB be generated by the Mailbox role server in the Accounting department and that the Marketing OAB be generated by the Mailbox role server in the Marketing department. Because OABs in this scenario only contain the relevant address lists and are generated close to the MAPI clients that will use them, OABs will be updated and distributed efficiently within the organization.

 CREATE A NEW OFFLINE ADDRESS BOOK

GET READY. Turn on the computer, and log in as the Administrator user account. Close any windows that appear on the desktop.

1. Click **Start**, **All Programs**, **Microsoft Exchange Server 2007**, and then click **Exchange Management Console**. The Exchange Management Console window appears.
2. In the console tree pane, expand **Organization Configuration** and highlight **Mailbox**.
3. In the action pane, click **New Offline Address Book**. The New Offline Address Book window appears as shown in Figure 6-10.

Figure 6-10

Creating a New Offline Address Book

![New Offline Address Book wizard window showing Introduction page with Name field, Offline address book generation server field with Browse button, Include the default Global Address List checkbox, and Include the following address lists option]

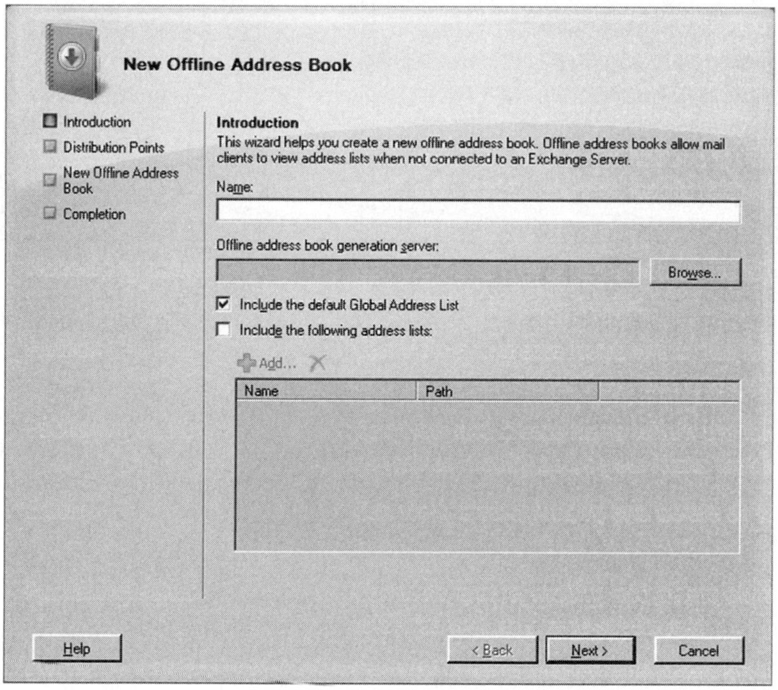

4. Supply an appropriate name in the Name dialog box. Next, click **Browse**, select the Mailbox role server that should be used to generate the OAB in the Select Mailbox Server window that appears, and click **OK**.
5. The Default Global Address List is included in the new OAB by default. However, you can deselect the related option to prevent this. To add additional address lists, select **Include the following address lists** and add the appropriate address lists by clicking **Add**.
6. Click **Next**. The Distribution Points page appears as shown in Figure 6-11.

Figure 6-11

Specifying Offline Address
Book Distribution Points

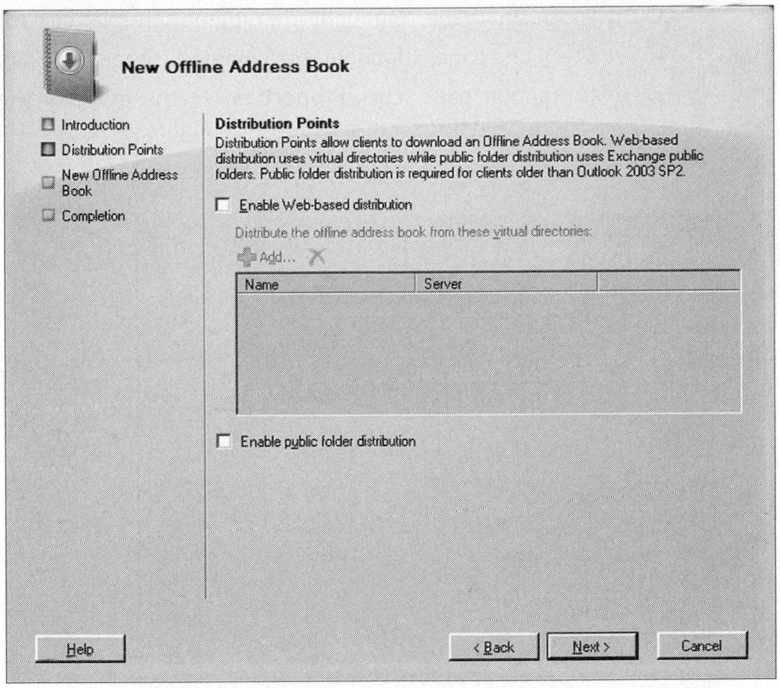

New Offline Address Book

- Introduction
- Distribution Points
- New Offline Address Book
- Completion

Distribution Points
Distribution Points allow clients to download an Offline Address Book. Web-based distribution uses virtual directories while public folder distribution uses Exchange public folders. Public folder distribution is required for clients older than Outlook 2003 SP2.

☐ Enable Web-based distribution

Distribute the offline address book from these virtual directories:

✚ Add... ✕

Name	Server	

☐ Enable public folder distribution

Help   < Back   Next >   Cancel

7. If you have Outlook 2003 or Entourage 2004 clients or earlier, you must select **Enable public folder distribution** to allow the OAB to be distributed alongside the default public folder tree. To optionally enable web-based distribution for your Outlook 2003 SP2, Outlook 2007, and Entourage 2008 clients, select **Enable Web-based distribution** and add the appropriate Web sites to the dialog box using the **Add** button. These Web sites must reside on a CAS role server within your organization.

8. Click **Next**. The New Offline Address Book page appears.

9. Review the summary of your settings and click **New**. The Completion page appears.

10. Click **Finish** to close the New Mailbox window.

11. Close the Exchange Management Console.

THE COMMAND
LINE WAY

You can also use the **New-OfflineAddressBook** cmdlet in the Exchange Management Shell to create OABs. For example, to create an OAB called Marketing Department Offline Address Book that includes the Default Global Address List and All Users address lists as well as specify that it should be generated on the Mailbox role server EXCH2, use public folder distribution and web-based distribution using the OAB virtual directory on the default Web site on EXCH2, you could run the following command in the Exchange Management Shell:

New-OfflineAddressBook –Name 'Marketing Department Offline Address Book' –AddressLists '\Default Global Address List', '\All Users' –Server 'EXCH2' –PublicFolderDistributionEnabled $true –VirtualDirectories 'EXCH2\OAB (Default Web Site)'

➔ CONFIGURE A MAILBOX DATABASE TO USE AN OFFLINE ADDRESS BOOK

GET READY. Turn on the computer, and log in as the Administrator user account. Close any windows that appear on the desktop.

1. Click **Start, All Programs, Microsoft Exchange Server 2007**, and then click **Exchange Management Console**. The Exchange Management Console window appears.

2. In the console tree pane, expand **Server Configuration** and highlight **Mailbox**.

3. In the result pane, highlight the appropriate Mailbox role server object.

4. In the work pane, highlight the appropriate mailbox database.

5. In the action pane, click **Properties**. In the property window that appears, highlight the **Client Settings** tab as shown in Figure 6-12.

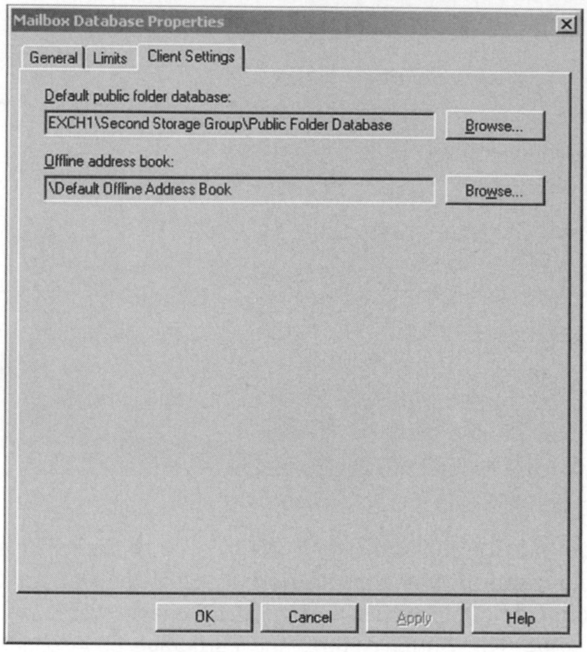

Figure 6-12

Configuring an Offline Address Book on a Mailbox Database

Mailbox Database Properties

General | Limits | Client Settings

Default public folder database:

| EXCH1\Second Storage Group\Public Folder Database | Browse... |

Offline address book:

| \Default Offline Address Book | Browse... |

| OK | Cancel | Apply | Help |

6. Click **Browse** next to the Offline address book dialog box, select the appropriate OAB in the Select Offline Address Book window that appears, and click **OK**.

7. Click **OK** to close the properties of the mailbox database.

8. Close the Exchange Management Console.

THE COMMAND
LINE WAY

You can also use the **Set-MailboxDatabase** cmdlet in the Exchange Management Shell to specify the OAB for an existing mailbox database. For example, to specify the Marketing Offline Address Book on the Marketing Mailbox Database, you could run the following command in the Exchange Management Shell on the Mailbox role server:

Set-MailboxDatabase 'Marketing Mailbox Database' –OfflineAddressBook 'Marketing Offline Address Book'

Over time, you may need to modify the properties of additional OABs to specify different client support, address lists, updated schedules, or distribution methods. After modifying an OAB, you can select **Update** from the action pane in the Exchange Management Console shown earlier in Figure 6-6 to regenerate and redeploy the OAB immediately. Alternatively, you can select **Set as Default** from the action pane to change the default OAB or **Remove** from the action pane to remove an OAB.

If your MAPI clients have difficulty obtaining an OAB, the server that is used to generate the OAB is likely on a remote network. To change the generation server for an OAB to a Mailbox role server that is closer to the MAPI clients, you can click **Move** in the action pane. This will open the Move Offline Address Book window shown in Figure 6-13 and allow you to select a different generation server.

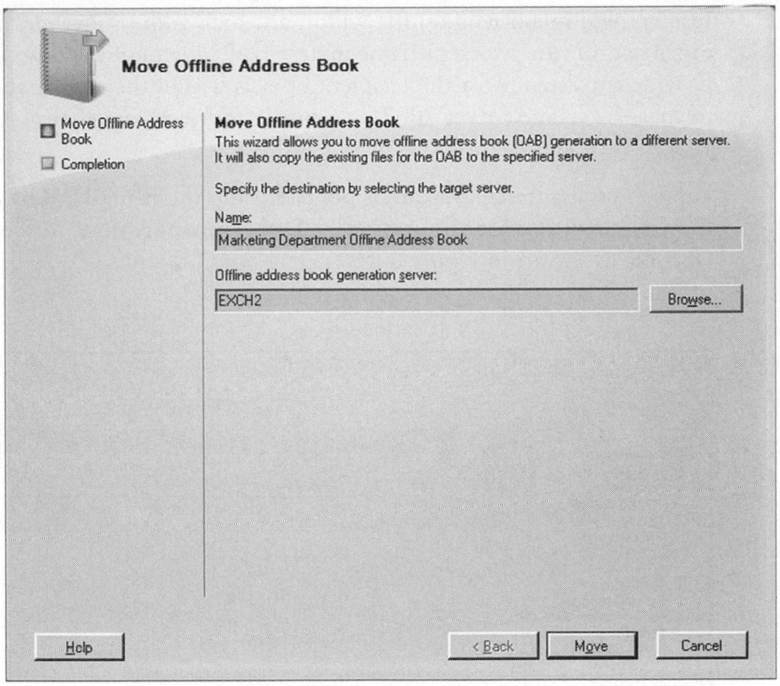

Figure 6-13

Specifying a New Offline Address Book Generation Server

You can also use the following cmdlets within the Exchange Management Shell to configure and manage OABs:

Get-OfflineAddressBook to view OABs settings.

Set-OfflineAddressBook to modify the properties of an OAB.

Move-OfflineAddress Book to modify the generation server for an OAB.

Update-OfflineAddress Book to regenerate an OAB.

Remove-OfflineAddress Book to remove an OAB.

To see the available options for these cmdlets, you can search for their names within Exchange Server 2007 Help.

■ Configuring Policies

In Lesson 5, "Working with Recipient Objects," you created resource-booking policies for use with resource mailboxes. This section examines email address policies that can be used to standardize email formats for recipient objects as well as messaging compliance policies that can be applied to mailbox users to enforce legal restrictions regarding the retention of email. ActiveSync policies will be covered in Lesson 12, "Providing for Mobile Access and Unified Messaging."

↓
THE BOTTOM LINE

Configuring Email Address Policies

CERTIFICATION READY?
Configure policies
3.4

As an Exchange administrator, you are responsible for ensuring a consistent format for email addresses within your organization. By creating email address policies within the Exchange Management Console or the Exchange Management Shell, you can ensure that recipient objects receive the appropriate email address automatically.

Just as the domain name suffix within an email address provides a consistent identity for the organization, the recipient name in an email address should also follow a standard format to provide consistency for the recipient objects within the organization. To provide this standard format, Exchange Server 2007 uses *email address policies* that automatically provide email addresses to recipient objects.

You can configure email address policies using the **E-mail Address Policies** tab under the **Organization Configuration** > **Hub Transport** node in the Exchange Management Console as shown in Figure 6-14.

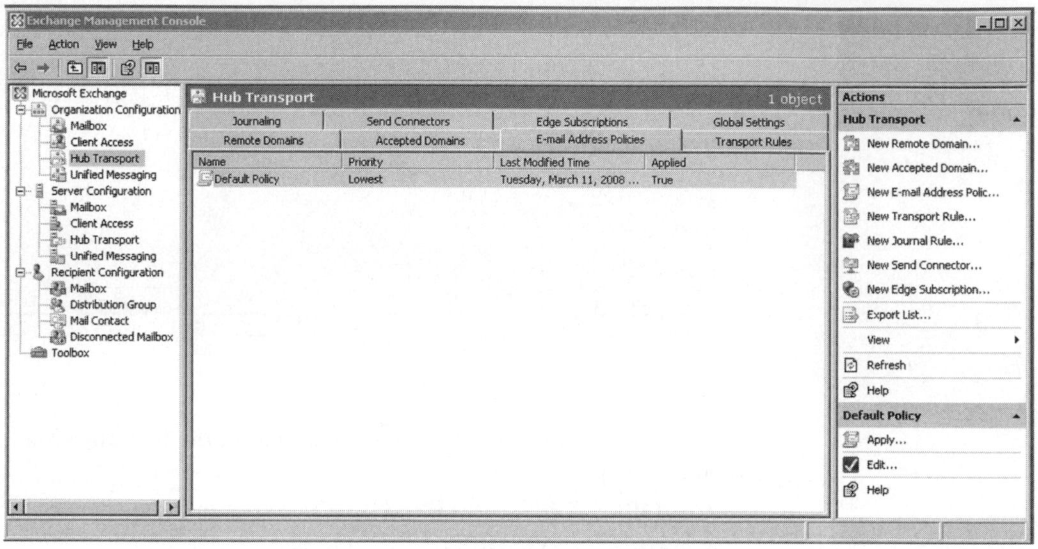

Figure 6-14

Viewing the Default Email Address Policy

As shown in Figure 6-14, there is a single default email address policy called Default Policy that is created after deploying Exchange. This policy provides the default email address of alias@domainname to all recipient objects in the Exchange organization. Furthermore, this policy is always given the lowest priority and cannot be deleted. If there are two email address policies that match a recipient object, only the highest priority email address policy will be applied. As a result, you can create additional email address policies that override the default email address policy.

Provided that you specify aliases that follow a predefined standard when creating recipient objects, the default email address policy will provide a standard look and feel to the email addresses within your organization. However, there are certain situations in which you may need to change the default email address policy or add additional email address policies.

If your organization requires a different email address format for different recipient types, departments, or divisions within the organization, you will need to create multiple email address policies. Each email address policy will contain a different email address format and apply to different recipient types, departments, or divisions.

In addition, some organizations may need to move to a different email address format due to growth. Say, for example, that your small organization uses email addresses in the form firstname@domainname to give a personal feel to the email addresses within the organization. However, as the organization grows and hires more members with the same first name, you will need to change the email format to something that uniquely identifies your members such as firstname.lastname@domainname. To do this, you could simply change the default email address policy to the new format. Alternatively, you could create an additional email address policy that applies the new email address format to all recipient objects with a higher priority than the default email address policy.

Accepted domains were discussed in Lesson 4, "Configuring a New Exchange Server."

Email address policies are also useful when organizations need to add additional email addresses to existing recipient objects due to the renaming or merging of divisions. You can simply modify an existing email address policy and add additional email addresses as well as specify the main email address used when the recipient replies to email. If the additional email addresses contain a new domain name, you must configure an accepted domain for them on your Hub role servers.

Moreover, some organizations simply change their email address format to reduce the number of spam messages that are sent to the organization. After modifying the email address format, spam messages sent to the original email address will be rejected if there is no recipient object with the target email address.

 CREATE A NEW EMAIL ADDRESS POLICY

GET READY. Turn on the computer, and log in as the Administrator user account. Close any windows that appear on the desktop.

1. Click **Start**, **All Programs**, **Microsoft Exchange Server 2007**, and then click **Exchange Management Console**. The Exchange Management Console window appears.
2. In the console tree pane, expand **Organization Configuration** and highlight **Hub Transport**.
3. In the action pane, click **New E-mail Address Policy**. The New E-mail Address Policy window appears as shown in Figure 6-15.

Figure 6-15

Creating a New Email Address Policy

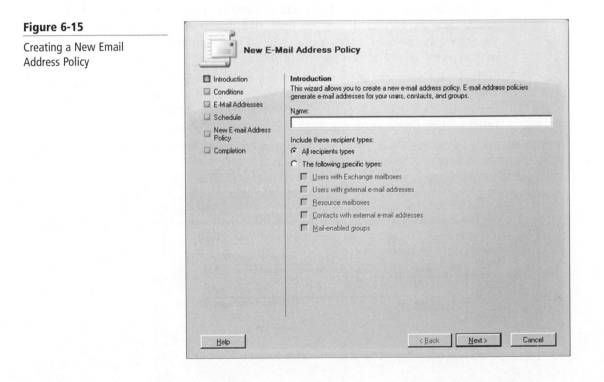

4. Supply an appropriate name in the Name dialog box. If the email address policy should only apply to specific recipient objects, click **The following specific types** and select the appropriate recipient object types.
5. Click **Next**. The Conditions page appears as shown in Figure 6-16.

Figure 6-16

Specifying Email Address Policy
Conditions

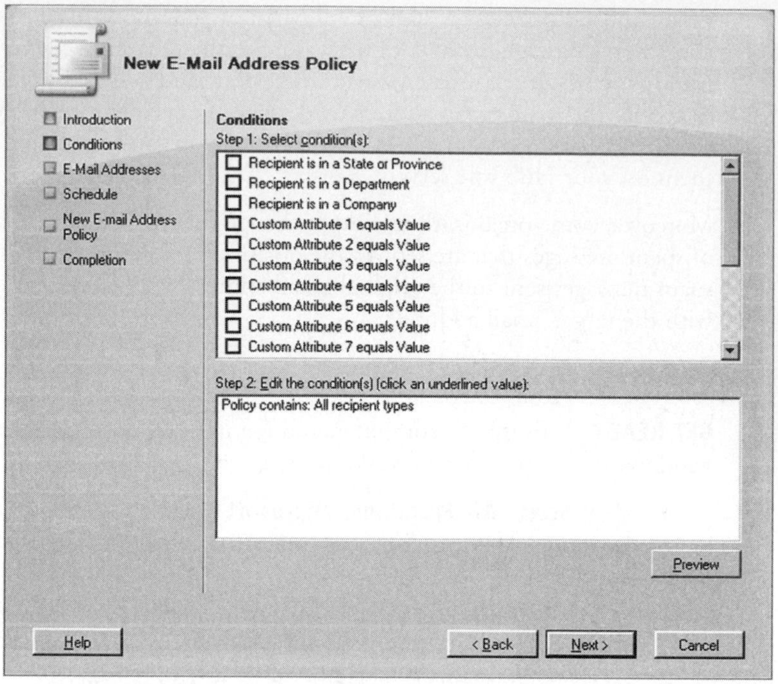

6. Select the recipient object attributes that the email address policy will apply to. Each attribute that you select will add a condition to the Step 2 dialog box. To add a value for each attribute, you must click **Specified** within the condition that was added to the Step 2 dialog box, type in the appropriate value in the window that appears, click **Add** and then click **OK**.

7. To test your settings by searching for the recipient objects that match your email address policy, you can click **Preview** in Figure 6-16 and review the information shown in the E-Mail Address Policy Preview window. When finished reviewing the results, click **OK** to close the E-mail Address Policy Preview window.

8. Click **Next**. The E-Mail Addresses page appears as shown in Figure 6-17.

Figure 6-17

Adding Email Address Formats

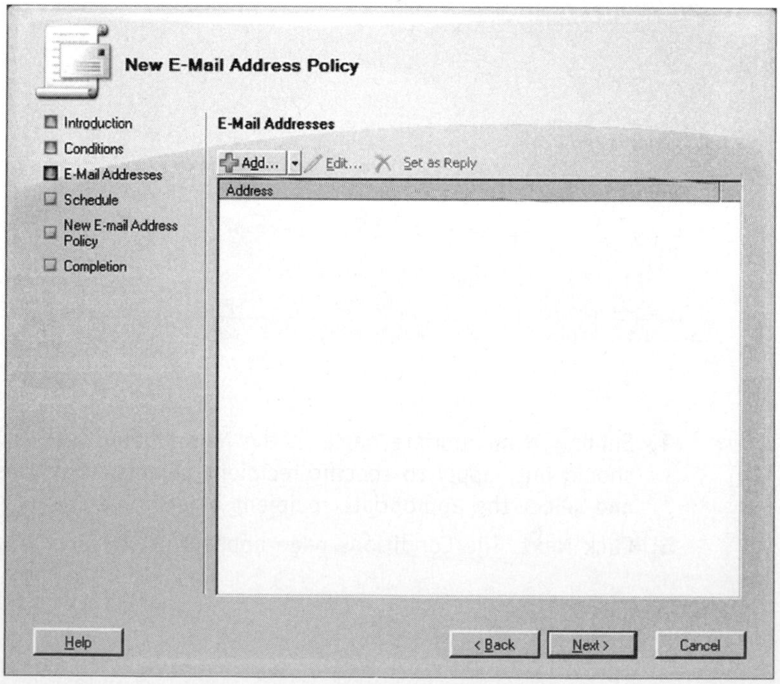

9. Click **Add** to add an email address format to your email address policy. The SMTP E-mail Address window appears as shown in Figure 6-18.

Figure 6-18

Selecting an Email Address Format

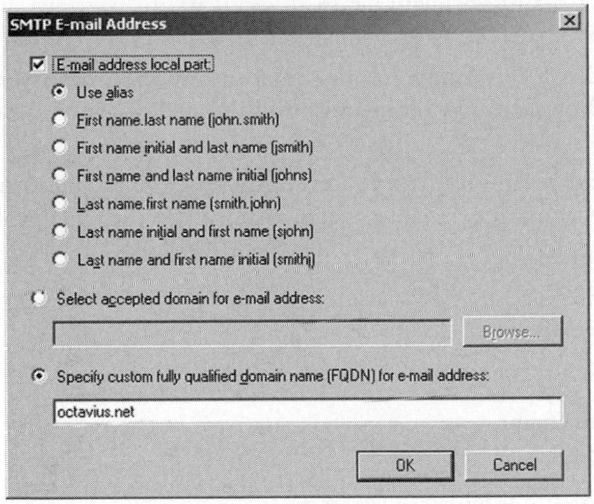

10. To specify the recipient name format within the email address, ensure that **E-mail address local part** is selected and choose the appropriate format underneath it.

TAKE NOTE*

You must ensure that the **E-mail address local part** option is selected when you create a new email address policy. This option is only deselected when modifying the domain name suffix for an existing email address policy.

11. Supply the correct domain name suffix for the email address format in the **Specify custom fully qualified domain name (FQDN) for e-mail address** dialog box. Alternatively, you can click **Select accepted domain for e-mail address**, click the **Browse** button, select the appropriate accepted domain in the Select Accepted Domain window that appears and click **OK**.

12. Click **OK** to close the SMTP E-mail Address window. If you wish to add additional email addresses to your email address policy, you can repeat Steps 9 through 11. If you have added multiple email addresses, select the email address format that recipients should use when replying to email and click the **Set as Reply** button as shown in Figure 6-17.

13. Click **Next**. The Schedule page appears.

14. By default, the email address policy will apply immediately to the Exchange organization. If you wish to apply the new email address policy to the system at a later time, click **At the following time** and select the appropriate time in the related drop-down boxes. You can optionally select **Cancel tasks that are still running after (hours)** and supply the maximum number of hours that the email address policy should take to apply.

15. Click **Next**. The New E-mail Address Policy page appears.

16. Review the summary of your settings and click **New**. The Completion page appears.

17. Click **Finish** to close the New E-Mail Address Policy window.

18. Close the Exchange Management Console.

THE COMMAND LINE WAY

You can also use the **New-EmailAddressPolicy** cmdlet in the Exchange Management Shell to create email address policies. For example, to create an email address policy called Standard Email Address Policy that has the highest priority and applies an email format of firstname.lastname@octavius.net to all recipient objects, you could run the following command in the Exchange Management Shell:

New-EmailAddressPolicy –Name 'Standard Email Address Policy' –Priority 1 –EnabledEmailAddressTemplates 'SMTP:%g.%s@octavius.net' –IncludedRecipients 'AllRecipients'

The %g and %s in the email address format used in the previous example represent variables. Some common variables that you can use in the email address format are:

%g   First name

%1g   First letter of first name

%3g   First three letters of first name

%i   Middle initial

%s   Last name

%1s   First letter of last name

%3s   First three letters of last name

%d   Display name

%m   Alias name

For additional options to the New-EmailAddressPolicy cmdlet, search for New-EmailAddressPolicy within Exchange Server 2007 Help.

After you create a new email address policy using the Exchange Management Shell, you must apply it using the **Update-EmailAddressPolicy** cmdlet for it to take effect within your Exchange organization. To apply the email address policy created in the previous example, you can run the following command in the Exchange Management Shell:

Update-EmailAddressPolicy –Identity 'Standard Email Address Policy'

After creation, you can modify email address policies by highlighting them under the **E-mail Address Policies** tab in the **Organization Configuration > Hub Transport** node within the Exchange Management Console and selecting the appropriate action from the action pane.

The **Apply** action will apply the email address policy within the Exchange organization, whereas the **Remove** action will delete the email address policy. If you have two or more email address policies in addition to the default email address policy, you can select the **Change Priority** action to modify the priority (1 is the highest priority, 2 is the second highest priority, and so on).

If you need to change an existing email address policy to apply to different recipient objects or use a different or additional email address, you can select the **Edit** action. This will start the same wizard used to create the email address policy and allow you to make the appropriate changes.

THE COMMAND LINE WAY

You can also use the following cmdlets within the Exchange Management Shell to configure and manage email address policies:

Get-EmailAddressPolicy to view email address policy settings.

Set-EmailAddressPolicy to modify the properties of an email address policy.

Remove-EmailAddress Policy to remove an email address policy.

To see the available options for these cmdlets, you can search for their names within Exchange Server 2007 Help.

Although email address policies provide standardization for the email addresses used within your organization, you can choose to override email address policies for specific recipient objects. This is necessary if you wish to modify the email addresses on a recipient object that were assigned by an email address policy or change the primary email address used when replying to email.

To override email address policies, you can simply uncheck **Automatically update e-mail addresses based on e-mail address policy** on the E-Mail Addresses tab of a recipient object as shown in Figure 6-19 for the mailbox user Jane Doe. Following this, you can delete existing email addresses, add additional email addresses that do not follow the format specified in an email address policy, and specify a different email address used when the recipient replies to email.

Figure 6-19

Overriding Email Address Policies

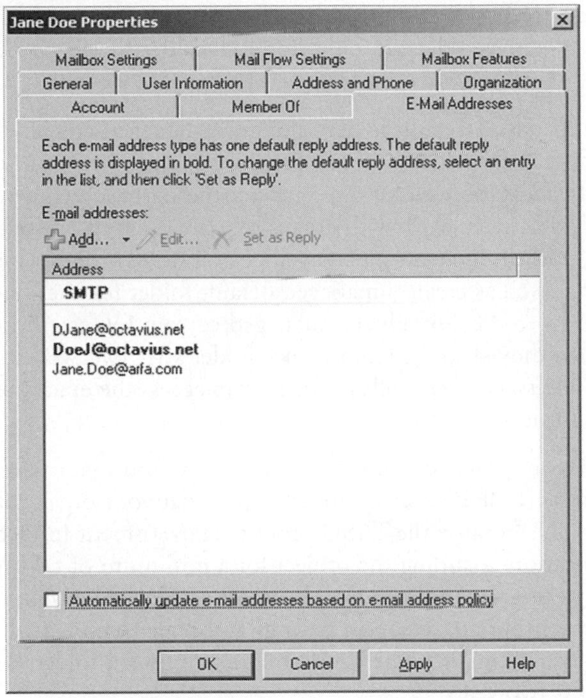

Configuring Messaging Compliance Policies

> Messaging compliance policies are common in most organizations and serve to protect vital emails from deletion for litigation purposes. To create a messaging compliance policy, you can configure managed folders and managed folder mailbox policies to archive email for specific time periods or configure journaling to archive emails in a separate mailbox. Messaging compliance configuration can be performed in both the Exchange Management Console and the Exchange Management Shell.

CERTIFICATION READY?
Configure transport rules and message compliance.
3.23

As organizations continue to take advantage of the digital age, laws and regulations regarding email retention are becoming more common. Depending on the type of organization, regional laws may require that certain emails be retained in the event they are required for litigation. Each country, region, and municipality has different guidelines for email retention for key organizations. In addition, a court ruling may require that copies of all information including email be kept for a certain number of years. This is common when litigation reveals missing documentation.

Regardless of the requirements, the process of storing emails for legal reasons is called *messaging compliance*. Using Exchange Server 2007, you can implement a messaging compliance policy to match the legal requirements of your organization. There are two Exchange Server 2007 features that you can use to create a messaging compliance policy: Messaging Records Management (MRM) and message journaling.

CONFIGURING MESSAGING RECORDS MANAGEMENT

MRM allows you to create *managed custom folders* that Outlook 2003 SP2, Outlook 2007, Entourage 2008, and OWA clients can use to store email or other items that need to be retained for a certain period of time. Managed custom folders appear under a Managed Folders section within the Mail Folders pane within Outlook, Entourage, or OWA. Any items stored within these managed custom folders cannot be deleted before the end of the time period.

Moreover, you can specify that email and other items that reside within existing default folders such as Inbox and Sent Items be retained for a certain period of time or moved to a managed custom folder for storage. These default folders are called *managed default folders*. Although you can create additional managed default folders, Exchange Server 2007 automatically creates a managed default folder for each folder that is normally displayed in Outlook, Entourage, or OWA.

You can use managed default folders alongside managed custom folders to automate the retention of email for legal purposes. Say, for example, that your organization must retain a copy of all emails received for one year. Furthermore, users in your organization usually do not need to actively work with emails that are older than two weeks. To provide message compliance, you could create a managed custom folder called Compliance that retains email for one year as well as create a managed default folder for the Inbox that moves items older than two weeks to the Compliance managed custom folder. All items that are received in the Inbox are then moved to the Compliance folder after two weeks, where they are retained for one year. If necessary, users will still be able to access the emails in the Compliance folder for reference or for legal reasons.

Managed custom folders can also be used to store information for legal purposes related to specific projects or divisions. Say, for example, that your organization is involved with a project called TASU. Because the TASU project is government funded, you are required to keep all communication regarding the project for a minimum of two years. To provide message compliance in this situation, you could create a managed custom folder called TASU that contains the appropriate retention settings and direct members of the TASU project to move any TASU-related emails to the TASU managed custom folder, where they will automatically be retained for two years.

Managed custom folders and managed default folders can be created and managed within the Exchange Management Console using the appropriate tabs under the **Organization Configuration > Mailbox** node. After creating a managed custom folder or managed default folder, you can specify the retention settings for items within the folder by highlighting the managed folder and selecting **New Managed Content Settings** from the action pane within the Exchange Management Console. In addition to retention settings, the New Managed Content Settings wizard also allows you to forward copies of items within the managed folder to another mailbox for archiving or monitoring.

⊙ CREATE A NEW MANAGED CUSTOM FOLDER

GET READY. Turn on the computer, and log in as the Administrator user account. Close any windows that appear on the desktop.

1. Click **Start, All Programs, Microsoft Exchange Server 2007,** and then click **Exchange Management Console.** The Exchange Management Console window appears.
2. In the console tree pane, expand **Organization Configuration** and highlight **Mailbox.**
3. In the action pane, click **New Managed Custom Folder.** The New Managed Custom Folder window appears as shown in Figure 6-20.

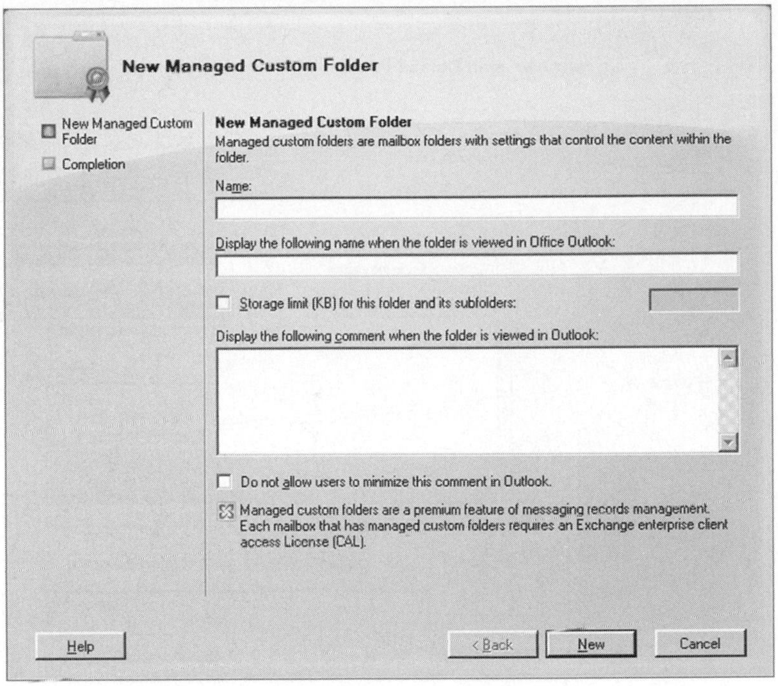

Figure 6-20

Creating a New Managed
Custom Folder

4. Supply an appropriate name for the managed custom folder in the first dialog box as well as a name that will appear in Outlook, Entourage, or OWA in the second dialog box.

5. To restrict the size of the managed custom folder, you can optionally select **Storage limit (KB) for this folder and its subfolders** and supply the appropriate value in the related dialog box.

6. Enter a description that will be shown in Outlook, Entourage, or OWA for the managed custom folder in the final dialog box. To ensure that the comment is always visible in Outlook, Entourage, or OWA, you can select **Do not allow users to minimize this comment in Outlook**.

7. Click **New**. The Completion page appears.

8. Click **Finish** to close the New Managed Custom Folder window.

9. Close the Exchange Management Console.

⊙ CREATE A NEW MANAGED DEFAULT FOLDER

GET READY. Turn on the computer, and log in as the Administrator user account. Close any windows that appear on the desktop.

1. Click **Start, All Programs, Microsoft Exchange Server 2007**, and then click **Exchange Management Console**. The Exchange Management Console window appears.

2. In the console tree pane, expand **Organization Configuration** and highlight **Mailbox**.

3. In the action pane, click **New Managed Default Folder**. The New Managed Default Folder window appears as shown in Figure 6-21.

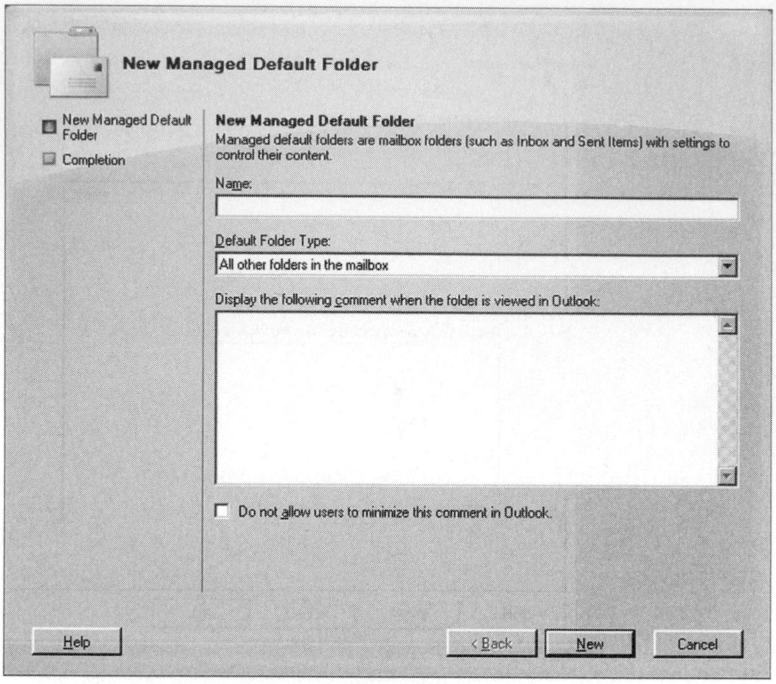

Figure 6-21

Creating a New Managed
Default Folder

4. Supply an appropriate name for the managed default folder in the Name dialog box as well as select the appropriate folder type (Calendar, Contacts, Drafts, etc.) from the Default Folder Type drop-down box. If the additional managed default folder should contain items of various types, you should select the **All other folders in the mailbox** type.

5. Enter a description that will be shown in Outlook, Entourage, or OWA for the managed custom folder in the final dialog box. To ensure that the comment is always visible in Outlook, Entourage, or OWA, you can select **Do not allow users to minimize this comment in Outlook**.

6. Click **New**. The Completion page appears.

7. Click **Finish** to close the New Managed Default Folder window.

8. Close the Exchange Management Console.

THE COMMAND LINE WAY

You can also use the **New-ManagedFolder** cmdlet in the Exchange Management Shell to create managed folders. For example, to create a managed custom folder called TASU with a storage limit of 600 MB that is displayed in Outlook, Entourage or OWA as TASU with an appropriate comment, you could run the following command in the Exchange Management Shell:

New-ManagedFolder -Name 'TASU' -FolderName 'TASU' -StorageQuota '600MB' -Comment 'This folder stores all internal communication regarding the TASU research project.'

To instead create a TASU managed default folder that stores all message types with an appropriate display comment, you could run the following command in the Exchange Management Shell:

New-ManagedFolder -Name 'TASU' -DefaultFolderType 'All' -Comment 'This folder stores all internal communication regarding the TASU research project.'

You can also use the **Get-ManagedFolder** cmdlet to obtain information about existing managed folders, the **Set-ManagedFolder** cmdlet to modify managed folder settings, or the **Remove-ManagedFolder** cmdlet to remove managed folders. To see more options that may be used alongside these cmdlets, search for the appropriate cmdlet within Exchange Server 2007 Help.

➔ **APPLY RETENTION SETTINGS TO A MANAGED FOLDER**

GET READY. Turn on the computer, and log in as the Administrator user account. Close any windows that appear on the desktop.

1. Click **Start**, **All Programs**, **Microsoft Exchange Server 2007**, and then click **Exchange Management Console**. The Exchange Management Console window appears.

2. In the console tree pane, expand **Organization Configuration** and highlight **Mailbox**.

3. To apply retention settings to a managed custom folder, click the **Managed Custom Folders** tab in the detail pane, highlight the appropriate managed custom folder, and select **New Managed Content Settings** in the action pane. Alternatively, to apply retention settings to a managed default folder, click the **Managed Default Folders** tab in the detail pane, highlight the appropriate managed default folder, and select **New Managed Content Settings** in the action pane. The New Managed Content Settings window appears as shown in Figure 6-22.

Figure 6-22

Creating a New Managed Content Settings for a Managed Folder

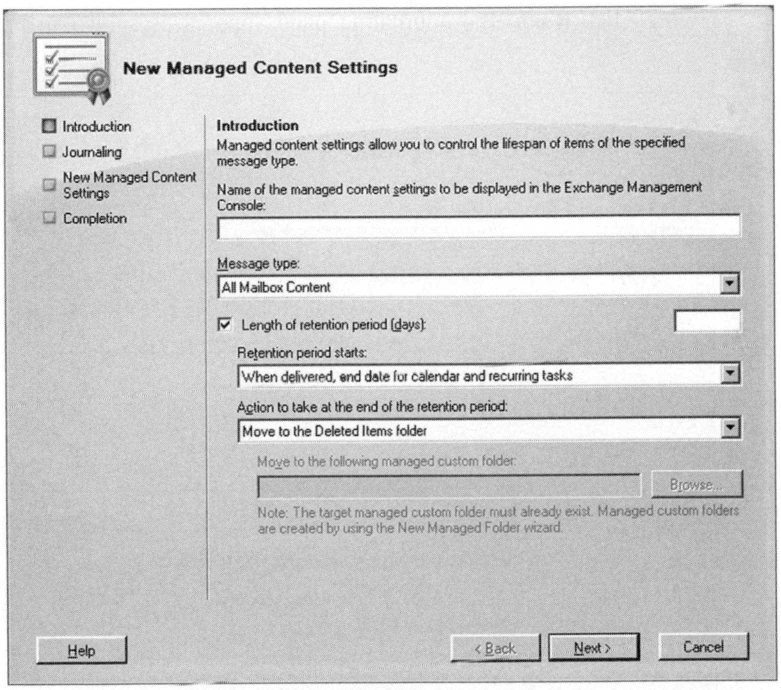

4. Supply an appropriate name for the retention settings in the first dialog box. By default, retention settings apply to all items within the managed folder. To only apply retention settings to a specific item type such as email or calendar items, select the appropriate item type from the **Message type** drop-down box.

5. Next, ensure that **Length of retention period (days)** is selected and supply the number of days in the associated dialog box that items within the managed folder should be retained for. By default, this number represents the number of days following the end date of a calendar item or the date on which an email or other item was received. If you want the number to represent the days after the item was moved to the managed folder, you can select **When item is moved to the folder** from the **Retention period starts** drop-down box.

6. By default, items are moved to the deleted items folder after the retention period. Alternatively, you can select a different action using the **Action to take at the end of the retention period** drop-down box:

   • **Move to a Managed Custom Folder** will move items to a managed custom folder where they will be processed according to the retention settings on the managed custom folder. After selecting this option, you must also click **Browse**, select the appropriate managed custom folder from the Select Managed Folder window that appears, and click **OK**.

   • **Delete and Allow Recovery** deletes the items in the same manner that Deleted Items are removed. Like other items that have been removed from the Deleted Items folder, you can recover them within the recovery time frame specified in mailbox database properties.

   • **Permanently Delete** deletes the item immediately without the possibility of recovery.

   • **Mark as Past Retention Limit** does not delete items from the managed folder. Instead, items are simply given a label after the retention period and can be manually removed by the user.

7. Click **Next**. The Journaling page appears as shown in Figure 6-23.

Figure 6-23

Specifying Journaling Options

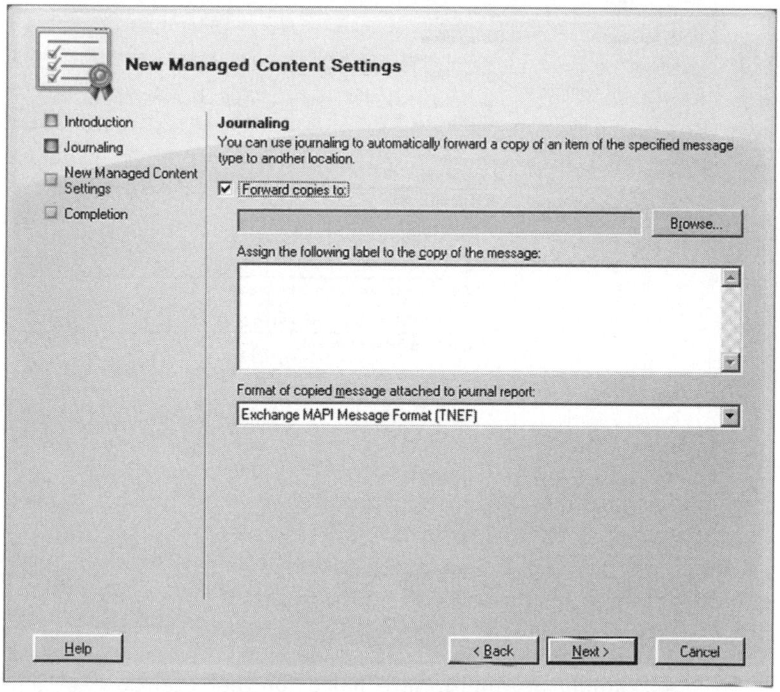

8. If you wish to forward a copy of all items in the managed folder to a particular mailbox for archiving purposes, ensure that **Forward copies to** is selected, click **Browse**, select the appropriate recipient object in the Select Recipient window that appears, and click **OK**. You can optionally supply a label that will be added to the item copies and select the item format. By default, Exchange MAPI Message Format is used when forwarding copies, but you can instead select **Outlook Message Format** in the associated drop-down box if the messages need to be read in a nonMAPI email client program.

9. Click **Next**. The New Managed Content page appears.

10. Review your settings and click **New**. The Completion page appears.

11. Click **Finish** to close the New Managed Content Settings window.

12. Close the Exchange Management Console.

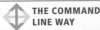

**THE COMMAND
LINE WAY**

You can also use the **New-ManagedContentSettings** cmdlet in the Exchange Management Shell to add a retention and forwarding setting on an existing managed folder. For example, you could create a new managed content setting configuration called "Retain for 2 years" that retains items in the TASU managed folder for 2 years (730 days) from the date the item was delivered. After 2 years, the items should be moved to the managed custom folder called Compliance, and email forwarding should not be enabled. The following command in the Exchange Management Shell will achieve these requirements:

**New-ManagedContentSettings -Name 'Retain for 2 years' -FolderName 'TASU'
-RetentionEnabled $true -AgeLimitForRetention '730.00:00:00' -TriggerForRetention
'WhenDelivered' -RetentionAction 'MoveToFolder' -MoveToDestinationFolder
'Compliance' -JournalingEnabled $false**

Similarly, you can use the **Get-ManagedContentSettings** cmdlet to obtain information about an existing managed content settings configuration or the **Remove-ManagedContentSettings** cmdlet to remove one. To see more options that may be used alongside these cmdlets, search for the appropriate cmdlet within Exchange Server 2007 Help.

After you have created managed folders and specified retention settings using the New Managed Content Settings wizard, you can administer them using the **Organization Configuration** > **Mailbox** node in the Exchange Management Console as shown in Figure 6-24.

Figure 6-24

Viewing Managed Folders

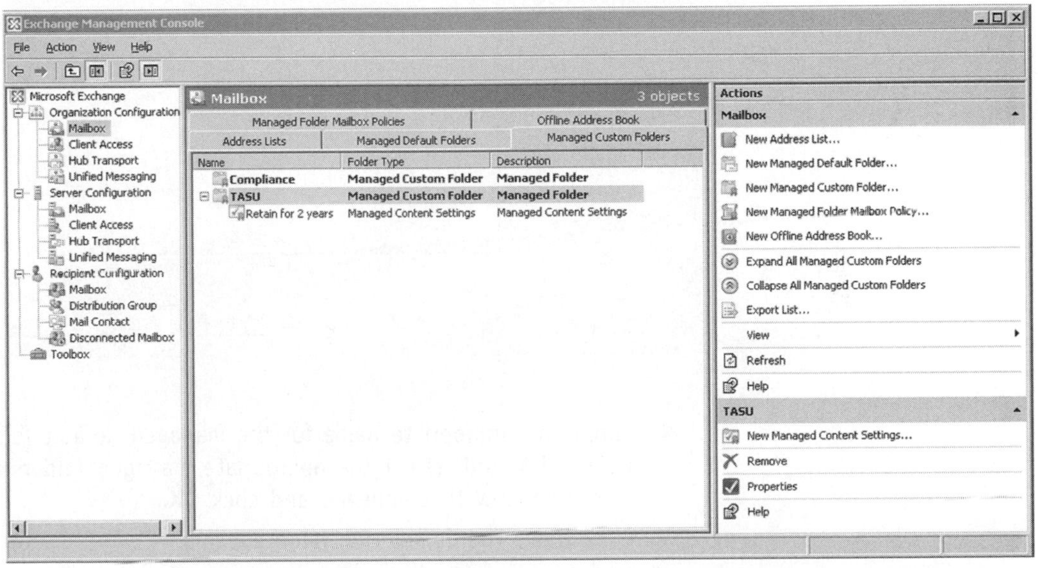

The Managed Custom Folders tab shown in Figure 6-24 indicates that there are two managed custom folders created called Compliance and TASU. In addition, the TASU managed custom folder contains a managed content settings configuration called Retain for 2 years. Managed default folders are displayed in the same way on the Managed Default Folders tab.

You can highlight managed folders and select **Properties** from the action pane to modify their settings or select **Delete** from the action pane to remove them. Similarly, you can highlight managed content settings and select **Properties** from the action pane to modify the retention settings or select **Delete** to remove them. In addition, you can add multiple managed content settings to a managed folder by selecting **New Managed Content Settings** from the action pane.

Once you have created the appropriate managed folders with the appropriate retention settings, you can add them to a *managed folder mailbox policy* that can be applied to new or existing mailbox users. Managed folder mailbox policies simply contain one or more managed folders and their related retention settings. As with managed folders, you can create managed folder mailbox policies using the **Organization Configuration** > **Mailbox** node within the Exchange Management Console.

→ CREATE A MANAGED FOLDER MAILBOX POLICY

GET READY. Turn on the computer, and log in as the Administrator user account. Close any windows that appear on the desktop.

1. Click **Start**, **All Programs**, **Microsoft Exchange Server 2007**, and then click **Exchange Management Console**. The Exchange Management Console window appears.

2. In the console tree pane, expand **Organization Configuration** and highlight **Mailbox**.

3. In the action pane, click **New Managed Folder Mailbox Policy**. The New Managed Folder Mailbox Policy window appears as shown in Figure 6-25.

Figure 6-25

Creating a Managed Folder Mailbox Policy

New Managed Folder Mailbox Policy

- New Mailbox Policy
- Completion

New Mailbox Policy
A managed folder mailbox policy groups together a set of managed folders so that you can add multiple folders to a user mailbox in a single step.

Managed folder mailbox policy name:

Specify the managed folders that you want to link to this policy:

⊹ Add... ✕

Folder	Description	Folder Type

Help   < Back   New   Cancel

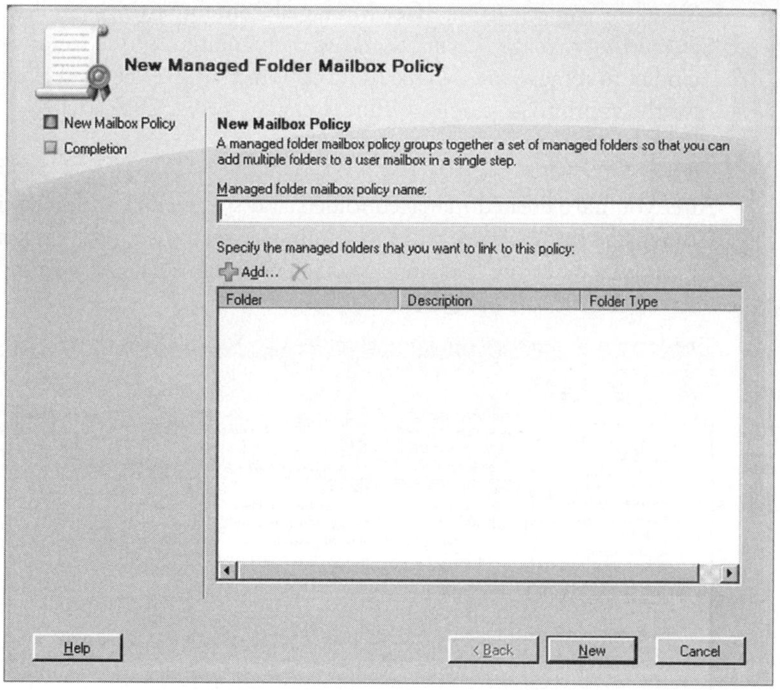

4. Supply an appropriate name for the managed default folder in the first dialog box. Next, click **Add**, select the appropriate managed folders in the Select Managed Folder window that appears, and click **OK**.

5. Click **New**. The Completion page appears.

6. Click **Finish** to close the New Managed Folder Mailbox Policy window.

7. Close the Exchange Management Console.

THE COMMAND LINE WAY

You can also use the **New-ManagedFolderMailboxPolicy** cmdlet in the Exchange Management Shell to create a managed folder mailbox policy. For example, to create a new managed folder mailbox policy called "TASU Project Members" that contains the Inbox managed default folder as well as the Compliance and TASU managed custom folders, you could run the following command in the Exchange Management Shell:

New-ManagedFolderMailboxPolicy -Name 'TASU Project Members' -ManagedFolderLinks 'Inbox', 'Compliance', 'TASU'

You can also use the **Get-ManagedFolderMailboxPolicy** cmdlet to obtain information about existing managed folder mailbox policies, the **Set-ManagedFolderMailboxPolicy** cmdlet to modify managed folder mailbox policies, or the **Remove-ManagedFolderMailboxPolicy** cmdlet to remove managed folder mailbox policies. To see more options that may be used alongside these cmdlets, search for the appropriate cmdlet within Exchange Server 2007 Help.

Once you have created managed folder mailbox policies, you can select them when creating new mailbox users within your organization as discussed in Lesson 5, "Working with Recipient Objects." Alternatively, you can apply your managed folder mailbox policies to existing mailbox users within your organization. To do this within the Exchange Management Console, simply navigate to the **Mailbox Settings** tab of mailbox user properties, highlight **Messaging Records Management**, and click **Properties**. The Messaging Records Management window that appears will allow you to select an appropriate managed folder mailbox policy as shown in Figure 6-26.

TAKE NOTE *

Managed folder mailbox policies can also be applied to resource mailboxes and linked mailbox users. Each mailbox user, resource mailbox, and linked mailbox user can only have one managed folder mailbox policy applied at any given time.

Figure 6-26

Specifying a Managed Folder Mailbox Policy for a Mailbox User

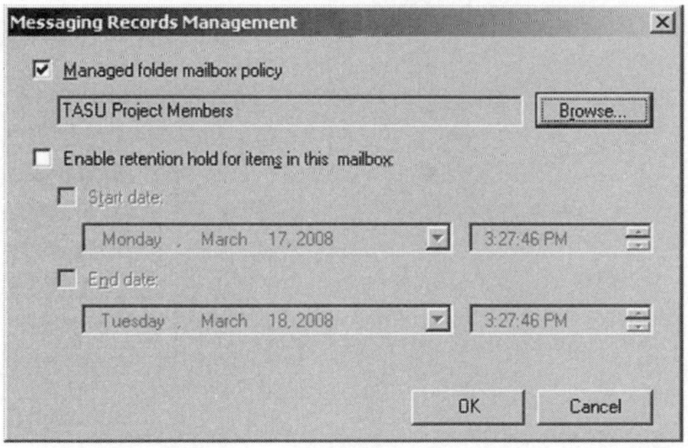

The mailbox user shown in Figure 6-26 currently has the TASU Project Members managed folder mailbox policy applied. To temporarily prevent this policy from applying to this mailbox user, you can select **Enable retention hold for items in this mailbox** and specify the appropriate time period. This is often used for mailbox users who are on vacation to prevent unnecessary policy processing.

You can also assign a managed folder mailbox policy to a user using the **Set-Mailbox** cmdlet in the Exchange Management Shell. For example, to apply the TASU Project Members managed folder mailbox policy to the Jeff Smith mailbox user, you can use the following command:

Set-Mailbox -Identity 'Jeff Smith' -ManagedFolderMailboxPolicy 'TASU Project Members'

Alternatively, to remove the managed folder policy and managed folders from Jeff Smith, you could use the following command:

Set-Mailbox -Identity 'Jeff Smith' –RemoveManagedFolderAndPolicy

It is important to ensure that mailbox users who receive a managed folder mailbox policy connect to their Exchange server using Exchange 2007, Exchange 2003 SP2, Entourage 2008, or OWA. Older MAPI clients such as Outlook 2000 or Entourage 2004 will receive an error when they attempt to connect to a mailbox that has a managed folder mailbox policy. If you wish to prevent users who have a managed folder mailbox policy from connecting to their mailbox using an incompatible MAPI client, you can restrict a mailbox to accept MAPI client version 11.8010.8036 or greater. For example, to prevent Jeff Smith from connecting to his mailbox from an incompatible MAPI client, you can run the following command in the Exchange Management Shell:

Set-CASMailbox -Identity 'Jeff Smith' -MAPIBlockOutlookVersions:'-11.8010.8036'

Managed folder processing is a resource-intensive task for Mailbox role servers within your organization and is disabled as a result. After specifying managed folder mailbox policies for mailbox users, you must enable the *Managed Folder Assistant* on the appropriate Mailbox role servers to activate managed folder processing and enforce the message retention settings that you specified on your managed folders.

To enable the Managed Folder Assistant in the Exchange Management Console, simply navigate to **Server Configuration** > **Mailbox**, highlight the appropriate Mailbox role server in the detail pane and click **Properties** from the action pane. On the **Messaging Records Management** tab of Mailbox role server properties, specify **Use Custom Schedule** as shown in Figure 6-27 and click **Customize** to schedule the Managed Folder Assistant using the Schedule window shown in Figure 6-28.

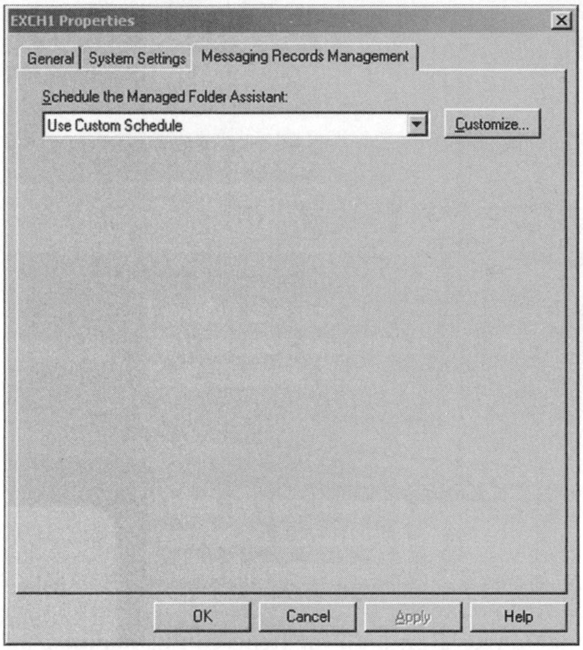

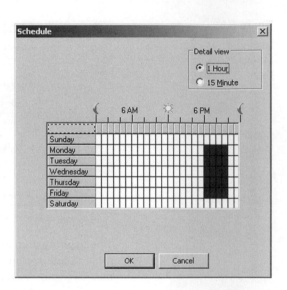

Figure 6-27

Configuring the Managed Folder Assistant

Figure 6-28

Specifying a Managed Folder Assistant Schedule

Because the Managed Folder Assistant will use a large amount of resources on your Mailbox role servers, it is best to schedule it to run after working hours. In Figure 6-28, the Managed Folder Assistant will be run at 6:00 p.m. Monday through Friday and will be stopped automatically if it is still running at 10:00 p.m.

After configuring and assigning managed folder mailbox policies, you may want to manually run the Managed Folder Assistant to test your policies. To start the Managed Folder Assistant immediately, you can run the **Start-ManagedFolderAssistant** command within the Exchange Management Shell.

Once the Managed Folder Assistant has run, Outlook, Entourage, and OWA users who have a managed folder mailbox policy will notice a Managed Folders section that contains the appropriate managed folders as shown for the user Jeff Smith using Outlook 2007 in Figure 6-29.

Figure 6-29

Viewing Managed Folders in Outlook 2007

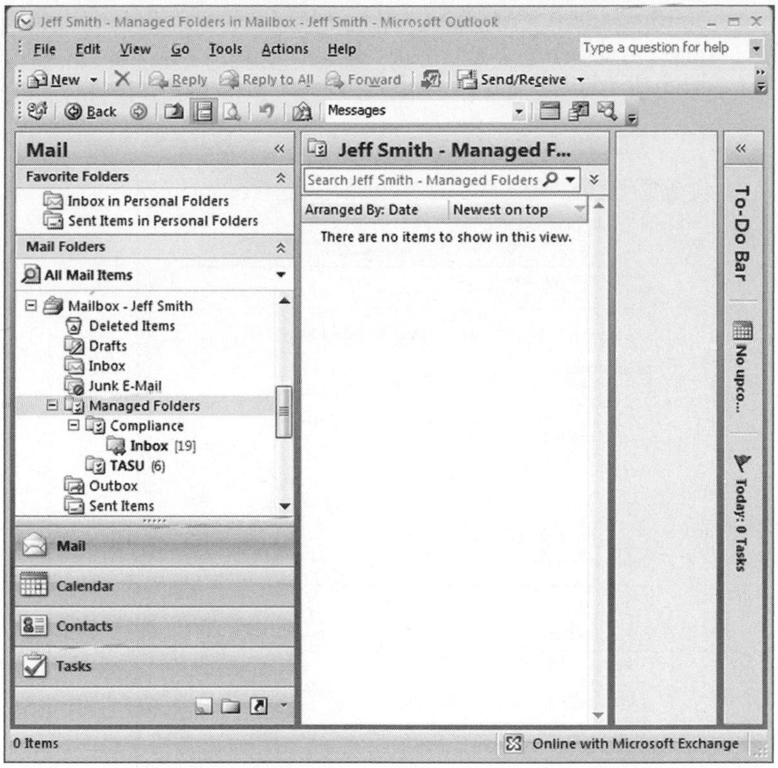

The managed folder mailbox policy applied to the Jeff Smith mailbox shown in Figure 6-29 creates two managed custom folders: Compliance and TASU. This policy also contains an Inbox managed default folder that is configured to move Inbox items that are more than two weeks old to the Compliance managed custom folder. An Inbox subfolder is automatically created under the Compliance managed custom folder to store any items that were moved from the user's Inbox.

CONFIGURING MESSAGE JOURNALING

Another method used to achieve message compliance involves archiving emails that are sent to or from certain recipient objects. This method is called *message journaling* and can be configured using a variety of different methods in Exchange Server 2007.

When you create a new managed content settings configuration for a managed folder, you can specify an email address on the Journaling page where copies of all items in the managed folder will be sent for archiving. Similarly, in Lesson 5, "Working with Recipient Objects," you learned how to configure a forwarding address in the properties of a mailbox user to forward a copy of emails addressed to the recipient to another mailbox. This target mailbox can also be used to store emails for message compliance purposes.

In addition to these methods, you can configure the *Journaling agent* for email archiving on your Hub role servers to satisfy your message compliance policy. There are two main types of message journaling that can be configured using the Journaling agent: *standard journaling* and *premium journaling*.

Standard journaling is available in all editions of Exchange Server 2007 and is used to archive all emails sent to or from a mailbox database. To configure standard journaling in the Exchange Management Console, view the properties of an existing mailbox database under the **Server**

Configuration > **Mailbox** node, enable **Journal Recipient,** and supply the appropriate recipient object as shown in Figure 6-30. All email that is relayed to or from a mailbox in the mailbox database will be copied to this recipient object for archiving.

Figure 6-30

Configuring Standard Journaling

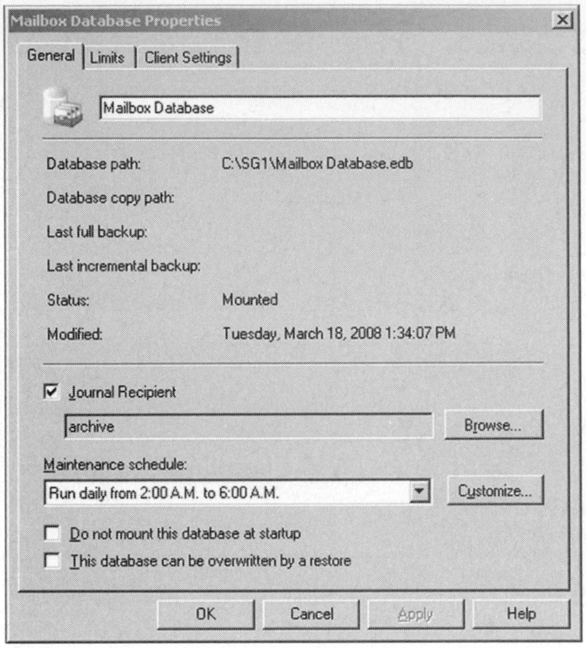

You can also configure standard journaling using the **Set-MailboxDatabase** cmdlet in the Exchange Management Shell. For example, to forward copies of all items sent to or from mailboxes within Mailbox Database 5 to archive@octavius.net, you could run the following command within the Exchange Management Shell:

Set-MailboxDatabase 'Mailbox Database 5' –JournalRecipient archive@octavius.net

Premium journaling is only available in the Enterprise edition of Exchange Server 2007 and can be used to archive messages that are sent to or from specific recipient objects. You can configure premium journaling by creating journal rules under the **Organization Configuration > Hub Transport** node within the Exchange Management Console. Once you have created journal rules, you can view, modify, disable, or remove them by selecting them under the **Journaling** tab in the result pane and selecting the appropriate action in the action pane.

⊙ CREATE A JOURNAL RULE

GET READY. Turn on the computer, and log in as the Administrator user account. Close any windows that appear on the desktop.

1. Click **Start, All Programs, Microsoft Exchange Server 2007,** and then click **Exchange Management Console.** The Exchange Management Console window appears.

2. In the console tree pane, expand **Organization Configuration** and highlight **Hub Transport.**

3. In the action pane, click **New Journal Rule.** The New Journal Rule window appears as shown in Figure 6-31.

Figure 6-31

Creating a New Journal Rule

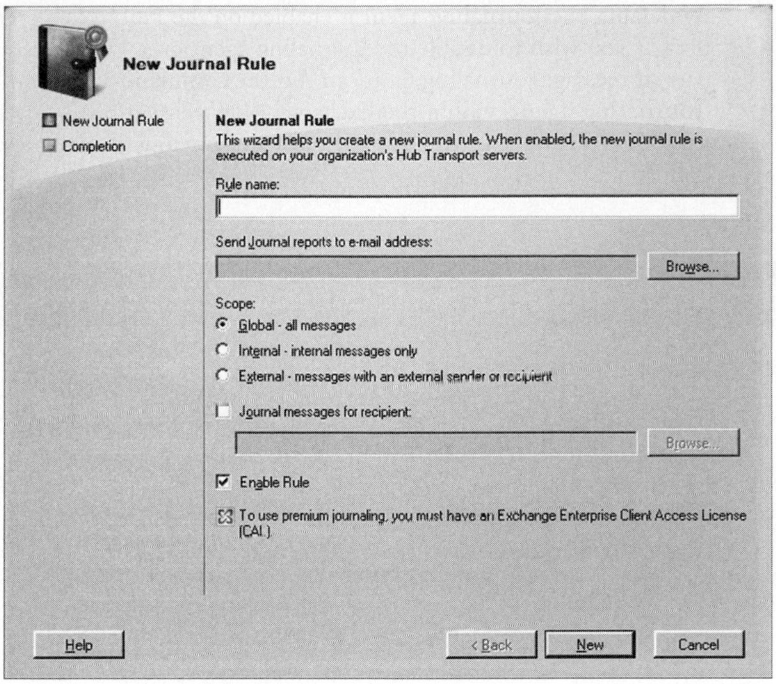

New Journal Rule

☐ New Journal Rule
☐ Completion

New Journal Rule
This wizard helps you create a new journal rule. When enabled, the new journal rule is executed on your organization's Hub Transport servers.

Rule name:

Send Journal reports to e-mail address:

Browse...

Scope:
○ Global - all messages
○ Internal - internal messages only
○ External - messages with an external sender or recipient

☐ Journal messages for recipient:

Browse...

☑ Enable Rule

☒ To use premium journaling, you must have an Exchange Enterprise Client Access License (CAL).

Help   < Back   New   Cancel

4. Supply an appropriate name for the journal rule in the Rule name dialog box. Next to the Send journal reports to e-mail address dialog box, click **Browse**. In the Select Recipient window that appears, select the recipient object that you wish to forward messages to for archiving purposes, and click **OK**.

5. Next, select **Journal messages for recipient** and click the related **Browse** button. In the Select Recipient window that appears, select the appropriate recipient object that the journaling rule should apply to and click **OK**.

6. By default, all messages that are sent to the recipient object specified in the previous step are forwarded to the archive email address. Alternatively, you can select **Internal—internal messages only** to only forward messages that are sent to or from recipient objects within the same Exchange organization or **External—messages with an external sender or recipient** to only forward messages that are sent to or from recipients objects in other organizations.

7. Ensure that **Enable Rule** is selected and click **New**. The Completion page appears.

8. Click **Finish** to close the New Journal Rule window.

9. Close the Exchange Management Console.

THE COMMAND LINE WAY

You can also use the **New-JournalRule** cmdlet in the Exchange Management Shell to create a journal rule. For example, to make a new journal rule called TASU Project Archive that forwards all internal and external messages sent to or from the TASU Project universal distribution group (email address = TASU.project@octavius.net) to the address archive-tasu@ octavius.net, you could run the following command in the Exchange Management Shell:

New-JournalRule -Name 'TASU Project Archive' –Scope 'Global' –Recipient 'TASU .project@octavius.net' –JournalEmailAddress 'archive@octavius.net' –Enabled $true

You can also use the **Get-JournalRule** cmdlet to obtain information about existing journal rules, the **Set-JournalRule** cmdlet to modify journal rules, or the **Remove-JournalRule** cmdlet to remove journal rules. In addition, you can temporarily disable and enable journal rules using the **Disable-JournalRule** and **Enable-JournalRule** cmdlets. To see more options that may be used alongside these cmdlets, search for the appropriate cmdlet within Exchange Server 2007 Help.

By default, the Journaling agent is enabled on the Hub role servers within your organization. If you wish to disable the Journaling agent on a Hub role server that will not participate in message journaling, you can run the command **Disable-TransportAgent –Identity 'Journaling agent'** within the Exchange Management Shell. Alternatively, you can run the **Disable-TransportAgent –Identity 'Journaling agent'** command to start the Journaling agent on a Hub role server.

■ Working with Mulitple Recipient Objects

THE BOTTOM LINE

You examined the procedures and tools used to create, modify, and manage recipient objects in Lesson 5, "Working with Recipient Objects." Although a good understanding of these procedures and tools is vital to any Exchange administrator, it is also important to understand how to create, modify, and manage multiple recipient objects at the same time to save administrative effort. In addition, you should understand how to create PowerShell scripts that can be used to manage multiple recipient objects as necessary or scheduled to perform regular administration of multiple recipient objects.

Modifying and Managing Multiple Recipient Objects

CERTIFICATION READY?
Implement bulk management of mail-enabled objects.
2.6

Although you can disable and remove multiple recipient objects in the Exchange Management Console, most bulk management tasks must be performed within the Exchange Management Shell. To perform bulk management in the Exchange Management Shell, you typically use the information stored within CSV files alongside cmdlets that can modify and manage recipient objects.

In Lesson 5, "Working with Recipient Objects," you learned how to modify and manage individual recipient objects using the Exchange Management Console as well as by using cmdlets within the Exchange Management Shell. However, in most organizations, you will be required to perform Exchange-related operations that affect several recipient objects. For example, your organization may need to implement email quotas on the users in a specific department or you may need to move several mailboxes to another Mailbox role server within the organization.

To perform these actions on each recipient object individually would be too time consuming and costly. As a result, Exchange Server 2007 allows you to modify and manage multiple recipient objects at the same time. This feature is called **bulk management** and is typically performed in the Exchange Management Shell using the same cmdlets that you learned in Lesson 5, "Working with Recipient Objects" alongside information stored in a **comma-separated values (CSV) file**.

A CSV file is simply a plain text file with a **.csv** extension that stores information for objects in comma-separated fields. These fields are defined in the first line of the file as depicted in the example CSV file shown in Figure 6-32.

Figure 6-32

An Example CSV File

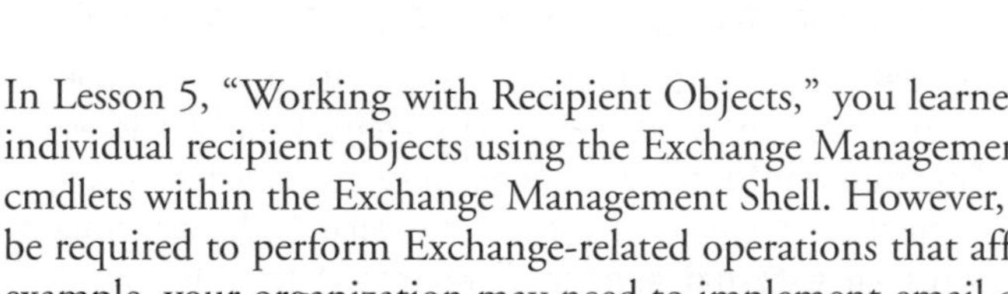

```
Example CSV File.csv - Notepad
File  Edit  Format  View  Help
field1name,field2name,field3name,field4name
object1value1,object1value2,object1value3,object1value4
object2value1,object2value2,object2value3,object2value4
object3value1,object3value2,object3value3,object3value4
object4value1,object4value2,object4value3,object4value4
object5value1,object5value2,object5value3,object5value4
```

CSV files used with the Exchange Management Shell cannot contain blank lines, trailing space characters at the end of a line, or space characters before or after the commas in each line. You can create a CSV file with any text editor such as Windows Notepad (**notepad.exe**) provided that you select a **.csv** extension. Because many text editors such as Notepad automatically add a **.txt** extension when you save the file, you should enclose the name in double quotes when you specify the file name in the Save As dialog box as shown in Figure 6-33. If you had typed **Example CSV File.csv** instead of **"Example CSV File.csv"** in Figure 6-33, the text editor will save the file as **Example CSV File.csv.txt** on the hard disk.

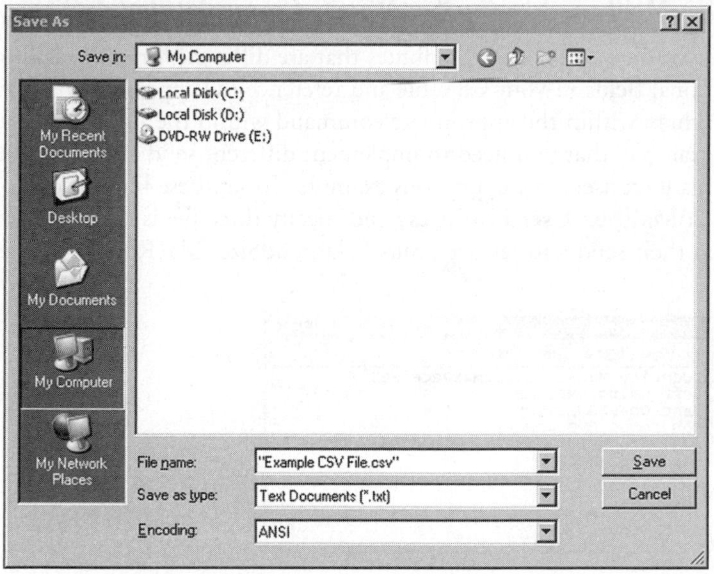

Figure 6-33

Saving a CSV File in Notepad

Each line under the first line of a CSV file can contain values that represent certain attributes for a specific recipient object. If you place 100 lines underneath the first line within a CSV file that contains information about 100 recipient objects, you can process all 100 recipients using a single command within the Exchange Management Shell.

The **Import-CSV** cmdlet can be used to read each line of a CSV file and send the appropriate values to another cmdlet that will modify or manage recipient objects using the piping feature of the Exchange Management Shell.

Say, for example, that you need to change the Custom Attribute 1 to TASU and the Office Attribute to Research for five mailbox users within your organization who have recently joined the TASU project in the Research office. Because the values for the Custom Attribute 1 and Office will be the same for all five users, you can simply create a CSV file called **C:\ Mailbox Users.csv** that lists the identity of each mailbox user you wish to modify as shown in Figure 6-34. The CSV file shown in Figure 6-34 only contains a single field called Identity, which can be identified within a cmdlet using the syntax **$_.Identity**.

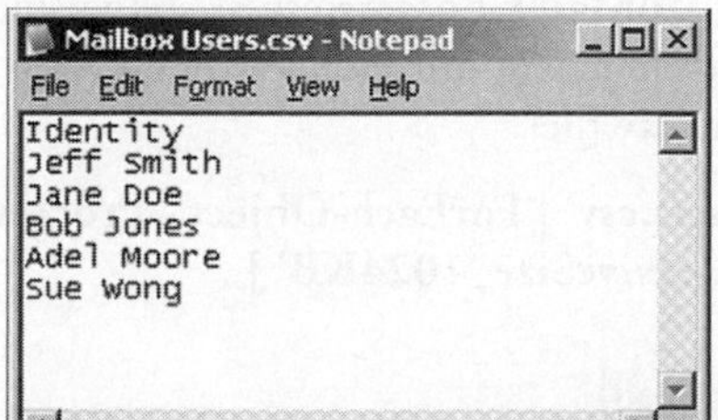

Figure 6-34

The Mailbox Users.csv File

Next, you can use the following command within the Exchange Management Shell to read the object lines within the **C:\Mailbox Users.csv** file and send each mailbox user's Identity to the **Set-Mailbox** cmdlet, which can be used to modify the appropriate attributes:

Import-CSV 'C:\Mailbox Users.csv' | ForEach-Object –Process { Set-Mailbox –Identity $_.Identity –CustomAttribute1 'TASU' –Office 'Research' }

The previous command is equivalent to running the following five commands in the Exchange Management Shell:

Set-Mailbox –Identity 'Jeff Smith' –CustomAttribute1 'TASU' –Office 'Research'

Set-Mailbox –Identity 'Jane Doe' –CustomAttribute1 'TASU' –Office 'Research'

Set-Mailbox –Identity 'Bob Jones' –CustomAttribute1 'TASU' –Office 'Research'

Set-Mailbox –Identity 'Adel Moore' –CustomAttribute1 'TASU' –Office 'Research'

Set-Mailbox –Identity 'Sue Wong' –CustomAttribute1 'TASU' –Office 'Research'

If you need to specify attributes that are different for each mailbox user, you can use additional fields in your CSV file and reference the appropriate fields using the **$_.fieldname** syntax within the appropriate command within the Exchange Management Shell. Say, for example, that you need to implement different send and receive size limits for each of the mailbox users in the previous example. To set these limits, you could create a CSV file called **C:\Mailbox User Limits.csv** and specify three fields that identify each user (Identity) as well as their send and receive limits (MaxSendSize, MaxReceiveSize) as shown in Figure 6-35.

Figure 6-35

The Mailbox User Limits.csv File

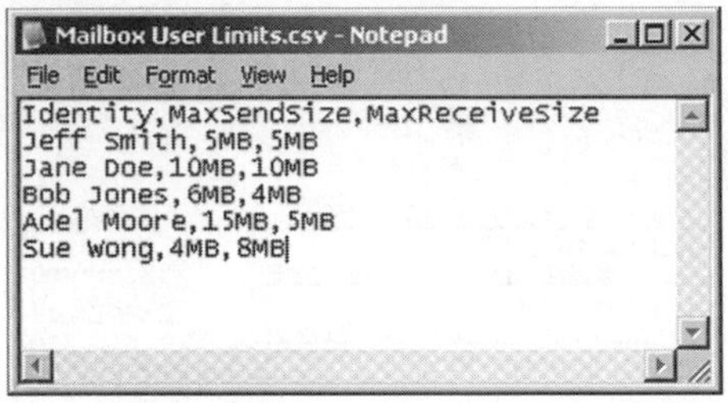

Next, you could run the following command within the Exchange Management Console to read each object line from the CSV file and configure the appropriate limits for each mailbox user using the Set-Mailbox cmdlet:

Import-CSV 'C:\Mailbox User Limits.csv' | ForEach-Object –Process { Set-Mailbox –Identity $_.Identity –MaxSendSize $_.MaxSendSize –MaxReceiveSize $_.MaxReceiveSize }

Because the **C:\Mailbox User Limits.csv** file used the Identity, MaxSendSize, and MaxReceiveSize fields, the command in the previous example had to use the variables **$_.Identity**, **$_.MaxSendSize**, and **$_.MaxReceiveSize** as arguments in order to obtain the correct values from the **C:\Mailbox User Limits.csv** file.

Bulk management is not limited to mailbox users. You can use CSV files within the Exchange Management Shell to bulk manage any recipient object using the appropriate cmdlets. For example, to modify the maximum receive size for email on a large number of mail contacts, you can create a CSV file that lists their identities and use the Import-CSV cmdlet to send the information to the Set-MailContact cmdlet with the appropriate options. For example, if you create a CSV file called **C:\Mail Contacts.csv** as shown in Figure 6-36, you could run the following command to set the maximum receive size to 1024 KB for each mail contact listed in the **C:\Mail Contacts.csv** file:

Import-CSV 'C:\Mail Contacts.csv' | ForEach-Object –Process { Set-MailContact –Identity $_.Identity –MaxReceiveSize '1024KB' }

Figure 6-36

The Mail Contacts.csv File

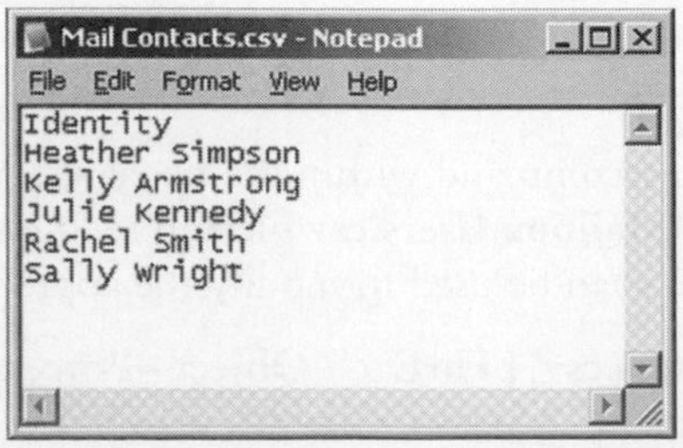

Alternatively, if each mail contact requires a different maximum receive size, you could add a second field to the **C:\Mail Contacts.csv** file called MaxReceiveSize that contains the appropriate values for each mail contact and replace '**1024KB**' in the previous Exchange Management Shell command with **$_.MaxReceiveSize** to use the appropriate values from the CSV file instead.

 TAKE NOTE*

Because it is difficult to remember all of the cmdlets that can modify and manage all recipient objects as well as their options, you should first research the appropriate cmdlet and options within Exchange Server 2007 Help. Once you have found the appropriate cmdlet and options, you can create a CSV file and run the appropriate **Import-CSV** command using the same syntax shown in the examples within this lesson.

In the previous three examples, we used cmdlets that started with Set- such as Set-Mailbox and Set-MailContact to modify existing recipient objects. However, you can perform bulk management with the other cmdlets used to manage recipient objects in the same way.

Say, for example, that you need to add several recipient objects to a mail-enabled universal distribution group called TASU Project Group. To do this, you can create a CSV file called **C:\TASU Members.csv** as shown in Figure 6-37 to list the appropriate recipient objects that should be added to the group.

Figure 6-37

The TASU Members.csv File

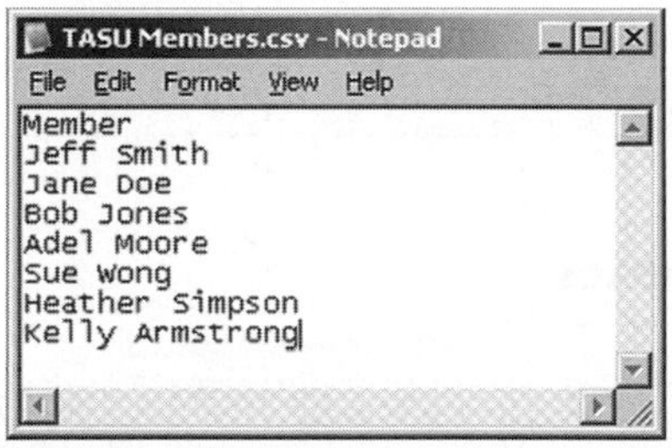

```
TASU Members.csv - Notepad          _ □ ×
File  Edit  Format  View  Help
Member
Jeff Smith
Jane Doe
Bob Jones
Adel Moore
Sue Wong
Heather Simpson
Kelly Armstrong
```

Next, you can pass the names of these recipient objects to the Add-DistributionGroupMember cmdlet to add them as group members using the following command within the Exchange Management Shell:

Import-CSV 'C:\TASU Members.csv' | ForEach-Object –Process { Add-DistributionGroup Member –Identity 'TASU Project Group' –Member $_.Member }

Because the **C:\TASU Members.csv** file uses the Member column, the command in the previous example had to use the **$_.Member** variable when referring to the members listed in the CSV file.

In addition, you can disable or remove multiple recipient objects by using the appropriate cmdlet alongside a CSV file that identifies the recipient objects. For example, to disable the mailbox users listed in the **C:\Mailbox Users.csv** file shown earlier in Figure 6-34, you could run the following command within the Exchange Management Shell:

Import-CSV 'C:\Mailbox Users.csv' | ForEach-Object –Process { Disable-Mailbox –Identity $_.Identity }

Alternatively, to remove the mail contacts listed in the **C:\Mail Contacts.csv** file shown earlier in Figure 6-36, you could run the following command within the Exchange Management Shell:

Import-CSV 'C:\Mail Contacts.csv' | ForEach-Object –Process { Remove-MailContact –Identity $_.Identity }

Although most bulk management must be performed within the Exchange Management Shell, you can disable or remove multiple recipient objects of the same type within the Exchange Management Console. In Figure 6-38, a filter was created to display only the mailbox users under the **Recipient Configuration** > **Mailbox** node that contained an Office attribute equal to Research. Next, you can use the **Ctrl-a** key combination to select all mailbox users as shown in Figure 6-38 and select the **Disable** or **Remove** action from the action pane to perform the related action on all of the selected mailbox users. Alternatively, to select only a subset of the mailbox users shown in Figure 6-38, you can hold the **Ctrl** key while selecting the appropriate mailbox users or hold the **Shift** key and select a range of mailbox users.

Figure 6-38

Managing Multiple Recipients

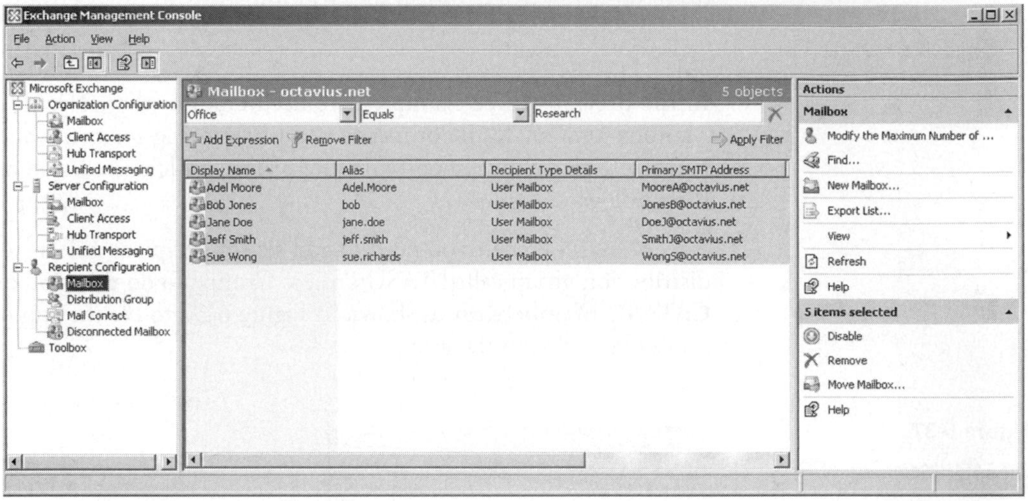

Moving Multiple Mailboxes

Bulk mailbox move operations are commonly performed by Exchange administrators using either the Exchange Management Console or Exchange Management Shell. To perform a bulk mailbox move operation within the Exchange Management Shell, you can use the Get-Mailbox cmdlet alongside the Move-Mailbox cmdlet or use the information stored within a CSV file to move mailboxes using the Move-Mailbox cmdlet.

As an Exchange administrator, there are many situations where you will need to move multiple mailboxes between Mailbox role servers or between storage groups on the same mailbox server. Before you retire an existing Mailbox role server, you must move the mailboxes on that server to another Mailbox role server. Additionally, you may need to move mailboxes between Mailbox role servers to load balance them or when a particular Mailbox role server is running low on hard disk space. Furthermore, you may need to move mailboxes to other storage groups that represent a specific department or contain mailbox restrictions that you wish to apply to a group of mailboxes.

Regardless of the reason, you can use commands within the Exchange Management Console to perform mailbox moves. The simplest method to move mailboxes is to send the output of the Get-Mailbox cmdlet to the Move-Mailbox cmdlet using the piping feature of the Exchange Management Shell.

For example, to move all the mailboxes in the Mailbox Database within the First Storage Group on the server EXCH1 to the Mailbox Database in the First Storage Group on the server EXCH2, you could use the following command within the Exchange Management Console:

Get-Mailbox –Database 'EXCH1\First Storage Group\Mailbox Database' | Move-Mailbox –TargetDatabase 'EXCH2\First Storage Group\Mailbox Database'

TAKE NOTE* When you move multiple mailboxes using the Exchange Management Shell, you will be prompted to confirm each mailbox move by pressing **Y**. Alternatively, you can press **A** to confirm all mailbox move operations.

In other situations, you may need to move mailboxes for users who provide a similar job function. To do this, you can specify filter conditions within the Get-Mailbox cmdlet. For example, to move only the mailboxes that have a corresponding mailbox user in the Marketing or Production departments to the Mailbox Database in the First Storage Group on the server EXCH2, you can use the following command within the Exchange Management Console:

Get-Mailbox –Filter { (Department – cq 'Marketing') –or (Department –eq 'Production') } | Move-Mailbox –TargetDatabase 'EXCH2\First Storage Group\Mailbox Database'

You can also specify to move the mailboxes for mailbox users who are located in a particular OU within AD. To move only the mailboxes that have a corresponding mailbox user located in the Marketing OU in the East OU in the octavius.net domain to the Mailbox Database in the First Storage Group on the server EXCH2, you can use the following command within the Exchange Management Console:

Get-Mailbox –OrganizationalUnit 'octavius.net/East/Marketing' | Move-Mailbox –TargetDatabase 'EXCH2\First Storage Group\Mailbox Database'

Instead of using the Get-Mailbox cmdlet, you can also place the names of the appropriate mailbox users within a CSV file that can be sent to the Get-Mailbox and Move-Mailbox cmdlets. This will save time if you already have a CSV file that lists mailbox users from another bulk management operation. For example, to move the mailboxes for the mailbox users defined in the **C:\Mailbox Users.csv** file shown earlier in Figure 6-34 to the Mailbox Database in the First Storage Group on the server EXCH2, you can use the following command within the Exchange Management Console:

Import-CSV 'C:\Mailbox Users.csv' | ForEach-Object –Process { Get-Mailbox –Identity $_ .Identity } | Move-Mailbox –TargetDatabase 'EXCH2\First Storage Group\Mailbox Database'

CSV files are also useful when you need to obtain mailbox information regarding specific mailbox users regardless of the location of their mailbox. For example, the following command will display the location of each mailbox for the users defined in the **C:\Mailbox Users.csv** file shown earlier in Figure 6-34:

Import-CSV 'C:\Mailbox Users.csv' | ForEach-Object –Process { Get-Mailbox –Identity $_.Identity } | Format-List

TAKE NOTE* You can use advanced options alongside the **Move-Mailbox** cmdlet within a bulk management command to perform advanced move operations such as moving mailboxes to another forest. These options were discussed in Lesson 5, "Working with Recipient Objects."

If you plan to move multiple mailboxes within the same forest and do not need to specify any advanced move options, you can also perform bulk mailbox move operations using the Exchange Management Console. Simply navigate to the **Recipient Configuration** > **Mailbox** node, optionally create a filter that narrows the list of mailbox users displayed, select the appropriate users while holding the **Ctrl** key or **Shift** key, and select **Move** in the action pane. The same Move Mailbox wizard discussed earlier in Lesson 5, "Working with Recipient Objects," will appear and prompt you for information regarding the move operation. On the Completion page, the Move Mailbox wizard will list each mailbox that will be moved as shown in Figure 6-39. When you click **Move** as shown in Figure 6-39, all of the selected mailboxes will be moved in a single bulk operation.

Figure 6-39

Moving Multiple Mailboxes

![Move Mailbox wizard showing summary of 5 mailboxes ready to be moved]

The following steps/items shown in the wizard screen:

- Introduction
- Move Options
- Move Schedule
- Move Mailbox
- Completion

Move Mailbox
The following mailboxes are ready to be moved. Click Move to continue.

Summary: 5 mailbox(es) will be moved.

Adel Moore
Parameters for move mailbox task are:
Server=EXCH2
Storage Group=First Storage Group
Mailbox Database=Mailbox Database

Bob Jones
Parameters for move mailbox task are:
Server=EXCH2
Storage Group=First Storage Group
Mailbox Database=Mailbox Database

Jane Doe
Parameters for move mailbox task are:
Server=EXCH2
Storage Group=First Storage Group
Mailbox Database=Mailbox Database

Jeff Smith
Parameters for move mailbox task are:
Server=EXCH2
Storage Group=First Storage Group

Select Ctrl+C to copy the contents of this page.

Help   < Back   Move   Cancel

Creating Multiple Recipient Objects

> The creation of multiple recipient objects can only be performed within the Exchange Management Shell. To perform a bulk create operation, you typically use information that is stored within a CSV alongside the appropriate cmdlet. You can also copy information stored in template recipient objects during a bulk create operation.

In addition to modifying and managing multiple recipient objects, you can create new recipient objects using bulk management techniques. Because the creation of recipient objects requires that a great deal of information be specified during creation, you can create a CSV file that has the appropriate information organized by fields. In addition, many other programs such as databases and spreadsheet applications store the information regarding these new recipient objects and can export this information to CSV files that you can modify and use for bulk recipient object creation.

Say, for example, that you recently received a spreadsheet that lists new contract members who will start work at your organization next week. Because these new contract members do not require an AD user account, you plan to creating mail contacts for them. To create these mail contacts in bulk, you could open the spreadsheet using the appropriate spreadsheet application, save the file as a CSV file, and modify it as needed so that you have a column that contains the name, first name, last name, alias, and external email address of each new mail contact. An example CSV file that may be used to create mail contacts is shown in Figure 6-40.

Figure 6-40

New Mail Contacts.csv File

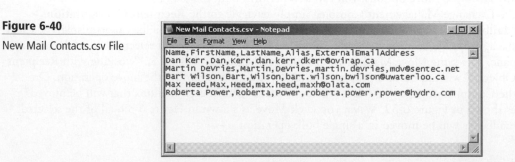

```
Name,FirstName,LastName,Alias,ExternalEmailAddress
Dan Kerr,Dan,Kerr,dan.kerr,dkerr@ovirap.ca
Martin DeVries,Martin,DeVries,martin.devries,mdv@sentec.net
Bart Wilson,Bart,Wilson,bart.wilson,bwilson@uwaterloo.ca
Max Heed,Max,Heed,max.heed,maxh@olata.com
Roberta Power,Roberta,Power,roberta.power,rpower@hydro.com
```

Next, you can use the Import-CSV cmdlet alongside the New-MailContact cmdlet to create the mail contacts within the Exchange Management Shell. For example, to create the mail contacts described in the **C:\New Mail Contacts.csv** file shown in Figure 6-40, you could run the following command within the Exchange Management Shell:

Import-CSV 'C:\New Mail Contacts.csv' | ForEach-Object –Process { New-MailContact –Name $_.Name –FirstName $_.FirstName –LastName $_.LastName –Alias $_.Alias –ExternalEmailAddress $_.ExternalEmailAddress }

TAKE NOTE*

It is considered good form to name template recipient objects with an underscore character at the beginning. This will ensure that the template recipient objects always appear at the top of the list when viewing recipient objects in both the Exchange Management Console and Exchange Management Shell.

You can also create mail-enabled groups, mail users, mailbox users, linked mailbox users, and resource mailboxes in the same way. However, when you create mail users and mailbox users, there is typically a large number of attributes for user account and mail settings that will need to be set during or after creation. To save time, you can first create ***template recipient objects*** that contain the appropriate attributes that are common among recipient objects with a particular job role or department. Template recipient objects are normal recipient objects that you use only for creating additional recipient objects. Any generic settings within the template recipient object, such as custom attributes, can be copied to new recipient objects during creation.

Say, for example, you need to create several mailbox users in the Marketing department with the same custom attributes. Before performing a bulk create operation, you could first create a template mailbox user called **_Marketing_MailboxUser_Template** and modify the appropriate custom attributes in the template mailbox user.

Next, you can create a CSV file that contains the appropriate name, first name, last name, user principle name, and alias for each new mailbox user as shown with the **C:\New Mailbox Users.csv** file in Figure 6-41.

Figure 6-41

New Mailbox Users.csv File

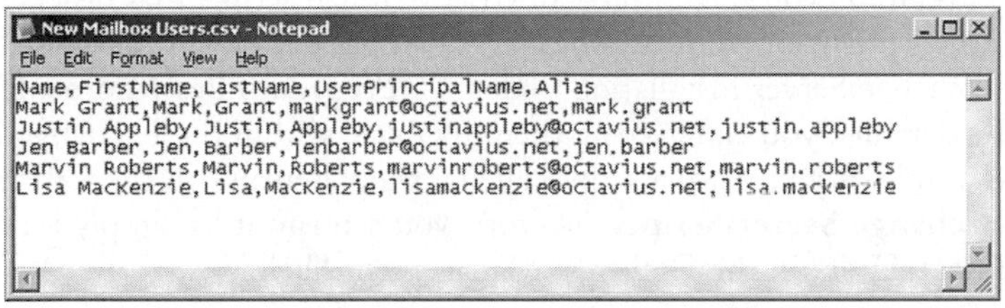

To create the mailbox users described in the **C:\New Mailbox Users.csv** file shown in Figure 6-41 under the East/Marketing OU of the octavius.net domain while using the settings within the **_Marketing_MailboxUser_Template** and specify that the mailbox be created in the Mailbox Database in the First Storage Group on the server EXCH2, you can run the following commands within the Exchange Management Shell:

$password = Read-Host 'Enter password' –AsSecureString

$template = Get-Mailbox '_Marketing_MailboxUser_Template'

Import-CSV 'C:\New Mailbox Users.csv' | ForEach-Object –Process { New-Mailbox –Name $_.Name –FirstName $_.FirstName –LastName $_.LastName –UserPrincipalName $_.UserPrincipalName –Alias $_.Alias –Database 'EXCH2\First Storage Group\Mailbox Database' –OrganizationalUnit 'octavius.net/East/Marketing' –Password $password –TemplateInstance $template }

The first command prompts you for an initial password that will be used for each mailbox user. The second command obtains a copy of the **_Marketing_MailboxUser_Template** mailbox user in the variable called **$template**. The third command performs the bulk creation of the mailbox users using the additional settings from the mailbox user template stored in the **$template** variable.

If you wish to set a different initial password for each user, you could instead add a Password field to the **C:\New Mailbox Users.csv** file with the appropriate values for each mailbox user and run the following commands to perform the bulk creation of the mailbox users:

$template = Get-Mailbox '_Marketing_MailboxUser_Template'

Import-CSV 'C:\New Mailbox Users.csv' | ForEach-Object –Process { $pw = ConvertTo-SecureString $_.Password –asPlainText –Force ; New-Mailbox –Name $_.Name –FirstName $_.FirstName –LastName $_.LastName –UserPrincipalName $_.UserPrincipalName –Alias $_.Alias –Database 'EXCH2\First Storage Group\Mailbox Database' –OrganizationalUnit 'octavius.net/East/Marketing' –Password $pw –TemplateInstance $template }

The **$pw = ConvertTo-SecureString $.Password –as PlainText –Force** section in the previous command obtains the plain text password from the Password field in the **C:\New Mailbox Users.csv** file, converts it to a secure string and stores it in the **$pw** variable for use with the **–Password** option of the New-Mailbox command.

Creating and Using PowerShell Scripts for Bulk Management

While bulk management commands within the Exchange Management Shell save administrative effort, they must be typed each time you use them unless you place them in a PowerShell script that is stored on the hard drive. To save time executing repetitive bulk management operations, you should understand how to create PowerShell scripts that can be executed as needed. In addition, PowerShell scripts can be scheduled to run in the future using the Windows Scheduled Tasks wizard.

TAKE NOTE*

Before downloading a PowerShell script from the Internet, you should first ensure that it is from a trusted source. Additionally, you should view the file within a text editor to ensure that you understand what the script does before executing it.

Like most other scripting languages, PowerShell has the ability to execute predefined script files. These scripts are simply text files that end with a **.ps1** extension and contain commands that will execute from within PowerShell or the Exchange Management Shell.

This allows you to run predefined PowerShell scripts that others have created to perform bulk management of recipient objects. If you place these scripts in the Scripts folder under your Exchange Server installation folder (**C:\Program Files\Microsoft\Exchange Server\Scripts** by default), you can execute them by name within the Exchange Management Shell. For example, if you place a script called CreateUsers.ps1 in the **C:\Program Files\Microsoft\Exchange Server\Scripts** directory, you can run it by simply typing **CreateUsers.ps1** or **CreateUsers** in the Exchange Management Shell.

By default, there are several predefined PowerShell scripts in the C:\Program Files Microsoft\Exchange Server\Scripts folder. However, these script files are typically used to monitor and manage Exchange Server processes rather than recipient objects.

To save administrative effort, you can also create your own PowerShell scripts that contain the bulk management commands you commonly use within your organization. Any bulk management command may be added to a PowerShell script and executed from within the Exchange Management Shell. Say, for example, that you create a PowerShell script called **C:\Program Files\Microsoft\Exchange Server\Scripts\OUMailboxMove.ps1** that contains the following lines:

Get-Mailbox –OrganizationalUnit 'octavius.net/East/Marketing' | Move-Mailbox –TargetDatabase 'EXCH2\First Storage Group\Mailbox Database'

You could simply type **OUMailboxMove** in the Exchange Management Shell to move any mailboxes for recipient objects in the East/Marketing OU in the octavius.net domain to the Mailbox Database in the First Storage Group on the server EXCH2 in your organization.

Unfortunately, it is unlikely that this same operation will be performed on the same OU and target database. As a result, you can pass *parameters* to a PowerShell script that define the variables used in the script. Say, for example, that you modify the C:\Program Files\Microsoft\Exchange Server\Scripts\OUMailboxMove.ps1 script so that it contains the following lines:

```
Param(

[string] $OrganizationalUnit

[string] $TargetDatabase

)
```

Get-Mailbox –OrganizationalUnit $OrganizationalUnit | Move-Mailbox –TargetDatabase $TargetDatabase

You can then run the command **OUMailboxMove –OrganizationalUnit 'octavius.net/East/ Marketing' –TargetDatabase 'EXCH2\First Storage Group\Mailbox Database'** to move the mailboxes for recipient objects in the East/Marketing OU in the octavius.net domain to the Mailbox Database in the First Storage Group on the server EXCH2.

However, you can supply any parameter for the OU or target database with the **OUMailbox Move** script. To move the mailboxes for recipient objects in the West/HR OU in the octavius .net domain to the Mailbox Database in the Second Storage Group on the server EXCH5, you could run the command **OUMailboxMove –OrganizationalUnit 'octavius.net/West/HR –TargetDatabase 'EXCH5\Second Storage Group\Mailbox Database'** within the Exchange Management shell.

Similarly, you can create PowerShell scripts that use information stored in CSV files. If you regularly create CSV files to set the maximum send and receive sizes for multiple mailbox users, you could create a PowerShell script called **C:\Program Files\Microsoft\Exchange Server\Scripts\MailboxSendReceiveLimits.ps1** and add the following lines:

```
Param(

[string] $CSVFile

)
```

Import-CSV $CSVFile | ForEach-Object –Process { Set-Mailbox –Identity $_.Identity –MaxSendSize $_.MaxSendSize –MaxReceiveSize $_.MaxReceiveSize }

If you create a CSV file that contains the Identity, MaxSendSize, and MaxReceiveSize fields, you could use it alongside the MailboxSendReceiveLimits.ps1 script within the Exchange Management Shell. For example, if you create the **C:\Mailbox User Limits.csv** file shown earlier in Figure 6-35, you could run the command **MailboxSendReceiveLimits –CSVFile 'C:\Mailbox User Limits.csv'** to set the maximum send and receive sizes for the mailbox users defined in the **C:\Mailbox User Limits.csv** file.

You can also schedule PowerShell scripts to run at a later time. However, PowerShell does not have a built-in scheduling utility. As a result, you must create a *batch file* that runs the PowerShell.exe command using the Exchange Management Shell plugin and the appropriate PowerShell script. Batch files are simply text files that use a **.bat** file extension and contain commands that can be executed directly from a Windows command prompt. When you execute a batch file, all commands within the batch file are executed within a Windows command prompt.

Suppose you create a batch file called **C:\PSLimits.bat** that contains the following PowerShell command that uses the Exchange Management Shell plugin (**C:\Program Files\Microsoft\ Exchange Server\Bin\ExShell.psc1**) to run the **MailboxSendReceiveLimits –CSVFile 'C:\Mailbox User Limits.csv'** script command used in the previous example:

PowerShell.exe –PSConsoleFile 'C:\Program Files\Microsoft\Exchange Server\Bin\ ExShell.psc1' –Command '. "MailboxSendReceiveLimits –CSVFile C:\Mailbox User Limits.csv" '

Next, you could simply type **C:\PSLimits.bat** at a Windows command prompt or the Run dialog box to manually execute the PowerShell script and set the mailbox send and receive limits specified in the **C:\Mailbox User Limits.csv** file.

In addition, you could schedule the C:\PSLimits.bat file to run at a later time using the Windows Scheduled Task Wizard (**Start > All Programs > Accessories > System Tools > Scheduled Tasks > Add Scheduled Task**). When you run the Windows Scheduled Task Wizard, you will need to specify the name and location of the batch file, the time it should run, and the credentials of the user that it will run as. After scheduling the C:\PSLimits.bat file to run at 8:32 a.m. on July 24, 2009, as the Administrator user using the Windows Scheduled Task Wizard, the Scheduled Tasks window will resemble that shown in Figure 6-42.

Figure 6-42

Viewing a Scheduled Task

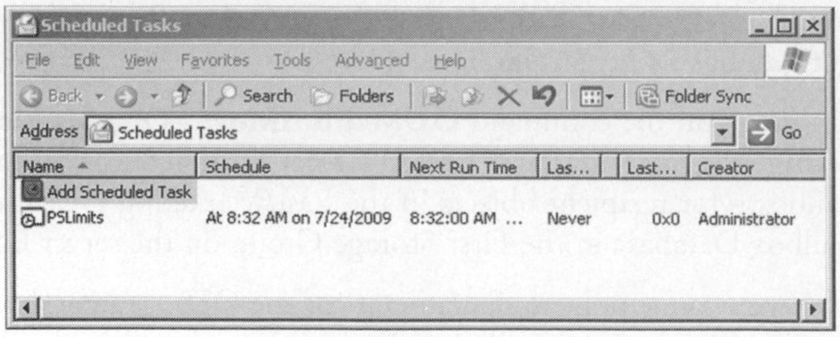

SUMMARY SKILL MATRIX

IN THIS LESSON YOU LEARNED:

- The recipient objects within your organization can be added to address lists to allow for fast searching within a MAPI client such as Outlook or Entourage. The Default Global Address List stores all recipient objects within the Exchange organization and cannot be removed or modified.

- To allow MAPI clients to access their address lists when they are not connected to their Exchange server, you can create OABs that contain the appropriate address lists. Each OAB must be generated by a single Mailbox role server within your organization. Mailbox users receive the OAB that is configured for use on their mailbox database.

- Recipient objects within your organization receive their default email address format of alias@domainname from the default email address policy. To control the format of email addresses for recipients within your organization, you can modify the default email address policy or create additional email address policies that override the default email address policy and apply to specific recipient objects.

- Messaging compliance policies are used to retain emails for legal purposes and consist of Messaging Records Management and message journaling.

- By using Messaging Records Management, managed custom folders and managed default folders may be given retention settings to prevent emails within them from being removed for a certain period of time. These managed custom folders and managed default folders can then be added to a managed folder mailbox policy that is applied to recipient objects. The Managed Folder Attendant process on each Mailbox server can then be configured to apply and enforce the managed folder mailbox policy.

- By using message journaling, you can configure the Journaling agent on your Hub role servers to send copies of email to a separate mailbox for archiving. Standard journaling archives all mail sent to and from a specified mailbox database, whereas premium journaling uses journal rules to determine which recipient objects should participate in email archiving.

- CSV files may be used alongside the appropriate cmdlet within the Exchange Management Shell to create, modify, and manage multiple recipient objects in a bulk operation. Multiple recipient objects may only be disabled or removed at the same time within the Exchange Management Console.

- You can use the Get-Mailbox cmdlet, CSV files and the Move-Mailbox cmdlet within the Exchange Management Shell to perform bulk mailbox moves. The Exchange Management Console can also be used to perform bulk mailbox moves within the same forest.

- For repetitive bulk management tasks, you can create PowerShell scripts that contain the appropriate Exchange Management Shell commands. PowerShell scripts may be executed within the Exchange Management Shell or added to a batch file that can be scheduled to execute at a later time using the Windows Scheduled Tasks wizard.

■ Knowledge Assessment

Fill in the Blank

Complete the following sentences by writing the correct word or words in the blanks provided.

1. Email address policies can be configured using the _____ node within the Exchange Management Console.

2. Managed default folders, managed custom folders, and managed folder mailbox policies are part of the _____ component within Exchange Server 2007.

3. When you create a new address list, you must specify the recipient object types that will be included as well as _____ that specify attributes for recipient objects that should be added to the address list.

4. To configure standard journaling, you can use the _____ cmdlet within the Exchange Management Shell.

5. To save time when creating multiple recipient objects, you can reference the settings stored in a _____.

6. After creating a new OAB, you must configure it for use in the properties of a _____.

7. Before creating an email address policy that contains a different domain name suffix, you must ensure that your Hub role servers are configured with the appropriate _____.

8. You can specify retention settings on a new managed folder by selecting the _____ action.

9. When creating a PowerShell script, you can define _____ to accept command line arguments that can be used by the cmdlets within the script.

10. The _____ cmdlet can be used to read the contents of a CSV file.

Multiple Choice

Circle the letter that corresponds to the best answer.

1. Only Version 4 MAPI clients can obtain an OAB using web distribution. Which of the following are Version 4 MAPI clients? (Choose all that apply.)
   a. Outlook 2007
   b. Entourage 2008
   c. Outlook 2003
   d. Entourage X

2. When used with the New-EmailAddressPolicy cmdlet, which of the following email address formats represents the first name of a user followed by the first three characters of the last name in the domain octavius.net?
   a. %g%3m@octavius.net
   b. %s%3g@octavius.net
   c. %m%3s@octavius.net
   d. %g%3s@octavius.net

3. You wish to ensure that any Sent Items for MAPI users within your organization are archived in a folder called Sent Item Archive for five years. Which of the following actions should you perform? (Choose all that apply. Each answer provides a part of the solution.)
   a. Create a managed default folder for Sent Items.
   b. Configure retention settings for the Sent Items managed folder that moves emails to the Sent Items Archive folder.
   c. Create a managed custom folder called Sent Item Archive and configure a five-year retention setting on it.
   d. Create a managed folder mailbox policy that includes the Sent Items and Sent Item Archive folders and apply it to the appropriate mailbox users.

4. You have defined a CSV file that contains the ProhibitSendQuota field. How can you call the values within this field in a command that receives the content of CSV file via Exchange Management Shell command piping?
   - **a.** $ProhibitSendQuota
   - **b.** -ProhibitSendQuota
   - **c.** $_.ProhibitSendQuota
   - **d.** | ProhibitSendQuota

5. Which of the following nodes within the Exchange Management Console may be used to manage address lists?
   - **a.** Organization Configuration > Hub Transport
   - **b.** Organization Configuration > Mailbox
   - **c.** Server Configuration > Hub Transport
   - **d.** Server Configuration > Mailbox

6. Which of the following cmdlets may be used to obtain a list of mailboxes for users within a particular department that will be sent to the Move-Mailbox cmdlet?
   - **a.** Get-Mailbox
   - **b.** Import-CSV
   - **c.** ForEach-Object
   - **d.** Set-MailboxDatabase

7. You have just created a PowerShell script called PSScript1.ps1. What directory should you place this script in so that you can execute it within the Exchange Management Console?
   - **a.** C:\Program Files\Microsoft\PowerShell
   - **b.** C:\Program Files\Microsoft\PowerShell\Scripts
   - **c.** C:\
   - **d.** C:\Program Files\Microsoft\Exchange Server\Scripts

8. After creating a managed folder mailbox policy and applying it to mailbox users, users do not receive their managed folder settings after they restart their email clients. What must you do to make the changes take effect? (Choose two answers. Each answer provides part of the solution.)
   - **a.** Enable the managed folder mailbox policy.
   - **b.** Configure the Managed Folder Assistant within the properties of the mailbox database that stores the related mailboxes.
   - **c.** Manually run the Managed Folder Assistant within the Exchange Management Shell.
   - **d.** Disable Cached Exchange Mode on each MAPI client.

9. Which of the following must you do to configure premium journaling using the Exchange Server 2007 Journaling agent?
   - **a.** Create journal rules.
   - **b.** Configure the properties of each mailbox that will participate in premium journaling.
   - **c.** Create a journal policy.
   - **d.** Configure the properties of the mailbox database that will participate in premium journaling.

10. You need to ensure that all recipient objects within your organization contain two email addresses. How can you achieve this? (Choose two answers. Each answer provides a complete solution.)
    - **a.** Modify the default email address policy and add an additional email address format.
    - **b.** Create a new email address policy with a lower priority than the default email address policy that contains two email address formats.
    - **c.** Create a new email address policy with a lower priority than the default email address policy that contains an additional email address format.
    - **d.** Create a new email address policy with a higher priority than the default email address policy that contains two email address formats.

True/False

Circle T if the statement is true or F if the statement is false.

T | F **1.** Premium journaling is only available in the Standard and Enterprise editions of
Exchange Server 2007.

T | F **2.** Any cmdlet that creates, modifies, or manages recipient objects can be used in a
bulk management command.

T | F **3.** A single managed folder can contain multiple managed content setting configurations.

T | F **4.** You can prevent a recipient object from applying email address policies.

T | F **5.** You can customize the Default Global Address List to include the recipients you
wish to display within MAPI clients.

T | F **6.** You can use the Exchange Management Console to perform bulk mailbox moves.

T | F **7.** Message compliance is used to enforce email retention required by law and regulation. As a result, it is rarely configured in most organizations today.

T | F **8.** A recipient object only applies the email address policy with the highest priority
that matches its attributes.

T | F **9.** Address lists may be created underneath existing address lists.

T | F **10.** When creating a new OAB, you must specify a CAS role server that will be used
to generate the list of recipients used within the OAB.

Review Questions

1. Explain why it is important to carefully plan the address lists and OABs that you use
within your organization.
2. Explain how creating PowerShell scripts for bulk management can save time and
administrative effort within an organization.

■ Case Scenarios

Scenario 6-1: Configuring a Messaging Compliance Policy

As the Exchange administrator for your organization, you have just been informed that your
organization must now keep emails regarding several of your key projects for a minimum of
seven years. In a short memo, explain the tasks that would need to be performed within your
Exchange infrastructure to create a messaging compliance policy that adheres to these needs.

Scenario 6-2: Performing Bulk Management

Recently, your organization has formed a Research division that will contain select users
from within the organization. This new Research division will contain its own Mailbox role
server for its members. You have been tasked with modifying the existing Exchange infrastructure to accommodate the new Research division. As a result, you will need to modify
the Department and Office attributes for all users as well as move their mailboxes to the
new Research Mailbox role server. Explain how you would perform these actions using bulk
management commands and write sample bulk management commands that may be used to
perform these actions.

7 LESSON

Working with Public Folders

LESSON SKILL MATRIX

TECHNOLOGY SKILL	OBJECTIVE DOMAIN	OBJECTIVE DOMAIN NUMBER
Creating Public Folders	Configure public folders.	2.4, 3.5
Configuring Public Folders	Configure public folders.	2.4, 3.5
Configuring Mail-Enabled Public Folders	Configure public folders.	2.4, 3.5
Working with Multiple Public Folders	Implement bulk management of mail-enabled objects.	2.6

KEY TERMS

administrative permission
client permission
content replica
default public folder
  subtree
Folder Assistant

moderated public folder
moderator
Outlook Form Designer
public folder hierarchy
Public Folder Management
  Console

public folder referral
Send As permission
system public folder
  subtree
Top Level Hierarchy (TLH)

■ Understanding Public Folders

THE BOTTOM LINE

Public folders provide a flexible means of storing different types of items that email users work with on a regular basis as part of their job role. Consequently, many organizations configure public folders as part of their Exchange infrastructure. As an Exchange administrator, you will likely need to create, configure, and manage public folders within your organization.

Public folders are folders that Exchange users can use to share information such as emails, notes, file attachments, tasks, calendars, journals, forms, and contacts with other Exchange users. In addition, you can use public folders to archive emails or to provide access to company information or documents. By mail-enabling public folders, you can also use them to store emails that are sent to a specific email address. Furthermore, you can restrict access to public folders and their content or hide them from address lists.

Outlook and Entourage are the most common programs used to access public folders. When you set up an Exchange account within Outlook and Entourage, public folders are displayed alongside your normal email folders for you to access. Additionally, you can use Outlook Web Access (OWA) to access and use public folders.

In previous versions of Exchange Server, you could use public folders to provide news-groups using the Network News Transfer Protocol (NNTP) for newsgroup clients such as Outlook Express. This feature is no longer available in Exchange Server 2007.

In many organizations, users are already familiar with email clients such as Outlook because they spend a great deal of time using it to support their job role. Because these users can access their email and public folders in the same client program, there is less of a learning curve in using public folders when compared to other technologies such as SharePoint and Groove 2007. However, although public folders provide an easy way of sharing or archiving files and information, they do not provide advanced document tracking features such as versioning. To provide these features, you will need to use other software that is specifically designed for document sharing such as SharePoint or Groove 2007. Similarly, technologies such as Messaging Records Management and message journaling are better suited for email archival when compared to public folders. Nonetheless, public folders provide a flexible mechanism for storing information and can prove very useful in many different situations.

Members of the Exchange Organization Administrator role or the Exchange Public Folder Administrator role can create, configure, and manage the public folders within your Exchange organization. To use the rights assigned to these roles, you must also be a local Administrator on the Mailbox server that contains the public folders.

Creating Public Folders

 **THE BOTTOM LINE** Although you can grant the ability to create public folders to others within your organiza-tion, you will likely need to create the initial public folder structure within your public folder databases. Public folders can be created within a public folder database on a Mailbox server within your organization using the Public Folder Management Console, Exchange Management Shell, Outlook, Entourage, or OWA.

Before you create public folders, you must first have a public folder database on a Mailbox role server that will be used to store them. On the Client Settings page during the Exchange Server installation, you were asked whether your Exchange organization will have client computers that are running Outlook 2003 and earlier or Entourage. If you selected Yes, a public folder database was automatically created during the installation. This is because public folders are used to store Offline Address Books (OABs), Exchange client configuration infor-mation, and calendar scheduling (free/busy) information used by Outlook 2003 and earlier clients as well as Entourage 2004 and earlier clients that are configured to use an Exchange account. Alternatively, if you selected No on the Client Settings page, a public folder database was not created during installation, and you must first create and mount a public folder data-base as discussed in Lesson 4, "Configuring a New Exchange Server."

Instead of using public folders, Outlook 2007 and Entourage 2008 MAPI clients use the Autodiscover and Availability services within Exchange 2007 to obtain Offline Address Books, schedule calendar appointments, and obtain configuration information.

By default, mailbox users can connect to a single public folder database using Outlook, Entourage, or OWA. The public folder database that mailbox users will receive is configured on the Client Settings tab of mailbox database properties. For example, the mailboxes stored within the Mailbox Database shown in Figure 7-1 are configured to use the public folders stored in the Public Folder Database in the Second Storage Group on the server EXCH1.

Figure 7-1

Specifying a Public Folder
Database

Mailbox Database Properties

General | Limits | **Client Settings**

Default public folder database:

EXCH1\Second Storage Group\Public Folder Database   [Browse...]

Offline address book:

\Default Offline Address Book   [Browse...]

[OK] [Cancel] [Apply] [Help]

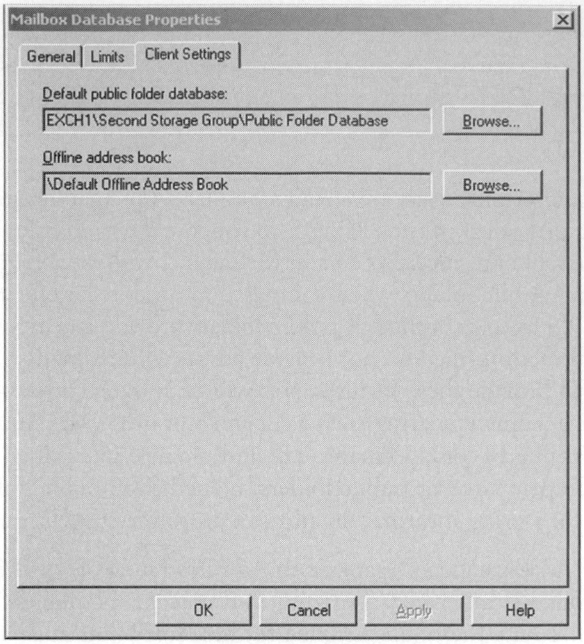

TAKE NOTE* Although mailbox users connect to a single public folder database by default, they will be able to see and access all of the public folders within the Exchange organization using **pub-lic folder referrals**. Public folder referrals are discussed in more detail later in this lesson.

Each new public folder database is configured to use the MAPI **Top Level Hierarchy (TLH)** tree structure. This allows you to create new public folders at the root of the database as well as under existing public folders.

In addition, MAPI TLH is divided into two subtrees. The **default public folder subtree** is used to store public folders for use by users, whereas the **system public folder subtree** stores the folders used to provide configuration, scheduling, and OAB information to MAPI clients. The folders under the system folder subtree cannot be accessed by users. They are automatically created and managed using Exchange Server and should not be modified.

TAKE NOTE* The default public folder subtree is also called the **Interpersonal Message (IPM) subtree**. The system folder subtree is often referred to using NON_IPM_SUBTREE.

You can create, configure, and manage public folders using Outlook, Entourage, or the **Public Folder Management Console** within the Exchange Management Console. To start the Public Folder Management Console, highlight the **Tools** node within the Exchange Management Console and double click **Public Folder Management Console** in the details pane. By default, the Public Folder Management Console displays the default public folder and system public folder subtrees on the current Exchange server as shown in Figure 7-2. You can manage any public folder database within the organization from within the Public Folder Management Console. Simply select **Connect to Server** in the action pane shown in Figure 7-2 and choose the appropriate server that contains the public folder database you wish to administer.

TAKE NOTE* The Public Folder Management Console is only available in Exchange Server 2007 SP1 or later.

Figure 7-2

Public Folder Management
Console

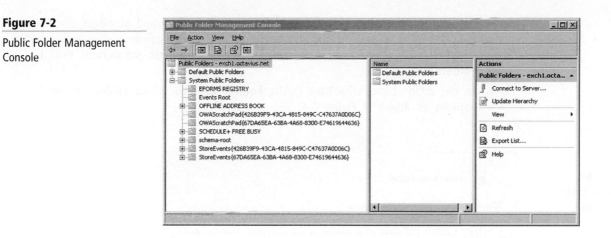

As shown in Figure 7-2, only the system public folders are created in a new public folder database. However, you can create new public folders under the default public folder subtree to match the needs of your organization. These folders can be created under the root (\) of the default public folder subtree or underneath existing public folders within the default public folder subtree. Figure 7-3 shows a public folder structure that has multiple levels within the public folder hierarchy under the root of the default public folder subtree.

In earlier versions of Exchange Server, you could create additional general-purpose public folder trees that could be accessed using OWA or NNTP clients. These general-purpose public folder trees are no longer supported in Exchange Server 2007, and all public folders that you create must reside under the default public folder subtree within a public folder database.

Figure 7-3

Viewing Public Folder Structure

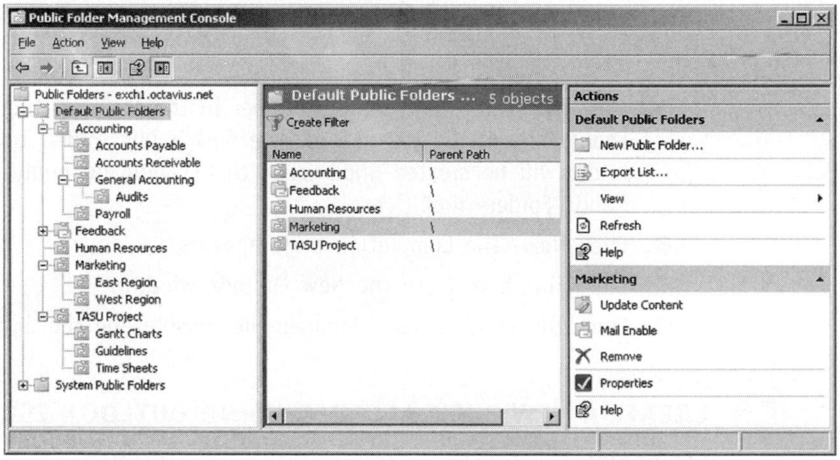

If you create a public folder within the Public Folder Management Console, it can only contain email and post items. Alternatively, if you create new public folders from within Outlook, Entourage, or OWA, you can select the type of content that will be allowed within the public folder.

CREATE A NEW PUBLIC FOLDER USING THE PUBLIC FOLDER MANAGEMENT CONSOLE

GET READY. Turn on the computer, and log in as the Administrator user account. Close any windows that appear on the desktop.

1. Click **Start**, **All Programs**, **Microsoft Exchange Server 2007**, and then click **Exchange Management Console**. The Exchange Management Console window appears.

2. In the console tree pane, highlight **Tools** and double click **Public Folder Management Console** in the detail pane. The Public Folder Management Console window appears.

3. Expand **Default Public Folders** in the console tree pane and highlight the folder under which you wish to create a new public folder. To create a new public folder underneath the root of the public folder tree, simply highlight **Default Public Folders**.

4. In the action pane, click **New Public Folder**. The New Public Folder window appears as shown in Figure 7-4.

Figure 7-4

Creating a New Public Folder in the Public Folder Management Console

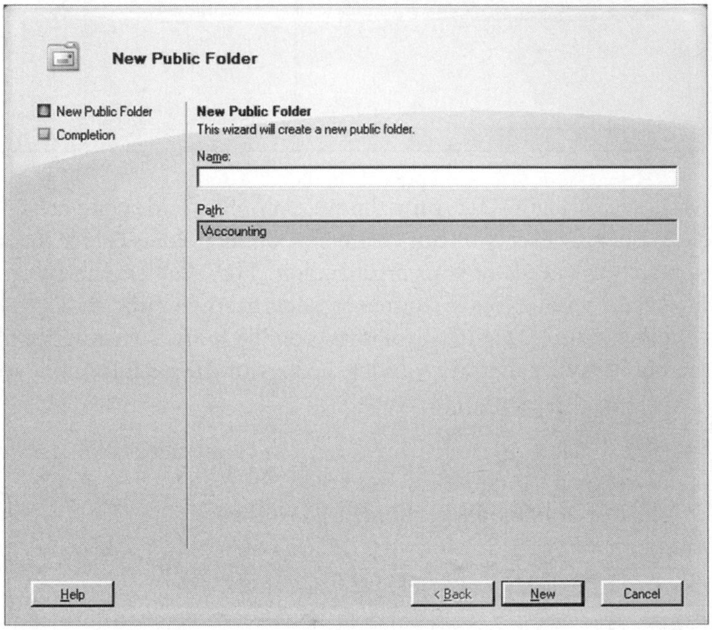

5. Type the name for the public folder in the Name dialog box. The Path dialog box should reflect the location for the new public folder. In Figure 7-4, the new public folder will be created underneath the Accounting public folder under the Default Public Folders root (\).

6. Click **New**. The Completion page appears.

7. Click **Finish** to close the New Mailbox window.

8. Close the Public Folder Management Console and the Exchange Management Console.

CREATE A NEW PUBLIC FOLDER USING OUTLOOK 2007

GET READY. Turn on the computer, and log in as the Administrator user account. Close any windows that appear on the desktop.

1. Click **Start**, **All Programs**, **Microsoft Office**, and then click **Microsoft Office Outlook 2007**. The Microsoft Outlook window appears.

2. Click on the Folder List icon in the lower left pane. In the Folder List window, expand **Public Folders**, **All Public Folders**.

3. Next, right click the folder under which you wish to create a new public folder and select **New Folder**. To create a new public folder underneath the root of the public folder tree, simply right click **All Public Folders** and select **New Folder**. The Create New Folder window appears as shown in Figure 7-5.

Figure 7-5

Creating a New Public Folder in Outlook

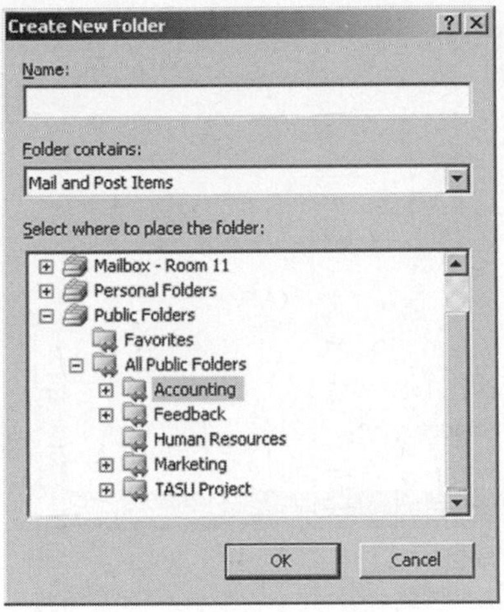

4. Type the name for the public folder in the **Name** dialog box. The dialog box at the bottom of the Create New Folder dialog box should reflect the location for the new public folder. To change this location, you can highlight the appropriate folder in this dialog box.

5. By default, public folders can store email and post items. To modify the type of items that should be stored in the public folder, you can select one of the following in the **Folder contains** drop-down box:

   • **Calendar Items**
   • **Contact Items**
   • **InfoPath Form Items**
   • **Journal Items**
   • **Mail and Post Items**
   • **Note Items**
   • **Task Items**

6. Click **OK**. Close Microsoft Outlook.

CREATE A NEW PUBLIC FOLDER USING ENTOURAGE 2008

GET READY. Turn on the Macintosh computer, and log in as the Administrator user account. Close any windows that appear on the desktop.

1. Click the Microsoft Entourage icon on the Macintosh OS X dock to open Microsoft Entourage 2008. Alternatively, you can navigate to **Macintosh HD**, **Applications**, **Microsoft Office 2008**, and then click **Microsoft Entourage** to open Microsoft Entourage 2008. The Microsoft Entourage 2008 window appears.

2. In the left pane, expand **Public Folders**, **All Public Folders**.

3. Next, right click the folder under which you wish to create a new public folder and select **New Folder**. To create a new public folder underneath the root of the public folder tree, simply right click **All Public Folders** and select **New Folder**. The Create New Folder window appears as shown in Figure 7-6.

Figure 7-6

Creating a New Public Folder in Entourage

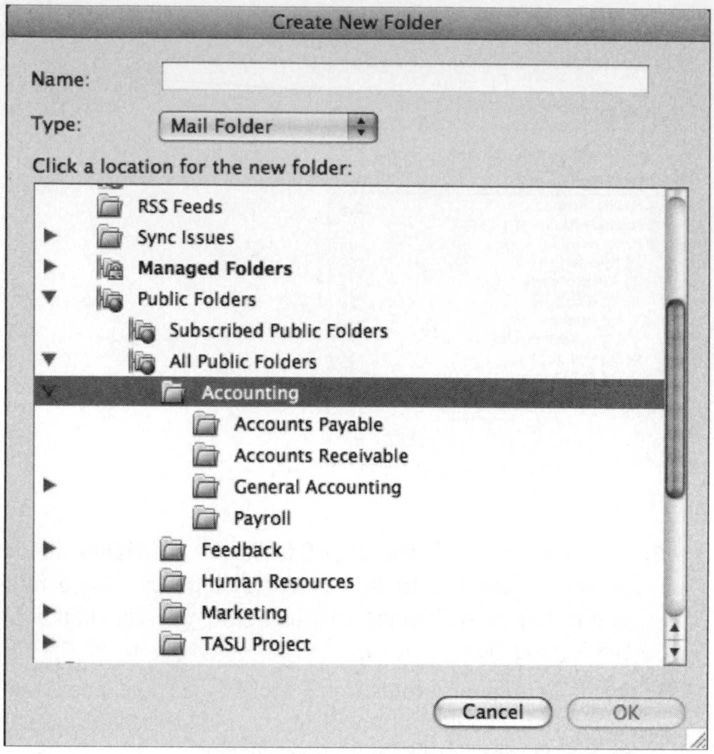

4. Type the name for the public folder in the **Name** dialog box. The dialog box at the bottom of the Create New Folder dialog box should reflect the location for the new public folder. To change this location, you can highlight the appropriate folder in this dialog box.

5. By default, public folders can store email and post items. To modify the type of items that should be stored in the public folder, you can select one of the following in the **Type** selection box:

   • **Mail Folder**
   • **Calendar**
   • **Address Book**

6. Click **OK**. Close Microsoft Entourage.

CREATE A NEW PUBLIC FOLDER USING OWA

GET READY. Turn on the computer, and log in as the Administrator user account. Close any windows that appear on the desktop.

1. Open your web browser and enter the URL **http://*server*/public** where *server* is the FQDN or IP address of the Mailbox role server that hosts the public folder database in which you wish to create public folders. When prompted to log in, enter your username and password and click **OK**.

2. In the left pane, click **Public Folders**.

3. Next, right click the folder under which you wish to create a new public folder, select **Create New Folder** and then select the type of folder that you wish to create:

   • **Mail Folder**
   • **Calendar Folder**
   • **Contact Folder**
   • **Task Folder**
   • **Notes Folder**

To create a new public folder underneath the root of the public folder tree, simply right click **Public Folders**, select **New Folder**, and then select the appropriate folder type.

4. Type the name for the public folder in the dialog box that appears next to the new public folder icon in the left pane and press **Enter**.

5. Close your web browser.

THE COMMAND LINE WAY

You can also use the **New-PublicFolder** cmdlet in the Exchange Management Shell to create a new public folder under the default public folder subtree. For example, to create a new public folder called Notes under the Accounting public folder under the root of the default public folder tree on the server EXCH2, you could run the following command in the Exchange Management Shell:

New-PublicFolder -Name 'Notes' -Path '\Accounting' -Server 'EXCH2'

If you omit the **–Path** option to the New-PublicFolder cmdlet, the new folder will be created under the root of the default public folder tree. Similarly, if you omit the **–Server** option to the New-PublicFolder cmdlet, the new public folder will be created in the public folder database on the closest Mailbox server. This server is located using site information stored in AD.

Once you have created public folders, you can view them using the **Get-PublicFolder** cmdlet. To view all of the public folders under the root (\), including subfolders, you can use the following command within the Exchange Management Shell:

Get-PublicFolder –Recurse | Format-List Name

Similarly, to view the details for public folder called Guidelines under the TASU Project public folder under the root (\) of the default public folder subtree on the server EXCH2, you could use the following command within the Exchange Management Shell:

Get-PublicFolder –Identity '\TASU Project\Guidelines' –Server 'EXCH2' | Format-List

Over time, you may need to monitor the size and number of items posted to a public folder. To do this, you can use the Get-PublicFolderStatistics cmdlet. To view the statistics for the TASU Project public folder under the root (\) of the default public folder subtree on the server EXCH2, you could use the following command within the Exchange Management Shell:

Get-PublicFolderStatistics –Identity '\TASU Project\Guidelines' –Server 'EXCH2' | Format-List

If you omit **–Identity '\TASU Project\Guidelines'** in the previous example, you will view statistics for all public folders on the server EXCH2.

■ Using Public Folders

THE BOTTOM LINE

Nearly everyone today has used an email program to send email to others. However, understanding how to use public folders is somewhat less common because public folders are only used within organizations and business environments that deploy Exchange Server, Outlook, Entourage, and OWA. To understand how to configure public folders, you must first understand their basic usage and function.

Outlook, Entourage, and OWA are the main client email programs you can use to access public folders in Exchange Server 2007. For Outlook users, public folders are automatically added to the folder list under an Exchange account in the left pane as shown for the Jeff Smith mailbox user in Figure 7-7. Depending on your version and configuration of Outlook, you may need to select the Folder List icon at the bottom of the left pane to view the default public folder subtree underneath your mailbox folder list in Outlook.

TAKE NOTE*

An easy way to identify the Folder List icon is to move your mouse over each icon in the lower left area of the Outlook window and observe the description labels that appear. The Folder List icon will have a description label of **Folder List** or **View Folders** depending on your version of Outlook.

Figure 7-7

Viewing Public Folder Items in Outlook

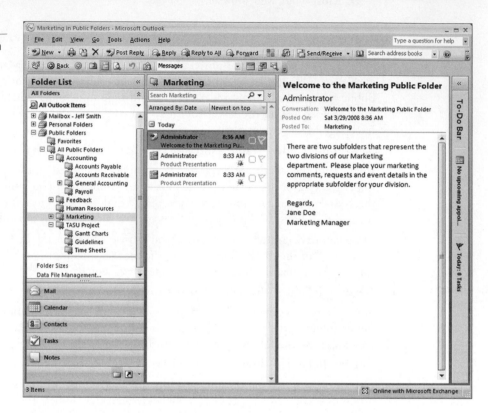

The **Mailbox—Jeff Smith** folder list normally contains the default email folders such as Inbox and Deleted Items, but has been collapsed in Figure 7-7 to show the public folders configured in the public folder database that is used by Jeff Smith's mailbox database. The root of the default public folder subtree is represented by the **All Public Folders** node in Figure 7-7. You can navigate the public folders underneath this node to view existing content. The Marketing folder highlighted in Figure 7-7 shows two meeting request emails from the Administrator regarding product presentations as well as a post item that welcomes visitors to the marketing public folder. You can double click any item within a public folder to view it or simply highlight it to view its contents in the right pane (reading pane) as shown with the welcome post in Figure 7-7.

To add existing items to a public folder, you can simply locate them in your mailbox folder list, right click them, and select Move to folder. You can then browse to an existing public folder and click **OK** to move the item to that public folder. This is often used for public folders that are designed to store copies of emails regarding company events or public folders used to archive important items. Provided that the public folder was created in Outlook and configured to contain the appropriate content, you can move email, post items, calendar items, contacts, tasks, notes, and journal items to a public folder. Email and post items are two of the most commonly configured content types used for public folders.

Alternatively, you can choose to add a new item to a public folder by selecting the appropriate public folder and clicking **New** in the upper left corner of Outlook. If your public folder is configured to contain email and post items, clicking **New** in the upper left corner will create a new post item by default as shown in Figure 7-8. However, you can select the drop-box icon to the right of the **New** button to select other item types. Post items are simply messages that can contain a subject line and message as well as attachments such as files and pictures. By clicking **Post** as shown in Figure 7-8, the post item will be stored in the appropriate public folder for others to view or respond to. After highlighting a post item, users can click **Reply** (shown in Figure 7-7) to reply to the original sender via email or the **Post Reply** button to post a related reply within the public folder itself.

Figure 7-8

Creating a New Post

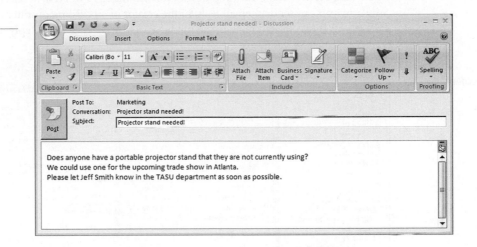

After creating an Exchange account in Entourage, you will see public folders alongside the other default mail folders provided that you manually specified a public folder server when you set up the Exchange account. To specify a public folder server for an Exchange account within Entourage, you can navigate to **Tools** > **Accounts**, double click your Exchange account and click the **Advanced** tab as shown in Figure 7-9.

Figure 7-9

Specifying a Public Folder Server in Entourage

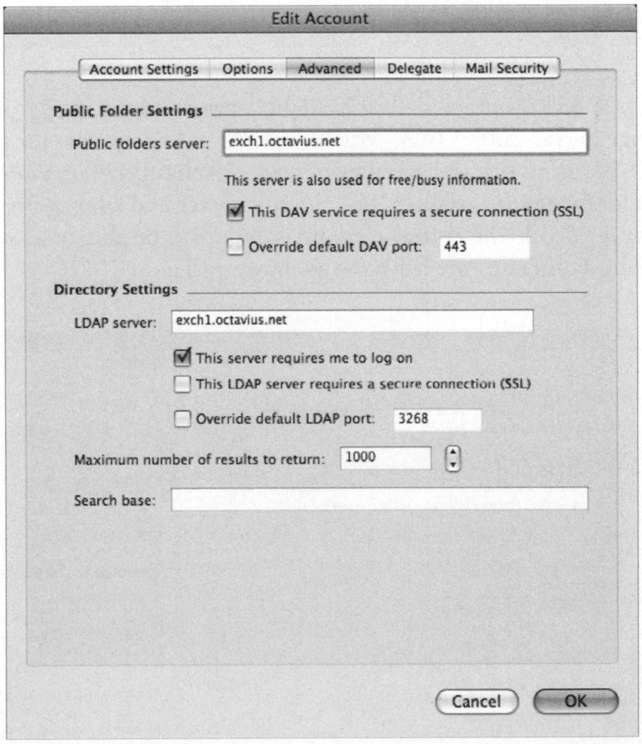

The server name or IP address that you specify in the Public folders server dialog box in Figure 7-9 does not need to be the same server configured on the Client Settings tab of the user's mailbox database as shown earlier in Figure 7-1. If you select a different server, then Entourage will locate the public folder database on that particular server. In addition, you must select **This DAV service requires a secure connection (SSL)** because all public folder access between Entourage and Exchange 2007 must be encrypted using SSL.

After you specify a public folder server in Entourage, the default public folder subtree will appear under the **All Public Folders** node within the left pane of Entourage as shown in Figure 7-10. As with Outlook, you can move items to public folders in Entourage as well as create a new post by clicking **New** or using the drop-down arrow to the right of **New** to select other message types. Similarly, you can send an email reply to the creator of an existing post item by clicking **Reply Directly** or post a related reply in the public folder by clicking **Post Reply** as shown in Figure 7-10.

Figure 7-10

Viewing Public Folder Items in Entourage

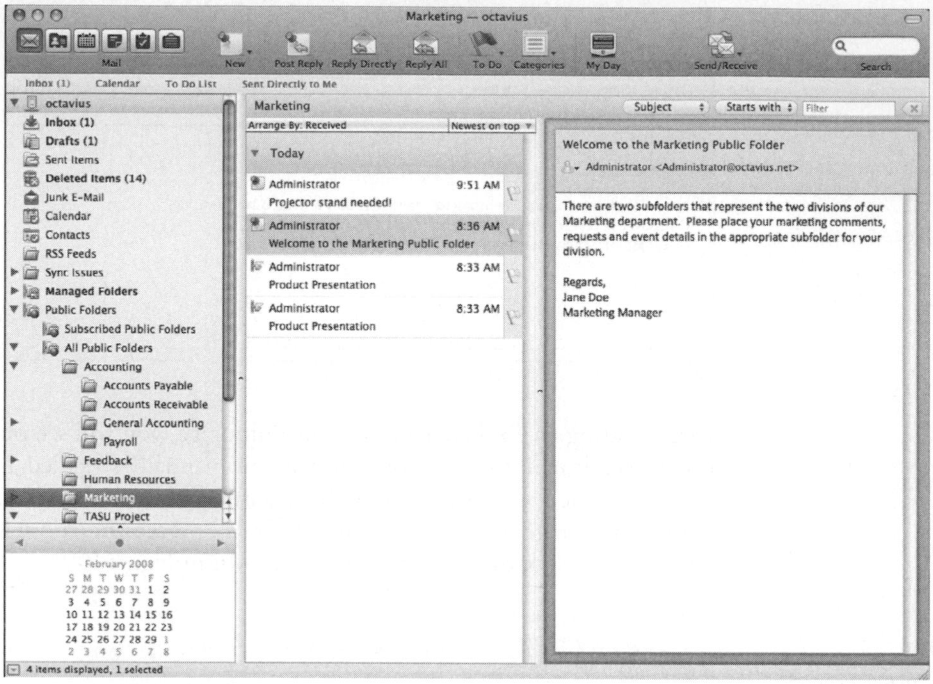

TAKE NOTE*

You can also access OWA using the URL **https://*server*/exchange** or **https://*server*/ public** and specifying the appropriate credentials at the logon screen.

If Outlook or Entourage are not available options for accessing public folders, you can use Exchange Server 2007 OWA, which contains native support for public folders. Simply access your OWA using the address **https://*server*/exchange/*user_name*** where *server* is the FQDN or IP address of your Mailbox or CAS role server and *user_name* is your account name. Once you provide the correct credentials, you will be able to access public folders by clicking on **Public Folders** in the left pane as shown in Figure 7-11.

Figure 7-11

Viewing Public Folder Items in OWA

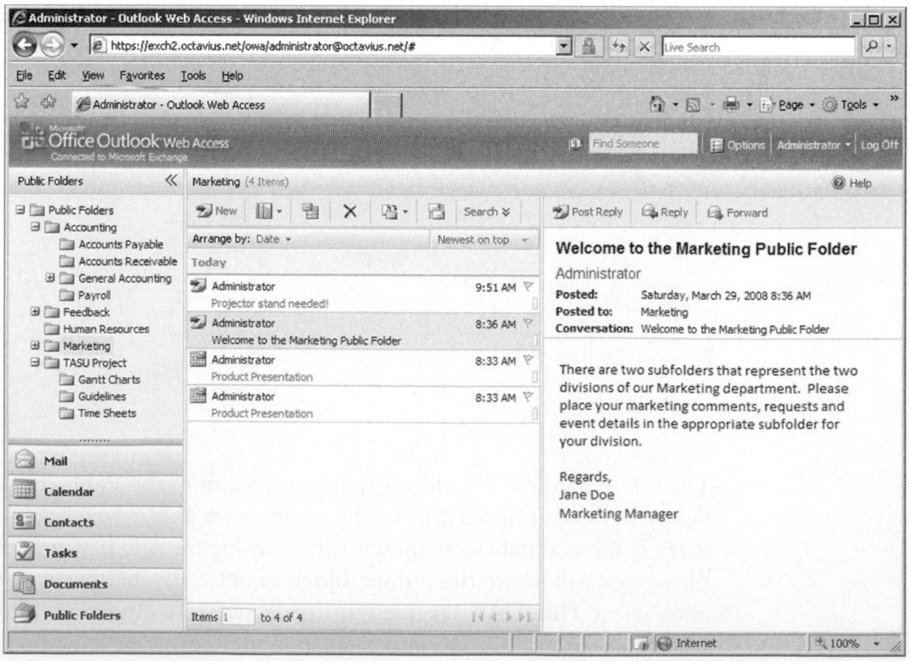

Although OWA is similar in functionality to Outlook and Entourage, you can only create new post items in a public folder by using the **New** button. However, you can perform most other public folder functions within OWA. For example, you can move existing items to a public folder within OWA as well as reply to public folder items using email with the **Reply** button or using a new post item with the **Post Reply** button.

■ Configuring Public Folders

↓
THE BOTTOM LINE

Public folders host a wide variety of configuration options that make them useful in a variety of situations. After creating public folders, you will need to modify the permissions on them as well as configure folder options, replication, and limits to meet the needs of your organization.

CERTIFICATION READY?
Configure public folders.
2.4, 3.5

Configuring Client Permissions

Client permissions give mailbox users within your organization the ability to view and manage the content within public folders as well as create new public folder content. In most situations, you will need to modify the default client permissions on public folders using Outlook or the Exchange Management Shell to ensure that the mailbox users within your organization have only the necessary access to public folder content.

TAKE NOTE*

Outlook is the only client program that can be used to configure public folder properties such as client permissions. You cannot use OWA to configure the properties for a public folder, and Entourage can only be used to view the configuration of public folders.

After creating public folders, any mailbox user within your organization can view items within the public folder as well as add new items and manage their own items. Depending on the intended use of the public folder, this may not be desirable. For example, if your organization uses public folders to store information for a particular department, only certain mailbox users should be able to store and view the information in that public folder. As a result, you can set *client permissions* on a public folder to specify the permissions that users have to the content within the public folder.

Client permissions can be configured on a public folder using Outlook or the Exchange Management Shell. To configure client permissions on a public folder in Outlook, simply right click the appropriate public folder, select **Properties**, and highlight the **Permissions** tab as shown in Figure 7-12.

Figure 7-12

Configuring Client Permissions

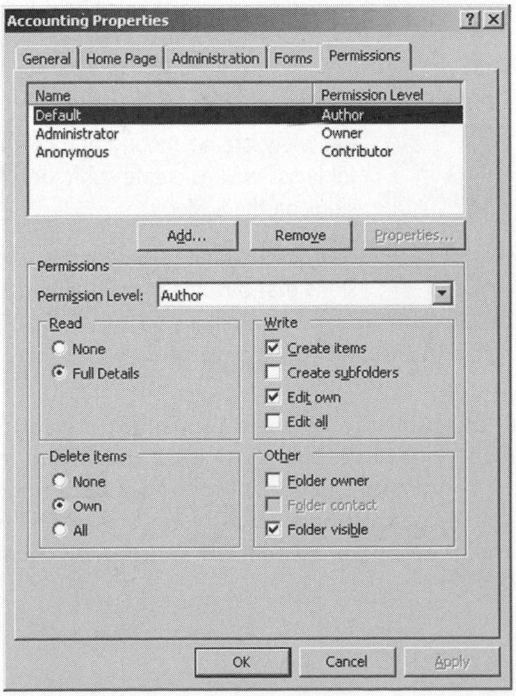

The client permissions for the Accounting public folder shown in Figure 7-12 can be used to determine whether a particular user can create, read, edit, and delete items within the Accounting public folder as well as create new public folders underneath the Accounting public folder. In addition, these client permissions can be used to determine whether the Accounting folder will be visible to the user in the default public folder subtree.

Because there can be many different combinations of client permissions, you can assign one of several *client permission levels* to a mailbox user or mail-enabled universal group as described in Table 7-1. These permission levels include common groups of client permissions that can be granted to a user or group.

Table 7-1

Public folder client permission levels

PERMISSION LEVEL	DESCRIPTION
None	Cannot view, create, modify, or delete any items within the public folder or view the public folder within the default public folder subtree.
Contributor	Can create new items in the folder, but cannot view other items in the folder or delete items. This permission level is appropriate when creating a drop-box folder that allows users to submit requests but not view or manage them afterwards.
Reviewer	Can view items within the folder only. This permission level is often assigned to users on public folders that provide information only.
Nonediting author	Can view and create items within the folder as well as delete items that they have created.
Author	Can view and create items within the folder as well as modify and delete items that they have created.
Publishing author	Can view and create items within the folder, create subfolders, as well as modify and delete items that they have created.
Editor	Can view, create, modify, and delete all items within the public folder.
Publishing editor	Can view, create, modify, and delete all items within the public folder as well as create subfolders.
Owner	Can view, create, modify, and delete all items within the public folder as well as create subfolders and modify the client permissions on the folder.
Custom	Used to designate a permission level that contains client permissions that have been manually specified.

The default client permission level granted to mailbox users is Author, which allows all other users to read all items in the folder as well as create and manage their own items. To restrict access to the content of a public folder, you should remove the **Default** user shown in Figure 7-12 or set the permission level to **None** for the **Default** user. Next, you can add the appropriate users or groups and assign the appropriate client permission level or custom client permissions.

TAKE NOTE*

Only mailbox users and mail-enabled universal groups within your Exchange organization can be assigned client permissions to public folders. When you click **Add** as shown in Figure 7-12 to add additional users or groups, you will not be able to select any mail users, mail contacts, and dynamic distribution groups.

In many organizations, the Exchange administrator does not handle the administration of public folder content and client permissions because it would be too time consuming. Instead, the manager of a department or project is often given the owner-client permission level. This user can then manage all content within the public folder, create subfolders, and assign client permissions to others as needed.

TAKE NOTE*

When you create a new public folder, it inherits its settings, including permissions, from its parent public folder. If you change the permissions on the parent public folder afterward, those permissions are not automatically set on its child public folders.

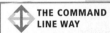

THE COMMAND LINE WAY

You can also use cmdlets within the Exchange Management Shell to manage client permissions on a public folder. To view existing client permissions on a public folder, you can use the **Get-PublicFolderClientPermission** cmdlet. For example, to view the existing client permissions on the Accounting public folder under the root of the default public folder subtree on the Mailbox server EXCH2, you could use the following command within the Exchange Management Shell:

Get-PublicFolderClientPermission –Identity '\Accounting' –Server 'EXCH2'

Similarly, you can use the **Add-PublicFolderClientPermission** cmdlet to add client permissions to a user or group. For example, to assign the author-client permission level to the mailbox user Jeff Smith to the same Accounting folder used in the previous example, you could execute the following command within the Exchange Management Shell:

Add-PublicFolderClientPermission –Identity '\Accounting' –Server 'EXCH2' –User 'Jeff Smith' –AccessRights 'Author'

To remove the client permissions for Jeff Smith to the Accounting public folder on EXCH2, you can use the **Remove-PublicFolderClientPermission** cmdlet in place of the **Add-PublicFolderClientPermission** cmdlet as shown in the following Exchange Management Shell command:

Remove-PublicFolderClientPermission –Identity '\Accounting' –Server 'EXCH2' –User 'Jeff Smith' –AccessRights 'Author'

When you use the **Remove-PublicFolderClientPermission** cmdlet, you will be prompted to confirm the removal.

Configuring Administrative Permissions

Unlike client permissions, administrative permissions allow users within your organization to administer various aspects of the public folders they have been granted access to. Administrative permissions can only be assigned using the Exchange Management Shell.

In addition to setting client permissions on a public folder to restrict content usage, you can also grant *administrative permissions* to users for individual public folders, which allows users to perform public folder administrative tasks. If you need to delegate the administration of public folders, it is good practice to grant administrative permissions to users for specific public folders rather than add them to the Exchange Public Folder Administrator role because Exchange Public Folder Administrator role members can modify the public folders on any public folder database within your organization.

The administrative permissions that can be granted to public folders in Exchange Server 2007 are listed in Table 7-2.

Table 7-2

Public folder administrative permissions

ADMINISTRATIVE PERMISSION	DESCRIPTION
None	Used to denote no administrative permissions on a public folder.
ModifyPublicFolderACL	Can modify the client permissions on a public folder (excluding client permissions for Administrative groups such as Domain Admins).
ModifyPublicFolderAdminACL	Can modify the client permissions on a public folder for Administrative groups such as Domain Admins.
ModifyPublicFolderDeleted-ItemRetention	Can modify the time period for deleted item retention within the properties of a public folder.
ModifyPublicFolderExpiry	Can modify expiry information within the properties of a public folder.
ModifyPublicFolderQuotas	Can modify quota limits within the properties of a public folder.
ModifyPublicFolderReplicaList	Can configure replication for a public folder.
AdministerInformationStore	Can modify all other properties for a public folder that are not granted by administrative permissions other than AllExtendedRights.
ViewInformationStore	Can view public folder properties.
AllExtendedRights	Can modify any public folder properties.

Administrative permissions can only be set and managed using cmdlets within the Exchange Management Shell. By default, members of the Exchange Public Folder Administrator role, the Exchange Organization Administrator Role, or the Domain Admins group can configure administrative permissions on public folders.

To view the existing administrative permissions on a public folder, you can use the **Get-PublicFolderAdministrativePermission** cmdlet. For example, to view the existing administrative permissions on the Marketing public folder under the root of the default public folder subtree on the Mailbox server EXCH1, you could use the following command within the Exchange Management Shell:

Get-PublicFolderAdministrativePermission –Identity '\Marketing' –Server 'EXCH1' | Format-List

You can also add the **–Owner** option to the **Get-PublicFolderAdministrativePermission** cmdlet to list the owner for a specific public folder. The owner of a public folder is the creator of the public folder. If a member of an administrative group such as Domain Admins creates a public folder, the group becomes the public folder owner.

To assign administrative permissions to a user or group for a public folder, you can use the **Add-PublicFolderAdministrativePermission** cmdlet. For example, to assign Fred Jones full administrative permission to the Marketing public folder used in the previous example, you could execute the following command within the Exchange Management Shell:

**Add-PublicFolderAdministrativePermission –Identity '\Marketing' –Server 'EXCH1'
–User 'Fred Jones' –AccessRights 'AllExtendedRights'**

Administrative permissions that are set on a public folder are not inherited by subfolders unless you add the **–InheritanceType 'All'** option to the **Add-PublicFolderAdministrative Permission** command.

To remove the administrative permissions that were assigned to Fred Jones in the previous example, you can simply replace the **Add-PublicFolderAdministrativePermission** cmdlet with the **Remove-PublicFolderAdministrativePermission** cmdlet as shown in the following Exchange Management Shell command. You will be prompted to confirm the removal.

**Remove-PublicFolderAdministrativePermission –Identity '\Marketing' –Server 'EXCH1'
–User 'Fred Jones' –AccessRights 'AllExtendedRights'**

Configuring Public Folder Options

From within Outlook, you can configure public folder options that affect how public folders appear within Outlook, Entourage, and OWA as well as the types of items that you can create within a public folder. In addition, you can use public folder options to modify public folder item processing or specify a public folder moderator.

In addition to setting client and administrative permissions, there are a number of options that can be configured within the properties of a public folder including view options, public folder moderators, processing options, and forms. Moreover, these options can only be configured by accessing the properties of the public folder within Outlook.

If you right click a public folder within Outlook and select **Properties**, you can provide a description for the public folder that will appear in Outlook, Entourage, or OWA as shown in the properties of the Time Sheets public folder in Figure 7-13. In addition, you can select view options or click the **Folder Size** button to view the size in KB used by the public folder and its subfolders.

Figure 7-13

Viewing Public Folder
Properties in Outlook

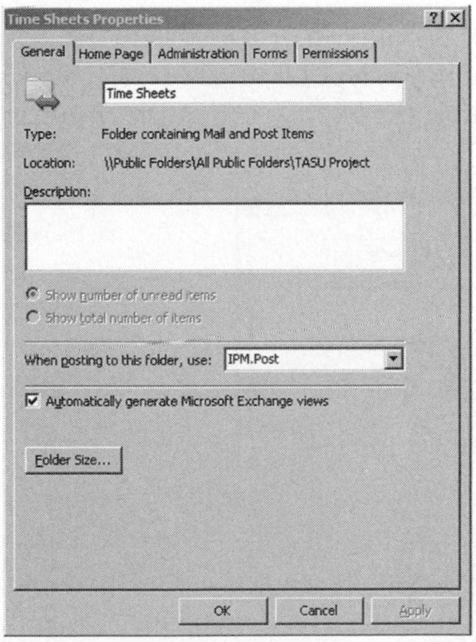

CONFIGURING FORMS

The General tab of public folder properties shown in Figure 7-13 allows you to select the default item type that is used when a user clicks the **New** button within Outlook, Entourage, or OWA. For public folders that allow email and post items, post items (IPM.Post) are created by default. However, you can also select a custom form that is based on an email message or post template. To create custom forms, you can use the ***Outlook Form Designer*** by navigating to **Tools** > **Forms** > **Design a Form** in the main Outlook window. Once your form has been designed, you can publish it and later select it using the drop-down box shown in Figure 7-13.

Say, for example, that your organization requires that project members post their time sheet information within the Time Sheets public folder. You could create a custom form called Time Sheet Form using the Outlook Form Designer to record the necessary information. Figure 7-14 shows a sample Time Sheet Form created in the Outlook Form Designer that is based on a standard post item template. After you are satisfied with the form layout, you can click the **Publish** button shown in Figure 7-14 and select the Time Sheets public folder.

Figure 7-14

Creating a New Custom Form

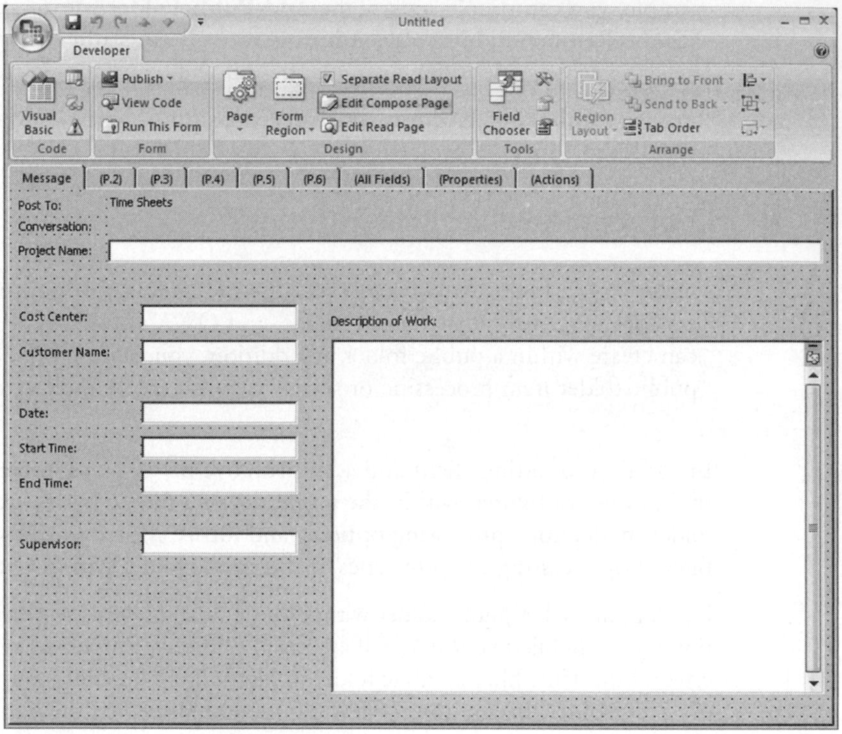

Now that you have published the Time Sheet Form to the Time Sheets folder, you can select Time Sheet Form as the default item type on the General Tab in the properties of the Time Sheets public folder shown in Figure 7-15. When project members need to post their time sheet

Figure 7-15

Specifying a Custom Form for a Public Folder

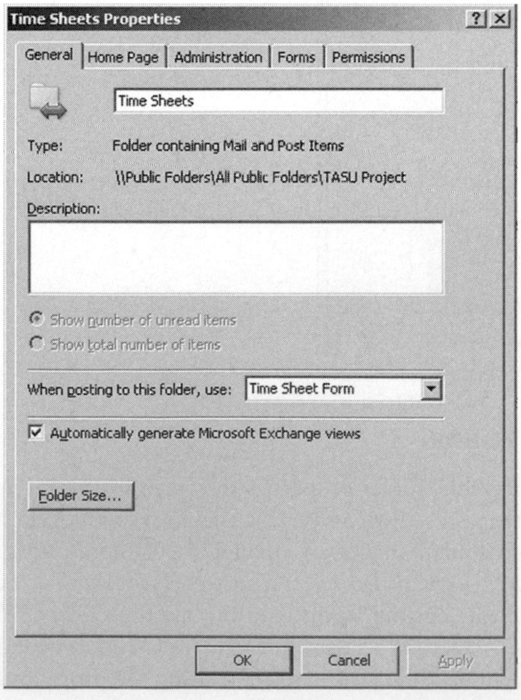

information, they simply select the Time Sheets folder in Outlook, Entourage, or OWA and click the **New** button. Instead of creating a new standard post item, they will receive the custom Time Sheets Form shown in Figure 7-16, where they can record the necessary time sheet information. When project members click the **Post** button in Figure 7-16, their time sheet information will be saved using the Time Sheet Form format as a post item within the public folder.

Figure 7-16

Creating a New Post Based on a Custom Form

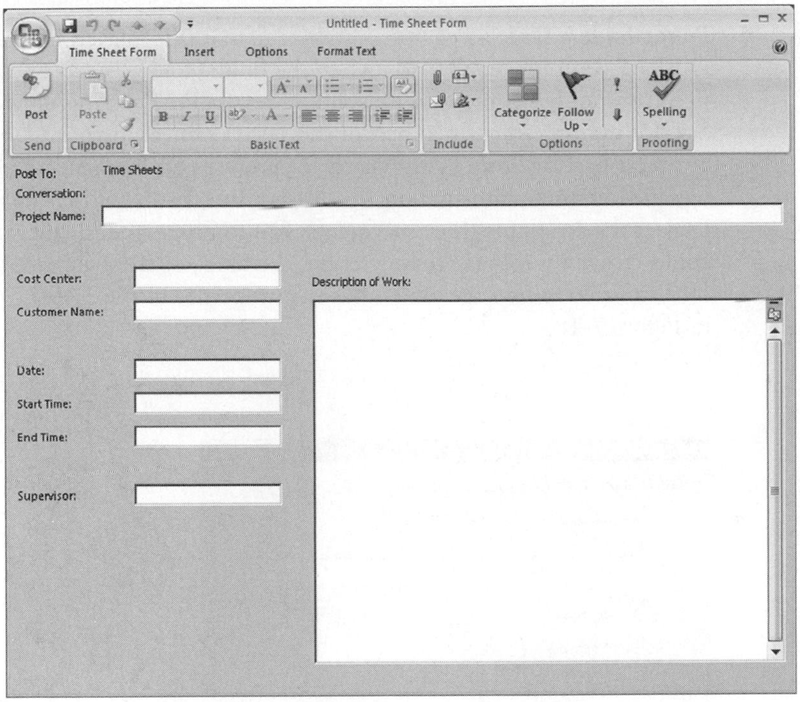

To ensure that project members do not see other time sheets, you could assign them contributor-client permissions to the Time Sheets folder. Similarly, to allow managers to view and manage the posted time sheets, you could assign them editor-client permission to the Time Sheets folder.

Although there can only be one default item type, a single public folder can contain multiple item types or forms. For example, if the Time Sheets public folder must contain post items based on the Time Sheet Form as well as standard post and message items, you can simply ensure that only those three item types are allowed on the Forms tab of public folder properties as shown in Figure 7-17.

Figure 7-17

Specifying Allowed Item Types and Forms

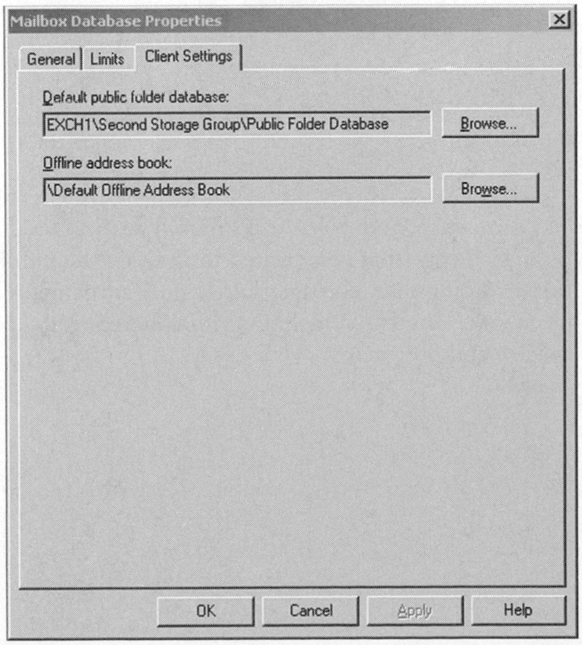

Because the Time Sheet Form is the default item type when creating a new item within the Time Sheets public folder, users must click the down arrow icon to the right of the **New** button in Outlook to select any additional item types such as standard post items or message items.

SETTING A HOME PAGE

Public folders can also contain a web page that is displayed instead of the item list within Outlook, Entourage, or OWA when the public folder is accessed. This is often useful when a public folder has subfolders that should be used for posting only certain types of information. Say, for example, that members of the TASU project in your company use public folders on a regular basis to store Gantt charts for project management, communicate guidelines, and record time sheet information. To support this, you could create a public folder called TASU Project that contains three subfolders: Gantt Charts, Guidelines, and Time Sheets. Next, you could create a web page that describes the usage of these subfolders and add the web page URL to the Home Page tab within the properties of the TASU Project public folder as shown in Figure 7-18.

Figure 7-18

Configuring a Public Folder Home Page

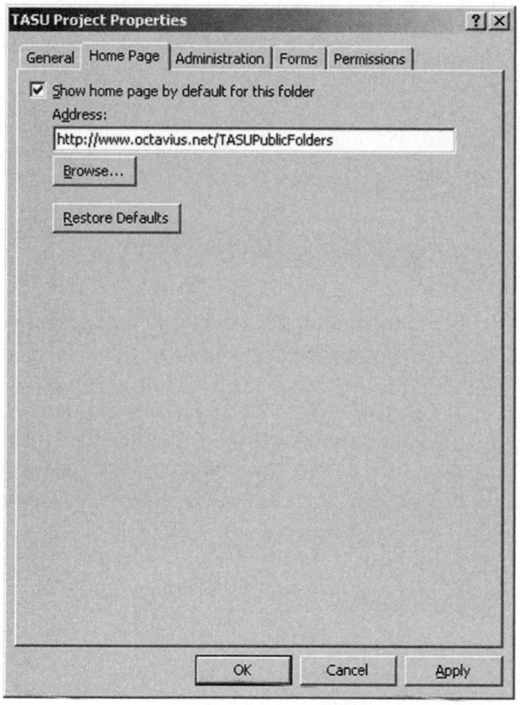

When Outlook, Entourage, and OWA users highlight the TASU Project public folder, they will be shown the web page that you created to indicate the public folder usage as shown in Figure 7-19. After reading the web page, TASU project members can then select the appropriate subfolder (Gantt Charts, Guidelines, Time Sheets) in the public folder list shown in Figure 7-19 to view and post items.

Figure 7-19

Viewing a Public Folder
Home Page

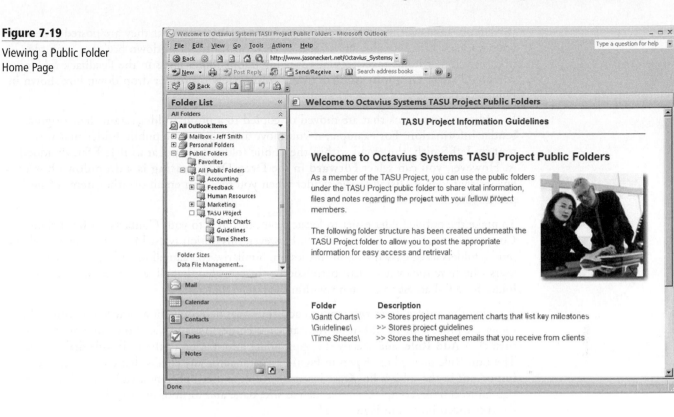

CONFIGURING ADMINISTRATIVE OPTIONS AND MODERATORS

The Administrative tab of public folder properties can be used to specify several different public folder options as shown with the Feedback public folder properties in Figure 7-20.

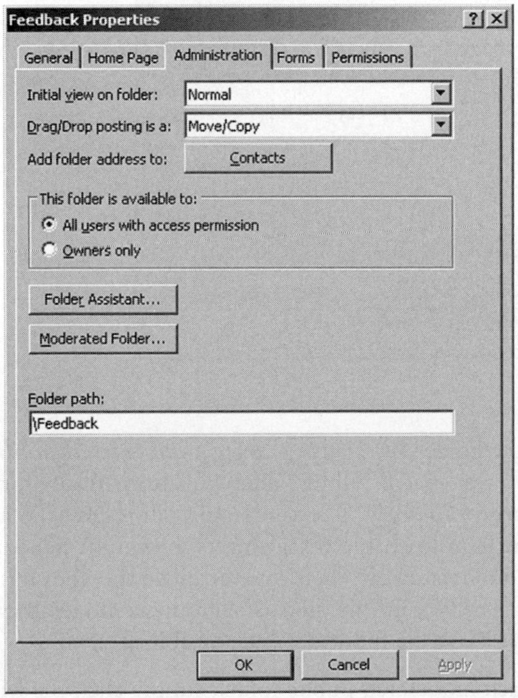

Figure 7-20

Configuring Administrative
Options

By default, items within public folders are listed in the order that they are posted unless you choose a different value in the **Initial view on folder** drop-down box. For example, to group similar items together when viewing public folder posts in the Feedback folder, you could select **Group by Subject** in the **Initial view on folder** drop-down box shown in Figure 7-20.

In addition, any items that are moved or copied to a public folder retain their original sender information. For example, if you move an email to the public folder that was sent by Jeff Smith, the email within the public folder will appear as if Jeff Smith added it. However, you can select **Forward** in the **Drag/Drop posting is a** drop-down box to ensure that you are listed as the sender when you move an email or other item to the public folder.

To make the public folder easier to locate, you can add it to your Contacts list by clicking the **Contacts** button shown in Figure 7-20. However, this option is used mainly by mail-enabled public folders as discussed later in this lesson. Similarly, you can allow public folder access to users who have the owner-client permission only, provided that all users who need to use the folder have full access to the items within the public folder.

By using the *Folder Assistant*, you can add rules that determine how new items within the folder are processed. To add rules, you can click **Folder Assistant** as shown in Figure 7-20, then click **Add Rule**, and specify the appropriate information in the Edit Rule dialog box. The Edit Rule dialog box shown in Figure 7-21 forwards any emails that contain the word **important** in the subject line (case insensitive) to the user Bob Jones. Rules can also be configured to contain complex criteria such as size, date, and form of information by selecting the **Advanced** button in Figure 7-21.

Figure 7-21

Adding a Folder Assistant Rule

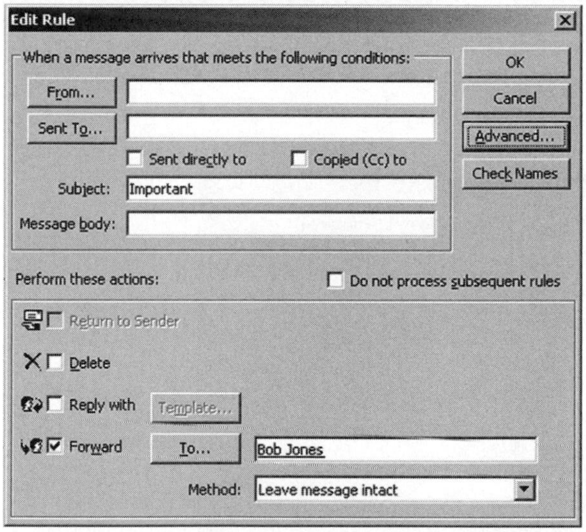

You can also use the Folder Assistant to create a *moderated public folder*. Any new items that are posted to a moderated public folder are automatically forwarded to a specific user called the *moderator* for review. The moderator will receive the item in his or her mailbox. After reviewing the item to ensure that it meets minimum standards and does not contain any profanity, the moderator can then copy or move the item into the public folder for others to access. You can specify multiple users or a group as moderators for a single public folder if several people must share the moderator responsibility.

To create a Feedback moderated public folder, simply click the **Moderated Folder** button as shown in Figure 7-20 and supply the appropriate information in the Moderated Folder window. The Moderated Folder window shown in Figure 7-22 forwards all new items posted to the folder to Adel Moore. Because Adel Moore is also listed in the Moderators dialog box, she can also move items back to the public folder after reviewing them.

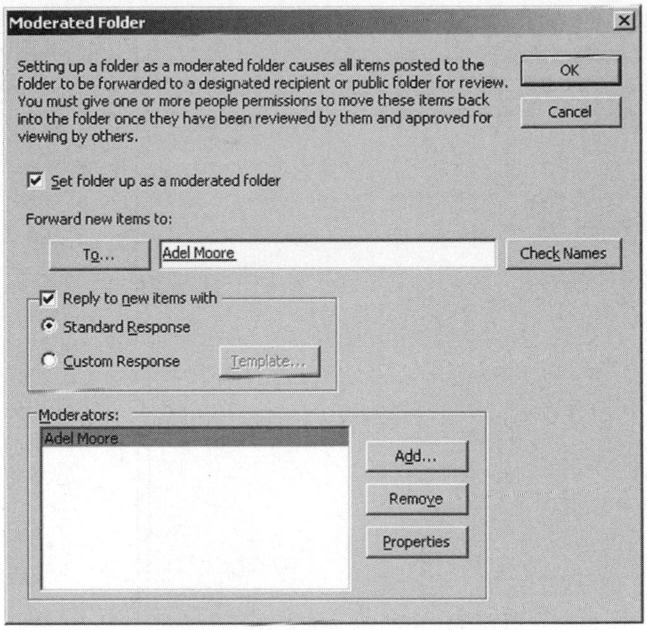

Figure 7-22

Configuring a Moderated
Public Folder

Any users who post a new item to the Feedback public folder will receive the following standard message to indicate that a moderator must first approve new items before they are posted:

Thank you for your submission. Please note that submissions to some folders or discussion groups are reviewed to determine whether they should be made publicly available. In these cases, there will be a delay before approved submissions can be viewed by others.

Alternatively, you can select **Custom Response** as shown in Figure 7-22 and click the **Template** button to modify the default message.

Configuring Public Folder Replication and Referrals

To ensure that public folders may be accessed across your Exchange organization, public folder databases replicate public folder lists and provide referrals to other public folder databases. In addition, you can configure the content of public folders to replicate between the public folder databases on the Exchange servers within your organization. You can configure public folder referrals and replication using the Public Folder Management Console and the Exchange Management Shell.

Recall that mailbox users who use an Exchange account in Outlook, Entourage, or OWA connect to the public folder database that is configured in their mailbox database properties. However, these same users will see all of the public folders within your Exchange organization under the All Public Folders node within Outlook or Entourage under the Public Folders section of OWA because public folder databases replicate their public folder lists to other public folder databases within the organization. The public folder list for a public folder database is called the *public folder hierarchy* and is replicated to all other public folder databases every 15 minutes by default. To modify replication of the public folder hierarchy, navigate to **Server Configuration** > **Mailbox** within the Exchange Management Console, access the properties of a public folder database, and highlight the Replication tab as shown in Figure 7-23.

To restrict replication to specific times, you can select a different **Replication interval** or click **Customize** to specify when public folder hierarchy replication will occur. Alternatively, you could use a **Replication interval** of Always Run as shown in Figure 7-23 and specify a different interval in the **Replication interval for "Always Run" (minutes)** dialog box. Public folder hierarchies are replicated using emails that are sent between Mailbox role servers. By default, if there is more than 300 KB of information, additional emails will be sent to relay the extra information. However, you can change this size limit using the **Replication message size limit (KB)** dialog box in Figure 7-23.

When you create new public folders, the public folder hierarchy will be automatically replicated to all other public folder databases according to the information that you specified on the Replication tab of the public folder database.

ANOTHER WAY

You can also replicate the public folder hierarchy immediately by selecting the **Public Folders** node in the Public Folder Management Console and clicking **Update Hierarchy** in the action pane.

Once the public folder hierarchy has replicated, mailbox users who are configured to use a different public folder database will see the new public folder in their own public folder hierarchy and can access your new public folder using a *public folder referral*. By using public folder referrals, Mailbox role servers can redirect mailbox users to the appropriate public folder database that contains the correct public folder.

Using public folder referrals to access public folder content can be quite slow, especially if the target public folder database is on a remote Mailbox role server. As a result, you can configure frequently used public folders to replicate their item content to another public folder database. Mailbox users who are configured to use a target public folder database will now no longer need to use public folder referrals to access the information in the public folder because their public folder database contains a copy of the items. Public folders that are replicated between public folder databases are called *content replicas*. When new items are created in a content replica, the new items are replicated to all other content replicas.

To configure content replication for a public folder, you can highlight the public folder in the detail pane within the Public Folder Management Console, click **Properties** from the action pane and add the appropriate public folder databases to the Replication tab. The Marketing public folder shown in Figure 7-24 replicates its contents between the public folder databases on the servers EXCH1 and EXCH2.

Figure 7-24

Configuring Public Folder Content Replication

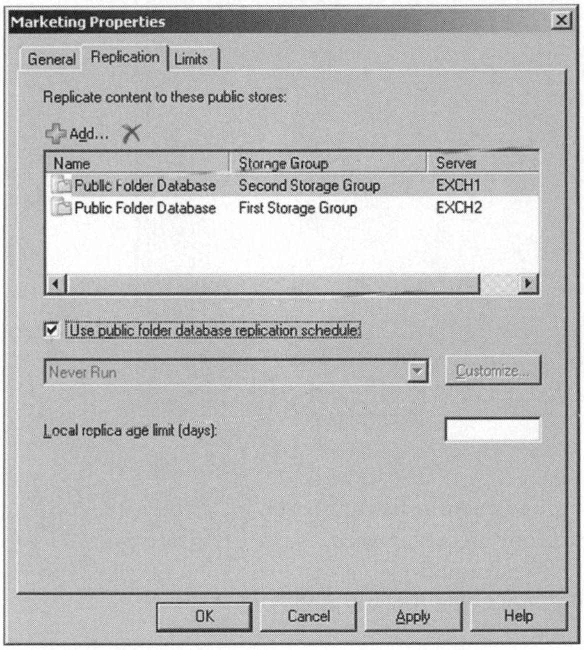

By default, public folders use the same schedule for replication specified on the Replication tab in the properties of their public folder database. However, for some public folders, you may need to deselect **Use public folder database replication schedule** and select or configure a different replication schedule. You can also configure the local public folder so that old items are automatically removed after a certain period of time using the **Local replica age limit (days)** dialog box in Figure 7-24. This will reduce the overall size of the local public folder as well as bandwidth that is needed to replicate its contents to other public folder databases.

Once you have configured content replication, you can highlight the public folder in the Public Folder Management Console and select **Update Content** from the action pane to replicate the contents immediately. Following this, new items that are added to the public folder will be replicated automatically using the schedule that you specified on the Replication tab of public folder properties.

Although content replicas reduce the number of public folder referrals, their replication will also use network bandwidth. As a result, it is important to keep the number of content replicas to a minimum. By default, if a mailbox user is given a public folder referral to a public folder that has content replicas, that mailbox user will be connected to the closest content replica using the site information stored in Active Directory (AD). Alternatively, you can manually choose the replicas that your Mailbox role server will refer mailbox users to using the Public Folder Referral tab of public folder database properties as shown in Figure 7-25.

Figure 7-25

Configuring Referrals on a
Public Folder Database

Public Folder Database Properties

General | Replication | Limits | Public Folder Referral

○ Use Active Directory site costs
○ Use custom list

⊕ Add...   ✎ Edit...   ✕

Name	Cost	

OK   Cancel   Apply   Help

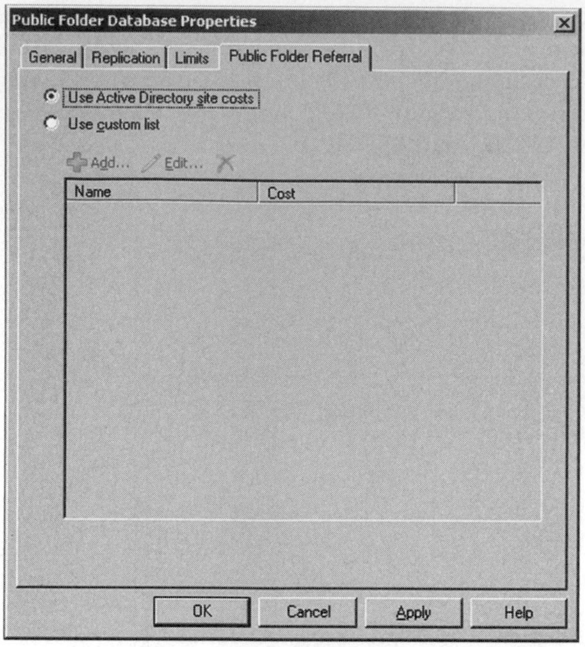

After selecting **Use custom list** in Figure 7-25, you can add the appropriate Mailbox servers and assign each one a cost between 1 and 100. Users who need access to a public folder that is not stored on your public folder database will be referred to the Mailbox server with the lowest cost that holds the desired public folder.

THE COMMAND LINE WAY

You can also use cmdlets within the Exchange Management Shell to configure and manage public folder replication. To configure the replication of the public folder hierarchy on your public folder databases, you can use the **Set-PublicFolderDatabase** cmdlet. For example, to specify that the public folder hierarchy in the Public Folder Database on your Exchange server replicates between 6:00 p.m. Saturday and 8:00 a.m. Sunday at 15-minute intervals and allows you to view the existing client permissions on the Accounting public folder under the root of the default public folder subtree on the Mailbox server EXCH2, you could use the following command within the Exchange Management Shell:

Set-PublicFolderDatabase –Identity 'Public Folder Database' –ReplicationSchedule 'Saturday.6:00PM-Sunday.8:00AM'

You can use different time formats alongside the **–ReplicationSchedule** option. For example, **'Sun.18:00-Sun.8:00'** would also specify replication between 6:00 p.m. Saturday and 8:00 a.m. Sunday, and **'Always'** would replicate at all times at 15-minute intervals. If your organization has multiple public folder databases and referrals are often granted to content in other databases, you can also use the **–CustomReferralServerList** option to manually specify the servers used during referrals and their costs. To configure the Public Folder Database on your Exchange server to send public folder referrals only to the server EXCH1 (cost=5) and EXCH2 (cost=10), you could run the following command:

Set-PublicFolderDatabase –Identity 'Public Folder Database' -CustomReferralServerList 'EXCH1:5','EXCH2:10'

To replicate the public folder hierarchy immediately, you can use the **Update-PublicFolderHierarchy** cmdlet. For example, to replicate the public folder hierarchy on the server EXCH1, you could run the following command in the Exchange Management Shell:

Update-PublicFolderHierarchy –Server 'EXCH1'

Additionally, you can configure content replicas for public folders using the **Set-PublicFolder** cmdlet. For example, to add replicas of the Marketing public folder under the root of the default public folder subtree on your Mailbox role server to the servers EXCH1 and EXCH2 using the replication schedule defined in your public folder database, you could execute the following command within the Exchange Management Shell:

Set-PublicFolder –Identity '\Marketing' –Replicas 'EXCH1,EXCH2' -UseDatabase ReplicationSchedule $true

If you decide to later specify a different replication schedule for the Marketing public folder of 7:00 to 9:00 p.m. on Saturday, you can run the following command within the Exchange Management Shell:

Set-PublicFolder –Identity '\Marketing' –ReplicationSchedule 'Saturday.7:00PM-Saturday.9:00PM'

The time formats that you can use following the **–ReplicationSchedule** option to the **Set-PublicFolder** cmdlet are identical to those for the same option in the **Set-PublicFolderDatabase** cmdlet. In addition, you can manually force content replication of a public folder by using the **Update-PublicFolder** cmdlet. To replicate the contents of the Marketing folder under the root of the default public folder subtree on the server EXCH1, you can run the following command within the Exchange Management Shell:

Update-PublicFolder –Identity '\Marketing' –Server 'EXCH1'

The Exchange Management Shell can also be used to control public folder replication across the entire Exchange organization. You can use the **Suspend-PublicFolderReplication** cmdlet without any options or arguments to temporarily stop all public folder replication in your Exchange organization. Afterwards, you can run the **Resume-PublicFolderReplication** cmdlet to resume public folder replication in your Exchange organization.

For a full list of options to the cmdlets mentioned in this section, search for the appropriate cmdlet in the Exchange Server 2007 Help.

Configuring Public Folder Limits

As with mailboxes, you can specify space usage and deletion limits for public folders to save space on the Mailbox servers within your organization. Public folder limits can be configured using the Public Folder Management Console or the Exchange Management Shell.

Depending on their usage and function, public folders may contain a large number of items, and these items could utilize a large amount of storage space on the Mailbox role servers within your organization. Some organizations implement a dedicated Mailbox role server that only contains a public folder database to store the public folders within the organization. This prevents public folder growth from affecting the mailbox databases used to store emails.

Other organizations that are unable to implement a dedicated public folder server store their public folder databases on the same Mailbox role servers that host mailbox databases. In this situation, it is good practice to store the public folder database and mailbox databases on each Mailbox role server on separate hard disks or RAID arrays. This prevents public folders from using hard disk space that may be required for email storage.

Regardless of public folder database structure, you should implement storage limits for the public folders within a public folder database to prevent unnecessary disk space usage. Although you can implement these storage limits using the Limits tab of the public folder database as discussed in Lesson 4, "Configuring a New Exchange Server," they are often configured on a public folder level because different public folders will likely require different storage limits.

To configure storage limits for a single public folder, highlight the public folder in the detail pane within the Public Folder Management Console, click **Properties** in the action pane and highlight the Limits tab. By default, public folders are configured to use the limits set on the Limits tab of their public folder database, but you can override this by supplying the appropriate values as shown for the Feedback public folder in Figure 7-26.

Figure 7-26

Configuring Public Folder
Limits

Feedback Properties

General | Replication | Limits

Storage quotas

☐ Use database quota defaults

☑ Issue warning at (KB):   204800

☑ Prohibit post at (KB):   256000

☑ Maximum item size (KB):   2048

Deleted item retention

☐ Use database retention defaults

Retain deleted items for (days):   1

Age limits

☐ Use database age defaults

Age limit for replicas (days):   7

OK   Cancel   Apply   Help

In Figure 7-26, the maximum size of a posted item is 2 MB (2048 KB). In addition, when the total size of the posts in the Feedback folder reaches 200 MB (204800 KB), the owner of the public folder receives an email indicating that the limit has been reached. When the total size of posts reaches 250 MB (256000 KB), users receive an error message when attempting to add items to the public folder and the public folder owner receives an additional email from the system indicating the limit.

The owner of a public folder is the creator of the public folder. If a member of an administrative group such as Domain Admins creates a public folder, the group becomes the public folder owner. If the Marketing public folder exists under the root of the default public folder subtree on the server EXCH1, you can use the following command within the Exchange Management Shell to view its owner:

Get-PublicFolderAdministrativePermission –Identity '\Marketing' –Server 'EXCH1' –Owner | Format-List

Figure 7-26 also indicates that items received from content replicas of the Feedback public folder are automatically deleted after 7 days to save space. Items that are deleted from a public folder are not permanently deleted immediately. Instead, public folder databases retain deleted items for 14 days by default. You can override this limit by specifying the appropriate number on the Limits tab of a public folder. The Feedback public folder shown in Figure 7-26 retains deleted items for 1 day.

TAKE NOTE*

To recover deleted items from within Outlook or Entourage, simply navigate to **Tools** > **Recover Deleted Items** and select the deleted items that you wish to recover. To recover deleted items within OWA, click **Options** in the upper right corner, select **Deleted Items** under the Options section in the left pane, and select the deleted items that you wish to recover.

THE COMMAND LINE WAY

You can also use the **Set-PublicFolder** cmdlet within the Exchange Management Shell to configure public folder limits. For example, to set the same limits for the \Feedback folder shown in Figure 7-26, you could use the following command within the Exchange Management Shell:

Set-PublicFolder –Identity '\Feedback' –MaxItemSize '2048' –StorageQuota '204800' –PostStorageQuota '256000' –AgeLimit '7' –RetainDeletedItemsFor '1'

■ Configuring Mail-Enabled Public Folders

↓
THE BOTTOM LINE

Public folders can be configured as recipient objects to accept email that is addressed to them. Instead of storing email in a mailbox database, public folders store email as items within their public folder database. You can mail-enable public folders and later manage them using the Public Folder Management Console or the Exchange Management Shell.

CERTIFICATION READY?
Configure public folders.
2.4, 3.5

Although you can store email within public folders, emails must be posted, moved, or copied to the public folder using Outlook, Entourage, or OWA. As a result, public folders are not recipient objects in their default configuration.

However, by mail enabling a public folder, you convert it to a recipient object that contains an email address. When you send email to the email address associated with the public folder, the emails are automatically posted to the public folder or sent to a moderator if a moderator is configured on the public folder. As a result, mail-enabled public folders do not require mailboxes.

Because mail enabled public folders are recipient objects, they will also have an associated object in AD as well as appear in the Global Address List. Moreover, mail-enabled public folders can be added to mail-enabled groups and custom address lists like any other recipient object.

There are several common uses for mail-enabled public folders. Some organizations use mail-enabled public folders to archive key emails. When users compose a new email that requires archiving, they can add the mail-enabled public folder to the **To** dialog box alongside other recipients. When the email is sent, a copy will be sent to the mail-enabled public folder recipient object and automatically stored in the public folder.

In addition, incoming email addressed to the mail-enabled public folder will also be stored in the public folder. Say, for example, that the Octavius organization encourages users who access their company Web site to send comments and feedback to feedback@octavius.net. By creating a public folder called Feedback and configuring it as a mail-enabled public folder with the email address feedback@octavius.net, the Feedback public folder will collect feedback emails from Web site users. Periodically, mailbox users within your organization who have the necessary client permissions to the public folder can view the feedback items within the folder, delete inappropriate items, and respond to other items as needed. In addition, you can configure *Send As permission* on the public folder to give certain mailbox users the ability to reply to email items within the folder as feedback@octavius.net. These mailbox users can then open an email item within a public folder using Outlook or Entourage, click the **Reply** button and specify feedback@octavius.net in the **From** dialog box. When the email is sent, it will appear as though it was from feedback@octavius.net rather than the actual mailbox user's email address.

➡ **MAIL ENABLE A PUBLIC FOLDER**

GET READY. Turn on the computer, and log in as the Administrator user account. Close any windows that appear on the desktop.

1. Click **Start, All Programs, Microsoft Exchange Server 2007**, and then click **Exchange Management Console**. The Exchange Management Console window appears.
2. In the console tree pane, highlight **Tools** and double click **Public Folder Management Console** in the detail pane. The Public Folder Management Console window appears.
3. Expand **Default Public Folders** in the console tree pane and highlight the folder that you wish to mail enable in the detail pane.
4. In the action pane, click **Mail Enable**.
5. Close the Public Folder Management Console and the Exchange Management Console.

TAKE NOTE*

To remove all email-related configuration for a mail-enabled public folder, you can select **Mail Disable** from the action pane.

You can also use the **Enable-MailPublicFolder** cmdlet within the Exchange Management Shell to mail enable an existing public folder. For example, to mail enable the Feedback public folder under the root of the default public folder subtree on your current Exchange server, you could run the following command within the Exchange Management Shell:

Enable-MailPublicFolder –Identity '\Feedback'

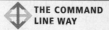
THE COMMAND LINE WAY

Alternatively, you can remove all email-related attributes from a public folder by using the **Disable-MailPublicFolder** cmdlet. For example, to remove all email attributes from the Feedback public folder used in the previous example, you could run the following command within the Exchange Management Shell:

Disable-MailPublicFolder –Identity '\Feedback'

CONFIGURE SEND AS PERMISSION FOR A MAIL-ENABLED PUBLIC FOLDER

GET READY. Turn on the computer, and log in as the Administrator user account. Close any windows that appear on the desktop.

1. Click **Start**, **All Programs**, **Microsoft Exchange Server 2007**, and then click **Exchange Management Console**. The Exchange Management Console window appears.

2. In the console tree pane, highlight **Tools** and double click **Public Folder Management Console** in the detail pane. The Public Folder Management Console window appears.

3. Expand **Default Public Folders** in the console tree pane and highlight the folder that you wish to configure Send As permission for in the detail pane.

4. In the action pane, click **Manage Send As Permission**. The Manage Send As Permission screen appears as shown in Figure 7-27.

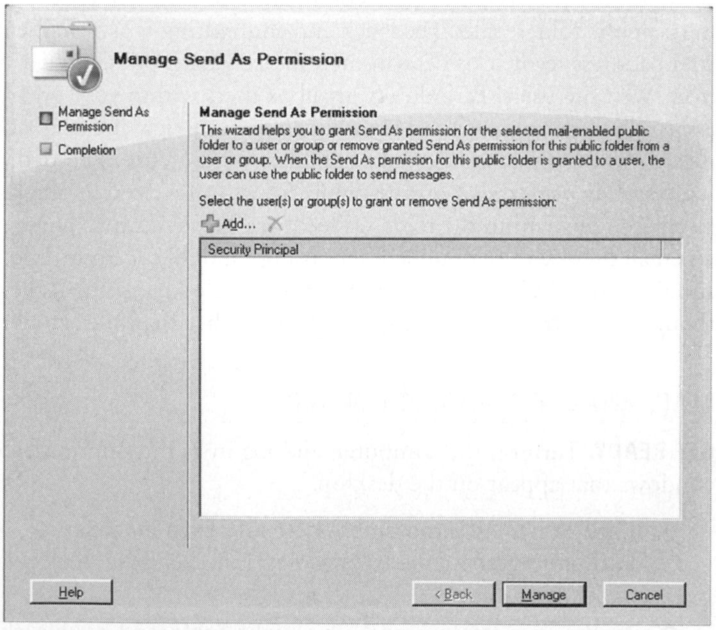

Figure 7-27

Configuring Public Folder Send As Permissions

Manage Send As Permission

Manage Send As Permission
This wizard helps you to grant Send As permission for the selected mail-enabled public folder to a user or group or remove granted Send As permission for this public folder from a user or group. When the Send As permission for this public folder is granted to a user, the user can use the public folder to send messages.

Select the user(s) or group(s) to grant or remove Send As permission:

Add... ✕

Security Principal

Help   < Back   Manage   Cancel

5. Click **Add**. Select the appropriate user or group in the Select User or Group window that appears and click **OK**.

6. Click **Manage**. The Completion page appears.

7. Click **Finish**. Close the Public Folder Management Console and the Exchange Management Console.

You can also use the **Add-ADPermission** cmdlet within the Exchange Management Shell to grant the Send As permission to a user or group for a public folder. The following command will assign Jeff Smith the Send As permission to the Feedback public folder when executed in the Exchange Management Shell:

Add-ADPermission –Identity 'Feedback' -User 'Jeff Smith' -ExtendedRights 'Send As'

It is important that you do not specify the path to the public folder when using the **Add-ADPermission** cmdlet as it only searches AD for the object name. To list the users and groups that have Send As permission for the Feedback public folder, you can use the **Get-ADPermission** cmdlet as shown:

Get-ADPermission –Identity 'Feedback' | Format-List User,ExtendedRights

Use the **Remove-ADPermission** cmdlet from within the Exchange Management Shell as shown to remove the Send As permission granted to Jeff Smith for the Feedback folder. You will be prompted to confirm the removal.

Remove-ADPermission –Identity 'Feedback' -User 'Jeff Smith' -ExtendedRights 'Send As'

THE COMMAND LINE WAY

You can access the properties of a mail-enabled public folder within the Public Folder Management Console; you will see the same General, Replication, and Limits tabs present in all public folder properties. However, you will also see Exchange General, E-Mail Addresses, Member Of, and Mail Flow Settings tabs as shown in Figure 7-28. These tabs contain the same recipient object attributes that you have examined in Chapter 5, "Working with Recipient Objects."

Figure 7-28

Mail-Enabled Public Folder Properties

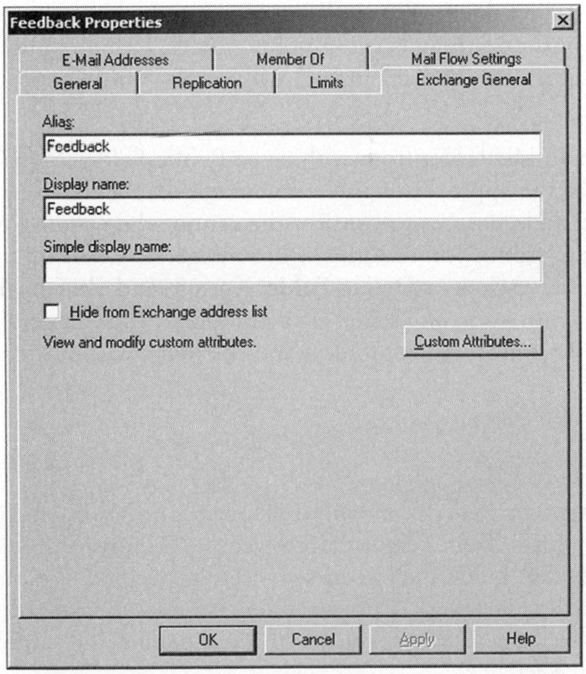

On the Exchange General tab, you can set the Alias and Display Name information as well as specify up to 15 custom attributes and hide the public folder from address lists. The Member Of tab lists groups to which the mail-enabled public folder belongs, and the E-Mail Addresses tab lists the email addresses used by the public folder. Unless modified, the default email address policy automatically assigns an email address of alias@domainname to the public folder. The Mail Flow Settings tab allows you to configure delivery options such as forwarding and Send On Behalf permission as well as message size restrictions and allowed senders.

To set any email-related properties for a public folder, you can also use the **Set-MailPublicFolder** cmdlet within the Exchange Management Shell. For example, to set the first custom attribute to TASU and the maximum item send limit to 2048 KB for the TASU Project public folder under the root of the default public folder subtree on your current Exchange server, you could run the following command within the Exchange Management Shell:

Set-MailPublicFolder –Identity '\TASU Project' –CustomAttribute1 'TASU' –MaxSendSize '2048'

You can also use the **Get-MailPublicFolder** cmdlet to obtain email-related information for a public folder. For example, the following command in the Exchange Management Shell will display the name and first custom attribute set on each public folder in the public folder database on your Exchange server:

Get-MailPublicFolder | Format-List Name,CustomAttribute1

■ Removing Public Folders

↓
THE BOTTOM LINE

Provided that you have the appropriate permission, you can remove public folders and their contents using the Public Folder Management Console, the Exchange Management Shell, Outlook, Entourage, or OWA.

TAKE NOTE*

You must first mail disable a mail-enabled public folder before removing it.

Although public folder are typically created by users who have the appropriate client permission underneath an existing public folder, only members of the Exchange Public Folder Administrator or Exchange Organization Administrator roles can remove a public folder.

To remove a public folder from within the Public Folder Management Console, you can highlight the appropriate public folder within the detail pane, select **Remove** in the action pane, and click **Yes** to confirm the action when prompted. Alternatively, you can delete a folder from within Outlook, Entourage, or OWA by right clicking it, selecting the appropriate **Delete** or **Delete Folder** option, and clicking **Yes** to confirm the deletion. When you remove a public folder using Outlook, Entourage, OWA, or the Public Folder Management Console, all subfolders and the items within them are automatically removed as well.

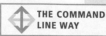

To remove a public folder from within the Exchange Management Shell, you can use the **Remove-PublicFolder** cmdlet. However, the **Remove-PublicFolder** cmdlet does not remove subfolders unless the **–Recurse** option is specified. For example, to remove the Feedback public folder and all of its subfolders under the root of the default public folder subtree on the server EXCH2, you could run the following command in the Exchange Management Shell:

Remove-PublicFolder –Identity '\Feedback' –Server 'EXCH2' –Recurse

After running this command, you will be prompted to confirm each deletion or press **A** to confirm all deletions. To test the removal of the Feedback public folder to see if you will receive any errors without actually removing the public folder, you can append the **–WhatIf** option to the previous command.

Working with Multiple Public Folders

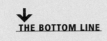

THE BOTTOM LINE

Like the recipient objects introduced in Chapter 5, "Working with Recipient Objects," you can create, configure, and manage multiple public folders using bulk management commands within the Exchange Management Console or by selecting several public folders within the Public Folder Management Console.

CERTIFICATION READY?
Implement bulk management of mail-enabled objects.
2.6

You can apply the bulk management techniques that you learned in Lesson 6, "Address Lists, Policies, and Bulk Management" to public folders and mail-enabled public folders. For most tasks, you can create CSV files and use the **Import-CSV** cmdlet within the Exchange Management Shell to send the information in the CSV file to the appropriate public folder cmdlet.

For example, to create the public folder structure shown in Figure 7-29, you could first create a CSV file called **C:\Public Folders.csv** that has two fields as shown in Figure 7-30. The first field could be called Name and list the names of each new public folder whereas the second field could be called Path and list the path that the public folder should be created under. Because public folder names can contain spaces, you should enclose each name and path within double or single quotes to ensure that the CSV file is processed correctly. In addition, public folders that need to be created under the root of the default public folder tree should list a path of "\".

Figure 7-29

Viewing Public Folder Structure

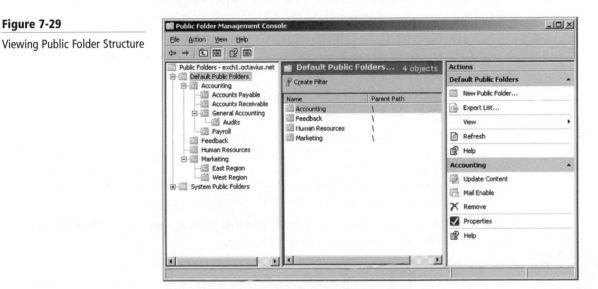

Figure 7-30

New Public Folders.csv File

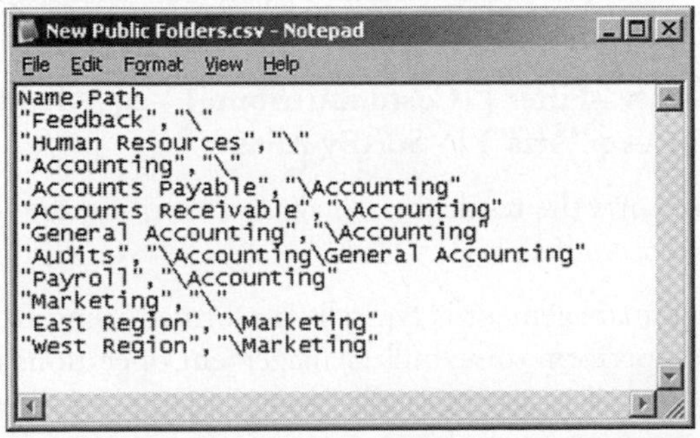

Next, you could run the following command within the Exchange Management Shell on the appropriate Mailbox role server to create the public folder structure:

Import-CSV 'C:\New Public Folders.csv' | ForEach-Object –Process { New-PublicFolder –Name $_.Name –Path $_.Path }

Once created, you can configure or manage these new public folders using bulk management commands. Because most cmdlets that configure and manage public folders require the path of the public folder, you could create a CSV file that lists each folder's path as shown in Figure 7-31 with the **C:\Public Folders.csv** file.

Figure 7-31

Public Folders.csv File

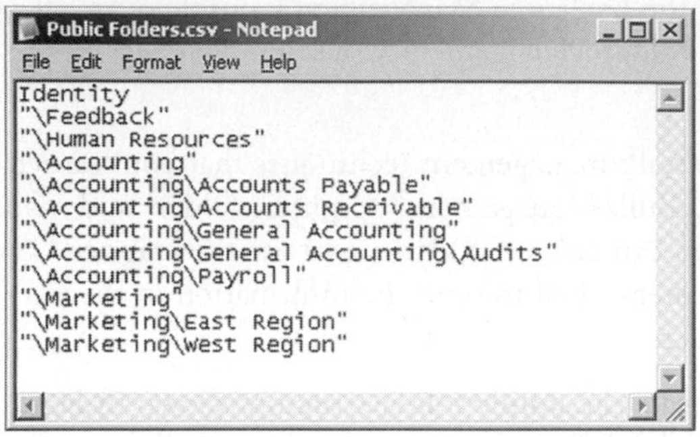

Next, to add content replicas for the public folders listed in the **C:\Public Folders.csv** file on the servers EXCH2 and EXCH3 and set a replication schedule between 10:00 p.m. Saturday and 6:00 a.m. Sunday, you could run the following command within the Exchange Management Shell:

Import-CSV 'C:\Public Folders.csv' | ForEach-Object –Process { Set-PublicFolder –Identity $_.Identity –Replicas 'EXCH2,EXCH3' –ReplicationSchedule 'Saturday.10:00PM-Sunday.6:00AM' }

In addition, you could use the following command in the Exchange Management Shell to mail enable the public folders listed in the **C:\Public Folders.csv** file:

Import-CSV 'C:\Public Folders.csv' | ForEach-Object –Process { Enable-MailPublicFolder –Identity $_.Identity }

To modify the email-related properties of the public folders listed in the **C:\Public Folders .csv** file, you must use the Set-MailPublicFolder cmdlet instead of the Set-PublicFolder cmdlet in the bulk management command. For example, to set the first custom attribute to Octavius for the mail-enabled public folders listed in the **C:\Public Folders.csv** file, you could use the following command within the Exchange Management Shell:

Import-CSV 'C:\Public Folders.csv' | ForEach-Object –Process { Set-MailPublicFolder –Identity $_.Identity –CustomAttribute1 'Octavius'

Not all public folder bulk management commands require the creation of a CSV file. For example, to view the mail-enabled public folders that have the first custom attribute set to Octavius or Arfa, you could use the **–Filter** option alongside the Get-MailPublicFolder cmdlet as shown in the following command:

Get-MailPublicFolder –Filter { (CustomAttribute1 –eq "Octavius") –or (CustomAttribute1 –eq "Arfa") } –SortBy Alias

This command also sorts the results by the alias name using the **–SortBy** option to the Get-MailPublicFolder cmdlet.

> TAKE NOTE*
>
> You can also create PowerShell scripts to manage public folders and mail-enabled public folders using the same syntax discussed in Lesson 6, "Address Lists, Policies, and Bulk Management."

Although most bulk management is typically performed using Exchange Management Shell commands, you can perform some bulk management operations using the Public Folder Management Console. You can optionally create and apply a filter in the detail pane of the Public Folder Management Console to narrow the list of public folders. Next, you can highlight several public folders within Public Folder Management Console while holding down the Shift or Ctrl keys and select **Update Content**, **Mail Enable**, **Mail Disable,** or **Remove** from the action pane to perform the related action.

SUMMARY SKILL MATRIX

IN THIS LESSON YOU LEARNED:

- Public folders provide a flexible means of storing email, calendar, journal, note, post, form, and task items within your organization for access by Outlook, Entourage, and OWA mailbox users. Public folders are also used to store calendaring, configuration information, and OABs for Outlook 2003, Entourage 2004, and earlier MAPI clients.

- Public folders are created within the default public folder subtree in a public folder database on the Mailbox role servers within your organization. The system public folder subtree stores public folders used internally by Exchange and should not be modified.

- When using OWA or an Exchange account in Outlook or Entourage, mailbox users automatically connect to the public folder database configured within their mailbox database properties.

- To create, configure, and manage public folders, you must be a member of the Exchange Public Folder Administrator role or the Exchange Organization Role as well as a local Administrator on the Mailbox role server that holds the public folder database.

- Client permissions are used to restrict access to public folder content whereas administrative permissions may be used to delegate administrative control to public folders.

- Custom forms can be used alongside public folders to create items that meet organizational needs.

- Public folders can contain custom view options as well as a home page that identifies the contents of subfolders.

- You can use the Folder Assistant to create filters that control the processing of items that are added to public folders. In addition, public folders may be configured to forward email to moderators who approve content before it is posted.

- Public folder hierarchies are replicated among the public folder databases within your organization. Users who need to connect to remote public folders are automatically referred to them by their public folder database server. You can also configure public folders to replicate their contents to other public folder databases as well as restrict the times for replication.

- To conserve space within a public folder database, you can specify limits for each public folder as necessary.

- Public folders may be mail enabled in order to receive email from other recipient objects. These emails are stored within the public folder alongside other items.

- The Public Folder Management Console is a graphical utility that may be used to create, configure, and manage public folders. It provides an alternative to the public folder cmdlets available within the Exchange Management Shell. In addition to these utilities, public folders can be created, configured, and removed within Outlook, Entourage, and OWA client utilities. Public folder options such as forms, home pages, view options, filters, and moderators can only be configured using Outlook clients.

- You can use the Public Folder Management Console or cmdlets within the Exchange Management Shell to perform bulk management of public folders. Public folder bulk management also supports the use of CSV files and the creation of PowerShell scripts.

Knowledge Assessment

Fill in the Blank

Complete the following sentences by writing the correct word or words in the blanks provided.

1. Before using public folders within _____, you must first configure a public folder server within the properties of the Exchange account.

2. The _____ is a graphical utility that may be used to create, configure, and manage public folders and is only available in Exchange Server 2007 SP1 and later.

3. To configure new public folder administrative permissions, you must use the _____ cmdlet within the Exchange Management Shell.

4. The _____ client permission grants all permissions to the content within public folders except for the ability to modify permissions.

5. To grant all administrative permissions on a public folder to a user, you can assign the _____ administrative permission to that user.

6. The _____ tab of public folder properties within Outlook may be used to configure how items are processed when moved or copied to a public folder.

7. When emails are sent to a mail-enabled public folder, they are stored within the public folder or forwarded to a _____, if one is configured.

8. To force content replication for a specify folder, you can select the appropriate folder within the Public Folder Management Console and select the _____ action.

9. You can specify a maximum item size for public folder posts on the _____ tab of public folder properties within the Public Folder Management Console.

10. The _____ can be used to create rules that specify how new posted items are processed within a public folder.

Multiple Choice

Circle the letter that corresponds to the best answer.

1. When you create a new public folder using the Public Folder Management Console, which of the following item types can be created in the public folder by default? (Choose all that apply.)
   a. email   b. calendar
   b. post   d. note

2. Which of the following client permission levels allows you to add items to a public folder but not view or manage other items that are in the public folder?
   a. contributor   b. author
   c. publishing author   d. editor

3. You wish to ensure that Bob Jones can modify the permissions that are set on the Comments public folder but not modify any permissions that have been assigned to Exchange administrators. Which administrative permission should you assign to Bob Jones for the Comments public folder?
   a. ModifyPublicFolderClientPermissions
   b. ModifyPublicFolderPermissions
   c. ModifyPublicFolderAdminACL
   d. ModifyPublicFolderACL

4. Which of the following MAPI clients use public folders to obtain OABs and calendaring information? (Choose all that apply.)
   a. Entourage 2004b   b. Outlook 2007
   c. Outlook 2003   d. Entourage X

5. Which of the following Exchange Management Shell commands will display all the public folders under the default public folder subtree on your current Exchange server?
   a. List-PublicFolder "\"
   b. Get-PublicFolder "\"
   c. List-PublicFolder –All
   d. Get-PublicFolder –Recurse | Format-List Name

6. You have recently opened a post item within a public folder using your Outlook MAPI client and wish to reply to the person who created the post item. Which button can you use to reply to the creator of the post item by posting a reply post item to the public folder rather than emailing the sender?
   a. Reply   b. Post Reply
   c. Create Reply   d. New

7. The arfa.com organization has a mail-enabled public folder called HRComments that stores comments and questions from users within the organization. As an HR manager, you plan on replying to some of these comments and questions but do not wish to let the sender know that the reply came from your email address. What permission must you have to the public folder to reply to comments and questions as HRComments@arfa.com?
   a. Owner   b. Send As
   c. Send On Behalf   d. Full Control

8. Your public folder database is quickly using the available space on your Mailbox server. After some investigation, you notice that many of the public folders contain items that are several weeks old. You would like to ensure that items older than 7 days are automatically deleted from the public folders within the public folder database. What should you do?
   a. Specify a **Local replica age limit** of 7 days on the Replication tab of public folder properties
   b. Check **Items must be deleted after 7 days** in the properties of the public folder database.
   c. Apply a filter that deletes items after 7 days on the **Administration** tab of public folder properties in Outlook
   d. Configure a maximum retention limit of 7 days using the **Set-PublicFolder** cmdlet.

9. You wish to create a custom form for use with a public folder. All new posts should use this form by default. Which of the following actions should you perform to provide this functionality? (Choose all that apply. Each answer provides a part of the solution.)
   a. Publish the form to the appropriate public folder.
   b. Specify the new form on the General tab of public folder properties within Outlook.
   c. Add the form to the Allowed Forms section on the Forms tab of public folder properties within the Public Folder Management Console.
   d. Create a new form using the Outlook Form Designer.

10. Which of the following cmdlets can be used to mail enable a public folder?
    a. Mail-Enable
    b. Mail-EnablePublicFolder
    c. Enable-PublicFolder
    d. Enable-MailPublicFolder

True/False

Circle T if the statement is true or F if the statement is false.

T | F   **1.** Each Exchange server within your organization can only have a single public folder database that contains a single public folder tree.

T | F   **2.** The public folder hierarchy is replicated between all Exchange folders within your Exchange organization by default.

T | F   **3.** You can only specify a single moderator within the properties of a public folder.

T | F   **4.** Client permissions are used to provide access to the content within a public folder as well as the ability to create subfolders.

T | F   **5.** The owner of a public folder is the person who created the public folder by default.

T | F   **6.** A mail-enabled public folder can be deleted using the **Remove-PublicFolder** cmdlet within the Exchange Management Shell.

T | F   **7.** Public folder home pages must be configured using an Outlook client.

T | F   **8.** Although multiple forms may be associated with a public folder, only one form may be selected as the default post item.

T | F   **9.** Public folder content replicas are configured within the properties of the public folder database.

T | F   **10.** You can configure size limits for a public folder using the Public Folder Management Console, Outlook, or the Exchange Management Shell.

Review Questions

1. Explain the purpose of the system public folder subtree within public folder databases.
2. Explain how content replicas may be used to improve public folder performance and reliability as well as reduce network traffic.

■ Case Scenarios

Scenario 7-1: Designing a Public Folder Proposal

As a new Exchange administrator within your organization, you are shocked to find that public folders are not used for collaboration or storage by any users within the organization. Moreover, the other Exchange administrators do not understand the benefits of using public folders and have only deployed public folder databases to fit the needs of older MAPI clients that require them for normal operation.

Prepare a proposal that you can present to the other Exchange administrators during the next department meeting that outlines some of the benefits of using public folders as well as the configuration options that may be used to control public folder usage.

Scenario 7-2: Implementing a Public Folder Structure

After hearing your proposal in Scenario 7-1, your department has approved the deployment of public folders and asked you to create and configure public folders for content sharing for each of the departments within your organization. Until the exact public folder needs of each department are determined over the next few weeks, you will start by creating a single public folder for each department and granting permissions for all users within the department so that they can add and manage their own items. Over the next few weeks, public folder users will email their public folder needs to a public folder using the email comments@domainname. Items within this folder will be read by all members of your IT department and used to determine the next steps to implementing additional public folders within your organization.

Explain how you would perform these actions using the various utilities available in Exchange Server 2007.

Configuring Email Protocols and Transport Rules

LESSON SKILL MATRIX

TECHNOLOGY SKILL	OBJECTIVE DOMAIN	OBJECTIVE DOMAIN NUMBER
Configuring Transport Rules	Configure transport rules and message compliance.	3.3
Configuring Client Access Protocols	Configure client connectivity.	3.6
Configuring the SMTP Protocol	Configure client connectivity.	3.6

KEY TERMS

Autodiscover service
Availability service
basic authentication
bounce message
Delivery Status Notification (DSN)
digest authentication
Edge Rules Agent

forms-based authentication
iCalendar
Integrated Windows Authentication
message classification
Non-Delivery Notification (NDN)
Non-Delivery Receipt (NDR)
Non-Delivery Report (NDR)

Out of Office Assistant
remote domain
Spam Confidence Level (SCL)
transport rule
Transport Rules Agent
Windows Rights Management Services
X.509 certificate

■ Configuring Client Access Protocols

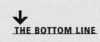 **THE BOTTOM LINE**

The CAS role servers within your Exchange organization provide access to email using a variety of different protocols including POP3, IMAP4, HTTP, MAPI, and Outlook Anywhere. The protocols used depend on the location of the email client computer as well as the email client programs used by users to access email. Moreover, each protocol offers unique configuration options that support its usage within the organization. Accordingly, a fundamental understanding of client access protocol configuration is key to deploying Exchange within any organization.

CERTIFICATION READY?
Configure client connectivity.
3.6

Configuring POP3 and IMAP4

POP3 and IMAP4 are commonly used to obtain email from Internet clients. You can configure the ports, authentication, encryption, protocol limits, and calendaring options used by these protocols on the CAS role servers within your organization. To configure the POP3 and IMAP4 protocols, you can use either the Exchange Management Console or cmdlets within the Exchange Management shell.

POP3 is the oldest and most common email protocol used by Internet email clients. Most ISPs offer POP3 services to their home and business clients, and all email client programs have built-in POP3 support.

POP3 is designed to download email from an email server to a client for viewing. Because POP3 only downloads email and does not open a persistent connection between the email client and server, POP3 is appropriate for clients with slow dial-up modem connections to the Internet.

When a POP3 client connects to an email server, it first checks for any new email since the last connection and then downloads it. Although this frees up space on the email server, it was designed for obtaining email from a single client computer. Say, for example, that you connect to your email server and download all of the email that you received during the day using POP3. Later, you connect to your email server from a different POP3 client and download any new emails you received since the last connection. These new emails are only stored on the POP3 client computer and not on the original computer that you used earlier. As a result, the emails you received during the day are spread across two different client computers and no longer remain on the email server.

To prevent this, most POP3 clients let you choose whether to allow email to remain on the email server after it has been downloaded. However, in most clients such as Outlook, Outlook Express, Entourage, and Windows Mail, this is not the default behavior and you must manually configure the account properties to allow emails to remain on the email server.

X REF

Configuring Outlook, Outlook Express, Entourage, and Windows Mail POP3 clients to store copies of email on the email server was covered in Lesson 4, "Configuring a New Exchange Server."

IMAP4 is a more sophisticated protocol than POP3. Instead of downloading email from the email server, it simply views emails that are stored on the email server using a persistent connection. Any emails viewed over an IMAP4 connection are cached to the email client and updated when the email client later reconnects to the email server. Say, for example, that you view emails over an IMAP4 connection and your IMAP4 email client caches those viewed emails to the client computer's hard drive. Next, you delete those same emails using a different MAPI client and then return to your IMAP4 client. When your IMAP4 client reconnects to the email server, it will notice that those items were moved to the Deleted Items folder and will update its own cache to match.

In addition, to save bandwidth, IMAP4 clients only view the headers of emails from the email server. The contents of the email are only retrieved from the email server and cached on the client computer when the email is opened.

Another important IMAP feature is native public folder support. Most IMAP clients also allow you to specify only those public folders that you want your IMAP client to synchronize automatically and download new items from to save bandwidth and storage.

After enabling the POP3 and IMAP4 services on your CAS role servers as discussed in Lesson 4, "Configuring a New Exchange Server," you can configure how CAS role servers respond to POP3 and IMAP4 requests. To do this within the Exchange Management Console, simply navigate to the **Server Configuration** > **Client Access** node, highlight the appropriate CAS role server in the detail pane, and select the **POP3 and IMAP4** tab in the work pane as shown in Figure 8-1. You must be a member of either the Exchange Organization Administrator role or the Exchange Server Administrator role for the CAS role server to configure POP3 and IMAP4 settings.

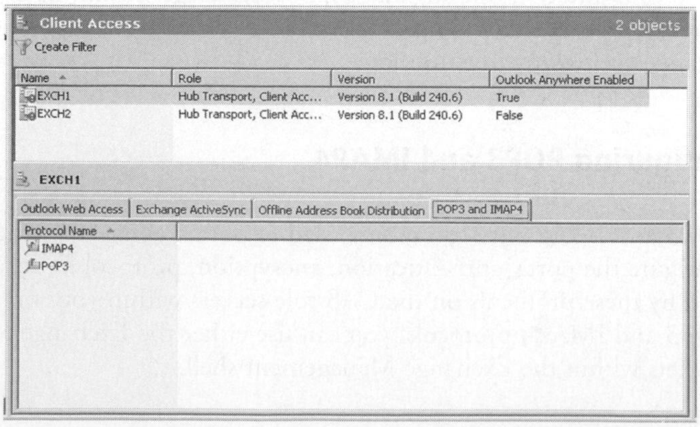

Figure 8-1

Configuring POP3 and IMAP4

> **TAKE NOTE** *
>
> You can only configure POP3 and IMAP4 within the Exchange Management Console using Exchange Server 2007 SP1 or later. If you run the original release of Exchange Server 2007, you must use cmdlets within the Exchange Management Shell to configure POP3 and IMAP4.

To configure the POP3 or IMAP4 protocols, you can highlight **POP3** or **IMAP4** in the work pane as shown in Figure 8-1 and select **Properties** from the action pane. The properties for both the POP3 and IMAP4 protocols are nearly identical. On the General tab of POP3 or IMAP4 properties, you can configure the banner that email client programs will receive when they first connect to the POP3 or IMAP4 server as shown for the properties of POP3 in Figure 8-2.

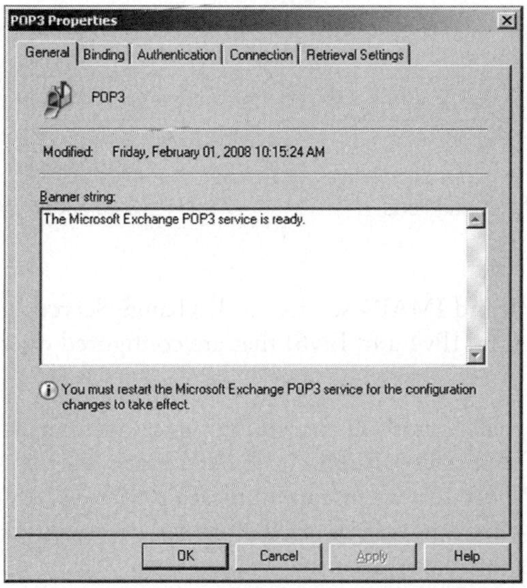

Figure 8-2

Configuring POP3 General
Settings

Although most email client programs do not display this message to the user, it is usually added to log files on the client computer and may assist in troubleshooting POP3 and IMAP4 connectivity problems. If the banner string shown in Figure 8-2 appears in the log file, it indicates that the email client program was able to successfully establish a connection to the POP3 service on the Exchange server. Because POP3 uses TCP port 110, you could also run the command **telnet server 110** (where server is the IP address or FQDN of the CAS role server) from a Windows command prompt on a client computer. If you see the banner string listed in Figure 8-2, the client computer is able to successfully interact with the POP3 service on your Exchange server. Alternatively, you could test an IMAP4 connection using the command **telnet server 143** (where server is the IP address or FQDN of the CAS role server) from a Windows command prompt on a client computer because IMAP uses TCP port 143 by default.

On the Binding tab of POP3 or IMAP4, you can configure your CAS role server to only listen on network interfaces that are configured with specific IP addresses as well as specify the ports that will be used by POP3 or IMAP4 connections. Figure 8-3 shows the default options on the Binding tab of POP3 properties, whereas Figure 8-4 shows the default options on the Binding tab of IMAP4 properties.

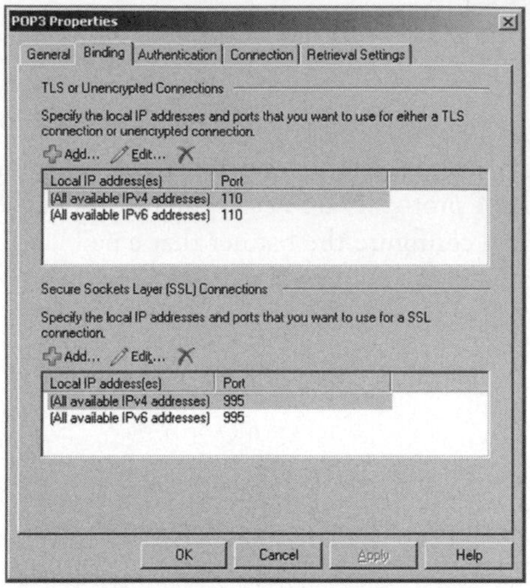

Figure 8-3

Configuring POP3 Interfaces and Ports

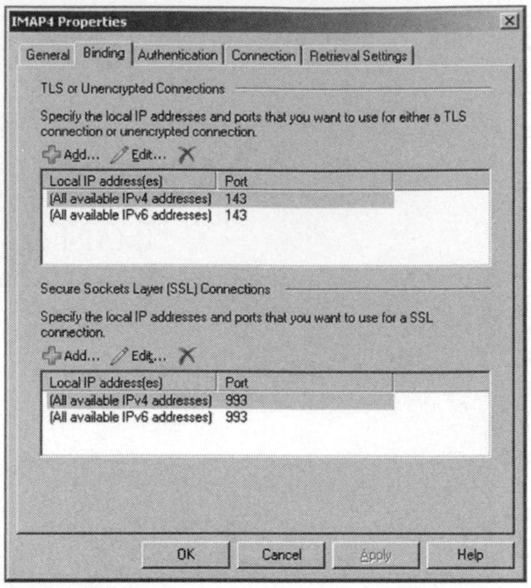

Figure 8-4

Configuring IMAP4 Interfaces and Ports

By default, the POP3 and IMAP4 services in Exchange Server 2007 are configured to listen to all IP addresses (IPv4 and IPv6) that are configured on network interfaces in your Exchange server.

POP3 email clients that do not use encryption typically contact the POP3 service on a CAS role server using TCP port 110. Similarly, IMAP4 email clients that are not configured for encryption use TCP port 143 when communicating with a CAS role server. However, you can configure email clients to encrypt POP3 or IMAP4 emails using either Secure Socket Layer (SSL) or Transport Layer Security (TLS).

SSL is the traditional technology used to provide encryption for POP3 and IMAP4 connections. SSL uses TCP port 995 for POP3S and TCP port 993 for IMAP4S by default. TLS is an enhanced version of SSL that can be used by newer email clients such as Outlook 2007 and Entourage 2008. Unlike SSL, TLS uses the same port as unencrypted traffic (TCP port 110 for POP3S and TCP port 143 for IMAP4S) by default.

Most Exchange servers only have a single network interface and contain clients that use the standard port numbers for POP3 and IMAP4. As a result, it is unnecessary to modify the settings on the Binding tab in most environments. However, if your Exchange server has several network interfaces and only services POP3 and IMAP4 clients on one of them using a nonstandard port, you can edit the default lines shown in Figure 8-3 and Figure 8-4 to reflect this. Simply click **Edit** in the appropriate section and specify a single IP address that the POP3 or IMAP4 service should bind to as well as a different port number to match the port number used by the POP3 or IMAP4 email clients.

X REF

Configuring certificates for use with SSL and TLS encryption is covered in Lesson 9, "Configuring Security."

In previous versions of Exchange Server, you needed to obtain an *X.509 certificate* in order to perform SSL or TLS encryption alongside the POP3 or IMAP4 service. However, Exchange Server 2007 automatically generates a sample X.509 certificate for use with SSL or TLS when you select the CAS role during the Exchange Server installation. This certificate is named according to your CAS role server's computer name and specified on the Authentication tab of both POP3 and IMAP4 properties. Figure 8-5 shows the Authentication tab of POP3 properties for the computer EXCH1. This sample certificate is only intended to provide support for SSL and TLS immediately following installation and should be replaced with a proper certificate.

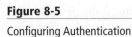

Figure 8-5

Configuring Authentication

POP3 Properties

General | Binding | Authentication | Connection | Retrieval Settings |

Logon Method

Specify the security settings to use for incoming connections.

○ Plain text logon (Basic authentication). No TLS connection is required for the client to authenticate to the server.

○ Plain text authentication logon (Integrated Windows authentication). No TLS connection is required for the client to authenticate to the server.

● Secure logon. A TLS connection is required for the client to authenticate to the server.

X.509 certificate name:

exch1

OK   Cancel   Apply   Help

Moreover, POP3 and IMAP4 clients must authenticate before obtaining email from a CAS role server. When a client authenticates to a CAS role server, the CAS role server contacts Active Directory (AD) to complete the authentication process. If the username and password supplied by the user are authenticated by AD, then the CAS role server will allow access to email for that user.

In Exchange Server 2007, clients are required to encrypt their logon credentials using TLS (Secure logon) as shown in Figure 8-5. If you select **Plain text logon (Basic authentication)** in Figure 8-5, email client programs will transmit the user's logon credentials to the CAS role server in plain text. In this case, anyone who can obtain a copy of the network traffic could potentially see the username and password of the user and should only be configured if the email client program does not support any other authentication method. Alternatively, if you select **Plain text authentication logon (Integrated Windows authentication)** in Figure 8-5, email client programs will encrypt the user's logon credentials using an NTLM hash or Kerberos before sending them to the CAS role server. However, this method requires that the email client computer be joined to the same AD domain as the Exchange server.

To modify connection settings for POP3, you can edit the default values on the Connection tab of POP3 properties as shown in Figure 8-6. Similarly, you can modify the default values on the Connection tab of IMAP4 properties to configure IMAP4 connections as shown in Figure 8-7.

POP3 Properties

General | Binding | Authentication | Connection | Retrieval Settings |

Time-out Settings

Authenticated time-out (seconds):   1800

Unauthenticated time-out (seconds):   60

Connection Limits

Maximum connections: 2000

Maximum connections from a single IP address: 2000

Maximum connections from a single user: 16

Maximum command size (bytes):   45

Command Relay

Proxy target port: 110

OK   Cancel   Apply   Help

IMAP4 Properties

General | Binding | Authentication | Connection | Retrieval Settings |

Time-out Settings

Authenticated time-out (seconds):   1800

Unauthenticated time-out (seconds):   60

Connection Limits

Maximum connections: 2000

Maximum connections from a single IP address: 2000

Maximum connections from a single user: 16

Maximum command size (bytes):   10240

Command Relay

Proxy target port: 143

OK   Cancel   Apply   Help

Figure 8-6

Configuring POP3 Connection Settings

Figure 8-7

Configuring IMAP4 Connection Settings

By default, POP3 and IMAP4 each allow up to 2,000 simultaneous connections per CAS role server. Although these 2,000 connections can be from a single IP address, only 16 of them can be from a single user. Furthermore, authenticated sessions will automatically end after 15 minutes (1,800 seconds) of inactivity, and unauthenticated sessions will automatically end after 60 seconds of inactivity. Unauthenticated sessions typically refer to the time period before a POP3 or IMAP4 client authenticates to the CAS role server.

By default, the POP3 service accepts POP3 requests that contain commands that are 45 bytes of size or less, whereas the IMAP4 service accepts IMAP4 requests that are up to 10 KB (10,240 bytes) in size. If your CAS role server receives a POP3 or IMAP4 request for email that resides in a mailbox on an Exchange 2003 server within your organization, it will redirect the request to the appropriate Exchange 2003 server using the port specified in the **Proxy target port** dialog box in Figure 8-6 and Figure 8-7.

The Retrieval Settings tab of POP3 or IMAP4 properties allows you to select the default email message format, sort order (Ascending or Descending), and calendar retrieval options for POP3 or IMAP4 connections. The Retrieval Settings tab of the default POP3 object is shown in Figure 8-8.

> **TAKE NOTE***
>
> You can configure the **Maximum connections** in Figure 8-6 and Figure 8-7 to accept up to 25,000 POP3 and IMAP4 connections per CAS role server.

Figure 8-8

Configuring Calendar and Format Settings

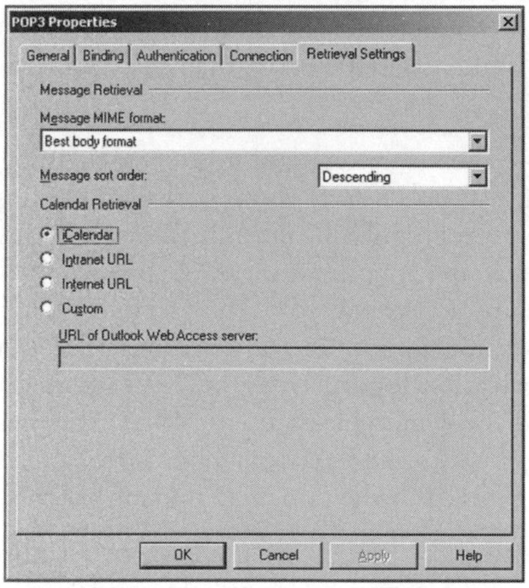

The Message MIME format drop-down box shown in Figure 8-8 allows you to select the same email message formats that you can configure within the properties of POP3 or IMAP4 on the Message Features tab of mailbox user properties as discussed in Lesson 5, "Working with Recipient Objects." By default, POP3 and IMAP4 email messages allow for Best body format, but you can choose Text, HTML, HTML and alternative text, Enriched text, as well as Enriched text and alternative text.

> **TAKE NOTE***
>
> If you specify POP3 and IMAP4 options on the Message Features tab within the properties of a mailbox user, those options will take precedence over any POP3 and IMAP4 options that you specify on your Exchange server.

The default method to obtain calendar information using POP3 or IMAP4 is the universal *iCalendar* standard. However, if you have Outlook 2007 or Entourage 2008 clients or later, you can specify that they obtain calendar information from an Intranet or Internet URL. Alternatively, you can select **Custom** in Figure 8-8 and specify the URL for OWA to obtain calendar information.

THE COMMAND LINE WAY

You can also use the **Set-POPSettings** cmdlet in the Exchange Management Shell to manage POP3 settings for the CAS role servers within your Exchange organization. Similarly, the **Set-IMAPSettings** cmdlet can be used to manage IMAP4 settings for the CAS role servers within your Exchange organization. For example, to set the maximum number of POP3 and IMAP4 connections to 25,000 on the server EXCH1, you could run the following commands in the Exchange Management Shell:

Set-POPSettings -Server 'EXCH1' –MaxConnections '25000'

Set-IMAPSettings -Server 'EXCH1' –MaxConnections '25000'

If you omit the **–Server** option to the cmdlets in the previous example, all CAS role servers will be affected. The Set-POPSettings and Set-IMAPSettings cmdlets can be used to configure any of the settings shown earlier within the properties of POP3 or IMAP4 in the Exchange Management Console. For more information on these cmdlets and their options, search for Set-POPSettings and Set-IMAPSettings within Exchange Server 2007 Help.

Configuring HTTP

Email clients typically access web-based email systems such as OWA using the Hypertext Transfer Protocol (HTTP). Like POP3 and IMAP4, you can configure protocol limits, ports, and authentication for HTTP as well as access restriction options and bandwidth limits. Although you can configure some HTTP options within the Exchange Management Console and Exchange Management Shell, some HTTP configuration must be performed using the Default Web site within the IIS Manager console.

Web-based email systems are fast becoming a common way of obtaining email on mobile computers because they only require a web browser. Client computers use their web browser to contact a web server that contains programs that allow you to retrieve and manage email from an email server as well as compose new emails that are sent by an email server. Moreover, web browsers communicate to these web servers using HTTP or HTTPS, which are unlikely to be restricted by firewalls. As a result, you can check email using a web-based email system from nearly any location and from free wireless connections when traveling with a mobile computer.

TAKE NOTE*

Although web-based email systems are common today, they are unlikely to replace email client programs because their interface, usability, and features are limited to those that can be displayed in a web page within the web browser. As a result, most organizations use web-based email systems as a backup method for obtaining email or for users who travel.

ANOTHER WAY

Recall that you can also use **https:// Mailbox_server/ exchange/username** or **https://Mailbox_server/ exchange** within the URL dialog box of a web browser to gain access to OWA.

In Exchange Server 2007, OWA is the program used alongside the Default Web site in IIS on each CAS role server to provide web-based email for clients with a web browser. OWA provides a Web site that allows users to obtain, manage, and compose emails that are then processed by the CAS role server that hosts OWA.

Moreover, the Default Web Site in IIS is configured to require SSL connections using an X.509 certificate that was generated during installation. As a result, users must use the URL https://CAS_server/owa in their web browser instead of http://CAS_server/owa when connecting to OWA in the default configuration. As with POP3 and IMAP4, the SSL certificate used by the Default Web Site is named for the server and only intended to provide support for HTTP+SSL (HTTPS) immediately following installation. Afterward, it should be replaced with a proper SSL certificate.

In Lesson 4, you learned how to configure OWA options such as WebReady document viewing and allowed file types using the **Server Configuration** > **Client Access** node within the Exchange Management Console. You can also configure the URL and authentication information used by OWA HTTPS clients by navigating to the same node within the Exchange Management Console as a member of the Exchange Organization Administrator role or the Exchange Server Administrator role for the CAS role server. Simply select the appropriate CAS role server in the detail pane, highlight **owa (Default Web Site)** under the Outlook Web Access tab in the work pane, and click **Properties** in the action pane. The General tab of owa (Default Web Site) properties allows you to set the default URL that internal and external clients will use when connecting to OWA as shown in Figure 8-9. For the server exch1.octavius .net shown in Figure 8-9, the default URL used by internal clients is https://exch1.octavius .net/owa. To allow for clients outside your organization to connect to OWA on your CAS role server using HTTPS, you must specify a URL in the External URL dialog box that users will use to connect. This URL must have a corresponding record in DNS and is automatically sent to the CAS role server in the HTTPS header from the web browser. If the CAS role server receives a different URL in the header, it will reject the HTTPS request. Consequently, if external HTTPS traffic must pass through a proxy server such as Microsoft ISA Server before it is forwarded to your CAS role servers, you must place the URL of the proxy server in the External URL dialog box in Figure 8-9 so that OWA does not reject the HTTPS request.

Figure 8-9

Configuring OWA URLs

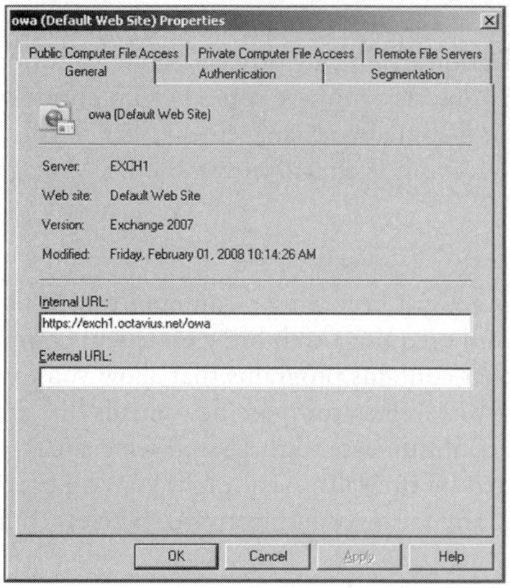

You can also configure the type of authentication method used by OWA on the Authentication tab of owa (Default Web Site) properties as shown in Figure 8-10. By default, OWA requires that users enter their credentials on the OWA logon form shown

Figure 8-10

Configuring OWA Authentication

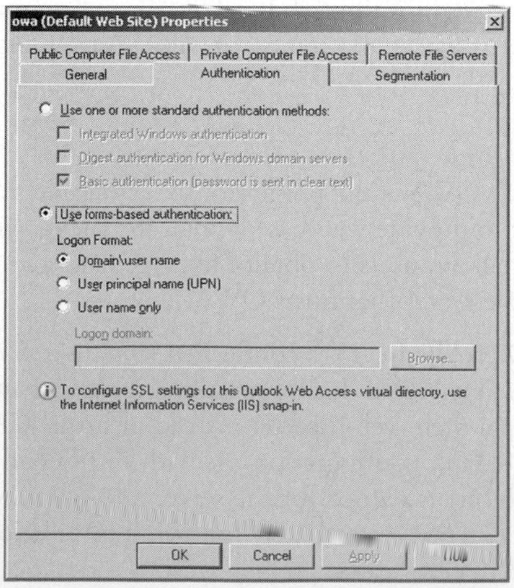

earlier in Figure 4-19. This type of authentication is called *forms-based authentication* and requires SSL. The default logon name format accepted on the OWA form is Domain\username (i.e., octavius.net\jeff.smith) but you can modify the format to use the UPN (i.e., jeff.smith@octavius.net) or the username only (i.e., jeff.smith). If you choose the username only format, you must click the **Browse** button in Figure 8-10 and select the domain that will be used for logons.

If you select **Use one or more standard authentication methods** in Figure 8-10, you can choose different logon methods to use instead of the OWA logon form shown earlier in Figure 4-19. *Integrated Windows Authentication* automatically passes your username and password to the CAS role server using an NTLM hash or Kerberos and requires that the client computer be joined to the same domain as the CAS role server. *Digest authentication* uses a digital hash to protect the password when sending the username and password to the CAS role server. *Basic authentication* sends the username and password to the CAS role server unencrypted and is a poor security practice if you are not using SSL on your CAS role server to protect HTTP traffic.

 TAKE NOTE*

To use digest authentication, user accounts must be configured to store passwords using reversible encryption on the Account tab of user account properties or within the Account Policies section of a GPO.

Because OWA uses the Default Web Site in IIS, you can configure other HTTP-related options within IIS Manager (**Start** > **All Programs** > **Administrative Tools** > **Internet Information Services (IIS) Manager**) provided that you are a member of the local Administrators group on the CAS role server. Expand the **Web Sites** folder under your CAS role server in IIS Manager, right click **Default Web Site**, and select **Properties**. On the Web Site tab of Default Web Site properties as shown in Figure 8-11, you can configure the port numbers and network interfaces used for HTTP connections. By default, HTTP connections are allowed on any IP address configured on network interfaces in your CAS role server. However, if your CAS role server has several network interfaces, you can direct IIS to only listen for HTTP connections on a single network interface by clicking **Advanced** and specifying a single IP address. Similarly, HTTP connections use TCP port 80 by default whereas HTTPS connections use TCP port 443. If the web browsers that connect to your CAS role servers use a nonstandard HTTP or HTTPS port, you can change these numbers. You can also modify the amount of time before idle HTTP sessions are automatically ended. The default is 120 seconds.

Figure 8-11

Configuring HTTP Interfaces and Ports

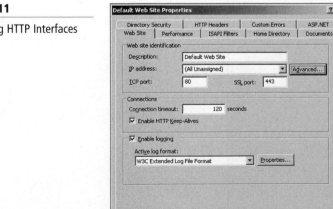

Additionally, you can limit the number of HTTP connections as well as the amount of bandwidth that HTTP traffic uses on your CAS role server using the Performance tab of Default Web Site properties as shown in Figure 8-12. Limiting the number and band-width of HTTP connections will prevent HTTP connections from adversely affecting the performance of other protocols on your CAS role server such as MAPI, POP3, and IMAP4.

Figure 8-12

Configuring HTTP Restrictions

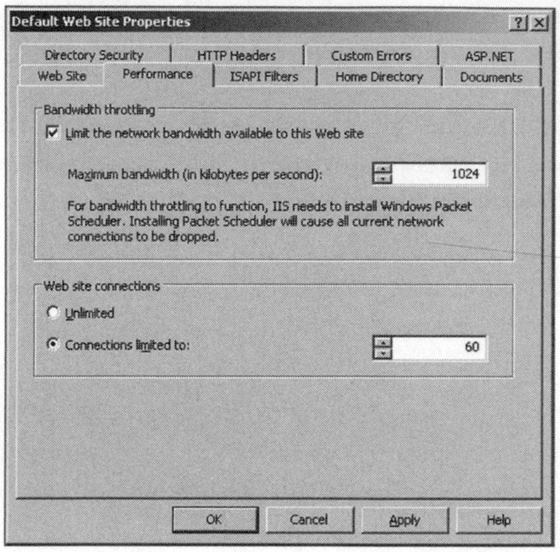

The Default Web Site listed in Figure 8-12 allows up to 60 concurrent HTTP or HTTPS connections and restricts the total bandwidth used by all 60 connections to 1024 KB per second. If you configure bandwidth throttling in Figure 8-12, you must also install the *Windows QoS Packet Scheduler*. To install the Windows QoS Packet Scheduler, you can navigate to the properties of your network interface (**Start** > **Control Panel** > **Network Connections** > **Connection_Name**), click the **Install** button and add the **QoS Packet Scheduler** service.

On the Directory Security tab of Default Web Site properties, you can configure authen-tication methods used by all virtual directories under the Default Web Site, IP address, and domain name restrictions, as well as the certificate used for SSL connections as shown in Figure 8-13. However, OWA authentication must be configured on the OWA virtual directory in the Exchange Management Console rather than within IIS Manager, and the default certificate configured in the Default Web Site should be replaced with a proper certificate.

Figure 8-13

Configuring Directory Security

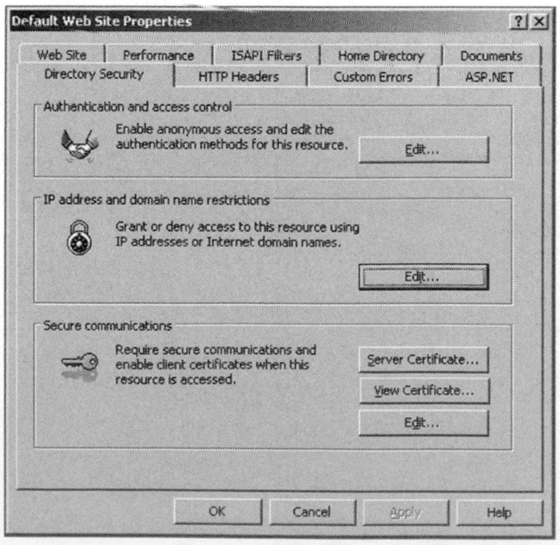

By default, all computers are allowed to connect to OWA on your CAS role server using HTTP/HTTPS. To restrict this, simply click the **Edit** button in the **IP address and domain name restrictions section** of Figure 8-13 and specify the appropriate information in the IP Address and Domain Name Restrictions window. You can specify computers by IP address, an IP network, or a domain name. In Figure 8-14, all computers are allowed to connect except for computers that have a DNS record in the arfa.com domain, computers that have an IP address on the 10.1.1.0 network (subnet mask 255.255.255.0), and the computer with the IP address 192.168.1.5. To restrict HTTP access to your CAS role server to certain computers only, you could instead select **Denied access** as shown in Figure 8-14 and add only those computers that require access.

Figure 8-14

Configuring IP Address and Domain Name Restrictions

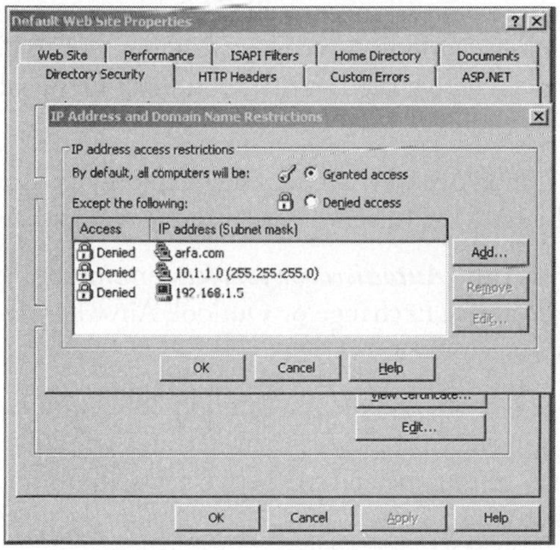

THE COMMAND LINE WAY

You can also use the **Set-OWAVirtualDirectory** cmdlet in the Exchange Management Shell to configure HTTP-related settings for OWA. For example, to configure digest authentication for OWA on the server EXCH1, you could run the following command in the Exchange Management Shell:

Set-OWAVirtualDirectory -Identity 'EXCH1\owa (Default Web Site)' -DigestAuthentication

For more information on the Set-OWAVirtualDirectory cmdlet and its options, search for Set-OWAVirtualDirectory within Exchange Server 2007 Help.

Configuring MAPI RPC and Outlook Anywhere

Exchange servers use the MAPI protocol to work closely with Entourage and Outlook clients within the local area networks (LANs) in your organization. As a result, MAPI RPC requires the least configuration of any email protocol. However, to use MAPI connections from remote networks using Outlook Anywhere, you will need to configure the Autodiscover and Availability services to allow for autoconfiguration, Online Address Book (OAB), and calendaring options using the Exchange Management Shell.

MAPI is similar to IMAP4 in structure and function. Like IMAP4, MAPI creates a persistent connection between the email client and server as well as allows for public folder support. However, MAPI protects the content of its emails so that they cannot be read in plain text when they are transferred across the network. In addition, because MAPI was developed by Microsoft, it contains additional features that work closely with Outlook and Entourage clients only.

Because MAPI connections are persistent and use RPCs to send information between the email server and client, they are appropriate for high-speed LAN use only. As a result, most Outlook and Entourage clients with an Exchange account (MAPI RPC) configured are within an organization and connect to the organization's Exchange servers using a LAN.

Email clients can also use MAPI RPC from across the Internet to connect to their Exchange server; however MAPI RPC must be contained within HTTP or HTTPS packets because most firewalls block RPC traffic. Outlook Anywhere is a protocol that tunnels MAPI RPC traffic within HTTP or HTTPS packets and is supported in Outlook 2003 and later MAPI clients.

By default, MAPI RPC is automatically configured on each CAS role server. As a result, internal MAPI RPC clients can connect to all CAS role servers within your organization by default. However, to allow Outlook Anywhere (RPC over HTTP) MAPI clients to connect to your CAS role server from across the Internet, you must first enable the Outlook Anywhere protocol.

Exchange Server 2007 adds two new services that can only be used by Outlook 2007, Entourage 2008, and later MAPI clients: the Autodiscover and Availability services.

MAPI clients can contact the *Autodiscover service* running on Exchange Server 2007 to automatically configure a new Exchange or Outlook Anywhere account by simply specifying the email address of the recipient.

When configuring a new email account in Outlook 2007, you are first prompted to supply your email address in the Add New E-mail Account window as shown in Figure 8-15. By default, your domain username and primary email address are supplied at this window. If you click **Next** in Figure 8-15, Outlook 2007 will contact the Autodiscover service on an Exchange server for the domain and set up the appropriate account settings as shown in Figure 8-16. Alternatively, if you select **Manually configure server settings or additional server types** and click **Next**, you will need to manually enter your account configuration information.

X REF

Enabling Outlook Anywhere on a CAS role server was covered in Lesson 4, "Configuring a New Exchange Server."

Figure 8-15

Autoconfiguring a New Outlook 2007 Account

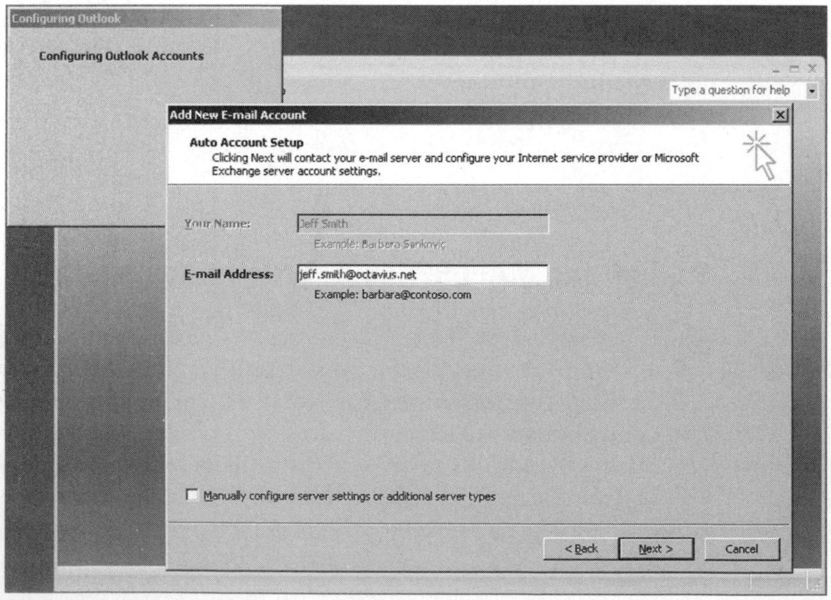

Figure 8-16

Completing the Autoconfigure Process

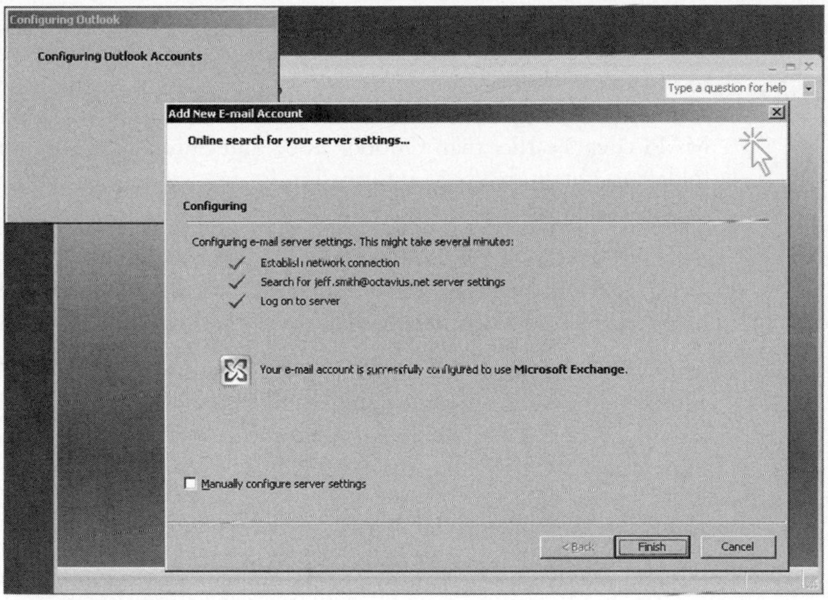

Similarly, when setting up a new Entourage 2008 account, you are first prompted to supply your email address so that Entourage can use the Autodiscover service to configure your email account settings as shown in Figure 8-17. Like Outlook 2007, Entourage 2008 also allows you to configure account settings manually by clicking the **Configure Account Manually** button shown in Figure 8-17.

Figure 8-17

Autoconfiguring a New Entourage 2008 Account

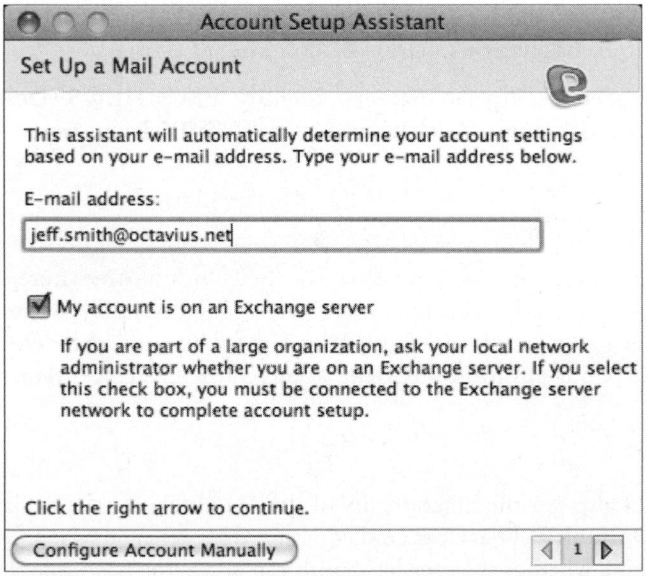

X REF

Configuring new email accounts in Outlook 2007 and Entourage 2008 was discussed in Lesson 4, "Configuring a New Exchange Server."

The Autodiscover service also reconfigures MAPI clients automatically when a mailbox is moved. For example, if Jeff Smith's mailbox is moved to a different Mailbox role server at a different site, Jeff Smith's MAPI client will automatically be configured to contact a new CAS role server close to the Mailbox role server in the destination site.

In addition, the Autodiscover service allows Outlook 2007, Entourage 2008, and later MAPI clients to obtain an OAB from the appropriate CAS role server directly. The MAPI client connects to the Autodiscover service, locates the URL for the closest OAB, and downloads it directly without relying on public folders. Previous versions of Outlook and Entourage must still reply on system public folders to obtain OABs.

Similarly, these same MAPI clients can also take advantage of the *Availability service* in Exchange Server 2007. The Availability service is used alongside the Autodiscover service to obtain free/busy information for calendar scheduling. In previous versions of Exchange, the free/busy service provided this information to MAPI clients using system public folders. MAPI clients earlier than Outlook 2007 and Entourage 2008 must still rely on system public folders to obtain free/busy information for use with calendar scheduling.

The Autodiscover and Availability services are contacted using virtual directories under the Default Web Site in IIS on the CAS role servers within your organization. For the CAS role server exch1.octavius.net, the default URLs for the Autodiscover and Availability services are **https://exch1.octavius.net/Autodiscover** and **https://exch1.octavius.net/EWS**.

After an Exchange Server installation, the Autodiscover services on the CAS role servers within your organization are automatically configured with the URLs for automatic configuration, OAB, and Availability service information. However, this information is only available to internal MAPI RPC clients.

To enable the Autodiscover and Availability services for external Outlook Anywhere (RPC over HTTP) MAPI clients, you must specify an external URL for Outlook Anywhere, Exchange Web Services, and the OAB. Following this, Outlook Anywhere clients will be able to use the Autodiscover and Availability services to autoconfigure email accounts and obtain OABs and calendar scheduling information by connecting to the appropriate external URL.

The following commands within the Exchange Management Shell configure the Autodiscover and Availability services for Outlook Anywhere using the server exch1.octavius.net and the HTTPS protocol. In order to run these commands, you must be a member of the Exchange Organization Administrator role or the Exchange Server Administrator role for the CAS role server.

Set-OutlookAnywhere -Identity 'EXCH1' -ExternalHostname 'exch1.octavius.net'

Set-OABVirtualDirectory -Identity 'EXCH1\OAB (Default Web Site)' -ExternalURL 'https://exch1.octavius.net/OAB' -RequireSSL:$true

Set-WebServicesVirtualDirectory -Identity 'EXCH1\EWS (Default Web Site)' -ExternalURL 'https://exch1.octavius.net/EWS/Exchange.asmx' -BasicAuthentication:$True

ANOTHER WAY

If you specified an external URL when you enabled Outlook Anywhere on your CAS role server, you do not need to execute the **Set-OutlookAnywhere** command afterward to set the external URL. Similarly, you can configure an OAB external URL in the properties of the **owa (Default Web Site)** object under the **Outlook Web Access** tab of **Server Configuration** > **Client Access** in the Exchange Management Console.

You can also test the functionality of the Autodiscover and Availability services using the **Test-OutlookWebServices** cmdlet within the Exchange Management Shell. For example, to determine whether the user Jeff Smith can access the CAS role server exch1.octavius.net using the Autodiscover and Availability services, you could run the following command within the Exchange Management Shell:

Test-OutlookWebServices –Identity 'Jeff Smith' –ClientAccessServer 'exch1.octavius.net' | format-list

If you omit the **–Identity** and **–ClientAccessServer** options to the **Test-OutlookWebServices** cmdlet, you will test the local CAS role server using the current user account.

■ Configuring the SMTP Protocol

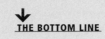

THE BOTTOM LINE

The Hub role servers within your Exchange organization use the Simply Mail Transfer Protocol (SMTP) to receive emails from POP3 and IMAP4 clients as well as relay emails to other email servers. Although email relay is largely configured using send and receive connectors, you can use the Exchange Management Console or Exchange Management Shell to configure remote domains, transport settings, and SMTP limits to alter the relay of SMTP email within your organization.

CERTIFICATION READY?
Configure client
connectivity.
3.6

SMTP is the protocol that email systems have largely been using since its formal standardization in 1982. As a result, it plays a vital role within any Exchange infrastructure. POP3 and IMAP4 clients send email to your Hub role servers using SMTP on TCP port 587 or 25, and Hub and Edge role servers relay email to other internal and external email servers using SMTP on TCP port 25.

The original SMTP protocol is only used by legacy email systems today. Instead, the newer Extended SMTP (ESMTP) protocol is used in its place and supports advanced functions such as authentication and encryption. In addition, these advanced functions are negotiated during an ESMTP session. When a computer starts an ESMTP connection to another computer, it first asks the other computer about the capabilities it supports and then adjusts its communication accordingly.

Nearly all email clients and email servers today support ESMTP and will fall back to using SMTP when communicating with other computers that do not support ESMTP. As a result, the term SMTP is commonly used when referring to either ESMTP or SMTP.

SMTP uses a series of text commands to send emails from one computer to another. Each time an SMTP command is sent, the other computer sends a reply to confirm that it received the SMTP command. Typical emails that are sent within an organization consist of over 20 separate SMTP commands.

As with POP3 and IMAP4, you can interact with the SMTP service on your Hub and Edge role servers using the **telnet.exe** command at a Windows command prompt. This is often useful in determining whether an email server supports SMTP or ESMTP. The first command in an SMTP session is HELO, whereas the first command in an ESMTP session is EHLO. Most email clients and servers today attempt an EHLO command when they communicate with SMTP. If successful, the other computer will respond with a list of the ESMTP features (such as authentication methods) that it supports. If the other computer only supports SMTP, then it will respond with an error code and the email client or server will then attempt a HELO command to see if the original SMTP protocol is supported.

If you type **telnet***server***25** (where *server* is the IP address or FQDN of the Hub or Edge role server), you will be able to type the EHLO command to see if the target email server supports SMTP. Figure 8-18, shows the output from the **telnet exch1.octavius.net 25** command. The 220 line appears after running the telnet command to display the banner information from the SMTP service. The HELO command that was typed at the prompt afterward resulted in

Figure 8-18

Interacting with the SMTP
Service

a 250 line that indicates that exch1.octavius.net supports SMTP. The EHLO command that was typed at the prompt following this resulted in several 250 lines that indicate the ESMTP features that exch1.octavius.net supports.

> ➕ **MORE INFORMATION**
>
> To see a complete list of SMTP commands, search for "SMTP Commands and Definitions" on the Microsoft Technet Web site at http://technet.microsoft.com.

X REF

The configuration of send and receive connectors was covered in Lesson 4, "Configuring a New Exchange Server."

The Hub and Edge role servers within your Exchange organization process internal and external SMTP email using the information stored in send and receive connectors. However, you can also configure general SMTP protocol settings using various nodes within the Exchange Management Console.

By navigating to **Organization Configuration** > **Hub Transport** within the Exchange Management Console as a member of the Exchange Organization Administrator role, you can configure the processing of items sent to specific domains as well as SMTP transport settings.

Under the Remote Domains tab as shown in Figure 8-19, you can configure the processing of messages and message formats. After installation, there is a Default *remote domain* that applies to email that is sent to any external domain on the Internet (*). If you highlight the Default remote domain and click **Properties** in the action pane, you can configure the processing of Out of Office messages that are sent by Outlook or Entourage clients within your organization as shown in Figure 8-20.

Figure 8-19

Viewing the Default Remote Domain

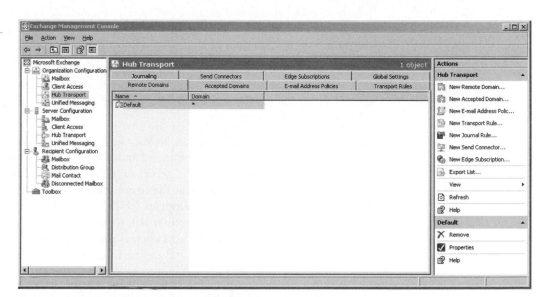

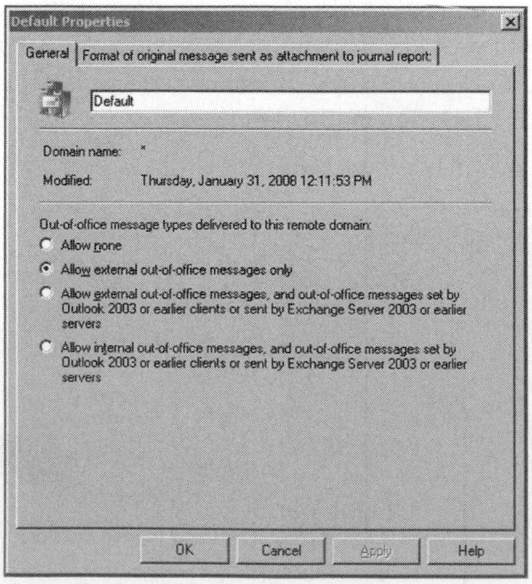

Figure 8-20

Configuring Out of Office Message Relay

Out of Office messages are often used to give senders immediate notification that their email may not be read until a specified time when users go on vacation or business trips. Outlook and Entourage clients can use the *Out of Office Assistant* (**Tools** > **Out of Office Assistant** in Outlook and **Tools** > **Out of Office** in Entourage) to configure an autoreply message. If the user specifies that he or she is out of the office in the Out of Office Assistant, this message will automatically be sent in response to any emails that are received. Moreover, the Out of Office Assistant allows you to specify a different message for internal senders who are part of your Exchange organization and external senders who are not part of your organization.

By default, the Default remote domain allows Exchange Server 2007 Out of Office messages from Outlook 2007, Entourage 2008, and later clients to be relayed to external senders only. If your organization has Exchange 2000 or 2003 servers or MAPI clients that run an earlier version of Outlook or Entourage, you must select the appropriate option in Figure 8-20 to allow for internal or external Out of Office messages from legacy clients and servers.

If you select the **Format of original message sent as attachment to journal report** tab shown in Figure 8-21, you can also specify relay options such as whether to allow delivery reports, rich text, or automatic replies for the remote domain.

Figure 8-21

Configuring Message Relay and Formats

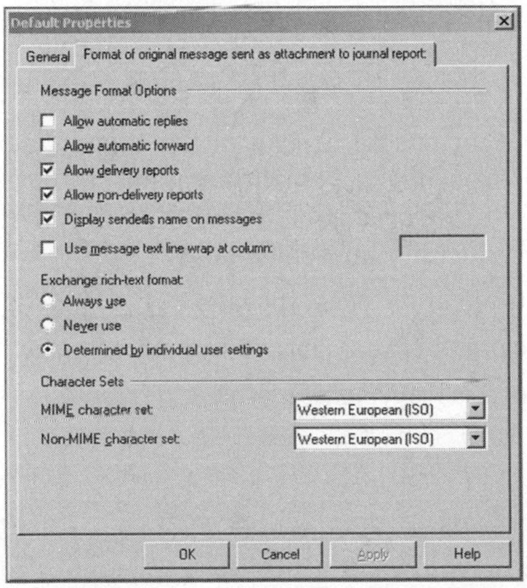

TAKE NOTE *

The **Format of original message sent as attachment to journal report** tab is mislabeled in Exchange Server 2007 SP1. The name of the tab should be **Message Format**, and the options specified on the tab apply to all SMTP email sent to the remote domain for which it applies.

If you wish to have different Out of Office or message format options for different external domains, you can create a new remote domain that applies to the correct external domain on the Internet and later specify the necessary options in the properties of the new remote domain. Any additional remote domains that apply to a specific domain will be used instead of the Default remote domain that applies to all domains on the Internet. For example, if you create a remote domain called Arfa that applies to all email sent to the arfa.com domain, its settings will always apply to emails that are sent to recipients in the arfa.com domain.

CREATE A NEW REMOTE DOMAIN

GET READY. Turn on the computer, and log in as the Administrator user account. Close any windows that appear on the desktop.

1. Click **Start**, **All Programs**, **Microsoft Exchange Server 2007**, and then click **Exchange Management Console**. The Exchange Management Console window appears.

2. In the console tree pane, expand **Organization Configuration** and highlight **Hub Transport**.

3. In the action pane, click **New Remote Domain**. The New Remote Domain window appears as shown in Figure 8-22.

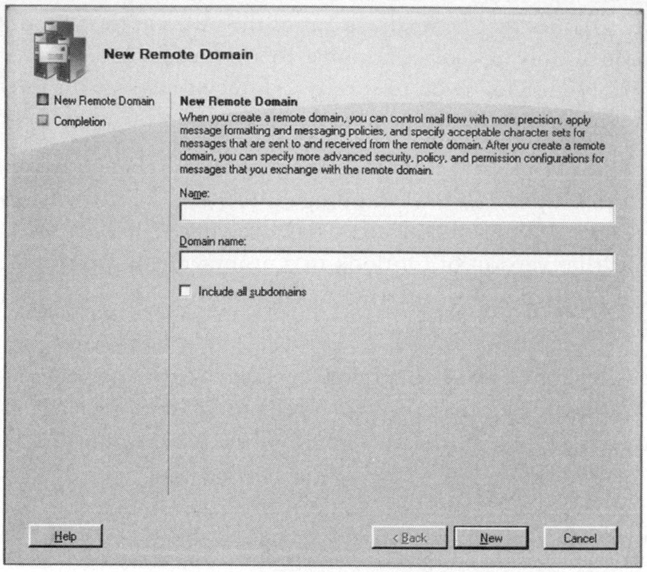

Figure 8-22

Creating a New Remote Domain

![New Remote Domain window screenshot]

4. Type a name for your remote domain in the **Name** dialog box and type the FQDN of the remote domain in the **Domain name** dialog box. If the remote domain should apply to all subdomains of the FQDN that you specified in the Domain name dialog box, select **Include all subdomains**.

5. Click **New**. The Completion page appears.

6. Click **Finish** to close the New Remote Domain window.

7. Close the Exchange Management Console.

THE COMMAND LINE WAY

You can also use the **New-RemoteDomain** cmdlet within the Exchange Management Shell to create a new remote domain and the **Set-RemoteDomain** cmdlet to specify SMTP options for the remote domain. For example, to create a new remote domain called Arfa that applies to the arfa.com domain and all subdomains, you could run the following cmdlet within the Exchange Management Shell:

New-RemoteDomain -DomainName '*.arfa.com' -Name 'Arfa'

Next, to prevent Out of Office messages to this Arfa remote domain, you could run the following command within the Exchange Management Shell:

Set-RemoteDomain 'Arfa' –AllowedOOFType 'None'

You can also set Out of Office message options on an individual mailbox user using the **Set-Mailbox** cmdlet. For example, to allow all external Out of Office messages for the user Jeff Smith, you could run the following command within the Exchange Management:

Set-Mailbox –Identity 'Jeff Smith' –ExternalOOFOptions 'External'

Additionally, the **Get-RemoteDomain** cmdlet can be used to obtain the configuration information for an existing remote domain and the **Remove-RemoteDomain** cmdlet can be used to remove a remote domain. For more information on the remote domain cmdlets in this section, search for their names within the Exchange Server 2007 Help.

In addition to remote domain options, you can configure SMTP transport settings under the **Organization Configuration** > **Hub Transport** node within the Exchange Management Console. If you click the Global Settings tab in Figure 8-19, highlight **Transport Settings**, and click **Properties** in the action pane, you can configure the default maximum size for items that are sent and received as well as the default maximum recipients per message as shown in Figure 8-23.

Figure 8-23

Configuring General Transport Settings

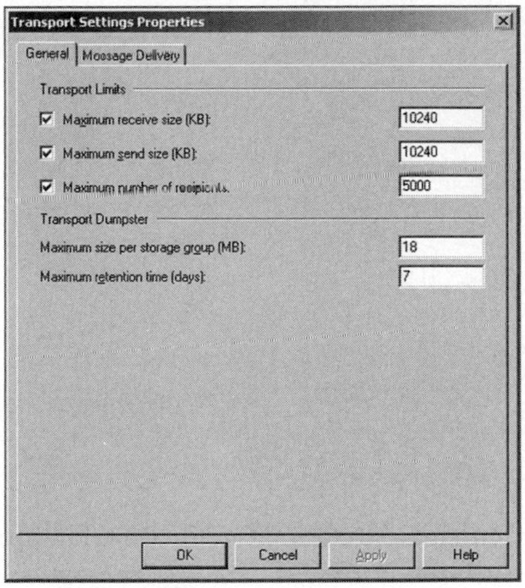

The Transport Dumpster settings shown in Figure 8-23 apply only to messages that have been sent from a mailbox that has been configured for Cluster Continuous Replication (CCR) and will be discussed in Lesson 13, "Providing for High Availability."

By default, incoming and outgoing SMTP messages can be 10 MB (10240 KB) in size and emails can be addressed up to 5,000 recipients. However, if you define the maximum receive size, maximum send size, and maximum number of recipients in the properties of a recipient object, it will override the limits that you set in the properties of Transport Settings.

On the Message Delivery tab of Transport Settings properties as shown in Figure 8-24, you can add the IP addresses of internal Hub role servers that will not participate in sender and spam filtering, as well as the **Delivery Status Notification (DSN)** codes that are allowed to be forwarded to recipient objects within your organization. DSNs are error messages that are sent by an email server to the sender of a message that could not be delivered. The DSN code is used to identify the type of error.

Figure 8-24

Configuring Message Delivery Options

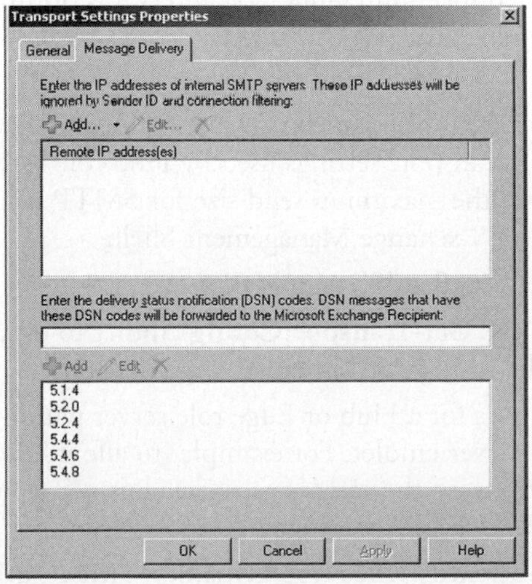

A DSN message is also called a **Non-Delivery Report (NDR)**, **Non-Delivery Receipt (NDR)**, **Non-Delivery Notification (NDN)**, or a **bounce message**.

Some SMTP settings can also be applied to individual Hub role servers within your organization. To configure these settings, you must be a member of the Exchange Organization Administrator role or the Exchange Server Administrator role on the Hub role server. Simply highlight the appropriate Hub role server in the detail pane under the **Server Configuration** > **Hub Transport** node within the Exchange Management Console and select **Properties** from the action pane. On the Limits tab of Hub role server properties, you can configure SMTP protocol parameters as shown in Figure 8-25.

Figure 8-25

Configuring SMTP Server Limits

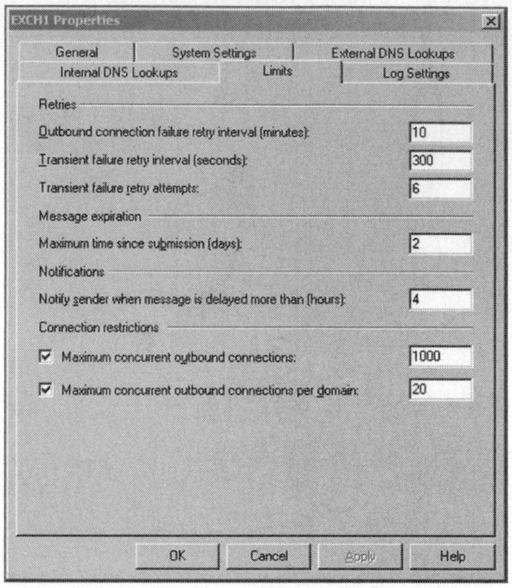

The default limits shown in Figure 8-25 indicate that the Hub role server will attempt to redeliver SMTP messages after 10 minutes if the first attempt could not be delivered due to network problems. If the redelivery fails, the Hub role server will attempt to redeliver the message up to 6 more times every 5 minutes (300 seconds). The senders of a message that is still stored in the SMTP queue after 4 hours will receive an email notification indicating that their email could not be delivered. If the email remains in the SMTP queue for 2 days, it will be automatically removed. In addition, the Hub role server allows for up to 1,000 concurrent SMTP sessions to other email domains on the Internet. However, only 20 concurrent SMTP sessions are allowed to the same email domain on the Internet.

You can also set SMTP limits on individual Edge role servers provided that you are a member of the local Administrators group on the Edge role server. Simply highlight **Edge Transport** in the console tree within the Exchange Management Console on the Edge role server, highlight the appropriate Edge role server in the detail pane, and select **Properties** from the action pane. The Limits tab of Edge role server properties contains the same configuration options as the Limits tab of Hub role server properties as shown in Figure 8-25. However, the default value for the Outbound connection failure retry interval is 30 minutes and the default value for the Transient failure retry interval is 600 seconds.

THE COMMAND LINE WAY

You can also use the **Set-TranportConfig** cmdlet within the Exchange Management Shell to configure the SMTP transport settings used by Hub role servers within your organization. For example, to set the maximum send size for SMTP relay, you could run the following cmdlet within the Exchange Management Shell:

Set-TransportConfig –MaxSendSize '20MB'

Similarly, you can run the **Get-TransportConfig** cmdlet to obtain the current SMTP transport settings used within your Exchange Organization.

To configure SMTP limits for a Hub or Edge role server within your organization, you can use the **Set-TransportServer** cmdlet. For example, to allow for a maximum of 300 outbound SMTP connections on the server exch1.octavius.net, you could run the following command within the Exchange Management Shell:

Set-TransportServer –Identity 'exch1.octavius.net' –MaxOutboundConnections '300'

To view SMTP settings for your Hub role servers you can also use the **Get-TransportServer** cmdlet. For more information on the Get-TransportConfig, Set-TransportConfig, Get-TransportServer, and Set-TransportServer cmdlets, simply search for their names within the Exchange Server 2007 Help.

Configuring Transport Rules

Transport rules may be used within an Exchange organization to modify th... email on the Hub and Edge role servers. Due to their complexity, you must fir...ing of stand the application and features of transport rules before creating or managing tr... within your Exchange organization.

Understanding Transport Rules

Transport rules function differently on the Hub and Edge role servers within your organization. Each transport rule is comprised of conditions and exceptions that match emails as well as actions that determine how to process those emails. A wide variety of criteria, as well as several different email processing actions, may be used within conditions and exceptions. Before you create transport rules on the Hub and Edge role servers within your organization, you must first understand the various components of transport rules and their usage.

Because Hub and Edge role servers perform all email relay within an organization, they are the ideal location to apply rules that modify emails and alter email processing. These rules are called *transport rules* and can be used to provide several important email-related functions within an organization. For example, you can create transport rules to prevent the relaying of email that contains inappropriate keywords or confidential information. In addition, transport rules can be used to add legal disclaimers to certain email messages, such as those that are sent outside the organization. You can also configure transport rules to archive key emails, forward sensitive emails to another person for inspection, reject emails, log message information, or mark emails as spam messages.

Hub and Edge role servers within your organization maintain separate transport rules. When you configure transport rules on a Hub role server, those rules are stored within AD and used by the *Transport Rules Agent* on all Hub role servers within your organization. Only members of the Exchange Organization Administrator role can create and manage transport rules on the Hub role servers within your organization. Alternatively, when you configure transport rules on an Edge role server, those rules are stored on the local Edge role server and used by the *Edge Rules Agent* on that server only. If you have multiple Edge role servers within your organization, you must configure transport rules separately on each one. To create and manage transport rules on an Edge role server, you only need to be a member of the local Administrators group on the Edge role server.

Although transport rules can be used to perform a wide variety of functions on emails that are relayed by your Hub and Edge role servers, they contain a large set of configuration options as a result.

Transport rules are composed of three components: conditions, exceptions, and actions. The *conditions* of a transport rule are used to determine the emails that the transport rule applies to. Because the conditions of a transport rule can match a large number of emails, you can specify *exceptions* that exclude certain emails based on a certain criteria. For example, if you wish to create a transport rule that applies to all emails that have the keyword "Project" in their Subject line from users within the organization, you could specify a condition that matches any emails that have the word "Project" in their Subject line and specify an exception that excludes any emails from external senders.

If you specify multiple conditions within a single transport rule, emails must match all of the conditions for the transport rule to be applied. Alternatively, if you specify multiple exceptions, emails need only match a single exception to be excluded from the transport rule. In addition, the available conditions and exceptions are different for transport rules configured on a Hub role server and Edge role server.

Although the wording of conditions and transport rules in the Exchange Management Console is different to identify their application, the criteria used for conditions and criteria are the same. Table 8-1 lists the criteria that you can use for conditions and exceptions within a transport rule as well as the servers that they apply to.

Table ‾‾‾‾‾ sed within transport rule conditions and exceptions
Criter‾‾‾

CRITERIA	SERVER ROLE	DESCRIPTION
From people	Hub only	Matches emails with specific senders that you specify.
From a member of a distribution list	Hub only	Matches emails with senders who are members of a distribution group that you specify.
From users inside or outside the organization	Hub or Edge	Matches emails from internal or external senders (you must choose either internal or external).
Sent to people	Hub only	Matches emails with specific recipients that you specify.
Sent to a member of a distribution list	Hub only	Matches emails with recipients who are members of a distribution group that you specify.
Sent to users inside or outside the organization	Hub only	Matches emails sent to internal or external recipients (you must choose either internal or external).
Between members of one distribution list and another distribution list	Hub only	Matches emails that are sent between members of two different distribution groups that you specify.
When any of the recipients in the To field are people	Hub only	Matches emails with specific recipients you specify provided that those recipients are listed in the To field of the email.
When any of the recipients in the To field are members of a distribution list	Hub only	Matches emails sent to recipients provided that those recipients are listed in the To field of the email and are members of a distribution group that you specify.
When any of the recipients in the Carbon Copy (Cc) field are people	Hub only	Matches emails with specific recipients you specify provided that those recipients are listed in the Cc field of the email.
When any of the recipients in the Cc field are members of a distribution list	Hub only	Matches emails sent to recipients provided that those recipients are listed in the Cc field of the email and are members of a distribution group that you specify.
When any of the recipients in the To or Cc fields are people	Hub only	Matches emails with specific recipients that you specify provided that those recipients are listed in the To field or the Cc field of the email.
When any of the recipients in the To or Cc fields are members of a distribution list	Hub only	Matches emails sent to recipients provided that those recipients are listed in the To field or Cc field of the email and are members of a distribution group that you specify.
Marked with classification	Hub only	Matches emails that contain a specific classification that was selected in Outlook or Entourage before the message was sent.
When the Subject field contains specific words	Hub or Edge	Matches emails that contain specific word(s) within the Subject field of the email.
When the Subject field or the body of the message contains specific words	Hub or Edge	Matches emails that contain specific word(s) within the Subject field or body of the email.
When a message header contains specific words	Hub or Edge	Matches emails that contain specific word(s) within the message header of the email.

Table 8-1

CRITERIA	SERVER ROLE	DESCRIPTION
When the From address contains specific words	Hub or Edge	Matches emails that contain specific word(s) within the From field of the email.
When any recipient address contains specific words	Edge only	Matches emails that contain specific word(s) within the To, Cc, and Bcc fields of the email.
When the Subject field contains text patterns	Hub or Edge	Matches emails that contain specific text pattern(s) within the Subject field of the email. Text patterns are strings that may contain portions of a word, an entire word, or several words and other characters.
When the Subject field or the body of the message contains text patterns	Hub or Edge	Matches emails that contain specific text pattern(s) within the Subject field or body of the email. Text patterns are strings that may contain portions of a word, an entire word, or several words and other characters.
When the message header contains text patterns	Hub or Edge	Matches emails that contain specific text pattern(s) within the message header of the email. Text patterns are strings that may contain portions of a word, an entire word, or several words and other characters.
When the From address contains text patterns	Hub or Edge	Matches emails that contain specific text pattern(s) within the From field of the email. Text patterns are strings that may contain portions of a word, an entire word, or several words and other characters.
When text patterns exist in any recipient addresses	Edge only	Matches emails that contain specific text pattern(s) within the To, Cc, or Bcc fields of the email. Text patterns are strings that may contain portions of a word, an entire word, or several words and other characters.
When any attachment file name contains text patterns	Hub only	Matches emails that contain specific text pattern(s) within the file name of any attachment included in the email. Text patterns are strings that may contain portions of a word, an entire word, or several words and other characters.
With a spam confidence level (SCL) rating that is greater or equal to the limit	Hub or Edge	Matches emails that have been given a **Spam Confidence Level (SCL)** that is higher than a number that you specify. The SCL is a numerical value between 0 and 9 that indicates the likelihood that a email message is spam. SCL values are typically added by antispam software components within Exchange Server 2007. A message with an SCL of 0 is highly unlikely to be spam, whereas a message with an SCL of 9 is almost certainly spam.
When the size of any attachment is greater than or equal to the limit	Hub or Edge	Matches emails that have attachments that are larger than the size that you specify in KB.
Marked with importance	Hub only	Matches emails that are marked with Low, Normal, or High importance (you must choose a level). Outlook or Entourage users can choose an importance level for emails before they are sent.

The *actions* within a transport rule determine the actions that are performed on messages that match the transport rule. The allowed actions that you can contain within a transport rule on a Hub role server are different from the actions that you can contain within a transport rule on an Edge role server. Table 8-2 lists the actions that can be performed as well as the servers they apply to.

Table 8-2

Transport rule actions

Action	Server Role	Description
Log an event with message.	Hub and Edge	Adds an event to the Application event log on the local computer with a custom message that you specify.
Prepend the subject with string.	Hub and Edge	Adds a string that you specify to the beginning of the text in the Subject line of the email.
Apply message classification.	Hub only	Automatically applies a message classification to the email that you specify.
Append disclaimer text using font, size, color, with separator and fallback to action if unable to apply.	Hub only	Automatically adds text to the beginning or end of the email message using a specific font and color according to the settings and text that you specify.
Set the spam confidence level to value.	Hub and Edge	Automatically sets the SCL on the email to the value that you specify.
Set header with value.	Hub and Edge	Sets the message header field for messages to the text that you specify. If a message header field does not exist, it will be created with the text that you specify.
Remove header.	Hub and Edge	Removes the specified message header field.
Add a recipient in the To field addresses.	Hub and Edge	Adds an additional recipient that you specify to the To field of the email.
Copy message to addresses.	Hub and Edge	Adds an additional recipient that you specify to the Cc field of the email.
Blind carbon copy (Bcc) the message to addresses.	Hub and Edge	Adds an additional recipient that you specify to the Bcc field of the email.
Drop connection.	Edge only	Stops the SMTP connection from the remote email server without sending an NDR.
Redirect message to addresses.	Hub and Edge	Sends the email to a different recipient that you specify. The original recipient does not receive a copy of the email and no NDR is sent.
Put message in quarantine.	Edge only	Sends the email to the spam quarantine mailbox instead of sending it to the original recipient. You can configure the location of the spam quarantine mailbox by using the -QuarantineMailbox option to the **Set-ContentFilterConfig cmdlet.**
Send bounce message to sender with enhanced status code.	Hub only	Deletes the email message and sends an NDR to the original sender.
Reject the message with status code and response.	Edge only	Deletes the email message and sends an NDR to the original sender with a specific DSN code that you specify.
Silently drop the message.	Hub and Edge	Deletes the email message without sending any notification to the sender.

Before you select the **Marked with classification** criteria or the **Apply message classification** action within a transport rule, you must first configure your Outlook clients to use *message classifications*. By default, there are several default message classifications that were originally designed to work alongside *Windows Rights Management Services* to restrict access to information. You can use these default message classifications alongside transport rules to restrict the processing of emails that contain specific classifications or create new message classifications that suit your organization's needs.

To create a new message classification called **Internal Use Only** that can be applied to emails that contain information that should not leave the organization, you could run the following command within the Exchange Management Shell:

New-McssageClassification -Name 'InternalUseOnly' -DisplayName 'Internal Use Only' -SenderDescription 'This category applies to information that should not be viewed by users who are not members of the organization.'

After creating a new message classification, OWA and Entourage 2008 MAPI users can then use this new classification when composing new emails. However, for Outlook MAPI clients, you must first export the message classification definitions to an XML file on your Exchange server. To create an XML file called C:\Classifications.xml that contains the message classifications from your Exchange server, simply run the following command within the Exchange Management Shell:

Export-OutlookClassification.ps1 > 'C:\Classifications.xml'

After you have created a message classifications XML file, you can copy it to each Outlook client computer and configure the appropriate registry keys to enable the message classifications.

CONFIGURE OUTLOOK 2007 TO USE MESSAGE CLASSIFICATIONS

GET READY. Turn on the computer, and log in as the Administrator user account. Close any windows that appear on the desktop.

1. Click **Start** and then click **Run**. Type **regedit** in the Run dialog box to open the Windows Registry Editor.

2. In the left pane, navigate to **HKEY_CURRENT_USER**, **Software**, **Microsoft**, **Office**, **12.0**, **Common**.

3. Right click **Common** in the left pane, select **New**, and then click **Key**. Supply the name **Policy** for the new key and press **Enter**.

4. Right click **Policy** in the left pane, select **New**, and then click **String Value**. Supply the name **AdminClassificationPath** for the new string value and press **Enter**.

5. Double click **AdminClassificationPath** in the right pane. In the Edit String window that appears, type the path to the message classifications XML file that you created on your Exchange server in the **Value data** dialog box and click **OK**. The Completion page appears. You must ensure that you use two backslash characters following the drive in the path name. For example, if the path name of the message classifications XML file is C:\Classifications.xml, you should type **C:\\Classifications.xml** in the **Value data** dialog box.

6. Right click **Policy** in the left pane, select **New**, and then click **DWORD Value**. Supply the name **EnableClassifications** for the new string value and press **Enter**.

7. Double click **EnableClassifications** in the right pane. In the Edit DWORD Value window that appears, type **1** in the **Value data** dialog box and click **OK**.

8. Right click **Policy** in the left pane, select **New**, and then click **DWORD Value**. Supply the name **TrustClassifications** for the new string value and press **Enter**.

9. Double click **TrustClassifications** in the right pane. In the Edit DWORD Value window that appears, type **1** in the **Value data** dialog box and click **OK**.

10. Close the Windows Registry Editor.

After configuring Outlook to use message classifications, you can add the appropriate message classification when composing a new email by selecting the icon shown in Figure 8-26.

Figure 8-26

Using Message Classifications
in Outlook 2007

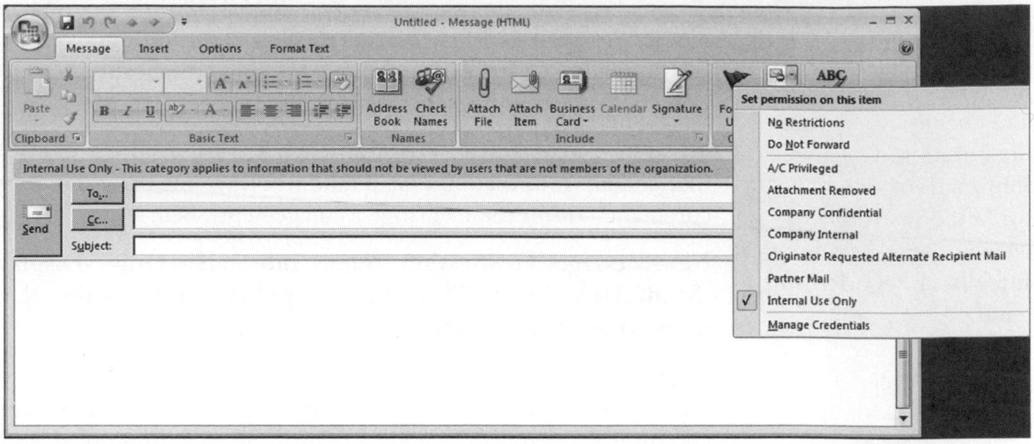

In Figure 8-26, the **Internal Use Only** message classification has been applied to the new email and the message classification description appears at the top of the email message. You can then create a transport rule on your Edge role servers to reject email messages that are sent to external recipients if the message contains the **Internal Use Only** message classification. To do this, you could create a transport rule on your Edge role servers that uses the **Marked with classification** criteria to match emails that use the **Internal Use Only** classification alongside the **Reject the message with status code and response** action.

When used alongside transport rules, message classifications provide a powerful and flexible way to restrict and process emails that are relayed by the Hub and Edge role servers within your organization.

Creating Transport Rules

You can create transport rules that provide email processing in a wide variety of environments for a wide variety of organizational needs. To create transport rules on a Hub or Edge role server, you can use either the Exchange Management Console or the Exchange Management Shell. Moreover, transport rules that are created on a Hub role server can be used by any Hub role server within your organization.

When you configure a transport rule for a Hub role server, that rule is applied to all Hub role servers within your organization to allow for email relay consistency. As a result, you can configure transport rules for Hub role servers using the **Organization Configuration > Hub Transport** node within the Exchange Management Console.

To configure transport rules within the Exchange Management Console on an Edge role server, you can navigate to the **Edge Transport** node. However, if you configure a transport rule for an Edge role server, that rule is applied to the local Edge role server only. If your organization has several Edge role servers that require the same transport rules, you can simply create the necessary transport rules on the first Edge role server and then use the **Export-TransportRuleCollection** cmdlet within the Exchange Management Shell to export the transport rules to an XML file that can later be imported to the other Edge role servers using the **Import-TransportRuleCollection** cmdlet.

To export the transport rules on the current Edge role server to the C:\EdgeRules.xml file, you could run the following command within the Exchange Management Shell:

Export-TransportRuleCollection C:\EdgeRules.xml

Next, you could copy the C:\EdgeRules.xml file to the same location on the other Edge role servers and run the following command within the Exchange Management Shell to import the transport rules:

Import-TransportRuleCollection C:\EdgeRules.xml

TAKE NOTE *

You can also use a UNC path (\\servername\sharename) alongside the **Export-TransportRule Collection** and **Import-TransportRule Collection** cmdlets.

Due to the large number of conditions, exceptions, and actions that are available within a transport rule, there are many different applications for transport rules on both the Hub and Edge role servers within your organization. As a result, we will examine two common applications of transport rules within this section:

- The addition of a legal notice disclaimer to all outgoing emails using a transport rule that applies to the Hub role servers within your organization
- The configuring of message screening for all messages from external senders that contain communication regarding the TASU project within your organization.

→ **CREATE A LEGAL NOTICE DISCLAIMER TRANSPORT RULE ON A HUB ROLE SERVER THAT APPLIES TO ALL EXTERNAL EMAILS**

GET READY. Turn on the computer, and log in as the Administrator user account. Close any windows that appear on the desktop.

1. Click **Start**, **All Programs**, **Microsoft Exchange Server 2007**, and then click **Exchange Management Console**. The Exchange Management Console window appears.

2. In the console tree pane, expand **Organization Configuration** and highlight **Hub Transport**.

3. In the action pane, click **New Transport Rule**. The New Transport Rule window appears as shown in Figure 8-27.

Figure 8-27

Creating a New Transport Rule

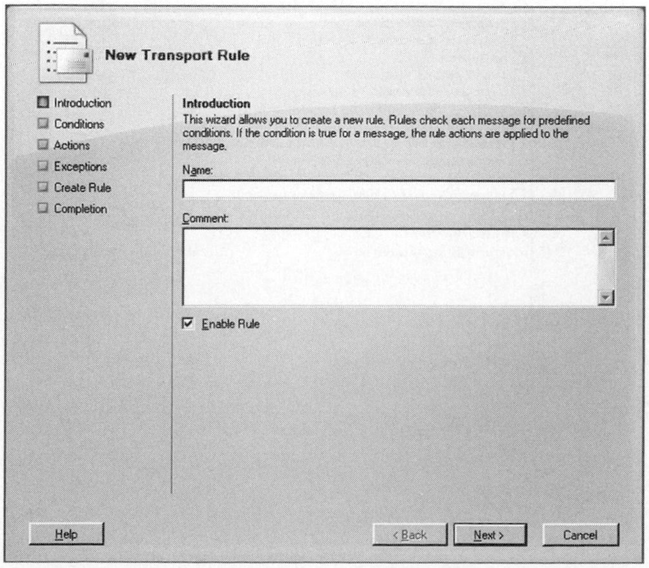

4. Supply an appropriate name for the transport rule in the **Name** dialog box as well as an appropriate description for the transport rule in the **Comment** dialog box. Verify that **Enable Rule** is selected to ensure that the transport rule is enabled after creation.

5. Click **Next**. The Conditions page appears as shown in Figure 8-28.

Figure 8-28

The Conditions Page

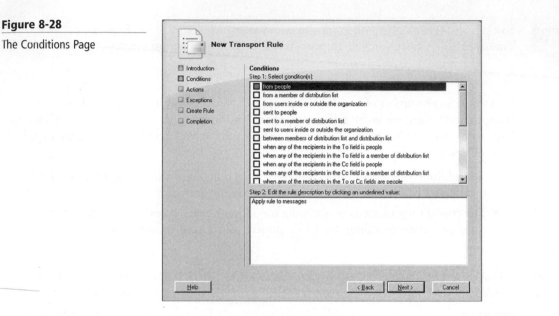

6. In the **Step 1: Select condition(s)** section, select **sent to users inside or outside the organization**. In the **Step 2: Edit the rule description by clicking an underlined value** click the **Inside** underlined word. In the Select scope window that appears, select **Outside** from the drop-down box and click **OK**. The Conditions screen will appear as shown in Figure 8-29.

Figure 8-29

Configuring Conditions

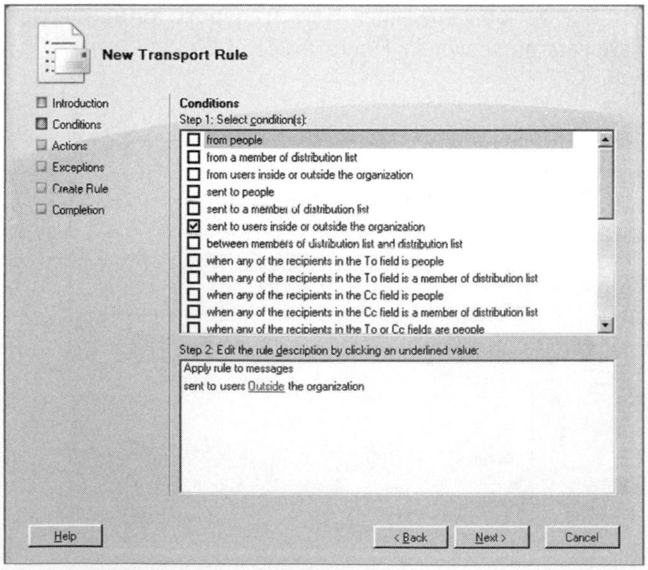

7. Click **Next**. The Actions page appears as shown in Figure 8-30.

Figure 8-30

The Actions Page

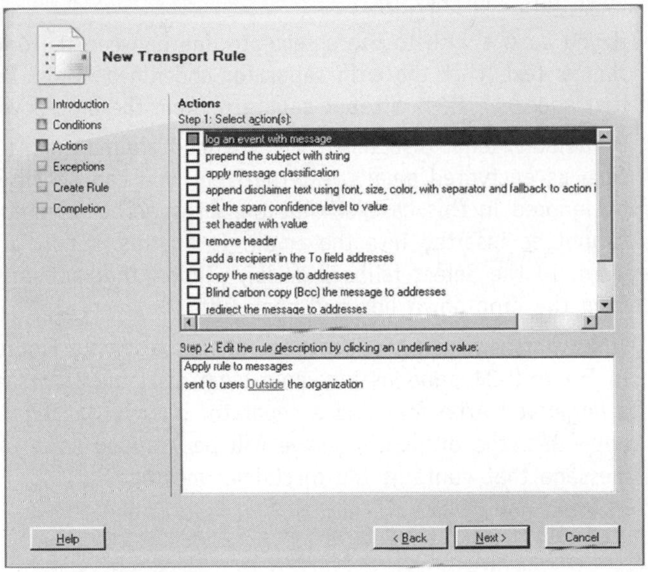

8. In the **Step 1: Select action(s)** section, select **append disclaimer text using font, size, color, with separator and fallback to action if unable to apply.**

9. In the **Step 2: Edit the rule description by clicking an underlined value** note that the disclaimer text is appended to emails with a separator line between the email and disclaimer text. In addition, the disclaimer text uses the smallest gray Arial font. If the disclaimer text cannot be inserted into the email message (i.e., if the message is encrypted), the email message will be wrapped as an attachment inside a new email that contains the disclaimer text.

10. Click the **disclaimer text** underlined words. In the Select disclaimer text window that appears, enter your legal disclaimer text in the **Disclaimer text** dialog box and click **OK**.

➕ MORE INFORMATION

Because legal disclaimer messages have been used alongside emails for many years now, they are usually common between organizations. Following is a typical legal disclaimer message:

This transmission (including any attachments) may contain confidential information, privileged material (including material protected by the solicitor-client or other applicable privileges), or constitute nonpublic information. Any use of this information by anyone other than the intended recipient is prohibited. If you have received this transmission in error, please immediately reply to the sender and delete this information from your system. Use, dissemination, distribution, or reproduction of this transmission by unintended recipients is not authorized and may be unlawful.

---

11. If you wish to attach the disclaimer to the beginning of the message, click the **append** underlined word. In the Select position window that appears, select **Prepend** from the drop-down box and click **OK**.

12. If you wish to use a font other than Arial for the disclaimer, click the **Arial** underlined word. In the Select font window that appears, select either **Courier New** or **Verdana** from the drop-down box and click **OK**.

13. If you wish to use a larger font size, click the **smallest** underlined word. In the Select font size window that appears, select the appropriate font size (**smaller**, **Normal**, **larger**, **largest**) from the drop-down box and click **OK**.

14. If you wish to change the font color, click the **Gray** underlined word. In the Select font color window that appears, select the appropriate font color from the drop-down box and click **OK**.

15. If you do not wish to use a separate line between the original email text and the disclaimer text, click the **with separator** underlined words. In the Select separator window that appears, select **without separator** from the drop-down box and click **OK**.

16. By default, legal disclaimers are wrapped around emails that cannot be modified such as encrypted emails. Alternatively, you can specify that the legal disclaimer be ignored in this case or that the message be rejected if the legal disclaimer cannot be inserted into the email. To do this, simply click the **wrap** underlined word. In the Select fallback action window that appears, select **ignore** or **reject** from the drop-down box and click **OK**.

17. When finished, your Actions page should resemble Figure 8-31. The Actions page in Figure 8-31 appends a sample legal disclaimer message to all messages using a larger red Arial font and a separator line. If the legal disclaimer cannot be appended, the original message will be wrapped as an attachment to a new email message that contains the disclaimer message.

Figure 8-31

Configuring Actions

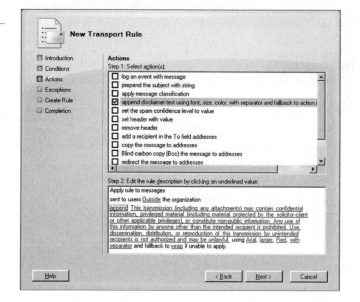

18. Click **Next**. The Exceptions page appears as shown in Figure 8-32.

Figure 8-32

The Exceptions Page

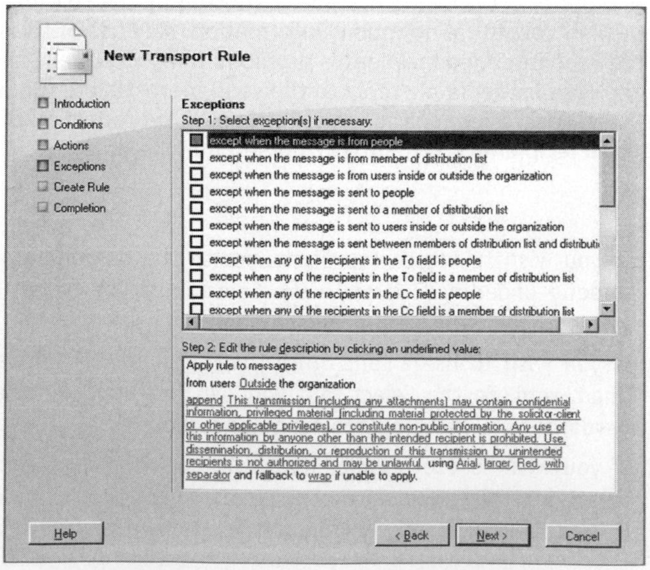

19. You can use the same process that you used on the Conditions tab to add criteria for emails that should be excluded from the transport rule. Because the legal notice disclaimer message should apply to all outgoing emails, you do not need to modify the Exceptions page.

20. Click **Next**. The Create Rule page appears.

21. Click **New**. The Completion page appears.

22. Click **Finish** to close the New Transport Rule window.

23. Close the Exchange Management Console.

 CREATE A MESSAGE SCREENING TRANSPORT RULE ON AN EDGE ROLE SERVER THAT APPLIES TO SPECIFIC RECIPIENTS

GET READY. Turn on the computer, and log in as the Administrator user account. Close any windows that appear on the desktop.

TAKE NOTE ✱ In this exercise, assume that you are the Exchange administrator for the octavius.net organization. The TASU project within your organization deals with confidential research that should not be sent to users outside of the organization. The project manager Jeff Smith intends to monitor all emails that leave the organization that mention the TASU project. To facilitate this, you need to create the appropriate transport rule on your Edge role servers.

1. Click **Start**, **All Programs**, **Microsoft Exchange Server 2007**, and then click **Exchange Management Console**. The Exchange Management Console window appears.

2. In the console tree pane, highlight **Edge Transport**.

3. In the action pane, click **New Transport Rule**. The New Transport Rule window appears as shown earlier in Figure 8-27.

4. Supply an appropriate name for the transport rule in the **Name** dialog box as well as an appropriate description for the transport rule in the **Comment** dialog box. Verify that **Enable Rule** is selected to ensure that the transport rule is enabled after creation.

5. Click **Next**. The Conditions page appears as shown in Figure 8-33.

Figure 8-33

The Conditions Page

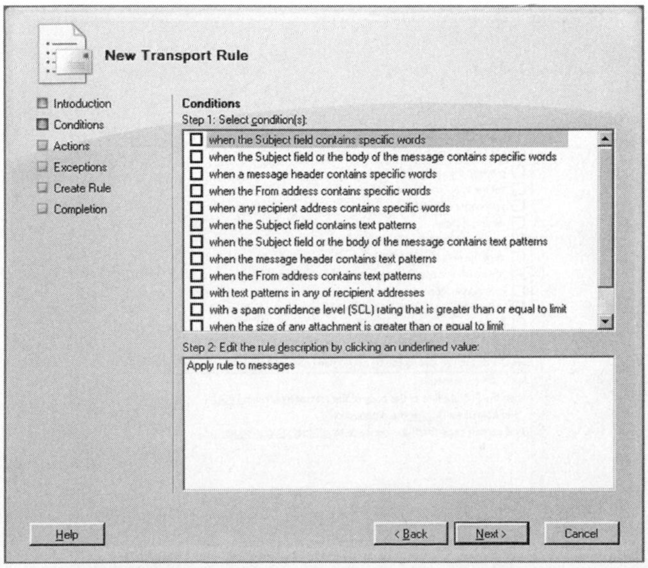

New Transport Rule

- Introduction
- Conditions
- Actions
- Exceptions
- Create Rule
- Completion

Conditions
Step 1: Select condition(s):

- when the Subject field contains specific words
- when the Subject field or the body of the message contains specific words
- when a message header contains specific words
- when the From address contains specific words
- when any recipient address contains specific words
- when the Subject field contains text patterns
- when the Subject field or the body of the message contains text patterns
- when the message header contains text patterns
- when the From address contains text patterns
- with text patterns in any of recipient addresses
- with a spam confidence level (SCL) rating that is greater than or equal to limit
- when the size of any attachment is greater than or equal to limit

Step 2: Edit the rule description by clicking an underlined value:

Apply rule to messages

Help   < Back   Next >   Cancel

6. In the **Step 1: Select condition(s)** section, select **when the Subject field or body of the message contains specific words**. In the **Step 2: Edit the rule description by clicking an underlined value** click the **specific words** underlined words. In the Specify words window that appears, type **TASU** in the dialog box, click **Add** and then click **OK**.

7. In the **Step 1: Select condition(s)** section, select **from users inside or outside the organization**. In the **Step 2: Edit the rule description by clicking an underlined value** click the **Inside** underlined word. In the Select scope window that appears, select **Outside** from the drop-down box and click **OK**. The Conditions screen will appear as shown in Figure 8-34.

8. Click **Next**. The Actions page appears as shown in Figure 8-35.

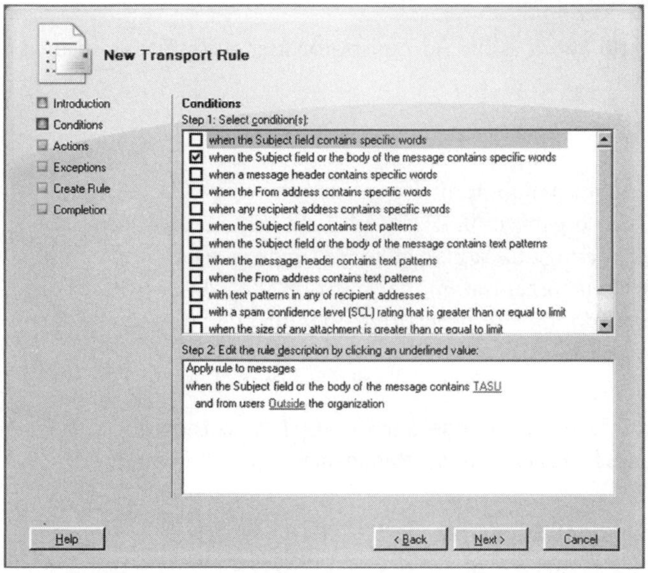

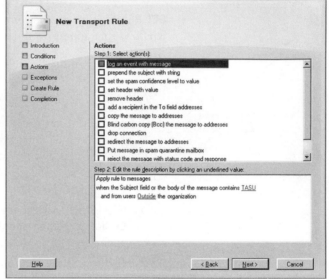

Figure 8-34

Configuring Conditions

Figure 8-35

The Actions Page

9. In the **Step 1: Select action(s)** section, select **Blind carbon copy (Bcc) the message to addresses**. In the **Step 2: Edit the rule description by clicking an underlined value**, click the **addresses** underlined word. In the Select recipients text window that appears, type **jeff.smith@octavius.net** in the dialog box, click **Add** and then click **OK**. The Actions page should resemble Figure 8-36.

Figure 8-36

Configuring Actions

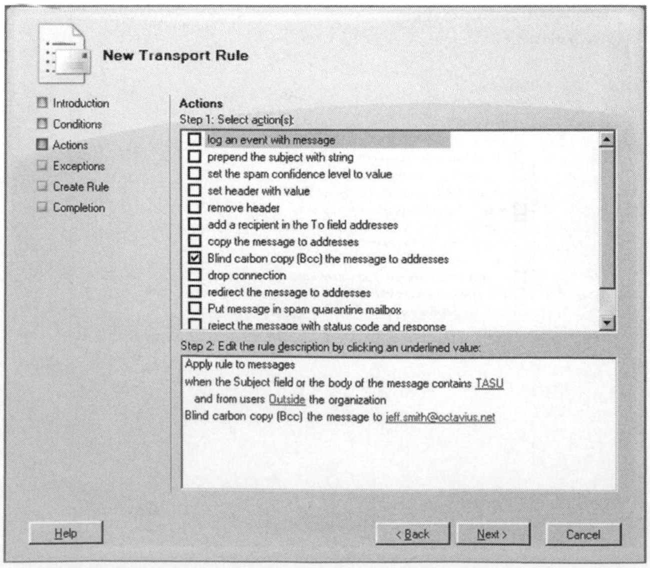

10. Click **Next**. The Exceptions page appears as shown in Figure 8-37.

Figure 8-37

The Exceptions Page

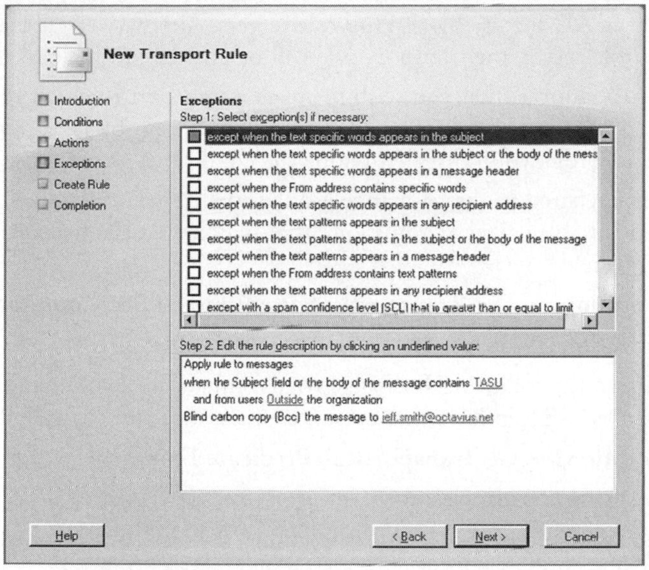

11. To exclude any emails that contain the word TASU that are sent to jeff.smith@ octavius.net from being forwarded again to jeff.smith@octavius.net, select **except when the text specific words appears in any recipient address** in the **Step 1: Select action(s)** section. In the **Step 2: Edit the rule description by clicking an underlined value**, click the **specific words** underlined words. In the Specify words window that appears, type **jeff.smith@octavius.net** in the dialog box, click **Add**, and then click **OK**. The Exceptions page should resemble Figure 8-38.

Figure 8-38

Configuring Exceptions

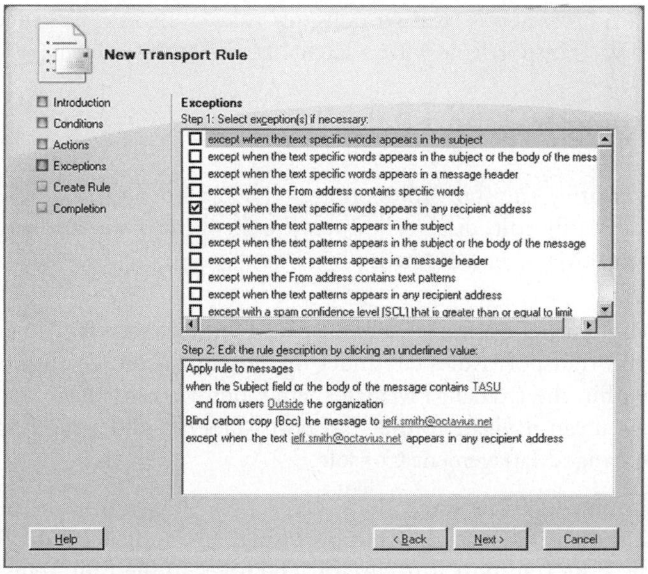

12. Click **Next**. The Create Rule page appears.

13. Click **New**. The Completion page appears.

14. Click **Finish** to close the New Transport Rule window.

15. Close the Exchange Management Console.

You can use the **New-TransportRule** cmdlet to create a new transport rule on a Hub or Edge role server. If this cmdlet is run from a Hub role server, the transport rule will be stored in AD for use by all Hub role servers. Alternatively, if this cmdlet is run from an Edge role server, the transport rule will be created on the local Edge role server only.

Say, for example, that you wish to create a transport rule that rejects emails that have the word TASU in the Subject field unless they are sent by Jeff Smith. Before creating this new transport rule, you must first define the conditions, exceptions, and actions using variables.

When executed in the Exchange Management Shell, the following commands create a condition variable called $Condition1 that matches emails that contain the word TASU in the Subject field:

$Condition1 = Get-TransportRulePredicate SubjectContains

$Condition1.Words = @('TASU')

Similarly, the following Exchange Management Shell commands create an exception variable called $Exception1 that excludes emails that are sent to Jeff Smith:

$Exception1 = GetTransportRulePredicate From

$Exception1.Addresses = @(Get-MailUser 'Jeff Smith')

To add an action variable called $Action1 that rejects messages and adds the text 'Only Jeff Smith can send TASU project emails.' to the NDR, you could execute the following Exchange Management Shell commands:

$Action1 = Get-TransportRuleAction RejectMessage

$Action1.RejectReason = 'Only Jeff Smith can send TASU project emails.'

Next, to create a new transport rule called Block TASU Project Emails using the conditions, exceptions, and actions defined earlier, you can execute the following Exchange Management Shell command:

New-TransportRule -Name 'Block TASU Project Emails' -Condition @($Condition1) -Exception @($Exception1) -Action @($Action1)

To learn more about creating transport rules using the Exchange Management Shell, search for New-TransportRule within Exchange Server 2007 Help.

THE COMMAND LINE WAY

Managing Transport Rules

After creating transport rules on the Hub and Edge role servers within your organization, you can easily edit, disable, and remove them using the Exchange Management Console or Exchange Management Shell.

After configuring transport rules on your Hub role servers, you can view and manage them using the Transport Rules tab under the **Organization Configuration** > **Hub Transport** node within the Exchange Management Console. To manage transport rules on an Edge role server, you can navigate to the Transport Rules tab under the **Edge Transport** node within the Exchange Management Console.

To edit the conditions, exceptions, and actions for a transport rule, simply select the appropriate transport rule under the Transport Rules tab, and click **Edit Rule** in the action pane to start the Edit Transport Rule wizard. The pages in the Edit Transport Rule wizard are identical to the pages that you used to create the transport rule.

Alternatively, you can highlight a transport rule in the Exchange Management Console and select the **Disable Rule** action from the action pane to temporarily disable the rule or select the **Remove** action from the action pane to delete the transport rule. In general, it is good practice to disable transport rules if you are not sure whether the rule may be needed in the future. In addition, disabling a transport rule may be useful when troubleshooting an email relay problem. If disabling the transport rule did not solve the problem, the problem is not related to the actions defined within the transport rule. To enable a disabled transport rule, you can select the **Enable Rule** action from the action pane.

If you have created several transport rules on your Hub or Edge role servers, they will be given a priority number that is used to determine the order in which they are processed by the Hub or Edge role server. Hub and Edge role servers first process the transport rule that has a priority number of 0, followed by the transport rule that has a priority of 1, and so on. To speed up transport rule processing, you should ensure that the transport rules that frequently match emails are listed with a lower priority number than transport rules that rarely match emails. To change the priority number, highlight the transport rule in the Exchange Management Console, select the **Change Priority** action from the action pane, and specify the appropriate priority number.

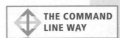

THE COMMAND LINE WAY

You can also use cmdlets within the Exchange Management Shell to manage transport rules on an Edge or Hub role server.

The **Get-TransportRule** cmdlet can be used to display the configuration of transport rules, and the **Set-TransportRule** cmdlet may be used to modify the configuration and priority of transport rules. Similarly, you can use the **Remove-TransportRule** cmdlet to remove transport rules or the **Disable-TransportRule** and **Enable-TransportRule** cmdlets to disable and enable transport rules respectively. For more information on the usage of these cmdlets, simply search for their names within the Exchange Server 2007 Help.

SUMMARY SKILL MATRIX

IN THIS LESSON YOU LEARNED:

- POP3 is the traditional email protocol used on the Internet to download email. IMAP4 is a newer email protocol used by Internet email clients that maintains a persistent connection to the email server for email viewing and provides support for additional features such as public folders.

- You can configure the authentication, encryption, ports, calendaring, and protocol limits used by both the POP3 and IMAP4 protocols using the name node within the Exchange Management Console or the appropriate cmdlets within the Exchange Management Shell. Only members of the Exchange Organization Administrator role or the Exchange Server Administrator role for the CAS role server are able to configure POP3 and IMAP4 settings.

- HTTP is used by email clients when accessing web-based email systems such as OWA. If you are a member of the Exchange Organization Administrator role or the Exchange Server Administrator role for the CAS role server that hosts OWA, you can configure some settings for HTTP such as authentication methods. Other HTTP settings such as protocol limits, ports, encryption, and access restrictions can be configured using the Default Web Site in IIS Manager provided that you are a member of the local Administrators group on the CAS role server.

- MAPI RPC is the most common email protocol used by Outlook and Entourage clients across a LAN. Outlook Anywhere provides MAPI RPC over HTTP for remote Outlook and Entourage clients. By default, MAPI RPC clients can take advantage of the Autodiscover and Availability services in Exchange Server 2007 to obtain autoconfiguration, OAB, and scheduling information. Alternatively, you must manually enable the Autodiscover and Availability services to work with Outlook Anywhere clients. To configure the Autodiscover and Availability services, you must be a member of the Exchange Organization Administrator role or the Exchange Server Administrator role for the CAS role server.

- SMTP is used by POP3 and IMAP4 clients as well as email servers to relay email. ESMTP is a newer implementation of SMTP that provides additional features such as authentication and encryption that are negotiated at the onset of an ESMTP connection. Most email client programs and email servers attempt to establish an ESMTP connection before falling back to an SMTP connection.

(continued)

- Provided that you are a member of the Exchange Organization Administrator role, you can configure SMTP transport settings as well as create and modify remote domains to control Out of Office message processing and SMTP message formats. In addition, you can modify the SMTP protocol limits on the Hub and Edge role servers within your organization. To modify SMTP protocol limits, you must be a member of the Exchange Organization Administrator role or the Exchange Server Administrator role for the Hub role server or a local Administrator on the Edge role server.

- By creating transport rules on the Hub and Edge role servers within your organization, you can modify the processing of email. Transport rules contains conditions and exceptions that are used to match emails as well as actions that may be used to delete, modify, monitor, or redirect emails.

- To create and manage transport rules on a Hub role server, you must be a member of the Exchange Organization Administrator role because transport rules are shared by all Hub role servers within the organization.

- To create and manage transport rules on an Edge role server, you must be a member of the local Administrators group on the Edge role server. Edge role transport rules are not shared by other Edge or Hub role servers within the organization. However, you can copy Edge role transport rules from one Edge role server to another to save time and administration.

■ Knowledge Assessment

Fill in the Blank

Complete the following sentences by writing the correct word or words in the blanks provided.

1. The _____ command in an ESMTP session determines the ESMTP features that the other computer supports.

2. The _____ service in Exchange Server 2007 allows for the autoconfiguration of MAPI account settings.

3. To configure the processing of Out of Office messages sent to a particular external email domain, you must create a new _____.

4. You can configure the maximum number of recipients in an SMTP message using the _____ tab of Transport Settings properties within the Exchange Management Console.

5. _____ is the default calendaring method used by POP3 and IMAP4 clients.

6. You can configure both POP3 and IMAP4 using the _____ node within the Exchange Management Shell.

7. If you configure bandwidth throttling for the HTTP protocol in the Default Web Site, you must also install the _____ in the properties of your network connection.

8. Transport rules use _____ and _____ to determine the emails that the transport rule should operate on.

9. The _____ cmdlet can be used to create additional message classifications that may be used to identify and process email using transport rules.

10. Transport rules that frequently match emails on your Hub and Edge role servers should be given a lower _____ number so that they are processed before other transport rules.

Multiple Choice

Circle the letter that corresponds to the best answer.

1. A Non-Delivery Report (NDR) is also referred to as a _____.
   - **a.** Delivery Status Notification (DSN)
   - **b.** Non-Delivery Receipt (NDR)
   - **c.** Bounce message
   - **d.** All of the above

2. What port should you configure on your IMAP4 clients so that they can connect to your Exchange server using SSL?
   - **a.** 110
   - **b.** 143
   - **c.** 993
   - **d.** 995

3. Which of the following protocols provides a persistent connection between the email client and server? (Choose all that apply.)
   - **a.** IMAP4
   - **b.** MAPI RPC
   - **c.** POP3
   - **d.** Outlook Anywhere

4. Which of the following email clients can use the Autodiscover and Availability services in Exchange Server 2007? (Choose all that apply.)
   - **a.** Entourage 2004
   - **b.** Outlook 2007
   - **c.** Outlook 2003
   - **d.** Entourage 2008

5. You configure digest authentication on your CAS role server, but HTTP clients are unable to connect using their credentials. What could be the problem?
   - **a.** Digest authentication requires SSL.
   - **b.** The AD user accounts are not configured to store passwords using reversible encryption.
   - **c.** HTTP cannot use Digest authentication.
   - **d.** The Default Web Site is not configured to use HTTP.

6. Which of the following protocols is best suited for remote clients who have dial-up Internet access?
   - **a.** POP3
   - **b.** IMAP4
   - **c.** MAPI RPC
   - **d.** HTTP

7. Which of the following cmdlets may be used to connect to the Autodiscover and Availability services for testing purposes?
   - **a.** Connect-Autodiscover
   - **b.** Get-OutlookConfiguration
   - **c.** Get-Autodiscover
   - **d.** Test-OutlookWebServices

8. Which of the following criteria can be used within a transport rule condition to match emails that have custom labels applied to them?
   - **a.** When a message header contains specific words
   - **b.** Marked with importance
   - **c.** Marked with classification
   - **d.** With a spam confidence level (SCL) rating that is greater than or equal to the limit

9. Which of the following transport rule actions can be used to send emails to another recipient and not to the original recipient listed in the email message?
   - **a.** Redirect message to addresses
   - **b.** Bcc the message to addresses
   - **c.** Add a recipient in the To field addresses
   - **d.** Copy message to addresses

10. Which of the following transport rule actions only apply to Edge role servers?
    - **a.** Silently drop the message
    - **b.** Reject the message with status code and response
    - **c.** Send bounce message to sender with enhanced status code
    - **d.** Put message in quarantine

True/False

Circle T if the statement is true or F if the statement is false.

T | F   1. You can set Out of Office message options on an individual mailbox using the Exchange Management Shell.

T | F   2. The Availability service can be used independently of the Autodiscover service.

T | F   3. The first command in any ESMTP session is HELO.

T | F   4. In order to run the **Set-IMAPSettings** cmdlet, you must be a member of the Exchange Organization Administrator role.

T | F   5. Forms-based authentication is used by default for OWA and requires SSL.

T | F   6. Integrated Windows Authentication encrypts logon credentials before sending them to the CAS role server.

T | F   7. POP3 + TLS connections use port 995 by default.

T | F   8. The X.509 certificate that is used for SSL and TLS connections alongside the POP3, IMAP4, and HTTP protocols is for temporary use only and should be replaced with a proper certificate for the organization.

T | F   9. Transport rules must be configured separately on each Hub role server within your organization.

T | F   10. In order to configure transport rules on the Edge role servers within your organization, you must be a member of the Exchange Organization Administrator role.

Review Questions

1. Explain how Exchange uses ESMTP to provide compatibility with other ESMTP and SMTP email systems.

2. Explain how the Autodiscover service may be used to reduce administrative effort within your organization.

■ Case Scenarios

Scenario 8-1: Selecting Email Protocols

Currently, your organization only allows internal access to the organization's email system using Outlook and Entourage clients and the MAPI RPC protocol. However, it has been decided that organization members should be allowed to connect to the organization's email system from home. For simplicity and administration, your organization will allow only a single protocol for home email clients. Because your organization uses public folders extensively and email is not to be downloaded to home email clients, you have narrowed your protocol selection to IMAP4 and Outlook Anywhere.

The IMAP4 and Outlook Anywhere protocols are similar in their purpose and function. Both protocols may be used to obtain email from remote clients using a persistent connection and both protocols support advanced features and public folders.

You must prepare a comparison of IMAP4 and Outlook Anywhere for your IT staff meeting tomorrow so that the members of your department can collectively decide on the protocol that will be allowed for home email clients. In a short memo, outline the pros and cons of using IMAP4 and Outlook Anywhere for home email access.

Scenario 8-2: Implementing Transport Rules

Your organization has recently discovered that important trade secrets have been leaked to competitors. It is believed that these trade secrets have been leaked unintentionally using regular email communication. As the Exchange administrator, you have been asked to determine whether Exchange Server 2007 can be used to minimize the chance that trade secrets are emailed to external recipients by accident. In a short memo, detail the various transport rules that can be created on the Hub and Edge role servers to address your organization's concerns.

Configuring Security

LESSON SKILL MATRIX

TECHNOLOGY SKILL	OBJECTIVE DOMAIN	OBJECTIVE DOMAIN NUMBER
Protecting against Viruses and Spam	Configure the antivirus and antispam system.	3.2

KEY TERMS

asymmetric encryption
Certificate Revocation List (CRL)
Certificate Services
certificate template
Certification Authority (CA)
connection filtering
cryptography
digital signature
encryption algorithm
enrollment
Forefront Security for Exchange
  Server (FSE)

Forefront Server Security
  Administrator
host-based firewall
method of least privilege
multifactor authentication
network-based firewall
practical security
private key
public key
public key certificate
Purported Responsible Address
  (PRA)

Realtime Block List (RBL)
Security Configuration Wizard
  (SCW)
sender ID
sender reputation
Spam Confidence Level (SCL)
Subject Alternative Name (SAN)
symmetric encryption
thumbprint
trusted root
virus definition
Windows Firewall

■ Understanding Security

↓ **THE BOTTOM LINE**

To protect the information that is stored on and relayed by email servers within your organization, you must implement various security technologies and configurations. However, you must first understand the various security threats and weaknesses that are common in email systems as well as the practices and procedures that can be used to minimize them.

No software is completely secure. There are always methods to manipulate software that is not desired or to access data that should not be accessed. However, the term *security* refers to the broad set of practices and procedures that you can use to minimize the chance that novice or advanced users will exploit your computer systems. Because these practices and procedures can take a great deal of time and money to implement, most organizations focus on implementing only those security practices and procedures that provide the most protection against exploits. This approach to security is called *practical security* and typically involves understanding the potential security risks for a particular organization, selecting the appropriate security technologies, and then implementing them. The security technologies, practices, and procedures selected will be relative to the level of risk as well as the amount of time and money that the organization can spend to protect against the risk. For example, financial institutions such as banks are more likely to have a larger security infrastructure than a manufacturing company because the likelihood and cost of a security breach is much higher.

Because email systems allow for communication, they also allow for unauthorized access to sensitive information. Sensitive information such as trade secrets could be sent to another person outside the organization within an email or as an attachment to an email. Moreover, sensitive information may be sent to others in the same organization who should not have access to it or be obtained by examining emails as they pass across networks. To minimize the possibility that this will happen, you can restrict access to the email system, encrypt email transfer, restrict email relay, limit permissions, control viruses and spam, stop unnecessary services, implement firewalls, and regularly update software.

RESTRICTING ACCESS TO THE EMAIL SYSTEM

Many organizations restrict access to the email system by preventing email access from outside the organization and forcing users to use an internal domain client computer to access email using a single protocol such as MAPI RPC. In addition, by implementing a policy whereby mailbox users must use complex passwords, change their password on a regular basis, and log in only during specific times, you minimize the chance that a member of your organization will guess another member's password and use it to exploit the email system. Similarly, by adopting a policy that requires mailbox users to be disabled when they leave the organization or take vacation will further prevent another member of the organization from using another user's email account. In organizations that require higher levels of security, users may be required to insert a *smart card* or use a *biometric thumbprint reader* on their workstation in addition to providing a username and password to log on to the domain or gain access to email. This approach to security is called *multifactor authentication* and minimizes the chances that unauthorized users will gain access to the computer system because multiple forms of authentication are required to do so.

ENCRYPTING EMAIL TRANSFER

Advanced users do not need to use another user's email account to view or send emails. Instead, they could use a *network protocol analyzer* program such as Wireshark to view the contents of POP3, IMAP4, HTTP, SMTP, and MAPI RPC traffic as it passes across a network from the client computer to the email server. To prevent this, you should always ensure that client computers access the email on their email server using encrypted versions of their email protocol. By default, MAPI RPC connections are encrypted and the default configuration of Exchange Server 2007 CAS role servers require POP3S, IMAP4S, HTTPS, and SMTPS using the default encryption certificate that is installed by Exchange. However, to allow for proper protocol encryption, you must replace the default encryption certificate on your Exchange servers with a signed certificate as discussed later in this lesson.

Recall that email servers relay email to other email servers across the Internet using SMTP. This email relay does not use encryption because it is too difficult to coordinate the usage of encryption certificates among all organizations in the world. However, because email servers relay SMTP email directly to the Internet from their organization's Internet connection to their ISP, it is unlikely that an advanced user will have the ability to view this SMTP traffic. Furthermore, today ISPs relay email directly to other ISPs on the Internet using private networks. Thus, the likelihood that an advanced user will be able to view unencrypted SMTP traffic as it passes from email server to email server across the Internet is very low.

Regardless, some organizations with higher security needs may encrypt email sent between partner organizations by creating special send and receive connectors in each organization that are configured to use TLS encryption alongside SMTP for email that is sent between the two organizations only. Still, other organizations may use general encryption technologies such as *Internet Protocol Security (IPSec)* or *Virtual Private Networks (VPNs)* to encrypt email traffic between partner organizations.

TAKE NOTE✳

Network protocol analyzers are commonly called *packet sniffers* because they capture (sniff) TCP/IP packets on the network.

RESTRICTING EMAIL RELAY

Regardless of whether your organization encrypts Internet email relay, you should also ensure that the email servers within your organization only relay necessary emails. By creating transport rules to monitor, log, and restrict email relay, you can help prevent sensitive information from being sent to the wrong recipients. For example, because most sensitive information will be recorded in files such as spreadsheets, you could create a transport rule that prevents emails and attachments from being sent outside your organization if they contain keywords that represent sensitive information. In addition, you can create transport rules that only allow certain users to send email to outside organizations or other users within the organization. This is important in preventing corporate fraud. For example, by preventing people in the Purchasing department (who create purchase orders for equipment and supplies) from communicating via email to users within the Accounts Payable department (who pay bills that have been received from other companies that are purchased from), you minimize the chance that someone in the Purchasing department will work with someone in the Accounts Payable department to commit fraud by agreeing to purchase equipment for noncorporate use.

TAKE NOTE *

You can use the Exchange Best Practices Analyzer tool introduced in Lesson 3, "Deploying Exchange Server 2007" to check the permissions assigned to Exchange servers. Access the **Best Practices Analyzer** under the **Toolbox** node within the Exchange Management Console and select a **Permission Check** scan type when prompted.

LIMITING PERMISSIONS

Many exploits that occur within organizations today are the result of poor permission assignments. Members of your organization should only have the permissions that they need to access data and no more. This practice is called the *method of least privilege.* For example, executive salary information may be stored within the HR public folder. If the Exchange Administrator or public folder owner does not modify the permissions to allow only HR staff to view the information in the public folder, then everyone within the organization will have access to the executive salary information due to the default permissions that are set on new public folders.

CONTROLLING VIRUSES AND SPAM

Viruses are small programs or program fragments that perform a wide variety of unwanted activities on your system. Some viruses slow the performance of your system whereas other viruses destroy valuable data. Still other viruses may be used to provide unauthorized access to your system by sending information to the Internet that others can use to exploit your system. Modern viruses are configured to replicate from computer to computer when the file that holds the virus is opened. Some viruses spread via email and are called *email bombs* as a result. When the file or file attachment that contains the email bomb is opened, the virus obtains a list of any email addresses it can find within your email client program (i.e., contact lists) and sends email to those recipients on your behalf along with the email bomb virus.

The best protection against viruses within your organization is antivirus software. Because most viruses are spread by email, installing antivirus software on the Edge or Hub role servers within your organization and regularly updating the virus database of your Edge or Hub role server will minimize the number of viruses within your organization. However, no antivirus software will catch every single virus. As a result, it is also important that you educate users about how to identify viruses and instruct them to delete any emails that appear to contain viruses. Because viruses are usually contained within email attachments, you should advise users to first determine whether an attachment is safe to open. In general, users should only open attachments if:

- They expected to receive the attachment, and it is from a trusted sender.
- The attachment is not an executable program (executable programs typically have a file extension of .exe, .bat, .vbs, .com, .ini, or .reg).
- The attachment does not have a suspicious filename (e.g., click_to_win.exe) or a file extension that does not match the filename (e.g., picture_of_ocean.vbs).

Spam, or junk mail, is simply unsolicited email from organizations on the Internet called *spammers*. In most cases, spam emails are from companies that you have never heard of or contacted in the past. Because different spam messages are often emailed to the same recipient and spammers trade their recipient lists with other spammers, you could receive hundreds of spam messages per day in your Inbox. Large numbers of spam messages waste time and productivity within organizations and are often cited as a primary reason why organizations change their email address formats.

Although spam messages can contain viruses, most spam messages are designed to sell questionable products, illegal services, and pornographic material. Consequently, spam is illegal in many regions and countries.

In addition, many spam messages contain hyperlinks that are used to verify that your email address exists to external organizations. These organizations will likely use this information to send more spam. Other spam messages attempt to lure users into filling out forms on Internet Web sites that contain their personal information. This information is often used to commit fraud or gain unauthorized access to a system because users often use personal information when generating account passwords. This type of spam is called a *phishing attack*.

To minimize the number of spam messages that your organization receives, it is important to install antispam software on the Edge or Hub role servers within your organization. However, because spam messages are often designed to resemble legitimate emails, antispam software cannot prevent all spam messages from entering your recipient's mailboxes. As a result, it is important to educate your users so that they can identify spam messages. Following this, it is vital that users understand that they should not respond to spam messages or click on any hyperlinks within the spam message itself.

A message is likely spam if it:

- Is from someone you do not know through a freely obtainable Internet account (e.g., hotmail, gmail, or yahoo);
- Is from scrambled, sales-oriented, or random-generated recipients (e.g., w8C4rsa29846@ hotmail.com or freequote@offers.com);
- Requests sensitive information using hyperlinks in the email itself that do not reflect the organization that sent the email;
- Contains a message that asks for help or assistance from an unknown person or organization;
- Contains an empty **To:** field; or
- Contains sales- or service-oriented information in the subject line (e.g., Make Quick Cash, Free Offer, Find Old Classmates).

The configuration of antivirus and antispam software is discussed later in this lesson.

STOPPING UNNECESSARY SERVICES AND IMPLEMENTING FIREWALLS

To gain access to a server, network users must interact with a network service that is running on the server. Each network service listens for incoming network traffic on specific port number(s) and processes any traffic that matches its port number(s). For example, the POP3 service on a CAS role server listens to TCP port 110 for unencrypted and TLS POP3 requests and TCP port 995 for SSL POP3 requests. If the POP3 service is stopped, then any incoming network traffic sent to the CAS role server on TCP port 110 or 995 will be discarded because there is no service that will respond to the request.

Similarly, if all services that listen to port numbers are stopped on a particular server, there is no possible way for a network user to access or exploit the server. However, to function, servers must provide certain network services to network users. Malicious network users can interact with these running network services to exploit the system if there is a weakness in the network service itself. Although many network services provide a high level of security, malicious network users will attempt to interact with all possible network services on your Exchange servers in hopes of finding a weakness. By stopping unnecessary services on your Exchange servers, you reduce the number of network services that malicious network users can attempt to exploit and hence reduce the *attack surface* of your Exchange servers. For example, if your CAS role server does not service POP3 clients, stopping the POP3 service and setting its startup type to Disabled will prevent malicious network users from interacting with your server via the POP3 service.

Another way to reduce the attack surface of your Exchange servers is to implement firewalls. Firewalls are software programs that prevent unnecessary network traffic from reaching computer systems. There are two main types of firewalls that you can use to protect Exchange Server: host-based firewalls and network-based firewalls.

A *host-based firewall* runs as a software component on the server itself to restrict incoming traffic destined for specific port numbers. However, host-based firewalls do not restrict outgoing traffic from the server itself and the associated responses from other servers. For example, if you implement a host-based firewall on your CAS role server that prevents traffic on TCP port 110 and 995, no network users can connect to your CAS role server on those ports regardless of whether the POP3 service is running. However, your CAS role server can connect to other servers using TCP port 110 and 995 and receive the associated responses through the firewall.

While host-based firewalls protect individual servers, **network-based firewalls** protect traffic passing from one network to another. As a result, they are typically comprised of software components on routers. By restricting network traffic on TCP port 110 and 995 from passing through your network-based firewall into your LAN, you prevent external network users from interacting with the POP3 services running on any server in your LAN. However, in this case, internal network users can still connect to the POP3 services running on any server in the LAN that does not have a host-based firewall that restricts POP3 traffic.

The configuration of services and firewalls is discussed in the next section of this lesson.

PERFORMING REGULAR SOFTWARE UPDATES

Although you can reduce the attack surface on your Exchange servers, malicious network users can still interact with those services that the server must host and attempt to locate a security loophole. Most network-based attacks attempt to interact with network services on servers in ways that the original developer of the network service did not expect. These types of attacks are commonly called **buffer overruns** and are designed to locate flaws in network services that allow a malicious network user unauthorized access to the system. The only solution to a network service weakness that can be exploited using a buffer overrun is to update the network service software to a newer version that does not contain the flaw. Program updates are continually created and released when weaknesses are found in network services. Consequently, it is important to update the software on your Exchange servers on a regular basis to ensure that the network services on them are not vulnerable to new buffer overrun attacks.

Although you can update Exchange Server 2007 using the setup program or the Windows Update Web site, you can also configure a **Windows Server Update Services (WSUS)** server on your network to automate the deployment of updates to the servers and workstations in your organization.

■ Reducing the Exchange Attack Surface

↓ **THE BOTTOM LINE**

A key component to any secure email system is the reduction of enabled services and open ports to minimize the number of ways that malicious users can interact with your email servers. You can achieve this by disabling unused services or by implementing host-based and network-based firewalls.

As mentioned in the previous section, reducing the attack surface is fundamental to ensuring that Exchange Server network exploits are minimized. The attack surface of a computer is simply the sum total of all the ways that a network user can interact with network services running on the computer. By stopping unnecessary services and implementing firewalls to restrict access to network services, you can minimize the attack surface on the Exchange servers within your organization. To perform these tasks, you must at a minimum be a member of the local Administrators group on the Exchange server.

You can stop unnecessary network services on an Exchange server by navigating to **Start** > **Administrative Tools** > **Services** in Windows, right clicking the appropriate network service in the Services window, and selecting **Stop** from the menu. To prevent the service from starting at boot time, you can also access the properties of the appropriate network service in the Services window and set its Startup type to **Disabled** as shown for the Telnet service in Figure 9-1.

Figure 9-1

Disabling a Service

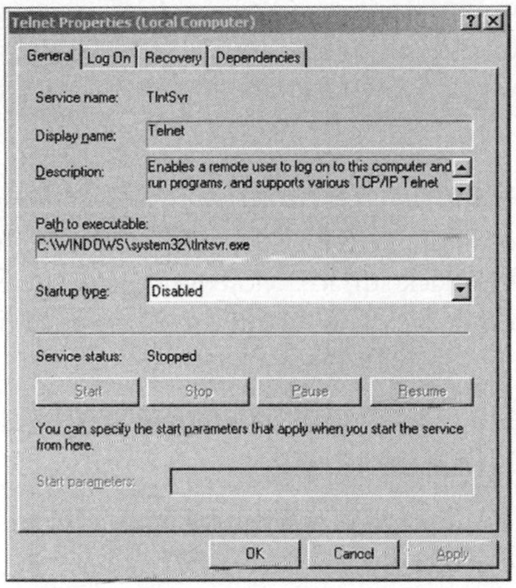

In addition to stopping unnecessary network services on your Exchange servers, you can implement a host-based firewall such as **Windows Firewall** to prevent all network requests from entering your Exchange server unless they are on a specific port number or destined for a specific service that your Exchange server provides. By default, host-based firewalls block inbound access to all protocols and allow exceptions for the protocols that you specify based on the program name or port number for a particular service. Table 9-1 lists common port numbers that are used by Exchange Server protocols.

Table 9-1

Common port numbers associated with Exchange Server protocols

PROTOCOL	PORT NUMBERS
ADAM (EdgeSync)	TCP 50389 (ADAM LDAP)
	TCP 50636 (ADAM LDAP with SSL)
HTTP (Outlook Web Access)	TCP 80 (unencrypted HTTP)
	TCP 443 (HTTP with SSL)
IMAP4	TCP 143 (unencrypted IMAP4 or IMAP4 with TLS)
	TCP 993 (IMAP4 with SSL)
MAPI RPC	UDP 135 (for service discovery)
	Random port number (for MAPI RPC data)
Outlook Anywhere	TCP 593 (for service discovery)
	TCP 80 (unencrypted HTTP)
	TCP 443 (HTTP with SSL)
POP3	TCP 110 (unencrypted POP3 or POP3 with TLS)
	TCP 995 (POP3 with SSL)
SMTP/ESMTP	TCP/UDP 25 (Internet email relay, legacy client access)
	TCP/UDP 587 (Client access)

If you use a host-based firewall on your Exchange server, you may need to open more ports than those listed in Table 9-1 if your server hosts additional network services. For example, if your Exchange server runs the DNS service, you will also need to open TCP and UDP port 53 to allow other computers to query your DNS service.

TAKE NOTE *

In case you disable too many network services or restrict too many ports, it is good practice to first configure the attack surface on a test Exchange server in a test environment before performing the same actions in a production environment.

The *Security Configuration Wizard (SCW)* component of Windows can be used to disable unused services as well as configure Windows Firewall on the Exchange servers within your organization to minimize the attack surface. Moreover, Exchange Server 2007 comes with templates that can be imported into the SCW to customize SCW settings for each server role.

INSTALL AND RUN THE SECURITY CONFIGURATION WIZARD TO REDUCE THE EXCHANGE SERVER ATTACK SURFACE

TAKE NOTE *

You must have Windows Server 2003 SP1 or Windows Server 2003 R2 or later to install the SCW.

GET READY. Turn on the computer, and log in as the Administrator user account. Close any windows that appear on the desktop.

1. Click **Start**, **Control Panel**, and then click **Add or Remove Programs**. When the Add or Remove Programs window appears, click **Add/Remove Windows Components** to open the Windows Components Wizard.

2. On the Windows Components page, select **Security Configuration Wizard** and click **Next**.

3. Click **Finish** to close the Windows Components Wizard. Close the Add or Remove Programs window.

4. Click **Start** and then click **Run**. In the Run dialog box, type **scwcmd register/ kbname:Ex2007KB/kbfile: "%programfiles%\Microsoft\Exchange Server\Scripts\ Exchange2007.xml"** and click **OK**. This command registers the Exchange Server 2007 services and features with the SCW.

5. Click **Start**, **Administrative Tools**, and then click **Security Configuration Wizard**. When the Security Configuration Wizard window appears, click **Next**. The Configuration Action screen appears as shown in Figure 9-2.

Figure 9-2

Creating a New Security Policy

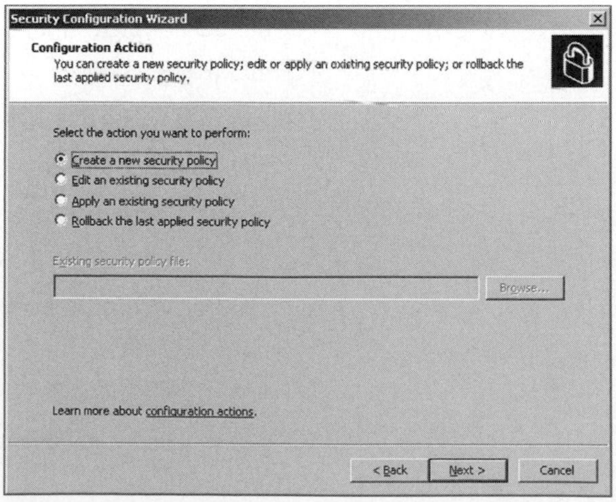

6. At the Configuration Action screen, ensure that **Create a new security policy** is selected and click **Next**. The Select Server screen appears as shown in Figure 9-3.

Figure 9-3

Selecting a Server

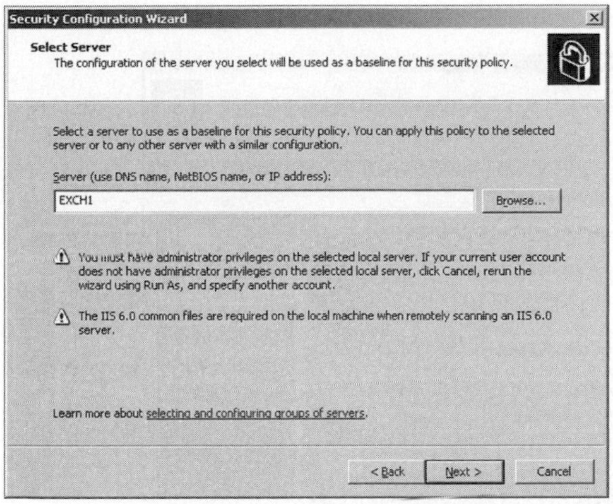

7. At the Select Server screen, type the NetBIOS name, IP address, or FQDN of the Exchange server that you wish to analyze. Alternatively, you can click **Browse**, select your server in the Select Computer window that appears, and click **OK**. If you select a different server than the local computer on which you are running the SCW, you must ensure that your local computer has IIS 6.0 installed.

8. When finished, click **Next**. The SCW will take a few moments to analyze the Exchange server on the Processing Security Configuration Database page. When it is finished, click **View Configuration Database** to open the SCW Viewer window.

9. In the SCW Viewer, expand the appropriate Exchange Server 2007 roles that are present on your Exchange server to view information regarding the installed services as well as the programs that listen on ports. Figure 9-4 shows the Exchange 2007 Hub Transport role expanded.

Figure 9-4

Viewing Server Details in the SCW Viewer

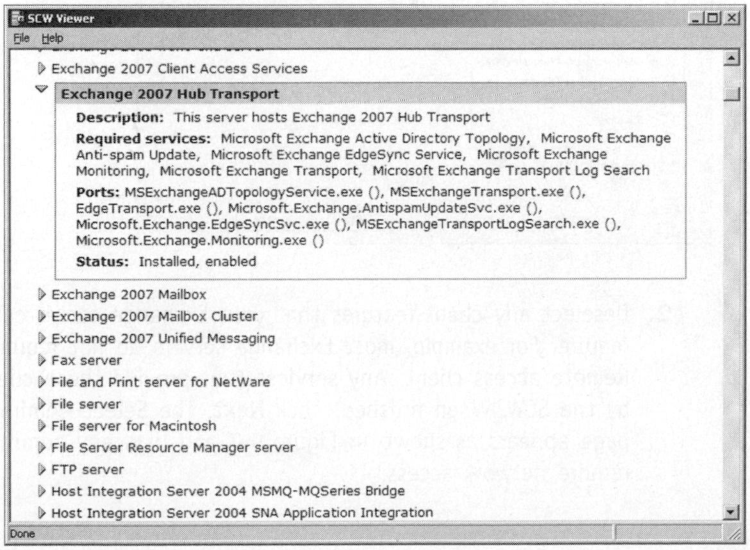

10. When finished, close the SCW Viewer window and click **Next** on the Processing Security Configuration Database page. When the Role-Based Service Configuration page appears, click **Next**. The Select Server Roles page appears and lists the installed server roles on your Exchange server as shown in Figure 9-5.

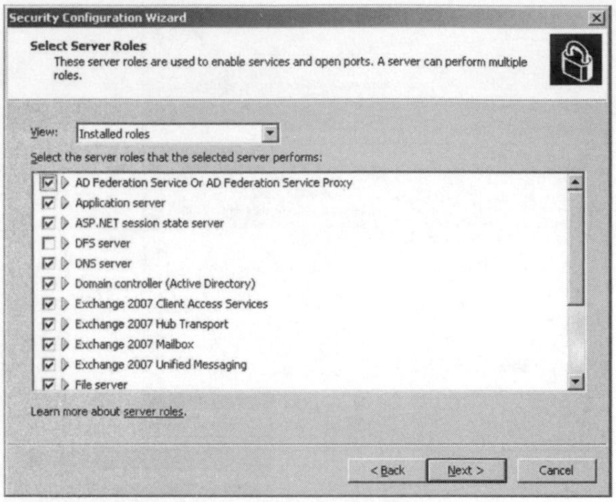

Figure 9-5

Selecting Server Roles

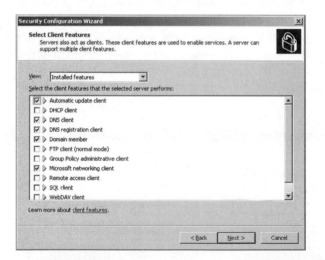

11. Deselect any server roles that your Exchange server currently has but does not require. For example, most Exchange servers do not require the Telnet server or File server services. Any services that you select here will be disabled by the SCW. When finished, click **Next**. The Select Client Features page appears and lists any client programs that are enabled on your Exchange server as shown in Figure 9-6.

Figure 9-6

Selecting Client Features

12. Deselect any client features that your Exchange server currently has but does not require. For example, most Exchange servers do not require the FTP client or the Remote access client. Any services that provide these client features will be disabled by the SCW. When finished, click **Next**. The Select Administration and Other Options page appears as shown in Figure 9-7 and lists any administrative programs that require network access.

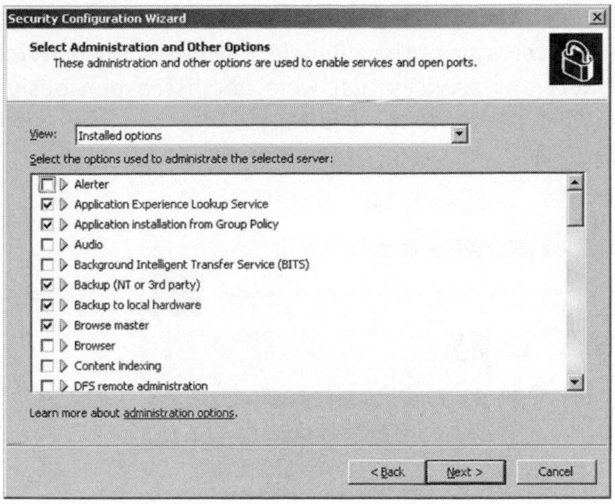

Figure 9-7

Selecting Administration
and Other Options

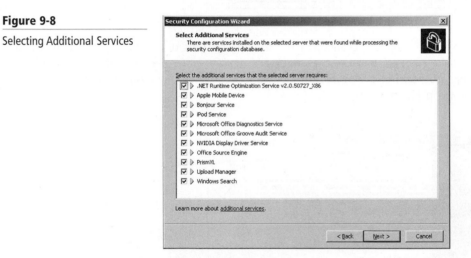

13. Deselect any administrative options that your Exchange server does not require. Any services associated with the administrative options that you deselect will be set to disabled by the SCW. Click **Next**. The Select Additional Services page appears as shown in Figure 9-8 and lists any third-party or additional Windows components that require network access.

Figure 9-8

Selecting Additional Services

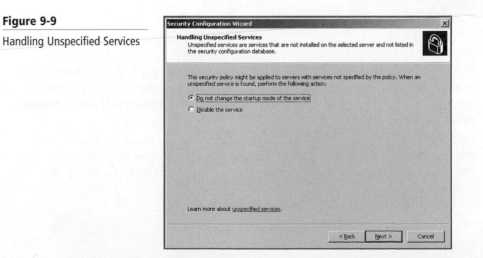

14. Deselect any additional software services that your Exchange server does not require. Any services associated with the additional software that you deselect will be set to disabled by the SCW. Click **Next**. The Handling Unspecified Services page appears as shown in Figure 9-9.

Figure 9-9

Handling Unspecified Services

15. By default, any services that were not detected by the SCW are left unchanged. However, you can optionally select **Disable the service** as shown in Figure 9-9 to disable any services that were not listed previously during the SCW. When finished, click **Next**. The Confirm Service Changes window appears as shown in Figure 9-10.

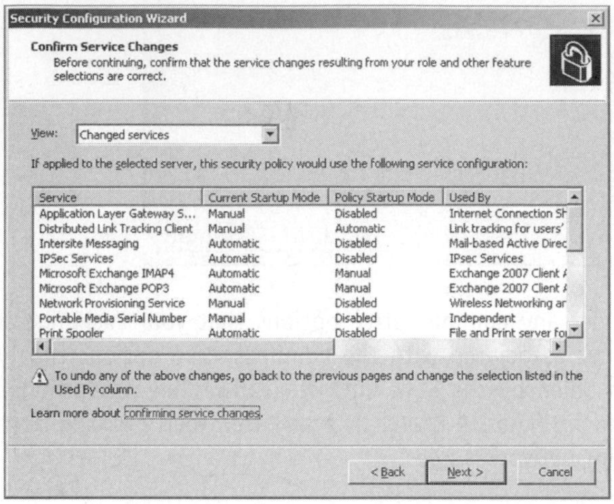

Figure 9-10

Confirming Service Changes

16. Review the proposed changes to the existing services on your computer. If you wish to make changes, you can click **Back** and modify your selections on the appropriate pages. Otherwise, click **Next**. The Network Security Configuration page appears as shown in Figure 9-11.

Figure 9-11

Specifying Network Security Options

17. By default, the SCW enables Windows Firewall and blocks any incoming traffic that is not specifically allowed according to your selections in the remaining pages of the SCW. If you do not wish to enable Windows Firewall, select **Skip this section** as shown in Figure 9-11.

18. Click **Next**. If you did not select **Skip this section** as shown in Figure 9-11, the Open Ports and Approve Applications page appears and lists the ports that match the enabled network services on your Exchange server as shown in Figure 9-12.

Figure 9-12

Specifying Open Ports and Approved Applications

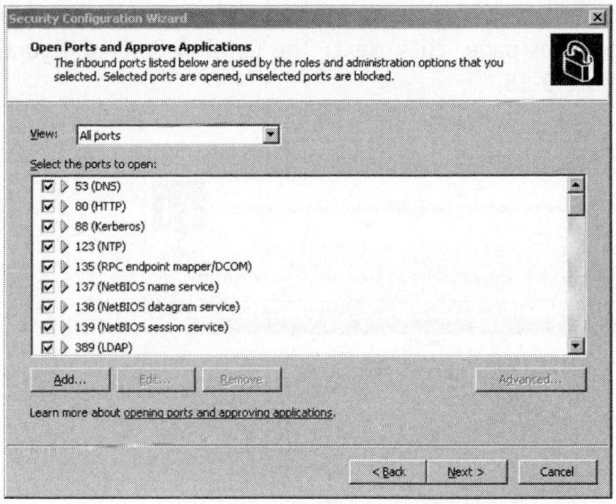

19. Deselect any ports that represent services that network computers should not use when contacting your Exchange server. For other services, you can specify the network interfaces that the service should be listed on as well as the remote clients that are allowed to interact with the service. Highlight the appropriate service and click **Advanced**. On the Remote Address Restrictions tab in the window that appears, you can choose to restrict access to specific remote hosts or networks that you specify by clicking **Add**. The **Remote Address Restrictions** tab shown in Figure 9-13 allows access to the DNS service for all computers on the 10.0.0.0 network as well as the host 192.168.1.55. If your Exchange server has multiple network interfaces, you can specify that the service only listen to requests from remote clients on a single network interface using the **Local Interface Restrictions** tab as shown in Figure 9-14. When finished specifying Advanced options, click **OK** to return to the Open Ports and Approve Applications page.

TAKE NOTE✱

When you click **Add** as shown in Figure 9-13, you can also require remote clients to use IPSec encryption or signing when interacting with the service. Exchange servers typically host several connections to clients and other servers. Because IPSec requires more resources per connection than SSL or TLS, IPSec is not a recommended option for securing traffic on your Exchange server.

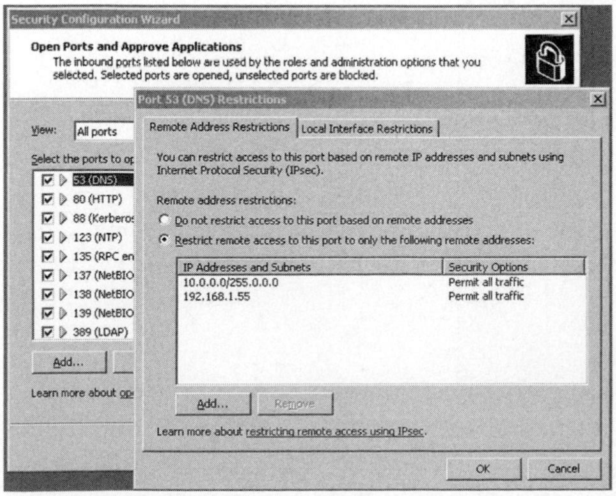

Figure 9-13

Configuring the DNS Port

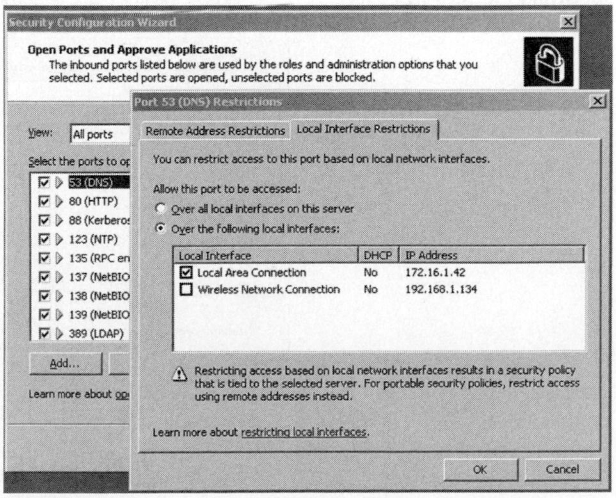

Figure 9-14

Specifying Network Interfaces for the DNS Port

20. When you are finished selecting port options on the Open Ports and Approve Applications page, click **Next**. The Confirm Port Configuration page appears as shown in Figure 9-15.

Figure 9-15

Confirming Port Configuration

Security Configuration Wizard

Confirm Port Configuration
Before continuing, confirm that the inbound port configuration resulting from your selections is correct.

If applied to the selected server, this security policy would use the following inbound port configuration:

Port	Protocol	Status	Security Options	Restrictions
53 (DNS)	UDP	Open		
53 (DNS)	TCP	Open		
80 (HTTP)	TCP	Open		
88 (Kerberos)	UDP	Open		
88 (Kerberos)	TCP	Open		
123 (NTP)	UDP	Open		
135 (RPC endpoint mapper/DCOM)	TCP	Open		
137 (NetBIOS name service)	UDP	Open		
137 (NetBIOS name service)	TCP	Open		
138 (NetBIOS datagram service)	UDP	Open		
139 (NetBIOS session service)	TCP	Open		

⚠ To change any of the above settings, go back to the previous pages and change the appropriate selections.

Learn more about confirming port configuration.

< Back   Next >   Cancel

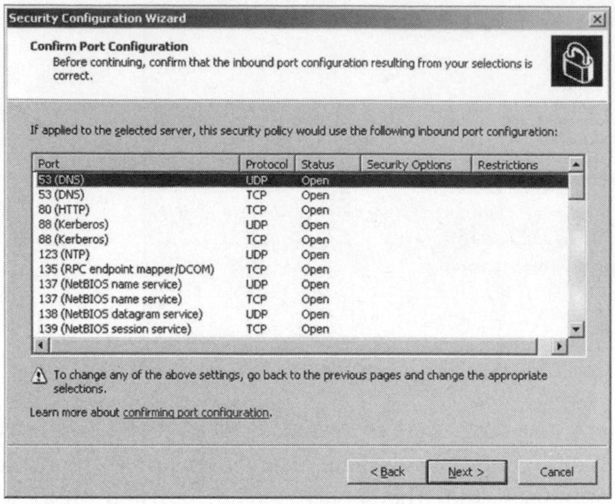

21. Review the port selections for Windows Firewall. If you wish to make changes, you can click **Back** and modify your selections on the previous page. Otherwise, click **Next**.

The SCW also allows you to specify registry keys that will prevent communication from unsecure clients, configure auditing of key events, as well as configure the usage of IIS. Because these parts of the SCW do not directly affect the attack surface of your Exchange server, we will skip their configuration.

22. At the Registry Settings page, select **Skip this section** and click **Next**.

23. At the Audit Policy page, select **Skip this section** and click **Next**.

24. At the Internet Information Services page, select **Skip this section** and click **Next**. When the Save Security Policy page appears, click **Next**. The Security Policy File Name page appears as shown in Figure 9-16.

Figure 9-16

Specifying the Security Policy File Name

Security Configuration Wizard

Security Policy File Name
The security policy file will be saved with the name and description that you provide.

Security policy file name (a '.xml' file extension will be appended if not provided):

C:\Exchange_2007.xml   Browse...

Description (optional):

View Security Policy   Include Security Templates...

Learn more about saving security policies.

< Back   Next >   Cancel

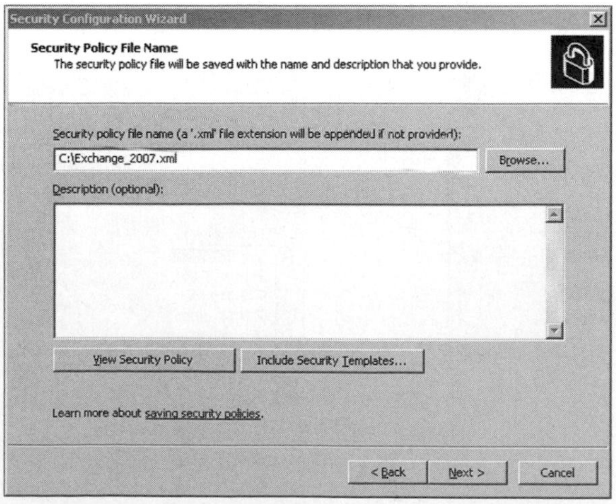

25. Supply the path name to an XML file that will store the settings that you configured in the SCW in the **Security policy file name** dialog box. This file can later be applied to other Exchange servers by running the SCW and selecting **Apply an existing security policy** on the Configuration Page as shown earlier in Figure 9-2.

TAKE NOTE *

After you have applied a security policy, you can run the SCW again and select **Rollback the last applied security policy** as shown earlier in Figure 9-2 to undo the settings configured by the security policy.

You can optionally supply a description of the policy in the **Description** dialog box. Click **View Security Policy** to review security policy settings or click **Include Security Templates** to add existing Windows security templates to the security policy.

26. When finished, click **Next**. Click **OK** to close the window that indicates that a reboot will be required after applying the policy. The Apply Security Policy window appears.

27. By default, the SCW does not apply the policy. To apply the policy immediately to your system, select **Apply now** and click **Next**. After the security policy is applied to your Exchange server, click **Next**. The Completing the Security Configuration Wizard page appears.

28. Click **Finish** to close the Security Configuration Wizard.

When reducing the attack surface of your Exchange servers, it is also important to restrict the network traffic that is allowed to pass into your LANs and reach your Exchange servers using network-based firewalls. Network-based firewalls typically offer advanced filtering options that are unavailable in host-based firewalls. For example, network-based firewalls can restrict traffic based on source and destination IP address, network, and MAC address as well as by protocol and port number. Although you can implement a Windows server running the ***Routing and Remote Access Service (RRAS)*** to perform routing and network-based firewall functionality within your organization, most organizations use network devices, such as hardware-based routers, to perform routing and network-based firewall functions for performance and cost purposes. These hardware-based routers often support ***Network Address Translation (NAT)***. NAT allows outgoing traffic from a network but only allows incoming network traffic that has been specifically configured to be forwarded to a particular computer on the internal network.

Network-based firewalls work together with host-based firewalls to provide a practical level of security for your network. If, for example, your organization has a single Exchange server on the internal LAN that hosts the Hub, CAS, and Mailbox roles as well as an Edge role server in the perimeter network that is used to filter inbound and outbound emails. Also, users within your organization use MAPI RPC within the internal LAN to obtain and send email using the internal Exchange server and can use IMAP4 with SSL (IMAP4S) from home clients to obtain email from the organization's CAS role email server across the Internet. In this situation, you can use network and host-based firewalls to reduce the attack surface of your Exchange servers as shown in Figure 9-17.

Figure 9-17

Firewall Configuration

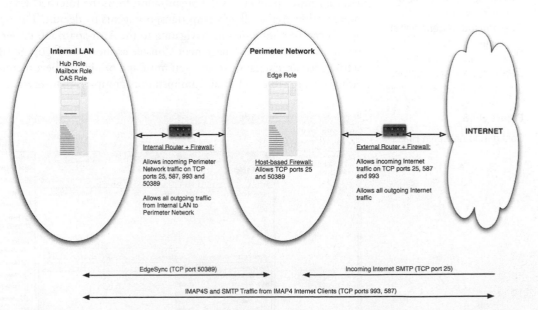

The firewall on the external router shown in Figure 9-17 is configured to allow only incoming SMTP (TCP port 25 for Internet email and TCP port 587 for IMAP4 client emails) and IMAP4S (TCP port 993) traffic to pass from the Internet into the perimeter network, but all outgoing Internet traffic is allowed. Similarly, the firewall configured on the internal router is configured to allow only SMTP

(TCP port 25 for email relay from the Edge role server and TCP port 587 for IMAP4 client emails), IMAP4S (TCP port 993), and EdgeSync (TCP port 50389) to pass from the perimeter network to the internal LAN, but allow all traffic from the internal LAN to pass to the perimeter network. Additionally, a host-based firewall on the Edge role server will prevent malicious users from interacting with services other than SMTP (TCP port 25) and EdgeSync (TCP port 50389). Because MAPI RPC clients must contact their CAS role server using a random port number, a host-based firewall is not configured on the Exchange server within the LAN.

■ Protecting against Viruses and Spam

↓ THE BOTTOM LINE

Spam messages and viruses are two of the most common problems that plague organizations today. By implementing antispam filters and antivirus software on key Exchange servers within your organization, you will minimize the amount of spam messages and viruses that are passed into your organization. Consequently, you will also minimize the time wasted by spam messages and virus infections as well as enhance the email experience for the users within your organization.

CERTIFICATION READY?
Configure the antivirus and antispam system.
3.2

Configuring Antispam Filters

Exchange Server 2007 may be used to protect against spam messages that are received from the Internet. Edge role servers within your organization automatically have several antispam agents enabled to combat incoming spam messages. Understanding how to configure these antispam agents is key to ensuring that most spam messages are removed before entering the organization while allowing legitimate email messages to reach the intended recipients.

✚ MORE INFORMATION

Antispam transport agents are used in addition to transport agents that provide for transport rules and journaling. You can view the list of all transport agents and the order in which they are applied on a Hub or Edge role server using the **Get-TransportAgent** cmdlet. To change the order that they are processed, you can use the **Set-TransportAgent** cmdlet.

To reduce the number of spam messages, Exchange Server contains several different *antispam transport agents* that email must pass through before reaching a mailbox. Each antispam transport agent is designed to filter emails based on different criteria such as sender, recipient, or email content.

Because most spam enters the organization from the Internet, Edge role servers within your organization enable all antispam transport agents by default. The settings for most of these agents can be configured by navigating to the **Anti-spam** tab under the **Edge Transport** node within the Exchange Management Console as shown in Figure 9-18. To modify antispam settings for an Exchange server, you must at a minimum be a member of the Exchange Server Administrator role and local Administrators group on that server.

Figure 9-18

Configuring Antispam Filters

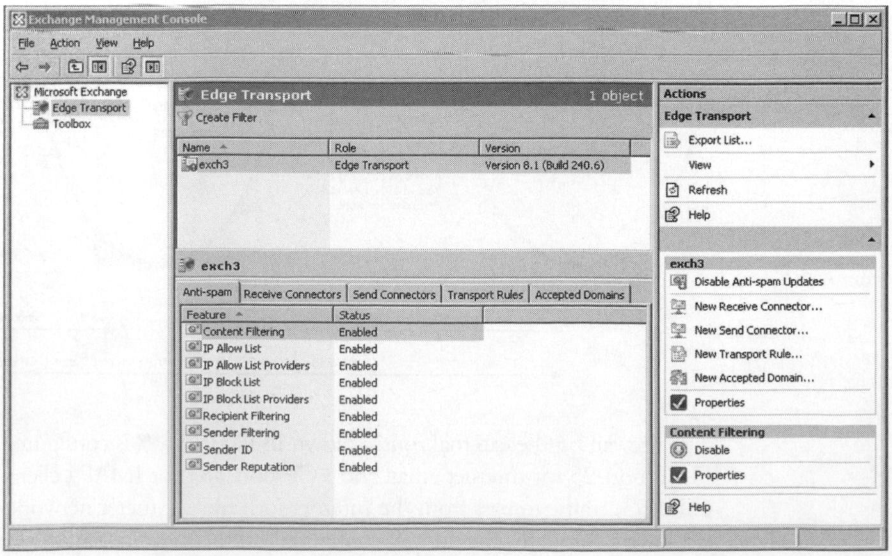

Each of the antispam features listed in Figure 9-18 can be disabled by highlighting the feature and selecting Disable from the action pane. Similarly, updated spam information and programs are automatically downloaded from the Microsoft Update Web site using the Automatic Updates feature of Windows and applied to your Edge role server. To prevent the automatic downloading of updates, you can select **Disable Anti-spam Updates** in the action pane shown in Figure 9-18.

If your organization does not use an Edge role server, you can enable a limited number of antispam transport agents on your Hub role servers by using the **Set-TransportServer** cmdlet within the Exchange Management Shell. For example, to enable the antispam transport agents on the server exch1.octavius.net, you could run the following command within the Exchange Management Shell:

Set-TransportServer –Identity 'exch1.octavius.net' –AntispamAgentsEnabled $true

After enabling the antispam transport agents on your Hub role server, you must restart the Exchange Server Transport service. Following this, you will see an Anti-spam tab under the **Server Configuration** > **Hub Transport** node within the Exchange Management Console. Unfortunately, the only antispam features that you can configure on your Hub role servers are the IP Allow List and IP Block List features shown earlier in Figure 9-18.

Configuring antispam settings is an art. Strict antispam settings will prevent some legitimate emails from reaching recipients whereas lenient antispam settings will allow some spam messages to reach recipients. As a result, it is important to continually refine your spam restrictions to ensure that members of your organization receive critical emails but only the occasional spam message.

FILTERING SPAM BY EMAIL CONTENT

To configure spam filtering by email content, you can highlight **Content Filtering** as shown in Figure 9-18 and select **Properties** from the action pane. On the **Custom Words** tab of Content Filtering Properties, you can specify a list of noncase-sensitive words or phrases that will be used to label messages as spam or not spam. As shown in Figure 9-19, any email messages that have "fast money," "make money," "no obligation," or "viagra" in the message body or subject line will be labeled as spam unless they contain "TASU" or "TPS Report."

On the Exceptions tab of Content Filtering Properties, you can add recipients within your organization who should be exempt from content filtering. This is appropriate for users who receive critical or time-sensitive emails that should never be accidentally removed by content filtering. As illustrated by Figure 9-20, any email addressed to **adel.moore@octavius.net** or **jeff.smith@ octavius.net** will not be examined by the content filtering antispam transport agent.

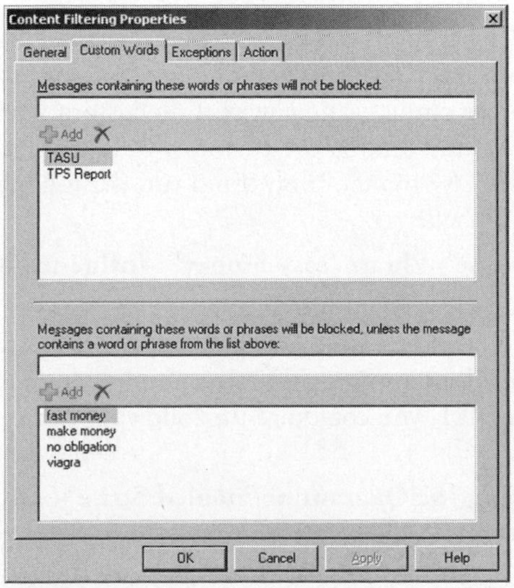

Figure 9-19

Specifying Custom Words

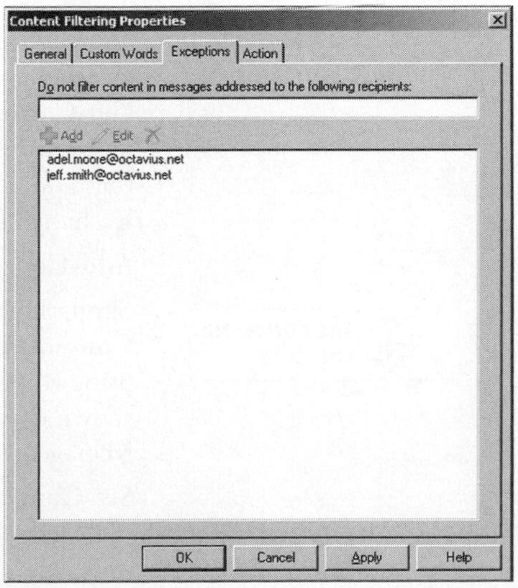

Figure 9-20

Specifying Exceptions

In addition to the words and phrases specified on the Custom Words tab of Content Filtering Properties, Exchange Server 2007 maintains a list of words and phrases that are commonly used within spam messages. These words and phrases are updated regularly and contain rankings that are used to determine the **Spam Confidence Level (SCL)**. The SCL is a number between 0 and 9 that represents the likelihood that a particular email is spam. An SCL of 0 is not likely to be spam whereas an SCL of 9 is almost certainly spam. Emails that contain words with a high-spam ranking and emails that contain multiple spam-related words are likely to have a high SCL. On the Action tab of Content Filtering Properties, you can configure how your Edge role server processes emails that have a certain SCL.

As shown in Figure 9-21, emails with an SCL of 9 are automatically deleted and an NDR is not sent to the original sender whereas emails with an SCL of 7 or 8 are automatically deleted and an NDR is sent to the original sender. Emails with an SCL of 5 or 6 are redirected to the quarantine mailbox (**spam-quarantine@octavius.net**) and an NDR is sent to the original sender. The quarantine mailbox is simply a mailbox that you create on a Mailbox role server to store potential spam messages. If an important email is accidentally sent to the quarantine mailbox due to content filtering, you can access the quarantine mailbox and forward it to the user who requested it.

TAKE NOTE*

The quarantine mailbox will accumulate many emails over time. As a result, you should create the quarantine mailbox in a separate mailbox database and ensure that the quarantine mailbox is monitored and emptied regularly.

Figure 9-21

Configuring Content Filter Actions

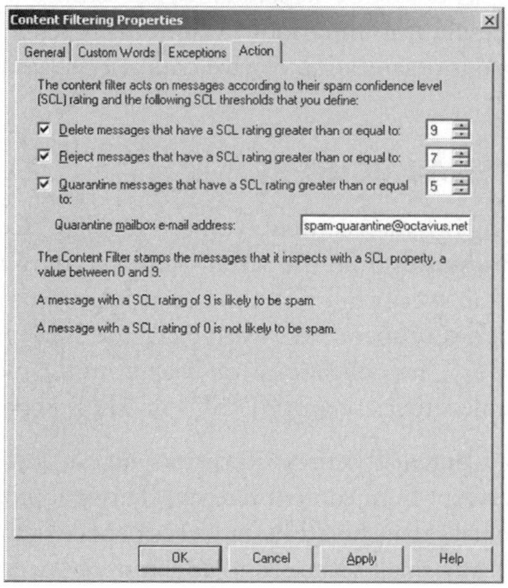

Content Filtering Properties

General | Custom Words | Exceptions | Action

The content filter acts on messages according to their spam confidence level (SCL) rating and the following SCL thresholds that you define:

☑ Delete messages that have a SCL rating greater than or equal to: 9

☑ Reject messages that have a SCL rating greater than or equal to: 7

☑ Quarantine messages that have a SCL rating greater than or equal to: 5

Quarantine mailbox e-mail address: spam-quarantine@octavius.net

The Content Filter stamps the messages that it inspects with a SCL property, a value between 0 and 9.

A message with a SCL rating of 9 is likely to be spam.

A message with a SCL rating of 0 is not likely to be spam.

OK   Cancel   Apply   Help

THE COMMAND LINE WAY

You can also use cmdlets within the Exchange Management Shell to configure content filtering. The **Add-ContentFilterPhrase** cmdlet can be used to add custom words, the **Get-ContentFilterPhrase** cmdlet can view existing custom words and the **Remove-ContentFilterPhrase** cmdlet can remove custom words. For example, to block messages that contain the phrase "easy money," you could run the following command within the Exchange Management Shell:

Add-ContentFilterPhrase –Phrase 'easy money' –Influence BadWord

Similarly, you can configure content filtering actions and exceptions using the **Set-ContentFilterConfig** cmdlet or view existing content filtering actions and exceptions using the **Get-ContentFilterConfig** cmdlet. For example, to configure the same settings shown earlier in Figure 9-21, you could use the following command within the Exchange Management Shell:

Set-ContentFilterConfig -SclQuarantineEnabled:$true -SclRejectEnabled:$true -SclDeleteEnabled:$true -SclQuarantineThreshold 5 -SclRejectThreshold 7 -SclDeleteThreshold 9 -QuarantineMailbox spam-quarantine@octavius.net

Exchange Server 2007 can also populate the exceptions list used in content filtering from the data stored within the Safe Senders list that is part of the Junk E-Mail feature of

Outlook 2007 and Entourage 2008. This information is replicated to Edge role servers using the EdgeSync protocol and used to enhance content filtering. To do this, you can run the **Update-Safelist** cmdlet. For example, to update the Safe Senders from the user Jeff Smith, you can run the following command within the Exchange Management Shell:

Update-Safelist -Identity 'Jeff Smith'

Alternatively, you can update the Safe Senders from all mailbox users within the organization using the following commands within the Exchange Management Shell:

AdminSessionAdSettings.ViewEntireForest = $True

Get-Mailbox -ResultSize Unlimited | Where {$_.RecipientType -eq [Microsoft .Exchange.Data.Directory.Recipient.RecipientType]::UserMailbox } | Update-Safelist

For more information on the content filtering cmdlets in this section, search for their names within Exchange Server 2007 Help.

FILTERING SPAM BY IP ADDRESS

Often, several spam messages are sent from a single IP address. This IP address represents the server that has relayed the spam messages directly to your Edge role server and is typically an anonymous remailer. Anonymous remailers are SMTP servers that accept email from unauthenticated clients or other email servers and forward it to its destination. Most spammers send email through several anonymous remailers to hide their identity because most anonymous remailers are in countries that do not have laws that prevent their use. Some spammers take advantage of legitimate email servers on the Internet to send spam. As a result, you can choose to block the IP address of the legitimate email server for a specific time. After this time, the organization that owns the email server will have remedied its spam situation and will later be able to send email to your organization.

Because of this, one of the most effective methods to reduce spam messages is to filter messages by IP address. This is often called *connection filtering*. If you highlight **IP Block List** as shown in Figure 9-18 and select **Properties** from the action pane, you can specify the IP addresses or IP address ranges of spam senders (including anonymous remailers) as well as the time period for which to block them on the **Blocked Addresses** tab. As Figure 9-22 illustrates, any emails will be deleted that originate from the IP address 233.14.8.1 indefinitely because there is no Expiration date.

Figure 9-22

Configuring Blocked Addresses

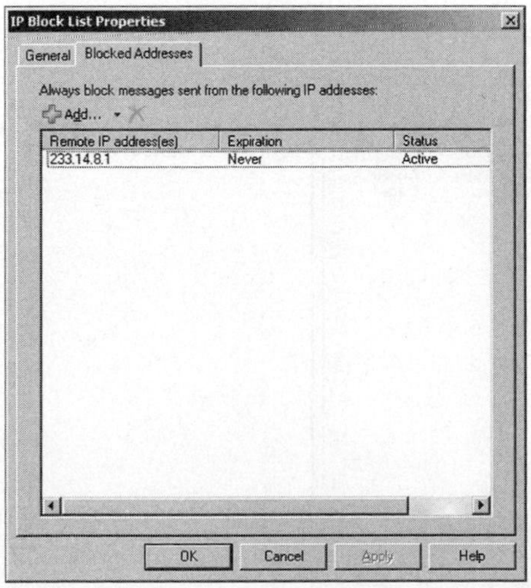

You can also provide IP addresses that should not be blocked by highlighting **IP Allow List** as shown in Figure 9-18, selecting **Properties** from the action pane, and adding the appropriate IP addresses or IP address ranges on the **Allowed Addresses** tab. IP addresses listed on the Blocked Addresses tab shown in Figure 9-22 take precedence over IP addresses listed on the Allowed Addresses tab. As illustrated by Figure 9-23, any messages from the IP address 64.114.88.12 and the IP address range 44.0.8.1 through 44.0.8.254 will be allowed unless they are also listed on the Blocked Addresses tab.

Figure 9-23

Configuring Allowed Addresses

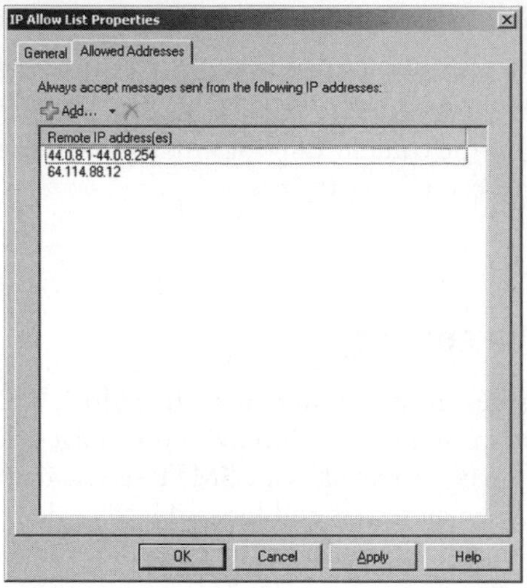

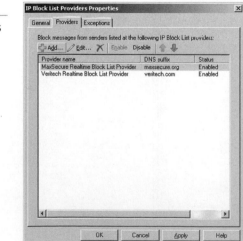

Blocking IP addresses is useful when you know the IP address of a sender that is propagating spam messages to your organization. However, determining the IP addresses to block is time consuming. As a result, many organizations subscribe to a *Realtime Block List (RBL)* provider that maintains a list of IP addresses of computers that are known to propagate spam. Your Edge role server can quickly query the RBL provider to see if certain sender's IP addresses are on the RBL. Any email from an IP address that is listed on an RBL is blocked from entering the organization. To configure one or more RBL providers, highlight **IP Block List Providers** as shown in Figure 9-18, select **Properties** from the action pane, and select the **Providers** tab. As Figure 9-24 illustrates, the MaxSecure RBL provider is used to determine whether incoming email messages are spam. If the IP address of the sender is not listed on the MaxSecure RBL, the Veritech RBL provider is queried. If the IP address of the sender is not listed on either RBL, the email is forwarded into the organization.

Figure 9-24

Specifying Block List Providers

You can modify the order that RBLs are queried by using the arrow icons shown in Figure 9-24. To add a new RBL provider, you can click **Add** and specify the name and domain name of the RBL provider in the Add IP Block List Provider window as shown in Figure 9-25. Some RBL providers provide different responses to identify whether the IP address is spam or not. For these RBL providers, you must enter the appropriate information under the Return status codes section in Figure 9-25. When an email is blocked because it is listed on an RBL, the sender receives an error message indicating the RBL that listed them. This allows legitimate organizations to contact the RBL and convince them to remove their IP address from the list. To customize the error message that is sent, you can click **Error Messages** shown in Figure 9-25.

Figure 9-25

Adding a Block List Provider

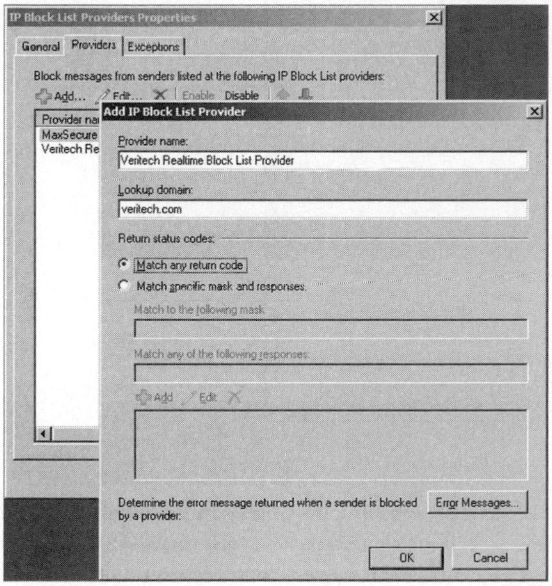

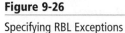

For users who receive critical or time-sensitive emails and should never be accidentally blocked by an RBL, you can add them to the Exceptions tab of IP Block List Providers properties. As shown in Figure 9-26, any email sent to the recipient **jeff.smith@octavius.net** will not be blocked even if the RBL lists the sender's IP address.

Figure 9-26

Specifying RBL Exceptions

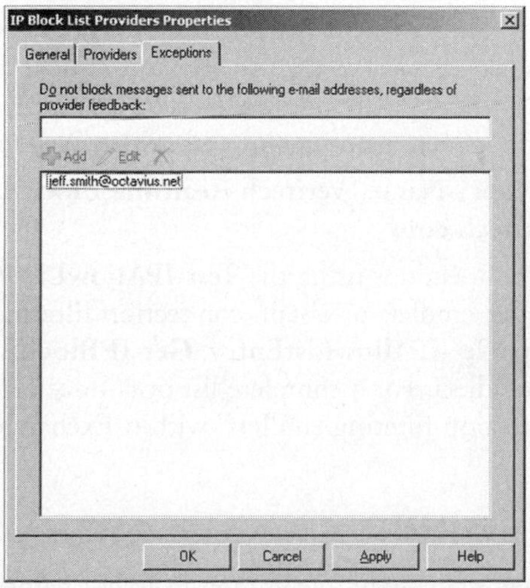

Some RBL providers offer a list of secure IP addresses that are not used by spammers. You can configure your Edge role server to query this list. Navigate to the properties of **IP Allow List Providers** shown in Figure 9-18, and add the appropriate entries on the **Providers** tab as shown in Figure 9-27. The entries on the Providers tab shown in Figure 9-27 are added in much the same way that you added RBL providers in the properties of IP Block List Providers. However, if the same IP address is both allowed and blocked by an RBL provider, emails will be blocked from entering the organization.

Figure 9-27

Configuring Allow List Providers

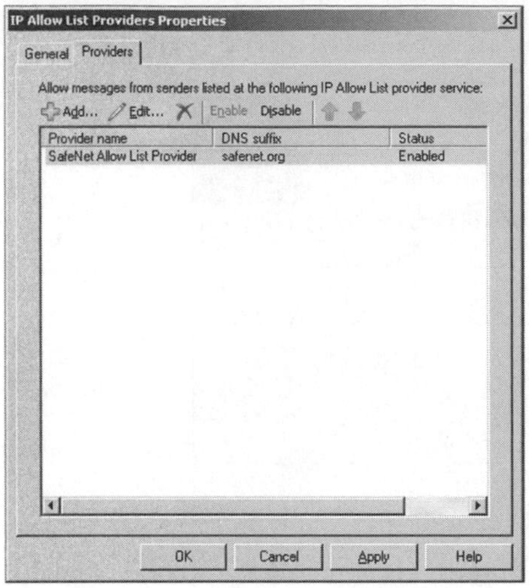

(image of IP Allow List Providers Properties dialog box)

IP Allow List Providers Properties

General | Providers |

Allow messages from senders listed at the following IP Allow List provider service:

Add... | Edit... | X | Enable Disable

Provider name	DNS suffix	Status
SafeNet Allow List Provider	safenet.org	Enabled

OK Cancel Apply Help

THE COMMAND
LINE WAY

You can also use cmdlets within the Exchange Management Shell to configure connection filtering. The **Add-IPBlockListEntry** and **Remove-IPBlockListEntry** cmdlets can be used to add and remove IP addresses to and from the IP block list respectively, whereas the **Add-IPAllowListEntry** and **Remove-IPAllowListEntry** cmdlets can be used to add and remove IP addresses to and from the IP allow list respectively. For example, to block the IP address 44.88.0.1 until 1:00 p.m. March 4, 2009, you could run the following command within the Exchange Management Shell:

Add-IPBlockListEntry –IPAddress '44.88.0.1' -ExpirationTime '3/4/2009 13:00'

Additionally, you can use the **Add-IPBlockListProvider** and **Remove-IPBlockListProvider** cmdlets to add and remove RBLs that are queried for blocked IP addresses respectively. Similarly, the **Add-IPAllowListProvider** and **Remove-IPAllowListProvider** cmdlets may be used to add and remove RBLs that are queried for allowed IP addresses. For example, to add the IP block list provider shown earlier in Figure 9-25, you could run the following command within the Exchange Management Shell:

Add-IPBlockListProvider –Name 'Veritech Realtime Block List Provider' –LookupDomain 'veritech.com'

You can also test RBL connections using the **Test-IPAllowListProvider** and **TestIPBlockListProvider** cmdlets or obtain connection filtering configuration using the **Get-IPBlockListEntry**, **Get-IPAllowListEntry**, **Get-IPBlockListProvider**, and **Get-IPAllowListProvider** cmdlets. For a complete list of connection filtering cmdlets and their usage, search for "connection filtering cmdlets" within Exchange Server 2007 Help.

FILTERING SPAM BY RECIPIENT

Recall that spammers often send email to common recipient names within the organization in hopes of contacting a valid recipient. When spammers obtain the address of a valid recipient (i.e., when a recipient clicks on a hyperlink within a spam message), they typically send multiple spam messages to that recipient. To filter spam by recipient, you can highlight **Recipient Filtering** shown in Figure 9-18, select **Properties** from the action pane, and specify the appropriate information on the **Blocked Recipients** tab as shown in Figure 9-28.

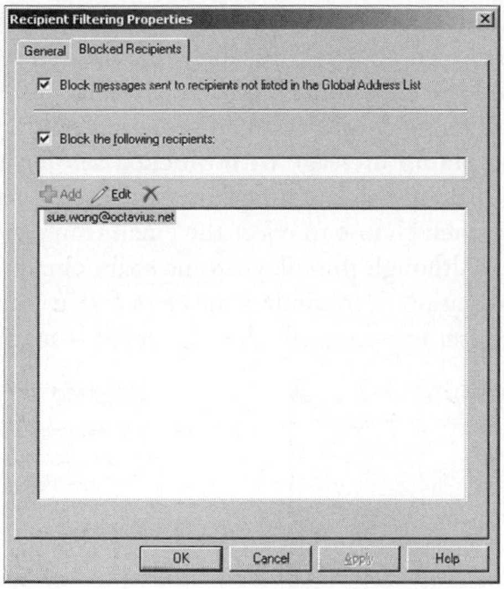

Figure 9-28

Specifying Blocked Recipients

The Edge role server does not forward any messages to the Hub role servers within your organization unless the recipients are listed in the Global Address List (GAL). This prevents your Hub role servers from relaying unnecessary email and improves the performance of your Exchange infrastructure. In addition, email sent to the recipient **sue.wong@octavius.net** will not be forwarded to the Hub role servers. Blocking recipients is commonly done when users complain that they receive too many spam emails. By assigning the recipient a different email address on the E-mail Addresses tab of mailbox user properties and blocking the recipient's old email address using Recipient Filtering properties, you will prevent these spam messages from entering the organization.

TAKE NOTE *

If you select **Hide from Exchange address lists** on the General tab of mailbox user properties, the mailbox user will not receive Internet email if **Block messages sent to recipients not listed in the Global Address List** is selected in Figure 9-28.

THE COMMAND LINE WAY

You can also use the **Set-RecipientFilterConfig** cmdlet to configure recipient filtering or the **Get-RecipientFilterConfig** to view the configuration of recipient filtering. For example, to block emails sent to the recipients **sue.wong@octavius.net** and **adel.moore@octavius .net**, you could run the following command within the Exchange Management Shell:

Set-RecipientFilterConfig –BlockListEnabled $true –BlockedRecipients 'sue.wong@ octavius.net,adel.moore@octavius.net'

For more information on the Set-RecipientFilterConfig and Get-RecipientFilterConfig cmdlets, search for their names within Exchange Server 2007 Help.

FILTERING SPAM BY SENDER

Another way to identify spam messages is to examine the sender's email address within the email itself. Often the same sender (i.e., **sales@bestoffers.org**) is used in multiple spam messages. Similarly, spammers often use freely obtainable email accounts to send spam (e.g., hotmail.com email accounts). To prevent messages from entering your organization by sender email address, you can highlight **Sender Filtering** shown in Figure 9-18, select **Properties** from the action pane, and specify the appropriate information on the **Blocked Senders** tab.

As Figure 9-29 shows, **john.smith@averitech.org** as well as blank senders or senders in the bestoffers.org and hotmail.com domains are labeled as blocked senders. By default, emails from blocked senders are deleted and the sender receives an NDR. However, you can choose to label emails from blocked senders as spam and forward them to mailboxes within your organization by selecting **Stamp message with blocked sender and continue processing** as shown in Figure 9-30. Outlook and Entourage users will see a warning indicating that the message is spam and can then choose to reject the email using the Junk E-mail feature of Outlook and Entourage. Although this allows some spam emails to be processed by Exchange servers within your organization, it minimizes the chance that important emails will be rejected by allowing the mailbox user to decide whether the email is spam.

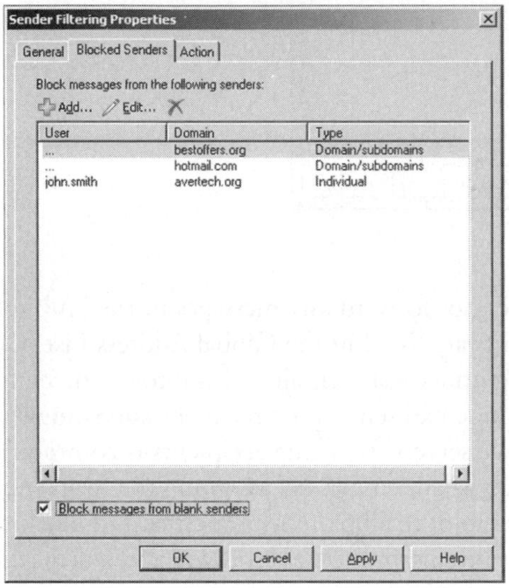

Figure 9-29

Specifying Blocked Senders

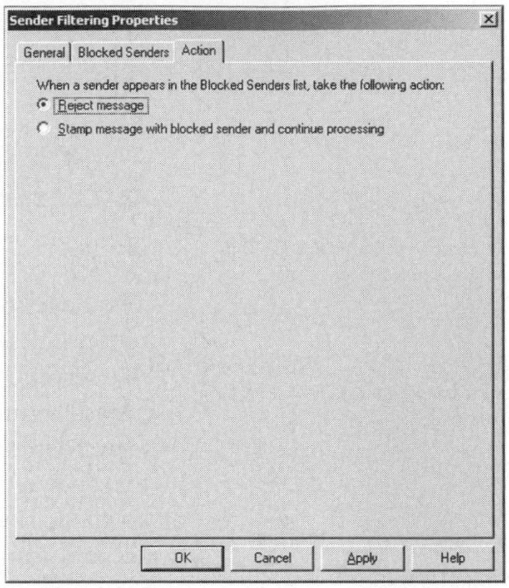

Figure 9-30

Configuring the Sender Filtering Action

Exchange Server 2007 also uses a complex *sender ID* algorithm that evaluates the senders listed within email header fields to calculate the ***Purported Responsible Address (PRA)***. The PRA is a measure of the likelihood that a message is spam based on email header information. You can specify how Exchange deals with email messages that are likely spam due to their PRA value by navigating to the properties of **Sender ID** shown in Figure 9-18 and selecting the appropriate action on the **Action** tab as shown in Figure 9-31. By default, if Exchange determines that a message is likely spam due to the PRA, it adds a warning to the email and proceeds to deliver it to the appropriate mailbox. However, you can select **Reject message** shown in Figure 9-31 to prevent the message from being delivered and send an NDR to the sender. Alternatively, you can select **Delete message** as shown in Figure 9-31 to delete the message without sending an NDR to the sender.

Figure 9-31

Configuring the Sender ID Action

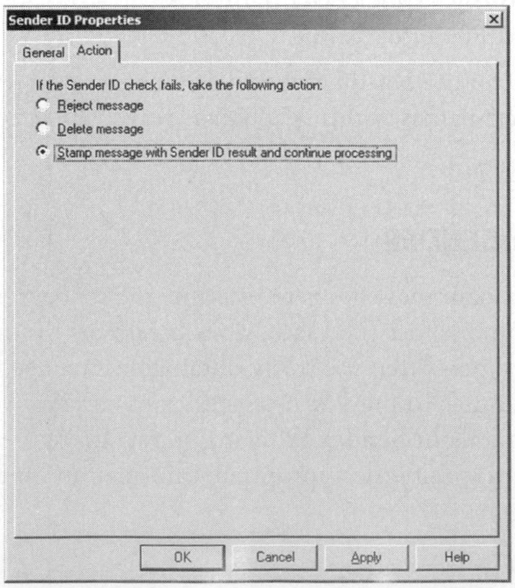

In addition to calculating the PRA, Exchange Server 2007 also monitors the SCL of emails that are determined to be spam and keeps track of the sender of the spam to determine the *sender reputation*. As the number of spam emails from a particular sender increases, the sender reputation declines. In addition, Exchange examines other aspects of the sender when determining the sender reputation including the SMTP traffic behavior and the DNS name of the sender.

You can configure sender reputation settings by highlighting **Sender Reputation** as shown in Figure 9-18 and selecting **Properties** from the action pane. On the **Sender Confidence** tab as shown in Figure 9-32, you can allow Exchange to test the sender's email server to determine whether it is an anonymous remailer. Email sent by an anonymous remailer automatically receives a poor sender reputation value.

Figure 9-32

Specifying an Open Proxy Test

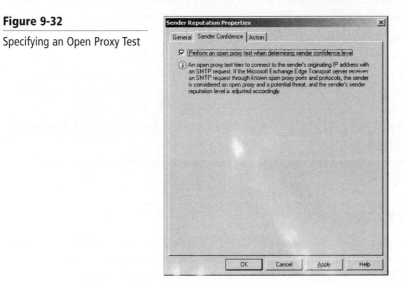

You can also control the processing of emails that have a poor sender reputation using the **Action** tab of Sender Reputation Properties as shown in Figure 9-33. By default, senders with a poor reputation are placed on the IP Block List for 24 hours if they have a poor sender reputation. The Sender Reputation Level Block Threshold value shown in Figure 9-33 is an arbitrary value that you can use to adjust how Exchange determines poor sender reputations. A higher threshold is more likely to give emails a poor sender reputation whereas a lower threshold is less likely to give emails a poor sender reputation.

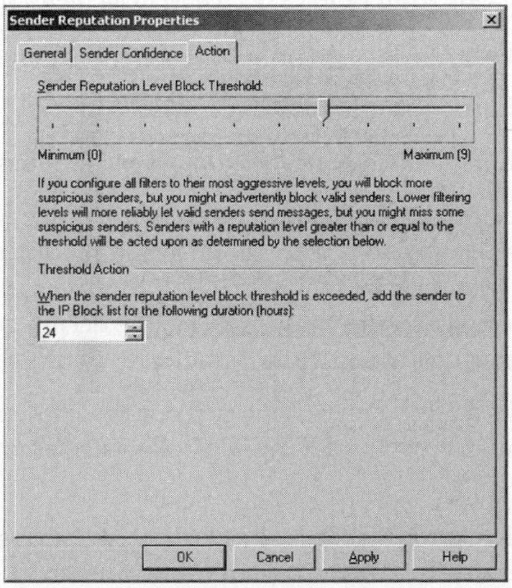

Figure 9-33

Configuring Sender Reputation Action

THE COMMAND LINE WAY

You can also use cmdlets within the Exchange Management Shell to configure sender filtering options. The **Set-SenderFilterConfig** cmdlet can be used to specify blocked senders and the **Get-SenderFilterConfig** cmdlet can be used to display blocked senders. For example, to reject emails from the same blocked senders as shown earlier in Figure 9-29, you could run the following command within the Exchange Management Shell:

Set-SenderFilterConfig –BlankSenderBlockingEnabled $true -BlockedDomainsAndSubdomains '*bestoffers.org,*hotmail.com' -BlockedSenders 'john.smith@averitech.org' –Action 'Reject'

The **Set-SenderIDConfig** cmdlet can be used to configure sender ID filtering and the **Get-SenderIDConfig** cmdlet can be used to view sender ID settings. For example, to reject messages that have an unacceptable PRA and send an NDR to the sender, you could run the following command within the Exchange Management Shell:

Set-SenderIDConfig -SpoofedDomainAction Reject

To configure and view sender reputation settings, you can use the **Set-SenderReputationConfig** and **Get-SenderReputationConfig** cmdlets respectively. For example, to set the same sender reputations settings shown in Figure 9-32 and Figure 9-33, you could run the following command within the Exchange Management Shell:

Set-SenderReputationConfig –OpenProxyDetectionEnabled $true -SrlBlockThreshold 6 -SenderBlockingEnabled:$true -SenderBlockingPeriod 24

For more information on these sender filtering cmdlets, search for their names within Exchange Server 2007 Help.

FILTERING SPAM BY ATTACHMENT

Edge role servers are automatically configured to filter emails based on the nature of the attachments that are included in the email. By default, Edge role servers filter email messages that contain common web application MIME types or common program extensions. However, you can modify this list or add entries that filter emails based on the name, extension, or MIME type of attachments using cmdlets within the Exchange Management Shell.

To view the current list of file names and MIME types that are filtered, you can run the **Get-AttachmentFilterEntry** cmdlet from within the Exchange Management Shell. There are over 60 file name extensions and MIME types that are filtered by default on an Edge role server.

Similarly, you can use the **Add-AttachmentFilterEntry** cmdlet to add a file name or MIME type to filter or you can use the **Remove-AttachmentFilterEntry** cmdlet to remove a file name or MIME type from being filtered. For example, to filter attachments called **readme.doc** as well as attachments that end with a **.bin** extension or have a JPEG image MIME type, you could run the following commands within the Exchange Management Shell:

Add-AttachmentFilterEntry –Name readme.doc –Type FileName

Add-AttachmentFilterEntry –Name *.bin –Type FileName

Add-AttachmentFilterEntry –Name image/JPEG –Type ContentType

All emails that are filtered by attachment are processed using the same action. By default, unacceptable attachments are removed from the email and the email is forwarded to the recipient within the organization with a notice indicating that the attachment was removed. You can use the **Get-AttachmentFilterListConfig** cmdlet to view the default action used for attachment filtering or the **Set-AttachmentFilterListConfig** cmdlet to modify the attachment filtering action.

For example, to reject all emails that have restricted attachments and send an NDR to the sender using a custom message, you could run the following command within the Exchange Management Shell:

Set-AttachmentFilterListConfig –Action Reject –RejectResponse "Your email has been rejected by octavius.net due to an unacceptable attachment."

Alternatively, you could configure emails that have restricted attachments to be deleted without sending an NDR using the following command within the Exchange Management Shell:

Set-AttachmentFilterListConfig –Action SilentDelete

To configure your Edge role server to delete restricted attachments from emails and forward them into the organization for delivery (the default action), you could run the following command within the Exchange Management Shell:

Set-AttachmentFilterListConfig –Action Strip

Configuring Forefront Security for Exchange Server Antivirus

Although there are many different antivirus software packages available on the market today that can be used alongside Exchange Server to remove viruses, Forefront Security for Exchange Server uses a variety of different virus-scanning engines and regular updates to minimize the number of viruses that enter your organization. In addition, Forefront Security for Exchange Server allows for advanced scanning options, manual virus scans, notifications, and detailed reporting.

Forefront Security for Exchange Server (FSE) is a powerful antivirus scanning and filtering software that can be used to scan email and public folder data that is processed by or stored on the Exchange servers in your organization.

At the time this was written, there were over 100,000 different active viruses for Windows operating systems and that number is continuously growing. This makes it more difficult to create an effective antivirus software program that catches all new viruses as they are released and is reflected by the large number of commercial antivirus software products available on the market today. One antivirus software product may not catch a specific newly released virus while another antivirus software product will. As a result, FSE uses several different licensed virus-scanning engines together from different antivirus companies to minimize the chance that a new virus will go undetected. These scanning engines are also configured to look for new *virus definitions* on the Internet every hour by default to protect against the latest virus attacks. FSE also allows you to customize the level to which virus-scanning engines analyze emails and attachments for viruses as well as the actions that can be performed on emails and attachments that contain viruses.

The functionality of FSE largely depends on the Exchange Server roles installed on the computer that hosts FSE. For example, if you install FSE on an Edge or Hub role server, it will scan email as it passes through the server. However, if you install FSE on a Mailbox role server, it will scan mailbox and public folder data stored on the Mailbox role server. To speed performance, FSE tags all messages that have been already scanned on one server role so that they are not scanned again when they reach other server roles within the organization that have FSE installed. For example, if an incoming email message is scanned by FSE on an Edge role server, the email message is not rescanned when it is passed to Hub or Mailbox role servers within your organization that host FSE unless you specify otherwise.

To install and manage FSE on an Exchange server, you must at a minimum be a member of the Exchange Server Administrator role and local Administrators group on that server.

INSTALLING FSE

Like other commercial antivirus software packages, Forefront is not free; it costs a great deal of money to keep antivirus programs and virus definitions updated to protect against new viruses. However, a 120-day evaluation of Forefront Security for Exchange Server is available for download from **www.microsoft.com/forefront/downloads.mspx**. At the end of the evaluation period, you can enter a valid license to continue using it rather than reinstalling a licensed version.

Forefront dramatically increases the processor and memory usage on your Exchange server. As a result, it is important to ensure that you allow for extra hardware during Exchange Server 2007 deployment to account for this. Microsoft recommends an additional 2 GB of RAM for Forefront in addition to the RAM required for server roles.

Any options chosen during the installation process can be modified afterward using the General Settings section within the FSE configuration utility.

 INSTALL FOREFRONT SECURITY FOR EXCHANGE SERVER

GET READY. Turn on the computer, and log in as the Administrator user account. Close any windows that appear on the desktop.

ANOTHER WAY

You can select **Remote Installation** instead of **Local Installation** to perform an installation of Forefront on another computer across the network.

1. Navigate to the folder that contains the 120-day evaluation of FSE that you downloaded or the folder that contains the licensed copy of FSE and double click **setup.exe**. When the Welcome page appears, click **Next**.

2. On the License Agreement page, click **Yes**.

3. On the Customer Information page, enter your name and company in the appropriate dialog boxes and click **Next**.

4. On the Installation Location page, ensure that **Local Installation** is selected and click **Next**.

5. On the Installation Type page, ensure that **Full Installation** is selected and click **Next**. The Quarantine Security Settings page appears as shown in Figure 9-34.

Figure 9-34

Specifying Quarantine Settings

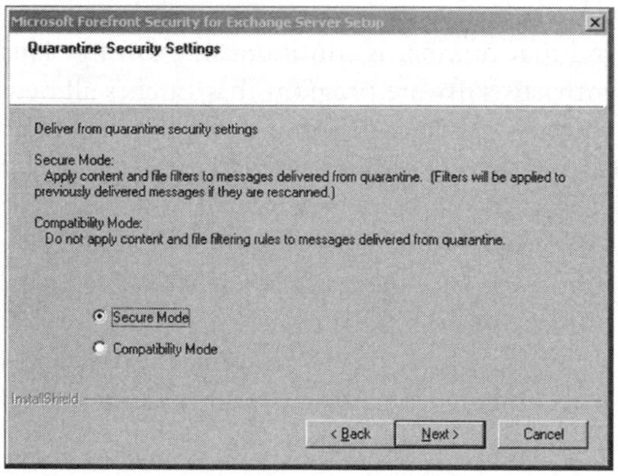

![Screenshot of Microsoft Forefront Security for Exchange Server Setup — Quarantine Security Settings dialog. Deliver from quarantine security settings. Secure Mode: Apply content and file filters to messages delivered from quarantine. (Filters will be applied to previously delivered messages if they are rescanned.) Compatibility Mode: Do not apply content and file filtering rules to messages delivered from quarantine. Secure Mode is selected. Buttons: Back, Next, Cancel.]

ANOTHER WAY

You can select **Client—Admin console only** instead of **Full Installation** to install the Forefront administration console only. This is often useful if you wish to remotely administer Forefront from a client computer. If there is a firewall between your client computer and Exchange server running Forefront, you must allow TCP port 135.

6. FSE is automatically configured to place infected messages in a quarantine folder. Messages can be moved from this quarantine folder if they need to be inspected for security reasons or if they were placed there accidentally. By default, FSE rescans any messages that are moved from the quarantine folder as shown in Figure 9-34. However, you can select **Compatibility Mode** if you do not want to rescan items that are moved from the quarantine folder. Click **Next**. The Engines page appears.

7. FSE uses up to five antivirus engines when scanning emails. The Microsoft Antimalware Engine is automatically chosen. Select up to four more antivirus engines as shown in Figure 9-35, and click **Next** when finished.

Figure 9-35

Selecting Virus-Scanning
Engines

8. At the Engines Updates Required page, read the update information and click **Next**. The Proxy Server page appears as shown in Figure 9-36.

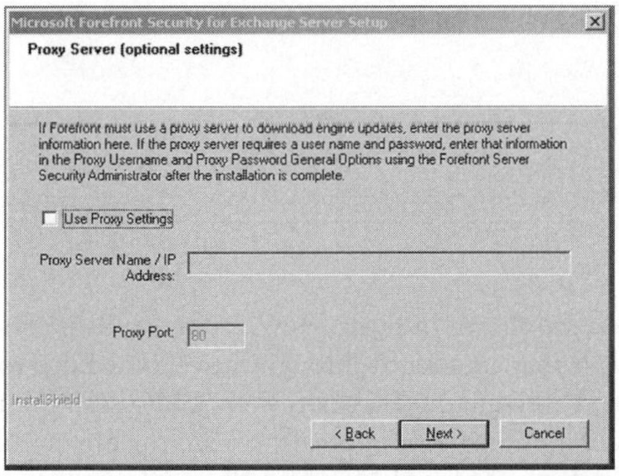

Figure 9-36

Specifying a Proxy Server

9. FSE must obtain virus updates by downloading them from the Internet. If your organization uses a proxy server to access the Internet, select **Use Proxy Settings** and supply the correct IP address or name of your proxy server as well as the port number in the dialog boxes provided and click **Next**. If your organization does not use a proxy server to obtain Internet access, click **Next**.

10. On the Choose Destination Location page, view the default destination folder that Forefront will be installed to. If you wish to change this location, click **Browse** and select a different folder and click **OK**. Click **Next**.

11. On the Select Program Folder page, view the default program folder on the Start menu that will be used to store the shortcut to the Forefront tools. If you wish to change this location, select an existing folder from the list or type a different name in the dialog box. Click **Next**.

12. At the Start Copying Files page, click **Next**.

13. At the Restart Exchange Transport Service page, click **Next** to restart the Exchange Transport Service to activate Forefront.

14. At the Recycling Exchange Transport Service page, click **Next**.

15. Click **Finish** to close the FSE setup window.

CONFIGURING FSE

After installing FSE, you can administer it using the *Forefront Server Security Administrator* utility (**Start** > **All Programs** > **Microsoft Forefront Server Security** > **Exchange Server** > **Forefront Server Security Administrator** by default). After opening Forefront Server Security

Administrator, you will be presented with the Scan Job Settings screen that may be used to configure email and public folder virus scanning as shown in Figure 9-37.

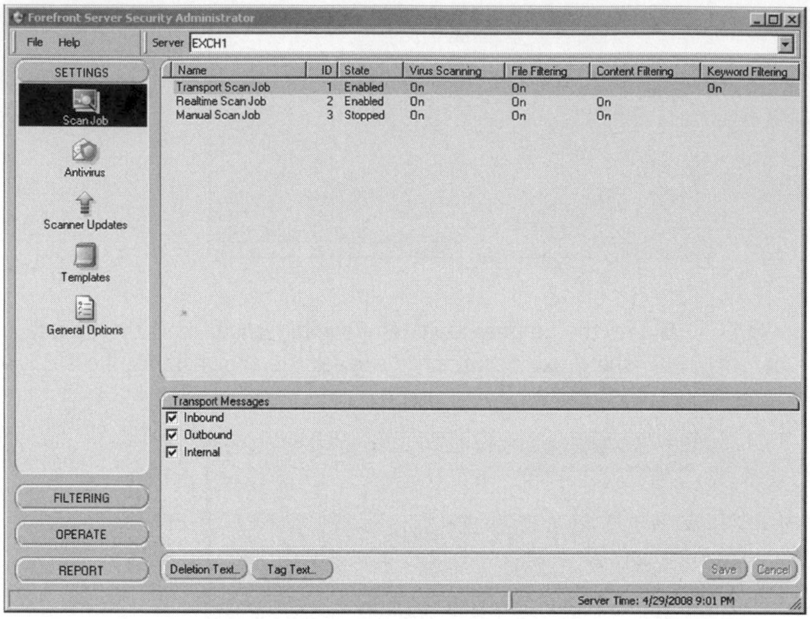

Figure 9-37

Configuring the Transport
Scan Job

The **Transport Scan Job** shown in Figure 9-37 is only available on Hub and Edge role servers because it scans emails that are relayed through the Hub or Edge role server. At the bottom of Figure 9-37, you can configure the Transport Scan Job to scan inbound and outbound Internet emails as well email that is only sent internally within the organization. The **Realtime Scan Job** and **Manual Scan Job** are only available on Mailbox role servers and can be used to scan emails and public folders that are stored within databases on the Mailbox role server. The Realtime Scan Job automatically scans emails and public folder items as they are stored or retrieved, whereas the Manual Scan Job can be run manually to scan the contents of mailboxes and public folders. If you highlight Realtime Scan Job or Manual Scan Job shown in Figure 9-37, you can configure FSE to scan all or selected mailboxes and public folders as well as disable the scanning of mailboxes or public folders as shown in Figure 9-38.

TAKE NOTE*

By default, FSE does not rescan messages that have already been scanned by FSE on the same or other server roles.

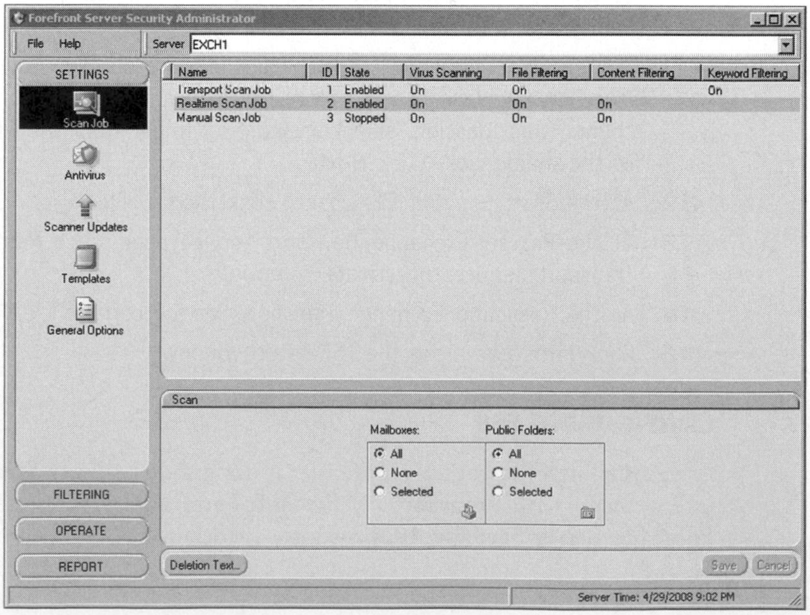

Figure 9-38

Configuring the Realtime
Scan Job

If you select **Antivirus** under the Settings section in the left pane shown in Figure 9-37, you can specify the virus-scanning engines used for each scan job as well as virus-scanning options as shown in Figure 9-39.

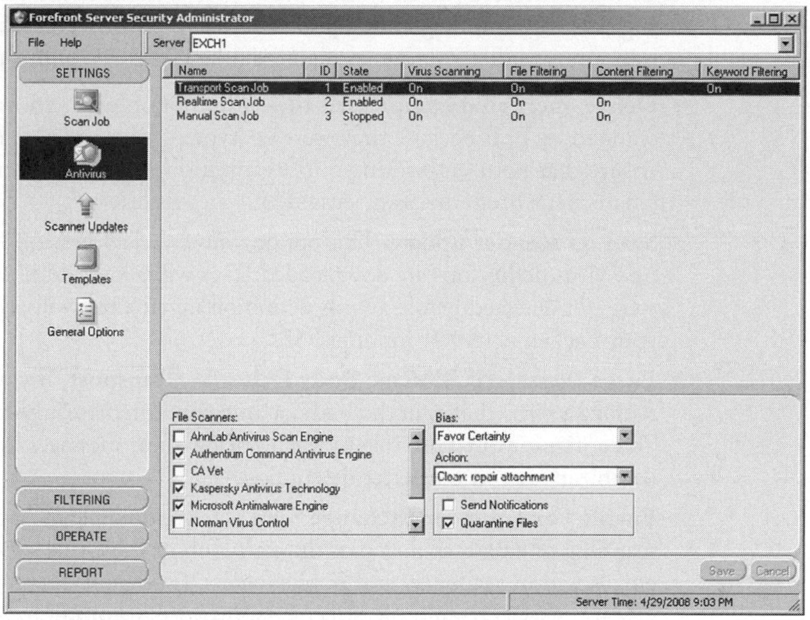

Figure 9-39

Configuring Antivirus Scanning

The Bias setting shown in Figure 9-39 determines how thorough each virus-scanning engine will be when scanning emails and attachments. There are five values for the Bias setting:

- **Max Certainty** (the most thorough and the most time consuming)
- **Favor Certainty**
- **Neutral**
- **Favor Performance**
- **Max Performance** (the least thorough and least time consuming)

When a virus is detected, the virus-scanning engines attempt to repair/remove the virus in the email or attachment (a process called *cleaning*). If the virus can be cleaned, the virus-free email is forwarded to the recipient. If the virus cannot be cleaned, the part of the email that contained the virus is replaced with a virus removal message or the attachment that contained the virus is deleted and replaced with another attachment that indicates the removal of a virus. However, you can modify this behavior by selecting a different Action as detailed in Figure 9-39. There are three possible Actions that can be used on virus-infected emails:

- **Skip: detect only** (which detects and labels viruses but does not remove them)
- **Clean: repair attachment** (the default action)
- **Delete: remove infection** (which removes the infected email or email attachment permanently)

Regardless of whether the virus can be cleaned or not, a copy of the virus-infected message is sent to the quarantine folder for later examination and, by default, a notification is not sent to the sender.

Other FSE settings can be configured by selecting the appropriate icon under the Settings section in the left pane shown in Figure 9-37. By selecting **Scanner Updates**, you can configure whether to download updated virus definitions for each virus-scanning engine and how often FSE should check for updates. By default, virus definitions are downloaded for all virus-scanning engines every hour. In the event of a new or serious virus attack, you can click the **Update Now** button on the Scanner Updates page to immediately update virus definitions.

To view additional scan jobs or modify existing scan job settings based on scan job templates, you can select the **Templates** icon in the left pane shown in Figure 9-37. To create a new scan job template, you can click **File** > **Templates** > **New** from the FSE window.

By selecting **General Options** from Figure 9-37, you can configure a large number of FSE scanning, logging, and diagnostic options as well as proxy server settings. Some of the more important options that you can configure on the General Options page include:

- **Delete encrypted compressed files.** This option will remove any files that could not be scanned by FSE because they were encrypted. If you enable this option, you must first ensure that no users within your organization use encryption certificates within their email client programs as discussed later in this lesson.

- **Scan on scanner update.** This option will rescan all previously scanned messages when new virus definitions are downloaded. This will allow additional viruses to be detected that were not detected before a virus definition update, but will also reduce the performance of your Exchange servers running FSE.

- **Purge Message if Message Body Deleted—Transport.** If your Edge role servers cannot remove a virus that is in the body of an email, it replaces the body with virus removal text. To configure your Hub role servers to delete these messages as they pass through the organization, you can select this option.

- **Enable Forefront for Exchange Scan.** This option allows you to enable or disable the scanning of emails as they pass through Hub or Edge role servers as well as the scanning of emails within mailboxes and public folders. By default, this setting is **Enable All**, but you can also select **Disable All**, select **Enable Store Scanning** to scan mailbox and public folders only, or select **Enable Transport Scanning** to scan email relayed on Hub and Edge role servers only.

FSE can also provide limited spam filtering for messages alongside the virus scanning provided by the Hub, Edge, and Mailbox role servers within your organization. Hub and Edge role servers can filter email based on keyword, attachment file name or extension, and sender. Mailbox role servers can filter email based on content (sender domain and subject line only), attachment file name or extension, and sender.

Although FSE maintains a regularly updated list of keywords, file names, and file extensions that should be filtered, you can add your own list of file names, file extensions, keywords, subject lines, sender domains, and allowed senders by navigating to the **Filter Lists** icon under the **Filtering** section in the left pane of the Forefront Server Security Administrator as shown in Figure 9-40.

Figure 9-40

Adding Entries to the Subject Lines Filter List

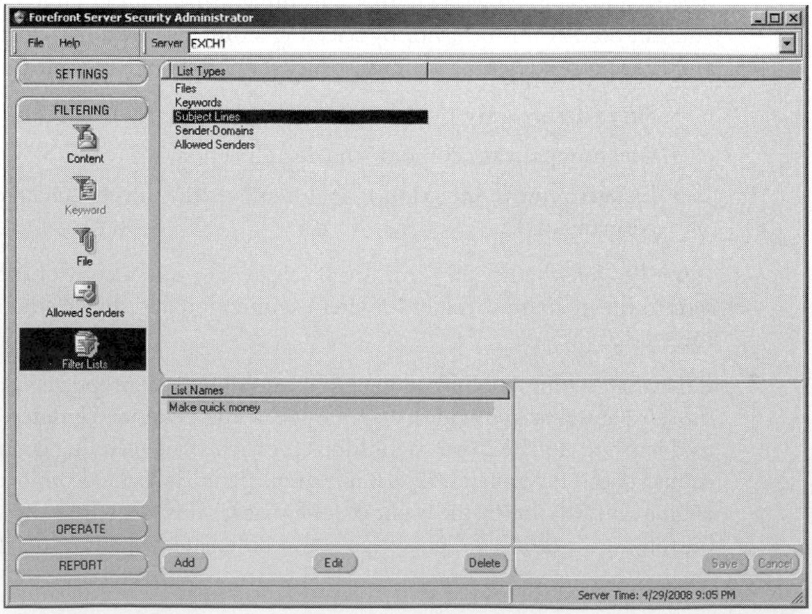

The subject line "Make quick money" was added to the list of subject lines shown in Figure 9-40. Following this, you can highlight the **Content** icon under the **Filtering** section shown in Figure 9-40 to configure how FSE handles emails that have a subject line of "Make quick money." As Figure 9-41 illustrates, if the Realtime Scan Job encounters the subject line "Make quick money," the email will be deleted immediately (**Purge: eliminate message**) and a copy will be sent to the quarantine folder for later examination if necessary.

Figure 9-41

Configuring Content Filtering

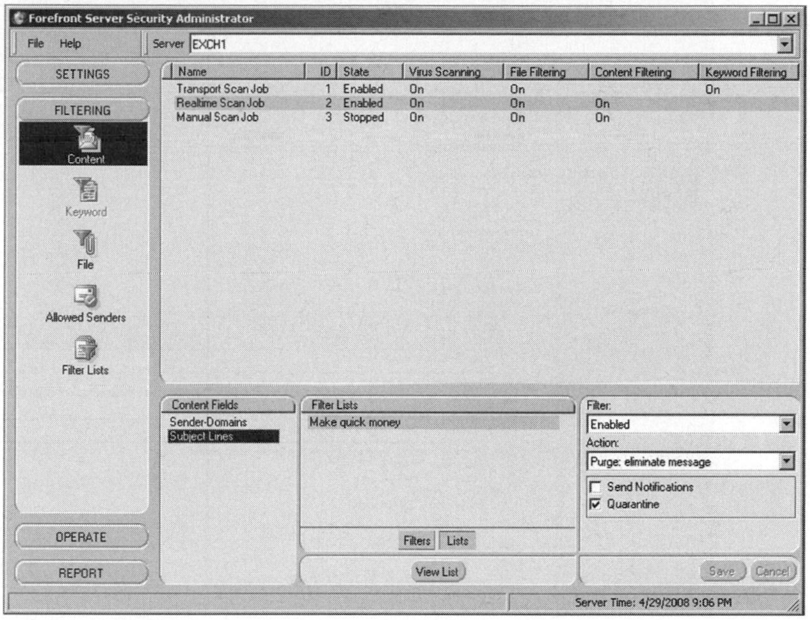

To run the Manual Scan Job in FSE, you can navigate to the **Run Job** icon under the **Operate** section in the left pane of the Forefront Server Security Administrator as shown in Figure 9-42, select the appropriate scanning options and click the **Start** button. Alternatively, the **Schedule Job** icon shown in Figure 9-42 can be used schedule a Manual Scan Job to run at a future time or on a regular basis, and the **Quick Scan** icon can be used to quickly scan certain mailboxes or public folders.

Figure 9-42

Running a Manual Scan Job

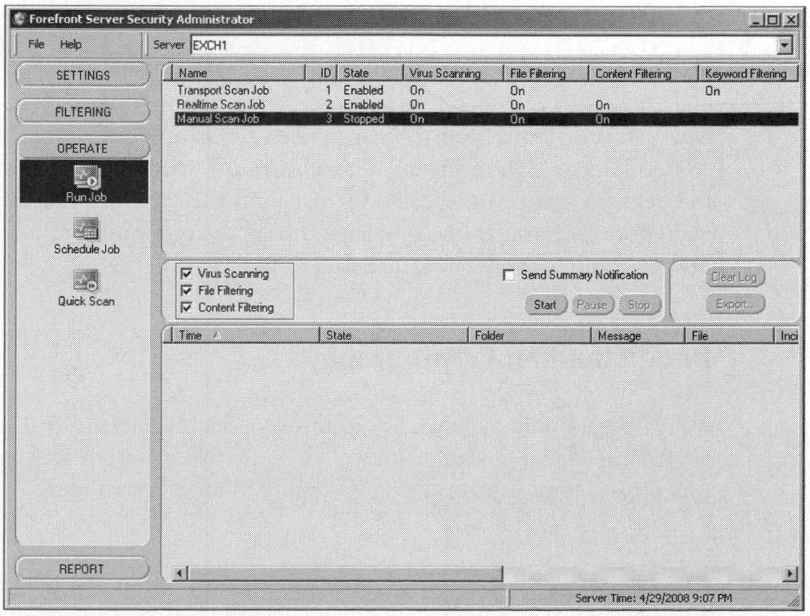

Under the **Report** section in the left pane of the Forefront Server Security Administrator, you can configure email notifications and view detected viruses as well as the contents of the quarantine folder. By highlighting the **Notification** icon as shown in Figure 9-43, you can add specific email addresses to custom error messages that indicate when FSE-related events occur. For example, Figure 9-43 shows that **administrator@octavius.net** is emailed each time a new virus is detected.

Figure 9-43

Configuring Notifications

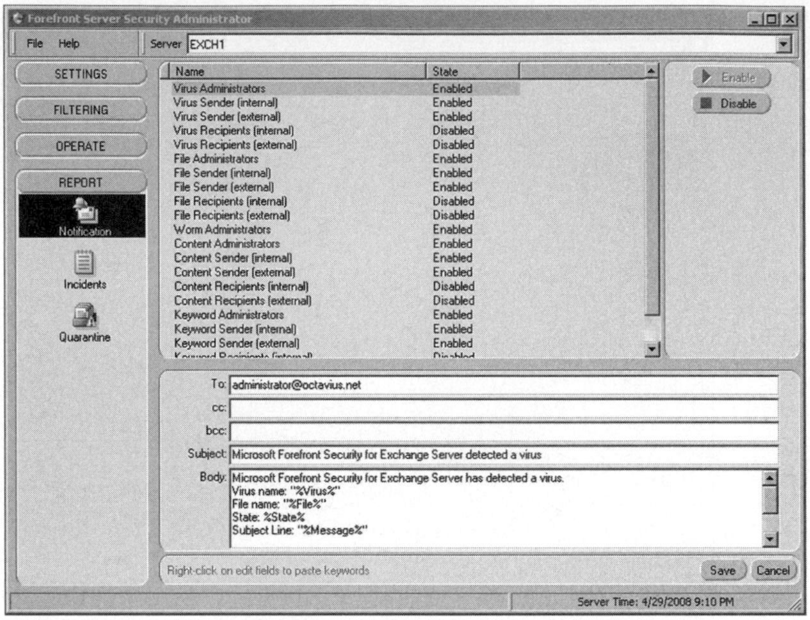

If you click the **Incidents** icon under the **Report** section shown in Figure 9-43, you can view the viruses that FSE has detected as well as a report that displays the number of viruses detected within emails and email attachments from mailboxes and public folders during a Realtime Scan Job or from a Transport Scan Job. Similarly, by clicking the **Quarantine** icon under the **Report** section shown in Figure 9-43, you can view quarantined messages as well as save quarantined items for later analysis or deliver them to their original destination if they were quarantined by mistake.

■ Configuring Protocol Encryption

↓
THE BOTTOM LINE

The best protection against unauthorized access to network data is the use of protocol encryption. By encrypting email protocols using SSL or TLS, the data that passes across the network will be unreadable by malicious users. Before you can configure protocol encryption, you must first understand basic encryption terminology and features as well as how encryption works to secure data.

Understanding Cryptography

Cryptography uses keys and algorithms to scramble data so that it is unreadable by anyone other than the intended recipient. There are two main types of cryptography that may be used to encrypt data; each one is specialized for different uses.

Cryptography is the practice of protecting information so that only certain users can read it. *Encryption* is the cryptography process whereby files, emails, and other data are converted to a format that is unreadable called *ciphertext*. Users can then use a *decryption* process to decipher the ciphertext and make the data readable again. The readable data is often called *plaintext*.

To encrypt information, you must use an *encryption algorithm*. An encryption algorithm is a mathematical formula or series of steps that can modify data. Because computers today can easily determine the steps in an encryption algorithm, nearly all encryption algorithms use a random component called a *key* to modify the steps within the algorithm. Suppose you create a simple encryption algorithm that multiplies a number by 2, subtracts 5, and then adds 3 to produce an encrypted number. If you perform this encryption algorithm on the number 20, you will obtain the number 38 as shown:

$$20 \times 2 - 5 + 3 = 38$$

Similarly, if you perform the same encryption algorithm on the number 44, you will obtain the number 86 as shown:

$$44 \times 2 - 5 + 3 = 86$$

With multiple examples, a simple computer program could easily determine the calculation used to encrypt the numbers. However, by multiplying each part of the equation by a random number called x, it becomes more difficult to determine the calculation (unless x is known). The equation now becomes:

$$plaintext \times 2(x) - 5(x) + 3(x) = ciphertext$$

If we assume that x is 5, then performing the encryption algorithm on the number 44 will produce the number 430 as shown:

$$44 \times 2(5) - 5(5) + 3(5) = 430$$

The x variable represents the encryption key. The larger the key, the more difficult it is to compare the plaintext and ciphertext to determine the encryption calculation. As a result, most keys are quite large. For example, if we use a key of 19827364 in the same encryption algorithm to encrypt the number 44, the resulting ciphertext (17051553304) will be very different than the original ciphertext (44) as shown:

$$44 \times 2(19827364) - 5(19827364) + 3(19827364) = 17051553304$$

In modern encryption algorithms, there are thousands of steps in the encryption algorithm and the randomly generated encryption keys are much larger than the key used in the previous example (19827364).

To decrypt the ciphertext in the previous example (17051553304), you could simply reverse the operations in the encryption algorithm using the same key (19827364) used to encrypt the original plaintext (44) as shown:

$$17051553304 - 3(19827364) + 5(19827364)/2(19827364) = 44$$

Because the encryption algorithm illustrated in the previous examples uses the same key to encrypt and decrypt, we call it a *symmetric encryption* algorithm. In symmetric encryption, a symmetric encryption algorithm is used alongside a key to encrypt plaintext. To decrypt ciphertext, the symmetric encryption algorithm is reversed and used alongside the same key. This process is illustrated in Figure 9-44.

Figure 9-44

Symmetric Cryptography

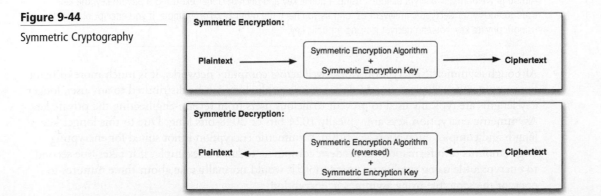

TAKE NOTE ✱

Each additional bit in the length of an encryption key doubles the strength of the encryption. For example, encryption that uses a 129-bit key is twice as difficult to decrypt as encryption that uses a 128-bit key.

Symmetric encryption is the simplest form of encryption used to protect information and the easiest encryption for modern computers to perform. As a result, symmetric encryption is ideal for encrypting large amounts of data quickly. The keys used by most symmetric encryption algorithms today are usually 128-bits or 256-bits long and are typically regenerated each time the encryption algorithm is used to encrypt information.

Unfortunately, symmetric encryption is ill suited to encrypting information that must be sent across a network because both the sender and recipient must first know the key. For example, if User A encrypts an email using symmetric encryption and sends it to User B, User B can only decrypt the file using the same key that was used to encrypt the file.

To solve this problem, you must use a method that allows User A to send the symmetric encryption key to User B across the network without allowing other users to view the symmetric encryption key. ***Asymmetric encryption*** addresses this problem by using different keys to encrypt and decrypt information.

In an asymmetric encryption algorithm, complex one-way mathematical functions are used to encrypt plaintext using a ***public key***, and a separate set of complex one-way mathematical functions are used to decrypt the associated ciphertext using a ***private key*** as illustrated in Figure 9-45. To provide this function, public and private keys must be generated at the same time on the same computer.

Figure 9-45

Asymmetric Cryptography

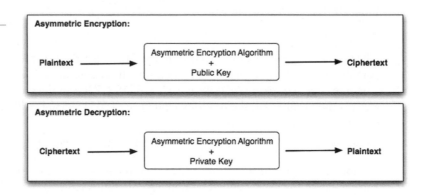

Each computer or user can generate a public/private key pair to use with asymmetric encryption. Public keys are normally given to any network user or computer that requests them. However, private keys are never disclosed.

Thus, if User A needs to send an encrypted message to User B, User A will first obtain User B's public key. Next, User A will encrypt the message using an asymmetric encryption algorithm alongside User B's public key. Because the resulting ciphertext was encrypted using User B's public key, only User B's private key can be used to decrypt it. As a result, User A can safely send the ciphertext across the network to User B and User B can use his or her own private key to decrypt the message.

➕ MORE INFORMATION

Although we normally encrypt plaintext using a public key and decrypt ciphertext using a private key, the key used to encrypt or decrypt is irrelevant as long as you have the other key. For example, if you encrypt plaintext using a private key, you can decrypt it using a public key.

Although asymmetric encryption works well across computer networks, it is much more difficult for computers to calculate. In addition, because public keys can be distributed to any user, longer key lengths are typically used to prevent malicious users from reverse-engineering the private key. Asymmetric encryption keys are typically 1024-bits or 2048-bits long. Due to this longer key length and complex encryption algorithm, asymmetric encryption is not suited for encrypting large amounts of information on modern computers today. For example, if it takes one second to encrypt a file using symmetric encryption, it would normally take about three minutes to encrypt the same file using asymmetric encryption.

Consequently, asymmetric encryption is often used to encrypt a small symmetric encryption key so that it can be sent to other users or computers across a network. The other users or computers can then decrypt the symmetric encryption key and use it for symmetric encryption. Because symmetric keys are typically small amounts of data that are 128-bits or 256-bits long, they can be encrypted using asymmetric encryption in less than one second on modern computers. The next section of this lesson examines how symmetric and asymmetric encryption work together for SSL and TLS.

Understanding SSL, TLS, and Certificates

SSL and TLS use the two different types of cryptography together to protect data transfer across the computer network. To ensure that malicious users cannot compromise the SSL and TLS encryption process, you must obtain a certificate from a Certification Authority.

Both SSL and TLS use symmetric encryption to protect data transfer and asymmetric encryption to protect the symmetric encryption key that is generated at the beginning of the SSL or TLS session. Exchange Server 2007 uses SSL and TLS to protect client email access using HTTP, POP3, IMAP4, and SMTP. Although most Internet email relay is unencrypted, Exchange Server 2007 can use TLS to protect SMTP email relay to other partner organizations on the Internet.

To use SSL or TLS, Exchange servers require a public and private key that will be used to protect the transmission of a symmetric key generated by the client computer for the HTTP, POP3, IMAP4, or SMTP session. Once the Exchange server and client computer have the same symmetric key, they will transfer information using symmetric encryption. This process is illustrated in Figure 9-46.

Figure 9-46

SSL and TLS Cryptography

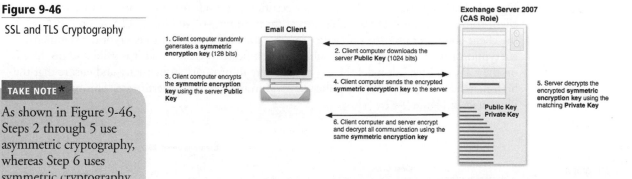

TAKE NOTE*

As shown in Figure 9-46, Steps 2 through 5 use asymmetric cryptography, whereas Step 6 uses symmetric cryptography.

Unfortunately, there is one security weakness to the process shown in Figure 9-46. A malicious user could intercept the Exchange server public key as it is sent from the Exchange server to the email client computer and substitute his own public key in its place. The client computer would have no way of knowing whether the public key it received was from the Exchange server or the malicious user. After the email client generates a symmetric encryption key, encrypts it using the malicious user's public key, and sends it on the network, the malicious user could intercept the communication and decrypt the symmetric encryption key using the associated private key. This process is called a *man-in-the-middle attack*.

To prevent man-in-the-middle attacks, public keys are typically sent to a trusted third-party computer called a *Certification Authority (CA)* for endorsement before they are used for SSL and TLS. This process is called *enrollment* and is usually performed immediately after a public/private key pair has been generated. Once the CA verifies the identity of the user or computer that generated the public key, the CA creates a *public key certificate* that includes:

- The name of the certificate and its possible uses,
- The public key,

- A digital signature,
- A time period for which the certificate is valid (typically one year), and
- The location of the Certificate Revocation List (CRL).

The most important part of a public key certificate is the digital signature. The *digital signature* in the public key certificate is a hash of the public key that is encrypted using the private key of the CA itself. Any computer or user can request the public key of the CA (called the *trusted root*) and decrypt the digital signature. If a digital signature can be decrypted by using the CA's public key, it proves that the CA's private key must have been used to create the digital signature. Additionally, this also proves that the CA verified the identity of the user or computer that generated the public key.

➕ MORE INFORMATION

A *hash* (also called a *checksum*) is a small calculation that is performed based on the contents of a file or piece of information. Hashes are often used to determine whether a file has been modified in transit. After a file has been received from another computer, the hash value for the file is verified against another hash calculation to ensure that the contents have not been modified.

TAKE NOTE*

Remember that CAs do not generate public/private key pairs. They only generate public key certificates from a public key that was generated on another computer.

Once a CA creates a public key certificate, it returns the public key certificate to the computer that generated the public key so that it can be used for SSL or TLS. Because the CA only creates public key certificates and does not participate in the encryption process, it maintains a list of any issued public key certificates that should not be used in a *Certificate Revocation List (CRL)*. The location of the CRL (typically a Web site) is listed within the certificate itself so client computers can check the CRL before using the public key in the certificate. Public key certificates are often added to the CRL when they are no longer used for a particular purpose or if the public key has been compromised by a malicious user.

Once an Exchange server has a public key certificate, it sends the public key certificate to the client computer instead of the public key at the beginning of an SSL or TLS session. Before the client computer uses the public key in the public key certificate to encrypt the symmetric encryption key, it first inspects the public key certificate to ensure that it is valid and not listed on the CRL and next decodes the digital signature to prove its authenticity and ensure that the hash matches the content of the public key within the public key certificate. This process is illustrated in Figure 9-47.

Figure 9-47

SSL and TLS Cryptography Using Certificates

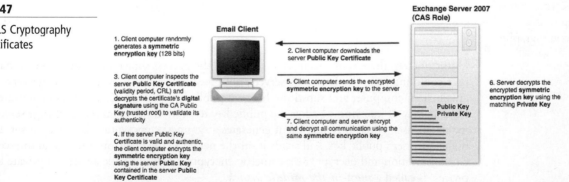

Configuring SSL and TLS Protocol Support

Although Exchange Server 2007 installs a self-signed certificate for use with SSL and TLS by default, you should replace this certificate with a CA-signed certificate from either a commercial CA or an enterprise CA within your organization.

By default, Exchange Server creates a public key certificate during installation that is digitally signed by the **Windows Certificate API (CAPI)** component of Windows on the Exchange server itself. As a result, this public key certificate is called a *self-signed certificate*.

By default, this self-signed certificate is configured for use with all SSL/TLS-capable services that are installed on your Exchange server. You can use the **Get-ExchangeCertificate** cmdlet within the Exchange Management Shell to list the default self-signed certificate as well as the services for which it is enabled. Figure 9-48 shows the output of the Get-ExchangeCertificate cmdlet on the server exch2.octavius.net. The Services column in the output of the Get-ExchangeCertificate cmdlet lists the services using single characters IMAP4 (**I**), POP3 (**P**), UM (**U**), HTTP (**W**), and SMTP (**S**). Thus the characters **IP.WS** in the Services column shown in Figure 9-48 indicates that the default self-signed certificate on the server exch2.octavius.net can be used to provide SSL/TLS for IMAP4, POP3, HTTP, and SMTP connections. The services available on your Exchange server depend on the server roles installed. The Hub role installs the SMTP service, the Mailbox and CAS roles install the HTTP service, the CAS role installs the POP3 and IMAP4 services, and the UM role installs the UM services.

Figure 9-48

Viewing Certificate Uses

You can view the self-signed certificate on an Exchange server by navigating to the Default Web Site from within IIS Manager. If you right click the Default Web Site, click **Properties**, and highlight the **Directory Security** tab, you can select the **View Certificate** button to view the default self-signed certificate. The default self-signed certificate for the computer exch2.octavius .net is shown in Figure 9-49.

Figure 9-49

Viewing the Default Self-Signed Certificate

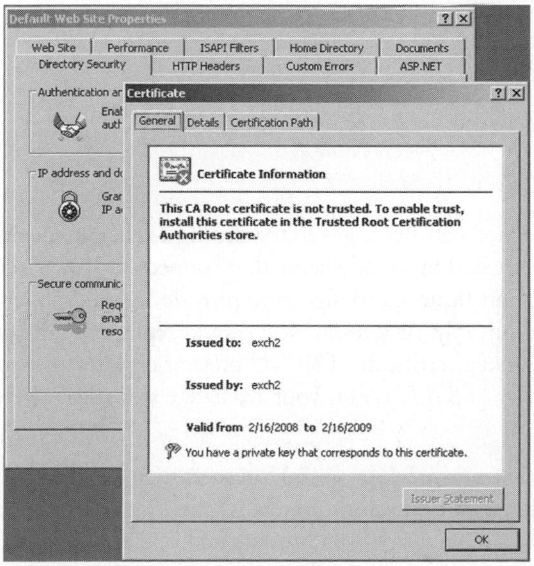

The red X icon shown in Figure 9-49 indicates that the computer does not have the trusted root (CA public key) used to verify the digital signature on the default self-signed certificate. As a result, when you use a web browser on the computer to access OWA on exch2.octavius.net, you will receive a certificate error as shown in Figure 9-50. Similarly, when you access a CAS role server using a POP3 or IMAP4 account that is configured for SSL or TLS, you will receive a similar warning about the default self-signed certificate as shown in Figure 9-51 using Outlook Express.

Figure 9-50

Internet Explorer Certificate Error

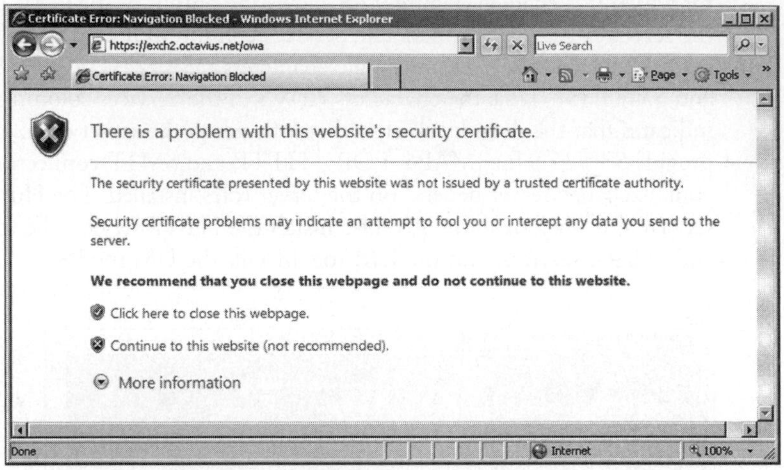

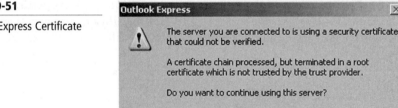

Figure 9-51

Outlook Express Certificate Error

Because the self-signed certificate generated during Exchange installation is not digitally signed by a CA, it is not trusted by email clients that connect to your Exchange servers. Instead, the default self-signed certificate was designed to provide SSL/TLS encryption immediately following Exchange installation only. As a result, you should replace the default self-signed certificate with a CA-signed public key certificate. This will prevent certificate errors on email clients as well as improve the security of SSL/TLS on your Exchange servers by preventing man-in-the-middle attacks.

There are many ***commercial CAs*** on the Internet, such as Verisign, eTrust, and Thawte that will issue public key certificates for a fee. Most client computers receive the trusted roots of these commercial CAs alongside web browser and operating system updates. This allows client computers to easily validate SSL or TLS public key certificates. As a result, paying a commercial CA to generate a public key certificate for SSL/TLS is commonly used if your servers need to perform SSL or TLS encryption with other computers on the Internet that are not part of your organization. For example, if your organization provides email access to home users, you would normally obtain a public key certificate that is signed by a commercial CA.

TAKE NOTE*

Commercial CAs are often called *public CAs*.

If your organization only uses SSL or TLS to encrypt communication between computers within the organization, then you can install a CA for use within your organization that can issue public key certificates for use with SSL/TLS. To ensure that each computer within your organization can verify the authenticity of these public key certificates, you must also import the trusted root of the organization's CA to each computer. You can import the trusted root certificate on each computer within your organization manually or by using a GPO.

Windows Server 2003 and 2008 have the ability to provide CA services within your organization using *Certificate Services*. When you install Certificate Services, you can create an *enterprise CA* or *stand-alone CA*. Only enterprise CAs can interoperate with AD and should be chosen to provide CA services within your Exchange organization. Moreover, large organizations can have several CAs configured in a CA hierarchy. The first CA deployed in a hierarchy is called the *root CA*, and other CAs that participate in the hierarchy are called *subordinate CAs*. In most organizations, only a single enterprise root CA is necessary for creating public key certificates.

You must at a minimum be a member of the Domain Admins group to install an enterprise CA. To configure certificates for use with an Exchange server, you must at a minimum be a member of the Exchange Server Administrator role and local Administrators group on that server.

TAKE NOTE *

Each Exchange server that participates in SSL/TLS encryption requires a different certificate. The same CA normally issues each of these certificates.

→ **INSTALL AN ENTERPRISE ROOT CA AND CONFIGURE CLIENT COMPUTERS WITH THE TRUSTED ROOT**

GET READY. Turn on the computer, and log in as the Administrator user account. Close any windows that appear on the desktop.

1. Click **Start**, **Control Panel**, and then click **Add or Remove Programs**. When the Add or Remove Programs window appears, click **Add/Remove Windows Components** to open the Windows Components Wizard.

2. On the Windows Components page, select **Certificate Services** and click **Yes** to acknowledge that the computer's name and domain membership can no longer be changed. Click **Next**. The CA Type page appears as shown in Figure 9-52.

TAKE NOTE *

Once you install Certificate Services on a computer to provide CA services, the computer's NetBIOS name, FQDN, and domain membership cannot be modified until you remove Certificate Services. This is because the name and domain membership of the CA are included in each public key certificate issued by the CA and used by computers to locate the CRL.

Figure 9-52

Creating an Enterprise Root CA

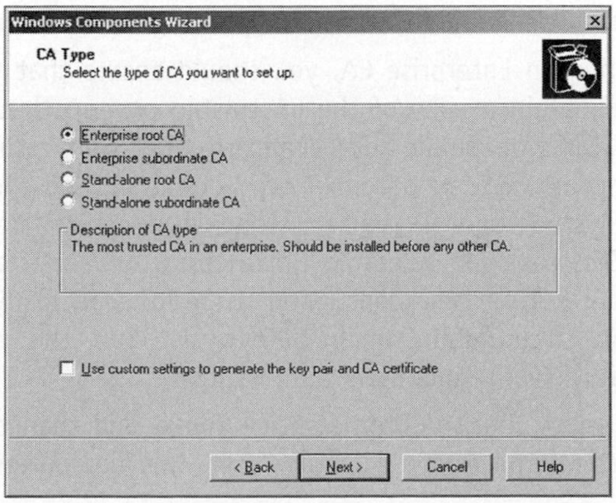

3. Ensure that **Enterprise root CA** is selected and click **Next**. The CA Identifying Information page appears as shown in Figure 9-53.

Figure 9-53

Adding CA Information

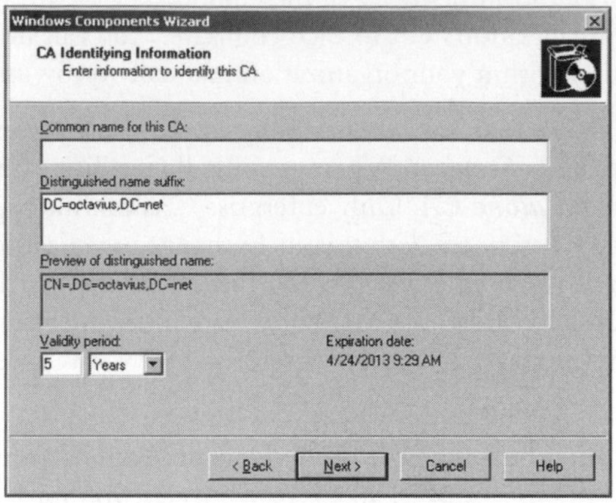

4. Type a descriptive name for your CA in the Common name for this CA dialog box. Normally the first CA in an organization is named for the organization. For example, Octavius Enterprise Root CA would be an appropriate common name for the Enterprise root CA in the Octavius organization.

5. By default, Enterprise root CAs generate their own public/private key pair for use when digitally signing public key certificates. The validity period for this public/ private key pair is 5 years by default, but you can change this value using the Validity period drop-down boxes shown in Figure 9-53.

TAKE NOTE*

The validity period for the CAs public/private key pair is used to determine the maximum validity period for public key certificates that are digitally signed by the CA. For example, if the CA certificate expires in April 2013, the CA cannot give a validity period beyond that date for any public key certificates that it digitally signs.

6. Click **Next**. After the CA public/private key pair is generated, the Certificate Database Settings page appears.

7. Review the default locations for the CA database and logs and click **Next**. When prompted to stop IIS to complete the installation of Certificate Services, click **Yes**.

8. Insert your Windows Server 2003 CD-ROM when prompted. When prompted to enable ASP, click **Yes**.

9. Click **Finish** to close the Windows Components Wizard window.

10. After installing an Enterprise CA, you should ensure that the computers within your organization obtain a copy of the CA trusted root so that they can validate the digital signatures on public key certificates that were issued by the CA. Although each client computer can obtain a copy of the trusted root by navigating to https:// *CA_name*/certsrv (where CA_name is the FQDN or IP address of the computer running Certificate Services) and selecting **Download a CA certificate, certificate chain, or CRL**, it would be too time consuming to perform on many computers. As a result, we will configure the Default Domain GPO to distribute the trusted root certificate for the CA to all domain computers automatically.

11. On your CA, click **Start**, **Administrative Tools**, and then click **Active Directory Users and Computers**. The Active Directory Users and Computers window appears.

12. Right click your domain in the left pane and click **Properties**. When the domain Properties window appears, highlight the **Group Policy** tab to view the Default Domain Policy as shown in Figure 9-54.

Figure 9-54

Viewing the Default Domain Policy

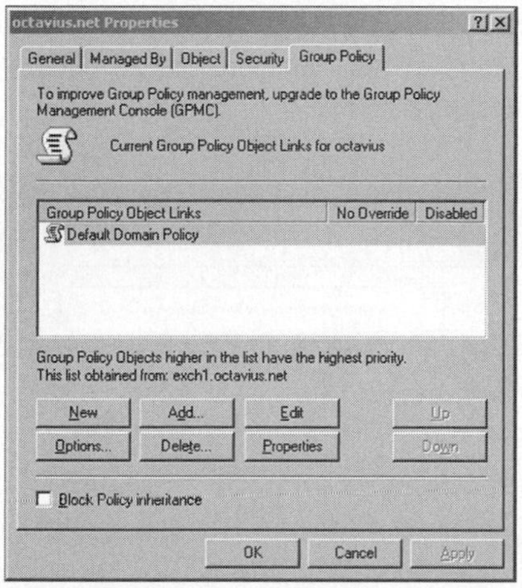

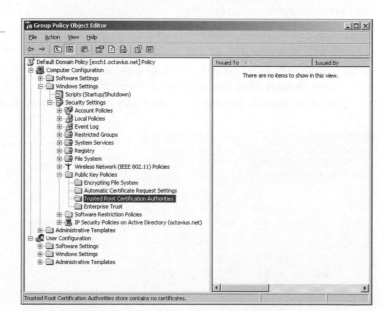

> **TAKE NOTE***
>
> If you have the Group Policy Management Console (GPMC) installed, you will not see the Default Domain Policy in the screen shown in Figure 9-54. Instead, you will need to click the **Open** button on the Group Policy tab to open the GPMC and expand your forest and domain in the left pane to view the Default Domain Policy.

13. Highlight **Default Domain Policy** and click **Edit**. The Group Policy Object Editor appears.

> **TAKE NOTE***
>
> If you have the GPMC installed, right click the Default Domain Policy in the left pane of the GPMC and select **Edit** to open the Group Policy Object Editor.

14. In the left pane of the Group Policy Object Editor, navigate to **Default Domain Policy** > **Computer Configuration** > **Windows Settings** > **Security Settings** > **Public Key Policies** > **Trusted Root Certification Authorities** as shown in Figure 9-55.

Figure 9-55

Configuring the Default Domain Policy

15. Right click **Trusted Root Certification Authorities** in the left pane and click **Import**. When the Certificate Import Wizard appears, click **Next**.

16. On the File to Import page, you must specify the trust root certificate of your CA. By default, the trusted root certificate is located on the root of C:\ on your CA and named *Server_CA-Name.crt*, where Server is the FQDN of your CA, and CA-Name is the name of your CA during installation. Figure 9-56 shows the location of the trusted root certificate for the Octavius Enterprise Root CA installed on exch1.octavius.net. Click **Browse**, select your trusted root certificate from C:\ in the Open window, and click **OK**. When finished, click **Next**.

Figure 9-56

Specifying a Trusted Root Certificate

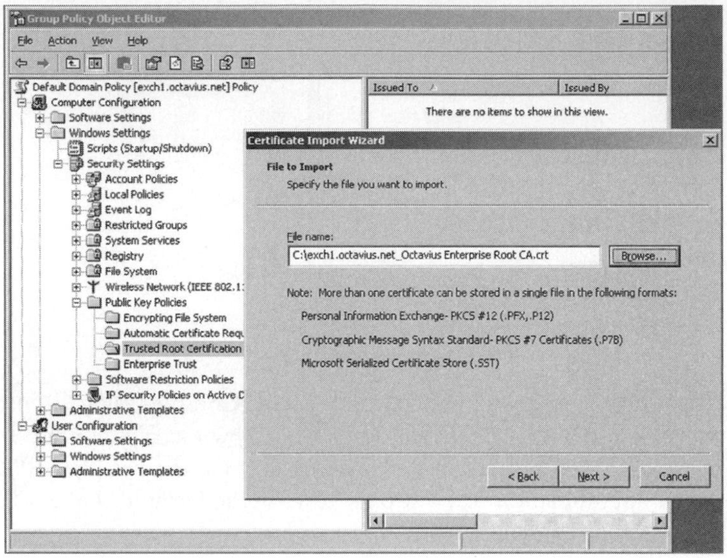

17. On the Certificate Store page, click **Next**. Click **Finish** to close the Certificate Import Wizard. Click **OK** to close the information dialog box.

18. Close the Group Policy Object Editor. Click **OK** to close the domain Properties window. Close the Active Directory Users and Computers window.

 REPLACE THE DEFAULT EXCHANGE SSL/TLS CERTIFICATE WITH A CERTIFICATE FROM AN ENTERPRISE CA

GET READY. Turn on the computer, and log in as the Administrator user account. Close any windows that appear on the desktop.

1. Click **Start**, **Administrative Tools**, and then click **Internet Information Services (IIS) Manager**. The Internet Information Services (IIS) Manager window appears.

2. In the left pane, expand your Exchange server and then expand **Web Sites**. Right click **Default Web Site** and select **Properties**. When the Default Web Site Properties window appears, highlight the **Directory Security** tab as shown in Figure 9-57.

Figure 9-57

Configuring Certificates in IIS Manager

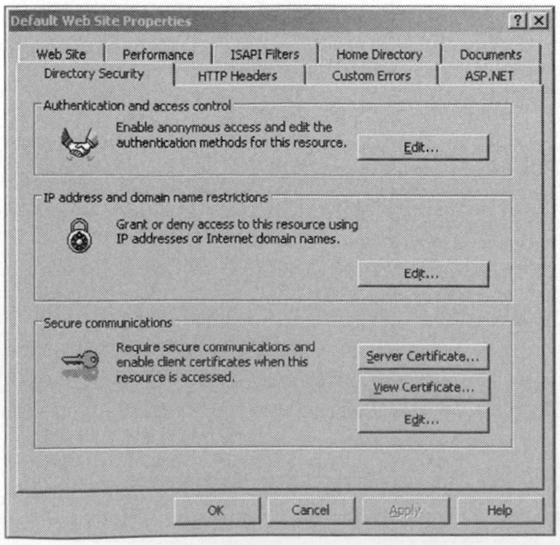

3. Click **Server Certificate**. When the Welcome to the Web Server Certificate Wizard page appears, click **Next** to start the IIS Certificate Wizard.

4. On the Modify the Current Certificate Assignment page, select **Remove the current certificate** as shown in Figure 9-58 and click **Next**. The Remove a Certificate page appears.

Figure 9-58

Removing an Existing
Certificate

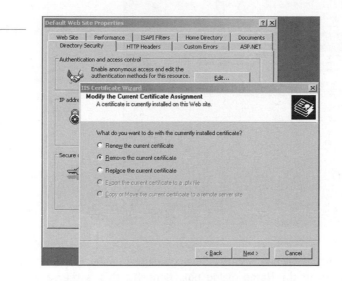

5. Review the details of the certificate that you are removing and click **Next**. Click **Finish** to close the IIS Certificate Wizard.

6. In the Default Web Site Properties window, click **Server Certificate**. When the Welcome to the Web Server Certificate Wizard page appears, click **Next** to start the IIS Certificate Wizard.

7. On the Modify the Current Certificate Assignment page shown in Figure 9-59, ensure that **Create a new certificate** is selected and click **Next**. The Delayed or Immediate Request page appears.

Figure 9-59

Creating a New Certificate

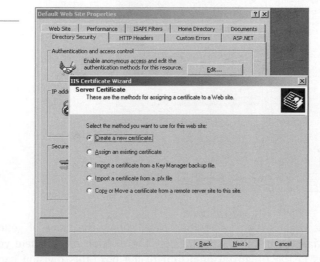

8. To enroll for a certificate from an Enterprise CA, ensure that **Send the request immediately to an online certification authority** is selected as shown in Figure 9-60 and click **Next**.

Figure 9-60

Sending a Certificate Request to an Enterprise CA

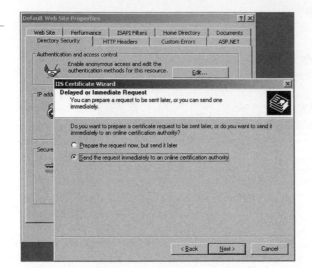

9. On the Name and Security Settings page, supply an appropriate name for your certificate in the **Name** dialog box. Normally, this is the same as the FQDN that email clients use when contacting your Exchange server for the server exch2.octavius.net as shown in Figure 9-61. You can optionally increase the key length to more than 1024 bits using the **Bit length** drop-down box, but this may exclude or reduce the performance of some SSL/TLS clients. Similarly, you can select the checkbox at the bottom of Figure 9-61 to select a different cryptographic algorithm provider, but this is necessary only for unusual situations. Click **Next** when finished.

Figure 9-61

Configuring the Certificate Name and Security

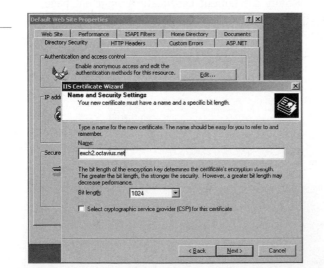

10. On the Organization Information page, supply the name of your organization in the **Organization** dialog box and supply the division name where your Exchange server resides in the **Organizational unit** dialog box. This division name is normally the same as the OU that contains the computer account for your Exchange server in AD. For example, if your Exchange server exists in the East OU of the Octavius organization, you could enter the values shown in Figure 9-62. Click **Next** when finished.

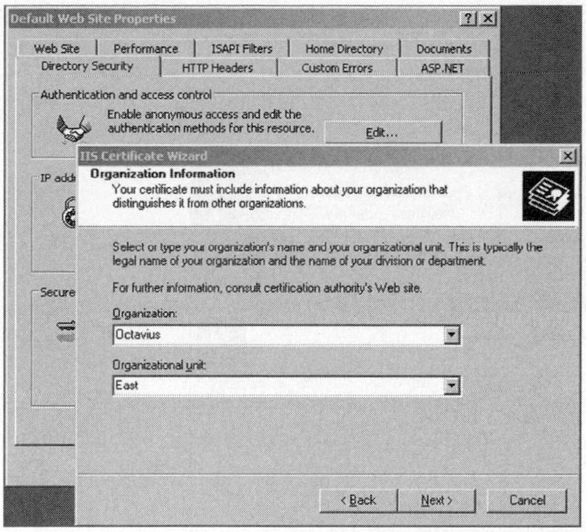

Figure 9-62

Specifying Organization Information

TAKE NOTE ★

If you configure client computers to contact your Exchange server by IP address or by using a different name than the one shown in Figure 9-63, clients will receive a certificate error in their application that indicates that the name on the SSL/TLS certificate does not match the server name.

11. On the Your Site's Common Name page, enter the FQDN or NetBIOS name that other computers will use when contacting your Exchange server in the **Common name** dialog box. For example, if you plan to configure client computers to contact exch2 .octavius.net, you would enter exch2.octavius.net in this dialog box as shown in Figure 9-63. Click **Next** when finished.

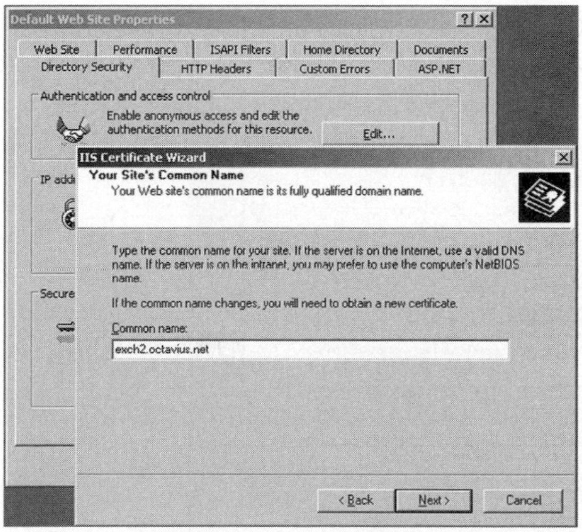

Figure 9-63

Configuring a Common Name

12. On the Geographical Information page, supply the appropriate information about your Exchange server's physical location in the appropriate drop-down or dialog boxes shown in Figure 9-64 and click **Next** when finished.

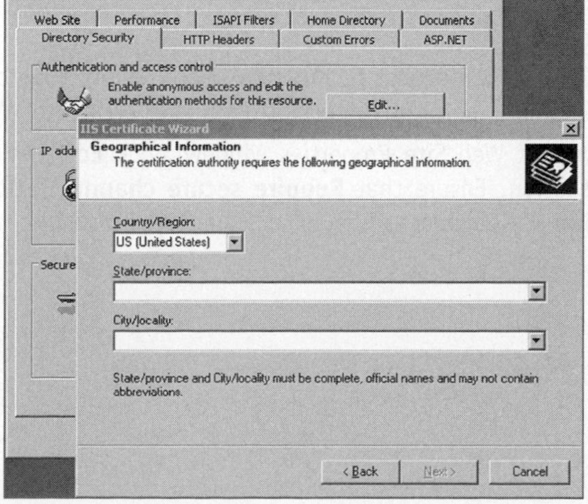

Figure 9-64

Specifying Geographical Information

13. On the SSL Port page, ensure that port 443 is listed in the dialog box as shown in Figure 9-65 and click **Next**.

Figure 9-65

Specifying the SSL Port for HTTP

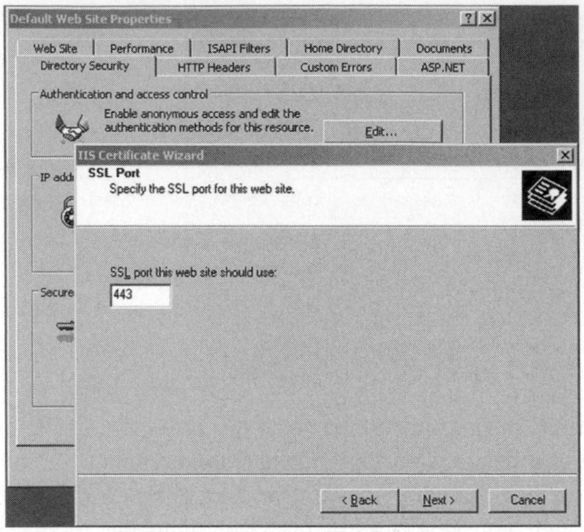

14. On the Choose a Certification Authority page, select your CA from the **Certification authorities** drop-down box as shown in Figure 9-66 and click **Next**.

Figure 9-66

Selecting an Enterprise CA

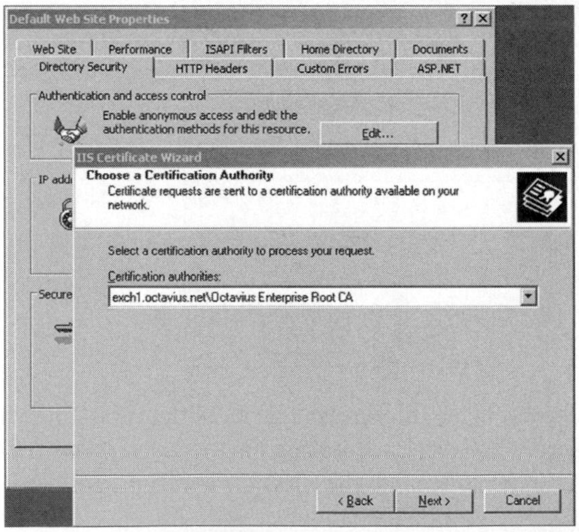

15. On the Certificate Request Submission page, review your certificate request settings and click **Next**. Click **Finish** to close the IIS Certificate Wizard.

16. In the Default Web Site Properties window, click **Edit** under the Secure communications section. Ensure that **Require secure channel (SSL)** and **Require 128-bit encryption** is selected as shown in Figure 9-67 and click **OK**.

Figure 9-67

Requiring SSL for HTTP

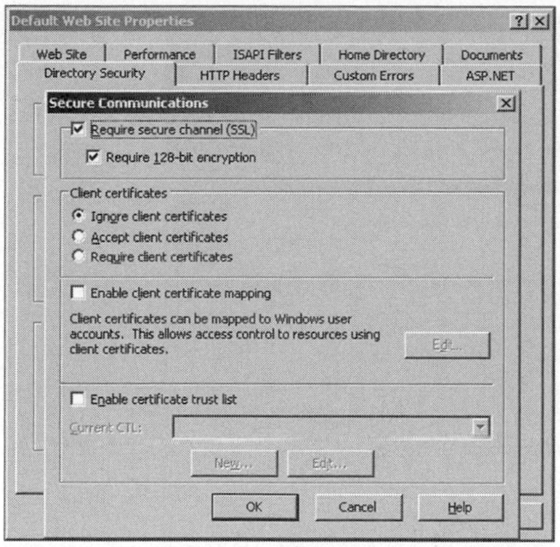

17. Click **OK** to close the Default Web Site Properties window and close IIS Manager.

 REPLACE THE DEFAULT EXCHANGE SSL/TLS CERTIFICATE WITH A CERTIFICATE FROM A COMMERCIAL CA

GET READY. Turn on the computer, and log in as the Administrator user account. Close any windows that appear on the desktop.

TAKE NOTE* The process within IIS Manager for obtaining a certificate from a commercial CA is similar to that for obtaining a certificate from an Enterprise CA. As a result, we focus on the differences within this exercise.

1. Click **Start**, **Administrative Tools**, and then click **Internet Information Services (IIS) Manager**. The Internet Information Services (IIS) Manager window appears.

2. In the left pane, expand your Exchange server and then expand **Web Sites**. Right click **Default Web Site** and select **Properties**. When the Default Web Site Properties window appears, highlight the **Directory Security** tab as shown earlier in Figure 9-57.

3. Click **Server Certificate**. When the Welcome to the Web Server Certificate Wizard page appears, click **Next** to start the IIS Certificate Wizard.

4. On the Modify the Current Certificate Assignment page, select **Remove the current certificate** as shown earlier in Figure 9-58 and click **Next**. The Remove a Certificate page appears.

5. Review the details of the certificate that you are removing and click **Next**. Click **Finish** to close the IIS Certificate Wizard.

6. In the Default Web Site Properties window, click **Server Certificate**. When the Welcome to the Web Server Certificate Wizard page appears, click **Next** to start the IIS Certificate Wizard.

7. On the Modify the Current Certificate Assignment page shown earlier in Figure 9-59, ensure that **Create a new certificate** is selected and click **Next**. The Delayed or Immediate Request page appears.

8. To enroll for a certificate from a commercial CA, ensure that **Prepare the request now, but send it later** is selected as shown in Figure 9-68 and click **Next**.

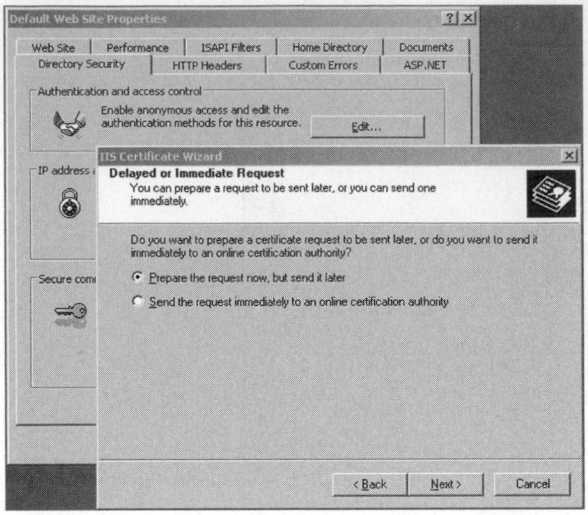

Figure 9-68

Sending a Certificate Request to a Commercial CA

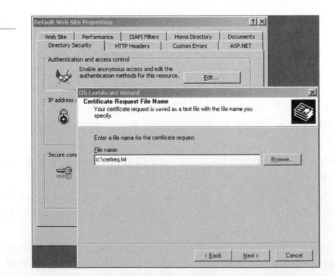

9. On the Name and Security Settings page, supply an appropriate name for your certificate in the **Name** dialog box (typically the FQDN of your Exchange server) and optionally modify the number of bits to use in the key as well as the cryptographic service provider as shown earlier in Figure 9-61.

10. On the Organization Information page, supply the appropriate organization and organizational unit names for your Exchange server as shown earlier in Figure 9-62 and click **Next**.

11. On the Your Site's Common Name page, enter the FQDN or NetBIOS name that other computers will use when contacting your Exchange server as shown earlier in Figure 9-63 and click **Next**.

12. On the Geographical Information page, supply the appropriate information about your Exchange server's physical location in the appropriate drop-down or dialog boxes as shown earlier in Figure 9-64 and click **Next**.

13. On the Certificate Request File Name page, enter the path to the text file that will contain the public key used to generate the certificate in the File name dialog box. The default name is c:\certreq.txt as shown in Figure 9-69. Click **Next** when finished.

Figure 9-69

Specifying the Certificate Request File Name

14. On the Request File Summary page, review your certificate request settings and click **Next**. Click **Finish** to close the IIS Certificate Wizard. Click **OK** to close the Default Web Site Properties window and close IIS Manager.

15. You must now contact the Web site for a commercial CA and request a certificate by following the steps outlined on the particular CA Web site. Part of this process will include

uploading the certificate request file (i.e., c:\certreq.txt) that contains your Exchange server's public key. In addition, you will be required to submit payment to the CA (typically using a credit card). The CA will then validate your identity using several methods (phone, records, physical meeting). After the validation process has completed (typically a few days), the CA will create a public key certificate file (with a .cer extension) that you can download from its Web site and import into IIS Manager.

16. Click **Start**, **Administrative Tools**, and then click **Internet Information Services (IIS) Manager**. The Internet Information Services (IIS) Manager window appears.

17. In the left pane, expand your Exchange server and then expand **Web Sites**. Right click **Default Web Site** and select **Properties**. When the Default Web Site Properties window appears, highlight the **Directory Security** tab as shown earlier in Figure 9-57.

18. Click **Server Certificate**. When the Welcome to the Web Server Certificate Wizard page appears, click **Next** to start the IIS Certificate Wizard.

19. On the Pending Certificate Request page, ensure that **Process the pending request and install the certificate** is selected as shown in Figure 9-70 and click **Next**.

Figure 9-70

Importing a Pending
Certificate Request

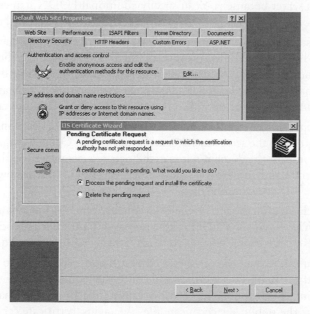

20. On the Process a Pending Request page, enter the path to the public key certificate file (*.cer) that you downloaded from the CA Web site in the **Path and file name** dialog box as shown in Figure 9-71 and click **Next**.

Figure 9-71

Specifying the Certificate File

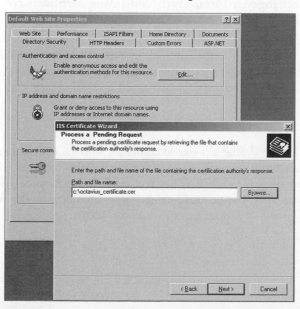

21. On the SSL Port page, ensure that port 443 is listed in the dialog box as shown earlier in Figure 9-65 and click **Next**.

22. Click **Next** on the Certificate Summary page. Click **Finish** to close the IIS Certificate Wizard.

23. In the Default Web Site Properties window, click **Edit** under the Secure communications section. Ensure that **Require secure channel (SSL)** and **Require 128-bit encryption** is selected as shown earlier in Figure 9-67 and click **OK**.

24. Click **OK** to close the Default Web Site Properties window and close IIS Manager.

THE COMMAND LINE WAY

You can also use cmdlets within the Exchange Management Shell to generate certificate requests and import them. To generate a certificate request that can be uploaded to a commercial CA for approval, you can use the **New-ExchangeCertificate** cmdlet. This is often useful if there are several names that Internet clients must use when contacting your Exchange server because you can specify additional FQDN names during the request that will be stored in the *Subject Alternative Name (SAN)* field of the certificate.

This is useful if you have remote Outlook or Entourage email clients. In order to use the Autodiscover service from a remote Outlook or Entourage client across a remote connection, you must also specify **autodiscover.domain** (where domain.com is your domain name) as an additional domain name during the certificate request or add the **–IncludeAutoDiscover** option to the New-ExchangeCertificate cmdlet.

For example, to generate a certificate request using a 1024-bit long key in the file c:\certreq.txt for the server exch2.octavius.net within Octavius organization (Country = US) that responds to the domain name exch2.octavius.net as well as the Subject Alternative Names exch2 and autodicover.octavius.net, you can use the following command in the Exchange Management Shell:

New-ExchangeCertificate -GenerateRequest $true -SubjectName 'C=US, O=Octavius, CN=exch2.octavius.net' -DomainName 'exch2,autodiscover.octavius.net' -PrivateKeyExportable $true –KeySize '1024' -Path 'c:\certreq.txt'

Next, you can upload the certificate request file (c:\certreq.txt) to a commercial CA and download the public key certificate file once the request has been approved. Following this, you can import the public key certificate using the **Import-ExchangeCertificate** cmdlet. To import the public key certificate file c:\octavius_certificate.cer and assign a friendly name of Exch2 Certificate, you could use the following command within the Exchange Management Shell:

Import-ExchangeCertificate -Path 'c:\octavius_certificate.cer' -FriendlyName 'Exch2 Certificate'

You can also use the New-ExchangeCertificate cmdlet to generate a new self-signed certificate or to request a certificate from an enterprise CA. For more information on the New-ExchangeCertificate and Import-ExchangeCertificate cmdlets, search for their names within Exchange Server 2007 Help.

After replacing the default self-signed certificate with a CA-signed certificate, you can view the new certificate by clicking on the View Certificate button on the Directory Security tab within the properties of the Default Web Site within IIS Manager as described earlier. The certificate should indicate that it was issued by the appropriate CA as shown for the SSL/TLS certificate shown in Figure 9-72 for the server exch2.octavius.net.

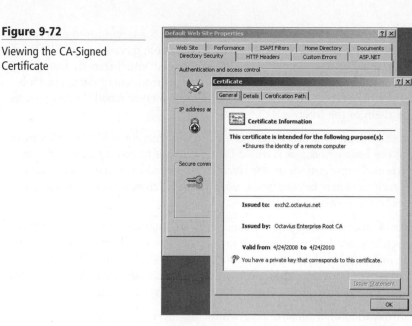

By default, the new CA-signed certificate is configured for use with the HTTP protocol as well as the POP3 and IMAP4 protocols if they were started on the Exchange server when the certificate was obtained. To configure this new certificate to be used for other protocols and services, you must first obtain the thumbprint for your new certificate by running the Get-ExchangeCertificate cmdlet as shown earlier in this section. Next, you can use the Enable-ExchangeCertificate cmdlet within the Exchange Management Shell to enable the certificate for use with other protocols and services. For example, to enable the command **Enable-ExchangeCertificate -Thumbprint** *thumbprint* **-Services 'IMAP, POP, UM, IIS, SMTP'** will enable the new CA-signed certificate with the specific *thumbprint* for use by IMAP4, POP3, UM, HTTP, and SMTP. However, because the HTTP protocol is already enabled after running the Web Certificate Wizard, you only need to enable any remaining protocols for use with a new CA-signed certificate. Figure 9-73 displays the Enable-ExchangeCertificate command needed to enable the exch2.octavius.net certificate for use with the additional protocols IMAP4, POP3, and SMTP as well as the output of the Get-ExchangeCertificate cmdlet afterward.

Figure 9-73

Enabling Certificate Use

When your public key certificate expires, you must renew the certificate or obtain a new one. If you are using a commercial CA, you typically obtain a new certificate using the same process discussed in this lesson. If you are using an enterprise CA, you can simply run the IIS Certificate Wizard again and select **Renew the current certificate** on the Modify the Current Certificate Assignment page shown earlier in Figure 9-58.

■ Configuring Email Encryption

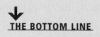
THE BOTTOM LINE

You can also use certificates to encrypt emails within email client programs. This ensures that messages remain encrypted as they are passed through several different email servers on the Internet. In addition, you can digitally sign emails to prove their authenticity by configuring email client programs to use certificates.

In the previous section, you learned how to configure SSL and TLS encryption to encrypt OWA traffic between web browsers on client computers to CAS role servers using HTTPS. In addition, this same SSL and TLS encryption can be used to protect email transfer from CAS role servers to email clients using POP3S and IMAP4S as well as from email clients to Hub role servers using SMTPS. However, CAS and Hub role servers decrypt emails before processing them and relaying them to the Internet.

Most email servers on the Internet will accept only anonymous unencrypted SMTP email from other emails servers on the Internet because it would be too difficult to coordinate certificates and trusted roots between all organizations on the Internet. As a result, sensitive emails that are forwarded to Internet recipients may be read by a third-party who has access to the traffic on the Internet as it passes between email servers.

To protect the contents of an email message as it passes across the Internet, you must encrypt the email message on the sender's email client before it is forwarded to an email server. The encrypted message will simply be forwarded to the destination email server on the Internet alongside other emails, however its contents will not be readable. When the encrypted message is delivered to the destination email client, that email client can then decrypt the encrypted message.

This process uses a combination of symmetric and asymmetric encryption in much the same way that SSL and TLS does. The original email message is encrypted on the sender's email client using a randomly generated symmetric key and this symmetric key is then encrypted using the recipient's public key. When the message reaches the destination email client, the recipient decrypts the symmetric key using his private key and then proceeds to use the symmetric key to decrypt the contents of the email message. When the recipient replies to the email message, this process is reversed.

To encrypt individual emails, you must configure your email client with a public-private key pair. There are many different technologies that can generate public-private key pairs for use with email encryption between email client computers. If your organization does not have a CA, you can add a *Pretty Good Privacy (PGP)* or *GNU Privacy Guard (GPG)* key pair that you generated using a PGP or GPG utility to your email client program. However, because PGP and GPG do not use CA-signed keys, you must manually approve other users' PGP or GPG keys before you can use them to send encrypted emails.

MORE INFORMATION

PGP is licensed for commercial use, but GPG is freely obtainable. To obtain a copy of GPG, visit **http://gnupg.org.**

If your organization has a CA, you can simply add a CA-signed *user certificate* to your email client program and ensure that the destination computer contains the trusted root of the CA. To allow users to obtain user certificates from an enterprise CA, you must log in as a user who is a member of the Domain Admins group and grant the appropriate users the Read and Enroll permissions on a *certificate template* that can be used for email encryption. Users can then use the Certificates MMC snap-in to request a certificate. If the user account has Read and Enroll permissions to the certificate template, AD generates a public-private key pair within the user account and automatically sends the public key to the enterprise CA. Once the Enterprise CA digitally signs the certificate, it is returned to the user account. Users can then add this user certificate to their email client program and use it for email encryption.

MORE INFORMATION

You can also use Group Policy to automatically issue certificates to users within your organization using a process called *autoenrollment*. For more information on how to configure autoenrollment, search for autoenrollment at **http://technet.microsoft.com**.

Instead of configuring your email client program for encryption, you can configure it to digitally sign all emails. Your email client will encrypt a hash of each email that you send using your private key. Others on the Internet can then verify the digital signature using your public key and prove that the email was sent by you and not modified during transit. Digital email signing can be done regardless of whether you use a CA-signed certificate, PGP, or GPG.

CONFIGURE USER CERTIFICATE TEMPLATE PERMISSIONS

TAKE NOTE✳

To perform these steps, you must already have an Enterprise CA installed within your forest.

GET READY. Turn on the computer, and log in as the Administrator user account. Close any windows that appear on the desktop.

1. On your Enterprise CA, click **Start** and click **Run**. In the run dialog box, type **certtmpl.msc** and press **Enter**. The Certificate Templates window appears.

2. In the right pane, right click **User** and click **Properties**. On the Security tab, ensure that Authenticated Users is allowed **Read** and **Enroll** permissions as shown in Figure 9-74.

Figure 9-74

Configuring a User Certificate Template

| User Properties | ? x |

General | Request Handling | Subject Name | Extensions | Security

Group or user names:

- Authenticated Users
- Domain Admins (OCTAVIUS\Domain Admins)
- Domain Users (OCTAVIUS\Domain Users)
- Enterprise Admins (OCTAVIUS\Enterprise Admins)

[Add...] [Remove]

Permissions for Authenticated Users | Allow | Deny
Full Control	☐	☐
Read	☑	☐
Write	☐	☐
Enroll	☑	☐

For special permissions or for advanced settings, click Advanced. [Advanced]

[OK] [Cancel] [Apply]

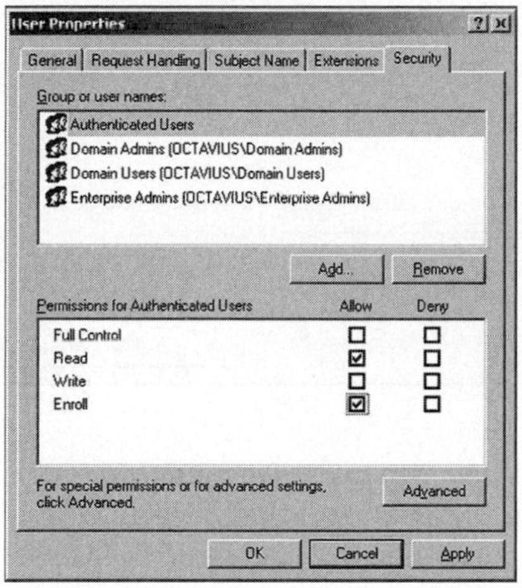

TAKE NOTE✳

If you wish to restrict the users who can obtain a user certificate, you can add the appropriate users as shown in Figure 9-74 and assign them Read and Enroll permissions instead.

3. Close the Certificate Templates window.

TAKE NOTE✳

If you configure the permissions on a different template than the one used in this exercise, you will need to add the template to the CA using the Certification Authority MMC snap-in (**Start** > **Administrative Tools** > **Certification Authority**).

REQUEST A USER CERTIFICATE

GET READY. Turn on the computer, and log in as any user account. Close any windows that appear on the desktop.

1. Click **Start** and click **Run**. In the run dialog box, type **certmgr.msc** and press **Enter**. The Certificates—Current User window appears.

2. In the left pane, expand **Personal** and **Certificates**.

3. Right click **Certificates**, select **All Tasks**, and click **Request New Certificate**. When the Certificate Request Wizard window appears, click **Next**.

4. On the Certificate Types page, select **User** as shown in Figure 9-75 and click **Next.**

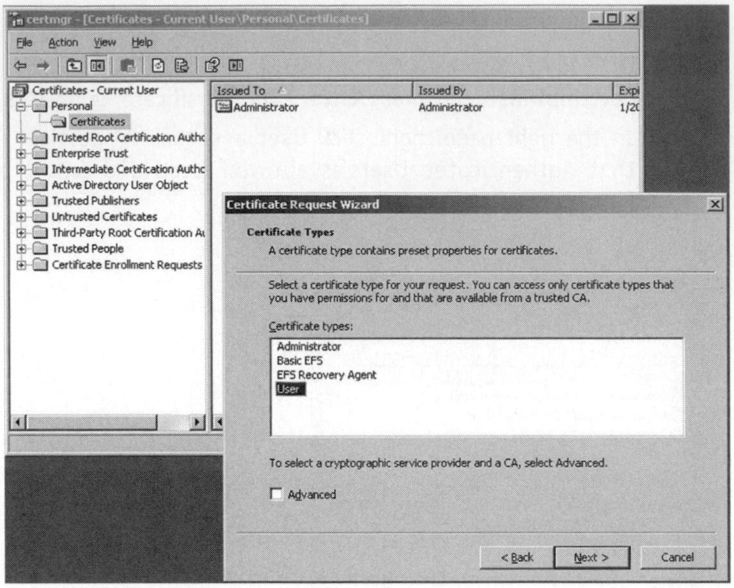

Figure 9-75

Creating a New Certificate Using a User Certificate Template

TAKE NOTE*

If you do not see User on the Certificate Types page, your user account does not have Read and Enroll permission to the User certificate template.

5. On the Certificate Friendly Name and Description page, supply an appropriate name for your certificate in the **Friendly name** dialog box as shown in Figure 9-76. Optionally, supply a description for your certificate in the **Description** dialog box and click **Next.**

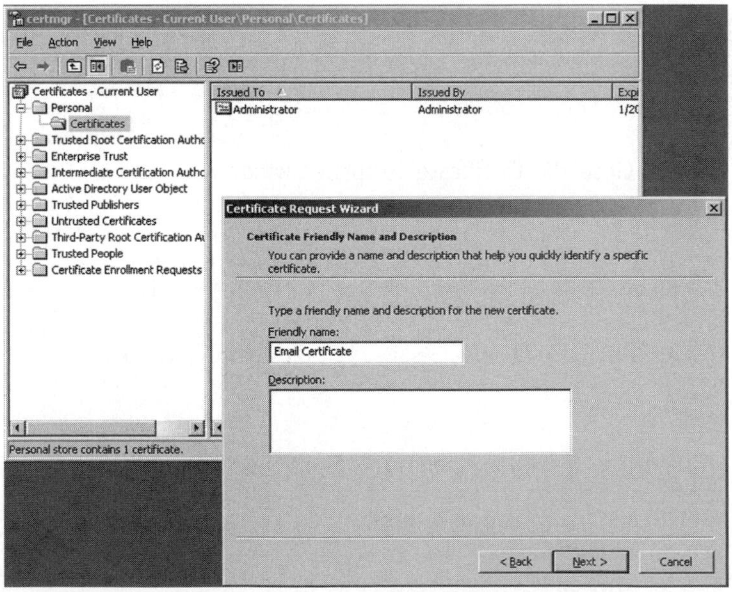

Figure 9-76

Specifying a Friendly Name and Description

6. Click **Finish** to close the Certificate Request Wizard. Click **OK** to close the result dialog box. You should now see a new certificate listed in the right pane of the Certificate—Current User window.
7. Close the Certificate—Current User window.

Once you have obtained a user certificate, you can configure your email client to use this certificate for email encryption or digital email signing. For Outlook 2007, you can navigate to **Tools > Trust Center**. When the Trust Center window opens, you can click **E-mail Security** in the left pane and select the appropriate options to allow for email encryption and digital signing as shown in

Figure 9-77. To select the certificate used for email encryption and digital signing, you can click **Settings** as shown in Figure 9-77 and choose the appropriate certificate to list in the **Signing Certificate** and **Encryption Certificate** dialog boxes as shown in Figure 9-78.

Figure 9-77

Configuring Email Encryption and Digital Signing in Outlook 2007

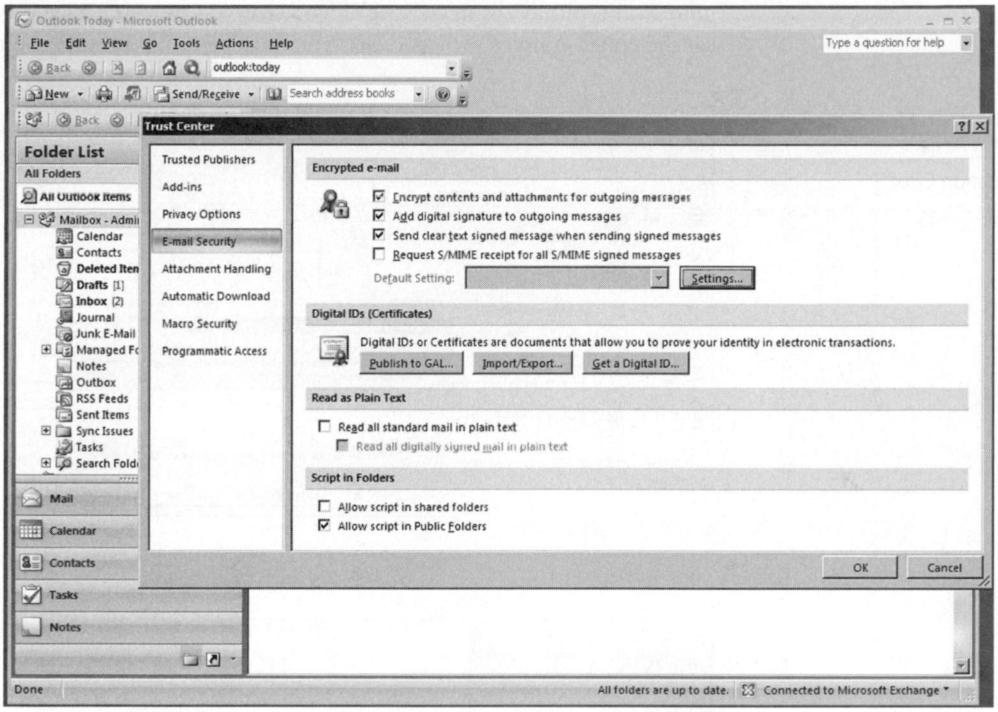

Figure 9-78

Selecting a Certificate in Outlook 2007

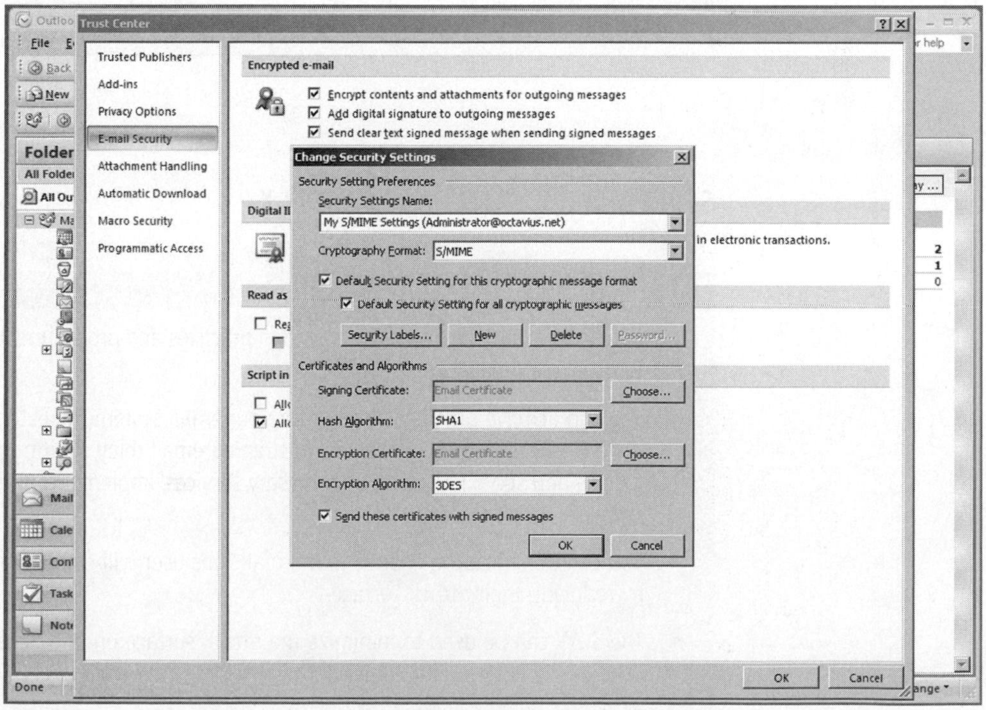

In previous versions of Outlook and in Outlook Express, you can configure email encryption and digital email signing by navigating to **Tool** > **Options** and selecting the **Security** tab. For Entourage clients, you can configure email encryption and signing by navigating to the **Mail Security** tab within the properties of the email account (**Tools** > **Accounts** in Entourage).

It is important to keep in mind that email encryption is a two-way process. If you enable email encryption in your email client program and attempt to send an encrypted email to a recipient who does not have a public-private key pair configured, you will receive an error message similar to the one shown in Figure 9-79 when attempting to send the email and will need to send the email unencrypted. Similarly, when you receive a digitally signed email, your email client program will typically display a special icon that you can use to see or validate the digital signature on the email message provided that you are able to obtain the public key of the sender.

Figure 9-79

Encryption Error

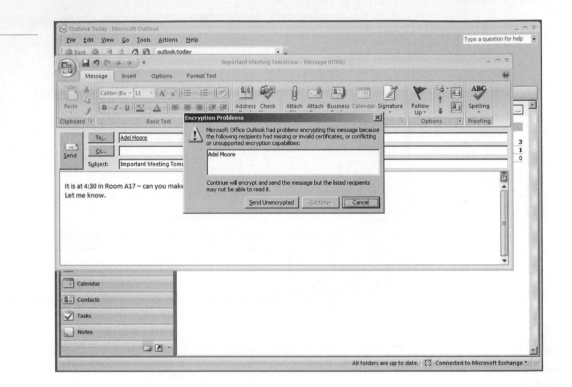

SUMMARY SKILL MATRIX

IN THIS LESSON YOU LEARNED:

- Practical security involves implementing practices and procedures that secure data according to organizational requirements.

- You can achieve practical security for your email system by restricting access to the email system, encrypting email transfer, restricting email relay, limiting permissions, minimizing viruses and spam, stopping unnecessary services, implementing firewalls, and updating software on a regular basis.

- You can minimize the chance that a malicious user will compromise your Exchange servers by reducing their attack surface.

- The SCW can be used to minimize the attack surface on an Exchange server by disabling unused services and implementing a host-based firewall.

- Network-based firewalls can be used to restrict the traffic that enters a network and thus reduce the Exchange attack surface.

- Antispam transport agents may be used to filter spam messages that enter your organization. These agents can filter spam messages by content, IP address, sender, recipient, and file attachment.

- Because nearly all spam enters your organization from the Internet, Edge role servers enable all antispam transport agents by default. You can optionally enable a limited number of antispam transport agents on Hub role servers.

- FSE is an antivirus software product that integrates with Exchange Server 2007 and uses up to five different antivirus-scanning engines that are updated on a regular basis. You can control the level of virus scanning as well as the processing of virus-infected files using FSE.

- When installed on a Hub or Edge role server, FSE scans messages that are relayed using a Transport Scan Job. Alternatively, FSE can scan mailboxes and public folders when installed on a Mailbox role server using the Realtime and Manual Scan Jobs.

- Cryptography protects data from access by unauthorized users by encrypting data using an algorithm and key. Symmetric cryptography uses the same key to encrypt and decrypt data, whereas asymmetric cryptography encrypts data using a public key and decrypts data using a private key. A digital signature is a hash that is encrypted using a private key. You can verify a digital signature using a public key.

- SSL and TLS use symmetric cryptography to encrypt email traffic on a network and asymmetric cryptography to protect the symmetric encryption key. To prevent a man-in-the-middle attack, public key certificates are used in place of public keys during the asymmetric encryption process.

- CAs create certificates by digitally signing public keys for other organizations. Commercial CAs are trusted by most applications, whereas enterprise CAs are trusted by an organization. You can install an enterprise CA within your organization to issue certificates for use with SSL and TLS. After obtaining a certificate, you can configure it for use with IMAP, POP, UM, HTTP, and SMTP.

- Email clients can be configured to encrypt the contents of emails before they are sent to an email server using user certificates. In addition, user certificates may be used to digitally sign emails that are sent by an email client.

■ Knowledge Assessment

Fill in the Blank

Complete the following sentences by writing the correct word or words in the blanks provided.

1. You can enable the _____ option in FSE to ensure that emails are rescanned following a virus definition update.

2. Filtering spam by IP address is commonly called _____.

3. The sum total of the number of ways that users can access your Exchange server is called the _____.

4. If you encrypt information using a public key, it must be decrypted using a _____.

5. The process of repairing a virus infection is called _____ .

6. To reduce the attack surface of a single Exchange server, you can run the _____ after registering the Exchange Server 2007 services.

7. The practice of limiting permissions is called _____.

8. You can configure content filtering to send copies of spam messages to a _____ mailbox.

9. You can obtain SSL and TLS certificates from a commercial or enterprise _____.

10. FSE can be configured to use up to _____ licensed antivirus engines for scanning emails.

Multiple Choice

Circle the letter that corresponds to the best answer.

1. Which of the following are good security practices with regards to Exchange? (Choose all that apply.)
   a. Limit access to email.
   b. Encrypt email traffic between clients and email servers.
   c. Ensure that client computers are regularly updated.
   d. Ensure that Exchange Server 2007 is regularly updated.

2. Which of the following scan jobs in FSE may be used to scan mailbox and public folder databases? (Choose all that apply.)
   a. Transport Scan Job
   b. Manual Scan Job
   c. Edge Scan Job
   d. Realtime Scan Job

3. After installing an enterprise CA within your organization, what must you install on all client computers so that they can validate CA-signed certificates?
   a. The CA private key
   b. The CA trusted root
   c. The CA digital signature
   d. The CRL

4. What must you obtain to configure digital email signing within Entourage?
   a. A CRL
   b. A digital signature
   c. A user certificate, PGP or GPG key pair
   d. A trusted root certificate

5. Which of the following bias settings would you configure within FSE to ensure that most viruses are detected?
   a. Favor Performance
   b. Max Certainty
   c. Max Performance
   d. Favor Certainty

6. Which of the following cmdlets may be used to update the Safe Senders list from an Outlook client?
   a. Set-ContentFilterConfig
   b. Update-Safelist
   c. Set-ContentList
   d. Update-ContentList

7. You have configured a CA-signed certificate for use with remote POP3 and IMAP4 clients. However, the autodiscover service on remote clients is unable to find your Exchange servers. How can you remedy the problem? (Choose two answers. Each answer is part of the solution.)
   a. Request a new SSL/TLS certificate using the New-ExchangeCertificate cmdlet
   b. Request a new SSL/TLS certificate using the Certificate Wizard
   c. Include an external URL in the certificate request
   d. Include a Subject Alternative Name (SAN) in the certificate request

8. Which of the following ports is used by EdgeSync traffic that is protected by SSL?
   a. 50636
   b. 443
   c. 995
   d. 993

9. Which of the following email addresses are likely from a spammer? (Choose all that apply.)
   a. bestoffer@acme.com
   b. A5829SGHW24@kei2.com
   c. julie@supersales.com
   d. hotbuys@hotmail.com

10. During the IIS Certificate Wizard, which value represents the URL of the Exchange server that users must use when accessing email?
    a. Organization
    b. Location
    c. Common name
    d. Subject Alternative Name (SAN)

True/False

Circle T if the statement is true or F if the statement is false.

T | F **1.** Host-based firewalls may be used to filter traffic that enters a network.

T | F **2.** Edge role servers have all antispam transport agents installed and enabled by default.

T | F **3.** You can configure one or more RBLs to aid in filtering spam by IP address.

T | F **4.** Attachment filtering can only be configured using cmdlets within the Exchange Management Shell on Hub role servers.

T | F **5.** You can reduce the attack surface of a computer by enabling SSL or TLS encryption.

T | F **6.** Educating users about how to identify spam and viruses is an important practice to minimize the spread of spam and viruses.

T | F **7.** If the sender reputation is too low, the sender's IP address will be added to the IP Block List for 24 hours by default.

T | F **8.** An SCL of 0 indicates that the email message is almost certainly spam, whereas an SCL of 9 indicates that the email message is not likely to be spam.

T | F **9.** All asymmetric encryption must use the public key.

T | F **10.** By regularly updating the software on your Exchange servers, you minimize the chance of buffer overruns.

Review Questions

1. Explain why continuous configuration of antispam filters is necessary within an organization.

2. Explain how protocol encryption can be used to provide security for local and remote email clients.

■ Case Scenarios

Scenario 9-1: Reducing the Classroom Attack Surface

The services that you disable and the firewalls that you configure are ultimately dependent on your network environment and the configuration of your Exchange servers. For your classroom or home network, diagram your network(s), routers, proxy servers (if used), Exchange servers (and roles), and Internet configuration. On your diagram, label where you should place network- and host-based firewalls. In addition, label the protocols that each Exchange server must use for normal functionality. When finished, use the SCW to reduce the attack surface on your Exchange server(s) and configure network-based firewalls on your network router(s) or proxy server(s) to minimize your Exchange attack surface.

Scenario 9-2: Responding to a New Virus Attack

FSE can remove or clean viruses for which it has virus definitions. However, when a new virus is released, that virus will not be detected by FSE until a new virus definition update is released that identifies the virus. Explain what you would do in the event of a new virus attack. Detail how you would determine the attack has occurred, the first actions that you should perform to minimize the impact of the attack as well as the actions that you should take to remove the virus using FSE.

10 LESSON

Backing Up, Restoring, and Repairing Exchange

LESSON SKILL MATRIX

TECHNOLOGY SKILL	OBJECTIVE DOMAIN	OBJECTIVE DOMAIN NUMBER
Backing Up Exchange Databases	Configure backups.	5.1
Backing Up Exchange Server Role Configuration	Configure backups.	5.1
Restoring Exchange Databases	Recover messaging data.	5.2
Restoring Mailboxes and Deleted Items	Recover messaging data.	5.2
Performing Dial Tone Recovery	Recover messaging data.	5.2
Restoring Exchange Server Roles	Recover server roles.	5.3

KEY TERMS

backup job
backup set
checkpoint file
circular logging
cleanup agent
cloned configuration
copy backup
dial tone recovery
differential backup
Extensible Storage Engine
  (ESE)

Extensible Storage Engine
  Utility
full backup
full-text index
hard recovery
incremental backup
Information Store Integrity
  Checker
message dumpster
Microsoft Exchange Information
  Store

normal backup
offline backup
offline defragmentation
online defragmentation
Recovery Storage Group (RSG)
streaming backup
system state
transaction log
Volume Shadow Copy Service
  (VSS)
Windows Backup

■ Backing Up and Restoring Exchange Databases

THE BOTTOM LINE

In any IT administration job role, one of the most critical and common tasks is protecting end-user data. This data includes emails and public folder items that are used within your organization. To protect this data, you must understand Exchange database structure, select the appropriate backup media and procedures, as well as know how to restore this data when necessary.

How Exchange Databases Work

Fundamental to knowing how to back up and restore Exchange databases is a good understanding of how Exchange databases work together with transaction logs and checkpoint files to store and retrieve data.

Recall that Exchange Server 2007 stores email and public folder items within *databases* on the Mailbox role servers within your organization. Databases consist of several organized *tables* of information. Each mailbox within a mailbox database is represented by several tables of information that contain emails organized by folder (e.g., Inbox, Sent Items), and each public folder within a public folder database is represented by a table in the public folder database that contains the appropriate public folder items.

Databases are well suited for storing email and public folder information because email and public folder items can be retrieved quickly from the structured tables within the database. However, databases are not as quick at storing email and public folder items because the appropriate tables must first be located and new table entries must be created before new items are stored within the database. As a result, email systems that store large quantities of new email and public folder items will exhibit poorer database performance. To minimize this performance cost, the *Microsoft Exchange Information Store* service in Exchange Server 2007 first writes new email and public folder items to a *transaction log*. Transaction logs are small files to which programs can quickly append information. The information in these transaction logs is then written (or *committed*) to the appropriate mailbox or public folder database a few moments later when the system load permits. Because it is faster to write to smaller files compared to larger ones, transaction logs are limited to 1 MB in size in Exchange Server 2007. In addition, transaction logs are not overwritten by default. Instead, when a transaction log reaches 1 MB in size, a new one is created.

After email or public folder items within the transaction log are written to the appropriate mailbox or public folder database, the associated email or public folder items within the transaction log are not deleted. Instead, entries are created in a *checkpoint file* that indicates the email and public folder items that were successfully written from the transaction log to the database. This allows for point-in-time restore operations because the checkpoint file can be used to locate specific email and public folder items within existing log files that should be recommitted to the mailbox or public folder database.

The components and processes within Exchange that perform these actions— *Extensible Storage Engine (ESE)*—are illustrated in Figure 10-1.

Figure 10-1

Database Components

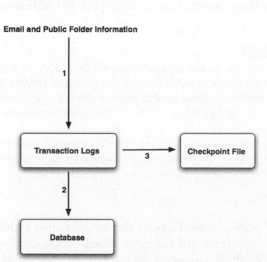

All mailbox and public folder databases must reside within a storage group, and each storage group can contain up to five databases. However, all databases within the same storage group must share the same transaction logs and checkpoint file. As a result, you must specify the location of the transaction logs and checkpoint file when you create a new storage group or move an existing storage group. The transaction logs and checkpoint file do not need to be on the same volume, but they usually are for easy management. To view the location of the transaction logs and checkpoint file, you can access the properties of the storage group on the appropriate server under the **Server Configuration** > **Mailbox** node within the Exchange Management Console. The properties of the First Storage Group are shown in Figure 10-2.

Figure 10-2

Storage Group Properties

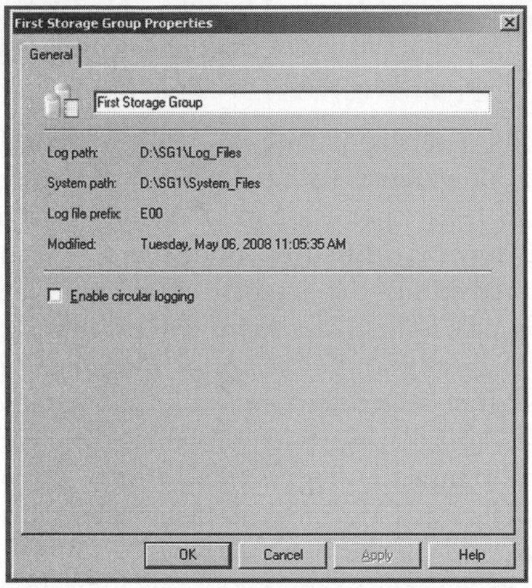

As illustrated in Figure 10-2, log files are stored in the D:\SG1\Log_Files folder. Moreover, each log file will be prefixed with the letters E00 to identify it as being part of the first storage group (the E01 prefix is used for the second storage group, and so on). The first log file will named E00.log, when the contents of this log file reach 1 MB, a new log file called E0000000001.log will be created. When the E0000000001.log file contains 1 MB of data, the file E0000000002.log will be created, and so on. Similarly, the checkpoint file for the First Storage Group shown in Figure 10-2 will be stored within the D:\SG1\System_Files folder and called E00.chk. If you select **Enable circular logging** (see Figure 10-2), new log files are not created when the E00.chk file reaches 1 MB in size. Instead, the E00.chk is overwritten to save disk space. Because *circular logging* prevents you from performing transaction log backups and does not allow for point-in-time restore operations, you should only select this option if your Exchange server is low on disk space and additional hard drives are unavailable.

➕ MORE INFORMATION

In addition to regular log files, the **Log files path** shown in Figure 10-2 will also contain an E00tmp.log file for storing temporary information as well as two reserve log files (E00res00001.jrs and E00res00002.jrs). These reserve log files are used to reserve disk space to allow the system to stop the database cleanly in the event that the volume containing the transaction logs runs out of space. These files are only for system use and are never backed up.

In addition to a checkpoint file, the **System path** shown in Figure 10-2 also contains a tmp.edb database file that is used to speed the access of information during mailbox and public folder store mounting. Because this database does not store email or public folder data, it is never backed up.

The mailbox and public folder databases that are contained within your storage groups are named when they are created and given an **.edb** extension. For example, the MailboxDatabase1.edb file represents the mailbox database called MailboxDatabase1 and the PublicFolderDatabase3.edb file represents the public folder database called

REF

The creation and management of storage groups and databases was discussed in Lesson 4, "Configuring a New Exchange Server."

PublicFolderDatabase3. When you create a new mailbox or public folder database, or move an existing one, you must specify the appropriate path for the database file. The path that you specify for database files need not be on the same volume as the storage group to which it belongs.

The current location of the mailbox and public folder databases on your server are listed under the **Database Management** tab for your server within the **Server Configuration** > **Mailbox** node of the Exchange Management Console.

The ESE structure for the first storage group that contains a mailbox and public folder database is illustrated in Figure 10-3.

Figure 10-3

ESE Structure

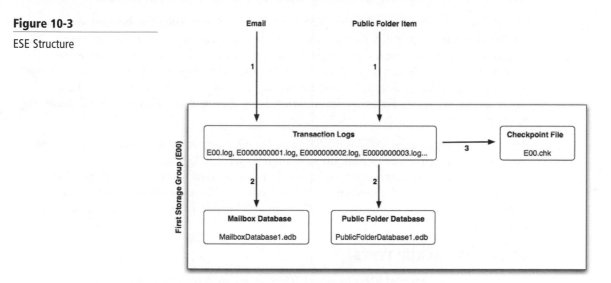

Understanding Database Backups

Planning for database backup is crucial to protecting the data that is most important to your organization. This planning involves selecting the appropriate backup media, program, and types used to create a backup set.

Before you back up Exchange databases, you must first choose a media type for the backup, the backup program that you will use, as well as the types of backups that need to be performed to ensure that backups are readily available when you need to recover data.

SELECTING MEDIA

In the past, magnetic tape media was commonly used to back up data because tapes could store large amounts of information for a low cost. However, it takes a great deal of time to back up data to a tape or recover data from a tape. As a result, most organizations that used tape media for backups performed full backups of data only on weekends because a daily backup after working hours would not be finished before the working hours began on the following day. In addition, copies of backups should be stored off-site in the event of a fire. For tape media, the process of duplicating tapes was time consuming. Furthermore, the data on tapes could easily be erased if the tapes were not stored in a cool, dry environment that was free of electromagnetic interference.

Because hard disk space is relatively inexpensive today and has a very fast transfer speed, most organizations use hard disk media to perform data backups. Moreover, backups are often performed to hard disk media that resides on a *Network Attached Storage (NAS)* device. NAS devices typically have several hard disks configured using fault-tolerant RAID and can be used to store backups from several computers on the network using standard Windows file sharing,

FTP, SSH, or HTTP. In addition, you can quickly restore a backup from a hard disk or NAS device from any computer on the network.

Hard disk media are much more tolerant of different operating environments (temperature, humidity, electromagnetic interference) and can be quickly copied to make off-site backups. Many organizations copy hard disk backups to optical media or upload hard disk backups to Internet-based backup providers for off-site storage.

SELECTING A BACKUP PROGRAM

Windows Backup ships with Windows Server 2003 and can be used to back up Exchange Server databases. We will focus on using Windows Backup throughout this lesson.

The **Volume Shadow Copy Service (VSS)** in Windows Server 2003 can be used alongside the Windows Backup utility to make point-in-time backups from files that are open, locked, or in use. However, the Windows Backup utility is not able to use VSS when backing up Exchange Server 2007 databases. Instead Windows Backup performs Exchange Server 2007 database backups by reading the contents of the database in much the same way that the Microsoft Exchange Information Store service does. This is called a **streaming backup**.

Because Exchange Server 2007 is a VSS-aware application, you can choose to use a third-party VSS-aware program to back up Exchange Server 2007 databases using VSS. Many commercial backup programs are expensive, but can be used for several different types of servers and data across the network. Before selecting a VSS-aware third-party backup program, you should first ensure that the program will be able to back up Exchange Server 2007 databases.

SELECTING BACKUP TYPES

The backup type that you select in your backup program determines which components of your databases will be backed up. Windows Backup supports the following four backup types when backing up Exchange databases:

- Full (Normal)
- Copy
- Incremental
- Differential

A **full backup** (also called a **normal backup**) backs up the databases that you select as well as the related transaction log files in the storage group. Because a copy of the transaction log files is stored in the backup media following a full backup, the original transaction log files are deleted to reduce disk space usage on your Exchange server. When you restore a full backup, you can choose to restore the database only or to restore the database and transaction logs. If you choose to restore the database and transaction logs, Windows Backup can replay the transaction logs to ensure that any uncommitted email or public folder items that were stored in the transaction logs at the time the backup was created are written to the database following the restore operation.

If you are using hard disk media for backup, you can likely perform full backups after working hours each day to provide a high level of protection for your Exchange databases. Alternatively, if you are using tape media, full backups are normally performed on weekends only.

A **copy backup** backs up the databases you select as well as the related log files, but does not remove the original transaction log files.

Due to their advanced structure, databases are much more likely to become corrupted than transaction logs. Consequently, databases are also more likely to cause errors on the file system on which they reside. As a result, many Exchange administrators choose to store mailbox and public folder databases on a different volume from their storage group to separate the database files from the transaction log and checkpoint files. In this case, if databases or database file systems become corrupted, you can configure Windows Backup to restore only the database files from a copy backup to save time. Following this, you can remove the checkpoint file to force the ESE to replay the recent email and public folder items stored in the uncorrupted log files to the restored database. This process is called a *hard recovery* because the original log files are replayed to a restored copy of the database. More important, this process saves time during a restore operation and also ensures that the most recent emails are not lost.

Incremental and differential backups only back up transaction log files, not Exchange databases. As a result, these backups take much less time than a full backup and are often performed daily when tape media is used as the backup medium. An *incremental backup* backs up the transaction logs that were created since the last full or incremental backup and then deletes those original transaction logs to save disk space. During a restore operation, you must select all incremental backups that you have created. Windows Backup then replays the restored transaction logs to ensure that the email and public folder items are committed to the appropriate databases.

A *differential backup* backs up only the transaction logs that were created since the last full backup and does not remove any transaction logs. As a result, successive differential backups will take longer to perform as time progresses. However, during a restore operation, you only need to select the last differential backup that you created because it includes the same information stored in previous differential backups. After restoring a differential backup, Windows Backup replays the restored transaction logs to ensure that the email and public folder items are committed to the appropriate databases.

Ultimately, the type of backup that you choose depends on the media on which you will store the backup as well as the recovery needs of your organization. For example, organizations that use hard disk media and require fast restore times in the event of data loss will likely perform a full backup of each database at the end of each day. In addition, these organizations may perform multiple copy backups during the day if email recovery is vital and the transaction logs are stored on a separate volume. Alternatively, organizations that use tape media and require fast backup times are more likely to perform incremental backups at the end of each weekday and a full backup on the weekend. Organizations that use tape media and require fast restore times will likely use differential backups each weekday and perform a full backup on the weekend. If multiple backup types are used together to backup data (e.g., weekday incremental backups and weekend full backups), the entire set of backups that must be used to restore data is referred to as a *backup set*.

Backing Up Exchange Databases

> You can use the Windows Backup program to perform regular backups of the Exchange databases within your organization. Moreover, you can monitor the progress of backups and search for backup errors following the backup procedure.

Windows Backup provides an easy graphical interface that allows you to quickly locate and back up an entire storage group or individual mailbox and public folder databases. In addition, Windows Backup allows you to schedule a backup to run at a later time or repetitively. For example, if you plan to perform daily incremental backups on Monday through Saturday and a full backup on Sunday, you could easily schedule two *backup jobs* within Windows Backup. The first backup job would perform incremental backups at a specific time on Monday through Saturday, and the second backup job would perform a full backup at a specific time on Sunday.

TAKE NOTE*

Full and incremental backups are the only two backups that delete original transaction log files after completion. If you never perform a full or incremental backup of your Exchange databases, the log files will use as much space as your databases on the volumes used by your Exchange servers.

TAKE NOTE*

If your storage groups use circular logging, you cannot back up Exchange transaction logs. As a result, incremental and differential backups are not permitted and you can only restore databases to the point in time that a full or copy backup was taken.

CERTIFICATION READY?
Configure backups.
5.1

TAKE NOTE ✱ You can also supply options to the Windows Backup command line utility (ntbackup.exe) to perform nongraphical backups. However, you cannot back up Exchange databases using this method.

Each mailbox or public folder database that will be backed up by Windows Backup must be mounted prior to running the Windows Backup program or the backup will fail. To dismount and back up Exchange databases, you must be a member of the Exchange Server Administrator role as well as a member of the local Administrators group on the Mailbox role server.

➕ **MORE** **INFORMATION**

You can also back up Exchange databases by dismounting the appropriate databases and manually copying the database and log files to another location (e.g., hard disk or tape device). This type of backup is called an ***offline backup*** and can be restored by copying the files back to their original location. Microsoft does not recommend offline backups because they often result in errors due to mismatched information between the restored files and Exchange Server 2007 information regarding them.

➡ **BACK UP EXCHANGE DATABASES**

GET READY. Turn on the computer that hosts the Mailbox role, and log in as the Administrator user account. Close any windows that appear on the desktop.

1. Click **Start**, **All Programs**, **Accessories**, **System Tools**, and then click **Backup**. If the Backup or Restore Wizard window appears, deselect **Always start in wizard mode** as shown in Figure 10-4 and click the Advanced Mode link. The Backup Utility window appears as shown in Figure 10-5.

◆ **ANOTHER WAY** You can also start the Windows Backup utility by typing **ntbackup.exe** within the Run dialog box on the Start menu.

Figure 10-4

Starting Windows Backup

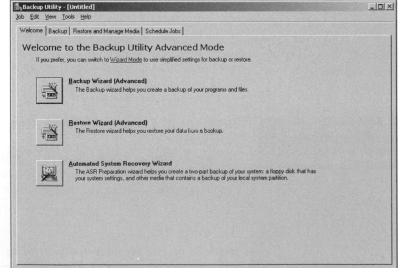

Figure 10-5

Windows Backup

2. Highlight the **Backup** tab. In the left pane, expand **Microsoft Exchange Server**, then the appropriate server, and **Microsoft Information Store**. Next, select the appropriate storage groups or databases that you wish to back up by placing a

checkmark in the appropriate check boxes. If you select a storage group, all databases within the storage group will be backed up. For example, Figure 10-6 shows
a backup that will include the Marketing Mailbox Database and Sales Mailbox
Database within the Third Storage Group on the server EXCH1.

Figure 10-6

Selecting Storage Groups and
Databases

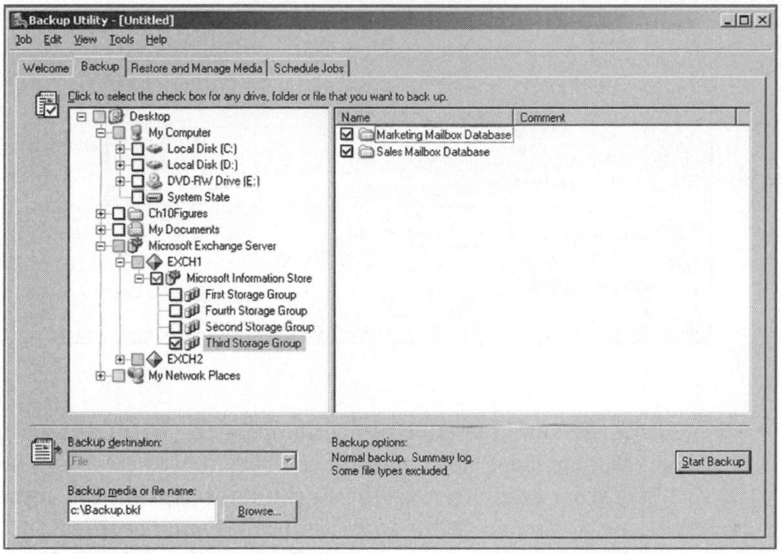

 You can select multiple mailbox databases from different storage groups on different servers
in a single backup job.

3. If you are backing up to a tape device, select the appropriate tape device in the
Backup destination drop-down box. Alternatively, if you are backing up to a file on
a hard drive or NAS device, select **File** in the **Backup destination** drop-down box
and type an appropriate path and filename that will store the backup in the **Backup
media or file name** dialog box. This file should have the .bkf extension. As Figure
10-6 illustrates, the backup will be stored in the file c:\Backup.bkf.

 If you are backing up data to a NAS device, the **Backup media or file name** dialog box
should contain the appropriate path to the NAS device and file. For example, to back up
data to the Exchange share on the NAS server called NAS1 using Windows file sharing,
you could enter **\\NAS1\Exchange\Backup.bkf**.

➕ **MORE INFORMATION**

You can also save your backup selections within the Windows Backup utility by clicking **Save Selections** from
the **Job** menu. This often saves time when performing similar backups in the future.

4. Click **Start Backup**. The Backup Job Information window appears as shown in
Figure 10-7.

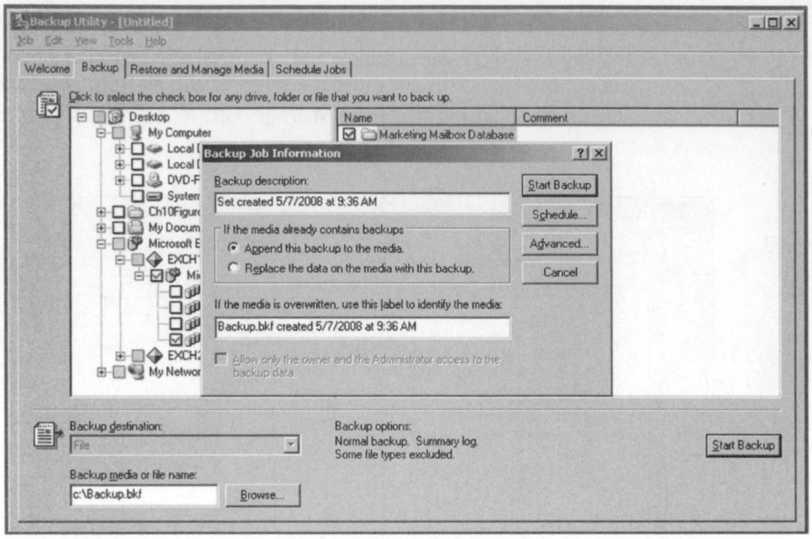

Figure 10-7

Configuring the Backup Job

5. By default, the Windows Backup utility creates a description of your backup job that includes the time that the backup was created, however, you can supply a custom description in the **Backup description** dialog box. In addition, backups are appended to the tape or file that you specified on the Backup tab earlier. Alternatively, you can select **Replace the data on the media with this backup** to overwrite the tape or file using the description shown in the dialog box at the bottom of Figure 10-7.

6. By default, Windows Backup performs a full (Normal) backup and does not verify the contents of the backup afterwards. However, you can click **Advanced** as shown in Figure 10-7 and select a different backup type or **Verify data after backup** as shown in Figure 10-8 and click **OK**.

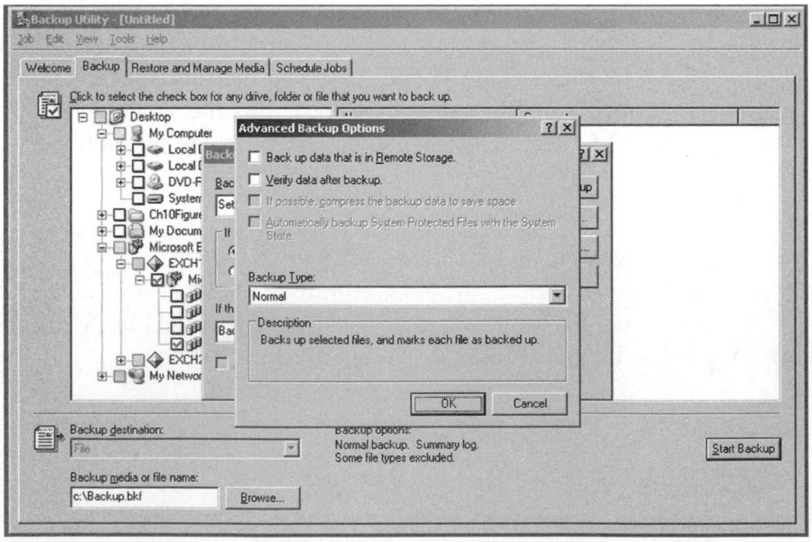

Figure 10-8

Configuring Advanced Backup Options

7. To schedule the backup job for a future time (e.g., after working hours), you can click **Schedule** as shown in Figure 10-7, save your backup settings and select a single time or repetitive schedule for the backup to run, and click **OK**.

> **+ MORE INFORMATION**
>
> If you chose to schedule your backup, you can use the **Scheduled Jobs** tab within the Backup Utility to view and manage your scheduled backup jobs.

8. Click **Start Backup.** When the backup completes, you can optionally click **Report** to view the backup log file. Next, click **Close** to close the Backup Progress window.

9. Close the Windows Backup utility.

You can also monitor the progress of a backup by viewing the appropriate event properties within the Application log of the Windows Event Viewer (**Start** > **Administrative Tools** > **Event Viewer**). Events with a Source of NTBackup and Event ID of 8000 indicate that a backup has started. Event IDs 8018 and 8019 indicate that errors occurred and Event ID 8001 indicates that the backup has completed as shown in Figure 10-9.

Figure 10-9

Viewing Backup Events

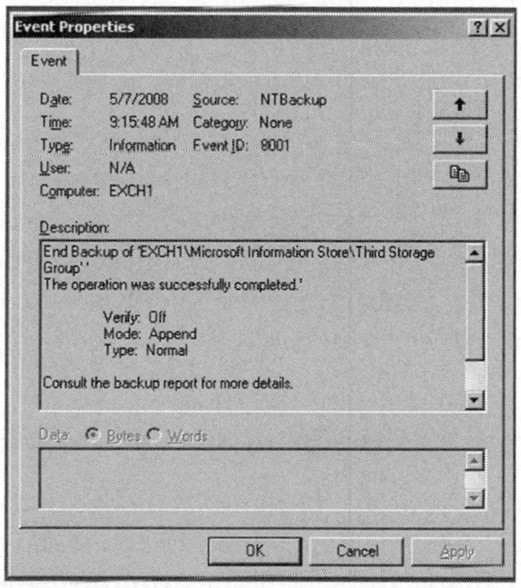

Alternatively, you can the following command within the Exchange Management Shell to view events that have an Event ID of 8001 from the Application event log:

Get-EventLog Application | where { $_.EventID –eq 8001 } | Format-List

If there are errors during a backup operation, you can view the backup log file to determine the cause of the error. By default, there is a new backup log file created during each Windows Backup session in the profile of the user who started the backup. For example, if Administrator ran the Windows Backup program, the backup log files will be stored in **C:\Documents and Settings\Administrator\Local Settings\Application Data\Microsoft\ Windows NT\NTBackup\data** and will be named **backup*XX*.log** where *XX* is a number that is incremented each time Windows Backup is run. An example backup log is shown in Figure 10-10.

Figure 10-10

Viewing the Backup Log

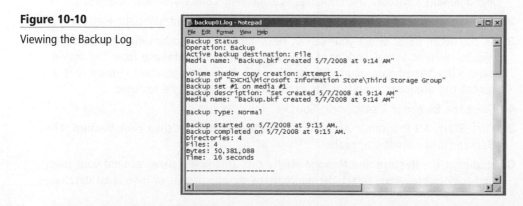

CERTIFICATION READY?
Configure backups.
5.2

Restoring Exchange Databases

Exchange databases can be restored using the Windows Backup program. However, the procedures that you use when restoring a database largely depend on the nature and type of backup as well as the goals of the restore procedure itself. Following a successful restore, you must re-create any full-text indexes used by the database.

Because databases have a complex structure and are used to continually store and access information, database corruption is not uncommon over time. When it happens, restoring a backup copy of the database is often the best solution.

Windows Backup can be used to restore a backup of mailbox or public folder databases that was created earlier using the same program. When restoring a database backup that includes the associated log files using Windows Backup, you can select the *Last Restore Set option* to ensure that Windows Backup replays the log files after the restore operation. If you are restoring multiple incremental backups following the restoration of a full backup, you only need to select the Last Restore Set option for the last incremental backup to replay all the log files in all incremental backups.

Before performing a restore operation, you must dismount each mailbox or public folder database that will be restored by Windows Backup. This can be done within the Exchange Management Console or by using the **Dismount-Database** cmdlet within the Exchange Management Shell. For example, to dismount the Sales Mailbox Database in the Third Storage Group on the server EXCH1, you could run the following cmdlet within the Exchange Management Shell:

Dismount-Database -Identity 'EXCH1\Third Storage Group\Sales Mailbox Database'

Following the restore operation, you can configure Windows Backup to automatically mount the restored database. Otherwise, you could remount the database manually within the Exchange Management Console or by using the **Mount-Database** cmdlet within the Exchange Management Shell. For example, to mount the Sales Mailbox Database in the Third Storage Group on the server EXCH1, you could run the following cmdlet within the Exchange Management Shell:

Mount-Database -Identity 'EXCH1\Third Storage Group\Sales Mailbox Database'

To restore Exchange databases, you must be a member of the Exchange Server Administrator role as well as a member of the local Administrators group on the Mailbox role server.

RESTORE EXCHANGE DATABASES

GET READY. Turn on the computer that hosts the Mailbox role, and log in as the Administrator user account. Close any windows that appear on the desktop.

1. Click **Start, All Programs, Microsoft Exchange Server 2007**, and then click **Exchange Management Console**. The Exchange Management Console window appears.
2. In the console tree pane, expand **Server Configuration** and highlight **Mailbox**.
3. In the detail pane, select your server. Next, highlight the appropriate database that will be restored in the work pane and select **Dismount Database** from the action pane. Click **Yes** when prompted to confirm the dismount operation. Ensure that you repeat the dismount operation for each database that will be restored.
4. Close the Exchange Management Console.
5. Click **Start, All Programs, Accessories, System Tools**, and then click **Backup**. The Backup Utility window appears.
6. Highlight the **Restore and Manage Media** tab. In the left pane, expand your media, and backup file. Next, select the appropriate storage groups or individual databases

and log files to restore. As shown in Figure 10-11, the Marketing Mailbox Database and Sales Mailbox Database from the Third Storage Group on the server EXCH1 will be restored along with the related log files to their original location.

Figure 10-11

Selecting a Backup to Restore

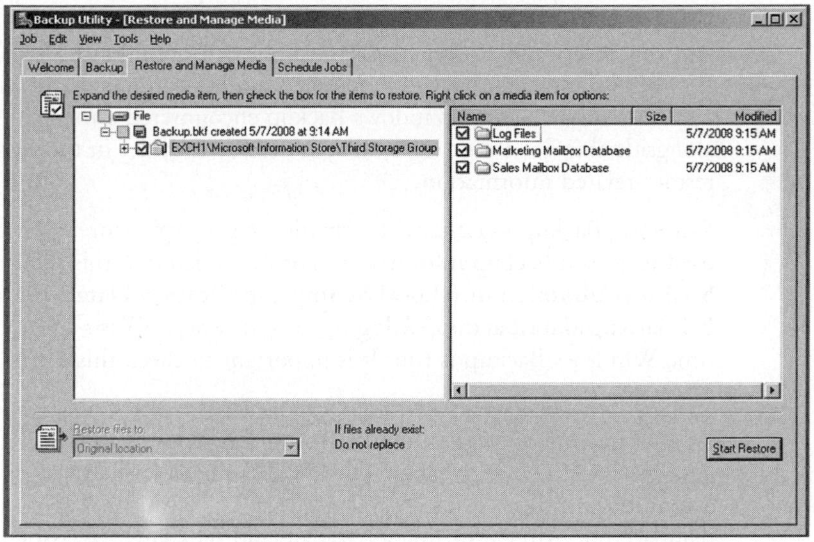

7. Click **Start Restore**. Ensure that your server is listed in the **Restore To** dialog box and enter a directory path (e.g., C:\Temp) that will be used as working space during the restore in the **Temporary location for log and patch files** dialog box as shown in Figure 10-12. If you are restoring log files, you should also select **Last Restore Set** to ensure that the log files are replayed following the restore operation. To mount the database following the restore operation, you can also select **Mount Database After Restore**.

⊕ MORE INFORMATION

One method that may be used to test a restore operation is to use a different server name in the **Restore To** dialog box shown in Figure 10-12. However, this requires an available Exchange server that has the same storage group and database structure created.

Figure 10-12

Specifying Restore Information

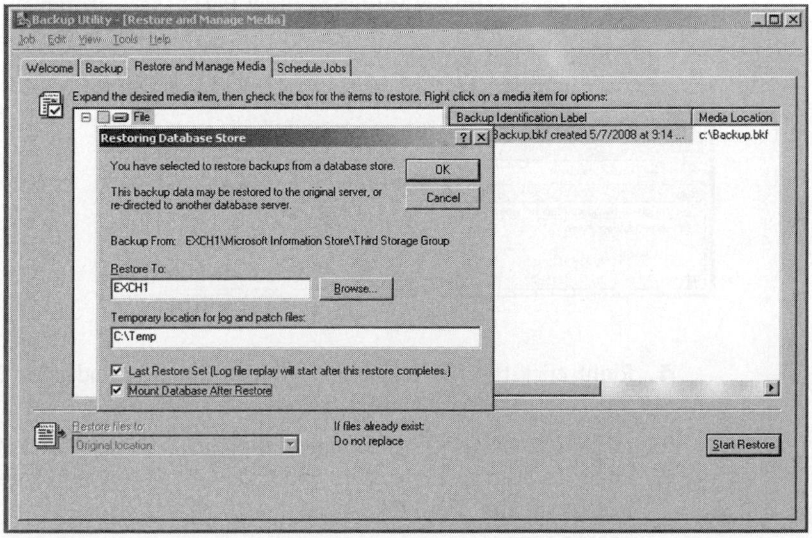

8. Click **OK**. When the restore operation has completed, you can optionally click **Report** to view the restore summary. Next, click **Close** to close the Restore Progress window.

9. Close the Windows Backup utility.

As with backups, you can also monitor the progress of a restore by viewing events with a Source of NTBackup within the Application log of the Windows Event Viewer. Events with an Event ID of 8002 indicate that a restore operation has started, and events with an Event ID of 8003 indicate that a restore operation has completed. As with backups, Event IDs 8018 and 8019 indicate that Windows Backup encountered errors. These Event IDs can be used alongside the Get-EventLog cmdlet as described earlier in this lesson to search for specific restore-related information.

Windows Backup writes any information regarding restore operations to the same log file used to record backup information. For Administrator, this file is **C:\Documents and Settings\Administrator\Local Settings\Application Data\Microsoft\Windows NT\ NTBackup\data\backup*XX*.log** by default, where *XX* is a number that is incremented each time Windows Backup is run. It is important to check this file if an error occurs to determine its cause.

During normal operation, the Microsoft Exchange Search Service automatically creates *full-text indexes* to speed searching for email and public folder items. These full-text indexes are stored in full-text index catalog directories within the same directory that holds the database file. After restoring a database and replaying the associated log files, these full-text index catalogs will not be synchronized to the content in the database and should be rebuilt.

➔ RE-CREATE A SEARCH INDEX

GET READY. Turn on the computer that hosts the Mailbox role, and log in as the Administrator user account. Close any windows that appear on the desktop.

1. Click **Start**, **All Programs**, **Accessories**, and then click **Command Prompt**. The Windows command prompt appears.

2. At the Windows command prompt, type **net stop MSExchangeSearch** and press **Enter** to stop the Microsoft Exchange Search service. Minimize the Windows command prompt.

3. Click **Start**, **My Computer**. Navigate to the directory that contains the restored database and locate the full-text index catalog directory. The full-text index catalog directory is named for the GUID of the database. Figure 10-13 shows the full-text index catalog directory for Mailbox Database 4 stored in C:\SG4\database.

Figure 10-13

Viewing an Existing Full-Text Index Catalog Folder

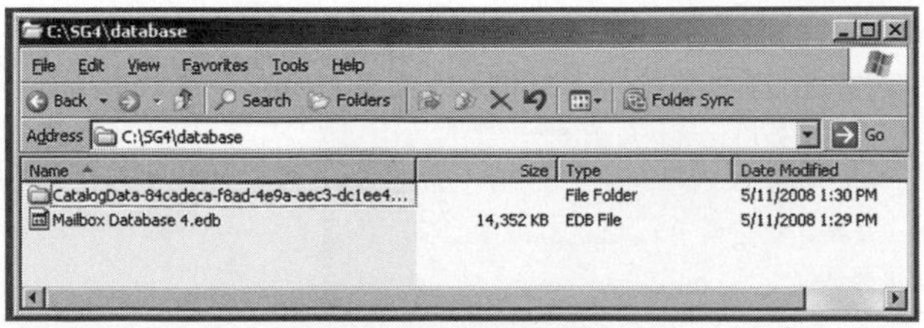

4. Right click the full-text index catalog directory and click **Delete**. Click **Yes** to confirm the deletion. Close the My Computer window.

5. Maximize the Windows command prompt, type **net start MSExchangeSearch** and press **Enter** to start the Microsoft Exchange Search service. A new full-text index catalog will be created the next time a search request is made using the Microsoft Exchange Search service.

ANOTHER WAY

> You can also run the **ResetSearchIndex.ps1** script followed by the appropriate database name within the Exchange Management Shell to recreate the full-text index catalog. To rebuild all full-text index catalogs, you could type **ResetSearchIndex.ps1 –all** within the Exchange Management Shell.

6. Close the Windows command prompt.

Using the Recovery Storage Group

> Recovery Storage Groups can be used during a database restore procedure to obtain a working copy of a mailbox database from a backup. Restoring a backup to a Recovery Storage Group can be used to test the successful creation of a backup as well as restore information to a mounted database. As a result, Recovery Storage Groups have several useful applications in most organizations and add flexibility to any restore procedure.

TAKE NOTE *

You can only create a single RSG on each Mailbox role server. Furthermore, you can only restore mailbox databases to an RSG.

To add flexibility and advanced functionality to database restore operations, you can create a *Recovery Storage Group (RSG)* on each Exchange Server 2007 Mailbox role server. RSGs can only be used for mailbox database restore operations and cannot be accessed by email clients or participate in policies, replication, or clustering. When you create an RSG, you configure it to impersonate an existing storage group that contains mailbox databases. Next, when you restore a backup of the original storage group's mailbox databases using Windows Backup, the restore operation will restore the mailbox databases to the RSG instead of the original storage group. During the restore operation, the mailbox databases within the original storage group do not need to be dismounted and can still be available to email clients while the backup is being restored to the RSG. After the restore operation has completed, you will have the original mounted mailbox databases as well as the backup copy of the mailbox databases in the RSG.

If, for example, you have four storage groups (SG1, SG2, SG3, and SG4) and you back up the contents of SG3 (Marketing Mailbox Database, Sales Mailbox Database, and Transaction Logs) to a file called Backup.bkf as illustrated in Figure 10-14, you could then use Windows Backup to restore the Backup.bkf file and overwrite the contents of SG3. However, this will require that the databases in SG3 be dismounted and unavailable to clients during the restore operation.

Figure 10-14

Backing Up SG3

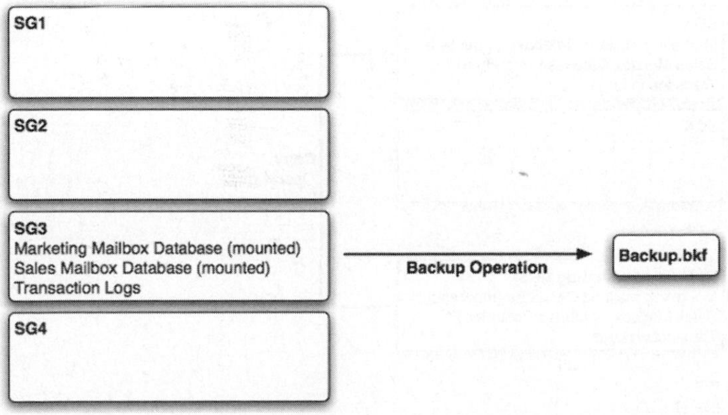

```
SG1


SG2


SG3
Marketing Mailbox Database (mounted)      Backup Operation  ───▶   Backup.bkf
Sales Mailbox Database (mounted)
Transaction Logs

SG4
```

If you instead create an RSG that impersonates SG3, restoring the Backup.bkf file using Windows Backup will automatically restore the mailbox databases and transaction logs to the RSG instead of to the original location (SG3) as illustrated in Figure 10-15.

Figure 10-15

Restoring SG3 to RSG

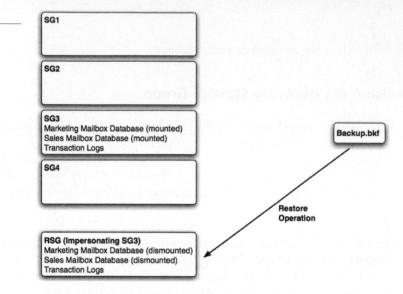

Following this restore, you can mount the mailbox databases in the RSG and copy the appropriate mailboxes or emails to the original storage group to restore data while the original mailbox database is mounted as shown in Figure 10-16. This minimizes the disruption to users who are currently accessing the original database. Alternatively, you could configure the properties of the original storage group to use the restored files within the RSG to allow quick recovery and minimize downtime. Copying data from the RSG to other storage groups and switching the location of a storage group to an RSG will be discussed later in this lesson.

Figure 10-16

Copying Data from an RSG

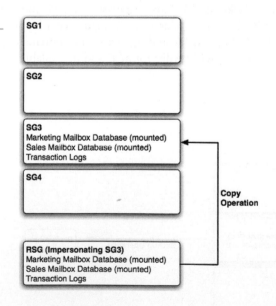

Many Exchange administrators mount the restored mailbox databases within the RSG to test the validity of the backup itself. If the backup restores successfully to the RSG and the mailbox databases can be mounted, then the backup was successfully created and can be used to restore a mailbox database at a later time. To test a backup using this method, you must first create an RSG and configure it to impersonate the original storage group. Next, you must restore the backup using Windows Backup as you normally would and then mount the mailbox databases within the RSG.

➔ RESTORE MAILBOX DATABASES TO AN RSG

GET READY. Turn on the computer that hosts the Mailbox role, and log in as the Administrator user account. Close any windows that appear on the desktop.

1. Click **Start, All Programs, Microsoft Exchange Server 2007**, and then click **Exchange Management Console**. The Exchange Management Console window appears.

2. In the console tree pane, highlight **Toolbox**. In the detail pane, double click **Database Recovery Management** under the Disaster recovery tools section.

3. When the Microsoft Exchange Troubleshooting Assistant window appears, enter a description for your actions in the dialog box at the top of the window and ensure that your Exchange server and domain controller are listed in the appropriate dialog boxes as shown in Figure 10-17. The Select one of the following tasks page appears as shown in Figure 10-18.

> **TAKE NOTE** *
>
> If you are logged on as a user that is not a member of the Exchange Server Administrator or Exchange Organization Administrator role, you must select **Show advanced logon options** as shown in Figure 10-17 and supply the credentials of a user that is a member of one of these roles.

Figure 10-17

Entering Server and User Information

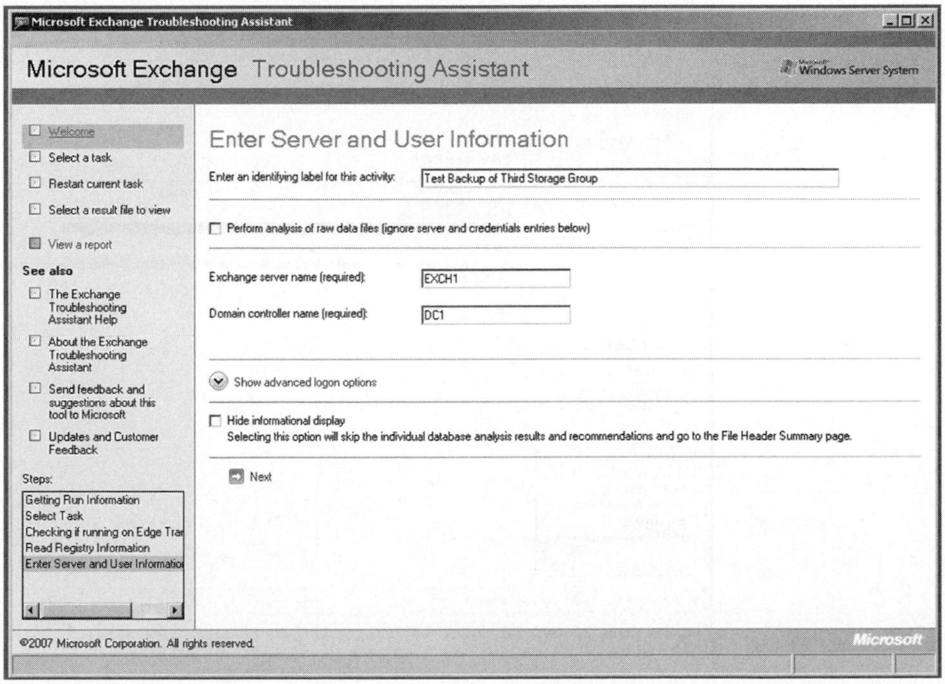

Figure 10-18

Selecting a Task

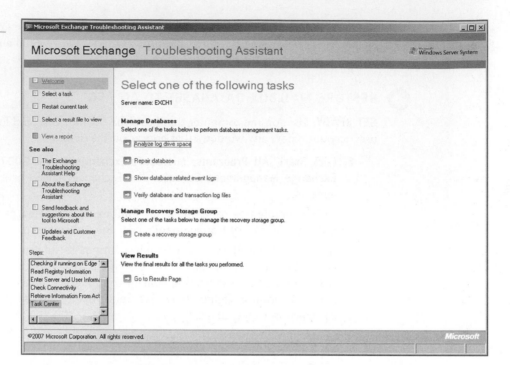

4. Click **Create a recovery storage group.** The Select the Storage Group to Link with the Recovery Storage Group page appears as shown in Figure 10-19.

Figure 10-19

Selecting a Storage Group to Impersonate

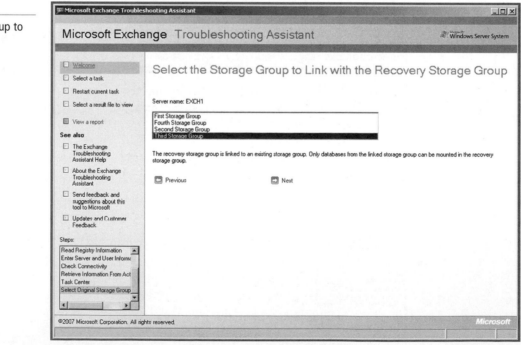

5. Highlight the storage group that the RSG will impersonate and click **Next.** In this example, as Figure 10-19 illustrates, the RSG will impersonate the Third Storage Group.

6. On the Create the Recovery Storage Group page as shown in Figure 10-20, supply a name for your RSG in the **Recovery storage group name** dialog box. By default, the database, checkpoint and log files used by the RSG will be stored within a subdirectory of the original database location with a directory name that indicates the date the RSG was created. As shown in Figure 10-20, the RSG will be located in the directory C:\SG3\ RSG20080511092310. If you wish to change the location, you can click the appropriate **Browse** buttons shown in Figure 10-20, select the appropriate directory, and click **OK**.

Figure 10-20

Specifying RSG Information

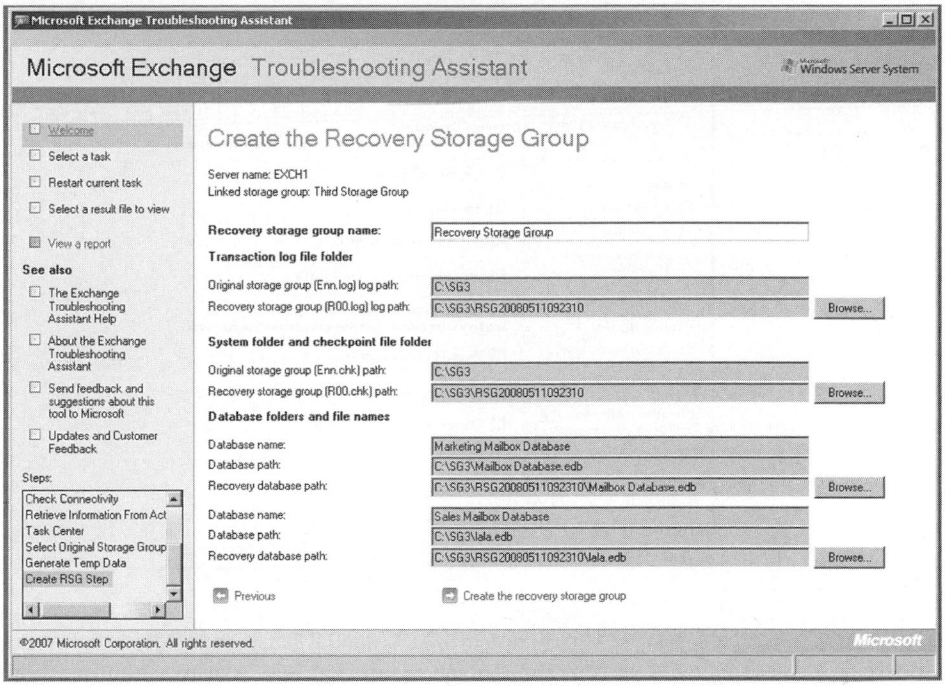

7. Click **Create the recovery storage group**. At the Create the Recovery Storage Group Result page, review the summary and click **Go back to task center**. Minimize the Microsoft Exchange Troubleshooting Assistant window.

8. Click **Start**, **All Programs**, **Accessories**, **System Tools**, and then click **Backup**. The Backup Utility window appears.

9. Highlight the **Restore and Manage Media** tab. In the left pane, expand your media, and backup file. Next, select the appropriate storage groups or individual mailbox databases and log files to restore as shown earlier in Figure 10-11. Although Windows Backup will appear to restore the backup to its original location, the backup will actually be restored to the RSG.

10. Click **Start Restore**. Ensure that your server is listed in the **Restore To** dialog box and enter a directory path (e.g., C:\Temp) that will be used as working space during the restore in the **Temporary location for log and patch files** dialog box as shown earlier in Figure 10-12. If you are restoring log files, you should also select **Last Restore Set** to ensure that the log files are replayed following the restore operation.

> **TAKE NOTE ***
>
> Do not select any public folder databases on the **Restore and Manage Media** tab. If you do, the restore operation to the RSG will fail.

> **TAKE NOTE ***
>
> Following the restore operation, Windows Backup will attempt to mount mailbox databases restored to the RSG if you select **Mount Database After Restore** as shown in Figure 10-12. However, it is a good practice to mount them manually to ensure that they are available.

11. Click **OK**. When the restore operation has completed, you can optionally click **Report** to view the restore summary. Next, click **Close** to close the Restore Progress window.

12. Close the Windows Backup utility. Maximize the Microsoft Exchange Troubleshooting Assistant window.

13. At the Select one of the following tasks page as shown in Figure 10-21, select **Mount or dismount databases in the recovery storage group.**

Figure 10-21

Selecting RSG Tasks

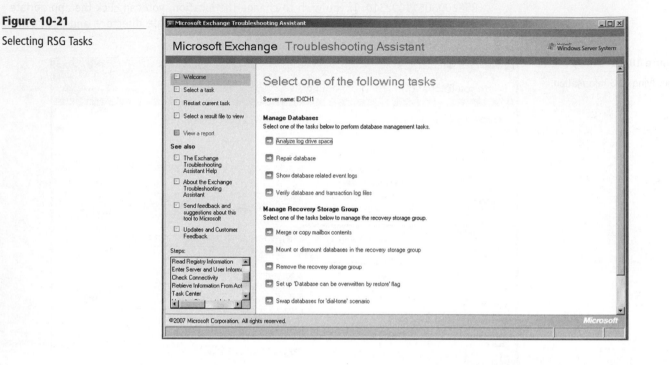

14. At the Mount or Dismount Database page select the appropriate mailbox databases within the storage group that you wish to mount as shown in Figure 10-22 and click **Mount selected database.** After the databases have been mounted, the Mount or Dismount Databases Report page appears.

Figure 10-22

Mounting Databases in the RSG

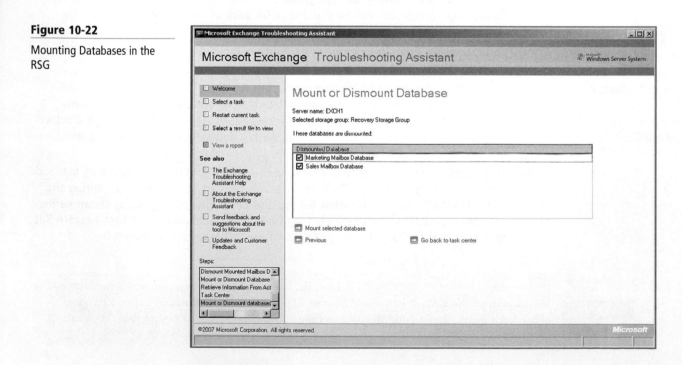

15. Close the Microsoft Exchange Troubleshooting Assistant window.

THE COMMAND
LINE WAY

You can also use cmdlets within the Exchange Management Shell to create and mount RSGs. For example, to create an RSG on the server EXCH1 that stores the transaction logs and checkpoint file within the D:\RSG directory, you could run the following command within the Exchange Management Shell:

New-StorageGroup -Name 'Recovery Storage Group' -Server EXCH1 –LogFolderPath 'D:\RSG' –SystemFolderPath 'D:\RSG' -Recovery

After restoring a backup to this RSG, you can use the following command within the Exchange Management Shell to mount it:

Mount-Database –Identity 'EXCH1\Recovery Storage Group'

CERTIFICATION READY?
Recover messaging data.
5.2

Performing Dial Tone Recovery

Dial tone recovery may be used to minimize email interruption to users during a restore operation that must be performed during working hours. To ensure that you can restore a database using dial tone recovery, you must first understand how dial tone recovery works using Recovery Storage Groups as well as the procedures used to complete the dial tone recovery process.

Because they are accessed more frequently, mailbox databases are much more likely to exhibit some form of corruption compared to public folder databases. Some mailbox database errors allow for most users to access their mailboxes, but produce database-level errors within the Application log of Event Viewer. Examples of this include events that indicate a page number mismatch (Event ID 475) or a bad page link (Event ID 447). Quite often, this type of database corruption only impacts a few users, but the entire mailbox database needs to be restored from a backup to remedy the error.

When you restore an entire mailbox database from a backup to its original location, the original mailbox database must first be dismounted and must remain dismounted until the restore operation is complete. For mailbox database corruption that only affects a few users, this means that all users will not have access to their email while the mailbox database is restored from backup. However, if you create an RSG, you can ensure that these users lose access to their email for only a few seconds by performing a *dial tone recovery*. In a dial tone recovery, the backup of the corrupted mailbox database is restored to the RSG while the corrupted mailbox database is still used by users. Next, the physical paths for the mailbox database configured in the original storage group and in the RSG are switched so that users are immediately redirected to the mailbox database in the RSG. For example, the Third Storage Group and related database files are stored in the C:\SG3 directory, and you restore a backup of the Third Storage Group to the RSG stored in C:\RSG as shown in the top half of Figure 10-23. After a dial tone recovery, the Third Storage Group will be configured to access its database files from the C:\RSG directory (that contains the restored files), and the RSG will be configured to access the corrupted database files in the C:\SG3 directory as shown in the bottom half of Figure 10-23. During the dial tone recovery, the mailbox databases will only be made unavailable to users for a few seconds while the database paths are switched.

TAKE NOTE *

You can also perform dial tone recovery to a different server, but you will need to reconfigure the email accounts on any email clients that do not support the Autodiscover service so that they can obtain email from the new location.

Figure 10-23

Dial Tone Recovery

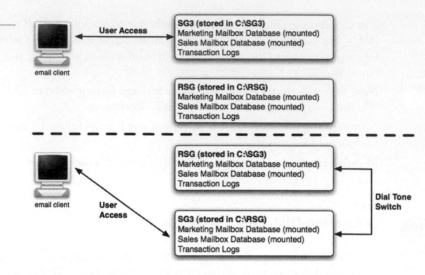

To perform a dial tone recovery for a corrupted mailbox database, you must first create an RSG and restore a backup of the corrupted mailbox database to the RSG using the same process described in the previous section. Next, you should copy the transaction logs from the original storage group directory to the RSG directory and then mount the mailbox database in the RSG as described in the previous section. When the mailbox database is mounted, any transaction logs in the RSG directory will be replayed to ensure that the latest emails will be available to the RSG (hard recovery).

Next, you can perform the dial tone recovery to switch the paths used by the original corrupted mailbox database and the restored mailbox database in the RSG.

⊕ **PERFORM A DIAL TONE RECOVERY**

GET READY. Turn on the computer that hosts the Mailbox role, and log in as the Administrator user account. Close any windows that appear on the desktop.

> To perform this exercise, you must first have an RSG that contains a restored copy of the appropriate mailbox database and that the restored copy of the mailbox database is mounted in the RSG.

1. Click **Start**, **All Programs**, **Microsoft Exchange Server 2007**, and then click **Exchange Management Console**. The Exchange Management Console window appears.

2. In the console tree pane, highlight **Toolbox**. In the detail pane, double click **Database Recovery Management** under the Disaster recovery tools section.

3. When the Microsoft Exchange Troubleshooting Assistant window appears, enter a description for your actions in the dialog box at the top of the window and ensure that your Exchange server and domain controller are listed in the appropriate dialog boxes as shown earlier in Figure 10-17.

4. At the Select one of the following tasks page shown earlier in Figure 10-21, select **Swap databases for 'dial-tone' scenario**. The Select a Mounted Database in the Recovery Storage Group page appears as shown in Figure 10-24.

Figure 10-24

Specifying a Mounted Database in the RSG for Dial Tone Recovery

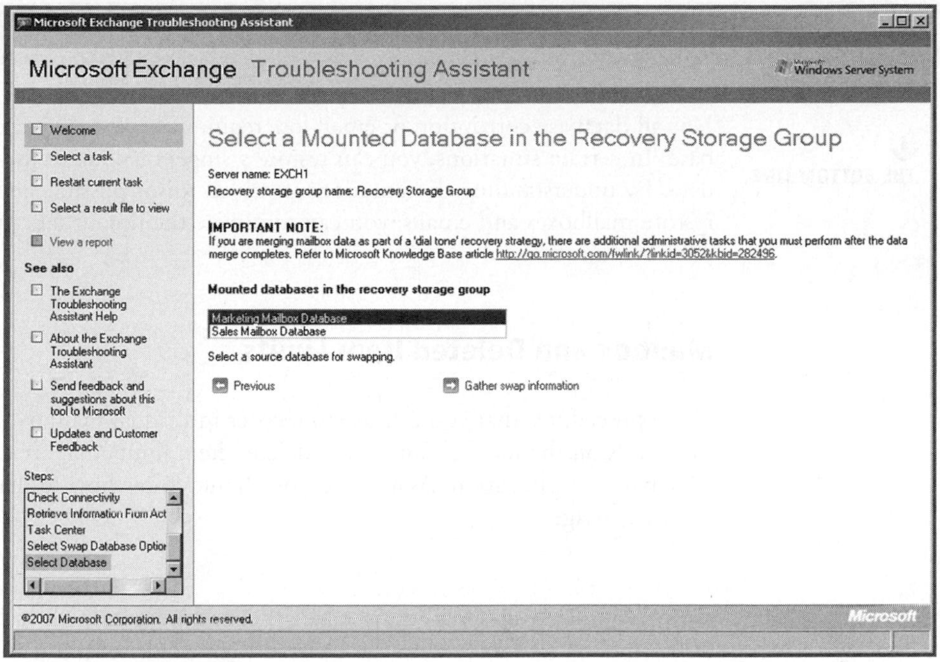

Microsoft Exchange Troubleshooting Assistant

Microsoft Exchange Troubleshooting Assistant

Windows Server System

- Welcome
- Select a task
- Restart current task
- Select a result file to view
- View a report

See also

- The Exchange Troubleshooting Assistant Help
- About the Exchange Troubleshooting Assistant
- Send feedback and suggestions about this tool to Microsoft
- Updates and Customer Feedback

Steps:

Check Connectivity
Retrieve Information From Act
Task Center
Select Swap Database Option
Select Database

Select a Mounted Database in the Recovery Storage Group

Server name: EXCH1
Recovery storage group name: Recovery Storage Group

IMPORTANT NOTE:
If you are merging mailbox data as part of a 'dial tone' recovery strategy, there are additional administrative tasks that you must perform after the data merge completes. Refer to Microsoft Knowledge Base article http://go.microsoft.com/fwlink/?linkid=3052&kbid=282496.

Mounted databases in the recovery storage group

Marketing Mailbox Database
Sales Mailbox Database

Select a source database for swapping.

Previous   Gather swap information

©2007 Microsoft Corporation. All rights reserved.   **Microsoft**

5. Highlight the appropriate database and click **Gather swap information.** The Select Database Swap Option page appears and indicates the file paths that will be changed. Review the information and click **Perform swap action.**

6. Close the Microsoft Exchange Troubleshooting Assistant window.

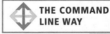

THE COMMAND LINE WAY

You can also use cmdlets within the Exchange Management Shell to perform a dial tone recovery. For example, to switch the file paths for Marketing Mailbox Database in the Third Storage Group on the server EXCH1 and the Marketing Mailbox Database restored to the Recovery Storage Group on the server EXCH1, you could use the following commands within the Exchange Management Shell:

Get-Mailbox –Database 'EXCH1\Third Storage Group\Marketing Mailbox Database' | Move-Mailbox -ConfigurationOnly –TargetDatabase 'EXCH1\Recovery Storage Group\ Marketing Mailbox Database'

Get-Mailbox –Database 'EXCH1\Recovery Storage Group\Marketing Mailbox Database' | Move-Mailbox -ConfigurationOnly –TargetDatabase 'EXCH1\ Third Storage Group\Marketing Mailbox Database'

X REF

Moving storage groups and mailbox databases was covered in Lesson 4, "Configuring a New Exchange Server."

Following a dial tone recovery, you can dismount all mailbox databases within the RSG and remove the RSG itself using the Database Recovery Management utility. Select the **Mount or dismount databases in the recovery storage group** option to dismount the appropriate mailbox databases in the RSG followed by the **Remove the recovery storage group** option to remove the RSG as shown earlier in Figure 10-21. Alternatively, you can use the Dismount-Database and Remove-StorageGroup cmdlets within the Exchange Management Shell to perform the same actions respectively.

If the new location of the mailbox database is not optimal, you can move the location of the storage groups and mailbox databases after working hours to a better location or to its original location.

■ Restoring Mailboxes and Emails

↓
THE BOTTOM LINE

Not all database corruption or email loss requires the restoration of an entire mailbox database. In certain situations, you can restore a single mailbox or individual emails to recover data. By understanding the situations in which this is possible and the procedures used to restore mailboxes and emails, you can minimize the time it takes to recover data within your organization.

Mailbox and Deleted Item Limits

The procedures that you can use to recover individual mailboxes and emails largely depends on the mailbox limits and deleted item limits that are configured within your Exchange organization. As a result, you should know how to determine these limits as well as their usage.

When you delete an email using a MAPI client program such as Outlook 2007 or Entourage 2008, that email is moved to the Deleted Items folder within your mailbox, where it can still be accessed or moved to other folders. In this respect, the Deleted Items folder is similar to the Windows Recycle Bin.

Periodically, MAPI client users should empty the items in their Deleted Items folder to conserve space on their Mailbox role server. When these users empty their Deleted Items folder, the items within are not immediately removed. Instead, they are moved to the ***message dumpster*** portion of their mailbox for a specific period of time and removed by the Exchange ***cleanup agent*** on a periodic basis.

Similarly, when you delete the mailbox for a mailbox user, the mailbox is moved to the message dumpster for a specific period of time before the cleanup agent removes it.

You can configure the amount of time that items will be retained in the message dumpster on the Limits tab of mailbox database properties as shown in Figure 10-25.

Figure 10-25

Mailbox Database Limits

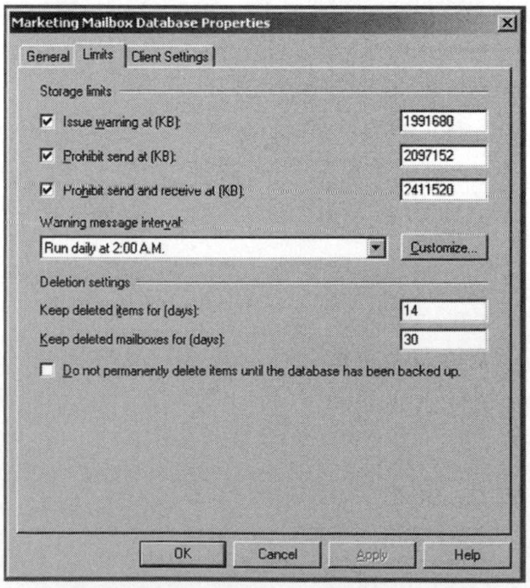

By default, deleted email items (removed from the Deleted Items folder) are retained for 14 days and deleted mailboxes are retained for 30 days before the cleanup agent removes them. If you select **Do not permanently delete items until the database has been backed up** (shown in Figure 10-25), deleted email items and mailboxes may exist for longer periods of time if you do not perform frequent backups.

You can override deleted email limits shown in Figure 10-25 on a user-by-user basis by specifying the appropriate settings in the Storage Quotas properties for the user. You can access these properties by navigating to the **Mailbox Settings** tab of mailbox user properties and double clicking **Storage Quotas**. The Storage Quotas shown in Figure 10-26 retain deleted items for 21 days or until the mailbox database is backed up.

Figure 10-26

User Limits

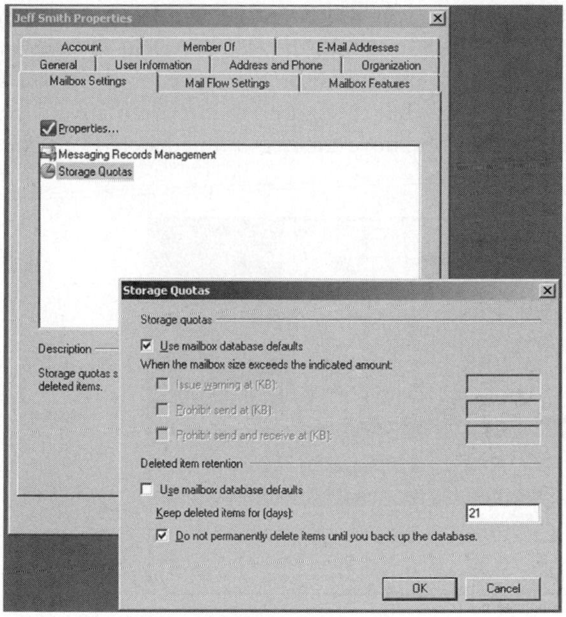

Figure 10-27

Viewing the Maintenance Schedule

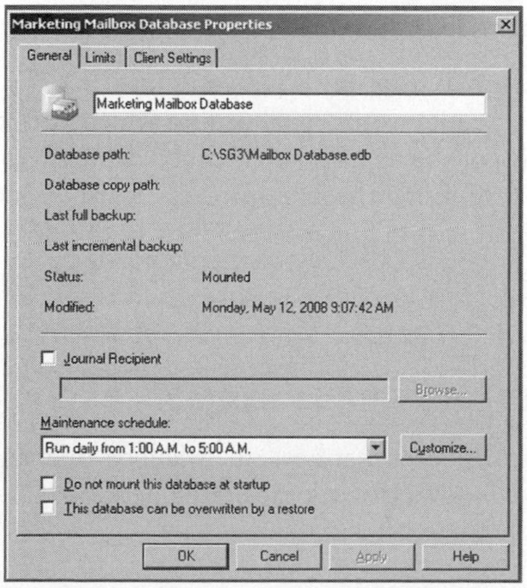

The procedures and cmdlets that may be used to configure mailbox limits for databases and users were discussed in Lesson 4, "Configuring a New Exchange Server," and in Lesson 5, "Working with Recipient Objects."

Additionally, you can also configure the schedule used to determine when the cleanup agent is run to remove deleted email items and mailboxes. By default, the cleanup agent runs from 1:00 a.m. to 5:00 a.m. each day, but you can click the **Customize** button on the General tab of mailbox database properties to modify the schedule as shown in Figure 10-27.

CERTIFICATION READY?
Recover messaging data.
5.2

Restoring Mailboxes and Deleted Items

Restoring disconnected mailboxes and deleted items within the mailbox and deleted item limit can easily be performed without restoring a backup. In other situations, you must restore a backup to the Recovery Storage Group and copy the appropriate mailboxes or emails to the necessary mailbox database.

X REF

Reconnecting mailboxes was covered in Lesson 5, "Working with Recipient Objects."

It is easier to recover a deleted mailbox or email item provided that you recover it within the mailbox and deleted item limits. If you remove the mailbox for a user, you can easily reconnect the deleted mailbox to another user account within the deleted mailbox limit (30 days by default).

Similarly, you can easily recover deleted email items provided that you do so within the deleted item limit (14 days by default). If you are using a newer MAPI client (Outlook 2003, Entourage 2004, or newer), highlight the **Deleted Items** folder in the left pane and click **Tools > Recover Deleted Items**. In the Recover Deleted Items window that appears, you can select the emails that you would like to recover and click on the **Recover Selected Items** icon (second icon from the left in Figure 10-28). Alternatively, you can click the black X icon shown in Figure 10-28 to remove the item immediately from your mailbox.

Figure 10-28

Recovering Deleted Items in Outlook 2007

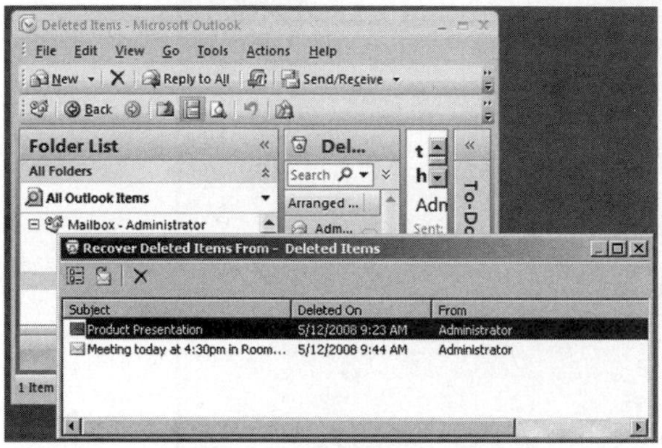

Deleted email items can also be recovered using Outlook Web Access (OWA). Click on the **Options** button in the upper right corner of the OWA window and select **Deleted Items** from the left pane.

Conversely, if you wish to restore mailboxes after the deleted mailbox limit, or restore specific emails after the deleted item limit, you will need to restore them from a backup. Luckily, you can easily restore the appropriate mailbox database to an RSG and copy the entire mailbox or individual email items from the RSG to the original database as shown earlier in Figure 10-16.

To restore mailboxes and email using an RSG, you must first create an RSG that impersonates the storage group that contains the mailboxes to which you wish to copy items. Next, you must restore a backup of the appropriate mailbox database to the RSG and mount the restored database in the RSG using the same process described earlier in this lesson. Following this, you can merge the contents of an entire mailbox in the RSG to the same mailbox in the original mailbox database, or you can copy selected items from the appropriate mailbox in the RSG to the original mailbox in the mailbox database.

RESTORE MAILBOXES AND EMAILS FROM AN RSG

GET READY. Turn on the computer that hosts the Mailbox role, and log in as the Administrator user account. Close any windows that appear on the desktop.

TAKE NOTE*

To perform this exercise, you must first have an RSG that contains a restored copy of the appropriate mailbox database, and the restored copy of the mailbox database must be mounted in the RSG.

1. Click **Start, All Programs, Microsoft Exchange Server 2007**, and then click **Exchange Management Console**. The Exchange Management Console window appears.

2. In the console tree pane, highlight **Toolbox**. In the detail pane, double click **Database Recovery Management** under the Disaster recovery tools section.

3. When the Microsoft Exchange Troubleshooting Assistant window appears, enter a description for your actions in the dialog box at the top of the window and ensure that your Exchange server and domain controller are listed in the appropriate dialog boxes as shown earlier in Figure 10-17.

4. At the Select one of the following tasks page shown earlier in Figure 10-21, select **Merge or copy mailbox contents**. The Select a Mounted Database in the Recovery Storage Group page appears as shown in Figure 10-29.

Figure 10-29

Selecting a Database in the RSG to Copy Data From

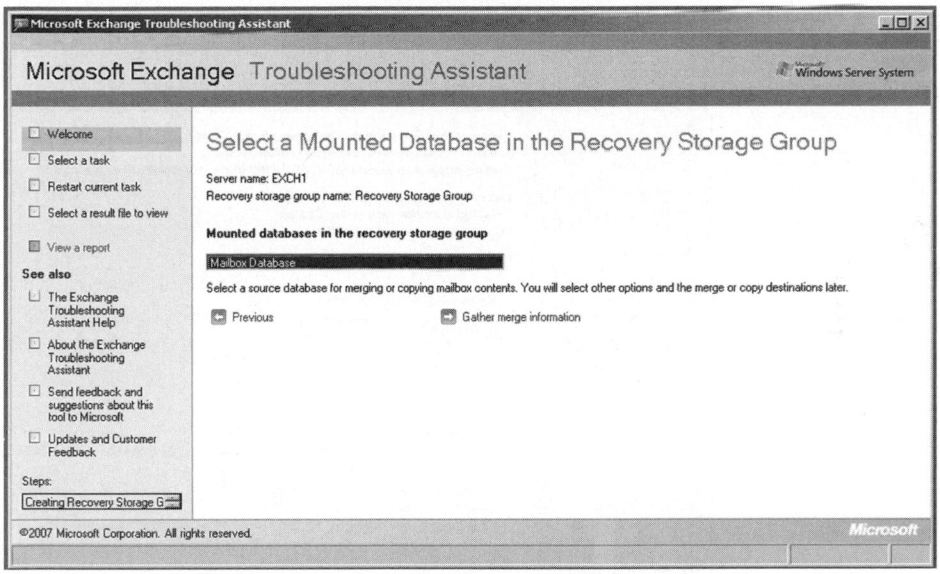

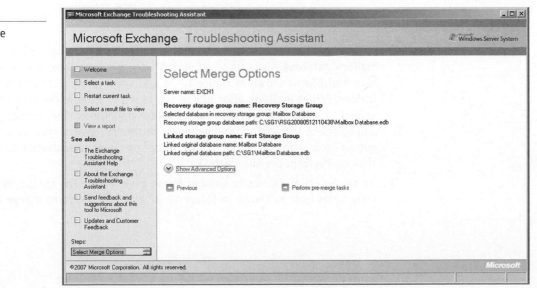

5. Highlight the appropriate database and click **Gather merge information**. The Select Merge Options page appears as shown in Figure 10-30 and displays information regarding the mailbox database in the RSG and original (linked) storage group.

Figure 10-30

Viewing RSG Database Information

6. If you plan on merging the entire contents of mailbox from the RSG with the mailbox in the original mailbox database, you can click **Perform pre-merge tasks** to advance to the next page. However, if you wish to copy only specific emails from the RSG to the original mailbox database or merge several mailboxes from the RSG into a single mailbox in the original mailbox database, you must click **Show Advanced Options** shown in Figure 10-30 and supply the appropriate information. For example, the advanced options shown in Figure 10-31 will copy only emails that were sent in January 2007 and have a subject line of TASU Update. If more than 5 corrupted messages are found, the copy operation will abort.

Figure 10-31

Specifying Advanced Options

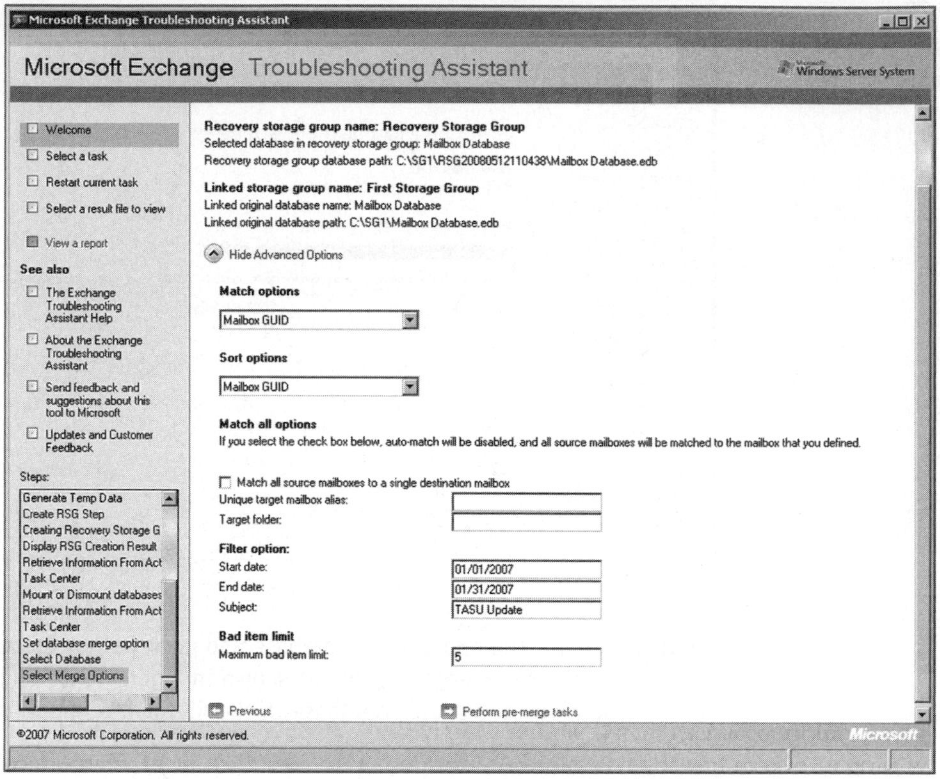

To copy email from several mailboxes in the RSG to a single mailbox in the target mailbox database, you can select **Match all source mailboxes to a single destination mailbox** as shown in Figure 10-31 and specify the name of the mailbox in the **Unique target mailbox alias** dialog box as well as the folder that the email will be copied to (e.g., Inbox) in the **Target folder** dialog box. The next page will prompt you to select the appropriate mailboxes in the RSG that should be copied to this target mailbox. After specifying advanced options, you can advance to the next page by clicking **Perform pre-merge tasks**.

7. On the Select Mailboxes to Copy or Merge page, select the mailboxes that you wish to copy items from as shown in Figure 10-32 and click **Perform merge actions**.

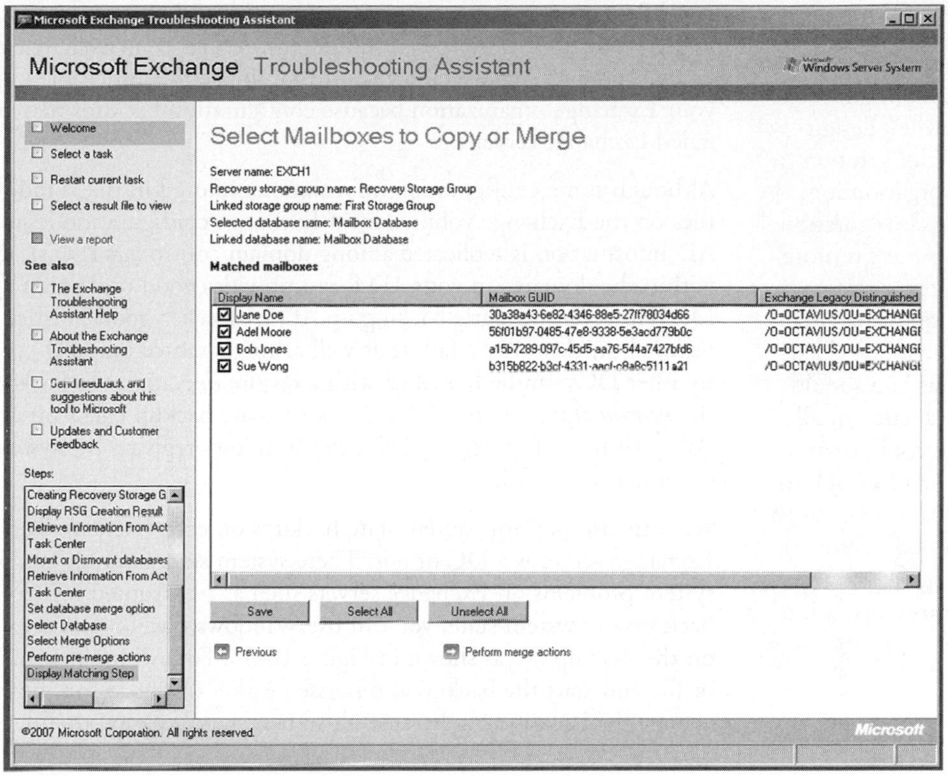

Figure 10-32

Specifying Mailboxes to Copy from the RSG

8. Close the Microsoft Exchange Troubleshooting Assistant window.

THE COMMAND LINE WAY

After you have mounted a recovered mailbox database within the RSG, you can use the **Restore-Mailbox** cmdlet within the Exchange Management Shell to copy mailboxes or emails from the RSG to the original mailbox database. For example, to restore any emails with the subject line "TASU Project Time Line" within Jeff Smith's mailbox in the RSG called "Recovery Storage Group 1" to Jeff Smith's current mailbox, you could use the following command within the Exchange Management Shell:

Restore-Mailbox -Identity 'Jeff Smith' -RSGDatabase 'Recovery Storage Group 1' -SubjectKeywords 'TASU Project Time Line'

For more information on the syntax and usage of the Restore-Mailbox cmdlet, search for Restore-Mailbox within Exchange Server 2007 Help.

■ Backing Up and Restoring Exchange Server Roles

↓
THE BOTTOM LINE

Although it is vital to protect the email and public folder data stored on the Mailbox role servers within your organization, you should also protect against the failure of a server role to ensure that your email infrastructure is available to the users who use it. To protect the server roles within your Exchange infrastructure, you must understand the files and settings that should be backed up as well as procedures and practices used to restore a failed server role.

CERTIFICATION READY?
Configure backups.
5.1

Backing Up Exchange Server Role Configuration

Although most Exchange configuration is stored within Active Directory (AD), different server roles also have valuable configuration data stored within the Windows registry and file system files. As a result, you should identify and back up those components to ensure that they can be restored in the event of a failure.

TAKE NOTE *

Do not rely solely on Exchange configuration backups when designing a backup solution for your organization. Restoring configuration information is far more prone to failure compared to restoring email and public folder data. As a result, you should carefully document all Exchange configuration changes in a logbook to ensure that an Exchange server can be re-created if an Exchange configuration restore operation fails.

In addition to protecting the email and public folder information on the Exchange servers within your organization, you should ensure that your Exchange configuration is protected using backups. This will allow you to minimize the noticeable impact of a failed server role in your Exchange organization because configuration backups may be used to quickly restore a failed Exchange server.

Although some configuration information is stored in the Windows registry and within data files on the Exchange volume, most Exchange configuration is stored within AD. Because AD information is replicated among domain controllers (DCs), deploying multiple DCs within the domains in your AD forest provides good protection against the failure of a single DC. However, regularly backing up AD is always a good practice to ensure that DCs can be restored quickly after a failure as well as to guarantee that AD corruption that is replicated to other DCs can be remedied with a restore operation. To back up AD, you can back up the *system state* on your DCs. A system state backup backs up the AD database and Group Policy (if the computer is a DC), the Windows registry, the system boot files, and several other key system files.

You can also perform system state backups on each Exchange server regardless of whether the Exchange server is a DC or not. These system state backups can be used to restore operating system problems on Exchange servers such as a corrupted registry or missing boot files. To back up the system state, you can use Windows Backup and select the System State option on the Backup tab as shown in Figure 10-33. Following this, you can select a backup media or file and start the backup as discussed earlier in this lesson, however you will not be able to change the backup type because all system state backups are full backups.

Figure 10-33

Selecting a System State Backup

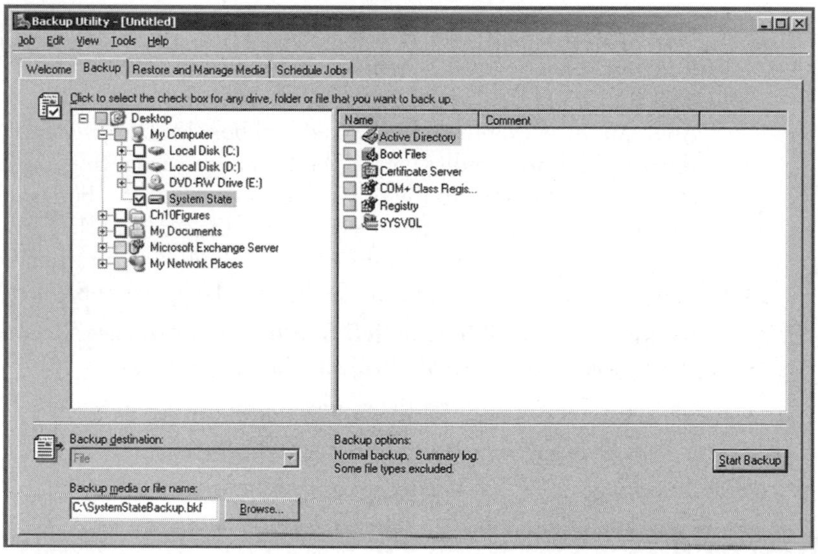

Because system state backups could take a long time to restore, you should also back up the Windows registry keys that store Exchange configuration information in case you need to quickly restore Exchange configuration information only. It is only necessary to back up these Exchange registry keys after making configuration changes to your Exchange server.

To back up the Exchange configuration within the Windows registry, you can open the Windows Registry Editor by typing **regedit.exe** (16-bit version) or **regedt32.exe** (32-bit version) at the **Run** dialog box on your Exchange server. Next, navigate to the following keys:

HKEY_LOCAL_MACHINE\SOFTWARE\Microsoft\Exchange

HKEY_LOCAL_MACHINE\SYSTEM\Current Control Set\Services

For each key, you can right click the key itself and choose **Export** as shown in Figure 10-34 and supply the name of the file that will store the configuration. This file will have a **.reg** extension and can be easily imported into the Windows registry later to restore the Exchange configuration.

Figure 10-34

Exporting Registry Keys

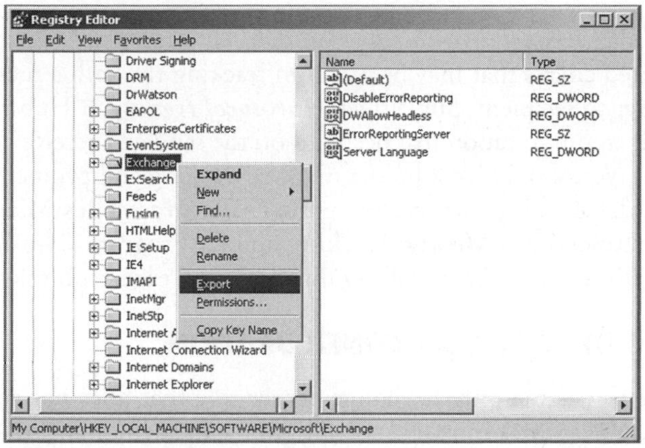

If your Exchange server has a certificate for use with SSL and TLS, you can also back up the public key certificate and associated private key in case they are corrupted or lost. If your public key certificate was signed by an enterprise CA within your organization, there is no need to back it up because you can easily obtain a new public key certificate from the enterprise CA at no cost. However, if your public key certificate was issued by a commercial CA for a fee, you should back it up so that you can restore it if necessary rather than pay for a new one.

TAKE NOTE *

Ensure that you store any exported certificates in a secure location to prevent them from being stolen and used to decode your protocol encryption. It is a good practice to move the exported certificates to removable media and store the removable media in a locked cabinet or desk.

The easiest way to export an SSL/TLS certificate is to use cmdlets within the Exchange Management Shell. Before you export a certificate, you must first obtain the thumbprint of the certificate. You can view the thumbprints of each certificate installed on your Exchange server by running the Get-ExchangeCertificate cmdlet within the Exchange Management Shell. Next, you can run the Export-ExchangeCertificate cmdlet to export the certificate to a file. Because this file will contain the public and private key, it must be protected with a password. For example, the following command will export the public key certificate and related private key that has the thumbprint d86cf4d4ba72552c6ba1493413bd5adc54a55c5f to the file C:\CertificateExport.pfx using a PKCS#12 format. You will be prompted to supply a username and password that will be used to protect the file.

Export-ExchangeCertificate -Thumbprint d86cf4d4ba72552c6ba1493413bd5adc54a55c5f –BinaryEncoded:$true -Path C:\CertificateExport.pfx –Password (Get-Credential) .password

In addition to backing up the system state and exporting Exchange registry keys and certificates, there are certain files and directories on the file system that should be backed up depending on the server roles that are installed on the Exchange server. These files and directories can easily be backed up within the Windows Backup program by navigating to their locations on the Backup tab.

BACKING UP MAILBOX ROLE CONFIGURATION

Mailbox role servers store most of their configuration within AD. However, the Offline Address Book (OAB) is stored on the mailbox role server itself. For MAPI clients older than Outlook 2007 or Entourage 2008, the OAB is stored within the default public folder database. Thus, to back up the OAB used by these clients, you can back up the default public folder database. However, Outlook 2007, Entourage 2008, and later MAPI clients obtain their OAB using the Autodiscover service. To back up the OABs used by these clients, you can back up the ExchangeOAB directory on your Mailbox role servers. By default, this directory is **C:\Program Files\Microsoft\Exchange Server\ExchangeOAB**.

BACKING UP HUB ROLE CONFIGURATION

Like Mailbox role servers, Hub role servers store most of their configuration within AD. Hub role servers also have a storage queue database that is used to store emails temporarily during the email relay process. Because these storage queue databases use circular logging, they cannot be restored from a backup and need not be backed up as a result.

However, the *message tracking logs* on each Hub role server include important information about routed emails that may be useful in tracking the path a message took when delivered from sender to recipient. Similarly, the *protocol logs* on all Hub role servers contain all of the SMTP communication that occurred on the send and receive connectors of those servers. As a result, you should back up the message tracking and protocol logs on each Hub role server. By default, these are located in the **C:\Program Files\Microsoft\Exchange Server\TransportRoles\Logs\MessageTracking** and **C:\Program Files\Microsoft\Exchange Server\TransportRoles\Logs\ProtocolLog** directories on each Hub role server.

BACKING UP EDGE ROLE CONFIGURATION

The Edge role is the only Exchange Server role that does not store its configuration within AD. Instead, it stores most of its configuration, such as antispam filter settings, on the local server and obtains some configuration from Hub role servers using the EdgeSync protocol.

To back up the local configuration settings on an Edge role server, you can save all Edge role settings in an XML-formatted file. This is often referred to as a *cloned configuration* because it can easily be used to restore Edge role server settings on the same Edge role server or on a new Edge role server within the organization that requires the same configuration.

To create a cloned configuration, you can run the ExportEdgeConfig.ps1 script within the Exchange Management Shell on your Edge role server. For example, to create a cloned configuration that is stored in the C:\EdgeBackup.xml file, you could run the following command within the Exchange Management Shell:

ExportEdgeConfig.ps1 –CloneConfigData 'C:\EdgeBackup.xml'

This cloned configuration file can then be copied to removable media or included with other file backups.

Like Hub role servers, Edge role servers maintain message tracking and protocol logs. Because these logs may contain important information, you should back them up on each Edge role server within your organization. By default, these are located in the **C:\Program Files\Microsoft\Exchange Server\TransportRoles\Logs\MessageTracking** and **C:\Program Files\Microsoft\Exchange Server\TransportRoles\Logs\ProtocolLog** directories on each Edge role server.

Edge role servers also log information regarding messages that were filtered by spam filtering agents within *agent logs*. These logs are located by default in the **C:\Program Files\Microsoft\Exchange Server\TransportRoles\Logs\AgentLog** directory on each Edge role server and should be backed up alongside the message tracking and protocol logs.

BACKING UP CAS ROLE CONFIGURATION

CAS role servers store their configuration in several locations. Most configurations are stored within AD, but some configuration is also stored within local configuration files as well as within IIS. Although you can back up the configuration of IIS within IIS Manager, restoring this configuration often causes problems because changes made to IIS are not synchronized with the related changes to AD. As a result, it is best to carefully document the configuration changes that you make within IIS Manager or to OWA on a CAS role server so that those settings can be re-created following a restore. This documentation should specifically include any virtual directories or additional Web sites that you created within IIS.

BACKING UP UM ROLE CONFIGURATION

Nearly all of the configuration information used by the UM role is stored within AD. However, your organization may use custom audio files (*.wav) that are used by the UM role when interfacing with the telephone system or when providing Outlook Voice Access. You can back up these custom audio files by backing up the Custom directory on your UM role server (**C:\Program Files\Microsoft\Exchange Server\UnifiedMessaging\Prompts\Custom** by default).

Restoring Exchange Server Roles

CERTIFICATION READY?
Recover server roles
5.3

> Provided that you have backed up the appropriate configuration for the server roles within your organization, you can restore a failed server role. The process used to restore the Hub, CAS, Mailbox, and UM server roles is fundamentally different than the process used to restore an Edge role server.

Like all computers, Exchange servers can encounter problems that prevent them from working. If the error is related to the Windows operating system, such as a corrupt boot file or registry key, restoring a system state backup using Windows Backup often remedies the problem. Similarly, if you suspect that the problem is related to incorrect Exchange information within the registry, you can double click on the exported registry keys (*.reg) that you created in the previous section to import them into the Windows registry.

However, in other situations, you may need to reinstall the operating system and reconfigure the Exchange server to restore it. This is common practice following a hard disk failure or after file system corruption. Because the CAS, Hub, Mailbox, and UM roles store most of their configuration within AD, the procedures that you use to restore these roles is different from those used to restore an Edge role server.

RESTORING A CAS, HUB, MAILBOX, OR UM ROLE SERVER

To restore a CAS, Hub, Mailbox, or UM role server using the information stored within AD, you must perform the following steps in this order:

TAKE NOTE *

Computer accounts have the same name as the computer name they represent. Thus, to reset the computer account for the server EXCH1, you should search for a computer account called EXCH1 within the Active Directory Users and Computers console.

1. Reset the computer account for the failed server within AD as described in Lesson 2, "Working with Active Directory."
2. Replace any failed hardware if necessary and reinstall the Windows operating system on the failed server role. During the installation, you must select the same computer name that was used previously.
3. Join the reinstalled server to the domain. When the server is joined to the domain, it will associate itself with the existing computer account that has the same computer name instead of creating a new computer account.
4. Install the necessary prerequisite software for the server role as described in Lesson 3, "Deploying Exchange Server 2007."
5. Run the **Setup.com /m:RecoverServer** command from the root of your Exchange Server 2007 installation media. This command will install Exchange Server 2007 on your computer using the server role configuration information stored within AD for the appropriate computer account.
6. Restore any additional role-based files or logs that you backed up for your server as discussed in the previous section. These files can be restored using Windows Backup.
7. Restore any certificates that you backed up for your server as discussed in the previous section. To restore an exported certificate, double click on the .pfx file that you created. The Certificate Import Wizard will launch to allow you to import the certificate and related private key.

X REF

If you are recovering a failed Mailbox role that participates in clustering, there are additional steps that may need to be performed. These steps are discussed in Lesson 13, "Providing for High Availability."

TAKE NOTE *

Computer accounts have the same name as the computer name they represent. Thus, to reset the computer account for the server EXCH1, you should search for a computer account called EXCH1 within the Active Directory Users and Computers console.

8. Review your printed documentation and make any remaining changes to the configuration of your server role that were not made during the recovery process.

RESTORING AN EDGE ROLE SERVER

Because Edge role servers are not joined to a domain, you can recover them by installing them as you normally would when adding an additional Edge role server, subscribe them to an existing Hub role server, and restore their configuration from backup. More specifically, you must perform the following steps in this order:

1. Replace any failed hardware if necessary and reinstall the Windows operating system on the failed Edge role server.

2. Replace any failed hardware if necessary and reinstall the Windows operating system on the failed server role.

3. Install the necessary prerequisite software for the server role as described in Lesson 3, "Deploying Exchange Server 2007."

4. Run the Exchange installation program and select the Edge role as described in Lesson 3, "Deploying Exchange Server 2007."

5. Enable the EdgeSync protocol by subscribing the Edge role server to a Hub role server using a subscription file as discussed in Lesson 4, "Configuring a New Exchange Server."

6. Restore the cloned configuration XML file that you created earlier using the ImportEdgeConfig.ps1 script. To do this, you must first validate the cloned configuration XML file and create an answer XML file that may optionally be used to customize the settings for your server (i.e., computer name). To validate the C:\EdgeBackup.xml cloned configuration XML file and create an answer XML file called C:\Answer.xml, you could run the following command within the Exchange Management Shell:

   ImportEdgeConfig.ps1 –CloneConfigData 'C:\EdgeBackup.xml' -isImport $false -CloneConfigAnswer 'C:\Answer.xml'

   Next, you can edit the Answer.xml file if you wish to add any additional server parameters such as computer name. Following this, you can import the C:\EdgeBackup .xml cloned configuration XML file and the C:\Answer.xml file using the following command within the Exchange Management Shell to restore the configuration of your Edge role server:

   ImportEdgeConfig.ps1 –CloneConfigData 'C:\EdgeBackup.xml' -isImport $true -CloneConfigAnswer 'C:\Answer.xml'

7. Restore the message tracking, protocol, and agent logs that you backed up for your server as discussed in the previous section. These files can be restored using Windows Backup.

8. Restore any certificates that you backed up for your server as discussed in the previous section. To restore an exported certificate, double click on the .pfx file that you created. The Certificate Import Wizard will start to allow you to import the certificate and related private key.

9. Review your printed documentation and make any remaining changes to the configuration of your server role that were not made during the recovery process.

■ Managing and Repairing Exchange Databases

↓ THE BOTTOM LINE

Exchange Server 2007 contains several utilities that may be used to check databases for corruption, defragment databases, as well as repair databases. A firm understanding of these utilities and their application is key to maintaining the health of your Exchange servers.

Because databases are complex storage mechanisms, they often encounter errors over time. As an Exchange administrator, you should understand how to detect these errors, how to determine the nature of the problem, and the procedures that can be used to remedy it. While you normally detect most Exchange database problems when they affect users within your organization, other errors will post events to the Application log in the Windows Event Viewer. When you encounter database related errors, you should first examine the nature of the problem before you attempt to remedy it. To detect most database problems, you can dismount the affected database and run the *Extensible Storage Engine Utility* (eseutil.exe) from the Windows command prompt. For example, to perform an integrity check on the table structure within the **D:\SG1\Mailbox Database.edb** database, you could dismount it and run the following command from the Windows command prompt:

eseutil.exe /g 'D:\SG1\Mailbox Database.edb'

The eseutil.exe utility can also be used to prevent future database problems. When information is removed from a database, Exchange automatically performs an *online defragmentation* procedure that removes the data from the appropriate tables. However, this online defragmentation leaves blank entries within the database, and the size of the database is not reduced. Over time, this makes it more difficult to store information within the database and increases the chance that the database will become corrupted. To prevent this, you can use the eseutil.exe utility to perform an *offline defragmentation* of your database. An offline defragmentation removes any blank entries within the database and reduces the database to a more manageable size. To perform an offline defragmentation of the **D:\SG1\Mailbox Database.edb** database, you could dismount it and run the following command from the Windows command prompt:

eseutil.exe /d 'D:\SG1\Mailbox Database.edb'

Table 10-1 lists some common options that may be used alongside the eseutil.exe utility to analyze, maintain, and repair databases.

TAKE NOTE*

In addition to the mailbox and public folder databases, you can use the eseutil.exe utility on the email queue databases used by the Hub and Edge role servers. These databases are located in the **C:\Program Files\ Microsoft\Exchange Server\TransportRoles\ data\Queue\mail.que** file by default on your Hub or Edge role server.

Table 10-1

Common eseutil.exe options

ACTION	DESCRIPTION
/cc	Replays transaction logs after a database restore operation that did not include the Last Restore Set option (hard recovery).
/d	Defragments the Exchange database by removing empty database pages as well as rebuilds database indexes.
/g	Checks the tables within the Exchange database for logical consistency.
/k	Verifies the checksums on all database components (database pages, transaction log files, checkpoint file).
/m	Displays the headers of the database files, transaction logs, and checkpoint files as well as displays recent backup information.
/p	Repairs the tables within the Exchange database. Any pages that cannot be repaired are removed.
/r	Replays existing transaction log files to bring a database to a consistent state (soft recovery).

As shown in Table 10-1, you can use the **/p** option of the eseutil.exe utility to repair a corrupted database. For example, to repair corrupted tables within the **D:\SG1\Mailbox**

Database.edb database, you could dismount it and run the following command from the Windows command prompt:

eseutil.exe /p 'D:\SG1\Mailbox Database.edb'

The eseutil.exe utility only understands how to work with and repair the individual tables within a database and does not understand the relationship between database tables within the database. As a result, many administrators only perform an **eseutil.exe /p** command on a database if restoring from a backup is not an option.

The *Information Store Integrity Checker* (isinteg.exe) understands the entire structure within an Exchange mailbox or public folder database and can safely be used to detect and repair Exchange problems with them. Because of this, it is a good practice to first attempt to repair a corrupted mailbox or public folder database using isinteg.exe before restoring the database from a backup.

As with eseutil.exe, you must first dismount the databases that you wish to analyze using isinteg.exe. When you run the isinteg.exe utility, you can specify different tests that should be performed. To perform all tests on a mailbox or public folder database on the server EXCH1 and fix any errors, you could run the following command at the Windows command prompt:

isinteg.exe –s EXCH1 –fix –test alltests

After running this command, you will be prompted to select the dismounted database on the server that you wish to analyze. After analyzing the database and correcting any errors, the isinteg.exe utility displays a report that indicates the type and number of errors corrected.

➕ MORE INFORMATION

The eseutil.exe and isinteg.exe commands are stored in the **C:\Program Files\Microsoft\Exchange Server\bin** directory and are added to the PATH variable in Windows by default so that you can execute them from any location.

For more information on the eseutil.exe and isinteg.exe utilities, search for their names within Exchange Server 2007 Help.

You can also use the Microsoft Exchange Troubleshooting Assistant to analyze, defragment, and repair Exchange databases. Navigate to the **Tools** node within the Exchange Management Console and select **Database Recovery Management** in the detail pane. After specifying a descriptive label and selecting the appropriate Exchange server and DC, you can select one of several tasks as shown in Figure 10-35.

Figure 10-35

Selecting Database Management Tasks

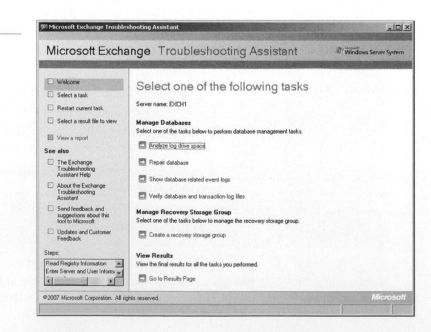

Under the **Manage Databases** section, you can select one of four tasks that can be used to manage your Exchange databases:

- **Analyze log drive space.** Displays the amount of disk space used by the log files within each storage group as well as the remaining available disk

- **Repair database.** Performs the **eseutil /p**, **eseutil /d**, and **isinteg –fix –test alltests** commands on the database that you specify.

- **Show database related event logs.** Searches the Application log within Event Viewer and displays any Exchange-created events.

- **Verify database and transaction log files.** Performs the **eseutil /g**, **eseutil /k**, and **eseutil /m** commands on the database that you specify as well as checks for missing or damaged log files.

To perform the database management procedures discussed in this section, you must be a member of the Exchange Server Administrator role as well as a member of the local Administrators group on the Mailbox role server.

SUMMARY SKILL MATRIX

IN THIS LESSON YOU LEARNED:

- The ESE first writes information to a transaction log before committing it to a mailbox or public folder database and updating the checkpoint file. Because all databases within the same storage group use the same transaction logs and checkpoint file, you should ensure that databases within the same storage group have similar backup schedules.

- Information within transaction logs can be used when restoring data. If circular logging is enabled in the storage group, data is not stored within transaction logs for recovery purposes.

- Most backups are performed to hard disk media using Windows Backup or a third-party backup program. Windows Backup does not support VSS for Exchange database backups.

- Full backups back up databases and transaction logs as well as clear existing transaction logs. Copy backups are like full backups but do not clear existing transaction logs and are often used to perform hard recovery. Incremental backups back up transaction logs since the last backup and clear them afterward. Differential backups back up transaction logs since the last backup but do not clear them afterward.

- Windows Backup may be used to create a backup as well as restore a backup. Before restoring a backup, the target database must first be dismounted. By selecting the Last Restore Set option when configuring a restore, transaction logs are replayed following the restore operation.

- You can create a single RSG on each Mailbox role server that impersonates an existing storage group for restore purposes. You can restore a backup to an RSG to obtain a working copy of a mailbox database from a backup. This working copy can then be used to perform a dial tone recovery, restore mailboxes and emails, or test a backup. Dial tone recoveries switch the working copy of the database within the RSG with the original database to minimize interruption to users.

- You can create RSGs, perform dial tone recoveries, and restore individual mailboxes and emails from an RSG using the Database Recovery Management tool within the Exchange Management Console or by using cmdlets within the Exchange Management Shell.

- You can recover deleted emails within Outlook, OWA, or Entourage within the deleted item limit time period. Similarly, you can recover deleted mailboxes within the Exchange Management Console or Exchange Management Shell within the deleted mailbox limit.

(continued)

- To ensure that your Exchange Server roles can be restored in the event of a server failure, you should back up the system state, Exchange registry keys, certificates used by the server role, as well as any role-specific files.

- You can restore the AD configuration for Hub, CAS, Mailbox, and UM roles by reinstalling the operating system and running the Exchange installation using the /m:RecoverServer option of the Exchange setup.com program. All other configuration must be re-created or restored from backup.

- Because Edge role servers do not store configuration information within AD, you can recover an Edge role server by re-creating it as you would a new Edge role server and restoring its configuration from a backup.

- The eseutil.exe utility may be used to verify, defragment, and repair databases at the table level. To verify and repair databases at the database level, you can use the isinteg.exe utility. The Database Recovery Management tool within the Exchange Management Console may also be used to verify, defragment, and repair Exchange databases.

Knowledge Assessment

Fill in the Blank

Complete the following sentences by writing the correct word or words in the blanks provided.

1. Selecting the _____ option during a restore operation replays transaction logs following the restore operation.

2. To create a cloned configuration on an Edge role server, you can execute the _____ script within the Exchange Management Shell.

3. A _____ refers to the sum total of all backups that work together to protect Exchange data.

4. The _____ option to the setup.com command on the Exchange Server 2007 installation media may be used to reinstall a server role using the configuration information within AD.

5. The _____ utility may be used to verify and repair email queue databases on a Hub or Edge role server.

6. Instead of using VSS, Windows Backup performs a _____ backup of the Exchange database.

7. If you enable _____ on a storage group, transaction logs cannot be used to restore data to a specific point in time.

8. The _____ cmdlet can be used to export a public key certificate and related private key on an Exchange server.

9. The process of replaying transaction logs against a database that has been restored from a backup is called _____ .

10. The _____ role does not store configuration information within AD.

Multiple Choice

Circle the letter that corresponds to the best answer.

1. Which of the following log files should be backed up on an Edge role server as part of a server backup procedure? (Choose all that apply.)
   a. Message tracking logs
   b. Event logs
   c. Agent logs
   d. Protocol logs

2. Which of the following actions should you perform prior to performing a dial tone recovery? (Choose all that apply.)
   a. Create an RSG that impersonates the appropriate storage group
   b. Copy transaction logs from the failed database to the RSG directory
   c. Restore the appropriate database backup to the RSG
   d. Mount the database within the RSG

3. Which of the following Event IDs indicate an error during a backup operation? (Choose all that apply.)
   a. 8000
   b. 8018
   c. 8001
   d. 8019

4. Your organization uses tape media to perform Exchange database backups. The IT manager has stressed the need for quick restoration of an Exchange database in the event of database corruption. In addition, restored information should be no more than one day old. Which of the following backup sets would meet these needs?
   a. Differential backups during weekdays and full backups on weekends
   b. Copy backups during weekdays and full backups on weekends
   c. Incremental backups during weekdays and full backups on weekends
   d. Full backups during weekdays and weekends

5. Which of the following items are included within a system state backup? (Choose all that apply.)
   a. The Active Directory database (DCs only)
   b. The Windows Registry
   c. System log files
   d. System boot files

6. Which option to the eseutil.exe command may be used to verify the checksums of database components?
   a. /g
   b. /k
   c. /m
   d. /d

7. Which of the following actions should be performed immediately following a restore operation? (Choose all that apply.)
   a. Mount the database
   b. Check the database for consistency
   c. Rebuild the full-text index catalog
   d. Defragment the database

8. Which of the following prefixes will be used to identify the transaction logs and checkpoint file for the second storage group on your Mailbox server?
   a. T01
   b. E01
   c. T02
   d. E02

9. One of the users within your organization asks you to restore an email that he deleted a few moments ago from his Deleted Items folder in Outlook 2007. What is the easiest way to restore this email?
   a. Restore the email from a backup that is mounted to the RSG
   b. Restore the mailbox from a backup that is mounted to the RSG
   c. Delete and reconnect the user's mailbox within the Exchange Management Console
   d. Use the Recover Deleted Items feature of Outlook 2007

10. What two actions will back up the OAB for current and legacy MAPI clients within your organization? (Choose two answers.)
    a. Backing up the public folder database
    b. Backing up the system state
    c. Backing up the Exchange registry keys
    d. Backing up the C:\Program Files\Microsoft\Exchange Server\ExchangeOAB directory

True/False

Circle T if the statement is true or F if the statement is false.

T | F   **1.** Transaction logs are shared by all databases within the same storage group.

T | F   **2.** You can only create a single RSG per Mailbox role server.

T | F   **3.** Log files are only removed from a storage group after a full backup.

T | F   **4.** To protect your server configuration, you should back up any certificates that have been issued by an Enterprise CA within your organization.

T | F   **5.** An offline defragmentation must be performed on a dismounted database, which reduces the overall size of the database by removing blank database entries.

T | F   **6.** The Restore-Mailbox cmdlet may be used to restore individual emails from a restored mailbox database within an RSG.

T | F   **7.** Before restoring a corrupted database from backup, you could run the isinteg.exe utility on the database with the –fix option to attempt to repair the corruption.

T | F   **8.** The ESE writes information to a transaction log after it has been committed to the database.

T | F   **9.** The isinteg.exe utility only checks table structure and does not understand the relationships between tables within an Exchange database.

T | F   **10.** You should always document the configuration of each server role in addition to backing up configuration settings.

Review Questions

1. Explain why the backup types that you select depend on the media used for backup.
2. Explain how dial tone recovery can be used to save your organization money in the event of database corruption.

■ Case Scenarios

Scenario 10-1: Designing a Database Backup Plan

One of the most important tasks that you will need to perform as an Exchange administrator is the design and execution of a backup plan that meets your organization's needs. Assume that you are an Exchange administrator for a medium-sized company that does not have a great deal of money to spend on protecting email data. Existing file backups are performed to tape media, and your organization will not be purchasing a NAS device for backup purposes in the near future. You have created a full backup of the mailbox databases on one of your Mailbox role servers and noticed that it takes about 15 hours to complete. Although email functionality is not critical for the daily function of your organization, backups should not be performed during working hours (9:00 a.m. to 5:00 p.m. Monday through Friday) and emails from the previous day should be recoverable in the event of data loss. Your supervisor has stressed that backup jobs should be completed in the least amount of time possible.

In a short memo, design a database backup plan that would suit the needs of your organization.

Scenario 10-2: Recovering Mailbox Data

For the backup plan that you created in Scenario 10-1, describe the process that you should perform if you suspect database corruption on one of your mailbox databases. Ensure that you describe the detailed steps to perform the restore procedure.

Monitoring Exchange

LESSON SKILL MATRIX

TECHNOLOGY SKILL	OBJECTIVE DOMAIN	OBJECTIVE DOMAIN NUMBER
Monitoring Email Queues	Monitor mail queues.	4.1
Monitoring System Performance	Monitor system performance.	4.2
Tracking Messages	Perform message tracking.	4.3
Monitoring Client Connectivity	Monitor client connectivity.	4.4
Creating Server Reports	Create server reports.	4.5
Creating Usage Reports	Create usage reports.	4.6

KEY TERMS

alert	message tracking log	remote delivery queue
capacity planning	performance baseline	rogue process
counter log	performance object	submission queue
email queue	pickup directory	System Monitor
Event Viewer	poison message queue	Task Manager
Exchange Troubleshooting Assistant	proactive monitoring	trace log
	protocol log	unreachable queue
mailbox delivery queue	Queue Viewer	
memory leak	reactive monitoring	

■ Monitoring System Performance

THE BOTTOM LINE

As your organization grows, so does the load on the Exchange servers within your organization. In addition, because Exchange servers are hardware and software configured to perform a certain task, the performance of your Exchange servers will suffer when hardware fails or software is misconfigured or crashes. Regardless of the cause of poor performance, regular monitoring of the Exchange servers within your organization is vital to planning for growth as well as troubleshooting server performance.

CERTIFICATION READY?
Monitor system performance.
4.2

After you have deployed Exchange Server 2007 on your network, you must maintain the integrity of your email system over time by monitoring the performance of your Exchange servers. Monitoring the performance of the Exchange servers within your organization can be reactive or proactive. *Reactive monitoring* is used to identify the source of a problem that has already affected the performance of a system, such as a heavy system load, runaway program, or failing hard disk. *Proactive monitoring* involves monitoring normal system performance at regular intervals over time. This type of monitoring may be used to identify potential problems before they affect the performance of the Exchange server or to create a performance baseline. A ***performance baseline*** is performance data for a particular server that is representative of normal system activity. By comparing baseline data to performance data gathered during reactive monitoring, you can often determine the source of a performance problem by identifying the differences between the performance baseline and the performance data that you gathered during reactive monitoring.

TAKE NOTE*

When a performance-related problem is identified and resolved, it should be documented to ensure that similar problems can be solved quickly in the future. To ensure that this documentation is not lost during a system failure, it should be printed and kept in a logbook rather than stored on the system itself.

There are six main utilities within Windows Server that may be used to perform reactive and proactive monitoring:

- Task Manager
- System Monitor
- Performance Logs and Alerts
- Event Viewer
- Exchange Best Practices Analyzer
- Exchange Troubleshooting Assistant

Monitoring Performance Using Task Manager

The Windows Task Manager is the quickest way to obtain realtime information about the performance of your Exchange server.

Task Manager is typically the first utility that is used by Exchange administrators to perform reactive monitoring of an Exchange server because it can quickly check server and network performance as well as manage the processes that are running on the system. You can start Task Manager within Windows using a variety of different methods:

- By pressing **Ctrl+Shift+Esc**
- By pressing **Ctrl+Alt+Del** and then clicking **Task Manager**
- By right clicking the Windows task bar and selecting **Task Manager** from the menu
- By executing **taskmgr.exe** in the Run dialog box or Windows command prompt.

Regardless of the method that you use to start it, Task Manager has five different tabs that may be used to monitor various areas of your system: Applications, Processes, Performance, Networking, and Users.

If your system is experiencing poor performance, you should first navigate to the Performance tab as shown in Figure 11-1.

Figure 11-1

Monitoring Performance Using Task Manager

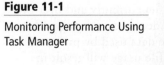

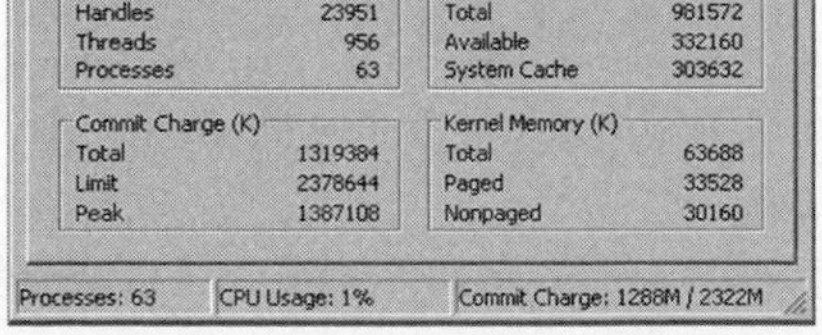

The Performance tab provides an overview of a system's current performance. The statistics shown on the Performance tab are not designed to give details on performance information for all system components, but they can be used to quickly check if there is a problem with your computer. At the bottom of the Performance tab (Figure 11-1), there are several statistics that may be used to quickly determine the state of your system. These statistics are described in Table 11-1.

Table 11-1

Performance tab statistics

STATISTIC	DESCRIPTION
Totals	Displays the total number of handles (connections to open files), threads (process components that are currently executing on the system), and processes currently running on the system.
Physical Memory	Displays the total amount of RAM in your system, the amount of available RAM to new processes, and the amount of RAM used by the operating system (called the system cache).
Commit Charge	Displays the amount of virtual memory from the page file (or swap file) that is currently committed to all processes currently running on the system, as well as the size limit of the page file and the peak usage of the page file in the past few minutes.
Kernel Memory	Displays the amount of memory that has been allocated to the Windows operating system kernel and related components, including the amount of RAM that is used (nonpaged) and the amount of virtual memory that is used (paged). Normally the kernel memory has little impact on system performance.

Most performance problems are the result of a high CPU utilization or not enough available RAM for applications that require it. As a result, these two items are represented by graphs within Task Manager for easy viewing.

The CPU Usage graph shown in Figure 11-1 indicates that the CPU is only used at 1% capacity at the current time. The CPU Usage History shows the CPU Usage over a past few minutes per processor or processor core. Figure 11-1 shows two CPU Usage History graphs because the computer that it is running on has two cores. If your system has consistently high CPU utilization (above 80%), your system may have one or more rogue processes. A *rogue process* is a failed process that has entered an endless resource loop that causes it to continually use up CPU resources.

The PF Usage graph and Page File Usage History graphs on the Performance tab (Figure 11-1) display the amount of space that is used within the page file currently and over the past few minutes respectively. As the amount of available RAM decreases, the *page file* (or *swap file*) on the hard disk is used more extensively to store the data used by processes. Because hard disks are much slower than RAM, extensive page file usage will result in poorer application performance as well as poorer hard disk performance. If your page file usage is high, your system may be running too many processes or may have a memory leak. A *memory leak* is a failed process that continues to use more and more RAM on your system. Eventually, a memory leak may cause your whole system to become unresponsive.

To identify rogue processes and memory leaks, you can navigate to the Processes tab of Task Manager as shown in Figure 11-2 and select **Show processes from all users** to view all processes on the system.

Figure 11-2

Managing Processes Using
Task Manager

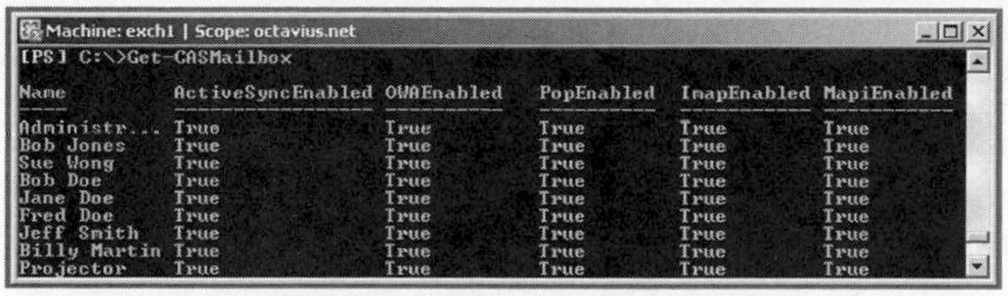

The Processes tab displays information about all of the processes currently running on the system including the percentage of CPU time and RAM that is being used by the process. If you double click on a column name on the Processes tab, the list of processes will sort by that column with the largest values displayed at the top. If you sort using the Mem Usage column, as shown in Figure 11-2, the processes that are using the most RAM will be listed at the top of the window and will allow you to identify memory leak processes that are using far more RAM than they normally should. Similarly, if you sort using the CPU column, you will see the processes that have the highest CPU usage and can identify a rogue process using an unusually large amount of CPU time. Once you have identified a rogue process or memory leak, you can remove the process by right clicking it on the Processes tab and selecting **End Process**.

TAKE NOTE *

You can add columns that contain additional information about processes on the Processes tab of Task Manager. Navigate to **View** > **Select Columns** within Task Manager and select the appropriate information.

The Applications tab of Task Manager is similar to the Processes tab. However, the Applications tab only displays the nonsystem programs that are currently running and their status (Running or Not responding). Because programs typically consist of multiple processes, there will be fewer entries on the Applications tab than on the processes tab. However, this tab is often used to end a stopped or hung program by program name. Users need to highlight their program and click **End Task**.

The Networking tab displays the speed, status, and network usage of each network adapter in your computer as shown in Figure 11-3. If your network utilization is close to 100% for your network adapters, your server is being flooded with network packets and cannot respond to them appropriately. This can be the result of too many SMTP or client requests on your Exchange server as well as network viruses or **Denial of Service (DoS)** attacks that flood your Exchange server with unnecessary traffic.

Figure 11-3

Monitoring Network
Bandwidth Using Task
Manager

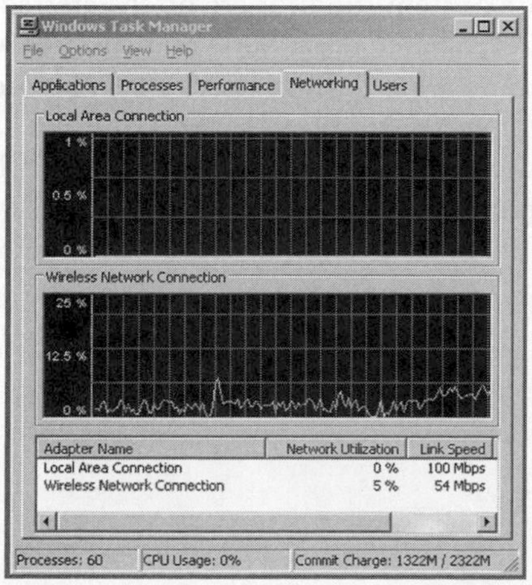

Although less likely, performance problems can also be the result of too many users accessing the Exchange server across the network. The Users tab in Task Manager allows you to view a list of users currently logged on to your server and disconnect them if necessary.

Monitoring Performance Using System Monitor

To obtain detail performance information from your Exchange server, you can use the System Monitor utility. System Monitor can be used to troubleshoot a performance problem, plan for future growth, or create a performance baseline to help in future trouble-shooting situations.

System Monitor is one of the most powerful monitoring utilities for obtaining performance data because it can measure hundreds of system statistics on the local computer or on computers across the network. You can use System Monitor to perform both reactive and proactive monitoring of the Exchange servers within your organization. You can proactively monitor the performance of your server on a regular basis to obtain a performance baseline. When performance problems occur, you can compare the current performance statistics with the normal performance statistics in the baseline. The statistics that differ between them are good indicators of the nature of the problem.

In addition, System Monitor can be used to detect trends that may lead to poor performance. If you notice that the performance of a hard disk is decreasing slowly over time with no additional system load or other related performance factors, you can replace the hard disk before it fails. Similarly, as your organization grows, the additional load on your Exchange servers will eventually lead to reduced performance. By monitoring your Exchange servers over time, you can better plan when new servers are required and obtain the appropriate funding before the existing servers reach their useful capacity. This practice is often called *capacity planning*.

Before you select the performance statistics to monitor within System Monitor, you must first understand the terminology that System Monitor uses to identify them. The *performance object* is the area of the system that should be monitored. The Processor performance object may be used to monitor the CPUs within your computer whereas the Physical Disk performance object may be used to monitor the physical usage of your hard disks. Once you have selected the appropriate performance object, you can select the appropriate performance statistic, or *counter*, within the particular performance object. For example, the % Processor Time counter within the Processor performance object monitors average CPU usage. Because your computer may contain multiple CPUs or CPU cores, you can optionally choose to monitor a single CPU by selecting an *instance* of the counter.

Performance statistics within System Monitor are often referred to using the format **performance object\counter**. The % Processor Time counter within the Processor performance object would be represented as **Processor\% Processor Time**. To denote the instance of a particular counter, you can use brackets following the performance object name. To refer to the % Processor Time counter for the first CPU within the Processor performance object, you could use the notation **Processor(0)\% Processor Time**. Alternatively, **Processor(_Total)\% Processor Time** would refer to the same counter averaged across all CPUs.

Table 11-2 lists the common objects and counters used to monitor the performance of a server system.

Table 11-2

Common System Monitor statistics

PERFORMANCE OBJECT	COUNTER	DESCRIPTION
Physical disk	Disk Reads/sec	Measures read activity on your hard disk.
Physical disk	Disk Writes/sec	Measures read activity on your hard disk.
Physical disk	Current Disk Queue Length	Measures the number of read-write requests waiting in system memory for disk operations. In general, if this number exceeds 2 for long periods of time, your hard disks cannot keep up with the number of system requests.
Physical disk	Avg. Disk Queue Length	Measures the average number of read-write requests that were queued in system memory for disk operations during the monitoring time.
Logical disk	% Free Space	Measures free space on a logical volume that you select as an instance. In general, this number should be greater than 15% to satisfy the needs for system caches and working space on a volume.
Logical disk	% Disk Time	Measures the percentage of time that a whole hard disk or single logical volume (e.g., C:\) is busy servicing read or write requests.
Memory	Available Bytes	Measures unused physical memory.
Memory	Cache Bytes	Measures physical memory available to services and hardware for caching.
Memory	Pages/sec	Measures the number of virtual memory requests that are sent to or received from the paging file (swap file) per second. In general, if this number is consistently over 20, your system may require more RAM to reduce page file use.
Network Interface	Bytes Total/sec	Measures the throughput of your network interface(s).
Processor	% Processor Time	Measures the percentage of time that a processor is busy servicing requests. If this number exceeds 80% over a long period of time, your CPU cannot adequately handle the number of processes that are executing on your system.
System	Processor Queue Length	Measures the total number of processes waiting for processor time in system memory for all CPUs on the system. As a result, you should divide this number by the number of CPUs or CPU cores on your system to obtain a single CPU value. If the single CPU value exceeds 2 over a long period of time, your system cannot adequately handle the number of processes that are executing on it.

System Monitor is part of the Performance console (**Start** > **Administrative Tools** > **Performance**). When you first open System Monitor, the **Memory\Pages/sec**, **Physical Disk\Av. Disk Queue Length**, and **Processor\% Processor Time** statistics on your local system are automatically monitored and displayed in graph format as shown in Figure 11-4.

Figure 11-4

System Monitor

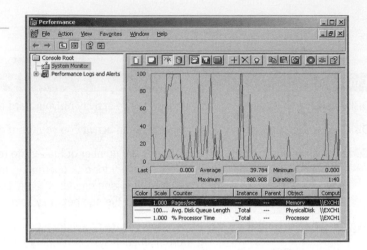

By default, each counter is given a different color and measurements are taken every second. You can modify this interval as well as the style and layout of the graph by clicking the Properties icon within System Monitor (fourth icon from the right in Figure 11-4). Similarly, by selecting the appropriate icon within System Monitor, you can change the graph view to a histogram or report view, add additional counters, remove existing counters, as well as freeze the display to temporarily stop monitoring.

If you click the + (add) button as shown in Figure 11-4, you can select a computer to monitor, a performance object, counters, and instances as shown in Figure 11-5. In the Add Counters window shown in Figure 11-5, the **Processor\% Processor Time** counter for the first CPU (instance 0) on the computer EXCH1 has been selected. You can click **Explain** in the Add Counters window to obtain a description of the counter or click **Add** to add the counter to the System Monitor window while keeping the Add Counters window open to add additional counters.

Figure 11-5

Adding a Counter

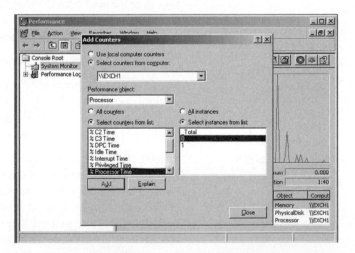

When you install additional system components, services, and applications such as Exchange Server 2007, performance objects and counters are typically added to System Monitor to aid in system monitoring. When you install the Hub, Mailbox, CAS, and UM roles, over 80 performance objects (with a **MSExchange** prefix) are added to System Monitor that together include over 1000 counters that can be used to monitor various Exchange components. Monitoring all of these components would be too time consuming to perform for most Exchange administrators and would be difficult to interpret. Instead, these performance objects and counters are available in case you need to monitor the performance of a specific Exchange component for capacity planning or troubleshooting. If you want to know the number of messages submitted to the Mailbox database in the First Storage Group on the Mailbox role server EXCH1, you could specify the **MSExchangeIS Mailbox** object on the server EXCH1 in the Add Counters window, select the **Messages Submitted/sec** counter, choose the **Fourth Storage Group-Mailbox Database** instance as shown in Figure 11-6, and click **Add**.

Figure 11-6

Adding an Exchange Counter

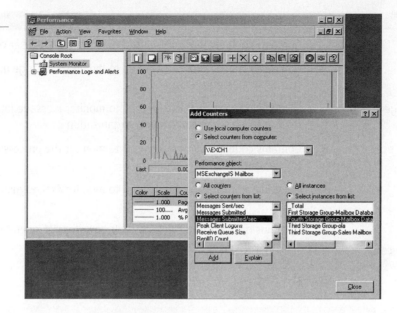

Table 11-3 lists some common performance objects that may be used to monitor the performance of Exchange components.

Table 11-3

Common exchange performance objects

OBJECT	DESCRIPTION
MSExchangeAutodiscover MSExchange Availability Service	Contains counters that can be used to monitor the Autodiscover and Availability services.
MSExchangeIS MSExchangeIS Client MSExchangeIS Mailbox MSExchangeIS Public MSExchange Store Driver	Contains counters that can be used to monitor the Microsoft Exchange Information Store service in general or for client-related, mailbox-related, or public folder-related operations only.
MSExchangeTransport SmtpRecieve MSExchangeTransport SmtpSend	Contains counters that can be used to monitor, receive, and send connectors on a Hub or Edge role server.
MSExchangePop3	Contains counters that can be used to monitor POP3 connections on a CAS role server.
MSExchangeIMAP4	Contains counters that can be used to monitor IMAP4 connections on a CAS role server.
MSExchangeEdgeSync Job	Contains counters that can be used to monitor EdgeSync replication between the Hub and Edge role servers within your organization.
MSExchange Sender Id Agent MSExchange Sender Filter Agent MSExchange Recipient Filter Agent MSExchange Content Filter Agent MSExchange Connection Filter Agent	Contains counters that can be used to monitor spam-filtering agents on the Hub and Edge role servers within your organization.

(continued)

Table 11-3 (continued)

OBJECT	DESCRIPTION
MSExchange OWA	Contains counters that can be used to monitor OWA user connections.
MSExchange Database	Contains counters that can be used to monitor Exchange mailbox and public folder database operations.
MSExchange Journaling Agent	Contains counters that can be used to monitor message journaling operations on the Exchange servers within your organization.
MSExchange Transport Rules	Contains counters that can be used to monitor the processing of Exchange Server transport rules.
MSExchange ActiveSync	Contains counters that can be used to monitor ActiveSync connections from mobile clients.
MSExchangeUMGeneral MSExchangeUMPerformance	Contains counters that can be used to monitor UM operations and the time that they take on UM role servers within your organization.

TAKE NOTE ✱

If you navigate to the **Toolbox** node within the Exchange Management Console and double click on **Performance Monitor** under the Performance Tools section in the detail pane, System Monitor is opened and several commonly used Exchange-specific counters are automatically added from the Exchange performance objects.

Once you have obtained the necessary performance data using System Monitor, you can save it to an HTML file (*.htm) or tab-delimited text file (*.tsv) that can be stored for later use as well as printed and placed in a logbook. To do this, right click any area within the System Monitor window, select **Save As**, and specify the correct format and filename.

Monitoring Performance Using Performance Logs and Alerts

Performance Logs and Alerts allow you to collect the same detailed performance information available from System Monitor as well as perform actions when a performance statistic reaches a critical value.

In addition to System Monitor, you can use the Performance Logs and Alerts utility in the Performance snap-in to monitor and obtain detailed performance information about the Exchange servers within your organization.

When you access the Performance Logs and Alerts utility, you can configure counter logs, trace logs, and alerts as shown in Figure 11-7.

Figure 11-7

Performance Logs and Alerts

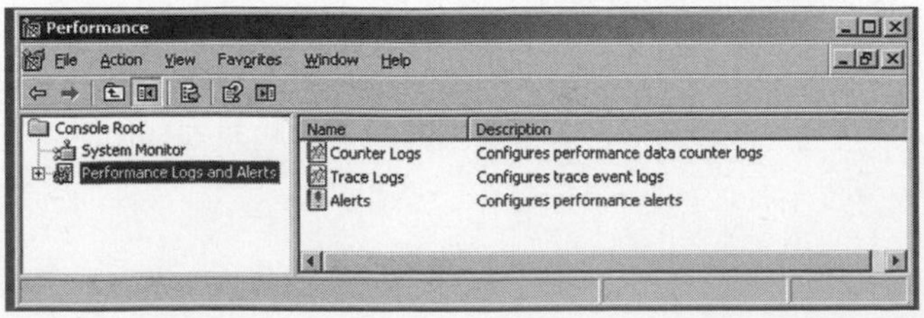

Counter logs monitor the same performance objects and counters that you specified in System Monitor for a specific period of time that you select. This monitoring information is then saved to an SQL database or a log file, where it can be later viewed using System Monitor or another program such as Microsoft Excel. *Trace logs* can be used to log system events as they occur, and *alerts* may be used to log information, send a notification, or run a program when a specific counter reaches a critical value called a *threshold*. Like counter logs, alerts can be configured for any performance object or counter available in System Monitor.

Both counter logs and alerts are useful when monitoring the performance of the Exchange servers within your organization.

⊕ CREATE A COUNTER LOG

GET READY. Turn on the Exchange server, and log in as the Administrator user account. Close any windows that appear on the desktop.

1. Click **Start**, **Administrative Tools**, **Performance**. When the Performance window appears, highlight **Performance Logs and Alerts** in the left pane.

2. In the right pane, right click **Counter Logs** and click **New Log Settings**. In the New Log Settings window that appears, type a descriptive name for your new counter log and click **OK**.

3. In the counter log window that appears, you can add individual counters to monitor by clicking the Add Counters button and selecting the appropriate counter as you would in System Monitor shown in Figure 11-5. Alternatively, you can click the Add Objects button to add all of the counters from a performance object that you specify. As Figure 11-8 illustrates, the Memory\Pages/sec, Physical Disk\Av. Disk Queue Length, and Processor\% Processor Time counters on the server EXCH1 have been added individually.

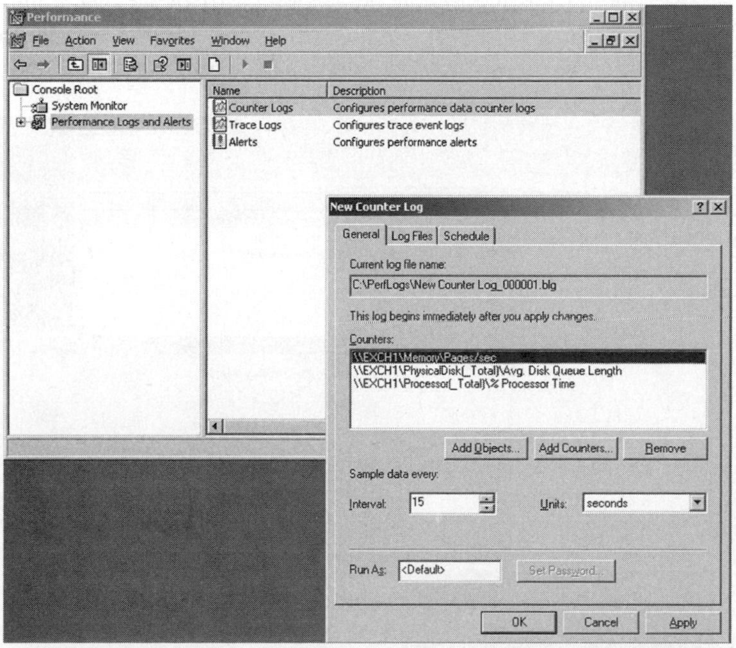

Figure 11-8

Configuring a Counter Log

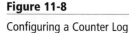

4. By default, counter logs take performance measurements every 15 seconds. However, you can select a different value in the **Interval** and **Units** dialog box shown in Figure 11-8 to modify this. In addition, the counter log runs as the local system user by default unless you provide a username in the **Run As** dialog box and specify the associated password by clicking the **Set Password** button.

5. Highlight the **Log Files** tab. By default, counter logs are saved in binary format to a numbered file in the C:\PerfLogs directory as shown in Figure 11-9. However, you can change the file naming structure or instead save counter logs to a tab- or colon-delimited text file or SQL database by selecting the appropriate options.

Figure 11-9

Configuring Counter Log File Format

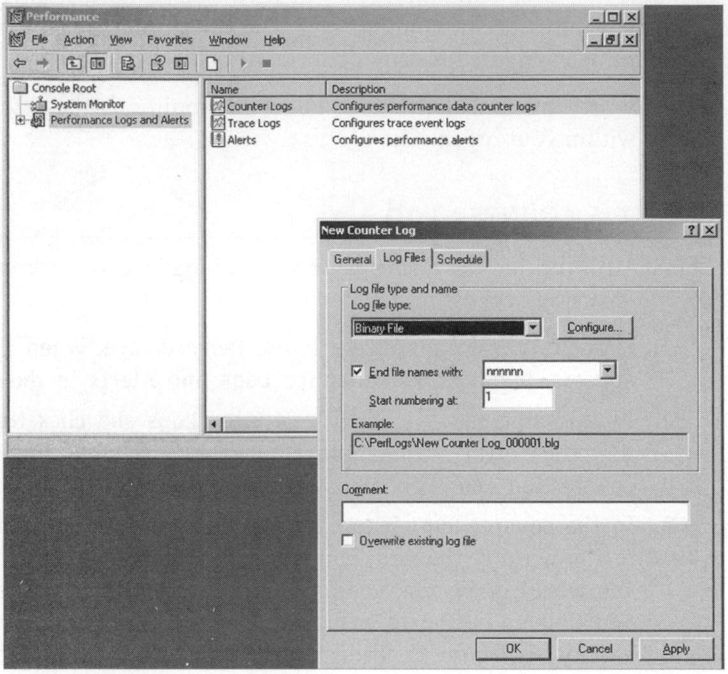

6. Highlight the **Schedule** tab. By default, counter logs start measuring performance continually after they are configured, but you can manually specify a specific time period for monitoring. As Figure 11-10 shows, the counter log will be set to monitor for a period of 1 day starting at 6:00 p.m. on January 1, 2009 and a new log file will be created for additional monitoring after this period.

Figure 11-10

Configuring a Counter Log Schedule

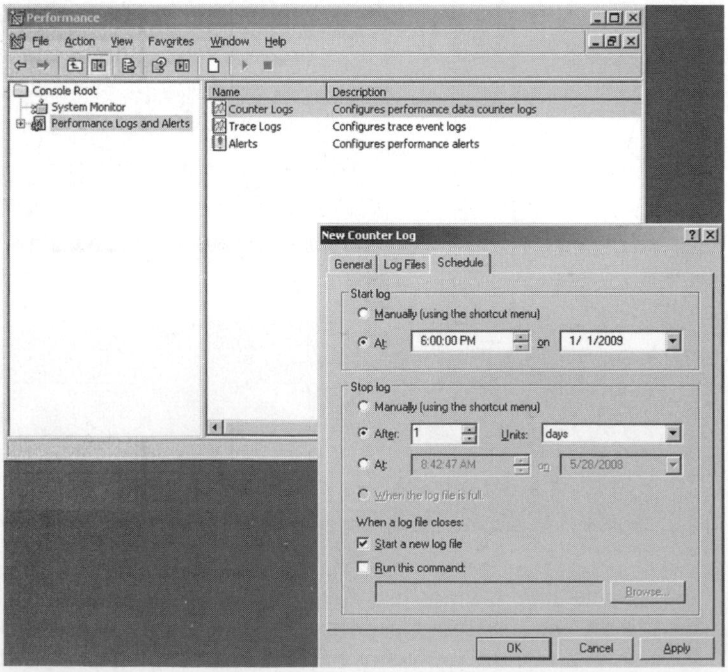

7. Click **OK**. If you are prompted to create the C:\PerfLogs folder, click **Yes**. Your counter log will be displayed in the right pane of the Performance console when you highlight **Counter Logs** in the left pane as shown in Figure 11-11. A green icon next to your counter log indicates that it is currently monitoring your system whereas a red icon indicates that monitoring is stopped. You can right click your counter log shown in Figure 11-11 and select **Start** or **Stop** to manually control when your counter log monitors system performance regardless of the schedule you specified.

Figure 11-11

Viewing Counter Logs

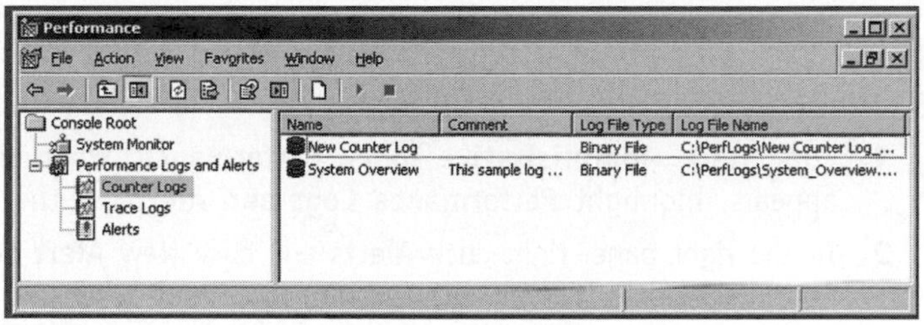

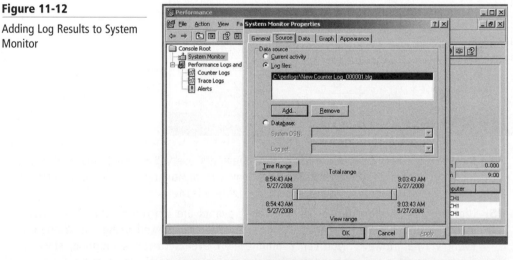

8. Close the Performance window.

Before you can analyze a counter log, you must first right click it in the Performance window and select **Stop** to close the open connection to the counter log file. Counter logs stored in binary format can be later analyzed in System Monitor, whereas counter logs stored in text format or within an SQL database must be read by another application such as Microsoft Excel. If you have created a counter log stored in binary format, you can view it in System Monitor by selecting the **View Log Data** icon (fourth icon from the left in Figure 11-4) and specifying the appropriate log file and time range in the System Monitor properties window as shown in Figure 11-12. Next, take the same counters stored within the counter log that you wish to monitor and add them to the data tab as shown in Figure 11-13. Click **OK** to view the performance information for that time period from the counter log.

Figure 11-12

Adding Log Results to System Monitor

Figure 11-13

Adding Counters to View Log Results in System Monitor

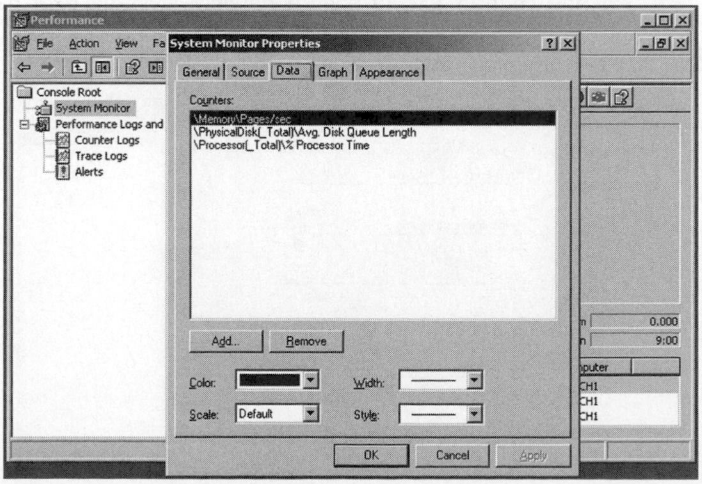

After you have reviewed the performance data from your counter log using System Monitor, you can save it to an HTML or tab-delimited text file within System Monitor as described in the previous section.

CREATE A PERFORMANCE ALERT

GET READY. Turn on the Exchange server, and log in as the Administrator user account. Close any windows that appear on the desktop.

1. Click **Start**, **Administrative Tools**, **Performance**. When the Performance window appears, highlight **Performance Logs and Alerts** in the left pane.

2. In the right pane, right click **Alerts** and click **New Alert Settings**. In the New Alert Settings window that appears, type a descriptive name for your new alert and click **OK**.

3. In the alert window that appears, you can add individual counters to monitor by clicking the **Add** button and selecting the appropriate counter as you would in System Monitor shown in Figure 11-5. Following this, you can specify the criteria that must be met for each counter to generate an alert event. As illustrated in Figure 11-14, an alert event will be generated if the Processor\% Processor Time counter is above 95.

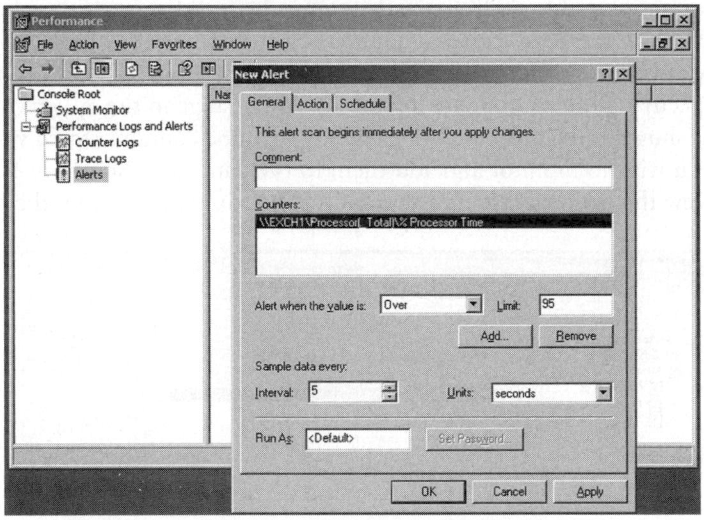

Figure 11-14

Configuring a Performance Alert

4. By default, alerts take performance measurements every 5 seconds and run as the local system user. As with counter logs, you can optionally modify these settings using the appropriate sections shown in Figure 11-14.

5. Highlight the **Action** tab. By default, alert events are written to the Application event log as shown in Figure 11-15 and can be later viewed using the Windows Event Viewer. However, you can configure alert events to run a program, start an existing counter log, or send a network message to a particular computer.

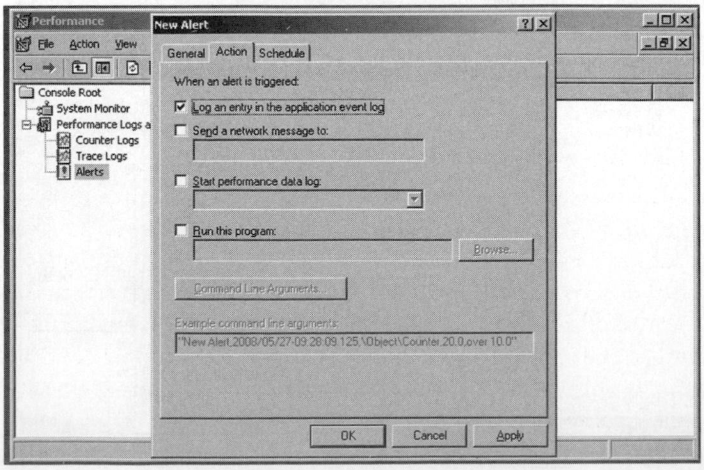

Figure 11-15

Specifying a Performance Alert Action

Microsoft*

TAKE NOTE ✱ If you select **Send a network message to** (see Figure 11-15), the server configured with the performance alert must have the Alerter service started and the destination computer receiving the message must have the Messenger service started. These services can be started using the Services console (**Start** > **Administrative Tools** > **Services**) on your Windows server.

6. Highlight the **Schedule** tab. By default, alerts start monitoring performance continually after they are configured, but you can manually specify a specific time period for monitoring. As shown in Figure 11-16, the alert will be set to monitor from 9:00 a.m. Monday May 26, 2008 through 5:00 p.m. Friday May 30, 2008.

Figure 11-16

Specifying a Performance Alert Schedule

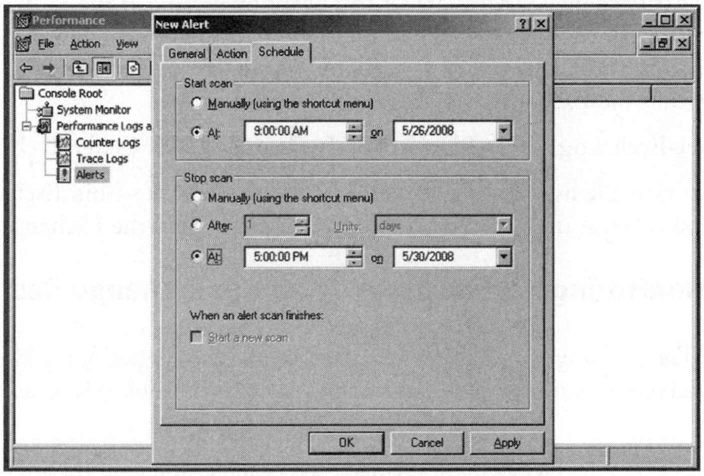

7. Click **OK**. Your alert will be displayed in the right pane of the Performance console when you highlight **Alerts** in the left pane. A green icon next to your alert indicates that it is currently monitoring your system, whereas a red icon indicates that monitoring is stopped. As with counter logs, you can right click your alert and select **Start** or **Stop** to manually control when your alert monitors system performance regardless of the schedule that you specified.

8. Close the Performance window.

Monitoring Performance Using Event Viewer

When Exchange services encounters errors, events are written to the Windows Event Viewer. The entries in the Windows Event Viewer can easily be used to determine the nature of these errors that ultimately result in poor performance.

The Windows *Event Viewer* is a powerful reactive monitoring and troubleshooting tool in Windows that can display information about the hardware, system services, and applications that are running on your server. When different components and services in Exchange Server 2007 experience problems leading to poor system performance, they write information about the nature of those problems to the Application log within Event Viewer. For example, if the POP3 service fails to start on a CAS role server within your organization, you can often find the cause by examining the Warning and Error events in the Event Viewer Application log. In addition, each event lists the Exchange component that generated it in the Source field as well as a number that represents the nature of the problem in the Event ID field. If the cause or nature of the error is not listed in the event itself, you can often enter the related event ID number in a search engine such as Google (**www.google.com**) or on the Microsoft TechNet Web site (**http://technet.microsoft.com**) to find more information about the problem and possible solutions.

TAKE NOTE ✱ By default, any user can view the contents of the Application log in Event Viewer.

By default, all Exchange Server 2007 services and components log minimal information to the Windows Event Viewer. However, if you are troubleshooting a performance problem that affects a certain component of Exchange, you should increase the level of logging to log more information to Event Viewer. This information may be helpful in determining the nature of the problem. There are five levels of event logging that can be configured for Exchange services:

- Lowest
- Low
- Medium
- High
- Expert

Most Exchange services are set to Lowest by default. If the POP3 service is experiencing performance issues, you could increase the default logging level to High to obtain more information that may be used to troubleshoot the POP3 problem and run the following command within the Exchange Management Shell:

Set-EventLogLevel –Identity 'MsExchange POP3\General' -Level 'High'

To view the list of available services and components within Exchange and event logging levels, you can run the **Get-EventLogLevel** cmdlet within the Exchange Management Shell.

Monitoring Performance Using the Exchange Best Practices Analyzer

The Exchange Best Practices Analyzer can be used to perform a Health Check on the Exchange servers within your organization and report any possible problems as well as remedies.

In Lesson 3, "Deploying Exchange Server 2007," you used the Exchange Best Practices Analyzer to analyze preinstallation requirements for Exchange Server 2007. You can also run the Exchange Best Practices Analyzer following installation to obtain and analyze performance information from the Exchange servers within your organization. Navigate to the **Toolbox** node within the Exchange Management Console and double click on **Best Practices Analyzer**. You can then start a Best Practices Analyzer scan using the same procedure discussed in Lesson 3, "Deploying Exchange Server 2007." However, you should ensure that the **Health Check** scan type is selected on the **Start a New Best Practices scan** page as shown in Figure 11-17.

Figure 11-17

Performing a Health Check Scan

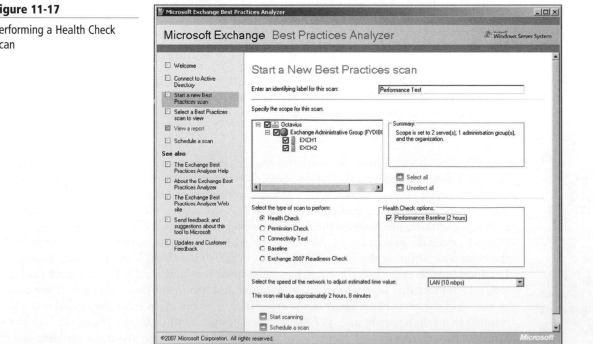

A Health Check scan in the Exchange Best Practices Analyzer examines key system files as well as events that are recorded in the Application event log to determine any performance or configuration problems. If you select **Performance Baseline (2 hours)** (see Figure 11-17), the Exchange Best Practices Analyzer will additionally test the activity of your Exchange server for up to two hours and examine the results within the Application event log.

If you click **Start scanning** (see Figure 11-17), the Health Check scan will run immediately. However, if you have selected the **Performance Baseline (2 hours)** option, it is a good practice to schedule the scan to run after working hours by selecting **Schedule a scan**.

After the Health Check scan has completed, you can view a report that lists any problems with the performance or configuration of your Exchange server organized by tabs. The All Issues tab shown in Figure 11-18 indicates that the SystemPages value is set too high and provides links to more information about the problem and how to resolve it.

Figure 11-18

Viewing a Health Check Report

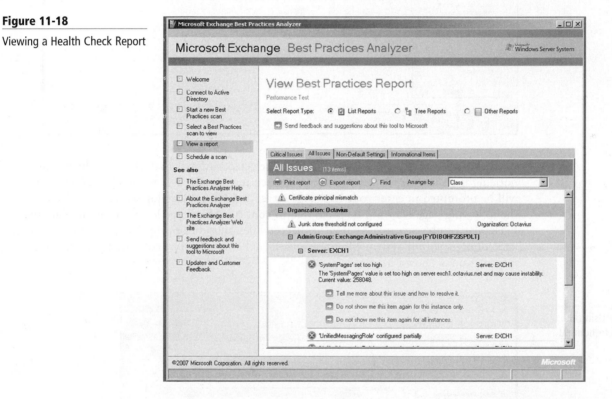

Monitoring Performance Using the Exchange Troubleshooting Assistant

By using the Performance Troubleshooter section of the Exchange Troubleshooting Assistant, you can quickly solve common performance problems. Based on your feedback, the Performance Troubleshooter automatically monitors key performance statistics and analyzes the results to identify the source of a performance problem.

The *Exchange Troubleshooting Assistant* is one of the most powerful tools for reactive monitoring in Exchange Server 2007 because it can automatically monitor and analyze performance information based on the nature of the performance problem. When one of your Exchange servers exhibits poor performance, you can start the Exchange Troubleshooting Assistant by navigating to the **Toolbox** node within the Exchange Management Console and double clicking on **Performance Troubleshooter** under the Performance tools section. When the Microsoft Exchange Troubleshooting Assistant opens, you can enter a name for your analysis, click **Next**, and select the nature of the performance problem as shown in Figure 11-19.

Figure 11-19

Selecting Performance Symptoms

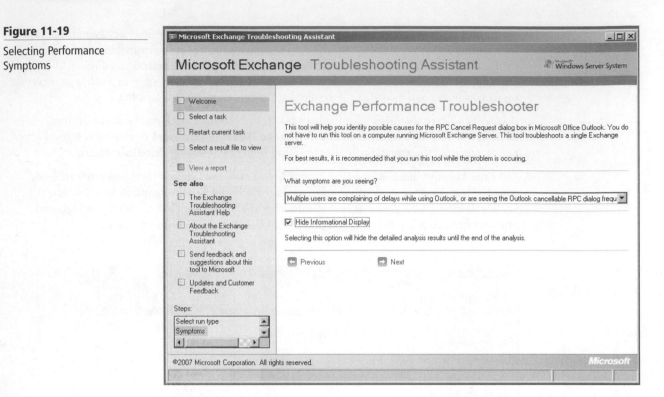

As illustrated by Figure 11-19, the symptom selected indicates that Outlook clients are noticing unusual delays when retrieving and sending emails. When you click **Next**, you will be prompted to enter your Exchange server and Global Catalog server names. On the following page, you will be prompted to confirm the storage location for any data the Exchange Troubleshooting Assistant collects while using the appropriate performance objects and counters within System Monitor, as well as the time to start collecting performance information as shown in Figure 11-20.

Figure 11-20

Collecting Data Using the Exchange Troubleshooting Assistant

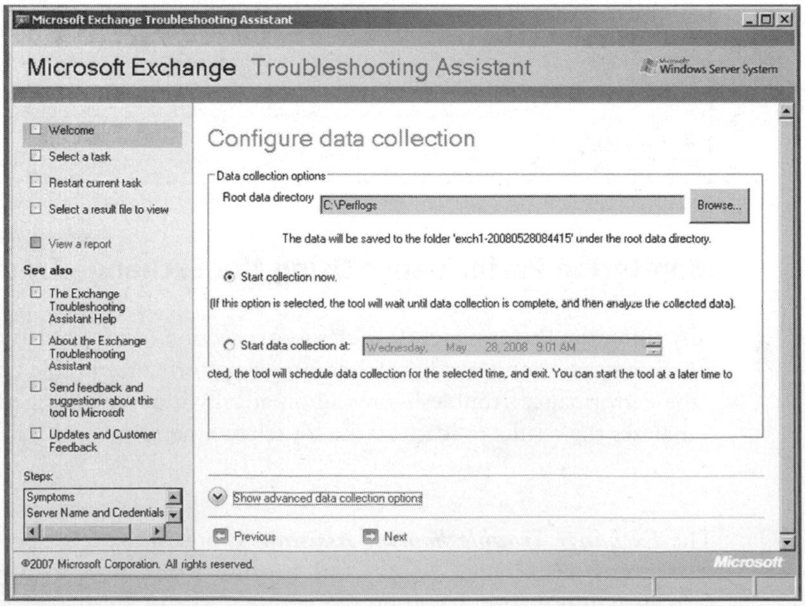

If you click **Next**, the Exchange Troubleshooting Assistant will start collecting data immediately from the Exchange server. It is best to ensure that this information is collected while the performance of the Exchange server is poor to allow the Exchange Troubleshooting Assistant to determine the areas of the server that are problematic. During the course of the collection, the Exchange Troubleshooting Assistant will periodically analyze the results and prompt you for more information that will be used to collect additional performance information. For example, in the screen shot in Figure 11-21, the Exchange Troubleshooting Assistant determined that there was an unusually large number of RPC requests, which indicated high client activity and required more information to determine the exact nature of the performance problem. After supplying this information, the Exchange Troubleshooting Assistant will continue collecting data to determine the exact nature of the problem.

Figure 11-21

Specifying Additional
Information

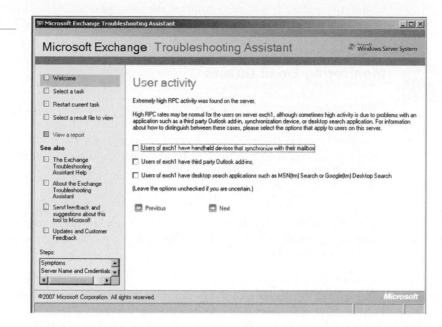

Once the Exchange Troubleshooting Assistant has finished collecting and analyzing performance data, it will present you with a report that organizes any problems by tabs. The report shown in Figure 11-22 indicates that one of the hard disks on the server is performing poorly and that there are too many clients currently connecting to the Exchange server. You can view more specific performance-related problems on the Performance Issues tab as well as possible solutions to the performance issues on the Recommendations tab. For the problems shown in Figure 11-22, replacing the affected hard disk and implementing an additional Exchange server to balance the traffic load are recommended.

Figure 11-22

Viewing Troubleshooting
Reports

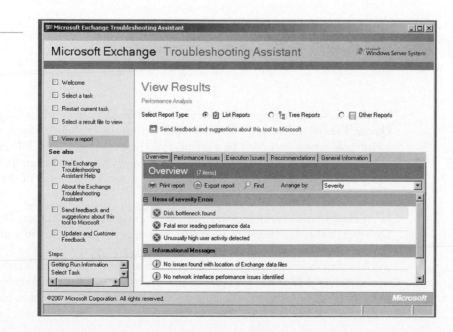

■ Monitoring Email

A key component to any Exchange administrator's job is monitoring email as it passes through the Edge and Hub role servers within the organization. More specifically, this includes monitoring email queues to identify email relay problems that prevent items from leaving the queue, as well as monitoring the message tracking logs to determine information about the emails that have already been relayed.

Monitoring Email Queues

You can easily monitor the email that is currently stored within the email queue databases on your Hub and Edge role servers by using cmdlets within the Exchange Management Shell or by using the graphical Queue Viewer utility. Before you monitor and troubleshoot email relay, you must first understand the types and function of the queues that are available in Exchange Server 2007.

Before emails are relayed by the Edge and Hub role servers in your organization, they are first stored in an *email queue* within an email queue database until the appropriate Exchange component can process them.

TAKE NOTE *

Non-Exchange programs can add email to the submission queue by placing email messages in the *pickup directory* on a Hub or Edge role server. By default, the pickup directory is C:\ Program Files\Microsoft\ Exchange Server\ TransportRoles\Pickup\.

When emails are first submitted to a Hub role server from other Exchange servers or email clients, those emails are stored in a *submission queue*. The *categorizer* component on each Hub or Edge role server examines the messages in the submission queue, expands any address lists, and then attempts to determine the target email server. If the target email server is within the same Exchange organization, the emails are placed in a *mailbox delivery queue* on the Hub role server where they can be delivered to the appropriate Mailbox role server using MAPI RPC requests. If the target email server is not within the same Exchange organization, the emails are placed in a *remote delivery queue* and the SMTP service then delivers the email to the target email server. If the target email server cannot be determined, or delivery fails for an extended period of time, then the emails are placed in an *unreachable queue*. Any emails that are potentially harmful to Exchange Server are placed in a *poison message queue* where they are suspended indefinitely.

TAKE NOTE *

The mailbox delivery queue only exists on Hub role servers within the Exchange organization. Any email that is sent between Hub and Edge role servers is placed within the remote delivery queue only.

You can view and manage the content of email queues on a Hub or Edge role server using the *Queue Viewer* utility in the Toolbox node within the Exchange Management Console. On a Hub role server, you must be a member of the Exchange View-Only Administrator role to view email queues and a member of the Exchange Organization Administrator role to manage email queues. On an Edge role server, you must be a member of the local Administrators group to view and manage email queues.

In an ideal environment, messages should be queued for a minimum amount of time. However, if there are network problems, messages could be stuck in a queue for a long period of time. If the target email server cannot be contacted, emails sent to a remote target domain will be stuck in the remote delivery queue. As a result, the Queue Viewer displays the submission queue as well as any messages within the mailbox delivery queue by target server name and any messages within the remote delivery queue by target domain name as shown in

Figure 11-23. If the number of target servers and remote domain names is large, you can click **Create Filter** (see Figure 11-23) to create a filter that narrows the list displayed using the criteria that you specify.

Figure 11-23

The Queue Viewer

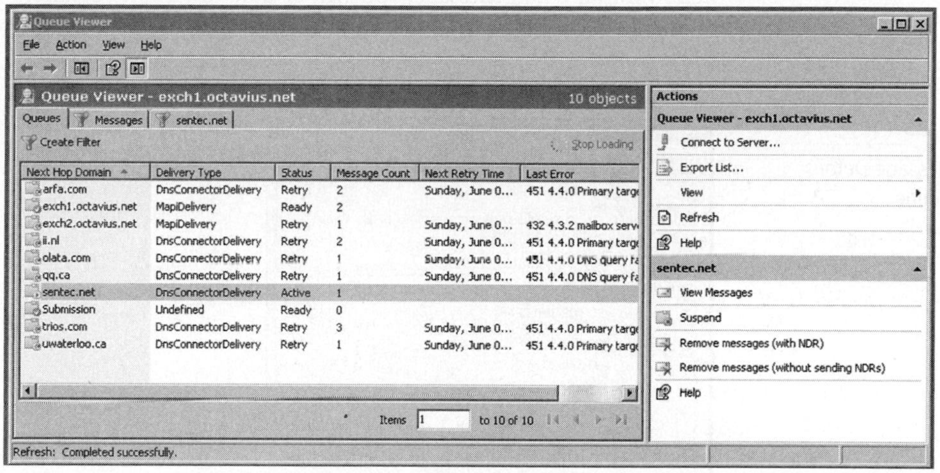

The unreachable and poison message queues only appear within the Queue Viewer when they contain messages.

The Queues tab shown in Figure 11-23 indicates that there are currently 0 messages in the submission queue, 3 email messages in the remote delivery queue (**DnsConnectorDelivery**) destined for a recipient in the trios.com domain, and two messages in the mailbox delivery queue (**MapiDelivery**) destined for the internal Mailbox role server exch1.octavius.net. The error number and message shown in the Last Error column can be searched within Exchange Server Help to determine why the messages are stuck in the queue. The **451** and **432** errors shown next to the trios.com domain and the exch2.octavius.net server indicate that an SMTP session could not be established to the target email server IP address. This type of problem may be the result of an unavailable target email server or network problems between the source and target email servers.

Moreover, the Status column shown in Figure 11-23 indicates the current state of the messages within the queue. The **Active** status indicates that Exchange is currently attempting to deliver messages whereas a status of **Ready** indicates that the messages are waiting to be processed in the mailbox or remote delivery queues. The **Retry** status indicates that Exchange has previously failed in delivering a message from the mailbox or remote delivery queue. If the problem persists for two days, those messages will be moved to the unreachable queue.

From the Queues tab shown in Figure 11-23, you can remove all the messages destined for a specific domain or Mailbox role server (with or without sending an NDR to the sender), as well as temporarily suspend or resume processing of the same messages by selecting the appropriate actions in the action pane. Alternatively, if you select **View Messages** in the action pane, an additional tab will be displayed to list the messages that are stored within the queue as shown for the trios.com remote delivery queue in Figure 11-24.

Figure 11-24

Viewing Details for a Single Queue

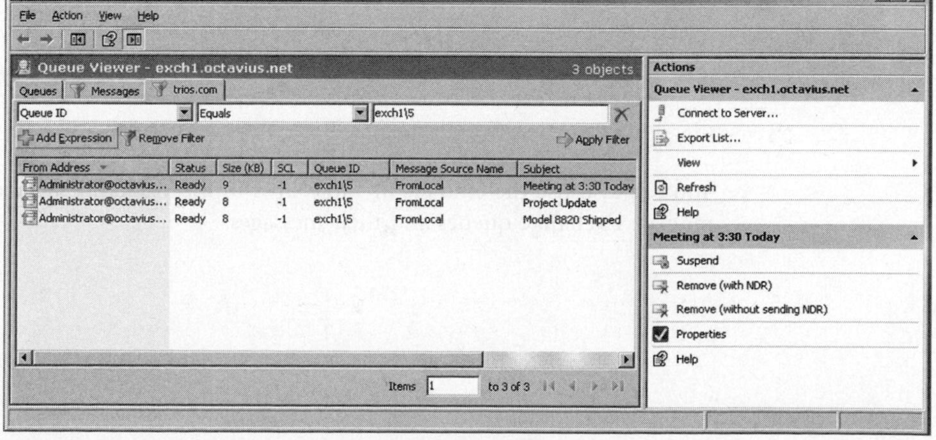

As with email queue entries, after highlighting an individual email message, you can remove it (with or without sending an NDR to the sender), as well as temporarily suspend or resume its processing by selecting the appropriate actions in the action pane. If you select the **Properties** action for an email message, you will be able to view its detailed information and recipients as shown in Figure 11-25.

Figure 11-25

Viewing Message Details within a Queue

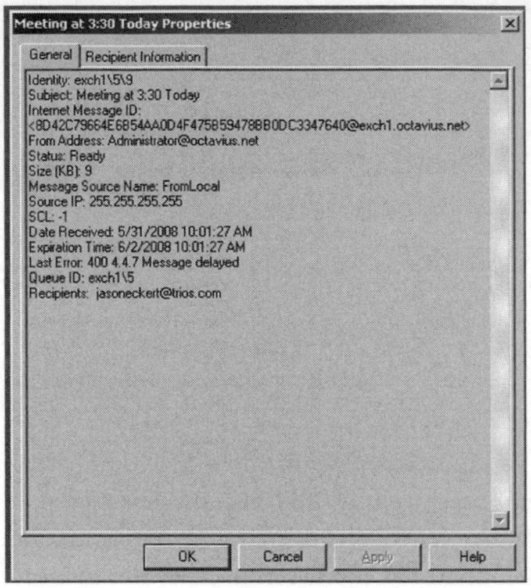

If you wish to search for messages that are not organized by destination domain or Mailbox server name, you can use the Messages tab of Queue Viewer as shown in Figure 11-26. Because the number of messages will typically be large, you should create a filter to narrow the list to only desired messages. The messages shown in Figure 11-26 include those received after 1:04 a.m. on May 31, 2008.

Figure 11-26

Viewing Queued Messages

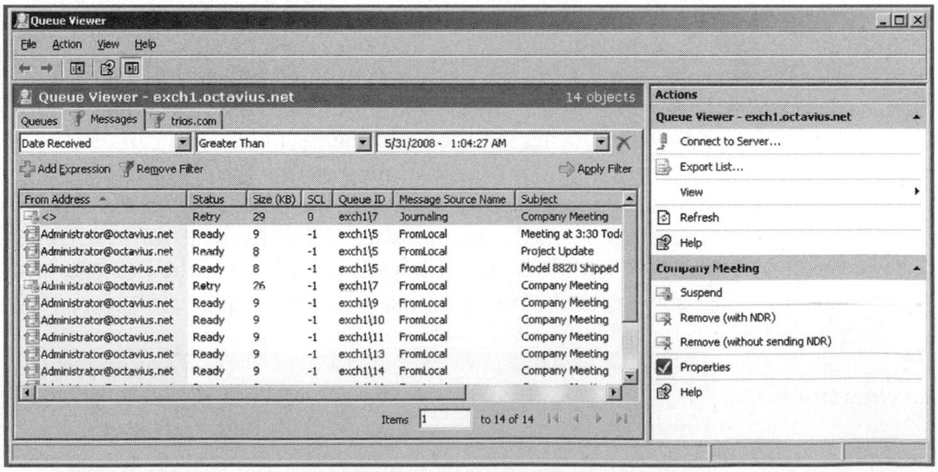

You can also use the cmdlets in Table 11-4 in the Exchange Management Shell to view and manage Exchange queues and their messages.

Table 11-4

Queue management cmdlets

CMDLET	DESCRIPTION
Get-Message	Lists email messages and message details in Exchange queues.
Remove-Message	Removes an email message from a queue. By default, an NDR is sent to the sender, but you can choose to modify this behavior using the –WithNDR $false option.
Suspend-Message	Suspends processing of an email message in an Exchange queue.
Resume-Message	Resumes processing of a suspended email message in an Exchange queue.
Export-Message	Saves a copy of an email message to a file in Outlook Email format (*.eml).
Get-Queue	Displays queue configuration.
Suspend-Queue	Suspends processing of all email messages in an Exchange queue.
Resume-Queue	Resumes processing of all suspended email messages in an Exchange queue.
Retry-Queue	Forces Exchange to retry delivery of messages in a queue that have a status of Retry. You can optionally specify the –Resubmit $true parameter to force the categorizer to reanalyze the email messages before the delivery.

Each of the cmdlets in Table 11-4 accept the **–Filter** option to allow you to specify the appropriate queues or messages. This is often useful when you need to view or remove specific email messages with certain properties shown in Figure 11-25. Available **–Filter** option operators include **–eq** (equals), **-ne** (does not equal), **-gt** (greater than), **-ge** (greater than or equal to), **-lt** (less than), **-le** (less than or equal to), **-like** (contains), and **–and** (used to combine criteria).

To view all email messages that have an SCL value of 7 or higher, you could run the following Exchange Management Shell command:

Get-Message –Filter {SCL –ge 7}

To remove those same email messages without sending an NDR to the sender, you could run the following Exchange Management Shell command:

Remove-Message –Filter {SCL –ge 7} –WithNDR $false

Similarly, to view all email messages that were sent from Administrator@octavius.net, you could run the following command within the Exchange Management Shell:

Get-Message –Filter {FromAddress –like Administrator@octavius.net}

This will produce output that will list each email message with the appropriate Identity (**server\queue_number\message_number**) as shown in Figure 11-27.

Figure 11-27

Viewing Queues Using the Exchange Management Shell

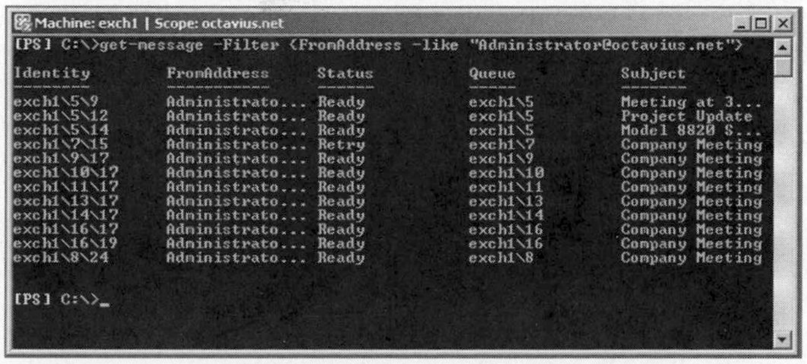

To remove an individual email message, you could then specify the appropriate Identity alongside the Remove-Message cmdlet. The following command will remove the third email message shown in Figure 11-27:

Remove-Message –Identity 'exch1\5\14'

Alternatively, you could run the following commands within the Exchange Management console to suspend the same email message (you will be prompted to confirm) and then export it to the file C:\Email_Audit.eml for later viewing:

Suspend-Message –Identity 'exch1\5\14'

Get-Message –Identity 'exch1\5\14' | Export-Message –Path 'C:\Email_Audit.eml'

Most email messages that are stuck in Exchange queues are the result of temporary network problems. After those problems have been solved, you could use the following command within the Exchange Management Shell to force outbound processing of all email messages that have a Retry status:

Retry-Queue –Filter {Status –eq "Retry"}

Alternatively, to force outbound processing only for email messages addressed to the trios.com domain that have a status of Retry, you could use the following command within the Exchange Management Shell:

Retry-Queue –Filter {NextHopDomain –eq "trios.com" –and Status –eq "Retry"}

In addition to using the Queue Viewer and queue management cmdlets, you can also use the Exchange Troubleshooting Assistant to troubleshoot queue-related problems. The Exchange Troubleshooting Assistant can be used to automatically analyze the contents of the queues on your Hub and Edge role servers as well as perform the appropriate tests to determine the cause of queue-related problems. Navigate to the **Toolbox** node within the Exchange Management Console and double click on **Mail Flow Troubleshooter** under the Mail flow tools section. When the Microsoft Exchange Troubleshooting Assistant opens, you can enter a name for your analysis and select an appropriate symptom as shown in Figure 11-28.

Figure 11-28

Starting the Mail Flow Troubleshooter

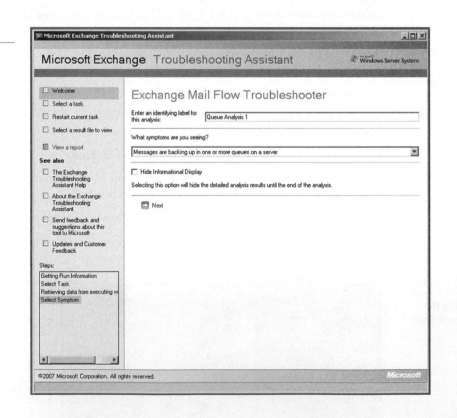

When you click **Next** (see Figure 11-28), you will be prompted to enter your Exchange server and Global Catalog server names. Following this, the Exchange Troubleshooting Assistant will analyze the contents of the queues and logs on the server. Based on the results, the Exchange Troubleshooting Assistant may also test DNS, Global Catalog, routing, and remote SMTP server connectivity, as well as the configuration of DNS, SMTP connectors, and third-party applications installed on the server. At various stages of the analysis, the Exchange Troubleshooting Assistant will display any errors that may indicate the root of the queue-related problem as shown in Figures 11-29 and 11-30 as well as a summary of all issues at the end of the analysis.

Figure 11-29

Viewing a DNS Report

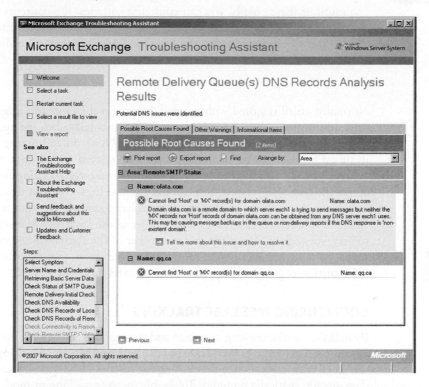

Figure 11-30

Viewing a Connectivity Report

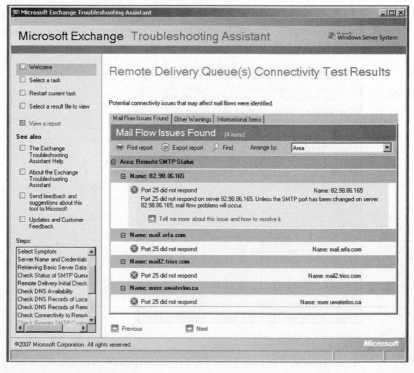

⊕ **MORE INFORMATION**

Because monitoring email queues can be time consuming, many Exchange administrators create performance alerts that send a network message to the Exchange administrator's workstation when the number of messages within email queues reaches a level that requires further investigation. One counter that can be used within an alert to monitor email queue size is **MSExchangesIS Mailbox\Messages Queued For Submission**.

CERTIFICATION READY?
Perform message tracking.
4.3

Tracking Messages

In a normal environment, most emails pass through the Edge and Hub role servers too quickly to be monitored by examining the contents of the email queue database. Instead, to monitor these emails, you can configure and view the contents of the message tracking logs on the Hub, Edge, and Mailbox role servers within your organization. Message tracking logs may be viewed using the Message Tracking graphical utility or cmdlets within the Exchange Management Shell.

Normally, email is stored within email queues on the Hub and Edge role servers within your organization for a short period of time before it is relayed to the appropriate destination. As a result, monitoring email queues is well suited for troubleshooting email relay problems and ill suited for monitoring the messages that are relayed within your organization. However, Hub, Edge, and Mailbox role servers maintain ***message tracking logs*** that list information about the messages relayed. You can query these logs to obtain detailed information about email relay or track the path that an email has taken within your organization. On a Hub or Mailbox role server, you must be a member of the Exchange View-Only Administrator role to view message tracking logs and a member of the Exchange Server Administrator role to manage message tracking logs. On an Edge role server, you must be a member of the local Administrators group to view and manage message tracking logs.

CONFIGURING MESSAGE TRACKING

By default, message tracking is enabled and message tracking logs are stored in the **C:\Program Files\Microsoft\Exchange Server\TransportRoles\Logs\MessageTracking** directory. A new log file is created each day or when the existing log reaches 10 MB in size and log files older than 30 days are automatically removed. To disable message tracking or modify the message tracking log directory path, you can navigate to the Log Settings tab within the properties of your Hub or Edge role server within the Exchange Management Console as shown in Figure 11-31.

Figure 11-31

Configuring Message Tracking Logs

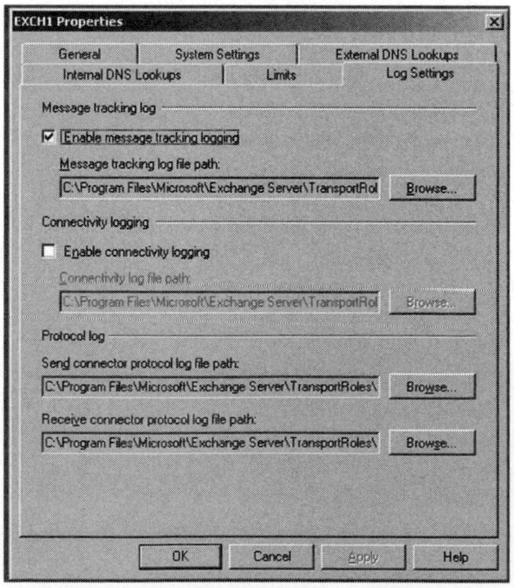

TAKE NOTE*

If you modify the message tracking log path, the target directory must grant the following NTFS permissions:

Administrator = Full Control

System = Full Control

Network Service = Read, Write, Delete Subfolders and Files

Alternatively, you could use the **Set-TransportServer** cmdlet within the Exchange Management Shell to configure message tracking on a Hub or Edge role server or the **Set-MailboxServer** cmdlet to configure message tracking on a Mailbox role server. These cmdlets accept the same options and can be used to configure all aspects of message tracking. To enable message tracking on the Hub role server EXCH1, set the message tracking directory to

D:\Message-Tracking, specify that new logs are created when existing logs reach 30 MB in size, limit the size of the message tracking log directory to 750 MB, and only remove logs that are older than 90 days, you could run the following command within the Exchange Management Shell:

Set-TransportServer EXCH1 -MessageTrackingLogEnabled:$true -MessageTrackingLogPath 'D:\Message-Tracking' -MessageTrackingLogMaxFileSize '30MB' -MessageTrackingLogMaxDirectorySize '750MB' -MessageTrackingLogMaxAge '90.00:00:00'

Although message tracking logs do not store the contents of email messages, they store the subject line of each email message by default. Because the subject line of email messages may contain confidential information, you could disable the message tracking logging of subject lines using the Set-TransportServer or Set-MailboxServer cmdlet. The following command disables subject line message tracking logging on the Mailbox role server EXCH3 when executed within the Exchange Management Shell:

Set-MailboxServer EXCH3 –MessageTrackingLogSubjectLoggingEnabled $false

VIEWING MESSAGE TRACKING LOGS

Because a typical Exchange server can easily process thousands of emails each day, it is too time consuming to analyze the contents of the message tracking logs manually. To analyze the message tracking logs on an Exchange server, you can use the **Get-MessageTrackingLog** cmdlet within the Exchange Management Shell or the Exchange Troubleshooting Assistant. To start the Exchange Troubleshooting Assistant for message tracking, navigate to the **Toolbox** node within the Exchange Management Console, double click on **Message Tracking** under the Mail flow tools section, and specify the appropriate parameters for selecting messages to track as shown in Figure 11-32.

Figure 11-32

Performing Message Tracking

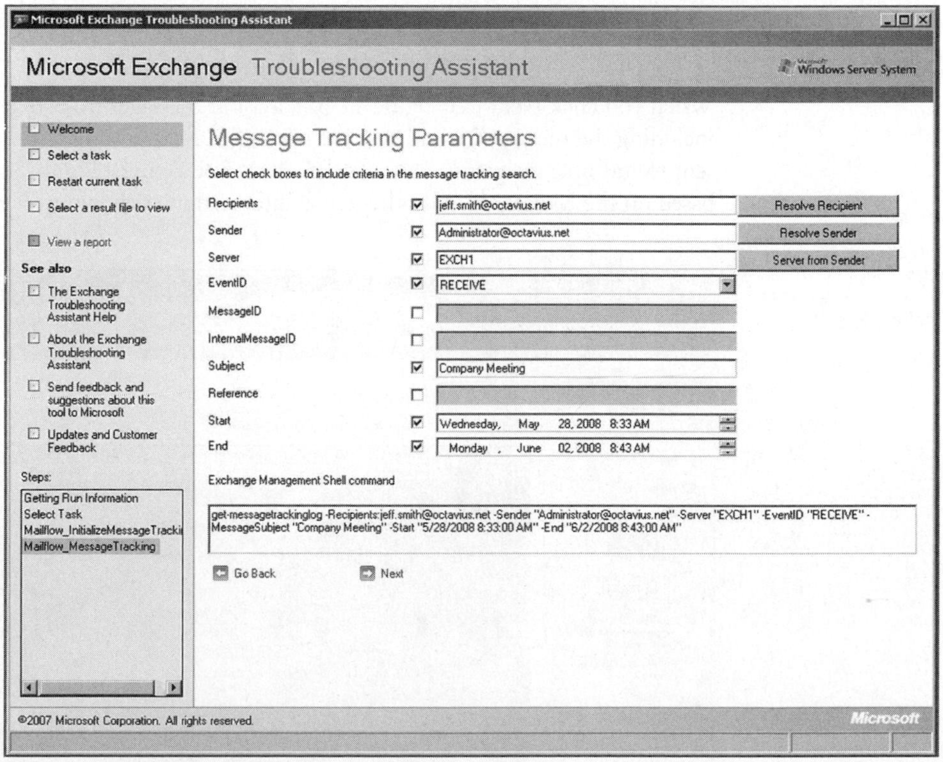

As illustrated by Figure 11-32, messages received by the server addressed to jeff.smith@ octavius.net and from Administrator@octavius.net with the subject line "Company Meeting" between May 28 and June 2 will be tracked. The EventID field within a message tracking analysis is used to identify the type of email message event to track. Table 11-5 lists the available events that can be chosen within the EventID field.

Table 11-5

Message tracking events

EVENT	DESCRIPTION
BADMAIL	Messages that cannot be delivered or returned.
DEFER	Messages that have been delayed for message delivery.
DELIVER	Messages that have been successfully delivered to a mailbox.
DSN	Messages that have generated a DSN (NDR).
EXPAND	Messages that have had a distribution group expanded by the transport server.
FAIL	Messages that cannot be delivered.
POISONMESSAGE	Messages that have entered the poison message queue.
RECEIVE	Messages that have been received by a transport server and have been entered into the queue database.
REDIRECT	Messages that were redirected to another recipient after an AD recipient lookup.
RESOLVE	Messages that were resolved to a different email address after an AD recipient lookup.
SEND	Messages that were sent to a target email server using SMTP.
SUBMIT	Messages that were submitted from a Mailbox role server to a Hub role server. SUBMIT messages are the only message type in a message tracking log on a Mailbox role server.
TRANSFER	Messages that were converted due to format, recipient, or spam agent limits.

When you click **Next** (see Figure 11-32), a list of messages from that time period will be displayed including the message identifier in the MessageId field as shown in Figure 11-33. If the email was sent to multiple recipients, you can click **Next** (see Figure 11-33) to generate an additional query based on the MessageId and other email information as shown in Figure 11-34.

Figure 11-33

Message Tracking Results

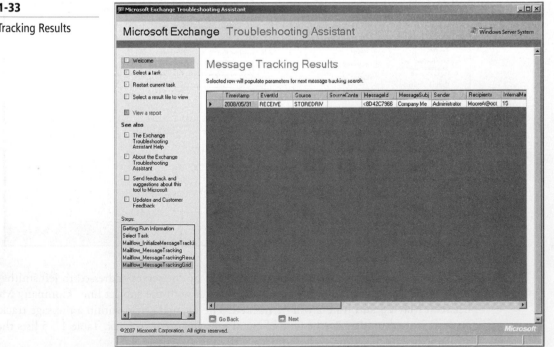

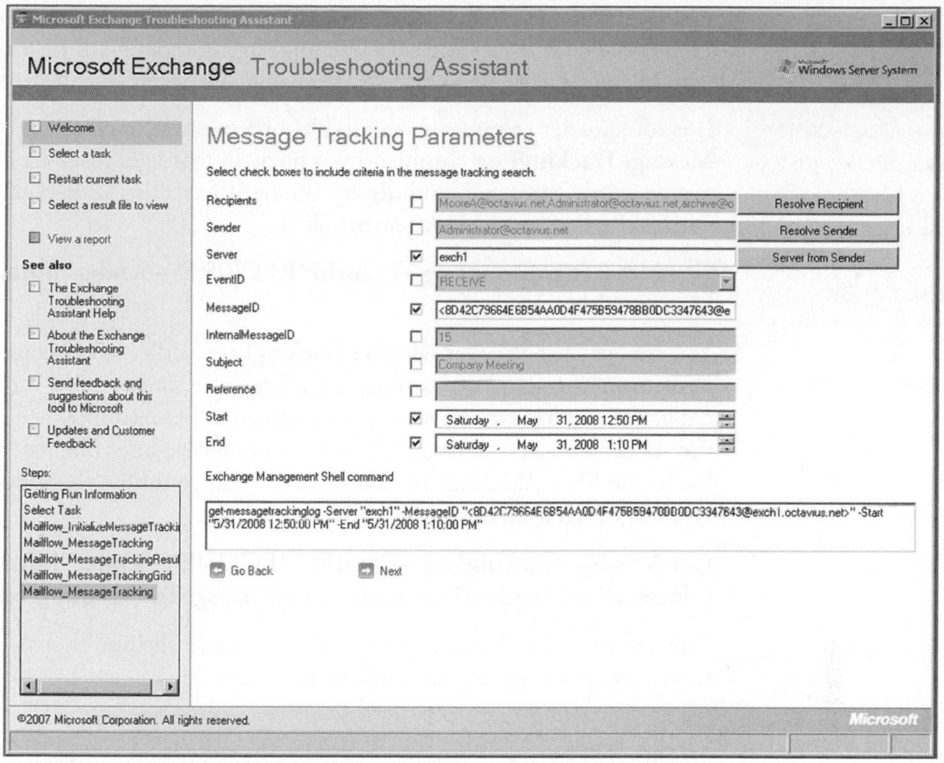

Figure 11-34

Performing Message Tracking
Using MessageID

When you press Next (see Figure 11-34), the second query will find all related email messages as shown in Figure 11-35.

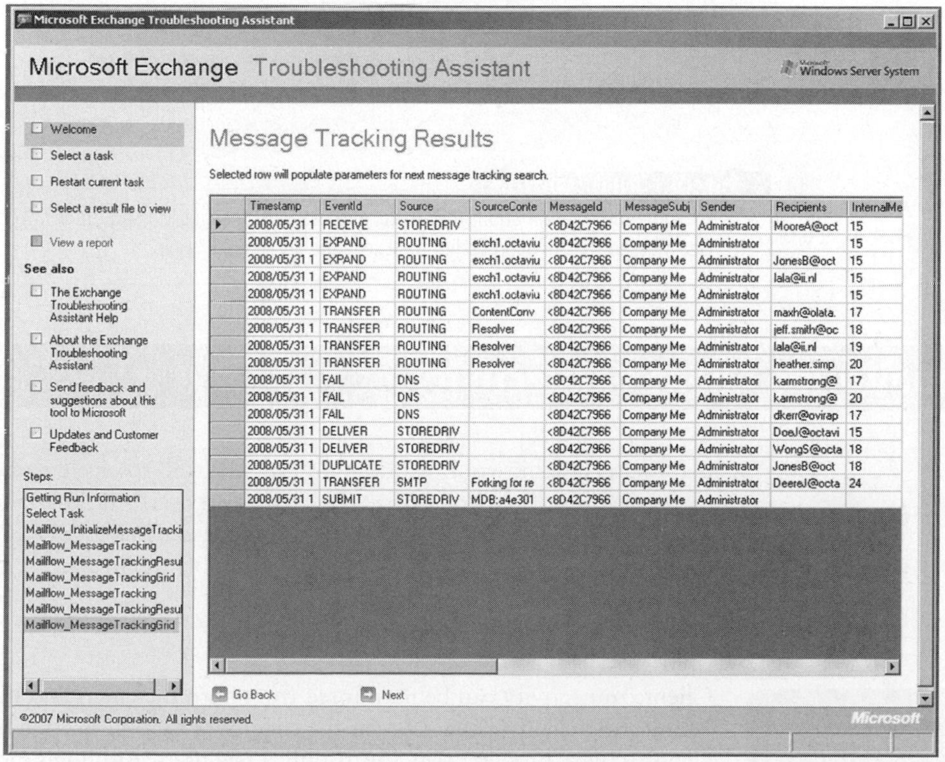

Figure 11-35

Viewing Similar Messages

TAKE NOTE *

The Get-Message
TrackingLog cmdlet
displays the first 1,000
log entries only. If you
anticipate a large
number of results, you
can use the **–ResultSize**
'Unlimited' option.

After selecting the appropriate message tracking parameters as shown in Figures 11-32 and
11-34, the related Get-MessageTrackingLog command will be displayed at the bottom of the
window and can be copied to the Exchange Management Shell or a text file for later usage.

It is often easier to interpret the results of a message tracking analysis using the **Get-
MessageTrackingLog** command. To track all messages received by the sender horace
.watersworth@mos.com and display the results as a list, you could use the following command
within the Exchange Management Shell:

**Get-MessageTrackingLog –EventId 'RECEIVE' –Sender 'horace.watersworth@mos.com'
| Format-List**

You can also use the Get-MessageTrackingLog cmdlet to generate a report of the emails that
pass through your Mailbox, Hub, and Edge role servers. This is often used when investigating
email activity for specific senders or recipients. For example, to track all messages received by
the sender horace.watersworth@mos.com and save only the Sender and Recipients fields in a
list to the file C:\MessageTrackingLog.txt, you could use the following command within the
Exchange Management Shell:

**Get-MessageTrackingLog –EventId 'RECEIVE' –Sender 'horace.watersworth@mos.com'
| Format-List Sender,Recipients > C:\MessageTrackingLog.txt**

This command will result in a text file similar to the one shown in Figure 11-36. You can
then view, print, or archive this text file.

Figure 11-36

Message TrackingLog.txt

```
MessageTrackingLog.txt - Notepad                                    _ □ ×
File  Edit  Format  View  Help
Sender      : horace.watersworth@mos.com
Recipients : {jason.eckert@trios.com}

Sender      : horace.watersworth@mos.com
Recipients : {MooreA@octavius.net, archive@octavius
             .net, bwilson@uwaterloo.ca, MartinB@octavius.net, DoeB@octavius.ne
             t, JonesB@octavius.net, cher@octavius.net, dkerr@ovirap.ca, Dord@o
             ctavius.net, DoeF@octavius.net, heather.simpson@arfa.com, Int-Mark
             eting@octavius.net, DoeJ@octavius.net, jeff.smith@octavius.net, je
             n.barber@octavius.net}

Sender      : horace.watersworth@mos.com
Recipients : {JonesB@octavius.net, WongS@octavius.net, DoeJ@octavius.net, jeff.
             smith@octavius.net, karmstrong@mips-in.com, MooreA@octavius.net, h
             eather.simpson@arfa.com}

Sender      : horace.watersworth@mos.com
Recipients : {jeff.smith@octavius.net, MooreA@octavius.net, DoeJ@octavius.net,
             JonesB@octavius.net, WongS@octavius.net}
```

✚ MORE INFORMATION

For more information about the syntax and usage of the Get-MessageTrackingLog cmdlet, search for
Get-MessageTrackingLog within the Exchange Server 2007 Help.

■ Monitoring Client Connectivity

↓
THE BOTTOM LINE

Before users within your organization can send and receive emails, their email client
programs must first connect to an Exchange server. To troubleshoot email access problems,
you must first understand the tools and procedures that can be used to monitor client
connectivity. In addition, monitoring the number of clients that connect can also be used
for capacity planning.

CERTIFICATION READY?
Monitor client
connectivity.
4.4

Client connectivity can be monitored from both the client and the Exchange server.
Monitoring client connectivity at the client workstation is often useful when troubleshooting
a connectivity problem that affects only a few users. Although monitoring client connectivity
on the Exchange server can be used to troubleshoot connectivity problems, it is often used to
audit client access requests as well as determine the number of client access requests for future
capacity planning.

Monitoring Client Connectivity from a Client Computer

Monitoring client connectivity from a client computer is often performed when trouble-shooting a connectivity problem that prevents a user from sending or receiving email. You can use standard Windows utilities or Outlook to test connectivity from a client computer.

When troubleshooting an email client that cannot retrieve or send email from an email server, you should first check the email account settings within the properties of the email client program to ensure that the information is correct. Next, you should test to see whether the email client can successfully contact the email server. To do this, you can perform the following actions in this order:

1. Open a command prompt and type **ping *IP_Address*** where ***IP_Address*** is the IP address of the Exchange server. If you do not receive any replies from the Exchange server, then the target Exchange server is unavailable or there is a network problem that is preventing TCP/IP packets from reaching the target server such as a firewall that blocks ICMP ping echo requests.

2. Open a command prompt and type **ping *name*** where ***name*** is the DNS or NetBIOS name of the Exchange server registered in DNS. If you do not receive any replies from the Exchange server, then DNS or NetBIOS name resolution problems are preventing your client computer from contacting the Exchange server. You should then check your Exchange server record in the DNS and WINS databases as well as clear any incorrect entries within your DNS and NetBIOS name caches on the email client computer. To clear the DNS cache, you can run the command **ipconfig/flushdns** from a command prompt. To clear the NetBIOS name cache, you can run the command **nbtstat –R** from a command prompt. You can also clear all caches on your computer by navigating to **Start** > **Control Panel** > **Network Connections**, right click the appropriate network connection, and select **Repair**.

3. To test IMAP4, POP3, or SMTP connections, open a command prompt and type **telnet *IP_Address port*** where ***IP_Address*** is the IP address of the Exchange server and ***port*** is the port number of the IMAP4, POP3, or SMTP service. If you are unable to receive a response from the server using the **telnet** command, the IMAP4, POP3, or SMTP service is unavailable on the server or a firewall is blocking traffic between the client computer and the Exchange server.

4. Temporarily stop or uninstall any firewall, firewall-related software, or IPSec encryption policies on the client computer to ensure that they are not preventing communication with the Exchange server.

TAKE NOTE*

The notification area of Windows is often called the system tray.

For Outlook clients, you can also obtain information about your connection to your Exchange server by opening the Connection Status window. While holding down the Ctrl key, right click the Outlook icon within the notification area in the lower right corner of the Windows desktop and select **Connection Status**. The Microsoft Exchange Connection Status window will open to display connection statistics as well as allow you to reconnect your email client to the Exchange server as shown in Figure 11-37.

Figure 11-37

Viewing Outlook Connection Status

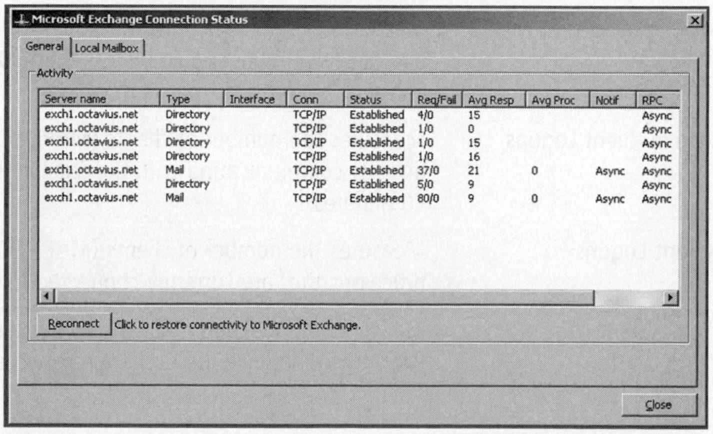

Sometimes, the Autodiscover service may cause problems with Outlook 2007 clients that prevent it from connecting to the correct Exchange server. To test the Autodiscover service from an Outlook 2007 client, hold down the Ctrl key, right click the Outlook icon within the notification area in the lower right corner of the Windows desktop and select **Test E-Mail AutoConfiguration**. In the Test E-Mail AutoConfiguration window that appears, click **Test** to ensure that your Outlook 2007 client is obtaining the correct information as shown in Figure 11-38.

Figure 11-38

Testing AutoConfiguration

Monitoring Client Connectivity from Exchange Server

System Monitor and counter logs can be used to monitor client connectivity from the Exchange servers within your organization to obtain capacity planning information. In addition, you can use protocol logging on your Hub role servers to monitor SMTP requests from POP3 and IMAP4 clients as well as cmdlets on your CAS role servers to monitor MAPI, Outlook Anywhere, OWA, POP3, and IMAP4 connectivity for troubleshooting purposes.

USING PERFORMANCE STATISTICS

The easiest way to obtain capacity planning information is by gathering and analyzing system statistics on the Exchange servers within your organization. By adding the appropriate counters within System Monitor or within a counter log, you can monitor the number and type of connections from client computers during a specific period of time. Table 11-6 lists some common counters that may be used to monitor client connectivity on the Exchange servers within your organization that host the CAS or Hub role.

Table 11-6

Common System Monitor statistics for monitoring client connectivity

PERFORMANCE OBJECT	COUNTER	DESCRIPTION
MSExchangeIS	RPC Requests	Measures the number of MAPI requests from email clients. The average of this number should be less than 30 on a typical Exchange server.
MSExchangeIS Mailbox	Active Client Logons	Measures the number of clients (MAPI, POP3, IMAP4) that were actively communicating with the Exchange server during the last 10 minutes.
MSExchangeIS Mailbox	Client Logons	Measures the number of clients (MAPI, POP3, IMAP4) and system processes that are currently connected to the Exchange server.
MSExchangeIS Mailbox	Peak Client Logons	Measures the maximum number of concurrent client logons (MAPI, POP3, IMAP4) since the Exchange services have been started.

Table 11-6

PERFORMANCE OBJECT	COUNTER	DESCRIPTION
MSExchangePOP3	Connections Current	Measures the number of currently open POP3 connections from client computers.
MSExchangePOP3	Connections Total	Measures the total number of POP3 connections from client computers since the POP3 service was started.
MSExchangePOP3	Active SSL Connections	Measures the number of currently open POP3 connections that use SSL or TLS from client computers.
MSExchangeIMAP4	Current Connections	Measures the number of currently open IMAP4 connections from client computers.
MSExchangeIMAP4	Total Connections	Measures the total number of IMAP4 connections from client computers since the IMAP4 service was started.
MSExchangeIMAP4	Active SSL Connections	Measures the number of currently open IMAP4 connections that use SSL or TLS from client computers.

It is important to monitor the number of concurrent client connections on your Exchange servers using the appropriate counters in Table 11-6 to determine the load that your Exchange servers are experiencing from client connections. As this load increases, you should carefully monitor CPU, disk, and memory counters to determine when it may be necessary to add additional CPUs, disks, memory, or deploy additional Exchange servers to distribute the load.

If your Exchange server has more hardware capacity than needed by the current system load, you can also modify client connection parameters to remedy connection errors. By default, the POP3 and IMAP4 services in Exchange Server 2007 each allow for a maximum of 2,000 concurrent connections, including a maximum of 10 concurrent connections from a single user and 20 concurrent connections from a single IP address. If POP3 and IMAP4 clients are unable to connect during peak usage times, you may need to increase the maximum number of connections that the POP3 and IMAP4 services will accept. If POP3 and IMAP4 clients reside behind a NAT router or proxy server (which connect to Exchange using a single public IP address), you may need to increase the maximum concurrent connections from a single IP address.

You can modify the maximum number of connections for the POP3 or IMAP4 service by accessing the Connection tab of POP3 or IMAP4 properties within the Exchange Management Console or by using the Set-POPSettings or Set-IMAPSettings cmdlets within the Exchange Management Shell as discussed in Lesson 8, "Configuring Email Protocols and Transport Rules."

USING PROTOCOL LOGS

You can also monitor the SMTP email requests sent by POP3 and IMAP4 clients by examining *protocol logs*. Protocol logs are comma-delimited text files that can be viewed easily using a text editor or imported into an SQL database or applications such as Microsoft Excel. By default, SMTP protocol logging is disabled for all send and receive connectors on the Hub and Edge role servers within your organization and must be enabled on a connector-by-connector basis. To enable and manage protocol logs on a Hub role server, you must be a member of the Exchange Server Administrator role. To enable and manage protocol logs on an Edge role server, you must be a member of the local Administrators group.

For example, your Hub role server (EXCH1) has a receive connector called 'Client EXCH1' that receives SMTP email from the POP3 and IMAP4 clients within your organization. To enable protocol logging on this connector, you can select **Verbose** in the properties of the connector under the **Server Configuration > Hub Transport** node within the Exchange Management Console as shown in Figure 11-39.

Figure 11-39

Enabling Protocol Logging

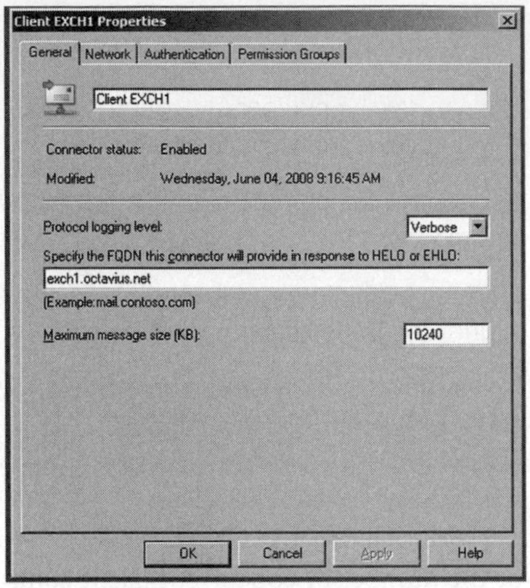

Alternatively, you could run the following command within the Exchange Management Shell to enable protocol logging on this connector:

Set-ReceiveConnector 'Client EXCH1' –ProtocolLoggingLevel 'Verbose'

The **–ProtocolLoggingLevel** option only accepts two values: **Verbose** (enable logging) and **None** (disable logging). By default, protocol logs for receive connectors are stored in the **C:\Program Files\Microsoft\Exchange Server\TransportRoles\Logs\ProtocolLog\ SmtpReceive** directory. A new protocol log file is created each day or when the existing log reaches 10 MB in size, and log files older than 30 days are automatically removed. You can change the location for protocol logs using the Logging tab of server properties within the Exchange Management Console as shown in Figure 11-31 or by using the Set-TransportServer cmdlet within the Exchange Management Shell. The Set-TransportServer cmdlet can also be used to modify other properties of protocol logging. To set the receive connector protocol logging directory to D:\SMTP-Receive-Log on the server EXCH1, specify that new logs are created when existing logs reach 30 MB in size, limit the size of the receive connector protocol log directory to 750 MB, and only remove logs that are older than 90 days, you could run the following command within the Exchange Management Shell:

Set-TransportServer 'EXCH1' -ReceiveProtocolLogPath 'D:\SMTP-Receive-Log' -ReceiveProtocolLogMaxFileSize '30MB' -ReceiveProtocolLogMaxDirectorySize '750MB' -ReceiveProtocolLogMaxAge '90.00:00:00'

⊕ **MORE INFORMATION**

Although not related to client connection monitoring, you can enable send connector protocol logging within send connector properties in the Exchange Management Console or by using the **Set-SendConnector** cmdlet. The location for send connector protocol logging can be set on the Logging tab of server properties in the Exchange Management Console or by using the **Set-TransportServer** cmdlet. The Set-TransportServer cmdlet may also be used to configure other protocol logging options for send connectors.

For more information on how to use the Set-SendConnector and Set-TransportServer cmdlets, search for their names within Exchange Server 2007 Help.

After you have configured protocol logging on your receive connector, you can examine the receive connector protocol logs. The top of the log file contains comment lines (starting with a # character) that define the data that is stored in each column as shown in Figure 11-40. Because each SMTP event during a client SMTP session is logged to the protocol log, the log file may contain thousands of entries. As a result, it is best to import the contents of the protocol log into another program that can be used to view and sort the entries.

Figure 11-40

Viewing a Protocol Log

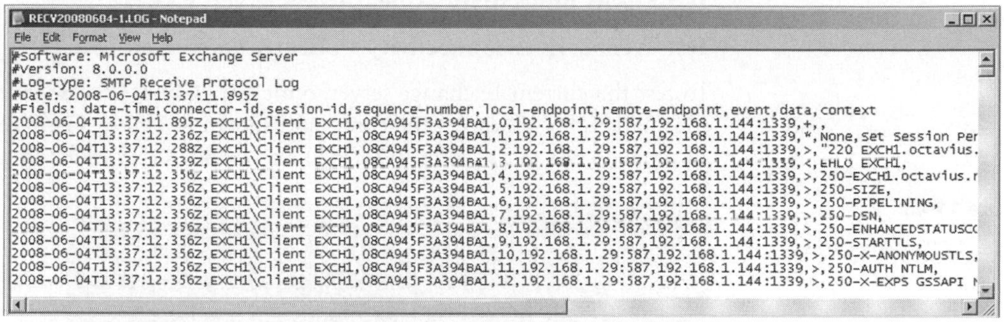

```
RECV20080604-1.LOG - Notepad
File Edit Format View Help
#Software: Microsoft Exchange Server
#Version: 8.0.0.0
#Log-type: SMTP Receive Protocol Log
#Date: 2008-06-04T13:37:11.895Z
#Fields: date-time,connector-id,session-id,sequence-number,local-endpoint,remote-endpoint,event,data,context
2008-06-04T13:37:11.895Z,EXCH1\Client EXCH1,08CA945F3A394BA1,0,192.168.1.29:587,192.168.1.144:1339,+,,
2008-06-04T13:37:12.236Z,EXCH1\Client EXCH1,08CA945F3A394BA1,1,192.168.1.29:587,192.168.1.144:1339,*,None,Set Session Per
2008-06-04T13:37:12.288Z,EXCH1\Client EXCH1,08CA945F3A394BA1,2,192.168.1.29:587,192.168.1.144:1339,>,"220 EXCH1.octavius.
2008-06-04T13:37:12.339Z,EXCH1\Client EXCH1,08CA945F3A394BA1,3,192.168.1.29:587,192.168.1.144:1339,<,EHLO EXCH1,
2008-06-04T13:37:12.356Z,EXCH1\Client EXCH1,08CA945F3A394BA1,4,192.168.1.29:587,192.168.1.144:1339,>,250-EXCH1.octavius.r
2008-06-04T13:37:12.356Z,EXCH1\Client EXCH1,08CA945F3A394BA1,5,192.168.1.29:587,192.168.1.144:1339,>,250-SIZE,
2008-06-04T13:37:12.356Z,EXCH1\Client EXCH1,08CA945F3A394BA1,6,192.168.1.29:587,192.168.1.144:1339,>,250-PIPELINING,
2008-06-04T13:37:12.356Z,EXCH1\Client EXCH1,08CA945F3A394BA1,7,192.168.1.29:587,192.168.1.144:1339,>,250-DSN,
2008-06-04T13:37:12.356Z,EXCH1\Client EXCH1,08CA945F3A394BA1,8,192.168.1.29:587,192.168.1.144:1339,>,250-ENHANCEDSTATUSCO
2008-06-04T13:37:12.356Z,EXCH1\Client EXCH1,08CA945F3A394BA1,9,192.168.1.29:587,192.168.1.144:1339,>,250-STARTTLS,
2008-06-04T13:37:12.356Z,EXCH1\Client EXCH1,08CA945F3A394BA1,10,192.168.1.29:587,192.168.1.144:1339,>,250-X-ANONYMOUSTLS,
2008-06-04T13:37:12.356Z,EXCH1\Client EXCH1,08CA945F3A394BA1,11,192.168.1.29:587,192.168.1.144:1339,>,250-AUTH NTLM,
2008-06-04T13:37:12.356Z,EXCH1\Client EXCH1,08CA945F3A394BA1,12,192.168.1.29:587,192.168.1.144:1339,>,250-X-EXPS GSSAPI N
```

USING CMDLETS

As a member of the Exchange Server Administrator role, you can also test client connectivity to the Exchange servers within your organization using cmdlets within the Exchange Management Shell on the server itself. For example, to ensure that MAPI requests can be processed by your server for all mailbox databases, you can run the **Test-MAPIConnectivity** cmdlet from the Exchange Management Shell on the Exchange server as shown in Figure 11-41.

Figure 11-41

Testing MAPI Connectivity

```
Machine: exch1 | Scope: octavius.net
[PS] C:\>Test-MAPIConnectivity | Format-list

Server       : EXCH1
StorageGroup : First Storage Group
Database     : Mailbox Database
Mailbox      : SystemMailbox{06C81C5F-2D28-40EA-9C43-AE7724E5977A}
Result       : Success
Latency      : 00:00:00.0084781
Error        :

Server       : EXCH1
StorageGroup : Fourth Storage Group
Database     : Mailbox Database 4
Mailbox      : SystemMailbox{84CADECA-F8AD-4E9A-AEC3-DC1EE4C60913}
Result       : Success
Latency      : 00:00:00.0079367
Error        :

Server       : EXCH1
StorageGroup : Third Storage Group
Database     : Marketing Mailbox Database
Mailbox      : SystemMailbox{BD5875C4-BCAD-41C8-AD7C-B9F8937DA59B}
Result       : *FAILURE*
Latency      : 00:00:00
Error        : Database is dismounted.
```

If a test fails, the Test-MAPIConnectivity output will identify the cause of the error. As Figure 11-41 illustrates, the Marketing Mailbox Database in the Third Storage Group failed a MAPI test because the database was dismounted.

If a particular client is having trouble connecting to your Exchange servers using MAPI, you can run the Test-MAPIConnectivity cmdlet for that user alone. For example, running the **Get-Mailbox 'Jeff Smith' | Test-MAPIConnectivity | Format-List** command in the Exchange Management Shell will test MAPI connectivity only for the user Jeff Smith and generate a list of the results as shown in Figure 11-42.

Figure 11-42

Testing MAPI Connectivity for a Single User

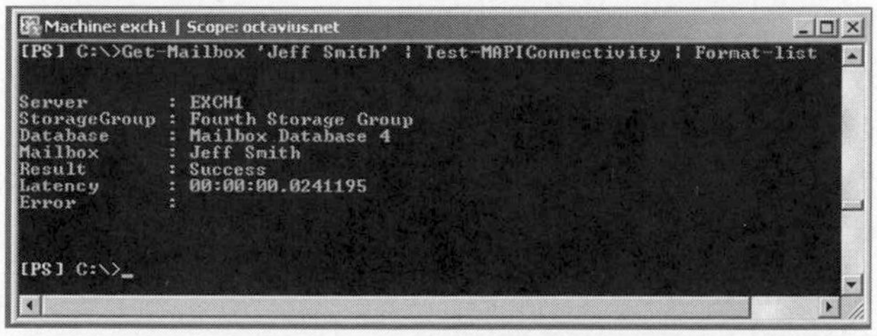

```
Machine: exch1 | Scope: octavius.net
[PS] C:\>Get-Mailbox 'Jeff Smith' | Test-MAPIConnectivity | Format-list

Server       : EXCH1
StorageGroup : Fourth Storage Group
Database     : Mailbox Database 4
Mailbox      : Jeff Smith
Result       : Success
Latency      : 00:00:00.0241195
Error        :

[PS] C:\>_
```

You can also test POP3, IMAP4, OWA, and Outlook Anywhere functionality using the **Test-POPConnectivity**, **Test-IMAPConnectivity**, **Test-OWAConnectivity**, and

Test-WebServicesConnectivity cmdlets within the Exchange Management Shell respectively. For example, the following commands will test the POP3, IMAP4, OWA, and Outlook Anywhere connectivity for all mailboxes on the CAS role server EXCH1:

Test-POPConnectivity –ClientAccessServer 'EXCH1'

Test-IMAPConnectivity –ClientAccessServer 'EXCH1'

Test-OWAConnectivity –ClientAccessServer 'EXCH1'

Test-WebServicesConnectivity –ClientAccessServer 'EXCH1'

To test the current Exchange server, omit the **–ClientAccessServer** option to each of these commands. For example, the command shown in Figure 11-43 tests POP3 connectivity for all users on the local server (EXCH1) and displays the results in a list format.

Figure 11-43

Testing POP3 Connectivity

The **Test-POPConnectivity**, **Test-IMAPConnectivity**, **Test-OWAConnectivity,** and **Test-WebServicesConnectivity** cmdlets use a sample system user account for testing client connectivity to all mailboxes on a specified CAS role server. If you receive an error when using these cmdlets, you may need to create a new system user account for testing by running the **New-TestCASConnectivityUser.ps1** script in the Exchange Management Shell.

TAKE NOTE*

Because POP3, IMAP4, OWA, and Outlook Anywhere connections are processed differently than MAPI connections, you must provide sample credentials along with the cmdlet if you wish to test POP3, IMAP4, OWA, or Outlook Anywhere connectivity for a single user. For example, to test Jeff Smith's ability to interact with the POP3, IMAP4, OWA, and Outlook Anywhere services on the CAS role server EXCH1 in the Octavius domain, you could run the following commands within the Exchange Management Shell:

Test-POPConnectivity –ClientAccessServer 'EXCH1' –MailboxCredential: (Get-Credential octavius\jeff.smith)

Test-IMAPConnectivity –ClientAccessServer 'EXCH1' –MailboxCredential: (Get-Credential octavius\jeff.smith)

Test-OWAConnectivity –ClientAccessServer 'EXCH1' –MailboxCredential: (Get-Credential octavius\jeff.smith)

Test-WebServicesConnectivity –ClientAccessServer 'EXCH1' –MailboxCredential: (Get-Credential octavius\jeff.smith)

After executing each of these commands, you will be prompted to supply the password for Jeff Smith.

■ Creating Reports

A vital part of any Exchange administrator's job is recording information related to the configuration and usage of the Exchange servers within the organization. This information is useful when troubleshooting problems, performing capacity planning, and acclimating new administrators to the structure of your Exchange organization. To create most reports, you must at a minimum be a member of the Exchange View-Only Administrator role. For Edge role servers, members of the local Administrators group can generate reports.

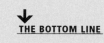

CERTIFICATION READY?
Create usage reports.
4.6

Creating Usage Reports

As an Exchange administrator, you must create regular reports that detail the usage of mailboxes, databases, queues, and protocols. This allows you to monitor storage capacity and limits as well as identify problems with client access and email queuing. Exchange Server 2007 comes with a rich set of cmdlets that may be used within the Exchange Management Shell to generate reports of mailbox, queue, and protocol usage. However, to generate a robust report, you must be able to select the appropriate data as well as display it in an easy-to-interpret way.

MAILBOX USAGE

To successfully manage the mailboxes and mailbox limits within your organization, you must first obtain information regarding mailbox usage. For example, in order to obtain the detailed information for Jeff Smith's mailbox including the last log on, database name, mailbox size, and item count, you could send the output of the Get-MailboxStatistics cmdlet to the Format-List cmdlet using the piping feature of the Exchange Management Shell. The following command within the Exchange Management Shell will achieve this and produce the output shown in Figure 11-44:

Get-MailboxStatistics –Identity 'Jeff Smith' | Format-List

Figure 11-44

Viewing Mailbox Statistics for a Single User

Because it is more practical to obtain a report that lists the mailbox details for each user, you can omit the **–Identity** option to the Get-MailboxStatistics cmdlet. In addition, you can use output redirection feature of the Exchange Management Shell to save a copy of the report to a file that could be printed or imported into another program. For example, to save the mailbox details for all mailboxes on your Mailbox role server in list format to a text file called 'C:\MailboxStatsList.txt', you could run the following command within the Exchange Management Shell:

Get-MailboxStatistics | Format-List > 'C:\MailboxStatsList.txt'

Following this, you could open the C:\MailboxStatsList.txt file in a text editor or word processor program as shown in Figure 11-45 to reformat it as necessary for presentation or printing.

Figure 11-45

MailboxStatsList.txt

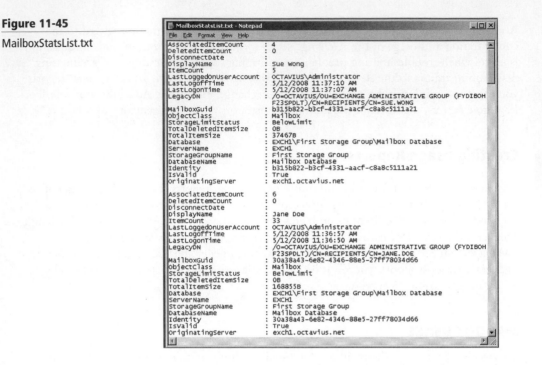

For quick comparison of values, it is often better to obtain output in table format. Table format is the default format for most cmdlets. For example, to save the mailbox details for all mailboxes on your Mailbox role server in table format to a text file called 'C:\MailboxStatsTable.txt,' you could run the following command within the Exchange Management Shell:

Get-MailboxStatistics > 'C:\MailboxStatsTable.txt'

However, if you open the C:\MailboxStatsTable.txt file in a text editor, you will see only the fields that could be displayed within the Exchange Management Shell terminal screen only. As a result, table format is useful when you need to display only a few fields. For example, the following command only displays the DisplayName, ItemCount, and TotalItemSize fields from the Get-MailboxStatistics command in the previous example:

Get-MailboxStatistics | Select-Object DisplayName,ItemCount,TotalItemSize > 'C:\MailboxStatsTable.txt'

Following this command, you can open the C:\MailboxStatsTable.txt file in a text editor to view a report that lists only three fields for each mailbox in table format as shown in Figure 11-46.

Figure 11-46

MailboxStatsTable.txt

```
MailboxStatsTable.txt - Notepad
File Edit Format View Help

DisplayName              ItemCount TotalItemSize
-----------              --------- -------------
Sue Wong                         5 37467KB
Jane Doe                        33 168855KB
Bob Jones                       10 80656KB
Adel Moore                       9 60565KB
Bob Doe                          9 68542KB
Administrator                  152 5958641KB
Billy Martin                    80 8431096KB
Jen Barber                       3 27356KB
Jeff Smith                      58 8334034KB
```

The list and table formats are well suited to importing data into a word processing document (e.g., Microsoft Word) or into a presentation (e.g., Microsoft PowerPoint). However, if you wish to perform detailed analysis, graphing, or calculation on this data using a spreadsheet program (e.g., Microsoft Excel) or database (e.g., SQL Server), it is best to save your output in comma-separated text file format (CSV) using the Export-CSV cmdlet. Although the

Export-CSV cmdlet preserves all data fields during export, it also adds a label header that identifies the program that generated it. Because this label header should not be imported into other programs, you can omit it by appending the **–NoType** option to the Export-CSV cmdlet.

To obtain mailbox details for all mailboxes on your Mailbox role server and save the output to the CSV file C:\MailboxStats.csv without a label header, you could run the following cmdlet within the Exchange Management Shell:

Get-MailboxStatistics | Export-CSV 'C:\MailboxStats.csv' -NoType

Next, you can open the MailboxStats.csv file in a spreadsheet program or import it into a SQL database for analysis. Figure 11-47 shows the C:\MailboxStats.csv file within Microsoft Excel.

Figure 11-47

MailboxStats.csv

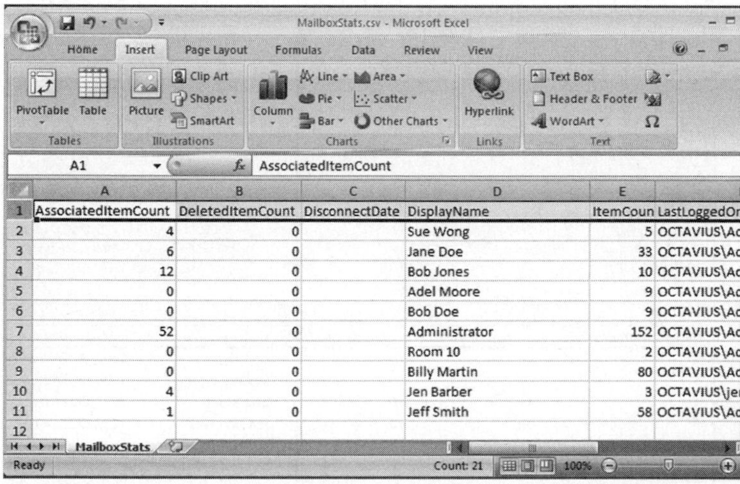

If you want to obtain mailbox details for mailboxes that reside within a single database or storage group only, you can add the appropriate option to the Get-MailboxStatistics cmdlet. The following command will save mailbox statistics to the C:\MailboxStats.csv file for mailboxes within the Sales Mailbox Database in the Third Storage Group on the server EXCH1 only:

Get-MailboxStatistics –Database 'EXCH1\Third Storage Group\Sales Mailbox Database' | Export-CSV 'C:\MailboxStats.csv' -NoType

In addition, to save mailbox details to C:\MailboxStats.csv for all mailboxes on all Exchange servers, you could run the following command within the Exchange Management Shell:

Get-ExchangeServer | Get-MailboxStatistics | Export-CSV 'C:\MailboxStats.csv' -NoType

In many situations, it is easier to narrow the list of useful information before analyzing it in a program such as Microsoft Excel by specifying selection criteria alongside the **Where** cmdlet. For example, to save the mailbox details for all disconnected mailboxes on your Exchange server to the file C:\LargeItemCount.csv, you could execute the following command within the Exchange Management Shell:

Get-MailboxStatistics | Where {$_.DisconnectDate –ne $null} | Export-CSV 'C:\ LargeItemCount.csv' -NoType

Similarly, you can easily specify selection criteria within the Exchange Management Shell to obtain a report for large mailboxes. For example, to save the details for mailboxes on your server that are larger than 500 MB to the file C:\LargeItemSize.csv, as well as save the details for mailboxes on your server that have more than 1,500 items to the file C:\LargeItemCount.csv, you could run the following commands within the Exchange Management Shell:

Get-MailboxStatistics | Where {$_.TotalItemSize –ge 500MB} | Export-CSV 'C:\ LargeItemSize.csv' -NoType

Get-MailboxStatistics | Where {$_.ItemCount –ge 1500} | Export-CSV 'C:\ LargeItemCount.csv' -NoType

Additionally, you can manipulate fields before saving data to a CSV file. For example, to sort the entries saved in the C:\LargeItemCount.csv file shown in the previous example numerically by ItemCount, you could run the following command within the Exchange Management Shell:

Get-MailboxStatistics | Where {$_.ItemCount –ge 1500} | Sort-Object ItemCount | Export-CSV 'C:\LargeItemCount.csv' -NoType

As a result, when you open the LargeItemCount.csv file in Microsoft Excel, you will notice that the entries are ordered numerically by the number of items within the ItemCount field as shown in Figure 11-48.

Figure 11-48

LargeItemCount.csv

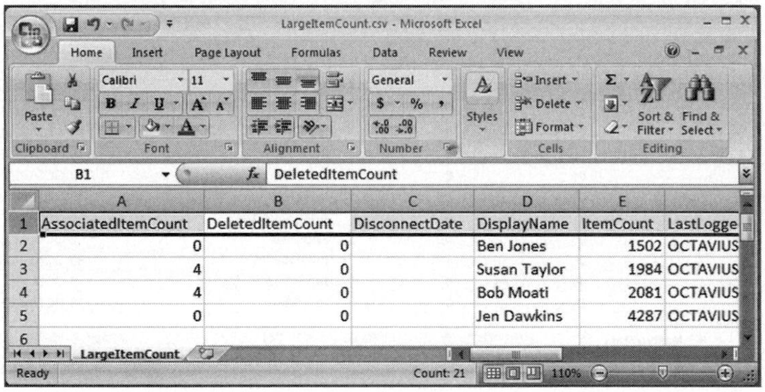

Similarly, you may only require certain information regarding mailboxes. For example, to save only the DisplayName, ItemCount, and TotalItemSize for mailboxes that have exceeded their storage limit on your Mailbox server to the file C:\OverLimit.csv, you could run the following command within the Exchange Management Shell:

Get-MailboxStatistics | Where {$_.StorageLimitStatus –ne "BelowLimit"} | Select-Object DisplayName,ItemCount,TotalItemSize | Export-CSV 'C:\OverLimit.csv' -NoType

When you open the C:\OverLimit.csv file, it will only display the appropriate fields as shown in Figure 11-49.

Figure 11-49

OverLimit.csv

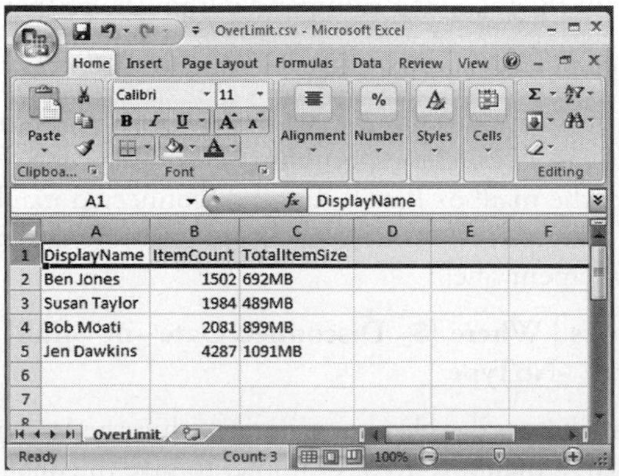

You can also obtain information about the quotas for the users within your organization by using the Get-Mailbox cmdlet. Because the Get-Mailbox cmdlet lists a large amount of configuration information for each mailbox, it is important to specify selection criteria that includes only quota-related information. For example, the following command saves the quota configuration information for all mailboxes on your Exchange server to the file C:\MailboxQuotas.csv:

Get-Mailbox | Select DisplayName,*Quota | Export-CSV 'C:\MailboxQuotas.csv' -NoType

When you view the C:\MailboxQuotas.csv file in Microsoft Excel, you will notice that only the DisplayName field and any fields that end with the word Quota are included as shown in Figure 11-50.

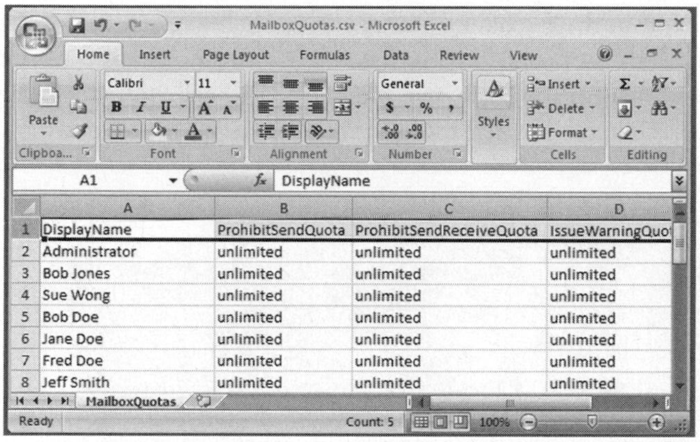

Figure 11-50

MailboxQuotas.csv

QUEUE USAGE

The easiest method for tracking queue usage is to examine the message tracking logs on your Exchange server as discussed earlier in this lesson. The Get-MessageTrackingLog cmdlet can be used to obtain information about the emails sent or received by your Exchange servers as well as to save that information to a text file or CSV file for later analysis. For example, to store the emails sent to jeff.smith@octavius.net to the C:\JeffSmithEmails.csv file, you could use the following command within the Exchange Management Shell:

Get-MessageTrackingLog –EventID 'RECEIVE' –Recipients 'jeff.smith@octavius.net' | Export-CSV 'C:\JeffSmithEmails.csv' -NoType

Additionally, it is important to understand the top senders and receivers within your organization. To determine the users who send and receive the most email, you can use the Get-MessageTrackingLog cmdlet to group results by sender for emails that are submitted to and received by the Exchange servers within your organization. The following commands within the Exchange Management Shell save the top senders to C:\TopSenders.csv and the top receivers to C:\TopReceivers.csv:

Get-MessageTrackingLog –EventID 'SUBMIT' | Group Sender | Export-CSV 'C:\ TopSenders.csv'-NoType

Get-MessageTrackingLog –EventID 'RECEIVE' | Group Sender | Export-CSV 'C:\ TopReceivers.csv' - NoType

You can also obtain information about the status of the queues on your Exchange server as well as the number of items in each queue by using the Get-Queue cmdlet within the Exchange Management Shell. For example, to list the target name, status, and number of items for each queue on your Exchange server and display the results in table format, you could use the following cmdlet within the Exchange Management Shell to produce output similar to that shown in Figure 11-51:

Get-Queue | Select NextHopDomain,Status,MessageCount

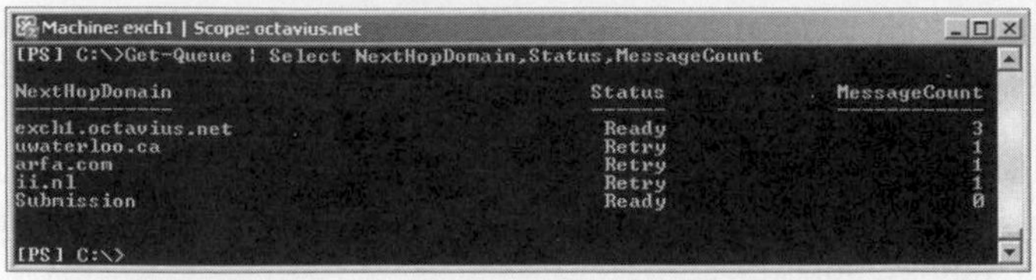

Figure 11-51

Viewing Queue Information

Alternatively, you can redirect the output of the Get-Queue command to a text file or to the Export-CSV cmdlet that will store the results in a comma-delimited text file.

PROTOCOL USAGE

To obtain detailed information about protocol usage, it is important to monitor client connectivity as described earlier in this lesson. However, you can also use the Get-CASMailbox cmdlet within the Exchange Management Shell to obtain information about the protocols that each mailbox user is allowed to use when accessing email. By running the **Get-CASMailbox** command within the Exchange Management Shell, you will receive information about the protocols that are enabled for each mailbox user within your organization as shown in Figure 11-52.

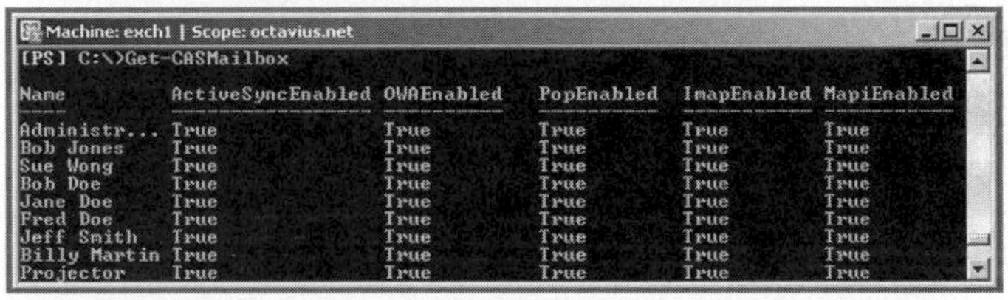

Figure 11-52

Viewing Protocol Usage

You can then use the Set-CASMailbox cmdlet to modify the protocols that mailbox users are allowed to use when interacting with the CAS role servers in your organization. The following command disables the POP3 and IMAP4 protocols for the user Jeff Smith:

Set-CASMailbox –Identity 'Jeff.Smith' –POPEnabled $false –IMAPEnabled $false

When the output is formatted as a list or saved to a CSV file, the Get-CASMailbox cmdlet will display much more information about each mailbox user. To obtain a report that indicates which mailbox users use the default settings for POP3, you could run the following command within the Exchange Management Shell:

**Get-CASMailbox | Where-Object {$_.POPEnabled –eq $true}
| Select DisplayName,PopUseProtocolDefaults | Export-CSV
'C:\POPDefaultUsers.csv' -NoType**

The C:\POPDefaultUsers.csv file will display a TRUE or FALSE value next to each mailbox user as shown in Figure 11-53.

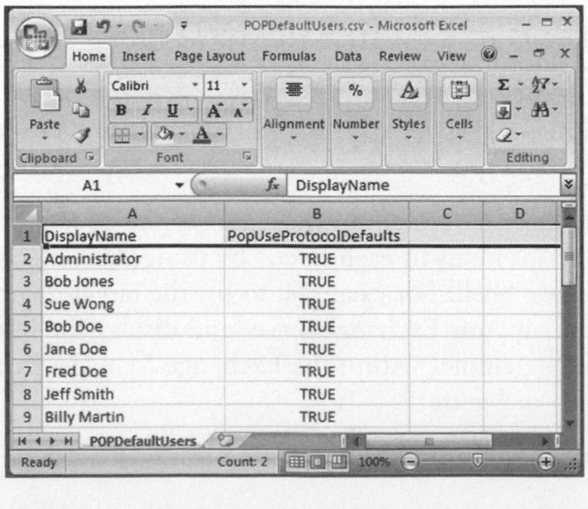

Figure 11-53

POPDefaultUsers.csv

Creating Server Reports

CERTIFICATION READY?
Create server reports.
4.5

In addition to creating usage reports, Exchange administrators should also create reports that list the configuration and health of the Exchange servers within the organization. For Hub and Edge role servers, it is also important to create reports that identify the nature of the spam and viruses that are filtered by Forefront Security for Exchange Server.

SERVER CONFIGURATION AND HEALTH

There are many cmdlets that may be used to obtain information about the configuration and health of your servers. As a result, it is best to use only those cmdlets to obtain information about the areas of your Exchange servers for which your organization requires documentation. Table 11-7 lists common cmdlets that may be used to obtain configuration information from various Exchange components. Table 11-8 also lists cmdlets that can be used to test various Exchange components and generate a health report.

Table 11-7

Common cmdlets used to obtain system configuration

CMDLET	DESCRIPTION
Get-POPSettings Get-IMAPSettings Get-OutlookAnywhere	Lists POP3, IMAP4, and Outlook Anywhere service configuration on a CAS role server.
Get-OWAVirtualDirectory Get-WebServicesVirtualDirectory Get-ActiveSyncVirtualDirectory	Lists the configuration information for the OWA, EWS, and ActiveSync virtual directories on a CAS role server. The EWS virtual directory is used for remote client connections.
Get-EmailAddressPolicy Get-ActiveSyncMailboxPolicy	Lists the configuration information for email address and ActiveSync policies configured within your Exchange organization.
Get-AttachmentFilterEntry Get-AttachmentFilterListConfig Get-ContentFilterConfig Get-IPAllowListConfig Get-IPAllowListEntry Get-IPAllowListProvider Get-IPAllowListProvidersConfig Get-IPBlockListConfig Get-IPBlockListEntry Get-IPBlockListProvider Get-IPBlockListProvidersConfig Get-RecipientFilterConfig Get-SenderIdConfig Get-SenderReputationConfig Get-SendFilterConfig	List the configuration of antispam agents on the Hub and Edge role servers within your organization.

(continued)

Table 11-7 (*continued*)

CMDLET	DESCRIPTION
Export-AutoDiscoverConfig Get-OutlookProvider Get-AvailabilityConfig	Lists the configuration of the AutoDiscover and Availability services on the CAS role servers within your organization.
Get-ExchangeServer	Displays configuration information for the Exchange servers within your organization.
Get-NetworkConnectionInfo	Displays configuration information for the network interfaces on the Exchange servers within your organization.
Get-EventLogLevel	Lists the event logging levels for the different components of an Exchange server.
Get-OrganizationConfig	Displays the configuration information for the Exchange organization within an Active Directory forest.
Get-StorageGroup Get-MailboxDatabase Get-PublicFolderDatabase Get-Queue	Lists the attributes and configuration information for the storage groups, mailbox databases, public folder databases, and queue databases on the Exchange servers within your organization.
Get-TransportAgent Export-TransportRuleCollection Get-TransportConfig Get-AcceptedDomain	Lists the configuration of transport agents and transport rules as well as SMTP transport configuration and accepted domains.
Get-SendConnector Get-ReceiveConnector	Displays the send and receive connectors on the Hub and Edge role servers within your organization as well as their configuration settings.
Get-ExchangeAdministrator	Lists the Exchange administrative roles configured within the Exchange Organization.
Get-TransportServer Get-UMServer Get-MailboxServer Get-ClientAccessServer	Displays the configuration stored within Active Directory for the Transport (Hub, Edge), UM, Mailbox, and CAS role servers within your organization.
Get-ManagedFolderMailboxPolicy	Lists the configuration of managed folder mailbox policies and managed folder settings within the Exchange organization.
Get-ManagedContentSettings	

Table 11-8

Common cmdlets used to generate server health reports

CMDLET	DESCRIPTION
Test-ActiveSyncConnectivity	Tests ActiveSync connectivity to one or more mailboxes within your Exchange organization.
Test-EdgeSynchronization	Tests Edge role servers to ensure that their configuration information is up to date using the EdgeSync protocol.
Test-ExchangeSearch	Verifies that the Exchange search service is running and Indexing database contents efficiently.
Test-Mailflow	Tests whether system email can be sent to the system mailbox on a Mailbox role server.
Test-MAPIConnectivity	Verifies that MAPI is working properly on the Exchange servers within your organization.
Test-OWAConnectivity	Verifies that OWA components are working properly on CAS and Mailbox role servers within your organization.
Test-ServiceHealth	Checks to see if all services that are set to start automatically at boot time are currently running on the Exchange server.
Test-SystemHealth	Tests the configuration and performance of your Exchange server as well as checks for system updates.
Test-UMConnectivity	Verifies that the UM components are functioning normally on a UM role server.
Test-WebServicesConnectivity	Tests Outlook Anywhere components on a CAS role server within your organization.

You can also generate server reports using graphical utilities. For example, after selecting performance counters within System Monitor, you can select the report view within System Monitor to list the values. Figure 11-54 shows the report view for the default performance counters added to System Monitor when you navigate to the **Toolbox** node within the Exchange Management Console and double click **Performance Monitor**.

Figure 11-54

System Monitor Report View

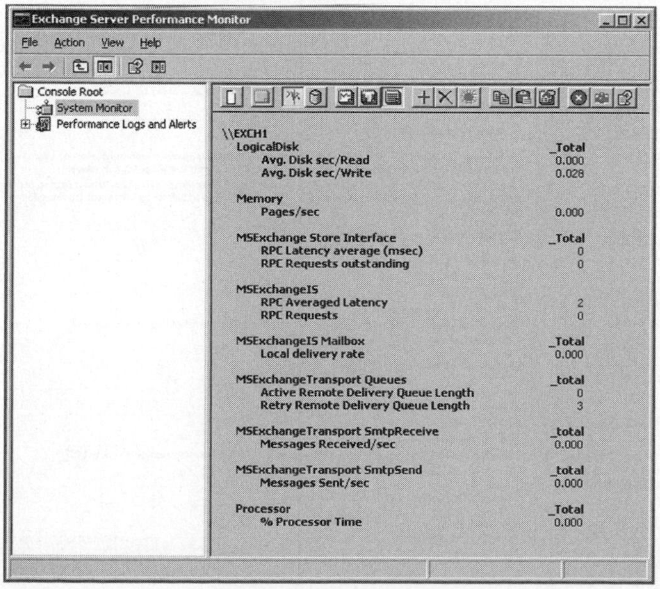

The other utilities available under the **Toolbox** node within the Exchange Management Console typically generate reports that can be exported to a file or printed from the utility itself. The Exchange Best Practices Analyzer displays a report following each scan as well as saves the scan results to an XML file for later use. To view previous scans, open the Exchange Best Practices analyzer and click **Select a Best Practices scan to view** from the Welcome page and navigate to the appropriate scan by date as shown in Figure 11-55.

Figure 11-55

Viewing Previous Scans

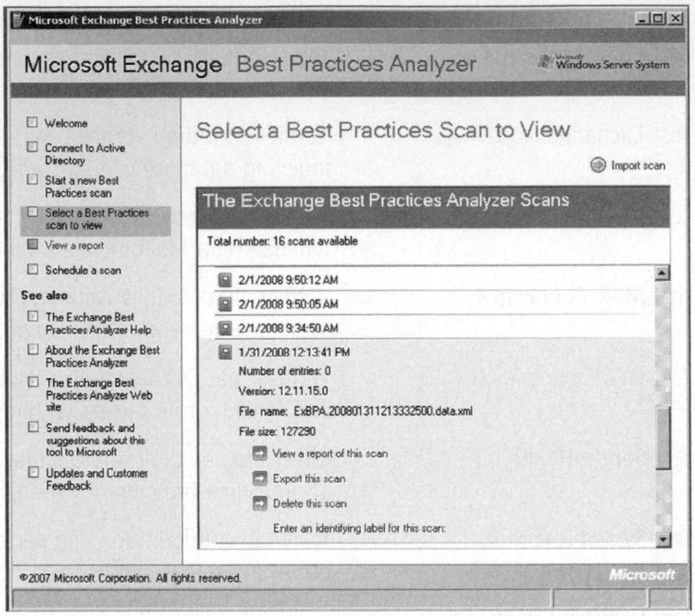

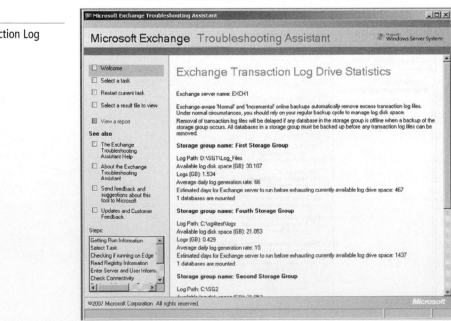

You can then choose to view the report from the scan or export the report to an XML file that can be interpreted by another program or imported into a database for further analysis.

Similarly, when you double click **Database Recovery Management**, **Database Troubleshooter**, **Mail Flow Troubleshooter**, **Message Tracking**, or **Performance Troubleshooter** from the **Toolbox** node within the Exchange Management Console, the Exchange Troubleshooting Assistant starts and provides you with one or more reports based on the nature of the activity. For example, when you open Database Recovery Management and select the task **Analyze log drive space**, the Exchange Troubleshooting Assistant will generate a report that lists the storage groups and space usage on your Mailbox role server as shown in Figure 11-56. This report can be printed for later use or copied to another program using the Windows clipboard.

Figure 11-56

Viewing a Transaction Log Report

Many organizations adopt third-party software that can be used to monitor several different server types within your organization from a central console. These utilities typically analyze server configuration, usage, and performance across the network and store the resulting data in an SQL database from which graphs and reports can be easily generated. Microsoft Operations Manager (MOM) and Microsoft System Centre Operations Manager (SCOM) are two products that can be used to monitor, manage, and generate reports for the various server types within your organization including Exchange Server 2007. For more information on these products, search for their names at www.microsoft.com.

VIRUSES AND SPAM

For the Hub and Edge role servers within your organization that have antivirus and antispam functionality, it is important to ensure that you also generate reports that identify the nature of virus and spam attacks so that you can take steps to mitigate similar attacks in the future.

You can generate reports that detail the nature of virus infections within Forefront Security for Exchange by navigating to **Reports** > **Incidents** within the Forefront Server Security Administrator as shown in Figure 11-57.

Figure 11-57

Viewing Incident Reports

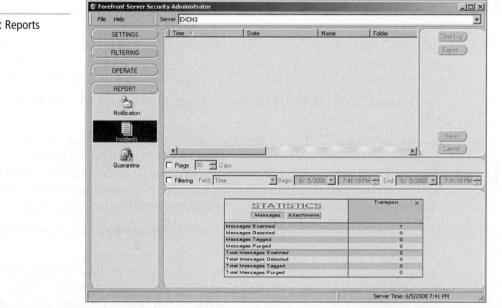

You can click the **Export** button shown in Figure 11-57 to save a copy of the report for later analysis or click **Quarantine** in the left pane to view the quarantined email messages and their senders.

Forefront Security for Exchange can also be configured to log virus detection, quarantine, and cleaning information to a log file. Navigate to **Settings** > **General Options** within Forefront Server Security Administrator and select **Enable Forefront Virus Log** as shown in Figure 11-58. Once enabled, virus information will be logged to **VirusLog.txt** in the Forefront installation directory (**C:\Program Files\Microsoft Forefront Security\ Exchange Server** by default).

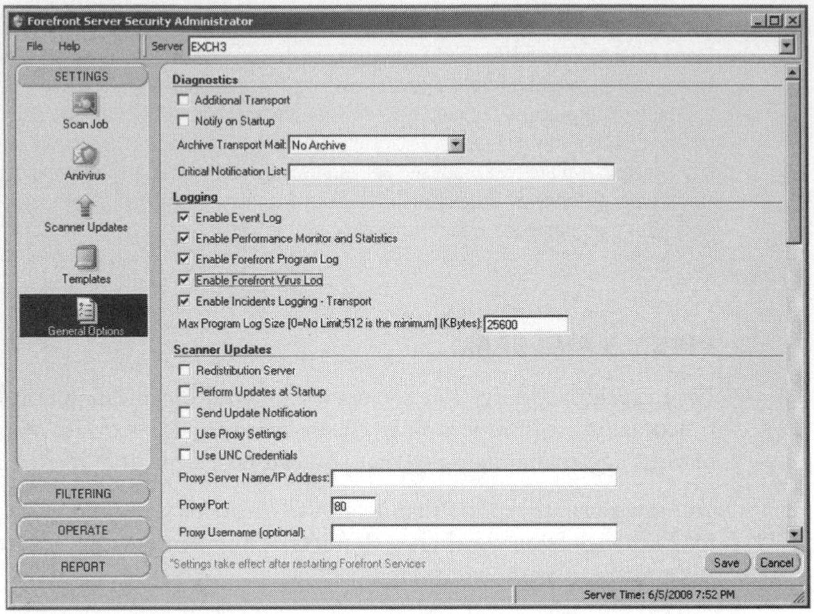

Figure 11-58

Configuring Virus Logging

To generate reports on spam, you can use one of several cmdlets within the Exchange Management Shell. One approach is to view messages with a high Spam Confidence Level (SCL) indicating that they are likely to be spam. To save all messages on the server EXCH1 with an SCL greater than or equal to 8 to the C:\HighSCLEmail.csv file for later analysis, you could run the following command within the Exchange Management Shell:

Get-Message –Server EXCH1 –Filter {SCL –ge 8} | Export-CSV 'C:\HighSCLEmail.csv' –NoType

If you have configured content filtering to send messages with a high SCL to a quarantine mailbox, you can also analyze the quarantine mailbox to understand how much spam your organization is receiving. The following Exchange Management Shell command saves the mailbox details (including the number of items) for the quarantine mailbox (email address = **spam-quarantine@octavius.net**) to the C:\SpamQuarantineStatistics.csv file:

Get-MailboxStatistics –Identity spam-quarantine@octavius.net | Export-CSV 'C:\SpamQuarantineStatistics.csv'

To see the messages that have been sent to the quarantine mailbox as well as their subject lines, you can use the Get-MessageTrackingLog cmdlet. The following Exchange Management Shell command saves all messages sent to the spam quarantine mailbox used in the previous example to C:\SpamQuarantineMessages.csv:

Get-MessageTrackingLog –EventID 'RECEIVE' –Recipients 'spam-quarantine@octavius .net' | Export-CSV 'C:\SpamQuarantineMessages.csv' -NoType

SUMMARY SKILL MATRIX

IN THIS LESSON YOU LEARNED:

- Ongoing monitoring of your Exchange servers allows you to create a performance baseline that can be used to troubleshoot future performance problems as well as detect problems before they affect the performance of your Exchange infrastructure.

- The Task Manager utility can be quickly used to verify a server performance problem as well as correct memory leak and rogue processes.

- System Monitor can be used to obtain performance statistics from nearly any hardware or software component. System Monitor includes several objects and counters that can be used to monitor the performance of Exchange Server 2007 components. The same objects and counters used within System Monitor may also be used within counter logs to monitor performance for long periods of time. You can also create alerts to perform actions when a counter reaches a threshold value.

- Increasing the event logging level for key Exchange components can also help in trouble-shooting performance problems by writing extra information to the Windows Event Viewer.

- You can also monitor and troubleshoot performance issues on your Exchange server by performing a Health Check scan within the Exchange Best Practices Analyzer or by running the Performance Troubleshooter component of the Exchange Troubleshooting Assistant.

- On transport servers, email is first stored within a submission queue before it is moved to a mailbox delivery queue for local mailbox delivery or to a remote delivery queue for remote SMTP delivery. If email cannot be delivered, it is stored within an unreachable queue or within a poison message queue if it affects the stability of Exchange server. You can monitor, manage, and troubleshoot the messages within these queues using the graphical Queue Viewer utility or cmdlets within the Exchange Management Shell.

- To obtain information regarding the email that passes through the transport servers within your organization, you can configure and analyze the message tracking logs on the Mailbox, Hub, and Edge role servers within your organization. You can perform message track-ing using the graphical Message Tracking utility or by using cmdlets within the Exchange Management Shell.

- When troubleshooting client connectivity problems, you can use standard Windows utilities or Microsoft Outlook from a client computer to test connectivity to an Exchange server. Alternatively, you can use cmdlets on the Exchange server to test client connectivity by protocol or analyze protocol logs to determine the cause of a client connectivity problem. Monitoring client connectivity using performance counters can also be used for capacity planning.

- Exchange Server 2007 has several cmdlets that may be used to generate detailed reports on mailbox, queue, and protocol usage as well as server health, server configuration, and spam. These reports can be saved in table, list, or CSV format. You can also export virus incident reports using Forefront Server Security Administrator or enable virus logging to generate detailed virus reports.

■ Knowledge Assessment

Fill in the Blank

Complete the following sentences by writing the correct word or words in the blanks provided.

1. Monitoring your Exchange servers to troubleshoot current performance problems is called _____ monitoring.

2. To specify the type of events that you wish to search for within the Message Tracking utility, you can select the appropriate _____.

3. You can view the connection and Autodiscover service status for an Outlook 2007 client by right clicking the Outlook icon in the Windows notification area while pressing the _____ key on the keyboard.

4. By performing a _____ scan within the Exchange Best Practices Analyzer, you can identify the configuration and system problems that slow the performance of your Exchange servers.

5. Messages that are potentially harmful to Exchange Server are automatically placed in a _____ queue.

6. By regularly monitoring concurrent client connections and server performance using various counters within System Monitor, you can easily determine when additional email servers are required within your organization. This process is called _____.

7. You can immediately retry delivery of messages stored in a queue with a "Retry" status using the _____ cmdlet within the Exchange Management Shell.

8. The _____ option of the Export-CSV cmdlet prevents a label header from being written to the CSV file.

9. To gather additional information about a performance problem using Event Viewer, you can increase the event logging level for a particular Exchange component using the _____ cmdlet within the Exchange Management Shell.

10. System Monitor statistics that monitor the performance of the IMAP4 service are stored within the _____ object.

Multiple Choice

Circle the letter that corresponds to the best answer.

1. Which of the following utilities within the Toolbox node of the Exchange Management Console can be used to automate the collection and analysis of performance data to troubleshoot an active performance problem?
   a. Performance Monitor
   b. Performance Troubleshooter
   c. Performance Analyzer
   d. Performance Logs and Alerts

2. Which of the following key combinations can be used to open the Windows Task Manager directly?
   a. Ctrl+Alt+Esc
   b. Ctrl+Shift+Delete
   c. Ctrl+Alt+Delete
   d. Ctrl+Shift+Esc

3. You have modified the default location for message tracking logs on your Exchange server. However, no new log files are created, and you receive errors within Event Viewer indicating that message tracking was unsuccessful in writing events to the message tracking log. What could be the cause of the problem?
   a. You have not enabled event logging on your Exchange server
   b. The NTFS permissions on the new message tracking directory
   c. The new directory is not on the system volume
   d. The Event Log service has not been restarted

4. Which of the following commands will only display the name and size of mailboxes on your Exchange server?
   a. Get-MailboxStatistics | For DisplayName,ItemCount,TotalItemSize
   b. Get-MailboxStatistics | Where DisplayName,ItemCount,TotalItemSize
   c. Get-MailboxStatistics | Select-Object DisplayName,ItemCount,TotalItemSize
   d. Get-MailboxStatistics | Format-List DisplayName,ItemCount,TotalItemSize

5. Which of the following describes the Avg. Disk Queue Length counter in the Physical Disk object for the second physical disk on your system?
   a. Physical Disk (1)\Avg. Disk Queue Length
   b. Physical Disk\Avg. Disk Queue Length (1)
   c. Physical Disk (2)\Avg. Disk Queue Length
   d. Physical Disk\Avg. Disk Queue Length (2)

6. You would like to ensure that your network workstation receives a message when the number of concurrent client connections reaches 800. What should you do?
   a. Create a counter log within Performance Logs and Alerts that monitors MSExchangeIS Mailbox\Active Client Logons and sends a network message to your workstation when the value is under 800.
   b. Create a performance alert within Performance Logs and Alerts that monitors MSExchangeIS Mailbox\Active Client Logons and sends a network message to your workstation when the value is under 800.
   c. Create a counter log within Performance Logs and Alerts that monitors MSExchangeIS Mailbox\Active Client Logons and sends a network message to your workstation when the value is over 800.
   d. Create a performance alert within Performance Logs and Alerts that monitors MSExchangeIS Mailbox\Active Client Logons and sends a network message to your workstation when the value is over 800.

7. You are analyzing the information within the Queue Viewer and notice an entry on the Queues tab that has a Next Hop Domain of **arfa.net**, a Delivery Type of **DnsConnectorDelivery**, and a Status of **Retry**. What does this mean?
   a. Email within the mailbox delivery queue destined for arfa.net was not delivered on its first attempt.
   b. Email within the remote delivery queue destined for arfa.net was not delivered on its first attempt.
   c. Email within the mailbox delivery queue destined for arfa.net was delivered on its first attempt.
   d. Email within the remote delivery queue destined for arfa.net was delivered on its first attempt.

8. Which of the following Exchange server roles contains a message tracking log? (Choose all that apply.)
   a. Hub   b. Mailbox
   c. CAS   d. Edge

9. A user in one of your departments is having trouble connecting to the Exchange server using MAPI RPC. No other users are experiencing the same issues. What would be your first course of action when troubleshooting this problem?
   a. Have the user attempt to connect to the Exchange server IP address using the ping utility.
   b. Have the user attempt to connect to the Exchange server FQDN using the ping utility.
   c. Check the functionality of the MAPI RPC protocol for all users using the Test-MAPIConnectivity cmdlet on the CAS role server.
   d. Check the functionality of the MAPI RPC protocol for the affected user only using the Test-MAPIConnectivity cmdlet on the CAS role server.

10. Your supervisor has asked you to report on the number of users who are allowed to use POP3 and IMAP4 to access email. What cmdlet can generate this report?
    a. Get-Mailbox   b. Get-CASMailbox
    c. Get-ProtocolUsage   d. Get-CASServer

True/False

Circle T if the statement is true or F if the statement is false.

T | F   1. Task Manager is often used to identify performance problems that result from rogue processes and memory leaks.

T | F   2. To identify the nature of a queue delivery problem, you can research the error number shown in the Last Error column for the appropriate queue listed on the Queues tab of Queue Viewer.

T | F **3.** By examining the statistics and contents of the spam quarantine mailbox, you can obtain valuable information about the spam that has been received by your organization.

T | F **4.** Frequent monitoring of server performance is required for capacity planning.

T | F **5.** The submission queue is used for delivering email to mailboxes within the organization using the SMTP protocol.

T | F **6.** Performance counters represent measurable statistics from performance objects.

T | F **7.** Protocol logs are enabled by default and track IMAP4, POP3, MAPI, and OWA connections.

T | F **8.** In order for a performance alert to send a network message from an Exchange server to a target workstation, the Exchange server must have the messenger service started and the target workstation must have the alerter service started.

T | F **9.** To test the functionality of Outlook Anywhere, you can use the Test-WebServicesConnectivity cmdlet within the Exchange Management Shell.

T | F **10.** When saving output from a cmdlet to a text file in table format, it is important to select a small number of fields that can be displayed within the Exchange Management Shell to ensure that information is not truncated.

Review Questions

1. Explain why taking a performance baseline will help in future troubleshooting situations.

2. Describe some common situations that would require you to extract information from message tracking logs.

■ Case Scenarios

Scenario 11-1: Troubleshooting Exchange Performance

All organizations experience performance problems over time. As a result, it is best to prepare a plan of attack in advance that you will use when solving performance problems reactively. In a short memo, list the tools and procedures in the order that you would use them to troubleshoot an Exchange server that exhibits poor performance.

Scenario 11-2: Preparing Server Documentation

Using the utilities and cmdlets described in this lesson, prepare a set of documentation in file and printed format for your Exchange server according to the roles that it hosts. Ensure that your system documentation includes a performance baseline; configuration documentation; system health; and normal mailbox, protocol, and queue usage.

Providing for Mobile Access and Unified Messaging

LESSON SKILL MATRIX

TECHNOLOGY SKILL	OBJECTIVE DOMAIN	OBJECTIVE DOMAIN NUMBER
Configuring Unified Messaging Support	Configure Exchange Server roles.	1.4
Creating and Applying ActiveSync Policies	Configure policies.	3.4
Configuring a UM Mailbox Policy	Configure policies.	3.4

KEY TERMS

ActiveSync policies
automated attendant
BlackBerry Enterprise Server
  (BES)
BlackBerry Infrastructure
BlackBerry Manager utility
BlackBerry Server Configuration
  utility
DirectPush
Email Transfer Protocol (ETP)
Internet Protocol (IP) gateway
IT policy
local wipe

long-standing HTTPS request
Mobile Data Service (MDS)
nonprovisionable device
Outlook Voice Access (OVA)
Personal Identification Number
  (PIN)
Personal Information Manager
  (PIM)
Private Branch eXchange (PBX)
Public Switched Telephone
  Network (PSTN)
remote wipe
roaming

Server Routing Protocol (SRP)
Session Initiation Protocol (SIP)
subscriber access number
UM auto attendant
UM dial plan
UM IP gateway
UM mailbox policy
Uniform Resource Identifier
  (URI)
Voice Over IP (VOIP)
Windows Mobile Device Center
wireless provider

■ Implementing Mobile Access

THE BOTTOM LINE

Many users require the ability to access email and calendar information from their mailboxes remotely using portable devices. As an Exchange administrator, it is important that you understand the different technologies that are used to provide mobile access to Exchange mailboxes as well as the practices and procedures used to implement them.

Understanding Mobile Access Technologies

Most wireless providers offer access to email systems such as Exchange from smartphone devices. ActiveSync can be used on many different smartphone models to access your CAS role servers directly from a wireless connection. Some smartphone models can also connect to the BlackBerry infrastructure to access mailboxes on the Exchange servers within your organization via a BlackBerry Enterprise Server.

Many users require the ability to communicate and access important information from any location. As a result, smartphones have quickly become the standard communication device for users when they are away from their computers. A *smartphone* is a wireless telephone device that also hosts applications that allow mobile access to information and services such as email, contacts, calendar, tasks, notes, and web pages. There are many different smartphone manufacturers, including Nokia, Apple, RIM, Sony, HTC, and Palm. Each smartphone connects wirelessly to a *wireless provider* such as AT&T to connect to the worldwide telephone network and the Internet.

In addition, you can configure most smartphones to interact with Exchange Server 2007 so that smartphone users can access their email, calendar, notes, and contacts in the same way they normally do using Outlook or Entourage. The two most common ways to integrate smartphones with Exchange Server 2007 is by using *ActiveSync* or by using the *BlackBerry Infrastructure*.

UNDERSTANDING ACTIVESYNC

ActiveSync is a Microsoft program that can be installed on a PC, Macintosh, or smartphone. When installed on a PC or Macintosh, ActiveSync can synchronize data on a smartphone or Personal Digital Assistant (PDA) device with the computer. However, when installed on a smartphone, ActiveSync can synchronize data to an email server product such as Microsoft Exchange Server or Kerio Mailserver. This synchronization process involves the coordination and communication of email and *Personal Information Manager (PIM)* data such as calendar items, contacts, address lists, and task items between the mailbox database on the email server and the smartphone. Exchange Server 2003 SP2 and Exchange Server 2007 have built-in ActiveSync support that can be used to synchronize email and PIM data with smartphones that run one of the following operation systems:

- Windows Mobile 5 (with the Messaging and Security Feature Pack)
- Windows Mobile 6
- Symbian
- Palm OS
- Macintosh OS X (iPhone)

> **TAKE NOTE** *
>
> Starting with Windows Vista, the ActiveSync Windows program is now referred to as the *Windows Mobile Device Center*.

When the Exchange servers in your organization receive new email items, those items are stored in the appropriate mailbox as well as sent to the appropriate smartphone using a technology called *DirectPush*.

DirectPush works by keeping an empty HTTPS session open between the smartphone and a CAS role server in your organization. When you configure a smartphone for DirectPush, you must supply the name or IP address of a CAS role server within your organization that can be contacted from across the Internet as well as the credentials for the appropriate AD user account. When the smartphone connects to a wireless provider, it authenticates to the CAS role server and sends a *long-standing HTTPS request* to a CAS role server within your Exchange organization. Long-standing HTTPS requests are HTTPS requests that are made to a web server to create a session only. When new email items arrive for the smartphone user on the Exchange server, the CAS role server immediately responds to the long-standing HTTPS request from the smartphone client and notifies it of any new email items. The smartphone then initiates ActiveSync synchronization to obtain the new email items and a new long-standing HTTPS request will be made to start the whole process again. This process is illustrated in Figure 12-1.

Figure 12-1

ActiveSync Components

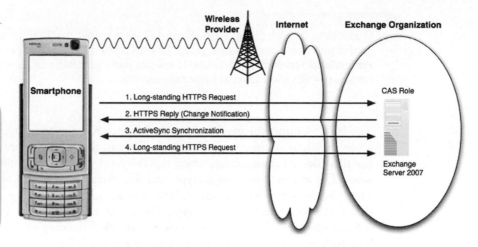

If the smartphone user replies to the email items or creates new email items, those items will then be resynchronized to the CAS role server using ActiveSync and sent to the appropriate recipients using email relay from within the Exchange organization. Similarly, if the HTTPS is disconnected, the smartphone will start a new session by sending a new long-standing HTTPS request.

One of the largest benefits of DirectPush is that it uses most of its bandwidth only when the smartphone synchronizes data with a CAS role server. The long-standing HTTPS session traffic typically uses less than 1 MB of bandwidth per month. This, in turn, translates to a lower wireless provider access cost for the smartphone user. Another benefit of DirectPush is that it is widely supported by a large number of smartphones today by manufacturers such as Nokia, Apple, Sony, HTC, and Palm.

You can configure the ActiveSync and DirectPush features in Exchange Server 2007 provided you are a member of the Exchange Organization Administrator role.

UNDERSTANDING THE BLACKBERRY INFRASTRUCTURE

Another way that smartphone users can access the mailboxes on their Exchange server is by connecting to the BlackBerryInfrastructure. Instead of connecting directly to Exchange through a wireless provider, BlackBerry users connect through a wireless provider to BlackBerry Infrastructure servers that work closely with the wireless provider. The BlackBerry Infrastructure servers then connect across the Internet to the ***BlackBerry Enterprise Server (BES)*** within your organization using the ***Server Routing Protocol (SRP)***. The BES in your organization then connects to the appropriate Exchange servers within your organization to send and retrieve email and PIM data. These components are illustrated in Figure 12-2.

Figure 12-2

BlackBerry Infrastructure Components

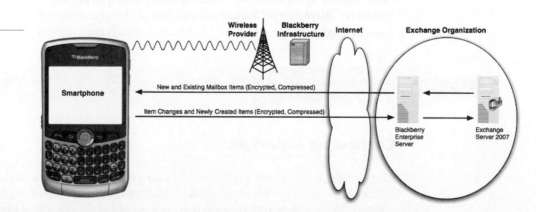

The BES monitors the mailboxes on the Mailbox role servers within your organization. When a new email arrives in your Exchange mailbox, BES compresses, encrypts, and forwards it to the BlackBerry Infrastructure, where it is delivered to the smartphone via the wireless network. The smartphone then decrypts and decompresses the email before displaying it to the smartphone user. When the smartphone user replies to an email or composes a new email, that email is compressed and encrypted on the smartphone before it is sent to the BlackBerry Infrastructure via the wireless network, where it is forwarded to the BES in your organization. The BES then decrypts and decompresses the email before it is forwarded to the appropriate Exchange servers within your organization for local or remote delivery.

A similar process is used for the other PIM information stored in your mailbox, such as calendar appointments, notes, and address lists. The arrows in Figure 12-2 show how this process works alongside the BlackBerry Infrastructure components.

One of the primary benefits of the BlackBerry Infrastructure is that it uses strong encryption. BlackBerry devices use either 168-bit 3DES or 256-bit AES symmetric encryption compared to the 128-bit RC4 encryption used by ActiveSync HTTPS.

Another key benefit of the BlackBerry Infrastructure is that it minimizes the use of bandwidth across the network. In addition to compressing all traffic, BES only delivers the first 2 MB of any large emails to smartphone users across the wireless network. When the smartphone user reads the first 2 KB, the next 2 KB of the email is then sent across the wireless network to the smartphone user, and so on.

By using the **Mobile Data Service (MDS)** component of BES, smartphone users can also access key applications within their organization from their smartphones. Additionally, the **BlackBerry Attachment Service** component of BES converts email message attachments into a custom format that can easily be displayed on the BlackBerry smartphone device. It works with a wide variety of media formats such as JPEG and MP3 as well as document formats such as Microsoft Office, Adobe Acrobat, and Corel WordPerfect.

The BlackBerry Infrastructure is owned and maintained by the Canadian organization **Research In Motion (RIM)**. As a result, nearly all devices that use the BlackBerry Infrastructure are BlackBerry smartphones manufactured by RIM. However, other supported third-party smartphones, such as the Palm Treo, can be BlackBerry enabled so that they can use the BlackBerry Infrastructure in the same way that BlackBerry smartphones do. These third-party smartphones must have **BlackBerry Connect** software installed and the wireless provider that they use must be configured to access the BlackBerry Infrastructure servers.

TAKE NOTE✳ You can obtain a list of smartphone models that can be BlackBerry enabled by visiting www.BlackBerry.com.

Configuring ActiveSync

By default, the CAS role servers within your organization provide the ability for ActiveSync clients to connect to their Exchange mailboxes. Before deploying ActiveSync smartphones within your organization, you should also understand how to configure ActiveSync support for mailbox users as well as configure ActiveSync policies that provide smartphone restrictions. In addition, you should understand how to configure the ActiveSync virtual directory as well as manage ActiveSync devices.

CONFIGURING ACTIVESYNC MAILBOX SUPPORT

Configuring ActiveSync and DirectPush is relatively easy using Exchange Server 2007 provided that you deploy smartphones that support it. By default, ActiveSync is enabled for all user accounts. However, it is considered good security practice to disable ActiveSync for any mailbox users who do not have smartphones. You can disable ActiveSync for specific mailbox users by navigating to the **Mailbox Features** tab of their mailbox properties within the Exchange Management Console, highlighting **Exchange ActiveSync** and selecting the **Disable** button as shown in Figure 12-3 for Adel Moore's mailbox.

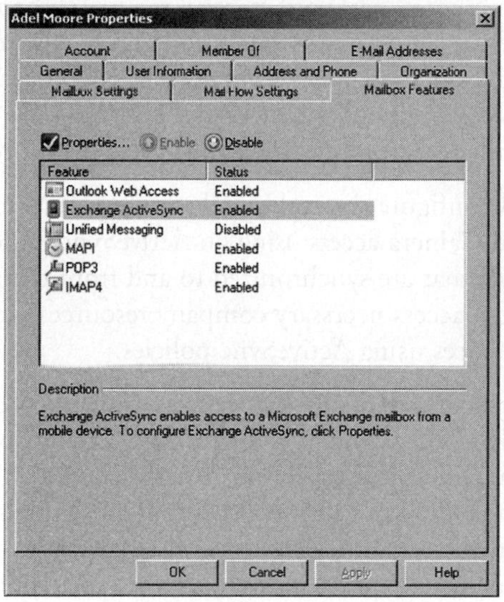

Figure 12-3

Configuring ActiveSync User Support

![Screenshot of the Adel Moore Properties dialog box showing the Mailbox Features tab with Exchange ActiveSync highlighted and enabled]

Alternatively, you can use the Set-CASMailbox cmdlet within the Exchange Management Shell to enable and disable the ActiveSync protocol for mailbox users. The following command within the Exchange Management Shell will disable ActiveSync for the user Adel Moore:

Set-CASMailbox –Identity 'Adel Moore' –ActiveSyncEnabled $false

Alternatively, you could disable ActiveSync for several mailbox users by placing their names within a CSV file that can be used with a bulk management command. The following command will disable ActiveSync for any users listed in the **Identity** field within the **C:\Mailbox Users.csv** file when executed in the Exchange Management Shell:

Import-CSV 'C:\Mailbox Users.csv' | ForEach-Object –Process { Set-CASMailbox –Identity $_.Identity –ActiveSyncEnabled $false }

Additionally, you can associate a mailbox with a single smartphone device to ensure that other smartphone devices cannot be used to access mailbox contents. To do this, you must first obtain the *smartphone device identifier (ID)* using the Get-ActiveSyncDeviceStatistics cmdlet after users have successfully synchronized their smartphone with their mailbox. The following command in the Exchange Management Shell will display the smartphone device ID that was last synchronized to the Jeff Smith mailbox (jeff.smith@octavius.net):

Get-ActiveSyncDeviceStatistics –Mailbox:'jeff.smith@octavius.net'

Following this, you can restrict Jeff Smith's ActiveSync synchronization to only a single device by running the following command within the Exchange Management Shell, where DEVICE_ID is the smartphone device ID that you obtained earlier using the Get-ActiveSyncDeviceStatistics cmdlet:

Set-CASMailbox –Mailbox:'jeff.smith@octavius.net' –ActiveSyncAllowedDeviceIDs: 'DEVICE_ID'

X REF

Bulk management commands and techniques were discussed in Lesson 6, "Address Lists, Policies, and Bulk Management."

TAKE NOTE ★

You can specify multiple device IDs alongside the **–ActiveSyncAllowedDeviceIDs** option to the **Set-CASMailbox** cmdlet to allow ActiveSync synchronization from multiple smartphones.

CREATING AND APPLYING ACTIVESYNC POLICIES

After you have ensured that the appropriate mailboxes have ActiveSync enabled, you can control how smartphones interact with your CAS role servers using *ActiveSync policies*.

ActiveSync policies can be used to control the security settings on your smartphone in much the same way that a Group Policy can be used to modify security settings on a client operating system. An ActiveSync policy can be used to force smartphone users to use device passwords. This prevents an unattended smartphone from being accessed by an unauthorized user. In addition, the ActiveSync policy can be used to enforce a minimum password length (maximum 18 characters), require encrypted password storage, require alphanumeric passwords, enable password recovery, as well as set password expiration and password history values to ensure that passwords are uniquely changed on a regular basis. Moreover, ActiveSync policies can also be used to set a time-out value that determines how long the smartphone device can be inactive before it is automatically locked using the device password.

You can also restrict and configure smartphone device features such as WiFi, Bluetooth, web browser, application, and Camera access using an ActiveSync policy, as well as control the size of emails and attachments that are synchronized to and from the smartphone. To ensure that smartphone users can only access necessary company resources, you can restrict access to file shares and SharePoint services using ActiveSync policies.

A wide range of ActiveSync-enabled smartphones are available today. As a result, not all smartphones may be able to enforce all of the settings that you specify within an ActiveSync policy. These smartphones are called *nonprovisionable devices*. You can specify whether you will allow nonprovisionable devices to connect to your CAS role server within an ActiveSync policy. Preventing nonprovisionable devices using an ActiveSync policy is appropriate for environments where security is important to ensure that smartphones that connect using ActiveSync have the latest security features.

To manage ActiveSync policies using the Exchange Management Console, navigate to the **Organization Configuration** > **Client Access** node as shown in Figure 12-4. In Exchange Server 2007 SP1, a default ActiveSync policy is automatically created and applied to all mailboxes. This default policy permits unrestricted smartphone device access and does not enforce device passwords. As a result, it is a good practice to modify the default policy or create additional mailbox policies that can later be applied to the appropriate mailbox users within your organization.

Figure 12-4

Configuring ActiveSync Policies

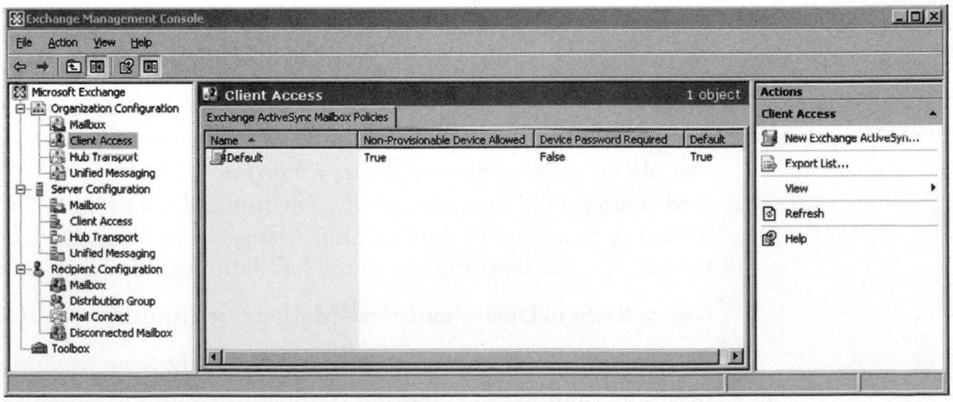

CREATING AN ACTIVESYNC POLICY

GET READY. Turn on the computer, and log in as the Administrator user account. Close any windows that appear on the desktop.

1. Click **Start, All Programs, Microsoft Exchange Server 2007,** and then click **Exchange Management Console.** The Exchange Management Console window appears.

2. In the console tree pane, expand **Organization Configuration** and highlight **Client Access**.

3. In the action pane, click **New Exchange ActiveSync Mailbox Policy**.

4. At the New Exchange ActiveSync Mailbox Policy window, specify an appropriate name in the **Mailbox policy name** dialog box and select the appropriate policy options. As shown in Figure 12-5, nonprovisional devices are allowed to connect, and all devices must have 6 character alphanumeric passwords that must be changed every 42 days to a new value that has not been used 5 times previously. In addition, devices will be automatically password-locked after 15 minutes and forgotten passwords can be recovered if necessary.

Figure 12-5

Creating a New ActiveSync Policy

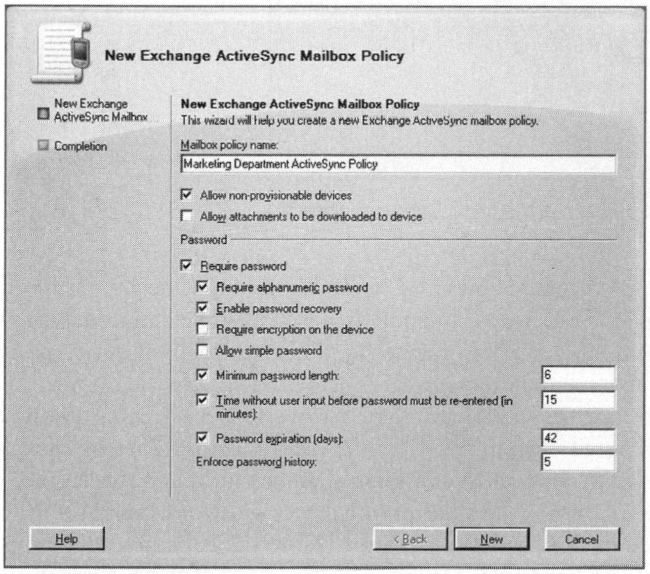

5. Review your settings and click **New**. The Completion page appears.

6. Click **Finish** to close the New Exchange ActiveSync Mailbox Policy window.

7. Close the Exchange Management Console.

THE COMMAND LINE WAY

You can also use the **New-ActiveSyncMailboxPolicy** cmdlet in the Exchange Management Shell to create a new ActiveSync policy. To create the same ActiveSync policy described in Figure 12-5, you could run the following command in the Exchange Management Shell:

New-ActiveSyncMailboxPolicy -Name 'Marketing Department ActiveSync Policy' -AllowNonProvisionableDevices $true -DevicePasswordEnabled $true -AlphanumericDevicePasswordRequired $true -MaxInactivityTimeDeviceLock '00:15:00' -MinDevicePasswordLength '6' -PasswordRecoveryEnabled $true -RequireDeviceEncryption $false -AttachmentsEnabled $false -AllowSimpleDevicePassword $false -DevicePasswordExpiration '42.00:00:00' -DevicePasswordHistory '5'

For more information on the syntax and usage of the New-ActiveSyncMailboxPolicy cmdlet, search for it within Exchange Server 2007 Help.

Not all ActiveSync policy settings can be configured during policy creation. As a result, it is important to review and modify the properties of an ActiveSync policy after creation. You can do this within the Exchange Management Console by highlighting the appropriate ActiveSync policy under the **Organization Configuration** > **Client Access** node and selecting **Properties** from the action pane. On the General tab of the ActiveSync policy properties, you can select whether nonprovisional devices will be allowed to connect to your CAS role server as well as whether smartphones will be allowed to access Windows file shares or SharePoint as shown in Figure 12-6.

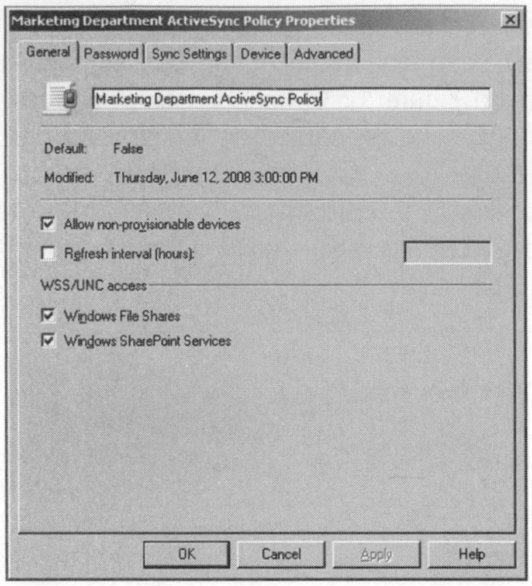

Figure 12-6

ActiveSync Policy Properties General Tab

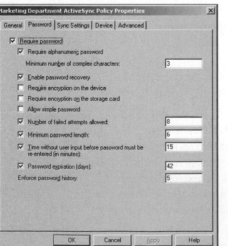

The Password tab allows you to modify the same device password restrictions that you configured when you created the policy as well as some additional password restrictions. As shown in Figure 12-7, you can further require encryption of device passwords that are stored on removable memory storage cards as well as specify the number of complex characters that must be part of an alphanumeric password. Because smartphone device passwords traditionally consisted of numbers only, the **Minimum number of complex characters** shown in Figure 12-7 refers to the number of alphabetical and special (i.e., *, &, $, #) characters that must exist within the smartphone device password. In addition, you can specify the number of failed device password attempts before the configuration and personal information is automatically deleted from the device (a process called *local wipe*) using the **Number of failed attempts allowed** option (the default value is 8).

Figure 12-7

ActiveSync Policy Properties Password Tab

You can use the Sync Settings tab of ActiveSync policy properties to control the amount of information sent between the smartphone and CAS role server during the synchronization process. In general, you should choose values that provide the necessary email and calendar functionality while preventing unwanted items from being synchronized across the wireless network. This will minimize the amount of wireless bandwidth used during synchronization as well as prevent the storage space on the smartphone from being exhausted by unnecessary emails and attachments. The settings shown in Figure 12-8 restrict synchronization of calendar items that are older than two weeks and email items that are older than three days. Moreover, emails that are larger than 2 MB (2048 KB) and attachments that are larger than 1 MB (1024 KB) will not be synchronized. Although HTML-formatted emails use more bandwidth than plaintext emails, they will be allowed because they support color, graphics, and different font styles that are useful when reading email content. To prevent synchronization problems, synchronization will not be allowed during roaming. ***Roaming*** is the switching of physical wireless connections during travel.

Figure 12-8

ActiveSync Policy Properties
Sync Settings Tab

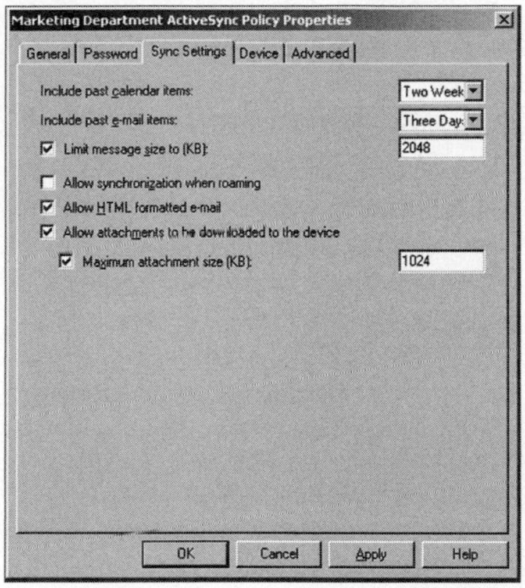

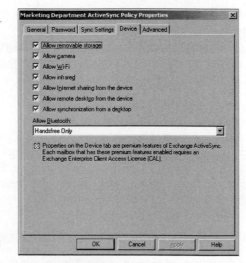

The Device and Advanced tabs shown in Figures 12-9 and 12-10 allow you to restrict the functions and features of the smartphones that apply the ActiveSync policy. On the Device tab shown in Figure 12-9, you can restrict access to smartphone device features such as a built-in digital camera to prevent smartphone users from exhausting the storage space on their smartphone with picture files. In addition, you can prevent smartphone users from sharing or accessing resources using WiFi, infrared, Bluetooth, Remote Desktop, or removable storage cards by deselecting the appropriate options. Because many smartphone users use Bluetooth-enabled handsfree headsets, it is good security practice to only allow Bluetooth for handsfree devices and not for other devices or file sharing as shown in Figure 12-9.

Figure 12-9

ActiveSync Policy Properties
Device Tab

There are thousands of third-party applications that smartphone users can download and install on their smartphones today. Unfortunately, these applications may gain access to personal information stored on the smartphone or waste valuable storage space that should be used for email. Fortunately, you can restrict the types of applications that are allowed to run on smartphones using the Advanced tab of ActiveSync policy properties as shown in Figure 12-10. You can prevent web browsers or applications that do not have a digital signature from executing on smartphones. In addition, if you click **Add** under the Blocked Applications section shown in Figure 12-10, you can specify the name of applications that you wish to block. Alternatively, you can click Add under the Allowed Applications section and browse to the executable files of applications that should be allowed. When you select an executable file, a hash of the file will be taken and compared to applications that are running on the smartphone to determine whether the application should be allowed. Moreover, you can prevent users from configuring email applications on the smartphone to obtain email from personal email accounts by deselecting **Allow consumer mail** as shown in Figure 12-10.

Figure 12-10

ActiveSync Policy Properties
Advanced Tab

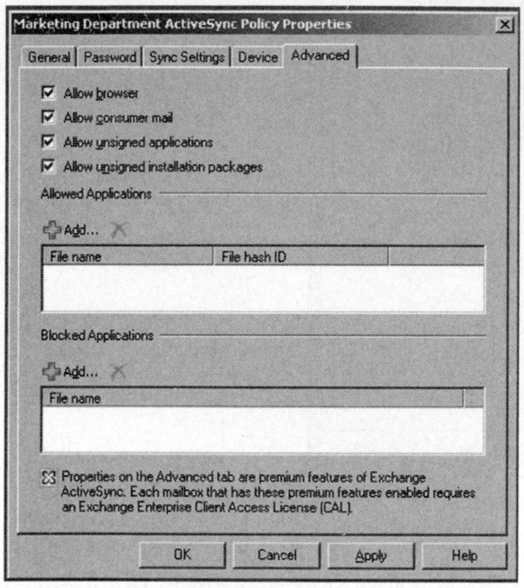

TAKE NOTE*

To restrict the features shown on the Device and Advanced tabs of ActiveSync policy properties, you must purchase Exchange Enterprise Client Access Licenses for each ActiveSync client connection.

THE COMMAND LINE WAY

You can also use the **Set-ActiveSyncMailboxPolicy** cmdlet in the Exchange Management Shell to modify ActiveSync policy settings. In addition to the settings that you can configure using the Exchange Management Console, the Set-ActiveSyncMailboxPolicy cmdlet can also configure additional ActiveSync restrictions. To prevent smartphone users from text messaging using the Marketing Department ActiveSync Policy, you could run the following command in the Exchange Management Shell:

Set-ActiveSyncMailboxPolicy -Name 'Marketing Department ActiveSync Policy' -AllowTextMessaging $false

In addition, you can use the **Get-ActiveSyncMailboxPolicy** cmdlet to view existing restrictions. For more information on the syntax and usage of these cmdlets, search for Set-ActiveSyncMailboxPolicy and Get-ActiveSyncMailboxPolicy within Exchange Server 2007 Help.

TAKE NOTE*

You can only apply a single ActiveSync policy to each mailbox user.

After you have modified your ActiveSync policy to include the appropriate settings, you can apply it to the appropriate mailbox users within your organization. By creating and applying different ActiveSync policies to different users, you can provide smartphone restrictions that are geared towards the different job roles within your organization.

APPLYING AN ACTIVESYNC POLICY TO A MAILBOX USER

GET READY. Turn on the computer, and log in as the Administrator user account. Close any windows that appear on the desktop.

1. Click **Start, All Programs, Microsoft Exchange Server 2007**, and then click **Exchange Management Console**. The Exchange Management Console window appears.

2. In the console tree pane, expand **Recipient Configuration** and highlight **Mailbox**.

3. In the result pane, highlight the user that you wish to assign an ActiveSync policy to and click **Properties** in the action pane.

4. At the mailbox user properties, highlight the **Mailbox Features** tab, select **Exchange ActiveSync**, and click **Properties**. The Exchange ActiveSync Properties window appears as shown in Figure 12-11.

Figure 12-11

Assigning an ActiveSync Policy to a User

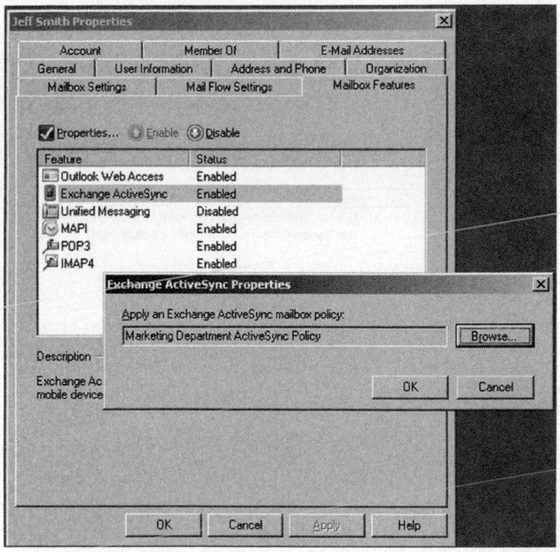

5. Click **Browse**, select the appropriate ActiveSync policy in the Select ActiveSync Mailbox Policy window that appears, and click **OK**.

6. Click **OK** to close the Exchange ActiveSync Properties window.

7. Click **OK** to close the user properties window.

8. Close the Exchange Management Console.

THE COMMAND LINE WAY

You can also use the **Set-CASMailbox** cmdlet in the Exchange Management Shell to assign an ActiveSync policy to a mailbox user. To assign the Marketing Department ActiveSync Policy to the user Jeff Smith, you could run the following command in the Exchange Management Shell:

Set-CASMailbox – Identity 'Jeff Smith' -ActiveSyncMailboxPolicy 'Marketing Department ActiveSync Policy'

Similarly, you could assign the same ActiveSync policy to all users with the following Exchange Management Shell command:

Get-Mailbox | Set -CASMailbox -ActiveSyncMailboxPolicy 'Marketing Department ActiveSync Policy'

If you have created an ActiveSync policy that defines the minimum restrictions for ActiveSync connections across your entire organization, you can set it as the default policy. The default ActiveSync policy is automatically configured for all mailbox users who do not have an ActiveSync policy manually configured using the Exchange Management Console or the Set-CASMailbox cmdlet. To set a policy as the default policy, select it under the **Organization Configuration** > **Client Access** node of the Exchange Management Console and click **Set as Default** in the action pane. Alternatively, you can use the Set-ActiveSyncMailboxPolicy cmdlet to set the default ActiveSync policy for your organization. The following Exchange Management Shell command sets the Marketing Department Mailbox Policy as default:

Set-ActiveSyncMailboxPolicy -Name 'Marketing Department ActiveSync Policy' –IsDefaultPolicy $true

CONFIGURING THE ACTIVESYNC VIRTUAL DIRECTORY

ActiveSync-enabled smartphones communicate directly with the ActiveSync virtual directory under the default Web site in IIS on the appropriate CAS role server. By default, the virtual directory is accessed from smartphones using https://CAS_server/Microsoft-Server-ActiveSync and can be configured by navigating to the **Server Configuration** > **Client Access** node within the Exchange Management Console, selecting the appropriate CAS role server in the detail pane, and highlighting the **Exchange ActiveSync** tab as shown in Figure 12-12.

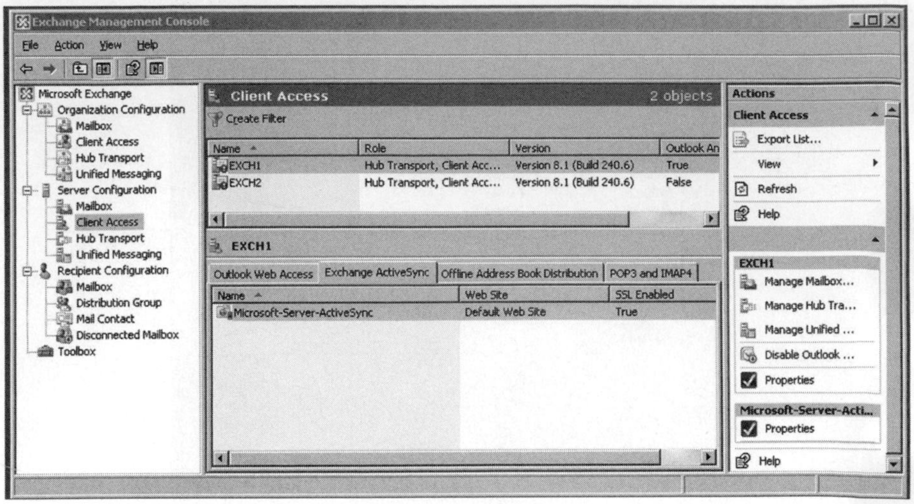

Figure 12-12

Configuring the ActiveSync Virtual Directory

To ensure that ActiveSync can use the Autodiscover and Availability services in Exchange Server 2007, select the Microsoft-Server-ActiveSync object shown in Figure 12-12, select **Properties** from the action pane, and supply the URL that smartphones will use when contacting their CAS role server in the **External URL** dialog box as shown in Figure 12-13.

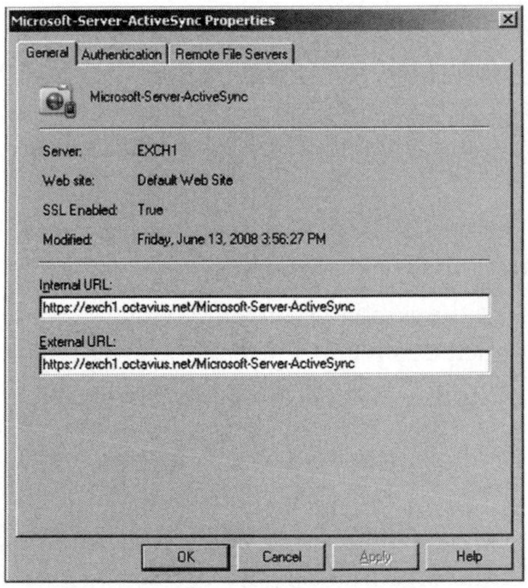

Figure 12-13

ActiveSync Virtual Directory Properties General Tab

By default, ActiveSync uses basic (clear text) authentication across the encrypted HTTPS session and does not accept authentication certificates from smartphone users. However, if your organization deploys authentication certificates to the smartphones within your organization, you can accept or require them during the authentication process by selecting the appropriate options on the Authentication tab of Microsoft-Server-ActiveSync properties as shown in Figure 12-14.

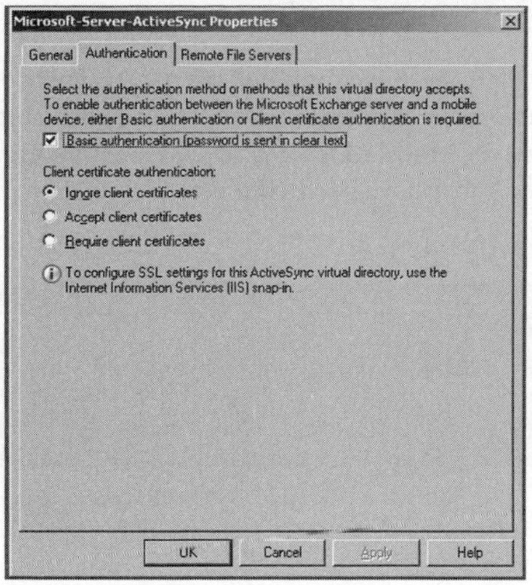

Figure 12-14

ActiveSync Virtual Directory
Properties Authentication Tab

Although ActiveSync
HTTPS requests will
work using a self-signed
SSL certificate, it is a
good practice to replace
the self-signed SSL cer-
tificate used for HTTPS
with a CA-signed certifi-
cate as discussed earlier in
Lesson 9, "Configuring
Security."

If you enabled access to Windows file shares in your ActiveSync policy as shown earlier in Figure 12-6, you can specify the names of file servers within your organization that ActiveSync users can access from their smartphone devices. To do this, configure the appropriate server names on the Remote File Servers tab of Microsoft-Server-ActiveSync properties as shown in Figure 12-15.

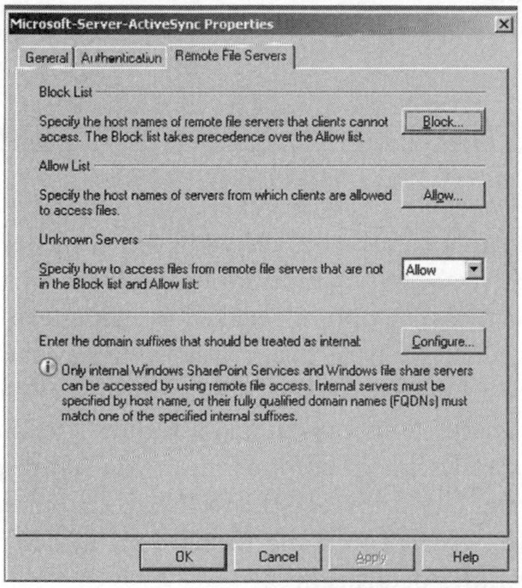

Figure 12-15

ActiveSync Virtual Directory
Properties Remote File Servers
Tab

By default, ActiveSync clients can access all internal file servers within your organization. However, you must click the **Configure** button as shown in Figure 12-15 and specify the domain name suffixes that should be treated as internal. To specify server names that ActiveSync clients should access, click the **Allow** button shown in Figure 12-15, and supply the appropriate server names in the window that appears. Alternatively, you can click the **Block** button and specify server names that ActiveSync clients cannot access regardless of whether they have been previously allowed. To block access to file servers that are not listed on the Remote File Servers tab, select **Block** in the drop-down box shown in Figure 12-15.

You can also use the **Set-ActiveSyncVirtualDirectory** cmdlet in the Exchange Management Shell to configure the settings for the ActiveSync virtual directory in IIS on the CAS role servers in your organization. To assign the external URL of https://exch1.octavius.net/ Microsoft-Server-ActiveSync to the server exch1.octavius.net in the Octavius organization, you could run the following command in the Exchange Management Shell:

Set-ActiveSyncVirtualDirectory -Identity 'octavius\microsoft-server-activesync'
–ActiveSyncServer 'https://exch1.octavius.net/Microsoft-Server-ActiveSync'
–ExternalURL 'https://exch1.octavius.net/Microsoft-Server-ActiveSync'

For more information on the usage of the Set-ActiveSyncVirtualDirectory cmdlet, search for its name in Exchange Server 2007 Help.

MANAGING ACTIVESYNC DEVICES

Once you have configured ActiveSync, mailbox users can synchronize information from their mailbox as well as manage their ActiveSync connection using Outlook Web Access (OWA). By navigating to **Options** > **Mobile Devices** in OWA as shown in Figure 12-16, you can view all ActiveSync devices that have been connected to your mailbox in the past.

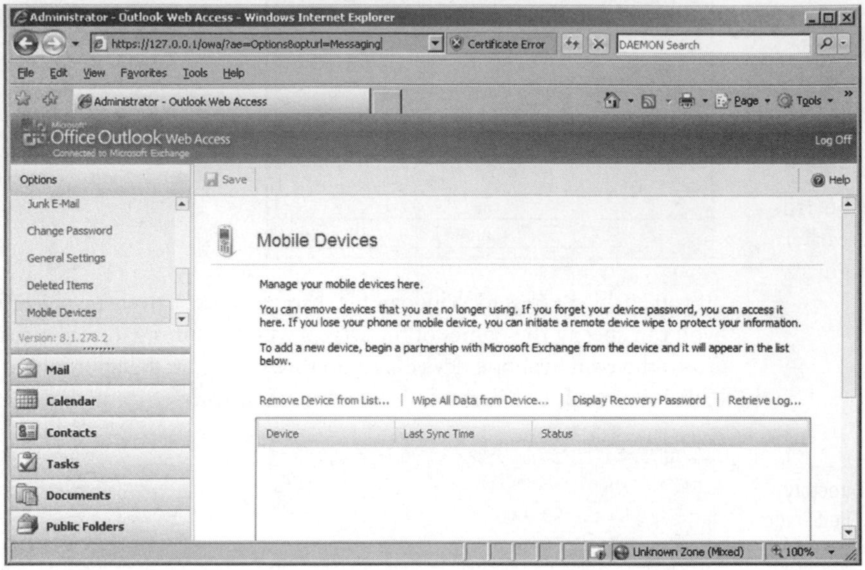

Figure 12-16

Managing Mobile Devices in OWA

TAKE NOTE

Before recovering a device password, you should first verify the user's identity. After recovering a device password for a user, you should ensure that the user immediately changes his or her device password to a new value to ensure device password privacy.

Newer smartphones that support password recovery will copy device passwords to their Exchange server during ActiveSync synchronization provided that their ActiveSync policy has the **Enable password recovery** option checked as shown earlier in Figure 12-7. In the event that users forget their device password, they can display the copy of it stored on the Exchange server by clicking **Display Recovery Password** shown in Figure 12-16. If OWA has been disabled or is inaccessible, users can instead ask their Exchange administrator to obtain their device password. As an Exchange administrator, you can display the device password for a mailbox user using the Get-ActiveSyncDeviceStatistics cmdlet within the Exchange Management Shell. The following command displays the device password(s) associated with the user Jeff Smith (jeff.smith@octavius.net):

Get-ActiveSyncDeviceStatistics –Mailbox:'jeff.smith@octavius.net' –ShowRecoveryPassword:$true

In the event that a smartphone is lost or stolen, you can also force Exchange Server 2007 to remove all configuration and personal information from the device provided that the device supports the *remote wipe* feature of DirectPush. Users can start the remote wipe process by clicking on **Wipe All Data from Device** as shown in Figure 12-16. Exchange administrators can also perform a remote wipe operation using the Clear-ActiveSyncDevice cmdlet from an Exchange server. However, the Clear-ActiveSyncDevice cmdlet requires the smartphone device ID. The first Exchange Management Shell command will obtain the smartphone device ID for Jeff Smith (jeff.smith@octavius.net). This smartphone device ID can then be used in the second command to perform a remote wipe of the specific device (where DEVICE_ID represents Jeff Smith's smartphone device ID):

Get-ActiveSyncDeviceStatistics –Mailbox:'jeff.smith@octavius.net'

Clear-ActiveSyncDevice –Identity 'DEVICE_ID'

To help in troubleshooting connections, you can also click **Retrieve Log** as shown in Figure 12-16 to obtain an email that lists the details of the last 15 ActiveSync connections. In addition, Exchange administrators can save a copy of this log using the Get-ActiveSyncDeviceStatistics cmdlet on an Exchange server. For example, to save the ActiveSync connection details for Jeff Smith's smartphone to a text file on C:\, you could run the following command within the Exchange Management Shell:

Get-ActiveSyncDeviceStatistics –Identity:'jeff.smith@octavius.net' -GetMailboxLog:$true -OutputPath:'C:\'

Configuring BlackBerry Infrastructure Support

To integrate your Exchange servers with the BlackBerry Infrastructure, you must first install and configure a BES within your organization as well as create and activate BlackBerry users. In addition, you can use IT policies to control BlackBerry devices for different BlackBerry users and groups within your organization.

INSTALLING BLACKBERRY ENTERPRISE SERVER

To connect your Exchange organization to the BlackBerry Infrastructure so that BlackBerry-enabled devices can access Exchange mailboxes, you must first install BES version 4.1.3 or later on a Windows 2000 Server or Windows Server 2003 computer within your organization that does not contain any Exchange Server 2007 roles or have Outlook installed.

TAKE NOTE*

The recommended minimum hardware requirements for a BES that will service 500 smartphones is a Pentium 4 with a 2 GHz or greater CPU and 1.5 GB of RAM.

Before the installation, you must install the **Microsoft Exchange Server MAPI Client and Collaboration Data Objects 1.2.1** program on the server to obtain the Collaboration Data Object (CDO) and MAPI DLL files. You can download the **Microsoft Exchange Server MAPI Client and Collaboration Data Objects 1.2.1** program from **www.microsoft.com**.

In addition, you should create a mailbox user in your Exchange organization (e.g., BESAdmin) that will be used by BES to connect to Exchange Server 2007 and perform administration. This BESAdmin user account should be placed in the local Administrators group of the server on which you will be installing BES and be granted the Exchange View-Only Administrator role within your Exchange Organization. The BESAdmin user account should also be granted the **Logon as a service** right to the server on which you will be installing BES. You can configure the **Logon as a service** right using the **Computer Configuration** > **Windows Settings** > **Security Settings** > **Local Policies** > **User Rights Assignments** node within a GPO that applies to the BES computer.

Next, you must grant special permissions to the BESAdmin user account for the mailbox servers within your organization. To grant the necessary permissions for the BESAdmin user to the EXCH1 Mailbox role server, you could run the following command within the Exchange Management Shell:

Get-MailboxServer –Identity 'EXCH1' | Add-ADPermission –User 'BESAdmin' –AccessRights GenericRead, GenericWrite –Extendedrights Send-As, Receive-As, ms-Exch-Store-Admin

Next, you can log on to the target server as the BESAdmin user account and run the BES installation program. During the BES installation, various other software components will be installed, including the Java Runtime Environment (JRE), the Apache web server, and the Microsoft SQL Desktop Engine (MSDE).

INSTALLING BLACKBERRY ENTERPRISE SERVER

GET READY. Turn on the Exchange server, and log in as the BESAdmin user account. Close any windows that appear on the desktop.

1. Navigate to the BES installation media and double click the **setup.exe** file. The BlackBerry Enterprise Server Installation window appears as shown in Figure 12-17.

Figure 12-17

Starting a BES Installation

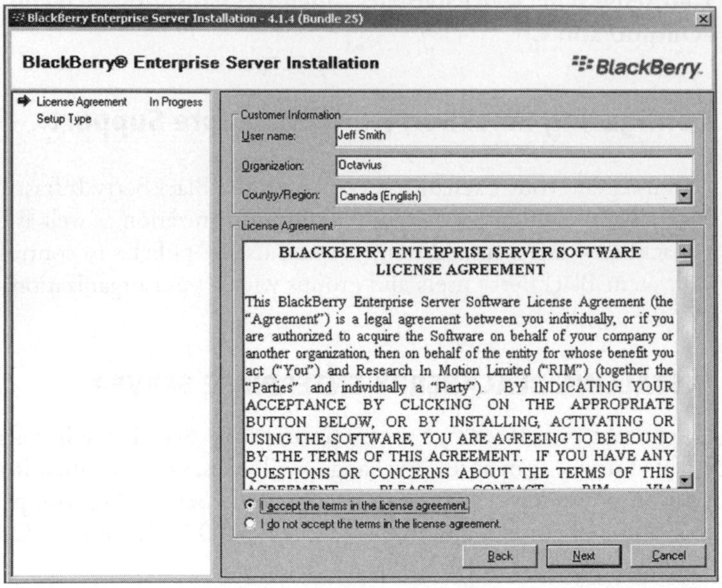

BlackBerry Enterprise Server Installation - 4.1.4 (Bundle 25)

BlackBerry® Enterprise Server Installation   **BlackBerry.**

➡ License Agreement   In Progress
   Setup Type

Customer Information
User name: Jeff Smith
Organization: Octavius
Country/Region: Canada (English)

License Agreement

BLACKBERRY ENTERPRISE SERVER SOFTWARE LICENSE AGREEMENT

This BlackBerry Enterprise Server Software License Agreement (the "Agreement") is a legal agreement between you individually, or if you are authorized to acquire the Software on behalf of your company or another organization, then on behalf of the entity for whose benefit you act ("You") and Research In Motion Limited ("RIM") (together the "Parties" and individually a "Party"). BY INDICATING YOUR ACCEPTANCE BY CLICKING ON THE APPROPRIATE BUTTON BELOW, OR BY INSTALLING, ACTIVATING OR USING THE SOFTWARE, YOU ARE AGREEING TO BE BOUND BY THE TERMS OF THIS AGREEMENT. IF YOU HAVE ANY QUESTIONS OR CONCERNS ABOUT THE TERMS OF THIS

⦿ I accept the terms in the license agreement.
○ I do not accept the terms in the license agreement.

Back   Next   Cancel

2. Supply the appropriate organization information as shown in Figure 12-17, select **I accept the terms in the license agreement**, and click **Next**.

3. At the Setup Type page, select BlackBerry Enterprise Server in the Setup Type dialog box and click **Next**.

4. At the Apache License page, select **I accept the terms in the license agreement** and click **Next**.

5. At the Preinstallation Checklist page, review any warnings or errors as well as any software that will be automatically installed on the server to support BES. The "Exchange Server is not detected" warning shown in Figure 12-18 is normal if your Exchange organization only contains Exchange Server 2007 computers. When finished, click **Next**.

Figure 12-18

Viewing BES Prerequisites

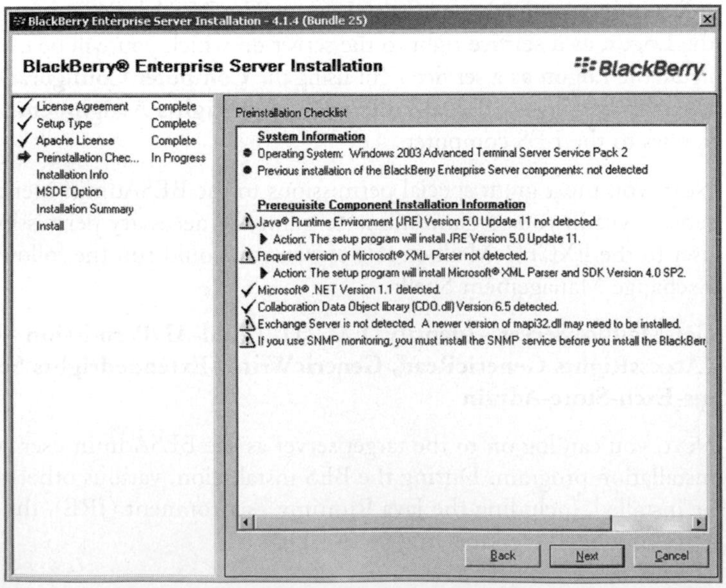

BlackBerry Enterprise Server Installation - 4.1.4 (Bundle 25)

BlackBerry® Enterprise Server Installation   **BlackBerry.**

✓ License Agreement   Complete
✓ Setup Type   Complete
✓ Apache License   Complete
➡ Preinstallation Chec...   In Progress
   Installation Info
   MSDE Option
   Installation Summary
   Install

Preinstallation Checklist

System Information
● Operating System: Windows 2003 Advanced Terminal Server Service Pack 2
● Previous installation of the BlackBerry Enterprise Server components: not detected

Prerequisite Component Installation Information
⚠ Java® Runtime Environment (JRE) Version 5.0 Update 11 not detected.
   ▶ Action: The setup program will install JRE Version 5.0 Update 11.
⚠ Required version of Microsoft® XML Parser not detected.
   ▶ Action: The setup program will install Microsoft® XML Parser and SDK Version 4.0 SP2.
✓ Microsoft® .NET Version 1.1 detected.
✓ Collaboration Data Object library (CDO.dll) Version 6.5 detected.
⚠ Exchange Server is not detected. A newer version of mapi32.dll may need to be installed.
⚠ If you use SNMP monitoring, you must install the SNMP service before you install the BlackBerr

Back   Next   Cancel

6. At the Installation Info page, ensure that your computer name is listed in the **Name** dialog box and supply the password for your BESAdmin user account in the **Password** dialog box as shown in Figure 12-19. Following this, you can optionally change the default location of the BES installation and log files. When finished, click **Next**.

Figure 12-19

BES Account and System Information

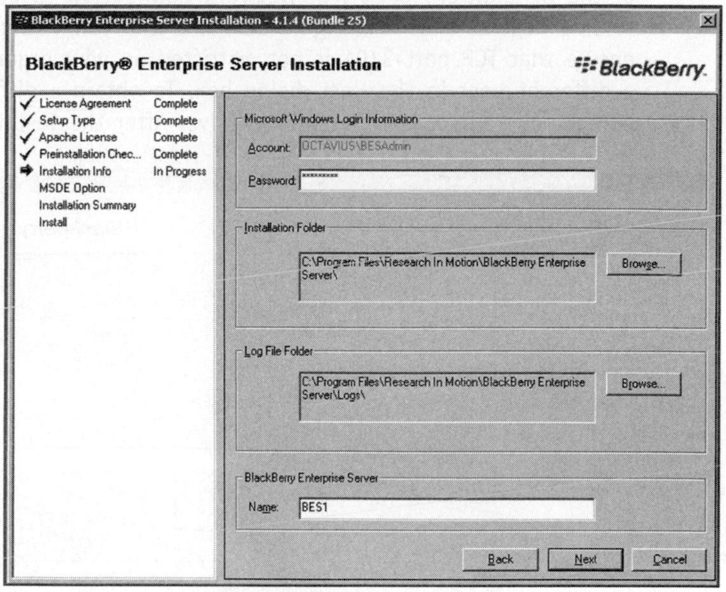

7. At the MSDE Option page, ensure that **Yes, I want to install MSDE 2000 locally** is selected and click **Next**.

8. At the Installation Summary page, review the summary of your selections and click **Next**.

9. At the Install page, click **Continue** to install BES. At the end of the installation process, click **Yes** to reboot your computer and continue the installation process by configuring BES settings.

10. After your computer has rebooted, log in as BESAdmin. The BlackBerry Enterprise Server Installation window will appear and prompt you to specify details regarding the SQL database used by BES as shown in Figure 12-20. If you have installed the MSDE locally, you do not need to modify the parameters on this page. Click **Next**. When prompted to create the BESMgmt database, click **Yes**.

Figure 12-20

BES SQL Configuration

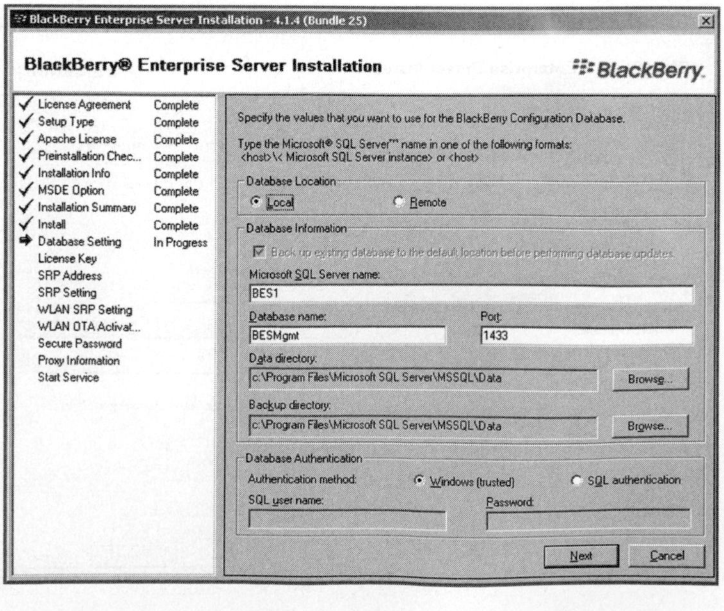

11. At the License Key page, enter your BES Client Access License key in the **CAL Key** dialog box and click **Next**. You can find this key on your installation media or supporting documentation.

12. At the SRP Address page, you will automatically be provided with a BlackBerry Infrastructure server host for the geographic location that you chose at the onset of the installation. Click **Test Network Connection** to ensure that you can connect to this host as shown in Figure 12-21. If the connection fails, you may need to ensure that TCP port 3101 is not restricted on your organizational firewall or supply a different host in the Host dialog box. To obtain a different host, you must contact your RIM support representative. After the test is successful, click **Next**.

Figure 12-21

SRP Configuration

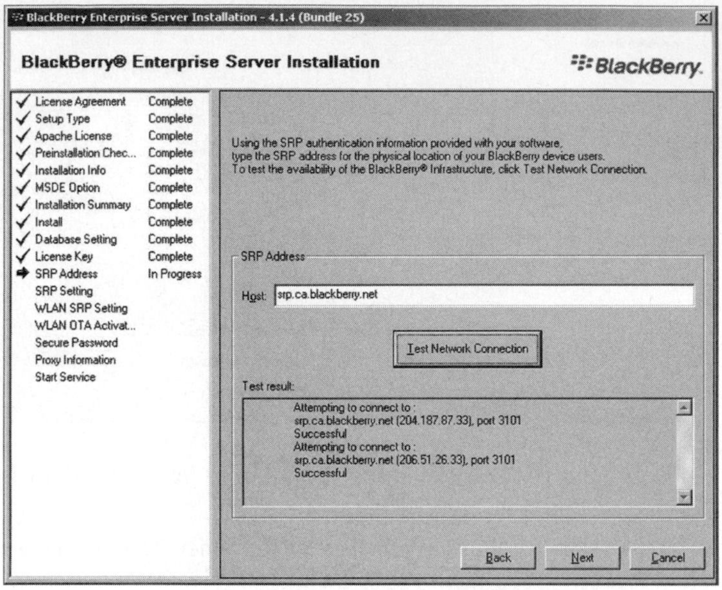

13. At the SRP Setting page shown in Figure 12-22, enter the SRP identifier, SRP authentication key, and host routing information in the appropriate dialog boxes. You can find these on your installation media or supporting documentation. This information is used to authenticate your BES to the BlackBerry Infrastructure when sending and receiving information using SRP. To ensure that you have entered valid information, click **Validate SRP key and ID**. If you receive a message indicating that your SRP key and ID are valid, click **Next**. Otherwise, ensure that you have typed the correct information and repeat this step.

Figure 12-22

SRP Authentication Configuration

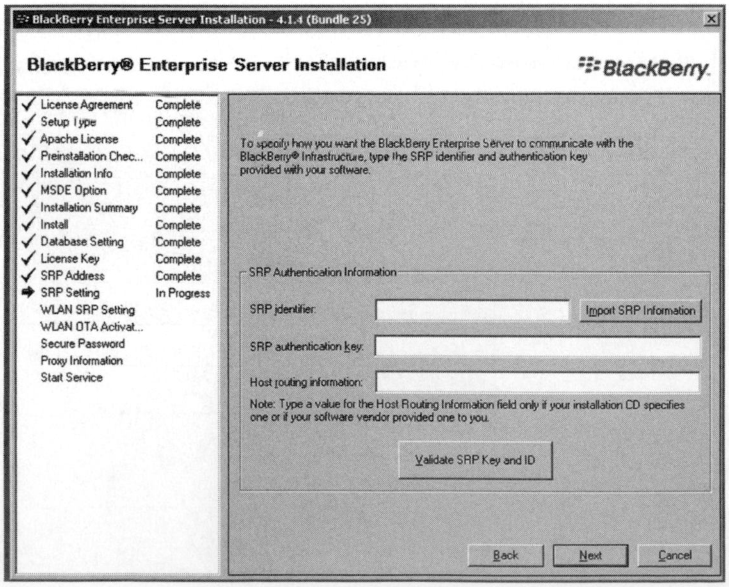

14. At the Microsoft Exchange Server window, supply an Exchange server and mailbox name (i.e., BESAdmin) to verify MAPI connectivity and click **Check Name**. If the MAPI connectivity test is successful, the Exchange server and mailbox names will be underlined. Click **OK**.

15. At the WLAN SRP Setting page, click **Next**.

16. At the WLAN OTA Activation page as shown in Figure 12-23, select **Allow wireless activation in my WLAN environment** if you wish to allow WiFi-enabled BlackBerry devices to be activated *over the air (OTA)* using a WLAN. If you select this option, you must also select to use MX records to resolve the target SMTP server or configure it manually as well as specify the recipient of any *Email Transfer Protocol (ETP)* messages during the activation process. When finished, click **Next**.

Figure 12-23

WLAN Activation Configuration

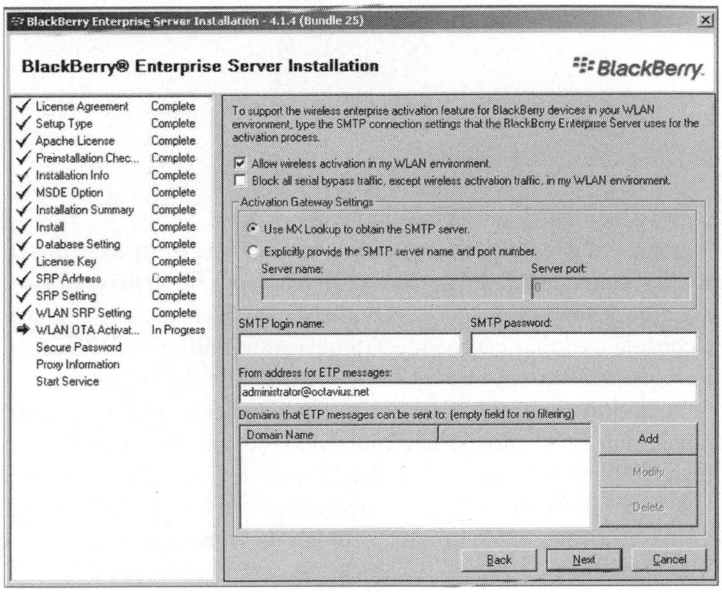

17. At the Secure Password page, optionally override default parameters used to secure communication between BES components and click **Next**.

18. At the Proxy Information page, optionally specify Proxy server configuration only if your BES server must pass through a proxy server to access the Internet and click **Next**.

19. At the Start Service page, click **Start Service** to start the BES components. Click **Finish**. You may be prompted to specify the credentials of a MAPI account used when connecting to Exchange Server 2007. This account should be your BES administrative account (i.e., BESAdmin).

After BES has been successfully installed, you can modify most parameters that you entered during the installation as well as specify additional server settings using the *BlackBerry Server Configuration utility* (**Start** > **All Programs** > **BlackBerry Enterprise Server** > **BlackBerry Server Configuration**). The BlackBerry Router tab of BlackBerry Server Configuration can be used to modify the BlackBerry Infrastructure server name and ports used for SRP as shown in Figure 12-24.

Figure 12-24

BlackBerry Server Configuration Utility

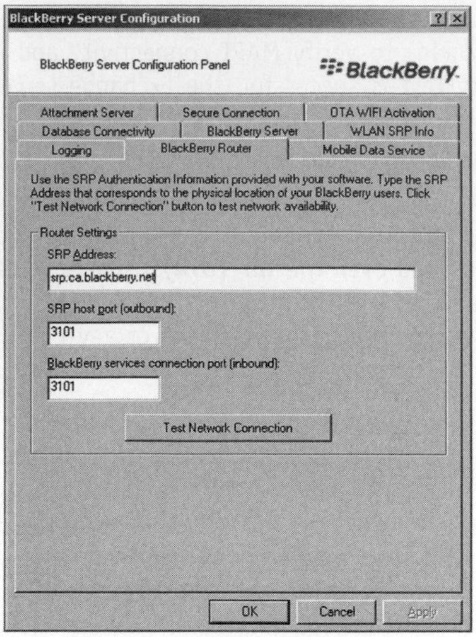

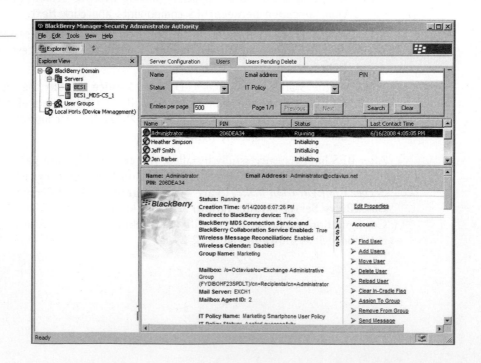

Nearly all day-to-day configuration of BES is performed using the ***BlackBerry Manager utility*** (**Start > All Programs > BlackBerry Enterprise Server > BlackBerry Manager**). The BlackBerry Manager is very similar to the Exchange Management Console in that it has a console tree that can be used to navigate to different BES areas, a detail pane that has tabs to organize features, and a work pane that lists the properties of the current item. Instead of an action pane, the BlackBerry Manager has a tasks area in the lower right portion of the screen that is used to execute common tasks for the currently selected item. In Figure 12-25, the BES1 server is selected in the console tree, and the Administrator user is selected on the Users tab of the detail pane. At the top of the Users tab, you can narrow the list of users displayed using search criteria in much the same way that filters do within the Exchange Management Console. The work pane at the bottom of Figure 12-25 lists the details for the Administrator user and the Account section of the tasks area in the lower right corner lists common Account tasks.

Figure 12-25

BlackBerry Manager Utility

Using BlackBerry Manager, you can configure BlackBerry users and groups as well as control their functionality using *IT policies* in much the same way that ActiveSync policies do.

ADDING BLACKBERRY USERS

After installing BES, you must add BlackBerry device users from your Exchange organization so that BES can monitor their mailboxes for new items that should be relayed to the BlackBerry device. You can add a new BlackBerry device user within the BlackBerry Manager utility by selecting your BES server under the **BlackBerry Domain > Servers** node in the console tree, selecting the **Users** tab and clicking **Add Users** in the tasks area as shown earlier in Figure 12-25. You can then select the appropriate mailbox users from the Global Address List in the Select Mailbox window as shown in Figure 12-26.

Figure 12-26

Adding a BlackBerry User

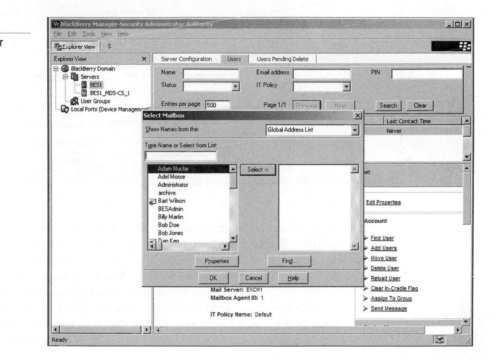

ACTIVATING BLACKBERRY USERS

Once you have added mailbox users from your Exchange organization to BES, you must activate them so that BES can communicate with their smartphone devices using the BlackBerry Infrastructure. There are four ways to activate a BlackBerry user:

TAKE NOTE *

You can obtain a copy of the BlackBerry Desktop Manager software from www.BlackBerry.com.

- BlackBerry smartphone users can log on to their AD domain from their workstation, connect their BlackBerry smartphone device to their workstation via a USB/serial cable and use the ***BlackBerry Desktop Manager utility***. During the installation of the BlackBerry Desktop Manager, you will be prompted to select Microsoft Exchange synchronization support, and when you connect your BlackBerry smartphone device to your computer and run the BlackBerry Desktop Manager, it will automatically activate your smartphone device according to your Outlook account information.

- BES administrators can connect BlackBerry smartphone devices to their administrative workstation using a USB/serial cable before deploying the device to users and use the BlackBerry Manager utility to assign the device to users. To assign a connected device to a user using BlackBerry Manager, navigate to your BES server under the **BlackBerry Domain > Servers** node in the console tree, select the appropriate user on the **Users** tab, and click **Assign Device** in the Device Management section of the tasks area as shown in Figure 12-27.

Figure 12-27

Assigning a BlackBerry Device

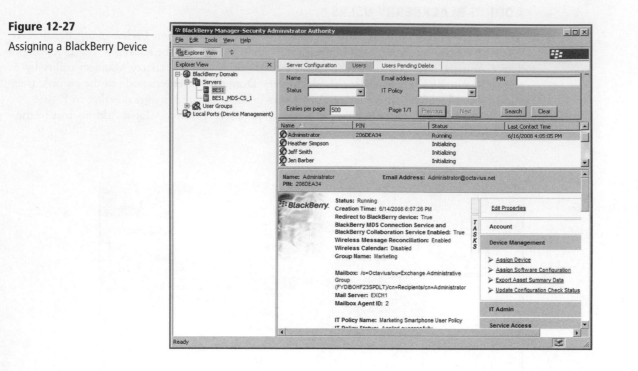

• BES administrators set an enterprise activation password. To set an enterprise activation password using BlackBerry Manager, navigate to your BES server under the **BlackBerry Domain > Servers** node in the console tree, select the appropriate user on the **Users** tab and click **Set Activation Password** in the Service Access section of the tasks area as shown in Figure 12-28. After you specify a password and time limit (48 hours by default), users can complete the enterprise activation process within the time limit by navigating to **Options > Advanced Options > Enterprise Activation** on their BlackBerry smart-phone and supplying their email address as well as their enterprise activation password.

Figure 12-28

Configuring BlackBerry Activation

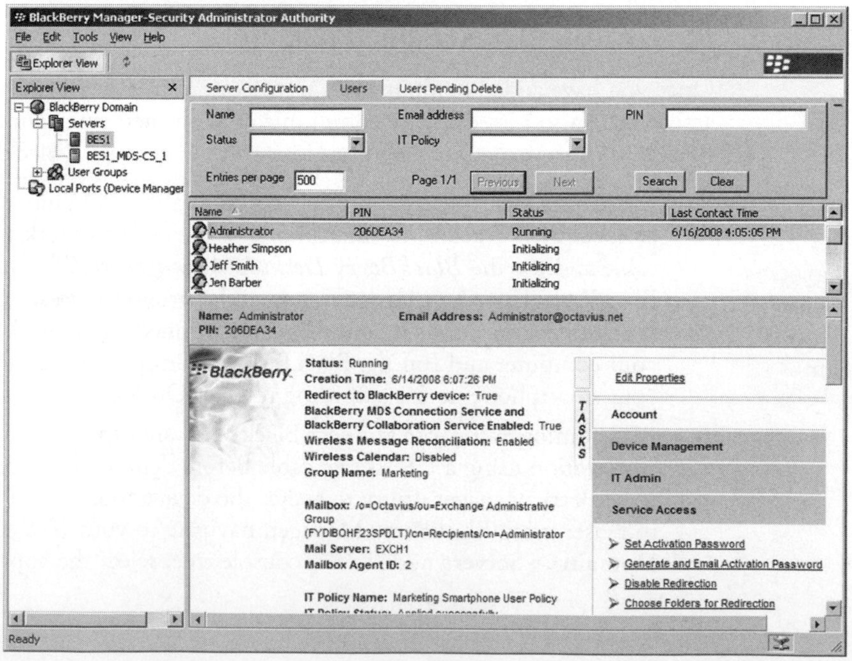

- BES administrators generate an enterprise activation password. To generate an enterprise activation password in BlackBerry Manager, navigate to your BES server under the **BlackBerry Domain** > **Servers** node in the console tree, select the appropriate user on the **Users** tab, and click **Generate an Email Activation Password** in the Service Access section of the tasks area as shown earlier in Figure 12-28. Users will receive an email indicating the password and process used to activate their BlackBerry smartphone as shown in Figure 12-29.

Figure 12-29

BlackBerry Enterprise
Activation Email

Once you have activated a user, the *Personal Identification Number (PIN)* from the associated BlackBerry smartphone device will show up alongside the user with a status of **Running** when listed in BlackBerry Manager as shown earlier for the Administrator user in Figure 12-28.

CREATING AND ASSIGNING IT POLICIES

Like ActiveSync policies, BES IT policies can be used to configure and restrict the settings on the BlackBerry smartphones within your organization. This includes restricting access to smartphone features such as WiFi and digital cameras as well as the configuration of security settings such as device password restrictions.

After BES installation, a default IT policy is applied to all BlackBerry users that allows complete smartphone functionality and provides a minimum level of security. You should create additional IT policies that define a more appropriate level of security and functionality.

CREATING AN IT POLICY

GET READY. Turn on the computer, and log in as the Administrator user account. Close any windows that appear on the desktop.

1. Click **Start**, **All Programs**, **BlackBerry Enterprise Server**, and then click **BlackBerry Manager**. The BlackBerry Manager window appears.

2. In the console tree pane, highlight **BlackBerry Domain** and select **Edit Properties** from the tasks area under the Global tab in the detail pane. When the Global Properties window appears, select IT Policy in the left pane as shown in Figure 12-30.

Figure 12-30

Global Server Properties

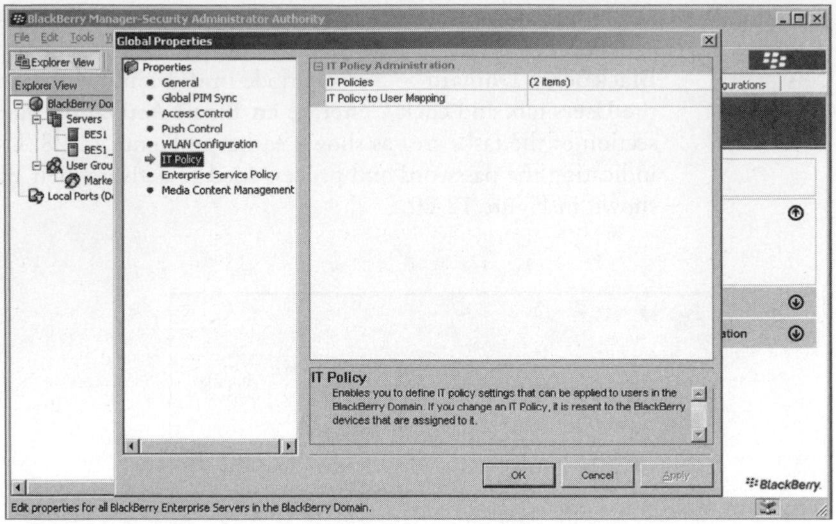

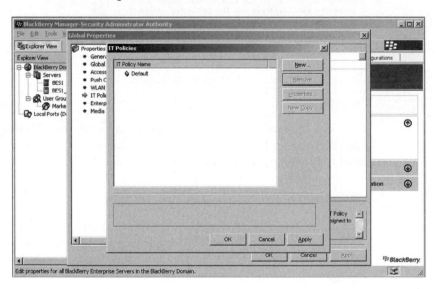

3. Double click **IT Policies** in the right pane. The IT Policies window appears as shown in Figure 12-31.

Figure 12-31

Configuring IT Policies

4. Click **New**. When the IT policy window appears, supply a name for the IT policy next to the **IT Policy Name** field as shown in Figure 12-32.

Figure 12-32

Configuring a New IT Policy

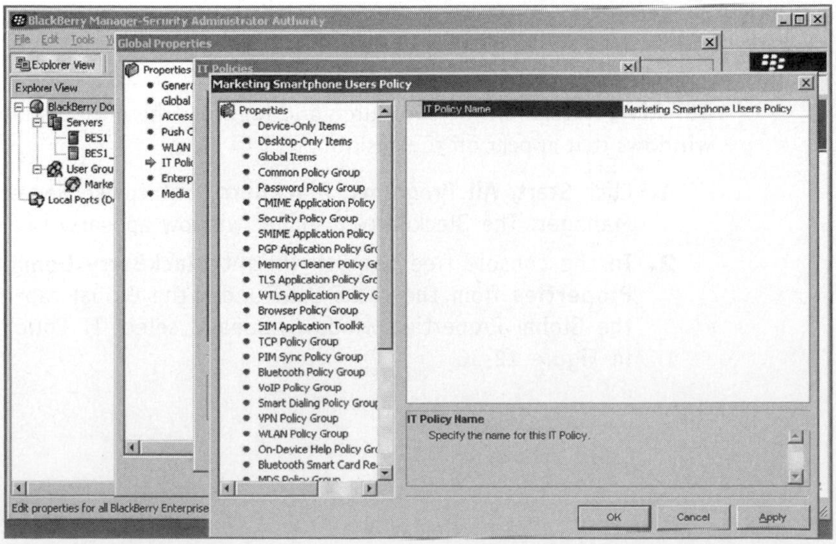

5. Navigate through the property objects in the left pane and specify any policy options in the appropriate fields in the right pane. Although IT policies contain far more options than ActiveSync policies, many of the settings are similar. The Password Policy Group settings shown in Figure 12-33 will force the smartphone to be locked after 15 minutes of inactivity. To unlock the smartphone, the user must type the smartphone device password. This password is not displayed on the screen as it is typed (Suppress Password Echo), and 8 invalid password attempts will force the removal of all configuration and personal data from the smartphone. If users change their device password, they must change it to a unique value that has not been used 6 times previously.

Figure 12-33

Password Policy Group Options

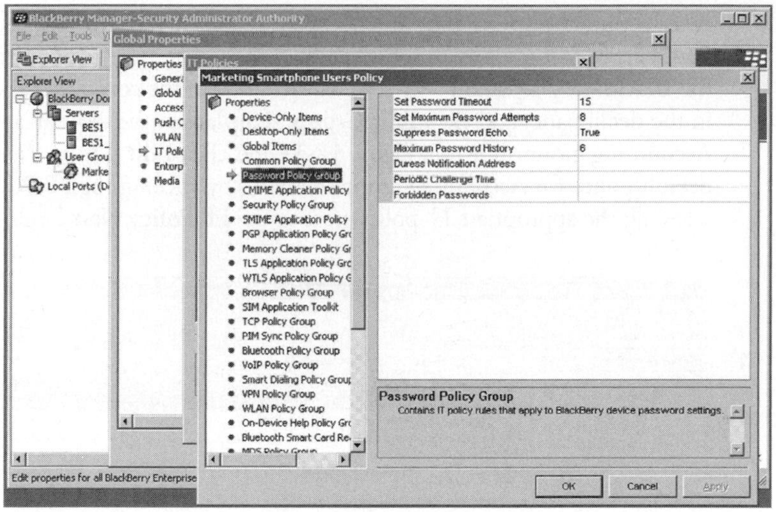

6. When finished specifying IT policy options, click **OK**.

7. Click **OK** to close the IT Policies window.

8. Click **OK** to close the Global Properties window.

9. Close the BlackBerry Manager.

After creating IT policies, you can assign them to the appropriate users. Select the appropriate users under the **Users** tab for your BES server as described earlier, click **Assign IT Policy** under the IT Admin section of the tasks area, and select the appropriate policy from the drop-down box in the Select IT Policy window as shown in Figure 12-34. Each user can only have a single IT Policy assigned to them. If you wish to assign the same policy to multiple users, hold down the **Shift** or **Ctrl** key while selecting users before you click **Assign IT Policy**.

Figure 12-34

Applying an IT Policy to a User

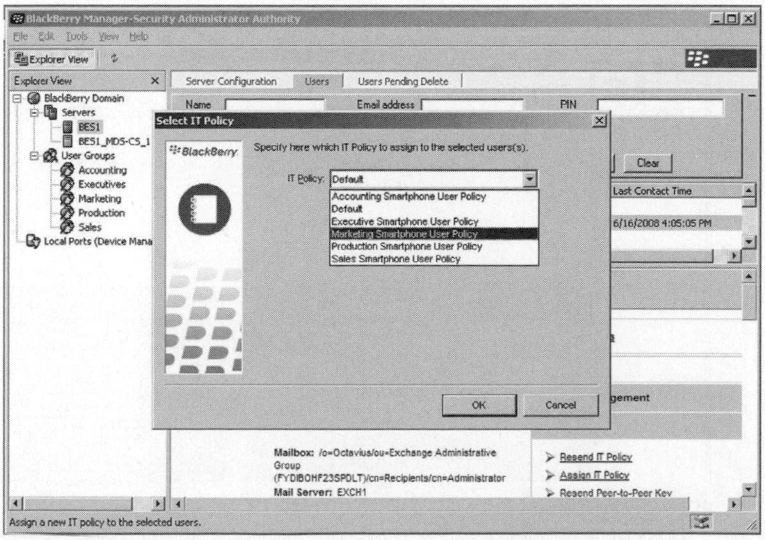

CREATING AND USING BLACKBERRY GROUPS

To simplify the management of BlackBerry users, you can create BlackBerry groups that contain users with the same restrictions and management requirements. To create a new BlackBerry group in BlackBerry Manager, navigate to **BlackBerry Domain > User Groups** node in the console tree, select **Create Group** from the tasks area, and supply a name and description for the group when prompted.

Following this, you can assign existing BlackBerry users to your new BlackBerry group within BlackBerry Manager by selecting them under the **Users** tab for your BES server, clicking **Assign To Group** in the tasks area as shown earlier in Figure 12-25, and specifying the appropriate group.

After adding the appropriate users to groups, you can apply IT policies to all current and future members of the group within BlackBerry Manager to save time managing IT policies. Navigate to the **BlackBerry Domain > User Groups** node in the console tree, select the appropriate group in the detail pane, and click **Edit Group Template** in the tasks area. For example, if you select the Accounting group shown in Figure 12-35 and click **Edit Group Template**, you can specify the default policy for Accounting group members by clicking the **IT Policy** object in the left pane and selecting the appropriate IT policy next to the **IT Policy Name** field as shown in Figure 12-36.

Figure 12-35

Viewing BlackBerry User Groups

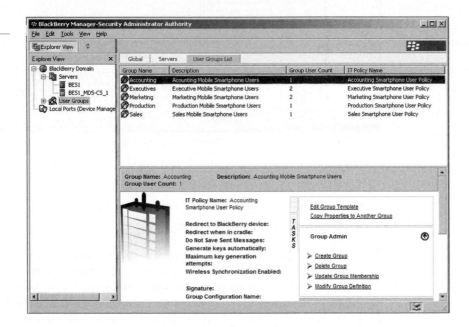

Figure 12-36

Setting the Default IT Policy for a Group

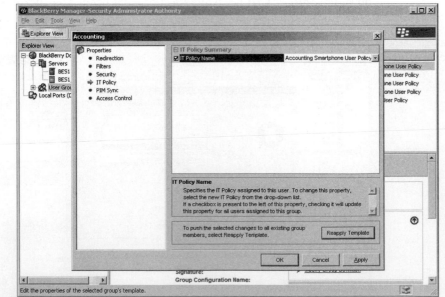

Afterwards, you can select the **BlackBerry Domain** > **User Groups** node within BlackBerry Manager as shown earlier in Figure 12-35 to view the list of groups, the number of members in each, as well as the default IT policy used for group members.

■ Implementing Unified Messaging

THE BOTTOM LINE

Many organizations are using Unified Messaging to consolidate their messaging and telephone infrastructures into a single unit for email, calendar, fax, voice mail, and telephone access. Before you implement Unified Messaging, you must first understand its components as well as the procedures used to configure the Exchange Server 2007 UM role.

Understanding Unified Messaging

UM role servers within your organization provide for Unified Messaging by connecting to the PBX system used to service your organization's telephone system. This allows voice mail and fax messages to be stored within Exchange mailboxes as well as the ability to access mailbox contents from a telephone connection using Outlook Voice Access.

TAKE NOTE ★

Public telephone networks are often called the *Public Switched Telephone Network (PSTN)*.

Most organizations use a *Private Branch eXchange (PBX)* to connect telephones within the organization to the public telephone network so that users within the organization can make outgoing telephone calls as well as receive incoming telephone calls. Each telephone in the organization is given a telephone extension number that can be used by internal and external callers to locate individuals within the organization. Most PBX systems also provide *automated attendants* (commonly called auto attendants) that provide instructions to callers about how to use the system, for example, "Press 1 for office hours," "Press 2 for reception," or "If you know the extension for an individual member of the organization, you can enter it at any time." Moreover, PBX systems can also be configured to receive faxes and store voice mail for users by extension number.

Newer PBX systems can also communicate to email servers within your organization across the existing IP network. The PBX component that is used to interface with your organization's IP network is called the *Internet Protocol (IP) gateway*.

By integrating your PBX system with your Exchange servers, voice mail and faxes can be stored within the appropriate Exchange mailbox and accessed from an email client. In addition, mailbox users can access their email, faxes, and calendar appointments from a remote telephone connection. This functionality is collectively referred to as *Unified Messaging (UM)*. Exchange Server 2007 implements UM using the UM role. UM role servers connect the Hub, CAS, and Mailbox Exchange server roles to the PBX system.

UM role servers can retrieve voice mail messages left for your telephone extension. These voice mail messages are first retrieved from the PBX using the *Voice Over IP (VOIP)* protocol and converted to SMTP email that is forwarded to the Hub role servers within your organization and ultimately delivered to your mailbox on the appropriate Mailbox role server. You can then view your voice mail alongside other emails using an email client such as Outlook or Entourage or by accessing OWA. Figure 12-37 illustrates the various UM components working together.

Figure 12-37

Unified Messaging Components

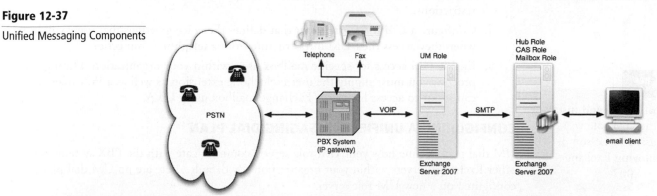

Using UM, you can also access the email, voice mail, and calendar items within your mailbox using an analog, digital, or cellular telephone by dialing a telephone number called the *subscriber access number* that is configured on your PBX to forward requests to *Outlook Voice Access (OVA)*. After entering your telephone extension number and a PIN that is configured for your mailbox on the telephone touchpad, OVA will use *Automatic Speech Recognition (ASR)* to allow you to speak your selections into your telephone. Alternatively, you can use the touchtone inputs on your telephone keypad to navigate the menu system.

By using OVA, you can:

- Listen to new and existing email and voice mail messages
- Forward or reply to email and voice mail messages
- Listen to your calendar appointments
- Accept or decline meeting requests
- Locate users in the global address list (GAL)
- Leave a voice mail message for another user

When OVA accesses the content of your mailbox, the *Text-to-Speech (TTS) engine* on the UM server converts the email and calendar items to speech audio. This speech audio is then sent to the PBX using VOIP, where it is then played for the telephone user.

Configuring Unified Messaging Support

In addition to configuring a PBX, you must also configure the UM role servers within your organization to provide for Unified Messaging. To do this, you should understand how to create and configure UM dial plans, UM IP gateways, UM mailbox policies, and UM auto attendants, as well as how to enable UM for mailbox users.

CERTIFICATION READY?
Configure Exchange server roles.
1.4

To configure UM within your organization, you must configure settings on your PBX and IP gateway as well as on the Exchange servers within your organization that host the UM role. Because there are many different PBX systems available from different manufacturers, the steps that you take to configure your organization's PBX to work with the Exchange Server 2007 UM role will ultimately depend on the type and model of the PBX that you have. As a result, we will focus on the PBX-general steps required to prepare Exchange Server 2007 for UM.

Before configuring UM in Exchange Server 2007, you must have one or more Exchange servers that host the UM role. Following this, you can use the Exchange Management Console or the Exchange Management Shell as an Exchange Organization Administrator to configure the UM role to work with your organization's PBX. To configure UM for your organization, you must perform the following tasks:

TAKE NOTE*
You can obtain information regarding the configuration of your PBX system from the PBX manufacturer. Often, this information is readily available in document form on the PBX manufacturer's Web site.

1. Configure a *UM dial plan* that contains UM role settings, and associate the dial plan with your UM role server.
2. Configure a *UM IP gateway* that identifies the IP gateway device that is used to connect Exchange Server 2007 to the PBX system as well as the UM dial plan it should use.
3. Configure a *UM mailbox policy* with the appropriate message, PIN, and dialing restrictions.
4. Configure a *UM auto attendant* that defines the voice greetings that users will hear when they access their UM infrastructure from a telephone connection.
5. Enable UM access for specific mailbox users within your organization. During this process, you must supply the user's telephone extension as well as a PIN that the user can input to access his or her Exchange mailbox using OVA.

Preparing for and installing the UM role was discussed in Lesson 3, "Deploying Exchange Server 2007."

CONFIGURING A UNIFIED MESSAGING DIAL PLAN

UM dial plans define how your UM role servers communicate with the PBX system and other Exchange servers within your organization. By default, there are no UM dial plans configured on a new UM role server.

CREATING A NEW UNIFIED MESSAGING DIAL PLAN

GET READY. Turn on the computer, and log in as the Administrator user account. Close any windows that appear on the desktop.

1. Click **Start**, **All Programs**, **Microsoft Exchange Server 2007**, and then click **Exchange Management Console**. The Exchange Management Console window appears.

2. In the console tree pane, expand **Organization Configuration** and highlight **Unified Messaging**.

3. In the action pane, click **New UM Dial Plan**.

4. At the New UM Dial Plan window, specify an appropriate name for your UM dial plan in the **Name** dialog box and specify the appropriate dial plan options. As shown in Figure 12-38, the Octavius Dial Plan accepts 3-digit telephone extensions and does not provide any VoIP security.

Figure 12-38

Creating a New Unified Messaging Dial Plan

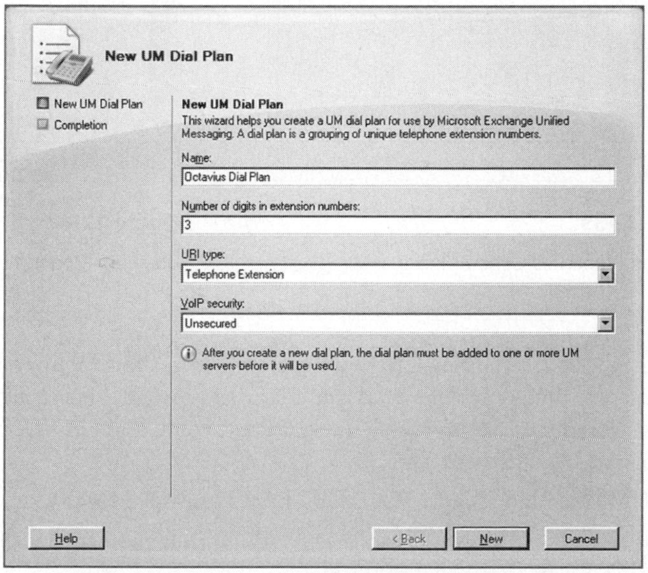

TAKE NOTE*

The *Uniform Resource Identifier (URI)* type shown in Figure 12-38 refers to the method used to contact phone recipients. In addition to regular telephone extension routing, you can also choose *E.164* or *Session Initiation Protocol (SIP)* if your PBX supports them.

New UM Dial Plan

New UM Dial Plan
This wizard helps you create a UM dial plan for use by Microsoft Exchange Unified Messaging. A dial plan is a grouping of unique telephone extension numbers.

Name:
Octavius Dial Plan

Number of digits in extension numbers:
3

URI type:
Telephone Extension

VoIP security:
Unsecured

(i) After you create a new dial plan, the dial plan must be added to one or more UM servers before it will be used.

Help   < Back   New   Cancel

5. Review your settings and click **New**. The Completion page appears.
6. Click **Finish** to close the New UM Dial Plan window.
7. Close the Exchange Management Console.

THE COMMAND LINE WAY

You can also use the **New-UMDialPlan** cmdlet in the Exchange Management Shell to create a new UM dial plan. To create the same UM dial plan shown earlier in Figure 12-38, you could run the following command in the Exchange Management Shell:

New-UMDialPlan -Name 'Octavius Dial Plan' -NumberOfDigitsInExtension '3' -URIType 'TelExtn' -VoIPSecurity 'Unsecured'

For more information on the syntax and usage of the New-UMDialPlan cmdlet, search for it within Exchange Server 2007 Help.

After creating a new UM dial plan, you must configure its settings. Select it under the UM Dial Plan tab within the **Organization Configuration > Unified Messaging** node of the Exchange Management Console and select **Properties** from the action pane. The settings that you configure within your dial plan will largely depend on the settings that are required by your PBX system. However, some settings within your UM dial plan are used to affect the functionality of your UM role server. For example, on the General tab of dial plan properties, you can configure whether users are allowed to receive fax transmissions that are sent to their telephone extensions as shown in Figure 12-39. Similarly, to use OVA, you must specify a subscriber access number that users can dial from a telephone to access the OVA system on the Subscriber Access tab of UM dial plan properties. On the Subscriber Access tab shown in Figure 12-40, users can access OVA by dialing 519-429-8177.

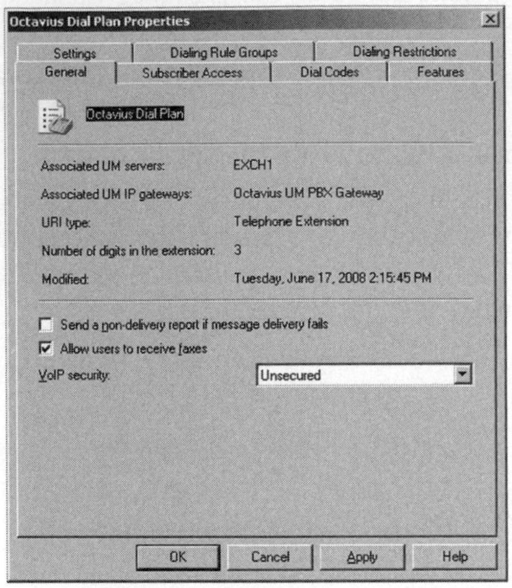

Figure 12-39

Dial Plan Properties General Tab

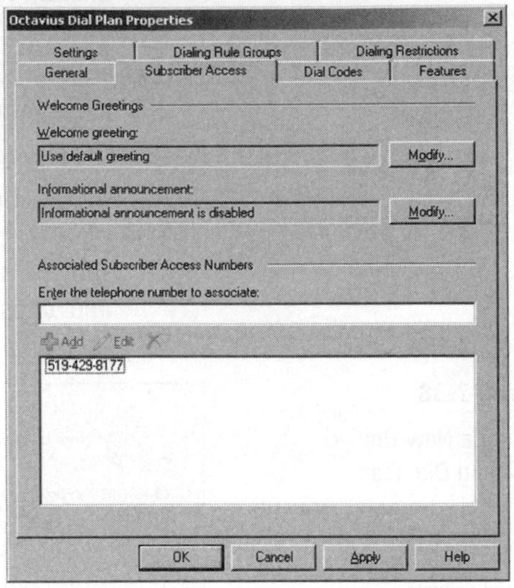

Figure 12-40

Dial Plan Properties Subscriber Access Tab

THE COMMAND LINE WAY

You can also use the **Set-UMDialPlan** cmdlet in the Exchange Management Shell to modify the properties of a UM dial plan. To prevent users from receiving fax transmissions using UM for the Octavius Dial Plan, you could run the following command in the Exchange Management Shell:

Set-UMDialPlan -Name 'Octavius Dial Plan' –FaxEnabled $false

For more information on the syntax and usage of the Set-UMDialPlan cmdlet, search for it within Exchange Server 2007 Help.

After configuring a UM dial plan with the appropriate settings to match your PBX, you must associate the dial plan with a UM role server to allow the UM role server the ability to access the information within the UM dial plan.

 ASSOCIATING A UNIFIED MESSAGING DIAL PLAN WITH A UM ROLE SERVER

GET READY. Turn on the computer, and log in as the Administrator user account. Close any windows that appear on the desktop.

1. Click **Start**, **All Programs**, **Microsoft Exchange Server 2007**, and then click **Exchange Management Console**. The Exchange Management Console window appears.

2. In the console tree pane, expand **Server Configuration** and highlight **Unified Messaging**.

3. In the detail pane, highlight your server and click **Properties** in the action pane.

4. In the properties of your UM role server, click on the **UM Settings** tab as shown in Figure 12-41. Click **Add**; select the appropriate dial plan in the Select Dial Plan window that appears, and click **OK**. You can optionally specify a different maximum number of phone and fax calls using the appropriate dialog boxes shown in Figure 12-41.

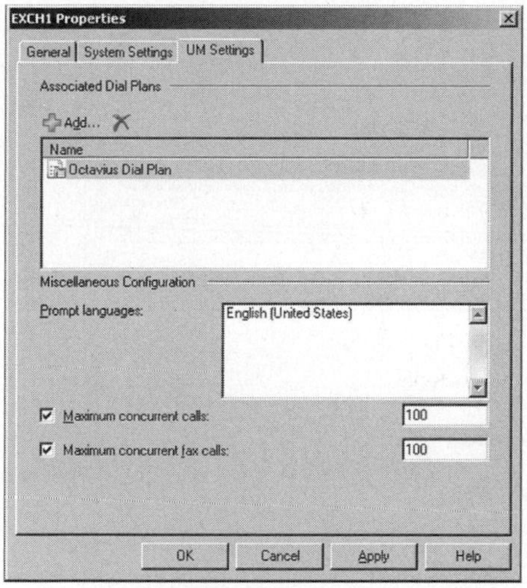

Figure 12-41

Associating a Unified Messaging Dial Plan with a UM Role Server

5. Click **OK** to close the server properties window.
6. Close the Exchange Management Console.

THE COMMAND LINE WAY

You can also use the **Set-UMServer** cmdlet in the Exchange Management Shell to associate a UM dial plan to a UM role server. To associate the Octavius Dial Plan with the server EXCH1, you could run the following command in the Exchange Management Shell:

Set-UMServer -Identity 'EXCH1' -DialPlans 'Octavius Dial Plan'

For more information on the syntax and usage of the Set-UMServer cmdlet, search for it within Exchange Server 2007 Help.

CONFIGURING A UNIFIED MESSAGING IP GATEWAY

To communicate with your organization's PBX, your UM server must be configured with the location of the PBX's IP gateway. To do this, you must create a UM IP gateway that lists the name or IP address of your PBX's IP gateway as well as the UM dial plan that will use it. Any UM role servers configured with this UM dial plan will be able to access the PBX's IP gateway.

CREATING A NEW UNIFIED MESSAGING IP GATEWAY

GET READY. Turn on the computer, and log in as the Administrator user account. Close any windows that appear on the desktop.

1. Click **Start**, **All Programs**, **Microsoft Exchange Server 2007**, and then click **Exchange Management Console**. The Exchange Management Console window appears.
2. In the console tree pane, expand **Organization Configuration** and highlight **Unified Messaging**.
3. In the action pane, click **New UM IP Gateway**.

4. At the New UM IP Gateway window, specify an appropriate name for your UM IP Gateway in the **Name** dialog box and supply the IP address or FQDN of the IP gateway device as well as the dial plan that should be used. In Figure 12-42, the Octavius UM PBX Gateway uses the IP address 10.3.111.250 and the Octavius Dial Plan.

Figure 12-42

Creating a Unified Messaging IP Gateway

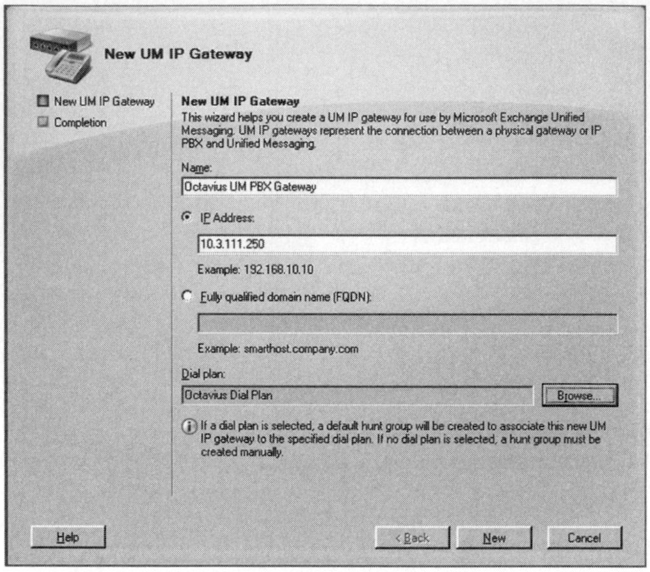

5. Review your settings and click **New**. The Completion page appears.

6. Click **Finish** to close the New UM IP Gateway window.

7. Close the Exchange Management Console.

> **THE COMMAND LINE WAY**
>
> You can also use the **New-UMIPGateway** cmdlet in the Exchange Management Shell to create a new UM IP gateway. To create the same UM IP gateway shown earlier in Figure 12-42, you could run the following command in the Exchange Management Shell:
>
> **New-UMIPGateway -Name 'Octavius UM PBX Gateway' -Address '10.3.111.250' -UMDialPlan 'Octavius Dial Plan'**
>
> For more information on the syntax and usage of the New-UMIPGateway cmdlet, search for it within Exchange Server 2007 Help.

CONFIGURING A UNIFIED MESSAGING MAILBOX POLICY

> **CERTIFICATION READY?**
> Configure policies.
> **3.4**

After you create a UM dial plan, a UM mailbox policy is automatically created and associated with your UM dial plan. You can modify this default UM mailbox policy or create a new one that is associated with your UM dial plan. To modify an existing UM mailbox policy, select it under the UM Mailbox Policies tab within the **Organization Configuration > Unified Messaging** node of the Exchange Management Console and select **Properties** from the action pane.

This UM mailbox policy defines the text included in email messages generated by your UM role server when sending voice mail or faxes to a mailbox as well as dialing restrictions. In addition, UM mailbox policies define the security settings used for PINs that are used to access OVA. The PIN Policies tab of the Octavius Mailbox Policy shown in Figure 12-43 requires that a PIN be a minimum of 6 digits in length and changed every 60 days. When changing a PIN, users cannot reuse their previous 5 PIN numbers. The PIN is automatically erased after 5 incorrect PIN attempts and the mailbox user is locked out after 15 incorrect PIN attempts.

Figure 12-43

Configuring PIN Settings in a
UM Mailbox Policy

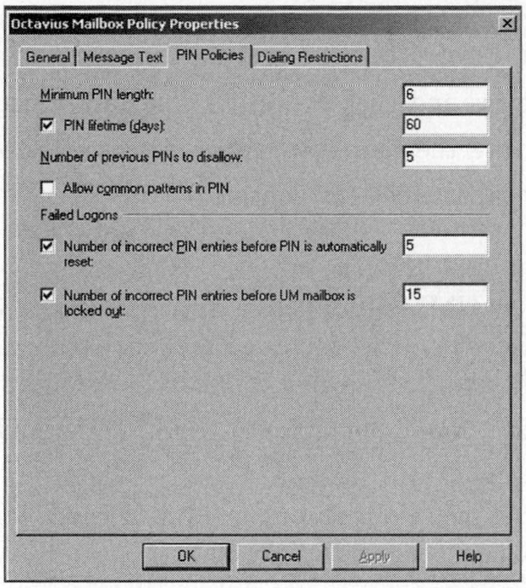

Octavius Mailbox Policy Properties

General | Message Text | PIN Policies | Dialing Restrictions |

Minimum PIN length: `6`

☑ PIN lifetime (days): `60`

Number of previous PINs to disallow: `5`

☐ Allow common patterns in PIN

Failed Logons

☑ Number of incorrect PIN entries before PIN is automatically reset: `5`

☑ Number of incorrect PIN entries before UM mailbox is locked out: `15`

OK | Cancel | Apply | Help

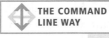

THE COMMAND
LINE WAY

You can also use the **Set-UMMailboxPolicy** cmdlet in the Exchange Management Shell to modify the settings within an existing UM mailbox policy. To set the same policy settings shown earlier in Figure 12-43, you could run the following command in the Exchange Management Shell:

**Set-UMMailboxPolicy -Identity 'Octavius Mailbox Policy' -MinPINLength 6
-PINLifetime 60 -PINHistoryCount 5 -LogonFailuresBeforePINReset 5
-MaxLogonAttempts 15**

For more information on the syntax and usage of the Set-UMMailboxPolicy cmdlet, search for it within Exchange Server 2007 Help.

➔ **CREATING A NEW UNIFIED MESSAGING MAILBOX POLICY**

GET READY. Turn on the computer, and log in as the Administrator user account. Close any windows that appear on the desktop.

1. Click **Start, All Programs, Microsoft Exchange Server 2007**, and then click **Exchange Management Console**. The Exchange Management Console window appears.

2. In the console tree pane, expand **Organization Configuration** and highlight **Unified Messaging**.

3. In the action pane, click **New UM Mailbox Policy**.

4. At the New UM Mailbox Policy window, specify an appropriate name for the UM mailbox policy in the **Name** dialog box as shown in Figure 12-44.

Figure 12-44

Creating a New Unified
Messaging Mailbox Policy

New UM Mailbox Policy

- New UM Mailbox Policy
- Completion

New UM Mailbox Policy

This wizard helps you create a new UM mailbox policy for use by Microsoft Exchange Unified Messaging. You must enter a name for this UM mailbox policy and associate this policy with a UM dial plan.

Name:

`Octavius Mailbox Policy`

Select associated dial plan:

`Octavius Dial Plan` | Browse...

Help | < Back | New | Cancel

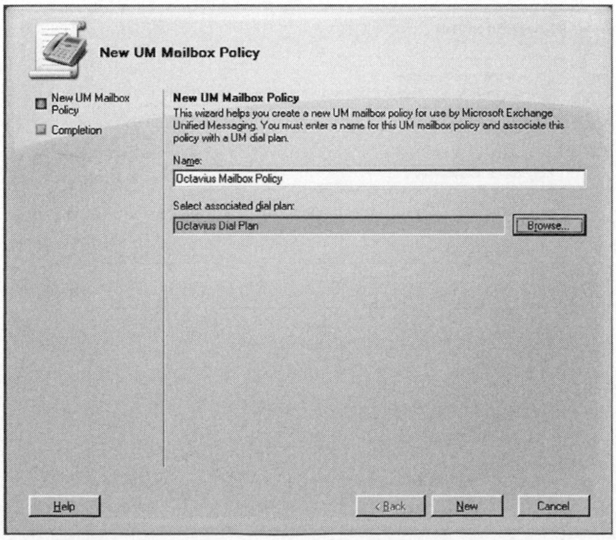

5. Next, click **Browse**, select the appropriate dial plan to associate with the new UM mailbox policy in the Select UM Dial Plan window that appears and click **OK**.

6. Review your settings and click **New**. The Completion page appears.

7. Click **Finish** to close the New UM Mailbox Policy window.

8. Close the Exchange Management Console.

THE COMMAND LINE WAY

You can also use the **New-UMMailboxPolicy** cmdlet in the Exchange Management Shell to create a new UM mailbox policy. To create the same UM mailbox policy shown earlier in Figure 12-44, you could run the following command in the Exchange Management Shell:

New-UMMailboxPolicy -Name 'Octavius Mailbox Policy' -UMDialPlan 'Octavius Dial Plan'

For more information on the syntax and usage of the New-UMMailboxPolicy cmdlet, search for it within Exchange Server 2007 Help.

CONFIGURING A UNIFIED MESSAGING AUTO ATTENDANT

Although most PBX systems have an auto attendant service, you may wish to create an auto attendant on your UM role server that contains greetings and voice prompts that guide telephone users through navigating the UM menu system. These greetings are stored as *.wav files on your UM role server. When you create a new UM auto attendant, you must also select a telephone extension number that is used to access the auto attendant UM menu system.

CREATING A NEW AUTO ATTENDANT

GET READY. Turn on the computer, and log in as the Administrator user account. Close any windows that appear on the desktop.

1. Click **Start**, **All Programs**, **Microsoft Exchange Server 2007**, and then click **Exchange Management Console**. The Exchange Management Console window appears.

2. In the console tree pane, expand **Organization Configuration** and highlight **Unified Messaging**.

3. In the action pane, click **New UM Auto Attendant**.

4. At the New UM Auto Attendant window, specify an appropriate name for the UM auto attendant in the **Name** dialog box as shown in Figure 12-45.

Figure 12-45

Creating a New Unified Messaging Auto Attendant

![New UM Auto Attendant window. This wizard helps you create a new UM auto attendant (AA) for use by Microsoft Exchange Unified Messaging. You must enter a name for this AA and associate the AA with a dial plan. You can also enter the extension number or numbers that callers will use to access this AA. Name: Octavius AutoAttendant. Select associated dial plan: Octavius Dial Plan, with Browse button. Extension numbers: 999. Checkboxes checked for Create auto attendant as enabled and Create auto attendant as speech-enabled. Buttons: Help, Back, New, Cancel.]

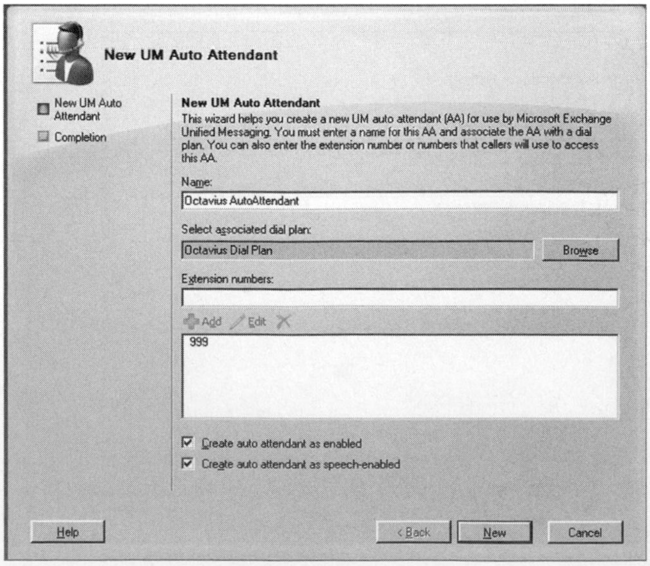

5. Next, click **Browse**, select the appropriate dial plan to associate with the new UM auto attendant in the Select UM Dial Plan window that appears and click **OK**.

6. In the **Extension numbers** dialog box, enter an extension number that users can input to access the auto attendant and click **Add**.

7. Ensure that **Create auto attendant as enabled** is selected to enable the auto attendant following creation. To additionally allow the auto attendant to respond to voice commands, ensure that **Create auto attendant as speech-enabled** is selected.

8. Review your settings and click **New**. The Completion page appears.

9. Click **Finish** to close the New UM Auto Attendant window.

10. Close the Exchange Management Console.

THE COMMAND LINE WAY

You can also use the **New-UMAutoAttendant** cmdlet in the Exchange Management Shell to create a new UM auto attendant. To create the same UM auto attendant shown earlier in Figure 12-45, you could run the following command in the Exchange Management Shell:

New-UMAutoAttendant -Name 'Octavius AutoAttendant' -UMDialPlan 'Octavius Dial Plan' -PilotIdentifierList '999' -Status 'Enabled' -SpeechEnabled $true

For more information on the syntax and usage of the New-UMAutoAttendant cmdlet, search for it within Exchange Server 2007 Help.

After you have created a UM auto attendant, you can modify it to specify custom greetings and menu prompts as well as specify greeting and menu options. To modify a UM auto attendant, select it under the UM Auto Attendants tab within the **Organization Configuration** > **Unified Messaging** node of the Exchange Management Console and select **Properties** from the action pane. By default, the UM auto attendant uses default greetings and menu prompts. However, you can specify different greetings, menu prompts, and options for different times and dates. To modify the default greetings and menu prompts used, you can click the appropriate **Modify** buttons on the Greetings tab of UM auto attendant properties as shown in Figure 12-46 to select the appropriate *.wav files.

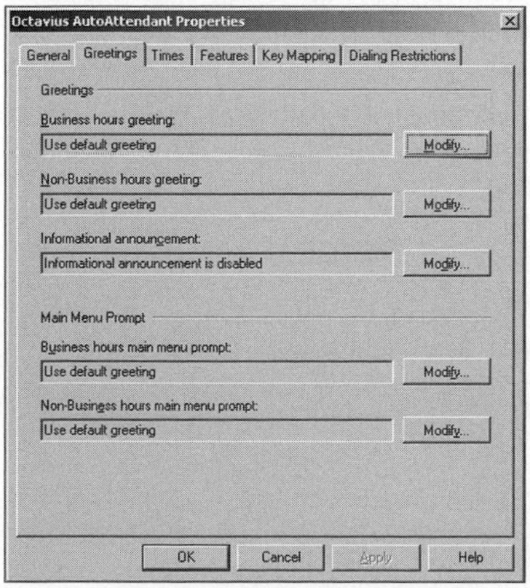

Figure 12-46

Unified Messaging Auto Attendant Properties Greetings Tab

ENABLING UM ACCESS

For mailbox users to access the UM features provided by the PBX and UM role servers within your organization, they must first be enabled for UM functionality. When you enable mailbox users for UM, you must supply their telephone extension number as well as a PIN that they can use to access OVA.

➡ ENABLING UM FOR A MAILBOX USER

GET READY. Turn on the computer, and log in as the Administrator user account. Close any windows that appear on the desktop.

1. Click **Start**, **All Programs**, **Microsoft Exchange Server 2007**, and then click **Exchange Management Console**. The Exchange Management Console window appears.

2. In the console tree pane, expand **Recipient Configuration**, **Mailbox** and highlight the appropriate mailbox user in the detail pane.

3. In the action pane, click **Enable Unified Messaging**. The Enable Unified Messaging window appears as shown in Figure 12-47.

Figure 12-47

Enabling Unified Messaging for a Mailbox User

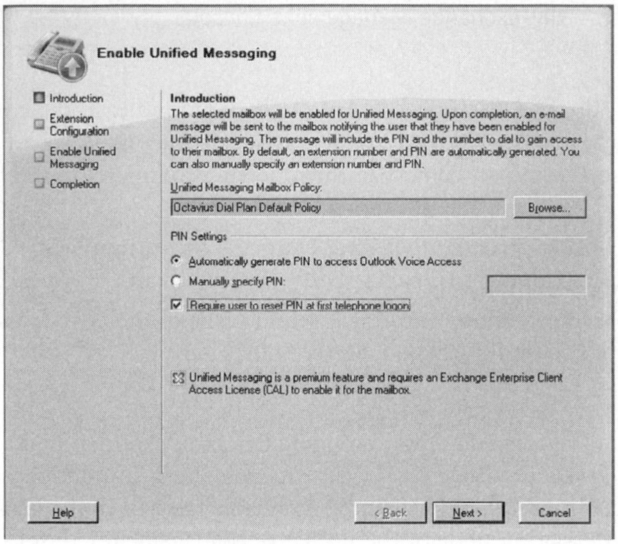

4. At the Enable Unified Messaging window, click **Browse**, select the appropriate UM mailbox policy to associate with the mailbox user in the Select UM Mailbox Policy window that appears and click **OK**.

5. Next, specify the PIN that the mailbox user can input to access his or her mailbox using the auto attendant and Outlook Voice Access. Alternatively, you can allow Exchange Server 2007 to generate a PIN that is emailed to the user and require that the user change this PIN on first use as shown earlier in Figure 12-47. When finished, click **Next**.

6. At the Extension Configuration page, specify the telephone extension that is used to contact the mailbox user in the dialog box as shown in Figure 12-48 and click **Next** when finished.

Figure 12-48

Specifying Telephone Extension Information

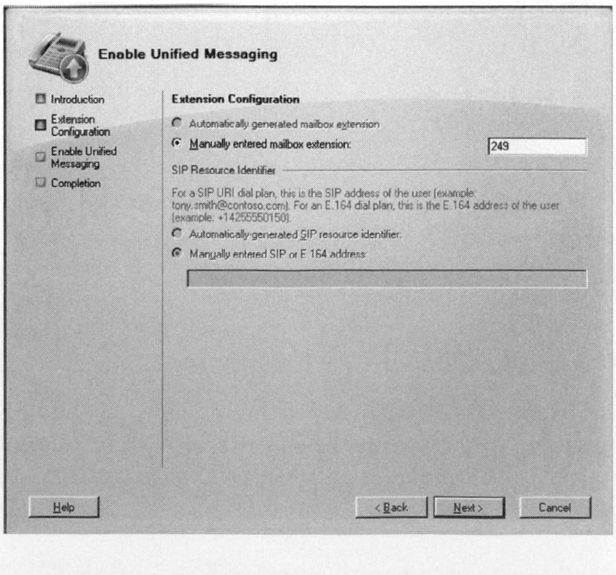

TAKE NOTE✱

If your UM dial plan uses the E.164 or SIP URI type, you will be prompted to supply the appropriate E.164 or SIP information in Figure 12-48.

7. At the Enable Unified Messaging page, review your settings and click **Enable**. The Completion page appears.

8. Click **Finish** to close the Enable Unified Messaging window.

9. Close the Exchange Management Console.

THE COMMAND
LINE WAY

You can also use the **Enable-UMMailbox** cmdlet in the Exchange Management Shell to enable UM for a mailbox user. To enable UM for the user Jeff Smith using the same options shown in Figures 12-47 and 12-48, you could run the following command in the Exchange Management Shell:

Enable-UMMailbox –Identity 'Jeff Smith' -PinExpired $true -UMMailboxPolicy 'Octavius Dial Plan Default Policy' -Extensions '249'

For more information on the syntax and usage of the Enable-UMMailbox cmdlet, search for it within Exchange Server 2007 Help.

SUMMARY SKILL MATRIX

IN THIS LESSON YOU LEARNED:

- An understanding of mobile technologies such as ActiveSync and BlackBerry Infrastructure are vital today when supporting mobile users who connect to their Exchange mailboxes using wireless smartphone devices.

- ActiveSync is supported on a wide variety of smartphone models. DirectPush works alongside ActiveSync to notify smartphone users of new mailbox items by using a long-standing HTTPS request.

- ActiveSync support is automatically enabled on all CAS role servers within your organization, but can be disabled for users who do not require mobile access. In addition, you can restrict ActiveSync access or use ActiveSync policies to control the configuration and security of smartphone devices. After deploying ActiveSync smartphones within your organization, you can recover smartphone device passwords, wipe smartphone data, and view ActiveSync logs from your Exchange server.

- BlackBerry-enabled smartphones connect to the BlackBerry Infrastructure via a wireless provider before connecting to a BlackBerry Enterprise Server (BES) within your organization. BES communicates directly with Exchange Server 2007 to access mailbox contents and monitors mailboxes for new items that are then relayed to the appropriate smartphone user. BlackBerry smartphone devices and BES work together to provide encryption and compression for all communication.

- To connect your Exchange servers to the BlackBerry Infrastructure, you must first install BES 4.1.3 or greater and configure it to communicate with the BlackBerry Infrastructure using SRP. Next, you must add BlackBerry users and activate their smartphone devices for use with BES. To control the configuration and security of BlackBerry smartphone devices, you can create IT policies. To simplify management, these IT policies can be applied to BlackBerry users or to BlackBerry groups that contain several users.

- Unified Messaging (UM) allows your organization to consolidate email, calendar, fax, voice mail, and telephone into a single infrastructure for access and manageability. Exchange Server 2007 uses the UM role to communicate with the PBX system within your organization to store voice mail and fax messages within Exchange mailboxes. In addition, the Outlook Voice Access component of the UM role allows users to access mailbox contents from a telephone connection.

- To configure UM, you must configure your PBX and UM role servers. For UM role servers, you must configure a UM dial plan to store UM configuration, a UM IP gateway to locate the PBX system, UM mailbox policies to control UM mailbox access, and UM auto attendants to define voice greetings and menu prompts. In addition, each mailbox user must be UM enabled to utilize the features provided by UM.

Knowledge Assessment

Fill in the Blank

Complete the following sentences by writing the correct word or words in the blanks provided.

1. The component of a PBX that integrates with your IP-based LAN is called the
   _____.

2. To connect Exchange Server 2007 to the BlackBerry Infrastructure, you must use BES
   version _____ or later.

3. UM role servers obtain voice mail from your organization's PBX system using the
   _____ protocol.

4. To access OVA, you must dial a _____ number.

5. BlackBerry device users can activate their own BlackBerry devices by plugging them into
   their workstation and running the _____ utility.

6. Information such as calendar items, contacts, address lists, and task items are commonly
   called _____ data.

7. Before installing BES, you must first install _____ to obtain the CDO and
   MAPI DLL files.

8. _____ is an ActiveSync component that alerts your smartphone device when
   new items arrive in your Exchange mailbox.

9. ActiveSync devices that cannot apply all ActiveSync policy settings are called
   _____ devices.

10. Mailbox users can access their UM-enabled mailbox by navigating the _____
    interface using voice commands or telephone keypad input.

Multiple Choice

Circle the letter that corresponds to the best answer.

1. Your organization uses a combination of ActiveSync and BlackBerry-enabled smartphone
   devices. In the past, contact information was stolen within your organization because
   smartphone users left their devices unattended. How can you combat this problem?
   (Choose all that apply.)
   a. Create an ActiveSync policy that forces smartphone users to input device passwords.
   b. Create an IT policy that forces BlackBerry devices to require device passwords.
   c. In the ActiveSync policy, specify that devices will be locked after 15 minutes of
      inactivity.
   d. In the IT policy, specify that devices will be locked after 15 minutes of inactivity.

2. Which of the following cmdlets will obtain the device ID for your ActiveSync-enabled
   smartphone?
   a. Get-ActiveSyncDeviceID
   b. Get-ActiveSyncDeviceStatistics
   c. Export-ActiveSyncDeviceID
   d. Export-ActiveSyncDeviceStatistics

3. How many ActiveSync policies can be applied to a single mailbox user?
   a. 1
   b. 2
   c. 8
   d. Unlimited

4. During the installation of BES, you enter your SRP server information and click **Test Network Connection**. However, the test fails. What is the most likely cause of this problem?
   a. You have not entered the correct SRP server name
   b. You have not entered the correct SRP key
   c. TCP port 3101 is not open on your organization's firewall
   d. TCP port 443 is not open on your organization's firewall

5. What is the easiest way to apply an ActiveSync policy to several users within your organization that do not already have an ActiveSync policy manually assigned to their mailbox?
   a. Create a template user that has the ActiveSync policy applied
   b. Set the ActiveSync policy as default
   c. Create a group for the users and set the ActiveSync policy on the group
   d. Apply the ActiveSync policy to all users and modify the permissions on the ActiveSync policy.

6. Which of the following items must you specify when you enable a user for UM?
   a. PIN information
   b. Telephone extension
   c. UM mailbox policy
   d. UM dial plan name

7. After installing BES, you have created BlackBerry users, IT policies, and BlackBerry groups that contain the appropriate users and apply the appropriate IT policies. However, your BlackBerry devices are unable to connect to BES. What should you do?
   a. Enter SRP server information within BES
   b. Register the users within Active Directory
   c. Assign the IT policies to the users rather than the group
   d. Activate the BlackBerry users

8. One of your ActiveSync users has lost her smartphone device. To ensure that the data on the device is not read by unauthorized persons, you wish to force the removal of all data from the device using remote wipe. How can you achieve this? (Choose all that apply.)
   a. Remove the ActiveSync device ID from your CAS role server using the Remove-ActiveSyncDevice cmdlet within the Exchange Management Shell.
   b. Obtain the smartphone device ID and run the Clear-ActiveSyncDevice cmdlet using this device ID from within the Exchange Management Shell on your Exchange server.
   c. Ask the user to initiate a remote wipe using the **Options** > **Mobile Devices** section of OWA.
   d. Configure an ActiveSync policy that performs a remote wipe operation and apply the policy to the user account.

9. You have forgotten your smartphone device password and wish to recover it using OWA. However, when you access the appropriate section within OWA, there are no passwords that can be recovered. What is the most likely cause?
   a. Password recovery was not enabled in the ActiveSync policy that applies to your mailbox user account.
   b. Your smartphone device is nonprovisionable.
   c. Your smartphone device does not support remote password recovery.
   d. Your user account is not a member of the Exchange Organization Administrator role.

10. Which option can you deselect within an ActiveSync policy to prevent users from configuring personal email accounts on their smartphones?
    a. Allow web browser
    b. Allow nonprovisionable devices
    c. Allow consumer mail
    d. Allow personal email accounts

True/False

Circle T if the statement is true or F if the statement is false.

T | F **1.** Most options selected during BES installation can be changed afterwards using the BlackBerry Manager utility.

T | F **2.** You can configure the servers that ActiveSync users can access in your organization in the properties of the ActiveSync virtual directory.

T | F **3.** Only RIM BlackBerry devices can access the BlackBerry Infrastructure.

T | F **4.** To access your mailbox from a telephone connection using UM, you must have a PIN that is preconfigured on your mailbox.

T | F **5.** ActiveSync is enabled for all mailbox users by default.

T | F **6.** BlackBerry devices communicate with the BlackBerry Infrastructure servers using a long-standing HTTPS request.

T | F **7.** You can generate or manually set an activation password for a BlackBerry user during the BES enterprise activation process.

T | F **8.** BES communicates with the BlackBerry Infrastructure using the Server Routing Protocol on TCP port 3101.

T | F **9.** You can customize the greeting and menu prompts used by the UM auto attendant by selecting the appropriate *.wav files within the properties of the UM auto attendant.

T | F **10.** By assigning multiple IT policies to a single user, you can control the configuration and security for the BlackBerry devices within your organization.

Review Questions

1. Explain why you should limit the size and number of attachments that are sent to smartphone devices within your organization using an ActiveSync or IT policy.

2. Explain why you should limit the features and programs that are available on the smartphone devices within your organization using an ActiveSync or IT policy.

■ Case Scenarios

Scenario 12-1: Comparing Smartphone Technologies

You are the network administrator for a small international goods manufacturer. Your organization is considering adopting smartphone devices to allow users to access their mailbox data while out of the office. You have informed your supervisor that there are two different technologies that can integrate with Microsoft Exchange Server 2007: ActiveSync and the BlackBerry Infrastructure. As a result, your supervisor has asked you to create a report that lists the pros and cons of each technology. Using the information within this lesson as well as the Internet, create a report that meets these needs.

Scenario 12-2: Configuring a PBX for Unified Messaging

In this lesson, we have examined the procedures used to configure UM role servers for Unified Messaging. Using the Internet, research the procedures used to configure a specific PBX system to work with the UM role servers within your organization using the PBX manufacturer's Web site. Summarize the steps in a short memo.

Providing for High Availability

LESSON SKILL MATRIX

TECHNOLOGY SKILL	OBJECTIVE DOMAIN	OBJECTIVE DOMAIN NUMBER
Providing High Availability for Mailbox Role Servers	Configure high availability.	5.4
Providing High Availability for Nonmailbox Role Servers	Configure high availability.	5.4

KEY TERMS

active node
active/passive server cluster
Cluster Continuous Replication
 (CCR)
Cluster Service
failover
heartbeat
high availability

LCR storage group
Local Continuous Replication
 (LCR)
log replay
log shipping
multicast mode
Network Load Balancing
 (NLB)

passive mailbox database
passive node
seeding
Single Copy Cluster (SCC)
Standby Continuous Replication
 (SCR)
unicast mode

■ Understanding High Availability

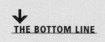

THE BOTTOM LINE

High availability strategies are used to eliminate or minimize downtime after a failure within your Exchange infrastructure to ensure that the users within your organization have continuous access to email and other messaging services.

After deploying Exchange Server 2007, it is important to create a strategy that will ensure that the Exchange servers within your organization continue to function when one or more servers or databases fail. This *high availability* strategy aims to provide continuous access to the Exchange infrastructure for the users within your organization.

Although high availability strategies may include restoring database backups and server roles, we will focus on configuring high availability using different technologies and procedures in this lesson. The types of high availability solutions that you can use ultimately depend on the server roles as well as the available hardware and software components on the Exchange servers within your organization.

■ Providing High Availability for Mailbox Role Servers

THE BOTTOM LINE

Because Mailbox role servers store mailbox and public folder data within your organization, you should ensure that they can still function after hardware or software failure to minimize the disruption to users within your organization. There are four different technologies that can be used to provide high availability for Mailbox role servers. Each technology has different hardware and software requirements and provides high availability in different situations.

CERTIFICATION READY?
Configure high availability.
5.4

Configuring Local Continuous Replication

You can configure Local Continuous Replication to copy a mailbox database to another hard disk using a single mailbox server. If the hard disk holding the mailbox database fails, you can quickly reconfigure your Mailbox role server to use the mailbox database copy to minimize downtime for the users within your organization. Unfortunately, Local Continuous Replication does not protect against the failure of the Mailbox server role itself.

Local Continuous Replication (LCR) allows you to quickly restore user access to mailboxes if a mailbox database becomes corrupted or if the hard disk that hosts the mailbox database fails. By using LCR, a mailbox database is continuously backed up to another hard disk. LCR creates a backup copy of a mailbox database within an *LCR storage group*. This backup copy of the mailbox database within the LCR storage group is called the *passive mailbox database* and can be stored on a separate hard disk within the same Mailbox role server or on a hard disk that is connected to the Mailbox role server using a fast interconnect such as USB.

When emails and other items need to be written to a mailbox, they are first written to transaction logs in the associated storage group before they are written to the appropriate mailbox database. When LCR is enabled for a storage group, the transaction logs are copied to the LCR storage group (a process called *log shipping*) where their contents are later written to the passive mailbox database (a process called *log replay*). Both log shipping and replay are separate processes that do not affect the ability for emails and other items to be written to mailboxes within the original mailbox database. As a result, log shipping and log replay of mailbox items are called asynchronous processes and often take place after the same mailbox items have already been written to the original mailbox database. Figure 13-1 illustrates the LCR process.

Figure 13-1

Local Continuous Replication

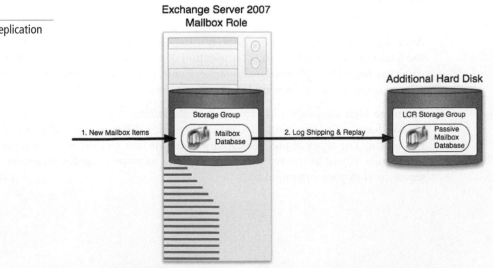

Exchange Server 2007
Mailbox Role

1. New Mailbox Items

Storage Group
Mailbox Database

2. Log Shipping & Replay

Additional Hard Disk

LCR Storage Group
Passive Mailbox Database

If the hard disk containing the original mailbox database fails, you can configure Exchange Server 2007 to use the passive mailbox database within minutes to minimize the downtime for the affected email users within your organization.

Although LCR can provide fault tolerance for mailbox databases in the event of a hard disk failure, it cannot be used with public folder databases. To ensure that the data stored within your public folder databases are fault tolerant, you can configure public folder replication between two or more Mailbox role servers. In addition, any storage groups that will be used for LCR can only contain a single mailbox database.

 CONFIGURING LOCAL CONTINUOUS REPLICATION

GET READY. Turn on the computer, and log in as the Administrator user account. Close any windows that appear on the desktop.

1. Click **Start**, **All Programs**, **Microsoft Exchange Server 2007**, and then click **Exchange Management Console**. The Exchange Management Console window appears.

2. In the console tree pane, expand **Server Configuration** and highlight **Mailbox**.

3. In the detail pane, highlight the appropriate Exchange server and select the appropriate storage group in the work pane.

4. In the action pane, click **Enable Local Continuous Replication**. When the Enable Storage Group Local Continuous Replication window appears, click **Next**.

TAKE NOTE ★

If the **Enable Local Continuous Replication** action is not available within the Exchange Management Console, the selected storage group contains more than one mailbox database and cannot be enabled for LCR.

5. At the Set Paths page, specify the directory that should contain the LCR storage group transaction logs and system files (e.g., checkpoint file) as shown in Figure 13-2. To do this, click the appropriate **Browse** button, navigate to the appropriate folder in the window that appears and click **OK**. As Figure 13-2 illustrates, LCR will copy transaction log files to the D:\LCR_LOGS directory and copy system files to the D:\LCR_SYSTEM directory. Click **Next** when finished.

TAKE NOTE ★

The directories that you specify as shown in Figure 13-2 can be on any hard disk device that has a local drive letter including internal, USB, and Firewire hard disks as well as hard disks that are located on NAS/SAN or iSCSI devices. You cannot choose the root directory of a volume when specifying a directory as shown in Figure 13-2.

Figure 13-2

Enabling Local Continuous Replication

Enable Storage Group Local Continuous Replication

- Introduction
- Set Paths
- Mailbox Database
- Enable
- Completion

Set Paths
Enter the path to the local continuous replication files for the storage group below.

Storage group name:

EXCH1\First Storage Group

Local continuous replication system files path:

D:\LCR_LOGS   Browse...

Local continuous replication log files path:

D:\LCR_SYSTEM   Browse...

Help   < Back   Next >   Cancel

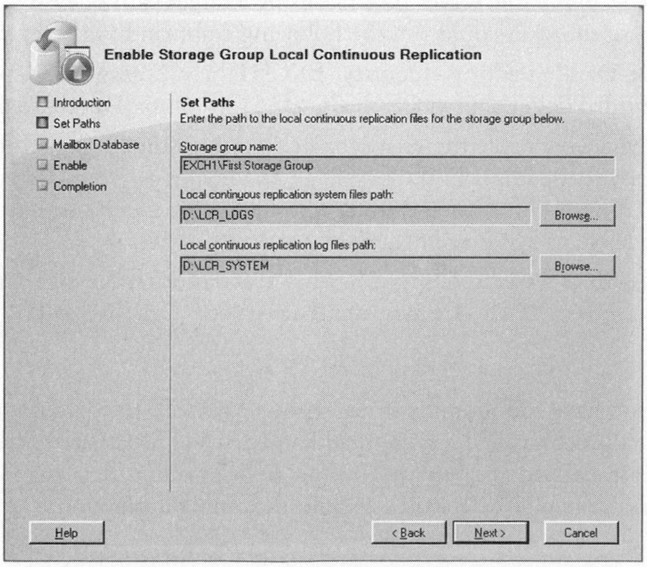

6. At the Mailbox Database page, specify the directory that should contain the passive mailbox database as shown in Figure 13-3. To do this, click the appropriate **Browse** button, specify the location and name for your passive mailbox database in the window that appears, and click **Save**. Click **Next** when finished.

TAKE NOTE*

As in Figure 13-2, the passive mailbox database specified in Figure 13-3 can be located on any hard disk device that has a local drive letter and cannot be within the root directory of a volume.

Figure 13-3

Specifying Mailbox Database Information

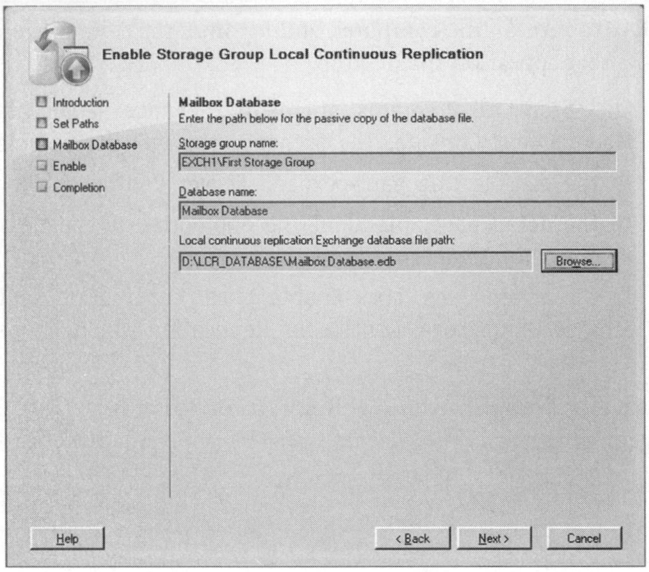

Enable Storage Group Local Continuous Replication

- Introduction
- Set Paths
- Mailbox Database
- Enable
- Completion

Mailbox Database
Enter the path below for the passive copy of the database file.

Storage group name:
EXCH1\First Storage Group

Database name:
Mailbox Database

Local continuous replication Exchange database file path:
D:\LCR_DATABASE\Mailbox Database.edb   Browse...

Help   < Back   Next >   Cancel

7. At the Enable page, review your selections and click Enable.

8. On the Completion page, click Finish to close the Enable Storage Group Local Continuous Replication window.

9. Close the Exchange Management Console.

THE COMMAND LINE WAY

You can also use the **Enable-DatabaseCopy** and **Enable-StorageGroupCopy** cmdlets in the Exchange Management Shell to enable a storage group and database for LCR. To create a passive mailbox database copy of the Mailbox Database within the First Storage Group on the Mailbox role server EXCH1 using a target path of D:\LCR_DATABASE\Mailbox Database.edb, you could run the following command in the Exchange Management Shell:

Enable-DatabaseCopy -Identity 'EXCH1\First Storage Group\Mailbox Database' -CopyEdbFilePath 'D:\LCR_DATABASE\Mailbox Database.edb'

Next, you can enable the First Storage Group on the Mailbox role server EXCH1 for LCR using a target path of D:\LCR_SYSTEM for storage group system files and a target path of D:\LCR_LOGS for storage group transaction log files by executing the following command in the Exchange Management Shell:

Enable-StorageGroupCopy -Identity 'EXCH1\First Storage Group' -CopyLogFolderPath 'D:\LCR_SYSTEM' -CopySystemFolderPath 'D:\LCR_LOGS'

After you have configured a storage group for LCR, the database is copied to the target LCR folder (a process called *seeding*), and any new log files that are created in the original storage group are shipped and replayed on the passive mailbox database. This ensures that the original and passive mailbox databases contain the same information.

You can temporarily disable LCR operations (log shipping and replay) for an LCR-enabled storage group by highlighting the appropriate storage group within the Exchange Management Console and selecting **Suspend Storage Group Copy** from the action pane. You can then supply a reason for disabling LCR operations as shown in Figure 13-4 and click **Yes** to stop LCR operations. Following this, you can resume LCR operations by highlighting the appropriate storage group within the Exchange Management Console, selecting **Resume Storage Group Copy** from the action pane, and clicking **Yes** when prompted.

Figure 13-4

Suspending Local Continuous Replication

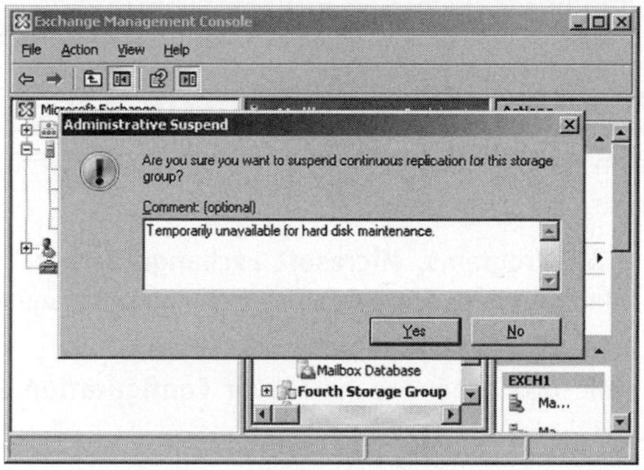

You can also use the Suspend-StorageGroupCopy and ResumeStorageGroupCopy cmdlets to temporarily disable and resume LCR operations for an LCR-enabled storage group respectively. The following command will disable LCR operations for the First Storage Group on the server EXCH1 with the reason "Temporarily unavailable for hard disk maintenance" when executed within the Exchange Management Shell:

Suspend-StorageGroupCopy -Identity 'EXCH1\First Storage Group' -SuspendComment 'Temporarily unavailable for hard disk maintenance'

To resume LCR operations for the same storage group, you could run the following command within the Exchange Management Shell:

Resume-StorageGroupCopy -Identity 'EXCH1\First Storage Group'

To view the status of your LCR configuration, you can use the Get-StorageGroupCopyStatus cmdlet. To list the status of the LCR configuration for the First Storage Group on the server EXCH1, you could use the following command within the Exchange Management Shell:

Get-StorageGroupCopyStatus –Identity 'EXCH1\First Storage Group' | Format-List

Alternatively, you can view the status of your LCR configuration by highlighting your LCR-enabled storage group within the Exchange Management Console, clicking **Properties** from the action pane and selecting the **Local continuous replication** tab as shown in Figure 13-5.

Figure 13-5

Viewing Local Continuous ReplicationStatus

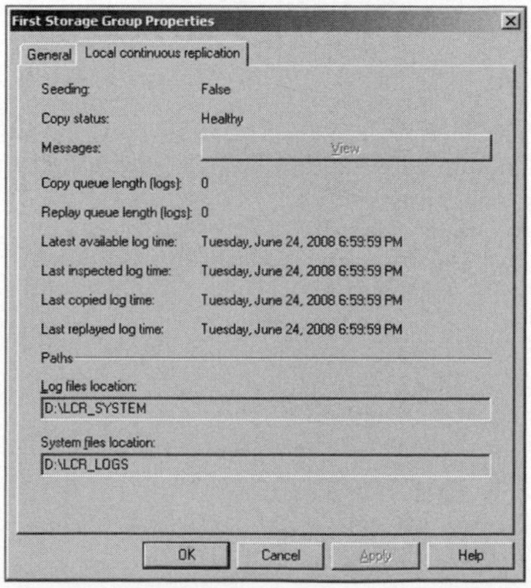

The Healthy Copy status (Figure 13-5) indicates that there are no problems with LCR log shipping and replay and that the passive mailbox database is free of structural errors. Figure 13-5 also indicates that the database is not currently seeding. Although the storage group shown displays the last time logs were shipped and replayed, there are no transaction logs waiting to be shipped (**Copy queue length**) or replayed (**Replay queue length**).

If the copy status shown in the output of the Get-StorageGroupCopyStatus cmdlet (or storage group properties shown in Figure 13-5) indicates that the passive mailbox database has failed, then you will need to reseed the passive mailbox database.

 RESEEDING AN LCR PASSIVE MAILBOX DATABASE

GET READY. Turn on the computer, and log in as the Administrator user account. Close any windows that appear on the desktop.

1. Click **Start, All Programs, Microsoft Exchange Server 2007,** and then click **Exchange Management Console.** The Exchange Management Console window appears.

2. In the console tree pane, expand **Server Configuration** and highlight **Mailbox.**

3. In the detail pane, highlight the appropriate Exchange server and select the appropriate storage group in the work pane.

4. In the action pane, click **Update Storage Group Copy**. The Update Storage Group Copy window appears as shown in Figure 13-6.

Figure 13-6

Reseeding a Database Copy

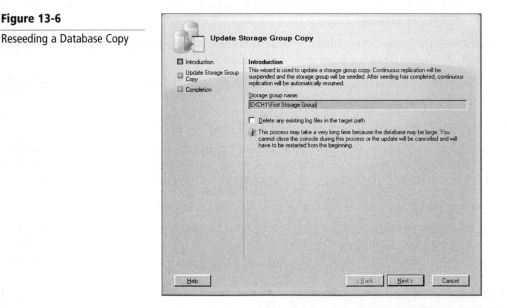

5. You can optionally choose to remove any transaction log files in the LCR storage group before reseeding by selecting **Delete any existing log files in the target path**. Click **Next** when finished.

6. At the Update Storage Group Copy page, review your selections and click **Update**. If you are prompted to overwrite the target database and transaction logs, click **Yes**.

7. On the Completion page, click **Finish** to close the Update Storage Group Copy window.

8. Close the Exchange Management Console.

THE COMMAND LINE WAY

You can also use the **Update-StorageGroupCopy** cmdlet in the Exchange Management Shell to reseed an LCR passive mailbox database that has LCR operations disabled. To reseed the passive mailbox database copy within the First Storage Group on the Mailbox role server EXCH1 and delete any existing LCR transaction logs, you could run the following commands in the Exchange Management Shell:

Suspend-StorageGroupCopy -Identity 'EXCH1\First Storage Group'

Update-StorageGroupCopy -Identity 'EXCH1\First Storage Group'

Alternatively, if the copy status indicates that the original mailbox database has failed, then you can reconfigure your storage group to use the passive mailbox database for mailbox storage instead. To do this, you must restore your storage group copy.

RESTORING A STORAGE GROUP COPY

GET READY. Turn on the computer, and log in as the Administrator user account. Close any windows that appear on the desktop.

1. Click **Start, All Programs, Microsoft Exchange Server 2007**, and then click **Exchange Management Console**. The Exchange Management Console window appears.
2. In the console tree pane, expand **Server Configuration** and highlight **Mailbox.**
3. In the detail pane, highlight the appropriate Exchange server, expand the appropriate storage group in the work pane, and select the mailbox database.
4. In the action pane, click **Dismount Database** and click **Yes** when prompted.
5. In the work pane, highlight the appropriate storage group and click **Restore Storage Group Copy** from the action pane. The Restore Storage Group Copy window appears as shown in Figure 13-7.

Figure 13-7

Restoring a Database Copy

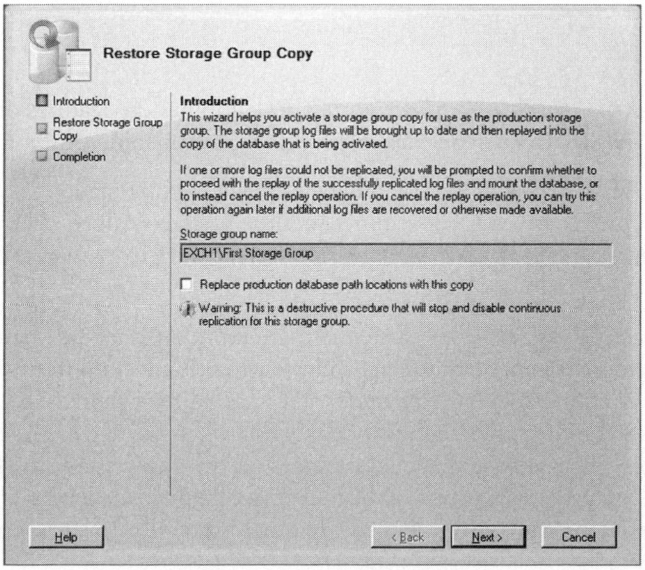

Restore Storage Group Copy

☐ Introduction
☐ Restore Storage Group Copy
☐ Completion

Introduction

This wizard helps you activate a storage group copy for use as the production storage group. The storage group log files will be brought up to date and then replayed into the copy of the database that is being activated.

If one or more log files could not be replicated, you will be prompted to confirm whether to proceed with the replay of the successfully replicated log files and mount the database, or to instead cancel the replay operation. If you cancel the replay operation, you can try this operation again later if additional log files are recovered or otherwise made available.

Storage group name:

EXCH1\First Storage Group

☐ Replace production database path locations with this copy

⚠ Warning: This is a destructive procedure that will stop and disable continuous replication for this storage group.

Help   < Back   Next >   Cancel

6. To configure the original storage group to use the LCR storage group and passive mailbox database, selecting **Replace production database path locations with this copy.** Click **Next** when finished.
7. At the Restore Storage Group Copy page, review your selections and click **Restore.**
8. On the Completion page, click **Finish** to close the Restore Storage Group Copy window.
9. In the detail pane, select the appropriate mailbox database and click **Mount Database.**
10. Close the Exchange Management Console.

THE COMMAND
LINE WAY

You can also use the **Restore-StorageGroupCopy** cmdlet in the Exchange Management Shell to configure a storage group that contains a dismounted database to use its passive mailbox database. To dismount the Mailbox Database within the First Storage Group on the Mailbox role server EXCH1 and restore the LCR storage group to the paths used by the passive mailbox database, you could run the following commands in the Exchange Management Shell:

Dismount-Database –Identity 'EXCH1\First Storage Group\Mailbox Database'

Restore-StorageGroupCopy -Identity 'EXCH1\First Storage Group' -ReplaceLocations

Mount-Database –Identity 'EXCH1\First Storage Group\Mailbox Database'

If you wish to permanently disable LCR for a storage group, you can highlight your LCR-enabled storage group within the Exchange Management Console, select **Disable Local Continuous Replication** from the action pane and click **Yes** when prompted. This will disable LCR entirely for the storage group as well as remove the LCR storage group and passive mailbox database. Alternatively, you could use the Disable-StorageGroupCopy cmdlet to remove an LCR configuration. To remove the LCR configuration for the First Storage Group on the Mailbox role server EXCH1, you could run the following command within the Exchange Management Shell:

Disable-StorageGroupCopy –Identity 'EXCH1\First Storage Group'

Configuring Cluster Continuous Replication

By using Cluster Continuous Replication, you can ensure that your Mailbox role servers and their databases are protected in the event of a hardware or software failure. Cluster Continuous Replication copies mailbox data between two servers that run the Windows Cluster Service. If the first server fails, the second server starts to service network requests automatically.

Cluster Continuous Replication (CCR) combines the features of LCR with the benefits of the Windows *Cluster Service* to provide high availability for your Mailbox role servers.

Like LCR, CCR uses log shipping and replay to copy mailbox data to a passive mailbox database copy. However, CCR requires that the passive mailbox database be on another Mailbox role server and that both Mailbox role servers participate in an *active/passive server cluster* using the Windows Cluster Service.

In an active/passive server cluster configuration, both servers share a common name and IP address that other computers will use when connecting to the cluster. However, only one of the computers (the *active node*) will respond to requests. The other computer (the *passive node*) will only start responding to requests when the active node has failed (a process called *failover*). Because the mailbox databases on the passive node are kept up to date via log shipping and replay, users will be able to access their mailboxes after failover. As a result, CCR ensures high availability when any vital hardware or software components fail on the active node.

Although CCR provides availability in the event of any hardware failure on the active node, it has additional requirements compared to LCR. To use the Windows Cluster Service in an active/passive configuration, CCR requires two Mailbox role servers that run the Enterprise edition of Windows Server 2003 or greater. These Mailbox servers cannot share hardware with other Exchange server roles and require a second network interface that is used for

TAKE NOTE*

Unlike LCR, CCR also provides for log shipping and relay of public folder databases.

intracluster communication. To provide for automatic failover, you must also configure a shared directory on another Exchange server within your organization that is used to monitor the active/passive server cluster. This Exchange server is called a ***file share witness*** and is typically a Hub, UM, or CAS role server in the same site as your Mailbox role servers.

TAKE NOTE＊   The type of server clustering used by CCR is properly called ***majority node set quorum with file share witness***.

A typical CCR configuration is illustrated in Figure 13-8.

Figure 13-8

Cluster Continuous Replication

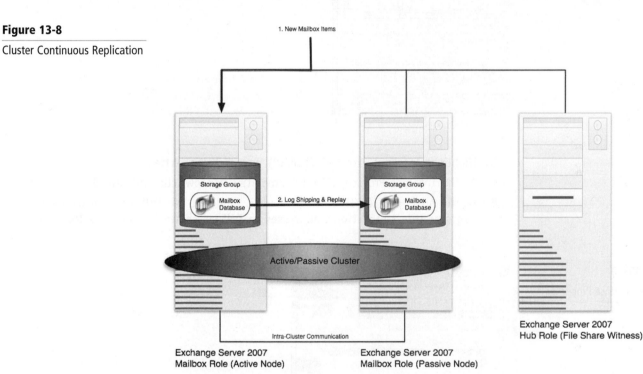

To configure CCR, you must first configure the Windows Cluster Service before deploying Exchange Server 2007 clustered Mailbox roles. More specifically, you must install two servers with an Enterprise edition of Windows Server or later. Each server must have two network interfaces: a ***public interface*** that is connected to the LAN within your organization as well as a ***private interface*** that connects the computers within the cluster together for intracluster communication. On the private interface for each server, you must disable the following components:

- File and Printer Sharing for Microsoft Networks,
- Dynamic DNS Update, and
- NetBIOS over TCP/IP.

PREPARING THE PRIVATE INTERFACE ON A CCR SERVER

GET READY. Turn on the computer, and log in as the Administrator user account. Close any windows that appear on the desktop.

 1. Click **Start**, **Control Panel**, **Network Interfaces**, and then click your private network interface.

2. At the interface properties window, deselect **File and Printer Sharing for Microsoft Networks** as shown in Figure 13-9.

Figure 13-9

Network Interface Properties

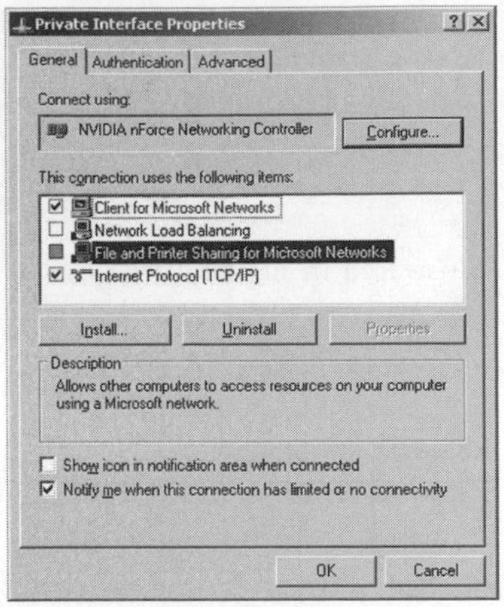

3. Highlight **Internet Protocol (TCP/IP)** and click **Properties**.

4. At the Internet Protocol (TCP/IP) Properties window, click **Advanced**.

5. At the Advanced TCP/IP Settings window, highlight the **DNS** tab and deselect **Register this connection's addresses in DNS** as shown in Figure 13-10.

Figure 13-10

Network Interface Properties

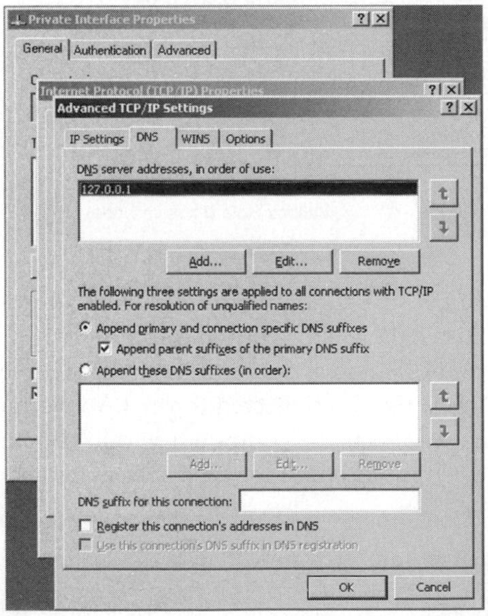

6. Highlight the **WINS** tab of Advanced TCP/IP Settings and select Disable NetBIOS over TCP/IP as shown in Figure 13-11.

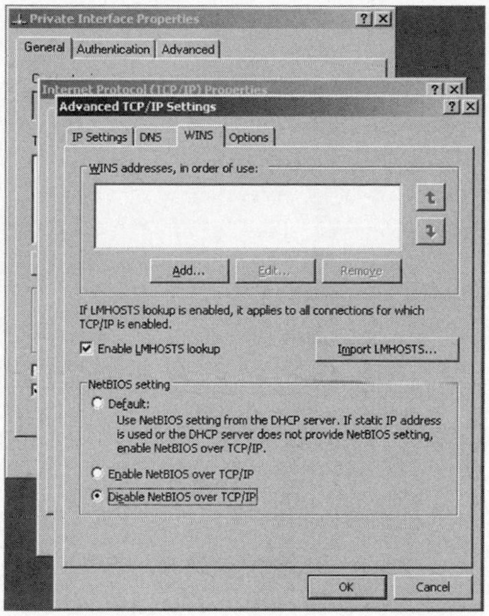

Figure 13-11

WINS Tab of Advanced TCP/IP Properties

7. Click **OK** to close the Advanced TCP/IP Settings window.

8. Click **OK** to close the Internet Protocol (TCP/IP) Properties window.

9. Click **OK** to close the properties of your private network interface.

After you have prepared your network interfaces, you can create a user account that the Windows Cluster Service will run as. This user account must at a minimum have the **Log On As A Service** right on the server prior to configuring the Windows Cluster Service. In addition, you must create a shared directory on an existing Hub, UM, or CAS role server that is within the same site as the CCR cluster. This share must assign Full Control share and NTFS permissions to the user account that will be used by the Windows Cluster Service.

Next, you can configure the Windows Cluster Service to support CCR. This configuration must occur on the computer that will become the active node of the cluster. During this process, you will create a new cluster configuration, add the passive cluster node, as well as configure the location of the file share witness.

 CONFIGURING WINDOWS CLUSTER SERVICE FOR CCR

GET READY. Turn on the computer that will become the active node, and log in as the Administrator user account. Close any windows that appear on the desktop.

1. Click **Start**, **All Programs**, **Administrative Tools**, and then click **Cluster Administrator**. The Cluster Administrator window appears.

> **TAKE NOTE***
>
> If the Cluster Administrator utility is not available on the Administrative Tools menu, you are not running the Enterprise or newer edition of Windows Server.

2. In the Open Connection to Cluster window, select **Create new cluster** from the Action drop-down box as shown in Figure 13-12 and click **OK**.

Figure 13-12

Creating a New Cluster

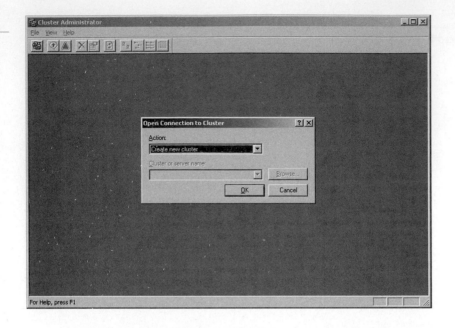

3. When the New Server Cluster Wizard window appears, click **Next**.

4. At the Cluster Name and Domain page, select the AD domain that the cluster will use in the **Domain** drop-down box and type an appropriate name for the cluster in the **Cluster name** dialog box as shown in Figure 13-13. When finished, click **Next**.

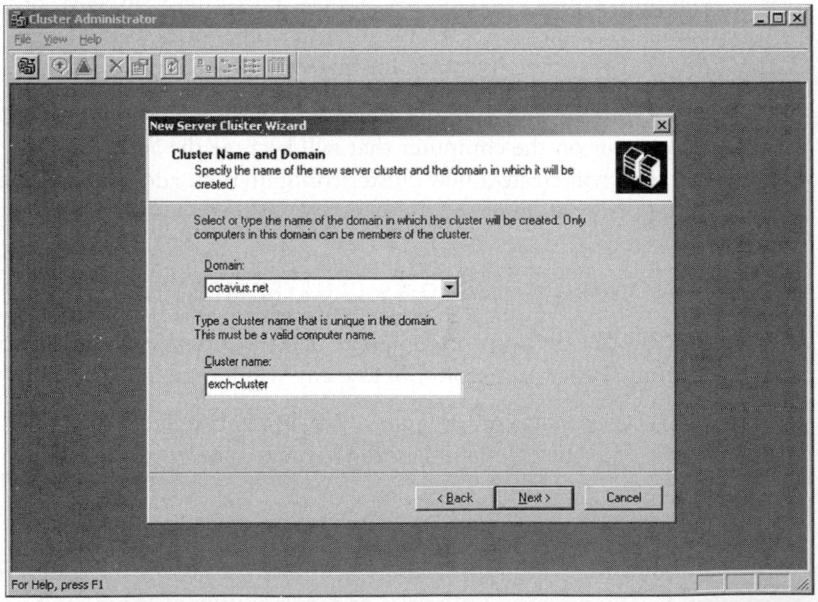

Figure 13-13

Specifying Cluster Name and Domain

5. At the Select Computer page, ensure that the name of the computer that will become the first node in the cluster is listed in the **Computer name** dialog box as shown in Figure 13-14 and click **Next**.

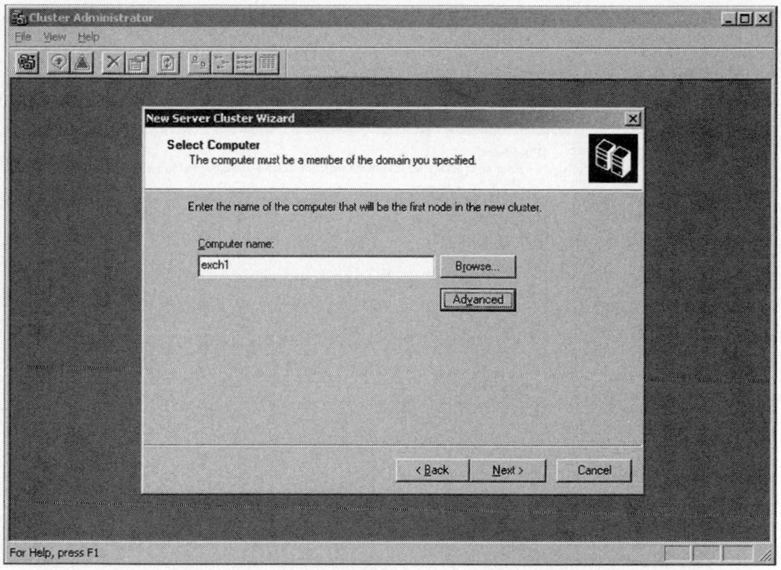

Figure 13-14

Specifying the First Cluster
Node

6. At the Analyzing Configuration page, the New Server Cluster Wizard checks for
   necessary prerequisites before creating the cluster as shown in Figure 13-15. Because
   CCR clusters do not use shared storage, you can safely ignore the warnings shown
   in Figure 13-15 that indicate there are no shared disk resources configured on your
   server. Click **Next** when finished.

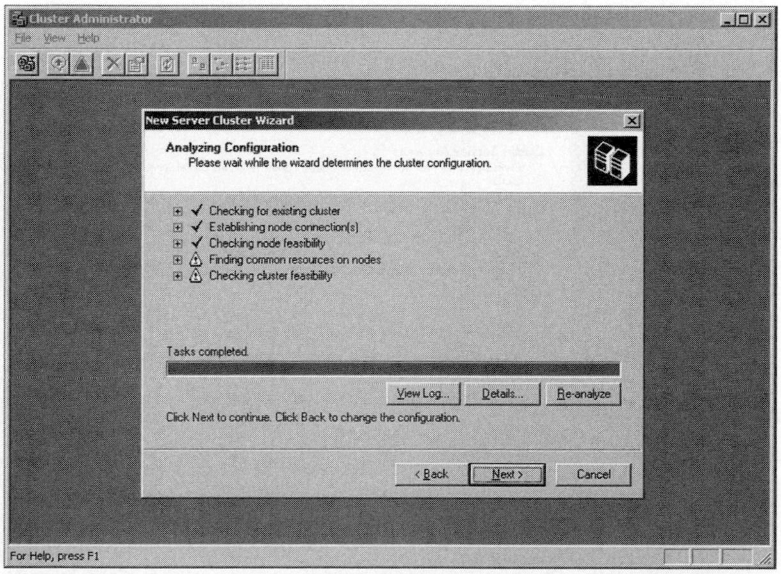

Figure 13-15

Analyzing Cluster Configuration

7. At the IP Address page, enter an IP address that will be used by the nodes within
   the cluster as shown in Figure 13-16. This IP address should be configured on the
   same network used by the public network interface of the server. Click **Next** when
   finished.

Figure 13-16

Specifying the Cluster IP Address

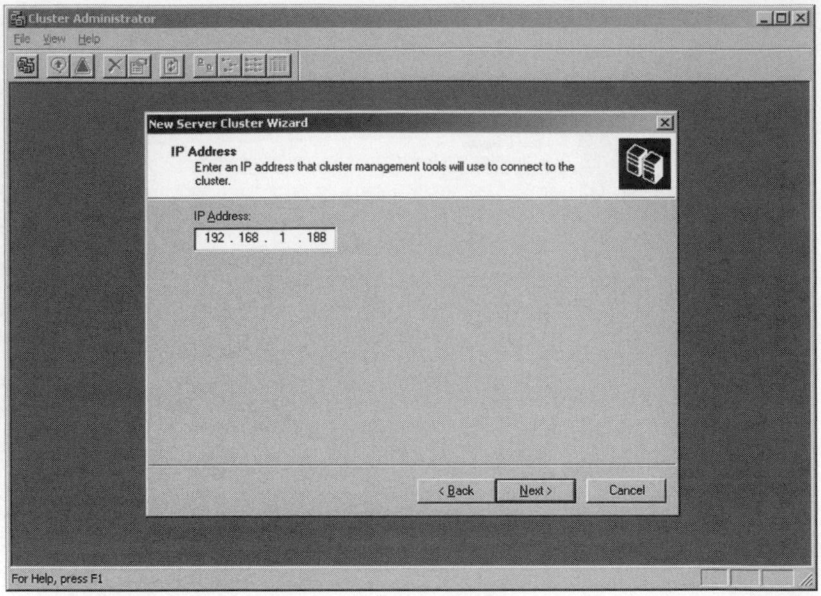

8. At the Cluster Service Account page, enter the credentials for a domain user account that the Windows Cluster Service will use as shown in Figure 13-17. This account should be granted at a minimum the **Log On As A Service** right on your server. Click **Next** when finished.

Figure 13-17

Specifying the Cluster Service Account

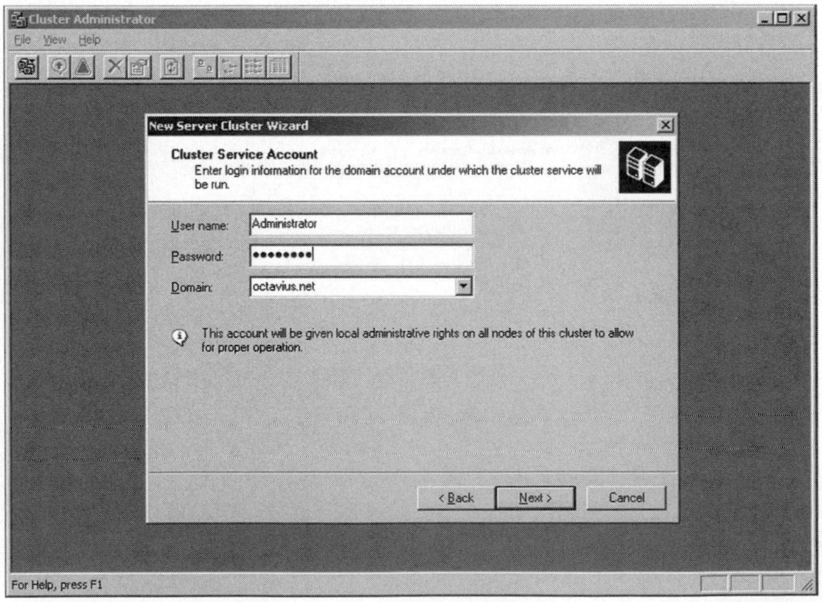

9. At the Proposed Cluster Configuration page as shown in Figure 13-18, review your selections and click **Quorum**. When the Cluster Configuration Quorum window appears, select **Majority Node Set** from the drop-down box as shown in Figure 13-19 and click **OK**. Click **Next** when finished.

Figure 13-18

Viewing the Cluster
Configuration Summary

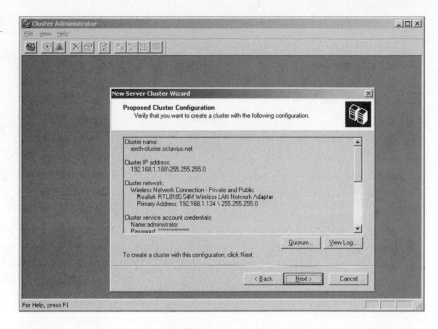

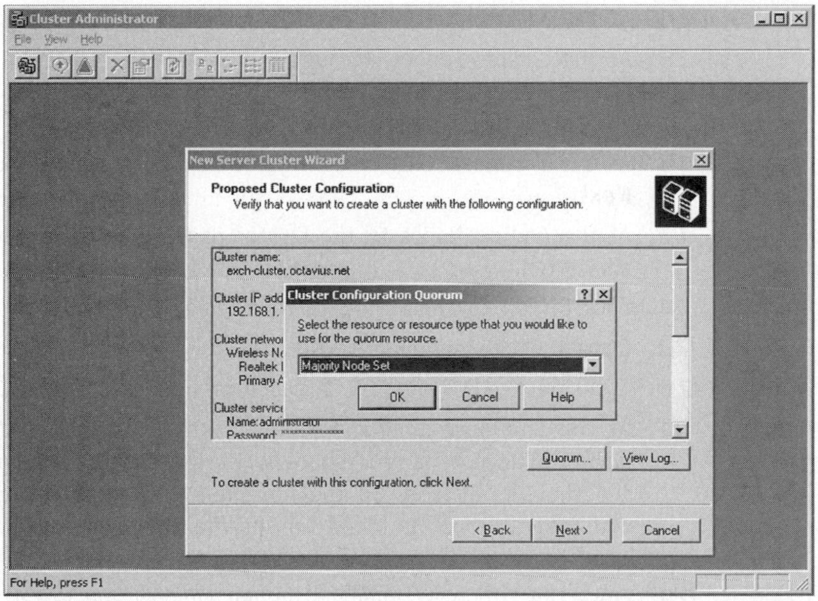

Figure 13-19

Specifying the Cluster
Configuration Quorum

10. Click **Finish** to close the New Server Cluster Wizard window.

11. In the left pane of the Cluster Administrator utility, right click the server that is the first node in the cluster, select New, and **Node**.

12. When the Add Nodes Wizard appears, click **Next**.

13. At the Select Computer page, supply the name of the computer that will become the second cluster node in the **Computer name** dialog box and click **Add** to place it in the Selected computers dialog box as shown in Figure 13-20. When finished, click **Next**.

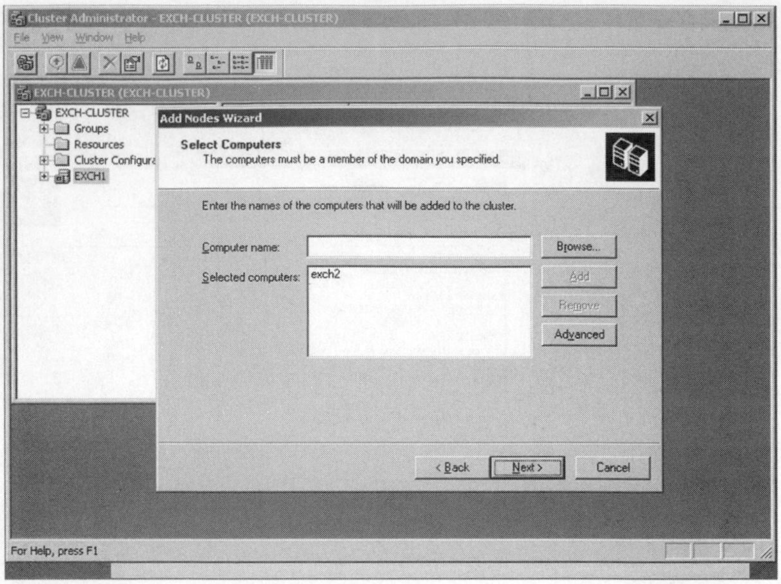

Figure 13-20

Adding an Additional Cluster
Node

14. At the Analyzing Configuration page, review the settings and click **Next**.

15. At the Cluster Service Account page, enter the credentials for a domain user account that the Windows Cluster Service will use on the second cluster node and click **Next** when finished.

16. At the Proposed Cluster Configuration page, review your selections and click **Next**.

17. At the Adding Nodes to the Cluster page, review the information displayed and click **Next**.

18. Click **Finish** to close the Add Nodes Wizard window.

19. Close the Cluster Administrator utility.

20. Click **Start**, **All Programs**, **Accessories**, and then click **Command Prompt**.

21. At the Windows command prompt, type **Cluster res "Majority Node Set" /priv MNSFileShare=\\server\share** where **\\server\share** represents the UNC path to the shared directory on the file share witness and press **Enter**. This command will register the file share on the file share witness with the active cluster node.

22. Close the Windows command prompt window and restart both cluster nodes.

After you have prepared the cluster, you can install Exchange Server 2007. You must first install Exchange Server 2007 on the active node followed by the passive node. The process for preparing for and installing Exchange Server 2007 is nearly identical to that described in Lesson 3, "Deploying Exchange Server 2007." However, during the graphical installation process you must select **Custom Exchange Server Installation** on the Installation Type page. Following this, you must select **Active Clustered Mailbox Role** on the Server Role Selection page to install Exchange on your active node as shown in Figure 13-21. This role cannot share hardware with other Exchange server roles.

Figure 13-21

Installing the Active Clustered
Mailbox Role

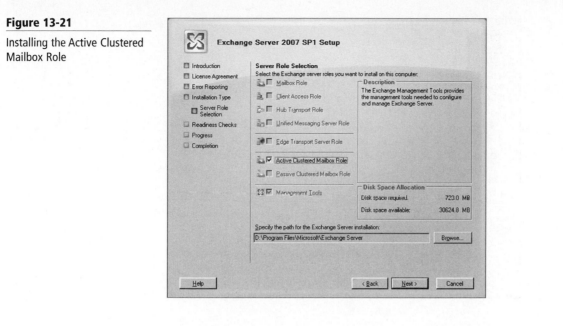

After selecting the Active Clustered Mailbox Role, you will be prompted later during the installation to specify the type of cluster (Cluster Continuous Replication), the server name for the active node, and the path for mailbox and public folder database files on the Cluster Settings page as shown in Figure 13-22. It is important to ensure that the path specified in Figure 13-22 remains identical on both the active and passive nodes of the CCR cluster.

Figure 13-22

Specifying Cluster Type and
Settings

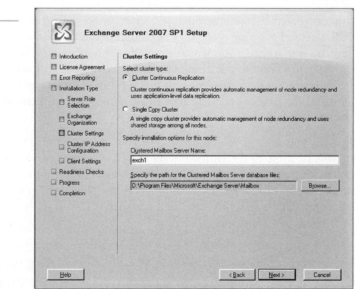

Additionally, you will be prompted to supply the IP address that will be used to contact your cluster node on the Cluster IP Address Configuration page as shown in Figure 13-23. This IP address cannot be the same as the IP address used to identify your cluster from your Windows Cluster Service configuration.

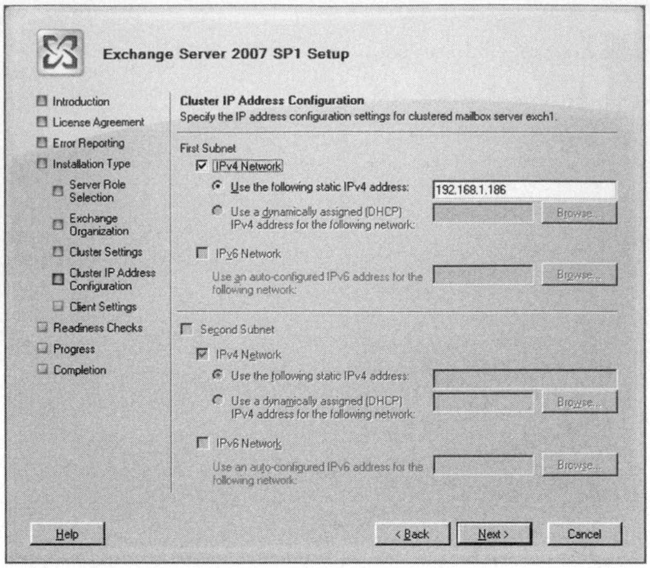

Figure 13-23

Specifying Cluster IP
Configuration

During the installation process, the Exchange Server 2007 installation program will configure the Windows Cluster Service with the resource information it requires for Exchange failover. After the installation has completed, you can repeat the process to install Exchange Server 2007 on your passive node. During the second installation, you need to select **Passive Clustered Mailbox Role** on the Server Role Selection page shown earlier in Figure 13-21. During the installation of the passive node, the Mailbox role configuration will be copied from the active node.

Once the configuration has completed, you must restart both cluster nodes to fully activate your CCR cluster. Following this, you can configure the databases on your Mailbox role servers in the same way that you would normally configure a nonclustered Mailbox role server. Any information written to the databases on the active node will automatically be copied to the same databases on the passive node using log shipping and replay. If the active node fails for any reason, the passive node will start servicing network requests using its own database copies and become the active node.

As with LCR, you can view the properties of your storage groups within the Exchange Management Console to determine the status of log shipping and replay. Highlight the **Cluster Continuous Replication** tab within storage group properties to view this information. Similarly, you can suspend and resume log shipping and replay, as well as reseed the passive database copy using the same methods that LCR uses. Select your storage group within the Exchange Management Console and click on of the following options in the action pane:

- **Suspend Storage Group Copy** to temporarily stop CCR log shipping and replay
- **Resume Storage Group Copy** to resume CCR log shipping and replay
- **Update Storage Group Copy** to reseed the passive database copy

Alternatively, you could use the Suspend-StorageGroupCopy, Resume-StorageGroupCopy, and Update-StorageGroupCopy cmdlets within the Exchange Management Shell to perform the same actions. The syntax of these cmdlets is the same for CCR and LCR configurations.

To obtain information regarding the cluster status of your CCR cluster node, you can access the **Clustered Mailbox Server** tab within the properties of your Mailbox role server as shown in Figure 13-24.

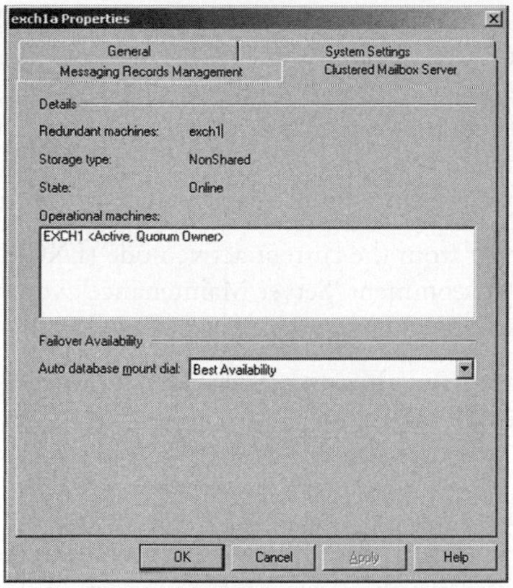

Figure 13-24

Viewing Clustered Mailbox
Server Status

Alternatively, you can use the Get-ClusteredMailboxServerStatus cmdlet within the Exchange Management Shell to view CCR cluster node status. The **Get-ClusteredMailboxServerStatus –Identity 'EXCH1A'** command shown in Figure 13-25 will display the status of the EXCH1A node.

Figure 13-25

Get-ClusteredMailboxServer-
Status Cmdlet

The **State** field shown in Figures 13-24 and 13-25 indicates the current status of the cluster:

- **Online** (the CCR cluster is functioning normally)
- **Partially online** (one CCR node/resource is offline)
- **Online pending** (one CCR node/resource is currently starting)
- **Offline** (the CCR cluster is not functioning)
- **Offline pending** (one CCR node/resource is currently stopping)
- **Failed** (the node has failed)

Over time, you will be required to perform maintenance on the nodes within your cluster, such as applying software updates. If you are performing maintenance on the passive node, you must first stop the CCR functionality. To stop CCR functionality on the server EXCH2B, you could use the following command within the Exchange Management Shell:

Stop-ClusteredMailboxServer –Identity 'EXCH2B'

After performing the maintenance, you must manually start the CCR functionality on the passive node. Although most maintenance requires you to reboot the Windows operating system afterwards, the passive node CCR functionality will not automatically start during the boot process after it has been stopped using the Stop-ClusteredMailboxServer cmdlet. To start CCR functionality on the server EXCH2B, you could run the following command within the Exchange Management Shell:

Start-ClusteredMailboxServer –Identity 'EXCH2B'

You cannot stop the CCR functionality using the Stop-ClusteredMailboxServer cmdlet to perform maintenance on the active node of a CCR cluster without affecting user access because the Stop-ClusteredMailboxServer cmdlet does not initiate failover to the passive node. Instead, you must first perform failover using the Move-ClusteredMailboxServer cmdlet to change the passive node to the active node and change the active node to the passive node. Next, you can perform maintenance on the passive node as described earlier.

To perform manual failover from the current active node (EXCH1A) to the current passive node (EXCH1B) using the comment 'Server Maintenance', you could run the following command within the Exchange Management Shell:

Move-ClusteredMailboxServer –Identity 'EXCH1A' –TargetMachine 'EXCH2B' –MoveComment 'Server Maintenance'

TAKE NOTE *

The failover process will take the databases on your Mailbox role server offline for up to one minute while the active and passive nodes are reconfigured. During this time, users will receive a notification within their email client program indicating that their Exchange server is temporarily unavailable.

You can also stop, start, and manually fail over a CCR cluster using the Exchange Management Console. Navigate to **Server Configuration** > **Mailbox**, highlight the active node server in the detail pane, and click **Manage Clustered Mailbox Server** in the action pane. When the Manage Clustered Mailbox Server window appears, you can select the appropriate action as shown in Figure 13-26.

Figure 13-26

Managing a Clustered Mailbox Server

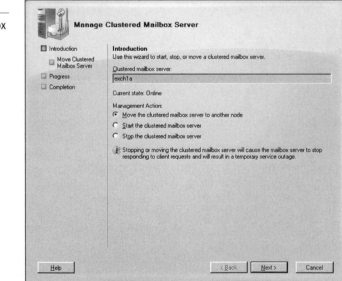

If you select **Move the clustered mailbox server to another node** in Figure 13-26 to perform failover, you will additionally be prompted for the target server name and comment.

Configuring a Single Copy Cluster

Single Copy Clusters use the Windows Cluster Service to maintain high availability in the event that a Mailbox role server fails. Instead of copying data between the two servers, Single Copy Clusters store their data on a shared storage device. If the first server fails, the second server starts to service network requests automatically. Unfortunately, Single Copy Clusters cannot protect against the failure of the shared storage device. The configuration and management of a Single Copy Cluster is very similar to that of Cluster Continuous Replication.

Previous versions of Exchange Server relied exclusively on the Windows Cluster Service to provide high availability without the use of log shipping and replay. You can implement the same type of high availability within Exchange Server 2007 by creating a ***Single Copy Cluster (SCC)***.

In an SCC, two Mailbox role servers are clustered using the Windows Cluster Service in an active/passive configuration. Like CCR, the active/passive cluster has a single name and IP address for access and a second network interface for intracluster communication. However, the Exchange databases and cluster configuration are stored on a ***shared storage device***. Fibrechannel Arrays, iSCSI, NAS, and SAN devices are commonly used for shared storage in an SCC. If the active node in an SCC fails, the passive node will start servicing network requests using the same databases on the shared storage device. A typical SCC structure is illustrated in Figure 13-27.

Figure 13-27

A Single Copy Cluster

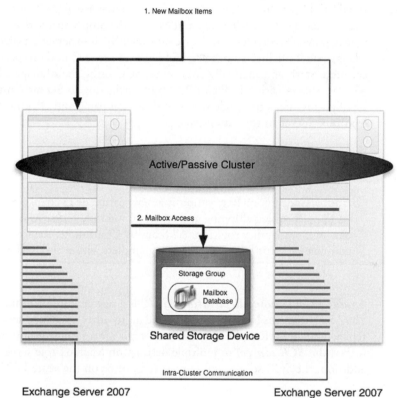

Although an SCC provides high availability in situations where a Mailbox role fails, it does not provide high availability if the shared storage device fails or if the databases on the shared storage device become corrupted. As a result, the shared storage device used by an SCC is a single point of failure. To minimize downtime following hard disk failure, many shared storage devices contain multiple hard disks that are configured in a fault tolerant RAID such as RAID 1 or RAID 5. Unfortunately, the added cost of shared storage and the possibility of a single point of failure make SCCs less attractive as a high availability method when compared to LCR and CCR.

The first step to configuring an SCC is to install a shared storage device and the associated software and drivers on each server. This procedure depends largely on the shared storage device type and manufacturer.

After configuring your shared storage device, the process for configuring an SCC is almost identical to the process for configuring a CCR cluster. Both nodes must have two network interfaces in the same configuration that CCR requires, as well as an Enterprise or later edition of Windows Server. However, when configuring the Windows Cluster Service, you must select the **Quorum** button on the Proposed Cluster Configuration page shown earlier in

Figure 13-18, and select your shared storage device instead of Majority Node Set from the drop-down box in the Cluster Configuration Quorum window shown earlier in Figure 13-19. Additionally, when you install Exchange Server 2007 on your active and passive SCR nodes, you must select **Single Copy Cluster** on the Cluster Settings page of the Exchange installation wizard as shown earlier in Figure 13-22.

Once the active and passive nodes of the SCC have been installed and restarted, you can configure and manage databases on your shared storage device from your active node Mailbox role server.

You can view the status of your SCC node by accessing the Single Copy Cluster tab of Mailbox role server properties within the Exchange Management Console. As with CCR, you can also use the Get-ClusteredMailboxServerStatus cmdlet within the Exchange Management Shell to obtain the status of your SCC node.

In addition, the procedures and tools used to manage an SCC are identical to those used to manage a CCR cluster. You can use the Stop-ClusteredMailboxServer, Start-ClusteredMailboxServer, and Move-ClusteredMailboxServer cmdlets within the Exchange Management Shell to stop, start, and fail over an SCC node respectively. Alternatively, you can stop, start, and manually fail over an SCC using the Manage Clustered Mailbox Server window shown earlier in Figure 13-26 by navigating to **Server Configuration** > **Mailbox**, highlighting the active node server in the detail pane, and clicking **Manage Clustered Mailbox Server** in the action pane.

Configuring Standby Continuous Replication

Standby Continuous Replication is a new feature of Exchange Server 2007 SP1 that allows you to perform log shipping and replay to multiple target Mailbox role servers to enhance your high availability solution. All Standby Continuous Replication configuration and maintenance must be performed using cmdlets within the Exchange Management Shell.

Standby Continuous Replication (SCR) is a new feature introduced in Exchange Server 2007 SP1 that can be used to replicate data to other Exchange servers using log shipping and replay. Unlike LCR and CCR, SCR can replicate a storage group on a Mailbox role server (called the *SCR source*) to multiple destination Mailbox role servers (called *SCR targets*). In addition, the SCR source and target need not be on the same LAN or site.

TAKE NOTE* Although there is no limit to the number of targets you can have for a single source, Microsoft recommends a maximum of four targets per source for performance reasons.

An SCR source can be a stand-alone Mailbox role server or a Mailbox role server that already uses a CCR or SCC configuration. However, any storage groups on the source that will be enabled for SCR must contain only a single mailbox database. An SCR target can be a stand-alone Mailbox role server or a passive node in a server cluster that has an unclustered Mailbox role installed and does not participate in CCR or SCC. Both the source and target Exchange servers must be running Exchange Server 2007 SP1 or later, and any database and log file paths must be the same on both the source and the target.

Although SCR is relatively easy to configure and manage, you must use cmdlets within the Exchange Management Shell. To enable SCR replication for the First Storage Group on the server EXCH1 with an SCR target of the server EXCH7, you could run the following command within the Exchange Management Shell:

Enable-StorageGroupCopy -Identity 'EXCH1\First Storage Group' -StandbyMachine 'EXCH7'

By default, any transaction logs that are shipped from the SCR source to the SCR target are replayed on the target database 24 hours later and not truncated. However, you can specify different values when you enable SCR using the format **Days.Hour:Minutes:Seconds** alongside the **–ReplayLagTime** and **–TruncationLagTime** options. To enable SCR replication for the First Storage Group on the server EXCH1 with an SCR target of EXCH7 as well as ensure that transaction logs are replayed 30 minutes after they are shipped and truncated 8 hours afterwards, you could run the following command within the Exchange Management Shell:

Enable-StorageGroupCopy -Identity 'EXCH1\First Storage Group' -StandbyMachine 'EXCH7' -ReplayLagTime 0.0:30:0 -TrucationLagTime 0.8:30:0

As with LCR and CCR, you can use the following cmdlets to manage SCR:

- **Get-StorageGroupCopy.** Displays the status and health of SCR log shipping and replay
- **Suspend-StorageGroupCopy.** Temporarily stops SCR log shipping and replay
- **Resume-StorageGroupCopy.** Resumes SCR log shipping and replay
- **Update-StorageGroupCopy.** Reseeds an SCR target database copy
- **Disable-StorageGroupCopy.** Disables an SCR target as well as removes the database and transaction logs on the SCR target Mailbox role server

However, when you use these cmdlets to manage SCR, you must specify the SCR target server using the **–StandbyMachine** option in addition to the name of the storage group. To remove the SCR configuration to the target computer EXCH7 for the First Storage Group on the server EXCH1, you could run the following command within the Exchange Management Shell:

Disable-StorageGroupCopy -Identity 'EXCH1\First Storage Group' -StandbyMachine 'EXCH7'

If you wish to use the information stored on an SCR target after a system failure, you can use Restore-StorageGroupCopy cmdlet to make the SCR target database mountable. If, for example, the Mailbox Database within the First Storage Group on the server EXCH1 becomes corrupted, you could make the SCR target database copy of this database on the server EXCH7 mountable by running the following command within the Exchange Management Shell:

Restore-StorageGroupCopy –Identity 'EXCH1\First Storage Group' -StandbyMachine 'EXCH7' –Force

Next, you can mount the SCR target database copy using the following command within the Exchange Management Shell:

Mount-Database –Identity 'EXCH7\First Storage Group\Mailbox Database'

If the SCR target database copy will not mount, you will need to run the **eseutil.exe** utility on it with the **/r** option to replay any recently shipped transaction logs and bring the database to a consistent state. The **eseutil.exe** utility was discussed in Lesson 10, "Backing Up, Restoring, and Repairing Exchange."

Finally, you can configure the properties of the EXCH1 Mailbox role server to redirect clients to the working copy of their mailbox database on EXCH7 using the following command within the Exchange Management Shell:

Get-Mailbox -Database 'EXCH1\First Storage Group\Mailbox Database' | Move-Mailbox -ConfigurationOnly -TargetDatabase 'EXCH7\First Storage Group\Mailbox Database'

➕ MORE INFORMATION

For additional information on how to deploy SCR in different environments, search for SCR at http://technet .microsoft.com or within the Exchange Server 2007 Help.

■ Providing High Availability For Nonmailbox Role Servers

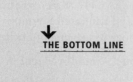

THE BOTTOM LINE

In addition to providing high availability for your Mailbox role servers, you should also provide high availability for the Hub, Edge, CAS, and UM role servers within your organization by implementing multiple Exchange servers that host these roles. If you deploy multiple Edge role servers, you must also configure DNS records for them. Similarly, to ensure high availability for CAS role servers, you can configure DNS or implement Network Load Balancing to redirect clients to another CAS role server in the event of a failure.

CERTIFICATION READY?
Configure high availability.
5.4

Although it is important to provide high availability for the Mailbox role servers within your organization, it is also important to provide high availability for the other Exchange server roles in your organization to ensure that a hardware or software failure does not affect the functionality of your Exchange infrastructure.

For Hub and UM role servers within your organization, you can provide high availability by deploying more than one server that contains the role. If each AD site within your organization has two or more Hub role servers, then the failure of a single Hub role server will not affect email relay because any available Hub role server can provide email relay within an AD site. Similarly, by configuring more than one UM role server to service a UM dial plan, the failure of a single UM role server will not affect your UM infrastructure.

You can also provide high availability for the Edge role servers within your organization by deploying more than one Edge role server subscribed to the Hub role servers within each AD site. If a single Edge role server fails, the Hub role servers will pass outgoing email through a different Edge role server associated with its AD site. However, to provide high availability for incoming Internet email, you must ensure that MX records exist for each Edge role server on your public DNS servers. When external email servers query the MX records for your organization, they will attempt to contact the first email server. If the first email server in the list is unavailable, the second email server in the list will be contacted, and so on.

By implementing several CAS role servers in your organization, email clients will be able to contact another CAS role server if the CAS role server configured within their email account settings fails. However, you will need to reconfigure the email account settings on each affected email client so that they can contact a CAS role server that is available. If your organization has many email clients, this could be time consuming. As a result, many Exchange administrators configure multiple CAS role servers and create A records for their IP addresses in DNS that have the same FQDN. The DNS console shown in Figure 13-28 indicates that there are three A records for cas.octavius.net that point to three different IP addresses:

```
cas.octavius.net    A          192.168.1.75
cas.octavius.net    A          192.168.1.76
cas.octavius.net    A          192.168.1.77
```

Figure 13-28

Viewing DNS A Records

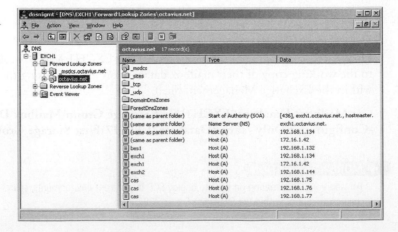

Following this, you can configure cas.octavius.net as the CAS role server name in the account settings on each email client. When an email client resolves the name cas.octavius.net using its DNS server, it will receive all three A records and will attempt to contact the first IP address in the list. If the first IP address is unavailable because the CAS role server has failed, the email client will attempt to contact the second IP address in the list, and so on. To provide load balancing of CAS role requests, the list of A records will be rotated for each name resolution request using the round robin feature of DNS.

The function and configuration of DNS A records, MX records, and round robin were discussed in Lesson 1, "Exchange Server 2007 Basics," and Lesson 4, "Configuring a New Exchange Server."

You will also need to configure the Autodiscover and Availability services on your CAS role servers with an internal and external URL that includes the name cas.octavius.net as well as replace the SSL/TLS certificate on each CAS role server with a certificate that includes the name of the CAS role server as well as the name cas.octavius.net within the Subject Alternative Name field.

The configuration of email account settings on client computers was discussed in Lesson 4, "Configuring a New Exchange Server." The configuration of the Autodiscover and Availability services was covered in Lesson 8, "Configuring Email Protocols and Transport Rules." The configuration of SSL/TLS certificates that use the Subject Alternative Name field was discussed in Lesson 9, "Configuring Security."

Instead of configuring multiple DNS A records for your CAS role servers to provide high availability, you can instead configure **Network Load Balancing (NLB)** on the CAS role servers in each AD site. NLB is available in both the Standard and Enterprise editions of Windows Server and can be configured after deploying the CAS role.

TAKE NOTE

Although it is possible to configure NLB for client Hub role servers that run Exchange Server 2007 SP1 or later, it can only be used to load balance requests from POP3 and IMAP4 clients that send email to the Hub role using SMTP.

In an NLB cluster, each of the nodes identify themselves using a single IP address and name in much the same way that a CCR or SCC does. To provide high availability for your CAS role servers, you can configure the name of the NLB cluster within the email account settings on each of your email clients.

When client computers contact the NLB cluster, each node in the NLB cluster receives the client request and independently decides whether it is their turn to respond to the request using an algorithm that is created during the creation of the NLB cluster. For example, if there are three nodes within an NLB cluster, the first node in the NLB cluster will configure itself to service the 1st, 4th, 7th, and 10th request; the second node in the NLB cluster will configure itself to service the 2nd, 5th, 8th, and 11th request; and the third node in the NLB cluster will configure itself to service the 3rd, 6th, 9th, and 12th request; and so on.

To ensure that the nodes within an NLB cluster are aware of the failure of another node, each node sends **heartbeat** packets every one second to the other nodes in the cluster. After five missed heartbeats, the other servers in the NLB cluster will recalculate their algorithm to exclude the failed NLB node. For example, if the third node in a three-node NLB cluster fails, the first node in the NLB cluster will reconfigure itself to service the 1st, 3rd, 5th, and 7th request; and the second node in the NLB cluster will reconfigure itself to service the 2nd, 4th, 6th, and 8th request; and so on.

TAKE NOTE* Although it is not mandatory, it is good form to use a second private network interface on each NLB node. As with CCR and SCC, this second network interface will be used for heartbeats and other intracluster communication.

TAKE NOTE*

You can configure up to 32 servers within a single NLB cluster.

The NLB cluster depicted in Figure 13-29 has three nodes that host the CAS role. Although each of these nodes receives requests from email clients, only one of them will respond according to their algorithm. In Figure 13-29, the third node determined that it should respond to the previous email client request.

Figure 13-29

CAS Role Network Load Balancing

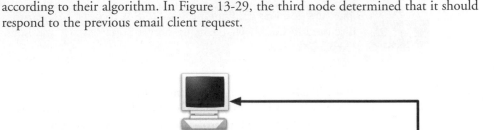
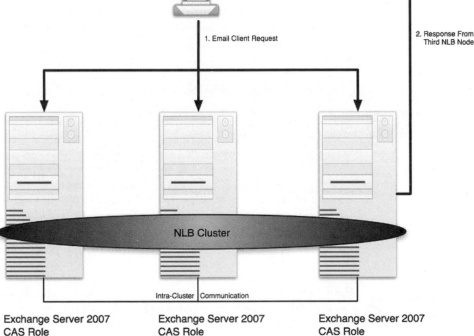

Before configuring an NLB cluster, you must first determine which mode the cluster should operate in. In *unicast mode*, the public network interface on each node within the NLB cluster is configured with the same hardware address. Because IP requests are ultimately sent to the hardware address of a network interface, this makes each node within the NLB cluster indistinguishable from one another. To manage individual cluster nodes that use unicast mode, you must have a second network adapter that does not participate in NLB.

Alternatively, when you configure an NLB cluster in *multicast mode*, the public network interface on each node retains the original hardware address and receives an additional hardware address that is the same for all cluster nodes. This allows for individual management of cluster nodes. Both unicast and multicast mode provide the same NLB functionality for CAS role servers.

 TAKE NOTE* A network interface hardware address is also called a **Media Access Control (MAC) address**.

→ **CONFIGURING NLB FOR CAS ROLE HIGH AVAILABILITY**

GET READY. Turn on the computer, and log in as the Administrator user account. Close any windows that appear on the desktop.

1. Click **Start**, **Administrative Tools**, and then click **Network Load Balancing Manager**.

2. When the Network Load Balancing Manager window appears, right click **Network Load Balancing Clusters** in the left pane and select **New Cluster**.

3. At the Cluster Parameters window, supply an IP address, subnet mask, and FQDN for the NLB cluster and then select a cluster mode as shown in Figure 13-30. Optionally specify a password used for remote management and click **Next**.

Figure 13-30

Specifying Cluster Parameters

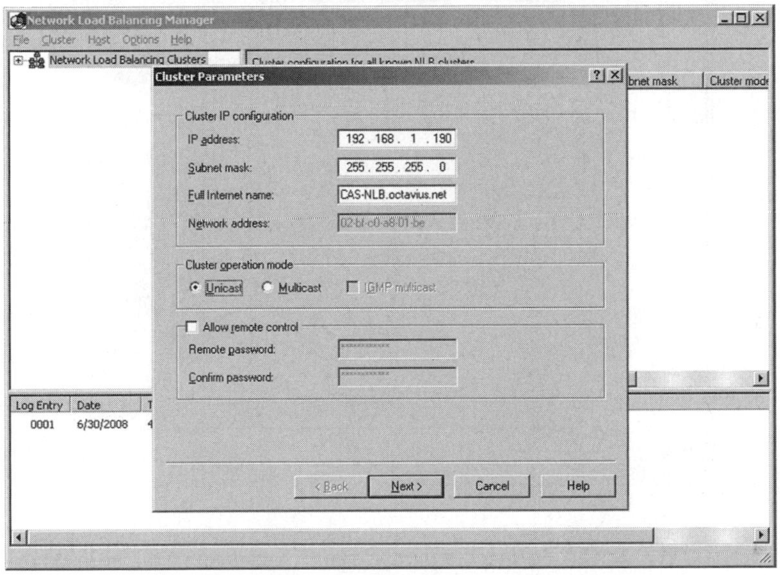

4. At the Cluster IP Addresses window shown in Figure 13-31, you can optionally add additional IP addresses that will be used to identify the cluster. Click the **Add** button, specify the appropriate IP information, and click **OK**. Click **Next** when finished.

Figure 13-31

Specifying Additional Cluster IP Addresses

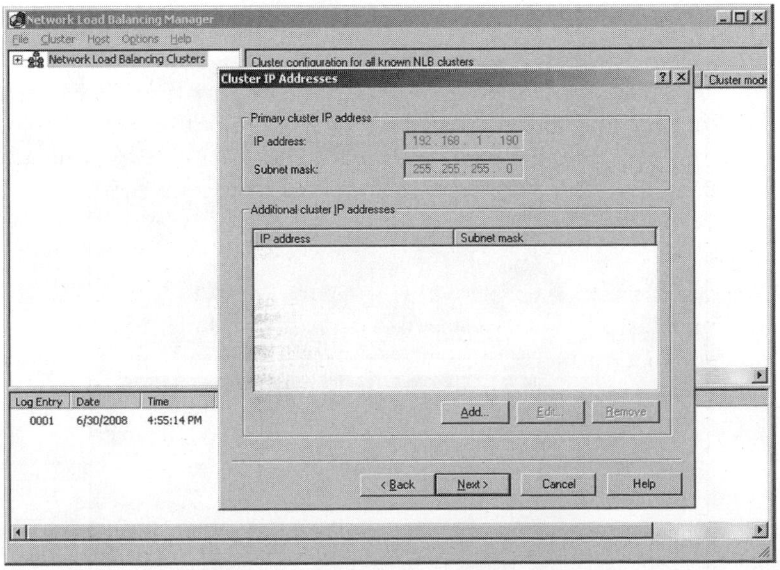

5. At the Port Rules window, you can specify the TCP and UDP traffic that the NLB cluster will accept from clients. By default, all TCP and UDP traffic on all ports are accepted as shown in Figure 13-32. However, you can remove the default rule and add rules that specify only the types of traffic that you expect to receive from your email clients by using the appropriate buttons. If your organization uses MAPI clients, it is best to leave the default selections because MAPI clients often select a random port number during connection. Click **Next** when finished.

Figure 13-32

Specifying Port Rules

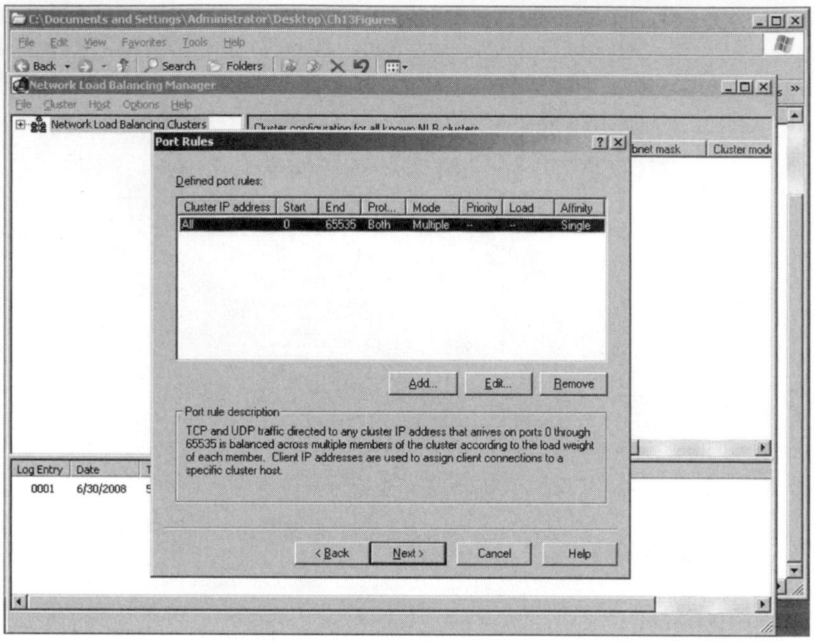

6. At the Connect window, type in the name of your first NLB node in the **Host** dialog box and click **Connect** to view the available network interfaces as shown in Figure 13-33. Highlight the network interface that should service email clients and click **Next**. This network interface will be configured to join the NLB cluster. As illustrated in Figure 13-33, the Public Interface is used for NLB and the Private Interface is used for intracluster communication.

Figure 13-33

Specifying a Cluster Node and Interface

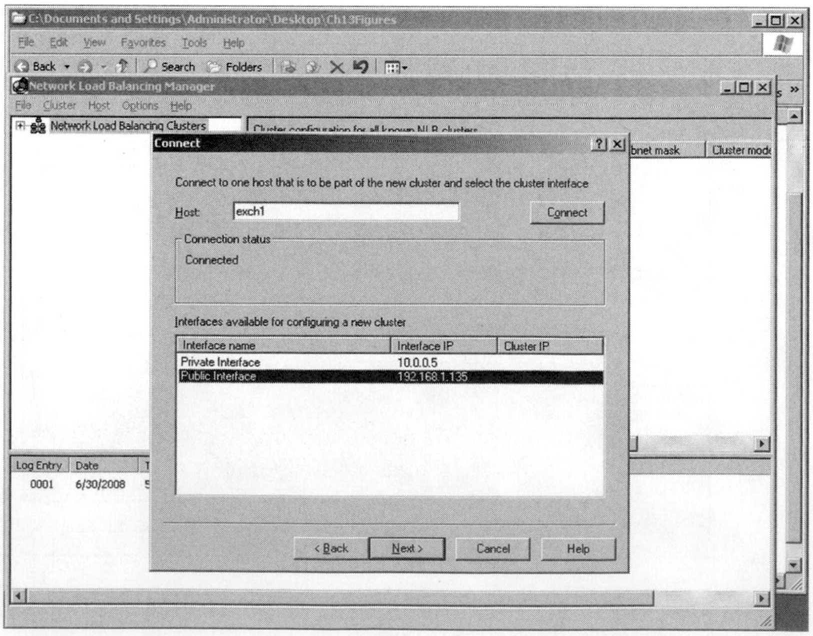

7. At the Host Parameters window, ensure that the **Priority** of your NLB network interface is **1**, the **Default state** is set to **Started**, and the original IP address of the NLB network interface is listed in the **Dedicated IP configuration** section as shown in Figure 13-34. Click **Finish** to create the NLB cluster. After the NLB cluster has been created, the Network Load Balancing Manager will display the NLB cluster name and IP as well as the first cluster node with a status of "Converged." In Figure 13-35, EXCH1 is the first cluster node in the NLB cluster called CAS-NLB .octavius.net using the shared IP address 192.168.1.190.

Figure 13-34

Specifying Host Parameters

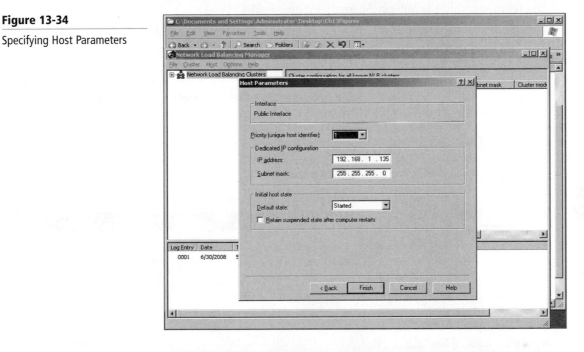

Figure 13-35

Network Load Balancing Manager

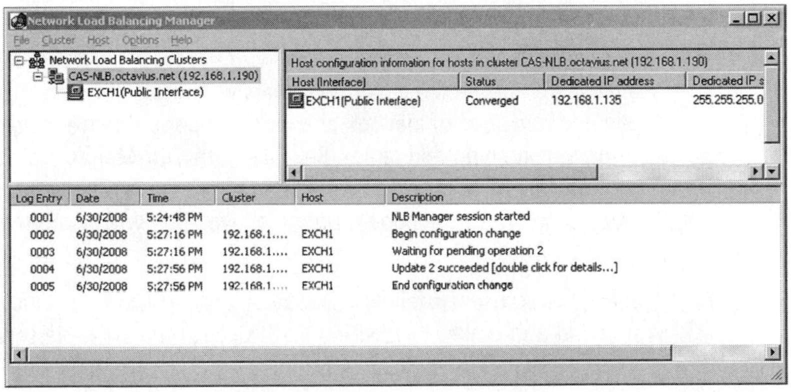

8. Right click your NLB cluster and click **Add Host To Cluster**.

9. At the Connect window, type in the name of your second NLB node in the **Host** dialog box and click **Connect** to view the available network interfaces as shown earlier in Figure 13-33. Highlight the network interface that should service email clients and click **Next**. This network interface will be configured to join the NLB cluster.

10. At the Host Parameters window, ensure that the **Default state** is set to **Started** and that the original IP address of the NLB network interface is listed in the **Dedicated IP configuration** section as shown earlier in Figure 13-34. However, change the **Priority** of the NLB network interface to **2** because the node is the second one in the cluster. Click **Finish**. Once the node has been successfully added to the cluster, the Network Load Balancing Manager should list the new node with a status of "Converged."

11. Repeat Steps 8 to 10 for any additional nodes within the cluster. At the Host Parameters window, ensure that you change the **Priority** section appropriately.

12. Close the Network Load Balancing Manager.

Once your CAS role servers have been added to the NLB cluster and your email clients have been configured to connect to the NLB cluster name, you will also need to configure the Autodiscover and Availability services with an internal and external URL that includes the name of the NLB cluster as well as replace the SSL/TLS certificate on each CAS role server with a certificate that includes the name of the CAS role server and the name of the NLB cluster within the Subject Alternative Name field.

After deploying NLB, you can easily manage your NLB cluster using the Network Load Balancing Manager. To remove an existing node from your NLB cluster and restore its original IP configuration, right click the appropriate computer within the Network Load Balancing Manager and select **Delete Host**. Alternatively, if you right click your NLB cluster within the Network Load Balancing Manager and select **Delete Cluster**, all hosts will be unconfigured from the NLB cluster, and the cluster will be removed.

SUMMARY SKILL MATRIX

IN THIS LESSON YOU LEARNED:

- By creating a high availability strategy, you can ensure that Exchange server roles remain available for user access following the failure of an Exchange server or database.

- There are four technologies that allow you to provide high availability for your Mailbox role servers: LCR, CCR, SCC, and SCR.

- LCR creates a continually updated copy of a mailbox database on a locally attached hard disk device. The mailbox database copy is updated using log shipping and replay and can be used as the production mailbox database in the event of a database failure.

- CCR combines the functions of LCR with the Windows Cluster Service to ensure high availability for the Mailbox role servers within your organization. CCR creates a continually updated copy of mailbox and public folder databases on another Mailbox role server using log shipping and replay. Because both CCR Mailbox role servers are also joined to an active/passive server cluster using the Windows Cluster Service, the failure of any hardware or software component on the active node will result in automatic failover to the passive node.

- You can also use the failover capabilities of the Windows Cluster Service without log shipping and replay. By creating an SCC, both Mailbox role servers are part of an active/passive server cluster that uses shared storage for mailbox and public folder databases. Failover automatically occurs when the active node fails and results in the passive node servicing requests using the mailbox and public folder databases stored on the shared storage device.

- SCR is a log shipping and replay technology that is only available in Exchange Server 2007 SP1 and later. You can create multiple copies of a mailbox database on several different target servers. In the event of a database failure, you can mount and access the mailbox database on a target server.

- You can provide high availability for the Hub, Edge, UM, and CAS role servers within your organization by deploying multiple Exchange servers that host each role. After deploying multiple Edge roles, you must ensure that multiple MX records exist within DNS so that external organizations can locate your Edge role servers. Similarly, you can use multiple DNS A records or implement NLB to ensure that clients can access another CAS role server in the event of a CAS role failure.

■ Knowledge Assessment

Fill in the Blank

Complete the following sentences by writing the correct word or words in the blanks provided.

1. By creating several DNS A records with the same FQDN that refer to different CAS role servers, DNS will use its _____ feature to load balance the requests across each server.

2. SCR can be used to create multiple copies of mailbox databases on servers called _____.

3. Most shared storage devices use _____ to provide fault tolerance in the event of a hard disk failure.

4. The _____ cmdlet may be used to manually initiate failover.

5. After deploying multiple Edge role servers, you must configure _____ records within DNS to allow the Edge role servers to be contacted by external organizations.

6. A single NLB cluster can have up to _____ nodes.

7. The user account that is used by the Windows Cluster Service must be granted the _____ right.

8. The process whereby a passive cluster node becomes active is called _____.

9. The mailbox database copy in an LCR configuration is called the _____ mailbox database.

10. If the output of the Get-StorageGroupCopyStatus cmdlet indicates that a passive mailbox database has failed, you should _____ the database.

Multiple Choice

Circle the letter that corresponds to the best answer.

1. Which of the following high availability technologies use log shipping and replay? (Choose all that apply.)
   - **a.** LCR
   - **b.** SCC
   - **c.** SCR
   - **d.** CCR

2. Which high availability technology can only be configured using cmdlets within the Exchange Management Shell?
   - **a.** LCR
   - **b.** SCC
   - **c.** SCR
   - **d.** CCR

3. Which high availability technology provides protection for a Mailbox role server but not for the mailbox and public folder databases on that Mailbox role server?
   - **a.** LCR
   - **b.** SCC
   - **c.** SCR
   - **d.** CCR

4. Which high availability technologies require the use of the Windows Cluster Service? (Choose all that apply.)
   - **a.** LCR
   - **b.** SCC
   - **c.** SCR
   - **d.** CCR

5. Which high availability technologies provide high availability for the mailbox databases on a Mailbox role server but not against the failure of the Mailbox role itself? (Choose all that apply.)
   - **a.** LCR
   - **b.** SCC
   - **c.** SCR
   - **d.** CCR

6. Which of the following cmdlets can you use to configure your Mailbox role server to use a passive mailbox database copy following a failure of the original mailbox database?
   a. Update-StorageGroupCopy
   b. Restore-StorageGroupCopy
   c. Resume-StorageGroupCopy
   d. Activate-StorageGroupCopy

7. Which of the following cluster states indicates that a cluster node or resource is currently stopping?
   a. Partially online
   b. Online pending
   c. Offline
   d. Offline pending

8. The cmdlets used to manage LCR and SCR are identical but used for different purposes. Which of the following cmdlet options can only be used to configure log shipping and replay for an SCR configuration?
   a. StandbyMachine
   b. SCR
   c. Target
   d. Copy

9. Which of the following should be disabled on the private interface of a CCR or SCC cluster? (Choose all that apply.)
   a. NetBIOS over TCP/IP
   b. Quality of Service (QoS)
   c. File and Printer Sharing for Microsoft Networks
   d. Dynamic DNS Update

10. What must you do after configuring an NLB cluster for your CAS role servers? (Choose all that apply.)
    a. Configure DNS A records for each cluster node
    b. Configure the account settings on email clients
    c. Configure a new SSL/TLS certificate
    d. Configure the Autodiscover and Availability services

True/False

Circle T if the statement is true or F if the statement is false.

T | **F**   **1.** CCR is only available in Exchange Server 2007 SP1.

T | **F**   **2.** SCC can be run in one of two modes: unicast mode or multicast mode.

T | **F**   **3.** You can use NLB to balance the load of requests and provide high availability for several CAS role servers.

T | **F**   **4.** CCR requires the configuration of a file share witness.

T | **F**   **5.** Exchange Server maintenance must be performed on the passive node of a server cluster.

T | **F**   **6.** The passive node within a server cluster must be installed before the active node.

T | **F**   **7.** The best way to provide high availability for the UM role servers within your organization is to deploy multiple UM role servers that share the same UM dial plan.

T | **F**   **8.** NLB must be configured before the installation of Exchange Server 2007.

T | **F**   **9.** An SCC requires the configuration of a shared storage device.

T | **F**   **10.** You can temporarily suspend and resume log shipping and replay using the Exchange Management Console or Exchange Management Shell.

Review Questions

1. Explain the difference between high availability and backup strategies.
2. Explain why CCR offers the most comprehensive high availability for your Mailbox role servers.

▪ Case Scenarios

Scenario 13-1: Creating a High Availability Strategy

Creating a high availability strategy is closely coupled with the needs and structure of your organization. Imagine that you are the network administrator for a medium-sized manufacturing company that has 500 users who require email access. Using the technologies and procedures described in this chapter, create a high availability strategy for this organization that will ensure continuous access in the event of a single server failure. Only select the technologies that are appropriate for your organization.

Scenario 13-2: Researching High Availability Technologies

In addition to the technologies presented in this lesson, there are several other software and hardware-based technologies (e.g., hardware-based load balancing) that can be used to provide high availability for your Exchange infrastructure. Using the Internet, research three of these technologies. For each, note their features, benefits, and costs compared to the technologies discussed in this lesson.

Objective Domain	Skill Number	Lesson Number
Prepare the infrastructure for Exchange installation.	1.1	3
Prepare the servers for Exchange installation.	1.2	3
Install Exchange.	1.3	3
Configure Exchange Server roles.	1.4	4, 12
Configure recipients	2.1	5
Configure mail-enabled groups.	2.2	5
Configure resource mailboxes.	2.3	5
Configure public folders.	2.4	7
Move mailboxes.	2.5	5
Implement bulk management of mail-enabled objects.	2.6	6, 7
Configure connectors.	3.1	4
Configure the antivirus and antispam system.	3.2	9
Configure transport rules and message compliance.	3.3	6, 8
Configure policies.	3.4	5, 6
Configure public folders.	3.5	7
Configure client connectivity.	3.6	4, 8
Monitor mail queues.	4.1	11
Monitor system performance.	4.2	11
Perform message tracking.	4.3	11
Monitor client connectivity.	4.4	11
Create server reports.	4.5	11
Create usage reports.	4.6	11
Configure backups.	5.1	10
Recover messaging data.	5.2	10
Recover server roles.	5.3	10
Configure high availability.	5.4	13

The *Microsoft Exchange Server 2007 Configuration* title of the Microsoft Official Academic Course (MOAC) series includes two books: a textbook and a lab manual. The exercises in the lab manual are designed for classroom use under the supervision of an instructor or a lab aide.

■ Classroom Setup

This course should be taught in a classroom containing networked computers where students can develop their skills through hands-on experience with Microsoft Exchange Server 2007. The exercises in the lab manual require the computers to be installed and configured in a specific manner. Failure to adhere to the setup instructions in this document can produce unanticipated results when the students perform the exercises.

Classroom Configuration

The following configurations and naming conventions are used throughout the course and are required for completing the labs as outlined in the lab manual.

The classroom network consists of a single instructor computer and several student computers. The student computers do not rely on the instructor computer for any labs in the lab manual. As a result, both the instructor computer and student computers have identical setup requirements. Furthermore, the instructor computer is optional; it may be used at the discretion of the instructor for demonstrating certain lab steps.

Each computer will need to have three fully updated instances of Windows Server 2003 SP2 hosted by three different virtual machines on the same computer using virtualization software such as:

- Microsoft Virtual PC
- Microsoft Virtual Server
- VMWare Server
- VMWare Workstation
- VMWare Fusion

This will allow both students and the instructor to interface with all three instances of Windows Server 2003 SP2 from the same computer during the exercises in this lab manual. Consequently, the host operating system that runs the virtualization software is irrelevant. Common host operating systems that can be used for virtualization include Windows 2000, Windows XP, Windows Server 2003, Windows Vista, Windows Server 2008, Linux, or Macintosh OS X.

Each computer that hosts the virtualization software should be configured with the correct IP information for classroom Internet access. Furthermore, the virtualization software on each computer should be configured to give Internet access to each virtual machine using NAT mode or Bridging mode.

Each instance of Windows Server 2003 SP2 hosted by the virtualization software should:

- Use the same password for the Administrator user for simplicity when switching from one virtual machine to another in the classroom environment.

- Have a different computer name that adheres to the following naming convention: StudentXX-A, StudentXX-B, and StudentXX-C, where XX is a unique number assigned by the instructor (typically the computer number within the classroom).

Include a single network interface that is configured with the correct IP address, subnet mask, and default gateway necessary to gain Internet access in the classroom. The network interface on StudentXX-A should also be configured with the DNS server used for Internet access within the classroom. The DNS server configured within the network interfaces on StudentXX-B and StudentXX-C should be the IP address of StudentXX-A.

Figure B-1 provides an example configuration for three instances of Windows Server 2003 on the first student computer using the 10.0.0.0 network, a classroom default gateway of 10.0.0.254, and a classroom DNS server of 10.0.0.253.

Figure B-1

A sample Student01 computer with three virtual machines

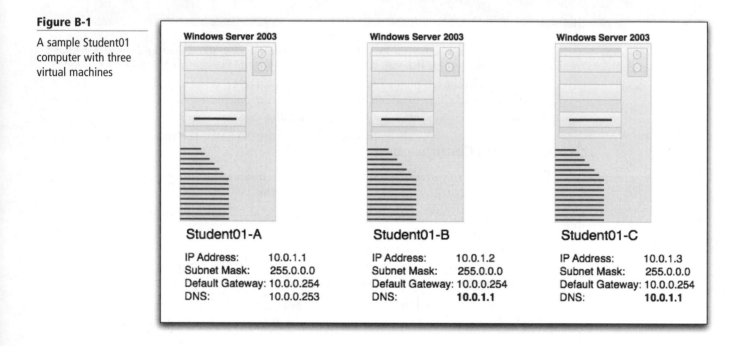

To support this classroom configuration, students configure their Windows Server 2003 virtual machines throughout the first three labs in the lab manual. Students configure the IP and name information for their virtual machines in Lab 1. In Lab 2, students configure the Active Directory service, and in Lab 3, students configure Exchange Server 2007 server roles.

The setup of the instructor computer, if used, will be identical to the student computer setup outlined in the lab manual. In addition, all labs within the lab manual are cumulative; before you begin a later lab, you must have completed all prior labs.

Classroom Computer Requirements

The host computer that will run the virtual machines in the classroom requires the following hardware and software:

Hardware Requirements

- Processor: 1 GHz (minimum); 2 GHz or faster (recommended)
- RAM: 2 GB (minimum); 4 GB or more (recommended)

  a. 2 GB of RAM leaves 512 MB for each of the three virtual machines plus 512 MB for the host OS

  b. 4 GB of RAM leaves 1024 MB of RAM for each of the three virtual machines plus 1024 MB of RAM for the host OS

- Disk space requirements: 40 GB (minimum); 80 GB or more (recommended)
  a. 40 GB leaves 10 GB for each of the three virtual machines plus 10 GB for the host OS
  b. 80 GB leaves 20 GB for each of the three virtual machines plus 20 GB for the host OS
- DVD-ROM drive
- Super VGA (800 x 600) or higher-resolution monitor
- Keyboard and mouse (or other pointing device)
- One network interface adapter

Software Requirements
- Microsoft Windows Server 2003, Enterprise edition
- Microsoft Exchange Server 2007, Enterprise edition

Classroom Computer Setup Instructions

Before you begin, do the following:

- Read this entire document.
- Verify that you have the Instructor CD provided with the course materials and the installation disk for Microsoft Windows Server 2003.

Installing Windows Server 2003

Using the following setup procedure, install Windows Server 2003 on each virtual machine.

> **TAKE NOTE***
>
> Before you install Windows Server 2003, you must start and configure your virtualization software. This will depend on the virtualization software that you plan to use. Consult your virtualization software guide for more information.

 INSTALL WINDOWS SERVER 2003

> **TAKE NOTE***
>
> These steps must be performed three different times in order to install three different virtual machines. It is unnecessary to provide the correct computer names and IP information during these steps since they will be configured during Lab 1 of the lab manual.

1. Boot the virtual machine from the Windows Server 2003 Installation disk. When you boot from the disk, the Windows Server 2003 Setup program starts.
2. At the Setup Notification screen, click **Enter**.
3. At the Welcome to Setup screen, click **Enter**.
4. At the Windows Licensing screen, press **F8** to accept the Windows Licensing Agreement.
5. At the partitioning screen, create a single partition that uses all of the space available to the virtual machine.
6. Select your C: partition and press **Enter** to install Windows Server 2003 on that partition.
7. Select **Format the partition using the NTFS file system** and press **Enter**. The partition will now be formatted and files will be copied to it. Following the copy operation, your virtual machine will be restarted.

8. Once the virtual machine has rebooted and the Windows environment has been loaded, click **Next** at the Regional and Language Options screen.

9. At the Personalize Your Software screen, enter your name in the Name box and your school or organization in the Organization box. Click **Next** when finished.

10. At the Your Product Key screen, enter the product key that came with your copy of Windows Server 2003. Click **Next** when finished.

11. At the Licensing Modes screen, ensure that **Per server** is selected and enter **50** in the concurrent connections box. Click **Next** when finished.

12. At the Computer Name and Administrator Password screen, enter the computer name **Student-A** if you are installing the first virtual machine, **Student-B** if you are installing the second virtual machine, or **Student-C** if you are installing the third virtual machine.

13. Enter the password of **secret** in both the Administrator password and Confirm password dialog boxes and click **Next** when finished. Click **Yes** when a message appears warning you about the simplicity of your password. Normally, you would select a complex password for Administrator in a production environment. However, we will use a simple password for convenience within the classroom environment.

14. At the Date and Time Settings screen, ensure that your date, time, and time zone are correct and click **Next**.

15. At the Networking Settings screen, ensure that **Typical settings** is selected and click **Next**.

16. At the Workgroup or Computer Domain screen, verify that **No, this computer is not on a network, or is on a network without a domain** is selected and click **Next**.

17. After the installation has completed, your virtual machine will automatically reboot. Remove the CD-ROM or DVD from your CD-ROM or DVD drive.

18. At the login dialog box, press Ctrl+Alt+Del and log in as the Administrator user (password > secret).

19. When the Manage Your Server screen appears, select the **Don't display this page at logon** checkbox in the bottom left hand corner of window and close the window.

20. Click **Start, All Programs, Activate Windows**. When the Activate Windows wizard appears, follow the directions to activate your copy of Windows Server 2003.

21. Install any updates needed to keep the operating system current.

A

A (host) Records DNS records used to associate IP addresses to host names during DNS forward lookup.

accepted domain A domain for which Exchange Server 2007 can accept and relay email.

Access Control List (ACL) A collection of rules that define the access that all users and groups have to an object.

action An event that occurs following the processing of a rule or filter.

Active Directory (AD) Microsoft's directory service that automates network authentication, management, and security.

Active Directory Domains and Trusts A Windows utility that manages Active Directory trust relationships and domain functional levels.

Active Directory Installation Wizard The program used to install Active Directory on a Windows server.

Active Directory Migration Tool (ADMT) A utility that can migrate or move objects from one Active Directory domain and forest to another.

Active Directory Sites and Services A Windows utility that manages site objects and Global Catalog functionality for an Active Directory domain.

Active Directory Users and Computers A Windows utility that manages Active Directory objects.

active node The functional node of a Windows cluster.

active/passive server cluster A Windows cluster type that uses an active node to service client requests as well as a passive standby node that is used if the active node fails.

ActiveSync A protocol used to synchronize email and other items between a smartphone device and Microsoft Exchange Server.

ActiveSync policy A set of rules that restrict the functionality of a smartphone device that uses the ActiveSync protocol.

address list A list of email addresses available to users when locating email recipients.

administrative permission A level of access that allows one to administer a

component of Exchange Server 2007 such as public folders.

administrative role A level of access for administrators within Exchange Server 2007. Different administrative roles allow different abilities within the Exchange Organization.

administrative templates A file that contains configurable Group Policy items. Different third-party vendors release administrative templates that you can use within a Group Policy.

agent log A log that contains events from the antispam agents within Exchange Server 2007.

alert A configurable notification that is triggered when a particular event occurs on a system.

alias The primary name of a recipient object. It is normally the portion of an email address before the @ symbol.

antispam transport agent The Exchange Server component that performs spam filtering.

asymmetric encryption A type of cryptography that uses a public key and private key to encrypt and decrypt data.

attack surface The sum total of the ways that an attacker can interact with a target computer across the network.

attribute A configurable property within an object.

authentication The process by which Active Directory verifies that the user matches the user account employed to gain access.

authoritative DNS server A server that hosts a zone for a domain in the Domain Name Space.

authorization The process of determining whether an identified user or process is permitted access to a resource and the user's appropriate level of access.

Autodiscover service An Exchange Server 2007 service that allows client computers to easily discover and configure the appropriate email account on their email client programs.

autoenrollment A feature of Windows Server 2003 certificate services that allows the users and computers within

your organization to receive certificates from a Group Policy.

automated attendant A Unified Messaging component that provides user interface prompts on the organization's telephone system.

Automatic Booking A feature of Exchange Server 2007 calendaring that allows appointments to be scheduled automatically in other recipients calendars.

Automatic Speech Recognition (ASR) A feature of Unified Messaging that allows users to speak commands into their telephone to navigate their voicemail and email items as well as respond to or create new email items.

Automatic Updates A Windows component that automatically installs Windows updates from the Windows Update servers on the Internet.

Availability service An Exchange Server 2007 component that updates free/busy calendaring information for mailbox users.

B

Backup Domain Controller (BDC) A Windows NT4 domain controller that contains a read-only copy of the directory database.

backup job A set of files and objects that are backed up at the same time.

backup set A set of files and objects that are backed up, managed, and restored as a single unit.

basic authentication An authentication method that does not encrypt the username and password as it passes across the network.

batch file A file that contains commands that can be executed at a Windows command prompt.

Berkeley Internet Name Domain (BIND) The standard used for the Domain Name System.

biometric thumbprint reader A device that reads human thumbprints to provide authentication on a computer system.

BlackBerry Attachment Service A component of BlackBerry Enterprise Server that expands and sends attachments to BlackBerry smartphones.

BlackBerry Connect A software component that can be installed on many third-party smartphone devices to allow them to use the BlackBerry Infrastructure.

BlackBerry Desktop Manager utility A software program used to manage BlackBerry smartphone devices that are connected to the computer via a USB, serial or Bluetooth connection.

BlackBerry Enterprise Server (BES) A server software suite that allows Exchange Server 2007 to interact with the BlackBerry Infrastructure.

BlackBerry Infrastructure The hardware and software components that allow wireless providers to send and receive emails and other data to and from BlackBerry smartphone devices.

BlackBerry Manager utility The software program used to create and manage BlackBerry Enterprise Server objects.

BlackBerry Professional Server (BPS) An alternative to BlackBerry Enterprise Server designed for smaller organizations.

BlackBerry Server Configuration utility The software program used to configure the different components of the BlackBerry Enterprise Server.

Book-In Policy A scheduling policy that allows users to automatically schedule a resource mailbox.

bounce message An error message indicating that an email could not be delivered.

bridgehead server A domain controller that is responsible for intersite replication.

buffer overrun A software exploit that sends undesirable information to an application in order to gain unauthorized access to the system or deny others service to the application.

bulk management The process of creating and managing several objects at the same time.

C

Cached Exchange Mode A feature of Outlook 2003 and later that can store frequently used information, such as address lists, on the hard drive of the client computer for future access.

Calendar Attendant The Exchange Server 2007 software component that processes calendar meeting requests.

capacity planning The process of planning for present and future growth within an organization.

categorizer An Exchange Server 2007 component that analyzes incoming information such as emails and directs them to the appropriate software component for processing.

Certificate Revocation List (CRL) A list of blacklisted certificates on a Certification Authority. The CRL is made available to certificate users for validation purposes.

Certificate Services The component of Windows Server 2003 that provides Certification Authority functionality.

certificate template A collection of settings that represent the features and function of a certificate.

Certification Authority (CA) A server that validates and digitally signs public key certificates to prevent man-in-the-middle cryptography attacks.

checkpoint file A file that contains entries to indicate the successful application of changes to a database.

checksum A calculation that renders a number that uniquely represents the size and contents of a file or data string. It is also called a hash.

child domain A DNS or AD domain that contains an existing domain name prefixed by a subdomain name. For example, subdomain.domain.com is a child domain for domain.com.

ciphertext Data that has been encrypted by an encryption algorithm.

circular logging A database feature that reuses transaction log files instead of creating new ones when they reach their maximum size.

classes Object types.

cleaning The process of removing a virus from a virus-infected file.

cleanup agent The Exchange Server 2007 component that locates and removes deleted items from a mailbox.

Client Access Server (CAS) An Exchange Server 2007 server role that allows email clients to interact with Exchange Server 2007 to send and receive email and other information.

client permission A permission that is granted to a user to allow them access to the contents of a public folder in Exchange Server 2007.

client permission level A set of client permissions that are granted to a user.

cloned configuration An Edge role configuration that can be copied and configured on another Edge role server.

cluster A group of computers that are configured to work together for fault-tolerance or performance purposes.

Cluster Continuous Replication (CCR) A type of Exchange Server 2007 clustering that continuously copies mailbox database changes from an active cluster node to a passive cluster node. Following an active node failure, the Cluster Service changes the passive node to the active node.

Cluster Service The Windows service that can be used to create a fault-tolerant server cluster.

cmdlets Commands that can be executed within the Exchange Management Shell.

comma-separated values (CSV) file A file that lists information for an object on a line-by-line basis organized by comma-delimited fields that are defined at the beginning of the file.

commercial CA A CA that issues digitally signed certificates for a fee. It is also called a public CA.

committed A database change that has been successfully written from the transaction log to the database.

common name (CN) An LDAP component that identifies the name of the object.

Computer Configuration The portion of a Group Policy that applies to the computer account within the Active Directory domain.

condition A criteria that must be met for a rule or filter to apply.

configuration partition The part of the Active Directory database that stores domain and forest information.

Configure Your Server Wizard A Windows utility that allows you to configure Windows server roles such as DNS and Active Directory.

connection filtering An Exchange Server 2007 spam filter that can be used to reject emails based on the IP of the source email relay computer.

connector An object that represents a connection to another computer.

container object An Active Directory object that contains other Active Directory objects.

content replica A copy of a public folder and its contents that is replicated across the network.

copy backup A backup type that is used to copy specified files to a target location.

cost A number that represents the value of an object, link, or component. Objects, links, and components with lower costs are typically chosen before those with higher costs.

counter A performance statistic within the Windows Performance MMC snap-in.

counter log A file that records Windows performance information over a long period of time. Counter logs are configured in the Windows Performance MMC snap-in.

cross forest trust A trust relationship between two different Active Directory forests that are at the Windows Server 2003 forest functional level.

cryptography The study and process of restricting the access of information to those who require it.

D

database A file that organizes data into records that contain common fields.

decryption The process of decoding encrypted data.

default public folder subtree The hierarchical public folder structure available for storing user-defined public folders in a public folder database.

Delivery Status Notification (DSN) A message that contains information regarding the successful or unsuccessful delivery of an email message.

demilitarized zone (DMZ) A public network within an organization that is connected to both the Internet and the private corporate network via a firewall. It is also called a perimeter network or screened subnet.

Denial of Service (DoS) A type of network service attack that prevents users from accessing the network service normally.

dial tone recovery A high availability recovery method that can be used to switch the production database with a backup copy of the production database that is mounted to the Recovery Storage Group.

differential backup A backup type that backs up files that have changed since the last full (normal) backup. Differential backups do not reset the archive bit on each file following the backup procedure.

digest authentication A type of authentication that reversibly encrypts passwords before they are sent across a network.

digital signature A CA-signed hash of a public key that is used to validate certificates.

direct file access An Exchange Server 2007 feature that allows OWA users to access and save files to their local computer.

directory partitions Divisions of the Active Directory database.

directory services A suite of services that allows for centralized authentication.

Active Directory is an example of a directory services suite.

Directory Services Restore Mode A Windows mode that does not start the Active Directory database. You can boot to Directory Services Restore Mode by pressing F8 during the Windows boot sequence.

DirectPush The technology that notifies smartphones of new email items and PIM data within ActiveSync.

distinguished name (DN) An LDAP name that includes the name of an object and its location within the LDAP database.

Distributed Authoring and Versioning (DAV) A technology that allows the editing of Web content on remote servers.

distribution group A group type that can be used to relay email to the members of the group.

DNS name resolution The process of obtaining the IP address or name of a computer from the information stored on a DNS server.

domain A portion of the Domain Name Space.

Domain Controller (DC) A computer that hosts the Active Directory database.

domain functional level A mode that indicates the level of backwards-compatibility for Active Directory domain controllers.

domain local An Active Directory group scope that requires the group be assigned permissions to the local domain in which the group was created.

Domain Name System (DNS) A system that associates IP address to Fully Qualified Domain Names and vice versa.

Domain Naming Master An Active Directory FSMO role that enforces the uniqueness of domain names within a forest.

domain partition The portion of the Active Directory database that stores domain objects such as users and groups.

dynamic distribution group A group within Exchange Server 2007 that generates its membership from specific criteria.

dynamic update The process whereby a computer automatically creates or updates its DNS records on a DNS server.

E

E.164 A standard that defines the format of telephone numbers.

Edge Rules Agent An Edge role software component that can be used to control the relay of emails based on user-defined rules.

Edge Transport Role (Edge) An Exchange Server 2007 server role that provides security for all inbound and outbound email for an organization.

EdgeSync The protocol used to transfer configuration information from the Hub role servers to the Edge roles within your organization.

Electronic mail (email) Personal messages that are sent across a computer network such as the Internet.

email address policy A set of rules within an Exchange organization that defines how email addresses are automatically configured for recipient objects.

email bomb A spam or email message that is sent to several recipients.

email protocols An email delivery mechanism used by email clients and servers.

email queue A temporary storage location for emails that are relayed by an email server.

email relay The process of sending email from one computer to another.

Email Transfer Protocol (ETP) The protocol used between the BlackBerry Infrastructure and the BlackBerry Enterprise Server within your organization.

encryption The process of transforming data so that it can only be read by certain intended recipients.

encryption algorithm The mathematical formula used to perform encryption.

enrollment The process whereby a user or computer generates a public/private key combination and sends the public key to a Certification Authority for approval and digital signing.

enterprise CA A Windows Certification Authority that is integrated with the Active Directory service.

Event Viewer A Windows utility that logs system, application, and security events for later use.

exception A condition that should not be applied to a rule or filter.

Exchange Best Practices Analyzer A utility that can be used to analyze the performance, configuration, and health of an Exchange Server 2007 computer.

Exchange Management Console (EMC) The graphical Microsoft Management Console snap-in utility used to manage Exchange Server 2007.

Exchange Management Shell (EMS) The command-line utility used to manage Exchange Server 2007 using cmdlets.

Exchange organization An object that represents Exchange Server computers within the same organization and Active Directory forest.

Exchange Organization Administrator An Exchange Server 2007 administrative role that has all rights to the Exchange organization.

Exchange organization model A value that represents the relative complexity of the Exchange organization when analyzed in the Exchange Best Practices Analyzer utility.

Exchange Public Folder Administrator An Exchange Server 2007 administrative role that has all rights to manage public folder databases and their contents within the Exchange organization.

Exchange Recipient Administrator An Exchange Server 2007 administrative role that has all rights to manage recipient objects within the Exchange organization.

Exchange resource forest An Active Directory forest that contains resources that are used by another Active Directory forest across a trust relationship.

Exchange Server Administrator An Exchange Server 2007 administrative role that has rights to manage the databases and configuration of a specific Exchange server.

Exchange Troubleshooting Assistant A graphical software utility that can be used to diagnose and remedy various Exchange Server 2007 configuration, communication, and performance problems.

Exchange View-Only Administrator An Exchange Server 2007 administrative role that has the ability to view the properties of all objects within the Exchange organization.

expansion server The Hub role server that is responsible for generating the list of recipient objects within a dynamic distribution group.

Extended Simple Mail Transfer Protocol (ESMTP) The latest protocol used to relay email messages from POP3 and IMAP4 to email servers, as well as from email servers to other email servers across the Internet.

Extensible Storage Engine (ESE) The database engine used by Exchange Server 2007.

Extensible Storage Engine Utility A command line utility that may be used to defragment, analyze, and repair Exchange Server 2007 databases.

external relay Email relay to an email server in a remote organization across the Internet.

external trusts Trust relationships between two Active Directory domains or between an Active Directory domain and a Windows NT4 domain.

F

failover The process whereby a passive cluster node starts responding to client requests when the active cluster node fails.

file share witness A cluster node used to monitor other cluster nodes within a server cluster.

filter A series of restrictions that are applied to data as it passes through a server or application program.

Flexible Single Master Operations (FSMO) A domain controller role that provides a unique function within an Active Directory domain or forest.

Folder Assistant The Exchange Server 2007 component that creates and configures managed folders within mailboxes.

Forefront Security for Exchange Server (FSE) A Microsoft virus-scanning and spam-filtering software product for Exchange Server 2007.

Forefront Server Security Administrator The graphical utility used to manage FSE.

forest The largest container object within Active Directory.

forest functional level A mode that represents the level of backwards compatibility for legacy domain controllers within an Active Directory forest.

forest root domain The first domain within an Active Directory forest.

forms-based authentication A type of authentication that allows users to enter their credentials within a form on a web page that is secured with SSL.

forwarding The process of forwarding email to another recipient object automatically.

Full Access permission A permission granted to a user that gives the ability to view, manage, and send email to another user's mailbox.

full backup A backup of all files or objects regardless of their state.

full-text index An ordered list of the text within email fields to speed searching.

Fully Qualified Domain Names (FQDNs) Computer names within the Domain Name Space that include a host name followed by a domain name.

G

global An Active Directory group scope that allows the group to be assigned permissions and rights in any domain.

global catalog (GC) An Active Directory database and service that records user and group object information for the forest to ensure quick access and searching.

Globally Unique IDentifier (GUID) A unique number assigned to every Active Directory object.

GNU Privacy Guard (GPG) An open source version of the PGP protocol.

group manager A user that is responsible for the maintenance of a group.

group nesting The process of adding one group to another.

Group Policy The feature of the Active Directory service that can be used to install software or modify the settings on the computers within a domain.

Group Policy Management Console (GPMC) An MMC snap-in utility that can be used to manage all of the GPOs within an Active Directory forest.

Group Policy Object Editor The MMC snap-in utility that can be used to modify the settings within a GPO.

Group Policy Objects (GPOs) An object that contains a set of configuration settings that are applied to users and computers.

group scope The Active Directory domains that can assign permissions to an Active Directory group.

H

hard recovery A process where transaction logs are replayed after restoring a database from an online backup.

hash A calculation that renders a number that uniquely represents the size and contents of a file or data string. It is also called a checksum.

heartbeat A small network packet that is sent between cluster nodes.

high availability The practice where procedures and technologies are implemented to ensure that user interruption is minimized after the failure of a server.

host-based firewall A firewall located on a single computer that functions to limit the traffic passing from the network to the services that run on the computer itself.

Hub Transport Role (Hub) An Exchange Server 2007 server role that is responsible for relaying email within an Exchange Organization.

Hypertext Markup Language (HTML) The language used to format web pages.

Hypertext Transfer Protocol (HTTP) The protocol used to display web pages.

I

iCalendar A standard for calendar data exchange.

In Policy A scheduling policy that allows users to schedule a resource mailbox after they receive approval.

incremental backup A backup type that backs up files that have changed since the last incremental or full (normal) backup. Incremental backups clear the archive bit on each file following backup.

Information Store Integrity Checker A utility that can be used to check the high-level structural integrity of an Exchange mailbox database and fix any errors.

Infrastructure Master An FSMO role that updates group membership across domains within a forest.

instance An installed copy of an application that can be executed alongside other applications.

Integrated Windows Authentication An NTLM-based authentication mechanism used on web servers.

internal relay Email relay to another Exchange server within the same Exchange organization.

Internet Information Services (IIS) The Windows services that provide for the Web (HTTP), FTP, NNTP, and SMTP protocols.

Internet Message Access Protocol Version 4 (IMAP4) A common email access protocol that email clients can use to obtain email from an email server using a persistent connection.

Internet Protocol (IP) gateway A UM device that allows for communication between an IP network and PBX.

Internet Protocol Security (IPSec) A TCP/IP driver module that encrypts and decrypts IP data between two computers on a network.

Internet Service Provider (ISP) An organization that provides Internet access to other organizations.

Interpersonal Message (IPM) subtree The default public folder hierarchy used to contain user-created posts and items.

inter-site transport The protocol used to replicate Active Directory information between sites.

IT policy A BES object that can be used restrict the functionality of BlackBerry smartphones within your organization.

J

Journaling agent The Exchange Server 2007 software component that provides for message journaling.

Just a Bunch of Disks (JBOD) A series of hard disk drives that are treated as a single contiguous volume. JBOD is also known as RAID level 1 or spanning.

K

Kerberos The authentication protocol used by Active Directory.

key A unique piece of information that is used alongside encryption algorithms when encrypting data.

L

Last Restore Set option A restore option within Windows Backup that replays restored transaction logs following a database restore.

LCR storage group A storage group that is configured for LCR.

leaf object An object within Active Directory that does not contain other Active Directory objects.

Lightweight Directory Access Protocol (LDAP) The protocol used to search the Active Directory database.

link state A method used in Exchange Server 2003 and earlier when determining the best route for email to take when it is transferred between routing groups within the Exchange organization.

linked mailbox user A disabled mailbox user that is associated with a user account in another forest.

Local Continuous Replication (LCR) A high availability method that uses asynchronous log shipping and replay on a remote server.

local group A group stored within the registry of a Windows computer.

local user account A user account stored within the registry of a Windows computer.

local wipe The process of removing all user data from a mobile smartphone device.

log replay The process of adding the information from transaction log files to an Exchange database a second time.

log shipping A system that copies transaction log files from one database to another for backup purposes.

long-standing HTTPS request An HTTPS request that has an extended time-out value. Long-standing HTTPS requests are used by ActiveSync.

M

mail contact A recipient object that represents an external email recipient. It includes the external recipient's email address and personal information.

Mail Delivery Agent (MDA) The X.400 component that receives email from other email servers and delivers it to a recipient's mailbox.

Mail eXchanger (MX) records DNS records that list the email server for a particular DNS domain.

Mail Transfer Agent (MTA) The X.400 component that transfers email from one email server to another.

mail user A recipient object within Exchange Server 2007 that represents an Active Directory user account with an external email address.

Mail User Agent (MUA) The X.400 component that allows a client computer access to email on an email server.

mailbox database A database that stores email for mailbox users.

mailbox delivery queue A temporary storage location for email that is to be delivered to a mailbox on a Mailbox role server within your organization.

Mailbox Role An Exchange Server 2007 server role that stores mailbox and public folder databases as well as provides access to their contents.

mail-enabled universal distribution group A universal group object within Active Directory that functions as a recipient object within Exchange Server 2007.

mail-enabled universal security group A universal group object within Active Directory that can be used for permissions and rights assignments as well as functions as a recipient object within Exchange Server 2007.

managed custom folder A nondefault mailbox folder that is assigned a managed folder mailbox policy.

managed default folder A default mailbox folder that is assigned a managed folder mailbox policy.

managed folder A mailbox folder that is assigned a managed folder mailbox policy.

Managed Folder Assistant The Exchange Server 2007 component that is responsible for creating and updating managed folders within mailboxes.

managed folder mailbox policy A policy that contains managed folders that can be assigned to a mailbox.

man-in-the-middle attack A type of attack where a hacker intercepts and modifies network traffic while it is in transit.

Manual Scan Job An FSE scan that can be manually performed on mailbox and public folder databases.

MAPI clients Client computers that run software (such as Microsoft Outlook and Entourage) and can connect to Exchange Server 2007 using the MAPI protocol.

MAPI RPC The RPC-based, Microsoft-specific client access protocol designed to integrate Microsoft Outlook and Entourage with advanced features in Exchange Server 2007.

master account A user account that has the ability to access a mailbox in a resource forest.

memory leak A condition where a process on the system continuously consumes more and more available memory.

message classification A classification that can be applied to email messages within Microsoft Outlook and Entourage.

message dumpster A temporary location for deleted mailboxes on a Mailbox role server.

message journaling The process of archiving or copying email messages to another recipient's mailbox.

message tracking log A log file that records the messages that have passed through the email message queues on a Hub or Mailbox role server.

Messaging Application Programming Interface (MAPI) The RPC-based, Microsoft-specific client access protocol designed to integrate Microsoft Outlook and Entourage with advanced features in Exchange Server 2007. It is often referred to as MAPI RPC.

messaging compliance A set of procedures and practices that an organization uses to ensure that its messaging system meets legal requirements.

Messaging Records Management (MRM) An Exchange Server 2007 feature that allows organizations to easily store and archive messages for periods of time as required by law.

method of least privilege A practice where users are only granted the minimum necessary rights or permissions to servers, objects, and resources.

Microsoft Exchange Information Store The Exchange Server 2007 component that manages access to mailbox and public folder databases on a Mailbox role server.

Microsoft Internet Security and Acceleration (ISA) Server A Microsoft proxy server and firewall product.

migration The process of moving a user, configuration, or role to another location or computer.

mirroring A hard disk configuration where data is written to two identical hard disks simultaneously. It is often referred to as RAID level 1.

Mobile Data Service (MDS) A BES component that allows for the deployment of applications to BlackBerry smartphones.

moderated public folder A public folder that is configured to pass new posts to a moderator for approval before they are added to the public folder.

moderator A user that receives new public folder posts for approval.

multicast mode A NAT mode in which each network interface that is joined to the NAT cluster retains its original network hardware (MAC) address.

multifactor authentication A form of authentication where more than one proof of identity is required.

Multipurpose Internet Mail Extensions (MIME) A standard that defines different content formats for use on the Internet.

N

Network Address Translation (NAT) A type of routing that allows several computers on a private network to access a public network using a single IP address.

Network Attached Storage (NAS) A hard disk-based storage device that can be accessed across a computer network.

Network Load Balancing (NLB) A clustering process that evenly distributes network requests amongst several identically configured servers.

network protocol analyzer A software program that captures and analyzes network traffic. It is also called a packet sniffer.

network-based firewall A firewall that resides on a network router and serves to restrict the flow of traffic from one network to another.

node A computer that participates in a cluster.

Non-Delivery Notification (NDN) An error message indicating that an email could not be delivered.

Non-Delivery Receipt/Report (NDR) An error message indicating that an email could not be delivered.

nonprovisionable device A smartphone that can not be configured by all of the settings within an ActiveSync policy.

normal backup A backup of all selected files and objects regardless of their archive bit. It is often called a full backup.

O

object An entity that represents a person, place or thing.

Offline Address Book (OAB) A set of address lists that are cached to an email client's hard drive for use when the email client loses network connectivity to its email server.

offline backup A database backup that occurs when the database is not used by any services.

offline defragmentation A process whereby blank records within an offline database are removed to reduce database size and ensure that database records are contiguous.

one-way trust A trust relationship used by Active Directory to allow users in one domain the ability to access resources in another domain that they have permission to.

online defragmentation The process whereby a database engine removes data from a database while the database is being used by other processes.

Out of Office Assistant A component of Microsoft Outlook and Entourage that allows users to configure a message that is automatically sent as a reply to emails received by the user's mailbox when the users is not available.

Out Policy A scheduling policy that allows users to automatically schedule a resource mailbox if it is available. If it is unavailable, they must obtain approval.

Outlook Anywhere A protocol that allows MAPI clients to obtain email from their Exchange Server 2007 computer from across the internet using HTTPS. It is also called RPC over HTTP/HTTPS.

Outlook Form Designer A Microsoft Outlook utility that can be used to design a custom form template for use with emails or public folder posts.

Outlook Voice Access (OVA) A UM voice-controlled system that allows users the ability to access, reply, and manage their email via a telephone.

Outlook Web Access (OWA) A Web site and related services that are hosted by a CAS role server to provide access to email via a web browser.

over the air (OTA) A process that occurs across a wireless network.

P

packet sniffer A software program that captures and analyzes network traffic. It is also called a network protocol analyzer.

page The smallest manageable unit within a database.

page file A file that Windows writes information to that could not be written to physical memory. It is also called a swap file.

Parallel Advanced Technology Attachment (PATA) A hard disk technology that transfers information across a parallel interface cable to the computer.

parameter A piece of information used to configure an object, computer, or software component.

parent domain A DNS or AD domain that contains child domains. For example, domain.com is a parent domain for subdomain.domain.com.

passive mailbox database An inactive, standby mailbox database copy that can be used if the original mailbox database fails.

passive node An inactive, standby computer within a server cluster.

PDC Emulator An FSMO role that manages time synchronization, password changes, and BDC replication within an Active Directory domain.

performance baseline A standard level of performance for a computer.

performance object A performance category used within the Windows Performance MMC snap-in.

perimeter network A public network within an organization that is connected to both the Internet and the private corporate network via a firewall. It is also called a DMZ or screened subnet.

permissions group A group of permissions that can be granted as a single unit.

Personal Identification Number (PIN) A unique number that identifies a BlackBerry smartphone within the BlackBerry Infrastructure.

Personal Information Manager (PIM) An organizer data category that includes contacts, address lists, memos, calendars, and tasks.

phishing attack A network attack where fraudulent emails are sent to recipients with the intent of obtaining personal information.

pickup directory A directory that contains email for pickup by a transport agent in Exchange Server 2007

plaintext Data that has not been encrypted.

poison message queue A temporary storage location for email messages that are potentially harmful to Exchange Server 2007.

Post Office Protocol Version 3 (POP3) A common email access protocol that can be used to download email from an email server.

postmaster A recipient object that users are directed to email when they encounter problems with their email functionality.

PowerShell A Windows command line management and scripting utility.

practical security A level of security that meets the needs of the organization.

premium journaling A type of email message journaling that journals messages that match a particular set of criteria.

prestaging The process of creating a computer object within Active Directory before the associated computer is joined to the Active Directory domain.

Pretty Good Privacy (PGP) A widely used technology used to encrypt and decrypt emails using asymmetric cryptography.

Primary Domain Controller (PDC) A Windows NT4 domain controller that contains a read-write copy of the directory database.

priority number A number that identifies the order for which DNS MX records should be processed following a DNS MX record lookup.

Private Branch eXchange (PBX) An internal telephone system within an organization.

private interface A network interface that does not receive client requests.

private key An asymmetric encryption key that can decrypt information that has been encrypted by the associated public key.

proactive monitoring A practice that involves monitoring servers and applications to ensure that problems can be identified shortly after they occur.

protocol log A log file on a Hub or Edge role server that contains SMTP and ESMTP information or each email that has been relayed.

public CA A CA that issues digitally signed certificates for a fee. It is also called a commercial CA.

public folder database A database that stores public folders and the related posts on a Mailbox role server.

public folder hierarchy A hierarchical structure used to organize public folders to ensure that users can quickly locate the information that they need.

Public Folder Management Console A graphical utility used to manage public folders in Exchange Server 2007 SP1 and later.

public folder referral A process whereby a Mailbox role server directs a client to another public folder database on a different Mailbox role server to obtain public folder content.

public folder A folder that can be used to store email, posts, tasks, notes, memos, calendars, and journal items.

public interface A network interface that receives client requests.

public key An asymmetric encryption key that is typically used to encrypt data using an asymmetric encryption algorithm.

public key certificate An object that contains a CA-signed public key.

Public Switched Telephone Network (PSTN) The public telephone network.

Purported Responsible Address (PRA) An identification that determines the likelihood that an email is spam based on header information.

Q

Queue Viewer A graphical utility that may be used to view and mange the email queues on an Exchange Server 2007 computer.

R

reactive monitoring A practice where servers and applications are monitored following the detection of a problem to determine the nature of the problem and identify its cause.

realm trust An Active Directory trust relationship between a Windows domain and a UNIX Kerberos realm.

Realtime Block List (RBL) A list of blacklisted email relays and senders.

Realtime Scan Job An FSE scan that is immediately performed on items that are sent and received by mailboxes and public folders.

receive connector An object that represents how email is received by an Edge or Hub role server.

recipient An entity that is the target of an email.

recipient object An object that can receive email within Exchange Server 2007.

recovery storage group (RSG) A temporary storage group that can contain a restored backup copy of another database for use in disaster recovery and restore procedures.

Redundant Array of Independent Disks (RAID) A standard used to define the methods used to create volumes from several different hard disks.

Relative Identifier (RID) The unique component of a SID within a domain.

remote delivery queue An email queue that contains emails that are destined for remote domains on the Internet.

remote domain An Exchange Server 2007 object that represents a domain on the Internet that is not part of the organization.

Remote Procedure Call (RPC) A communication technology that allows commands to be executed on a remote computer.

remote wipe A process whereby the information on a smartphone device is removed using a command issued across a wireless network.

Research In Motion (RIM) The company that produces BlackBerry smartphone devices and hosts the BlackBerry Infrastructure.

Resource Booking Attendant The Exchange Server 2007 component that controls the resource booking process.

resource booking policy A set of rules that determines who can schedule resource mailboxes and whether approval is required.

resource mailbox A mailbox that is used for resource scheduling within MAPI clients.

Rich Text Format (RTF) A common cross-platform text format that allows for text formatting and styles.

RID Master An FSMO role that generates Relative Identifiers for objects within a domain.

roaming The process of switching to a different wireless infrastructure using a wireless device.

rogue process A process on a computer that consumes a large amount of CPU cycles.

root CA The first CA in a CA hierarchy.

round robin The process whereby a list of multiple DNS A records for a host are rotated for each name resolution request.

Routing and Remote Access Service (RRAS) The Windows server service that provides routing, VPN, and dial-in access.

routing groups Objects used within Exchange Server 2000/2003 to represent a set of Exchange server computers within the same site or fast LAN.

RPC over HTTP/HTTPS A protocol that allows MAPI clients to obtain email from their Exchange Server 2007 computer from across the internet using HTTPS. It is often called Outlook Anywhere in Exchange Server 2007.

S

schema The list of all object types and attributes within Active Directory.

Schema Master The FSMO role that has the ability to modify the Active Directory schema.

schema partition The portion of the Active Directory database that stores the Active Directory schema.

SCR source The original production database in an SCR configuration.

SCR target A standby database copy in an SCR configuration.

screened subnet A public network within an organization that is connected to both the Internet and the private corporate network via a firewall. It is also called a perimeter network or DMZ.

Secure Extended Simple Mail Transfer Protocol (ESMTPS) A version of the ESMTP protocol that uses cryptography.

Secure Hypertext Transfer Protocol (HTTPS) A version of the HTTP protocol that uses cryptography.

Secure Internet Message Access Protocol Version 4 (IMAP4S) A version of the IMAP4 protocol that uses cryptography.

Secure Password Authentication (SPA) An NTLM-based authentication mechanism used to authenticate an SMTP session with a remote SMTP server.

Secure Post Office Protocol Version 3 (POP3S) A version of the POP3 protocol that uses cryptography.

Secure Simple Mail Transfer Protocol (SMTPS) A version of the SMTP protocol that uses cryptography.

Secure Socket Layer (SSL) A technology used to provide encryption for a wide range of Internet protocols such as HTTP.

security The robustness of a computer, system or software program against unauthorized access.

Security Accounts Manager (SAM) The portion of the Windows registry that contains local user accounts and user accounts within a Windows NT4 domain.

Security Configuration Wizard (SCW) A Windows software utility that can be used to stop unneeded services, modify operating system security, and configure Windows Firewall.

security group An Active Directory group type that can be assigned permissions and rights to resources.

Security IDentifier (SID) A unique identifier assigned to a user account for use in permissions and rights assignments.

seeding The process of copying database contents to a standby database copy.

seize The process where a Windows domain controller forcibly obtains an FSMO role.

self-signed certificate A public key certificate that is digitally signed by the host that generated it.

Send As permission A permission that allows a mailbox user to send emails using another mailbox user in the From field.

send connector An object that represents how email is sent by an Edge or Hub role server.

Send On Behalf permission A permission that allows a mailbox user to send emails on behalf of another user in the From field.

sender The person or object that is listed in the From field of an email.

sender ID An email authentication technology that helps to reduce phishing attacks by verifying sender relay information.

sender reputation A measure used by the antispam agents on an Edge role server that identifies spam by combining several factors.

Serial Advanced Technology Attachment (SATA) A hard disk technology that transfers information across a serial interface cable to the computer.

server role A role that defines the functionality of an Exchange Server 2007 computer.

Server Routing Protocol (SRP) The protocol used to transfer information between the BlackBerry Infrastructure and a BlackBerry Enterprise Server.

service record (SRV) A DNS record that is used to list services that are available on a specific computer.

Session Initiation Protocol (SIP) A protocol used to establish multimedia and voice sessions across the Internet.

shared storage device A hard disk-based storage device that is connected to two or more cluster nodes.

shortcut trust A manually created trust relationship between two domains in the same Active Directory forest.

Simple Mail Transfer Protocol (SMTP) The legacy protocol used to relay email messages from POP3 and IMAP4 to email servers, as well as from email servers to other email servers across the Internet.

Single Copy Cluster (SCC) Two or more computers that are configured as a cluster using the Windows Cluster service.

single sign-on A feature of directory services such as Active Directory that allows users to authenticate to a single domain controller in order to access all of the required services on the network.

site A physical location within an organization.

site link An object that is used to represent the physical connection between sites.

site object An object that represents a physical location with a fast interconnect.

Small Computer Systems Interface (SCSI) A hard disk technology that is commonly used within server computers due to its fast transfer speed.

smart card A physical card that stores a private key used for multifactor authentication.

smart host A third-party email server that queues and filters email.

smartphone A mobile telephone device that offers data services such as email access and web browsing.

smartphone device identifier (ID) A number used to uniquely identify a smartphone device.

spam Unsolicited commercial email.

Spam Confidence Level (SCL) A number that represents the likelihood that an email message is spam. Higher SCL numbers represent higher spam liklihoods.

spammer A person or organization that sends spam messages on the Internet.

spanning A hard disk configuration that allows a single volume to span multiple hard disk drives. It is a form of RAID 0.

stand-alone CA A Windows CA that is not integrated with Active Directory.

standard journaling A type of message journaling in which a copy of all email messages for a mailbox database are sent to a specified mailbox.

Standby Continuous Replication (SCR) An Exchange Server 2007 configuration that performs log shipping from one mailbox database to a number of standby databases on different Mailbox role servers.

Storage Area Network (SAN) A series of network-available storage devices that are available to computers for storage via a fast interconnect.

storage group A storage area that is used to contain one or more public folder or mailbox databases as well as the associated transaction logs and system files.

streaming backup A backup method that does not take advantage of the Windows Volume Shadow Copy service.

striping A hard disk configuration that divides data so that it is evenly stored across several hard disks that operate as a single volume. It is a form of RAID 0.

striping with parity A type of striping that writes parity information to ensure that information can be recovered in the event of a single hard disk failure. It is also called RAID 5.

Subject Alternative Name (SAN) An additional name that is assigned to a public key certificate.

submission queue A temporary storage location for emails that have been submitted to a Hub or Edge role server for processing and relay.

subnet object An Active Directory object that represents an IP network used by a site object.

subordinate CA A CA that has been installed following the root CA in a CA hierarchy.

subscriber access number The number used by UM users when accessing OVA.

subscription file A file that contains the information used to activate and configure EdgeSync for an Edge role server.

swap file A file that Windows writes information to that could not be written to physical memory. It is also called a page file.

symmetric encryption A type of cryptography that uses a single key when encrypting and decrypting data.

System Monitor The Windows graphical performance monitoring utility within the Performance MMC snap-in.

system public folder subtree A public folder hierarchy used to store system information for MAPI clients such as offline address book information.

system state The configuration information used on a Windows computer, including the Windows registry, Active Directory, IIS metabase, and boot files.

T

tables The organizational unit used within a database. Each database table can contain rows (records) of information that are categorized by column (field).

Task Manager A small, graphical, real-time performance monitoring utility within Windows.

template recipient object A recipient object that is copied to create new recipient objects that share the same properties.

Text-to-Speech (TTS) engine A UM software component that translates text to spoken words that are sent to a telephone user.

threshold A value within a performance alert that triggers an event.

thumbprint A unique identifier for a public key certificate.

ticket A set of data used by Kerberos to provide authentication information to Active Directory domain members.

token A set of data used by NTLM to provide authentication information to Active Directory domain members.

Top Level Hierarchy (TLH) The default public folder hierarchy format used within Exchange Server 2007 public folder databases.

trace log A log file that is used to record system events within the Windows Performance MMC snap-in.

transaction log A file that temporarily stores information that must be written to a database.

transitive trust A trust relationship that can be used by other trust relationships.

Transport Layer Security (TLS) A security technology based on SSL that can be used to secure a wide range of network protocols such as SMTP and ESMTP.

transport rule A rule that can be used to modify the processing of email relay on an Edge or Hub role server.

Transport Rules Agent The Exchange Server 2007 component that is responsible for enforcing transport rules during email relay.

Transport Scan Job An FSE virus scan that runs in real time on a Hub or Edge role server to scan emails as they are relayed.

tree A group of Active Directory domains within the same forest that share the same domain name suffix.

trust An association between two Active Directory, NT4, or Kerberos domains that allows for remote resource access. It is also called a trust relationship.

trust relationship An association between two Active Directory, NT4, or Kerberos domains that allows for remote resource access. It is also called a trust.

trusted root The public key certificate of a CA. It is used to validate CA-signed certificates.

two-way trust A trust relationship used by Active Directory to allow users in one domain the ability to access resources in another domain that they have permission to and vice versa.

U

UM auto attendant A UM object that is used to process and respond to incoming telephone calls from a PBX.

UM dial plan A UM object that represents the configuration of the PBX systems within a single organization.

UM IP gateway A UM object that represents the IP address and configuration of an IP PBX gateway device within an organization.

UM mailbox policy A policy that is assigned to a mailbox user in Exchange Server 2007 to enable them for UM funtionality.

unicast mode A NAT mode in which each network interface that is joined to the NAT cluster uses the same virtual hardware (MAC) address.

Unified Messaging (UM) The Exchange Server 2007 component that allows for integration with an organization's PBX.

Uniform Resource Identifier (URI) A unique number used to identify resources on the Internet.

universal A type of Active Directory group scope that allows the group to be assigned rights and permissions within any native mode domain in the forest.

Universal Group Membership Caching (UGMC) A feature of an Active Directory site that allows domain controllers within the site to cache universal group memberships to speed logon times in a native mode domain.

unreachable queue A temporary location for email messages that could not be routed to their destination on a Hub or Edge role server.

user account template A user account that is copied to configure new users with the same settings.

user certificate A public key certificate that is assigned to a user account.

User Configuration The portion of Group Policy that is applied to users that log in to a domain computer.

User Principle Name (UPN) The unique name assigned to a user account in an Active Directory forest.

V

Virtual Private Networks (VPN) A virtual network that encrypts all traffic as it passes through an existing network.

virus definition An entry within antivirus software that provides the necessary information needed to detect the virus during a virus scan.

Voice Over IP (VOIP) A technology that allows spoken information to be sent across an IP network.

Volume Shadow Copy Service (VSS) A Windows services that can be used to efficiently back up open files.

W

WebReady Allows OWA users to access and view attachments in various formats such as Microsoft Office Word.

Windows Backup The file and service backup program in Windows Server 2003. You can use Windows Backup to back up and restore Exchange Server 2007.

Windows Certificate API (CAPI) The Windows API used to provide asymmetric cryptographic operations such as public and private key generation.

Windows Firewall A firewall software that ships with Windows XP and later operating systems.

Windows Mobile Device Center A Windows Vista software program that allows users to synchronize data from a mobile smartphone or PDA to their computer.

Windows QoS Packet Scheduler A Windows software component used for network bandwidth management and control.

Windows Rights Management Services A Windows service that works alongside applications to restrict access to sensitive information.

Windows Server Update Services (WSUS) A server software component that automates and simplifies the distribution of updates to the computers within your organization.

wireless provider A network provider that offers wireless service over long distances. There are many wireless providers in North America including AT&T, Rogers, and Bell.

X

X.400 A commonly used legacy email standard.

X.500 A commonly used directory service structure standard.

X.509 certificate A public key certificate that adheres to the X.509 standard for public key cryptography.

Z

zone A file or object that contains resource records for a portion of the Domain Name Space.